D0794439

COLLINS/Fontana

WAR PAPERS

INTRODUCTION BY
LUDOVIC KENNEDY

FRONT PAGES
REPRODUCED FROM THE
JOHN FROST
HISTORIC NEWSPAPER SERVICE

FIRST PUBLISHED IN 1989
BY FONTANA PAPERBACKS
8 GRAFTON STREET, LONDON W1X 3LA

TYPESETTING AND REPRODUCTION BY H&J GRAPHICS, LONDON
COVER REPRODUCTION BY COLOUR PLANNERS plc, LONDON
COVER PHOTOGRAPH FROM THE KEYSTONE COLLECTION

PRINTED AND BOUND IN GREAT BRITAIN BY
WILLIAM COLLINS SONS & CO. LTD. GLASGOW

PRODUCED FOR FONTANA PAPERBACKS BY
GLAZER AND POMFRET

COMPILED AND DESIGNED BY
STANLEY GLAZER

INTRODUCTION
BY
LUDOVIC KENNEDY

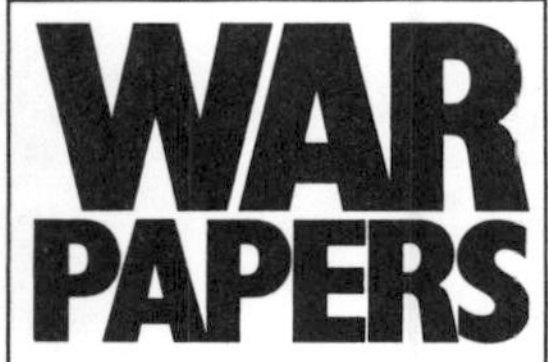

THIS COLLECTION OF FRONT PAGES of newspapers published during the second world war has been culled from many sources; mostly from popular Fleet Street papers such as the *Daily Mirror, Daily Mail, Daily Express, Daily Sketch, Daily Herald* and *News Chronicle* (all of which cost a penny throughout the war) but also from farther afield such as the *New York Post, New York Journal American, Stars and Stripes, Union Jack, Tunis Telegraph*, and many others.

For those like myself who lived and saw service throughout the war, the collection makes nostalgic reading. For those (now the great majority of the population) who were not born until after it, the book provides a graphic and easy to follow guide of how the war progressed from its beginnings in September 1939 to its conclusion in Europe in May 1945 and in the Far East the following August.

For me, during those momentous years, certain events are etched more vividly in my mind than others. The first was the outbreak of the war itself. As people can tell you today where they were when they heard of the death of President Kennedy, so people of that time can tell you where they were when they heard of the outbreak of war. I was in Edinburgh, staying in my grandmother's flat, and as I listened on the radio to Prime Minister Neville Chamberlain's sombre closing words – ". . . *and that consequently this country is at war with Germany*" - I wondered with great intensity and some unease what the war would bring. And that unease increased when a short time later we heard for the first time the mournful wail of the air-raid sirens, and hand in hand my grandmother and I stole down to the cellar. Was Edinburgh about to be destroyed? Was I about to be killed, and if not now, on some future occasion? We were entering into the unknown with a vengeance.

My next great moment of recall was the aftermath of Dunkirk, the miraculous rescue operation by which, in the early summer of 1940, more than 330,000 troops of the British Expeditionary Force were delivered from capture by the Germans. "Tired, dirty, hungry" said the *Daily Express*, "they came back unbeatable". But now a question-mark arose in the minds of many. Hitler had made himself master of Europe from the North Cape to the Pyrenees, and his battle-scarred and victorious troops faced us only twenty miles away across the Channel. We were alone and, with so much of our military equipment abandoned in France, largely unarmed. Would it be only a matter of time before Hitler did to us what he had already done to Belgium and France, Denmark and Norway? The thought of the Wehrmacht marching through the towns and villages of England was a grim one; yet did not at the time seem fanciful.

On both sides preparations went ahead. The Germans began assembling invasion barges and other craft in the ports of

"Was I about to be killed, and if not now, on some future occasion? We were entering into the unknown with a vengeance."

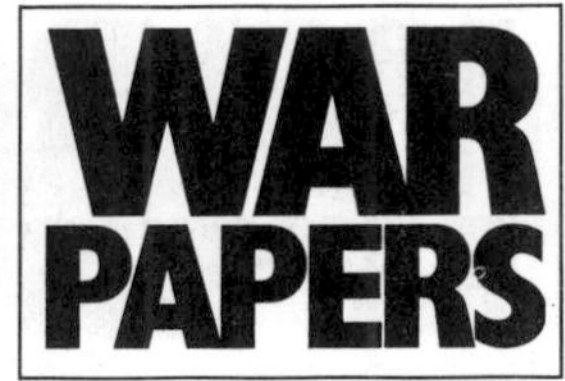

"Then Winston Churchill spoke, not only for himself and the government but for us all."

northern France, and Hitler, who had always hoped to avoid war with England, offered us one last chance of negotiating a peace before unleashing his forces.

On our part all signposts in southern England were ordered to be removed lest they be of help to German parachutists, and from the Wash to Rye a strip of land twenty miles in from the coast was declared forbidden to holiday-makers. The thoughts of those of us who were away on service at the time (I was in a destroyer at Scapa Flow) and whose families lived in the south naturally turned towards them and how they might manage if Hitler came.

Then Winston Churchill spoke, not only for himself and the government but for us all: *"We shall go on to the end, we shall fight in France, we shall fight on the seas and oceans, we shall fight with growing confidence and growing strength in the air, we shall defend our island, whatever the cost may be, we shall fight on the beaches, we shall fight on the landing ground, we shall fight in the fields and in the streets, we shall fight in the hills; we shall never surrender."*

It was, said the *Daily Mirror*, the greatest speech ever made by a Prime Minister of Great Britain, and today, fifty years later, one would not wish to say otherwise. And when we heard it, we knew in an instant, that everything would be all right; not only that if Hitler's troops did try and come, we would drive them back, but also that however long it took and whatever the setbacks, we would in the end win the war. And we were not at all surprised (although obviously relieved) to learn a little later that Hitler had abandoned his plans for invasion and the invasion craft had been dispersed. For Hitler had discovered what Napoleon had discovered 137 years earlier – that without a navy to match the Royal Navy, an invasion of England was impossible. Then Admiral Lord Vincent had told a nervous House of Lords, "I do not say they cannot come, my Lords. I only say they cannot come by sea." True in 1803, and again in 1940.

During the next four years the war on many fronts raged to and fro; Hitler's attack on Russia at first succeeding but then, like that of Napoleon in 1812, exhausting itself and leading to retreat; Rommel's early successes with the Afrika Corps bringing him almost to the gates of Cairo before the tide turned and first Montgomery's Eighth Army and later the Allied forces under General Eisenhower that had landed in Tunisia forcing him out of Africa altogether; similarly the devastating initial advances of the Japanese being finally checked, and both at sea and on land the Americans, with their vast military and economic resources, taking the initiative.

Which brings me to the third event which I see as clearly as on the day it happened – the invasion of Europe on June 6th 1944. I have cause to remember it, as I was lucky enough to be there. My

job was to escort to Portsmouth some twenty Press correspondents, allocate them to various ships in the invasion force and then embark myself in one of the headquarters ships. As with the declaration of war and the aftermath of Dunkirk, it was the apprehension of what the future might bring that has stayed in my mind. There were many who believed the casualties would be massive, that we might not even succeed in gaining a foothold on the shore, that before the day was out the approaches to the beaches would be littered with sunken ships. In the end the landings were accomplished without too much opposition and, although one or two ships were torpedoed by submarine, not a single enemy plane was seen anywhere near the fleet. What I had not expected that morning when I went down to the wardroom after the first landings was to find breakfast going on as usual and to hear the white-coated steward say as I sat down, "Porridge or cereals this morning, sir?" For all that was happening outside, we might still have been alongside the jetty at Portsmouth.

And as my first most vivid memory of the war had been hearing the declaration of it, so my last was hearing the end of it. At the time I was in a troopship passing through the Mediterranean on my way to Italy to take up an appointment as first lieutenant of a destroyer. Ever since leaving Liverpool the ship had been blacked out from stem to stern as all shipping in wartime always was. But when the news came through that all hostilities had officially come to an end, orders were given for the ship's scuttles and deadlights to be pulled back so that lights from a hundred portholes could blaze out triumphantly across the darkling sea. There could have been no more dramatic or immediate evidence that five years of war was finally over.

The first impression of anyone coming fresh to these front-pages for the first time will, I feel sure, be an awareness of the over-optimism of so many of the reports. I doubt if the writers of the reports were themselves optimistic, for newspapermen are a notoriously hard-bitten breed. But newspapers were and are commercial enterprises and what wartime readers wanted to hear was news to cheer and not depress. There are many examples. Soon after the battleships *Prince of Wales* and *Repulse* had been sunk off Malaya and the Japanese were rampaging down the peninsula, the *Sunday Pictorial* could write: *"The news from the Pacific was better last night – five Japanese planes were shot down."* And because, following on the loss of the battleships, the surrender of our great base of Singapore seemed both possible and yet unthinkable, the *Daily Sketch* could fly a headline the day before it happened:

SINGAPORE'S 400 SHELLS AN HOUR
ON JAPS. LINES STABILISED

Another example was the *Daily Mirror*'s

"The surrender of our great base of Singapore seemed both possible and yet unthinkable"

“Readers of popular newspapers like nothing more than stories about heroes, and, with a war on, the demand often led to reporters inventing them.”

headline on the Combined Operations raid on Dieppe in August 1942,

BIG HUN LOSSES IN
9 HOUR DIEPPE BATTLE

when in fact the operation was an unmitigated disaster with huge Canadian casualties and comparatively few German ones. Again when the first of the V1 flying bombs came over, the *Daily Mail* reported:

PILOTLESS ATTACK MAY NOT LAST.
TOO COSTLY TO GERMAN MATERIAL

In fact attacks by the V1's and later by the much more dangerous V2 rockets (for the first you knew about them was when they exploded) continued to be a worry until the invasion forces had over-run their launching sites in Belgium and Northern France.

The readers of popular newspapers like nothing more than stories about heroes, and, with a war on, the demand often led to reporters inventing them. On September 9th 1940 the front page of the *Daily Mirror* produced two. *"All Londoners deserve the V.C."* was one American broadcaster's tribute to the stoicism of those enduring the blitz, while the headline:

COULDN'T FLY – SAVED PLANE

told of how a 22-year-old navigator *"whose flying experience was practically nil"* landed his plane safely after his pilot had been killed. In fact he was a qualified pilot and couldn't have flown the plane at all if he hadn't been. Also in these pages will be found the hoariest aeroplane story of them all – that of the pilot who rather than let his damaged plane fall on a town, crash lands beyond it, when in fact what he is trying to do is save himself, his crew and his plane.

Yet of all the dottiest invented hero stories to be found in these pages, my favourite comes from the *Daily Mirror* of August 16th 1940:

"When a German raider dropped a bomb down the funnel of a trawler in the Channel, the skipper ran from the bridge, carried the bomb from the engine-room to the deck and threw it overboard.

It exploded a second before it hit the water and the ship was undamaged."

How the skipper avoided being burned to death fetching the bomb from the furnace, or else being blown up when the bomb exploded is not explained!

But the commonest and most understandable forms of falsification were those concerning claims for aircraft destroyed and U-boats sunk. These were less the fault of the newspapers as of the service ministries who accepted too readily claims that were too often the result of self-delusion and wishful thinking. The *Daily Mail* for instance claimed at the end of August 1940 that the RAF had shot down a thousand enemy planes in that month alone and nearly 10,000 since the beginning of the war – figures which post-war analysis showed to be wildly exaggerated. It was the same with the Battle of the Atlantic. On May 13th 1943 the *Daily Mirror* claimed that in a recent convoy battle we

had sunk ten U-boats whereas in fact we had sunk six. The *Daily Express* too claimed in July 1940 that *"Britain's new terrifying weapon is a gun that fires steel cables to ensnare German planes".* If such a weapon ever did exist, nothing more was heard of it. Other bizarre claims were those of the *New York Post* in September 1940 that London was being shelled by 90 mile guns (a ballistic impossibility) and a report in the *Daily Mail* of March 7th 1941 that 18 Dutchmen had been sentenced to death for putting vitriol in German soldiers' cocktails!

Some reservations should also be made when reading correspondents' "I was there" stories. For example (from the *Evening Standard* of June 7th 1944 *"It is now exactly 7.25am and through my glasses I can see the first wave of assault troops touching down on the water's edge and far up the beach."* He may well have been there and saw what he said he saw, but he (and others who filed similar despatches) may equally well have been told it. It cost money for newspapers to retain correspondents in the field and those who didn't file "I was there" stories were likely to be soon recalled.

One of the most pleasurable things for me in browsing through this collection is being reminded of events I had quite forgotten. One was the news, published in all newspapers, that within a few days of the outbreak of war we had dropped *six million* propaganda leaflets over Germany – presumably in the naive belief that people might band together to persuade Hitler, then at the zenith of his power, to sue for peace. What a waste of effort and money! I was so glad to be reminded of the extraordinary proposal that our government made to Russia in September 1940 that (a) we would recognise *de facto* the integration of the Baltic States (which Russia had just overrun) within the Soviet Union, (b) we would guarantee that Russia (then neutral) should participate with us in any post-war peace settlement and (c) we would not in any way be associated with an attack on Russia. As Stalin was no less a villain than Hitler and as the two of them had recently signed a non-aggression pact, such kow-towing seems shameful.

Two other small items that struck me at the time but which I had since forgotten: the German radio announcing after Hess had disappeared but before he had landed in Scotland that he had committed suicide; and a picture in all the papers in June 1945 (ie, a month after the European war had ended) of a 16-year-old German named Heinz Petry being led away by his American captors to be shot for spying. It shocked me greatly at the time and 44 years later I find that it still has the power to.

How many events that took place in the war but are not to be found in these pages because of wartime censorship, it is hard to say. But I can speak of at least three. In the *New York Post* of April 25th 1940 Leland Stowe reported that 1,500

"One of the most pleasurable things for me in browsing through this collection is being reminded of events I had quite forgotten."

"The off-beat human stories . . . the invention of "a victory bicycle" to save petrol."

raw British troops had been sent to Norway without anti-aircraft weapons, supporting aeroplanes, or artillery. It was, he said, *"a bitterly disillusioning and almost unbelievable story".* My ship was in Norwegian waters at the time and I know the story to be broadly true, but obviously there could be no place for it in British papers.

Another story that remained unwritten occurred during the chase and sinking of the battleship *Bismarck* in which my ship also took part. It was that the pilot of the Catalina aircraft that had resighted the *Bismarck* after she had been lost for two days was not an RAF man but an American naval officer – one of some 23 whom President Roosevelt had allowed to be seconded to the RAF to teach our pilots how to fly Catalinas. Nothing very remarkable in this, you may think, but at that time America was still neutral and the presence of the Americans as active participants in the war was a clear breach of the U.S. Neutrality Act – which might have led Hitler, had he heard of it, to take counter measures. So that when Godfrey Winn, a famous English journalist of the time went to Catalina's base in Northern Ireland to interview the crew, he found a scoop on his hands which he was unable to use.

Yet the most glaring omission of all from British wartime newspapers was any mention of the destruction of two thirds of the Arctic convoy, PQ17, next to the sinkings of the *Prince of Wales* and *Repulse* the Royal Navy's greatest disaster of the war. This came about because the First Sea Lord, Admiral of the Fleet Sir Dudley Pound, ignored the advice of his intelligence chiefs that although the battleship *Tirpitz* had come to anchor in northern Norway and was in a position to attack the convoy, they would know from radio reports and agents messages the moment she had sailed. Disregarding this advice, Pound ordered the convoy to scatter with the result that, without the help of the *Tirpitz* U-boats and aircraft sent to the bottom more than twenty valuable ships. So great a setback was not allowed to be published at the time: had it been, Pound's head would have rolled, and he was a man whom Churchill relied on.

Yet what has given me as much pleasure as the front page headlines have been the off-beat human stories which rarely find their way to the front page. Two from New York came soon after America's entry into the war. One announced the formation of no less than 48 special ambulances to rescue dogs and cats injured in air-raids. The other was about the invention of "a victory bicycle" to save petrol. To demonstrate the bicycle "the U.S. Price Adminstrator Leon Henderson scorched along a Washington street on the bicycle with a cigar in his mouth and a pretty typist in the handle-bar basket".

I was pleased that the call-up of a Canadian farmer called Donald Duck was thought worthy of a mention; also the story of Margaret Horton, a Women's

Auxiliary Air Force mechanic who was working on the tail of a Spitfire when it suddenly took off. *"She clung on for ten minutes until the extra weight was noticed by the pilot".* He managed to land safely and poor Margaret was taken to hospital with shock and bruises.

Two other stories I noticed were that towards the end of the war a Swedish fireworks firm was taking heavy orders for fireworks showing the faces of Stalin, Churchill and Roosevelt; and the discovery by British troops in Germany of a document addressed to the members of a German parachute regiment. This said that rumours that Hitler flew into rages, tore the curtains, bit the carpet and rolled on the floor were quite untrue, although – and this was a nice touch – suggesting that with all he had to put up with, it would have been understandable if he had done all these things.

Yet among the many front-page headlines of this collection, many of them telling of great historical events, my favourite remains these two from the *Shields Evening News,* a distillation of what Winston Churchill said to the House of Commons and a paradigm of fanciful sub-editorial invention: they appeared in the issue of July 27th 1943.

PREMIER SAYS KEYSTONE OF FASCIST ARCH HAS CRUMBLED: ENTIRE EDIFICE DOOMED

ITALIANS TO STEW IN THEIR OWN JUICE WHILE WE HOT UP THE FIRE

I have too gained pleasure, and I hope the reader will, from some of the advertisements, many of them advocating the virtues of products long forgotten: "Serve Kep with savouries": "Erinmore cigarettes – did you say 10 for 6d?": Free running Sifta Salt – never cakes": "How Lucozade stops vomiting": "Yeast-Vite for Sleeplessness": "Take Elasto the wonder drug and stop limping"; and – a reminder of the times, the current cinema – *Tartus* with Robert Donat and Valerie Hobson held over for a 4th week, and, for a *6th week*, Bing Crosby and Dorothy Lamour in *Dixie.*

If I have one regret of this admirable collection it is that many of the stories – especially the major ones – are completed on some inner page and we are left, as it were, dangling in space. Two examples of this are the communique from the Admiralty about the Bismarck operation and a speech in which Winston Churchill refers to the Empire being in peril, though we do not learn how. But then the purpose of this book is not to tell the full story of the events of those turbulent years, rather to mark out the principal peaks and valleys so that the reader who is so inclined may fill the gaps in his knowledge elsewhere.

It all happened a long time ago, and for those of us who lived through it, it *seems* a long time ago. But – and I hope this is as true for those to whom the period is history as to those of us to whom it was reality – the pages that follow bring it all vividly and dramatically to life.

"It all happened a long time ago . . . The pages that follow bring it all vividly and dramatically to life."

THE STAR. FRIDAY, SEPTEMBER 1, 1939.

LONDON'S FOOTBALL PROSPECTS
By JACK INGHAM
Page Nine

THE LONDONER'S EVENING PAPER
No. 15,983. ONE PENNY. FRIDAY, SEPTEMBER 1, 1939. RADIO : Page Two. WEATHER : Mainly Cloudy.

POLAND INVADED

Warsaw And Other Towns Bombed: Anglo-Polish Treaty Invoked

COMPLETE MOBILISATION

—Official

KING SIGNED ORDER IN COUNCIL ORDERING COMPLETE MOBILISATION OF ARMY AND AIR FORCE.

THE KING ALSO SIGNED PROCLAMATION WHICH, IN EFFECT, ORDERS COMPLETE NAVAL MOBILISATION. HE ALSO SIGNED OTHER PROCLAMATIONS DEALING WITH EMERGENCY.

Swiss Mobilise

Swiss Government to-day ordered general mobilisation to-morrow.—Exchange.

MOBILISATION AND MARTIAL LAW IN FRANCE: "STATE OF SIEGE"

Nazi Troops March Into Poland At 5.45 a.m.

BRITAIN IS DETERMINED

Germany invaded Poland to-day. Warsaw and many other Polish towns have been bombed by German warplanes.

The Polish Ambassador called on Lord Halifax, the Foreign Secretary, and invoked the Anglo-Polish Treaty.

The French Cabinet to-day decided to order general mobilisation, proclaim martial law and declare a state of siege throughout France and Algiers.

As his troops marched into Poland, Hitler, in an address to the Reichstag, said that Poland was fighting on German territory last night and Germany had been "shooting back since 5.45 this morning." He added: "From now on bomb after bomb is falling."

The British Cabinet met at 11.30 a.m. and an authoritative statement issued soon afterwards said that, if the Proclamation to the German people by Hitler (issued to-day) should mean, as it would seem to mean, that Germany had declared war on Poland, Britain and France were inflexibly determined to fulfil to the uttermost their obligations to Poland.

The King held a Privy Council at Buckingham Palace to-day. Both Houses of the British Parliament will meet at 6 o'clock to-night.

NEWS that Germany had invaded Poland was broadcast by the official Warsaw radio and announced by the Polish Embassy in Paris almost simultaneously.

Then an official at the Polish Embassy in London confirmed that Germany had begun an offensive along the entire Polish front.

The official added: "I think the European war will start to-day. Poland will fight to the end for victory."

It was also stated at the Embassy that the bombed cities and towns included Warsaw, Vilna, Cracow, Posnan, Ptzew, Grodno, Torun, Katowice and Gdynia.

Many lives, it was added, were lost in Warsaw, including those of women and children.

Long-wave Polish radio stations were being jammed by Germany, and the short-wave stations had been cut off.

"FULL-SCALE ATTACK"

The Warsaw radio statement said that Germany had launched a full-scale attack.

According to a British United Press message, Warsaw was raided at 9 a.m., and the "All clear" was sounded at 9.40. People then went about their business.

A Paris message says that the Polish Official News Agency there carries reports from Warsaw that the main German offensive is directed at Czestochowa, north of Katowice, while a secondary

(CONTINUED ON BACK PAGE.)

GERMAN AND POLISH DIPLOMATS AT DOWNING-ST.

The German Charge d'Affaires, Dr. Kordt, called at No. 10, Downing-street, to-day, while the Polish Ambassador was with Mr. Chamberlain. Dr. Kordt was received by the Premier and Lord Halifax and stayed for twenty minutes.

MINISTERS in charge of all the defence departments met at the Cabinet offices in Richmond-terrace this morning.

Dominions High Commissioners were received by Sir Thomas Inskip, the Dominions Secretary.

Mr. Arthur Greenwood, who this morning saw the Prime Minister, called a meeting of Labour's national executive this afternoon. The Parliamentary Labour Executive were meeting later.

FROM THE ROYAL MEWS

Women and children of the Royal Mews were being evacuated to-day into the country. Horses are also to go.

19 LONDON UNDERGROUND STATIONS TO BE CLOSED

LONDON TRANSPORT announced to-day that it will be necessary to close immediately until further notice the following Underground stations so that certain work may be done:

Arsenal.
Balham.
Bank (Central Line).
[illegible]-street.
Chancery-lane.
Charing Cross (Bakerloo and Northern lines).
Clapham Common
Green Park.
Hyde Park Corner
King's Cross (Piccadilly and Northern Line).
Knightsbridge.
[illegible]
Old-street.
Oval.
Oxford-circus.
Tottenham Court-road.
Trinity-road.
Waterloo (Northern Line)

Subways for interchange between lines will be kept open at the Bank, Oxford-circus and Tottenham Court-road.

On the Northern line there will be no trains until further notice between Kennington and Strand.

ALTERNATIVE SERVICES

Holders of season tickets to closed stations may retain their tickets and complete their journey from the nearest open station, by bus, tram or trolley-bus, but owing to the exceptional circumstances accommodation on the alternative road services cannot be ensured.

If they wish, season ticket holders may surrender their tickets at any ticket office, or by post to the Commercial Manager, London Transport, 55, Broadway, S.W.1—and they will, in due course, receive a full refund for the unused period from the date of surrender.

LEFT LUGGAGE TO BE REMOVED

No tickets will be issued to closed stations, but only to the nearest open station.

Ordinary single and return and workmen's tickets will not be accepted on the alternative road services.

Luggage and other articles which have been left in cloakrooms at the closed stations will be removed to the Lost Property Office, 200 Baker-street, W., where they may be claimed Mondays to Fridays between 10 a.m. and 7 p.m.

London's Children Were Grand

EVACUATION of thousands of London children was carried out to-day without a hitch.

There were smiles everywhere, and hardly a tear.

And soon from the reception areas came reports of the warm and friendly welcomes that were given to the little ones on their arrival.

The evacuation was a triumph of good organisation.

A visitor to London would hardly have realised that it was happening at all. Not one big traffic hold-up was reported, and people had remarkably little difficulty in catching trains and buses.

Those City and West End workers who took the advice of London Transport to be at work by nine o'clock found in many cases that they were actually at the office ahead of normal time.

Full Story and Pictures.—Page Seven

NEW 2s. 6d. STAMPS

King George VI 2s. 6d. postage stamps will be on sale on Monday. After that the King George V 2s. 6d. stamps will be sold until exhausted.

The design of the new stamp is the same as that of the 5s. denomination recently issued, and the colour is brown.

WHERE BRITAIN STANDS

THE CABINET MET AT NO. 10, DOWNING-STREET THIS AFTERNOON.

LATER THE KING HELD A PRIVY COUNCIL. THOSE PRESENT WERE LORD RUNCIMAN, LORD ZETLAND, LORD NEWTON, AND CAPT. CROOKSHANK.

WHEN PARLIAMENT MEETS THIS EVENIING SPECIAL EMERGENCY LEGISLATION WILL BE PASSED AFTER MR. CHAMBERLAIN HAS DESCRIBED WHAT HAS TAKEN PLACE SINCE TUESDAY.

IT IS POINTED OUT IN OFFICIAL CIRCLES IN LONDON THAT IF THE PROCLAMATION TO THE GERMAN PEOPLE BY HERR HITLER, WHICH HAS ALREADY BEEN ANNOUNCED, SHOULD MEAN, AS IT WOULD SEEM TO MEAN, THAT GERMANY HAS DECLARED WAR ON POLAND, IT CAN BE STATED ON THE HIGHEST AUTHORITY THAT GREAT BRITAIN AND FRANCE ARE INFLEXIBLY DETERMINED TO FULFIL TO THE UTTERMOST THEIR OBLIGATIONS TO THE POLISH GOVERNMENT.

The official view is this:

"The German account of the course of the negotiations is wholly misleading. On August 29, the German Chancellor informed Sir Nevile Henderson that he expected a Polish plenipotentiary to appear in Berlin by the following day with full powers to negotiate a settlement. He added that in the meantime he hoped to elaborate proposals.

"In other words, the Polish Government were expected to submit to the procedure imposed on the President of Czecho-Slovakia (Dr. Benes), and to despatch an emissary to Berlin who was to accept terms, the character of which was wholly unknown to the Polish Government.

"The Polish Government have not unnaturally been unwilling to place themselves in this humiliating position.

"It is not customary, even in the case of peace terms imposed on a defeated Power, to demand that negotiators should not be allowed to refer for instructions to their Government.

MISLEADING GERMAN STATEMENTS

"It is impossible to comment at such short notice on the misleading statements of the German Government, but the general attitude of the British Government may be briefly defined as follows.

"If the German Government had been sincerely desirous of settling the dispute by negotiation, they would not have adopted this procedure, which has the character of an ultimatum.

CIVILISED GOVERNMENT

"They would, on the contrary, have opened negotiations with the Polish Government in accordance with the normal procedure of [illegible] the place and time for the opening of negotiations.

"The Polish Government, in the opinion of H.M. Government, were fully justified in declining to submit to the treatment which the German Government endeavoured to impose on them.

"As regards the terms now published, which have never been hitherto communicated to the Polish Government, the Government can only say that these terms should, of course, have been submitted to the Polish Government with time to consider whether or not they infringed Poland's vital interests, which Germany, in a written communication to the British Government, had declared her intention of respecting."

HITLER TELLS ITALY "WE WILL CARRY OUT OUR TASK ALONE"

WITHIN a few hours of Germany's attack on Poland, Hitler in the Kroll Opera House, Berlin, to-day told the Reichstag."

"I am not going to ask help from Italy. It is a matter for Germany to solve alone.

"The German Army to-day is better than that of 1914.

"Since 5.45 this morning Germans have been bombing Poland.

"If anything happens to me Goering is to be my successor and after that Hess.

"I have given instructions to the German Air Force to bomb only military objects, but if the enemy acts otherwise they will reply in the same way.

"An iron discipline is to be imposed on German women."

Hitler spoke for 36 minutes. He ended with the cry, "Sieg Heil" (Hail Victory), and moved the bill for the reunion of Danzig with the German Reich. The bill was voted on at once and passed.

Full report of Speech on Page Three.

ROOSEVELT'S PLEA

PRESIDENT ROOSEVELT to-day appealed to "potential participants in a European war" to give a pledge against bombardment of civilians or open towns.

The appeal, addressed to Britain, France, Italy, Poland and Germany, said:—

"I am therefore addressing this urgent appeal to every government which may be engaged in hostilities publicly to affirm its determination that its armed forces shall in no event and under no circumstances undertake bombardment from the air of civilian populations or unfortified cities, on the understanding that the same rules of warfare will be scrupulously observed by all their opponents.

"I request an immediate reply."

AIR WARNING SYSTEM IN OPERATION

LOCAL authorities have been instructed to put the air raid warning system into full operation, it is announced by Sir John Anderson, the Lord Privy Seal.

This means that, from now on, the sounding of all factory sirens and hooters is prohibited, except for giving air-raid warnings.

An air-raid warning on a factory hooter or siren is given by a series of short blasts. The "raiders passed" signal, as in the case of police sirens, is given by a long, steady blast lasting two minutes.

How to be safe in an air raid.—Page Six.

DAILY HERALD, September 4, 1939.

Daily Herald

No. 7349 MONDAY, SEPTEMBER 4, 1939 ONE PENNY

WAR DECLARED BY BRITAIN AND FRANCE

The Fleet Moves Into Position

GREAT BRITAIN DECLARED WAR ON GERMANY AT 11 O'CLOCK YESTERDAY MORNING.

Six hours later, at 5 p.m., France declared war.

Britain's resolution to defend Poland against Nazi aggression was described by the newly-formed Ministry of Information in one of its first announcements, as follows:—

"At 11.15 this morning (Sunday) Mr. R. Dunbar, Head of the Treaty Department of the Foreign Office, went to the German Embassy, where he was received by Dr. Kordt, the Charge d'Affaires.

"Mr. Dunbar handed to Dr. Kordt a notification that a state of war existed between Great Britain and Germany as from 11 o'clock B.S.T. this morning. This notification constituted the formal declaration of war."

Navy Fully Mobilised

The King broadcast to the nation last night. A copy of his message, with facsimile signature, will be distributed to every household in the country.

Britain's Navy is fully mobilised and is at its war stations in full strength, supplemented by a number of fully commissioned armed merchant ships as auxiliary cruisers.

The convoy system for merchant shipping has been introduced.

The King has made the following appointments: Commander-in-Chief of the British Field Forces, General Viscount Gort, V.C.; Chief of the Imperial General Staff, General Sir Edmund Ironside; Commander-in-Chief of the Home Forces, General Sir Walter Kirke.

The Empire has sprung to Britain's support, "Australia is at war," declared Mr. Menzies, the Commonwealth Prime Minister, broadcasting last night.

"Where Britain stands," he said, "there stands the people of the Empire and the British world."

"All Possible Support"

The New Zealand Government has sent a telegram 'immediately associating' itself with the British Government. "All possible support" is assured.

The Viceroy of India has issued a proclamation announcing the outbreak of war.

It is understood that the Japanese Government has given the British Government assurances of Japan's neutrality.

Hitler left Berlin last night for the Polish Front, where he is to assume command of the German armies.

Sir Nevile Henderson, the British Ambassador, and M. Coulondre, the French Ambassador, took their leave of Herr von Ribbentrop, German Foreign Minister, yesterday. Neither envoy saw Hitler.

To-day has been declared a Bank Holiday. It affects only banks and does not apply to any other business. The banks will reopen to-morrow.—*Details on Page 8.*

Petrol is to be controlled and rationed from September 16. One grade only will be supplied. It will be called "Pool Motor Spirit," and will cost 1s. 6d. a gallon.

All cinemas, theatres and other places of entertainment are closed until further notice.

Premier Sees King

The Prime Minister, who, in a broadcast to the nation, had declared: "We have resolved to finish it," visited the King at Buckingham Palace last night. War Minister Hore-Belisha also saw the King.

Mr. Arthur Greenwood, Acting Leader of the Opposition, in a broadcast, said: "If we do not overthrow the forces of dictatorship now, our turn will come sooner or later."

WAR CABINET OF NINE

Churchill Is Now First Lord

By MAURICE WEBB
"Daily Herald" Political Correspondent

BRITAIN'S new War Cabinet, which will have full control of the conduct of hostilities, was set up yesterday.

Mr. Winston Churchill is one of the nine members. He has been appointed First Lord of the Admiralty.

Lord Hankey, who is Minister without Portfolio, is the only other member who was not in the late Government. Sir Samuel Hoare leaves the Home Office to become Lord Privy Seal, in which post he will have special emergency duties.

The full War Cabinet is as follows:

Prime Minister ...... **Mr. Neville Chamberlain.**
Foreign Secretary ......**Lord Halifax.**
Defence Co-ordination Minister ...... **Lord Chatfield.**
Chancellor of the Exchequer ...... **Sir John Simon.**
First Lord of the Admiralty ...... **Mr. Winston Churchill.**
War Secretary ...... **Mr. Leslie Hore-Belisha.**
Air Minister ......**Sir Kingsley Wood.**
Lord Privy Seal ...**Sir Samuel Hoare.**
Minister without Portfolio ...... **Lord Hankey.**

At the request of the Prime Minister all the members of the late Government placed their resignations in his hands to enable reconstruction to take place.

Sweeping Changes

The War Cabinet is an inner body on the lines of that set up in December, 1916. It is the supreme authority for all matters connected with the conduct of the war.

Sweeping changes have been made in the general Cabinet.

Mr. Anthony Eden comes back to the Front Bench with special access to the War Cabinet as Dominions Secretary in place of **Sir Thomas Inskip**, who goes to the House of Lords as Lord Chancellor in place of Lord Maugham.

Lord Runciman is replaced as Lord President of the Council by **Lord Stanhope**, who was First Lord of the Admiralty.

(Continued on Page 7, Col. 5.)

Unthinkable We Should Refuse The Challenge

—THE KING

Broadcasting last evening from his study at Buckingham Palace, the King said:—

IN this grave hour, perhaps the most fateful in our history, I send to every household of my people, both at home and overseas, this message, spoken with the same depth of feeling for each one of you as if I were able to cross your threshold and speak to you myself.

For the second time in the lives of most of us we are at war.

Over and over again we have tried to find a peaceful way out of the differences between ourselves and those who are now our enemies.

But it has been in vain.

We have been forced into a conflict. For we are called with our Allies to meet the challenge of a principle which, if it were to prevail, would be fatal to any civilised order in the world.

* * *

IT is the principle which permits a State, in the selfish pursuit of power, to disregard its treaties and its solemn pledges; which sanctions the use of force or threat of force against the sovereignty and independence of other States.

Such a principle, stripped of all disguise, is surely the mere primitive doctrine that might is right; and if this principle were established throughout the world the freedom of our own country and of the whole British Commonwealth of nations would be in danger.

But far more than this—the peoples of the world would be kept in the bondage of fear and all hopes of settled peace and of the security of justice and liberty among nations would be ended.

This is the ultimate issue which confronts us.

For the sake of all that we ourselves hold dear and of the world's order and peace, it is unthinkable that we should refuse to meet the challenge.

* * *

IT is to this high purpose that I now call my people at home and my peoples across the seas who will make our cause their own.

I ask them to stand calm and firm and united in this time of trial.

The task will be hard. There may be dark days ahead and war can no longer be confined to the battlefield.

But we can only do the right as we see the right and reverently commit our cause to God.

If one and all we keep resolutely faithful to it, ready for whatever service or sacrifice it may demand, then, with God's help, we shall prevail.

May He bless and keep us all.

POLES SMASH WAY INTO E. PRUSSIA

OFFICIALS in Warsaw stated late last night that the Polish army has smashed a way across the Northern border into East Prussia, after driving the Germans from several Polish towns in bitter fighting.

On the Northern Front the Poles are reported to have defeated the German effort to drive a barrier across the upper part of the Corridor. The Germans fell back behind their frontiers.

The Poles say they have broken through the German fortifications as far as the railway terminus of Deutsch Eylau.

One of the most important towns recaptured is stated to be Zbaszyn.

Early to-day an official Polish communiqué admitted, however, that Polish troops had been compelled to abandon Czestochowa, about 17 miles from frontier of Upper Silesia.

(Continued on Page 2; Earlier fighting details on Page 10)

London Hears Its First Raid Warning

LONDON was calm yesterday when it heard its first air raid warning.

This is the official statement issued by the Air Ministry:—

At 11.30 a.m. yesterday an aircraft was observed approaching the South Coast.

As its identity could not be readily determined an air-raid warning was given.

It was shortly afterwards identified as a friendly aircraft and the all-clear signal was given.

(Full Story on Page Seven.)

BLACK-OUT TIME TO-NIGHT—7.40

BREMEN REPORTED TAKEN

THE 50,000-ton German liner Bremen is reported to have been captured by British warships.

A report to this effect was broadcast from a French wireless station last night and picked up in New York.

A "high French source" was quoted as saying that the Bremen was taken at 4 p.m., the area not being given, and was being taken to a British port.

The Ministry of Information announced last night that the Admiralty knew nothing about the capture of the Bremen.

The Bremen was built in 1929 for the North German Lloyd line at a cost of more than £1,250,000.

With a crew of about 1,000 hands she has accommodation for more than 2,000 passengers.

Maginot Line

CIVILIANS LEAVE

PARIS, Sunday.

THE area to the rear of the Maginot Line has been completely evacuated by civilians.—British United Press.

CHILDREN GO

Evacuation of London has been carried out more rapidly than was expected and the number remaining to be evacuated to-day is smaller than on previous days.

The number evacuated from the capital up to Saturday night, the latest figure available, is 485,900.

* * *

A Dutch steamer reports that four German submarines are fuelling at Curacao, the Dutch colony off the coast of Venezuela.

* * *

Moscow civilians in the Red Army Reserve yesterday began registration at specified stations. It is believed similar steps were taken in other large centres (Reuter says).

DAILY MIRROR, Monday, September 4, 1939

Daily Mirror

No. 11,152 ✦ ONE PENNY
Registered at the G.P.O. as a Newspaper.

BRITAIN'S FIRST DAY OF WAR: CHURCHILL IS NEW NAVY CHIEF

BRITAIN AND GERMANY HAVE BEEN AT WAR SINCE ELEVEN O'CLOCK YESTERDAY MORNING. FRANCE AND GERMANY HAVE BEEN AT WAR SINCE YESTERDAY AT 5 P.M.

A British War Cabinet of nine members was set up last night. Mr. Winston Churchill, who was First Lord of the Admiralty when Britain last went to war, returns to that post.

Full list of the War Cabinet is:—

PRIME MINISTER: Mr. Neville Chamberlain.
CHANCELLOR OF THE EXCHEQUER: Sir John Simon.
FOREIGN SECRETARY: Viscount Halifax.
DEFENCE MINISTER: Lord Chatfield.
FIRST LORD: Mr. Winston Churchill.
SECRETARY FOR WAR: Mr. Leslie Hore-Belisha.
SECRETARY FOR AIR: Sir Kingsley Wood.
LORD PRIVY SEAL: Sir Samuel Hoare.
MINISTER WITHOUT PORTFOLIO: Lord Hankey.

There are other Ministerial changes. Mr. Eden becomes Dominions Secretary, Sir Thomas Inskip goes to the House of Lords as Lord Chancellor, Lord Stanhope, ex-First Lord, becomes Lord President of the Council, Sir John Anderson is the Home Secretary and Minister of Home Security—a new title.

None of these is in the Cabinet, which is restricted to the Big Nine. These are the men who will be responsible for carrying on the war.

But Mr. Eden is to have special access to the Cabinet.

The Liberal Party explained last night that although Sir Archibald Sinclair had been offered a ministerial post, the Party had decided at this moment not to enter the Government.

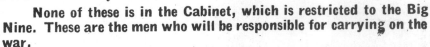

POLES ATTACK

POLISH troops are fighting on German territory, according to a Warsaw message.

A Polish counter-attack pushed back the Germans and penetrated East Prussia near Deutsch Eylau, it was claimed.

The Polish Embassy in London described a Nazi report that troops had cut the Corridor as "entirely false."

Later (according to the Havas Agency) the Polish Radio announced that Poland had retaken the frontier station of Zbazyn.

The German News Agency claimed that Nazi troops operating on the Southern front had taken the town of Radomsko.

Radomsko, north of the industrial region round Kattowitz, is about forty miles from the Polish frontier.

1,500 Raid Casualties

The Poles' latest estimate of casualties in German air raids was issued last night in Warsaw.

It is alleged that 1,500 people were killed or injured in German air bombardment of open towns and villages during Friday and Saturday. A considerable proportion of the victims were women and children.

[The German Government had secured from

Contd. on Bk. Page, Col. 1

"BREMEN IS CAPTURED"

—French Report

The £4,000,000 German liner Bremen was reported to have been captured yesterday and taken to a British port.

A report from a high French source stated that the Bremen was captured at 4 p.m., but the area in which the liner was captured was not mentioned.

A French Government radio station broadcast the report which was picked up by the Mutual Broadcasting System of America.—Associated Press and British United Press.

Petrol Will Be Rationed

The first meeting of the new war Cabinet took place last night. Mr. Churchill was the first to leave and the crowd broke into a cheer as he walked out. Mr. Hore-Belisha was driven away by a woman chauffeur in uniform.

The Premier went from Downing-street to Buckingham Palace where he stayed with the King for three-quarters of an hour.

It was announced last night that as from September 16 all petrol will be rationed. In the meantime all car owners are asked not to use their cars more than is vitally necessary.

To-day all banks throughout Britain will be closed.

Australia yesterday declared war on Germany. "Where Britain stands, stand the people of the Empire and the British world," said Prime Minister Menzies in a broadcast message last night.

New Zealand has cabled her full support to Britain. There is a rush of recruits in Canada. At Toronto a queue of 2,000 men lined outside the Recruiting Office.

Japan has assured Britain of her neutrality in the present war.

Britain's last two-hour ultimatum to Germany was revealed to the people of Britain in a memorable broadcast from Downing-street by Mr. Chamberlain at 11.15 yesterday morning. By that time

cont'd in Col. 4, Back Page

The King to His People

"The task will be hard. There may be dark days ahead. . . . But we can only do the right as we see the right, and reverently commit our cause to God. If one and all we keep resolutely faithful to it, ready for whatever service or sacrifice it may demand, then, with God's help, we shall prevail."

These words were broadcast by the King last night. And to every household in the country a copy of his message, bearing his own signature facsimile, will be sent as a permanent record. The full speech is on page 3.

2nd DAY OF THE SECOND GREAT WAR

LINER SINKING 'DELIBERATE'

SEE THIS PAGE

DAILY SKETCH

No. 9,465 TUESDAY, SEPTEMBER 5, 1939 ONE PENNY

PREMIER BROADCASTS IN GERMAN

RADIO: PAGE 20

R.A.F. RAIN LEAFLETS OVER GERMANY

ROYAL AIR FORCE 'planes flying by night dropped 6,000,000 leaflets in Germany.

This was revealed last night in a Ministry of Information communiqué stating:—

"On the night of the 3-4th September aircraft of Royal Air Force carried out extensive recconnaisance over Northern and Western Germany. They were not engaged by enemy aircraft. More than six million copies of a note to the German people were dropped over a wide area."

The Admiralty announced that naval activity continues on all seas, but without major operations.

ATHENIA OUTRAGE

It was added that the torpedoing of the liner Athenia, bound for Canada with many Americans aboard, was a deliberate disregard of a declaration voluntarily made by Germany in 1930.

This was to the effect that she renounced of her own free will the right to make use of unrestricted submarine warfare in any future campaign. (See Page 5).

'TIGER' IN COMMAND

THE Commander of Britain's Forces in the Field, General Lord Gort, V.C.

Aged only 53, he has won the nickname of the "Tiger" for his ferocity in seeing that tasks he imposes are not only done, but done well.

HITLER'S RECORD OF TREACHERY—SEE MIDDLE PAGES

8th DAY OF THE SECOND GREAT WAR

FAMOUS LINER CHEATS U-BOATS:

See Page Five

FRENCH TAKE 350 SQUARE MILES

—PAGE TWO

No. 9,470 MONDAY, SEPTEMBER 11, 1939 ONE PENNY

RADIO: PAGE 10

WARSAW DEFIANT

NAZI LINE BENT

WARSAW has not fallen and Poland's Army shows no sign of cracking, it was stated officially in London last night.

The Ministry of Information said that "in spite of the German Government's claim, they have not entered Warsaw. This is confirmed by the Polish Government's own wireless bulletins from Warsaw.

THEIR TOUGHNESS

"One thing stands out clearly—the heroic resistance offered by the Polish Armies against tremendous odds, their exceptionally high moral, and their toughness and steadiness in retreat.

"Germany has had to mass 70 divisions against Poland. Yet the Polish Army has withdrawn in an orderly manner and with a steadiness which must excite admiration among its beholders.

"It is too soon yet to talk of what will happen to Warsaw. What is certain is that the Polish Army is firmly in being."

"WE are now reaching the first German line of resistance, and we are operating against the advanced positions of the Siegfried Line," states the semi-official Paris newspaper "Le Temps," quoted by B.U.P.

"These positions," adds the newspaper, "have been dented at one point by one of our divisions in a brilliant attack."

The intensification of the fighting on the Western Front seems near to attaining the desired objective of retarding German action on the Polish front, for reports reaching Paris by way of Belgium say that the German roads leading to the Western Front are jammed with troops and supplies coming from the east.

ALL GAINS HELD

French General Staff Communiqué No. 13, issued yesterday, says the French are holding the gains previously reported. The communique adds:

"The Germans yesterday carried out counter attacks against numerous points of our front."

A FINE ADVANCE ON THE FOOD FRONT

The Army goes marketing, and, as you see (left), Covent Garden at once capitulates. There is indeed plenty of everything (second picture), and prices are lower than at this time last year. Also the women porters are towers of strength who bear crates of vegetables on their heads (right) like a feather.

BLACK-OUT ZERO HOUR TO-NIGHT

Daily Express
WORLD'S LARGEST DAILY SALE

No. 12,265 | Tuesday, September 12, 1939 | One Penny

"The British, this time wonderfully prepared, are already fighting by our side"

BRITISH TROOPS IN FRANCE

'In large numbers' says Paris radio

TROOP TRAIN CHEERED

From GEOFFREY COX and GEORGE MILLAR
Daily Express Staff Reporters

PARIS, Monday.

"BRITISH TROOPS ARE FIGHTING IN FRANCE." THIS WAS THE MESSAGE GIVEN OVER THE RADIO FROM PARIS TONIGHT BY ROLAND DORGELES, FAMOUS FRENCH WAR AUTHOR.

M. Dorgeles declared that this time the British soldiers are "wonderfully prepared." He said: "They are already fighting in large numbers by our side, and their numbers will increase continually."

To this the French Commissariat of Information added: "It has been impossible for military reasons to give precise information regarding British troops in France. . . . The support that Britain will be able to give us will be infinitely greater than in 1914."

Everywhere in France the first British troops have been received by the people with cheers and handshakes.

Here is a scene in a French village this morning. A long British troop train rumbled through. The villagers rushed to the station as a few watchers on the platform shouted "Les Anglais!"

Infantrymen in khaki leaned from the carriages, waved cheerily and shouted to the French people. From the compartments at the end of the train officers saluted smilingly.

The grey-haired stationmaster told onlookers: "I fought beside the British at the Somme. My son has already gone to the Maginot. He'll be with them now."

General Viscount ("Tiger") Gort, V.C., is Commander-in-Chief of the British Field Forces, and this time there will be no "muddling through."

Everywhere the network of the British military machine is preparing the way for the Expeditionary Force.

Thousands of technicians, the R.A.S.C., and the R.A.M.C. are now working according to plans discussed by France's General Gamelin and General Gort in their first staff talks twelve months ago.

In a village inn today four English officers bent over papers strewn over the kitchen table. From a café one could hear the murmur of their voices.

HARVESTING

Old peasants rumbled through the dusty street in carts for the harvesting. Boys drove cattle through the village to gorge on clover patches.

An ultra-smart Parisienne evacuee picked her high-heeled way to morning Mass. The maid asked the bar for "Three teas and one beer for the English officers."

A British airplane rose from behind the poplars and flew east.

In a new hut alongside the village garage six British Army mechanics fixed new machinery. A French staff colonel drove up and joined the parley in the kitchen.

Two hundred miles away in a big seaside resort there was no room for civilian guests. Every hotel had been requisitioned.

Now let us turn to the situation at the front.

The French, firing from new trench lines in the zone between

CONTINUED ON BACK PAGE

FRENCH PUSH ON 12-MILE FRONT

FRENCH troops were digging a new front line in the Saar sector last night after fresh advances which are described in war communiqué No. 16:—

"Despite enemy resistance, our attacks are continuing to make considerable progress along a front of about twenty kilometres (12½ miles) east of the Saar."

It is believed that "the Saar" here refers to the Saar River which runs parallel to the Siegfried Line at a distance varying from five to twenty miles behind the German frontier.

The French advance was accompanied by fierce hand-to-hand fighting. The first attacks, launched at midday, at once relieved German pressure on the French left flank.

To clean out the German positions tanks and trench mortars were used.

Germans expecting a big battle

From MONTAGUE LACEY *Daily Express Staff Reporter*

AMSTERDAM, Monday.

IT is reported here today that Germany is expecting a big Western Front battle soon.

A high German military officer in Berlin is quoted as saying that the situation on the Western Front is much like that on both sides of the Somme in the last war before the beginning of the enormous combined French and British offensive.

Now, as then, there have been week-long gropings, scoutings and local activities by advanced troops, intended to discover the strongest and weakest places in the hostile lines.

NO WEAK POINTS

This time, says the officer, one may only look for the less strong points—the weak points do not exist.

Germany is seriously prepared for an attack on the Siegfried Line, and there is, therefore, enormous military activity.

It is also stated that the announcement of Soviet mobilisation has created a big impression throughout Germany.

We fight to bitter end

—Mr. EDEN

"The people of this country are ready to fight a very long war to the bitter end to rid the world of Hitlerism and all that Hitlerism implies."—*Mr. Anthony Eden on the radio last night. See Back Page.*

Hitler to his fans

"NO FLOWERS, BY MY REQUEST"

NO flowers may be thrown at Hitler during his visits to the front, says an order from the "Fuehrer's headquarters," quoted by the German radio yesterday afternoon. The order added: "Flowers should be handed to the troops."

Hitler again flew over the front in Poland yesterday.

A row in the Nazi command

Admiral (Tirpitz) Raeder backs "Sink at sight" policy

From SELKIRK PANTON
Daily Express Staff Reporter

COPENHAGEN, Monday.

JUST as Grand Admiral von Tirpitz, the ex-Kaiser's naval chief, clashed with his Government over the question of unrestricted U-boat warfare, so a conflict has now broken out between the Nazi naval staff and political leaders over the torpedoing of the Athenia.

Reports reaching me from Berlin state that the German Foreign Office and other propaganda officials are alarmed at the reaction of the world to the sinking of the Athenia, and, by claiming that Churchill sank the ship, tried to wash their hands of the whole affair.

Grand Admiral Erich Raeder, Hitler's navy chief, countered with the claim that the only hope of breaking the British blockade lay in unrestricted U-boat warfare. He protested against the clumsy efforts of Dr. Goebbels to cast the blame elsewhere.

He said the U-boat commander's worst fault, if any, was that he had carried out too literally Hitler's express orders to sink without warning.

He added that the commander should be rewarded with the Iron Cross for drawing first blood, even if only neutral women and children were the victims.

GERMAN WARSHIP BLOWN UP

From SELKIRK PANTON
Daily Express Staff Reporter

COPENHAGEN, Monday.

A GERMAN torpedo boat threading its way through the German minefield laid between Denmark and Sweden at dawn today struck a mine and sank within a few minutes.

The loss was reported by a Swedish steamer, and the people of Trelleborg, a town at the southernmost end of Sweden, who saw the warship sink — Germany's first naval loss in the Baltic.

They saw the torpedo-boat, an old type, suddenly enveloped in a great spout of water, then heard the boom of the bursting mine. As the water subsided the ship disappeared.

A German trawler is believed to have saved ten of the crew of about fifty. The Swedish steamer was unable to approach the ship because of the minefield.

SUNK, THEN HELPED BY U-BOAT

The crew of the British steamer Olivegrove (4,060 tons)—in two ship's boats—row towards the American steamer Washington which took them to Southampton. The Olivegrove was sunk by a U-boat. One of these lifeboats, containing seventeen men, was towed ten miles towards the shore by the submarine.—*The bo'sun tells the story: Page Five.*

BERLIN PROMISES BLOCKADE REPLY

BERLIN (via New York), Monday.—In a semi-official quarter in Berlin tonight a vigorous counter-attack—presumably by submarines—was promised against the British blockade. Germany would take the following action, it was stated:—

"Draft a list of contraband goods similar to that announced by Britain;

Use every means to prevent war materials and foodstuffs reaching Britain directly or through neutral Powers;

Draw up a black list of commercial firms dealing with Britain. —British United Press.

NOT SO BLACK SOON

Daily Express Political Correspondent

POSSIBILITY of relaxing some of the severe lighting restrictions is being considered by the Government. Any relaxation, it is expected, will relate solely to public lighting.

As a considerable increase in street accidents has resulted from the black-out, the Government's expert advisers may suggest a resumption of street-lighting under proper safeguards. Motor vehicles may be allowed slightly stronger lighting.

Present restrictions on the lighting of buildings will be retained.

THE EASTERN FRONT

Nazi army tired out

Daily Express Military Correspondent

THE Germans have withdrawn from Warsaw, while to the south-west of the city a battle is being waged along a 180-mile front. The German High Command have admitted a reverse.

There are two reasons for the Germans' withdrawal — apart from the heroic resolution of the Poles in the defence of their capital.

One of them is technical, the other human.

The technical reason is that German tactics—the means by which individual commanders carry out their orders—sometimes conflict with German strategy, the plan of campaign of the High Command.

That is what has happened on the Warsaw front.

The German strategist always tries

CONTINUED ON BACK PAGE

STOP PRESS WAR NEWS

Central 8000

Gen. Weygand off to help Warsaw

General Weygand is preparing to go to aid of Warsaw. French Embassy in Ankara (Turkey) last night admitted that they could not refute news that Weygand was hurrying to rescue of Warsaw, but refused details.

He will travel with a Polish general.

Poles have saved their army, says Moscow radio

Moscow radio last night took favourable view of Poland's position, said:—

"The Poles have succeeded in saving their army. They have done this by manœuvring at night and fighting by day. All now depends on capacity of the Polish leaders. German planes are looking feverishly for new secret Polish air stations."

WARSAW PALACE BOMBED

Warsaw has suffered very heavily from extensive air bombardments in the last twenty-four hours.

Among the buildings destroyed, according to Polish radio reports, says Reuter, is the famous Belvedere Palace in the Lazienki Park, where Pilsudski lived.

10th day of the war against Hitlerism

BLACK-OUT TO-NIGHT 7.9

HITLER'S ADJUTANT MYSTERY: BACK PAGE

DAILY SKETCH
No. 9,476 MONDAY, SEPTEMBER 18, 1939 ONE PENNY

WHAT SOLDIERS' DEPENDENTS WILL GET

—PAGE FOUR

RADIO: PAGE 11

TWENTY-FOUR DAYS AFTER—

—SIGNING OF SOVIET-NAZI PACT

RUSSIA MARCHES

ARMIES MEET TO-DAY

WARSAW FALL NEAR

MOSCOW. – Russian armies marched into Poland at dawn yesterday to occupy the Polish Ukraine and White Russia.

Last night the Russian and German armies were advancing towards each other on an 800-mile front.

They expected to meet this morning—probably at Brest-Litovsk.

BERLIN—Warsaw has asked for German envoys to be sent to discuss terms of surrender.

CERNAUTI (Rumania) — The British and French diplomatic missions have reached here. High officials of the Polish Foreign Office also arrived. It was reported that Colonel Beck, Polish Foreign Minister, was among them, but this could not be confirmed.

LONDON—The Ministry of Information announced that the Soviet Government had informed the British Ambassador in Moscow that they will pursue a policy of neutrality in relations between the Soviet and Great Britain.

LONDON — Premier and Lord Halifax in consultation throughout yesterday on development of situation. Other Ministers also met.

MOSCOW—Warning of the Soviet march was handed to the Polish Ambassador on Saturday night. The text of this Note has been communicated to the British Ambasador. It says that the Polish Government having "disintegrated," the Soviet Government cannot leave its kindred peoples defenceless.

It was reported last night that there were no signs of serious resistance by the Poles to the Russian march.

ROME — Many diplomats here thought Russia's entry into the European conflict would tend to weaken the Italo-German alliance.

ANKARA — The Turkish Foreign Minister, it is officially announced, will leave for Moscow early this week at the Soviet's invitation. A new agreement is forecast.

CERNAUTI (Rumania) — German 'planes bombed the 50-mile strip of the Polish-Rumanian frontier yesterday, destroying a bridge across the Dniester.

Full Story, Page Three.

POLES PRAY FOR THEIR COUNTRY

News that their homeland had been invaded on another frontier found London's Poles in prayer. Their Ambassador and members of the military mission attended Mass at the Polish Church in North London. Here are some of them. Cardinal Hinsley was also present.—("Daily Sketch.")

NEWS CHRONICLE, Saturday, Sept. 23, 1939.

News Chronicle

No. 29,139 ONE PENNY SATURDAY, SEPTEMBER 23, 1939

POSTAGE IN U.K. CANADA, AND NEWFOUNDLAND 1d. OTHER PLACES ABROAD 1d

BARGAINS BY POST
See Page Two

Russia Gets Two-Thirds of Poland

Area of Poland to be under German occupation (shaded horizontally) includes rich industrial and textile areas of Silesia, Kielce, Lodz, Warsaw, Bydgoszcz, Bielsko, Sandomierz and Poznan, with Poland's only port, Gdynia. Russia's share contains Drohobycz and Jaroslav oilfields (1938 production 502,000 tons of crude oil), and main agricultural and forest regions. The Curzon Line was suggested as the frontier between Poland and Russia at the Peace Conference of 1919, which Poland rejected

NEW FRONTIER PASSES THROUGH WARSAW

How Poland was distributed in 1914: German (black), Austro-Hungarian (white), Russian (grey). Rumanian (vertical shading)

Stalin Gets The Oil; Hitler the Steel

RUSSIA WILL GAIN ABOUT TWO-THIRDS OF POLAND AND APPROXIMATELY HALF THE POPULATION UNDER THE AGREEMENT REACHED BY BERLIN AND MOSCOW ON THE LINE OF DEMARCATION BETWEEN THE ZONES TO BE OCCUPIED BY THE TWO INVADING ARMIES.

This line, announced yesterday in a joint communiqué, follows the rivers Pissa, Narew, Vistula and San and gives to Russia 96,467 square miles of territory and to Germany 52,584 square miles. The population in both areas is approximately 16,000,000.

The Soviet frontier now advances west to Modlin, the famous fortress at the junction of the Narew and Vistula, 15 miles north-west of Warsaw, and passes through Warsaw itself to the confluence of the Vistula and the San.

Rumanian Border Covered

It then follows the course of the San through Przemysl to Sanok and the Hungarian frontier near Lupkow.

Russia, therefore, occupies not only the whole length of the Polish-Rumanian frontier, but also the whole length of the frontier with Sub-Carpathian Ukraine.

The partition of Warsaw, through which the Vistula flows, gives to Germany the west bank, on which is the main city. Russia gets the east bank, where lies the suburb of Praga, about half the size of Warsaw proper.

In the north the Russian frontier starts on the Polish-East Prussian border, about 20 miles north of Novogrod.

Industrial Gains

In the industrial partition the Soviet has gained:

OILFIELDS: These are all in Galicia, in the Drohobycz area. In 1938 Poland had 27 refineries employing 3,200 workers. Total crude oil production was 502,000 tons. Refined products included: Petrol, 141,000 tons; oil, 141,000 tons; gas oil and fuel oil, 91,000 tons.

TIMBER: Poland's timber exports in 1938 were 1,689,422 tons.

AGRICULTURE: The fields of Poland in 1937-38 yielded 2,171,000 tons of wheat, 7,000,000 tons of rye, 1,300,000 tons of barley, 34,000,000 tons of potatoes.

Coal and Iron

Germany obtains all Poland's coal mines, all the heavy industrial area, including most of the newly-developed "industrial" triangle of Sandomierz, in which, during the past two years, Poland has invested large sums, and most of the textile regions.

This is what these acquisitions mean to Hitler:

HEAVY INDUSTRIES.—Principal coal mines are in Silesia and Kielce; main metallurgical centres are Warsaw, Lodz, Bydgoszcz and Poznan; armament centres are Sandomierz and Radom. Iron and steel production in 1937 (metric tons) was: Pig iron, 724,000; steel, 1,145,000; rolled iron and welded, 1,047,000.

TEXTILES: In this Russia, which takes over Bialystok, has a share. Main centres now German are Lodz and Bielsko. In 1936 Poland had 1,875,625 spindles and 61,351 looms in the cotton industry and 791,453 spindles and 13,520 looms in the woollen trade.

How Towns Went

The principal towns falling to the partitioning Powers are:

To Russia:

BIALYSTOK: Population 60,000; second only to Lodz as textile centre; specialised in imitation "Harris Tweed."

VILNA: Capital of mediæval Lithuania. Ceded to Lithuania after the war, but seized by

TURN TO BACK PAGE, COL. THREE

ALLIED WAR CHIEFS MEET IN "A SUSSEX ROOM"

THE Allied Supreme War Council met yesterday in a small committee room in Sussex.

Britain's representatives were: The Prime Minister, Lord Halifax (the Foreign Secretary) and Lord Chatfield (Minister for Co-ordination of Defence).

France was represented by M. Daladier (the Premier), [illegible] Minister of [illegible] Gamelin (Commander-in-Chief of the French Armed Forces) and Admiral Darlan (Chief of Naval Staff).

A Ministry of Information announcement says:

"Two sittings were held, one in the morning, and one in the afternoon.

"Developments which have taken place since the meeting of September 14 were reviewed, and their effect on the future course of events estimated.

"There was complete agreement on the course to be followed, both to meet these developments and to give effect to the Allied plans.

"The Supreme War Council considered the question of munitions and supplies, and agreement was reached on procedure for co-ordinating and perfecting the arrangements to be made by the two Governments."

POLICE GUARD

Police officers only were responsible for guarding the conference building during the meetings and the building at which the members had a simple luncheon.

M. Daladier and the French party landed at an airport and drove to the meeting place.

The British delegation travelled by special train.

The door of the room adjoining that in which the meetings were held was kept locked and detectives remained on guard.

TRAFFIC JAMMED

When the War Council broke up for luncheon, Mr. Chamberlain, with M. Daladier, strolled downstairs and into the street by a side entrance.

A small crowd recognised them and cheered.

"God bless you both,' shouted women. Both statesmen smiled and waved their thanks.

The French delegation returned by air.

News that they were in the building quickly spread and 50 minutes later, when the conference ended, thousands of people had gathered outside and traffic was jammed

BUTTER CONTROL

BUTTER supplies are to be requisitioned and the distribution controlled as from today.

This is to facilitate equitable distribution pending the introduction of rationing, announces the Ministry of Information.

An order has been made requisitioning all butter in registered cold stores in Britain, all imports of butter arriving and all butter manufactured in Britain after last night.

Requisitioned butter will be disposed of by the Ministry of Food through agents for distribution through normal trade channels.

West End Film Hours

THE Home Office last night intimated to the film industry that general opening of West End cinemas until 10 p.m. could not be granted at the present time.

It is, however, suggested by the Home Office that cinema owners might devise a scheme by which some of the West End cinemas could be opened until 10 p.m.

The film industry is considering this suggestion.

Madame Pilsudski

STOCKHOLM, Friday.—The widow of Marshal Pilsudski, accompanied by her two daughters, arrived here from Poland by air this afternoon, according to the "Aftonbladet." It is understood that Madame Pilsudski is going to London.—Reuter.

Dr. Benes and His Generals

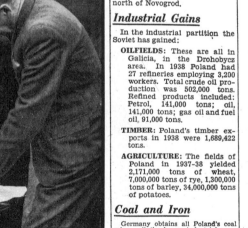

Dr. Benes in London yesterday with three chiefs of the new Czecho-Slovak Legion now being formed in Britain. Left to right: Colonel Moravec, General Serge Ingr, Dr. Benes and General Rudolf Viest

Unknown Submarines In U.S. Waters

WASHINGTON, Friday.

PRESIDENT ROOSEVELT startled his Press conference at the White House today by announcing that two submarines, "nationality unknown," had been sighted near the coast of the United States.

One was seen in the Pacific off the point where Alaska meets the Canadian border. The other was in the Atlantic off Boston, about 75 miles south of Nova Scotia.

There have been rumours before of submarines in American waters, but this official notice by the President that he had received "authentic information" is a very different matter.

The President's study was crowded with more newspapermen than I have ever seen in it before and the announcement about the submarines, though made by Mr. Roosevelt in an unemotional, almost conversational, tone caused a perceptible stir.

There were quick questions.

Were the submarines within the orbit of the newly-instituted navy patrols now ranging the United States coasts? The President said the patrols were operating along the coastline from its most northern point on the Atlantic side, right down to the Caribbean Sea, but there was no patrol at present on the Pacific Coast.

We tried to get more specific information on the probable identity of the submarines.

"Might they be Canadian?" somebody asked. Mr. Roosevelt brought this line of questioning to an abrupt close by saying "They *might* be Swiss."

We Are Now In The Fight

—Dr. Benes

DR. EDOUARD BENES, former President of Czecho-Slovakia, held a conference with two of his former generals and a colonel in a Putney house yesterday.

"My people, in every part of the world, are now with me in the fight," Dr. Benes told the News Chronicle.

"In my country the people continue to resist, and we who are outside Czecho-Slovakia will fight and work to free our country and make a new Europe. This pledge we will fulfil whatever the cost."

Dr. Benes will not serve with his army abroad but will remain in London, where his services will be needed.

★

Soon after war broke out Mr. Chamberlain wrote to Dr. Benes:

"The sufferings of the Czech nation are not forgotten, and we look forward, through the triumph of the principle for which we have taken up arms, to the relief of the Czech people from foreign domination."

LATE NEWS

Gasbags For Cars Here Soon

LONDON gas companies are preparing for the supply of gas in bags for commercial vehicles and private cars.

Arrangements will be made for filling the bags at the works and depots of the companies and at many garages and service stations through whom it is expected the bulk of the fuel will be supplied.

It is also hoped to make early arrangements with automobile engineers for the fitting of gas carburettors alongside the existing petrol ones.

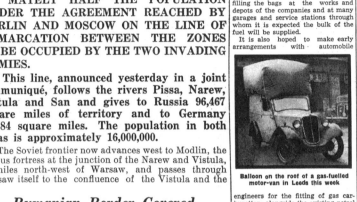

Balloon on the roof of a gas-fuelled motor-van in Leeds this week

Manufacture and fitting of the bags will be undertaken by firms with the necessary facilities, and it is hoped that the gas will be retailed at a price comparing favourably on a mileage basis with that of petrol.

Technical questions to be settled before supplies are available are now being discussed, and a more definite announcement will be made soon.

At a London garage last night I was given a rough quotation of £15 for altering a medium-powered car to burn gas (writes the Motoring Correspondent). For the use of compressed gas, a cylinder can be fitted to the car and the necessary alterations made to the engine for about £50.

BLACK-OUT TIME TONIGHT IS 6.57 TOMORROW 6.54

CLOSING PRICES

FINAL NIGHT

Evening Standard

Black-out To-night 6.27
Sunrise To-morrow ...... 7.10 a.m.

No. 35,910 LONDON, FRIDAY, OCTOBER 6, 1939 ONE PENNY

HITLER: COLONIES AND WORLD CONFERENCE

"Peace" Terms Are His Last Offer: He Wants To Make New Polish State

THREATS OF DESTRUCTION IN BATTLE: 'WE AWAIT THE ENEMY'

"IF THE ALLIES DO NOT AGREE WITH MY DEMANDS IT WILL BE MY LAST OFFER.

"ON THE WEST WE AWAIT THE ENEMY."

HITLER MADE THESE DECLARATIONS IN HIS MUCH-TRUMPETED "PEACE PLAN" SPEECH TO THE REICHSTAG THIS AFTERNOON. THE CHIEF POINTS OF HIS PLAN ARE:

The return of colonies—"the most important German political demand." This demand is not an ultimatum, and should not be carried out by force.

The colonial claim is justified by the necessity of a new distribution of the world's raw materials.

The creation of a just and enduring German frontier.

The various races throughout German sovereign territory and throughout South-Eastern Europe to be put in order.

The building up of a Polish State whose security will be guaranteed by Germany and Russia, and the Government of which will allow no intrigues against either of those countries.

THE GREAT NATIONS TO MEET IN CONFERENCE. IT IS IMPOSSIBLE TO CALL SUCH A CONFERENCE UNDER THE PRESSURE OF WAR OR EVEN MOBILISED ARMIES.

The rules of war must be rectified. The purposes of the air force, submarine warfare, and of contraband must be definitely fixed so as to make war less terrible for those not taking part in it.

After Hitler had outlined these proposals he said: "Should Mr. Churchill refuse this, then this, my declaration, will be the last. Mr. Churchill may be convinced that Great Britain will be victorious. I do not doubt that Germany will be victorious.

"MAY GOD HELP SO THAT MY THOUGHTS ARE UNDERSTOOD AND SO THAT NOT ONLY GERMANY, BUT ALL THE NATIONS OF EUROPE MAY ENJOY PEACE."

Other points from the speech were:

Germany has no claims against France and no claims will ever be raised against France.

There can be only real peace in Europe and the world when Britain and Germany come to agreement. "Never have I tried to oppose British interests."

"The present conditions on the Western Front cannot last. One day France will destroy Saarbruecken, and Germany will in return bomb Mulhausen. And so it will continue. More and more guns will be brought into the battle, and destruction will increase. Whatever the guns do not destroy will be exterminated by bombers."

Speech in full begins on PAGE TWO.

HITLER'S SPEECH

(See Page One)

Following is the text of the concluding passages in Hitler's speech:

"Later more remote aims will be undertaken and the air force will make its annihilating appearance.

"It will be a grim business, and this war of annihilation will not be confined to the Continent, but will reach out to the sea. To-day there are no longer any islands.

"One day the only frontier between Germany and France will be a frontier dividing graveyards.

"If, however, the attitude of Churchill is victorious, then we shall fight. Neither armed force nor time will conquer Germany. A November 1918 will not occur again. I do not doubt for one moment that Germany will win.

"Fate will show who is right. One thing is certain, there have never been in the history of the world two victors, but there have often been two conquered. May those reject my hand who are prepared to accept the responsibility for it."

Raising his voice, Hitler concluded: "As leader of the German people I can thank God that He has shown the justice of our cause in the first month and I pray Him to guide us further on our way."—Reuter.

CINEMA "SHUTTLECOCK" BEGINS TO-NIGHT

FIVE West End cinemas will open until 10 p.m. for a week beginning to-night. Next Friday they will close at 6 p.m. and another six will open until the late hour.

The two groups will take alternate weekly spells of late opening until further notice.

The following will open late from to-night until next Friday: Plaza, Odeon, Warner Theatre, Ritz and Rialto.

Next Friday and for the week following these will open late: The Pavilion, Empire, Gaumont Palace, Leicester-square Theatre, the Paris and the Forum.

On Sundays the 10 o'clock group will open from 4.30 to 10 and the second group from 2 p.m. to 6.

Ten news reel theatres in this West End area will open until 10 p.m. continuously.

The Home Office order was made to-day.

"Germans Do Not Want War," Says Officer

"The German people do not want war. I do not want it myself, but I am only carrying out my duty."

This statement was made by a German submarine officer after his ship had sunk the British steamer Blairlogie on September 11.

It was reported by Ronald Farrell, 19-year-old Glasgow University student, who worked as a cabin boy in the Blairlogie during the summer vacation. He arrived at his home at Hamilton to-day.

(Stop Press also Back Page and Page 11.)

French Thrust Again, May Outflank Nazis

ANOTHER "QUIET NIGHT"

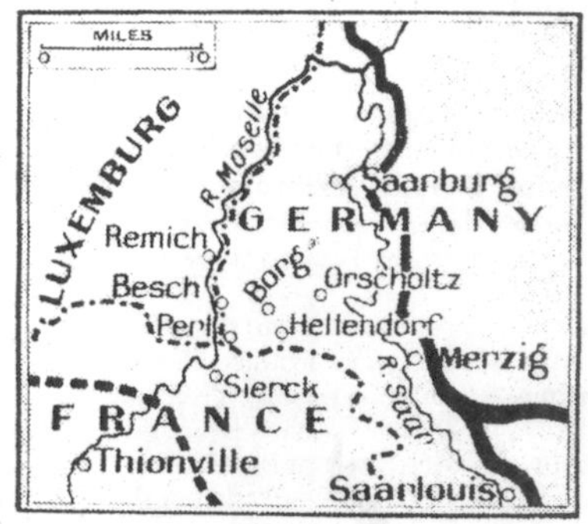

French War Communiqué, No. 65, issued to-day, says:

"A QUIET night. Patrols were active, particularly to the south-west of Saarbruecken."

A new French thrust in the Moselle-Saar corridor, immediately east of Luxemburg, is being strenuously resisted by the Germans.

By a surprise attack in the Borg district near the Luxemburg frontier, the French have succeeded in totally occupying the Borg Forest. Shock troops have now consolidated positions won in this area.

The French advance is a threat to any German plan to violate the neutrality of Luxemburg—to give themselves more room to manœuvre.

Moreover, should they succeed in reaching the environs of Beuren, which is about six miles from the French frontier, advanced works of the Siegfried Line situated further south risk being threatened from the flank and being taken at one bold stroke.

The whole pocket or corridor between the Saar and the Moselle would then be in danger.

Domination of this pocket, which some military observers believe to be well within sight, would enable the French to wheel round to the east and concentrate on a vast new sector.

In the district of the latest advance the French lines lie far beyond Perl. They fringe Besch, then follow the wood east of this village and on through the Borg Forest to the south of Orscholtz, ascend the wooded heights nearby and run on to the little hamlet of Hellendorf, south of the Orscholz.

(Reuter message.

Sunday Express

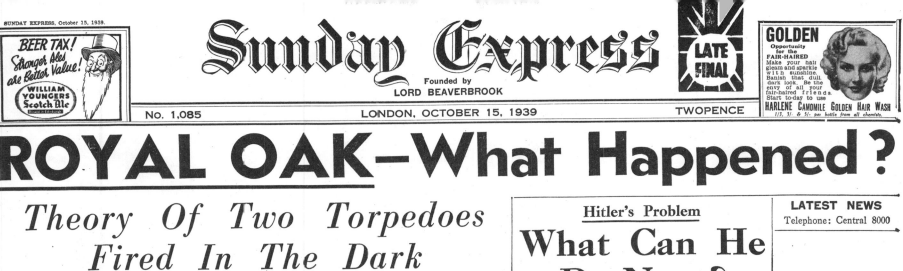

Founded by LORD BEAVERBROOK

No. 1,085 | LONDON, OCTOBER 15, 1939 | TWOPENCE

ROYAL OAK—What Happened?

Theory Of Two Torpedoes Fired In The Dark

How Did The U-Boat Get So Close?

By H. C. FERRABY
Sunday Express Naval Correspondent

ALTHOUGH the Admiralty yesterday still kept secret every detail of the torpedoing of the Royal Oak, it is surmised from calculations based on the time of the first announcement of the disaster that the sinking took place between Friday midnight and 2.30 a.m. yesterday.

THE TOTAL LOSS OF LIFE IS APPROXIMATELY 800 OFFICERS AND MEN. THE COMPLEMENT OF THE SHIP WAS ABOUT 1,200, AND THERE ARE 396 SURVIVORS SO FAR AS IS AT PRESENT KNOWN.

It is on the West Country that the tragedy falls most heavily. The Royal Oak was a West Country ship in every sense of the word, for not only was she built by West Country hands at Devonport Dockyard, but almost throughout her career she was manned by crews from the West Country port.

Where was she lost? How? Why? These are the questions that were eagerly asked throughout Britain yesterday.

For the present there is no official reply. The Admiralty possibly have sound reasons for temporary silence.

I can envisage circumstances surrounding the loss in which it would be quite against the public interest in wartime to make any hasty disclosures.

Silence, however, inevitably means Rumour. All yesterday Rumour was already running around with wild suggestions. I venture to contradict a few of them because they are wild and senseless.

The Royal Oak was not sunk by air attack. The Admiralty phrase "it is believed by U-boat action" did not satisfy some people, who thought it was put out as a cover for a bad air defeat. That is not the case.

When more details are available we shall, certainly, find that the Royal Oak was a victim of submarine attack. And in view of her construction we may expect to learn that more than one torpedo was put into her.

Time Of Disaster

How on earth could such a thing happen? The only condition under which I can see it happening is—darkness.

Some time in the dead of night a U-boat, with a stroke of luck, might find herself close enough to a battleship, say 600 to 700 yards away, to get off both port and starboard tubes at her simultaneously.

WHY DO I SUGGEST DARKNESS? THE ADMIRALTY ANNOUNCEMENT OF THE LOSS WAS MADE AT 10.30 YESTERDAY MORNING. NOW, THE ADMIRALTY IS VERY PROMPT IN ISSUING NEWS OF LOSSES DUE TO ENEMY ACTION, HOWEVER SLOW THE SYSTEM MAY BE IN GETTING OUT FULLER DETAILS AFTERWARDS. SO I DEDUCE THAT THE SINKING OF THE ROYAL OAK OCCURRED DURING THE NIGHT.

MAKING ALLOWANCES FOR THE TIME NECESSARY TO CODE AND DECODE MESSAGES AND FOR THE EXACT WORDING OF THE OFFICIAL ANNOUNCEMENT TO BE SETTLED, I PUT THE PROBABLE TIME OF SINKING SOME EIGHT HOURS EARLIER.

It is quite certain that the Royal Oak was not lost or even attacked at the time the Admiralty made its sensational disclosures on Friday evening about the sinking of three U-boats in one day.

That means that her loss was not connected with those sinkings. All those three U-boats, we shall find later, were lost some hours before the attack on the Royal Oak.

Why did the torpedoing occur? That is a question that will have to be the subject of a judicial inquiry. There will be much evidence to be considered before it can be answered.

Ark Royal Again

Germany had no news yesterday from the U-boat which attacked the Royal Oak. The German radio was dependent on the B.B.C. broadcast for its news. It was officially stated in Berlin: "We must wait for a report from whatever German units may have been involved."

The German radio then promptly trotted out its old question, "Where is the Ark Royal?" The answer, as they know perfectly well, is that the Ark Royal is afloat and at work.

With jubilant and screaming headlines across the front pages Berlin evening newspapers announced the disaster.

Commenting, the Boersen Zeitung said:—

"This represents another bitter lesson for those English circles who believe they can wage a war of starvation against Germany without much risk. In the great war our U-boats sank some old ships of line, but never succeeded in destroying a modern English battleship as now."

The New York correspondent of the Sunday Express cabled last night that German circles there were claiming that 70,000

CONTINUED ON BACK PAGE

(Survivors' List—Page Thirteen.)

'Bitter Lesson,' say Nazis

Night Of Alarm In Berlin

HEAVY gunfire was heard in Berlin coming from a distance late last night. Searchlights swept the sky. No air raid alarm was sounded, states British United Press.

As soon as the gunfire was heard the Berlin radio transmitters ceased broadcasting. Radio authorities said there was a "technical hitch."

Searchlights were switched off about forty minutes later.

The gunfire came from west of the city.

It lasted for about ten minutes, but searchlights remained very active for some time all over the city.

The sound of the firing was very distinct and the flashes of the guns were clearly visible.

After a period of quietness the firing broke out an hour later. The flashes were again visible, this time to the north of the city.

The gunfire ceased after about fifteen minutes. The Propaganda Ministry admitted that it might have been caused by enemy reconnaissance planes flying at a high altitude.

Nothing was heard in Hamburg.

The Sunday Express learns that the R.A.F. were not concerned in raid on Berlin.

It Is A War

Not one bomb has yet been dropped by either French or German airplanes operating on the Western Front, it was stated yesterday (says Reuter) by the French Ministry of Information.

Last night's French communiqué said: "Enemy patrols have shown themselves active to the west of the Saar, as well as to the south of Zweibruecken. They were repelled. Fairly active artillery fire to the south-west of Saarbruecken."

The King And Queen

The King and Queen returned to London last night from Windsor Castle.

Let's Send Them All!

Berlin radio said last night that the British Ministry of Information had opened a branch at Tokyo.

Hitler's Medal Goes To Lindbergh's Head

COLONEL LINDBERGH, honoured and decorated visitor of Hitler's, fervent admirer of Nazi strength, is now apparently developing the Hitler mind.

He declares that Canada has no right to go to war unless with the permission of the United States.

In a broadcast to the American people yesterday, he said: "I desire the utmost friendship with the people of Canada.

"If their country is ever attacked, our navy will be defending their seas, our soldiers will fight on their battlefields, our fliers will die in their skies.

"But have they the right to draw this hemisphere into a European war simply because they prefer the Crown of England to American independence?

"Sooner or later we must demand the freedom of this continent and its surrounding islands from the dictates of a European Power."

The repeal of the present arms embargo, he declared, would not assist democracy in Europe, "because I do not believe that this is a war for democracy."

Promptly there came this stinging reply from Senator Pittman, Chairman of the Senate Foreign Affairs Committee:—

"Apparently Lindbergh approves of the brutal conquest of the European democracies by the totalitarian States."

The Toronto Daily Star calls the speech "presumptuous, offensive and pure Hitlerian doctrine." It dismisses it with the comment "fortunately it does not represent the attitude of the vast majority of Canada's good neighbours."

Hitler's Problem

What Can He Do Next?

'Pale With Anger' As Pessimism Spreads

Sunday Express Diplomatic Correspondent

HITLER is all in a pother over the contemptuous turning down of his peace offer. Messages from Berlin yesterday describe him as "pale with anger."

The Berlin correspondent of the Swedish Tidningen says "the language used in German official quarters in abuse of Mr. Chamberlain" is of a virulent and vituperative nature, the like of which the staid Wilhelmstrasse building has never known before."

But Hitler's need for peace is so great that in a most unusual, un-Hitlerlike way he is apparently preparing to swallow the insult to his pride and keep on trying.

The explanation may lie in this comment from the Berlin correspondent of the Copenhagen Politiken:—

"German military circles are aiming at the earliest possible conclusion of the war, as there is no doubt that a long-drawn-out blockade does not fit in with their staff's calculations."

TURKEY LOYAL

All week-end Hitler is holding conference after conference with his advisers, who are said to be "at sixes and sevens" regarding the next most suitable move.

One of the points troubling them a great deal is this Istanbul statement quoted by Paris Radio.

"RUSSIA IS BELIEVED TO HAVE GIVEN TURKEY AN ASSURANCE THAT SHE WILL NOT TAKE PART IN THE WAR ON THE SIDE OF GERMANY."

The Berlin correspondent of the Amsterdam Telegraaf says: "It is especially among the army, navy, and air force that expressions of anxiety over the situation are heard." He describes the prevailing feeling as "one of pessimism."

What is Germany's next move likely to be?

This is the position as it is seen in the best-informed diplomatic quarters in London. There are four courses now open to Hitler:—

1. HE MAY MAKE ANOTHER PEACE EFFORT, THIS TIME WITH THE ALLIES' IRREDUCIBLE MINIMUM DEMANDS IN MIND;

2. HE MAY LAUNCH A STRONG ATTACK ON THE WESTERN FRONT;

3. HE MAY BEGIN A CONCENTRATED ATTACK ON BRITISH AND FRENCH SHIPPING, AND PORTS; OR

4. HE MAY SIT BACK BEHIND THE SIEGFRIED LINE AND DO NOTHING.

There is reason to believe that different trusted advisers of Hitler favour each of these plans. Which will carry the day is still a matter of doubt.

A "counter blockade," consisting of increased air activity against shipping coming to Britain, is thought to be the most likely development.

HITLER MAKING HIS WILL

According to the Stockholm newspaper Aftonbladet, people close to Hitler declare that he has drafted a political testament which is to be delivered to his designated successor (Field-Marshal Goering).

This document is believed to comprise some thirty typed pages.—Reuter.

Is He The Messenger?

MUCH interest was taken yesterday in the hurried arrival in England of Signor Bastianini, the new Italian Ambassador.

Lord Halifax sent a car to Folkestone to meet him, and he was whisked to London without delay.

Story and Picture on the Back Page.

LATEST NEWS
Telephone: Central 8000

RADIO . . . PAGE 2

DAILY MIRROR, Tuesday, Oct. 17, 1939.

Daily Mirror

No. 11,189 ✦ ✦ ONE PENNY

Registered at the G.P.O. as a Newspaper.

FIRST BOMBS ON BRITAIN: 4 NAZI PLANES DOWN

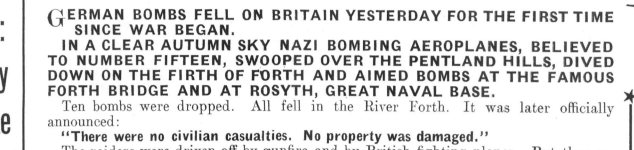

The Boy Heroes of Britain: A Story to Make You Proud (See P. 11)

GERMAN BOMBS FELL ON BRITAIN YESTERDAY FOR THE FIRST TIME SINCE WAR BEGAN.

IN A CLEAR AUTUMN SKY NAZI BOMBING AEROPLANES, BELIEVED TO NUMBER FIFTEEN, SWOOPED OVER THE PENTLAND HILLS, DIVED DOWN ON THE FIRTH OF FORTH AND AIMED BOMBS AT THE FAMOUS FORTH BRIDGE AND AT ROSYTH, GREAT NAVAL BASE.

Ten bombs were dropped. All fell in the River Forth. It was later officially announced:

"There were no civilian casualties. No property was damaged."

The raiders were driven off by gunfire and by British fighting planes. But they returned again and again to attempt to bomb their objectives in the river.

FOUR RAIDING PLANES WERE BROUGHT DOWN; ONE IN THE RIVER NEAR ROSYTH, ONE IN THE FISHING VILLAGE OF CRAIL IN FIFE, ONE ON THE NORTH SIDE OF THE FORTH NEAR FORTH BRIDGE.

Edinburgh first knew of the raid when anti-aircraft guns opened fire in the streets of the city.

There had been no raid warning. Men and women ran into the streets to watch one of the most thrilling air combats ever fought over British soil.

One Nazi raider, separated from his companions swooped low on the city, twisting and turning to dodge the bursting shells.

Once he came as low as 200ft. above the roofs, then climbed back to disappear behind a hill, followed by the bursts of white smoke.

"I was sitting at home with my sister," Miss J. Kerr, of South Queensferry, said, "when we heard the noise of many planes. I said, 'That's the sound you'll hear when the Germans come.'

"I looked out of my window, and to my amazement saw two big black aeroplanes.

"They dived on Forth Bridge and we saw the bombs hurtling down. Great spouts of water splashed up as the bombs fell, but the bridge was undamaged.

"At once our guns opened fire. Then British planes appeared. In what seemed only seconds they were on the tails of the raiders.

Trains Ran On

"One German plane rose straight in the air and swung back over my house.

"A British machine was above it, firing all the time. Then the German machine quivered and seemed to stagger away

All the time the raid was in progress trains continued their normal service over Forth Bridge.

Passengers in the 2.30 train from Edinburgh to Dunfermline were told at Dalmeny that a raid was on. Most of them decided to stay in the train. One, Mr. David Archibald, of Dunfermline, said:

"The train travelled very slowly across the bridge. Two planes, one on the north and the other on the south side of the river, dived over the bridge, dropping bombs."

Another witness of the attack said that two bombers came over from the direction of Rosyth and swooped low over the bridge. A bomb fell and a huge column of water shot into the air.

One of the German raiders circled and returned to attack the bridge.

"Two British fighters made to attack them,

Continued on Back Page

WARSHIP HIT IN ATTACK

OFFICIAL news of the raid, released last night, said:

"Today, October 16, between 9 a.m. and 1.30 p.m., several German aircraft reconnoitred Rosyth.

"This afternoon, about 2.30, a series of bombing raids began.

"These were directed at the ships lying in the Forth and were conducted by about a dozen machines.

"All the batteries opened fire upon the raiders and the Royal Air Force fighter squadron ascended to engage them.

"No serious damage was done to any of his Majesty's ships.

"One bomb glanced off the cruiser Southampton causing slight damage near her bow and sank the Admiral's barge

"There were three casualties on board the Southampton and seven on board the cruiser Edinburgh from splinters.

"Another bomb fell near the destroyer Mohawk which was returning to harbour from convoy escort.

"This bomb burst on the water and its splinters caused twenty-five casualties to the men on the deck of the destroyer. Only superficial damage was caused to the vessel.

"On the other hand, four bombers at least out of the twelve or fourteen were brought down, three of them by fighters of the R.A.F.

"The first contact between R.A.F. aircraft and the enemy raiders took place off May Island, at the entrance to the Firth of Forth at 2.35 p.m., when two enemy aircraft were intercepted.

"They were driven down by our aircraft from 4,000ft. to within a few feet of the water and chased out to sea.

"Another enemy aircraft was engaged ten minutes later over Dalkeith. It fell in flames

"Within a quarter of an hour a sharp combat took place off Crail and the second raider crashed into the sea.

"A third German aircraft was destroyed in the pursuit.

"Two German aviators had been rescued by one of our destroyers, of whom one has since died.

"No civilian casualties have been reported and none occurred in the Royal Air Force."

Not So Lucky..

Nazi planes carry this "Good-Luck" pennant — a Chamberlain umbrella broken by machine-gun bullets. Goering gives it to his airmen.

British Naval Win

A GERMAN warship was sunk in a battle with British ships and planes off the Norwegian coast, according to fishermen who watched the action.

The story is told in the *Gula Tidende*, of Bergen, Norway.

The fishermen, returning to the Norwegian mainland from Vaagsoe Island, say that the battle took place on Saturday. It lasted for two hours.

They heard heavy gunfire and saw columns of smoke, and through a telescope saw one warship engaged in a running fight with three others, which were British, and a number of aircraft. The lone warship appeared to be trying to escape to Norwegian territorial waters.

The fishermen report that the warship was badly damaged and seemed to be settling in the water. They think that the ship sank.

After the battle another warship arrived and the three other warships disappeared to the west.

"Repulse, Hood Hit"

The Nazis indulged in an orgy of naval claims yesterday. After the German Supreme Command claimed that the U-boat that had sunk the Royal Oak had "severely damaged H.M.S. Repulse and put her out of commission," the German radio claimed that H.M.S. Hood, the largest battleship in the world, had been "severely damaged" when aircraft dropped two 600lb. bombs on her in the North Sea.

The claim, already disproved, that the Ark Royal had been sunk was repeated yet once more.

A Correction

Later the German Supreme Command issued a "corrected" communique which said that the Repulse had been "torpedoed," but the effect of the alleged action was not given.

A note, issued on the authority of the Admiralty, said:—

"The Admiralty have no comment to make on the German wireless communique that the Repulse has been damaged and rendered unfit for action by the same U-boat which attacked the Royal Oak.

"Naval circles in London pooh-pooh this message, which is regarded as another typical example of German propaganda."

NAZIS OPEN ATTACK

On a front of about four miles the Germans last night launched an attack supported by artillery fire immediately to the east of the Moselle.

This news was contained in the official French communique, after a day of waiting for zero hour all along the Western Front (see page 2.) The communique continued:—

"They occupied the height of the Schneeberg, on which we had a light line of observation posts supported by land mines.

"Caught under our fire the enemy attack came to a halt and even had to withdraw to the north of Apach, in which village they had momentarily penetrated."

GESTAPO GAOL HITLER'S FRIEND

The Paris radio reports that Leni Riefenstahl, the German film star, and friend of Hitler, has been arrested by the Gestapo, says British United Press.

Fraulein Riefenstahl was chosen by Hitler to do the official film of the Olympic Games which took place in Germany in 1936.

DAILY MIRROR, Monday, October 23, 1939

Daily Mirror

No. 11,194 ✦ ✦ ONE PENNY

Registered at the G.P.O. as a Newspaper

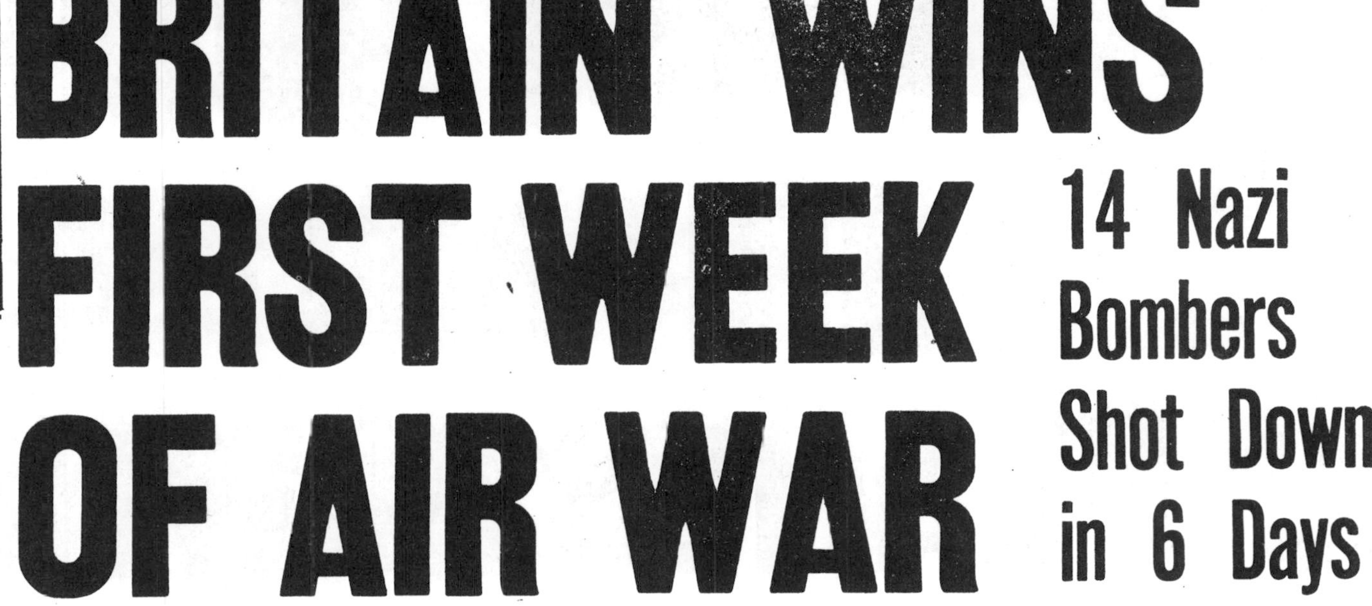

BRITAIN WINS FIRST WEEK OF AIR WAR

14 Nazi Bombers Shot Down in 6 Days

EVERY ENEMY AIR RAID ON THE BRITISH COAST HAS BEEN DRIVEN OFF WITH HEAVY LOSS TO THE GERMANS. ANOTHER NAZI BOMBER — THE FOURTEENTH IN SIX DAYS—WAS SHOT DOWN YESTERDAY IN THE SEA OFF THE EAST COAST OF SCOTLAND.

As sirens shrieked a warning to towns along the Scottish coast two German machines appeared.

At once British fighters went up. There was a furious battle in the sky. In a few minutes one raider was down.

A collapsible rubber boat was seen to leave the wreck.

And as British planes repulsed the latest attempt to raid our shores ships of the first British convoy to be attacked from the air arrived in port, with seamen who had a tale to tell.

They told of two different attacks at a convoy spread out to form a large target for bombers. Both attacks failed miserably.

Gunfire from the ships and the furious attack of our fighting planes, summoned quickly to the scene, brought down four Nazi raiders. The rest ran for home.

One of the eye-witnesses said: "Three planes dived on us from one side and two from another. Before you could say Jack Robinson the guns of the escorting ships started to rattle.

"Not one bomb was dropped. I think the Nazis were scared with the reception they got.

"Within seconds, it seemed, British fighters were above us chasing off the enemy

"I saw one of the Nazi planes caught by shell fire. It just fluttered its wings and dropped into the sea."

Nazis Poor Shooting

Another said: "I went to the gun station I had the enemy planes sighted lovely. I say I could have blown them out of the sky

"We asked could we fire. but were not allowed.

"If I had been at the breech instead of the sights I don't think I could have resisted.

"A vessel to the rear of us let fire as the bombers dived over us

"Talk about the pictures. It was the most exciting thing I have ever seen, but if I had been the gunner of a German plane and I could not do better than he did—well, I'd eat my hat, and I only had a fortnight's course."

Two hours later the enemy planes returned to the attack on the convoy This time only one bomb was seen to drop

"A Direct Hit"

"It dropped only one bomb," the same sailor went on.

"It landed not far from a warship I think and then—bang, the plane had caught a direct hit from one of the warship's guns.

"Our fighters were over us like lightning. think they must have scared the Nazi pilots."

A member of another crew in the convoy said: "The warship escorting us gave the Nazi planes ten minutes of hell

"They must have been scared stiff, but in two raids, only one bomb dropped—and it was the last that plane ever dropped."

"It was just an incident in our work." a member of another crew said.

"As a matter of fact, I had been asleep and just went on deck out of curiosity.

"If it is the best the Nazis can do to stop our convoys. then we have no need to worry"

Mr. Kenneth Luke, chief officer of one ship in the convoy, said:—

"At 12.30 p.m three German bombers appeared to the east flying very high and they dived down over the escort ships which immediately opened anti-aircraft fire.

"I saw one of the German machines lurch

Continued on Back Page

If I Go —Hitler Warns

HITLER conferred all day yesterday with the Nazi State Governors and Party leaders he had summoned to Berlin from all over Germany.

German officials in Berlin describe the meeting as "a conference of historic importance," and it is certain that Hitler was forced to reveal his desperate military and economic position.

For the British and French pact with Turkey has been a major blow to Germany. It strengthens the appeal of the Ribbentrop group who urge Hitler to secure Russia's active help "at any price."

There is no doubt that when the party leaders met yesterday, Hitler sounded them on the probable public reaction to a more pronounced pro-Moscow policy, and the general effect of war on the public morale.

It is known, too, that Hitler took care to share the responsibilities of the war.

"Stick Together" Plea

He told his party chiefs that the Allies seek an end of Hitlerism—and the death of Nazism meant the end of their careers. This warning that "if I go you go" was followed by an appeal to stick together in the hour of fate.

Hitler has already addressed his Army chiefs in the same vein warning them the end of the Nazi regime, through an allied victory, will be the end of the German army too.

In his discussions with his naval and military leaders and the ambassadors from Turkey. Russia and Italy, Hitler has given his assurance that he will do all he can to get the active help of Moscow and Rome without committing himself too far

But the Fuehrer had to admit that his attempt even to bring Moscow and Rome into a joint consultation has dismally failed.

NEW SOVIET-NAZI MOVES

A NEW and extensive trade agreement between Germany and Russia is expected to be signed in the next few days.

The Soviet Union will buy from Germany considerable equipment for the Soviet Navy and the mercantile marine.

This was reported last night after a Moscow announcement that a Soviet trade mission, headed by P. P. Tevosyan, Commissar for the shipbuilding industry, will leave for Berlin in the near future to supervise the transport of German exports to the U.S.S.R.

Herr Ritter, a special member of the German trade delegation in Moscow, left for Berlin yesterday by plane after the completion of the first stage in the Soviet-German trade negotiations.

A joint communique said the talks have been "proceeding favourably, according to expectations."

From General to Private

General Clement de Grancourt, whose last command in the French Army was over a brigade in Syria, has just rejoined the Colours as a private for the duration of the war.

NICE RAVING, DR. GOEBBELS

DR. Goebbels, Germany's Propaganda Minister, excelled himself last night in the maddest and wildest speech of his career.

He devoted himself wholly to an attack on Mr. Churchill. To listeners he seemed to "froth at the mouth" in his anger.

"We shall get you one day and force you to answer our questions," he screamed almost hysterically.

"None of your lies can make us silent," Goebbels shouted. "Don't pose to be a decent gentleman. Give an answer. A neutral witness, Henderson, gave clear proof that you ordered the sinking of the Athenia by three British destroyers

[Unfortunately the "neutral witness" happens to have the typically German name of Gustav.]

"And now my questions! How dared you to speak in your first communique thus:—Athenia was sunk by a German torpedo when you the First Lord of the British Admiralty knew that three British destroyers had sunk her.

"Where have you, Mr. Churchill, found these criminal witnesses.

"We know we can't expect to hear the truth from you, Mr. Churchill. This would be against your character and your nature and besides this truth would be the death sentence of your political career and therefore let me help you a bit, Mr. Churchill.

Goebbels then gave his "detailed account" of the sinking of the Athenia

"You took care," he shouted, "that American citizens should he on the Athenia because you wanted to have American victims of your crime.

"Acused. Winston Churchill. First Lord of the Admiralty. it's up to you now."

CONGRATULATIONS, DR. GOEBBELS—A MAGNIFICENT EFFORT. THE ONLY THING THAT PUZZLES AMERICA NOW IS WHY NONE OF HER MANY CITIZENS ON BOARD SAW THE DESTROYERS. PERHAPS THEY ON THE OTHER SIDE OF THE SHIP WERE. YES?

BLACK-OUT ZERO HOUR TO-NIGHT UNTIL 7.57 A.M.

Daily Express

WORLD'S LARGEST DAILY SALE

No. 12,309 — Thursday, November 2, 1939 — One Penny

Here is your BUTTER ration (actual size) for a week

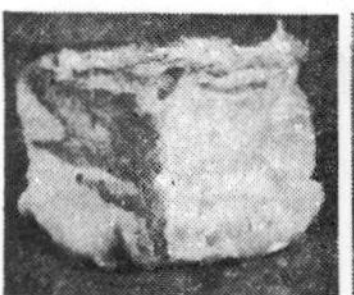
SUNDAY

MONDAY

TUESDAY

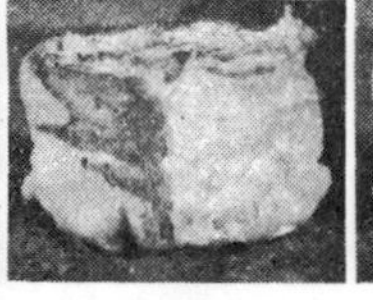
WEDNESDAY

THURSDAY

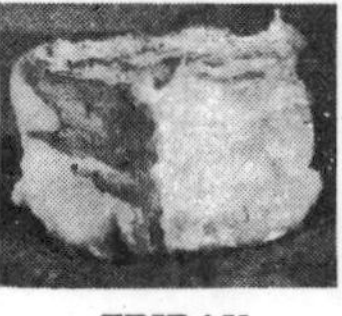
FRIDAY

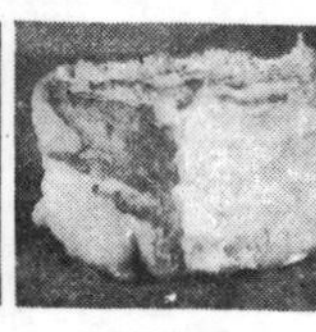
SATURDAY

HAM, TOO

Half a coupon for a ham sandwich

But none for butter in a restaurant

WHEN BUTTER AND BACON ARE RATIONED, HAM WILL BE RATIONED, TOO.

The rations announced last night will probably begin on December 16. They will be a quarter of a pound each of butter and bacon for every individual. That means a pound of bacon and a pound of butter for a family of four.

Ham will be treated as part of the bacon ration; bacon coupons will have to be given up from your ration book when you buy ham.

Margarine will not be rationed. Nor will pork, sausages, meat, or any other food—yet.

There will be three kinds of ration books—a general one for men, women and children over six years old; a child's book for children under six; and a traveller's book for people who do not permanently live at home.

TRAVEL COUPONS

A traveller who is away from home for most of the week will have to carry a special ration book, and the coupons used will be deducted from his or her family's allowances.

If you eat meals in a restaurant every day you will get more than your ration in butter.

No coupon will be required for any butter provided at a meal in a café, hotel or restaurant, as a fairly normal supply of butter will be allowed to catering establishments.

Housewives will have to register with grocers to obtain butter, bacon and ham.

Officially a ham sandwich will be a meal. You will have to give up half a coupon for it, whether you eat it at a railway station buffet or a West End snack bar.

FACING REVOLT

If you buy a meal away from home which includes bacon or ham you must produce your ration book and allow the caterer to tear out part or the whole of a coupon, according to the size of the meal.

Mr. W. S. Morrison, the Food Minister, faces a revolt over his rationing plan, and he may yet have to postpone it until after Christmas.

Broadcasting last night he admitted that there was no great urgency for the rationing of butter and bacon.

He said there was no need for general food rationing at present: "I see no reason to expect any shortage of meat, and I do not see any reason why we should at present impose rationing.

"There are many unrationed things to take the place of bacon on our breakfast table," he declared. "To replace any deficiency of butter we must turn to margarine. There is no scarcity of fats. The margarine now on sale has the same vitamin qualities as butter. You may call them 'sunshine' qualities."

M.P.s are sharply criticising his statement in the Commons yesterday that there were no Government

BACK PAGE, COLUMN SIX

RATIONS The answers to your questions

? How big a ham sandwich can I get for half a bacon coupon?—A sandwich containing two ounces of ham.

? Can I order bread and butter or a roll and butter in a restaurant without giving up a coupon?—Yes.

? Can I get butter without a coupon at a staff canteen?—Yes, at all catering establishments.

? Are fried eggs and bacon or fried eggs and ham exempt?—No, you must give up a coupon for them if you order them in a restaurant.

? If bacon and ham are rationed, what about pork?—Pork is not rationed. Nor are pork sausages, pigs' trotters, liver, kidneys, chitterlings, and other offals.

? If I live in London, my wife and family (evacuated) in, say, Exeter, do we register with two grocers, and what amounts of butter and bacon do we get individually?—Yes, you register in London, your wife in Exeter, and the ration is four ounces of butter and four ounces of bacon a person a week.

? If butter is rationed what about margarine and lard?—You can buy as much margarine, lard and cooking fats as you require, without coupons.

? What was the British butter ration in the great war?—Rationing began on February 25, 1918. Each person was allowed four ounces of butter OR margarine a week.

? What is the German butter ration now?—Between three and four ounces a person a week—when they can get it.

And this is how far it goes—

Butter ration is a quarter of a pound weekly. That is enough, each day, to spread thinly five slices of bread—each four by three inches.

Here's your week's BACON

Bacon ration is a quarter of a pound a week. Four slices—each a tenth of an inch thick. Four-sevenths of a rasher a day. In the picture, *left*, is a side view of a ration rasher "life-size."

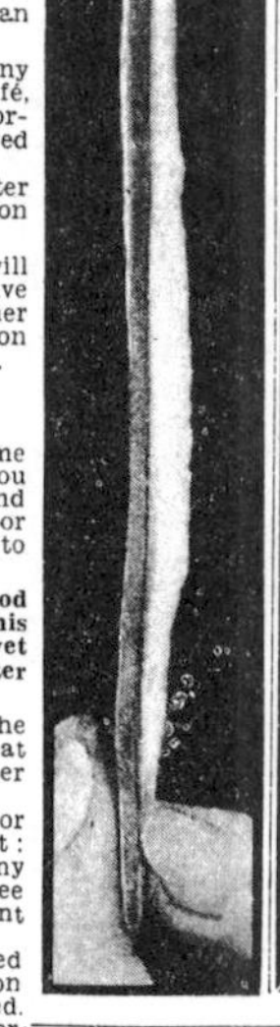

Treasure, 'spy' girl, found gassed

Daily Express Staff Reporter

A GIRL known as "Treasure," who is alleged to have said she was a German spy, was found dead yesterday in a flat in Alexandra-road, Kilburn, N.W.

She was to have given evidence today in a blackmail case at Birmingham. Her real name was Mrs. Mabel Muffett.

Lying by her side on a made-up bed on the floor was another dead girl named Williams, whose name was mentioned when the case opened in Birmingham last week. Both girls were about twenty-two.

Both "Treasure" and Miss Williams were in their dressing-gowns. They had been dead several days, apparently from gas poisoning.

Police believe that as soon as "Treasure" returned from Birmingham, they decided to commit suicide together.

Constables forced their way into the flat after the landlady had noticed milk bottles accumulating outside.

A number of letters found in the flat have been handed to the coroner.

"Treasure" gave evidence in a

BACK PAGE COL. FOUR

DANGER-ZONE SCHOOLS AGAIN

SOME schools in evacuation areas are to be reopened. Mr. Kenneth Lindsay, Parliamentary Secretary to the Board of Education, said in the House of Commons yesterday that in many cases it may be necessary to work a double-shift system.— *Details on Page Seven.*

Staff chief is to leave War Office

Lieutenant-General Sir Ronald Adam, deputy-chief of the Imperial General Staff, is leaving the War Office to take up a command.

With Lord Gort and Lieutenant-General H. R. Pownall, Director of Military Operations and Intelligence, this means that the three most important General Staff officers—the Cabinet's chief advisers on military matters—have gone away within two months of the declaration of war.

Nazi raider crashes

LUXEMBURG, Wednesday.—While watching planes raiding French territory, inhabitants of the Luxemburg town of Esch-sur-l'Alzette saw one machine crash.—Reuter.

Rooms to let to view raids

"PEOPLE in South Queensferry are letting rooms for week-ends at high premiums to visitors who take them in the hope of seeing air raids over the Forth," said Major Monteith Carstairs at Lanark County Council's education committee meeting yesterday.

4 a.m. EDITION

Finland mines port Soviet wants

"Independence is not for sale"

COPENHAGEN, Thursday Morning.

MINES have been laid at Hangoe, Finnish port at the mouth of the Gulf of Finland which the Soviet wishes to be ceded to her, announces the Finnish Legation in Copenhagen.

The channel between the islands of Hastos and Busoe has been closed.—British United Press.

Finland answered back over the radio late last night to the "malicious attacks made on the Finnish State in Soviet broadcasts."

Speaking in Russian from a station near the frontier, the announcer said Finland could never agree to a pact such as Stalin has forced on smaller Baltic nations.

Finland's Foreign Minister, Dr. Erkko, also broadcast to the Finnish people and to the 100,000 Finnish Army on the frontier that Finland's independence was not for sale.

"Stalin's demands," he declared, "may be a small thing to a great nation like Russia, but to us they are very big indeed.

"A way can and must be found for Finland and Russia to live together, but no pressure can change our resolution. The country is determined to defend itself."

Neutrals bark

"When our answer to Russia is published tomorrow the world will know how far we have gone for peace."

[M. Paasikivi, Finnish Special Envoy, arrives with the reply in Moscow this morning.]

Sweden, Finland's closest neighbour, and other neutral States come out strongly this morning against the Russian demands.

After last night's meeting of the Swedish Foreign Affairs Committee it was stated in Stockholm at 1.30 a.m. that a Soviet naval base on the Finnish coast would be a grave threat to the Scandinavian countries.

Norway's Government newspaper Arbejder Bladet sees the Soviet claims as an ultimatum which renders further talk practically useless, and continues:—

"It is not the spirit of Lenin that marks Russian foreign policy but the spirit of Peter the Great."

Russia buys rubber in U.S. for Nazis

Daily Express Staff Reporter

NEW YORK, Wednesday.—Despite warnings by President Roosevelt, Acting-Navy Secretary Edison and Assistant War Secretary Louis Johnson, the Soviet Union, through Amtorg, the Russian trading company, have bought up several thousand tons of rubber believed to be intended for Germany. Amtorg are said to be seeking 10,000 tons or more through New York jobbers.

That Man has "decided" again

'A QUIET WINTER'

MESSAGES from Berlin last night indicated that there will be no German attack on the Maginot Line until the Spring.

Hitler, it was said, has reluctantly abandoned his plan for a smashing frontal attack to restore German prestige.

The decision followed a day of anxiety for German army chiefs. Hitler, who has hardly left the Chancellery during the past two weeks, locked himself in his study and refused to see any one.

The Fuehrer broke his solitude only when he summoned his military chiefs suddenly for a one-hour conference at which huge-scale maps of the Western Front were inspected.

He studied detailed reports of the small-scale trial attacks on the French lines in the Moselle sector—attacks carefully staged by forces ranging from sixty to 1,000 men during the past few days under differing weather conditions.

Results of these trial attacks have convinced the German General Staff that a big-scale attack would be terribly costly.

It is expected that Hitler will now lay plans for a quiet winter on the war front and concentrate on new diplomatic moves to strengthen his position before the spring.

Tailpiece

While Hitler was planning a quiet winter for the troops, his own Nazi newspaper, Voelkischer Beobachter, was pressing on the nerve war—"Blitzkrieg for Britain."

The newspaper said yesterday:—

"Our proud young manhood are burning to deal those blows against Britain which are necessary finally to cure her of her presumptuousness, to put her back within the limits set for her by nature and her actual achievements."

*** Hitler turns hate on France, Page Two.

NUFFIELD JOINS AIR MINISTRY

Daily Express Staff Reporter

LORD NUFFIELD has joined the Air Ministry as Director-General of Maintenance, without remuneration.

Sir Kingsley Wood, the Air Minister, made this official announcement last night.

Lord Nuffield will be responsible for the vast organisation that is to maintain Britain's air strength, and he will also be responsible for repairs to damaged aircraft.

He has consented to go to the Air Ministry at Sir Kingsley's personal and urgent request.

His assistant, Mr. Oliver Boden, who becomes Deputy Director-General, has also given his services free. Mr. Boden is vice-chairman of Morris Motors.

The Air Ministry official statement says: "Lord Nuffield will be responsible to the Air Council through the Air member [Air Vice-Marshal W. L. Welsh] for the supply and organisation that have been established, and are in the course of rapid expansion for the repair of aircraft and ancillary equipment to the R.A.F.

'SUPERVISION'

"He will also exercise general supervision under the Air Ministry for the supply and organisation of the supply services of the R.A.F. with a view to their co-ordination with the repair services."

Lord Nuffield's co-operation with the Government in many departments of defence work has been increasingly cordial since the settlement of his dispute with the Air Ministry in 1936 about the "shadow factory" scheme.

STOP PRESS

MID-AIR MURDERER GETS LIFE-SENTENCE

MACON (Missouri), Thursday.—Ernest Pletch, twenty-nine-year-old pilot, who confessed to murder in mid-air of Flying Instructor Carl Givens, has been sentenced to life imprisonment.—British United Press.

61st day of the war against Hitlerism

Arsenal films stolen

SCOTLAND-YARD have been notified of the loss of a set of photographic negatives belonging to the War Department.

It is understood that the negatives were given to a messenger at a military establishment outside London on Tuesday afternoon.

The messenger had instructions to take them to an arsenal, but when he arrived at the arsenal it was found the negatives were missing from a roll of documents he was carrying.

It is believed the negatives relate to a gun.

WORLD'S LARGEST DAILY SALE

No. 12,315 Thursday, November 9, 1939 One Penny

4 a.m. EDITION

A defiant shriek "I'm ready for a five-year war!" then—

HITLER ESCAPES EXPLOSION IN A BEER CELLAR

6 dead, 60 hurt: Reported attempt with time-bomb

27 MINUTES AFTER HIS SPEECH

TWENTY-SEVEN MINUTES AFTER HITLER ENDED A HYSTERICAL SPEECH IN THE BUERGERBRAU BEER CELLAR AT MUNICH LAST NIGHT—A SPEECH IN WHICH HE CRIED THAT HE WAS READY FOR A FIVE-YEARS' WAR WITH BRITAIN—THE BUILDING WAS SHAKEN BY AN EXPLOSION WHICH KILLED SIX MEMBERS OF THE "OLD GUARD" OF THE NAZI PARTY, AND INJURED SIXTY OTHER PEOPLE.

HITLER HAD ALREADY LEFT AND WAS NOT HURT. HE LEFT EARLIER THAN HE ORIGINALLY INTENDED AS HE WAS SUMMONED BACK TO BERLIN BY IMPORTANT STATE BUSINESS.

The identities of the dead and injured are unknown, it is officially stated, says the British United Press from Berlin this morning.

Police admitted that the explosion was due to an "explosive body"—not to a defective boiler, as was suggested at first. The official statement says that the outrage was inspired by foreign agents, and a reward of £25,000 has been offered for the discovery of the perpetrators.

Munich-Berlin phone cut

New York radio stations go so far as to report that the explosion was caused by a time-bomb, placed in position by some one posing as a Nazi Storm-trooper.

Neither Goering nor Ribbentrop attended the meeting, but Hitler's deputy, Rudolf Hess, Dr. Goebbels and the Nazi Labour Front leader, Dr. Ley, were all there.

After the explosion, reports from Berlin said that telephone communications with Munich had been "interrupted by a disturbance." The Havas Amsterdam correspondent says they were cut.

The official statement issued by the German Ministry of Propaganda in Berlin this morning says:—

"The Fuehrer arrived in Munich yesterday in connection with the anniversary of the Old Guard for a short visit. Instead of Hess, the Fuehrer himself made a speech in the Buergerbrauhaus.

"Since affairs of state compelled the Fuehrer to return in the course of the night, he left the Buergerbrau sooner than was expected, and entered the train which was held in readiness.

"Shortly afterwards an explosion took place in the Buergerbrau cellar, killing six Old Guards and injuring more than sixty others.

"The attempt seems traceable to foreign instigation, and has aroused fanatical indignation in Munich.

"To ascertain the perpetrators a reward of £25,000 is offered."

Hitler has been a target for assassins ever since his rise to power six years ago.

In March 1933 twenty people were arrested and charged with plotting his death. Churches were occupied by police. Sewers were searched.

In June 1934 Hitler, alleging that he had discovered a conspiracy among his own Nazi Party, destroyed seventy-seven of its leaders in the famous "blood purge."

Since then many similar attempts have been reported, and there was a mass trial in which several hundred plotters were concerned.

FOREIGN PAGE DOG COMES TO THE FRONT PAGE

"Vot, mein Fuehrer has to five years' hard labour himself sentenced! . . ."

'We will never capitulate'

HITLER'S speech was a furious attack on Britain which reached its climax in eleven words: "The rest will be said in language that the English understand.

To his brown-shirted followers, who met again in the Munich beer cellar where they plotted to seize power in 1923, Hitler gave this promise:—

"No matter how long the war may last Germany will never capitulate.

"England claims to be prepared for a three-year war. On the day when England declared war on Germany I gave Goering orders to prepare for a war of five years."

Mad cheering could be heard over the radio as Hitler went on:—

"We have developed all Germany's resources down to the last detail. They will never lay us low, economically or militarily.

"There can be only one victor, and that is us."

The voice that, at the start of the speech, seemed tired and hesitant, was almost hysterical as Hitler went on:—

"Germany is filled with an unconquerable will. When Britain today says that she is fighting for culture and the freedom of civilisation, we merely laugh.

'Britain does not want peace. We heard that again yesterday. I have already spoken in the Reichstag, and I have nothing to add.

"Our strength against outside enemies is as great and steadfast as it was in our internal struggle.

PAGE TWO, COLUMN FOUR

MR. CHURCHILL declared in the House of Commons yesterday:—

"Our struggle at sea will be long and unrelenting, but in the end

WE SHALL BREAK THEIR HEARTS!

"I feel after the ninth week of the war that so far as the sea is concerned—and the sea has often proved decisive in the end—we may cherish good hopes that all will be well."

Full report begins on Page Five.

THEY'RE STILL AT SIXES AND SEVENS

The thin dotted line between Black-out and Light on Kilburn High-road last night at six. Shops on the West Hampstead side are open now until seven o'clock. Those across the road, in Willesden, are "curfewed" at six. *"It's like having one blind eye, walking down that way," says Hilde Marchant on Page Seven.*

BRUSSELS: Report from Henry Fast, Daily Express Correspondent

Holland fears attack is now imminent

HOLLAND is in imminent danger. Pressing demands have been made at The Hague by Germany. An attack on Holland was planned for today; it has now been put off, but only, perhaps, for a few days.

The Dutch answer has been morally the new peace appeal; materially, the opening on a large scale of the sluices which flooded some of the frontier regions.

There was little doubt yesterday that the peace appeal of King Leopold and Queen Wilhelmina was largely a diplomatic move to strengthen the international position of Holland and Belgium.

Such a move meets Germany's desire for peace, and the hope expressed by Hitler that neutral countries should offer to evolve a peace plan.

According to one of my informants Germany has asked Holland not only for military air bases, but also for the control of the port of Flushing.

These demands have been flatly refused by the Dutch, who have also told Germany they will resist

BACK PAGE, COLUMN FOUR

3 Kings join plea

KING CHRISTIAN OF DENMARK, King Haakon of Norway, King Gustav of Sweden, and President Kallio of Finland, sent telegrams to Queen Wilhelmina and King Leopold yesterday congratulating them on their peace plan and wishing it success.

Planes over Belgium were not British

BRUSSELS, Wednesday.

The Belgian Defence Ministry tonight said violations of Belgian territory by planes had been proved, and it was known that the planes were neither British nor French.

About a dozen planes flew over Belgium yesterday, it was added, and apparently took photographs.—Exchange.

French order U.S. guns

NEW YORK, Wednesday. — The French Government have placed an order for £187,000 worth of machine guns from the Auto-Ordnance Corporation of America.—British United Press.

Daily Express WARTIME NET SALE

THE restriction in the return of unsold copies which was imposed by all newspapers in October has had its effect on net sales.

Some newspapers have suffered more than others.

THE DAILY EXPRESS SOLD 2,521,061 COPIES EVERY DAY THROUGHOUT OCTOBER.

The Daily Express, therefore, not only continues to have the world's largest daily net sale, but is now the only daily newspaper in Great Britain with a net sale in excess of 2,000,000 copies a day.

Auditors' Certificate

We have examined the books and accounts of the London Express Newspaper, Limited, and certify that the average net daily sale of the Daily Express at the recognised trade terms or published prices (as defined by and arrived at in accordance with the instructions of the Audit Bureau of Circulations Limited) during the month of October 1939 was 2,521,061 copies.

Deloitte, Plender, Griffiths & Co., Chartered Accountants.

November 6, 1939.

City of Flint to sail

NEW YORK, Wednesday.—United States Lines tonight radioed Captain Joseph Gainard, master of the City of Flint, now in Bergen, Norway, to sail back to New York with her holds empty.

It is presumed that her cargo, which includes tractors and leather, will be sold in Norway.

R.A.F. BAG TWO NAZI PLANES

TWO R.A.F. pilots of the Coastal Command, patrolling over the North Sea yesterday, won a fight with three Nazi planes.

PILOT No. 1 reported by radio, "I have made contact with the enemy." One minute later his radio flashed: "I have destroyed one enemy seaplane."

Back at his base, he said: "The fight took place 100 feet above the sea. A Heinkel seaplane came out of the clouds above and behind me.

"He tried to get on my tail. I did a steep turn, and my air gunner and I got in bursts at close range. The enemy plane dived into the sea and sank."

PILOT No. 2 sighted a German flying boat at 100 feet and dived five times to attack. Several bursts of fire entered the flying boat's engines, and the rear gunner's cockpit was seen to be empty after the second dive.

After the fifth dive the flying boat went down, partly out of control.

The British rear gunner reported the approach of a second Nazi flying boat during the fight. The pilot waited till he had settled the first machine; then he turned on the second and silenced its front guns.

He made three close circuits while his rear gunner shattered the enemy's wings and engines. Then, without a bullet left, he turned for home.

Nazis send Rumania oil shares soaring

BUCHAREST, Wednesday. — Oil shares in the Bucharest Stock Market opened 16 per cent. above yesterday's prices, after having doubled in price in the last fortnight—because of attempts by Germans to corner crude oil supplies.—British United Press.

Britain fixes trade pact with Bulgars

A trade and payments agreement between Britain and Bulgaria was announced by the Foreign Office last night. The terms are set out in a series of Notes exchanged by Lord Halifax, Foreign Secretary, and the Bulgarian Minister in London, M. Momtchilov.

Dominion celebrates 100 years as nation

WELLINGTON, Wednesday.—Lord Galway, Governor-General, today opened New Zealand's Centennial Exhibition at Wellington, celebrating the Dominion's first hundred years as a nation.—Reuter.

ROYAL OAK SCANDAL

Who was to blame? SEE OPINION, PAGE SIX

Daily Express Naval Reporter

ONE of the five subsidiary channels into Scapa Flow was left insufficiently blocked. That is the incredible fact that stands out from yesterday's official explanation of the loss of the Royal Oak.

It is a solution of the mystery that no student of naval affairs considered possible.

The whole lesson of 1914 was that Scapa was vulnerable unless all channels but those actually used by the Fleet were completely blocked to all ships.

The two channels for the Fleet were guarded in the last war by nets, minefields, and electrical detectors. As the U-boats found when these were in place, it was not possible for a submarine to get in without the watchers knowing that it was near the channel.

To leave one of the lesser approaches incompletely blocked after six weeks of war was not taking a legitimate war risk. It was a gamble with the lives of the officers and men of the Home Fleet.

WHY THE DELAY?

It was obvious last autumn that Scapa might be needed as a war base at any moment, and the most immediate task was to ensure that the harbour was submarine-proof.

The secondary channels into the Flow could be completely closed at any time without causing difficulty to the small amount of traffic going in and out of Scapa.

It is an appalling thought that the provision of the necessary blockships was so much delayed that the war had been in progress for forty-two days before the last of them arrived.

STOP PRESS

FINNS SEIZE GERMAN SHIP

HELSINKI, Thursday. — The German steamer Ottawa has been detained by Finnish authorities as a reply to capture of the Finnish steamer Otava by Germans.—British United Press.

68th day of the war against Hitlerism

CO-OP BOSS IS ANGRY WITH THE DAILY EXPRESS

—See Page Twelve

WORLD'S LARGEST DAILY SALE

No. 12,333 | Thursday, November 30, 1939 | One Penny

Russia breaks off relations with Finland: Roosevelt offers to help, but half an hour later Molotov says:—

"RUSSIA WILL ACT"

Finns fear invasion this morning

SOVIET REPORTED MOVING UP MORE TROOPS

FROM HELSINKI EARLY TODAY CAME MESSAGES THAT THE FINNISH CABINET, AFTER DISCUSSING AT AN EMERGENCY MIDNIGHT MEETING MOLOTOV'S RADIO WARNING THAT "RUSSIA WILL ACT" EXPECT A SOVIET INVASION AT ANY HOUR.

Finland took Russia's threat calmly. There was no excitement or panic in Helsinki. At midnight orchestras were still playing dance music in the cafés. But the people were saying to one another: "Now it has come."

M. ELJAS ERKKO, *Finland's "Strong Man"—and Foreign Minister.*

The Finns are wondering where Russia will strike first. One report says that Soviet troops are being moved up to the frontier north of Leningrad.

Finland's Cabinet meeting was called after a night of swiftly rising crisis.

At EIGHT-THIRTY President Roosevelt offered the "good offices" of the American Government in helping to settle the dispute. At NINE O'CLOCK Molotov, Russia's Premier, announced over the radio that Russia would take immediate measures against Finland and that the Red Army, Navy and Air Force were ready for all emergencies.

At TEN O'CLOCK the Finnish radio, replying to Russia's denunciation of the non-aggression pact with Finland, said: "The Government suggest that an arbitration committee be called immediately if all other diplomatic means fail.

"Alternatively a neutral committee should be called. If either of these committees decides that Russia is threatened, or that Leningrad is not sufficiently safeguarded, we, in order to prove to Russia that we are prepared to do everything for peace, will withdraw our frontier guards to ensure the safety of the city."

NO TIME TO REPLY

At TEN THIRTY M. Potemkin, Russia's Foreign Vice-Commissar, handed a Note to the Finnish Minister in Moscow, Baron Koskinen, telling him formally that Russia had broken off diplomatic relations.

Baron Koskinen was not even given a chance to hand over the Finnish Note—the official reply to Molotov's Note denouncing the non-aggression pact—which arrived in Moscow yesterday.

Russia's official Tass Agency said that Baron Koshinen was told Russia could no longer maintain normal relations with Finland "because of the increasing attacks of Finnish troops on Soviet territory."

At MIDNIGHT Molotov's speech was rebroadcast to the world in Finnish, English, French, German and Swedish.

TWO MONTHS' TALK

Here are main points of Molotov's speech: "You know already that for the last two months negotiations have been going on with regard to safeguarding the safety of Leningrad and the Soviet Union.

"Instead of talking in a friendly way Finland has rejected all our proposals without any concessions. During the last two days terrible

BACK PAGE COL. ONE

IS there a man or woman in this country—poor, injured, destitute it may be—who does not know very well that the stake for which we are fighting is going to be for the benefit of every single citizen in this land?

—Sir John Simon in the House last night.

Bigger dole by Christmas

OLD AGE PENSIONS TOO?

By WILLIAM BARKLEY
Daily Express Parliamentary Reporter

SOCIALIST demands for bigger pensions and other State benefits were met in Parliament last night by a grave statement from Sir John Simon, the Chancellor of the Exchequer.

Possibly a small increase in old age pensions, charged mainly to industry, may be agreed. An increase is to be made in relief scales paid by the Unemployment Assistance Board —increases which the Board recommend, if accepted by the Government, will be operated before Christmas.

Otherwise, the Chancellor told Parliament that in a fight for our lives it is a delusion to think that all standards of living will not be affected.

'Not rich alone'

He cannot, he said, finance the war by soaking the rich alone. He faced the risk of "fearful strains and trials" as great in men and money as the last war.

Democracy, to win, must even do without rises of wages. Defeat would mean the rule in Britain of the German concentration camp and the German Gestapo.

In putting over the unpalatable case, Sir John Simon had a parliamentary triumph. His speech was sensitive, his manner ingratiating, his argument buttressed with such formidable figures that he dominated Socialist critics into silence without once raising his voice.

He began by appealing to trade union members who had most influence with wage earners to set the desires for bigger social services against his survey. This was under six heads:—

(1) Before September our ex-

PAGE TWO, COLUMN FIVE

2,000,000 AFFECTED

THERE are at least 2,000,000 people affected by Sir John Simon's promise to increase the "dole."

Latest returns, issued by the Unemployment Assistance Board in the middle of this year, show that the average number of recipients of relief at any time is about 585,000 but each has at least two dependants.

Applicants for relief are usually workers who have exhausted unemployment benefit, which is usually paid for about twenty-six weeks to thirty weeks after a job has been lost.

Hitler wants their gold wedding rings

AMSTERDAM, Wednesday.—German wives are to be asked to offer their gold wedding rings and jewels to a "Hitler Fund" to be used to pay for imports from Russia, say reports from Berlin tonight.—Exchange.

Home is the sailor—home from the sea (and the Rawalpindi)—Page Three; Cambridge talkers won't fight, and fighters won't talk—Page Four; Gentlemen, you may now swear (William Barkley's birthday message for Mr. Winston Churchill)—Page Six; "My Horrible Budget" (by Sir John Simon)—Page Eight.

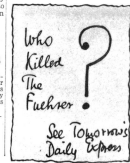

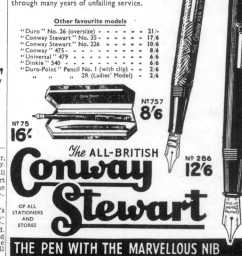

Who Killed The Fuehrer? See Tomorrow's Daily Express

COMBAT —BEFORE BREAKFAST

HERE, in pictures, is the vivid story of the battle yesterday, off Northumberland, between an R.A.F. fighter and a German Heinkel bomber.

The German bomber first appeared flying east from behind a bank of cloud.

The fighter pilot ducked back into the clouds for about thirty seconds. When he came out, the enemy was immediately above him.

The bomber dived and the fighter followed, with tracer bullets from the enemy flashing over his cockpit. He fired a burst and the German was silenced. He then closed in to 150 yards, still firing, when the enemy turned on his side and dived vertically into cloud.

A great column of smoke issued from the German machine. Suddenly the British pilot realised his own danger. In the gloom he saw the sea coming up to hit him.

Just in time he pulled up . . . and climbed again. He then flew home to breakfast. Searchers have not been able to find any trace of the German bomber.—*Drawings by Montague Black, F.R.A.S.*

AND YESTERDAY, TOO—*There was an air battle above a south-east Scottish town and over the Firth of Forth area. It ended in the flight of the raiders, hotly chased by R.A.F. fighters.*

4 *Nazi bombers out of*→ 6 *shot down by warships*

FOUR seaplane bombers out of six were shot down or made forced landings yesterday in a two-hour battle with a cruiser and two destroyers off the south-west coast of Norway.

The nationality of the attacked warships has not been confirmed. It is possible they were units of Allied patrols blocking any possibility of the pocket-battleship Deutschland's return to Kiel.

One plane, a giant German bomber, landed crippled off Mandal, Norway's most southerly town, and the crew of four were interned.

Four more Nazi airmen were picked up twenty-five miles west of Mandal by a Norwegian steamer. They were transferred to a Norwegian destroyer.

A third German seaplane with four men aboard was wrecked later at Suderoe, Faroe Islands.

And the crew of a fourth, in a rubber raft, landed at Stad, on the west coast of Norway.

People in Stad heard heavy gunfire in the morning. Crowds rushed to the beach and saw the warships' guns blazing to beat off bombers that swooped and dived and circled and dropped bombs all around them.

ARCTIC OCEAN · ICELAND · ATLANTIC OCEAN · Faroe Islands · STAD · Shetland Is · Orkney Is · NORWAY · SWEDEN · FINLAND · NORTH SEA · SKAGERRAK · DENMARK · BALTIC SEA · Kiel Canal · BRITISH ISLES · HOLLAND · BELGIUM · GERMANY · FRANCE · MILES 0 100 200 300 400

SAW SHIPS FIRE

The keeper of the lighthouse on the Stad Peninsula saw the whole battle.

On the telephone last night he told Selkirk Panton, Daily Express staff reporter in Copenhagen, that he first heard the firing shortly after ten o'clock. The ships were then about nine miles away.

"Through my glasses," he said, "I saw the ships setting up a terrific fire. But the planes dived low time after time.

"One destroyer had been hit, but it was still able to manœuvre and carried on the fight."

Three seaplanes, apparently crippled, then gave up the battle and tried to escape, losing height all the way.

Later he saw some of the airmen reaching land on rubber rafts.

Channel service has started again

After being suspended the Channel service between Belgium and England was resumed yesterday. One of the mail boats arrived safely at an English port last night with sixty-eight passengers.

R.A.F. MAN FLIES ONE-WING PLANE

'What a nit-wit I should have been—'

ONE of the R.A.F. planes that flew over north-west Germany on Monday returned, according to the story told last night, ALMOST WINGLESS.

Only the framework of one wing was left; half of the other wing had gone, too—damaged, it is said, by lightning or anti-aircraft fire.

Two young New Zealand pilots—one a schoolmaster, the other a wool buyer—were flying the plane.

No. 1 pilot says "a blinding yellow flash was followed by a big bang" when they were flying at about 2,000 feet.

The plane began to go round and round in uncontrollable circles and to drop at an alarming rate. Believing that they were going to fall into the sea, the second pilot, also the navigator, went aft to get the dinghy ready.

He then found that practically all that was left of the top of the port wing was the framework, that the fabric was stripped off the starboard wing.

When they landed, the pilot's right arm was temporarily paralysed. "The instinct of self-preservation pulled us through," he said.

"Anyhow, what a nit-wit I should have been to let her fall into the sea after pulling her out of that fall through space."

STOP PRESS

Germans say: We approve Russian aims

German radio at 1.20 this morning said:

"Soviet desire to have access to Baltic is understood here. Since last war Britain has hinted she has claims on islands in Baltic People in Berlin think that bases which were once Russian are more vital for Russians than for independence of Finland."

RAIDER OVER SHETLANDS

Unidentified plane, believed to be hostile, was seen over south coast of Shetlands yesterday. British fighters patrolled islands and plane disappeared in haze. No air raid warning was given.

Warship saves steamer's crew

Liverpool steamer Ionian (3,114 tons) has been sunk off East coast. All crew—thirty-eight officers and men—were landed at North-East coast port last night by British warship. Seaman Hendrikus McIntyre and Fireman George Young, both of Hull, were slightly injured. Captain William Smith, of Wallasey, was knocked out when saloon fittings fell on him.

Ionian, an Ellerman liner, was completed only last year.

U.S. FUEHRER GUILTY

Fritz Kuhn, Fuehrer of German-American Bund, found guilty of stealing funds of the organisation.

89th day of the war against Hitlerism

Ex-MP risks £500 fine

Sir William Lane-Mitchell, seventy-nine-year-old Conservative ex-M.P. for Streatham, S.W., took his seat from force of habit in the House of Commons last night.

By doing so, he risked a fine of £500, and caused one of the greatest personal sensations known in the House for some time.

For he is no longer an M.P. His appointment as Steward of the Bailiff of the Manor of Northstead was announced in the London Gazette yesterday morning. This automatically puts him out of Parliament.

Mr. A. P. Herbert was actually proposing a cheer for the ex-M.P. when Captain David Margesson, Government Chief Whip, saw the mistake and hurried over to Sir William.

Experts are now trying to decide whether a special Act of Parliament will be necessary to save Sir William from the £500 penalty.

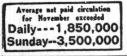

Average net paid circulation for November exceeded
Daily---1,850,000
Sunday--3,500,000

DAILY  NEWS

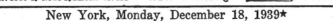

Copr. 1939 by News Syndicate Co. Inc. NEW YORK'S PICTURE NEWSPAPER Trade Mark Reg. U. S. Pat. Off.

★★★ FINAL

Vol. 21. No. 151 New York, Monday, December 18, 1939★ 56 Pages 2 Cents IN CITY LIMITS | 3 CENTS Elsewhere

SPEE BLOWN UP BY CREW

Story on Page 3

(Associated Press Radiofoto)

Spee Goes To Her Death

At 4.19 yesterday afternoon the Nazi pocket battleship Graf Spee steamed past these spectators on her way to a rendezvous with death. At 5.55 these same spectators had grandstand seats at her suicide. Flame and smoke rocketed up from the powerful vessel and in less than ten minutes she had been sent to the bottom by her crew. —*Story p. 3.*

DAILY EXPRESS. Friday, December 29, 1939.

BLACK-OUT
ZERO
HOUR
TO-NIGHT
UNTIL 7.56 A.M.
MOON RISES 8.21
MOON SETS 9.55

FOUNDED BY LORD BEAVERBROOK

NORTHERN EDITION

No. 12,356 — Friday, December 29, 1939 — One Penny

Women and children escape from bombed house

Morrison announces his new food plans, and tells housewives potatoes and raisins are good substitutes

SUGAR, MEAT WILL BE RATIONED

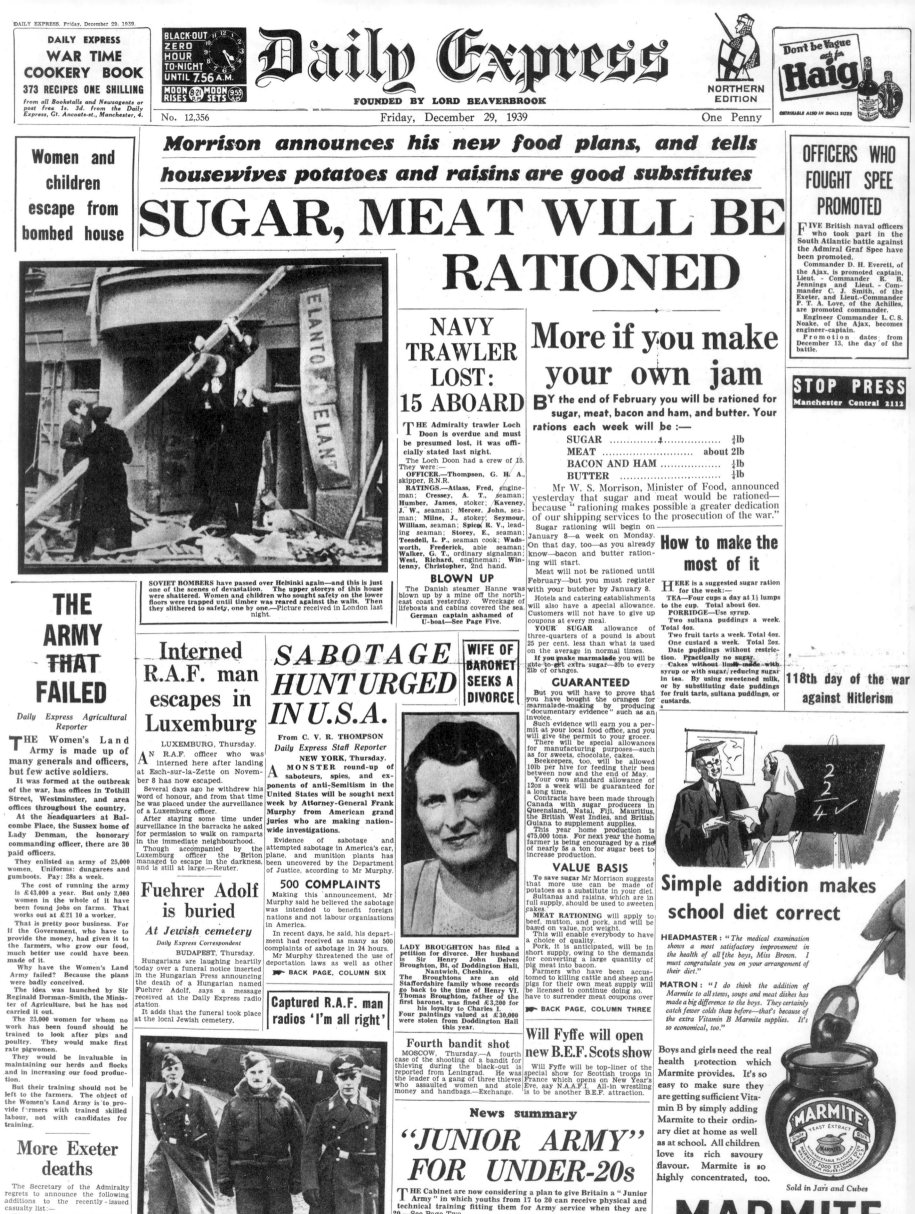

SOVIET BOMBERS have passed over Helsinki again—and this is just one of the scenes of devastation. The upper storeys of this house were shattered. Women and children who sought safety on the lower floors were trapped until timber was reared against the walls. Then they slithered to safety, one by one.—Picture received in London last night.

NAVY TRAWLER LOST: 15 ABOARD

THE Admiralty trawler Loch Doon is overdue and must be presumed lost, it was officially stated last night.

The Loch Doon had a crew of 15. They were:—

OFFICER.—Thompson, G. H. A., skipper, R.N.R.

RATINGS.—Atlass, Fred, engineman; **Cressey, A. T.,** seaman; **Humber, James,** stoker; **Kaveney, J. W.,** seaman; **Mercer, John,** seaman; **Milne, J.,** stoker; **Seymour, William,** seaman; **Spice, R. V.,** leading seaman; **Storey, E.,** seaman; **Teesdell, L. P.,** seaman cook; **Wadsworth, Frederick,** able seaman; **Walker, G. T.,** ordinary signalman; **West, Richard,** engineman; **Wintenny, Christopher,** 2nd hand.

BLOWN UP

The Danish steamer Hanne was blown up by a mine off the north-east coast yesterday. Wreckage of lifeboats and cabins covered the sea.

German captain ashamed of U-boat—See Page Five.

More if you make your own jam

BY the end of February you will be rationed for sugar, meat, bacon and ham, and butter. Your rations each week will be :—

SUGAR	¾lb
MEAT	about 2lb
BACON AND HAM	¼lb
BUTTER	¼lb

Mr W. S. Morrison, Minister of Food, announced yesterday that sugar and meat would be rationed—because "rationing makes possible a greater dedication of our shipping services to the prosecution of the war."

Sugar rationing will begin on January 8—a week on Monday. On that day, too—as you already know—bacon and butter rationing will start.

Meat will not be rationed until February—but you must register with your butcher by January 8.

Hotels and catering establishments will also have a special allowance. Customers will not have to give up coupons at every meal.

YOUR SUGAR allowance of three-quarters of a pound is about 25 per cent. less than what is used on the average in normal times.

If you make marmalade you will be able to get extra sugar—3lb to every 2lb of oranges.

GUARANTEED

But you will have to prove that you have bought the oranges for marmalade-making by producing "documentary evidence" such as an invoice.

Such evidence will earn you a permit at your local food office, and you will give the permit to your grocer.

There will be special allowances for manufacturing purposes—such as for sweets, chocolate, cakes.

Beekeepers, too, will be allowed 10lb per hive for feeding their bees between now and the end of May.

Your own standard allowance of 12oz a week will be guaranteed for a long time.

Contracts have been made through Canada with sugar producers in Queensland, Natal, Fiji, Mauritius, the British West Indies, and British Guiana to supplement supplies.

This year home production is 475,000 tons. For next year the home farmer is being encouraged by a rise of nearly 5s a ton for sugar beet to increase production.

VALUE BASIS

To save sugar Mr Morrison suggests that more use can be made of potatoes as a substitute in your diet.

Sultanas and raisins, which are in full supply, should be used to sweeten cakes.

MEAT RATIONING will apply to beef, mutton, and pork, and will be based on value, not weight.

This will enable everybody to have a choice of quality.

Pork, it is anticipated, will be in short supply, owing to the demands for converting a large quantity of pig meat into bacon.

Farmers who have been accustomed to killing cattle and sheep and pigs for their own meat supply will be licensed to continue doing so. have to surrender meat coupons over

BACK PAGE, COLUMN THREE

How to make the most of it

HERE is a suggested sugar ration for the week:—

TEA—Four cups a day at 1½ lumps to the cup. Total about 6oz.

PORRIDGE—Use syrup.

Two sultana puddings a week. Total 4oz.

Two fruit tarts a week. Total 4oz.

One custard a week. Total 2oz.

Date puddings without restriction. Practically no sugar.

Cakes without limit made with syrup or with sugar, reducing sugar in tea. By using sweetened milk, or by substituting date puddings for fruit tarts, sultana puddings, or custards.

OFFICERS WHO FOUGHT SPEE PROMOTED

FIVE British naval officers who took part in the South Atlantic battle against the Admiral Graf Spee have been promoted.

Commander D. H. Everett, of the Ajax, is promoted captain, Lieut. - Commander R. B. Jennings and Lieut. - Commander C. J. Smith, of the Exeter, and Lieut.-Commander P. T. A. Love, of the Achilles, are promoted commander.

Engineer Commander L. C. S. Noake, of the Ajax, becomes engineer-captain.

Promotion dates from December 13, the day of the battle.

STOP PRESS
Manchester Central 2112

118th day of the war against Hitlerism

THE ARMY THAT FAILED

Daily Express Agricultural Reporter

THE Women's Land Army is made up of many generals and officers, but few active soldiers.

It was formed at the outbreak of the war, has offices in Tothill Street, Westminster, and area offices throughout the country.

At the headquarters at Balcombe Place, the Sussex home of Lady Denman, the honorary commanding officer, there are 30 paid officers.

They enlisted an army of 25,000 women. Uniforms: dungarees and gumboots. Pay: 28s a week.

The cost of running the army is £43,000 a year. But only 2,000 women in the whole of it have been found jobs on farms. That works out at £21 10 a worker.

That is pretty poor business. For if the Government, who have to provide the money, had given it to the farmers, who grow our food, much better use could have been made of it.

Why have the Women's Land Army failed? Because the plans were badly conceived.

The idea was launched by Sir Reginald Dorman-Smith, the Minister of Agriculture, but he has not carried it out.

The 23,000 women for whom no work has been found should be trained to look after pigs and poultry. They would make first rate pigwomen.

They would be invaluable in maintaining our herds and flocks and in increasing our food production.

But their training should not be left to the farmers. The object of the Women's Land Army is to provide farmers with trained skilled labour, not with candidates for training.

Interned R.A.F. man escapes in Luxemburg

LUXEMBURG, Thursday.

AN R.A.F. officer who was interned here after landing at Esch-sur-la-Zette on November 8 has now escaped.

Several days ago he withdrew his word of honour, and from that time he was placed under the surveillance of a Luxemburg officer.

After staying some time under surveillance in the barracks he asked for permission to walk on ramparts in the immediate neighborhood.

Though accompanied by the Luxemburg officer the Briton managed to escape in the darkness, and is still at large.—Reuter.

Fuehrer Adolf is buried

At Jewish cemetery

Daily Express Correspondent

BUDAPEST, Thursday.

Hungarians are laughing heartily today over a funeral notice inserted in the Hungarian Press announcing the death of a Hungarian named Fuehrer Adolf, says a message received at the Daily Express radio station.

It adds that the funeral took place at the local Jewish cemetery.

SABOTAGE HUNT URGED IN U.S.A.

From C. V. R. THOMPSON
Daily Express Staff Reporter

NEW YORK, Thursday.

A MONSTER round-up of saboteurs, spies, and exponents of anti-Semitism in the United States will be sought next week by Attorney-General Frank Murphy from American grand juries who are making nation-wide investigations.

Evidence of sabotage and attempted sabotage in America's car, plane, and munition plants has been uncovered by the Department of Justice, according to Mr Murphy.

500 COMPLAINTS

Making this announcement, Mr Murphy said he believed the sabotage was intended to benefit foreign nations and not labour organisations in America.

In recent days, he said, his department had received as many as 500 complaints of sabotage in 24 hours.

Mr Murphy threatened the use of deportation laws as well as other

BACK PAGE, COLUMN SIX

Captured R.A.F. man radios 'I'm all right'

WIFE OF BARONET SEEKS A DIVORCE

LADY BROUGHTON has filed a petition for divorce. Her husband is Sir Henry John Delves Broughton, Bt, of Doddington Hall, Nantwich, Cheshire.

The Broughtons are an old Staffordshire family whose records go back to the time of Henry VI. Thomas Broughton, father of the first baronet, was fined £3,200 for his loyalty to Charles I.

Four paintings valued at £30,000 were stolen from Doddington Hall this year.

Fourth bandit shot

MOSCOW, Thursday.—A fourth case of the shooting of a bandit for thieving during the black-out is reported from Leningrad. He was the leader of a gang of three thieves who assaulted women and stole money and handbags.—Exchange.

Will Fyffe will open new B.E.F. Scots show

Will Fyffe will be top-liner of the special show for Scottish troops in France which opens on New Year's Eve, say N.A.A.F.I. All-in wrestling is to be another B.E.F. attraction.

More Exeter deaths

The Secretary of the Admiralty regrets to announce the following additions to the recently-issued casualty list:—

H.M.S. Duchess.—Missing, believed drowned: Anderson, R. H., ordinary seaman, C/SSX 21970.

H.M.S. Exeter.—Previously reported as wounded in action, now reported as having died of wounds: Legg, Frank, P.O. cook, D/M 52427; Powton, F. G., chief P.O. cook, D/M 37983; Collins, Anthony C. P., chief shipwright, 2nd class, D/M 14336.

SERGEANT H. ROUSE (centre), of the R.A.F., pictured in Germany with his Nazi guards. He was captured after the war's biggest air battle over Heligoland when 12 German planes were brought down. Sergeant Rouse made a forced landing on an island off the north German coast. Last night Hamburg broadcast a message from him, sending his love to his mother and telling her that he was uninjured.

News summary

"JUNIOR ARMY" FOR UNDER-20s

THE Cabinet are now considering a plan to give Britain a "Junior Army" in which youths from 17 to 20 can receive physical and technical training fitting them for Army service when they are 20.—See Page Two.

THE Government of Eire last night offered a reward of £1,000 for information leading to the recovery of the ammunition stolen by armed raiders from the arsenal in Phœnix Park, Dublin.—**Page Eight.**

HILDE MARCHANT talks to the man who looks like Hitler.—**Page Five.**

A STOCKTON-ON-TEES aircraftman heard by telegram yesterday that he had become the youngest D.F.M. in Britain. Story and picture—**Page Five.**

ANOTHER 60,000 civil servants are to leave London for the provinces.—**Page Five.**

THOUSANDS of wool workers may lose their jobs in the height of the greatest textile boom since the last war.—**Page Five.**

BLACK OUT
ZERO
HOUR
TO-NIGHT
UNTIL 7.37 A.M.
MOON RISES 4.54 A.M.
MOON SETS 1.52 P.M.

No. 12,363 Saturday, January 6, 1940 One Penny

SENSATIONAL GOVERNMENT CHANGES

NEW MINISTER FOR WAR Mr. Oliver Stanley

former President of the Board of Trade.

NEW INFORMATION MINISTER Sir John Reith

former Imperial Airways and B.B.C. chief.

NEW BOARD of TRADE PRESIDENT Sir Andrew Duncan

former chief of four big industries.

We hired the money: they hired the soldiers

by Lord Beaverbrook

Page Six

HORE-BELISHA RESIGNS

Generals resented his drastic reforms

By GUY EDEN
Daily Express Political Correspondent

MR. LESLIE HORE-BELISHA, WAR MINISTER, RESIGNED FROM THE WAR CABINET LAST NIGHT. MR. OLIVER STANLEY, PRESIDENT OF THE BOARD OF TRADE, SUCCEEDS HIM.

Refusing the offer by the Prime Minister of the post of President of the Board of Trade—outside the Cabinet—Mr. Hore-Belisha is leaving the Government altogether.

The news of Mr. Hore-Belisha's dismissal will come as a great shock to the public this morning, for there had been not the least idea that he was not in the highest favour.

Then why did he resign?

That is the question the whole country will be asking.

And this is the answer:—

The generals were displeased with him. They objected to his reforms, and also to his drastic changes, in the face of opposition, which they say created resentment.

So they made representations to the Prime Minister, who still retains his confidence in Mr. Hore-Belisha, as his letter accepting the War Minister's resignation shows.

Mr. Chamberlain says he is an admirer of Mr. Hore-Belisha's work. But he felt himself unable to resist the pressure, and in a Cabinet "reconstruction" offered a post of lesser importance.

POPULAR WITH PUBLIC

Most observers thought Mr. Hore-Belisha sure to retain his office for the duration of the war. In the public estimation he stood higher than any Minister save one—Mr. Winston Churchill.

Mr. Hore-Belisha was looked on as second man in the War Cabinet for energy and drive—whether his judgment was good or not. Some thought he was the best of the Government's team of broadcasters, and it was felt that his ability in this was of great advantage to the Government.

Before he went to the War Office his success as Minister of Transport was greatly admired, and in the office he gave up last night he had a fine record of achievement.

He brought about the dismissal of the old generals. He doubled the Territorial Army. He was right about the need for conscription—and got it through Parliament.

He popularised the Army. He raised the Army's pay. He improved the marriage allowances.

HE PROPHESIED WAR

And the confidence the public felt in his administration at the War Office was due largely to the fact that he rightly prophesied war. They believed that, since he prophesied war, he had prepared for it.

The public astonishment will not be lessened by the announcement that Mr. Oliver Stanley is to go from the Presidency of the Board of Trade to succeed Mr. Hore-Belisha as War Secretary and a member of the War Cabinet.

Sir Andrew Rae Duncan is to be the new President of the Board of Trade, and Sir John Reith will be Minister of Information, in place of Lord Macmillan, whose resignation was also announced last night.

Neither Sir Andrew nor Sir John has a seat in Parliament. I understand a seat in the House of Commons will probably be found for Sir John Reith, and that Sir Andrew may accept a peerage.

But interest will continue to centre in the position of Mr. Hore-Belisha. As soon as Parliament reassembles—and it was

BACK PAGE, COLUMN FIVE

He says 'CANNOT TAKE NEW JOB'

HERE is Mr. Hore-Belisha's letter of resignation (dated yesterday) to the Prime Minister.

My dear Prime Minister,

I wish I had felt able to accept the important office which you have been good enough to offer me in your reconstructed Government, but for the reasons I gave to you verbally this morning, I regretfully cannot see my way to do so.

I shall, however, naturally, give all the support in my power to the firmest conduct of the war until it is brought to a successful issue. I am glad to think that there is no difference of policy between us.

On the personal side, I recall the kindness you have shown to me in our relationship during the many years we have been together.

In my work, particularly at the War Office, I have relied on your understanding co-operation in the inspiring task of reorganising and preparing the Army for war.

Yours very sincerely,
(Signed)
Leslie Hore-Belisha.

PREMIER'S REPLY—

MY dear Leslie,

It was with very great regret that I received your decision not to accept the office which I offered you in the course of the reconstruction of the Government which I have in hand.

At the same time, I fully understand and respect the reasons you gave me.

I should like now to pay my sincere tribute to your work at the War Office, and to the important reforms you have carried out.

It is a great satisfaction to me that there is not now, and never has been, any difference between us on policy, and in particular on the necessity for prosecuting the war with the utmost determination to a successful issue.

I should like also to thank you for the loyal support you have always given me, and for those pleasant personal relations which have characterised our association over so many years.

Yours ever,
(Signed)
Neville Chamberlain.

Macmillan says 'JOB WAS FULL OF PROMISE'

THIS is the letter Lord Macmillan sent to the Premier yesterday from the Ministry of Information:—

My dear Prime Minister,—

You have been good enough to tell me that impending changes which you have in view, as well as the embarrassment which has been caused by the fact that I have not a seat in the House of Commons, render it expedient that I should place my appointment at your disposal.

I should not for a moment stand in the way of any step which would promote the efficiency of the Ministry, and I readily leave myself in your hands.

I confess that it is with some regret that I relinquish the task which you did me the honour to entrust to me at the outbreak of the war, for I have found it most interesting, and latterly full of the promise of increasing usefulness. But I shall always recall with pleasure my brief experience of office under you.

Yours sincerely,
(Signed) Macmillan.

The Premier's reply is on Back Page.

MR. STANLEY HAS 'FLU

MR. OLIVER STANLEY was not receiving visitors last night. He lay upstairs in his Westminster home, a 'flu victim. His butler shepherded away callers. "Mr. Stanley is indisposed," he replied, when a Daily Express reporter asked to see him, "but you can tell people he's going on all right."

★

Mr. Stanley is taking on the job his father, Lord Derby, held from 1916 to 1918, and from 1922 to 1924.

Two earlier members of the family also held the office—Lord Stanley of Bickerstaffe, Earl of Derby, in 1833 and 1841, and Lord Stanley of Preston, Earl of Derby, in 1878.

GERMANY reports it WITHOUT COMMENT

NEWS of Mr. Hore-Belisha's resignation was given to the German public last night fifteen minutes after the announcement had been released in London for publication abroad.

No comment was added, even in broadcasts early this morning.

AMERICA says— 'The biggest bombshell'

A New York message last night described Mr. Hore-Belisha's resignation as "The biggest political bombshell of the war."

Canada not told

OTTAWA, Friday Night. — The changes in the British Government caused surprise in Ottawa tonight. The Canadian Government, it is said, were not advised that any changes were impending. — British United Press.

WILLIAM POWELL MARRIES BEAUTY AGED 20

Daily Express Staff Reporter

NEW YORK, Friday.

WILLIAM POWELL, forty-seven-year-old screen star of "Thin Man" fame, went off today to Hidden Well Ranch, near Las Vegas, Nevada, and married Diana Lewis, film beauty, aged twenty.

This is Powell's third marriage. It took Hollywood by surprise, although it was known that the couple had recently been dining and dancing together.

Miss Lewis is petite, auburn-haired, and blue-eyed.

She was married in a printed flower dress, with a turban to match, and Powell wore a grey sports suit and a blue sweater.

Powell was formerly husband of Carole Lombard, who was his second wife. The marriage was dissolved in 1933. He was later reported to be engaged to Jean Harlow, and when she died in 1937 he had a nervous breakdown.

Picture of the new Mrs. Powell—Page Seven.

Busmen get 4/- a week more pay

LONDON TRANSPORT BOARD'S 50,000 workers are to receive more pay. Men will get 4s. more under a new agreement reached last night. Women will get lesser increases.
—See *PAGE SEVEN.*

FINNS admit Russian push to the West.—*PAGE TWO.*

MAYFAIR-in-the-Shires is doing its bit to entertain the troops.—*PAGE THREE.*

WEST END club had girl of fourteen as dance hostess.—*PAGE FOUR.*

O. D. GALLAGHER tells the story of the Black Watch on Western Front patrol.—*PAGE FIVE.*

THE MEDAL which ranks next to the V.C. is one which hardly anybody knows. Its name is on—*PAGE SEVEN.*

SHOW GIRL loses two jobs trying to help her mother—*PAGE ELEVEN.*

STOP PRESS

SEARCH FOR SOLDIER IN BLAZING HUTS

When huts at military camp in eastern counties town caught fire at midnight, search was made for a lance-bombardier understood to be trapped in one of huts.

U.S.-ARGENTINA TRADE TALKS FAIL

BUENOS AIRES, Saturday.—Officially announced negotiations for trade agreement between Argentina and United States have broken down following imposition by United States of restrictions on Argentine products.—Reuter.

Four children drowned

Four children were drowned yesterday afternoon in a pool not far from their home at Coseley, near Wolverhampton—Desmond Gordon Fletcher, aged eight; his sister Irene, aged ten; Joseph Gerald Flavell, aged nine, and Norman Fellows, aged thirteen.

Arthur Edwin Bennett, aged fifteen, dived into the pool, found one child, and applied artificial respiration in vain. Police found the three other children.

BLACK-OUT ZERO HOUR TO-NIGHT UNTIL 6.49 A.M.
MOON RISES 9.0 A.M. MOON SETS 11.45 P.M.

Daily Express

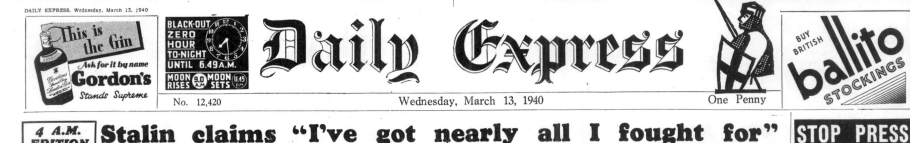

No. 12,420 | Wednesday, March 13, 1940 | One Penny

4 A.M. EDITION

Stalin claims "I've got nearly all I fought for"

REDS "CEASE FIRE" AT NOON TODAY

Karelian Isthmus ceded, Hangoe base leased

WILL FINN M.P.s AGREE?

MOSCOW ANNOUNCED EARLY THIS MORNING THAT THE WAR IN FINLAND, WHICH BEGAN WITH THE SOVIET ARMY'S INVASION 104 DAYS AGO, WILL END AT MIDDAY TODAY.

Although Helsinki so far has not confirmed it, Moscow claims that a peace treaty has been signed with Finland. Under it Stalin gets almost everything he demanded when he went to war.

The Karelian Isthmus (where Finland's main defences stand) and the long defended city of Viipuri, with the whole shore of Lake Ladoga, are ceded to Russia.

Hangoe, Finland's Gibraltar (main demand made by Stalin and from which he has never deviated), is leased to Russia for thirty years.

Russia is given free transit rights through Petsamo into Norway.

The new frontiers are to be fixed within ten days.

Soviet planes can fly across northern Finland to Norway without interference.

All Stalin has not got is actual possession of Petsamo. The old non-aggression pact is resurrected.

Will the Finnish Parliament agree? At two o'clock this morning they were still debating the terms. A five-eighths majority is needed for ratification.

Stalin's terms in full

MOSCOW radio interrupted a special concert at three o'clock this morning to announce the signing of the treaty at 2.30 a.m. These are the terms :—

1 Military operations shall cease at once.

2 Finland to cede the whole of the Karelian Isthmus, with the city of Viipuri, the whole of Viipuri Bay with its islands, the territory west and north of Lake Ladoga, including the towns of Kakisalmi, Sortavala and Suojaervi, the territory north of Markajaervi and Kuolajaervi, and a number of islands in the Gulf of Finland.

3 The precise line of the frontier to be fixed by a joint commission within ten days after the signing of the treaty.

4 Both countries give a pledge of non-aggression against each other, and pledge not to conclude any alliances or to take part in any coalitions directed against the other signatory.

5 Finland to lease to Russia the peninsula of Hangoe for thirty years, with the area five miles south and east of Hangoe and three miles west and north of Hangoe, with all islands situated in this area, for a yearly payment of £38,000.

6 Finland agrees to the establishment at Hangoe of a Soviet military base for protective purposes, in accordance with which Russia has the right to place there a number of troops and air units.

Finland to remove all her troops from the peninsula of Hangoe within ten days, after which it is to come under Soviet administration.

7 Russia obtains the right of free transit through the Petsamo region into Norway and back, and the establishment of a consulate at Petsamo. Goods from Russia to Norway, or from Norway to Russia, which are sent through Petsamo are to be free of transit duties.

8 Soviet non-military planes obtain the right of free movement over the Petsamo region for the purpose of communication between Russia and Norway.

9 Russia agrees to withdraw all her troops from the Petsamo area.

Finland must not keep in the waters of Petsamo more than fifteen war vessels up to 400 tons each, any submarines or warplanes, and must not build any naval bases or shipyards beyond what are necessary for the upkeep of the warships situated there.

10 Finland agrees to grant a right of way between Russia and Sweden by the shortest route. For this purpose a new railway is to be built jointly by the two countries, possibly during 1940, between Kandalaksha (Russian White Sea port) and Kemijaervi (railway junction linking Finland with Sweden).

11 The two countries undertake to negotiate a new trade treaty.

The treaty was signed for Russia by Premier Molotov, M. Zhdanov, a member of the Supreme Council, and Brigade Commander Vassilievski; for Finland by all four members of the delegation—Dr. Ryti (Prime Minister), M. Paasikivi (Minister without portfolio), General Walden, and M. Voionmaa (a Finnish M.P.).

A Helsinki despatch to Paris early today said that the Finnish War Minister, M. Niukkanen, and the Education Minister, M. Hannula, had resigned.

FINNS BLAME IT ON THE SWEDES

From GEOFFREY COX,
Daily Express Staff Reporter

HELSINKI, Wednesday Morning.

THE Finnish Parliament is sitting throughout the night in secret session to discuss the Russian peace proposals. All day yesterday Dr. Risto Ryti, Finland's Premier, kept on his peace talks with Stalin.

Dr. Ryti and his three colleagues are in constant contact with the other members of the Finnish Cabinet and heads of the political parties.

Strict secrecy is maintained here officially, but one thing is certain—the Finns did not attempt to make any immediate acceptance of the Allies' offer.

This offer has been in their hands for at least a fortnight. We informed them through diplomatic channels that we were ready to give help if they asked for it.

If by now no such Finnish appeal has reached the British authorities here, Sweden is undoubtedly responsible for this.

Her refusal to let Allied fighting men pass has hamstrung the scheme

BACK PAGE, COLUMN TWO

This is what Stalin wanted

THROUGH the long, bitter Moscow negotiations of October and November which preceded the invasion of Finland on November 30, Stalin demanded :

1 **That Finland should cede a twenty-mile-wide strip of the Karelian Isthmus.**

2 **Four islands in the Finnish Gulf, including the Finnish holiday resort of Hogland, should be handed over to secure the sea approaches to Kronstadt, the Red Navy's "Portsmouth."**

3 **"Finland's Gibraltar," the peninsular fortress of Hangoe, should be leased to Russia for thirty years.**

4 **Petsamo, Finland's Arctic outlet, was to be handed over, with the eastern half of the Rybachi (Fishermen's) Peninsula.**

5 **In return, Russia offered to strengthen her old pact of non-aggression with Finland, and to cede a large area of Russian Karelia—north of Lake Ladoga—which is largely sub-Arctic desert.**

—and— this is what he gets

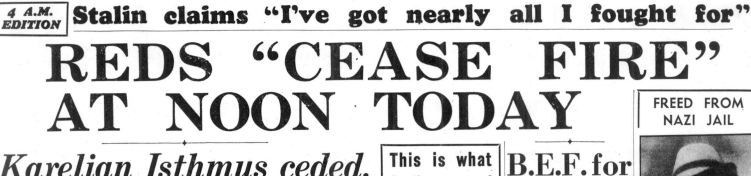

Among Finn concessions : The Karelian Isthmus and a base at Hangoe.

B.E.F. for Finland still stands

By GUY EDEN.

IT is now possible to reveal that a high British Army officer spent some time in Finland, making preparations for possible action, and that detailed plans of campaign were drawn up.

A strong B.E.F. was formed and specially trained in the forms of warfare necessary for a campaign in ice-bound Finland. This force is still in being.

M. Daladier, the French Premier, revealed in the Chamber last night that 50,000 French troops had been ready for the last fortnight to go to Finland's aid if direct appeal were made from Helsinki.

MANNERHEIM

There has been constant contact for weeks past between Marshal Mannerheim, the Finnish Army chief and the British General Staff.

The attitude of Sweden, however, made decisive action impossible. For that reason, Mr. Chamberlain's pledge of aid to the Finns had to be in less definite terms than he wished.

Finland, having been declared by the League of Nations to be the victim of aggression, was entitled to appeal for aid to other members of the League.

Britain and France, members of the League, were authorised to go to Finland's assistance, without formally declaring war on Russia.

Sweden was entitled, without sacrificing her neutrality, to permit Allied forces to pass through her territory, on the way to defend Finland.

Britain and France waited for the formality of an appeal from Finland so as to bring their action within the procedure of the League of Nations, and thus legalise it.

The geographical position of Finland made the co-operation, or at least the acquiescence, of Sweden essential to any Allied action.

Sweden resisted all pressure or persuasion in favour of permitting organised Allied forces through her country.

FREED FROM NAZI JAIL

Mrs. Peggy Ward, wife of a London musician, reached Amsterdam yesterday after nearly four months in a Nazi criminal jail. They stripped her ten times before letting her go—without money.
Story on Page Seven.

STOP PRESS

Army opposing the peace

HELSINKI, Wednesday.—Many indications in Helsinki show that strong opposition to reported peace is developing in Finnish Parliament's debate. Army circles are reported to be leading the opposition.—British United Press.

TROOPS TO WITHDRAW HALF A MILE

Moscow statement this morning said both sides were to withdraw their troops half a mile behind positions held at cessation of hostilities.

Soviet troops to leave Petsamo region by April 10.

Disputes over troop withdrawals to be submitted to mixed Russo-Finnish military commission.

CANADA DOUBLES AIR FORCE

OTTAWA.—War establishment of Royal Canadian Air Force has been increased by nearly 14,000 men to 30,400, Mr. Rogers, Defence Minister, announced in Ottawa last night.—Reuter.

CHIEFS OF THE A.T.S. ATTACKED BY M.P.

CRITICISM of those responsible for running the A.T.S. was made by Sir Joseph Nall, Manchester Conservative M.P., in the House of Commons last night.

He said there was need for direction at the top of the A.T.S.—a need for something a little more in touch with the ideas of present-day girls serving in it.

The Air Ministry was administering its women's service in a more enlightened way than the War Office.

He added: "It is high time those who joined the A.T.S. over a year ago were given their second uniform. It is a matter of administration. The A.T.S. are adequately fed and adequately housed."

Mr. Oliver Stanley, War Secretary, said the A.T.S. had done invaluable work and he would certainly look into the comfort of the billeting and medical arrangements affecting them.

*** Chief Controller of the A.T.S. is Dame Helen Gwynne-Vaughan, who, in the last war, formed the W.A.A.Cs and later became commandant of the Women's R.A.F. Chief Commandant for the City of London is Lady Trenchard. Commander of the A.T.S. in France is Mrs. Fuller-Maitland.

B.E.F. PASSES 300,000 MARK

The B.E.F. in France is now more than 300,000 strong.

Mr. Stanley, War Secretary, said in Parliament yesterday that the number of troops had doubled since October. On October 11, the last time figures were given, B.E.F. strength was put at 158,000.

Roosevelt peace plan expected

Daily Express Political Correspondent

INFORMED diplomatic quarters in London regard it as certain that, as a result of the report of his special envoy, Mr. Sumner Welles, President Roosevelt will frame a peace plan for submission to the belligerent nations.

It is believed that the President's plan will include adjustment of economic problems, and a world conference at which all nations shall have the right to raise their grievances.

Mr. Welles leaves London tomorrow for another talk with Mussolini in Rome, and he will return to the U.S.A. in six days' time.

Premier to make statement today

MR. CHAMBERLAIN will make a statement about Finland in the Commons this afternoon. If the position has clarified sufficiently he will reveal the part Britain and France have played in recent events.

Some Government M.P.s were inclined last night to criticise Ministers for their failure to "do something" to help. The Prime Minister is likely to deal with this aspect of the question.

KEEP THE CHILDREN AWAY AT EASTER

BECAUSE the risk of air raids must be regarded as greater during Easter than it was at Christmas the Government urges parents not to bring home their evacuated children during the holidays.

"The responsibility for dangers which may ensue on failure to act on this advice must rest with parents," says the Minister of Health.

Local authorities in evacuation areas have been asked to send a leaflet to parents earnestly advising them not to bring back their children.

R.A.F. sink another U-boat

AN Air Ministry communiqué revealed last night that an R.A.F. plane bombed a U-boat during a reconnaissance flight over the Heligoland Bight on Monday, and is believed to have sunk it.

The submarine was seen travelling slowly on the surface towards home in the Schillig Roads at the mouth of the River Elbe.

Four 250lb. bombs were dropped on it. At least one scored a direct hit just ahead of the conning tower.

The pilot reports that before he flew off to continue his reconnaissance he saw the bow and the stern of the submarine rise above the surface the centre part being submerged.

Only last week another U-boat was bombed and sunk by the R.A.F. in the same area.

BEHAR BROTHERS CEASE TO BE OFFICERS

TWO brothers, David and Robert Behar, dismissed, without reasons being given, from the Ministry of Supply, were listed in the London Gazette last night as second lieutenants in the Royal Artillery, and in each case it was announced they would relinquish their commissions today.

David's appointment was dated January 9; Robert's February 1. A War Office official said: "The fact that these men were not gazetted before has no special significance."

SUBURBS win the first day of meat rationing. —PAGE THREE.
NEW NAME found for the unmarried wife. —PAGE FIVE.
MRS. DAWE catches two Dartmoor men. —PAGE SEVEN.
GERMAN BOMBER fights Belgian 'planes. —BACK PAGE.

WEATHER

Partly cloudy tonight and tomorrow. Cooler tonight. Northwest winds. Temperature tonight in the city and suburbs about 40.

New York Post

Founded 1801. Volume 139. No. 122.

NEW YORK TUESDAY APRIL 9 1940

SPORTS FINAL

THREE CENTS

OSLO FALLS TO GERMANS; SEA, AIR BATTLES RAGING

Nazis Demand Balkans Yield Control of Danube

LONDON, Apr. 9 (UP)—A battle between British and German warships was reported in progress off the coast of Norway late today and the British Press Assn. announced that "good news may be forthcoming."

Details of the battle were not immediately available.

An official Foreign Office spokesman cautioned correspondents to be patient about naval developments in Scandinavian waters.

"When a warship is at sea, it has to keep its radio silent, unless it wants to reveal its whereabouts to the enemy," he said. "So we do not get the news ourselves immediately. Very probably you will get a very good story within the next 12 hours."

By WM. STONEMAN
Special Cable
Copyright, 1940, New York Post and Chicago Daily News, Inc.

LONDON, Apr. 9.—Insistent reports prevailed in London late this afternoon that a first-class naval battle had taken place off the Norwegian coast between the British fleet and units of the German navy which were intercepted as they raced for home. Officials stated

Continued on Page 4, Col. 4

Bulletin

A Berlin broadcast picked up in New York this afternoon declared the German High Command "had found it necessary to bomb severely several cities and towns in the northern region" of Scandinavia.

STOCKHOLM, Apr. 9 (UP).—Germany today occupied a protesting Denmark without resistance, invaded Norway in a lightning offensive on the southern and western coasts and challenged the combined Allied naval and aerial forces in the North Sea.

A naval battle was reported raging off the Norwegian coast. Allied and German airplanes fought over Oslo, the Norwegian capital, and at several points off the coast.

The British and French governments announced their intention to rush "full aid" to Norway.

The Supreme War Council of the Allies met in London, with both Premier Reynaud and Defense Minister Daladier attending.

The Norwegian army fought back against the German invasion, which struck with lightning speed from Oslo in the south to far-northern Narvik in a "protective" campaign to win vitally important aerial and submarine bases just across the North Sea from the British Isles.

Oslo fell after being surrounded by German troops, and the fighting at that point ceased at 10 a. m. (New York time).

German troops occupied the Norwegian capital, surrounding the public buildings and communications centers. Fleeing residents were ordered to return to Oslo.

The Norwegian government, at war with the Reich, fled to Hamar, north of the capital.

The cabinet resigned to make way for a coalition national defense government.

With general mobilization ordered, the Norwegian army took its stand at a defense line between Oslo and Hamar to protect the government.

Sweden also ordered general mobilization and the Swedish parliament was called into emergency session. It was said authoritatively that the government had decided to resist all attacks.

The Swedish legation in Paris received unconfirmed reports that German troops had landed on Swedish territory. The legation said also that the Swedish government had urged evacuation of the larger cities.

The Nazi invading forces already had moved into all important areas of Denmark, passing through Jutland to Aalborg, the main town in Northern Jutland. German planes landed on Danish soil, from which they will be in a position to raid Allied shipping in the North Sea and the British Isles.

Nazi Battle Cruiser Reported Sunk

Advices received in Stockholm said the German invasion of Norwegian coastal points was carried out with

Continued on Page 8, Col. 1

Sunk?

STOCKHOLM, Apr. 9 (UP).—It was reported here today that Norwegian coastal artillery had sunk the 26,000-ton German battleship Gneisenau in Oslo Fjord.

The Gneisenau was reported damaged by British bombers in a raid on Wilhelmshaven Sept. 4, second day of the war, but had since been sighted at sea with its sister ship Scharnhorst, according to a British submarine commander.

Stocks Climb, Then Dive

Germany's invasion of Scandinavia brought violent movements to the world's financial and money markets today.

In New York, stocks shot up more than 6 points, reacted sharply around noon, then rallied again in the heaviest trading since last September.

The list closed mixed, with war issues up spectacularly and so-called domestic issues off.

More than 2,000,000 shares

Continued on Page 20, Col. 6

Two Sections 24 Pages

Nazis Nearer Us

By FLETCHER PRATT
N. Y. Post Military Expert

Out of the welter of censored reports and uncertainties today, three facts emerge with startling clarity Germany is now within easy distance of winning the war. The Allies have only themselves to blame for the latest development. Finally, the U. S. has been brought to the edge of war.

The last of these statements has a sound of almost ridiculous exaggeration today, with the news from northern Europe still so new that to us in America it is something consisting of words without relation to living individuals. Yet no effect of this latest development could be clearer.

The various polls of American public opinion on the war have shown very clearly that the sentiment for the Allies has been geographically well concentrated along the Atlantic seaboard. Isolationist and pacifist sentiment has similarly shown a geographical concentration in the belt of midwestern states from Indiana to Montana, from Missouri to Minnesota.

The last census reports show more than 1,500,000 persons of Scandinavian birth resident in these states; of persons of Scan-

Continued on Page 4, Col. 2

RACE RESULTS ON PAGE 18

Berlin Seeks Danube Grip

BELGRADE, Apr 9 (AP). The German government, it was learned on high authority today has demanded that Yugoslavia, Hungary, Bulgaria and Rumania accept German river police along the entire length of the Danube River to secure this vital supply route for Germany.

The demand was made

Continued on Page 8, Col. 1

British Fight at Oslo

By OLAV MYRE

OSLO, Apr. 9 (UP).—German and British planes battled over Oslo today and reports circulated that a great Allied air fleet was speeding over the North Sea to the Norwegian capital.

I saw German planes dive low over the Oslo airfield and release bombs which scored direct hits on Norwegian planes but the Norwegian airforce fought back valiantly.

I believe I saw four German planes crash and probably two Norwegian craft that went down.

The German bombing planes scored direct hits on six Norwegian planes on the Fornebo airfield, on the outskirts of Oslo, where they fought with the Norwegian craft.

There was no confirmation of reports that other Allied planes were en route to Oslo, but persistent rumors were that 600 to 700 British and French craft were coming.

About 20 houses on the outskirts of Oslo were damaged by German bombs in an air raid before German forces marched into the capital.

Late today a German destroyer, badly damaged apparently by Norwegian coastal guns in Oslo fjord, steamed slowly into Oslo harbor, where it anchored.

TROJAN HORSE IN NORWAY

STOCKHOLM, Apr. 9 (UP).—Germany today rewrote military history when she used the famed Trojan horse tactic, by which the Greeks took Troy, to capture principal Norwegian ports on the northern and western coasts, facing the North Sea and the British Isles.

Disguised as seamen, German marines sprang into action at such ports as Narvik, Bergen and Stavanger, at the moment the Nazis decided to take over, and hurled hand grenades at port officials who resisted them.

Nazis had been trading regularly with northern and western Norwegian ports, especially Narvik, where they picked up iron ore for shipment to Germany. To all appearances, the German ore ships were ordinary merchant vessels. But when the hour struck, orders from Berlin transformed the "Trojan horse" detachments into fighting units which already were in position to strike a mortal blow.

WEATHER
Partly cloudy, not much change in temperature and moderate winds tonight and tomorrow; warmer and fair Saturday, lowest temperature tonight 42.

New York Post

Founded 1801. Volume 139. No. 136.

NEW YORK THURSDAY APRIL 25 1940

SPORTS FINAL
LATE SPORTS RESULTS PAGES 17 AND 18
THREE CENTS

LELAND STOWE RADIOS:

BRITAIN SENT 1,500 RAW TROOPS WITHOUT ARTILLERY OR PLANES TO NORWAY---AND SLAUGHTER

By LELAND STOWE
Special Radio to The Post
Copyright 1940, New York Post and Chicago Daily News

EXCLUSIVE

GAEDDEDE, Norwegian-Swedish Frontier, Apr. 25.—Here is the first and only eyewitness report on the opening chapter of the British expeditionary troops' advance in Norway north of Trondheim. It is a bitterly disillusioning and almost unbelievable story.

The British force which was supposed to sweep down from Namsos consisted of one battalion of Territorials and one battalion of the King's Own Royal Light Infantry. These totaled fewer than 1,500 men. They were dumped into Norway's deep snows and quagmires of April slush without a single anti-aircraft gun, without one squadron of supporting airplanes, without a single piece of field artillery.

Ill-equipped, they were thrown into the snows and mud of 63 degrees north latitude to fight crack German regulars—most of them veterans of the Polish invasion—and to face the most destructive of modern weapons. The great majority of these young Britishers averaged only one year of military service. They have already paid a heavy price for a major military blunder which was not committed by their immediate command, but in London.

Unless they receive large supplies of anti-air guns and adequate reinforcements within a very few days, the remains of these two British battalions will be cut to ribbons.

Here is the astonishing story of what has happened to the gallant little handful of British expeditionaries above Trondheim:

After only four days of fighting, nearly half of this initial BEF contingent has been knocked out—either killed, wounded or captured. On Monday these comparatively inexperienced and incredibly underarmed British troops were decisively defeated. They were driven back in precipitate disorder from Vist, three miles south of the bomb-ravaged town of Steinkjer.

As I write, it is probable that the British field headquarters has been withdrawn northward and that the British vanguard has been compelled to evacuate one or several villages. Steinkjer was occupied by the Germans Tuesday.

I was in Steinkjer Monday evening just before the British lines were blasted to pieces. I was the only newspaper correspondent to enter the burning town and the only correspondent to visit British advance headquarters and to pass beyond to the edge of the front's heavy firing zone.

A score of buildings were flaming fiercely on the town's waterfront from a second bombing two hours earlier. In the midst of the smoky ruins I heard machine-gun cracking at high tempo in the hills just beyond the town. Shell explosions rapped the valley regularly with angry echoes. This was the first sustained battle between German and British troops on Norwegian soil. Already the conflict was snarling hot.

A battalion of 600 territorials was fighting desperately to hold Vist, the point of their farthest southward advance toward Trondheim. As Monday's twilight closed they were completely done in. For hours they had been torn and broken under the terrible triple onslaught of German infantry, tri-motored bombers and naval artillery firing from destroyers at the head of Breitstadfjord.

Within two hours the British troops were in flight. They had no chance whatever of standing off from bombs and three- or six-inch shells with nothing but Brenn machine guns and rifles. Before 11 o'clock that night I talked with the nerve-shattered survivors of the British battalion. We found two truckloads of them several miles above their headquarters and on their way north away from the front.

One of the officers told me the battalion had lost more than 200 in killed and that one entire company had been captured. He could not estimate the number of missing, but said that perhaps 150 of the battalion's 600 might be rallied later on.

"We have simply been massacred," he declared. "It

Continued o' Page 12, Col 1

Germans Push 125 Miles in Day; Motor Troops Reported in Roros

BERLIN, Apr. 25 (UP).—The official news agency DNB claimed today that German bombing planes, flying at low altitude, had dispersed concentrations and remnants of the main Norwegian army around Dombas.

By PETER C. RHODES
STOCKHOLM, Apr. 25 (UP)—Two German columns pounding northward through Central Norway were reported today to have smashed Allied defenses northeast of Lillehammer and at Roros in a drive toward the west coast port of Trondheim.

(The Associated Press said the Roros column had advanced 125 miles from Orphus since yesterday.)

British and Norwegian troops falling back northwestward from Lillehammer were reported to have encountered severe German air bombardment in the region of Otta and it was believed they had retired still further toward the railroad junction of Dombas. The exact positions of the Allied forces in this sector, however, were obscure.

(German official dispatches reported that the German column northeast of Lillehammer had reached Ringebu, 25 miles from Otta, and that Nazi planes had bombed and cut Allied railroad lines to their coastal bases.)

In addition to the German column advancing northwest from Lillehammer toward Dombas, a fast motorized detachment was striking northward from Rena and Koppang and was reported by the newspaper Allehanda to have occupied Roros, only 75 miles southeast of Trondheim.

Reports from Fjallness on the Swedish-Norwegian border said Allied troops had reached the vicinity of Roros and joined with Norwegians in battle with the Germans.

The Allies were said to have occupied the hills overlooking Roros where the Germans apparently had halted to await reinforcements.

Allied troops which had landed at Andalsnes had split at

Continued on Page 9, Col. 1

F. D. R. Proclaims State of War Exists Between Nazis and Norway

WARM SPRINGS, Ga., Apr. 25 (AP).—President Roosevelt today proclaimed a state of war in existence between Germany and Norway and the neutrality of the U. S. in the conflict.

Another proclamation barred submarines of the belligerents from American ports and territorial waters.

In an executive order, Mr. Roosevelt prescribed regulations governing enforcement of U. S. neutrality in the fighting between Germany and Norway.

One result of the proclamation and order was to apply the cash and carry plan to Norway, who now will be able to obtain war supplies in this country only by paying cash and transporting them in non-American vessels.

The cash and carry provisions of the Neutrality Law previously had been applied to Germany.

Texts of the documents were to be released in the State Dept. in Washington. A bare summary was given out here.

No mention was made of Denmark by White House officials and there were no indications whether similar proclamations would be issued in the case of that nation.

How Trondheim Fell: U. S. Captain's Diary

Capt. William A. McHale, master of the Moore-McCormack freighter Mormacsea, today brought into New York the first uncensored eyewitness account of the fall of Trondheim to the Germans.

Before sailing for Scandanavia Feb. 19, Capt. McHale promised the children of the Richard E. Byrd school, in Glen Rock, N. J., to write a day-by-day account of his voyage. The children had "adopted" the ship and were to use the diary for geography study.

But when the Mormacsea docked at Canal St. today, the captain's story proved to be more than a schoolboy lesson. Confirming in detail Leland Stowe's report of wholesale treason and espionage that paved the way for Norway's invasion, it is a document of historical significance.

Diary Tells Story

The diary of Captain McHale, who is a 44-year-old veteran of the last war and lives with his wife and two children in Glen Rock, tells itself as well as words can:

"APR. 9. TRONDHEIM: 5 A. M.—Somebody knocked at my door and said: 'We have a boat and would like to come alongside of you. Will it be alright?'

"As I was half asleep I answered, 'Yes, certainly,' thinking it was some small Nor-

Continued on Page 2, Col. 1

Adonis Seized Power In McCooey Decline

By EDWARD P. FLYNN
Copyright, 1940, by New York Post, Inc.

It was the decay of the Brooklyn Democratic organization of John H. McCooey in the early '30s which gave Joe Adonis his opportunity to make himself one of the most powerful men in the politics of the borough.

He had already entrenched himself in the 8th A. D., where gangsterism had been inseparable from politics for years, but that was not enough for him.

Adonis shrewdly saw that McCooey was growing old, that his grip on the organization was slipping, that long success had made him too complacent. And he realized these fact, at a time when to all outward appearances the fat, benevolent-looking Brooklyn leader was at the height of his power.

The first sign of the impending disintegration of the McCooey machine came in 1931

Continued on Page 24, Col. 1

Acts on Adonis

It was learned this afternoon from official sources that Mayor LaGuardia is about to issue special instructions to the police department concerning the activities of Joe Adonis.

Commissioner of Investigation Herlands has been conducting an extensive inquiry into the operations of the White Auto Sales Co. in Brooklyn, one of the many enterprises with which Adonis is connected. This company and Adonis' connection with it has been described in The Post's series of articles on the Brooklyn crime boss.

"95 p.c. Out" In Taxi Strike

Both sides showed determination today to carry on a finish fight in the strike of the Transport Workers Union (CIO) against the Parmelee and Terminal taxicab systems.

Union officials claimed that 5,663 men, representing approximately 95 per cent of the two companies' employees, had registered at strike headquarters.

Spokesmen for the two companies declared that the strike was not nearly that effective,

Continued on Page 5, Col. 1

F. D. R. Warns Pay Law Foes

WASHINGTON, Apr. 25 (UP).—President Roosevelt today declared it would be "a great mistake" to adopt the proposed Barden amendments to the wage-hour law.

Mr. Roosevelt's views were communicated to Rep. Norton (D-N.J.) chairman of the House Labor Committee, who made them public.

The Barden amendments are the most drastic of three sets of

Contitnued on Page 15, Col. 7

EVENING STANDARD, May 10, 1940

LATE SPECIAL

Evening Standard

Amusements 10
Radio 10

BLACK-OUT 9.5 pm, 4.47 am.
MOON Rose 7.37 am; Sets 11.24 pm.

No. 36,093 LONDON, FRIDAY, MAY 10, 1940 ONE PENNY

NAZIS INVADE HOLLAND, BELGIUM, LUXEMBURG: MANY AIRPORTS BOMBED

Allies Answer Call for Aid: R.A.F. Planes are in Action

HITLER HAS INVADED HOLLAND, BELGIUM AND LUXEMBURG. HIS PARACHUTE TROOPS ARE LANDING AT SCORES OF POINTS AND MANY AIRPORTS ARE BEING BOMBED.

THE DUTCH HAVE OPENED THEIR FLOOD-GATES AND CLAIM TO HAVE BROUGHT DOWN A DOZEN BOMBERS.

It was confirmed in official quarters in London shortly after 8a.m. to-day that appeals for assistance have been received from both the Belgian and Dutch Governments, and that these Governments have been told that H.M. Government will, of course, render all the help they can.

Every airport in Belgium has been attacked by Nazi airplanes, it is announced in Brussels.

BRUSSELS IS BEING "BOMBARDED TERRIFICALLY," SAYS A NEW YORK MESSAGE.

A Zurich report states that casualties in the first raid over Brussels amounted to 400 dead and wounded.

Lyons Airport Bombed

Other reports say that Antwerp and the airport at Lyons (France) have been bombed.

THE BELGIAN ARMY IS RESISTING THE GERMAN INVASION, IT IS OFFICIALLY ANNOUNCED IN PARIS. GENERAL MOBILISATION HAS BEEN PROCLAIMED.

BRUSSELS RADIO ANNOUNCE THAT ALLIED TROOPS ARE ON THE WAY TO BELGIUM'S AID.

French, Belgian and British airplanes have been sighted over Holland, states an official Dutch announcement.

"These airplanes," it was added, "belong to our Allies and they are enthusiastically greeted as a sign of friendship."

The Dutch Legation in London announce:

"Our appeal for aid sent to the Allied Governments has been answered. Britain and France are going to our assistance immediately."

Belgium, too, appealed for help. The Luxemburg Government have fled.

(Continued on PAGE TWO)

HITLER IS FOLLOWING THE SCHLIEFFEN PLAN—SPECIAL ARTICLE AND MAP, PAGE SEVEN.

You Must Carry Your Gas Mask

A.R.P. Should Be On Alert

—Says Ministry

The Minister of Home Security states that in the light of to-day's events in Holland and Belgium, it is very necessary that all civil defence and A.R.P. services should be on the alert.

The carrying of gas masks by the public is once more necessary. They should acquaint themselves with the position of shelters and first aid post in their neighbourhoods.

Householders are recommended to overhaul their domestic preparations against air attack.

Anti-aircraft guns over a wide area around the mouth of the Thames were in action at dawn to-day when five German airplanes, believed to be Heinkel bombers, flew over the coast and passed over several towns.

The sound of heavy firing awakened thousands of people, who hurriedly dressed and went into the streets to catch a glimpse of the raiders.

No air raid warning was sounded, but wardens were on duty and shepherded everyone indoors.

Five airplanes, flying in an arrow-head formation, were seen. They were flying at about 10,000 feet. Their course was clearly marked by the puffs and flashes of the bursting shells from the anti-aircraft batteries.

They were flying due east. A few

(Continued on Back Page, Col. Three)

Daily Mail
FOR KING AND EMPIRE
LATE WAR NEWS SPECIAL
NO. 13,745 * * TUESDAY, MAY 14, 1940 ONE PENNY

2,000 TANKS IN BIG BATTLE

Fierce Action North-West of Liége

BRILLIANT FIGHT BY THE FRENCH

From WALTER FARR, Daily Mail Correspondent

PARIS, Monday.

BETWEEN 1,500 and 2,000 tanks are engaged in a great battle between French and German motorised forces north-west of the Belgian fortress of Liége. The Germans are making their main attack in this sector, and their advance is being held.

To-night's French communiqué, referring to this battle, said counter-attacks led mainly by tanks, inflicted heavy losses on the enemy.

Reports reaching Paris say the French are putting up a brilliant fight and that their motorised units are clearly superior.

German armoured columns are debouching from Maastricht, Hasselt, and Tongres, but latest reports indicate that Liége, which the enemy claim to have taken, is still resisting.

Following the falling back of the Belgian troops to the north-west the Liége fortress stands at the head of a salient jutting out from the main Belgian defences.

Every bridge over the Meuse at Liége has been blown up. Every road has been destroyed by the Belgians. Only one big fort has fallen into enemy hands.

Again and again German motorised columns are renewing their attacks, only to be stopped by devastating attack by R.A.F. and French 'planes.

The French communiqué summed up the position on all fronts:

"German troops to-day continued their mass attacks in both Holland and Belgium. In Holland they made some advance, especially south of the Lower Meuse.

"The Germans made a particularly important effort in the Belgian Ardennes, where they achieved some progress.

"Our cavalry elements (light mechanised units), having fulfilled the delaying action with which they were charged, fell back on the Meuse, which the enemy had reached at one point.

"The enemy exerted strong pressure on Longwy. His attacks were repulsed, as were those launched east of the Moselle and in the region of the Saar.

"Nothing to report on the Rhine. Allied and enemy aircraft continued their supporting actions of their land forces. Fifteen enemy aircraft were shot down during these engagements.

"Behind the lines enemy air action, though repeated, caused only damage of little importance from the military point of view."

The Belgian communiqué said: "Our troops were engaged in hard fighting all day. Everywhere they offered fierce resistance to the enemy.

"A village which had fallen into the hands of the enemy was reoccupied following counter-attacks led by Belgian units and supported by Allied tanks."

The official German News Agency claimed that strong motorised forces had made contact with the troops landed round Rotterdam by air.

There was no confirmation of this success in the Dutch communiqué. The farthest point reached by the Germans in Central or Southern Holland, according to the Dutch, was Langstraat, a series of villages along the River Meuse.

Dutch Defence

In making their claim the German agency said additional troops had been landed by 'plane, and the area between Moerduk and the Hague was thereby dominated by German forces.

"By new methods of warfare the Germans have succeeded in forcing their way into the enemy's position in a way which will be decisive for the military situation in Dutch territory."

The Dutch have now evacuated their territory situated to the east of the Zuyder Zee.

This part of Holland has no defence line at the frontier with Germany and is being taken over by the enemy with little difficulty.

The fighting in Holland is therefore confined mainly to checking the German assault on the square made by Amsterdam, Utrecht, Groningen, and Rotterdam,

Infantry Ready to Strike

Belgium 'Push'

From PAUL BEWSHER, with the B.E.F.

BELGIUM, Monday.

BRITISH infantry were preparing to-day to take their part in stemming the tide of the German mass attack in Belgium.

Within a short time the whole force of the British Army here will be opposed against the invaders. Heavy and light artillery are being quickly put into position.

The advance stream of armoured cars and light tanks, the modern equivalent of the light cavalry patrols, are already in contact with the enemy.

Engagements have taken place with enemy forces and our units, imbued with the old cavalry spirit, have met with much success.

Where They Fight

The fighting is taking place in beautiful rolling valleys amid wooded hills.

This scene of full spring beauty provides a sad contrast, making the horror of the invasion still greater.

Shells are bursting in fields full of spring flowers. Tanks are hiding beneath flowering chestnut and lilac trees.

The very loveliness of the surroundings has made our men still more determined to resist to the utmost the invaders who have hammered their brutal way into the peaceful country.

Everybody knows that they are probably up against one of the hardest tasks the British Army have ever faced in their long history.

Heavy sacrifices will have to be made.

But every single soldier I have met is fully prepared to take the supreme risk in order to help destroy the evil thing.

Difficulty does lie ahead, but our men in the field have the blazing light of indignation and determination to illuminate the darkness.

Satisfactory Results

Up to the moment very little information about the fighting is available.

In these engagements between tanks and armoured cars over a wide area the action is so moving and scattered that it takes some time before reports can be sent back.

I understand, however, that the situation is proceeding as satisfactorily as can be expected.

News that both British and French troops are now in contact with the Germans has done much to cheer the Belgians.

To-day everywhere I went in a 200-miles tour of the forward area I found a slightly greater optimism.

At the same time everyone realises that the Germans are launching an attack in which they are using every scrap of their terrific power in a do-or-die attempt to break right through into France.

Not One 'Plane

A few miles behind the front I found a battalion installed. Although they had not been in position for more than a few hours they had settled down just as if they were in barracks.

The sergeant-major told me that the battalion had travelled by road through Belgium to the village without being attacked in any way by German aircraft. They had not suffered the smallest casualty.

This is the story everywhere.

Throughout my tour to-day I did not see a single German machine or hear one anti-aircraft gun.

One reason, undoubtedly, is the success of the Royal Air Force, who have shown their mastery over the Germans in an incredible fashion.

FIGHTERS CLAIM 68 'PLANES

From NOEL MONKS, Daily Mail Correspondent

WITH THE R.A.F. IN FRANCE, Monday.

GERMAN bombers made massed raids on British and French aerodromes in France to-day. A few minutes ago the fifth "All clear" was sounded throughout the Champagne country. There are still several hours of daylight.

Although I have not been allowed to visit the places raided, I am told officially that no serious damage was done, nor were any of our personnel hurt.

In at least three of the raids Hurricane fighters attached to the Advanced Striking Force made things so hot for the raiders that high explosive bombs were jettisoned in open fields.

Seven Heinkels were shot down by fighters and three more by anti-aircraft units.

The fierce attacks against British bases in France are striking evidence of the havoc our bombers have been causing among enemy troops in Belgium and Holland.

Low-diving bombing attacks on German mechanised and infantry columns have been carried out almost continuously in the last 24 hours, and the story of the most successsful of these raids has just come in.

A French unit desperately holding up an advance by German mechanised troops in Holland sent an SOS for aerial support.

In less than an hour a whole flight of our bombers were diving on the Germans, bombing and machine-gunning them. The hard-pressed French unit were able to consolidate their position. All

Turn to BACK Page

The battle for Liége.

I Saw the Terror in Holland

RALPH IZZARD, the *Daily Mail* Correspondent in Amsterdam, arrived back in England yesterday—one of the last Britons to leave the city.

He brought back a vivid eye-witness account of the invasion of Holland—the terror from the air, the incessant bombings, the parachute attackers, the Fifth Column menace.

"The day I left Amsterdam there were so many raid alarms we lost count....

"To understand the parachute menace you have to realise that any of the soldiers you meet may be an armed German.

"Parachutists taken prisoner were brought into the town with faces torn and bleeding. The women had attacked them with their nails.

"A Fifth Columnist stood on the roof of the Hotel Europe and let off a direction flare. Civic Guards chased him over the roof tops."

These are some of the things Izzard tells in his story in **Page FIVE.**

FOUR MORE MINISTERS CHOSEN

FOUR more appointments to the Government were announced last night. They were:

Secretary for India and for Burma: Mr. L. S. Amery (Cons.), aged 66.

Minister of Health: Mr. Malcolm MacDonald (Nat. Lab.), 39.

Minister of Labour and Minister of National Service: Mr. Ernest Bevin (Lab.), 56.

Minister of Food: Lord Woolton, 56.

Mr. Churchill's Government now has 19 Ministers, including the five members of the War Cabinet.

Mr. Bevin, once a Somerset farm boy, now secretary of the Transport and General Workers' Union, has become a Privy Councillor on his appointment.

A seat in Parliament will have to be found for him and it is expected that he will take the late Mr. George Lansbury's place as M.P. for Bow and Bromley.

This would mean that Mr. Bevin will be in the House almost immediately.

Rebel Leader

Mr. Amery was one of the leaders of the Government back bench "rebels" whose vote in the critical division last week was largely responsible for the change of Premiership.

He is a former Colonial Secretary and Dominions Secretary.

Mr. Malcolm MacDonald is transferred from the Colonial Office.

It is expected that another post will be found for Mr. Ernest Brown, the displaced Minister of Labour, who has held that office for a record period of five years.

It was announced from 10, Downing-street last night that the King has conferred a viscounty on Sir John Simon on his appointment to be Lord Chancellor.

CHURCHILL'S ORDER OF THE DAY

WHAT is our policy? I say it is to wage war—war by sea, land and air; war with all our might and with all the strength that God can give us . . . what is our aim? It is victory, victory at all costs, victory in spite of all terrors; victory, however long and hard the road may be.

Mr. Churchill's speech to the House of Commons is in PAGE SIX

QUEEN WILHELMINA IN LONDON

Welcome by the King

By Daily Mail Reporter

QUEEN WILHELMINA of the Netherlands arrived in London last night—a refugee. She stepped from a special train at Liverpool-street Station with a Service gas-mask slung across her shoulder.

She looked tired and travel-stained. The King, in the uniform of Admiral of the Fleet, was first to greet her. He strode quickly up to her, took her hand, and kissed her on both cheeks.

Then she caught sight of her daughter, Princess Juliana, and her son-in-law, Prince Bernhard, who had arrived in London earlier in the day. And suddenly she seemed quite at home on this strange, rather sombre, London railway station.

Smiled in Her Sorrow

The Princess rushed up to her mother and kissed her warmly several times. Then the Prince also kissed her.

The King watched the family reunion with a smile. Then—her face very serious, and family

Turn to BACK Page

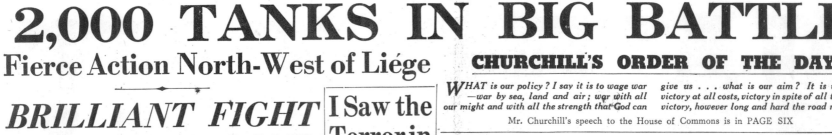

After 42 years on Holland's throne — Queen Wilhelmina becomes a refugee.

Earlier yesterday Princess Juliana reached London. With her from the train walked her elder daughter, Princess Beatrix — one hand in her mother's, the other "waving to the people." Behind them is Lord Harewood, who met the party.—"Daily Mail" picture.

She found refuge in France —wired picture as the Grand Duchess Charlotte of Luxemburg set foot on French soil.

HOLLAND'S RULERS MOVE

THE Dutch Government have transferred their seat elsewhere in order to give greater freedom of action, according to a proclamation, broadcast by the Amsterdam radio, from General Winkelman, Commander-in-Chief of the Dutch forces.

The new whereabouts of the Netherlands Government has not yet been established. In some circles it is believed to be the town of Alphen, in Holland.

An unconfirmed report that the Dutch Government was transferring its seat to London had late last night received no substantiation.

The King in Dorset

The King and Queen left London for Dorset last night, the *Court Circular* announced.

They were attended by Lady Nunburnholme and Lieut.-Col. the Hon. Piers Legh.

Princess Elizabeth and Princess Margaret went riding in Windsor Great Park yesterday and had a picnic in Windsor Forest.

Billeting Pay Up

Increased billeting rates for evacuated school children were announced last night. From May 31 householders are to receive:

For children between 10 and 14, 10s. 6d. a week; between 14 and 16, 12s. 6d.; over 16, 15s.

The present rates are: Up to 14, 10s. 6d. for a single child; 8s. 6d. each where more than one are billeted; over 14, 10s. 6d. in all cases.

The Ministry of Health also announced last night further proposals for accommodating children in hostels.

This accommodation would be provided only where billeting difficulties could not be solved in any other way.

B.B.C. Say 'Disregard Broadcast'

The B.B.C. announced last night on the authority of the Air Ministry that a notice broadcast at 7.15 p.m. had been put out through a misunderstanding, and should be disregarded.

The notice stated that all men in the Royal Air Force Volunteer Reserve not on leave, and those carrying out civilian duties, should report to their bases as soon as possible.

No German Trains Reach Bâle

ZURICH, Monday.—Contrary to the announcement of the Bâle railway authorities that traffic with Germany via Bâle would be resumed to-day, it is learned that no trains have arrived from Berlin.

The Germans say that trains running to Bâle were again machine-gunned during the night by French aeroplanes, and that it is doubtful whether traffic to Bâle can be kept up.—*Exchange.*

Grain Store Fire

Four hundred tons of grain and meal were destroyed when fire broke out at a two-storey warehouse in Boundary-street, Liverpool, yesterday.

I'LL ASK MY PEOPLE TO WORK LIKE HELL—Bevin

MR. ERNEST BEVIN, speaking for the first time as Labour Minister, said at Bournemouth last night: "I hope the War Cabinet will not allow vested interests to stand in the way of maximum production, nor must profit or anything else stand in the way. If this is the policy of the Government I will ask my people to work like hell to save the lives of our lads."

Mr. Bevin was speaking at a dinner of the Transport and General Workers' Union, of which he has for years been general secretary. He commented that he had heard a lot of talk about equal sacrifices, and went on:

"We at the T.U.C. have had all this talk about spirals. The working classes are generous to a fault, but it is not by mucking about with pennies of their wages that you get the best out of the workers."

"I can promise the trade unions group that I will not let them rust. There must be in the workshop, among shop stewards and others, a feeling that they are part of the Government, and then they will stick it through to the end."

Anti-Parachute Corps Planned

Britain is to recruit a home defence guard of men over military age to deal with possible parachute invaders.

Mr. Anthony Eden, the War Minister, said in the House of Commons yesterday that he hoped to give details at an early date.

*** Crack shots over 50 will be recruited.—Page Three.

Britain Ready for First Refugees

The first Dutch and Belgian refugees arrived in Britain yesterday.

Arrangements have been made for refugees to be received at centres in London, Lancashire, Cheshire, West Yorkshire, Scotland, and Wales.

*** Full details are in Page THREE.

LATEST

GAS WARNING TO CIVILIANS

Daily Mail Radio Station

Several times last night Belgian and French radio stations broadcast urgent instructions to civil population on what to do in gas attacks.

A 2

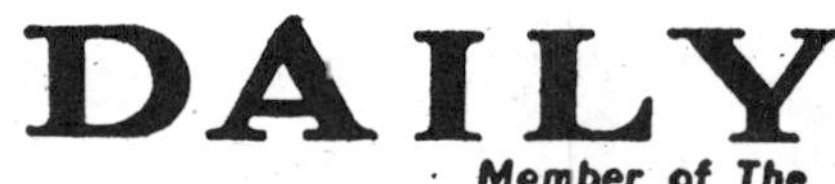

MIRROR

Member of The Associated Press

WEATHER SHOWERS, COOLER (Details on Page 6.)

Copyright, 1940, Daily Mirror, Inc.

3 Cents Outside City Limits

Vol. 16. No. 282 C New York, Friday, May 17, 1940 FINAL EDITION ★★★

NAZIS CUT DEEP INTO FRANCE

In Control, Says Paris; British Hold Louvain

F. D. R. ASKS BILLION AND 50,000 PLANES

Stories on Pages 2 and 3—Late War Bulletins on Back Page

BELGIAN ARMY SURRENDERS!

IN THE NEWS

MISS IDA KOVERMAN, the extremely able assistant of Mr. Louis B. Mayer at the Metro-Goldwyn-Mayer Studios, wishes your columnist to publish a poem which he wrote in one of his less lucid intervals.

She thinks the poem would give some variety to the column and would not entirely disgrace it.

Perhaps the lady is right about the need of variety. One cannot always be discussing war and politics, and all the depressing and distressing things of life.

One should occasionally dilate on the more cheerful aspects of existence—even on the emotional and sentimental phases of our being.

But a poem, um uh! That may be crowding the mourners,—that may be pressing an assumption too far.

There is a very distinct possibility that those readers who have complied—perhaps with considerable difficulty—with your columnist's request not to shoot the organist,—as he is doing the best he can,—may not be able to restrain themselves any longer.

However, those chances have to be taken and there is always the likelihood, too, that they may miss.

Everyone must have a lot of confidence in Miss Koverman's judgment.

She passes upon all sorts of scenarios,—good, bad and indifferent.

She estimates the value of various performers and performances.

She reviews finished products.

She bestows rewards and recompense.

She doubtless has in her desk a chaplet of bays for aspiring poets.

So here goes. With one twang of the lyre, your columnist is going to enter the lists to compete with Homer, Hesiod, and Horace.

He is going to dare the danger.

He is going to mount his unpracticed Pegasus even if he falls off and breaks his literary neck.

He is going to woo the fair Calliope even at the risk of being ignominiously and humiliatingly rejected.

The verse Miss Koverman alludes to was written at Wyntoon in the depths of the forest that flanks the tumultuous McCloud River.

Even if the poem were good—many times as good as it is—it could not express the beauty and tranquility of the forest, the majesty of those tall trees that tower to heaven and point the way, and lift the soul, to higher thoughts and things.

In their mysterious shadowy depths of the forest it is the softly whispering voices of the trees that speak serenely to the spirit of man and seem to say:

I am the forest of fir and pine,
Shadow and silence and peace are mine.
Mine are the springs and the rills and brooks,
Which, rising in quiet hidden nooks,
Join hands with the river and joyously flow
To the wide spread plains which lie below.
Mine is the green of the stalwart trees,
And the scarlet and golden harmonies
Of the tenderer shrubs which lay away
Their garments of green for a Summer day.
Mine are the paths by the riverside,
And the high steep trails over which you ride,
And the soft sweet meadow upon whose breast
You lie you down in delight to rest.
Mine is the glint of the golden sun
Which sifts through the trees till the day is done;
Then the cool calm darkness—all too soon
Dispersed by the light of the silvery moon.
Mine is the warmth of the Summer glow,
Mine is the chill of the Winter snow.
Mine is the magic of sun and air,
Which cures every ill and dispels every care.

• • •

ENVOI

I am the forest of fir and pine,
Which soothes and stimulates more than wine.
You need no nepenthe of vat or vine,
For the solace of silence and peace are mine.

WAR AT A GLANCE

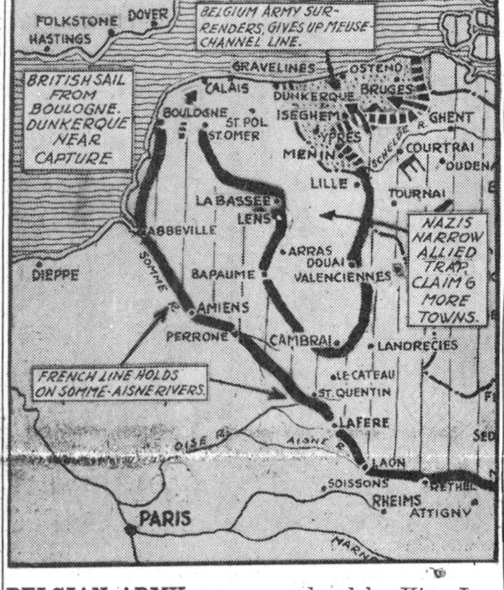

BELGIAN ARMY was surrendered by King Leopold. Nazis claimed rout at Bruges in Channel march.

NAZIS SMASHED through Flanders defenses; claimed six more towns, including Douai. "Ring" around trapped troops tightened.

SOMME-AISNE line held. Some British sailed from Boulogne.

Navy Rescues British Troops

By ROBERT G. NIXON,
International News Service Staff Correspondent.

LONDON, May 28.—A presumably large number of British troops were safely evacuated from Boulogne before surrender of King Leopold of Belgium gravely compromised the position of Allied forces in France and Belgium, it was officially revealed today.

British authorities released a graphic eye-witness description telling how the British troops, performing their work under "hellish fire," after demolition squads had paved the way for an escape.

Lauds Heroism of Navy

"The behavior of our troops in the face of attack by greatly superior enemy forces, assisted by aircraft, tanks and field guns, was truly wonderful," the British eyewitness said.

"Particularly admirable was the role of officers and men of destroyers of the royal navy, who

Continued on Page 2, Column 5.

Belgians Still Fight

LONDON, May 28 (By International News Service).—The Exchange Telegraph Company today quoted Premier Hubert Pierlot as announcing in a broadcast that the Belgian Army will continue to fight despite surrender of King Leopold.

A Reuter's dispatch from Paris said it was learned the Belgian Cabinet has decided that Leopold's capitulation against the advice of his government is unconstitutional.

CHARACTER QUALITY New York ENTERPRISE ACCURACY
Journal AND American
AN AMERICAN PAPER FOR THE AMERICAN PEOPLE
B 3
No. 19,155—DAILY | In Two Sections—Section One | TUESDAY, MAY 28, 1940 | DAILY 3 Cents | SATURDAY 5 Cents | SUNDAY 10 Cents

FINAL
COMPLETE
LATEST STOCKS

Path to Sea Opened By Leopold's Action

By JOHN MacVANE, International News Service Staff Correspondent.

PARIS, May 28.—Capitulation of the Belgian army to the German invaders under orders of King Leopold was announced by French Premier Paul Reynaud in a nation-wide radio broadcast today.

Reynaud revealed the Belgian capitulation in a bitter address excoriating Belgium—particularly King Leopold.

He said Leopold had "given up" the fight "without consideration for the Allies" and charged that Leopold took the decision "against the unanimous advice of his Ministers."

The Belgian Government will continue to fight, the French Premier asserted.

"The responsible Ministers of the Belgian Government," Reynaud said, "added they would place their services in the common cause.

"All forces of the country are still at their disposal. They are willing to raise a new army and collaborate in the task of arming France."

Flays King's Lack of Gratitude

Making no effort to conceal the seriousness of this newest war development, Reynaud told the French people:

"I must announce to the French people a grave event which occurred during the night.

"Frenchmen no longer can count on the support of the Belgian Army.

"Since 4 o'clock this morning (11 p. m., Monday,

Continued on Page 3, Column 1.

'Shame' Cries Commons for Leopold's Act

LONDON, May 28 (By International News Service).—Cries of "shame" today greeted Prime Minister Winston Churchill's announcement in the House of Commons that King Leopold of Belgium had surrendered to Nazi Germany.

"The House must prepare itself for hard and heavy tidings," he warned.

By CHARLES A. SMITH,
International News Service Staff Correspondent.

LONDON, May 28.—Frank admission that the surrender of King Leopold of Belgium has placed the British Army in France in an extremely precarious position was made today by Alfred Duff Cooper, British Minister of Information.

In a broadcast to the British people a few hours after the Belgian Monarch capitulated, Duff Cooper asked the people of Britain to reserve judgment on King Leopold's act.

"I do not think we should at

Continued on Page 4, Column 3.

Nazis Claim Douai Fall

BERLIN, May 28 (By International News Service). — By smashing through strong Allied frontier fortifications, German troops have crossed the Scheldt Canal west of Valenciennes and have captured Orchies and Douai, the official German communique announced today.

By PIERRE J. HUSS,
International News Service Staff Correspondent.

BERLIN, May 28.—Capitulation of the Belgian Army will enable the Reich to intensify and redouble its military campaign against the Allied forces, authoritative German quarters declared today.

This declaration was made after Chancellor Hitler's headquarters at the front announced that King Leopold of the Belgians had decided to give up "senseless resistance" against German might and ask for an armistice.

In reply, it was announced, Germany demanded and received the unconditional surrender of the Belgian army.

An authoritative commentary on the situation said:

"The Belgian capitulation is of enormous mili-

Continued on Page 4, Column 1.

Lindbergh Disowned By Lafayette Fliers

PARIS, May 28 (By International News Service).—The Trench and Air Association of American Volunteers, composed of combatants in the French army from 1914-1918, today ejected Col. Charles A. Lindbergh from honorary membership because of his speech criticizing President Roosevelt's war defense address recently.

An official statement issued by the organization characterized Lindbergh's speech as an "insult" to the memory of the Lafayette Escadrille.

The announcement said:

"In a moment of enthusiasm, mistaken but understandable, the

Continued on Page 6, Column 7.

Stocks Crash $1-8

The stock market crashed $1 to $8 a share today on news of the Belgian surrender to the Nazis. Scores of issues hit new lows for the year or longer, and included many of the market's leaders.

(For details see Financial Pages.)

THE WEATHER

Showers today and tomorrow.

Sun rises 5:29 a. m.; sun sets 8:17 p. m. High tide at Governors Island, 2:20 a. m. and 3:02 p. m.

HOURLY TEMPERATURES

2 a. m.	61	7 a. m.	58
3 a. m.	60	8 a. m.	58
4 a. m.	58	9 a. m.	58
5 a. m.	58	10 a. m.	58
6 a. m.	58	11 a. m.	61

(Complete Weather Table on Page 8)

TODAY'S INDEX

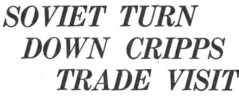

DAILY EXPRESS, Thursday, May 30, 1940.

Daily Express

PETS CORNER
Buzz!
Bee quicker!
Bee smarter!
FIELD-DAY
Olive Oil BRUSHLESS SHAVE

No. 12,486 Thursday, May 30, 1940 One Penny

Allies stem German onslaughts in history's greatest rearguard battle

B.E.F. FIGHTS DOWN NARROW CORRIDOR TO DUNKIRK

French stand-and-die troops battle in Lille

MARINES ENTRENCHED ALONG THE COAST

DOWN A RAPIDLY DWINDLING CORRIDOR, THIRTY MILES AT ITS WIDEST, THE B.E.F. AND ITS FRENCH ALLIES ARE SMASHING A WAY TO THE SEA THIS MORNING IN THE MOST GLORIOUS REARGUARD ACTION OF ANY WAR.

Two-thirds of the ports on which our armies in Flanders were based have fallen into enemy hands since the Belgian betrayal. Dunkirk remains, and it is towards this last link with England that the British troops are making their fighting withdrawal.

From now on the fate of the B.E.F., which has borne the brunt of battle for the last ten days, is largely dependent on the Navy and the R.A.F.

Already the R.A.F. have slowed down the German pursuit by plastering their lines with bombs and ground-strafing their advance troops. Over Dunkirk alone yesterday more than twenty enemy raiders were brought down by Defiants and Hurricanes.

Midnight reports pictured the B.E.F. fighting back in a compact wedge with its widest side on the thirty miles of coastline round Dunkirk.

GALLANT ACTION

The wedge narrowed down towards Lille, nearly fifty miles behind, where French divisions were carrying out a gallant delaying action at the risk of being cut off.

The main body of British troops had already reached positions of comparative safety. They had retired into a corridor between the rivers Aa and Scarpe.

Three parallel barriers cover the withdrawal—the River Lys, over which most of the B.E.F. has already fallen back; the River Yser; and finally the broad canal which runs close up behind Dunkirk.

The French covering army under General Prioux, which carried the fight into the streets of Lille to gain time for the British withdrawal, is now in the gravest peril.

General Prioux is trying desperately to cut a path through the Germans who have thrown themselves across his lines to Dunkirk.

ENEMY ON HILLS

Strong enemy forces are established at Cassel and Mount Kemmel—hills dominating the Flanders plains—with orders to stop Prioux's march at any cost.

Prioux's main hope rests on a French fleet under the command of Vice-Admiral Abrial, which is raining shells on the German rear.

Warships of many classes are waiting for Prioux's gallant men at the coast.

The fate of this hemmed-in Army was described in Berlin last night as "dire and certain."

"They can only surrender or die," a German war correspondent said. "The German Army will see to it that everything around the French will crash and burn—to the last house, if necessary."

In the fortified area of Dunkirk (which the Germans claimed yesterday to have entered) Allied naval forces, including French marines, are now firmly entrenched. British and French units were also reported last night to be still in possession of part of Calais.

"SUPPLIES SATISFACTORY"

Dunkirk is being further fortified by French and British naval engineers, and the admiral commanding the operations reported last night that he was "satisfied" with the supply situation.

Ships are reported to be bringing a steady stream of food and war supplies to Dunkirk.

Allied air forces are co-operating in keeping communications open around the port.

According to the German High Command some of the French troops concerned in the rearguard action have already been encircled south of Lille in an area of twelve square miles.

A strong break through the entire line at Lille is claimed by Berlin, which goes on to declare: "We are continuing our action with the object of destroying the British Army."

Ostend, Zeebrugge and Bruges and Armentieres are among yesterday's Berlin claims.

The French War Ministry spokesman said last night that on the central front the "quite heavy" action begun yesterday to wipe out German bridgeheads on the south side of the Somme was completed yesterday afternoon, with many Germans taken prisoner.

He estimated that the Belgians who surrendered on Tuesday composed half of the Allies armies in the north.

HEROISM WORTHY OF TRADITIONS

LAST night's French communiqué stated :—

French and British troops, fighting in Northern France, are undergoing with a heroism worthy of their traditions a struggle of exceptional intensity.

For fifteen days they have been giving battle, cut off from the bulk of our armies by German forces constantly reinforced.

Attacked incessantly on their two flanks, east and west, they are disputing the ground with the enemy, hanging on to territory and counter-attacking with both stubbornness and bravery.

"CEASE FIRE!"

While they withstood these attacks, the Belgian Army, which was under the direct command of King Leopold III. and defended positions on the River Escaut [Schelde] and the coast north-east of Ostend, received from its King the order to cease fire, opening to the enemy a route to Ypres, Furnes and Dunkirk.

From that moment our troops, under the command of Generals Blanchard and Prioux and in close collaboration with the British Army of Lord Gort, have had to face increased danger.

Displaying in these grave circumstances an indomitable resolution, they are endeavouring to move towards the coast, where there is very heavy fighting.

STRONG SUPPORT

The French Navy is giving them powerful support in the defence of ports and communication lines.

Under the command of Admiral Abrial, the Navy is employing a very great number of ships and is engaged in supplying the fortified camp of Dunkirk and the troops based on it.

Land and naval aviation is co-operating constantly.

On the Somme front fierce attacks by our troops have allowed us today to reduce the bridgeheads which the enemy had occupied south of this river.

We took several hundred prisoners.

Nothing of importance to report on the rest of the front.

"I.R.A. READY"

PHILADELPHIA, Wednesday.—"Fifty thousand men of the I.R.A., equipped with weapons obtained in the United States, are ready to strike for freedom from Britain when Britain is invaded by Germany," says Mr J. J. Duignan, of Philadelphia, who describes himself as "leader of Pennsylvania I.R.A. veterans."—British United Press.

—THE KING— TO THE B.E.F.

Our hearts are with you

THE King sent this message yesterday to Lord Gort, Commander-in-Chief of the B.E.F.:—

"ALL your countrymen have been following with pride and admiration the courageous resistance of the B.E.F. during the continuous fighting of the last fortnight.

"Placed by circumstances outside their control in a position of extreme difficulty they are displaying a gallantry that has never been surpassed in the annals of the British Army.

"The hearts of every one of us at home are with you and your magnificent troops in this hour of peril."

Lord Gort's reply :

"The Commander-in-Chief with humble duty begs leave on behalf of all ranks of the B.E.F. to thank your Majesty for your message.

"May I assure your Majesty that the Army is doing all in its power to live up to its proud tradition, and is immensely encouraged at this critical moment by the words of your Majesty's telegram."

SOVIET TURN DOWN CRIPPS TRADE VISIT

Will talk through Ambassador

MOSCOW, Wednesday.

THE Soviet radio announced tonight that the sending of Sir Stafford Cripps—now on his way to Moscow—as special trade envoy was "unacceptable" to the Soviets.

M. Molotov, the Soviet Premier, through the London Embassy, said Russia could not accept Sir Stafford Cripps or any other person (says Associated Press). If the British Government really wanted to conduct trade negotiations it could do so through the British Ambassador, Sir William Seeds, or another Ambassador appointed in his place.

And, writes Daily Express Political Correspondent Guy Eden, Sir Stafford is likely to be made British Ambassador to Moscow—with a special mission to conclude a trade agreement between the two countries.

SPEED-UP TALKS

When he left London on Monday it was proposed that he should be a special representative of the British Government to carry on the trade talks, and that a diplomat should be appointed Ambassador to work with him.

But the Soviet Government asked for Sir Stafford to be given full Ambassadorial rank, believing that this would help to speed up the talks.

Sir Stafford will not give up his parliamentary seat, will not draw an Ambassador's salary, but will have all his official expenses paid.

a penny or two cheaper." Cheese has a high energy value (four times as much as eggs, for instance) and tops the list of foods which are rich in calcium and phosphorus. Combine it with potatoes (like this recipe) and you have a really first-class nutritious dish.

POTATO GRATIN: You will want: 2lbs. old potatoes, 2 onions, an egg, 1 pint milk, ¼lb. grated cheese (Parmesan or Gruyère is best, but mild Cheddar will do quite as well).

FIVE members of the former pro-Nazi organisation, The Link, have now been interned under Section 18B of the Defence Regulations.

Other former principal members of the organisation have, it is understood, received official warning concerning their future activities.

The Link, according to the then chairman, Admiral Sir Barry Domvile, was dissolved in September.

French general jailed

PARIS, Wednesday.—Medical Corps General Henri Bodet was sentenced by the Paris Military Tribunal today to six months' imprisonment for abandoning his post on the night of May 15, when the Germans broke through in the Sedan sector.—Associated Press.

STOP PRESS

U.S. SPEEDS PLANE DELIVERY METHOD

Daily Express Staff Reporter

NEW YORK, Wednesday.—Mr. Cordell Hull, U.S. Secretary of State, tonight gave Neutrality Act ruling which speeds up plane shipments to Allies by ending "tow-rope delivery." American pilots may now fly planes to Eastern Canada ports for shipment to Europe. Hitherto they have had to land on U.S. side of Canadian border, where tow-ropes were fixed for Canadians to drag them across.

Big air order transferred

Australia waives claim

Mr. S. M. Bruce, High Commissioner for Australia, has informed the Minister of Aircraft Production that the Australian Government proposes to transfer to the British Government its claims upon an important aircraft order now being completed in the U.S.A.

The Minister of Aircraft Production has gladly accepted this proposal. He is deeply grateful to the Australian Government for a splendid act of generosity.

THE Daily Express news map today shows the advances claimed by the Germans since the surrender of Leopold, and how the French formed a rearguard protecting a British fighting withdrawal. At a late hour last night the French claimed that their troops were still battling in Calais, and that Dunkirk was entirely in Allied hands.

—After Quisling—

Captain Mutterer

Daily Express Correspondent

BERNE, Wednesday.

CAPTAIN MUTTERER, a captain on the Swiss General Staff, has been sentenced to six years' imprisonment and dismissed from the Swiss army because he copied secret orders and plans.

Mutterer, who had been given a confidential task in the section of the General Staff dealing with defence plans, copied some and took them home.

The anti-spy squad tracked him, but the military tribunal could not prove he had had relations with a foreign Power or agent.

German 'tourists'

SOFIA, Wednesday.—Bulgaria today gave Germany permission to send large numbers of tourists to Varna, the Black Sea resort. The tourists are expected to include several thousand wounded soldiers.—Reuter.

TWO MORE BUDGETS

There may be two more Budgets this year—one in about two months' time and another before December.

Sir Kingsley Wood, Chancellor of the Exchequer, in Parliament yesterday forecast an increase in taxes "in the near future," but promised a short period to allow the country to adjust itself to the burdens already placed on it by last month's Budget.

Chancellor says: "I know you will not flinch."—*See Page Two.*

Lord Beaverbrook goes to the Palace

The King received Lord Beaverbrook at Buckingham Palace last night on his appointment as Minister of Aircraft Production.

Mr. Eden, War Minister, was also received by the King during the day.

Aliens curfew

Every alien will have to stay at home all night after Monday, by order.

Curfew hours in London will be midnight, elsewhere 10.30 p.m., to six a.m.

See Page Five.

News  Chronicle

No. 29,355 ONE PENNY WEDNESDAY, JUNE 5, 1940 RADIO, PAGE 7 * POSTAGE IN U.K., CANADA, AND NEWFOUNDLAND .. 1d OTHER PLACES ABROAD 1d

"We shall defend our island whatever the cost may be. We shall fight on the beaches, we shall fight on the landing grounds, in the fields, in the streets and in the hills. We shall never surrender."—Mr. Churchill

335,000 MEN EVACUATED

Men of the B.E.F. assembled with French troops on the beach at Dunkirk, ready to be taken off by the Navy.
MORE PICTURES OF THE EVACUATION ARE ON THE BACK PAGE.

Dunkirk at Last Abandoned: The Withdrawal Complete

LAST night the French Admiralty and the British War Office announced that Dunkirk has now been abandoned by the Allies after the most remarkable withdrawal in military history.

In the House of Commons during the afternoon Mr. Churchill (whose speech is fully reported on this page and Page Three) declared that no fewer than 335,000 British and French troops had been evacuated from the port.

B.E.F. losses were: 30,000 killed, wounded and missing; 1,000 guns and all transport and armoured vehicles lost.

In a special broadcast to the German people last night the German High Command said the Nazi losses between May 10 and June 1 were: 10,252 killed, 8,463 missing, 42,523 wounded.

Between May 10 and June 1, said the German communiqué, 432 German planes were lost. The German Air Force shot down 1,841 enemy planes and at least 1,600 more were destroyed on the ground.

If Allies Don't Accept Peace—

The communiqué ended with a warning to the Allies that if they still rejected peace, the struggle would go on until they (the Allies) were annihilated.

Admiral Abrial, commanding the French Forces at Dunkirk, was the last to leave. He did so at seven o'clock yesterday morning.

Completion of the evacuation, the News Chronicle is officially informed, means that no troops were left behind.

The French Admiralty's communiqué announcing the abandonment of Dunkirk, said: "During the night of June 3-4 the last of the land and naval forces which, under the command of Admiral Abrial, were defending Dunkirk to permit the withdrawal of the Allied armies of the North, were all embarked in good order, after having rendered the port unusable.

"By their close co-operation, British and French marines have thus completed an operation unique in history—an operation which has enabled more than 300,000 men of the Allied armies to be rescued.

French Lost Eight Warships

"Three hundred French warships and merchant vessels of various sizes, with 200 smaller boats, as well as numerous formations of the naval air arm, took part in this operation.

"We lost the torpedo boats Jaguar and Chacal, the destroyers L'Adriot, Bourrasque, Foudroyant, L'Oragan and Sirocco, and the supply ship Niger.

"Most of the crews were saved.

"The French Admiralty knows that the success of such an enterprise necessarily entails the sacrifice of a certain number of naval and air units. The crews themselves also realise it. They did their duty as a matter of course."

Our Losses Are Small In Comparison

The British War Office, announcing the completion of the withdrawal last night, said:

"The outstanding success of these operations, which must rank as one of the most difficult operations of war ever undertaken, has been due to the magnificent fighting qualities of the Allied troops; to their calmness and discipline in the worst of conditions; to the devotion to duty of the Allied navies, and to the gallantry and exertions of the Royal Air Force.

"As the result, although our losses have been considerable, they are small in comparison to those which a few days ago seemed inevitable.

"South of the Somme our troops are now operating in conjunction with the French.

"Today has been a quiet day on the British front."

Last night's French High Command communique said: "Our soldiers returning from the North, whose energy remains intact, are ready for fresh battles.

"Fighting occurred this morning on the Lower Somme, in which we took some prisoners."

Submarine Sinks Greek Ship

VIGO, Tuesday.—The Greek steamer Yonna (1,040 tons) has been sunk by a submarine 120 miles off Cape Finisterre.

Survivors were brought ashore today by the Spanish ship Razo.

It was off Cape Finisterre that the Argentine ship Uruguay was sunk recently.—Associated Press.

[No ship Yonna is mentioned in "Lloyd's Register."]

Call-Up Speed-Up This Month

Mr. Anthony Eden, War Minister, stated in the Commons yesterday that the calling up of men for the Army was being accelerated to the maximum number which could be trained, and the calling up this month would give an intake of about double the normal rate.

LATE NEWS

U.S. Minister's Warning

NEW YORK.—"If England and France are conquered, Americas will be next objective," said Mr. Wallace, U.S. Secretary of Agriculture, in a broadcast. He called for economic as well as military preparedness.—Reuter.

Italy is Still Prepared —Says Rome

Commenting on yesterday's Italian Cabinet meeting, Rome Radio broadcast in English: "Results of this meeting are by no means to be taken as indication Italy has changed intentions. She is still prepared to take up arms and fight for her rights at any time she thinks fit."

Fair broadcast summary of Churchill's speech came as eye-opener to Italian public, who for days past read of nothing but German victory and annihilation of Allied northern army. Remark generally heard was that Hitler had won the battle, but that did not mean he had won war.—Reut

LONDON BLACK-OUT TIME
9.41 p.m.—4.15 a.m.

Reynaud Tells Italy, Door Open

Telephone communication between Italy and France has been cut, it was announced in Rome last night, says B.U.P.

M. REYNAUD, the French Prime Minister, in a statement to the Senate Foreign Affairs Commission in Paris yesterday, said:

"If Italy enters the war she will be doing so deliberately for the sole purpose of waging war."

He recalled that both before and since September 1 last the French Government had made known to the Italian Government its willingness to open discussions aimed at finding a friendly basis for an equitable settlement of all questions outstanding between the two countries.

"These overtures," M. Reynaud said, "remained without response, but the attitude which the Italian Government felt called on to adopt made no difference to the feelings of the French Government."

FOUND NO ECHO

A statement to this effect was brought to the notice of the Italian Government.

It was also widely reproduced in the French Press without finding any echo in the Italian Press.

During the last few days the French Government, in full accord with the British Government, had renewed its demarches in this sense.

"Signor Mussolini," M. Reynaud continued, "is well aware of these demarches, and the spirit in which they are made.

"He knows that there is nothing provocative in our attitude; nor in that of our British friends, and we have never closed, and do not now close, the door to any negotiations."—Reuter.

Repeated What Haw-Haw Said: Court Charge

A man will be charged at Mansfield (Notts) today with being responsible for a rumour that he had heard from a German broadcast by "Lord Haw-Haw" that the Germans were going to attack a Mansfield school.

This was stated yesterday by Mr. J. L. Nicol, Regional Information Officer, at the inaugural meeting at Nottingham of the North Midland Regional Advisory Committee, which will function under the jurisdiction of the Ministry of Information.

PREMIER PREDICTS ANOTHER BLOW AT THE ALLIES SOON

By E. CLEPHAN PALMER
The Parliamentary Correspondent

THE full gravity of the military position was brought before the House of Commons last night by the Prime Minister in a speech of matchless oratory, uncompromising candour and indomitable courage.

Sometimes he sent a chill through the crowded House, as when he spoke of the "colossal military disaster" in France and Flanders, and of our determination "to defend our island home and ride out the storms of war . . . if necessary, for years, if necessary, alone." He was grim then.

He stressed, however, that the British Empire and the French Republic, linked together, would defend to the death their native soils.

Always the darkness of the picture he drew was relieved by his faith in the people of Britain—his confidence that, whatever happened, they would refuse to accept the possibility of defeat.

Even if the worst happened—

"We shall defend our island whatever the cost may be. We shall fight on the beaches, we shall fight on the landing grounds, in the fields, in the streets, and in the hills. We shall never surrender."

The House did not cheer. It was, it seemed, a moment for something deeper than cheers. The tense silence was unbroken till Mr. Churchill said:

"Even if—which I do not for a moment believe—this island or a large part of it were subjugated and starving, then our Empire beyond the seas, armed and guarded by the British Fleet, will carry on the struggle until, in God's good time, the New World, with all its power and might, sets forth to the liberation and rescue of the Old."

The B.E.F. Will Be Rebuilt

This confidence that a German victory was unthinkable—not only to ourselves, but to the United States—was loudly cheered.

So was the Premier's determination that the British Expeditionary Force should be rebulit and re-equipped to fight again in France, in spite of its losses:

30,000 killed, wounded or missing; 1,000 guns, and all transport and armoured vehicles lost.

He paused a moment to bring still nearer to the House the cost of the heroic retreat. Glancing along the Treasury bench, he said in a low voice: 'The President of the Board of Trade (Sir Andrew Duncan) is not in his place. His son has been killed."

A Miracle of Deliverance

He spoke of the epic of Dunkirk as a "miracle of deliverance by which 335,000 men, British and French, have been taken out of the jaws of death back to their native land." But it was not to be confused with victory. Wars were not won by evacuation.

The only victory—beyond the countless individual victories over fear and death—he found in the air

Turn to Back Page, Col. Four

Churchill Assures United States

By VERNON BARTLETT

AMONG diplomats in the Gallery the reaction to the Prime Minister's speech in the House of Commons was one of unreserved welcome.

Several of them had feared that he might succumb to the temptation to disguise the magnitude of the disaster under moving phrases about the heroism and organisation with which the B.E.F. faced up to it.

Such an attitude would have convinced many neutrals, including those in the New World to whom Mr. Churchill appealed in his concluding sentence, that the British public was still considered too weak for any diet but the soft, soothing, reassuring lies it received from the previous Government.

HELP WELCOMED

The moving phrases were certainly there, but so, also, were two arguments of the first importance at the present time. One, that those Americans who believe any assistance they might send us would arrive too late are misled—they will still find us fighting.

Two, that with the best will in the world the disgraceful gaps in our defences coupled with those honourable ones left by the evacuation from Dunkirk cannot be made good for some time.

And since during that time the Nazis may be expected to strike with their greatest possible vigour, assistance would be doubly welcome immediately.

ROUSED ANXIETY

The Prime Minister's reference to the possibility of fighting alone has naturally aroused a lot of anxious speculation, despite his tributes elsewhere in his speech to France.

The reason for it is presumably the recognition that France has lost more heavily in men and perhaps in material than we have, and may none the less have to bear almost the entire brunt of a new German offensive within the next few days.

It is increasingly probable that she would also be attacked from the rear by Mussolini's unhappy Italians.

Also the resurrection in Spain of the one cry which might win very widespread Spanish support of all

Turn to Back Page, Col. Three

Reprisals For Bombs On Paris

IN reprisal for Monday's raid on Paris—which killed 254—French planes bombed military objectives at Munich and Frankfurt-on-Main, including an important Nazi aircraft engine factory.

This was announced by the War Ministry spokesman in Paris last night.

British planes, it was announced, also undertook reprisals, bombing railway stations, oil refineries and other industrial objectives in the "forge of the Reich": the Ruhr region.

PARIS TIME BOMBS

Paris casualties totalled 906, and 195 of the dead were civilians, 59 being military. Of the 652 people wounded 545 were civilians.

Twenty-five German bombers were brought down. Time bombs dropped on Monday were still exploding yesterday morning.

Fires were started by incendiary bombs in Le Havre. High explosive bombs were also dropped. Houses were hit.

When oil depots and storage tanks in Western Germany were attacked by R.A.F. heavy bombers on Monday direct hits with high explosives and incendiary bombs were registered on many targets.

OIL TANKS FIRED

Last night's British air communiqué said aerodromes occupied by the enemy in North-West Germany and Holland were also bombed.

At least three big tanks were fired at Ghent, and oil stocks seized by German forces destroyed.

It was announced in Berlin that eight persons were killed when an Allied plane raided a suburb of Munich at 2 a.m. One bomb, it was said, struck a factory, causing substantial damage.

Foreign Messages from Reuter, B.U.P. and Associated Press

Paris Raid Damage Pictures: Page Two

Inside News

Soviet Accept Cripps

THE British Government is prepared to enter into fully normal diplomatic relations with Russia. This was announced by Mr. R. A. Butler, Under-Secretary for Foreign Affairs, in the House of Commons yesterday.

Mr. Butler said that he hoped to be able to give a reply today on the subject of diplomatic representation by an Ambassador in Moscow.

This is believed to foreshadow official confirmation of the appointment of Sir Stafford Cripps as full-time Ambassador to the Kremlin.

Moscow radio broadcast an official Foreign Office announcement last night saying that the Soviet Government had no objection to the appointment of Sir Stafford Cripps as British Ambassador to Russia in place of Sir William Seeds. Nor did M. Molotov, Soviet Foreign Commissar, foresee any objection to the appointment of M. Labonne as French Ambassador in place of M. Naggiar.

DAILY MIRROR, Wednesday, June 5, 1940.

Daily Mirror

JUNE 5

No. 11,385 ✦ ✦ ONE PENNY

Registered at the G.P.O. as a Newspaper.

WE NEVER SURRENDER

DUNKIRK —LAST MEN GO

THE French Admiralty announced yesterday that the last land and naval forces defending Dunkirk were embarked during the night.

The port had previously been made useless to the Germans.

The French Navy, it was added, had lost in the Dunkirk operations seven destroyers—Jaguar, Chacal, Adroit, Bourrasque, Foudroyante, Ouragan and Sirocco—and the supply ship Niger.

Confirming the completion of the evacuation, a British communique said: "Our losses, though considerable, are small in comparison to those which a few days ago seemed inevitable."

The French communique states:

"Three hundred French warships and merchant vessels of various sizes, with 200 smaller boats, as well as numerous formations of the Naval Air Arm, took part in this operation.

"Most of the crews of our lost naval vessels were saved.

3 Admirals Land

"Other ships were damaged, but some have already put to sea again.

In addition to making Dunkirk unusable as a port, the Allied forces destroyed war material which could not be removed.

"When the Germans enter they will find almost nothing," French reports stated.

Three admirals of the French Navy and three French generals arrived at a south-east coast port yesterday with French troops evacuated from Dunkirk. They travelled to London to visit the Admiralty and War Office

254 KILLED IN PARIS AIR RAID

Death-roll in Monday's Paris air raid was 254, of whom 195 were civilians and fifty-nine soldiers, says the Paris War Ministry. It adds: 652 were wounded—545 civilians, 107 soldiers.

MILITARY objectives in Munich, Frankfort-on-Main and the Ruhr were bombed by Allied warplanes as a reprisal for Monday's raid on Paris, the official Havas Agency announced last night.

It has now been established that twenty-five of the German bombers taking part in yesterday's raid were brought down.

A Berlin report yesterday stated that a "suburb of Munich" was bombed by an Allied plane, and eight people were killed. One bomb, it was stated, hit a factory, causing much damage.

R.A.F. fighters maintained offensive patrols throughout Monday and early yesterday in the Dunkirk area.

In Germany refineries, oil tanks, supply depots and marshalling yards in the Ruhr Valley, Rhenish Prussia and in the neighbourhood of Frankfort were among the important military objectives attacked.

"EVEN if large tracts of Europe fall into the grip of the Gestapo and all the odious apparatus of Nazi rule, we shall not flag or fail. We will go on to the end, and will fight in France, on the oceans and in the air. We will defend our island, whatever the cost, and will fight on the beaches and landing grounds, in the fields and streets and we shall never surrender.

"Even if this island or a large part of it were subjugated, our Empire abroad, armed and guarded by the British Fleet, would carry on the struggle until, in God's good time, the new world, with all its force and men, set forth to the liberation and rescue of the old world."

That proclamation of the unbreakable Allied will to fight on for freedom was made by Mr. Winston Churchill in his speech to the House of Commons yesterday—the greatest speech ever made by a Prime Minister of Britain.

Standing as the staunch embodiment of that will to fight, he declared:—

"I have myself full confidence that if all do their duty, and if nothing is neglected, and the best arrangements made—as they are being made—we shall prove ourselves once again able to defend our island home.

"We shall ride out the storms of war and outlive the menace of tyranny, if necessary for years."

A roar of cheers answered his superb, stark confidence.

"That is the resolve of the Government—every man of it—and that is the will of Parliament, and the nation," said Mr. Churchill.

"The British Empire and the French Republic, linked together in their cause and in their need, will defend to the death their native soil, aiding each other like good comrades to the utmost of their strength."

THESE were other vital points in the Prime Minister's speech (the full report of which begins on page 3):

Thankfulness at the escape of the B.E.F. must not blind us to the fact that what happened in North France and Belgium was a colossal military disaster.

✦ ✦ ✦

We must expect another blow almost inmediately

✦ ✦ ✦

We have more military forces in this country now than ever before. This will not continue. We shall not be content with a defensive war. We shall build up the B.E.F. once again under its gallant Commander-in-Chief, Lord Gort.

✦ ✦ ✦

Meantime we must bring Britain's defences to the height of efficiency.

IRONSIDES FOR HOME DEFENCE

SMALL bodies of highly mobile and strongly-armed troops—to be called "Ironsides"—are being organised for home defence by General Sir Edmund Ironside, Commander-in-Chief, Home Forces. There will be many hundreds of these formed from the Regular Army.

The War Office, announcing this last night, says that Sir Edmund has sent to each "Ironside" a copy of the following saying by Oliver Cromwell:—

"Your danger is as you have seen: and truly I am sorry it is so great. But I wish it to cause no despondency, as truly I think it will not: for we are British. . . . It's no longer disputing, but out instantly all you can."

The name Ironside, first given to Cromwell himself by Prince Rupert after the battle of Marston Moor in 1644, was later given to the troopers of his cavalry — those "God-fearing men," raised and trained by him in an iron discipline.

It traditionally implies great bravery, strength or endurance.

400,000 Local Defence Volunteers

Lord Croft, Under-Secretary for War, stated in the House of Lords last night that 400,000 had volunteered for the L.D.V.

He protested against suggestions that officers who had come forward were too old.

"It is no mere outlet of patriotic emotion that we are endeavouring to recruit," he said, "but a fighting force which may be at grips with the enemy next week or even tomorrow.

Lord Strabolgi said that besides making open spaces unusable for the landing of invading planes we should do the same with large spaces of water.

Lord Breadalbane suggested that each local area should have a lorry armoured against splinters and bullets and armed with a couple of guns

RUMOUR-MONGER TO BE CHARGED

A CHARGE of being responsible for a rumour that he had heard from a German broadcast by Lord Haw-Haw that the Nazis were going to attack a Mansfield school is being brought today against a man at Mansfield.

This was stated today by Mr. J. L. Nicol, Regional Information Officer, at the inaugural meeting at Nottingham of the North Midland Regional Advisory Committee, which will function under the jurisdiction of the Ministry of Information.

Mr. Nicol added: "A Ministry official will attend."

This will be the first case of its kind under the new regulations.

LIVESTOCK LEAVES COAST

As a precautionary measure, the numbers of livestock in certain areas in South-East England are being reduced, says the Ministry of Agriculture. Some store animals, particularly ewes and lambs, are being transferred to other counties.

Stock fit for immediate slaughter is being bought by the Ministry of Food. The dispersal is not in any way extensive, and will not have any effect upon supplies of home-killed meat in those areas

The Noble Story of Calais

Given an hour to surrender, 4,000 British and French troops, ordered to hold Calais to the end, spurned the demand to give in and kept the German hordes at bay for four days.

Then silence fell on the port.

Thirty unwounded survivors were taken off by the Navy.

This noble story of the heroic defence of Calais is told on page 3.

Pictures of the Evacuation: Pages 8 & 9

BLACK-OUT 9.44 p.m. to 4.15 a.m.
Sun rises 4.45 a.m. sets 9.14 p.m.
Moon rises 10.59 a.m. sets 12.35 a.m.

LONDON ITALIANS ROUND-UP PAGE FIVE

No. 9,702 (E*) TUESDAY, JUNE 11, 1940 ONE PENNY

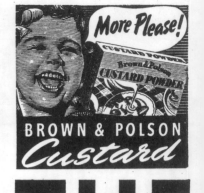

ITALY TAKES THE PLUNGE INTO THE WAR AT MIDNIGHT

HOUR BY HOUR

4 p.m. ITALY DECLARES WAR ON FRANCE AND BRITAIN AS FROM MIDNIGHT.

5.50 Announced Paris placed in state of defence.

6.0 Mussolini to Rome crowd: "The hour of destiny has arrived."

7.0 Ribbentrop gloats: "Victory is guaranteed."

7.5 ANNOUNCED TO-DAY'S SECRET SESSION OF PARLIAMENT POSTPONED.

7.30 Official London statement: "Allies' preparations complete."

7.45 Officials say Turkey resolved to fulfil pact with Allies. M. REYNAUD TELLS FRANCE: "THE WORLD WILL JUDGE THIS ACT."

8.0 Telephones between Turkey and rest of Europe cut.

9.0 Duff Cooper broadcasts. He says: "Mussolini will leave nothing behind him but the curses of those he has betrayed.

10.0 French G.H.Q. announce Germans across the Seine west of Paris.

10.30 Bulgaria announced she looks to Russia for protection. Turkish and Greek frontiers guarded.

12.15 a.m. Roosevelt declares: "Full speed ahead to aid Allies."

ITALY IS TO-DAY AT WAR WITH FRANCE AND BRITAIN, AFTER EIGHT HOURS' NOTICE OF HER DECISION.

At 4 p.m. yesterday Count Ciano informed the Allied Ambassadors in Rome that Italy would enter the war on the side of Germany at midnight.

At 6 o'clock Mussolini proclaimed to a war-fevered crowd that Italy had made her "irrevocable" decision.

IT WAS MET BY THE FIRMEST REPLIES BOTH FROM LONDON AND PARIS. IN LONDON IT WAS OFFICIALLY STATED THAT THE ALLIES KNEW HOW TO MEET SWORD WITH SWORD.

PRESIDENT ROOSEVELT, BROADCASTING EARLY TO-DAY, REVEALED THAT MUSSOLINI HAD TURNED DOWN HIS OFFER TO MEDIATE ON ITALY'S CLAIMS, AND SAID THAT HE HAD GIVEN THE ORDER "FULL SPEED AHEAD" FOR ARMAMENTS FOR THE ALLIES.

Violent fighting was continuing last night along the whole Weygand Line, and Paris was placed in a state of defence as the Germans were reported across the Lower Seine at certain points.

—See Pages Two and Three.

New theatres of war are opened up by Italy's entry into the conflict.

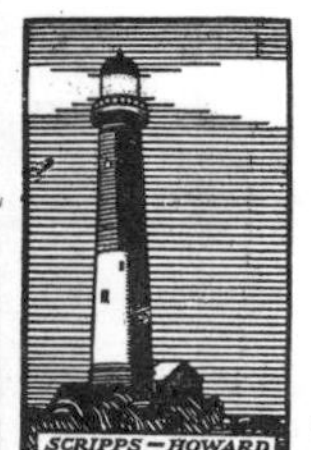

New York World-Telegram

Local Forecast: Light showers tonight and tomorrow; warmer tomorrow.

VOL. 72—No. 298.— IN TWO SECTIONS—SECTION ONE NEW YORK, MONDAY, JUNE 17, 1940. Entered as second-class matter, Post Office, New York, N. Y.

CLOSING WALL ST. PRICES

Real Estate, Page 28

PRICE THREE CENTS

FRANCE ASKS PEACE

Berlin to Ask Total Surrender

Britain to Continue Fight Alone

By the United Press.

France asked Adolf Hitler for "peace with honor" today, but Great Britain fought on alone.

Hitler was reported by Nazi sources as likely to accept nothing but complete capitulation. He arranged to meet with Premier Mussolini to discuss the French proposal broadcast by Premier Marshal Henri Philippe Petain as German armies thundered southward through the beaten and exhausted ranks of poilus.

Leaders of the British government took the position that the fight must go on and that France probably would join other refugee governments to carry on outside French soil, especially with the French naval forces that are so vital to Britain. But that may depend on the meeting between Hitler and Mussolini.

In Berlin it was stated that Germany would regard France's capitulation as a question of complete and unconditional surrender rather than a matter for negotiation.

Reports that negotiations for France's capitulation were being carried on were questioned by well-informed German sources which pointed out that high Nazi quarters recently had emphasized that only total surrender would be acceptable.

No information to show that fighting in France had ceased was received in the German capital where the oficial news agency reported that a French counter-attack had been smashed and huge quantities of war materials, including several big railroad guns, had been captured near Sens, southeast of Paris.

The advance of German armies through France continued at a headlong pace despite the broadcast of aged Marshal Petain, the man who said at Verdun a quarter of a century ago: "They shall not pass." The city of Orleans, relieved by Joan of Arc in a historic battle five centuries ago, fell to the German mechanized columns, the Rhone valley resounded to their thunderous advance and the Maginot Line became what Germans called a "mouse trap" for French soldiers as a result of a Nazi push to the Swiss frontier.

GERMAN BOMBERS BLAST RETREATING FRENCH ARMY

German bombers were everywhere. They blasted the retreating fragments of the French army and poured tons of high explosive on refugee-packed Tours, where the government first fled on abandoning Paris.

Meantime in Bordeaux the fateful decision was being made.

A censored United Press dispatch from Bordeaux indicated that the French people were restive.

Political views that had been buried during the crisis, it said, are now coming to the front again and "class opinions" may eventually become more grave. The dispatch referred to reports that caused the public wrath to rise, but the nature of the reports was not passed by the censorship.

All day yesterday conference followed conference. Premier Paul Reynaud gave the Cabinet President Roosevelt's pladge of "redoubled aid" so long as France resisted—a reply to Reynaud's final

(Continued on Page Two.)

Duce Leaving To See Hitler

By JOSEPH W. GRIGG, JR.,
United Press Staff Correspondent.

BERLIN, June 17.—Adolf Hitler will meet with Benito Mussolini to discuss the French proposal for peace, the German wireless disclosed today as Nazi sources reported belief that only complete capitulation would be accepted by the Axis Powers.

[An authoritative source in Rome said Mussolini would leave his capital tonight to meet Hitler somewhere in Germany or France. They were expected to discuss the next logical phase of the war—an offensive against Great Britain.]

Authorized sources said that the German offensive into France continued "on all fronts" and that there had been no armistice yet, although the French had begun in contact with Hitler's headquarters—apparently through Spanish diplomatic channels.

[A Madrid dispatch said Germany invited Spain to participate in peace negotiations with France.]

"The fighting obviously must continue until Hitler has time to discuss the conditions with Mussolini," it was stated. "No harm will come to French units that capitulate at once."

ORLEANS TAKEN BY GERMANS, THEY TELL OF PETAIN'S PLEA.

Officially there was no comment on the French proposal and the High Command's communique said that the beaten French armies had been smashed on all fronts and were being pursued southward after encirclement of the Maginot Line and capture of the historic city of Orleans, 70 miles south of Paris on the Loire River.

The following communique was issued at Hitler's headquarters:

"Marshal Petain, Premier of the newly formed French government, declared by radio to the French people that France must now lay down her arms.

"In this speech he pointed out that steps ought to be taken informing the Reich government of this decision

(Continued on Page Two.)

Text of Petain Statement

The best available translation of Premier Petain's speech so far is that read from London by the official British wireless and recorded at Columbia Broadcasting System's short-wave listening station. Said the British wireless.

French Men and Women: At the call of the French President I have assumed the leadership of the government of France.

I have been thinking of those who have been fighting, true to their old military traditions, against an enemy of huge numerical superiority. I also think of those old combatants whom I commanded during the last war. I have given myself to France to better her situation at this grave hour.

At this moment I think of the unfortunate refugees, the men and women on the roads, driven away from their homes by the misfortunes of war.

I express to them my sincerest sympathy and compassion. It is with a heavy heart that I tell you today that we must stop the fight.

I sent a message to the enemy yesterday to ask him if he would meet with me, as between one soldier and another, after the fight, and honorably, to seek a way to put an end to hostilities.

Let all Frenchmen gather around the government over which I preside during these sad hours. And let them do their duty (one word inaudible) their faith in the destiny of their country.

Realism - - For You!

On the first page of the second section of this newspaper Gen. Hugh Johnson has an article today which should be read and pondered by every man of military age in this country—by his parents, his wife, or his sweetheart.

You may not like it. You may not agree with it. But you should read it and measure it, not by your emotion, your hopes or your desires, but by the facts, the uncontested facts as they have been revealed in the news columns of the daily press over the last few years.

The General, whose record for correctly calling the turn on coming events is well known to the readers of the World-Telegram, pours more water on the wheel of realism. —THE EDITOR.

12 Die as 2 Bombers Crash in Queens

BULLETIN.

The death toll in the crash of two army bombers in Queens today was raised to 12 when another burned body was found in the wreckage.

Two army bombers from Mitchel Field collided in the air today while on a practice flight, burst into fire and plunged flaming into a quiet Queens neighborhood, scattering charred and mangled bodies over streets and lawns.

Eleven officers and men were killed and two housewives were injured as the bombers crashed, spraying houses with flaming sheets of gasoline, starting four fires in that trim row of bungalows only two blocks from crowded Hillside Ave., almost on the boundary between the Queens Village and Bellerose sections of Queens.

Searchers say there may be one or two more dead in the twisted piles of junk that were $170,000 worth of Douglas medium bombers until their wings touched in the air and housewives looked up in terror at the sound the women of Europe have come to know so well, the scream of diving bombers.

They saw the blazing planes hurtling at them. They saw men try to bail out and fall with their

(Continued on Page Eight.)

Hitler to Occupy Versailles Palace

By the United Press.

ROME, June 17.—The newspaper La Tribuna said today that Adolf Hitler was expected momentarily in Paris "and perhaps has already arrived."

CCC to Enroll 100,000

By the Associated Press.

WASHINGTON, June 17.—The Civilian Conservation Corps announced today that it would begin enrolling 100,000 men July 1. They will replace men who have left to accept jobs.

World-Telegram Index

Roosevelt Seeks Trade Solidarity

Asks 22 Western Nations Join to Preserve Market

BULLETIN.

WASHINGTON, June 17.—Senator Connally (D., Texas), a member of the Foreign Relations Committee, told the Senate today that the United States should send warships immediately to protect British and French possessions in the Western Hemisphere.

By T. F. REYNOLDS,
United Press Staff Correspondent.

WASHINGTON, June 17.—President Roosevelt moved today to place all nations of the Western Hemisphere, including Canada, on an economic offensive designed to offset the implications of Germany's military victory over France.

He proposed swift creation of a central trading agency for all of the Americas to compel Germany, Italy and other totalitarian coun-

(Continued on Page Eight.)

The Weather

(Official United States Forecast.)

New York and Metropolitan Area—Light showers tonight and tomorrow; warmer tomorrow; light to moderate southerly winds.

Lowest temperature expected tonight, 68.

New Jersey—Cloudy with light showers tonight and in the northern portion tomorrow; slightly warmer in the interior tomorrow.

Connecticut—Cloudy with light showers tonight; tomorrow partly cloudy and warmer, with light showers.

Seaboard—The winds are light or moderate and mostly southerly from Eastport to Key West.

TODAY'S READINGS.

	Temp.	Hum.		Temp.	Hum.
Midnight	66	..	7 a. m.	63	91
1 a. m.	66	..	8 a. m.	65	90
2 a. m.	65	..	9 a. m.	68	80
3 a. m.	64	..	10 a. m.	70	68
4 a. m.	63	..	11 a. m.	72	61
5 a. m.	63	..	12 Noon	74	59
6 a. m.	62	92			

Highest and lowest temperatures a year ago, 88—62.

Additional weather data on page 2.

EVENING STANDARD, June 17, 1940

LATE NIGHT FINAL

Evening Standard

Amusements 8
Radio 9

BLACK-OUT 9.47 pm, 4.14 am
MOON Rises 6.31 pm ; Sets 3.47 am

No. 36,125 LONDON, MONDAY, JUNE 17, 1940 ONE PENNY

FRENCH STOP FIGHTING: PETAIN'S STATEMENT

'I Have been in Touch with the Enemy during the Night'

"A WAY TO END HOSTILITIES"

"I MUST TELL YOU THAT TO-DAY THE FIGHTING MUST CEASE. DURING THE NIGHT I HAVE BEEN IN TOUCH WITH THE ENEMY TO SEE WHETHER THEY CAN AGREE WITH ME, AN OLD SOLDIER, A MEANS OF PUTTING AN END TO THE HOSTILITIES"

Marshal Petain, the new French Premier, made this announcement to the French nation at 12.30 p.m. to-day.

He said: "Frenchmen! At the call of the President of the Republic, I have assumed the Government of France. I am sure of the faith of our soldiers, who have been fighting with admirable heroism against an enemy superior in numbers and in arms.

"WE ARE FULL OF ADMIRATION FOR THEM. I AM SURE OF THE SUPPORT OF EX-SERVICE-MEN OVER WHOM I HAVE THE HONOUR TO PRESIDE, AND I AM SURE OF THE FAITH OF THE NATION AS A WHOLE. I WILLINGLY MAKE THE GIFT OF MY PERSON TO LESSEN YOUR SUFFERINGS.

"I am thinking of all those unfortunate refugees who have been marching on the roads, and I should like to express to them my compassion and the care I feel for them.

"Let the people of France group themselves round the Government. Let them obey it with faith in our destiny."

"Unanimous Respect"

Earlier to-day French radio quoted this communiqué, which was issued last night after the meeting of the French Council of Ministers:

"In the present circumstances the Council of Ministers, on the proposal of M. Paul Reynaud, has deemed that the Government of France should be entrusted to a high personality enjoying the unanimous respect of the nation.

"In consequence M. Reynaud offered to the President of the Republic the resignation of the Cabinet.

"M. Albert Lebrun accepted the resignation, paying homage to the patriotism which dictated it, and appealed immediately to Marshal Petain, who accepted the task of forming a new Cabinet.

"The President of the Republic has thanked Marshal Petain, who, assuming the heaviest responsibility ever borne by a French

(CONTINUED ON BACK PAGE)

MARSHAL PETAIN

B.E.F. STILL OPERATING

Fighting on In Normandy

It was stated authoritatively in London before Marshal Petain broadcast to the French nation to-day that at the moment the main question is one of high policy rather than military operations.

The B.E.F. is still operating in Normandy with the French, but there are no details available to say exactly what they are doing.

There is little news of French military operations, but it seems that there is very little going on in the west.

The Germans have concentrated their efforts in the east, where they are now massing their armoured divisions and are apparently attempting a pincers movement around the Maginot Line.

Although there is no confirmation, there are indications that the French are leaving part of the Maginot Line after rendering it useless.

MAN IN CAR INSPECTED ARMY POSTS

Suspected He Has Forged Papers

Because of information received from the War Office, Scotland Yard to-day issued instructions to all police stations to watch for a grey saloon motorcar of German make.

The car, driven by a man wearing British Army uniform, was seen at a number of military posts near London during the week-end.

The driver is believed to have forged papers. He inspected a number of the posts.

The number of the car is officially allotted to a commercial vehicle.

Suspicion Aroused

Suspicion was aroused when it was noticed that the man was alone in the car. It is customary for officers carrying out such inspections to be driven by a private or N.C.O.

It was also discovered that no official instructions had been given for any officer to make such an inspection.

The main gained little information from the posts to which he gained admittance.

Sentries at barricades and Defence Volunteer men have also been told to challenge the driver of a car which answers the description.

"Ring Completed," Say Germans

To-day's German High Command communiqué, quoted by Associated Press, stated:

"Fast moving troops reached the Swiss border near Pontarlier, south-east of Besancon, thereby closing the ring around the enemy forces in Lorraine and Alsace.

"This completes the enclosure of all the French forces defending the Maginot Line, including evidently heavy fortifications in the vicinity of Nancy, Epinal and Belfort—a zone in which it was unofficially estimated at the beginning of the western campaign that upwards of 1,000,000 men were concentrated."

Bomb on the South Coast

The Air Ministry and Ministry of Home Security announced early to-day:

There was some enemy activity on the South Coast last night. One aircraft dropped a bomb which caused negligible damage. There were no casualties.

It is understood that the German airplane was picked up by searchlights and attacked by anti-aircraft fire.

The bomb dropped on downland. The only damage was broken windows in several houses about a quarter of a mile away. No air-raid alarm was given.

Another bomb was dropped on a golf course.

Shot at by Sentry

While Stanley Hartland, aged 44, a civilian shipwright, of Alexandra-avenue, Gillingham, was out walking late last night he did not reply to the challenge of a sentry.

The sentry, after challenging again, fired and Hartland was struck by a bullet in the leg.

Enemy Airplanes Over Bordeaux

Enemy airplanes were reported over Bordeaux early to-day, says a New York message.

No sirens were sounded. The authorities tried to avoid possible panic among the thousands of refugees now crowded into the town.

Information has reached Washington that Mr. William C. Bullitt, U.S. Ambassador to Paris, is safe and at liberty, says this New York message.

Paris Council Chief Killed

M. Raymond Laurent, former president of the Paris Municipal Council, has been killed during an air raid in France.—British United Press.

ORDER TO MAKE CARS UNUSABLE WHEN LEFT

It is likely that the Minister of Home Security will shortly issue an order compelling motorists to make their cars unusable when the vehicles are parked where parachutists may get at them.

U.S.A. Police Arrest Nazi Leaders

U.S.A. police seized two of the most prominent American Nazis at Reading, Pennsylvania, without disclosing what charges were being made against them, says a British United Press message.

The arrested Nazis are Gerhard Wilhelm Kunze, acting national leader of the German-American Bund and the secretary-treasurer, Gustav Elmer.

Japanese Women Leaving Britain

Women members of the staff of the Japanese Embassy in London are leaving this country towards the end of the month.

It was stated at the Embassy to-day that this step was decided on some time ago and is not because of the present situation.

Rail Shopmen Get Another 3s.

Under a settlement reached in London to-day the war advance for railway shopmen is to be increased to 8s. a week, to take effect from June 3.

This means an addition of 3s. to the existing war advance.

BLACK-OUT 9.48 p.m. to 4.14 a.m.

Sun rises 4.44 a.m. sets 9.18 p.m.
Moon rises 7.38 p.m. sets 4.16 a.m.

CALL-UP OF 3 CLASSES: BACK PAGE

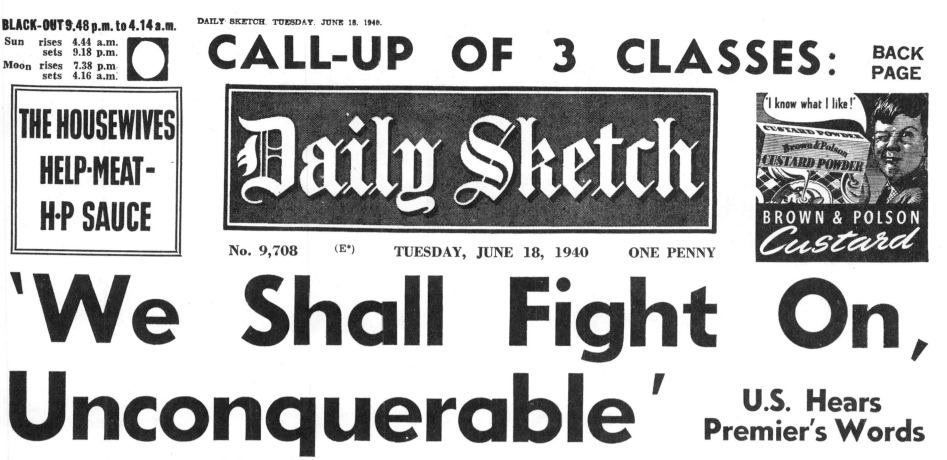

No. 9,708 (E*) TUESDAY, JUNE 18, 1940 ONE PENNY

'We Shall Fight On, Unconquerable'

U.S. Hears Premier's Words

In a short, historic broadcast last night, relayed to the United States, the Prime Minister, Mr. Churchill, said this concerning Marshal Petain's declaration that the French must cease fighting:

● "The news from France is very bad, and I grieve for the gallant French people who have fallen into this terrible misfortune. Nothing will alter our feelings towards them or our faith that the genius of France will rise again.

● "What has happened in France makes no difference to British faith and purpose. WE HAVE BECOME THE SOLE CHAMPIONS, NOW IN ARMS, TO DEFEND THE WORLD CAUSE.

● "We shall do our best to be worthy of this high honour. We shall defend our island, and, with the British Empire around us, we shall fight on unconquerable until the curse of Hitler is lifted from the brows of men.

● "We are sure that in the end all will be well."

* * *

● In Berlin it was stated that pending an armistice, the German advance into France continued in full force.

● Mussolini, accompanied by Count Ciano, left Rome at 8.30 p.m. to meet Hitler about the armistice terms.

* * *

● M. Baudouin, new French Foreign Minister, last night said: "We are ready to lay down our arms if we can get an honourable peace, but we are never ready to accept shameful conditions which would mean the end of spiritual freedom for our people."

See also Pages 2 and 3.

EVERY MAN—TO ARMS!

France's decision to "cease the fight" led yesterday to a great rush in London of men and women eager to serve. The new R.A.F. recruiting inquiry bureau (left) was thronged.

* *

Britain stands fast — resolved to resist any attempt at invasion, by air or sea. Our island home becomes a fortress.

* *

Standing with us is the Empire and all its vast resources. See middle pages.

DAILY MIRROR, Wednesday, June 19, 1940.

Daily Mirror

JUNE 19

No. 11,397 ✦ ✦ ONE PENNY
Registered at the G.P.O. as a Newspaper.

LEADERSHIP, GIVE US LEADERSHIP

1,750,000 MEN FOR DEFENCE

Strength of the defence forces now in Britain, Mr. Churchill stated, are:
1,250,000 Regular soldiers,
500,000 Local Defence Volunteers.
The Dominion Armies.
Large numbers of men in addition would soon be trained and equipped.

DICTATORS FIX TERMS

HITLER and Mussolini, after a four hour conference at Munich, agreed last night on the attitude of both their Governments toward France's request for armistice terms.

It was reported in Rome that the Dictators had ordered their armies to take positions for a final attack on France if their terms should be refused. Earlier, Berlin declared the terms would be unconditional surrender—or "destruction of the French system."

For two and a half hours the Dictators conferred alone. Then they called in Von Ribbentrop and Ciano, their Foreign Ministers, and their Chiefs of Staff. Both Hitler and Mussolini left Munich when the talks ended

FIGHT ON—PETAIN

MARSHAL PETAIN last night ordered all French and Allied combatants on land, sea and air to keep on fighting.

He said armistice negotiations had not even begun, and warned the Allied soldiers that German forces were using the white flag to take important points without fighting.

And there were indications that the French were regrouping their forces on a new line with an east wing based on the Jura Mountains—which cover the southern end of the Maginot Line.

The French military spokesman said the Army was resisting strongly along the Loire on a line through Tours, Blois and Orleans. He declared that heavy losses were inflicted on the Germans on Monday

French troops blew up the four-mile railway tunnel under Gold Mountain, in the Jura, through which famous expresses travelled in peace-time. The eastern mouth of the tunnel lies on the Swiss side of the mountain.

Refugees Barred

Petain's Government took action against the refugee problem, which has hampered resistance.

Civilians in the war zone were told to stay at home and leave the roads clear for the army.

All French towns of over 20,000 inhabitants were declared open towns, to provide shelter from battle and bombardment.

The commander of the powerful French forces in Syria, General Mittelhauser has issued a proclamation that the fight continues on land, sea and air.

Foreign messages: Reuter, British United Press, Associated Press, Exchange.

TAKE DOWN ROAD SIGNS

Every road or street noticeboard or direction post which could assist an invading enemy in discovering his whereabouts must be removed at once.

Failure to comply with this new Home Office order is an offence under the defence regulations

The Premier leaving Downing-street for the House.

Invasion— New Ways Expected

★

Germany Has Most Bombers

★

Churchill's Speech— Page Two

"THE battle of France is over. I expect that the battle of Britain is about to begin."

Thus, Mr. Churchill in the House of Commons yesterday, and now there can be no illusions in anybody's mind about the ordeal before us.

Mr. Churchill spared the feelings neither of the politicians who have failed us, nor of the public who must face the dangers to come.

"Hitler," he said, "knows he will have to break us in this island or lose the war."

He explained that the Navy makes a mass invasion impossible, but that "the Navy have never pretended to be able to prevent raids by 5,000 or 10,000 men thrown ashore at several points on some dark night.

He went on to "the great question of invasion from the air, and the impending struggle between the British and German Air Force."

Our Air Force could deal with any air invasion "until our Air Force has been definitely overpowered."

We must expect enemy bombers now. There may be raids by parachute troops and attempted descents by air-borne soldiers. They would get a warm welcome.

"But," he went on, "the great question is—Can we break Hitler's air weapon?"

He paused, and there was a deep regret for the past in his voice as he added, "It is a very great pity we have not got an Air Force at least equal to that of the most powerful enemy." In his broadcast speech last night he added a further comment on this. "We were promised that five years ago," he said.

R.A.F. Hope of Improvement

His next words were a tribute to the gallantry of the R.A.F. who at Dunkirk undoubtedly beat the German Air Force, inflicting a loss of three or four to one.

"We hope," he said amid cheers, "to improve on that rate."

In his other glance at the past Mr. Churchill said:—"There are many who wish to hold an inquest on the conduct of the Governments and of the Parliaments during the years that led up to this catastrophe.

"They seek to indict those who are responsible for the guidance of our affairs. This also would be a foolish and pernicious process. There are too many in it."

"There are too many in it." That makes tragic reading, Mr. Churchill. It tells a tale of deception and cowardice.

But you ask us to forget the past, and we respect you.

Therefore, until the future becomes the past, we leave it at that.

Having dealt with the politicians of the past, Mr. Churchill turned to the people of the present.

He did not underrate the ordeal before us, but believed that our countrymen and women would prove capable of standing up to it.

"Much will depend on themselves. Every man and woman will have the chance to show the finest qualities of our race, and render the highest service to the cause, and all will be helped to remember 'He nothing common did or mean upon that memorable scene.'"

You need not worry about the men and women of Britain, Mr. Churchill.

The common people of the land have the courage.

Give them arms and give them leadership and they will not fail as they have been failed.

BUT ABOVE ALL GIVE THEM—

LEADERSHIP

RAF BOMB 10 NAZI TOWNS

BOMBERS of the R.A.F. attacked military objectives in Germany at Gelsenkirchen, Homburg, Wanne Eickel, Essen, Dollbergen, Hamburg, Aachen, Duisberg, Rheydt, Cologne and Coblenz.

The raids, the Air Ministry stated last night, were carried out on Monday night

In the Ruhr Valley oil storage centres at Gelsenkirchen, Homburg and Wanne Eickel were subjected to a series of attacks.

High explosive and incendiary bombs were dropped on the Homburg oil tanks.

The raids lasted for nearly three hours, and the many fires started in the target area culminated in one great conflagration which, after burning strongly for about twenty minutes, died away leaving a column of black smoke towering nearly 2,000ft. into the air.

Repeatedly Hit

Two separate fuel installations were attacked at Gelsenkirchen, a great industrial centre to the north-east of Essen Both targets were repeatedly hit.

Oil tanks were set alight and an enormous green flash lit up the centre of the largest refinery.

Successive relays of aircraft set more tanks alight and demolished buildings, railway lines and junction. Strong opposition was encountered from the ground defences, but though two of the aircraft engaged in this operation were hit, both were able to complete their task and to return safely to their base.

BLACK-OUT 9.48 p.m. to 4.15 a.m.
Sun rises 4.44 a.m. sets 9.18 p.m.
Moon rises 8.37 p.m. sets 5.31 a.m.

IF INVADERS COME: Page Five

No. 9,709 (E*) WEDNESDAY, JUNE 19, 1940 ONE PENNY

BATTLE OF BRITAIN: R.A.F. ON OFFENSIVE

Dictators Talk Four Hours: French General's Appeal From London

SEE INSIDE PAGES

LET us brace ourselves to our duty and so bear ourselves that if the British Commonwealth and Empire lasts for a thousand years, men will still say: THIS WAS THEIR FINEST HOUR

—The Premier, last night

Let All The Children Go To Safety

THE six-day evacuation from London has ended. These boys and girls have been sent by their parents to the West Country. But about 340,000 children remain in Greater London.

Arrangements should be made at once to remove all children from crowded cities—if necessary to Canada, which has offered to shelter thousands.

France's Foreign Minister has said that his country "has merely asked Germany under what conditions she would consent to stop the slaughter of French children." We shall fight all the better if we know that the children are safe.

Daily Mail
FOR KING AND EMPIRE
NO. 13,777 THURSDAY, JUNE 20, 1940 ONE PENNY

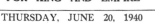

LATE WAR NEWS SPECIAL

MASSED BOMBING BEGINS

Raids from Scotland to Channel

'Business Only' in this Area

The new defence zone banned to holiday-makers.

Keep Out Order on E. Coast

Holidays Banned

ALL holiday-makers and those on pleasure trips are now banned from entering a 20-miles wide strip of country from the Wash to Rye, Sussex, under a defence area order made last night.

Regional civil defence commissioners will have power to control all people entering the area.

Sir John Anderson, Home Secretary and Minister of Home Security, last week appealed to the public not to make unnecessary journeys into the area. The response was excellent.

All Questioned

Now, however, it is desirable that every movement should be controlled.

All visitors are now liable to be asked by the police or military to explain their presence in the area.

If they have no business or other satisfactory reasons they will have to leave.

Those living within the area will not be affected, and there will be the least possible interference with business and other legitimate activities.

Lists of railway stations in the defence area will be posted at all other stations in the country.

A Ship to Safety for Your Child

IF you would like to send your child to safety in the Dominions—where the first batch of 20,000 are soon to go for the duration of the war—you will find full details in Page FIVE.

Points from the scheme are:

Passage will be free both ways.

The only parents who will be allowed to go with them are the widows of men killed in the present war.

The children will not go to institutions, but to private homes.

Parents will be expected to contribute for their keep the amount they now pay for children evacuated within this country. As a general rule this is 6s. a week.

In cases where this amount cannot be paid special arrangements will be made.

'Egypt Will Keep Her Promises'

CAIRO, Wednesday.—Ali Maher Pasha, the Egyptian Prime Minister, told the Chamber of Deputies to-night that the Government would never adopt a policy other than the maintenance of Egypt's independence and rights, and at the same time "the fulfilment of our obligations."

"The task is grave," he said. "I appeal for all help for the Government at this critical hour."—*Reuter.*

⁂ Egypt's Crisis Ends—Page TWO.

Hitler Awaits the French

VENUE KEPT SECRET, ITALIANS BARRED

FRENCH delegates were on their way last night to meet the German representatives. The meeting will be held on German-occupied territory. It is not yet known where the French delegates crossed the line.

According to unconfirmed reports in Bordeaux, three French negotiators—General Huntziger, M. Baudouin, the Foreign Minister, and M. Leon Noel—have been appointed.

M. Noel, a cousin of M. Flandin, a former Premier, was the French Ambassador in Warsaw. General Huntziger, a member of the Supreme War Council, was head of the French military mission in Prague until the Munich settlement of 1938.

In Berlin it was announced that Italy will not be represented when the French plenipotentiaries arrive to hear the terms.

"Italian interests are in good hands as a result of the Munich meeting," it was said in official Berlin quarters. Mussolini arrived back in Rome last night with Ciano and Von Mackensen, Hitler's Rome Ambassador. There were no public ceremonies connected with their return.

'ALL FOR THE AXIS'

In Rome, the *Popolo di Roma* published a version of the terms to be imposed on France.

France, it said, is to hand over to the Axis Powers all her gold and foreign credits, and French territory is to be partitioned between the Italian and German armies.

In addition, all French raw material is to be surrendered and all French commercial and industrial resources are to be available for the Continental blockade of Britain.

But this report was repudiated at once in Berlin. "It is pure bluff," said well-informed officials.

Meanwhile, French officials continue to insist that the peace must be an honourable one.

"If an end is to be put to hostilities we are firmly resolved to accept nothing but honourable terms," said the French radio commentator last night.

"Failing such terms," he said, "the Government will continue the struggle. France will not capitulate unconditionally."

Although the conditions Hitler will demand have not yet been disclosed, the German radio last night revealed how little Marshal Pétain can hope for the "honourable peace" which he sought.

"Only German arms will dictate the conditions in Europe," said Deutschlandsender, "and these arms will continue to dictate as long as it is the wish of our Führer.

"Europe will be completely changed. The German arms will destroy everything to the last bastion of whatever country opposes Hitler's will."

A Rome radio report last night stated that immediately on his return to his headquarters, the Führer ordered the German advance to be accelerated along all fronts.

BRITISH PLAN

In Bordeaux, the French official spokesman said that although France had asked Germany for terms the Government were still considering the British offer of a Franco-British union.

Marshal Pétain received Señor Lequerica, the Spanish Ambassador, who is acting as intermediary. He is reported to have announced Germany's willingness to meet French representatives and talk terms.

It is believed that negotiations for an armistice will take place either at Paris or Versailles. The Germans would prefer Versailles.

Meanwhile, the Germans continue to advance through France. They made a rapid push yesterday to the westwards, apparently to make sure of the whole of the Channel coast to increase their threat to Britain.

CHANNEL PUSH

The French armies, separated at various points, still form four groups. The Germans continue to bear on the first French army group in the region of Rennes, in the direction of St. Malo.

In the area which separates the army in Brittany from the army on the Loire the enemy did not exert any great pressure.

On the Loire the Germans attacked at points between Orleans and Nevers. In general the French are holding on, particularly in the region of Tours.

In the east, German motorised units have reached the Jura mountains near La Cure and Mijoux, north-west of Lake Geneva, it is learned in Geneva.—*Reuter, B.U.P., and Exchange.*

'France is Ready to Fight on'

M. HENRI HAUCK, Labour Attaché in the French Ministry of Information, told the Fabian Society in London yesterday: "As a French Socialist I am sure the Government presided over by Marshal Pétain does not represent the feeling of the mass of the working class in France.

'Our Colonies'

"We do not know yet if this Government presided over by a very aged Marshal of France will be strong enough to resist German pressure, but the position of this Government is very far from representing the true spirit of France.

"Whatever may happen now in France or Bordeaux, whatever terms the French Government will accept, there are in the French colonies, in the whole of the French Empire, in foreign countries, and especially in this country, French people who will not accept any treaty of peace whatever it may be, but will want to carry on the fight at the side of the Allies."

Pownall is New L.D.V. Chief

Lieut.-General H. R. Pownall, formerly Lord Gort's Chief of Staff, has been appointed Inspector-General of the Local Defence Volunteer Force, it was announced last night.

This is a new post necessitated by the growing importance of the L.D.V.s.

General Pownall's new job will be similar to the post of Inspector-General to the Forces. He will inspect and check the organisation, equipment, and training, and ensure that all are up to standard.

GARDEN BOMB

THIS picture of what happened when a bomb exploded in a back garden during the big raid points its own moral. The damage caused is clearly shown. But the occupants of the house were in their Anderson shelter, which stood up to all the shock and blast. Other pictures in Page THREE and BACK Page.

250 RAF Bombs on Bremen

R.A.F. heavy bombers have carried out their biggest series of raids over Germany, straddling the whole of North-West Germany, the Rhineland, and the Ruhr in one series of continuous attacks lasting from midnight to dawn.

More than 250 bombs were dropped on Bremen in ten minutes, causing many explosions and fires among oil tanks.

Then, in many other areas, oil supply centres, railway marshalling yards, power stations, and rail communications were subjected to fierce bombardment.

Besides Bremen, the principal centres attacked were Hamburg, Frankfurt, Hanover, Cologne, Essen, Dusseldorf, Castrop, and Sterkrade.

Targets in and near all these towns were relentlessly attacked in the face of strong opposition from anti-aircraft guns and searchlight batteries.

Arms Works Fired

The raids took place on Tuesday night, and are described in an Air Ministry bulletin issued last night.

Despite the large force of raiders and the fierceness of the opposition only three 'planes were lost.

In Hamburg, which was raided for four hours, salvos of bombs repeatedly straddled a large oil depot near the docks.

Fires were so widespread that the homeward-bound attackers could see them as they crossed the German coast 80 miles away.

At Schilau, nearby, direct hits on a power station resulted in vivid zig-zag flashes which lit up the whole target area.

Explosions and fires were caused when high explosive bombs were dropped on a petrol refinery at Castrop, to the north-west of Dortmund, in the Rhineland.

At Cologne a large munitions works was set ablaze and left with the flames reaching hundreds of feet.

In the raids on Hanover, oil storage tanks at Misburg, near by, were also systematically bombed.

A direct hit on a large build-

Turn to BACK Page

R.A.F. HAS YET MORE 'PLANES

LORD BEAVERBROOK, Minister of Aircraft Production, announced last night that the R.A.F. is stronger than when Hitler launched his great offensive.

"Aircraft production in this country," he said, "in every category, has since May 10 exceeded the total casualty list, including casualties sustained through accidents at home.

"The aircraft available of every type now in use exceeds the number of machines at the disposal of the Air Force when the battle broke out.

"In addition to production, repairs have replenished stocks. There is now on hand a very good surplus stock of engines.

"The public should give thanks for this immense effort to all the aircraft factories and engine shops and their workers, who have striven by night and day, without time off for recreation, without any regard for the pleasures and amenities of life.

"Their conduct is beyond praise. We can place our future in their keeping with confidence."

Madrid Plot Discovered

From Daily Mail Correspondent

MADRID, Wednesday.—A vast underground organisation has been discovered by the police in Madrid. Large numbers have been arrested, and a quantity of firearms and explosives seized.

She Walked On to Mined Bridge

Major Rowland Lancaster Willott, R.E., had lit the safety fuse in the centre of the last bridge over the River Escaut when he saw an aged Belgian woman walking on to the opposite end.

He dashed back under fire and carried the woman to safety—then he fired the full charge, electrically.

Major Willott, it was announced last night, has been awarded the D.S.O.

⁂ Other B.E.F. and R.A.F. Awards.—Page FIVE.

JAPAN 'WARNS' FRANCE

Daily Mail Correspondent

TOKIO, Wednesday.

TENSION over the position of French Indo-China mounted to-day with a direct protest by Japan against the passage of arms for General Chiang Kai-shek's forces.

The protest was delivered by Mr. Tami, Vice-Minister for Foreign Affairs.

He summoned M. Arsène Henry, the French Ambassador, and asked that steps should be taken immediately to secure the voluntary suspension of "assistance extended by French Indo-China to the Chungking Government."

Later the Domei Agency commented: "Qualified observers believe that if French Indo-China persists in extending assistance to the Chungking Government, Japanese expeditionary forces will be compelled to take such action as is strategically deemed necessary."

A message from Chungking says there are fears that a Japanese drive overland from Nanning into Indo-China, supported by naval action off Haiphong, is imminent. It is understood here that Japan has already made representations to Berlin and Rome concerning Indo-China.

⁂ Shanghai Demand to Allies—Page TWO.

WAVE ON WAVE THROUGH NIGHT

HITLER last night launched his greatest air attack of the war on Britain. Swarms of raiders swooped on the east coast of Scotland, on Yorkshire and on its coast; on Co. Durham, down to Lincolnshire and as far south as towns on the south-east coast.

While wave upon wave of German bombers were launching their attack, Hamburg and Bremen radio went off the air, indicating the presence of British 'planes.

The alarms in Yorkshire were over a wide area. Some unidentified 'planes were reported flying high.

Heavy explosions were heard some distance from a Lincolnshire coast town.

Earlier there had been considerable air activity, and large numbers of British 'planes were heard flying out over the sea. After the alarms British fighters were heard also going out to sea.

Numbers of people were caught in the streets in the coast towns. Many were returning from cinemas.

People who had gone to bed early, after being up during Tuesday night's raid, were awakened by the sound of their hurrying feet as they ran for shelter.

"PLANES HERE NOW"

Soon after the alarm a resident at one Yorkshire resort told a *Daily Mail* reporter: "There are heavy 'planes going overhead now at a great height.

"They have come from the sea and are obviously German. One 'plane flew high over our town and the sound of A.A. fire can be heard."

The Air Ministry issued the following communiqué late last night:

"Enemy aircraft crossed our east and south coasts late to-night.

"Air raid warnings were sounded in a number of districts.

"Anti-aircraft defences are in action at several points."

Great Barrage

The sound of bombs exploding was heard in one area. "Our A.A. guns put up a great barrage," said a watcher. "Soon after the alarm we heard 'planes, and the guns began to fire. The bombs seemed to be falling to the east.

"The guns continued to fire for some time and then stopped for a few minutes only to restart again.

Soon after the alarm at a north-east coast town one German bomber flew over the town. The 'plane was twice picked up by searchlights and anti-aircraft shells exploded around its wings.

Four Waves

British fighters came over, and from the sound of machine-gun fire a fierce fight was being fought some distance from the town. A few minutes later four waves of bombers swept over the district. Heavy explosions were heard.

An air raid alarm was sounded in Norfolk late last night. Many 'planes had been over the town some time earlier. Then another 'plane was heard.

This flew inland, but apparently it was British and the searchlights made no attempt to pick it up.

At a south-east coast town the droning of 'planes could be heard overhead at a great height. British fighters of the coastal patrol went up, searchlights were in action.

Nazi Radio Dumb

To the south the sound of anti-aircraft fire was heard.

Later an air-raid warning was sounded in an area on the east coast of Scotland. The all-clear was sounded in about half an hour.

After a 'plane had passed over a Yorkshire town a general warning was sounded in other towns in the county.

For some it was the first warning they had heard since the war began.

Early to-day sirens sounded at another south-east coast town. 'Planes could be heard flying high. There was no anti-aircraft fire

There appear to have been air raid alarms in Germany.

For the third night running the programmes of the Hamburg and Bremen wireless stations were interrupted last night, says *Reuter*. Both stations were off the air at 12.15 a.m.

Britain Has 'Iron Rations'

Secret reserves of "iron rations" have been established in various parts of Britain in case people have to be evacuated from their own localities, it was revealed by Lord Woolton, the Food Minister, in the House of Lords last night.

Full story—Page THREE.
2d.-a-Pint Milk Scheme—Page FIVE.

LATEST

'PLANE DOWN

Unconfirmed report states that a raider crashed in the sea off a coast town.

A4

SOLDIERS HELD, RIFLES TAKEN

Two British soldiers were disarmed in the Whiterock district of Belfast yesterday by a number of men who seized their rifles and escaped in a car.

Later the whole district was cordoned off by military police who made a house-to-house search.

Soldiers with Bren guns were mounted in the district early to-day.

B4

Sunday Dispatch

Radio Page 9.

139th Year. No. 7,234. JUNE 23, 1940. POSTAGE IN U.K., EIRE, CANADA, AND NEWFOUNDLAND .... 1d. OTHER PLACES ABROAD .... 1d. TWOPENCE.

U.S.A. BY CHURCHILL

FRENCH SIGN ARMISTICE

British Government's Grief And Amazement

Churchill Appeals To Frenchmen: 'Fight On'

THE FRENCH PLENIPOTENTIARIES SIGNED AN ARMISTICE WITH GERMANY AT 5.30 LAST NIGHT AT COMPIEGNE, FRANCE, WHERE THE 1918 ARMISTICE WAS SIGNED

"The Armistice will not take effect until six hours after a separate French-Italian agreement has been reached," stated a Berlin broadcast, which added that the French plenipotentiaries were expected to arrive at the appointed meeting place in Italy to-day.

No information about the terms of the armistice were known last night.

"Against Their Ally"

"The British Government have heard with grief and amazement that the terms dictated by the Germans have been accepted by the French Government at Bordeaux," says a statement issued to-day by Mr. Winston Churchill,, the Prime Minister.

"They cannot feel that such or similar terms could have been submitted to by any French Government which possessed freedom, independence, and constitutional authority.

"Such terms, if accepted by all Frenchmen, would place not only France but the French Empire entirely at the mercy and in the power of the German and Italian dictators.

"Not only would the French people be held down and forced to work against their Allies, not only would the soil of France be used with the approval of the Bordeaux Government as a means of attacking their Allies, but the whole resources of the French Empire and of the French Navy would speedily pass into the hands of the adversary for the fulfilment of his purpose.

"His Majesty's Government believe that whatever happens they will be able to carry the war wherever it may lead, on the seas, in the air, and upon land to a successful conclusion

When Great Britain is victorious, she will. inspite of the action of the Bordeaux Government, cherist the cause of the French people, and a British victory is the only possible hope for the restoration of the greatness of France and the freedom of its people. Brave men from other countries overrun by Nazi invasion are steadfastly fighting in the ranks of freedom.

"His Majesty's Government call upon all Frenchmen outside the power of the enemy to aid them in their task and thereby render its accomplishment more sure and more swift.

"They appeal to all Frenchmen, wherever they may be, to aid to the utmost of their strength the forces of liberation, which are enormous and which, faithfully and resolutely used, will assuredly prevail."

According to reliable reports from Bordeaux, where the French Cabinet is sitting in permanent session reviewing Hitler's peace terms, most of yesterday was spent in discussing the question whether the French Government should withdraw to Northern Africa to enable the French Air Force and the Fleet to continue resistance.

A powerful section of the French Government is understood to be opposed to complete surrender.

According to the French radio last night Pétain has made counter-proposals to Germany.

General de Gaulle, M. Reynaud's Military Adviser, broadcasting in French in the B.B.C. European news bulletin last night, appealed to all Frenchmen to rally to the British and fight on—whatever the decision of the Pétain Government, "which has no right to surrender." His speech is reported in Column 1, Page 12.

Reports have been received in London from all parts of the French Empire making it clear that feeling in French colonies is strongly in favour of continuing the war. Various Governors-General and commanders of troops have indicated that they are prepared to continue to fight side by side with the British Empire.

"As Soldier To Soldier"

Berlin radio last night broadcast a recording of the proceedings in the railway carriage in Compiègne:

"General Huntziger, who signed for France, speaking in a slow, hesitant, but firm voice, said:

"'The French Government has agreed to the terms of the armistice, but before signing the document, I wish to say a few personal words.

"'At the moment when the French delegation puts its signatures to this document, being forced to agree to conditions through military misfortune, the delegation wishes to point out that France has the right to expect from Germany a peace which would secure good-neighbourly relations with her great neighbour.

"'As soldier speaking to soldier, I hope that French soldiers will never have to regret that they laid down their arms for the peace to come.'

"General Keitel, the German Commander-in-Chief, in a brief statement, said: 'I confirm the acceptance of the French Government in signing this armistice agreement. As a soldier I have little to say except that the victor knows how to honour a courageous, defeated foe.'

"After the signature of the armistice, General Keitel asked the French and German delegates to rise, and then said, 'At this moment it is our duty to remember those brave soldiers of our countries who have spilled their blood on the battlefields. We have risen to honour their memory.'"

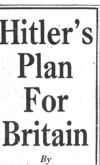

Hitler's Plan For Britain

By MADAME TABOUIS

● **HITLER, on June 4, informed his staff and his colleagues of his plans for the coming months.**

● **After reminding them that he would be in Paris on June 15, as he had arranged with Göring, Goebbels, and Himmler, he declared that he would not give Britain time to organise herself, that he would attack her round about July 2, according to the plan previously arranged.**

● **Therefore, he explained, France must be put out of any state capable of resisting, at least on the European Continent.**

● **The war against Britain would be carried on with the most extreme energy, including parachute invasion, bombing, and so on, and, Hitler thinks, ought to be terminated successfully towards the end of July. Hitler counts on speed of attack to succeed in winning before aid can come from America and the Dominions.**

● **The Führer then made it clear that diplomatic attacks against the U.S.S.R. would begin as from the first days of August; the Ukraine and the Baltic States should fall about August 15 under the attack of French divisions marching behind German tanks.**

● **The Führer then apparently explained the absolute necessity for the Reich not to lay down arms until after this campaign against Russia.**

● **Granted that there would be peace towards the end of the year, a peace establishing the means of existence of "Deutsch Europa," the campaign could not be of long duration.**

● **According to him, the American Continent would soon attack a Continent of Europe that had passed under the sovereignty of the Reich, in order to strike down the latter, and that would be the great struggle which the Third Reich would have to wage for its existence.**

● **To be able to resist victoriously, the Reich had need of the mineral and oil resources of Russia, as well as the certainty that the Third Reich would never have to defend its frontiers on the east against any enemy attack.**

● **After having declared that "Deutsch Europa" would be, after his victory over the Russians, stronger than the American Continent, the Führer explained at length how he would apply as soon as possible all that has been prepared in the various departments for the material and moral organisation of Europe.**

Madame Tabouis tells how she escaped from the Nazis—Page THREE.

NAZIS BOMB US AGAIN

During an air raid on the east coast early yesterday morning, an elderly couple living in a village took refuge in their Anderson shelter. A bomb crashed four yards in front of the entrance, but except for a slight cut on the nose the occupants were unhurt. The couple are seen at the entrance of the shelter.

The picture above shows the devastating effect a German bomb had on a house in Suffolk, in which three people were killed. A.R.P. workers are searching the wreckage.

ITALIAN "SUB" GIVES IN

—To A British Trawler

THE British trawler Moonstone, on patrol off Aden, has captured one of the biggest of Mussolini's submarines.

An Admiralty announcement last night stated that the Moonstone saw the periscope of the submarine and at once attacked with depth charges.

These brought the submarine to the surface.

The submarine engaged the trawler with her entire armament—torpedoes, two 3in. guns, and smaller guns.

THEIR "PRIZE"

The Moonstone replied with her 4in. gun and a Lewis gun, scoring hits.

The submarine then surrendered and was brought into Aden as a prize.

There were no British casualties. The Italian captain and several officers were killed.

Three officers and 37 ratings were taken prisoner.

JAPANESE MASSING TROOPS

JAPANESE troops, estimated last night to number 3,000, are massing on the borders of the British colony at Hong-kong.

Not far away Japanese warships, including aircraft carriers, have concentrated in the vicinity of Indo-China, it is reported from Shanghai.

It is expected that they will make an attempt to land there immediately they are assured of the definite capitulation of the French.

It is believed that the Japanese movements near Hong-kong are a prelude to protests concerning the alleged passage of supplies to Chungking, via Burmah.

A British Army officer in Hong-kong told the *B.U.P.*: "The Japanese are occupying certain areas adjacent to the colony for the purpose of mopping up Chinese guerrillas. The Japanese Army had advised the British authorities of their intention to do so."

BOUQUET FOR HITLER

A message for Hitler offering congratulations on the "Great achievements of the German Reich," was delivered to the German Ambassador, General Ott, in Tokio yesterday, on behalf of the "League of Diet Members for the Attainment of the Objective of the Sacred Campaign in China."

The league comprises 251 of the total of 446 members of the Japanese Diet.

"PEACE TALKS IN BERLIN"

HITLER PLANS TO CALL A EUROPEAN PEACE CONFERENCE IN BERLIN AS SOON AS A SETTLEMENT IS REACHED WITH FRANCE, ACCORDING TO A DISPATCH FROM LELAND STOWE FROM ISTANBUL TO THE "NEW YORK POST" YESTERDAY.

Mr. Stowe, whose source is a high Nazi official, states that the Hitlerian plan of Continental Europe will be outlined at this party, from which British and Russian representatives will be barred.

> *LELAND STOWE.*
>
> **gave to the world first news of our losses in Norway.**
>
> **He is a leading American journalist who went to Germany in 1933, and published a book—"Nazi Germany Means War." In it he forecast that the Hitler régime created a "grave menace to European peace."**

The Führer intends to establish his own model of a political and economic European federation, which will be sub-divided into three or four groups of nations, each linked along economic and geographical lines. All Governments would be modelled on Nazi lines, and their national armies would be abolished.

The aim of the federation would be to checkmate the "Anglo-American economic bloc," because Hitler expects the United States to enter the war, which would mean prolonged hostilities.

Once France is definitely out of the war, Germany will concentrate on aeroplanes and abandon tank construction, as an Anglo-American alliance would threaten to achieve superiority in the air.

All the details of Hitler's plan are not yet known, but the main bloc around Germany would be France, Switzerland, Holland, Belgium, and Denmark, all stripped of armies, but "protected" by Germany.

Mr. Stowe's informant also revealed that Germany intends to try to break England's resistance mainly by violent aerial bombardments.

Carol's Party Is Only One In Rumania

King Carol of Rumania has appointed M. Ernest Urdarjano, Minister of the Royal Household, to be chief of the headquarters staff of the new single "Party of the Nation," which has been formed under the King's personal leadership.

The new party, which is strongly Fascist, will keep the motto, emblem, and uniform of the National Renaissance Front, which it supplants.

THE BLACK OUT TO-NIGHT
London and South Coast } 9.51 p.m. to 4.13 a.m.

Scharnhorst Torpedoed

SCHARNHORST, 26,000-TONS CRACK GERMAN BATTLE-CRUISER, HAS BEEN TORPEDOED AND BOMBED OFF TRONDHEIM, NORWAY. SHE SUFFERED "CONSIDERABLE DAMAGE."

In the same action a Nazi destroyer was also torpedoed.

Heavily escorted by destroyers and screened by no fewer than 50 Messerschmitt fighters, Scharnhorst was spotted by the British submarine as she slunk out of Trondheim Fiord—obviously on her way to a port where she could repair the damage done by a heavy British bomb which hit her on June 13.

The submarine, at once attacking, scored a hit with one torpedo.

Relays of British bombers, informed by the submarine of the attack, shadowed the Nazi squadron for nearly nine hours until the light was suitable for a bombing attack.

Then they smashed through the screen of fighters and "an avalanche of light and heavy anti-aircraft shells."

At least three direct hits were made with heavy bombs. Two struck alongside Numbers One and Two gun turrets. The other smashed on to the stern, from which a great quantity of debris rose in the air.

An aerial torpedo hit one of the escorting destroyers.

At least two of the Messerschmitts were destroyed and others damaged. Five of our aircraft failed to return.

Scharnhorst, launched only in January of last year, ran away, badly damaged, when attacked by the Renown in Norwegian waters in April.

LATEST NEWS

5

PRISONERS NAMED

New list of British prisoners broadcast on German radio last night:

Pilot Officer R. G. Wood, Flying Officer N. Forbes, Leading Aircraftman J. H. Mackenzie, Pilot Officer T. A. Whiting, Pilot Officer H. E. Farhurst, Pilot Officer W. Stapleton, Flying Officer T. C. Bretherton, Sergeant M. A. Oliver, Pilot Officer B. A. James, Sergeant C. Merton, Pilot Officer Sedgwick Webster, Sergeant J. Horton, Richard Whitehurst, Kernside, Glasgow; Harry Moreby, Panforth, near Wakefield.

DAILY SKETCH, MONDAY, JUNE 24, 1940.

BLACK-OUT 9.49 p.m. to 4.16 a.m.
Sun rises 4.16 a.m. sets 9.19 p.m.
Moon rises 11.40 p.m. sets 10.50 a.m.

BALLOON BARRAGE GETS TWO NAZIS: BACK PAGE

No. 9,713 (E*) MONDAY, JUNE 24, 1940 ONE PENNY

GERMANY'S TERMS

Complete Capitulation of France

SHE MUST HAND OVER STOCKS, MATERIAL AND TERRITORY FOR WAR ON BRITAIN; FLEET TO BE CALLED TO HOME PORTS AND DISARMED

Here are the terms of Germany's armistice with France:

1—Germany will occupy the whole of the West Coast of France and all territory north of a line from Geneva to Tours. France will pay for the occupation.

2—The French armed forces are to be demobilised and disarmed. Only a small force in unoccupied France will be allowed, the size of this force being fixed by Germany and Italy.

3—Germany may demand the surrender in good condition of all artillery, tanks, aircraft and munitions.

4—No French forces may leave French soil. No material may be conveyed to Great Britain. No French merchant shipping may leave harbour, and ships outside France must be recalled.

5—All establishments and stocks must be handed over intact. The same applies to ports, fortifications, naval yards, railways and communications. All wireless stations in unoccupied territory must stop.

6—THE FRENCH GOVERNMENT MUST FACILITATE TRANSPORT OF MERCHANDISE BETWEEN GERMANY AND ITALY.

7—German prisoners of war must be released, but all French prisoners of war will remain in captivity until peace is signed.

8—THE FRENCH FLEET IS TO BE RECALLED TO FRENCH TERRITORIAL WATERS AND THERE TO BE DISARMED AND INTERNED UNDER GERMAN AND ITALIAN CONTROL IN PORTS WHICH THE GERMAN AND ITALIAN GOVERNMENTS WILL SPECIFY.

A CERTAIN PART OF THE FLEET, WHICH THE GERMAN AND ITALIAN GOVERNMENTS WILL DETERMINE, WILL, IT IS STATED, BE LEFT FREE FOR THE SAFEGUARD OF FRENCH INTERESTS IN THE COLONIAL EMPIRE.

9—The armistice will enter into force as soon as the French Government have concluded a similar agreement with the Italian Government.

10—The armistice is valid until peace is signed, but may be denounced at any moment by Germany if the French Government do not fulfil it.

SEE ALSO PAGE TWO

● What Hitler is leaving of France to Frenchmen. The shaded portion of the map is the area to be occupied by the German Army.

The Evening Post

Vol. 51 No 8 (Telephone Central 27.) JERSEY. TUESDAY JULY 9 1940. ONE PENNY.
Sole Proprietors, Printers and Publishers: W. E. GUITON & Co., 2, Charles Street, St. Helier.

Orders of the Commandant of the German Forces in Occupation of the Bailiwick of Jersey.

Dated the 8th day of July, 1940

1. **The German Commandant is in close touch with the Civil Authorities and acknowledges their loyal co-operation.**
2. **The Civil Government and Courts of the Island will continue to function as heretofore, save that all Laws, Ordinances, Regulations and Orders will be submitted to the German Commandant before being enacted.**
3. **Such legislation as, in the past, required the Sanction of His Britannic Majesty in Council for its validity, shall henceforth be valid on being approved by the German Commandant and thereafter sanctioned by the Bailiff of Jersey.**
4. **The orders of the German Commandant heretofore, now and hereafter issued shall, in due course, be Registered in the records of the Island of Jersey, in order that no person may plead ignorance thereof. Offences against the same, saving those punishable under German Military Law, shall be punishable by the Civil Courts, who shall enact suitable penalties in respect of such offences, with the approval of the German Commandant.**
5. **Assemblies in Churches and Chapels for the purpose of Divine Worship are permitted. Prayers for the British Royal Family and for the welfare of the British Empire may be said. Church Bells may ring ten minutes before Service. Such Assemblies shall not be made the medium for any propaganda or utterances against the honour or interests of, or offensive to, the German Government or Forces.**
6. Cinemas, Concerts and other Entertainments are permitted, subject to the conditions set out in Order No. 5 above.
7. Prices must not be increased or decreased. Any shopkeeper offending against this Order is liable to have his shop closed and also to pay any fine that may be imposed by the Competent Authorities.
8. The sale and consumption of wines, beer and cider is permitted in such premises as are licensed by the Civil Authorities.
9. Holders of Licences for the sale of such intoxicating liquors (wines, beer or cider), shall take the most rigid precautions for the prevention of drunkenness. If drunkenness takes place on such licensed premises, then without prejudice to any other civil penalty, the Island Police shall and are hereby empowered to close the premises.
10. All traffic between Jersey and Guernsey is prohibited, whether direct or indirect, for the time being (other Regulations will follow).
11. The Rate of Exchange between the Reichsmark and the Pound has been fixed at Eight Marks to the Pound.
12. The continuance of the privileges granted to the civilian population is dependent upon their good behaviour. Military necessity, however, may, from time to time, require the Orders now in force to be made more stringent.

For and on behalf of the German Commandant of the Channel Islands

(Signed) **GUSSEK, Hauptmann,**
Commandant, Jersey.

Average net paid circulation for June exceeded
Daily---1,950,000
Sunday-3,500,000

DAILY NEWS
Copr. 1940 by News Syndicate Co. Inc. NEW YORK'S PICTURE NEWSPAPER Trade Mark Reg. U. S. Pat. Off.
FINAL
Vol. 22. No. 22 New York, Saturday, July 20, 1940★ 28 Pages 2 Cents IN CITY LIMITS | 3 CENTS Elsewhere

YIELD OR DIE, HITLER ROARS AT BRITAIN

Story on Page 3

(Acme radiofoto FLASHED HERE YESTERDAY)

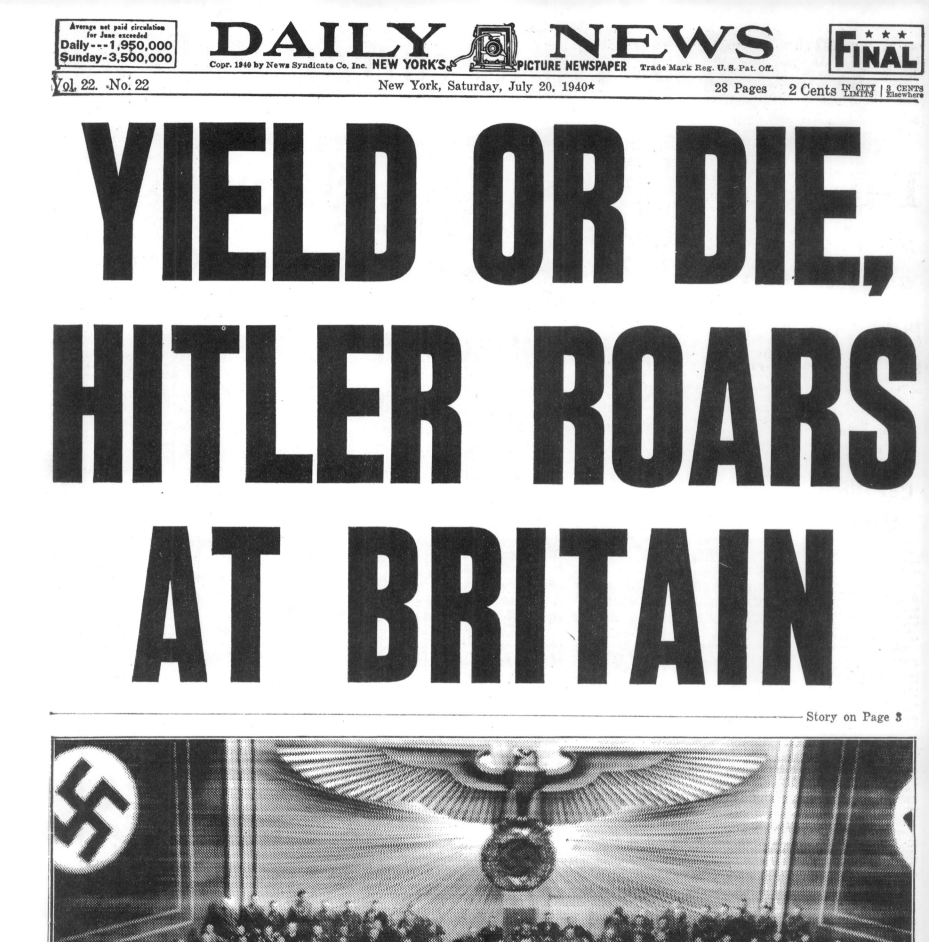

"One More Appeal to Reason." Speaking before the German Reichstag, Hitler yesterday offered England "peace or destruction." "I feel myself obliged to make one more appeal to reason to England," he said, "not as a victor but for the triumph of common sense." He made it clear that a rejection of this appeal would result in a "final" attack on England. *—Story on page 3; other picture on page 14. See map on page 12.*

BLACK-OUT
ZERO HOUR
TO-NIGHT
UNTIL 5.15 A.M.
MOON RISES 5.17
MOON SETS 2.13

Daily Express

No. 12,550 | Tuesday, August 13, 1940 | One Penny

The Battle of Britain is on: Hitler throws in more and more bombers

BIGGEST AIR RAIDS OF ALL

R.A.F. shoots down 39 more Nazis and loses only nine fighters

PORTSMOUTH HEAVILY BOMBED

Daily Express Air Reporter BASIL CARDEW

HITLER intensified his mass air raids on British ports still further yesterday. Even more aircraft than he used in the mass attacks on Thursday and Sunday were sent against Portsmouth and the Kent coast.

All day long there were terrific battles over the Channel and along the coast. And last night the Air Ministry announced we had shot down thirty-nine more Germans and had lost nine R.A.F. fighters. The German official news agency claim seventy-one British planes down, and admit nineteen Germans missing.

After dark last night the raiders returned—over the south-east, the south-west, north-east, and Wales. At midnight it was reported that bombs had been dropped in one south-east area.

Although fewer German aircraft were shot down yesterday the ratio in favour of the R.A.F. is almost doubled. On Thursday it was nearly three and a half to one; on Sunday it dropped to two and a half to one; and yesterday it was nearly four and a half to one.

Here is the battle-record since the mass raids began :—

	German losses.	British losses.
Thursday	61	18
Friday	1	0
Saturday	1	1
Sunday	61	26
Monday	39	9
Total	163	54

Altogether bombers and fighters raided an area of 400 miles yesterday—far more widespread than the day before—extending from the north-east area of England, round the coast and into Wales.

They dropped bombs in Portsmouth dockyard area, sank two small boats, set fire to a store, damaged a jetty.

They hit a railway station and fired a brewery. They hit a church in the Isle of Wight, and damaged several R.A.F. airfields on the mainland.

The more widespread attack was one reason why fewer raiders were shot down.

An R.A.F. fighter pilot said to me last night: "Jerry's bombers split up more yesterday and he was harder to find. On Sunday they concentrated and were better targets."

The Germans tried out two new tricks yesterday.

(1) Just before the start of the day's battles a large squadron, flying too high to be identified, set up a smoke screen.

Clouds of thick white smoke poured from the planes. They dropped no bombs, but they laid a fifteen-mile screen for the first bombing raiders who followed five minutes later.

(2) German pilots shot down in the sea used a green vapour, which can be seen five miles away, as a distress signal.

A fighter pilot who took part in yesterday's battles last night de-

BACK PAGE, COLUMN FOUR

Afterthoughts on raiding Britain by FIVE CAPTURED RAIDERS

Here are stories sent from five south-east coast towns last night :—

THE REALIST

A BADLY wounded German airman came down by parachute in a field. A farm groom covered him with a shotgun. The airman flung up his hands.

And then he said: "No more fighting. English too good."

THE PHILOSOPHER

CRIPPLED by a British fighter, a Messerschmitt made a forced landing in a field of cabbages. The thirty-year-old pilot, an officer wearing several decorations, stepped out with his hands above his head, gave himself up to a farm hand.

And then he said: "These Spitfires are very good. They were too fast for me. So I'm out of it now."

THE FINANCIER

RIDDLED with Hurricane bullets and shrapnel, a Heinkel bomber crashed in a field. All five of the crew parachuted and were captured. The pilot was the last to be found.

And then he said: "A shell got the port engine. A shell got the middle engine. A million marks gone!"

THE GROUSER

ANOTHER Messerschmitt made a forced landing among corn stooks at Berwick, eight miles from Eastbourne. He was wounded in the shoulder. He was taken prisoner by an Army sergeant.

And then he said: "That's what we get for coming to England."

AND THE ITALIAN

A JUNKERS 88 was shot down over Portland. One of the four airmen, who all parachuted to safety, was an Italian. He fell in the sea and was rescued.

And then he said: "Yes, I am an Italian. I was fighting for the Germans."

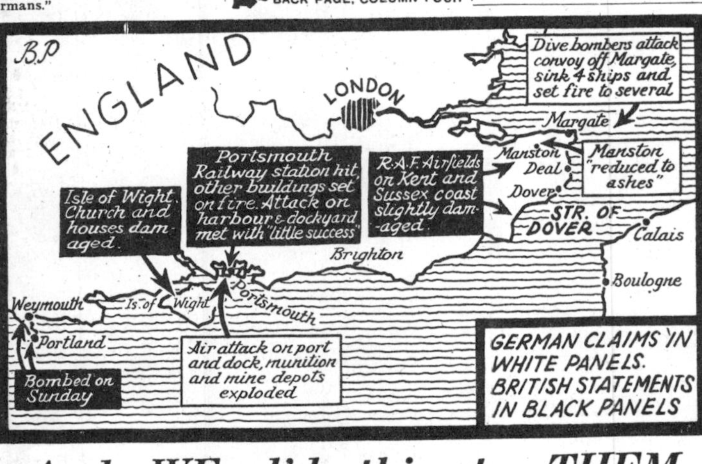

B.P.

Bombed on Sunday
Air attack on port and dock, munition and mine depots exploded
GERMAN CLAIMS IN WHITE PANELS. BRITISH STATEMENTS IN BLACK PANELS

And WE did this to THEM

THE crew of an R.A.F. aircraft which bombed a synthetic oil plant at Dortmund, in the Ruhr, during Sunday night, reported that they saw and HEARD an explosion of exceptional violence.

The attack took place in darkness and cloud, but soon after midnight an early raider saw four of his bombs fall on the oil plant, to be followed by a big blue flash.

An hour later another aircraft took up the attack. After a salvo of its heavy bombs had struck the plant, there was a violent explosion, and even though they were flying at several thousand feet the crew could hear it above the roar of their engines.

In most cases the engines drown the noise of the explosions.

That was the high spot of a series of raids which cost us three planes.

Oil was again the main objective. The plants at Gelsenkirchen and Wanne Eickel were heavily bombed. Other aircraft attacked the depot at Cherbourg, where tanks were set on fire.

Accurate bombing from high altitudes was a feature of daylight raids by medium bombers, when, for the third day running, Le Bourg airfield in Guernsey was bombed.

He gave his life to save town . .

"AN R.A.F. plane, flames spreading from airscrew to tail, came crashing towards the centre of a south-east town. The pilot stuck to his controls, skimmed rooftops—by feet, it seemed—and sacrificed his life by crashing into the sea."

You remember the story. Here is the hero—Flying Officer D. N. Grice, of Park-hill, Ealing. He was twenty-eight; was married nine months ago to Miss Margaret Peal, of Ealing.

The mayor of the town he saved has received subscriptions from many citizens who wish the heroism of Flying Officer Grice to be commemorated.

DOCTOR OPERATED AS BOMBS BURST

Daily Express Staff Reporter BERNARD HALL

PORTSMOUTH, Monday.

TWENTY-FIVE bombers, remnants of a much larger force broken up and dispersed over the Channel by the R.A.F., carried out the twenty-minute raid on Portsmouth at noon today.

I watched part of the raid from the centre of the city. Anti-aircraft fire from shore batteries and warships was terrific. Hardly had the first raider arrived when the sky for miles was a closely woven pattern of white and black shell-bursts—thousands of them.

French naval ratings shot off the tail of one machine. It crashed, and a German parachuted from it into the middle of a street. Four other Nazis were captured—two on mudfloats in the harbour. Six German bombers were shot down.

ON DENSE AREA

Twenty-one bombs fell in the most densely populated areas of the city; some of the bombers machine-gunned the ground as they passed.

A railway station was partly destroyed. Among the casualties was a four-month-old baby, one of three members of a family who were killed. But the record of escapes is astonishing.

An elderly surgeon, a specialist famous in the south, was carrying out a critical mastoid operation on a woman patient. A bomb burst in a narrow street a few yards outside the hospital. With his staff of five the surgeon carried on, and completed the operation.

The nurses' wing of the hospital caught fire. But it was empty. The night-duty nurses who had been sleeping there were all out. In the flooded corridor outside one room I found a book. It was entitled "With Four Walls: a classic of escape."

HOSES IN POND

The bomb burst a water main, and the crater filled with a constantly renewed supply of water. Firemen used the "pond" for their hoses to put out the blaze.

At this very point Lord Nelson left his hotel on that famous morning in 1805 to sail for Trafalgar. The path he took down the street to Sally Port was littered today with wreckage and splinters.

Nearby, an old parish hall used as a rest-room by A.R.P. staff was hit and set on fire. But the staff had just left it to go on duty. They returned to salvage their property.

A church was hit. But the vicar was at a cemetery conducting a funeral. His wife and child took refuge in the basement of the vicarage and escaped injury.

A big bomb fell in the middle of a road near a park. But it missed buildings on both sides. Windows were splintered.

One other oddity of the raid: the Guildhall clock has a twisted hand. It was hit by a bomb fragment.

And that is all. Net result: damage to war effort, slight; morale of the population stronger than ever.

Tip for next time: Keep under cover.

3 lbs. 13 ozs. of shell

Misses a gardener

While a gardener in a south-eastern coastal town was weeding yesterday, a piece of shell whistled over his bent back and buried itself beside him.

The shell fragment was 7ins. long, 2¼ins. wide and 1¼ins. thick, and weighed 3lbs. 13ozs.

Crown Princess will be Roosevelt's guest

STOCKHOLM, Monday.—The Norwegian legation in Stockholm announced today that Crown Princess Martha and her children—Regnhild (aged ten), Astrid (seven), and Harald (three)—have left Stockholm for the United States, where they will be the guests of President Roosevelt.—A.P.

Aliens' camps visited

Mr. Osbert Peake, Under-Secretary of Home Affairs, returned to England yesterday after a two-day visit to aliens' camps in the Isle of Man.

'Britain's new terrifying weapon'

NEW YORK, Monday.

AMERICAN newspapers, finding their most exciting news today in Britain's defeat of German air attacks, prominently display stories of a "new and terrifying British weapon."

They say Britain has a gun which fires steel cables to snare German planes, and that the new one-inch pom-pom gun may supply an answer to the dive bomber.

Berlin claims of staggering victories in today's air battles are generally discounted in the New York evening papers, whose headlines emphasise the Nazi losses while the German figures for British planes shot down are printed in small type.

BALLOON TRY-OUT

Sailors who man the ships that guard and feed industrial Britain believe that the side which finds the answer to the dive-bomber has won the war—and they think Britain has found or is finding it, writes an A.P. war correspondent.

The answer would be an anti-aircraft gun plus the balloon barrage, which convoys appear to be trying out. The balloons keep the bombers high enough to prevent accurate bombing and if they come low the new guns get them.

The gun is a many-barrelled pompom which lets off a bundle of inch or more shells, constructed so delicately that they explode on the slightest contact.

U.S. mission 'a step towards war'

Says American admiral

Daily Express Staff Reporter

NEW YORK, Monday.—One of the most significant steps taken by President Roosevelt according to Admiral Yates Sterling, U.S. Navy (retired), is the despatch to London of the special naval mission headed by Rear-Admiral Robert Ghormley.

Admiral Sterling writes today: "Our present mission may be for the purpose of finding out just how seriously Britain needs our active help in much greater volume than we have been giving up to date.

"An increasing section of American naval opinion in my observation tends to the belief that we cannot afford to have Britain defeated and her fleet made derelict.

"This trend is towards American participation in the war if the possibility of a British defeat seems imminent. Admiral Ghormley's mission may be the preliminary step towards that eventuality."

Even conversation rationed in Paris

Daily Express Correspondent

GENEVA, Monday.—Goods are not the only things restricted in France. Conversation between shopkeeper and customer has also been reduced, says the Petit Parisien, which gives the following list of expressions in the daily life of France since the German invasion :—

Shopkeeper: I've sold out.
Car owner: Not a single drop. And how about you?
Housewife: Have you any butter?
Baker: Give me your ration coupon.
Grocer: No sugar.
Coal merchant: I am expecting fresh supplies.

Russia expecting bumper harvest

Pravda, official newspaper of Russia's Communist Party, reported yesterday that the Soviet harvest this year is likely to be much better than that of most European countries.

Crops are extremely good, the newspaper said, but difficulty was being experienced in getting farmers to deliver their quota of grain to the State.

Nazis jail rumour-monger for life

BERLIN, Monday. — An Austrian, Eduard Grabher, has been sentenced to the maximum penalty, penal servitude for life, by the Nazi People's Court for spreading rumours in Switzerland that Germany intended to invade that country, says the German News Agency tonight.

After the Austrian anschluss, Grabher fled to Switzerland, where he told an officer of the Swiss Army that German troops and military detachments were ready to invade Switzerland. Later he was expelled from Switzerland.—Reuter.

Finns found league to fight for liberty

A League of "Veterans" of last year's Russo-Finnish war has been founded "to strengthen the unanimous will of the Finnish people to defend their independence in any circumstances," said Helsinki radio last night.

British officer killed

SIMLA, Monday.—Captain H. L. V. Russell and one Indian soldier were killed in a recent engagement with hostile tribes on the Bannu-Miran Shah road (North-West Frontier), it was announced in Simla today. Fourteen Indians were wounded, and one is missing.—Reuter.

Hollywood recruits

NEW YORK, Monday.—Patric Knowles and Colin Tapley, young British film actors in Hollywood, left for Ottawa today to offer themselves to the Royal Canadian Air Force.

ALBANIANS KILL 400 ITALIANS

Belgrade report

BELGRADE, Monday.

AN unconfirmed report from the Albanian frontier received in Belgrade states that 10,000 Albanians are in revolt, and that 400 Italian soldiers have been killed in Albania.

Three Italian warships with troops aboard are said to have arrived at Durazzo, the Albanian port, yesterday.

M. Musa Juka, former Albanian Minister of the Interior, is reported to be among the rebels.—B.U.P.

Italian plots exposed.—Page Two.

Former A.R.P. chief held

Daily Express Staff Reporter

BOURNEMOUTH, Monday.

MR. H. G. D. BARRETT, who was appointed as area A.R.P. staff officer for Bournemouth, Christchurch and Poole in October 1938, and who resigned early last June, has been arrested by the Bournemouth police.

When he resigned no statement about the reason was made.

Before coming to Bournemouth Mr. Barrett was A.R.P. organiser for St. Pancras, N.W. He had previously travelled extensively in France, Spain and Germany, where he is understood to have studied air raid precautions. He holds a B.Sc. degree.

Three little girls buried alive

They were filling sandbags

Three little girls helping to fill sandbags in Fordham, Cambs, yesterday, were buried alive when a wall of the pit gave way. Three other children partly buried were rescued.

Those killed were Pauline Cole, aged nine; Vera Margaret Parr, nine, and Irene May Plumb, ten.

162 seavacuees arrive

NEW YORK, Monday.—Four hours late, the liner Scythia (19,761 tons) docked in New York today with 162 British child refugees, all accompanied, and 612 other passengers.—A.P.

STOP PRESS

MOUNTAIN GRAVE FOR SIR ABE BAILEY

CAPETOWN, Monday.—Sir Abe Bailey will be buried at Muizenberg on Thursday afternoon on the mountainside above his house.—Reuter.

FRICK TO INSPECT OCCUPIED FRANCE

Dr. Frick, German Minister of the Interior, has arrived in Strasbourg to make a tour of inspection of the occupied western territories.—Reuter.

B.B.C. FADES OUT

B.B.C. Home Service programme was faded out on certain wavelengths just before eleven o'clock in interests of national security. It was still possible to get clear reception on an alternative wavelength.

Mr. Coward has plans for "after the war"

NEW YORK, Monday.—Mr. Noel Coward, planning to leave tomorrow for Hollywood [illegible] British children, said today that he has set aside his plans for new plays until the war is finished.

Dive bombers attack convoy off Margate, sink 4 ships and set fire to several
Margate
Manston
Deal

Manston "reduced to ashes"
Portsmouth Railway station hit, other buildings set on fire. Attack on harbour & dockyard met with little success
R.A.F. Airfields on Kent and Sussex coast slightly damaged
Isle of Wight Church and houses damaged
STR. OF DOVER
Calais
Brighton
Boulogne
Weymouth
Is. of Wight

Then, he says, he is going to an isolated corner of the world, not only to resume his writing, but "to get my nerves unstrung."—A.P.

DAILY MIRROR, Friday, August 16, 1940.

Daily Mirror

AUG. 16

No. 11,447 ONE PENNY

Registered at the G.P.O. as a Newspaper.

144 DOWN OUT OF 1,000

SUPPLY MUDDLE: OFFICIAL

WAR production is frequently left to face not merely competition between the Ministries, but even between different departments of the same Ministry—all pressing for orders to be completed.

This criticism of the lack of coordination in the present system of priority of supplies is made by the Select Committee on National Expenditure in a report issued last night.

A contractor told the committee that—if he followed every order he received about the urgency of various articles—he would have his shops full of half-finished stuff, owing to continued switching from one job to another.

The committee recommend that the priority organisation, the Raw Materials Department and the Salvage Organisation should be separated from the Ministry of Supply and placed under a separate Minister or a Parliamentary Secretary to the Minister of Defence.

This new and compact department would not be a user of any of the materials handled and would be able to allocate them to the best possible use.

Increased Costs

Unless rapid decisions are taken, the committee say, delays in production and increased costs are inevitable.

Whatever new organisation is adopted, it must command the respect of all departments and have overriding powers.

If factories are to be kept at greatest production with least cost it is suggested, both planning and priority periods should as far as possible be for not less than three months.

The committee heard evidence from Mr. Arthur Greenwood, Minister without Portfolio, who presides over the Production Committee of the Cabinet, and Colonel J. J. Llewellin, in charge of the Central Priority Department of the Ministry of Supply.

PARACHUTES A VAIN NAZI RUSE

THE dropping of parachutes by enemy aircraft during the night of August 13 was no more than a clumsy effort on the part of the enemy to undermine the British morale, the Ministry of Information said last night.

A large number of parachutes were dropped in widely-separated areas.

In many instances the harness had not been undone, and in some places empty parachutes were seen falling.

In addition, bags containing instructions purporting to be operation orders were found. At least one bag was dropped in a place and under circumstances which make it obvious that the Germans intended the bag to fall into the hands of the military authorities.

Contd. on Back Page, Col. 4

This bus was damaged in the Croydon raid.

Plane Trap Is Secret

A PLANE trap erected by the Ministry of Transport caught a German bomber yesterday and wrecked it.

All the crew were killed.

British military authorities have no intention of giving away to the enemy details of the plane trap.

The trap is the latest British "hush-hush" defence weapon, as the Nazis have already learned to their cost.

More news of its formidable and effective nature can be expected soon.

Threw Bomb Overboard

When a German raider dropped a bomb down the funnel of a trawler in the Channel, the skipper ran from the bridge, carried the bomb from the engine-room to the deck, and threw it overboard.

It exploded a second before it hit the water, and the ship was undamaged.

The skipper's courage saved the ship and the lives of all but one of his crew.

He picked the bomb from the bilge, and staggered with it up the companion-way.

A HUNDRED AND FORTY-FOUR ENEMY RAIDERS WERE BROUGHT DOWN UP TO MIDNIGHT YESTERDAY.

That was Britain's answer at the end of the day of the greatest air attacks of the war, in which the German "blitz" swept the length of Britain.

Twenty-seven R.A.F. fighters were lost in the mighty defence battles, but eight of the pilots are safe.

For hour after hour through the day, and then into the night, our fighters swept against the huge raiding squadrons.

The German Air Force used more than a thousand bombers and fighters in the attacks.

Croydon Aerodrome, London's airport before the war, was raided last night. "Bombs were dropped on and around the aerodrome," said the Air Ministry later. "Some damage was done, but details are not yet available."

Sirens were sounded in a wide area of Greater London.

Many towns were attacked during the day, and a number of people killed. R.A.F. aerodromes in the south-east and in the north-east were bombed.

Heavy attacks on south-east areas went on into the evening hours. All the time German machines were being shot out of the sky.

Over one coast district R.A.F. fighters and the guns smashed up a three-hour attack by 250 raiders.

Once again there was a spell in which German planes were dropping out of the sky at the rate of one a minute.

14 Dive-Bombers

At another point the destruction of several barrage balloons cost nine raiders. People in yet another district saw eight of a big attacking squadron destroyed.

It was the most gruelling day for the R.A.F. fighters. And their greatest.

Fourteen dive-bombers, protected by fighters, attacked Croydon Aerodrome. High explosive "screamers" and incendiary bombs were dropped.

Some people were killed and a number injured.

The raiders were first seen when they started to dive about three miles from the aerodrome. People in the streets saw them come to a few hundred feet before the bombs were released.

Within a few seconds anti-aircraft guns put up a fierce barrage. R.A.F. fighters swept to the attack. Three of the raiders are believed to have been smashed.

One bomb narrowly missed a gas-works, but houses in an adjoining road were hit.

Main casualties of the raid were caused by a bomb which wrecked a building where men were working.

Hours afterwards rescue workers were still digging in the debris for bodies of the victims.

Not far away a bomb dropped only a few yards from a bus and blew out a 30ft. wide crater.

Passengers were injured by flying glass as all the bus windows were blown out. Part of the engine was

Contd. on Back Page, Col. 2

TRAIN BOMBED: SEVERAL KILLED

SEVERAL passengers were killed by bomb splinters when a train was stopped during a raid over north-east England yesterday.

In the same area an express train was machine-gunned by a German plane.

A passenger, David Stafford, was injured in the leg. Carriage windows were broken.

News Chronicle

No. 29,425 ONE PENNY MONDAY, AUGUST 26, 1940 RADIO, PAGE 2 *

POSTAGE IN U.K. .. 1½d. ALL PLACES OUTSIDE UNITED KINGDOM .. ½d.

SCREAMING BOMBS ON LONDON LAST NIGHT

89 Raiders Shot Down In Two Days: 24 In One Battle

LONDON had two air raids during the night. In the first, just before midnight, there was no damage and no casualties and the all-clear was sounded an hour later.

The second alarm was given two hours after the first. It lasted half an hour. Screaming bombs were heard to fall in the area, but early today no damage or casualties had been reported.

Just before the first alarm was given it had been officially announced that on Saturday and yesterday 89 German planes had been shot down—50 on Saturday and 39 yesterday, including 24 in one battle off the Dorset coast.

Our losses in the two days were 30 fighters. The pilots of 15 of them are safe.

SCREAMING BOMBS

Five screaming bombs were dropped on a South-Western town last night by two enemy planes which appeared over the town just after dusk from different directions.

They dropped bombs simultaneously in different parts of the town.

Two men were killed and several people injured.

Formations of German bombers, accompanied by Messerschmitt fighters, were intercepted by British Spitfires above the clouds when they crossed the S.E. Coast last night.

A series of dog-fights developed and within ten minutes a Messerschmitt 109 was shot down in flames into a field. The pilot, who baled out, was killed when he struck the ground after his parachute had failed to open.

BLOWN TO PIECES

A Dornier bomber was blown to pieces in mid-air when its cargo of bombs were exploded by a Spitfire's bullets.

When the sirens first wailed in London last night crowds in the streets made for shelters quickly. Many people who flocked to Underground stations were asked by officials if they were travelling to a particular destination. Those who were not were told to go to the nearest public shelter.

The Air Ministry and the Ministry of Home Security announced last night that bombs were dropped in the Scilly Isles, where one person was killed.

Although in Saturday's big raids there was widespread damage in savage attacks on the civilian population at Ramsgate, Portsmouth, a village in the South-East, areas in the Midlands, in the North and on London suburbs, there were astonishingly few fatal casualties.

FEW KILLED

"The fatal casualties in the London area in all the week-end raids did not reach double figures," a Ministry of Home Security official said to the News Chronicle last night.

Hitherto, in the majority of recent raids, some semblance of a desire to hit targets of a military character in this country has been apparent.

But as local reports came pouring in yesterday it became clear that of the hundreds of bombs dropped during the night only a very small proportion was intended to strike a blow at military objectives.

CINEMA HIT

An Air Ministry and Ministry of Home Security communiqué yesterday stated:

"It is now confirmed that during the raid on Portsmouth a number of casualties was caused, some of them fatal.

"The majority of these were in a cinema which received a direct hit. Damage was also done to private property and business premises.

"It is now known that in addition to the attack already reported on Manston aerodrome, casualties were also caused at another R.A.F. aerodrome.

"Elsewhere in England sporadic attacks were made over a wide area.

SAVAGERY AND HEROISM

Saturday's attack on Ramsgate illustrates not only German savagery but also the way in which people in all the bombed areas have met the attacks.

Although a large number of houses and shops were damaged or destroyed, yesterday the inhabitants of the town were returning to their normal life in the best of spirits.

No gas was available for cooking, and spirit stoves and oil stoves of every description were being raked out of lumber rooms to do service once more.

The result of the bombing was that the German airmen well deserved the criticism that "they were rotten shots." It is the cot-

Turn to Back Page, Col. Three

Air War on Britain Enters a New Phase

By RONALD WALKER, The Air Correspondent

The German night air raids on Britain during the week-end were the most intensive and widespread yet attempted.

They confirm the forecast I made on Saturday that the enemy is changing his tactics and that the air war on Britain has entered still another phase.

Saturday's two mass raids were not on the previous scale, and the change of tactics to night bombing is clear evidence that Britain as an intended victim has proved to be unwilling and surprisingly difficult.

But while accepting this tribute to the R.A.F. and our ground defences, we must expect from now on night raids growing in intensity until the enemy again learns that the cost of battering Britain into submission is too high even for the Luftwaffe.

SMALL FORMATIONS

For the first time the City of London was bombed during the week-end. Bombs also fell in the suburbs and many parts of the country. In the main the damage was to civilians and their property.

The bombs were dropped not by large formations of aircraft such as stormed our defences from August 8 to 18. The raiders were single machines or small formations which were able to sneak through the defences at night, taking advantage of cloud, as they did on Saturday night, to hide from the searchlights and guns.

In one respect the Germans are consistent. They remain faithful to the practice which became familiar in their assaults on Poland, Norway, Holland, Belgium and France of feeling for the soft spot.

By sea, land and air the Nazi forces have never willingly gone into action against a side known to be strong and holding a chance of victory. They have always groped for the soft spot in the enemy's defences.

WANTED QUICK WIN

When found, as the Germans found the soft spot of France in the Sedan area, they have struck with all the triumphant might of a Goliath defeating a David.

With the collapse of France, Germany turned the full attention of her air force on to Britain on the night of June 18. Already the Luftwaffe had had a good taste of the quality of the R.A.F. at Dunkirk. Obviously the German air staff was not making the mistake of accepting Britain, her air force and defences as an easy "push over."

Germany wanted another quick victory, but for week after week small raids or armed reconnaissances, mostly by day, came with the evident intention of finding the soft spot.

Whether the pilots collectively reported the discovery of a suitable soggy patch will not be known until after the war. Perhaps impatience alone dictated the launching of the mass daylight attacks which began on August 8 and ended so abruptly on August 18.

Those raids came up against a particularly hard spot. Southern England and the sea approaches were littered with fallen Nazi aircraft. The damage we sustained was inconsiderable compared with the enemy losses.

Certain definite conclusions can be drawn from the progress of the air war to date. The R.A.F. and our ground defences forced the enemy to the decision that mass air attacks by day were not to gain the quick results required.

The alternative was to try and copy the R.A.F. and embark on a policy of night bombing. This was a real change of policy, for the German air staff had always been in favour of precision bombing by day.

ACTING ALONE

Equally definite is the fact that the Luftwaffe has failed as a lightning decisive weapon against Britain. In previous campaigns, beginning with Poland, the Luftwaffe struck hard and without mercy on military and civilians alike; but its savage attacks were always supported and followed up by land forces.

Here the German Air Force is left to act alone. In Europe it was the spearhead of attack. The R.A.F. has blunted that spearhead.

But this is not the moment, as some people appear to think, for enjoying success. The spearhead of German attack is still there and can easily be sharpened again.

We are now beginning the real trial of strength.

I HAVE SEEN THE DAMAGE FOR MYSELF,
By E. P. Montgomery
Page Four

LONDON SKYLINE

The figure of Justice on the dome of the Old Bailey silhouetted against the glare in the sky after the raid on London. People saw searchlights sweeping in all directions above the City and heard a whistling bomb fall and explode. Then in one area low clouds were lit up by the glow of a fire

Land Mine Kills Peer And Sister

When a land mine exploded on the South-East Coast yesterday, Lord North and his sister, Lady Cynthia Williams, were killed, and Lady North was seriously injured.

She was taken to hospital. Last night she was still unconscious and in a critical condition.

The three were taking a walk yesterday morning and one of the party is believed to have trodden on the mine.

The explosion was heard many miles away.

IMPERSONATED IN HOAX

Lord North, aged 38, was the eldest son of the Earl of Guilford.

He was impersonated as part of a hoax in a publicity affair in Philadelphia some eight years ago.

Educated at Eton, he served with the 2nd Life Guards and the Sussex Yeomanry.

Lady North is the elder daughter of Sir Merrik Burrell.

Hitler Arrives At 'Western Front H.Q.'

From Our Own Correspondent

BUDAPEST, Sunday. — German propaganda messages announce Hitler's arrival at "Western Frontier Headquarters" for the launching of the long-predicted offensive against England.

A.R.P. in Hungary, Rumania

Last night's news from the troubled Balkans was:

RUMANIA-HUNGARY

As the result of German pressure talks between Hungary and Rumania will be resumed in Budapest on Wednesday. But tension between the two countries remains.

Hungary has called up more reserves, ordered air-raid precautions and taken other defence measures.

In Rumania opposition to territorial changes grows. Air-raid shelters are to be completed by September 15. (See Page Three.)

TURKEY-RUSSIA

Reports that the Soviet Government has demanded the right to send warships through the Dardanelles in the event of war were denied both in Ankara and Moscow.

It is learned in Istanbul that the last of the British big guns for the defence of the Straits has arrived in Turkey.

It is also reported that the most important railway bridges and railway centres are under military guard.

GREECE-ITALY

Greece has called up 14 classes of reservists in Epirus district. Private vehicles are being requisitioned.

Gayda, in the "Voce d'Italia," declared that "it will not be many days before the British find themselves up against some new surprise."

Sir Michael Palairet, British Minister in Athens, has reported to London on his talks with General Metaxas, the Greek Premier.

News Chronicle Correspondent, Reuter, B.U.P., A.P. and Exchange.

2,200 Ships Convoyed Only 9 Lost

Toronto, Sunday.—Of 2,200 ships convoyed from Canada since the war began to July 31, only nine have been lost, said Col. J. L. Ralston (Defence Minister) at the Canadian National Exhibition.—A.P.

Bomb Explosions Heard North of Berlin, Says New York Report

Berlin had an air raid alarm just after midnight (11 p.m. B.S.T.) last night, and Bremen, Cologne, Munich and Leipzig radio stations were off the air at 9.45 p.m., a quarter of an hour earlier than usual. Bombs were heard first North of Berlin, according to messages reaching New York. Over Boulogne a brilliant display of searchlights and flares could be plainly seen from the English Coast.

FOR two and a half hours on Saturday night and early yesterday morning bombers of the R.A.F. hovered over big arms and chemical production works in Germany, carefully placed their heavy loads and waited to see the havoc they caused.

At the same time other British bombers were hitting hard at targets in Italy, France, Belgium and Holland.

In Italy targets at Milan (where the Caproni works are) and at Sesto Calende (site of the Savoia aircraft works) were attacked.

The chief objective in Germany was the great Daimler-Benz plant at Stuttgart, where the Nazis produce a big proportion of their armoured cars. It is one of the most important arms works in Western Germany. It was very heavily attacked.

Arriving over the factories at 11.30 p.m., the raiders carried out methodical bombing here for more than an hour, and in orderly succession the pilots delivered their attacks, undeterred by heavy anti-aircraft fire and concentrations of searchlights.

Fire soon broke out and, as more bombs fell, spread rapidly until the main group of buildings was seen to be blazing. As the flames spread, a series of heavy explosions was observed. One of the biggest explosions of all occurred ten minutes after the aircraft had left for

Turn to Back Page, Col. Five

LATE NEWS

BRITISH SHIP'S SOS: RADIO REPORT

NEW YORK.—According to Mackay Radio, British steamer giving letters GLZB sent out message 8.30 p.m. (B.S.T.) saying she had been attacked by a submarine off Irish coast and was sinking rapidly.—Reuter.

BERLIN RAID ALARM

At least ten heavy explosions were heard to the north-west of Berlin in the first ten minutes after air raid alarm was sounded. Reverberations felt in centre of Berlin.—B.U.P.

LONDON BLACK-OUT TIME
8.30 p.m.—5.34 a.m.

He Has Made His Last Strafe

Emblem on the fuselage of a Messerschmitt 109 fighter (below) shot down in South-East England includes Mr. Chamberlain's umbrella and the slogan "Gott Strafe England." And on the fighter's tail three white marks together with dates indicate the air combat victories claimed by the pilot. The dates are 7.7.40, 29.7.40, 15.8.40

Italian Planes Kill Sudanese Children

CAIRO, Sunday. — A communiqué from British G.H.Q. today states:

"Enemy aircraft carried out indiscriminate bombing of the town of Omdurman in the Sudan. Three Sudanese children were killed and six other persons wounded.

"On other fronts there is nothing to report."—Exchange.

Cabinet Will Have Final Say On Rail Fares

By a Political Correspondent

The Charges (Railway Control) Consultative Committee today begin their public inquiry into the proposals to increase railway charges, referred to them by the Minister of Transport, Sir John Reith.

In view of the widespread opposition to the proposals and the effect they are likely to have on the cost of living, if accepted, it is certain that when Sir John Reith receives the Committee's report, he will ask the War Cabinet for its guidance.

[*The railway companies and London Passenger Transport Board have asked for increase of 6.8 per cent. on present charges to operate from October 1. This would bring the total increase on pre-war rates to 17½ per cent.*]

The Country Is Against Stricter Press Control

THE people of this country generally do not think it would be wise for the Government to impose any stricter control and censorship of the Press than exists at present. Indeed, it is the view of many that even the present standard of strictness might be relaxed with advantage.

The exact proportions of the opinions of the country on censorship of the Press are revealed by a Gallup Survey recently taken by the British Institute of Public Opinion. This question was put to a sample of the adult voting population all over the country:

"Do you think that stricter control and censorship of the Press by the Government would be wise?" Of the total number questioned:

19% said ... Wise
68% said ... Unwise
13% said ... Don't know

Comments made to the interviewers in course of the questioning showed that most who defended control and censorship and who wanted it made stricter did so largely on security grounds.

"Definitely wise," said one man, and commented: "We must give the enemy absolutely no chance of getting any information."

It was evident, however, that the example of what too strict control and censorship had done to other countries, particularly to France, had had a strong influence on forming the majority opinion that it would be unwise for the Government to interfere further with the freedom of the Press.

"Look at France. That's what censorship did." "We would become like Germany." "Censorship is Hitler's game. We don't want to play his game, do we?" Comments like these were typical of many.

Others felt that stricter control and withholding of news from the people of this country would be unwise from the morale point of view. "We don't want things kept from us," said one person in this category.

No. 12,576 Thursday, September 12, 1940 One Penny

Mr. Churchill (in a broadcast last night reported on Page Five) gave warning that invasion may be attempted soon and made this call to the nation:

Every man—and woman—will therefore prepare himself to do his duty, whatever it may be, with special pride and care . . . With devout but sure confidence I say that God defends the right.

TERRIFIC LONDON BARRAGE MEETS GREATEST RAID

While Navy and RAF pound massed Nazi invasion fleet

SUPER-BLITZ GETS A SHOCK

HITLER'S PLANS FOR INVADING BRITAIN ARE NEARING COMPLETION.

Mr. Churchill last night said the invasion may be launched at any time.

Next week must be regarded as "very important."

Germany, he said, is massing barges and ships in ports from Hamburg down to the Bay of Biscay. Preparations have also been made to carry a force from Norway.

While the Army stands confident and ready for the assault, the Navy and R.A.F. are shelling and bombing every one of Hitler's invasion ports. Barges and harbours are being continuously and heavily bombarded. This has been going on since Tuesday night.

LONDON BLITZ NIGHT No. 5 WAS A SENSATION.

It began at 8.34 after three daylight raids. Goering intended it to be a Super-Blitz night.

He sent over bigger-than-ever formations of bombers, and sent fighters to protect them.

AND WHAT A SURPRISE THEY HAD!

All round them broke the biggest anti-aircaft barrage London has ever seen.

From every part of London A.A. guns flashed and roared. Only a few raiders got through to drop bombs on inner London. Most had to drop their bombs haphazard on the outskirts. And all the time the intense gunfire drowned the noise of the bombs.

The indiscriminate bombing of London now stands revealed by the Premier as part of the invasion plan.

CHANNEL BASES SHELLED

HERE is the full story, told last night in Admiralty, R.A.F. and German communiqués, of the terrific massed attacks made against Hitler's invasion bases.

Navy is there

"Strong and repeated offensive actions are being taken by our naval light forces against German shipping movements, ports and concentrations of shipping," said the Admiralty.

"These operations have inflicted losses upon the enemy, as well as damage to port facilities which would be vital to him in the event of an attempt to invade England.

"Further details cannot be given without disclosing information which would be useful to the enemy."

R.A.F. blast docks

EARLIER it was announced by the Air Ministry that for hours, up to dawn yesterday, R.A.F. bombers unloaded high explosive and fire bombs on Hitler's invasion harbours, causing heavy damage.

A large part of the dock area round the Carnot Basin at Calais Harbour was left in flames. One fire alone blazed along 200 yards of the water front.

Bombs were dropped clean on to barges tightly packed along the whole east side of the basin, and the explosions threw debris high into the air.

Barges in another basin were hit, and then a large merchant ship suddenly burst into flames.

For three hours the pounding of the dock area went on. A railway was hit and fires were started round lock gates.

Our pilots dived low through thick cloud to pick out their targets, braving fierce shelling from the ground.

Six E-boats—fast motor torpedo-boats—at Dieppe were bombed, despite heavy fire from the ground and a patrol of Messerschmitt fighters.

After the bomb explosions, two of the E-boats had disappeared.

Ostend harbour was continually bombed for eight hours. Heavy loads of high explosive straddled barges in the port, and direct hits were made on a number of ships.

German ships in Boulogne harbour were attacked, and other bomber squadrons unloaded on to the docks at Flushing.

Enemy fighters tried to find the raiders, but the R.A.F. pilots gave them the slip in the clouds.

From all these raids, and an attack on Berlin (reported on Page Three), four of our planes did not return.

The Nazi story

A GERMAN communiqué last night admitted the naval attack.

"Shortly after midnight last night," it said, "British warships approached the French Channel coast and opened fire.

"German coast artillery fired on the British warships, and several German motor speedboats, which were patrolling in the neighbourhood, joined in the action.

"A fire on one of the six enemy destroyers was noticed. Soon afterwards, the British ships ceased firing and disappeared into the darkness."

Gunfire louder than the bombs

FEWER searchlights—but MANY more guns—greeted the German raiders when they approached London last night within a few minutes of the sirens at 8.34.

It was the fiercest anti-aircraft barrage ever heard in London.

Chains of shells burst high in the sky, a curtain of steel. The sky must have been full of flying shrapnel.

It spattered on the rooftops at times like machine-gun fire.

The bombers and their escorting fighters were seen plainly in the moonlight, but when they disappeared their course was easily followed—not by their bomb flashes but by the red pin points of bursting shells.

With every minute the barrage increased, the gun flashes making an almost constant glow, the thunder of the guns shaking houses, even drowning the bomb explosions.

SOME OF THE GUNS SEEMED HEAVIER THAN ANY HEARD BEFORE. IT APPEARED TO BE A NEW SUPER-BARRAGE.

INCENDIARIES

The bombers could not face it and swung away east. Incendiaries whizzed down, but so far the raiders did not appear to have dropped high explosives.

One later raider, following the same route, was forced off his course too. He turned—straight into another barrage, and turned back again.

But as the first waves of the Germans, driven from London, made for home, the whistle of bigger bombs was heard.

They fell in south-east, south-west and west.

Then, mingling with the fireworks of the guns, watchers saw "Molotov breadbaskets" bursting to the south-east. Within a few minutes at least twelve were seen.

Bombs, including incendiaries, were dropped in three South London districts and in one area in West London.

And many of the bombs dropped in and out of London seemed to be a new type. They exploded with a vivid white flash followed by a very sharp crack after which, in every case, there was a succession of staccato reports like machine-gun fire.

There was no lull in the battle for more than an hour. Wave after wave of Germans met the barrage and were beaten back. Only an odd plane got through to drop his bombs, climb out of sight, and make off for home.

The lull lasted only five minutes. Flashing anti-aircraft guns down the Thames Estuary heralded yet another wave of attackers on their way to London.

Before they arrived the super-barrage was in full swing again, lashing hundreds of shells into the raiders' path.

"No aerial barrage of the last war compares with this," was the verdict of all who saw the red pin points peppering the skies.

In every part of London, in the suburbs and on the outskirts as far as the eye could see, A.A. guns were flashing. North, south-east and west their shells burst.

Reflections of the gun flashes danced off window panes. Great purple flashes ran along the horizon.

At the height of the battle another heartening note was added to the gun thunder—the whine of a plane diving steeply. If it crashed the noise was drowned by a new burst of gunfire.

Large formations or stragglers, they all got the same treatment, a withering "creeping barrage" right up the course of the Thames.

Soon after midnight the great barrage died down. It had become clear that the waves of the raiders were being forced to drop their bombs outside the London area.

MORE VIOLENT

Soon, however, the barrage opened up again, more violent than ever. A German plane flying comparatively low appeared over the Central London area.

Its course was marked by a continuous line of bursting shells. Flashes from the guns grew so great as the raider flew over the central area that the whole district was almost continually lit up. And the raider, harassed by the barrage, sheered away, followed by the bursting shells.

London had three alerts before the Great Night Battle began.

In the second Marshal Goering's "Yellow Nosed" Squadron—famed in Germany as the most daring fighting unit he possesses—were beaten by British Spitfires and Hurricanes when they led an attempt to penetrate the London defences.

The first warning, at 11.54 a.m., lasted sixteen minutes, the second was from 3.20 to 4.42, the third from 5.04 to 5.15.

Newspaper office bombed

A LONDON newspaper office was slightly damaged by a high explosive bomb early this morning. Windows were shattered and a water tank on the roof was burst.

No one was hurt.

Other bombs hit an A.F.S. station and a hall in the London area.

It was revealed last night, too, that Bond-street and the Burlington Arcade were damaged in Tuesday night's raid on London.

MORE GUNS—AND WHY

Daily Express Air Reporter

AN intensely powerful barrage of gunfire such as London heard last night not only keeps raiders at a great height but it makes districts where they are concentrated too hot for the enemy to linger.

It does NOT mean that attackers are prevented from dropping bombs, but at the heights they are forced to fly bombing becomes more difficult as the pilots are continually harassed.

It also becomes far less accurate, —*though this does not count for much when bombing is intended to be inaccurate.*

Wardens in some districts last night are reported to have warned people to stay indoors and not to be alarmed by the noise of the gunfire.

The sound of the guns shuld be reassuring. It is certainly a wise precaution for people to stay under cover when the air is full of falling shrapnel. Many casualties have been caused in raids by people forgetting that their own guns can be a danger to them.

And what of the lack of searchlights last night?

Searchlights have distinct disadvantages as well as advantages. If raiders keep above their range they can be a positive aid to the enemy by lighting up his target, as well as giving him directional aid for flying over a city.

90 DOWN

400 people killed on Monday night

NAZI squadrons tried twice yesterday afternoon and evening to thrust home attacks on airfields and on the London docks.

They paid with the loss of at least ninety aircraft—one of the most smashing defeats of the war.

As many of the planes brought down were bombers, Goering lost well over 200 airmen.

The two raids lasted altogether about two hours, so that the "death rate" was 45 an hour.

This news was issued after midnight. Earlier, it was stated that our losses were seventeen fighters, with three pilots safe. Here is the communiqué issued by the Air Ministry and Ministry of Home Security:—

Fuller reports are now available of last night's [Tuesday] enemy activity over the London area. Although much damage was done to private property, it was less than on previous nights and the casualties were fortunately very much less severe.

Incendiary bombs started many fires, but only one major fire was caused and all are under control. The work of the fire services has again been beyond praise, and their arrangements for mutual assistance are working smoothly.

Full reports of casualties are not yet available, but eighteen persons are known to have been killed and 280 injured in the London area.

School falls on families

Total casualties on Monday night are now reported to be in the neighbourhood of 400 killed and 1,400 injured—the majority of the fatalities occurring when an elementary school in the East End of London, which was affording temporary shelter to families whose homes had been destroyed, was hit and collapsed.

There was little enemy activity over this country today (Wednesday) until about 3 p.m., when a large number of enemy aircraft approached the London area. The enemy was driven off, but reports so far received show that some damage was done, mainly in three districts south of the river.

Particulars of casualties are not yet available.

Fighters have a grand day

Bombs were also dropped in another attack on a town on the south coast, where some casualties are reported, a number of which were fatal.

Reports up to 7.30 p.m. showed that of seventy-three enemy aircraft then known to have been destroyed by our fighters, forty-three were bombers, nineteen fighter-bombers, and eleven fighters.

A.A. batteries along the Thames are also believed to have shot down several.

Berlin has guest

Serrano Suner, Spanish Minister of the Interior, and brother-in-law of General Franco, has arrived in Berlin for a visit of several days, Berlin announced last night.

DOVER SHELLED: WE SHELL CONVOY

Daily Express Staff Reporter FRANK BUTLER

DOVER, Wednesday.

GERMAN long-range guns and dive-bombers opened a fierce attack on Dover this afternoon, apparently to cover the movement of at least twelve Nazi ships which were seen sneaking along the coast towards Boulogne harbour.

Big guns on the British shore answered the German shelling, and at once a smoke screen was flung out by the Nazi ships.

Later, large forces of R.A.F. bombers headed towards the French coast, and it appeared that many bombs were dropped east of Calais.

Salvos of six shells at a time were hurled at Dover by the Nazis; and a dozen German heavy bombers flew high over the town while the shelling was going on.

Bombs were dropped at random. Shops and houses were hit, and fires started.

The combined attack was the severest Dover has known since the war began. A few people are reported killed and some injured.

More guns barked — anti-aircraft guns on the English coast—and one shell burst clear on a bomber and blew it to bits.

The rest of the raiders droned away, but the German shelling continued for three-quarters of an hour.

The people of Dover were grand.

With shells bursting all round, A.R.P. workers, firemen and police went about

→ BACK PAGE, COL. FIVE

PALACE BOMB

Explodes near the King's sitting-room

Daily Express Staff Reporter HILDE MARCHANT

BUCKINGHAM PALACE has been bombed. A time bomb dropped into the Terrace on the North Wing just outside the King's sitting room. The King and Queen, who have used the Palace regularly throughout the raids, were away for the night.

It exploded at 1.30 on Tuesday morning. Both the King and Queen spent the night in the country, and members of the Palace staff were sleeping safely in shelters well away from the spot. No one was injured.

The swimming pool and corner of the terrace were wrecked. There is practically no glass left in the back of the Palace, and the explosion broke windows on the Park side.

The Germans seem to have made two attempts to bomb the Palace for there is another huge crater fifty yards outside the Palace grounds.

I went to the Palace yesterday morning to see the damage. There is a crater eighteen feet deep and forty feet wide.

WALLS TORN

It must have been a large bomb—probably 250 pounds—for thick pillars ten feet high and the heavy stone balustrade of the terrace had collapsed into the crater.

The wall of the swimming pool was torn wide open and the green painted steel diving steps were twisted like sticks of liquorice.

Walls were charred with black smoke and one heavy piece of stone had been blown over the Palace and had landed eighty yards away.

The King and Queen came back to the Palace the following day to look at the wreckage. The day before the King had been round the East End to look at the wrecked homes of the working-class people there.

Now they looked at their own home, with one wall wrecked, the windows of their rooms blown wide open to the sky and the wreckage all round the garden.

The furniture did not suffer much damage, but in the Chinese room I saw the frame of one of the tapestries had been broken.

Wire netting over the windows had prevented the glass blowing inwards, but a glass porch over the

BACK PAGE, COL. THREE

STOP PRESS

Raider's crew caught in North London

Enemy plane was brought down in North London early this morning. Its crew were captured.

Relays of single raiders were flying at about ten-minute intervals over central London area. Germans appeared to be using very fast machines which sped back and forwards.

Hardly had drone of one machine died away before it was followed by another. Some of planes had steadier and faster engine beat than usually associated with night raiders. Terrific gunfire still in progress in late morning.

Fire bomb falls in Goebbels's garden

BERLIN, Wednesday.—The official German News Agency says tonight:—

"During the British raid on Berlin last night a 15lb. incendiary bomb fell ten feet from Dr. Goebbels' residence and tore a deep hole in the garden."—B.U.P.

Invasion ports—bombarded

What we did to Berlin—*See pages 3 & 5*

DAILY MIRROR

Member of The Associated Press

WEATHER SHOWERS, COOLER (Details on Page 6)

(Copyright, 1940 Daily Mirror, Inc.)

3 Cents Outside City Limits

2¢

Vol. 17. No. 73 C New York, Monday, September 16, 1940 FINAL EDITION, 6 A.M. ★★★★

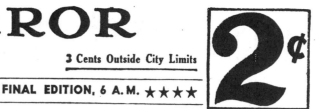

BRITISH DOWN 175 RAIDERS

Nazis Attack London at 10-Minute Intervals--See Story on Page 3

(British Press Combine)

Moving Target

The man the Nazis hate most of all, Winston Churchill, moves serenely through a bombed London area, personally checking on damage. Yesterday he put a huge "175" on his scoreboard of Nazi planes downed in one day. Please note that the British censor has blocked out all signs which might be clues to this location.

WEATHER

Partly cloudy with moderate temperatures and diminishing northwest winds tonight and tomorrow. Lowest temperature expected tonight about 45 degrees.

New York Post

7 SPORTS COMPLETE FINANCIAL

Founded 1801. Volume 139. No. 258.

NEW YORK TUESDAY SEPTEMBER 17 1940

THREE CENTS

GERMANS CLAIM:

LONDON SHELLED BY 90-MILE GUNS

BERLIN, Sept. 17 (AP).—Germany's long-distance guns on the French channel coast have begun to shell London, informed German sources disclosed tonight. The nearest point in France is about 90 miles from London.

The guns are super-cannon, hitherto unused, these sources said, and their firing at present is more or less limited to range-finding.

However, their use is expected to increase daily.

The strictest secrecy prevails concerning the calibre of the guns. Informed sources, however, said that some used during the World War would fire 75 miles (one was employed against Paris). Since then, they added, science has made great strides and the somewhat longer distance from Calais to London is "no problem."

From newsreel pictures which have been shown in Germany it appears that these new guns have barrels resembling a telescope.

That is, each section is slightly thinner than the preceding one, with the sections connected by strong buttresses.

The newsreel pictures show these barrels actually swaying in the air after a shot has been fired.

(Last June 4, German officers in Calais, the Nazi-held French port closest to England, showed Louis Lochner, Associated Press correspondent in Berlin, a long-range cannon which they declared could shoot into London any time Adolf Hitler gave the order.)

Distance Guns Belittled, Though Invasion Is Nearer

By FLETCHER PRATT

New York Post Military Expert

The German announcement that London is being shelled with big cannon from 90 miles away means that a mass attempt to invade England is probably a matter of days, perhaps of hours, in spite of the weather.

The military effect of such weapons is small, and certainly does not pay the cost of building them. This was demonstrated by the 75-mile gun that shelled Paris during the World War. Actually, there were at various times 12 of those guns, as many as six of them in action at once. All were wretchedly inaccurate.

The best figures show that one-third of the shells they fired missedy the whole city of Paris and only one of all those shells did any damage that might be considered military by the widest definition. That one struck a subway entrance and caved it in.

A gun firing this distance cannot be aimed in any proper sense. The shell has to travel through many layers of air, clear up into the stratosphere, then descend through other layers of air. All these layers have wind currents of varying direction and intensity and during its long upward and downward flight these carry the shell far from the point at which it was directed.

In addition, guns of such extreme range require huge powder charges, and the barrel of the piece must be tremendously long—90 to 120 feet. The tremendous explosion generated by the powder charge rapidly scores and tips even the hard steel of the gun-liner.

Measure Velocity at Start

In the long-range gunning of Paris, German artillery officers had to discover how far their shells went by means of a pressure guage inserted in the side of the barrel, which told what velocity of that particular shell had been when it left on its flight.

From this they formed an estimate of the necessary increase in the charge for the next shot. At the end of 50 shots the guns were no longer serviceable. There has been no improvement in artillery to justify the belief that the gun being used against London will be any more durable.

All this adds up to the fact that the Nazis cannot possibly obtain direct military results from their huge artillery, though they may have trebled or quadrupled the dozen guns shot at Paris.

The big guns are simply a piece of frightfulness, put into action partly for moral effect, partly to distract British airmen and artillery that might be out on other tasks.

Moral effect was regarded as important in Germany in the world war and this is probably the case today. But there is no use playing for the moral effect unless it is to be exploited by military means. The Paris guns opened up simultaneously with the big German line drive for Paris.

The fact that the London guns are in action probably means that an invasion attempt is scheduled for the earliest possible moment; and it would be no surprise to see it accompanied by a drive through Spain against Gibraltar.

Gales Scatter Nazi Invasion Fleet

LONDON, Sept. 17 (UP).—Providential gales — such as those which helped disperse and sink the Spanish Armada—scattered a German invasion fleet in the English Channel last night, an Air Ministry announcement disclosed today.

British reconnaissance fliers today quickly the new concentration points of the Nazi armada. the Ministry said.

The Ministry said:

"From dawn today (Tuesday) reconnaissance aircraft of the coastal command were combing the enemy coast line over the entire Channel area.

"Searches on a large scale had been organized overnight to ascertain the changes in disposition of German sea forces.

Forced to Seek Shelter

"These changes were imposed on the enemy in consequence of a strong westerly wind which swept the Channel throughout the night.

"It blew with gale force in exposed places where German surface craft had been last sighted.

"Most of the channel was very rough and as was expected the enemy ships and small craft had scattered and scurried to seek shelter. The new positions were located quickly today by the coastal command.

"Today coastal command aircraft gave escort to many large convoys of merchant vessels and there has not been a single enemy attempt at molestation by air or sea."

The Ministry also said the RAF had carried out daylight attacks on Germany's invasion bases at Calais, Ostend and Dunkerque yesterday.

Dutch Island Raided

A separate raid was made on the Dutch island of Walcheren, where a concentration of German barges was found in a canal and attacked by low-flying bombers.

"A convoy of 12 barges and 3 escort vessels," said the Ministry, "was intercepted and bombed off Zeebrugge. An attack also was made on three self-propelled barges patrolling off Ostend harbor which hove to and opened fire on sighting our aircraft. Haamstede Airdrome on the Dutch island of Schouven was raded."

A salvo of bombs was seen to burst along a quay at Calais, it was said.

MEN AGAINST AMERICA--Envoys Head 5th Column

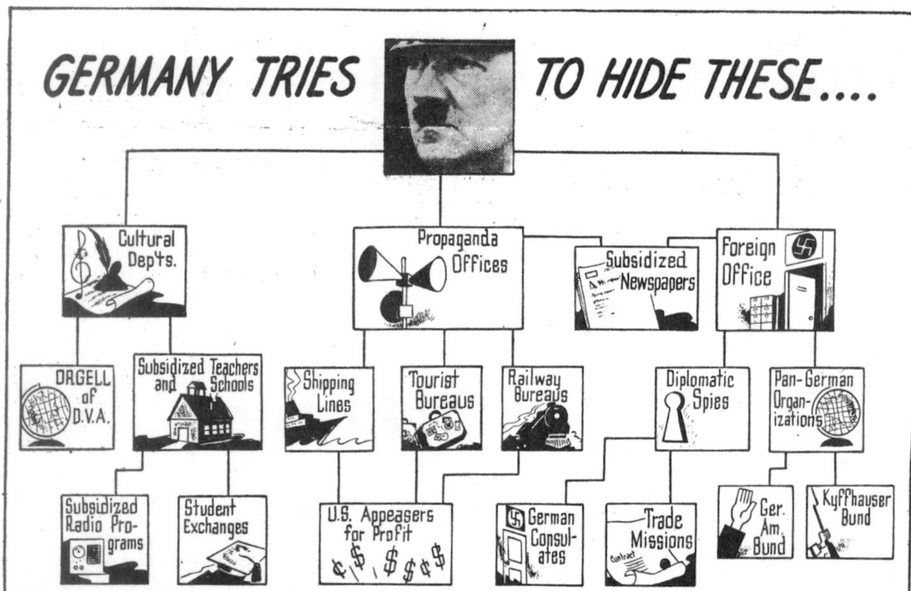

Copyright, 1940, by N. Y. Post

The editors and reporters of the Paris Soir paid slight attention to the new elevator operator. He was a little Alsatian, very subdued, unfailingly polite and adept in the handling of his lift. In Paris he was as small a cog as the city's wheels had—until Paris fell.

Then one morning the little Alsatian went upstairs in the elevator. He did not run it; he merely rode in it. He stepped off at the editorial room floor, took over the office of the editor-in-chief and sat down to present the policies of the victorious Hitler.

He was a fifth columnist. So was Herr Otto Abetz, who served as French correspondent for Hermann Goering's Essener National Zeitung, left Paris before the war and returned to Vichy as German ambassador to the Petain government. So were butchers and teachers and doctors; men about town and sewer rats; ditch diggers and druggists.

Most impressive of all the truths about this new technique of warfare is this: Nobody ever realized how effective the fifth column was, in the countries whose downfall it assisted, until it was too late to do anything about it.

Why? How can a country become ridden with dissident elements to its own destruction? It is very simple, really. The fifth column consists of men, like the little Alsatian in the Paris Soir. They do a vast number of things for a living.

Some of them are natives of the countries they served and are either naturalized or not, as expediency dictates. Others are natives of the countries they attack, disloyal to its institutions because they are eager for money or power, or because they are honestly convinced that another system is better than their own.

Chief among these men are the diplomatic representatives, propagandists and tourist bu-

Continued on Page 13, Col. 1

'He's Burning Us,' Gangster Sobs

Goldstein Begs Magoon to 'Tell Truth'

Something the movies have overlooked came to pass today in County Court, Brooklyn.

Before the startled eyes of a blue ribbon jury two gangsters, heretofore pictured as jovial, carefree members of the murder ring, burst into tears.

It happened at the trial of Harry (Pittsburgh Phil) Srtauss and Martin (Buggsy) Goldstein, who are charged with strangling one Irving ((Puggy) Feinstein while the raido played, and then making a bonfire of him in a vacant lot.

"Lives Depend on Truth"

Seymour Magoon, admitted member of the ring, was called as a state's witness. As Magoon placed his hand on the Bible to be sworn, Goldstein stood and shouted: "For God's sake, tell the truth, Seymour. Our lives depend on you telling the truth."

Goldstein stood with his manacled hands extended in an attitude of supplication; the tears welled in his eyes. Magoon's face grew red; he, too, began to weep, but Judge Fitzgerald called the whole thing off by ordering Goldstein to sit down.

But when Magood had told his story, Goldstein rose again

Continued on Page 3, Col. 5

INDEX TO POST FEATURES

Two Sections 16 Pages

U. S. Probes Von Spiegel

By STANLEY G. THOMPSON

Post Staff Correspondent

WASHINGTON, Sept. 17.—Secretary Hull said today that publication by the New York Post of a threatening letter sent to G. F. Neuhaeuser, San Antonio editor, in 1938, by German Consul General von Spiegel of New Orleans had caused the State Dept. to reopen the baron's case, already twice before the department.

Hull indicated that the letter, in addition to Spiegel's attempt to bribe the heads of two universities to make changes in their German departments and Spiegel's "off the record" state-

Continued on Page 3, Col. 2

RACE RESULTS ON PAGE 7

Last Stand of Jock Evans, Who Kept Traffic Away From a Time Bomb at Crossroads

By ROBERT J. CASEY

Special Cable to The Post

Copyright, 1940, New York Post and Chicago Daily News, Inc.

EXCLUSIVE

HOTSPOT, Southeast England, Sept. 17.—In the larger matters of threatened invasion by aerial bombs and artillery fire people have given little thought to Jock Evans upon whose thin breast nobody will ever pin any medals, even posthumously.

He will never have a public funeral with muffled drums, muted trumpets and such like tokens of civic gratitude. It is most unlikely that he will ever have any funeral at all.

The future historian looking over this war with the proper perspective, without worry about his own comfort or his own skin, may consider this unimportant. But from where this observer sits in the rockpile at the end of the trajectory, Jock Evans seems something more than one man who may have been over-heroic and over-stubborn at the same time.

So far as concerns the elements that have made England to date, he was an architect's model for the spirit of the British Empire.

Jock Evans, to get on with it, was, in his most recent career, an Air Raid Precautions warden. In a year's drill in how to put on the gas mask, how to revive fainting women, how to direct people to the nearest shelter, he would never have shown more than ordinary aptitude.

In the years before the war he had done nothing to distinguish himself. He had some sort of dock job where the dust hadn't been too good for his lungs. Because of bad eyes and other deficiencies, he had been rejected for military service even at the end of the last war when medical examiners hadn't been so particular.

Jock Evans was on duty the night the big crump fell in the garden by the crossroads.

He had been on duty most nights in the past month, with seldom an all-clear. He had phoned to the central control at 11 p. m. that he had seen a bright light somewhere. His superiors, remembering Jock, suspected it might be somebody with a too bright cigar.

He had stationed himself near the telephone kiosk on the edge of an outlying suburb where the artillery shells still land each day when the town is shelled. He had had no occasion to move from his post at midnight when the big crump fell.

The big crump was a time bomb—and a big one.

He told this to his chief in his report a minute later.

"Where is it?" inquired his chief.

"In the garden," said Jock.

Then the order "Get people out, empty nearby

Continued on Page 8, Col. 8

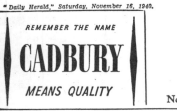

DAILY HERALD

EXTRA LATE EDITION

No. 7725 SATURDAY, NOVEMBER 16, 1940 ONE PENNY

Midlands City Is Now Like A Bombarded French Town

COVENTRY HOMELESS SLEPT BY ROADSIDE THIS MORNING

NOT A MORTAL BLOW —WORK WILL RESTART

By F. G. H. SALUSBURY, "Daily Herald" War Correspondent

COVENTRY, Friday Night

COVENTRY HAS BEEN THE VICTIM OF THE MOST CONCENTRATED, IF NOT THE WORST, RAID SINCE THE WAR BEGAN.

I HAVE JUST COME BACK FROM THE CENTRE OF THE CITY, WHICH NOW LOOKS EXACTLY LIKE ONE OF THOSE FRENCH TOWNS THAT WERE LAID LEVEL DURING THE LAST WAR BY AN INTENSIVE BOMBARDMENT.

The cathedral is in ruins, except for its tower, and over a large area surrounding it there lies the stench of burning houses.

The number of casualties cannot yet be determined, but it is certainly large. *(Preliminary reports, says the Ministry of Home Security, indicate that the number of casualties may number 1,000.)* The damage which has been inflicted on this city must run into millions of pounds.

I was told by one of the inhabitants that the noise of falling bombs was practically continuous, and that after a short time everyone was literally dazed by the noise.

I approached the city from Rugby, and a few miles out of Coventry I encountered the first large body of refugees walking along the roadside exactly as the Belgians and French escaped from the last German invasion.

Children were being carried in their fathers' arms, and pushed along in perambulators. Luggage was piled high in perambulators.

There were suitcases and bundles on people's shoulders; little families trudged along hand in hand with rugs, blankets, and, in fact, anything they could have salved from their ruined homes.

There were also many motor cars parked by the roadside, in which people would pass the night despite the intense cold.

UNDER THE HEDGEROWS

Nevertheless, those with motor cars will be luckier than those without. For despite the hospitality of surrounding towns and villages, it will have been impossible for everyone to get a bed or even shelter.

I saw several people making preparations to lie down under the leeside of buildings or against hedgerows.

Very soon after the raid began the Germans succeeded in starting their first large fire, and from then onwards they had no difficulty in sighting their targets.

Fires in the centre of the city multiplied and spread rapidly despite most magnificent work by the fire brigades' auxiliary fire services and the A.R.P.—indeed, all the services which could be called out to deal with this tragedy.

It was a miracle that the firemen confined the fires as they did. In one place they had to blow up a large building with dynamite to check the path of the flames.

Extra police and A.R.P. also rushed in.

Every conceivable assistance to Coventry has been rendered by her neighbours. But nothing can minimise the appalling extent of the tragedy, which has rendered scores of thousands of people homeless and severely damaged the heart of the city.

On my way to the cathedral I encountered a girl of, perhaps, 12 years of age, and I asked her what she was doing.

The air was thick with smoke and a fire was still blazing in a house not 20 yards away.

"Oh," she said, "I'm just having a look round." I asked her where she was going to sleep that night and she replied, "Why? Here, of course. We were lucky."

"Have you got any water or gas?" I asked. "No," she said, "but we'll do some cooking on an oil stove and the water will turn up from somewhere."

WORKMEN WERE THERE

Then she admitted with a smile that she had been very frightened last night and resumed her tour of inspection.

There was, of course, no work done in Coventry to-day, largely owing to the failure of the power supplies, though I understand there are some factories which manufactured their own electricity.

Nevertheless, the workmen were there, ready to start again if it had been possible.

This is not a mortal blow to our war production by any means, and I should not be surprised if quite soon work is resumed in Coventry to some extent.

The authorities are doing everything possible to get homeless people and refugees out of the city into neighbouring towns and rest centres, but their main difficulty is with transport.

There is nothing like enough transport for the people who wish to be moved, and the result, as I have said, is in these pathetic streams of refugees walking along the roads.

Nevertheless, the spirit of the people, without any exaggeration, is magnificent.

I even saw many smiles.

In every heart there is no fear, only a most passionate hatred of the enemy, and a determination to carry on at all costs.

In fact, the spirit of battered Coventry was very well expressed by a Union Jack which I observed stuck over the shattered doorway of an otherwise completely ruined building.

(Continued on Back Page)

Three famous spires of Coventry—Christ Church, Holy Trinity Church and the Cathedral.

RAF STRIKES AT BERLIN

WHILE the Germans were concentrating their hate on Coventry, R A F bombers were pounding the great Berlin railway stations and goods yards.

Heavy explosive and incendiary bombs caused fires that could be seen for many miles. The damage will increase the transport chaos in Germany already caused by the R A F. (See Page Six.)

Dusk To Dawn Raid

NAZIS SAY 30,000 FIRE BOMBS FELL

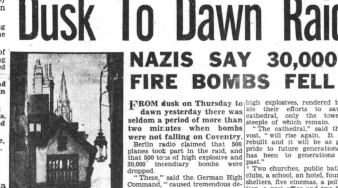

Old houses in Bayley-lane.

The Council House, opened by the King—then Duke of York—in 1920.

FROM dusk on Thursday to dawn yesterday there was seldom a period of more than two minutes when bombs were not falling on Coventry.

Berlin radio claimed that 500 planes took part in the raid, and that 500 tons of high explosive and 30,000 incendiary bombs were dropped.

"These," said the German High Command, "caused tremendous devastation" and fires that were visible from the Channel coast 125 miles away.

The raid was described by Berlin as a reprisal for the R A F attack on Munich, and was held to be the greatest bombardment in the history of air warfare.

Apparently the Luftwaffe was striving to make Coventry a second Guernica.

At times the attack took the form of dive-bombing and machine-gunning.

"The people of Coventry," the Ministry of Home Security stated, "bore their ordeal with great courage."

To this an official added, "There will be many stories to be told when it is possible to collect them."

Few shops were open in the city yesterday, but in the window of a fruit store, which had been damaged by blast, was the notice, "Business as usual. Nuts to Hitler!"

Died On Duty

Casualties included members of the Civil Defence fire and police services, who are known to have lost their lives while engaged on duty.

Among the places damaged. apart from the 14th century cathedral, was the operating theatre of a hospital, but the hospital—hit three times—was working yesterday as a clearing station.

An isolation hospital was hit, and in one ward some casualties were caused.

Five policemen—three specials and two regulars—were patrolling one street when a bomb was heard falling.

The three specials threw themselves down and the two regulars fell on top of them in an attempt to shield them. The bomb fell almost directly on them and all were killed.

One of the most tragic stories was that of a young Coventry man who had been working in Birmingham and returned to his home town to help with rescue work.

At the very first address to which he was sent he helped to recover the body of his young wife.

The Provost, the very Rev. R. T. Howard, and a party of cathedral watchers attempted to deal with 12 incendiary bombs.

They tackled them with sand and attempted to smother them until a shower of other incendiaries, accompanied this time by high explosives, rendered impossible their efforts to save the cathedral, only the tower and steeple of which remain.

"The cathedral," said the Provost, "will rise again. It will be rebuilt and it will be as great a pride to future generations as it has been to generations in the past."

Two churches, public baths, two clubs, a school, an hotel, four public shelters, five cinemas, a police station, a post office and two first-aid posts were damaged.

Steps were being taken yesterday to shepherd the homeless to emergency feeding centres.

Terrific Din

A policeman suffered injury to his eyes while dealing with one of the many incendiary bombs.

A reporter who watched the raid writes that at times the din was terrific.

The flash and crash of the barrage mingled with the whistle of falling bombs and explosions.

A pall of smoke lay over the town, and the red glare in the sky outdid the full moon in brilliance.

Stabbing through this scene, searchlights endeavoured to catch and hold the raiders in their beams.

(Continued on Back Page)

21 Down—Three In Last Night's Raid

AFTER a day in which eighteen German bombers and fighters were shot down in raids on Britain —for the loss of one Spitfire and one pilot—London had its worst night blitz for several weeks.

Three more enemy planes were destroyed in the night raids.

London anti-aircraft guns put up the heaviest barrage for weeks when relays of raiders attacked the capital in the early hours this morning.

Raids were widespread over the country. The West Midlands were again bombed, and several towns in the Home Counties.

But London appeared to be the butt of the main attack.

During the first few hours of the the night only single bombers came over, because of bad weather conditions.

80 BOMBERS

They tried without success to ring London with fires.

But when the clouds cleared the raiders came in greater strength and dropped oil bombs and incendiaries, as well as sticks of high explosives.

They repeated their tactics of trying to start a circle of fires.

An A.R.P. worker said, "For the first time the planes came over in formation. Within a few minutes I counted 80 heavy bombers.

"They were flying in close formation from the south due north.

"For numbers it is the worst night of my experience, and hundreds of German planes have been active over the area."

PLANE BLEW UP

A plane was seen to blow up in the sky at Debden, near Saffron Walden, Essex. There was a terrific explosion as parts of it hit the ground.

A second plane was brought down in Essex on Latters Priory Farm, Harlow.

(Continued on Back Page, Col. Six)

STOP PRESS

BERLIN RAIDED AGAIN

NEW YORK, Friday

German broadcast intercepted by National Broadcasting Company said large numbers of British planes attacked Berlin to-night, and six were brought down in Berlin and six near the Channel.

BRITAIN'S OFFER TO RUSSIA

GREAT BRITAIN is still awaiting Moscow's reply to the proposals made to Russia last month.

There were three main items in the proposals it was learned in London last night. They were:

De facto recognition of the incorporation of the Baltic States in the Soviet Union;

A guarantee that Russia would be a participant in any peace settlement after the war; and

An assurance that Britain would not be associated in any attack against Soviet Russia.

The proposals were submitted to M. Vishinsky, the deputy Commissar for Foreign Affairs, on October 22.

AN ITALIAN LIE

The Admiralty states there is no truth in the claim that an Italian submarine has torpedoed a British battleship of the Ramillies class.

Greeks Launch A New Attack

GREEK infantry at dawn yesterday launched a new attack on the Italian positions.

Preceded by a night of careful preparation, it was possibly the most determined attack which the war has seen so far (says a Reuter message from Athens).

The Greeks made the attack with bayonets among the rocky heights north-east of Koritza, the keypoint in Southern Albania.

Their chief objective was the mountain of Ivan, 6,000 feet high, overlooking Koritza.

Bayonet Fighting

Following a further assault with bayonets in the afternoon, the Greeks occupied a great deal of this mountain region.

During the day ten Italian large-calibre guns fell into their hands.

By the occupation of Ivan the Greeks will control still one more important road out of Koritza, making it much more difficult for the Italians to retain the town.

Koritza is not only the largest town of Southern Albania, with a population of 30,000, but it is also a centre of communications.

Its capture would offer the Greeks an entrance to the route leading north to Elbassan, the strategic centre of Albania.

This is where King Zog used to maintain most of his forces before the Italian invasion.

Italy's Offensive

In the Kalamas River sector (wires D. J. Travlos, "Daily Herald" correspondent at Athens) the Greek advance has reached the border line.

In the middle sector, where the Greeks are fighting on Albanian territory, they are reported to be shelling a road running parallel with the frontier.

The cutting of this road would be a serious threat to Italian supplies in this region.

Predictions that an Italian offensive against Greece is imminent were made by some observers on the Jugoslav border yesterday (reports Associated Press).

They based their view on two developments.

There was brisk artillery and air activity on the northern Greek-Albanian border and a change in Italian troop dispositions.

Egypt's New Premier

Hussein Sirry Pasha has been appointed Prime Minister of Egypt in succession to Hassan Sabry Pasha, who collapsed and died while reading the Speech from the Throne on Thursday.

As Minister of Public Works he came to England in 1938 to study London local government. He has also been Minister of Defence.

November 16, 1940
London Blackout
5.38 p.m.—7.53 a.m.
MOON RISES 6.32 p.m.;
SETS 10.11 a.m. To-morrow

Daily Mail

FOR KING AND EMPIRE

NO. 13,941 ** TUESDAY, DECEMBER 31, 1940 ONE PENNY

LATE WAR NEWS SPECIAL

Hitler Planned Monday Swoop

London was to Blaze First

By NOEL MONKS, Daily Mail Air Correspondent

HITLER meant to start the second Great Fire of London as the prelude to an invasion.

This was the belief held in well-informed quarters in London yesterday.

The Nazis planned to set big fires burning all over London before midnight.

Relays of bombers laden with H.E. would then have carried out the most destructive raid of the war. The New Year invasion was to have followed.

The R.A.F. have given more attention to the invasion ports this past week than for two [illegible] more. Clearly there [illegible]ons for supposing [illegible] still going ahead [illegible] plans.

THE FACTS

Here are the real facts of Sunday night's fire-raising raid, as told me yesterday:

It was one of the biggest night attacks on Britain since September.

No R.A.F. night fighters were operating over the London area, though some were doing so between London and the coast.

Soon after 10 p.m. the German Air Command sent out instructions for all the bombers then engaged to return to their bases, as the weather had taken a turn for the worse and fog was blotting out their aerodromes.

It was the weather, then, and not our night fighters, that saved London from an even worse attack. The view is held that the assault was intended to be the fiercest of the war.

Up to 1,000 bombers were to have been used during the night.

One explanation given for the sudden silence of London's inner A.A. barrage is that in the light of the fires by which most of London was lit up, to continue firing would have disclosed the positions of the guns.

Some of the German fighter-bombers came down to a lower height over London than ever before. They were able to do this because:

(1) The guns had stopped firing, and

(2) Flames lit up the barrage balloons, and the raiders could fly between them.

It is estimated that more than 10,000 incendiary bombs were dropped on the capital within three hours.

Until a late hour last night no raids had been reported from any part of Britain.

Because of bad weather across the Channel most of the R.A.F.'s operations on Sunday night had to be cancelled.

Churchill Sees London's Ruins

MR WINSTON CHURCHILL, accompanied by his wife, visited the ruins of London's famous Guildhall yesterday and spent two hours walking through the City.

As they walked along people cheered. One man shouted, "God bless you, sir." Mr. Churchill smiled and lifted his hat.

They inspected a deep, underground shelter. To shouts of "Good luck" from the crowd, Mr. Churchill replied, "Good luck to you."

As they left this shelter a woman ran forward and asked: "When will the war be over?"

Mr. Churchill paused, turned to the woman, and said. "When we've beaten 'em."

Mr. Churchill looked grim and determined as he noted the damaged churches and other buildings.

The news of his visit spread, and after a while a crowd of cheering Londoners were accompanying him on his tour.

Morrison on Radio To-night

MR. HERBERT MORRISON, Minister of Home Security, will broadcast after the B.B.C.'s six o'clock news bulletin this evening.

He will detail further measures being taken to assist fire fighting during air raids, and it is believed that he will deal with the need for greater fire-watching precautions at unoccupied or temporarily unoccupied business premises.

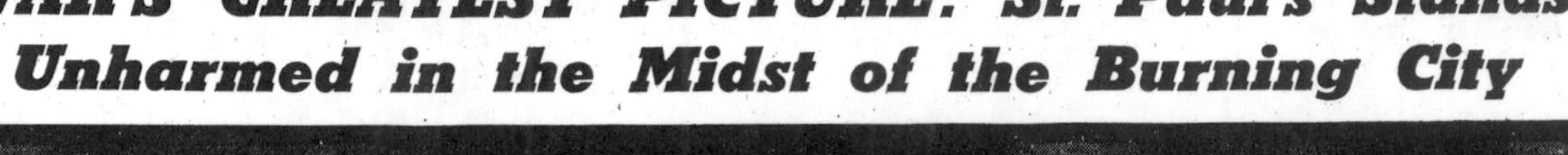

WAR'S GREATEST PICTURE: St. Paul's Stands Unharmed in the Midst of the Burning City

ROAR of gun barrage mingled with roar and crackle of flames; raiders droned overhead. Daily Mail cameraman H. A. Mason stood on a City roof to get this awe-inspiring picture of the second Great Fire of London—St. Paul's Cathedral ringed with flame. "I focussed at intervals as the great dome loomed up through the smoke," he said. "Glare of many fires and sweeping clouds of smoke kept hiding the shape. Then a wind sprang up. Suddenly the shining cross, dome, and towers stood out like a symbol in the inferno. The scene was unbelievable. In that moment or two I released my shutter." Here is his picture, one that all Britain will cherish—for it symbolises the steadiness of London's stand against the enemy: the firmness of Right against Wrong.

***** Other pictures showing the raid havoc are in the BACK Page.**

HAVOC COULD HAVE BEEN SAVED

By Daily Mail Reporter

MANY of Sunday night's fires in the City of London could have been avoided if fire-watching regulations had been properly observed.

That is the opinion of Commander A. N. G. Firebrace, the London Fire Brigade chief, who has just been transferred to the Home Office to help in organising local brigade duties through the country.

"It should be a point of honour," he declared, "for every firm to say: 'I will *not* let this place burn down, both for my own sake and for the sake of my neighbours.'"

Commander Firebrace was present at an urgent conference called yesterday by Mr. Herbert Morrison at the Home Office to consider the problems arising out of the fires.

Others present were Sir Philip Game, Commissioner of Police for the Metropolis, General Sir William Bartholomew, chief of civil defence for the London area and A.R.P. experts.

Even on Sundays

The whole available details of the raid were reported to Mr. Morrison, who will broadcast this evening during the 6 o'clock news.

The work of the firemen on duty throughout Sunday night was directed personally by Mr. F. W. Jackson, now in charge of the London Fire Brigade.

Mr. Jackson was having a brief holiday about 50 miles away from London when news of the raid reached him. He drove at once to London at the fullest possible speed, and was on duty all night.

Here is what another of Britain's fire-fighting experts said about the absence of spotters:

"If a proper fire-watching staff had been on duty at all the buildings affected nearly all the fires would have been prevented.

"It is terrible to see a little fire start, and then in half an hour to see the whole roof ablaze.

"What is needed is not merely one roof-spotter—you want a man on watch on the roof and then a party of half a dozen or so below who can be called up at once in an emergency.

"Employees of the various firms should in every case form a rota and stay behind—even on Sundays—so as to *ensure* that their building cannot be destroyed by a few small incendiary bombs."

The Second Great Fire of London, and Where Were the Roof Spotters?—Page THREE. Pictures—BACK Page.

'Spain to Fortify Canary Islands'

Daily Mail Radio Station

General Franco has signed a decree providing for the fortification of the Canary Islands, according to a Moscow report quoted by the Belgrade radio last night.

Berlin Radio Went 'All Quiet'

Berlin radio eliminated all reference to the destruction of churches and historic buildings in its broadcast account last night of the fire raid on London. Neither did it follow its usual practice of giving interviews with raiding pilots.

Bremen Radio's English announcer described it as a fierce mass attack, concentrated in the space of a few hours.

"A great number of fires were caused in a relatively small space," he said, "although the attack was pressed home with strong formations it came as a surprise to the enemy, and the German Luftwaffe sustained no losses."

No reference was made to the whereabouts of the fires other than "the eastern part of London."—*B.U.P.*

Four Raiders in Pacific'

Daily Mail Radio Station

Four German raiders are now operating in the Pacific between Australia and China, states a Shanghai report quoted by the Moscow radio.

Up to date, it was asserted, 13 ships have disappeared in those waters. The ships have been of British, Dutch, and Norwegian nationality.

100 to 1 Backing for Roosevelt

From Daily Mail Corresponden

WASHINGTON, Monday.

PRESIDENT ROOSEVELT is "tremendously pleased" at the reaction to his speech, in which he pledged more aid to Britain and declared that the Axis could not win the war.

The President's secretary, Mr. Stephen Early, said to-day that the address had brought a greater response than any previous Roosevelt talk.

Within 40 minutes of its end the President received 600 messages. They were 100 to 1 in favour.

This is how it was received by:

Senator Alben Barkley, leader of the Democratic Party in the Senate: A magnificent clarification of our objectives.

Senator Warren R. Austin, leader of the Republican Party Minority in the Senate: A remarkably fine presentation of the situation.

The New York Sun: Deadly, implacable hostility towards the dictatorships sounded in every phrase.

New York Post: One of the major declarations in the history of our republic. It may still save our peace and our world.

'End of Hitler'

Ralph Ingersoll, editor of P.M.: The end of Hitler is very near now. If he thinks he has a chance after Roosevelt's speech last night, he is even crazier than he sounds.

Mr. Arthur Purvis, head of the British Purchasing Mission in the United States, attended a conference at the White House to-day with President Roosevelt and Mr. Henry Morgenthau, Secretary of the Treasury, on the production of material for Britain.

"We had a general discussion on supply matters," Mr. Purvis said later. "President Roosevelt's loan and lease plan opens up a new chapter."

China Seeks U.S. Planes

From Daily Mail Correspondent

NEW YORK, Monday. — The United States Government are reported to be considering the release of 400 warplanes to China for use against the Japanese.

Major-General San-chu Mow, head of the Chinese Air Force, is in Washington conferring with Administration officials and Army and Navy leaders.

Some of the foremost American strategists favour the transfer of at least 400 of the latest type pursuit and bomber planes, including six Flying Fortresses.

According to a *Reuter* report from Chungking, the Anglo-Chinese short-term credit guarantee agreement has been extended for six months to facilitate Chinese purchases from Great Britain.

500 Were Killed in Manchester

Mr. R. H. Adcock, Manchester's Town Clerk, revealed last night that in the severe raids on the city a week ago, about 500 people were killed.

He made the statement to check rumours. In one case it was rumoured that hundreds were killed in a shelter, when in fact only a few were injured.

America Moves

BIG ARMS FLOW HAS BEGUN

From Daily Mail Correspondent

NEW YORK, Monday.

THE United States Defence Commission announced to-day that they had approved arms contracts worth £2,500,000,000.

Monthly production had now risen to 2,400 aircraft engines, 700 warplanes, 100 tanks, and 10,000 automatic rifles.

Present British and American orders on hand total 50,000 planes, 130,000 aero-engines, 9,200 tanks, 2,055,000 guns, 380 naval vessels, 200 merchant ships, 50,000 lorries, and other equipment.

The United States Government were building 40 war factories, including the first plant for mass-producing tanks.

LATEST

MORE U.S. AID FOR GREECE

Washington, Monday.

Mr. Morgenthau, Secretary of the Treasury, indicated to-day that President Roosevelt may extend his "loan or lease" plan to Greece and China, in addition to Britain.—Exchange.

ADMIRAL LEAHY REACHES EUROPE

Vichy, Monday.—Admiral Leahy, the new American Ambassador to the French Government at Vichy, has arrived in Lisbon on board the United States cruiser Tuscaloosa, states a Havas despatch.—Reuter.

News Chronicle

No. 29,566 SATURDAY, FEBRUARY 8, 1941 RADIO PAGE 3 * ONE PENNY

THE WHIRLWIND TRIUMPH OF BENGHAZI

Italians Caught on Two Sides by Brilliant Pincer Move

From BERTHA GASTER
News Chronicle Correspondent

CAIRO, Friday.

IN A SEVEN-DAY WHIRLWIND CAMPAIGN, THE IMPERIAL ARMY OF THE NILE HAS SWEPT THROUGH THE 175-MILE STRETCH OF HILL AND DALE OF CENTRAL CYRENAICA, SHOT PAST VILLAGES AND SETTLEMENTS IN ENDLESS SUCCESSION, SMASHED ENEMY AERODROMES IN A SERIES OF DEVASTATING RAIDS, AND TAKEN BENGHAZI.

Despite the broken morale of the Italians and the lack of any effective air opposition, the rapidity of the latest success is greater than anyone dreamed.

It was expected that progress over the plateau, where the country is eminently suitable for defensive fighting, would be slow and protracted. In fact, the rate of advance has been about as quick as troops could make it on ordinary line march without opposition.

On Thursday night our planes were still bombing Benghazi and the neighbouring aerodrome of Benina. Today both are in our hands, and the occupation of one-third of Libya is complete.

It is 60 days since the campaign against Sidi Barrani began. In that time we have advanced 440 miles from Mersa Matruh, over hitherto impregnable desert, captured three well-defended strongholds, taken more than 110,000 prisoners, and brought Mussolini's North African Empire crashing about his ears.

Brilliant Improvisation

And it is no secret that the original intention of the British leaders was limited to smashing Graziani's preparations for an attack on Egypt and pushing the Italians back to the frontier.

The rest of this amazing campaign has been one brilliant improvisation after another, often by the men on the spot.

The final assault on Benghazi was made in the face of a furious, blinding sandstorm.

In achieving this victory, which surely will go down in history as one of the most shattering and complete of all time, our casualties, as far as can be told, are at present under 2,000.

Once the advance started, the momentum gradually increased until the last lap—Derna-Cyrene-Benghazi—achieved in the extraordinary time of one week.

Swept Round Mountain Plateau

It may now be revealed that the fall of Benghazi yesterday afternoon was mainly due to a masterly flanking movement by our armoured formations, which swept round the whole mountain plateau of Jebel Akhdar by the desert track, splitting off southwards from Bomba.

Beating down a slight attempt at resistance at Mechili, 50 miles south, they ploughed their way for five days across the waterless desert in blinding sandstorms, while the Australians were racing through the uplands to the north behind the fleeing Italians.

By a masterpiece of timing they came out on the coastal road leading to Tripoli, south of Benghazi, somewhere in the neighbourhood of Solluch, and cut the Italian retreat as the Australians came up from the north and hemmed in both sides.

With the last lifeline to Tripoli straddled by the waiting tanks of the British the Italians in Benghazi threw in their hands with

Turn to Back Page, Col. Three

—Italian Prisoners— For the Land

"I hope to get several thousand Italian prisoners of war to work on the land in gangs," Mr. R. H. Hudson, Minister of Agriculture, told farmers at Devizes.

The Man

General Sir Archibald Wavell, 57-year-old C.-in-C., Middle East, since 1939. Son of a major-general, he was pupil of Allenby, whose biography he wrote. In the extracts serialised in the News Chronicle recently, Gen. Wavell stated

His Theory . . .

To the uninitiated, pursuit seems the easiest possible form of war. . . Yet the successful or sustained pursuits of history have been few, the escapes from a lost battle many.

A force retreating falls back on its depots and reinforcements; unless it is overrun it is growing stronger all the time. And there are many expedients besides fighting by which it can gain time: bridges or roads may be blown up, defiles blocked, supplies destroyed.

The pursuer soon outruns his normal resources. . . But the chief obstacle he has to overcome is psychological. The pursued has a greater incentive to haste than the pursuer and, unless he is demoralised, a stronger urge to fight. . .

While coolness in disaster is the supreme proof of a commander's courage, energy in pursuit is the surest test of his strength of will.

TRAPANI PALERMO MESSINA
SICILY
SICILIAN CHANNEL
BIZERTA
TUNIS
PANTELLERIA
MALTA
BENGHAZI TO SICILY 450 MILES
TUNIS
TRIPOLI
CYRENE
DERNA
TOBRUK
BARDIA
SOLLUM
SIDI BARRANI
MERSA MATRUH
ALEXANDRIA
BENGHAZI
BENGHAZI TO MERSA MATRUH 440 MILES
TRIPOLI TO BENGHAZI 600 MILES
CAIRO
LIBYA
EGYPT

Churchill to Broadcast Tomorrow Night

The Prime Minister, it was announced last night, will speak at 9 p.m. in the Home and Overseas Services.

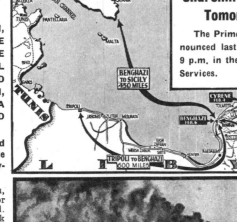

Here is part of the booty which fell into British hands at Tobruk. Line after line of Italian mechanised transport vehicles stand abandoned in the desert outside the town. Over the town itself roll clouds of smoke from burning oil and petrol dumps. Another picture on Back Page.

Italians Are Dispirited And Resentful

From Our Own Correspondent

NEW YORK, Friday.

SIGNS that the Fascist regime in Italy is fighting desperately to maintain its hold on a dispirited and resentful people continue to appear between the lines of news messages cabled from Rome.

Today and yesterday there have been more of the famous "student demonstrations," which Mussolini has been wont to stage whenever it becomes necessary to whip up a semblance of enthusiasm for one of his projects.

It is not long ago that "student demonstrators" were parading through the streets of Rome howling "Tunisia, Jibuti, Corsica!"

United Press reports that an extra guard of 500 fully armed troops was placed today around the United States Embassy in Rome. This might have indicated how roused and dangerous the demonstrators were, if one of the correspondents had not previously said that the total number of students taking part in the demonstration was about 500.

Significant also is the broadcast by Signor Ansaldo, in which he said that many Italians are now understanding "the terrible seriousness" of war, but added: "We cannot state that all Italians are equal to the moment—no, not at all."

IN GERMANY

From Berlin there continues to come news which shows how necessary the Nazis feel it is to soften the recent revelation that the United States is helping Britain.

The Blackshirt paper "Schwarze Korps" denounces the school of thought that fears a repetition of the events of the last war and promises, even if America should intervene, it would make no difference to the outcome of the war.

A cable from the German frontier comments on the "reserve" with which the German Press is now treating the war news, and boldly expresses the belief it is because of the growing desire for peace among the German people.

Vichy Report of Volpi Visit

Count Volpi has visited Vichy to ask the Spanish Ambassador to approach Sir Samuel Hoare, British Ambassador in Madrid, about evacuating Italian civilians from Abyssinia, it is learned in Vichy, says B.U.P.

Well-informed Rome circles deny the Volpi mission; Radio Vichy says Rome's denial is that Count Grandi is negotiating.

What the World Thinks

"Our congratulations to our great Ally. Well done!"

Radio Athens broadcast this message last night.

Here are other comments on the British capture of Benghazi:

BERLIN: "It's for our Allies to react before us."

Nazi newspapers do not even mention the Benghazi area.

SOVIET IMPRESSED

MOSCOW: Soviet radio devoted considerable attention to the news, the announcer emphasising Benghazi's strategic and naval importance.

He spoke of the great distances across the desert that the British troops had to cover.

The British communique was read, with London comments.

NEW YORK: "The Sun" hails "the smashing victory of General Wavell," and considers that the campaign is now at an end. A push towards Tripoli, adds "The Sun," would entail a new campaign, with different strategy.

AUSTRALIA: "A magnificent effort: Our forces must have had a motor race: Extraordinary how the Italians cleared out!" was the comment of Major-General V. A. H. Sturdee, Commander-in-Chief of the Australian Imperial Force, at Melbourne.

CANADA: "History will put a low estimate on the Duce," says the "Toronto Star." "Throughout Africa the initiative is now with the British and their native Allies. It was Mussolini's greed that got them into this position."

Says the "Montreal Star": "The campaign stands as one of the most brilliant achievements of all in the long and glorious annals of British arms. It definitely marks the decline, and in all probability the disappearance, of Italy's African empire."—B.U.P. and Reuter.

155 Held Under Defence Act Freed

A report by the Home Secretary last night stated that 155 persons detained under the defence regulations were released during December. In the same period 14 more persons were detained, making a total of 1,089.

NEWS CHRONICLE PICTURES OF LIFE IN A CORVETTE, BRITAIN'S NEW WARSHIP, HAVE BEEN HELD OVER BECAUSE OF PRESSURE ON SPACE

DESTROYER SHOT DOWN DORNIER

Attempting to attack a convoy, a Dornier twin-engined bomber was shot down by H.M.S. Vanity (Commander H. J. Buchanan, D.S.O., R.A.N.).

"A direct hit was made on the enemy aircraft, which crashed into the sea," said an Admiralty communiqué issued last night. "There were no survivors

"No damage or casualties were sustained by the convoy or H.M.S. Vanity."

Vanity is a destroyer launched in 1918, carrying a crew of 134.

Bombs Killed Eight

After dropping bombs which killed eight people and injured others at an East Anglian coast town yesterday afternoon, a raider is believed to have been brought down by ground defences.

As the plane was making off, two objects were seen to fall from it.

Later, two bullet riddled pieces of aluminium were found.

Onlookers saw smoke trailing from the tail, and one said that the plane was falling when lost to sight.

Gunned Streets

A plane which dropped several bombs on a North-East Scotland town also machine-gunned the streets.

One woman was removed to hospital. Another person received minor injuries

A single enemy raider appeared over an Eastern coastal district yesterday afternoon. Two bombs were dropped, but no damage is reported.

Up to a late hour London was raid-free for the fifteenth night out of the last 19. No raids were reported from other parts of Britain.

Lord Moyne May Succeed Lord Lloyd

Lord Moyne, it is understood, has been chosen to succeed Lord Lloyd as Secretary for the Colonies. An official announcement of Lord Moyne's appointment will probably be made shortly

As Mr. Walter Guinness, M.P. for Bury St. Edmunds, he was Minister for Agriculture, and is now Joint Parliamentary Secretary for Agriculture. He was in the Commons for 24 years before being created a baron in 1932.

Bread Prices Fixed

From Monday the prices of all types of bread must not be higher than on December 2.

This Order is complementary to the Government's offer of a subsidy of a halfpenny a quartern for bread sold at 8d. a quartern or less.

Weygand Says: We Keep Bizerta

GEN. WEYGAND broadcast from Algiers yesterday a denial of reports that France would permit Germany to use Bizerta, base in Tunisia, with a view to eventual action in Libya.

The General also denied, according to the Havas Agency, that negotiations had taken place with a view to the cession of Bizerta or the landing of German troops at the port.

Admiral Darlan, Vichy navy chief, is expected back in Vichy from Paris this morning.

It is believed that his return will be the signal for "reorganisation" of the Petain Government.

Many in Vichy expect collective resignation of the Cabinet.

Admiral Darlan is understood by reliable circles in Vichy to

Turn to Back Page, Col. Six

Milch Warns Germany

"DANGER hovers over everybody in Germany," declared Field-Marshal Milch, Goering's deputy, last night in a broadcast from all German stations.

His talk contained hints that the Germans may expect more intensified raids by the R.A.F.

"If our night rest is sometimes disturbed," he said, "you may rest assured that during the day preceding the alarm London has had six Alerts and then an uninterrupted night-raid from 6 p.m. to 6 a.m."

On the whole Germany had suffered merely pinpricks.

He regretted however, that the German workers spent half of their nights in shelters and had to work the next day.

SHELTER ACCIDENTS

The damage in Berlin was mainly to roofs and bore no proportion to the damage caused in London.

Eighty per cent. of the German casualties caused through air-raids were people who did not take cover in shelters or were killed by unfortunate accidents in shelters.

The Marshal said Germans must take new measures to make shelters blast- and splinter-proof. He continued:

HITLER EXPECTS . .

"When an alarm is sounded, the Fuehrer expects you to go down to your shelter without penalties for failing to do so. Enemy planes may drop H.E. and fire bombs without being heard.

"Unconditional confidence in our leaders and complete faith in the efficiency of our Luftwaffe will guarantee that the enemy will never succeed by air raids in shaking our people's conviction that victory is assured."

Field-Marshal Milch urged the organisation of more fire-fighters, men and women, but added: "It may be dangerous, as British planes often swoop low on our towns and machine-gun fire must be expected."

Goering Sent R.A.F. a Radio Message —Berlin Report

Goering sent a wireless message to the R.A.F. after the death in action of Captain Wieck, Nazi air ace, last November, Berlin radio announced yesterday

Two days later came a reply that Wieck was neither in a British prison camp nor could his name be found in the list of identified German casualties the announcer said.

Wieck's machine, the radio added, was seen to crash into the Channel after a fight with a Spitfire. Another pilot reported that Wieck baled out, but German rescue launches found no trace of him or his plane. —Reuter.

Greek Bayonets Pursue Italians

Large forces of Italian infantrymen were mown down by devastating Greek fire on the Albanian battlefront, Athens radio said last night.

A bayonet charge drove the Italians back beyond their lines, many being captured.

New Italian Attack Smashed: Page Three

Hitler Reported In Vichy

From Our Own Correspondent

NEW YORK, Friday. — The "Chicago Daily News" Rome correspondent learns that Senor Serrano Suner, Spanish Foreign Minister, has gone to Vichy "to join the German Chancellor there in bringing pressure on Pétain."

It is also suggested that Mussolini may join the conference.

There is no other indication from any source that Hitler is in Vichy or is going there

Invasion Ports Battered Again

From Our Own Correspondent

DOVER, Friday Night.

One of the biggest attacks on the invasion ports in Northern France is now in progress.

For some time our bombers have been in action over Calais and Boulogne.

From the cliffs of Dover, despite the fog, constant flashes can be seen lighting the sky like summer lightning. Star shells and streams of flaming onions are pouring into the sky. A fierce fire is reflected in the clouds.

The reverberations of exploding bombs can be heard and felt along the Kent coast, where thousands are watching the scene.

Thursday night's raids on invasion bases: Page Six

LATE NEWS

Death Sentence On "Brave Englishman"

Percy William Olaf de Wet, an Englishman whom the Germans described as a "brave and curious man," has been sentenced to death by the People's Court in Berlin after a secret trial at which he was found guilty of being a spy in the pay of the French.

LONDON BLACK-OUT
Tonight 6.31 p.m.-7.56 a.m.
Tomorrow 6.33 p.m.-7.55 a.m.

DAILY MIRROR, Monday, Feb. 10, 1941.

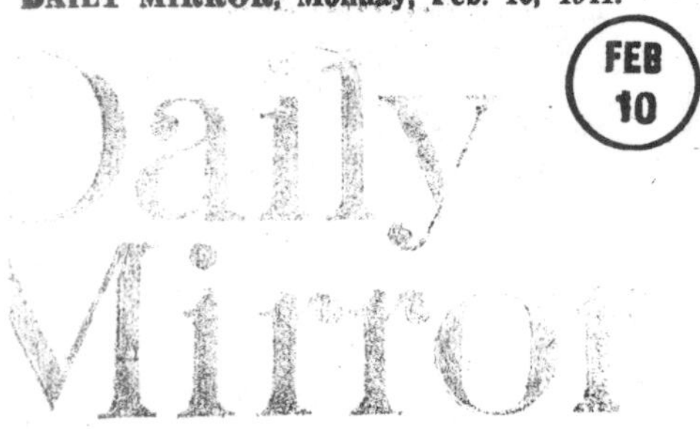

FEB 10

No. 11,597 ONE PENNY
Registered at the G.P.O. as a Newspaper.

NAVY BATTERS GENOA WITH 300 TONS OF SHELLS

WARSHIPS of the British Mediterranean Fleet battered the Italian naval base of Genoa at dawn yesterday, hurling 300 tons of shells on docks, factories, ships, railways and oil plants.

Two of our most powerful ships, the 32,000-ton battle cruiser Renown and the 31,000-ton battleship Malaya, led the attack.

Between them they carry fourteen 15-inch guns, each throwing a shell weighing 1,920lb. These were in action.

The aircraft carrier Ark Royal was there, too. Her planes bombed as the big guns plastered their targets.

And our total casualties were one Swordfish aircraft and her crew, reported missing.

The action was as glorious a feat as that performed by Drake in 1587, when he sailed into Cadiz and singed the King of Spain's beard.

For in shelling the Duce's chief seaport yesterday, the Fleet sailed deep into waters which Mussolini has exclusively regarded as his own.

By this attack the Navy proved its ability to operate successfully in the seas all around Italy.

The Admiralty stated last night that the bombardment and bombing were more successful than at first thought. The communique stated:

"Our forces, under the command of Vice-Admiral Sir James Somerville, consisted of Renown, Malaya, Ark Royal and the 9,100-ton cruiser Sheffield, with light forces in company.

"Military targets in and around the port of Genoa were subjected to a bombardment in which over 300 tons of shells were fired.

"The following results were observed: The Ansaldo electric works and the Ansaldo boiler works were heavily hit and large fires started.

"The main power station of the port, which also supplies power for the railways, was severely damaged and set on fire.

"Many hits were made on the dry docks and on warehouses and harbour works surrounding the inner harbour. Here, too, considerable fires broke out.

"The main oil fuel installation and oil tanks were repeatedly hit, as were a number of supply ships and the main goods yard of the railway.

"Several tons of bombs and a large number of incendiaries were dropped by naval aircraft on the oil refinery of the A.N.I.C. at Leghorn, and other targets in the vicinity.

"Other naval aircraft attacked Pisa, where the aerodrome and railway junction were hit. This railway junction is the intersection of the main west coast railway from Genoa to Rome and the south, and one of

Continued on Back Page, Col. 5

175 Miles Onward

ARMY of the Nile has advanced 175 miles along the Libyan coast from Benghazi. General "Electric Whiskers" Berganzoli, second only to Graziani, is one of seven generals captured with Benghazi. **(See Back Page.)**

Premier Tells Reason

GENOA was shelled and shattered by the Navy yesterday because a Nazi German expedition might sail from there to attack General Weygand in the French colonies of Algeria and Tunisia.

Mr. Churchill revealed this last night in a broadcast which was heard throughout Britain and the United States.

"It is right that the Italian people should be made to feel the sorry plight into which they have been led by Mussolini," the Premier said.

"If the cannonade of Genoa, rolling along the coast, reverberating in the mountains, has reached the ears of our French comrades in their grief and misery, it may cheer them with a feeling that friends, active friends, are near and that Britannia rules the waves."

During the winter Germany had the power to drop four tons upon us to our one on them.

"We are arranging so that presently this will be rather the other way round, but meanwhile London and our big cities have had to stand their pounding.

"They remind me of the British squares at Waterloo. They are not squares of soldiers, they do not wear scarlet coats: they are just ordinary English, Scottish and Welsh folk, men, women and children standing steadfastly together.

"But their spirit is the same, their glory is the same, and in the end their victory will be greater than famous Waterloo."

Referring to Italy's invasion of Greece, the Premier described Mussolini as "the crafty, cold-blooded black-hearted Italian, who had sought to gain an empire on the cheap." His forces were ignominiously hurled back while Generals Wavell and Wilson had received vast reinforcements in Egypt.

Then came our victory at Sidi Barrani. Wavell saw his chance.

"At that time I ventured to draw

Continued on Back Page, Col. 1

SPEECH WILL HASTEN U.S. AID

Moved by Churchill's plea, "Give us the tools and we will finish the job," Administration leaders in Washington last night predicted that the British Aid Bill will be made law on March 1, leading to the release of an enormous flood of war materials to Britain.

"Churchill's message is superb," said Mr. Sol Bloom, chairman of the Foreign Affairs Committee of the House of Representatives. "It is a complete assurance that democracy is still more than a match for the dictators."—British United Press and Associated Press.

MASTER OF THE "MED."

Admiral Sir Andrew B. Cunningham ("A.B.C." to the Navy), Commander of the Mediterranean Fleet.

Last week he swept the Italian seas for Musso's fleet—and couldn't find it.

So he sent his ships, under command of Vice-Admiral Sir James Somerville, to Genoa, big port of Italy, and bombarded it.

Daily Mail
FOR KING AND EMPIRE
NO. 13,998 ** FRIDAY, MARCH 7, 1941 ONE PENNY

LATE WAR NEWS SPECIAL

NORWAY RAID: FULL STORY

Amazing Scenes After Island Swoop

EXCITED CROWDS SWARM ABOARD

By Daily Mail Reporter

MORE than 300 Norwegian patriots, including many fishermen's wives, have been brought to Britain by the British warships which raided the Lofoten Islands, German fish-oil centre, off the coast of Norway, on Tuesday.

There were extraordinary scenes on the island as soon as the British force had overcome the German guards.

Crowds of Norwegians, cheering lustily, swarmed to the boats.

With such encouragements as "Any more for England?" and "Nice day for a sail, lady," grinning British sailors found themselves hauling aboard their ships men and women with their dearest possessions in bundles on their backs.

The emigrants' joy reached its height when they found fellow-countrymen aboard. For Norwegian troops and Marines, who had been in training in Britain, took part in the raid.

An eye-witness of the raid reveals that a number of fish oil factories and a power station were destroyed at each of the four principal ports of the Lofoten Islands, and oil storage tanks were set on fire.

Seventeen men of the German Air Force were captured when preparations were found being made to build a naval air station. The British troops and Free Norwegian troops fought with "tommy" guns.

This was the first time a Norwegian unit had taken part in Allied operations since Norway had to be abandoned last year.

Very different were the spirits of the patriots as they sailed to Britain from those of the 215 Germans and 10 Quislings who had been aiding the enemy, who came here as prisoners.

Norwegians in London are hoping to give an official welcome to some at least of the patriots.

What is to be the fate of the Quislings is being discussed between the Norwegian and British authorities in London.

One possible course of action is to hold them as hostages against the lives of loyal Norwegians now lying under sentence of death on charges of espionage.

The following eye-witness account of the raid was received last night from *Reuter's* Special Correspondent aboard one of the British warships which took part:

I am writing as we steam away from the scene of operations, but as use of our wireless would reveal our position, it cannot be transmitted yet.

NO CASUALTY

Great pillars of smoke and flame dwarfing the snow-covered mountains which drop sheer into the sea along this part of the fiords testify to the destructiveness of the raid.

One dense black column is billowing up to 6,000ft. far above the clouds, another envelops the mountains for miles in a foglike pall.

The operation took the Germans completely by surprise. For hours ships were on "Hitler's back doorstep." But no attempt was made to interfere with them.

It may be considered as a further sign that, on land as well as on sea and in the air, Britian has now passed from the defensive to the offensive in Europe.

There is great satisfaction among our men at the completion of their task. In the four principal fishing ports of the Lofoten Islands, 80 miles up the fiords leading to Narvik, fish oil factories and a power station were destroyed and oil storage tanks burned.

The fish oil is important to the Germans as it is used as glycerine in making explosives.

Nine German merchant ships, a Norwegian ship, and an armed German trawler, totalling 18,000 tons, were sunk. Two hundred and fifteen Germans and ten Quislings were taken prisoner, while one German naval officer and six ratings were killed.

We suffered no casualty or loss.

VOLUNTEERS

In addition to prisoners, hundreds of Norwegian volunteers for the Navy were brought back.

A number of hand-picked and specially trained troops took part in this first landing on Norwegian soil since we evacuated it last year. With them were a number of Norwegian naval ratings, troops, and guides.

Fine weather helped the coup.

BACK Page, Column THREE

LOFOTEN ISLANDS
VESTERAALEN IS.
AND FIORD
NARVIK
SVOLVAER
WEST FIORD
BODO
NORWAY
SWEDEN

Lofoten Islands — lonely centre of the three-fold attack.

What RAF Did to HAMM

(See Back Page Picture)

BELOW is published the first picture to bring home the real striking power of the R.A.F. on Germany. It shows a colossal fire raging throughout a German town after one of the R.A.F.'s heavy raids. The shot is from the current "March of Time" film. How it was obtained is told in the BACK Page.

Vital Oil Plant was One Target

HERE is one of the important fish-oil plants destroyed during the raid. Germans were producing glycerine for explosives here and the damage done is an irreparable loss.

'Declare Your Policy!'

British Demand to Yugoslavs

By Daily Mail Special Diplomatic Correspondent

BRITAIN has asked Yugoslavia to declare her position. The Yugoslavs have been told, courteously but firmly, that it is important that their policy should be known.

hey are warned that they cannot be "on both sides" at once.

his, I understand, is the effect of a communication made to the Yugoslav Government by Mr. Ronald Campbell, British Minister to Belgrade.

r. Campbell will undoubtedly add that any giving way to German pressure—in the way that Rumania and Bulgaria gave way—must eventually mean a break with Britain.

he reply is expected soon. When it is received it will enable British policy to be formulated.

e overwhelming sentiment of the Yugoslav people and the armed forces is known to be against any surrender to the Nazis.

is obvious that the Germans are working hard on the timidity of certain politicians to produce Yugoslav compliance with their wishes.

ritain, while recognising the difficulties of the situation, expects Yugoslavia to hold fast.

Regent Holds Hours Talks

From Daily Mail Correspondent

BELGRADE, Thursday.

ugoslavia faces decisions of the most fateful importance amounting to a national emergency. This was shown by a special meeting called at the Royal Palace this afternoon.

ince Regent Paul and the other two Regents conferred with the Premier, M. Tsvetkovitch, the Vice-Premier, and leader of the Croats, Dr. Machek, Minister for War, General Peshich, and the Chief of the Yugoslav General Staff.

e meeting, which lasted five hours, followed a long morning session of the Government which began at 8 a.m.

is reported here that Queen Maria, mother of the young King Peter, who is due to assume full royal powers six months from today, on his eighteenth birthday, is now on her way back to this country after an absence of nearly two years.

e left Yugoslavia early in 1939 to undergo an operation in Switzerland and later visited London with her two younger sons.

hile every hour brings fresh evidence of this country's expected stand against German pressure. British here are packing to leave, and the first dozen entrained to-night. Noon saw the exodus of a number of Britons from Zagreb.

e impression in political circles here is that the country is seeking compromise with Hitler by which any form of military action or use of transport facilities would be avoided.

Bulgaria: Mass Nazi March-in

e march of German troops into Bulgaria is now assuming the "proportions of a mass movement towards the Greek-Bulgarian frontier," said Ankara radio last night, according to a *Reuter* message.

l means of conveyance, including trains, lorries, and buses, it was added, are being utilised.

e announcer suggested that Germany was out to fight Britain wherever she found it possible to do so, and was "doubtless seeking the weakest point in the British chain of defence."

is believed that German troops are now all along the Turkish frontier, although it is reported that they are not in any great strength.

rom diplomatic quarters *B.U.P.* learns that Hitler's hasty message to Ismet Inönu professed the German desire for closer relations with Turkey, offered to send a highly placed German statesman to Ankara for discussion, and protested that Germany had not the remotest intention of threatening Turkey.

Greece Prepares

reece faces the threat from the north with calmness and resolve. A Belgrade message quoted by New York radio last night said that six divisions, approximating 90,000 men, have been massed along the Greek-Bulgarian frontier north of Salonika.

n *A.P.* Belgrade message says that the civilian population of Thrace and Eastern Macedonia have been evacuated to safer areas.

Weygand Tells Petain 'Army Restless'

From Daily Mail Correspondent

VICHY, Thursday.

GENERAL WEYGAND arrived at Vichy airport from North Africa late this afternoon and immediately motored to the Parc Hotel to see Marshal Pétain. His talk with the marshal lasted 2½ hours.

He is believed to have given an account of his efforts to keep the French North African Empire together, despite restlessness in the Army caused by the successes of General de Gaulle's forces against the Italians.

He is understood to have warned Marshal Pétain that the position in French Africa may change radically if:

1. The Axis attempt to increase the present German aid to Italy in Libya, or

2. Libya were to collapse and the British forces reach the border of French Tunisia.

The general is expected to return to Africa by the beginning of next week at the latest.

Six Months

General Weygand's visit to Vichy is his first since he went to North Africa six months ago.

It had been previously suggested that he had refused to travel to Vichy

General Weygand was smiling as he stepped down at the airport.

His arrival in Vichy was "officially" reported last night, but a French official to-day explained that yesterday's announcement was "just a blind."

"Air movements of important officials over the Mediterranean have been kept strictly secret since the plane in which Jean Chiappe was travelling to Syria was shot down," he said.

Vichy Yields to Japanese

From Daily Mail Correspondent

TOKIO, Thursday.—A joint Japan-French Indo-China-Thailand (Siam) communiqué issued here to-day announced that France and Thailand have agreed on all the principal points of Japan's mediation plan.

The Franco-Thai armistice has been extended indefinitely.

FOG BLANKETS STRAIT

Thick fog blanketed the Strait of Dover last night Visibility was restricted to less than 100 yards A light southerly wind was blowing.

'Give Army More Pay'

Civilians who cannot spend as much as they earn should take a lower rate of pay and soldiers should receive more—just as soldiers' and civilians' rations are now being equalised.

This suggestion was made by Major Vyvyan Adams (Cons., Leeds) in the House of Commons yesterday.

He added that he could not see "why the troops of the Mother Country receive less than the magnificent troops from Australia."

Eden and Dill In Cairo

CAIRO, Thursday.—Mr. Anthony Eden, the Foreign Secretary, and General Sir John Dill, arrived in Cairo to-night from Greece.

The Irak Foreign Minister has arrived here.—*A.P. and Exchange.*

U.S. Navy: 372,760

WASHINGTON, Thursday.—The House of Representatives naval committee to-day approved the Bill authorising a United States naval force of 300,000 men, 12,760 officers and 60,000 marines.—*Exchange.*

NO 'SAFETY GIRLS' FOR THE ATS

From Daily Mail Correspondent

CARLISLE, Thursday.

GIRLS who fill cinemas and tea-shops in Lakeland and will not join the war effort were denounced to-day by Company Commander Vera Lewis of the A.T.S.

She left London for the north-west to organise a recruiting drive through Cumberland, Westmorland, and North Lancashire.

That was 12 days ago. In that time not one woman has volunteered to serve.

Leisured Women

Company Commander Lewis told me to-day:

"There are hundreds of leisured women in this district, and I am bitterly disappointed that not one of them has come forward. It is disgraceful and disgusting.

"I see them in shops, in cafés, in cinemas, but never in the A.T.S. or in munition works.

"Surely it is time their conscience was stirred?

*** Bevin says girls must work —Page FIVE.

Paul Mitchell Escapes

Paul Mitchell, aged 21, escaped from military custody at Kingston, Surrey, early yesterday. A charge of false pretences has been made against him.

Mitchell was wearing battle dress when he got away from the camp.

Oranges Are Coming

Britain is to continue to import oranges, Major Lloyd George told M.P.s yesterday. To bring the juice, highly concentrated, would economise in shipping space, he said, but there were other considerations involved and these were being investigated.

Poison in Germans' Cocktails

Dutch Accused

AMSTERDAM, Thursday.

A SECRET Dutch organisation is putting vitriol in cocktails meant for German soldiers. This was revealed yesterday when a German court-martial here passed the death sentence on 18 Dutchmen, all alleged members of the organisation.

Another 19 alleged members were sentenced to various terms of imprisonment or fined.

The organisation is the Geuzen, the name by which Netherlands soldiers were known in the war of freedom against Spain.

Its aim was said to be to make the life of the German troops in Holland as difficult as possible.

'For Britain'

The men before the court-martial were charged with plotting to assassinate German soldiers by the use of poisoned finger-nails, poisoned pencils, and the vitriol cocktails.

Plans and drawings found on them, said to refer to dispositions of the German Army, were alleged to be intended for Britain.

The official prosecutor said he "regretted that German soldiers in Holland had been pushed into water and drowned or had fallen victims to snipers' bullets."

The Dutchmen denied that they knew the identity of their chief. He is said to be 43 and is known as "Colonel Verdun."

The Nazi president of the court-martial said that other "sabotage cases" were awaiting trial.

'Play With Life'

He reminded the Dutch people that they should not forget that everyone who, "even in his thoughts," was plotting against the Germans was "playing with his own life."—*A.P.*

Meanwhile, many more fires than usual have broken out recently in Holland, and nearly all are classed "Cause unknown," says *Vrii Nederland*, the Free Dutch newspaper.

A fire in a big garage at Zaandam used by the German Army did considerable damage to motors and tyres.

Air Chief is Killed

Air Vice-Marshad C. D. Breese has been killed on active service in a flying accident. He was born in 1889.

He became a qualified pilot 28 years ago and in 1936 was appointed Air Officer Commanding No. 23 Training Group.

The following year he went to No. 17 Training Group, and in September 1938 he was put in charge of No. 18 (Reconnaissance) Group

Lights Mystery at Old Bailey

Soon after three well-known members of London's underworld had been found guilty by the jury at the Old Bailey yesterday, every light in the Recorder's crowded court went out.

Women had been screaming to the court, and one had been led out shouting at the same time that her husband collapsed in the dock.

Scotland Yard are investigating the theory that the lights were deliberately cut off. On the switch-box being examined it was found to have been interfered with.

Full report in Page THREE.

Short Alert in London Area

There was a short Alert in the London area early last night.

Enemy planes were reported over north-east coast towns.

A plane machine-gunned a town in the west of England during the evening and dropped bombs in one district. One person was killed

THE KING MEETS SHOP STEWARDS

THE King and Queen during their tour of Edinburgh yesterday talked about trade union matters to three factory shop stewards, Andrew Beatson, Tom McGregor, and T. A. Brown.

"Do you enjoy being a shop steward?" the King asked McGregor, who smiled and said: "It is very entertaining, your Majesty."

"How is that?" asked the King.

"I mean when we have to go in to the board-room and have our little tiffs with the managing director."

The King asked Beatson if they had much trouble, and the shop steward told the King: "Oh, no, sir; we have little bits of bother sometimes, but the management are very good."

Three artisans, representing the factory workers of Glasgow, were among the guests at the luncheon to the King and Queen during their tour of the city on Wednesday, it was revealed last night.

They were Miss Agnes Simpson, head furnisher in a carpet factory, Mr. Harry Taylor, a shipwright, and Mr. William Jamieson, a turner.

They received an invitation to have luncheon in the city chambers with a "prominent young couple." Only after they had arrived at the chambers did they learn that they were to meet the King and Queen.

The King and Queen chatted with them and asked about the work they were doing and the arrangements for the welfare of the workers in the factories.

AMERICA MOVES

Italian Consuls Told to Quit

From Daily Mail Correspondent

WASHINGTON, Thursday.

STRONG action was taken by the United States Government to-day against Italian consulates and their personnel in key centres of American industry throughout the country.

The State Department announced that Italy has been requested to close her consulates at Detroit (Michigan) and Newark (New Jersey), "for reasons of national policy," and to withdraw the personnel.

Later Mr. Cordell Hull, the Secretary of State, revealed that he had sent a Note to Italy requesting her to restrict the movements of all her consular staffs in the United States.

The action does not suspend diplomatic relations between the United States and Italy—but it leads to that end.

A break will be inevitable if the Italians show any resentment.

'Stay-put' Request

Mr. Hull's Note asks that consular officials should confine their movements to the area under their jurisdiction.

This does not apply to Italian diplomats in Washington, however, but the Italian Embassy has been asked to keep the State Department informed of the movements outside the city of military and naval personnel attached to the Washington embassy.

There is reason to believe that the closing of the Italian consulates is the result of the German occupation of Italy.

The view is held that it was the occupation of large sections of Italy, particularly Sicily, by German troops which prompted the Italian Government to ask for the closing of the United States consulates at Palermo and Naples.

LATEST

'NAZIS BUILDING 40 AERODROMES'

Budapest, Thursday.—Reports from Bucarest say that Germany is rushing the building of 40 aerodromes in Bulgaria and Rumania.—B.U.P.

SLAVS 'GUARD INDEPENDENCE'

Belgrade radio announced last night that the Prime Minister and Foreign Minister, in a communiqué, said: "Present developments are being followed closely. The independence and entity of Yugoslavia are ever before us."

2

News Chronicle

No. 29,615 MONDAY, APRIL 7, 1941 ONE PENNY

NAZIS INVADE YUGO-SLAVIA, GREECE

BRITISH IN ACTION Says Rome

Greeks Destroy 10 German Tanks

Latest news from the Balkan war front: Greek forces on the Bulgarian frontier met violent attack, destroyed 10 German tanks, took prisoners, yielded some ground, but held up the enemy.

THE German Army invaded Yugo-Slavia and Greece at 5.30 a.m. yesterday. Later the British Government announced that Imperial troops had landed in Greece.

The British statement said:

"After the entry of German troops into Bulgaria had brought to a head the long-threatened German invasion of the Balkans, his Majesty's Government in the United Kingdom, in full consultation with the Dominion Governments concerned, have sent an army to Greece comprising troops from Great Britain, Australia and New Zealand to stand in line with the soldiers of our brave ally in defence of their native soil.

"The British Air Force, which has for some time been operating in Greece against the Italians, has been strongly reinforced."

Late last night Rome reported that the German troops were meeting with tenacious resistance from British forces, particularly in the Struma Valley.

Italian troops, said Rome Radio, had attacked in Southern Yugo-Slavia.

Greeks Tell Of First Day's Battle

The Greek High Command communiqué, broadcast by Athens Radio, late last night stated:

"Powerful forces, equipped with the most modern war machines and supported by tanks, abundant heavy artillery and numerous aircraft, this morning suddenly and repeatedly attacked our positions, defended only by very small Greek forces.

"A very violent struggle occurred all day in the main zone of the Bulgarian frontier area, particularly in the district of Beli and the Struma Valley.

"Our forces on this front waged a very hard fight against the aggressors with their restricted means.

"As much of the small Greek air force as could be spared from the Italian front aided our heroic troops.

"Our air formations, despite very heavy shelling by artillery and dive-bombing by enemy aircraft, have resisted with the exception of one, which fell after a particularly strong enemy attack.

Germans Taken Prisoner

"Ten enemy tanks were destroyed by our artillery and anti-tank guns. Five or six enemy planes were shot down by our air force and anti-aircraft artillery.

"A number of prisoners was taken.

"Some areas of national territory were evacuated in order to avoid unnecessary sacrifice. The enemy has made some progress, but has been held up on the front concerned.

"On the Italian front in Albania there has been patrol and artillery activity."

An Athens spokesman, amplifying the official communiqué, said that the German attackers left bodies piled high before the Greek defenders without being able to make a real advance.

Berlin Admits Resistance

The Germans early this morning stated that they dive-bombed Belgrade three times during the day. They claim that 33 "enemy" planes were shot down in combat and 48 destroyed on the ground. Nazi losses were given as four machines.

Previously, the German radio

Turn to Back Page, Col. Four

VANGUARD OF 300,000 FIGHTERS

A British expeditionary force, estimated by a high Yugo-Slav military source to be the vanguard of an army of 300,000 men, was reported to have landed in Greece and to have been actively preparing anti-aircraft defences against the awaited clash with the German armies.

Belgrade diplomatic sources said that the troops were concentrating on the defence of the Greek mainland and her ports, communication lines and airfields against Nazi bomber attacks, while additional troops were being disembarked.

Most of the troops were described as anti - aircraft divisions, which were quickly setting up gun emplacements and detection instruments at all key points in the southern half of Greece.

THE VANGUARD

Neutral diplomats who arrived in Yugo-Slavia from Athens said that 100,000 British troops had landed at a southern Greek port with mechanised equipment.

The figure of 150,000 was mentioned in a dispatch from the Associated Press Belgrade correspondent, who said this army included seven full divisions in addition to great numbers of R.A.F. engineers and other experts.

His information came direct from Athens, and it was stated that there were a great many troops in and around Salonika, but not on the Yugo-Slav frontier.

FIVE SHIPS A DAY

Five British ships were arriving daily from Africa loaded with men and material, neutral diplomats stated.

They added that British troops penetrated north into the Greek mainland as far as a line running from the Ægean port of Volos to Corfu.

According to a traveller arriving in Istanbul from Greece, "large numbers" of British troops were leaving Athens in trains for the North, presumably for the Bulgarian and Yugo-Slav frontiers.

The British troops were said to have marched cheering down the gangplanks of ships and to have swung off happily to their pre-arranged quarters. All hotels in Southern Greece had been requistioned for British staff headquarters and for officers.

LIGHT AND HEAVY TANKS

British equipment, according to these sources, consisted of a vast number of anti-aircraft guns, anti-tank guns, many thousands of light and heavy tanks and a great number of flame throwers.

The diplomat added that many shiploads of munitions and other war material had been landed at five ports, but so far few warplanes had been brought to the Greek mainland.

Meanwhile, fresh Australian and New Zealand troops were said to be pouring into Cairo to reinforce the Army of the Nile, and possibly to be transported later to the Balkans.—Associated Press.

Germany Bans Dancing

By order of Himmler, the German Gestapo chief, all public dancing in Germany has been banned, the German radio announced last night.

The ban will take effect immediately. No new dancing licences will be issued and licences already granted are being withdrawn. — Reuter.

Axis Ships Seized By Uruguay

Uruguayan police have taken four Italian and Danish ships into protective custody.

The Uruguayan Cabinet had previously decided on action that would conform with that taken by the United States.

The crews of the Danish ships, who were wearing pro-British badges, refused to go to the same hotels as the Italian seamen.

Argentina and Chile are now the only two South American maritime countries which have not followed the example of the United States in seizing Axis shipping.—Associated Press.

Soviet Press Acclaims Pact With The Serbs

From Our Own Correspondent

MOSCOW, Sunday.

Moscow's pact of friendship and non-aggression with Yugo-Slavia is published and commented on in today's Soviet Press.

In a prominent place in Pravda's first page is a large photograph of yesterday's signing ceremony, at which Stalin, Molotov (Soviet Foreign Minister) and M. Gavrilovitch (Yugo-Slav Minister) were present.

This is followed by the text of the pact, the most interesting point of which reads:

"In the event of either signatory becoming the victim of aggression by a third Power, the other signatory undertakes to maintain a friendly policy towards the other."

STROVE FOR PEACE

Thus the Soviet Union is pledged to pursue a friendly attitude to Yugo-Slavia in her present situation.

Pravda comments editorially: "The signature of the pact is important not only for the development of friendly Soviet-Yugo-Slav relations, but as a mark of the common effort of the Soviet and Yugo-Slavian Governments to strengthen peace and prevent the further spreading of war.

"The latest events in Yugo-Slavia have clearly shown that the Government of Yugo-Slavia is striving for peace, that it does not want the country to be dragged into the vortex of war.

BACKED BY PEOPLE

"Events have also shown that in its internal policy the Simovitch Government aimed to consolidate the internal forces of the country. In that, as in its foreign policy, the Government is supported by the great majority of its people."

Izvestia says: "The new Government of Yugo-Slavia, only a few days after its accession to power, was forced to adopt a number of preventive measures like the proclamation that Belgrade, Zagreb, Ljubljana were open towns, black-outs in Belgrade, etc.

"This shows what an alarming situation was created on the Yugo-Slav frontiers, notwithstanding the fact that in a number of documents General Simovitch's Government stressed and continues to stress its desire to live in peace and friendship with all its neighbours.

WARMEST SYMPATHY

"The attempts of the new Yugo-Slav Government to maintain peace could not but arouse the warmest sympathy in the Soviet Union."

In addition to the clause given above, the treaty contains the following points:

"Both sides agree to refrain from any aggression and to respect the other's independence, sovereignty and territorial integrity.

"The treaty is laid down for five years and, if not denounced by either of the signatories within a year before its termination, it will automatically be prolonged for another five years.

"The treaty comes into force at the moment of signing and must be ratified in the shortest possible time. The exchange of the document of ratification will take place in Belgrade"

VERNON BARTLETT on **PAGE TWO** discusses the new attack on Yugo-Slavia and Greece and the treaty signed by the Moscow-Belgrade Governments. He sums up with these words:

"Germany, despite her great territorial gains, has never stood more nearly alone than she does today."

See Page Five for summaries of Germany's final Notes to Yugo-Slavia and Greece and Hitler's order of the day to his advancing armies.

Germany's first move has been an air attack on the open town of Belgrade. The population of Yugo-Slavia is widely dispersed, and this largely discounts the value of air raids (writes H. D. Harrison).

Nazi land forces will undoubtedly attack in the north from the Hungarian and Rumanian plains. Here, the first Yugo-Slav line of defence will be the River Danube. Between Zagreb and Belgrade there are only three bridges over the Danube, and if threatened they will be blown up.

From Bulgaria, the only practicable lines of attack are through the valley of the Nisheva and, in the extreme south, along the valley of the Strumitza. There are 100 bridges and viaducts along the ten miles of narrow gorges, and once these were destroyed the passage of motorised forces would be slow and difficult.

South of the Nisheva valley, the frontier was chosen especially for its impassable nature as a defence against Bulgaria.

Yugo-Slavia could attack Italian forces in Albania from Podgoritza (in Montenegro), along the valley of the White Drin up from Prizren, or by the road between Lake Ochrid and Lake Prespan.

Addis Taken: 700-Miles Push In A Month

Duke Of Aosta's Gratitude

THE following message was given verbally to Lieut.-General A. G. Cunningham, G.O.C., East Africa, by the Italian envoy before the entry of the Imperial troops into Addis Ababa:

"His Royal Highness the Duke of Aosta wishes to express his appreciation of the initiative taken by General Wavell and General Cunningham regarding the protection of women and children in Addis Ababa, demonstrating the strong bonds of humanity and race still existing between the nations."

ADDIS ABABA, CAPITAL OF ABYSSINIA, HAS BEEN OCCUPIED BY IMPERIAL FORCES, IT WAS ANNOUNCED OFFICIALLY YESTERDAY.

The race to the city was won by South African troops, after one of the swiftest advances in military history.

Crossing the Abyssinian frontier from Somaliland on March 7, they covered 700 miles in exactly four weeks—an average of 25 miles a day.

Nothing could stop them—powerful enemy forces, bad country roads, blasted and torn by the retreating Italians.

Finally, the way to the capital was opened after they had forced a crossing over the River Awash, 90 miles from Addis Ababa. They covered the distance in two days.

The city, it was learned in Cairo last night, was captured without bloodshed. A military spokesman said the Italians had retreated beyond the capital. The South Africans met no resistance after crossing Awash River.

The Duke of Aosta, Viceroy of Abyssinia and Commander-in-Chief, was reported to be still in the country, though not at Addis Ababa.

Swift Moves On Other Key Towns

Yesterday's Cairo communiqué shows that the other forces converging on Addis Ababa from the north, following up the retreating Italians after taking Keren and Adowa, are rapidly approaching Dessie, 150 miles from the capital, and Gondar, 40 miles from the northern shore of Lake Tana.

The temporary hold up on the route to Massawa has been overcome, and the fall of this important port on the Red Sea coast may be expected in two or three days.

A Cairo message last night reported that Free French Forces were only eight miles away, and Empire troops 10 miles away.

Its possession will facilitate the withdrawal of the successful British troops from Abyssinia and Eritrea, when mopping up operations have been concluded, for service against the German divisions in Libya.

It was in May, 1936, that Mussolini completed his conquest of Abyssinia. Italian troops entered Addis Ababa on May 5.

Today Emperor Haile Selassie is ready to return in triumph. The ceremonial entry may be delayed until the anniversary date in May, though it is probable that he may fly to the capital from the Debra Markos area (where his patriot troops are advancing) at an early date.

The Emperor will find by his side Ras Seyum, Mussolini's "hope" for the position of puppet Emperor.

Massing Of Our Forces In Libya

Meanwhile, in Libya, where the advance by German and Italian tanks was reported over the week-end to have been successfully held, the concentration of British troops is proceeding smoothly.

On Friday night R.A.F. bombers made a heavy raid on Tripoli, causing explosions on the south-eastern mole, hitting the power station, and starting fires among barracks and stores. All our planes returned safely.

Our special correspondent in Cairo cables:

Although he is accumulating forward bases on his march from Tripoli, the enemy's lines of communication are lengthening dangerously, and he is already 436 miles from his base, with little opportunity of obtaining stores, replacements or reinforcements, except from the rear.

One decisive factor is certain to be air strength, and the British pilots have had the fullest possible desert training. As regards the sea, the enemy has no fleet to support him, whereas the Mediterranean Fleet is stronger than ever. The advance may arouse temporary fears locally, but the High Command view the situation with unbounded confidence.

Raiders Over Merseyside

Raiders over **Liverpool** and other **Merseyside** towns early this morning were met by a fierce barrage from the ground defences.

There was no activity for some time, then a raider tried to sneak in over the area, and was chased off.

A single enemy raider crossed the **Scottish East Coast** last night, dropped flares, and machine-gunned a town, but injured nobody.

London had its 17th bomb-free night.

Other Raids News: Back Page

Naval Yacht Sunk

The Admiralty reports the sinking of H.M. yacht Wilna (Temporary Lieutenant L. W. Cleverly, R.N.R.). There were no casualties.

ITALY'S ETHIOPIAN ARMY IS MELTING AWAY

From Our Own Correspondent

CAIRO, Sunday.

The capture of Addis Ababa has struck a last blow at the crumbling morale of the Italian troops in Abyssinia, and their position is nearly hopeless.

There are still strong forces up and down the country but the two main armies from Keren and Harar are swiftly disintegrating.

The troops from Addis Ababa may barricade themselves in Gondar, or may withdraw towards Dessie.

Even Gondar is likely soon to be between two fires.

With disciplined troops it might be possible to salvage something temporarily from the wreck, but there is every evidence that the native troops are melting away and surrendering on the slightest excuse.

The morale of the Italians themselves is on the verge of collapse.

Matsuoka Cuts Visit

"Mr. Matsuoka has had to cut short his visit to Europe, since important affairs of State demand his return to Tokio," according to the Swiss radio, quoting a message from Moscow.

Matsuoka, on his way back to Tokio after visiting Rome and Berlin, was expected to reach Moscow today, and to spend three days there.—Reuter and Associated Press.

LATE NEWS

ITALIANS BOMB YUGO-SLAV PORTS

Yugo - Slavia's Adriatic ports of Split and Kotor attacked by Italian planes, says official Italian agency.

Fram Kulovetz, Public Works Minister and leader of Slovene Party, reported killed in raid on Belgrade says Berne dispatch quoting Ljubljana radio.—Reuter.

Black-out Times

	p.m.	a.m.
Liverpool	8.27	6.00
Manchester	8.24	5.57

Moon sets 4.37 a.m. tomorrow. Full moon on Friday.

DAILY MIRROR, Monday, May 12, 1941.

Daily Mirror

MAY 12

No. 11,674 ONE PENNY

Registered at the G.P.O. as a Newspaper.

ABBEY, HOUSES OF PARLIAMENT BOMBED

124 in ten nights is our toll of night raiders, 33 being shot down on Saturday night and early yesterday.

WESTMINSTER Abbey, the Houses of Parliament and the British Museum were damaged during the Luftwaffe's mass attempt to burn London on Saturday night and early yesterday.

But night fighters of the R.A.F. made the Nazi Air Force pay. They shot down thirty-one of the record bag of thirty-three moon raiders. A.A. guns got the other two.

These losses bring the total of raiders shot down in the first ten nights of May to 124.

Assuming that each plane carried a crew of five, this means that the Luftwaffe has lost over 600 trained men, approximately 160 of them on Saturday night.

Some of the German crews were burned to death in the fires they had started.

One R.A.F. pilot caught a bomber going home, and saw it plunge in flames into a fire burning on the ground.

A French flight lieutenant and a Czech sergeant pilot bagged one raider each.

Another pilot destroyed two bombers within a few minutes after a chase to the Dutch coast. He caught up with the first at only 300ft. as it neared an aerodrome. It blew up in a great mass of flame

Another bomber took off from the drome—and was sent plunging to earth with a single long burst. The fighter, now down to 50ft., climbed quickly as "flak" exploded all round him.

It was another spite raid. The German High Command communique said that the Luftwaffe

Continued on Back Page

Early morning tea—but not according to custom. These two London women made the best of a bad night . . . stranded in the street during the blitz they made the "usual" over a fireplace of bricks and burning wood.

Turks Gravest Hour

ANKARA radio, after reporting that Axis had overcome all resistance on the Greek islands, where they bombed small ports ruthlessly and concentrated big forces, said last night:

"We face, perhaps, the gravest hour in the history of our nation. Never before were we so endangered and challenged by so imminent a peril.

"But Ataturk got us out of a more hopeless situation. We maintained our freedom by cool Turkish bravery. So shall we overcome our peril this time."

German troops are massed in Greece and the Greek islands ready to attack Syria, according to an Ankara report of the Soviet Tass agency.

New York radio, announcing this, added that according to informed circles Germany has asked Turkey for a free passage for her troops. Ankara denies such a demand.

HUSKINSON STILL HELPS

LYING in hospital where specialists are fighting to save his sight, Air Commodore Patrick Huskinson is still designing his "Beautiful Bombs."

Some of his colleagues (the "Boys in the Back Room") visit him in hospital. In detail they explain each new design, and Husky, memorising a blue-print he has never seen, suggests improvements.

The doctors say there is a good chance of saving his sight, but it will be a long job. He was blinded by blast while watching bomb flashes during a heavy raid last month.

R.A.F. Is Paying Back

FOUR enemy aircraft were destroyed in combat during heavy R.A.F. raids on Germany on Saturday night.

A strong force of bombers attacked the shipyards and industrial quarters of Hamburg.

Smaller forces raided the ports of Bremen, Emden and Rotterdam and "objectives in Berlin."

Other aircraft attacked enemy shipping. A naval vessel was hit and two supply ships were damaged.

In the brilliant moonlight many combats took place between our bombers and enemy fighters.

Seven of our bombers are missing.

Other Docks, Too

Raids on docks and shipping were carried out by aircraft of the Coastal Command. No planes were lost during these operations.

Germany's version of the Berlin raid was: "Some planes tried to reach the capital, but only a few reached the environs of Berlin and none the centre of the city."

The communque says: "Strong units of enemy forces attacked Hamburg last night. Many fires occurred and damage was caused nearly exclusively to residential quarters.

"Civilians were killed and wounded."

BOMBED BACK TO LIFE

Two women live to tell London's most curious blitz tales—one was bombed "back from the dead" and the other had to be fed through a sponge

AT the height of Saturday night's raid a warden guided an old woman to the house she was trying to find.

The young woman who opened the door shrieked as though she had seen a ghost.

"Mother, you . . ." she cried. "We thought you were dead."

The old woman, Mrs. Eliza Hill, was thought to have been killed in a previous raid. Instead, she had been in hospital suffering from loss of memory.

Shock of the latest raid restored her memory.

✦ ✦ ✦

Thirteen hours after she had been buried in her basement flat in a block destroyed by a heavy bomb, rescue workers tunnelling through the debris reached Mrs. J. O'Leary and found her still alive.

She was pinned under a mass of debris and could not move.

More than anything else she wanted a cup of tea.

The tea was fetched, but the problem was how to get it to her. Only her face was clear of the rubbble, and the ceiling had fallen within a few inches of her lips.

So a sponge was dipped in the cup, and while the rescue squad tunnelled and hacked and sawed to free her, Mrs. O'Leary sucked her morning cup of tea through a sponge.

✦ ✦ ✦

Albert and Ernest Hurst, 21 and 25, were in their parents' dug-out in a London suburb when they heard that a light was showing from a house nearby.

They went to warn the occupier, but a bomb fell while they were on the way and both were killed. Their parents are uninjured.

✦ ✦ ✦

A twenty-two-year-old London A.R.P. girl—Violet Malthouse—was still buried with her mother and grandmother under her ruined house after wardens had been working frantically for sixteen hours to release her yesterday.

Violet has been responsible for saving many lives in previous raids, and wardens would not give up hope of bringing her out alive.

"She has been the greatest little pal we've ever had," said one of the men.

LAWRENCE OF IRAQ

LAWRENCE of Arabia's colleague in the last war is stated to be in charge of British forces which have driven back rebels in Western Iraq.

The officer is named as Captain Abu Heneik, who seems to be Major J. B. Glubb, who is known as Abu Heneik ("Father of the Chins") because of an old war wound.

Iraqi rebels fleeing from Habbaniyah, the R.A.F. base sixty miles from Bagdad, are being pursued by British patrols.

BLAMED WOO-WOO FOR THE BOMB

An L.C.C. ambulance driver, Mr. Wells, was firewatching outside his home when a bomb crashed on it.

He knew that his two-year-old baby Kenneth was asleep on the first floor, and dug frantically to find him.

"They tried to stop me, as the wreckage was tumbling down," he said. But he found the child at last—safe. He was under his bed, which had been turned upside down

The first thing Kenneth said was, "Woo-woo has turned my bed over." Woo-woo is his dog.

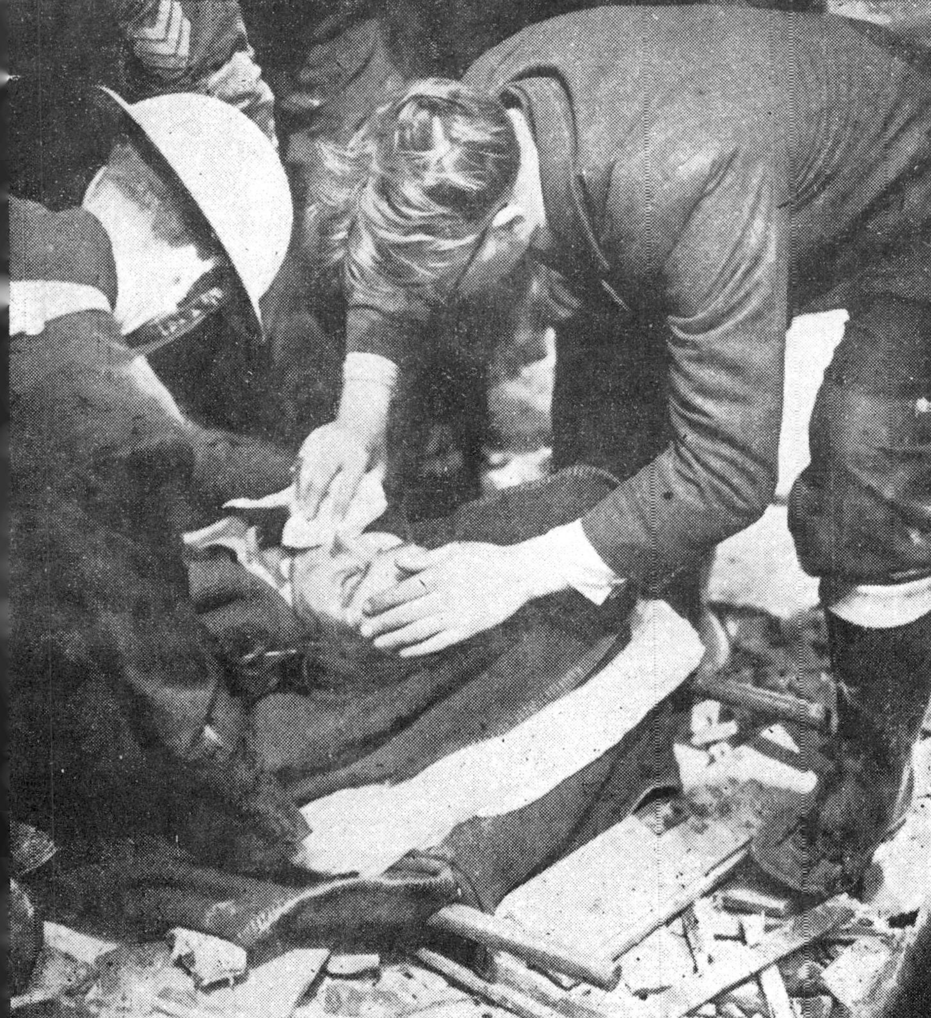

For thirteen hours Mrs. J. O'Leary lay—pinned beneath the debris of her home. What she wanted more than anything else, was a cup of tea. She got what she wanted—but only by sucking a sponge dipped in the tea !

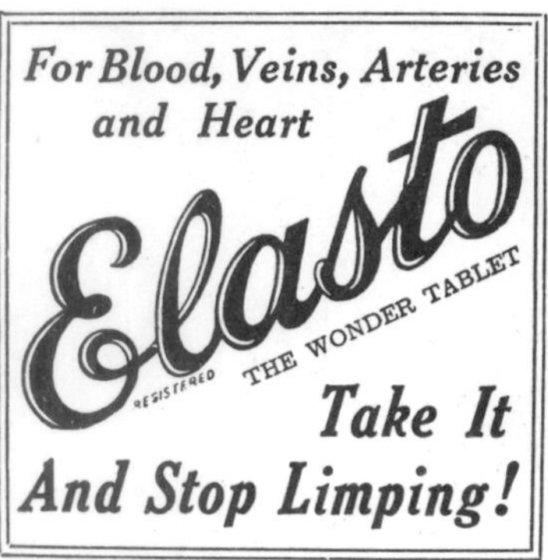

No. 9,987 (E*) TUESDAY, MAY 13, 1941 ONE PENNY

HESS, HITLER'S DEPUTY, PRISONER IN GLASGOW

'Shadow of The Fuehrer' Takes Off

Nazi Radio Said He Went Mad and Killed Himself

Rudolph Hess seen off on a flight by his wife.

RUDOLF HESS, Hitler's deputy and "dearest friend," has landed in Scotland in a Messerschmitt 110 and given himself up.

This was officially announced from No. 10, Downing-street last night.

It followed an earlier statement broadcast from the German radio that Hess had gone mad, vanished in a plane, and was believed to have committed suicide.

Berlin radio added that Hess left messages stating his intention to kill himself.

Then at 11.20 p.m. the following message from Downing-street blew the German statements sky high. It read:

Rudolf Hess, the Deputy-Fuehrer and Part-Leader of the National Socialist Party, has landed in Scotland in the following circumstances:—

On the night of Saturday, 10th, a Me. 110 was reported by our patrol to have crossed the coast of Scotland and was flying in the direction of Glasgow.

Since a Me. 110 would not have the fuel to return to Germany, this report was at first disbelieved.

He Brought Photographs

However, later on a Me. 110 crashed near Glasgow with its guns unloaded. Shortly afterwards a German officer was found with his parachute in the neighbourhood suffering from a broken ankle.

He was taken to hospital in Glasgow. Here he first gave his name as Horn.

Later he stated that he was Rudolf Hess.

He brought several photographs of himself of different ages, apparently in order to establish his identity.

These photographs were seen to be photographs of Hess by several people who knew him.

Accordingly an officer of the Foreign Office who was closely acquainted with Hess before the war has been sent up by plane to see him in hospital.

The official Nazi communiqué was:

"Party Comrade Rudolf Hess, who had been forbidden by the Fuehrer to undertake flying because of his illness, which had been getting worse for many years, succeeded in defiance of this in taking possession of a plane.

Fuehrer's Orders

"Last Saturday at 6 p.m. Rudolf Hess took off at Augsburg on a flight from which he has so far failed to return.

"The letter which he left was so confused that it shows signs of mental disturbance.

"This letter leads to the assumption that Hess fell victim to madness.

"The Fuehrer ordered the arrest of those party comrades

Continued on Back Page

MOMENTOUS CALL BY ROOSEVELT SOON

THE reason why President Roosevelt has cancelled his speech to the Pan-American Conference is not known, but it is not believed to be because of his recent indifferent health.

Circumstances are such, it is felt, that only a speech of the highest importance could be delivered at the present moment, states Reuter.

Will Not Be Hurried

Apparently the President is not yet ready to make his next important pronouncement on the war. He refuses to be pushed by public sentiment as expressed in the Press and on public platforms, which openly expected a momentous declaration to-morrow.

Newspapers continue to stress the seriousness of the shipping situation. Some writers declare that the policy of providing ships for Britain without giving the necessary protection for them is merely a waste of precious capital.

Navy Smash Benghazi At 'Point-Blank'

BRITISH warships heavily bombarded Benghazi, the enemy's port in Libya, on Saturday night and caused terrific damage at point-blank range, an Admiralty communiqué revealed last night.

"During Saturday night, May 10, powerful units of our light forces carried out an intensive bombardment of Benghazi from point-blank range," states the communiqué. "Damage was caused to shipping and military objectives.

SUNDAY NEWS

Copr. 1941 by News Syndicate Co. Inc. NEW YORK'S PICTURE NEWSPAPER Trade Mark Reg. U. S. Pat. Off.

5 CENTS PAY NO MORE

Vol. 21. No. 5 New York, Sunday, May 25, 1941★ 88 Main+8 Manhattan+16 Comic+16 Coloroto Pages

1,300 DEAD AS HOOD SINKS IN BATTLE

Story on Page 3

DEATH of a TITAN

Britannia, self-proclaimed ruler of the waves, made one of its most somber announcements of the war yesterday. London acknowledged the German claim that the British battle cruiser Hood (shown here), had been sunk by the Nazi battleship, Bismarck, in an engagement somewhere between Iceland and Greenland. H. M. S. Hood, world's largest battleship, was struck a fatal blow in one of its magazines. The titanic fighting ship exploded. Virtually all of her 1,341 officers and men were lost. —*Story on page 3.*

Turn to Center Fold for a Complete Diagram and Fighting Layout of the Hood.

Daily Mirror

MAY 28

No. 11,688 ✦ ONE PENNY

Registered at the G.P.O. as a Newspaper.

AVENGED

BISMARCK'S END: FULL STORY

She Met Bismarck

One of the British ships which met the Bismarck, Mr. Churchill stated in the House yesterday, was the Prince of Wales. One of our newest battleships (commissioned in 1939), she is 35,000 tons, with ten 14in. guns, sixteen 5.25 guns—and that's her in the picture below.

GERMANY'S great new battleship Bismarck has been sent to the bottom. The Royal Navy has avenged the Hood.

The Bismarck was grimly hunted, slowed down and then smashed in an eighty-hour battle of naval determination and strategy which showed the world that no enemy capital ship can challenge the Royal Navy on the high seas and live to get back to port.

The Bismarck, heading from the northern seas for Brest or St. Nazaire, was hounded down by naval planes. Four torpedoes were ripped into her huge hull. The battleship was brought to a standstill. Then our warships came up to finish off one of the shortest-lived capital ships ever.

Here is the official Admiralty communique giving full details of the action:

Air reconnaissance by Coastal Command aircraft revealed that the German battleship Bismarck and the cruiser Prince Eugen, which they had previously located in the Norwegian port of Bergen, had sailed.

Certain dispositions were therefore ordered, and as a result H.M.S. Norfolk (Captain A. J. L. Phillips, R.N.), wearing the flag of Rear-Admiral W. F. Wake-Walker, C.B., O.B.E., and H.M.S. Suffolk (Captain R. M. Ellis, R.N.) were ordered to take up a position in the Denmark Straits.

On the evening of May 23, Admiral Wake-Walker reported sighting an enemy force of one battleship and one cruiser proceeding at high speed south-westwards.

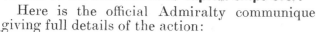

Prince of Wales Damaged

Visibility in the Denmark Straits was bad and extremely variable. The range of the enemy was only six miles when he was first sighted, and storms of snow and sleet and patches of mist at times reduced the visibility to one mile. Despite the difficulties of the visibility, H.M.S. Norfolk and H.M.S. Suffolk shadowed the enemy successfully throughout the night.

Meanwhile, other units of the Royal Navy were taking up dispositions at high speed with a view to intercepting the enemy and bringing him to action with our heavy forces.

Early in the morning of May 24, H.M.S. Hood (Captain R. Kerr, C.B.E., R.N.), wearing the flag of Vice-Admiral L. E. Holland, C.B., with H.M.S. Prince of Wales (Captain J. C. Leach, M.V.O., R.N.) in company, made contact with the enemy. Action was immediately joined.

During the ensuing engagement Bismarck received damage and was at one time seen to be on fire. H.M.S. Hood, as had already been announced, received a hit in the magazine and blew up. H.M.S. Prince of Wales sustained slight damage.

The chase was continued on a south-westerly course, with H.M.S. Norfolk and H.M.S. Suffolk shadowing the enemy and maintaining contact despite all his efforts to shake off the pursuit. It appeared at this time that the enemy's speed had been slightly reduced and reconais-

Contd. on Back Page, Col. 4

500 PLANES IN RAID ON FLEET

FIVE hundred German planes attacked the British Fleet in the Mediterranean, incessantly bombing our warships in the greatest sea and air battle of all time.

It was fought after the destruction of the German troop convoy bound for Crete.

Scores of enemy planes were clawed out of the sky by the Navy's A.A. gunners who faced without flinching the intense fury of a bombardment that lasted all day.

And the German pilots machine-gunned British sailors—survivors from the six warships which were sunk—as they struggled in the water. And the six warships—without exception—were sunk by the bombers.

A correspondent on board a British battleship in the battle described the Luftwaffe's attack as the most sustained ever carried out by the Germans against the British Fleet.

Streams of German bombers and dive bombers took part. The air was filled with the scream of bombs and the roar of planes as the Germans came swooping from the skies to drop their bombs.

Swam for Lives

They scored hits on one destroyer and a cruiser, forcing our men in the water to swim for their lives.

Then the Germans deliberately turned their attack upon them, bombing and machine-gunning them as they tried to reach the nearby coast of Crete.

The battle reached its peak on Thursday in the Kithera Straits, between the western end of Crete and Greece, when 100 bombers of all descriptions attacked incessantly from 5.30 a.m. until 8.15 p.m.

It began when the Battle Fleet was pushing its way through the Kithera Straits to help the cruisers which had broken up the attempted German landing from the sea.

Two cruisers had been damaged by bombs during the attack, but the German planes

Contd. on Back Page, Col. 1

ADMIRAL WENT DOWN

ADMIRAL LUETJENS went down with the Bismarck.

This was announced yesterday by the German High Command in a statement which said:

"The thoughts of the entire German people are full of pride and grief or Admiral Luetjens, Captain Lindeman and all the members of the brave crew of the battleship, Bismarck, who succumbed in their glorious fight off Iceland."

At 11.42 on Monday night, according to an earlier statement, Admiral Leutjens sent this report to the High Command:

"Ship incapable of manoeuvres. Will fight to the last shell. Long live the Fuehrer.—(Signed), Chief of Fleet."

RAF Smash Air Troops

BOTH British and German reinforcements have reached Crete, where severe fighting for possession of the island is proceeding.

Latest news of the battle is contained in this Cairo communique last night:

"Supported by further intensive bombing, German troops in the area west of Canea (Khania) launched another attack yesterday evening, which enlarged their penetration into our defences, necessitating the withdrawal of our troops to positions in the rear.

"German reinforcements continue to reach the island by air, and heavy fighting is continuing."

Say Nazis Lost 18,000

The R.A.F. are inflicting heavy losses on the enemy

Fighter aircraft carried out a successful attack at Maleme on Monday, where they shot down five Ju. 52s laden with troops.

A number of additional Ju. 52s were shot down by our fighters, three of which failed to return.

Our fighters also attacked about a hundred Ju. 52s closely concentrated on the ground at Maleme, inflicting heavy damage.

Cairo sources say that the Germans, so far, have lost at least 18,000 men in their attempts to capture Crete.

British Troops Land in Crete—page 3.

BLACK-OUT ZERO HOUR TO-NIGHT UNTIL 5-03 A.M.
MOON 1·07 RISES P.M. MOON 2·39 SETS A.M.

Daily Express

No. 12,798 — Monday, June 2, 1941 — One Penny

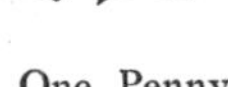

ONE MINUTE NEWS →

CRETE: About 15,000 British troops are evacuated, and, with the Navy's assistance, taken to Egypt. R.A.F. escorting planes shoot down five German bombers and two Italian machines.

R.A.F. CHANGES bring Air Chief Marshal Sir Arthur Longmore back from Middle East air command to become Inspector-General. He is succeeded by Air Vice-Marshal A. W. Tedder.

IRAQ: Armistice terms include return of Iraqi troops to peace-time stations, release of British prisoners, internment of Axis prisoners. Five hundred Bagdad Britons are freed.

THE NAVY BRINGS 15,000 TROOPS OUT OF CRETE

Hitler GAINS the island—but LOSES 18,000 men, 600 planes

Express Staff Reporter ALAN MOOREHEAD — CAIRO, Sunday.

THE Navy has brought 15,000 British and Empire troops out of Crete. Against the fury of the German air-borne invasion it would have been suicidal for them to continue the struggle without the support of masses of R.A.F. fighters.

They had fought with magnificent heroism since that dawn on Tuesday of the week before last, when paratroops and glidatroops descended on Maleme airfield, near Suda Bay.

They destroyed or wrecked 600 of Hitler's best invasion planes. They killed 18,000 of Hitler's best shock troops. They fought day and night without rest, on the airfields, on the beaches, in the hills.

Even in the British warships they had not seen the last of the Luftwaffe. Strong bomber formations attacked them. But escorting R.A.F. planes fought them off.

Five German Junkers 88's and two Italians—one S 79 and one Cant 1007 — were sent crashing into the Mediterranean.

Many others, severely damaged, are unlikely to have reached their bases.

The German airfields in Crete had been previously strafed. Three machines were set on fire at Maleme. At Candia six Ju 88's were machine-gunned, and runways and buildings were left blazing.

It is not yet known how many troops we had in Crete or whether the evacuation has been completed.

1 IN 10 SHOT

This was the story of the German losses told to me tonight by a high R.A.F. officer who lived through the battle from its first moments and visited most sectors of the fighting:—

"The paratroops were badly shot up. I saw one in ten crash to death with an unopened 'chute.

"They dropped from 300 feet and were only a few seconds in the air, but we shot at least a second man in every ten as he fell.

"At least one more man broke an ankle or leg or wrist.

"At Retimo and Candia 80 per cent. of the paratroops were killed.

"But what the paratroops failed to do German dive-bombers and high-level bombers—Junkers 87s and Heinkels—and fighters strafing along the ground did succeed in doing.

"They forced us off Maleme, and once the Nazis took Maleme the tide of battle turned.

SHOT TO PIECES

"Nothing stopped the Germans landing troops on Maleme then.

"We laid an artillery barrage across it. I saw the first 12 Junkers 52s, each carrying 30 men, land in that barrage, and they were smashed to pieces.

"That did not stop them. They went on landing, one plane regularly every three minutes, losing one, then getting another down, then losing another.

"It was carnage. But still they came. I estimate that the Germans used 1,000 planes.

"None of our men feared the paratroops, once they were aground, or the regular shock-troops either.

"Once they got split up they seemed to lose their confidence.

"Hitler's gliders must also have come far below his expectations. I

→ BACK PAGE, COL. FIVE

—CRETE—

Vengeance brings no-one back, and dries no tears;
Nor heals one wound, nor one heart's bitterness.
Yet they shall be avenged—all their lost years,
All that they suffered. We can do no less.
It was not for an island that they died,
But for a world—a world where men are free.
Let the world well remember that they cried:
"Give us machines!" And let that grim call be
Our watchword. Steel for steel, and flame for flame;
Fury for all Hell's fury. Thus the slain
Who held the rocks of Crete in Freedom's name
Through those black hours shall not have died in vain.

By Colin Wills, the Australian broadcaster in London, in a broadcast last night.

The lesson: More and more airfields

Express Military Reporter

CRETE has not been in vain. The "fiercest fight" in this war—to quote the War Office—probably indeed one of the bitterest fights in history, has won us three advantages:—

1 It has given General Maitland Wilson, commanding in Palestine, precious days to make his dispositions for the coming German onslaught on the Middle East.

While we have held up the Germans for nearly a fortnight battling for possession of Crete—they expected to take it in 48 hours—reinforcements have poured into the Middle East, both men and materials. Machines were the crying need.

There is good ground now to suppose that General Wilson has a sufficiency, at any rate, for the present.

The credit side

2 Crete has enabled us to smash a large part of Hitler's shock invasion force—his paratroops, glidatroops, and transport carriers.

The German killed and wounded are specialists, whose training takes six months. Hitler is believed to have 50,000 of them.

Most of the 600 aircraft Hitler is believed to have lost are troop-carriers. He is known to have massed 1,200 of them in South-Eastern Europe. Therefore a big dent has been made.

3 Hitler has shown his hand by his invasion of Crete. Leaving out the use of gas, he has demonstrated probably the worst he can do.

It has taught one great lesson—that airfields must be held at all costs, so that the R.A.F. can operate fighters to support both Army and Navy.

Now count the losses.

Crete is of great strategic importance to Hitler in his attempt to gain control of the Mediterranean. It is a menace, if it can be organised as a bomber base, to Alexandria, 340 miles away, where our Eastern Mediterranean Fleet is based.

It gives Hitler a better chance to reinforce General Rommel in Libya. Tobruk is 200 miles' flying away.

Hitler's aim

With the loss of Suda Bay our patrols of enemy traffic to North Africa cannot be so effective.

Crete gives Hitler the second point of his operational triangle for the attempt to drive eastwards. Rhodes is one, Crete the second, Cyprus the third.

With all three in his possession he would shut the British Fleet out of the Ægean Sea, where his new invasion preparations are going forward.

General Freyberg (who left Crete with his troops, it is understood) could not fight on any longer without effective air support.

The evacuation is little short of a miracle. Mr. Churchill himself said there was no retreat from the island.

The Navy had already suffered grievous losses in preventing the Germans from landing by sea. Yet without a real port to operate from they tackled this herculean task and brought back a large part of the British force.

The Germans claim to have taken 10,000 prisoners. It may be true. A considerable proportion of them will be Greeks. But it must be expected that some thousands of our Empire soldiers have been killed or wounded.

In such bitter fighting with the super-killing weapons that the Germans brought with them it is remarkable that they were not higher.

AFTER 12 DAYS...

This communiqué was issued last night by the War Office:

AFTER 12 days of what has undoubtedly been the fiercest fighting of this war, it was decided to withdraw our forces from Crete.

Although the losses inflicted on the enemy's troops and aircraft have been enormous, it became clear that our naval and military forces could not be expected to operate indefinitely in and near Crete without more air support than could be provided from our bases in Africa.

Some 15,000 of our troops have been withdrawn to Egypt, but it must be admitted that our losses have been severe.

Nazis preparing Syria landings

Bribing the Arabs

ANKARA, Sunday.—Germans are reported to be preparing to land forces in Syria.

Barracks have been evacuated by French troops and many boats are being assembled north of Tripoli and are being overhauled under German supervision.

Germany's Near Eastern expert, von Hentig, is reported to have returned to Syria.

Influential Arabs are receiving special excess food rations from the Germans, while others have been given large sums of money.—Reuter.

Navy watches for the Prinz Eugen

Express Naval Reporter

All through the week-end the Royal Navy and the R.A.F. maintained their cordon to intercept the Bismarck's consort, the 10,000-ton 8in.-gun cruiser Prinz Eugen.

The next front?

BIG R.A.F. CHANGES

TEDDER
New Air Commander-in-Chief, Middle East.

Longmore leaves C.-in-C. job

Express Air Reporter

THREE hours after the official news that Crete had been evacuated it was announced that Air Chief Marshal Sir Arthur Longmore, 56-year-old R.A.F. Commander-in-Chief in the Middle East, has been appointed Inspector-General to the R.A.F.

Sir Arthur returned to England at the beginning of last month and has been home since that time. He has had several consultations with the Prime Minister, Sir Archibald Sinclair, the Air Minister, and other Ministers on defence matters in the Middle East.

LONGMORE
Inspector-General

His command in Cairo goes to Acting Air Marshal Arthur William Tedder, a fifty-year-old spare, lean Scot, who has been Sir Arthur's deputy since last December.

He was the second man to be sent out to assist Sir Arthur. The first, Air Marshal Boyd, was taken prisoner by the Italians before he reached Cairo.

Air Marshal Tedder served with the Dorset Regiment in the last war before he transferred to the old Royal Flying Corps. He is a great technician and was Director-General of Research before returning to operational service. He did valuable work at the Ministry of Aircraft Production.

'SPECIAL DUTY'

Other R.A.F. High Command changes were also announced last night:—

Air Vice-Marshal A. T. Harris, aged 49, is given secret "special duty" with the rank of air marshal. He is one of the great experts in the R.A.F. on Palestine and Iraq.

Air Marshal Tedder's place as deputy commander in the Middle East is to be taken by Air Vice-Marshal Roy Maxwell Drummond, D.S.O., an Australian, aged 47, who was the senior officer there.

In the last war he transferred from the Australian Expeditionary Force to the R.F.C. He served with the Australian Air Board for several years till being given a command in England.

A new deputy chief of the Air Staff is also appointed—Air Vice-Marshal Norman Howard Bottomley, D.S.O., who was awarded the C.B. for distinguished services in an operational command last March.

Don't be a food hog, and don't be a clothes horse: See Opinion

CLOPONS MONDAY

Price-and-coupon labels in shop windows now: Clothes may be cheaper

MANY retail store executives will spend today, Whit Monday, when their shops are shut, working out a new system of values for window tickets. For in future all clothes, except hats, displayed in Britain's shop windows will bear two marks, their price and their value in clopons—clothes coupons.

This will be among the first results of the Rationing of Clothing and Footwear Order, announced yesterday by Mr. Oliver Lyttelton, President of the Board of Trade, and put in force at once.

Shop girls will have to learn the new code of clopons.

They will have to know into which of 26 main categories all the 3,000 types of articles sold in a modern store are placed.

Mr. Lyttelton's advisers believe that the rationing will work fairly, because it will guarantee clothes and shoes for all.

They suggest that the prices of less expensive goods will tend to drop.

Fashion experts say they will now concentrate on export goods. Women in this country will obviously turn to utilitarian designs—heavier shoes and warmer, hard-wearing clothes.

Traders expect a lull in sales for the next two or three weeks while the public gets used to the new system.

Your marge suit may cost you a bet less—Page Three.

16-NIGHT SILENCE ENDED

London hears guns

EARLY this morning London had its first alert for sixteen nights, after three weeks without a night raid.

Gunfire was heard on the outskirts.

Raiders were also reported over north-east and north-west England.

Bombs were dropped on one town in the north-west.

There was no bombing in Britain during daylight yesterday. Three raiders were shot down on Saturday night, when people were killed in an attack on Merseyside. The raid was not heavy.

15
15
47
90
156

JAN. FEB. MAR. APR. MAY.

THAT is how Nazi night raiders have been falling to our air defences during each of the first five months of this year.

The total number of enemy aircraft destroyed in the Battle of Britain last month was 239—156 at night and 83 during the day.

Nearly twice as many enemy machines were brought down at night in May as by day.

Night fighters claimed 98 of the night victims; A.A. fire accounted for 24; balloon barrage and "other means" destroyed 21.

Thirteen of the night victims were brought down over enemy or enemy-occupied territory—eight by night fighters and five by our night bombers.

Our losses during the month were 18 over Britain (nine of the pilots saved) and 68 over enemy and enemy-occupied territory and at sea—a total of 86 against 239.

Extra pay for ARP leaders

Post wardens and head wardens—full-time men who hold responsible jobs and are paid only £3 10s. a week like the men they command—are to get more money.

The Ministry of Home Security announced that from yesterday an extra 2s. 6d. will be paid to the first higher rank in the civil defence services (say leader of a first-aid party or senior warden), and a further 2s. 6d. for post or head wardens or ambulance section leaders.

Supervisors receive an extra 2s. 6d. or 5s., according to the number of parties under their control. Women higher ranks will also get rises above their basic pay. £2 7s.

Housewife thought it out

By HILDE MARCHANT

THREE women and four men advised Mr. Oliver Lyttelton on the basis of the new clothes ration. For six months they have travelled the country, talking to shoppers and shopkeepers.

They looked into shortage of supplies in big stores, little stores and village general shops.

Often they went in as ordinary shoppers to test the complaints of local people.

The three women were chosen to represent a fair cross-section—they were a business woman, a housewife, and a buyer who could balance the difficulties on both sides of the counter.

BUYERS HELPED

The four men were buyers, with two from the clothing trade to give a more specialised outlook.

The seven made detailed reports to the Board of Trade on their shopping. They did not know that a system of rationing was being considered on their information.

One of the women who made this survey said yesterday: "I studied all types of shoppers, but mainly the woman who runs her household on £3 to £4 a week.

"I do not think this group will be affected at all by rationing. The £5 group will be cut by about a quarter, while the other classes will be cut considerably.

"In my travels around the country I found that the bulk of the cheaper clothes for working families is strong and hard-wearing."

STUDIED TYPES

The woman buyer who went round studied the types of clothes that were being bought, and talked to retailers about the main shortages which the quota had created—the Government had already cut down supplies to the trade.

The housewife studied the domestic difficulties in clothing children and working men and women.

A Board of Trade official explained in detail yesterday the principles on which the ration has been formed. He said:—

"We studied the reports of our seven investigators very carefully.

"Under the quota system it was found that people with money to spare could stock up their wardrobes, while people who had to buy carefully over a longer period had to go short.

"The position was being reached that unless a system of rationing was introduced there would be unfair prices and unfair distribution."

Designers have still been left with a certain initiative in fashion

→ BACK PAGE, COL. SIX

Major Glubb alive

The War Office issued last night an official denial of German reports that Major Glubb, commander of the Arab Legion of Transjordan, is dead.

CURT NOTE TO VICHY

Sfax bombs protest rejected

REPORTS from Vichy last night said that Britain has "curtly rejected" Darlan's protest about the British bombing last week of the harbour of Sfax, in Tunisia.

The protest was sent through the Vichy Embassy in Washington.

Last night, R.A.F. Cairo headquarters announced a second attack on the Italian transport lying in Sfax harbour which was the target of our first raid.

Smoke poured from the ship after three direct hits had been followed by a low-level machine gunning attack, the communiqué said.

According to the German-controlled Paris newspapers, General Weygand has ordered the immediate reinforcement of North Africa's air defences "against British attacks."

Armed liner is sunk

The armed merchant cruiser Salopian (Captain Sir J. M. Alleyne, D.S.O., D.S.C.) has been sunk, the Admiralty announced last night.

Sir John Alleyne, then Lieutenant Alleyne, was navigator of the Vindictive when she was sunk as a blockship in Ostend Harbour on May 10, 1918.

He received the D.S.O. for his part in the raid.

Iraq is opened to our troops

Express Staff Reporter — CAIRO, Sunday.

BRITAIN'S 30-day war against the Iraqi rebels ended with an armistice at the gates of Bagdad today and a triumphal entry into the city.

Outstanding point of the armistice terms is that Britain regains the right, provided under the Anglo-Iraq treaty, to send troops through the country.

This is of great importance, since Iraq borders on Axis-dominated Syria. It was the refusal of this right by the fugitive quisling Rashid Ali which caused the revolt.

Other terms are:—

1 Iraq returns to its status as an independent country.

2 Rebels all over the country to lay down their arms, and Iraq Army units to return to their stations.

3 All Axis agents, agitators, soldiers and airmen, to be interned by the new Iraqi Government.

4 All British prisoners to be freed.

Extra British troops now needed in Iraq will be able to take up garrison duty as provided by the treaty.

It is stated the important Mosul oilfields in the north are in the control of the governor of the area, who has opposed Rashid Ali's revolt from the start.

The oilfield is reported to be undamaged.

Dawn armistice drama—Back Page.

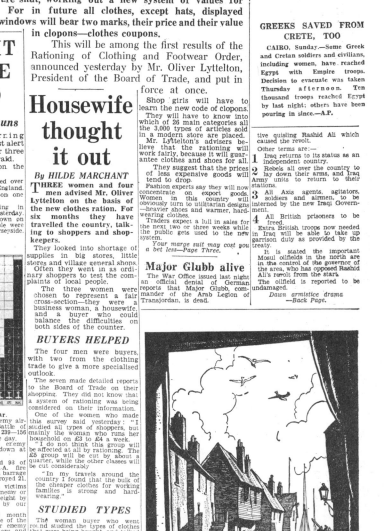

3 A.M. LATEST

GREEKS SAVED FROM CRETE, TOO

CAIRO, Sunday.—Some Greek and Cretan soldiers and civilians, including women, have reached Egypt with Empire troops. Decision to evacuate was taken Thursday afternoon. Ten thousand troops reached Egypt by last night; others have been pouring in since.—A.P.

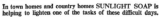

WEATHER
Clear this afternoon, tonight and tomorrow. Somewhat cooler tonight; moderate temperature tomorrow. Lowest tonight, about 60 degrees. High tomorrow, 75.

New York Post

SPORTS EXTRA

Founded 1801. Volume 140, No. 187.

NEW YORK WEDNESDAY JUNE 25 1941 THREE CENTS

LENINGRAD SET ABLAZE

Russians Bomb Helsinki and Six Nazi Cities

REPORT FINNS DECLARING WAR

RED PLANES IN THE SUNSET

BOMBERS AND FIGHTER PLANES of the Russian air force, shown during recent maneuvers. Russia claims planes like this have bombed Warsaw and Lubin in Poland, Constanta, Rumania, Konigsberg, capital of German East Prussia, and the former Free City of Danzig.

BERLIN, June 25 (AP).—Authorized German sources said Finland had declared herself at war with Russia today and that fighting was going on in full force.

HELSINKI, June 25 (AP).—Russia hurled a wholesale air offensive against Finland today, and the Finns made a second sharp protest to Moscow against what they called the Soviet's unprovoked attack.

Bombs were dropped on Helsinki twice, and swarming flights of Russian bombers and fighters caused four alarms in the capital before noon.

Bombs fell also in other Finnish cities, some of them heavily battered by Russian air attack in the Soviet-Finnish war of 1939-40.

[Almost all the larger cities and towns of Finland were bombed repeatedly by the Russians today, DNB reported at Berlin.]

Forest Fire Outside Capital

A forest fire was burning outside Helsinki as a result of the air bombardment, but no important targets were said to have been hit and damage was slight.

Reliable reports said big Russian guns at the naval base of Hango had been firing at taggets to the west.

[This would indicate action against German naval or air units in the northern Baltic. Hango is on Finland's southwest coast, but was leased to Russia after the Russian-Finnish war.]

The Finns showed no signs of panic as the Russians attacked Helsinki. Many ran into shelters, but the streets were crowded with spectators shading their eyes to watch.

Crowds cheered as one bomber was shot down by a Finnish fighter and the rest scattered under heavy ground fire.

F. D. R. Calls on Americans To Rededicate Selves July 4

WASHINGTON, June 25 (UP).—President Roosevelt today compared America's present crisis with the trying days of 1776 and called upon Americans to redeidicate themselves on July 4 to the basic principles enunciated in the Declaration of Independence.

Leningrad Reported In Flames

LONDON, June 25 (AP).—A Reuters, British news agency, dispatch from Stockholm said a heavy Nazi air attack was reported on Leningrad and that extensive and fierce fires were believed to have broken out in that city, the second largest in Soviet Russia.

RAF Steps Up Terrific Raids

LONDON, June 25 (AP).—RAF bombers roared across the Channel twice today, once briefly in the morning and then in a heavier daylight smash this afternoon, following up their 14th successive night assault on western Germany.

Terrific blows apparently were beign hit at targets between Boulogne and Callais in the afternoon raid, carried out by a large formation of bombers escorted by clouds of powerful fighters.

Observers said the rumble of explosions came from scattered directions and the RAF was said unofficially to have taken a heavy toll again of German fighters over the Channel.

While the main bomber formations swept into France, British fighters darted on patrol, often breaking away from their units to engage German planes.

Earlier details on Page 2.

Fred Snite May Take A Walk

DAYTON, Ohio, June 25 (UP).—Fred B. Snite Jr., "the boiler kid," visited relatives in Dayton today and planned to try out a portable respirator, worn under his street clothes, which would permit him more freedom of action, possibly including walking.

Leningrad in Russia, Warsaw in German Poland and Constanta in Rumania were reported in flames this afternoon as both German and Russian air forces sowed destruction from Finland to the Black Sea.

Six cities in Germany or German-held territory were strafed by the Russians, who also struck four times at Helsinki, the Finnish capital.

German sources said Finland was now at war with Russia.

The Luftwaffe bombed the principal cities of the Ukraine, White Russia and Latvia.

On land the Germans reported satisfactory gains, apparently in Lithuania, Russian Poland and the Ukraine. Rumanian sources said the Russians would be driven out of Bessarabia within a week.

A Nazi military spokesman said successes "baffling the imagination" would be announced in detail tomorrow.

Moscow, admitting some German penetration, reported counter-attacks and said the Germans were being held, with heavy losses in several areas.

MOSCOW, June 25 (AP).—Trading blow for blow with the Luftwaffe, the Red Air Fleet reported today it had left Warsaw and Constanta in flames, raided Danzig and East Prussia and destroyed 381 German planes against a three-day loss of 374 of its own aircraft.

Along the 1,350-mile land battlefront, a Soviet communique declared, the Red Army repulsed the Nazis with heavy losses in several sectors and counter-attacked sharply at several points.

The Russians were fighting fiercely to check Nazi drives into the Baltic states and old northeast Poland, and in the south they were holding German and Rumanian troops to a standstill on the banks of the Prut River.

The Red Army, aided by dive bombers and charging cavalry, was reported today to have smashed back a German drive across the Prut and to have inflicted heavy losses on Nazi mechanized columns, the United Press said.

The headlong clash of the two largest armies in Europe was reported heavy in casualties and destruction, with big guns in action and powerful motorized and mechanized divisions following up the first shock of advance units.

Nazi Parachutists Dropped

German parachutists and communications-wrecking details have been dropped behind the Russian lines, the Soviet communique declared. It alleged they were in "the uniform of Soviet militiamen" and said they would be mopped up.

The communique said the Germans had driven into Sovietized Lithuania in the direction of Kaunas, the capital; into the northern section of Sovietized eastern Poland toward Grodno, Wolkowysk and Kobryn, and into Sovietized southeastern Poland in the direction of Wlodzibierz and Brody.

All these penetrations, whose depth was not specified, were meeting "stiff resistance," the communique said. It reported that thrusts in the Siauliai area of Lithuania "have been repelled with heavy losses" and said "counter-attack of our mechanized units in this direction have destroyed tank formations of the enemy and a mechnized regiment has been entirely annihilated."

Fierce Fight at Grodno

"Fierce fighting' was reported under way in the defense of Grodno, Vilna and Kaunas against German thrusts northeast from East Prussia and into the 200-mile wide strip of Sovietized Poland north of the vast Pinsk marshes.

Heavy losses also were said to have been inflicted on the Germans in a continuing battle between large tank formations in the Nazi push toward Brody, northeast of Lwow.

The Russians admitted that the Luftwaffe had bombed the Crimean port of Sevastopol twice and that there had been repeated raids on Minsk, capital of White Russia; Kiev, capital of the Ukraine; Riga, capital of Sovietized Latvia; and the Latvian port of Libau.

Striking back, the Red Air Force was reported to have bombed Constanta and the town of Sulina three times.

Also reported bombed three times is as many days were Danzig, Koenigsberg in East Prussia, and Lublin and Warsaw in the German Government General of Poland. Gasoline supplies at Warsaw w ere reported set afiire.

Most Destroyed on Ground

The Russians said most of the 374 planes they had lost were destroyed on the ground by Nazi bombers striking at dawn Sunday in the first hours of the war. They claimed the Soviet Air Force shot down 161 German planes in aerial battles and destroyed at least 220 others on airdromes.

The communique declared specifically that both Finland and Rumania had lent their territory to the German army and air force for the fight.

"Not only are raids by the German air force carried out from Rumanian territory on Soviet towns and armies," the communique said, "but German troops with the co-operation of the Rumanian armies are also conducting a land offensive.

"The repeated attempts of the German-Rumanian armies to take possession of Cernauti (on the Prut river in Bucovina, which the Red Army took from Rumania last year along with Bessarabia) and gain a foothold on the eastern bank of the River Prut have not been successful."

The communique said German planes striking from Finland twice raided Soviet territory, once attempting to raid Kronstadt, near Leningrad, Russia's second largest city. It added that "some units of the German Army tried to cross the Soviet frontier" from Finland.

Moscow Features News

MOSCOW, June 25 (AP).—Moscow newspapers printed under large headlines today the news that frozen Soviet assets in the U. S. had been freed, and that President Roosevelt had pledged all possible aid to Russia.

The dispatches were received too late for editorial comment, but the general reaction appeared to be one of warm appreciation.

Map on Page 4

Rickenbacker Employees Endow Hospital Blood Bank

ATLANTA, June 25 (AP).—Employees of Eastern Air Lines today endowed a "blood bank" for Piedmont Hospital where EAL's president, Eddie Rickenbacker, has been since Feb. 28 when he was injured in a transport plane crash near here.

Rickenbacker made the gift on behalf of the men just before he left the hospital and boarded a plane for New York.

Woman, 64, Leaps 15 Floors to Death

The burden of life suddenly became too great today for Mrs. Minnie Brothers, 64, who had raised several children, had seen them all happily married, and found herself an old woman, ill, with no reason to go on living.

In her 15th floor room at the Hotel Greystone, 214 W. 91st St., she penned several notes, one of which read:

"To my dear children: I am tired of being sick and a burden to you. I am sorry I have to do this. My love to all of you. Mother."

Then, police said, she walked to a window of the room and leaped to a rear court.

Police located one of her sons, Arthur J. Brothers, an attorney, of 11 Broadway, and he identified his mother's body.

INDEX

WAR MAPS

A Private Without Privacy

His Name Is on Every Army Form

Special to The Post

SAN DIEGO, Cal., June 25.—A Kalamazoo, Mich., recruit was sent to a desk at the Coast Artillery Replacement Center here to fill out the usual array of forms. At the desk, for illustrative purposes, were sample forms filled out in the name of "John Doe."

When the recruit turned in his form the top sergeant hit the ceiling.

"What do you mean, filling these things out in the name of 'John Doe' — just like the samples?" the sergeant demanded.

"Because,' replied the recruit, "my name IS John Doe."

His father's name, he added, is John O. Doe.

Sand in Soup

FORT BLISS, Tex.—A 124th Cavalry trooper grumbled that there was sand in his soup.

"Did you join the Army to serve your country or to complain about the food?" demanded the cook.

"To serve my country," the trooper retorted—"not to eat it!"

First Aid Station

MANCHESTER, Tenn. — An 11th Infantry medical detachment, engaged in maneuvers near here, set up a first-aid station at night, without the slightest notion where they were.

But dawn disclosed that they'd established themselves smack in the middle of a country graveyard.

Truck Wheel Runs Amok

Hurls Man 15 Ft., Hits Baby Carriage

The right rear wheel of a large Consolidated Edison Co. truck parted company with the truck in 4th Av. at 19th St., Brooklyn, this morning and this is what happened:

The wheel caromed off Israel Backal, 60, standing on the sidewalk in front of his confectionery store at 664 4th Av. and threw him 15 feet through the doorway into the store. He struck a soda fountain stool, breaking the metal shaft in two.

The wheel rolled next door into a baby carriage in which Lucille O'Shea, 2, was resting in front of her home at 662 4th Ave., overturned the carriage, threw Lucille out and turned over on the sidewalk beside her.

At Methodist Hospital Backal was treated for head injuries and Lucille for a chest injury. Charles T. Merritt, 542 Parkside Av., Brooklyn, was the truck driver.

Of Us They Sing

The Moscow radio was heard last night by NBC broadcasting the tune, "Columbia, the Gem of the Ocean."

Two Sections 20 Pages

U. S. to Shun Strike Areas

WASHINGTON, June 25 (AP).—Communities that have a reputation for strikes and other labor disturbances may find themselves unable to get new defense orders and plant locations under a government policy disclosed today.

Market Leaders

(Sales in hundreds)

Stock Div.	Sales	High	Low	1:15	Net ch'ge
Allied C & D 6..	4	153	152	152¼	
Am Car & Fdy..	14	31⅜	31¼	31¼	− ¾
Am Smelt & R 2	14	41⅝	41¼	41¼	−1
Am Tel & T (9)	2	156	156	156	− ⅜
Anaconda 1a ...	16	27⅜	27¼	27¼	− ¼
Atch T & S F 1e	10	29	28¾	29	
Bendix Avia 2a..	1	36¼	36¼	36¼	+ ¼
Beth Steel 3a...	28	74	73⅛	73⅛	− ½
Boeing Airplane.	46	17	16½	16⅝	+ ⅛
Caterpillar T 2..	4	48	47½	47½	− ½
Ches & Ohio (3)	3	36½	36¼	36½	+ ¼
Chrysler (3a)...	17	57¾	57¼	57¼	− ¼
Cons Aircraft 2a.	13	30⅜	30	30	− ¼
Cons Edis (2)...	8	18¾	18⅝	18¾	− ⅛
Crucible Steel...	7	38½	38⅛	38⅛	− ⅛
Doug Aircraft 5e	7	73¾	72¼	73¼	+ ¾
DuPont 7.......	6	154½	153	154½	+1
East Kodak (6).	1	134½	134½	134½	+ ⅝
Gen Elec 1.40...	17	32⅝	32⅜	32½	+ ⅛
Gen Motors 1¾a	20	38⅝	38⅜	38½	− ⅛
Gen S Cast pf..	*300	68⅜	67½	67¾	− ¼
Gr Nor Ry pf 1a.	5	26	25¾	26	+ ⅛
Int Nickel 2.....	17	25½	25⅜	25⅜	− ½
Intl Pap & P....	5	14¾	14½	14¾	+ ⅛
Int P&F pf 8¾n.	7	66¼	65¾	65¾	
Kennecott 1b....	11	37¼	36⅞	37⅛	− ⅛
Lockheed A 1½e	20	25⅜	25	25	+ ⅛
Loft, Inc ½e....	15	22	21¾	21⅞	+ ⅛
Mart Glenn 1½a	5	28¼	27½	28	+ ½
Mont Ward 2....	16	35⅜	35⅛	35⅛	− ⅛
N Y Central.....	55	12⅜	12¼	12¼	
Nor Am Av 1¼e.	5	14⅜	14⅛	14⅛	
Paramount .40a..	58	11½	11⅛	11½	+ ⅜
Penn R R 1a....	7	23⅜	23¼	23¼	− ¼
Phelps Dodge 1..	25	29¾	29½	29⅝	− ¼
Pullman (1).....	7	27¼	26¾	27	− ¼
Republic Stl 1a.	9	19⅜	19⅛	19⅛	− ¼
Savage Arms 2½a	42	15⅜	15⅛	15¼	+ ¼
Sears Roeb 3...	8	72¾	72	72	+ ¼
Socony Vac (½).	30	9	8⅞	9	
Southern Pac....	34	11⅝	11⅜	11⅝	+ ⅛
Std Oil N J 1b..	28	40⅛	39⅞	40	
Tex Corp 2......	13	39½	39¼	39½	+ ¼
Un Car & C 2¼a	11	71⅞	71½	71¾	+ ½
Unit Aircraft 2a.	19	40¼	39⅞	40	+ ¼
U S Rubber ½a.	27	23⅜	22⅞	22⅞	− ⅜
U S Steel 2a....	51	56¾	56⅛	56⅛	− ⅜
West Union 1a..	3	24⅜	24¼	24¼	+ ⅛
West El&Mfg 2a.	3	94¾	94¾	94¾	+ ⅝
Young S&T 1¼a	12	36⅜	36	36¼	− ⅛

Baa! Says Rogers to Bethel

Connecticut Village Gets His Goat

Special to The Post

BETHEL, Conn., June 25.—Henry Huddleston Rogers Jr., 37, son of the late Col. Henry Huddleston Rogers, moved here about three months ago with his wife, a former hat-check girl, and has been at odds with his neighbors ever since.

They complain that he maintains 12 dogs, leaves the lights on in his house all night, allows the motors of several cars to run all night, has built a picket fence which varies in height from four to 12 feet, and keeps sheep on his lawn.

The Village Board of Commissioners finally passed a zoning ordinance prohibiting the keeping of sheep, pigs or goats in the town, and today Rogers struck back at them in the following poem:

Our city fathers, have you heard,
Have passed an edict (Oh, my word!)
You cannot keep upon your lawn
Two little lambs, just newly born.
No lamb chops in two hundred feet
Of a dwelling place upon the street.
So. mowing a lawn, I have to sweat,
For into the mountains you go, my pet!
Has our Council ever heard
That out of Washington came the word
That you must conserve your fuel and heat
So that this winter you might eat
A piece of meat, my sweet?
And onto your yard and vacant lot
Put the meat you like a lot

This world is bloody and full of tears,
This silly edict will stand for years.
I respectfully join my little lamb,
Spic and span.
In saying, "Baa! Baa! Baa!"

Rogers appended the following to his poem: "P. S. In case you don't know, my police dog had a romance with Mickey Rooney's dog and presented me with twelve pups, which are doing nicely. They will have to be exiled to Siberia, since some one claims I am running a kennel. My good gosh!"

WEATHER

Scattered showers and continued warm tonight and tomorrow, light winds. Lowest temperature tonight about 68 degrees. High tomorrow about 85 degrees.

New York Post

SPORTS FINAL 7

LATE SPORTS RESULTS ON PAGE 15

Founded 1801. Volume 140. No. 191.

NEW YORK MONDAY JUNE 30 1941 THREE CENTS

REICH ARMY SPOKESMAN INTIMATES:

HALF WAY TO MOSCOW

Germans Claim Capture of Lwow and Minsk

7 Spies Plead Guilty; FBI Seizes 2 More On Incoming Ships

By JOHNSTON D. KERKHOFF

Seven of 25 persons accused of belonging to a spy ring unexpectedly pleaded guilty when arraigned in Brooklyn today, and the others were held in $25,000 bail each.

While the arraignments were being held before U. S. Commissioner Epstein, FBI agents went down the bay on Coast Guard cutters and seized two stewards from incoming liners.

Those who pleaded guilty included Axel Wheeler-Hill, brother of James Wheeler-Hill, former German-American Bund secretary. It was in Axel Wheeler-Hill's apartment that agents found a short wave radio during the week-end roundup of suspects.

Another who pleaded guilty was a model, Lilly Barbara Carola Stein, who allegedly had moved in society circles collecting information.

The others:

Hartwig Richard Kleiss, seaman; Erwin Wilhelm Siegler, former chief butcher on the S. S. America; Franz Stigler,

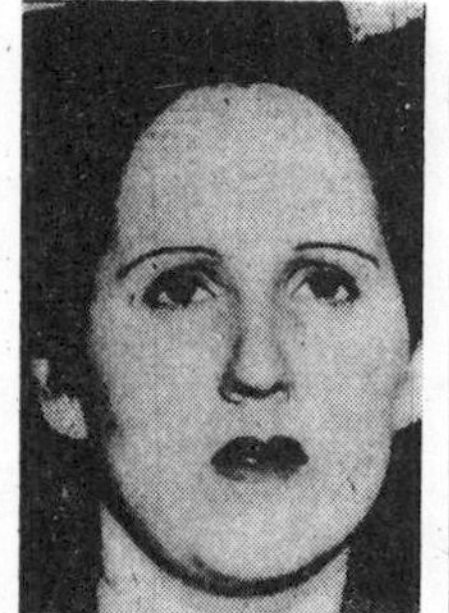

LILLY BARBARA Carola Stein, artists' model, was among 29 persons arrested on espionage charges by the FBI.

former chief baker on the America; Leo Waalen, German citizen, and Alfred E. Brokhoff, waterfront mechanic.

Each prisoner was transferred to Brooklyn in an automobile, and with each one rode three to five FBI agents. All were handcuffed.

More Arrests Indicated

The agents activity down the bay indicated that the roundup was not yet over. As one government official said: "I don't want the public to think that these are the only spies in the country."

Eight FBI agents first boarded

Continued on Page 10, Col. 6

Don't Write To Uncle Sam For a Mate

WASHINGTON, June 30 (AP).—The Census Bureau said today it didn't mind telling lonely women where detached males were running loose, but from there on it's up to the girls.

After revealing in a press release last week that men are in the vast majority in several American possessions, the bureau received hundreds of letters from women wanting names and street addresses of likely prospects.

The letters came from nearly every state east of the Mississippi River. They inquired about Guam, Alaska, Puerto Rico and Hawaii, and particularly about the Panama Canal Zone.

The bureau replied it is against the law to reveal individual names from census records.

Brenda Weds—'Simply'

The Champagne Will Cost Only $750

Brenda Diana Duff Frazier, who has got along pretty well despite the burden of being called Glamour Girl No. 1, becomes Mrs. John Simms (Shipwreck) Kelly today in what the society editors refer to as a simple ceremony.

She wears a $500 wedding gown, there are only 250 guests invited to the reception, and the champagne bill, it is figured, won't be more than $750.

The simplicity extended to Hal Phyfe, family photographer, who said that all other cameramen would be barred. "Anyone who tries to crash will be smashed by 'Shipwreck,'" was Phyfe's zero hour warning.

The wedding is being solemnized at 4:15 p. m. by the Rev. Father Joseph F. Flannelly, of St. Patrick's Cathedral, in the Carlton House living room of Miss Frazier's mother, Mrs. Frederic N. Watriss. There are only 20 guests.

Miss Frazier is being given in marriage by her stepbrother, Frederic Whitney Watriss. Sergeant T. Suffern Tailer is Kelly's best man.

At 5 p. m. there is to be a reception in the Crystal Room of the Ritz-Carlton. Following the reception, the couple will fly to California, and will spend their honeymoon in Honolulu.

In the fall they plan to take an apartment here. Next June when Miss Frazier is 21, she will come into about $4,000,000.

Murray Korman Photo.

BRENDA FRAZIER

Jackson Approved For Court

Senate Committee Acts Unanimously—Rejects Tydings Charge He's 'Unfit'

WASHINGTON, June 30 (AP).—The Senate Judiciary Committee approved unanimously today the nomination of Attorney General Jackson to be an associate Justice of the Supreme Court.

The committee rejected charges by Sen. Tydings (D.-Md.) that Jackson was unfitted for service on the court "by character, philosophy and judicial temperament."

Tydings said that Jackson had rejected his request that Drew Pearson and Robert Allen, columnists, be prosecuted for a 1939 radio broadcast in which they said Tydings had called on the WPA to build a road and a yacht basin on his estate.

Chairman Hatch (D.-N. M.) of the subcommittee put into the record a letter from Jackson to Tydings declining to prosecute Pearson and Allen. The letter, dated June 11, 1940, said:

"You have told me that you have other cases that you would also want prosecuted after this one. To use the power of the government in a campaign of this kind would, in my opinion, discredit the law enforcement agencies if unsuccessful, and, if successful, would constitute harassment not consistent with our support of freedom of the press. That this freedom is sometimes abused does not lessen the necessity for its protection."

Jackson followed Tydings to the witness stand and said the Justice Dept. had declined to prosecute because it wished to keep the government "out of the numerous fights between newspapers and men in public life."

Calls Tydings Beneficiary

The Attorney General said an investigation by the FBI had shown that WPA improvements ha dnot been made on the Senator's property "but a road was built to the Tydings estate and a yacht harbor adjacent to it."

"The inference is clear that you were a beneficiary," he snapped when Tydings challenged him to prove that WPA work had improved the Senator's property. Tydings said the work actually decreased the value of the property.

A few minutes after the committee had acted, Tydings announced in the Senate that he would oppose the nomination when it reached the floor.

Why It's So Humid

Today's humidity can be blamed on the ocean, according to James H. Kimball, head of the Weather Bureau.

It's so humid because the wind is coming in from the Atlantic," he said.

"I think the high humidity is possibly caused by its accumulation during the last five days when the temperature was above normal," he explained. "The air was dry until yesterday, with a fairly good breeze, and the sudden change has made it so noticeable."

The temperature, which was 77 at midnight, got down to 75 at 5:45 a. m., and then started right back up again, and by 8 a. m. it was 80. Yesterday's temperature at that hour was only 75.

Hourly temperatures today and yesterday were:

	Today	Yest.
Midnight	77	77
1 a. m.	78	76
2 a. m.	77	75
3 a. m.	78	74
4 a. m.	77	74
5 a. m.	77	74
6 a. m.	76	73
7 a. m.	78	74
8 a. m.	80	75
9 a. m.	82	77
10 a. m.	80	78
11 a. m.	80	79
Noon	82	80
1 p. m.	85	80

FIGHTING ON BORROWED LAND

NAZI FORCES HAVE KNIFED THROUGH the outer layer of Soviet defenses, built on territory annexed since 1939, and have captured Minsk (2), in Russia proper, Berlin announces. Advance units have driven on to a point "within sight of Smolensk," 200 miles on the road to moscow, a spokesman says. A German column advancing on Leningrad has taken Libau, naval base on the Latvian coast; other forces have captured Lwow (3) on the road to Kiev. In the southern sector along the Prut River to the Black Sea (4), the Russians claim complete success in stopping the invasion, and the Nazis make no claims of gains there.

U. S. Nurses on Lost Ship

Marine Believed Killed in Sinking

WASHINGTON, June 30 (AP).—While withholding official confirmation of the sinking, Sumner Welles, Acting Secretary of State, said today American Red Cross nurses were on board a ship reported to have been sunk in the Atlantic with the possible loss of an American marine.

Asked at a press conference about an authoritative report that the ship, carrying 10 U. S. Marines to London, was lost, Welles said he did not believe the Navy was in a position yet to make an official statement.

Welles added that American nurses were aboard the same vessel with the marines traveling to England to help the expanded services of the American Embassy including communications and fire prevention.

Under the Neutrality Act, Welles explained, the President had the power to make exceptions to permit Americans in certain instances to travel on belligerent ships.

The marines were on a Dutch vessel, now in British service, which was torpedoed somewhere in the Atlantic, the official said.

Only Saturday the announcement was made here that three officers and 60 enlisted men of the Marine Corps were being sent to London "to facilitate communications between the various U. S. offices located there."

Barrymore Runs Into a Zombie, a Fist and a Bouncer

The Great Profile Slips (While Ducking) After Blonde's Escort Swings

Special to The Post

HOLLYWOOD, June 30.—John Barrymore was struck by a zombie, a young man in a night club and a bouncer early today. He wound up on the sidewalk, loser on all three counts.

The affair took place at Earl Carroll's night club and theatre, where Barrymore had gone to attend the marriage of a pair of jitterbug champions by the Rev. R. Anderson Jardine, who married the Duke and Duchess of Windsor and thereby landed in Hollywood.

As he entered, "Think-a-Drink" Hoffman, who reads your mind and then mixes the drink you are thinking of, was doing his stuff.

"Think Again"

Barrymore thought of a zombie. Hoffman read his mind, and said, "You could get drunk on what youre thinking of. That's powerful stuff. You'd better think again."

Barrymore insisted he wanted a zombie, and Hoffman warned him again of the drink's potentialities and said the limit was one to a customer.

"I ought to know," said the Great Profile. "I was married to one for several years."

He finally got the drink, gulped it down, and weaved his way through the club, stopping to chat with an unidentified blonde. Her escort, Clarence Reed, resented a remark, and warned Barrymore to go away.

"His remark wouldn't bear repeating in nice society," Reed said later.

He "Just Slipped"

Barrymore repeated the remark and Reed let go a haymaker. The Profile ducked, and the blow merely grazed his chin. Barrymore went down, but ringsiders insisted he had slipped in ducking, and had not been floored by Reed. He was up at the count of one, ready to turn the other profile, when Marcel Lamaze, maitre d'hotel, and a squad of bouncers appeared.

Before you could say, "Elaine Barrie," the Profile was down again, this time on the sidewalk in front of the club.

He missed the wedding.

THE GREAT PROFILE—FLOOKED

THE GERMANS ANNOUNCE capture of Minsk, and intimate that Nazi forces are within sight of Smolensk, half way to Moscow. On the road to Leningrad, capture of the Latvian naval base of Libau is announced, and Lwow (Lemberg) on the road to Kiev, has fallen. Further encircling movements, trapping large sections of the Soviet armies, are indicated.

MOSCOW REPORTS annihilation of a German landing party trying to win a foothold at Viipuri, on the Gulf of Finland, and claims that the Red Army is standing off Nazi attacks all along the front. It says advance panzer divisions have been trapped.

LONDON ADMITS that the position of Soviet forces is very serious.

THE DECISION hinges on which side can maintain contact with, and reinforce, its advance units which are behind the enemy's lines.

STRIKING AT the German rear, the RAF launched a daylight offensive against Bremen and Oldenburg.

BERLIN, June 30 (AP).—The German advance is half way from Minsk to Moscow, a military spokesman intimated today.

The spokesman claimed that Minsk had fallen and the panzer divisions were racing for Moscow, 450 miles away. He hinted that the vanguard was in sight of Smolensk, only 250 miles from the Soviet capital, and said that encirclement of Soviet troops on the central front was proceeding rapidly.

Announcement of the fall of Minsk followed a communique from Adolf Hitler's field headquarters that Lwow, 50 miles from the German frontier in Sovietized Poland, had fallen at 4:20 a. m., and other claims of Russian defeats.

The German armored divisions admittedly have left many Russians behind them to the west, and it was acknowledged that the country across which they have sped cannot be regarded as German-occupied.

The High Command said that Libau ,important Baltic naval base just north o fthe Lithuanian border, had been seized by Nazi troops. DNB, authoritative news agency, reported isolation of a Red division "somewhere o nthe Baltic coast." The Slovak High Command claimed a break-through of the Soviet front at several points with a continuing advance.

The German radio earlier had claimed capture of Luck, 100 miles northwest of Lwow, but this was not confirmed. The objective in the Nazi drive in the Luck-Lwow sector was believed to be Kiev, 250 miles east of Lwow.

Panzer Force Trapped, Say Russians

MOSCOW, June 30 (AP).—The Red Army still is standing off heavy attacks on the Minsk front in White Russia and farther south at the Luck-Lwow gateway to the Ukraine, a Soviet communique said today. The repulse of German attempts to land at Viipuri also was reported.

Destruction of 53 German warplanes in air battles yesterday and the loss of only 21 Russian craft was announced.

German penetrations in Lithuania to the Dvinsk area—a third of the way to Leningrad—and across Sovietized Poland to the Minsk area—almost a third of the way to Moscow—were acknowledged, but in the Minsk drive German panzer advance forces have been trapped, the Red Army declared.

From the Luck-Lwow area to the Black Sea, along the southern flank of the battlefront, a communique said German and Rumanian attempts to smash through into the Ukraine and to cross the Prut River into Bessarabia had been repulsed in fierce fighting.

Describing the German High Command's claims yesterday of vast gains and great destruction as "a manifest lie and boastful humbug," the Moscow communique listed these figures for the two sides:

Tanks destroyed, or captured—2,500 German, up to 900 Russian; planes destroyed—1,500 German, 840 Russian; prisoners—30,000 German, 15,000 Russian.

(The German summary of the first week of fighting said the Nazi war machine had destroyed 2,233 Russian tanks, 1,297 armored cars and 4,107 planes, taken 40,000 prisoners, sunk four Soviet destroyers, three submarines and a torpedo boat and seriously damaged the 8,800-ton cruiser Maxim Gorky.)

48,400 Tons of Shipping Claimed by Germans

BERLIN, June 30 (AP).—German bombers and submarines have sunk 48,400 tons since the last report June 22, the High Command announced today.

Pants Ration Cuts Harry To the Quick

LONDON, June 30 (AP).—This is the sad saga of Harry Chambers and his pants.

Six weeks ago Harry sent the pants to the cleaner, who lost them. The cleaner reimbursed him but Harry can't buy a new pair because he lacks the necessary clothing coupons.

So he wrote the proper authorities of his plight and asked for emergency coupons.

He's just heard from them: "Kindly show how many pairs of trousers you still possess on the reverse of the enclosed form."

They'll get this answer:

"I am sitting here looking half like a nudist. You know which half. Please hurry with those coupons."

ants in your pants?
NO!- ants ATE my pants!

5th Av. Bus Line Gives Jobs to 10 Negro Youths

Ten Negro youths, who will be placed as apprentices in the shops of the Fifth Av. Coach Co. called on Mayor LaGuardia at Summer City Hall today with John E. McCarthy, president of the company.

The Mayor wished the youths luck, and commented that their placement was in line with the President's order that there be no racial discrimination in the mechanical defense program.

15 Missing, 18 Burned In Mine Dust Blast

INDIANA, Pa., June 30 (UP).—A dust explosion ripped through an isolated section of the Rochester and Pittsburgh Coal Co.'s McIntyre mine, 12 miles west of here today, severely burning 18 miners and leaving 15 or 16 unaccounted for.

INDEX

WAR MAP

76

Two Sections 18 Pages

NEWS CHRONICLE, Monday, July 14, 1941

News Chronicle

No. 29,698 MONDAY, JULY 14, 1941 RADIO PAGE 2 * ONE PENNY

BRITAIN AND SOVIET SIGN PACT

No Separate Peace: All Aid

BRITAIN AND THE SOVIET UNION HAVE SIGNED AN AGREEMENT WHEREBY EACH WILL SUPPORT THE OTHER IN EVERY WAY IN THE WAR AGAINST HITLERITE GERMANY, AND NEITHER WILL SIGN A SEPARATE ARMISTICE OR PEACE EXCEPT BY MUTUAL AGREEMENT.

The agreement was signed on Saturday in Moscow by M. Molotov and Sir Stafford Cripps. It was the result of negotiations between Sir Stafford and Stalin, who was present at the ceremony.

The pact, it was stated in London, does not mean an alliance, but the term "co-belligerents" was used to describe the relations between Britain and Russia.

The statement announcing the pact is headed "An Anglo-Russian Agreement" and declares:

"Agreement for joint action by his Majesty's Government in the United Kingdom and the Government of the U.S.S.R. in the war against Germany.

"His Majesty's Government in the United Kingdom and the Government of the U.S.S.R. have concluded the present agreement and declare as follows:

"(1) The two Governments mutually undertake to render each other assistance and support of all kinds in the present war against Hitlerite Germany.

Pact in Force Immediately

"(2) They further undertake that during this war they will neither negotiate nor conclude an armistice or treaty of peace except by mutual agreement.

"The contracting parties have agreed that this agreement enters into force as from the moment of signature and is not subject to ratification.

"It was concluded on the evening of July 12, 1941, and was signed by authority of his Majesty's Government in the United Kingdom by Sir Stafford Cripps, his Majesty's Ambassador, and by authority of the Government of the Union of Soviet Socialist Republics by M. V. Molotov, Deputy President of the Council of the People's Commissars and People's Commissar for Foreign Affairs.

"The agreement was concluded in English and Russian."

Among those representing Britain at the signing of the agreement were Lieut.-General F. M. Mason Macfarlane, head of the Military Mission, and Mr. Laurence Cadbury, head of the Economic Mission.

HITLER STILL FOLLOWS THE SCHLIEFFEN PLAN

By the Military Critic

What is in the minds of the German High Command?

Hitler and his generals do not despise history. Their modern technique is new flesh covering the skeleton of older strategies.

General von Schlieffen, who succeeded Field Marshal Moltke and became Chief of the German General Staff in 1891, is still considered to have been Germany's greatest military genius. He made the spine of his strategy the overwhelming of the flanks as opposed to frontal attack. Recently the German plans have all been variations of this theme.

Yesterday's German communique claims that the Stalin Line has been pierced at all decisive points. But to pierce a modern front may mean no more than piercing butter with a pin.

In the first phase of this campaign the northern and southern turning movements failed. The enemy may now be thinking on a smaller scale. What was originally to have been one bite they may plan to achieve in two or more.

The first bite may lie between Pskov and Vitebsk. The second will be south of the Pripet Marshes with Kiev as its centre.

Berlin Says Road To Moscow is Open

WHILE Berlin yesterday claimed that the Stalin Line had been pierced "at all decisive points," Moscow admitted heavy fighting in the directions of Pskov, Vitebsk and Novgorod-Volynsk, but declared that there had been no important change in the front.

Last night the official German News Agency issued this sweeping statement:

"Complete German victory is now assured. Leningrad is immediately threatened and the occupation of Kiev is imminent.

"The route to Moscow is opened up and there are no further natural or artificial barriers.

"Supply lines for the Panzer divisions are assured."

The German radio stated that the Nazi air force "played a big part in piercing the Russian line, bombing and machine-gunning Soviet troops." Round Smolensk, it was stated, 77 tanks and 400 lorries were destroyed.

Latest news from the sectors of the front covering these cities is:

LENINGRAD: Moscow reported stubborn fighting near Pskov, close to the Estonian frontier. Berlin stated that east of Lake Peipus "German tank divisions are advancing on Leningrad."

MOSCOW: The Soviet communique stated that there had been heavy fighting in the direction of Vitebsk, halfway between the Latvian frontier and Smolensk. The Germans claimed that Vitebsk had been in their hands since Friday.

North of the Pripet Marshes, said Berlin, strong fortified posts along the Dnieper had been captured, "thus advancing the centre of the German offensive 125 miles east of Minsk."

According to 'Pravda," Pinsk, west of the Pripet Marshes, is still in Soviet hands.

KIEV: Moscow admitted strong fighting near Novgorod-Volynsk, in the Ukraine. Berlin claimed that German-Rumanian armies had thrown the Russians back on a broad front beyond the Dniester and now stood "immediately before Kiev."

Berlin Admits Damage at Ploesti

The Soviet Air Force has again raided Ploesti, centre of the Rumanian oil industry. German circles in Ankara admit that Ploesti has been seriously damaged as a result of the Russian raids.

Texts of the Russian and German war communiques are:

MOSCOW (Morning)

"During July 12 stubborn fighting took place between our troops and enemy troops in the directions of Pskov, Vitebsk and Novgorod Volynsk.

"These encounters caused no important change in the front.

Aerodromes and Harbours Bombed

"Our air force operated against the enemy's mechanised units, and struck blows at his air force on aerodromes, covered operations of our troops, bombed harbour works and transport at Constanza and Sulina (on the Black Sea) and oil wells at Ploesti in Rumania.

"According to incomplete data 102 German aircraft were destroyed during the day.

"Guerilla detachments operating behind the lines of German occupation are carrying out incessant attacks on enemy communication lines, destroying munitions and fuel trains, discovering and exterminating

Turn to Back Page, Col. Four

Premier's Speech To Be Broadcast Today

A speech by the Prime Minister at a public luncheon today will be broadcast in the Home Service of the B.B.C.

Mr. Churchill is expected to begin his speech between 1.55 and 2.10 p.m.

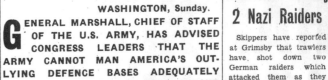

Moscow Not an Ally But "Co-Belligerent"

By VERNON BARTLETT

Yesterday, exactly three weeks after the Prime Minister in one of his most notable broadcasts had assured the nation that the British Government would do everything it could to further practical collaboration with the Government of the Soviet Union bringing about the defeat of Germany, a very important joint declaration was announced simultaneously in London and Moscow.

Its text is terse and emphatic. Each Government will render to the other all the help possible to hasten victory. Neither Government will negotiate an armistice or a treaty of peace without the other's consent.

People were asking yesterday whether the Soviet Union is now to be looked upon as an allied or an associate Power. Such questions are as foolish as some of the arguments deduced to show why the national anthem of the country, whose soldiers are giving the Germans much the hardest fight they have had so far, should not be broadcast.

SAME AS U.S. IN 1917

Fortunately these questions make no difference one way or the other to the fact that Hitler has plunged his country into that war on two fronts which his countrymen most hoped to avoid.

We should not have won the last war without American co-operation, but the United States was never an allied Power. Our close alliance with France has not prevented that country from falling into the hands of men who order their armies to fight for Germany against us.

In the search for a phrase which will satisfy everybody it has been suggested that the British and the Russians are "co-belligerents." That, or any other phrase, will do to remind Hitler of his failure to weaken our war effort by drawing a Red bogey across the track.

While it has not yet been possible for the British to carry out great operations in the West to distract German attention from the Eastern front, the intensive air attacks have been of great value.

It is in the air that the Russians most need help. Either the Germans must withdraw some of their squadrons from the East, or they must submit their factory workers—the men most likely to be angered by Hitler's attack on Russia—to bombardment of increasing intensity in the Ruhr and the Rhineland.

The reference in the joint declaration to "Hitlerite Germany" would suggest that at any rate the Russians still hope to split public opinion inside Germany.

DOMINIONS KNEW

The Dominion Governments have, of course, been kept fully informed of the discussions that led to this joint declaration.

Similar information has been given to the Government of the United States, where Mr. Hoover's ready acceptance of Hitler's claim to be the defender of civilisation against Communism has done a good deal to confuse public opinion.

Some at least of that confusion should be dissipated by this joint declaration of co-operation between two victims of Hitler's insane ambitions: Britain, alleged by the Germans to be dangerously reactionary, and Russia, alleged by them to be dangerously revolutionary.

72 p.c. in U.S. Hope Russia Will Win

From Our Own Correspondent

NEW YORK, Sunday.

A Gallup Survey published today shows that 72 per cent. of American voters would like to see Russia beat Germany (with 4 per cent. for Germany, 17 per cent. believing it makes no difference, and 7 per cent. undecided), but that only 22 per cent. expect Russia to win.

Forty-seven per cent. expect a German victory, 23 per cent. are undecided, and 8 per cent. predict a stalemate.

An interesting revelation of the poll is that there is little difference between the opinions of rich and poor, Protestants and Catholics—an indication that American opinion has not been split on either class or religious lines.

SYRIAN ARMISTICE INITIALLED

Following the initialling of the Syrian armistice terms, the documents have been referred back to the respective Governments, it was officially announced in Cairo last night.

The final decision is therefore still awaited.

Meanwhile the suspension of hostilities remains in force.

Britain's terms were accepted by General Dentz's representatives at Acre, Palestine, on Saturday night, after negotiations lasting nearly 12 hours.

FIRST SINCE WATERLOO

Details have not been published, says Reuter, pending a formal ratification of the agreement.

The negotiations were the first armistice talks between the British and French since the Battle of Waterloo.

The Military Critic writes:

The announcement of the armistice in Syria is doubly welcome, because it opens the way to the restoration of friendship with our late allies and provides a respite for the Imperial forces.

The situation in Libya will to some extent be favourably affected by the close of operations in Syria. The ground forces involved have been relatively small, and probably most of these will be needed where they are as troops of occupation.

MORE PLANES FOR LIBYA

The air force, on the other hand, with its superior mobility, can quickly effect a change of place and sufficient aircraft may be spared to strengthen air support in Libya if needed.

On the Egyptian-Libyan frontier the enemy is reported to be preparing extensive field fortifications in the region of Sollum and Halfyia Pass. This may mean they have decided to content themselves with static warfare during the next two or three months of extreme heat. It remains to be seen which side will take the offensive. The decision does not necessarily rest with the enemy.

News Chronicle Special Correspondent describes the Syrian armistice talks on Page Four

British Commercial Plane Down in Sea

Lisbon, Sunday.—A British twin-engined plane, believed to be a commercial machine, crashed into the sea this afternoon near Espozende, North Portugal, it is learned in Lisbon.

The machine is believed to have been on its way to Lisbon from London, and it is feared that all the occupants were drowned.—B.U.P.

British Overseas Airways, who control the only passenger plane service from this country to Lisbon, told the News Chronicle last night: "The crashed machine was not one of ours."

Italy's Missing Half Million

Italy's casualties in land operations up to the end of June total 582,000.

For Fire Service

Two fresh appointments to the headquarters of the new Fire Service are Mr. F. W. Delve, to be Deputy Inspector-in-Chief, and Mr. A. P. L. Sullivan, to be Deputy Chief of the Fire Staff.

U.S. Staff Chief Wants Longer Army Service

DEFENCE BASES WEAKNESS

WASHINGTON, Sunday.

GENERAL MARSHALL, CHIEF OF STAFF OF THE U.S. ARMY, HAS ADVISED CONGRESS LEADERS THAT THE ARMY CANNOT MAN AMERICA'S OUTLYING DEFENCE BASES ADEQUATELY UNLESS CONSCRIPTS ARE HELD BEYOND THE PRESENT ONE-YEAR LIMIT.

This follows the War Department's request for legislation on these lines and for the lifting of the ban on sending conscripted men overseas.

Tomorrow President Roosevelt will hold a conference at which leaders of the two parties in both Houses will express their views.

On Wednesday the Senate Military Affairs Committee will open public hearings on the subject.

Congress Leader Gives Warning

The non-interventionist group is now attempting to prove that feeling against the proposals is so great that the Administration could not get them through Congress even at the expense of a bitter fight.

The opposing group (of which Representative May, chairman of the House Military Affairs Committee, is a member) regards the danger as too acute for temporising. If information in the possession of the War Department could be released, said Representative May yesterday, it would "knock the hats off Congress."

Senator Has Compromise Plan

An appeal for a compromise is being put forward by Senator George, Chairman of the Senate Foreign Relations Committee. He appears to favour first the introduction of a system by which conscripted men would volunteer to serve an additional one, two or three years and, second, an amendment to present legislation making service in Iceland legal but denying the Administration the right to send conscripted men to other outposts.

Meanwhile, the controversy whether British troops are or are not leaving Iceland and whether they should or should not leave goes on here.

Senator Bone has advanced the view that a joint occupation by British and American troops is "fraught with danger," since the Germans have "the right" to attack if the British are there.

News Chronicle and A.P.

Sino-British Alliance Soon, Says Tokio

Tokio, Sunday.—A British military alliance with the Chinese Government in the near future is predicted in a Nanking dispatch to the Domei (Japanese) agency.

According to informed circles, says the message, the Chief of Staff of the British Forces in the Far East will visit Chungking in the middle of July to put the finishing touches to the agreement.—Reuter.

Fire Destroys Many Tons of Food

Many tons of food belonging to Messrs. Sainsbury, provision merchants, were destroyed by fire at Saffron Walden on Saturday night.

Bulgarian Troops On Turkish Frontier

Istanbul, Saturday (Delayed).—Travellers arriving here reported tonight that large numbers of Bulgarian troops had been concentrated on the Turkish frontier.—A.P.

Straits Brilliant

In the Straits last evening the weather was brilliantly fine.

The French coast was clearly visible, and white concrete buildings could be seen near Cap Gris Nez.

June Heat Record: Page Three.

Channel Shelling

German long range batteries shelled British shipping in the Channel during Saturday night

Trawlers Destroy 2 Nazi Raiders

Skippers have reported at Grimsby that trawlers have shot down two German raiders which attacked them as they were fishing in the North Sea.

R.A.F. Men Flew Through Storms to Bomb Bremen

Flying through heavy thunderstorms, Bomber Command planes raided Bremen and other places in North-West Germany on Saturday night.

Some exceptionally heavy bombs as well as incendiaries were used in the industrial areas and shipyards, says the Air Ministry.

Big fires broke out. One crew reported they could not see their own bomb bursts so heavy was the general strafing by our machines.

One pilot reported that his aircraft had been hit in about 20 places while he was making several runs over his target to make sure of his aim.

Two of our planes are missing. Berlin claimed that only slight damage was caused at Bremen, and that German defences prevented British bombers from reaching the city area of Hamburg.

The last three big raids on Munster caused terrific damage in nearly every part of the town, says Exchange from Zurich, and the authorities have ordered the evacuation of the town.

In the week ended at dawn yesterday the enemy (excluding the Russian campaign) lost 135 planes. Our losses were 96, with eight pilots safe.

NAZIS LOSE 2,170 PLANES

Moscow, Sunday.—The Soviet Army organ, "Red Star," estimated that since the beginning of the war against the Soviet Union Germany had lost 2,170 planes and had failed in the effort to gain mastery of the air.—A.P.

LONDON BLACK-OUT
10.57 p.m.—5.14 a.m.

B.B.C. Asks 'What is the Russian Anthem?'—Plays March

Before playing the Allied National Anthems the B.B.C. last night gave a recording of the "rousing military march and call to battle" broadcast by Moscow radio in connection with M. Stalin's recent wireless speech.

Earlier in the day, after the Anglo-Soviet agreement had been announced, a News Chronicle reporter asked the B.B.C. if the "Internationale" would be included among the Allied anthems.

"We shall certainly play one of the Russian anthems," said an official. "The question is what is the Russian anthem?"

The B.B.C. considered the matter for hours before stating no official announcement could be made before the nine o'clock news.

Afterwards a B.B.C. official said: "You must ask the Ministry of Information why the 'Internationale' was not played."

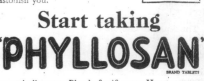

Said a Government official at the Ministry of Information: "The decision was taken in high quarters not to broadcast the 'Internationale' because in this country, at any rate, it has an international and subversive significance, and is, therefore, not considered suitable to be included among the national anthems. But I imagine the Russians will be shaking with laughter about it."

Daily Mirror JULY 15
No. 11,729 ✦ ONE PENNY
Registered at the G.P.O. as a Newspaper.

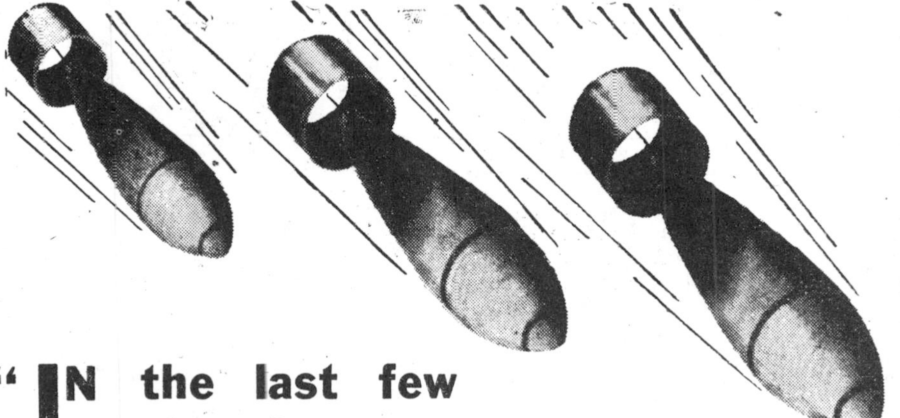

MR. CHURCHILL'S SMILE AS HE TALKED ABOUT THE BOMBS WE ARE NOW DROPPING ON THE ENEMY.

NAVY, RAF HIT 13 AXIS SHIPS

BOMBS

"IN the last few weeks alone we have thrown upon Germany about half the tonnage of bombs thrown by the Germans upon our cities during the whole course of the war. This is only the beginning . . ."

Mr. Churchill said this yesterday afternoon.

Speech Reported on Page 3

BRITAIN'S battering of Axis supply lines on land and sea continues with calculated ferocity.

Eight more enemy ships have been destroyed by our planes and submarines, it was officially announced yesterday. Two others were listed as "damaged and probably sunk," and three more suffered direct hits by bombs.

At the same time our bombers maintained their onslaught on docks, railways, locomotive sheds and factories in enemy - occupied territory.

Eight of the thirteen Axis ships hit by British bombs and torpedoes were attacked in the Mediterranean area of operations. The Navy's share of the "bag" was five.

Submarine Uses Gun

Here is the Admiralty communique, issued last night:—

"The Commander - in - Chief, Mediterranean, has reported further successes by submarines under his command.

"The Italian tanker Strombo (5,232 tons), which had put into Istanbul seriously damaged by a torpedo from one of our submarines, has now been sunk while on her way back to Italy to undergo repairs.

"A heavily-laden supply ship of about 5,500 tons sailing in convoy and escorted by an armed merchant cruiser and a destroyer has also been sunk.

"A large sailing vessel transporting enemy troops and military stores has been sunk in the Ægean.

"Another submarine, finding

Continued on Back Page

FORCE NAZIS TO ADOPT NEW ATTACK

STUBBORN Russian resistance to their tank attacks has forced the Germans to adopt new tactics, Moscow stated yesterday.

The Nazis are now sending batteries of anti-aircraft guns and squadrons of Messerschmitts with their tanks.

This means a sacrifice of speed in an effort to combat the Soviet warplanes which are still pressing home their attacks against the tanks.

Another new move on the part of the Germans is that they appear to be concentrating their action in the daylight hours, and resting at night

94 Planes Bagged

After their extravagant claims of the week-end, the German High Command yesterday sang small, but a Berlin radio commentator claimed last night that the Stalin Line had been pierced at four points.

The official Nazi news agency declared that tank forces were advancing on Leningrad.

The Russian communique said that no large-scale fighting had taken place during the previous night. The Russians added:—

"There was no significant change in the positions of the troops.

"Throughout the night our

Continued on Back Page

'MILLION CASUALTIES? GERMANY CAN STAND IT'

Rome radio, commenting on a Moscow report that 1,000,000 German soldiers had been put out of combat, said:—

"This figure is not far from the real number of German casualties, but Germany can stand this and other things."

And a Berlin military spokesman described the German losses as "really small."

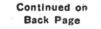

Berlin Listened for the "Internationale"

Berlin radio yesterday gave prominence to the refusal of the B.B.C. to play the "Internationale."

"Instead of the Russian national anthem," the announcer said, "a harmless military march was played."

COLONEL'S BAT(H)MAN

Scene: Minehead (Somerset) bathing pool.

A LARGE Army lorry pulls up at the entrance with curtains drawn across the back. Jumping from his seat, a private soldier pulls them on one side, and then stands stiffly to attention.

Out clamber a Colonel, an elderly woman and two girls in A.T.S. uniform. Collecting their bathing dresses, the Private follows the four into the pool.

After a suitable interval, he returns with a pile of wet bathing gear and escorts the party back into the Army lorry, pulling the curtains together behind them with another salute.

Then, with its precious but hidden cargo, the lorry sets out to return to its base miles away.

✦ ✦ ✦

The War Office has issued stringent orders to the Army about economy in petrol.

BRITISH SLOOP SUNK

The sloop H.M.S. Auckland (Commander M. S. Thomas, D.S.O., R.N.) has been sunk, the Admiralty stated last night. Next of kin of casualties have been informed.

We Send Bombers by the Hundred Now

SOME of the R.A.F. bombers now penetrating night after night deep into the heart of Germany are carrying three times the load that our planes took over a year ago.

In addition, while the raiders we sent over twelve months ago could be numbered by the score, they can now be numbered by the hundred.

With our latest monsters like the Halifax, the Short Sterling and the Avro Manchester it would be possible to send fewer planes than we sent last year and yet do more damage. As it is, while the Whitleys, Wellingtons and other stock bombers are going over in ever increasing numbers they are frequently accompanied by the new devastating types.

Ports Attacked

A month's survey of the R.A.F. offensive shows the terrific battering the Germans are getting, and also shows that we are till following the long-term plan made early in the war.

Stopping traffic from seaports is one of the main objects of our plan. During the last month we have made sixty-ine raids on seaports in German and German-occupied territory, and thirty-seven attacks on coastal shipping.

Behind the ports we have made twenty-seven attacks on railway centres and goods yards. There have been nine successful raids on power stations, seven on specific munition works, seven on oil plants, and seventy-three on industrial targets.

Here are the month's losses: German losses over Britain, 56; R.A.F. losses over Britain, 1 (pilot safe). German losses over Europe, 314; R.A.F. losses over Europe, 268.

The mere fact that the Air Ministry is prepared to lose 269 planes in a month indicates the terrific proportions which the R.A.F. have reached in both planes and personnel—and more and heavier stuff is on the way.

Hun Threat to Use Gas

GERMANY is preparing to use poison gas, judging by the Nazi-controlled Paris radio

Quoting Stockholm reports that the Russians have used poison gas on the Finnish front, the announcer said:—

"Should the reports be confirmed, then it is clear that the German High Command will know how to take reprisals against that breach of international law.

"In any way, the German chemical industry is of the highest degree of development, and the Russians will never be able to produce such huge quantities as the Germans may produce."

GERMAN'S SABOTAGE CALL TO GERMANS

Over Moscow radio last night, Michel Niederkirchner, who in peace time had a job in a Berlin steel factory, broadcast to Berlin steelworkers a call to sabotage Nazi war production.

"Remember, friends," he said, "each cartridge which does not explode is a shot into the heart of Hitler."

SPAIN GENERAL IN BERLIN

General Grande, leader of the Spanish volunteers going to fight against Russia, flew to Berlin yesterday, accompanied by officers.

'ITALIANS MARCH—TO FRESH GAOLS'

Moscow radio last night referred to the departure of Italian troops — Mussolini's "crusaders"—to the Russian front, and declared: "Italy, a country beaten by the British on land, sea and in the air, is marching against Russia now, under the pressure of Hitler.

"From the Russian front also they will find their way to prisoners' camps—as they have found their way from all the other fronts to the British prison camps in India."

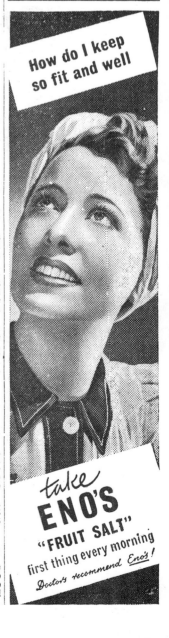

CLOSING PRICES

EVENING STANDARD, August 14, 1941.

FINAL NIGHT EXTRA

Evening Standard

Amusements 6
Radio 7

BLACK-OUT 8.55 pm to 5.14 am.
MOON rises 11.33 pm, sets 2.31 pm.

No. 36,486 | LONDON, THURSDAY, AUGUST 14, 1941 | ONE PENNY

ROOSEVELT & CHURCHILL: HISTORIC MEETING AT SEA

MUNITION PROBLEMS TACKLED: JOINT WAR AIMS

Beaverbrook and High Service Officers Were Present

"THE AGGRESSOR NATIONS MUST BE DISARMED"

"The President of the United States and the Prime Minister, Mr. Churchill, representing his Majesty's Government in the United Kingdom, have met at sea."

This dramatic news was announced to the world this afternoon simultaneously both in London and the United States. Mr. Attlee, Lord Privy Seal and Deputy Prime Minister, made the announcement in his eagerly awaited broadcast to the world.

SPEAKING FROM DOWNING-STREET, MR. ATTLEE SAID THAT MR. CHURCHILL AND MR. ROOSEVELT HAD BEEN ACCOMPANIED BY OFFICIALS OF THEIR TWO GOVERNMENTS, INCLUDING HIGH RANKING OFFICERS OF THEIR MILITARY, NAVAL AND AIR SERVICES. THE OFFICIAL STATEMENT SAID:

"The whole problem of the supply of munitions of war, as provided by the Lease-Lend Act, for the armed forces of the United States and for those countries actively engaged in resisting aggression has been further examined.

Talks in Washington

"Lord Beaverbrook, the Minister of Supply of the British Government, has joined in these conferences. He is going to proceed to Washington to discuss further details with appropriate officials of the United States Government. These conferences will also cover the supply problem of the Soviet Union.

"The President and Prime Minister have had several conferences. They have considered the dangers to world civilisation arising from the policy of military domination by conquest upon which the Hitlerite government of Germany and other governments associated therewith have embarked, and have made clear the steps which their countries are respectively taking for their safety in facing these dangers.

Seek No Aggrandisement

"They have agreed upon the following joint declaration:

The President of the United States and the Prime Minister, Mr. Churchill, representing his Majesty's Government in the United Kingdom, being met together, deem it right to make known certain common principles in the national policies of their respective countries on which they base their hopes for a better future for the world.

1—Their countries seek no aggrandisement, territorial or other.

2—They desire to see no territorial changes that do not accord with the freely expressed wishes of the people concerned.

3—They respect the right of all peoples to choose

(Continued on Back Page, Col. Two)

INVITATION CAME FROM ROOSEVELT

A picture of Mr. Attlee in Downing-street just before his broadcast to-day.

By Our Political Correspondent

I understand that the first step towards the historic meeting of President and Premier was taken by Mr. Roosevelt. He sent an invitation to Mr. Churchill.

They have been in constant touch through radio telephone and diplomatic channels and the exchange of personal messages since Mr. Churchill became Premier.

But as American and British co-operation became closer, and with the German attack on Russia, and Japan's threats in the Pacific raising new issues and new problems, it was felt that a personal meeting between the two leaders would be a great aid to a complete mutual understanding of the policies of the two nations.

Planned in Secret

Therefore, when Mr. Roosevelt's invitation came, Mr. Churchill responded at once.

The conveyance of the Prime Minister and his party across the submarine-infested Atlantic presented a big problem for the authorities, and in their discussions on the best and safest means of travel Mr. Churchill took an authoritative part.

The voyagers set out, of course, in absolute secrecy. The absence of the Premier from the war debate in the Commons caused some surprise, but only from the political point of view.

Reports from America stirred up speculation as to the whereabouts of the President, who had gone on a yachting cruise but was reported to have left his yacht and boarded a warship.

This story was in turn discounted by some on the theory that a President does not leave the Western Hemisphere, but

(Continued on Back Page, Col. One)

Her Nest Egg at 103

Annie Emily Jane Lugard, of Oak Park-road, Dawlish, Devon, who was 103, left £34.

NEW YORK HAD WEEK OF GUESSES

The greatest personal drama of the war—the rumoured meeting between President Roosevelt and Mr. Churchill—has been openly talked of in New York for days.

What all America has been trying to guess has been *where* the meeting was taking place and what was being said behind the curtains of secrecy, says Reuter.

It is disclosed here that the meeting was prompted by the President. This news came as a complete surprise.

Rumours of a meeting between the two world leaders first became current on August 6 and were given a place in the headlines of the New York Press.

Potomac Clues

Chief interest centred in the position of the President's yacht, Potomac.

On August 6 a brief message from the Potomac said that Mr. Roosevelt was "enjoying his cruise off New England."

It was on this day that the rumours of the meeting began to spread through America.

On the following day a cryptic official despatch from Potomac gave wings to the rumours which began to greatly excite America. The message said:

"All members of the party are showing the effects of the sunning. Fishing luck is good. No destination has been announced. . . ."

Then Silence

On the same day (August 7) the Washington correspondent of the New York Herald Tribune said that a mass of circumstantial evidence had been piled high to indicate that four of the highest ranking United States military and naval men had joined President Roosevelt at sea "for conference with Mr. Churchill and members of a British mission."

Last Saturday another humorously cryptic message was received from the President's yacht:

"The ship is anchored in fog. Prospects for fishing appear poor to-day. Everything quiet on board; no especial news."

Silence then descended upon the yacht.

Hopkins Again?

Yachtsmen reaching the Massachusetts coast said they had seen the President's yacht off Nantucket Island, with the President's ensign flying.

The master of one yacht told how, shortly after passing the Potomac, he had seen a large Canadian vessel, camouflaged, and with its name painted out, heading into Nantucket Sound along a route not usually followed.

One theory was that the meeting was arranged following information which Mr. Harry Hopkins, the President's personal friend and envoy, brought back from Moscow.

Getting It Hot

Some of the men in a new batch of German and Italian prisoners in London were wearing tropical outfits and sun helmets.

Libya: No Change

To-day's Cairo communiqué stated: "Libya: No change in the situation."

H.G. Will Be "Scorched Earth" Men

Evening Standard Reporter

If the Germans invade Britain the Home Guard will carry out the "scorched earth" policy that has been so successful in Russia.

They will act as saboteurs and harass the enemy in the same

LORD BRIDGEMAN

way as Stalin's guerrilla forces.

This was stated to-day by Lord Bridgeman, Director-general of the Home Guard, in a review of the lessons that have been learned from the recent big Home Guard exercises.

He pointed out how the training of the Home Guards had been adapted to meet the lessons learned from the Nazi invasion of Holland, Belgium and France and of the capture of Crete.

"Now," he said, "the lessons of the Russian campaign are beginning to come in, and they are most interesting to the Home Guard—particularly the message of Marshal Budenny emphasising the importance of sabotage behind the enemy lines.

"That is a task for which the Home Guard will be particularly suitable. They will carry out all those harassing operations inside the enemy lines which will keep the enemy preoccupied and nervous.

"We in the Home Guard are watching the sabotage campaign in Russia very closely."

I asked Lord Bridgeman if definite instructions had been given to the Home Guard as to how they were to carry out the policy of sabotage in the event of an invasion.

"Have they been told," I asked, "what to destroy, how to destroy it, and when to destroy it?"

He replied: "I can only say that certain instructions have already been issued. They are part of the general instructions to troops issued by the Commander-in-Chief of the Home Forces."

R.A.F. Again in Channel Sweep

The noise of many R.A.F. fighters was heard on the South-east Coast this afternoon as a large force of them made over the Channel towards the French coast.

They appeared to be making for Le Touquet, or further south, and it is believed that they carried out a sweep in that vicinity.

NEWS CHRONICLE, Friday, November 7, 1941.

LATE LONDON EDITION

News Chronicle

No. 29,798 FRIDAY, NOVEMBER 7, 1941 RADIO PAGE 2 ONE PENNY

Finnish Radio This Morning : FINLAND GOING OUT OF THE WAR

"MILITARY operations are drawing to a close as far as our country is concerned," declared a speaker on the Finnish radio this morning.

"Even though the war goes on between the great Powers, Finland will not carry on any longer than is necessary for her own safety and defence, while it is realised that our frontiers cannot finally be determined until the coming peace conference."

This followed radio reports from Stockholm that the Finnish Premier, who visited Stockholm and talked with leading Swedish statesmen concerning the American note to Finland, left Stockholm again by air for Helsinki.

According to a Helsinki message early today, the Finnish Social Democratic Party has asked the Government to find out the views of Parliament in secret session before an answer is sent to the United States note calling on Finland to end the war with Russia.

Stalin Says: "Second Front Will Lighten Our Burden"

IN A ROUSING SPEECH WHICH THE GERMANS TRIED IN VAIN TO JAM, STALIN LAST NIGHT CALLED FOR MORE TANKS, MORE PLANES AND GUNS FOR THE "COMPLETE DESTRUCTION" OF THE NAZI INVADER, AND A VICTORY EFFORT WHICH SHALL LIBERATE ALL PEOPLES FROM HITLER'S YOKE.

Addressing primarily the Moscow Soviet, in session to celebrate the twenty-fourth anniversary of the October Revolution, but speaking, in fact, to the Soviet peoples "living in unbreakable friendship," as well as their Allies, he explained the reasons for Red Army reverses — and promised the Nazi invaders annihilation.

"Doubtless the absence of a second front in Europe against the Germans very such lightens the position of the German armies," he said.

"But there can be no doubt that the appearance of a second front on the European Continent—and it must certainly appear in the immediate future—will very considerably lighten our position."

Prolonged cheering marked the beginning and end of the speech—his first since his address to the Soviet peoples on July 3.

Here is the full text:

"Twenty-four years have passed since the Socialist order was established in our land.

"We have spent more than four months in a fierce struggle against the German invaders. The war has stopped our peaceful construction. We are faced with the task of winning this war.

Miracles of Heroism

"Our Army is performing miracles of heroism, but the enemy does not stop. The German Fascist invaders are plundering our country. They are seizing the best lands of our peasants. They are torturing our peasants and our women and children.

"The enemy is throwing ever-new forces into the front, making every effort to seize Leningrad and Moscow, for he knows [illegible] winter will be bad for him.

"The French Government allowed themselves to be frightened by the spectacle of revolution. They went on their knees to Hitler and refused to defend their own country.

"Despite the efforts of Hess, not only did Britain and America not join the campaign of the German Fascist invaders against our country, but, on the contrary, found themselves in the same camp as the Soviet Union against Hitlerite Germany.

"It appears that the German policy of frightening with the spectre of revolution has exhausted itself and is no longer of any use in the new situation. And not only is it of no use, but it is also dangerous in some respects. The war will have the direct opposite result.

"Hitler's position is not stable. His rear is not stable because of the firm stand of our Red Army. Here, also, Hitler miscalculated.

"Any other State having losses in territory that we have had would not have withstood it, but would have fainted away. Our misfortunes, however, have not weakened this country. They have strengthened it.

"The Germans considered that they could finish the Soviet campaign in a month and a half, and announced this everywhere. But their plan miscarried. They did not manage to finish the war in the West, and their plans for the war in the East also did not materialise.

"Fundamentally More Solid"

"The Germans thought that the Soviets were disorganised behind their lines and that disturbances would occur. They were mistaken.

"Peasants and workers are helping. Never has the morale of the Red Army been as strong as now. If the Soviet State has stood firm it shows that it is fundamentally more solid than other countries.

"The Germans thought that their Army and Navy would destroy ours. But our Army and Navy, although they are not veterans like the Germans, for they have only been fighting four months, and although they lack the cadres which the bellicose Germans have been able to have in their armed forces, are morally stronger because they are defend-

Turn to Back Page, Col. Three

"Misfortune has strengthened the U.S.S.R."

LIFE AT PIER HEAD CORNER

Sailors Ashore Are Forgotten Men

By LOUISE MORGAN

LIVERPOOL, Thursday.

APPOINTED to Liverpool by the Ministry of Labour last March, Mr. R. M. K. Buchanan, regional seamen's welfare officer, has resigned on the ground that his reports have been pigeon-holed. Mr. Buchanan is an ex-lieutenant R.N.

From what I saw in my first half-hour, I guessed why he had resigned. For days and nights I have studied the life of the small, packed corner near the pier head where the men of the Merchant Navy await their next ship. It is hardly better than a concentration camp, except that there is no barbed wire.

All day, in rain and wind, you will find sailors, many of them shipwrecked survivors, sheltering behind buildings near the Pool, as they wait for news of ships. They look like marionettes after the show, lifeless bundles of clothes. There is no room where they can shelter, read, play games or get a hot meal.

SAME OLD YARNS

Hundreds of others wander aimlessly about the streets, or just sit, depressed and apathetic, on their narrow bunks in crowded hostels, thinking "What next?" and finding no answer.

A lad of 19 whom I found on his bunk with his head between his hands said: "Same old faces, same old yarns for three months at sea, and now the same old faces, same old yarns ashore."

After the children of the shelters, sailors at this port are the most bored people I have seen since the war began. No wonder they long to be back at sea. The terrors of torpedoes, exposure, starvation, thirst, or even sharks seem less than the miseries of nothing-to-do and nowhere-to-go.

They should have a sports ground, cinema shows, dances, good canteens, rest and recreation centres, and, above all, the chance of meeting and dancing with the right kind of girls.

Some of these things could be provided by the Mersey Mission, the Liverpool Sailors' Friend and the Sailors' Home—the three old-established societies which have been doing excellent work for the past 100 years and have exceptionally large reserves.

NOT NEEDED

But an official of one of them said to me: "Sailors don't need recreation centres. Give a sailor a pack of cards and that's all he wants. Sailors don't like to be interfered with."

Two of the most prominent "amusements" available are the very things these societies wish to save the men from—drink and prostitutes.

At one notorious spot on the boundary of Bootle and Seaforth these "amusements" abound. You have only to visit the public-houses, crowded with sailors of all ages, or to watch the police of Bootle chasing the women over to Seaforth and the police in Seaforth chasing them back.

Here and there, a few improvements are on the way, and a large empty hall near the Pool is being converted into a canteen and waiting-room. But nothing on an adequate scale is thought of.

I shall next report on the housing conditions.

Now read on the Back Page how these men live at sea—the story of a running battle lasting three nights, between a pack of U-boats and a convoy.

STRONG COUNTER-BLOWS BY MOSCOW ARMIES

This morning's Soviet communique: Fifty-six German planes were destroyed on Wednesday for the loss of 17 Soviet planes; 34 German planes were destroyed near Moscow yesterday.

From DENIS WEAVER
News Chronicle Special Correspondent

STOCKHOLM, Thursday.

ON the eve of the anniversary of the Russian Revolution 24 years ago and the successful defence of Madrid in 1936, the battle for Moscow enters its most critical phase today, with Soviet troops strongly counter-attacking in many sectors around a wide arc of German pressure extending from the north-west to the south.

While today's Russian communiqué speaks of undiminished fighting at every point, Berlin is discreetly silent. This fact is interpreted in Berlin messages as meaning that the German High Command have definite plans and do not wish to disclose them to the enemy, but it is considered here as more probably meaning that they are stymied at present and do not know what to say.

At Mojaisk, midpoint of the arc of the attack, the Germans are definitely on the defensive today—a telling tribute to the sweep and power of Russian artillery fire.

SOVIET COUNTER-THRUST

Fresh attempts to cross the Upper Volga further north and the River Nara met with failure.

Volokolamsk, where Von Bock has been seeking to probe for holes in the defences during the past week without success, has been the scene of a two-day Russian counter-drive which tonight shows no sign of slackening in intensity.

Only at Tula, the most important railway junction and strategically valuable base 100 miles to the south, is the position mentioned by Moscow as being "still grave."

Here frontal attack has alternated with flank attack for a fortnight now without, as yet, any decisive German break-through or decisive Russian counter-thrust.

ZHUKOV'S BRILLIANCE

Military experts here consider that General Zhukov's defence of Tula is one of the most brilliant actions in the whole brilliant story of the defence of Moscow. For, outnumbered in tanks and occupying positions not strengthened by any natural obstacles, and with a more or less open road to Moscow behind him, the Russian commander has succeeded thus far in holding the full pressure of German attack after attack delivered with punch and skill and persistence.

Berlin messages tonight assert that the Germans are now attempting to close in on Moscow by tightening the ring of encirclement to which Von Bock has been driven by the initial failure of the main attack from the west.

No explanations, however, are given regarding how this is to be

Turn to Back Page, Col. Seven

PLEDGE WILL BE FULFILLED —Eden to Molotov

Britain will honour her pledge to the Soviet, says Mr. Eden in a message to M. Molotov on the occasion of the 24th anniversary celebrations of the Soviet National Day.

The Government and the whole British people are united in wholehearted admiration of their ally, says the message, and they deplore the sacrifices which the civilian population have had to undergo. They remain convinced that their bravery and sacrifices will not prove vain.

The message concludes: "His Majesty's Government have pledged their utmost support to the Soviet Government, and they and the British people will ensure that this pledge is fulfilled.

"Thus the combined efforts of the two countries will defeat the common enemy. Thus will we achieve the common aim of all those leagued against Germany, to preserve freedom and civilisation and to build a better future."

B.B.C. Transmitted Stalin's Speech

Stalin's voice was broadcast from London during the night.

In its 11 p.m. European news bulletin the B.B.C. transmitted recorded passages from his speech as well as part of Mr. Roosevelt's broadcast.

The original speech was not heard clearly in London owing to German jamming.

Ninety-nine Lives Lost in the Reuben James

Ninety-nine lives were lost in the sinking of the U.S. destroyer Reuben James, torpedoed on Atlantic convoy duty, according to the revised figures issued in Washington.

Japan's Special Envoy To U.S.

By E. P. MONTGOMERY, the Diplomatic Correspondent

Diplomatic circles in London yesterday were speculating on the probable Japanese motive in sending Mr. Saburo Kurusu, ex-Japanese Ambassador in Berlin, on a special mission to Washington.

Opinion is generally inclined to regard his mission as merely a Japanese gesture to fill in time and to keep up the appearance of negotiating with Washington until the ultimate decision is reached where and when the next Japanese aggression is to take place.

The view is hardening in London that this aggression will take the form of an attack northwards into Yunnan from the Indo-China frontier with the object of capturing Kunming and cutting the Burma Road, and may be timed to start before the end of the year.

NOT RISKING ALL

It is believed that Japan is not yet ready to risk all-out war with the United States and Great Britain—as Germany is anxious to see her do—by attacking Thailand and Burma directly. Nor that she will risk an attack on Russia in Siberia until the outcome of the war between Germany and Russia is more certain.

Chief Tank Engineer

Lord Beaverbrook, Minister of Supply, has appointed Mr. W. A. Robotham, head of the tank development department of Rolls Royce, to be chief engineer on tank design under Mr. Oliver Lucas, the Controller-General of Research and Development, Ministry of Supply.

New 10% Milk Cut Next Week

The Ministry of Food is making a further cut of 10 per cent. in the milk supply from Sunday, a total reduction of 15 per cent. on the basis of sales for the week ending October 25.

"This step," says the Ministry, "is necessary to ensure supplies to priority classes such as children, adolescents, schools, hospitals, invalids and expectant mothers.

"It follows that the reduction in supplies to adults and other non-priority classes will be considerably greater than 15 per cent."

Milkmen in some areas may begin to leave tinned milk on your doorstep.

U.S. Lends Russia £250,000,000

A LEASE-LEND loan of £250,000,000 for Russia was announced by the State Department in Washington last night.

The loan was arranged in communications between Stalin and President Roosevelt, the announcement said, and Stalin had accepted "with sincere gratitude."

The President's offer specified that the indebtedness incurred by the Soviet Union should not be subject to interest and that repayment should not begin until five years after the end of the war.

In a letter to Stalin Mr. Roosevelt expressed the hope that arrangements would be made by the Soviet Union to sell to the United States such available raw materials and commodities as the U.S. might urgently need, and that the proceeds from such sales should be credited to the Soviet Government's account.

"I want to tell you," the President wrote, "of the appreciation of the U.S. Government for the expeditious handling by you of the Moscow supply conference, and to assure you we will carry out to the limit all the implications of it."

[Roosevelt says "America insists on the right to join in the common defence."—See Back Page.]

Litvinov Envoy To Washington

M. Maxim Litvinov has been appointed to succeed M. Constantin Oumansky as Soviet Ambassador to the United States, it is announced in Kuibishev.

M. Litvinov, who is 65, was formerly Ambassador to Britain. Later he served as Soviet Foreign Commissar from 1930 to 1939, with peace by collective security as his policy.

On his eclipse in 1939, when Molotov took over and signed the Nazi-Soviet Pact, Litvinov was removed from the Communist Party's Central Committee, but his influence since has been steadily growing.

The appointment of Litvinov, who with Mr. Roosevelt personally negotiated the recognition of the Soviet Union by the United States, is seen by Washington observers to indicate the great importance Stalin now attaches to close collaboration with America.

Ministry Lifts Ban on Visits to Coast

The ban on visits to the coast from the Wash to the Thames and from Littlehampton to Hastings was suspended at midnight last night.

In making this announcement, which affects many holiday resorts such as Brighton, Worthing, Hastings, Eastbourne, Felixstowe and Cromer, the Ministry of Home Security states that the ban will be reimposed on February 15, or earlier if necessary.

Moreover, anyone now entering the areas with the idea of taking up permanent residence there should first apply to the police for permission, otherwise he may find himself turned out when the ban starts again.

No extra transport will be provided for the areas concerned.

The ban remains in force in the Isle of Wight, practically the whole of Kent, and that part of Sussex east of Hastings.

Bomb Damage In S.E. Last Night

High-explosive bombs were dropped last night in East Anglia and South-East England.

Damage was slight and few casualties were reported. Our night fighters were active.

Raiders were also reported in the South-West.

A.A. guns were active in one area of the Thames Estuary. Firing was sharp, with 10-minute intervals. No bombs fell.

Americans Say "Free Trade Now"

New York, Thursday.—The National Foreign Trade Council—the most influential trade body in the import and export business—has called on the Governments of the United States and Britain "to seek now—**without waiting for peace**—to reach an accord on the principle of greater freedom of trade based on non-discrimination and equality of opportunity."

FILM UNION LEADERS GUILTY

From Our Own Correspondent

New York, Thursday.—Movie union leaders William Bioff and George Browne were found guilty today of extorting 550,000 dollars (about £140,000) from the cinema industry executives under threats of calling strikes.

LONDON BLACK-OUT
5.54 p.m.—7.34 a.m.
Moon rises 7.54 p.m.
New Moon, Nov 19

A corvette, sister ship of the Gladiolus

A Very Gallant Little Vessel is Sunk

Ship of Heroes, Terror of U-Boats

THE corvette Gladiolus—ship of heroes and terror of U-boats—has been sunk. She numbered among her crew one D.S.O., two D.S.C.s, four D.S.M.s and six officers and men mentioned in dispatches.

Lieut.-Commander H. M. C. Sanders, D.S.O., D.S.C., who commanded the Gladiolus, won the D.S.O. and D.S.C. for successful action against submarines.

During the night of June 30, 1940, U-26 torpedoed a ship of the convoy which H.M.S. Gladiolus was escorting. Gladiolus at once counter-attacked with depth charges. U-26 was so damaged that she was forced to surface, when she was sighted and attacked by a Sunderland flying-boat. The Germans then scuttled their U-boat. For this Lieut.-Cmdr. Sanders got the D.S.C.

On September 9, 1941, Lieutenant-Commander Sanders was awarded the D.S.O. "for enterprise, skill and devotion to duty in action against enemy submarines."

NOTORIOUS COMMANDER

This time the Gladiolus shared with two other corvettes the destruction of U-56 on June 27, 1941. This U-boat was commanded by Kapitan-Leutnant Wohlfarth who, with 40 of his ship's company, survived her destruction.

This U-boat captain is particularly notorious, since it was the U-boat under his command which on March 10, 1941, shelled and set on fire the unarmed Icelandic fishing trawler Reykjaborg, killing all but three of her crew.

In a subsequent description of his exploit on the German wireless Wohlfarth boasted that "it was a most beautiful sight to see her burning in the dusk."

MANY OTHER FIGHTS

In addition to her successes in action with U-26 and U-56, H.M.S. Gladiolus took a leading part in many other encounters with U-boats, and for their part in these several actions there were awarded to the ship's company of H.M.S. Gladiolus a total of one D.S.O., two D.S.C.s and four D.S.M.s.

In addition six officers and men were mentioned in dispatches.

H.M.S. Gladiolus was built at Smith's Dock, Middlesbrough.

Sunday Dispatch

141st Year. No. 7,306. 2d. NOVEMBER 9, 1941. Radio Page 7.

Pilots Tell The Whole Story Of The

HEAVIEST RAF RAID EVER

ODESSA LOOKS LIKE VAST 'BROKEN TOY'

THE "immense chaos" left behind by the Russians at Odessa is described by a correspondent of the Vichy News Agency who inspected Odessa from the air.

"Three weeks after the occupation by Rumanian troops smoke still rises from the ruins," he writes.

"From a plane the city looks like an immense broken toy. Not a ship can be seen on the sea. Surrounding country and villages have been turned into a vast desert over which silence has closed down.

"Places frequently mentioned in communiqués now exist merely as burnt-out walls.

"Trenches zig-zag across fields strewn with smashed-up tanks, abandoned guns, broken - down trees, animals' skeletons, destroyed munition wagons, and all the mournful debris of battle.

TRAINS WRECKED

"Not one house in five still has a roof. Not one factory chimney remains. Blown-up gasometers have crashed on to houses. Entire trains are overturned on their tracks.

"The beautiful avenues leading to the sea are blocked with debris and rubbish. Barricades of sacks of earth and overturned tramcars are still there.

"It is dangerous to enter buildings that are still intact. Every day there are terrific explosions as delayed action bombs go off.

"Yesterday a house blew up in the centre of the city near the Opera House, which was destroyed several days ago. It is believed that Russians may still be hiding in the catacombs. Several thousand people are still living in the city's ruins.

"In the harbour a forest of chimneys and masts emerges from the water. The entrances to the basins are mined and blocked by sunken ships."

'GREAT WARRIOR'

Winston— 'THE OLD WARHORSE' —Says Stalin

THIS is how the leaders of the Allied nations have recently spoken of each other:

Joseph Stalin (*by Winston Churchill*)—"That great warrior."

Winston Churchill (*by Joseph Stalin*)—"The old warhorse."

Stalin's apt phrase was quoted yesterday by Lord Beaverbrook when he described how he told Stalin that Churchill had said Britain would "take a chance" in depriving herself of aluminium in order to supply Russia.

The Prime Minister paid his tribute to Stalin in a speech at Sheffield yesterday.

The Premier was addressing thousands of workers from the balcony of Sheffield Town Hall.

He said: "None of us can say at what moment the bugles shall sound the 'Cease fire,' but we may be sure that however long and hard it may be the British Commonwealth of Nations will come through united, undaunted, stainless, unflinching.

"Many disappointments have occurred, very often many mistakes, but when we look back to 15 months ago and remember that then we were alone and almost unarmed and we now see our great forces developing their strength with great weapons;

INSPIRATION

"When we look across the wide stretches of European lands and see that great warrior Stalin at the head of his valiant Russians;

"When we look westward across the ocean and see Americans sending their war vessels out to rid the seas of pirates in order that they may carry to the fighting front line, without regard to the opposition they may encounter, weapons, munitions, and food we require;

"When we see this, it is a message of inspiration because we are sure that before we get to the end of the road we shall all be together.

"The work of everyone is of vital importance. This is a struggle for life. A struggle in which every man and woman, old and young, can play a hero's part."

Earlier, Mr. Churchill said to workers in a factory. "Everyone who keeps his time is doing his best to rid the world of this curse of war and Hitlerism. I am proud to come among you, because I am told you have lost only four and a half hours' time during air raids, although since January there have been 120 alerts.

"This is the way to stand up to it, as the artillerymen do with their guns, as the airmen do in cutting them down from the high air. You are doing your bit in the same way.

"Their work cannot begin until yours has finished. We have only to hold together, to go safely through the dark valley, and then we will see if we can make something lasting of our victory."

Professor Joad Explains

LAST week the *Sunday Dispatch* appealed to Professor C. E. M. Joad, star of the B.B.C. Brains Trust, to withdraw his name from an appeal urging that Britain and Germany should come to an agreement to stop night bombing.

We gave convincing reasons why night bombing by Britain should be continued.

Mr. Noel Pemberton-Billing, Independent candidate in the Hampstead by-election, wrote to Professor Joad challenging him to a public debate on the question.

Professor Joad replied that his many engagements prevented a debate of this kind, but, he added, "the considerations which have influenced me, such as they are, are set out in an article in next Sunday's *Sunday Dispatch*."

The article by Professor Joad is in Page 4.

No Rush To The Coast

THERE was no rush to Britain's "reprieved" south-east and south coast yesterday. Most of the resorts reported a trickle of visitors, but there was no difficulty anywhere in feeding them.

Motorists were stopped on the road to East Anglian towns and told that although the ban on visitors had been lifted, motor-cars were still banned. Permits would be issued only to holders of "E" supplementary petrol allowances.

Brighton is expecting amny more visitors in the coming weeks. The manageress of a sea-front hotel told the *Sunday Dispatch*: "The ending of the ban will probably be our salvation."

Mr. J. Kennedy Alerton, town clerk of Worthing, said: "I have had many letters from Londoners who wish to visit us. We shall probably have a big influx of visitors during the winter."

Afternoon trains at Southend brought several suitcase visitors.

Man Gives 373 Blood Transfusions

A man named Antonio Francisco has given 373 blood transfusions at the Coimbra Hospital in Lisbon since he walked into the hospital two years ago and volunteered for this service.

Nothing is known as to where he lives, or whether he is rich or poor.

Germany May Allow French Convoys

"This possibility is not out of the question," said German officials in Berlin yesterday, when asked about reports that Germany might allow French warships to convoy French food ships and other transports through the British blockade.

The officials said that they could not, at present, give a full statement on this subject.—*B.U.P.*

Teachers Give £750

The executive of the National Union of Teachers yesterday agreed to give £500 to Mrs. Winston Churchill's Russian Red Cross Fund and £250 to the Red Cross Book Appeal Fund for British prisoners.

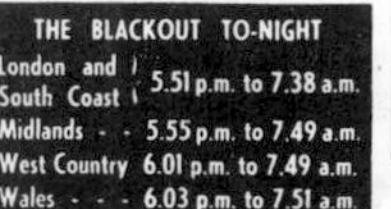

THE BLACKOUT TO-NIGHT	
London and South Coast	5.51 p.m. to 7.38 a.m.
Midlands	5.55 p.m. to 7.49 a.m.
West Country	6.01 p.m. to 7.49 a.m.
Wales	6.03 p.m. to 7.51 a.m.

Berlin Hammered Despite Appalling Weather; 500 Planes—37 Missing

FLYING IN APPALLING WEATHER CONDITIONS, WITH THE TEMPERATURE OFTEN 34 DEGREES BELOW ZERO, THE ROYAL AIR FORCE HAS DELIVERED THE HEAVIEST BOMBING ATTACK EVER CARRIED OUT ON GERMANY.

At least 500 of our biggest bombers, the "Sunday Dispatch" learns, took part in the raid—on Friday night. The chief objective was Berlin, which was subjected to the most severe attack it has ever experienced, both from the viewpoint of the numbers of machines and their bomb tonnages.

Berliners spent hours in their shelters as the city rocked with the exploding bombs. And it appeared as if they might have a second night of it, for at 7 o'clock last night Berlin Radio went off the air.

A total of 37 of our bombers are missing from the raid, most of them having been forced down through suddenly deteriorating weather conditions over the Continent. The losses were not due to any improvement in the enemy's defences. The weather was, in fact, almost too bad for night fighters to be able to operate.

The Air Ministry communiqué describing the raid stated:

> Berlin, Cologne, and Mannheim were the main objectives assigned for operations on the heaviest scale by Bomber Command last night. Very bad weather was encountered over the interior of Germany, but Stirling, Halifax, Wellington, and Whitley bombers reached the Berlin area in large numbers and dropped their bombs in spite of thunderstorms and severe icing.
>
> At Cologne, Manchesters and Hampdens had good success. Several other towns in Germany were bombed as well as the docks at Boulogne and Ostend. Mines were also laid in enemy waters.
>
> A number of our bombers were forced down by the weather during the return journey. A total of 37 of our aircraft are reported missing.

Four of the missing bombers are known to have force-landed on the Continent. In each the crews, all of whom were safe, set fire to their machines. One of them came down in Sweden, one in Norway, and two in France.

The Nazi High Command communiqué yesterday admitted Berlin had been bombed during widespread raids on German territory, but a military spokesman said "only seven people had been killed and 32 injured in the capital." At first they claimed six of our machines had been forced down; later they made it 19, and still later 27, a figure to which they adhered, even though we admitted 37.

Although not mentioned in the R.A.F. communiqué, the Swedish Radio yesterday stated that British planes flew over Oslo Fjord and dropped bombs near the fortress of Akershus. "Three Hampden-type machines were shot down by gunfire," it added. "Four airmen, two of them injured, were captured, while another two were found dead."

'Burnt' By Sextant

Here is the story of the raids—as told by the crews:—

The observer of a Wellington bomber described how broken cloud gradually thickened as they flew, until towards Berlin he could see nothing of the ground. Occasional gaps in the higher cloud were of no use because they were blocked by layers below. He had to steer entirely by the stars.

"The temperature was as low as 34 degrees below zero," he added. "When I went to the Astro-dome [the small transparent look-out post on the top of the fuselage] to take some sights, to keep my hands more free I wore only my silk inner gloves.

"It was agonising just to touch the sextant, and the pain bit into my fingers as though they were being scalded. I could not hold on to the sextant for more than 30 seconds, and afterwards it took me ten minutes to get the circulation back in my hands. When I went to pick up my leather gloves they were frozen as stiff as a board.

"I saw long icicles on the bottom of the pilot's oxygen mask. He broke one off and threw it at me to show he was keeping cheerful."

The navigator of another plane found unbroken layers of cloud until he was near Berlin. "Most of it," he said, "was flat and thick like a woolly blanket. There was a brilliant moon and plenty of stars. It looked cold, and it was cold. The windows frosted up and moisture inside the aircraft froze. Where I work is about

Continued in Page Eight.

These are a plane-spotter's caricatures of the R.A.F. planes which took part in Friday night's raid. By exaggerating detail the cartoonist helps to identify the aircraft. Left to right they are: Wellington II, Stirling, and Whitley.

—PETAIN'S MONEY—

MONEY in this country stated to belong to 85-years-old Marshal Pétain is shortly to be discussed in Parliament.

Mr. S. S. Silverman, Labour M.P. for Nelson and Colne, has given notice to ask the Chancellor of the Exchequer whether he has inquired into the amount and nature of the personal funds deposited here by Pétain, whether Pétain has been allowed to transfer either capital or dividends to France, and, if so, what were the circumstances entitling the Marshal to these exceptional privileges.

Some months ago it was reported that before the Munich crisis in 1938 the Marshal bought a life annuity in London. It amounted to a few hundred pounds a year, and was believed to have been added to later by other annuities bought in London by the Marshal's brokers.

After France fell the income from these annuities was "frozen." It went into the hands of the Custodian of Enemy Debts.

This "frozen" income began to accumulate, and in the early months of this year efforts were made on behalf of Pétain to secure its release. Pressure, it was stated, was exerted both in Paris and in London to bring this about.

A big American banking interest was understood to be carrying out negotiations on Pétain's behalf. His agents had approached the American Embassy in Vichy. The insurance company concerned could not act without sanction of the Custodian of Enemy Debts.

The possibility of an appeal direct to Mr. Winston Churchill for the release of the money was mentioned. Pétain was said to be relying on the income from these London annuities for his normal living expenses, because he is not a wealthy man.

This was last May. In January, four months earlier, a statement issued in Vichy disclosed that for the ensuing three months Pétain was to have an allowance of 954,000 francs.

This allowance worked out at the rate of about £20,000 a year—approximately the sum paid to the former President of the Republic.

Vichy explained that out of this sum the Marshal had to keep up his household and secretariat, and that the rest was spent "to help those in need whom the Marshal meets on his travels through France, or as answers to the many letters he receives."

U.S. WARSHIPS TO OPERATE FROM ICELAND NAVAL BASE

COLONEL KNOX, United States Secretary for the Navy, yesterday announced the establishment of a naval operating base in Iceland, which thus becomes one of the United States Navy's most important operations centres.

Rear-Admiral James L. Kauffman has been appointed Commandant of the base.

"The command of the base shall include all United States naval shore activities and United States naval local defence forces, district naval craft, and any additional units as may be assigned by the Atlantic Fleet," says the announcement.

This means that warship operations will be conducted from Iceland.

GOVERNMENT RESIGNS

The Iceland Government, headed by Prime Minster Herman Jonasson, has fallen for the second time in 16 days, when the Coalition it represents was split by Jonasson's Progressive Party.

Progressives introduced a Bill limiting the cost of living, thus breaking the political truce.

The Bill was defeated, and Jonasson handed in his resignation.

Steps towards forming a new Government will probably be taken this week-end.

R.A.F. SWEEP OVER FRANCE AGAIN

Sky Was Alive With Our Machines

WAVE upon wave of R.A.F. bombers and fighters crossed the south-east coast at 20-minute intervals yesterday in another great daylight sweep.

It was just before midday that the first squadrons swept over the coast Channelwards. All were flying so high that they could not be seen, but judging by the roar of their engines they must have been in considerable force (says a *Sunday Dispatch* observer).

For a long time the sky appeared to be alive with machines, and the drone of their engines was heavy and incessant.

People stood in groups on the sea front straining their eyes to get a glimpse of this passing air armada, but the machines were at too great a height to be seen.

That the attack was much farther inland than usual was borne out by the fact that no explosions were heard on this side of the Channel.

FROM BOULOGNE

Many Spitfires and Hurricanes were among the aircraft that passed over the south-east coast at Dungeness and swept out across the Channel.

There was a light haze over the Strait and the French coast was hidden from this side. Within an hour there was a procession of groups of fighters coming back from the French coast, many from the direction of Boulogne.

Last night the German News Agency, quoted by *Reuter*, said:

"A mixed formation of British planes attempted to cross the Channel at noon in the direction of the Occupied Territory."

"In air combats over Calais German fighters, according to reports so far received, shot down 14 planes without loss to themselves."

Eire To Send Us 'Ready Meals'

Lord Woolton is completing negotiations for the purchase of the whole of Eire's exportable surplus of canned steak and canned "ready meals"—amounting to 60,000,000lb.

The steak is valued at the full rate of 16 points per lb. under the new "points" rationing scheme which begins on Monday week; while the "ready meals" are scheduled at 8 points.

Lost—855,000 Days

DURING the first nine months of this year 855,000 working days were lost owing to trade disputes, states the Ministry of Labour Gazette.

This is over 100,000 more than in the period January to September, 1940.

The largest number of people affected was in the coal mining industry, where nearly 115,000 were involved. The engineering and shipbuilding industries lost 354,000 working days.

'You Will' Not 'Will You?' Wanted

After two years of war against the most formidable military machine ever mis-begotten by men, the people of Great Britain were tired of appeals and exhortations, said Commander Stephen King-Hall, M.P., at Ilfracombe yesterday.

"They want orders and not bromides or rhetoric," he declared. "There is too much 'Will you?' and not enough of 'You will.'" If the swastika ever flew over this country they would ask themselves in whispers whether everything had been done to avert the disaster. It would be too late to ask those questions then.

Enemy Lie Low In Middle East

Yesterday's Middle East communiqué from General Headquarters, Cairo, stated: There was no enemy air or artillery activity during the night November 6-7. Our patrols carried out extensive reconnaissances without interference, and gained valuable information regarding the enemy defences opposite our southern sector.

During the night November 6-7 our patrols in the frontier area between Halfaya and Sidi Omar made contact with enemy patrols at a number of points. In these patrol clashes we sustained three casualties.

They Want To Lift Bell-ringing Ban

Seventy of Britain's leading campanologists (bell-ringers) want the church bells to ring again, and they are to appeal to the authorities to lift the ban.

The bell-ringers, who met in London yesterday to celebrate the 300th anniversary of the Society of College Youths say the embargo, enforced when invasion seemed imminent, could be raised for half an hour on Sunday morning.

The Right To Torpedo

The Nazi official paper, *Voelkischer Beobachter*, said yesterday that Germany was entitled to torpedo without warning any United States armed merchantman—and added: "Roosevelt knows that merchantmen cannot reckon on special treatment within the blockade zone or in British ports."

LATEST

2

"PORTUGUESE SHIP ORDERED TO GIB."

Breslau radio claimed late last night that the Portuguese coastal steamer Marie Louise had been stopped by a British warship in Portuguese territorial waters and ordered to proceed to Gibraltar.—B.U.P.

FIERCE CRIMEA BATTLES

Moscow night communiqué stated: Our troops fought the enemy on all fronts to-day. Particularly fierce fighting went on in Crimean sector.—Reuter.

Milkona

CROWSON and Son, Ltd., of Smithfields, E.C., and the British Doughnut Co., Ltd., of Gloucester-gate, N.W., were summoned at Saffron Walden yesterday for giving to a certain food product, "Milkona," a label calculated to mislead as to its nature, substance, and quality. They were also summoned for giving false warranty in writing.

The hearing was adjourned until December 3. Supt. Faulkner said he understood there was a similar prosecution at Northampton on December 2.

A Group That Needs Watching

THE Government should watch *Socialist Appeal*, the propaganda journal of a group whose forces are drawn from the "Trotskyist" elements, who broke away from orthodox ("Stalinist") Communism, and also certain elements in the Independent Labour Party.

These forces have nothing to do with the British Socialist and Labour movements or with the Communist Party of Great Britain. They work on their own, but they have "spiritual" links with those people, of varying political complexion, who advocate a negotiated peace and disguise their real aims under the pretence of calling for a "People's Government." This phrase will be recognised by anybody who has heard the German radio ghost interjecting with exhortations for the formation of a People's Government here.

The *Socialist Appeal* group attempt to influence munition workers against a greater war effort in the factories; and the method is to try to throw a spanner into the scheme for joint committees of workers and managements for the speeding up and increase of production.

The following is a recent example: At a meeting at the Stoll Theatre in London a propagandist of the *Socialist Appeal* declared: "Where production committees are set up the bosses will attempt to use them as a means to paralysing independent action on the part of the working-class and can only agree to production committees if they are completely under their control. The bosses will make use of the workers on the committees precisely as the capitalist Government uses the Labour leaders to impose restrictive legislation which would not otherwise be possible."

Socialist Appeal has three main lines of attack, as follow:

1.—That it is useless to have victory without revolution.
2.—That the British Government is waging a capitalist war.
3.—That the "all aid to Russia" appeal is a "Stalinist racket."

The first point is an echo of the old Trotskyist arguments—i.e., that there must be "permanent revolution" throughout the world, as opposed to the Stalinist argument that Russia could maintain her own Communist State in a capitalist world. The third point is an echo of the old Trotsky-Stalin feud. The phrase "Stalinist racket" is also an indirect way of alleging that "Stalin has sold out to Churchill and the *capitalists*."

All this may sound academic to the non-Communist world. But it is very real to people versed in Communist ideology.

This being the case, it is not difficult to see why the people behind the propaganda of the *Socialist Appeal* are making use of the old Stalinism - versus - Trotskyism feud among Communist workers. It is an adroit and clever technique. And it is, moreover, completely in line with the Nazi technique of exploiting differences with a view to creating disunity and breakdown from within.

Copies of the *Socialist Appeal* have been circulated among munition workers, and it has been on sale outside public buildings in London. Its use of the word "Socialist" is deliberately calculated to mislead.

Doubtless many innocents are being taken in by this propaganda. Especially the half - baked and muddle minded. But there is nothing half-baked or muddle-minded about the propaganda itself or the aims of its promoters.

During the period of the Russo-German Pact, the policies of the Soivet Union and of Britain in regard to this war were opposed. Since the German attack on Russia and the Anglo-Russian Alliance the policies of London and Moscow have come into harmony.

Orthodox Communists are now supporting the Government's war effort, but the forces behind the *Socialist Appeal* are not promoting the ideology or policy of any one party. They represent people of various political origins who—some of them wittingly and others unwittingly and for a variety of reasons—are playing the Nazi game of campaigning against the victory of Britain and her Allies.

This is a jumble of Left-wingism, Pacifism, pro-Germanism, disguised Fascism, downright roguery, and mere boneheadedness; the sort of political scrambled egg which is the delight of the astute wagers of political warfare in Berlin.

It has been necessary to give these details about policies and ideologies in order to explain the methods being used by the promoters of the *Socialist Appeal*, and to give some idea also of the kind of political confusion which they are endeavouring to exploit for defeatist ends.

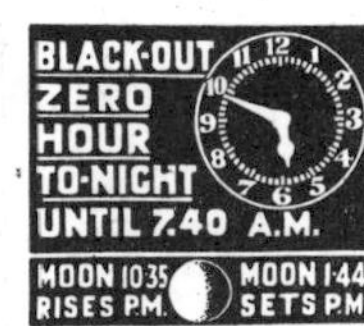

Daily Express

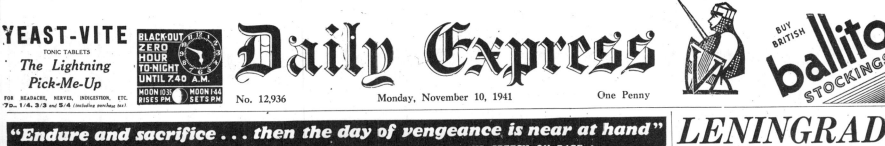

No. 12,936 Monday, November 10, 1941 One Penny

"Endure and sacrifice . . . then the day of vengeance is near at hand"

THIS IS LORD BEAVERBROOK'S WARNING. WILLIAM BARKLEY REPORTS HIS SPEECH ON PAGE 3

THE NAVY swoops off Taranto, smashes all ten ships in two Italian convoys, sinks an Italian destroyer and damages another. No British loss—not even a ship's paint scratched.

THE RUSSIANS open attack eastwards from Leningrad, and continue counter-attacks on Moscow front, where Germans prepare new push. Nazis claim Crimea progress.

TARANTO! THE NAVY SINKS 10 OUT OF 10

The eve

of victory —if you play your part

Women at War Reporter
HILDE MARCHANT

THIS is the eve of November the Eleventh, the eve of the day which represents Victory.

It is a victory which can only be repeated if every man and woman in Britain will now put forward the greatest effort for this country.

We appeal to every woman in this country to make up her mind tonight to take a part in the war effort.

There are many types of jobs waiting for women to do. I have told you of the work waiting in munitions, the services and child welfare.

Yet there are still too many idle hands. This week-end the West End of London has been packed with women shop-gazing, drinking tea, chatting in hotel lounges.

Yesterday, as I walked around the cinema belt, I saw girls queueing in the streets and others queueing at cafés, and I wondered how many could honestly give the answer—"I have earned my day off. I have done a week's hard war work."

Some of the women who wandered round the West End yesterday were munition workers having a day off. Their consciences are clear. Some were girls from the services who had changed into civilian clothes for a few hours. They are entitled to their leisure.

NOV. 10
GET INTO THE WAR
TODAY

Some were women who give part-time work as wardens and welfare workers. They, too, have no cause to question their right to a few hours' relaxation.

But to the others who merely climaxed an idle week with an idle day in town, rode on buses which were conducted by women, wasted the time of waitresses, I say this :—

Once again our country has reached the eleventh hour. History will repeat itself only if every woman in this country rises up and creates a greater victory.

Here is yet another way you can serve Britain :—

The Ministry of Health is now calling for thousands of women nurses.

The wounded soldiers, sailors and airmen need your care and patience. The children in the evacuated towns and villages need their health watched.

Civil defence services need thousands of women to care for the winter's air-raid casualties.

There are several branches of the nursing services. The Civil Nursing Reserve needs nursing auxiliaries. This is open to women of 18 to 55, without previous nursing experience. There is a short course of training in a hospital, then you are sent to first-aid posts in factories or towns, or air-raid shelters.

NOV. 10
GET INTO THE WAR
TODAY

Or you may work on casualty evacuation trains, rest centres, or the reception areas.

The uniform, a coat of grey-blue gabardine edged with red braid, a blue felt hat, and white indoor coat, is provided free. You will receive free board, lodging and laundry, and will be paid £55 a year.

This is the appeal the Ministry of Health makes to you :—

"Already 25,000 Nursing Auxiliaries are serving their country. If you will take up nursing for the period of war and will sacrifice personal convenience to your country's needs, and go wherever the sick and wounded and children need you—become a Nursing Auxiliary."

You can serve the wounded of this war by offering your name at a labour exchange.

Women of Britain — dedicate November 11, 1941, by volunteering to serve your country to the day of a New Victory.

Little ships defy big guns, destroy two convoys

IN a David and Goliath battle off Taranto, almost on the anniversary of the great Taranto victory last year, a tiny British naval force has sunk two Italian convoys of ten ships under the guns of Italian cruisers twice the size of our largest ship engaged.

One escorting Italian destroyer was also sunk, another was seriously damaged, and a third was later seen to be in tow.

This is the biggest Axis convoy yet sunk in the war. It follows the terrific blitz the R.A.F. has been giving Italian cities and ships, and adds to the heavy toll the Navy has already taken of Axis tonnage on the supply route to Libya.

The action took place at 1 a.m. yesterday after Maryland patrolling aircraft had spotted one Italian convoy. Our ships were the 5,270-ton cruisers Aurora and Penelope and the 1,920-ton destroyers Lance and Lively. Opposed to them were two Italian 10,000-ton cruisers of the Trento class and at least four destroyers.

NOT EVEN A SCRATCH

In command of our small force was 42-year-old Captain William Gladstone Agnew, of Aurora, one of the youngest captains in the Navy, and outstanding gunnery expert. He joined action at once against the larger and more heavily armed Italian escorts.

After sinking both convoys, and sending an Italian destroyer to the bottom of the Mediterranean, our ships returned unharmed without even a scratch on their paint.

Here is the full story of the battle, told by the Admiralty last night :—

"Two convoys of enemy supply ships have been annihilated in the Central Mediterranean and severe loss inflicted on their escorts in a brilliant and determined action by H.M. ships.

"On Saturday afternoon an enemy convoy consisting of eight supply ships escorted by destroyers was sighted south of Taranto by a Maryland aircraft on reconnaissance.

SECOND CONVOY JOINS

"A patrolling force consisting of the cruisers H.M.S. Aurora (Captain W. G. Agnew, R.N.), and H.M.S. Penelope (Captain A. D. Nicholl, R.N.), and the destroyers H.M.S. Lance (Lieut.-Commander R. W. F. Northcott, R.N.), and H.M.S. Lively (Lieut.-Commander W. F. E. Hussey, R.N.), was directed to intercept.

"This force, under the command of Captain Agnew, made contact with the enemy at about 1 a.m. on Sunday.

"It was then found that the large convoy of eight supply ships, escorted by destroyers, was being joined by another convoy of two supply ships escorted by two destroyers.

"The operation was being covered by two powerful 10,000-ton eight-inch gun cruisers of the Trento class.

BACK PAGE, COL. FOUR

AT 1 O'CLOCK IN THE MORNING—

—from this cruiser, the 5,270-ton AURORA, Captain W. G. Agnew, R.N., gave the order that led to the sinking of two Italian convoys.

INSIDE RUSSIA

THE Daily Express news service from Russia is the greatest in the world.

On PAGE TWO TODAY Ralph Ingersoll, noted New York editor who went round the world for the Daily Express, tells of the hour he spent with Stalin.

TOMORROW on the same page Quentin Reynolds, Daily Express Special Correspondent in Russia, describes a visit he made to a Russian arms factory hidden in the steppes, where he watched shells and bombs pouring out a thousand miles behind the front,

Mrs. Agnew dropped her stitches

"It was so thrilling"

Express Staff Reporter

THE wife of the captain of the cruiser Aurora was sitting at home knitting herself a jumper when she heard of her husband's exploit. The news made her drop several stitches—"it was so unexpected and thrilling," she said last night.

"I had not the faintest idea where he was," Mrs. Agnew said. "An air mail letter from him the other day merely said 'Just off again.' I certainly did not expect to hear of him again so soon—and with such news.

"His success is dumbfounding. It sounded too good to be true.

"I often knit things for Bill, but this was a jumper for myself, so dropping the stitches didn't matter so much, though I will treasure this jumper as a memory of a great occasion.

"It is amazing getting news like this while sitting at home alone on a Sunday evening, and to think that the action took place only a few hours before while we were asleep.

Drives ambulance

"I expect all the wives and families of the men with him will be just as thrilled and excited."

Captain Agnew is a Londoner—his father was principal of Agnew's, Bond-street art dealers—and he has a brother, Lieut.-Commander Hugh L. Agnew, also in the Navy.

"My husband, when he was promoted just over a year ago, was the second youngest captain in the Navy," Mrs. Agnew said. "He has had plenty of action in this war, and his speciality is gunnery.

"He has a marvellous eye, and is an all-round sportsman. He represented the Navy at Rugby and lawn tennis.

"Nowadays he is keen on squash and golf. He loves to potter about the garden, but he gets in as much golf and walking as he can."

While Mrs. Agnew was speaking on the telephone, neighbours who had heard the news began calling to congratulate her. "I shall be under fire all the evening," she said, "but it will be worth it."

Mrs. Agnew's own war job is ambulance driving.

To the wife of **Captain A. D. Nicholl**, of the Penelope, the news was also "all rather sudden" because she, too, had no idea where her husband was.

Plays a trumpet

"So far as I know," she said, "this is the first important action he has been in since the war began."

Captain Nicholl is 44, and his home is at Radlett, Herts.

Friends phoned **Mrs. Hussey**, wife of the 33-year-old commander of the destroyer Lively to tell her the news.

"I just didn't believe it, at first, but I was delighted when it was confirmed," she said.

She has two children, Christabel, not quite 12 months old, and Andrew, aged four. They are living at Chester.

"No, I did not wake Andrew to tell him the news," she said, "but he will be thrilled to hear of it in the morning."

Mrs. Hussey revealed that her husband has one hobby—"he plays a trumpet."

Lieut.-Commander Hussey won the D.S.C. in November 1939 for anti-submarine work and has been mentioned in despatches twice.

He is a native of Cheltenham, and entered the Navy, via Dartmouth, at the age of 13.

Berlin off at 7.30

Berlin Radio went off the air soon after 7.30 last night.

ASSASSIN ON A BICYCLE

BAGDAD, Sunday.

FAKHRI BEY NASHASHIBI, leader of the moderate Arab Defence Party, who was "condemned to death" by Palestine extremists in 1939, was shot dead by a man on a bicycle in a Bagdad main street today.

Two shots were fired as Fakhri Bey came out of his hotel. The assassin escaped.

Fakhri Bey, who was 45, came to London in 1939 to attend the Palestine conference on the future of his country.

He had his death warrant in his pocket. It was signed by a "general" of the extremists, led by the ex-Mufti of Jerusalem, who is now in Berlin.

While Fakhri Bey was in London his cousin was shot dead and another cousin wounded. Fakhri Bey was wounded by a gunman in 1937.—Reuter.

William Tell banned

BERLIN, Sunday.—Schiller's play, "William Tell," has been banned by the Nazis, because it "puts the Swiss in a too heroic light."—A.P.

The absent guest

THE LUFTWAFFE

Express Special Correspondent
QUENTIN REYNOLDS

KUIBISHEV, Sunday.

ONE invited guest failed to appear at the celebration of the 24th birthday of Soviet Russia in Kuibishev Square.

The British Ambassador (Sir Stafford Cripps) was there. The American Ambassador (Mr. Laurence Steinhardt) was there.

So were 100,000 Soviet soldiers, workers and peasants with many Soviet leaders.

The invited guest that did not appear was the Nazi Air Force.

Two weeks ago the Soviet authorities announced that the official celebration would be held in Kuibishev, and not in Moscow.

HATS WAVED

It was a clear-cut challenge to the Luftwaffe to attend this demonstration 500 miles east of Moscow.

Here was a chance for the German airmen to destroy Government leaders, high-ranking military leaders, and at least one army division with a great mass of tanks, guns and other equipment.

Clouds and slight overcast provided a perfect setting for dive-bombing. But the only aircraft to appear were 300 Red Air Force bombers and fighters, which flew over the square at 500 feet in perfect formation.

For three and a half hours the parade went on. The invited guest was still absent.

'R.A.F. raids Oslo twice'

Two British raids on Oslo were reported yesterday. Boston radio quoted news from Oslo that our bombers were there yesterday afternoon.

A Stockholm message said that many heavy bombers attacked Akershus fort and the German administrative buildings early on Saturday.

Bomber down

An enemy bomber was destroyed last night.

German planes raided a south-east coast town, where houses were wrecked and occupants escaped with slight injuries; and a town in the Thames Estuary, where there were no casualties.

—167—168—

Benghazi raids Nos. 167 and 168 (in daylight), within a few hours of each other, were announced last night.

"Stop broadcasts"

ANKARA, Sunday.—The Axis has asked Turkey to stop Ankara radio transmitting broadcasts to America.—Express.

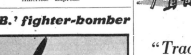

The new 'H.B.' fighter-bomber

FIRST picture of a one-man bomber, its bomb-beams filled, ready for the take off. This bomber is a fighter. . . . An "H.B."—one of the Hurricanes that have been adapted for attacks in daylight on Channel invasion ports and enemy shipping.

Some of them were in successful week-end sweeps. Once these machines unload their bombs they regain their speed as fighters, and Luftwaffe interception planes have little chance with them.

From France to join A.T.S.

Mrs. Evelyn C. Hutchison, in Monte Carlo, heard a British radio appeal for A.T.S. recruits. She decided to get out of Vichy France and join up.

She reached Portugal, then sailed in a British ship. Now she is in Britain, ready to enlist.

NO GOOSE-STEP For 'free' Nazis

A German broadcaster said last night that Hitler's men do not goose-step in Russia because :—

"The severe discipline of the drill ground had to become the voluntary subordination of the free soldier, or the army could never have measured its strength with the Soviet giant."

LENINGRAD ARMY ATTACK

Nazis claim: Nearer Sebastopol

Express Staff Reporter E. D. MASTERMAN

STOCKHOLM, Sunday.

GENERAL BONDAREV, the Leningrad commander, reinforced by 20,000 or 30,000 fresh troops, today opened an attack east of the city with several of his elite motorised divisions.

He struck towards Shlisselburg, town 30 miles from Leningrad, where the River Neva flows into Lake Ladoga.

The German forces menaced Shlisselburg some weeks ago, but, unable to continue their advance, dug in east of the town.

General Bondarev's aim is to establish the strongest possible positions along the shores of Ladoga, in view of the menace to Leningrad from this direction when the ice on the lake is strong enough to bear armoured columns.

His attack follows the smashing of the German offensive launched a few days ago with 100,000 men. It indicates that he still has immense forces at his disposal.

LENINGRAD weather : North-east gale; several degrees colder.

Again the Germans claimed that Leningrad was heavily shelled and was bombed by day and by night.

They admitted "three desperate Soviet counter-attacks" in the Leningrad zone, but claimed that

BACK PAGE, COL. FIVE

Frustration

REPORT last night by a German newspaperman at the front :—

The ocean of mud in the Ukraine is unimaginable. On this and other fronts the Luftwaffe is unable to build advance airfields.

Men sink into the swamps up to their knees, vehicles up to their axles.

Admission

BERLIN'S newspaper Boersen Zeitung, also complaining of "these enormous distances, these smashed roads, this scorched-earth destruction," said that the Red Army was the most stubborn and best-equipped that the Germans had yet faced.

Wonder

A VICHY news agency correspondent who visited Tiraspol, on the river Dniester said:—

"Of the 70,000 population more than 60,000 evacuated with the Soviet troops.

"Rumanian troops found not a stick of furniture in the houses, not one serviceable utensil.

"One wonders how the Russians were able to carry out such a complete removal. They took off everything, including beds and tables."

FINNS SAY 'NO' Answer soon to U.S.

Helsinki radio said last night: "The United States has exerted pressure on the Finnish Government to end the war with Russia. We will answer the American demand shortly—and the answer will be in the negative."—B.U.P.

M.C. for Tobruk Pole

CAIRO, Sunday.—First awards to Polish troops at Tobruk, announced today, include a Military Cross and two Military Medals.—A.P.

4 A.M. LATEST

FIRST INDIAN V.C.s PRESENTED

NEW DELHI, Monday.—Viceroy, Lord Linlithgow, accompanied by General Wavell, Commander-in-Chief India, today presented first two V.C.s won by Indians in this war. Recipients were Lieutenant P. S. Bhagat and widow of late Subedar (N.C.O.) Richpal Ram.

Both V.C.s were won in Abyssinia. Ram was killed and Bhagat wounded.—A.P.

ARK ROYAL SUNK!

NAZIS' FAVORITE TARGET: ENGLAND'S GIANT AIRCRAFT CARRIER, THE ARK ROYAL, OFTEN BOMBARDED, FALLS PREY TO TORPEDO

B 2

NIGHT EDITION

No. 19,684—DAILY | In Two Sections—Section One | FRIDAY, NOVEMBER 14, 1941 | DAILY 3 Cents | SATURDAY 5 Cents | SUNDAY 10 Cents

IN THE NEWS

THE two vital articles following are contributed by Mr. Jose Rodriguez and by Mr. Charles S. Ryckman in support of the contentions advanced in this column.

SPEAKING with scientific authority, Dr. Ruth Alexander, the noted New York economist, presented to the Teachers' Institute at Santa Barbara a factual and unanswerable indictment of Marxism that could well be expanded into a text on political economy superior to any now in use by our public schools.

"The Marxian idea is called progressive by some. In the light of history it is retrogressive. Collectivism is nothing new. It has appeared during the last 6,000 years whenever men became afraid of freedom.

"Despotism is the most timid of all forms of government and because of that it must resort to violence and paternalism.

"The security under it is not an implement of creation but an impediment to creation."

Turning to the comparative merits of free enterprise and Marxism, Dr. Alexander said:

"The American system is the only type left that has FREEDOM in contrast to the SECURITY which subjects of a dictatorship feel they have.

"The American ideal of freedom has not been attained elsewhere since the days of the Roman Empire.

"It is a medium between tyranny and anarchy.

"It is built solely on the foundation of private enterprise.

"Capitalism didn't cause poverty or business cycles, it inherited them.

"It was only under free enterprise that the great extremes of feudal times were approximately equalized."

This is an objective, accurate reading of history.

It poses the hard facts of actual results against doctrinal appeals to fear, passion and prejudice.

Americans, as people, are eating the cake of free enterprise.

Yet nevertheless there are some so blind to reality that they prefer to toy with the recipes of visionary doctrine, no matter how indigestible or unpalatable they have proved to unhappy peoples who have been forced to swallow them.

It is more than high time that Americans look about them to perceive and count their blessings, repudiating with natural scorn the tawdry bait of impractical and ruinous theory.

The healthy body of American society and economy has no need for the witch medicine of Marxism.

JOSE RODRIGUEZ.

THE railroad controversy which has provided an ominous background for all other national activity for many months is now approaching a crisis.

Unless there is an abrupt departure from existing attitudes, all rail transporta-

Continued on Page 2, Column 5.

REDS PIERCE LENINGRAD LINES

Bureau Help Saves Plan For School

Carrying forward its work on behalf of small business, the New York Journal - American today made possible resumption of electrical work on a school serving 700 children in North Tarrytown, N. Y., which had been halted for three months because of priority restrictions.

Through the effort of this newspaper's Industrial Service Bureau, co-operating with the OPM, the contractor received an official A-10 priority rating from Washington.

This enabled him to obtain special copper wire to repair the 25-year-old lighting and ventilation system in the North Tarrytown Grammar School.

RATING FORWARDED.

The school, a three-story brick structure, is located at the corner of Beekman ave. and Pocantico st., in North Tarrytown. The contractor is Schwer Bros., 176 Cortland st., North Tarrytown.

Signed by Priorities Director Donald M. Nelson, the all-important rating was at once forwarded to a copper wire supplier who earlier refused to accept the order on behalf of the North Tarrytown Board of Education because of the lack of a preference rating.

As a result, the school's 700

Continued on Page 11, Column 1.

Cite Big Reles Bribes

Abe Reles' payments for police "protection" in his $1,000,000 loan shark racket reached the staggering total of $500,000—fully half of the racket's proceeds—it was learned today.

According to information in the hands of Special Prosecutor Amen, vast sums of this money actually were paid to policemen by Reles himself long before he turned State's informer against his one-time underworld companions.

The pudgy little racketeer, killed when he fell from a sixth-story window of the Half Moon Hotel in Coney Island while attempting to escape Wednesday, made these personal visits after receiving mysterious telephone calls, it was learned.

PAID OUTSIDE STORE.

Amen turned down all inquiries regarding this phase of the investigation with a flat "no comment."

In another major development of the Reles investigation, the five police guards who were assigned to the gangster at the time of his death all faced charges of neglect of duty.

Regarding the "protection" fund, investigators discovered that Reles' personal payments usually were made outside a candy tsore at 779 Saratoga ave., Brooklyn.

This store was operated by 70-

Continued on Page 4, Column 4.

Nazis Yield After Infantry, Air Attack

By Associated Press.

A Russin brak through the German siege lines outside Leningrad was reported by the Moscow radio, the BBC said today in a broadcast heard here by CBS.

"The Moscow radio says that in the Leningrad area Russian infantry, with artillery and dive-bombing aircraft support, stormed the enemy lines and broke through to the rear, in the face of strong resistance," the BBC said.

Huge Victory Claimed by Reds, INS Reports

KUIBYSHEV, Nov. 14 (INS).—A tremendous new Soviet victory on the northwestern Moscow front, where Red Army forces were declared to have recaptured 20 villages, was reported by the Russian (Tass) news agency today.

The dispatch said the German offensive on the right flank of Kalinin, northwest of Moscow, had been checked and that the Soviets then counter-attacked, recapturing the villages and inflicting huge losses on the Nazis.

GAIN AT TULA.

Tass also reported Soviet forces in a powerful counter-offensive recaptured a number of villages below Tula, south of Msocow, and that 2,000 enemy soldiers were killed or wounded.

(The British radio, in a broadcast heard by CBS, quoted a Kuibyshev report which said the Russians had repelled 15 attempts in three days by two German divisions to cross the River Oka in the Tula sector and that the Germans are now on the defensive.)

The Red Army newspaper Red Star said the Germans also had been driven fro mthe eastern bank of the Nara River in the direction of Maloyaroslavetz, and that the Nazis still were rushing up reinforcements to the Moscow front.

HAND-TO-HAND FIGHTING.

The High Command's noon war communique merely said fighting continued on all fronts throughout the night.

. escribing the action at Malayaroslavitz, the Moscow radio said that in hand-to-hand fighting, Russian forces disclosed German units from a fortified hill commanding the battlefield.

Secret Plane Mission

WITH ARMY IN THE FIELD, Nov. 14 (AP).—Sudden withdrawal of combat planes for a secret destination has cut into the air power which the Army, the Navy and the Marine Corps has ready for maneuvers in the Carolinas, it was learned today.

An unimpeachable authority disclosed that aerial units? already here for the Army General Headquarters war games Nov. 15-30, have been recalled without explanation.

"We don't know where they hav gone, but our best guess is overseas," a high officer said.

He would not say whether the planes were Army, Navy or Marine. How many there were or whether the pilots also were sent on the mission. His position was so high that the information could not be challenged.

400 PLANES ASSIGNED.

About 400 planes originally were assigned for the maneuvers.

Another interesting disclosure on air power was an authoritative report on the results of battle experience in the Middle East, and Army live-bomb tests in the United States.

Maj.-Gen. Charles L. Scott, commander of the Armored Corps, the strongest offensive force the Army has ever put into field exercises, disclosed that so little damage has been done to tanks with anything less than 100-pound bombs that tank columns are regarded as inopportune targets.

Gov. Edison Urges Daily Peace Prayer

TRENTON, Nov. 14 (AP).—New Jersey's citizenry was urged yesterday by Governor Edison to pray for peace each day at noon.

Navy Rushes Arming of U. S. Ships

By WILLIAM S. NEAL,
International News Service Staff Correspondent.

WASHINGTON, Nov. 14.—The Navy today ordered immediate preparations to arm American merchant ships as President Roosevelt—happy over his greatest Congressionau victory on foreign policy—awaited delivery of the bill repealing all major shipping restrictions in the Neutrality Act.

The final seal of Congressional approval was written by the House after a hectic battle in which it approved Senate amendments to its armed ship bill by a vote of 212 to 194. Mr. Roosevelt is expected to sign the measure Monday.

Congress, by repealing the Neutrality Act ban on arming merchant ships and sending them through combat zones to belligerent ports, gave Mr. Roosevelt vast authority in the field of world relations.

He may now send American ships from U. S. ports, laden with munitions, to the docks in Liverpool, to China, to Russia or any belligerent port.

He may, legislative experts say, use his authority as commander-in-chief to order the American Navy and air service to convoy ships through submarine infested zones.

In its action, Congress turned its back on a unique experiment to keep the nation out of foreign wars. It repealed all major provisions of an act first enacted six year ago.

It abandoned law to keep merchant ships out of war zones and thus avoid incidents which may cause war in favor of a policy of permitting the President to order

Continued on Page 8, Column 1.

Final Coal Peace Parley Up Today

By JACK VINCENT,
International News Service Staff Correspondent.

WASHINGTON, Nov. 13.—Declaring "coal must be mined, President Roosevelt today met the threatened strike crisis head-on before sending a special communication to Congress asking for legislation to curb labor turmoil.

He gave John L. Lewis and steel companies owning coal mines a last chance to settle their "union shop" dispute at a White House conference during the day.

The conference, bringing together ranking CIO leaders and topflight steel executives, was timed so that Lewis could confer beforehand with the full policy committee of 200 of his United Mine Workers' Union.

Summoned before the President were: Lewis; Philip Murray, CIO president and a vice-president of the Mine Workers; Thomas Kennedy, Secretary-Treasurer of the Mine Workers; Benjamin Fairless, of U. S. Steel; Frank Purnell, of Youngstown Sheet and Tube; and Eugene Grace of Bethlehem Steel.

While Lewis has set Saturday midnight for granting of his de-

Continued on Page 6, Column 5.

Charm Girl!

Winner of contest to select New York City's most Charming working girl is announced on Page 3.

Steinhardt Plane Safe in Iran Port

CAIRO, Nov. 14 (UP).—An official announcement said today that the plane carrying Maxim Litvinoff, Russian ambassador to the United States, and Laurence Steinhardt, U. S. ambassador to Russia, has landed safely at Pahlevi, Iranian port on the Caspian Sea.

The statement said it was understood the plane was forced off its course over the Caspian Sea, apparently by bad weather.

Pehlevi is 175 miles North of Tehran.

The diplomats were due at Tehran last night and some fears had been expressed for their safety.

Aircraft Carrier Torpedoed

LONDON, Nov. 14 (AP).—The aircraft carrier Ark Royal, which the Germans often had reported sunk, now really has been lost—victim of a German submarine—the British Admiralty announced today.

The communique said the 22,000-ton floating airfield sank somewhere on some undisclosed date while in tow after having been torpedoed.

She was the third aircraft carrier lost by Britain in the war and the newest of them all·

Details of Sinking Withheld

Whether the Ark Royal actually sank from the torpedo hit of hits the Admiralty did not say. Fro mthe wording of the communique she might conceivably have been only crippled by the U-boat attack and sunk by other means, possibly further sea or air assault.

Loss of the Ark Royal was the greatest single blow suffered by the British Navy since the avenged sinking of the battle cruiser Hood, by the German battleship Bismark, between Greenland and Iceland last May 24.

Infirmed sources said the Ark Royal probably was sunk within the past few days.

The communique said that most of her crew — normally 1,575 men—had been taken off beforehand and that casualties were expected not to be heavy.

2 OTHERS SUNK.

The other British aircraft carriers sunk where the 22,500-ton Courageous which was torpedoed by a U-Boat Sept. 17, 1939, just two weeks after the outbreak of the war, and her sistership, the Glorious, which went down June 8, 1940, off northern Norway in a battle with the German battleships Scharnhorst and Gneisenau.

They were built in 1916. The Ark Royal was built in 1937.

The Ark Royal was reported at least once to have been sunk and repeatedly to have been damaged during the many naval engagements in which she participated sinc th start of th war.

The Germans insisted she had been sunk by bombs durnig the first month of the war. Three times after that the Italians claimed to have damaged her badly during air attacks in the Mediterranean between Sardinia and Gibraltar.

In the first days of the war the Ar Royal was credited by the British with capturing a German ship as a prize off Norway. Later, when the carrier entered the harbor at Rio De Janiero to take on fuel and supplies, a seaman said she had been struck by a bomb off Norway but was not put out of action.

The Ark Royal's planes carried out a major aerial attack on Sardinia a year ago, only a few days after she had been reported without confirmation to have been set afire by a bomb hit at Gibraltar.

The Italians said she was damaged seriously during the Sardinia operation, but she went into action again less than three months later, participating in the British shelling and bomb attack on Genoa.

Her planes took part in the far-flung Atlantic search in which the German battleship Bismarck was trapped and sunk last Spring.

Her complement of officers and men before the war was 1,575,, but this number probably was increased. Before the war she carried 60 planes.

SECOND LOSS IN WEEK.

The Ark Royal was the second of Britain's most widely known warships whose loss was announced by the Admiralty this week.

The other was the destroyer Cossack which ran the German prison ship Altmark into a Norwegian Fjord and rescued 300 imprisoned British seamen, led the British flotilla which penetrated Narvik Fjord, and was in on the sinking of the German battleship Bismarck. Her loss was reported Monday.

THE WEATHER

Today: Fair and warmer.

Tomorrow: Partly cloudy and continued moderately warm.

Sun rises, 6:41 a. m.; sun sets, 4:39 p. m. High tide Governors Island, 3:44 a. m., 3:50 p. m.

HOURLY TEMPERATURES

9 p. m.	48	2 a. m.	46
10 p. m.	47	3 a. m.	45
11 p. m.	47	4 a. m.	44
Midnight	46	5 a. m.	45
1 a. m.	46	6 a. m.	45

TODAY'S INDEX

Complete Weather Report on Page 30

The New York Journal-American has the largest circulation of any evening newspaper in America.

It is the only New York evening newspaper possessing the three great wire services—ASSOCIATED PRESS—INTERNATIONAL NEWS SERVICE—UNITED PRESS.

No. 12,947 Saturday, November 22, 1941 One Penny

Libya battle goes 'extremely well': Enemy tank losses (130 German, 50 Italian) are treble ours: deep advances

ROMMEL SURROUNDED

Germans must fight way out or surrender to British

R.A.F. DESTROYS SUPPLY PLANES

EXPRESS SPECIAL CORRESPONDENT CAIRO, SATURDAY MORNING.

EARLY TODAY A CAIRO MILITARY SPOKESMAN GAVE OUT THE TREMENDOUS NEWS THAT GENERAL ROMMEL'S TANK FORCES IN LIBYA ARE SURROUNDED. BROKEN INTO TWO GROUPS, THEY ARE TRYING DESPERATELY TO BREAK OUT OF THE BRITISH RINGS, BUT ALL THE TIME THEIR POSITION IS BECOMING "MORE UNFAVOURABLE."

The larger group is in the Gambut-Fort Capuzzo area near the Egyptian frontier. The smaller one is south of Tobruk.

Three separate attacks were made by the Germans about 45 miles west of Fort Capuzzo in an effort to smash through. Each time they were beaten back with substantially heavier tank losses than those of the British.

The greatest desert battle ever fought is at its height. It is going "extremely well for General Cunningham and the initiative remains with the British."

Tank casualties generally are three to one in our favour. On the vast battlefield between the Egyptian frontier and Tobruk Rommel has lost 50 per cent. of his strength.

In Cairo, it is pointed out that the German forces east of Tobruk must either attempt to fight through the British lines and join the Axis troops west of Tobruk—or surrender.

It would be most difficult for them to smash through on the south and east, while Tobruk is still the formidable barrier which the Axis has been trying to break down for seven months.

POUNDED BY NAVY

The Germans, who have few ways of receiving supplies, are meanwhile being pounded by the Navy.

Transport planes try to take up material which cannot be got over the bombed and shot away German land lines, but the R.A.F. is taking heavy toll of them. Some planes with trains of loaded gliders set out from Crete, flying only 500 feet above the sea. They met a similar end.

Co-operation between our air and ground forces is particularly close. The Army speaks in the highest terms of the very active assistance of the R.A.F. during the tank battles. Performance of American tanks has proved first-class.

Earlier, the communiqué from General Auchinleck's headquarters announced the destruction of 130 German tanks.

It said: The battle in Cyrenaica was joined in earnest yesterday (Thursday) afternoon. Following their rapid advance on the two previous days, our armoured forces on November 20 engaged German tanks in strength in the vicinity of Sidi Rezegh (10 miles from Tobruk's outer defence lines).

After losing 70 tanks and 33 armoured cars the German forces withdrew, leaving several hundred prisoners in our hands.

FINALLY DRIVEN OFF

Between this area and Sidi Omar (on the frontier) a further British armoured formation came into action against yet another concentration of German tanks which had advanced southwards from the Bardia-Gambut area.

During the first action on November 19 the enemy sustained 26 tank casualties against 20 of our own.

Yesterday morning the action was resumed, as the result of which the enemy was finally driven off in a north-easterly direction, losing a further 34 tanks.

In the Bir el Gobi area (40 miles south of Tobruk) the situation is less clear, except for the fact that an Italian armoured division originally deployed in this area has apparently exerted no influence on the battle now proceeding.

It will be remembered that this Italian armoured division was attacked and severely handled by British armoured forces on November 18, during their initial advance towards Sidi Rezegh.

Heavy pressure continues to be exerted upon the enemy holding defences between Halfaya (Hellfire Pass) and Sidi Omar.

'MAIN LINE' THREAT

Meanwhile, Imperial forces supported by further British tank formations are steadily making ground northward in a movement west of the latter locality.

In other parts of this huge battle arena strong British armoured and mechanised columns have made deep penetrations in a number of directions all threatening the enemy's main line of communications.

Throughout yesterday our air forces were active over the whole battle area. Fighter sweeps engaged enemy formations attempting to bomb our armoured forces, and intercepted enemy reconnaissance aircraft.

Our fighters also attacked enemy dive-bombers at their base with great success.

Our bombers carried out repeated attacks upon the two main enemy armoured concentrations.

Their support of our own armoured forces about Sidi Rezegh was particularly effective. At least 24 enemy aircraft were destroyed and many severely damaged.

We're using secret weapons, too

THE British are employing new devices and tactics, which cannot yet be divulged, in the advance into Libya, says an A.P. correspondent at the front.

The numbered arrows in the map below correspond with the advances made in the first, second and third days of the drive.

BOMBED BY R.A.F. — OUR FIGHTERS DESTROY 15 PLANES — BENGHAZI AND TRIPOLI ALSO BOMBED — AUSTRALIAN AND NAVAL AIRMEN STRAFE ALONG COAST — BOMBED BY R.A.F. — 70 GERMAN TANKS WIPED OUT — 24 GERMAN PLANES SHOT DOWN — 60 NAZI TANKS DESTROYED

DERNA — Martuba — Bomba — Tmimi — MEKILI — Gazela — TOBRUK — Acroma — Gad el Ahmar — El Adem — Rezegh — Gambut — BARDIA — S. Azeiz — Ft Capuzzo — SOLLUM — SIDI OMAR — Tengeder — Bir el Gobi — Gabr Saleh — Ft Sheferzen — CYRENAICA — EGYPT — Ft Maddelina — 0 10 20 50 Miles

GAINS ALL ALONG

Airfield pilots captured

Express War Reporter ALAN MOOREHEAD

With the British Army, Thursday (delayed).

BRITISH and Axis armies are locked together now at three main points. One is at Bir el Gobi, the second is at Sidi Rezegh, the third is in the direction of Fort Capuzzo.

At noon today the position was this—

GOBI: A division of Italian tanks gave battle to one arm of our armoured forces.

Fifty Italian tanks — one brigade—were wiped out. Their crews were killed. Burned-out steel carcases are lying out there in the sand for any one to see

This happened yesterday. The Germans rushed down armoured reinforcements overnight and with them now our tanks are in battle.

REZEGH: The second branch of the British armoured force stole upon an airfield in murky, rainy weather yesterday and captured 19 German aircraft, mostly Stukas, which were caught unawares.

FLUNG BACK

Fifty Germans—pilots and ground crews—were taken prisoner.

The enemy this morning made an infantry attack in an attempt to regain the airfield. They were flung back, and fighting now rages in the direction of Tobruk.

CAPUZZO: About 100 German tanks shot south from the coast, their object being to damage our flank and force an unexpected battle.

The third branch of our armoured force went out to meet them.

These were American tanks and from a few miles away I watched them go into battle for the first time.

They have emerged this morning in command of the battlefield with 15 enemy tanks destroyed for certain and the rest in retreat.

That, briefly, was the situation two days after we had made contact with the enemy.

The essential point is that Rommel has decided to stand and fight it out.

The first round is ours.

We are hotly on the offensive, gaining ground all the time.

Our aim is to wipe out the German armoured formations, and our

→ BACK PAGE, COL. SIX

'Relief of Tobruk any minute'

ADMIRAL OF THE FLEET SIR DUDLEY POUND, First Sea Lord, speaking at Bath last night, said:—

"Just before I came to this meeting I was told it was expected that Tobruk would be relieved almost immediately."

He added that the word "relieve" was entirely wrong.

"It is," he said, "a case of Tobruk bursting forth at a very inconvenient moment for the Germans."

Another Expressman on his travels

Convoy reaches Archangel

From WALTER KERR
(Express and N.Y. Herald-Tribune Reporter)

ARCHANGEL, Friday.

A LONG line of heavily escorted merchant ships pulled alongside the docks of Archangel recently after a trip through Arctic waters, bearing munitions of war from Great Britain to the Soviet Union.

On the snow-covered wharves were Russian troops ready to help in the unloading of airplanes, tanks, guns and ammunition. They stared at the ships, pointed to the huge crates lashed to the decks and then went on with their jobs.

Our last day at sea was passed in a channel of thin ice that moved sluggishly with the tide and the current of the North Dvina River, where it empties into the White Sea between solid masses of ice on the banks.

Skies were overcast, and the thermometer registered ten degrees of frost.

Behind us were days of steady sailing from England. During those days not one German submarine, surface ship or bomber challenged the convoy.

24-HOUR GUNS

It probably would have been suicide to have tried. The escorting vessels and the merchantmen were well armed, and their guns were manned 24 hours a day by crew and "passengers."

The passengers included several Russian officers, two members of the R.A.F., British tank experts, a few Polish officers and five newspapermen, three of them Americans.

The important fact is that the convoy got through, and the munitions it brought are significant. In Russia now will be Hurricane fighter planes equipped with their own guns and their own ammunition.

There are British-made tanks—enough of them to be of great value for a time in some sector of the front. There are sub-machine-guns from the U.S.A., tons of warm clothing and tons of food.

(World Copyright)

4 A.M. LATEST

NAZIS ON DEFENSIVE IN KARELIA

MOSCOW, Friday.—On certain sections of Karelian front Germans and Finns have been forced on defensive, but they are fighting fiercely to capture one important position, says Moscow newspaper Red Star. A battalion of Finnish troops launched against the objective yesterday were forced to retreat to the original positions after heavy fighting, leaving many killed and wounded.—B.U.P.

Enemy admits

'Extremely strong attack'

Express Radio Station

BOTH Berlin and Rome last night paid tribute to Britain's great push in Libya.

Said a military spokesman in Berlin: "An extremely strong offensive; it cannot be regarded purely as a propaganda affair."

Asserted Bremen Radio: "Britain appears to be charging up a blind alley."

MOODY MARIUS

Said the Italian News Agency Stefani: "Britain is employing superior forces."

Moody Marius—Marius Appellius, Italy's Radio Talker No. 1—did most of the talking from Rome.

It began as a pep talk, but developed into an uneasy and cautious warning in mournful tones. Said Marius:—

"It is a long war and a very hard war, and what is more, we are all in it this time. Either we all win or we lose, and lose everything.

"It is quite possible that the enemy will make progress in such and such a sector.

"KNOWS ALL"

"But don't draw any conclusions from the initial stages of this new campaign. You can have complete confidence in the Axis troops in Africa, whose command has foreseen everything and has left nothing to chance.

"Victory is certain. One day —one fine day—the streets of London will yet hear the rhythm of marching Axis troops."

The Italian communiqué said: "There were further developments on the Libyan front on Thursday.

"After having tenaciously held the enemy attack, our troops counter-attacked and repulsed the enemy armoured units, destroying numerous tanks and capturing prisoners.

"On the Tobruk front, there were violent artillery duels."

Drizzle

Dover Straits last night: *Drizzle.*

AXIS LOSE ONE TANK IN SEVEN

Express Military Reporter MORLEY RICHARDS

THE tank test has begun. British tanks v. German tanks. There can be no doubt at all from last night's communiqué that thus far the Imperial panzers have come off best.

Destruction of 130 German tanks and approximately 50 Italian, means that General Rommel has lost practically one-seventh of his total strength.

It includes some 400 Italian tanks.

There are roughly 400 tanks in a division, and Rommel possesses three—two Nazi and one Italian.

The enemy have been unable to keep clear of the fast Imperial thrusts of the Eighth Army armoured formations searching for them in the vast desert spaces.

General Auchinleck's communiqué shows that there are two enemy tank concentrations. One was east of Tobruk based on Bardia. The other was well to the west of Tobruk

The Italians were south of Tobruk and have obviously gone off westwards with the probable hope of linking up with Rommel's 15th Division in the vicinity.

Evidently the 21st Division moving from Bardia was wheeling around to the south-west with the intention of joining the main force when the Imperial columns caught them.

2 A.M. COMMENTARY

That is the proof that our attack did achieve complete surprise. The enemy could not get out of the way in time and are being struck before the two divisions could unite.

Having gone round the rear of Sidi Omar it now becomes plain that General Cunningham's columns are driving towards the road that will cut the 17-mile long supply line from Sollum to Bardia, thus isolating both enemy garrisons.

The communiqué does not say where the other Axis main communications have been threatened, but British tanks, keeping up their 50-mile-a-day dash, were

BACK PAGE, COL. FOUR

PETAIN TO MEET HITLER

Express Staff Reporter

NEW YORK, Friday.

INFORMATION in Washington today is that Marshal Petain and Admiral Darlan are to meet Goering in Occupied France next week, and then go on to meet Hitler.

Object of these conferences is believed to be a German demand for further Axis "protection" of French North Africa, in return for concessions to Petain in Occupied France.

Reports from France, following the dismissal of General Weygand as Vichy Delegate-General in Africa, indicate that Petain will be unable to count on the support of Weygand's army in any deal Petain may conclude with Hitler.

A German radio message picked up in New York refers to "anxiety over the arrival of British reinforcements at Sierra Leone." The German message adds: "According to latest reports six more British warships have anchored at Freetown, and 20 British bombers, complete with ground personnel, are said to have been landed."

OPINION

By the First Lord

Mr. A. V. Alexander, First Lord of the Admiralty, praised yesterday's Daily Express Opinion column when he spoke at a luncheon of the City Livery Club.

Given the use of sea power, he said, we could choose a theatre of war in which we could strike best, and through sea power we should bring this tremendous struggle to the end we all desired.

Mr. Alexander added that his listeners would no doubt have seen the remarkable article in the Daily Express, which put the case extremely well, and which was sound, thoughtful, and constructive.

Report on Back Page.

Malta scatters them

MALTA, Friday.—A communiqué issued today said that in the last 24 hours the alert sounded six times when enemy aircraft crossed the coast. The bombs dropped caused no damage but one serious casualty. One plane is believed to have been destroyed, three were damaged.—A.P.

69 to 14 is R.A.F.'s score in battle

Express Air Reporter BASIL CARDEW

THE Imperial air forces, in their third night and day of battle in Cyrenaica, established nearly a three to one superiority in planes destroyed, according to the R.A.F. official Middle East communiqué last night.

Twenty-four machines were shot down or smashed up against the loss of nine of ours. Our score to date is 69 to 14.

The communiqué names Me. 110 fighters and Ju. 88 bombers, and large formations of Stuka dive-bombers escorted by Me. 109s. Against all these our fighters were particularly successful, making the kind of sweeps the Germans know so well in Northern France.

In the late afternoon of Thursday, Royal Australian Air Force planes combined with Fleet Air Arm machines in tackling the big formation of Me. 109 fighters skynursing the Ju. 87 bombers.

The fighters were severely mauled, many seriously damaged, and were unable to keep the attackers off the Junkers. So two of the Ju. 87s went down.

One bomber party found numbers of dispersed 20-seater Ju. 52 troop-carriers standing on the ground. Two were left blazing and many others damaged.

Another prong of our air attack went to Derna, Bardia, Benghazi, and Tripoli, North African ports.

Long-range bombers formed the third air claw, attacking Messina, the air and sea port in Sicily, and Naples and Brindisi, convoy despatch centres.

Blenheims attacked shipping in the Gulf of Sirte, flying low through intense fire. Bombs dropped from mast height left a 5,000-ton vessel listing heavily and a schooner low in the water.

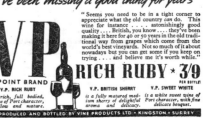

GERMANS BREAK RUSSIAN LINE AT TULA IN NEW MOSCOW THRUST: PAGE 4

Sunday Dispatch

141st Year. No. 7,308. 2d. NOVEMBER 23, 1941. Radio Page 7.

Libya Is 'Developing Most Satisfactorily'—Official

TOBRUK MEN BREAK OUT

Destruction Of Enemy Tanks Continues As Nazis Try To Pierce Our Wedge

"TAKEN ALL ROUND, THE WHOLE SITUATION IN LIBYA IS DEVELOPING MOST SATISFACTORILY," STATED A CAIRO MILITARY SPOKESMAN YESTERDAY AFTERNOON. AN AUTHORITATIVE COMMENT IN LONDON WAS: "THE BATTLE IS GOING FINE."

While the great battle of tanks was still raging west of Tobruk, it was learned in Cairo yesterday that a strong force from Tobruk itself is battling its way south-eastwards to link up with the spearhead of the main British Army ten miles away at Sidi Rezegh Aerodrome.

By nightfall on Friday this Tobruk force, which was headed by many tanks, had captured an enemy position three miles south-east of the perimeter and was making "steady progress in the face of heavy opposition."

The initial advance was made over ground which the enemy had mined. Since, however, this fact had been previously discovered by reconnaissance parties, there was little difficulty in getting through.

As the battle developed yesterday—with fewer tanks engaged owing to the previous day's losses—it became possible to obtain a clearer view of the strategy.

The British have driven a big wedge nearly to Tobruk. To the east are General Rommel's panzer divisions, almost, if not quite, cut off, their only direct path being through the few miles' gap between the Tobruk force and the British spearhead at Sidi Rezegh. That is if the gap still exists.

These forces are, in the words of a Cairo military spokesman yesterday, "doing their damnedest to break through to the west. Time and again they have been beaten back—and with each attempt we continue to destroy more of their tanks. But they will fight to the last one.

GEN. CUNNINGHAM'S OBJECTIVE

"Our objective is not Tobruk or the capture of prisoners, but the destruction of every German tank in Libya. That is what we are doing at the moment."

Enemy forces on the west of our wedge are being held back.

"Up to yesterday one-third of the whole Axis tanks in Libya had been destroyed," continued the spokesman.

Twenty-four hours previously it had been stated in Cairo that half the enemy tanks in action had been destroyed. The new proportion obviously takes into account the tanks the enemy had in reserve in supply bases.

It is impossible to give figures, but the strength of an Afrika panzer division is probably less than that of an ordinary German panzer division. There are supposed to be two German tank divisions and one Italian tank division operating in Libya.

When the enemy panzer divisions have been finally destroyed it will be comparatively easy to round up the German mechanised troops still holding their original positions at Halfaya Pass and at Capuzzo, already under pressure both from the west and south.

There was no official news of British losses in the battle, but it was pointed out in London that General Cunningham could not have achieved the destruction of a third of the enemy tanks without suffering casualties himself.

The R.A.F. is maintaining and increasing its supremacy in the air. The weather has been on the British side, for a great number of the enemy aerodromes have been waterlogged since the great storm in which the British offensive began.

MR. ALEXANDER OPTIMISTIC

Mr. A. V. Alexander, First Lord of the Admiralty, and General Sir Thomas Blamey, the Australian Army C.-in-C., were very optimistic yesterday.

Mr. Alexander said: "Such signals as I have received confirm that things are going very well."

General Blamey said: "The destruction of half the enemy's effective tank strength means that Britain has won the tank battle on which the result of the whole offensive hinged. There still remains the Italian infantry and motorised forces to deal with, although these should not offer very stubborn resistance, as the Allied forces possess most considerable reserves."

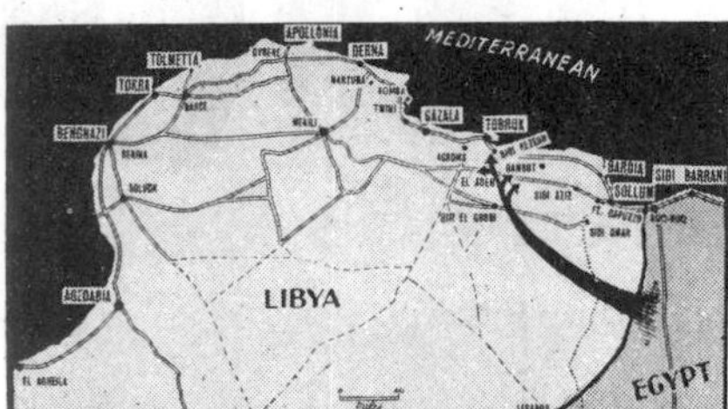

BRITISH ADVANCE LIKE ARMY IN A SUPER FILM

Flying Fortresses took a prominent part in the Battle of Libya, said B.U.P. last night, reporting that ten enemy aircraft were destroyed yesterday against five of the R.A.F.

THE Luftwaffe in Cyrenaica was almost entirely grounded last Monday—eve of the great Empire invasion of Libya—by torrential rains, it was revealed yesterday by *A.P.*

This left the Axis with hardly any air protection while British armoured forces crossed the frontier to engage the panzer divisions and British planes bombed enemy establishments and communications almost unopposed.

The R.A.F. was operating mainly from desert airfields far inland, where there was little rain and no trouble in getting planes into the air.

SEAS OF MUD

At first it was thought the rainstorm would benefit the enemy. But as skies were virtually clear of Axis planes on Tuesday and Wednesday it became plain that the storm was a great stroke of luck.

Rain turned the dry sands of the coastal airfields, which the Germans used almost exclusively, into seas of mud.

This defeated the Luftwaffe's Stukas more decisively than they had ever been defeated. They were stuck in the mud.

In all that time four Messerschmitts were the only German planes to cross over the frontier.

LIKE FILM ARMY

Describing the stirring scenes of the first advance, one *A.P.* correspondent reports:

The largest mechanised armoured force Britain has ever placed in the field invaded Libya.

Hundreds of new tanks, many American, rattled through gaps cut in Mussolini's wire fence north of Fort Maddalena, while whole squadrons of Hurricanes and Tomahawks ruled the skies above them.

Tuesday evening found the British land armada roughly 70 miles within the Libya frontier.

Hundreds of tanks and thousands of lorries made an unforgettable sight streaming through dense clouds of dust across the rolling landscape of rocks and sand.

Cecil de Mille could not have done better.

American medium tanks, the crews of which call them "Our Honeys,' made a brave sight as they deployed across the desert. Heavy guns and anti-tank batteries moved, protected by scores of carefully camouflaged armoured cars.

Fast little scout cars, which British soldiers call "Dingoes," fussed around like sheepdogs, keeping the great columns on the move.

"HEAVY FIGHTING"

Yesterday's Berlin communiqué made only slight mention of the campaign.

It stated: "In North Africa German and Italian troops have been engaged in heavy fighting with strong British tank formations on a broad front since November 19."

That was all.

Rome radio claimed the British objective in Libya is the domination of the Mediterranean. That, it said, made the battle so vital.

The radio also said Britain wants to show the world she is not inactive while Axis forces are fighting Russia, that she wants to eliminate Italy as a military Power, that she wants to end hostilities in the Mediterranean area, and thus be able to send troops to the Caucasus.

"These are only preliminary aims," said the spokesman. "The real objective is the conquest of all Libya and the entire domination of the Mediterranean.

"The Italian and German forces are continuing the fight with tenacity and determination, and the Italian and German nations are awaiting the outcome calmly."

'FIGHTING HARD'

Later it was claimed: "Both the Italian and the German troops are putting up a stiff resistance.

"They are fighting hard, confident of ultimate victory."

The Italian communiqué said the battle was continuing with undiminished violence.

It was claimed that losses in men and material are being inflicted on the British forces.

It stated: "At dawn yesterday the battle in Marmarica restarted and continued with violence during the whole day.

"Our land and air forces have been engaged in hard battles with the enemy forward posts, on which further considerable losses in men, material, and armoured vehicles have been inflicted.

"Repeated attempts of the enemy

Continued on Page 8.

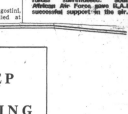

A glimpse of what the R.A.F. has been doing in the past week before and during the 8th Army's brilliant advance. This road is south of Benghazi. The vehicles are part of an enemy column. One has run off the road, another is "on its way out."

LATEST

U.S. AID CHIEF IN CAIRO

Brigadier-General Maxwell, head of the United States Military Mission to the British Forces in Africa, arrived by air in Cairo yesterday with five aides-de-camp. Mission will take charge of all phases of American aid to the British forces on the African continent. —A.P.

ITALIANS ROUTED

Strong enemy positions at Kulkaber and Ferroaber, east of Lake Tana were heavily attacked on November 21, says joint communiqué issued by Command and Air Headquarters yesterday. Italian forces surrendered. South African Air Force gave R.A.F. successful support in the air.

GERMANS CLAIM ROSTOV IS THEIRS, LAUNCH BIGGEST DRIVE ON MOSCOW

GERMANY hopes to pursue a winter campaign in the Caucasus, despite the terrible conditions of ice and snow that will prevail there for the next three or four months.

This is indicated by dispatches from Stockholm yesterday, which say that German troops are being given special training in mountain warfare.

The report also links up with the German claim yesterday to have captured Rostov, which guards the approaches to the Caucasus.

A Berlin communiqué stated:

"Formations of mobile troops and armed S.S. troops under the command of General von Kleist captured the town of Rostov, on the lower part of the Don.

"The Luftwaffe, under the command of Ritter von Greim, played an important part in the operations."

The claim is not confirmed from any Russian source.

A *Red Star* correspondent reported yesterday:

"The defenders of Rostov are fighting courageously, but are being forced to retreat under the pressure of numerically superior enemy forces, especially of tanks.

"In two days only our troops destroyed over 50 enemy tanks and large numbers of German infantry and artillery. Our troops are dealing telling blows at the enemy's flanks

TWO BATTALIONS LOST

"On November 20 the Germans lost two infantry battalions, over 100 lorries, and several tanks."

Rostov is a big industrial centre and has a pipe-line from the Caucasian oil fields. It has a peacetime population of about 500,000.

Even if the German claim is correct Rostov stands on the west bank of the swiftly-flowing Don, and the Germans would have to force a crossing of the river before they could drive on to the Caucasus.

Simultaneously the Germans have launched a great new attack on Moscow. Moscow yesterday admitted tank infiltration of the Russian lines near Tula, south of the city.

The battle now raging at the approaches to Moscow is probably the biggest of the campaign, said the special correspondent of *Pravda* yesterday.

"The Germans attacked in all sectors on Friday. In the Volokolamsk direction and on the southern flank of the Kalinin direction (north-west of the capital) the Germans concentrated large forces of tanks and infantry and began an attack.

PINCERS MOVE

"The Fascists are resorting to their usual tactics of the pincer movement.

"Our troops are fighting incessantly, retreating to new lines, fortifying themselves there, and checking him with counter-attacks.

"In the Volokolamsk direction the tank battle lasted 20 hours.

"In the Mojaisk direction the Germans threw four divisions against our lines. Disregarding losses they were incessantly launching new attacks.

"Our troops are holding their line and are dealing heavy blows to the enemy. In one sector alone the Fascists lost 20 tanks and about one and a half infantry battalions."

In the Tula direction, 100 miles south of Moscow, *Pravda's* special correspondent reports that violent fighting is continuing and the situation remains tense.

TANKS GET THROUGH

"Despite the heroic resistance of our troops the enemy succeeded in pressing them back in several places, while in some sectors his tanks infiltrated through our line eastward and northward," says the report.

The writer adds: "We have become stronger than we were one month ago, and if it was possible to hold the enemy then, it must be possible to hold him now and to inflict on him such a blow that he will be defeated."

Berlin yesterday stated that a son of M. Molotov, the Russian vice-Premier, had been taken prisoner at Tula.

Vichy radio stated yesterday that British planes are now in action in the Crimea.

Messages from Reuter, A.P., and Exchange.

DAVID, AGED 80, SAILED TO BRITAIN

To Prove Goebbels Is Wrong

DAVID WATT is 80. He is a New Yorker and a riveter by trade. He wanted to see whether Dr. Goebbels's tall talk about Britain's plight was true.

So white-haired David decided to come over to see for himself and get the truth for his mates in the New York shipyard where he works.

David Watt could not afford to pay his passage. So he signed as an ordinary seaman on a merchant vessel. He wasn't scared of U-boats.

A NEW SHIP

Off Freetown, West Africa, he contracted malaria and was put ashore. But as soon as he was on his feet again, he signed on with an Allied ship and eventually arrived at a Scottish port.

He spent a fortnight ashore, which convinced him that all his suspicions regarding Dr. Goebbels had been well founded.

So said David: "I'm going right back to tell the folks at home that you people are nothing short of miraculous, and that the way you are sticking it is wonderful.

"You will never knuckle down to them."

And now, 80-years-old David is working his passage home across the Atlantic—our unpaid ambassador in New York.

Calm Off Dover

Intervals of bright sunshine in the Strait of Dover yesterday; weather slightly colder; wind in the south-east. Sea calm, visibility improved, but light mist obscured the French coast.

News From The Stores

Stagg and Russell, Page 3; Pontings, 5; Barkers, 7; Pettits, 7.

Overwork?

Professor Giovanni de Agostini, Italian map-maker, has died at Milan.

A VERY PECULIAR ELECTION

THE most peculiar Parliamentary by-election of modern times is being fought at Hampstead, where votes will be cast next Thursday for four candidates—an official Conservative and three Independents.

This four-cornered fight is for the seat made vacant by the death of Mr. George Balfour, Conservative member since 1918.

* * *

PECULIARITY No. 1 is the length of time between the occurrence of the vacancy and next Thursday's polling. Mr. Balfour died on September 19. The writ for the election of his successor was not issued until November 11.

This delay contrasts with what happened at Brighton, when Lord Erskine resigned his seat.

His decision was announced on November 11. That day the new House of Commons writ was issued. On November 15 Major A. A. H. Marlowe was returned unopposed, and on November 18 he took his seat in the House.

* * *

PECULIARITY No. 2 became apparent when the Hampstead Conservative Association tackled the business of finding the official Government candidate. Forty men offered themselves — an unprecedented number.

One by one their names were gone through. Finally the association's chairman, Flying Officer Charles Challen, was chosen. Against him there entered the lists: Mr. Noel Pemberton - Billing (National Independent), Mr. W. R. Hipwell (Independent), and Mr. Arthur Dollond ("No-party All-out Aid for Russia").

* * *

PECULIARITY No. 3 concerns the attitude of Colonel James Rowbotham, Hampstead's chief A.R.P. warden. He was one of the 40 aspirants to official Government candidature.

He was interviewed by the Selection Committee. And he announced that if the association chose as candidate a man from outside the borough he, too, would stand—as an Independent supporting the Government.

The choice of Flying Officer Challen on October 25 made that unnecessary. A local paper, published on October 31, quoted Colonel Rowbotham as saying he would support Flying Officer Challen to the full. The colonel did not repudiate that interview.

Yet when nomination day—November 19—arrived his name appeared on the first nomination paper as nominator not of Flying Officer Challen—but of W. R. Hipwell, the Independent.

Colonel Rowbotham gave this explanation to the *Sunday Dispatch*: "Mr. Hipwell offered to withdraw in my favour and to support me if I stood as an Independent candidate. As a reciprocal act of courtesy I have signed his nomination papers."

The colonel added that he had never said he would support Challen. But the local newspaper repeats in a later issue that he told its representative he regarded Mr. Challen as an excellent candidate and would support him to the full. Mr. Hassan, assistant chief warden, follows the colonel as seconder of Mr. Hipwell.

* * *

PECULIARITY No. 4 concerns the electioneering literature of "Non-party All-out Aid for Russia" candidate Dollond. He stands, he says, for "taking advantage of Hitler's turned back to attack him." He also states: "I do not stand for ill-considered improvised attack in the West."

He further asserts: "I come before you at the request of leading members of all parties . . ." and then goes on to say: "I am fighting this election absolutely alone—I have no party ties, owe allegiance to no political party whatever; no party or person is financing my fight, sponsoring me, or giving my campaign official party support."

* * *

PECULIARITY No. 5 is that the four candidates sometimes share one meeting. When an audience of Hampstead women was addressed, the candidates followed each other at half-hour intervals.

Last night a meeting of wardens and Civil Defence workers heard speeches by all four candidates.

That meeting was arranged by Colonel Rowbotham, but the hall was paid for by Mr. Pemberton-Billing. He had already engaged it for an earlier meeting, and was willing to let the hall be used for the later joint four-candidate meeting.

* * *

PECULIARITY No. 6 (in view of past elections) is the fact that the Hampstead Communists have issued a statement urging support of the Government and Flying Officer Challen.

"Now is no time for divisions in the ranks of the people," says their statement. "The Prime Minister and the Government need all the strength that a united, determined people can give them if the opponents of Anglo-Soviet unity are to be overcome and the war waged effectively."

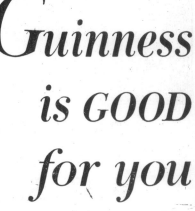

DAILY NEWS

Copr. 1941 by News Syndicate Co. Inc. NEW YORK'S PICTURE NEWSPAPER Trade Mark Reg. U. S. Pat. Off.

Vol. 23. No. 130 New York, Monday, November 24, 1941★ 44 Pages 2 Cents IN CITY LIMITS | 3 CENTS Elsewhere

BRITISH TAKE BARDIA, 15,000 PRISONERS

Story on Page 3

(By Associated Press)

Lion Roars Back. British forces shown entering the Italian desert stronghold of Bardia, Libya, after its capture Jan. 5, 1941, yesterday made a triumphant return to the city which had been in Axis hands since April 13. The glory of recapturing the town went to New Zealand troops. *—Story on page 3.*

A U. S. Ship Is Torpedoed!

Turn to the Center Fold for Two Pages of Remarkable Pictures

EXTRA!

WAR!

Chronicle Home Carrier Service

If for any reason your Chronicle is not received please call City Circulation Department, phone DOuglas 1414, before 10 a. m. daily and 11 a. m. Sunday and your Chronicle will be delivered promptly

San Francisco Chronicle

THE CITY'S ONLY HOME-OWNED NEWSPAPER

COMPARATIVE TEMPERATURES	High	Low		High	Low
San Francisco	60	50	Denver	69	25
San Jose	61	39	New York	56	44
Los Angeles	79	56	Chicago	35	26
Seattle	—	—	New Orleans	61	52
Honolulu	77	70	Salt Lake	44	20

Local Forecast: Fair
Complete Report on Page 10

FOUNDED 1865—VOL. CLIII, NO. 146 CC SAN FRANCISCO, MONDAY, DECEMBER 8, 1941 DAILY 5 CENTS, SUNDAY 10 CENTS: DAILY AND SUNDAY PER MONTH, $1.30

JAPAN ATTACKS U. S.!

Hawaii and Manila Bombed; Chute Troops Off Honolulu!

Bulletins

HONOLULU, Dec. 7 (AP)--A naval engagement is in progress off of Honolulu, with at least one black enemy aircraft carrier in the action against Pearl Harbor defenses.

Some aerial dogfights are in progress in the skies over Honolulu.

At 9:30 a. m. Honolulu time (noon Pacific standard time) the attack still was in progress.

What damage was done by the swift surprise raid was not immediately apparent. But reports said enemy bombers scored a hit at Hickam Field, army airport, and another on an old tank at the Pearl Harbor Naval Base.

At least two nine-plane formations of four-engined black bombers flew over Honolulu and Pearl Harbor. Each plane bore Japan's Rising Sun insignia.

There was a report from persons who came past Pearl Harbor that one ship there was lying on its side in the water and four others were on fire. This could not be immediately confirmed.

WASHINGTON, Dec. 7 (AP)—The White House announced at 3:35 p. m. (EST) today that the army had just received word that an American vessel, believed to be a cargo ship, had been sending out signals of distress approximately west of San Francisco.

Whether it had been torpedoed was not immediately learned.

The Time

War planes were roaring out of the night in the Pacific.

When first reports were received here at 11:29 yesterday (Sunday) morning, it was 8:29 Sunday morning in Hawaii and 3:29 Monday in Manila.

Eyewitness Reports Sound Of Terrific Cannonading In Pearl Harbor Area

HONOLULU, Dec 7 (UP)---Parachute troops were sighted off Harbor Point today.

By. EUGENE BURNS

HONOLULU, Dec. 7 (AP)--At least two Japanese bombers, their wings bearing the insignia of the Rising Sun, appeared over Honolulu at about 7:35 a. m. (Honolulu time) today and dropped bombs.

The sound of cannons firing comes to me here in Honolulu as I telephone this story to the San Francisco Associated Press office.

Reports say the Japanese bombers scored two hits, one at Hickam Field, air corps post on Oahu island, and another at Pearl Harbor, setting an oil tank afire.

Shortly before I started talking on the trans-pacific telephone, I saw a formation of five Japanese planes flying over Honolulu.

The sound of cannonading coming from the direction of Pearl Harbor has been continuing for an hour and a half. So far, there are no reports of casualties. No bombs have fallen in Honolulu itself, so far as I coud determine before making this call.

There is much commotion going on, with planes in the air and anti-aircraft firing.

The citizens of Honolulu have been cleared from the streets by military and naval units, assisted by

Continued on Page 11, Col. 2

THIS IS WHERE IT STARTED: The Japanese yesterday attacked Hawaii and all naval bases in the Philippines. Japanese troops were also reported en route to Thailand.

Bolivia Gets Lease-Lend

WASHINGTON, Dec. 6 (AP)—The United States signed a lease-lend agreement with Bolivia today. Details were withheld, but [illegible] reported to allot from $10,000,000 to $15,000,000 to Bolivia.

35 Cars of Nazi Wounded Daily

TORONTO, Dec. 6 (AP)—Norwegians who arrived here recently for training in the Free Norwegian armed forces said today that as many as 35 carloads of German wounded have arrived in Norway daily from the Russian front.

FDR Calls Cabinet; Army and Navy Ordered To Battle Stations

WASHINGTON, Dec. 7 (AP)—The President decided today after Japan's attack on Pearl Harbor and Manila to call an extraordinary meeting of the Cabinet for 8:30 o'clock tonight and to have congressional leaders of both parties join the conferenc at 9 p. m.

By the Associated Press

WASHINGTON, Dec. 7-Japanese airplanes today attacked American defenses bases at Hawaii and Manila, and President Roosevelt ordered the army and navy to carry out undisclosed orders prepared for the defense of the United States.

The White House said Japan had attacked America's vital outposts in the Pacific--Hawaii and Manila--at 3:20 p. m. (EST) and that so far as was known the attacks were still in progress.

Announcing the President's action for the protection of American territory, Presidential Secretary Sephen Early declared that so far as is known now, the attacks were "made wholly without warning--when both nations were at peace--and were delivered within an hour or so of the time that the Japanese Am-

Continued on Page 11, Col. 3

No. 12,960 Monday, December 8, 1941 One Penny

On the 826th day of the battle, war speeds right round the world

JAPS DECLARE WAR

'We fight Britain and America from dawn'

NAVY BATTLE IN PACIFIC

JAP PLANE CARRIER SUNK: U.S. BATTLESHIP ABLAZE

350 killed in a surprise raid on Hawaii airfield

PARATROOPS AT KEY BASE

Express Staff Reporters CHARLES FOLEY and NEWELL ROGERS

NEW YORK, Sunday.

PRESIDENT ROOSEVELT TONIGHT REPLIED TO JAPAN'S UNDECLARED WAR ON THE UNITED STATES BY DECREEING GENERAL MOBILISATION AND ORDERING THE ARMY AND THE NAVY TO PUT INTO OPERATION PLANS ALREADY PREPARED TO MEET JAPANESE ATTACK.

He was acting as Commander-in-Chief of the American armed forces. Tomorrow, a hastily convened session of Senate and Representatives will hear a message from the President asking for an immediate declaration of war against Japan.

Japan's war will be many hours old before her formal declaration—timed by Tokyo for dawn tomorrow—becomes operative.

Imperial Headquarters in Tokyo announced last night that from that time Japan will consider herself at war with America and Britain "in the Western Pacific."

Japanese paratroops were landing and bombs from carrier planes were still crashing on America's key Pacific outposts as War Secretary Stimson and Navy Secretary Knox put their machines into operation.

RAID BY 150 PLANES

Clouds of smoke lay over Pearl Harbour, Hawaii, home of the U.S. Pacific Fleet.

A great oil storage tank in the harbour was ablaze. So were installations on the Navy's Hickam airfield nearby.

A direct hit on the Hickam barracks is reported to have killed 350 men. Another, by an air-launched torpedo, set the battleship Oklahoma (29,000 tons) ablaze as she lay in harbour.

More than 150 Japanese planes were diving and turning above the harbour, releasing a rain of bombs, despite the losses inflicted on them by the swarm of American fighters which flashed among them.

Many of the raiders crashed in flames. Two were brought down over Honolulu, holiday paradise which received scores of bombs. "Heavy damage and grievous loss of life" are reported from the crowded city.

The Governor of the island was telephoning to President Roosevelt, giving him an account of the raid when a second wave of bombers swept over Honolulu.

Schools all over the island were requisitioned and turned into hospitals for the injured.

Radio announcers ordered the citizens—a third of them Japanese-born—to stay in their homes, but thousands of them flocked to the hills to get a grand-stand view of the raids.

Outside the harbour squadrons of the Japanese and American fleets were engaged in pitched battle.

At least one aircraft-carrier was with the Japanese squadron. Its planes were engaged in trying to silence the shore batteries which cover Pearl Harbour's approaches when it was sunk.

Nearly 5,000 miles away to the west, Manila, capital of the Philippines and bastion of the democracies on the South Asiatic battle-front, was also under air bombardment.

GUAM ATTACK

Guam, lonely island base in mid-Pacific, was attacked by another Japanese air fleet.

President Roosevelt dramatically broke the news of the attacks to the world when he summoned reporters to the White House this evening.

There Mr. Stephen Early read to them a bulletin prepared by the President, which said:—

> An air attack has been launched by the Japanese on the Hawaiian base of the United States Fleet at Pearl Harbour and on all military and naval activities on Oahu Island (main isle of the Hawaiian group).
>
> A second attack has been launched on army and navy bases at Manila, Philippine.

Mr. Early made it clear that the attacks were still in progress.

Within a few minutes came news that Bangkok, capital of Thailand, was being bombed from the air and shelled from the sea.

The war came even closer to America's home shores with an announcement from the White House that a U.S. Army transport had been torpedoed midway between

BACK PAGE, COL. FIVE

ADMIRAL OSAMI NAGANO
Japanese Navy chief. Came to London in 1935 for the Naval Limitation Conference.

PARLIAMENT CALLED FOR TODAY

Express Political Correspondent
GUY EDEN

DOWNING-STREET announced last night that both Houses of Parliament had been summoned to meet at three o'clock this afternoon.

A statement will be made in both Houses—by Mr. Churchill in the Commons.

Mr. John Winant, the American Ambassador, called on the Premier shortly after nine o'clock last night.

Mr. Churchill, at the Mansion House on November 11, gave this solemn pledge:—

"I TAKE THIS OCCASION TO SAY—AND IT IS MY DUTY TO SAY—THAT SHOULD THE UNITED STATES BECOME INVOLVED IN WAR WITH JAPAN THE BRITISH DECLARATION WILL FOLLOW WITHIN THE HOUR."

Call to Germany

As a member of the Axis, Japan will presumably be entitled to call upon Germany and Italy to declare war on America.

The intensive diplomatic activity of the Nazis in recent weeks is believed to have been with the aim of helping Japan by distracting attention of Britain and her Allies and bottling up anti-Axis forces far from Europe.

Invasion ports bombed by R.A.F.

The R.A.F. attacked the invasion ports last night in brilliant moonlight. Heavy A.A. fire extended from Dunkirk to Calais.

A German raider dropped incendiary bombs over an East Coast town, causing small fires which were soon put out.

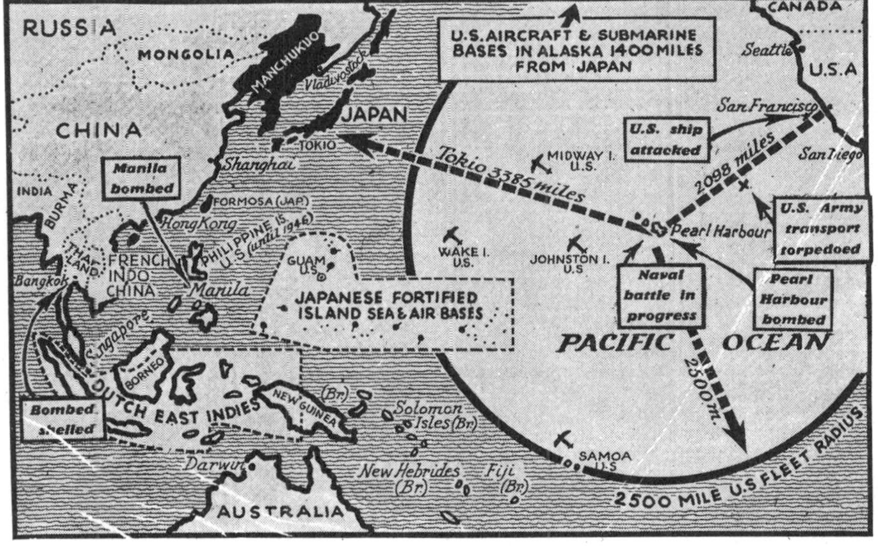

WHERE THE PACIFIC BASES LIE . . .

JAPAN has at least 15 fully developed naval bases in the Pacific, with two more under construction in Indo-China. In the mandated Caroline and Marianne Islands she has established two strategically important naval bases. She has been coveting naval and air bases in Thailand, nearer Singapore.

There are ten British naval bases in the Pacific extending in a rough half-circle from Burma, via Australia, to New Zealand.

Seven of America's naval bases in the Pacific lie along her own coast with only two of old standing flung far out—Pearl Harbour, 2,093 miles from San Francisco; 3,385 from Tokyo, and a base in the Philippines, 7,154 miles from America.

The U.S.A. has six other bases under construction or prepared.

Pearl Harbour, a few miles from Honolulu, is heavily guarded and surrounded by masses of barbed wire. The U.S. Navy has its own air base, occupying the whole of Ford Island.

Honolulu could not believe it

Express Radio Station

A HONOLULU correspondent of the NBC broadcast to New York this eye-witness account of the Japanese attack on Pearl Harbour:—

"Hawaii was raided at eight o'clock this morning. First reports were heard from the radio station.

"When bombs began to fall the people knew that Japan had begun to try to eradicate America's outposts in the Pacific.

"First the Japanese attacked Pearl Harbour. An attorney who was up in his private plane says that one or two Japanese planes gave him a salute with machine-gun bullets as they approached Honolulu.

"Next the Japanese attacked the Hickam Airfield. Considerable damage was done to planes and to the field. There is still great activity going on clearing the debris.

TORPEDOES

"In Pearl Harbour the American battleship Oklahoma was set on fire.

"The Army has issued orders for all civilians to remain off the streets.

"The first raiders carried torpedoes.

"Everyone was taken by surprise, and still finds it difficult to believe that these beautiful islands should have been attacked.

"Many planes were shot down, and the A.A. gunnery was very heavy.

"It is thought that the planes came from the south. Squadrons of Japanese planes came in dropping bombs and incendiaries over the city. Some bombs fell before the Governor's mansion, killing one man.

"In the Pacific Heights, the beautiful residential district there was heavy bombing.

"On Waikiki the people stayed out in the streets to watch the raiders, and some were killed by bombs."

Singapore at battle stations

Express Staff Reporter
O. D. GALLAGHER

SINGAPORE, Monday morning.

BRITAIN'S war machine in the Far East was ready for the clash—to the last detail.

Coded messages flashed all day yesterday between British G.H.Q. in Singapore and the American service chiefs at Manila, Philippines.

Significantly, Britain's first Far East "operational communiqué" was issued.

It reported the discovery by R.A.F. reconnaissance aircraft of two heavily escorted Japanese convoys—probably containing at least a division of troops—sailing north-west near Cambodia Point, southern extremity of Indo-China.

The presence of the convoys in these waters, together with the menacing disposition of the 125,000 Japanese in Indo-China, revealed the measure of the threat to Thailand.

Dictator's powers

In Singapore it is believed the convoys may be making for Koh Kong, island off the Indo-China coast only ten miles from the Thai frontier. The Japanese have been at work for months preparing the island as a base for land, sea, and air forces.

Thailand's uneasiness was expressed at an emergency session of the National Assembly, called in Bangkok yesterday. Premier Luang Bipul Songram was voted dictatorial powers.

Throughout Malaya police contacted all aliens, warning them that they could not leave the colony without permission.

At Hongkong general mobilisation was proclaimed.

Mr. Duff Cooper, representing the British War Cabinet in the Far East, has called a meeting of representatives of all the British possessions in the Orient, to be held at Singapore today.

'WE'RE IN IT AT LAST'

Express Foreign Editor CHARLES FOLEY

NEW YORK, Sunday.

AS suddenly, as treacherously as she flung herself on Czarist Russia a generation ago, Japan today struck at America without warning when President Roosevelt was awaiting a reply to his personal appeal to the Mikado for peace.

Ten minutes ago a Western Union cable operator, Tom Walsh, opened the door of this office. His face was white and he was clutching at his collar.

"They've done it!" he said. And then we knew that America was in the war for keeps.

Football scores were being read over the radio when the first news flash broke in—"The Japanese are bombing Pearl Harbour."

Bombs and fire

The reaction of the people on this sunny Sunday afternoon was one of utter incredulity.

Now messages are coming in faster than we can follow them.

"Manila bombarded."—*So they are going for the spearhead of American power in the Pacific, as well as trying to break the shaft of the spear with an attack on the Hawaiian Islands further out.*

"Smoke of A.A. guns is rising from Pearl Harbour."—*Do guns really smoke like that?*

"And heavy smoke can be seen going up from Ford Island, the U.S. naval and air base on the island of Oahu."—*So the smoke means bombs and fires after all.*

"Police as well as firemen have been called out in Honolulu."—*This suggests fear of*

BACK PAGE, COL. SIX

LONDON JAPS 'SHOCKED'

FIVE secretaries and attachés in golfing flannels sat playing a Japanese card game in the Japanese Embassy in London at 8:55 last night. They switched on the radio.

Six minutes later five astonished men laid down their cards. They heard the news of the attack on Pearl Harbour, stared at each other, one cried: "It can't be true!"

Dapper Mr. Kaira Matsui, third secretary who came to this country at the collapse of France, said to an Express Reporter: "The news came as a complete shock to all of us. But I still can't believe it, I can't believe it."

Mr. Kamimura, chargé d'affaires at the Embassy, was in the country for the week-end. Mr. Shigemitsu, the Ambassador, has been in Japan since June 1940.

'Lick hell . . .'

Senator Burton K. Wheeler, the Isolationist leader, said at Bitlings, Montana: "The only thing now is to do our best and lick hell out of them."

'Got it at last'

The German radio said: "Roosevelt has at last got the war he has always looked for."

Canada stands by

At Victoria, British Columbia, all Royal Canadian Air Force personnel in the Western Air Command were ordered to report immediately. All leave was cancelled.

Mr. Mackenzie King, the Canadian Premier, held a Cabinet meeting at midnight.

Nazi dump explodes

STOCKHOLM, Sunday.—An ammunition dump exploded today at Bergen, Norway, killing 15 German soldiers and two officers. Norwegian patriots are blamed.—Reuter.

JAPS SEIZE SHANGHAI, SINK BRITISH WARSHIP

SHANGHAI, Monday.

THE British gunboat Peterel, lying off the Shanghai Bund, was sunk by a Japanese battery on the south bank of the Whangpo River early today, after a brief exchange of fire.

Soon afterwards Japanese marines stormed into the International Settlement and set up machine-gun posts at all road crossings.

The Peterel (310 tons, two 3inch guns) has a normal complement of 55 officers and men.—B.U.P.

World war news: Latest

SINGAPORE BOMBED: "TWO CRUISERS SUNK"

Columbia radio reports Singapore bombed by Jap planes this morning. Two cruisers sunk, according to unquoted radio source.

Jap newspaper Osaka Mainichi reports Japanese naval force engaged in second sea battle with mixed British-American fleet in Western Pacific.

Report from Shanghai says Japanese have occupied Wake Island, American civil air base in mid-Pacific.

Learned in Washington that four Japanese submarines were destroyed at Hawaii.

Black-out ordered throughout Panama Canal Zone.—Express, Reuter and B.U.P. messages.

On the other battle fronts

'HEADWAY' IN LIBYA

A GREAT tank and infantry battle is raging in Libya.

Express War Reporter Alan Moorehead cables that "the news is much better, we are making headway."—Full story, Page Three.

Fresh drive on Moscow

FOURTH week of Hitler's greatest offensive against Moscow opened yesterday with still more furious attacks, the Soviet radio announced last night.

Russia's midnight communiqué said: "In several sectors of the western (Moscow) front our troops repelled fierce enemy attacks, inflicting heavy losses, and made gains of territory."

Moscow halts tank drive—Back Page.

More attacks on Paris Germans

VICHY, Sunday.—Two more German soldiers were attacked in Paris during the week-end. In one case a lieutenant was shot and is expected to die.

A bomb at midday today badly damaged a Montparnasse restaurant which had been taken over by the Germans. There were no casualties.—B.U.P.

Starlit Straits

Straits of Dover last night: Fine, starlit, much colder.

News Chronicle

No. 29,826 | WEDNESDAY, DECEMBER 10, 1941 | RADIO PAGE 2 | ONE PENNY

Japanese Say Troops Have Landed In The Philippines

Manila Bombed: Battle Still Rages For Key Malayan Airfield

JAPAN claimed last night that she had landed troops in the Philippines, that she had occupied an important strategic point in Northern Malaya and that her naval planes had bombed British destroyers at Hong Kong.

While British forces were still fighting Japanese troops in Northern Malaya, the enemy were also reported to have launched an attack on the Burma Road.

Manila, in the Philippines, had its first bombing attack yesterday and the Japanese dropped leaflets announcing that the population would be "freed from American suppression."

An attempted invasion of Hong Kong at two points was repulsed by British artillery, said a Hong Kong communique.

From Singapore, nearly 1,500 miles away, came reports of severe fighting continuing in the area of Kota Bharu, North Malaya, and a denial of Japanese reports that a landing had been made in South Malaya.

A Chungking cable said last night that a conference between Marshal Chiang Kai-shek and Anglo-American military leaders resulted in the suggestion that an Allied C.-in-C. might lead the combined forces fighting Japan in Southern China.

The claim that Japanese troops had made a successful landing in the Philippines was made by a Japanese military spokesman in Shanghai, according to Berlin radio.

Late last night Manila reports said that a small Japanese force had landed at Lubang, a tiny island off the North-West Coast of Mindoro, about 100 miles south of Manila.

MIDWAY ISLAND SHELLED

The radio quoted the Japanese spokesman as adding: "There have been no Japanese losses during the landings in Malaya, Thailand and the Philippines." The main Japanese force, it was added, had now marched into Bangkok (capital of Thailand).

The Japanese attack on the Burma Road, lifeline over which supplies go to China, was made known by Berlin radio, which claimed that the Japanese had begun an offensive against Burma and were advancing towards the Road.

The main battle front, however, is still in Northern Malaya, where the Japanese were able to land forces under the cover of gunfire from their warships.

Japanese ships, it was also claimed, had shelled the American Pacific base of Midway Island, setting hangars and fuel depots on fire.

The Japanese are using considerable aircraft to cover the landing of troops in Southern Thailand and Northern Malaya. Twenty-five additional Japanese transports had been sighted proceeding southwards along the Thai coast.

More detailed reports flashed to London from all points of the Pacific battle front were:

MALAYA: British Send Reinforcements

"Fighting in North Malaya has been severe, and is still confused," said the midday Singapore communique. British reinforcements should reach the area during the day.

"The Japanese have succeeded in making additional landings. Fighting for control of Kota Bharu aerodrome is particularly severe and lasted throughout the night."

The communique added that the Japanese engaged a considerable number of aircraft in an endeavour to obtain a measure of air superiority so as to cover their landings in Southern Thailand and continued their efforts to gain control of Kota Bharu aerodrome.

Air reconnaissance established that 25 further transports were proceeding down the coast of Thailand escorted by warships and apparently preparing to land additional troops in the Songkla and Kota Bharu area.

The Singapore midday communique added that pre-arranged reinforcement and reconnaissance plans between Australia, the Philippines and the Netherlands East Indies had been "fully implemented."

"The fullest co-operation between the A.B.C.D. Powers in the Far East has been manifested in these first two days of conflict," it said.

The communique concluded: "It is too early yet to forecast what the Japanese main plan is, but there are indications that following the collapse of resistance in Thailand and the heavy scale of his air effort from bases in Indo-China, the enemy is prepared to engage considerable forces in an endeavour to obtain control in Northern Malaya.

"This move was always foreseen to be a likely one and the dispositions of our forces before the outbreak of war were designed to meet it."

The official denial of a Japanese landing in South Malaya came after Tokio had claimed that "Japanese troops are now attacking the Singapore area, while Japanese air units are carrying out daring raids on British air bases in Malaya. A number of British planes, it is claimed, have been destroyed."

PHILIPPINES: Manila Has Its First Air Raid

Japanese planes bombed Manila yesterday. The southern end of the city was the main target, and fires there were visible from other parts. Anti-aircraft guns went into action.

This is the first actual air attack made on Manila, the capital of the Philippines, although Japanese planes have been very near to it and have attacked other targets in the islands. It is on the south-west coast of Luzon, on the west side of Manila Bay. Its population is 285,000, and a cathedral, the archbishop's palace, a university and the mint are among the

Turn to Back Page, Col. Three

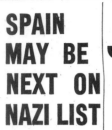

Fighting continues in Southern Thailand and in Northern Malaya. Fiercest battle is for Kota Bharu, vital airfield in Kelantan State, whose Sultan has handed over his administration to Britain "to ensure rapidity of action."

Ronald Walker, News Chronicle Air Correspondent, on the background of the air war in this region: Back Page.

SPAIN MAY BE NEXT ON NAZI LIST

By VERNON BARTLETT

THERE was much speculation yesterday about the significance of the Berlin military spokesman's statement that large-scale operations in Russia "have finished for the winter."

This may, of course, be intended to put the Russians off their guard. But, coupled with the fact that Hitler's puppets in Japan have attacked the Americans and not the Russians, it suggests that German divisions are to be removed from the Eastern Front for work elsewhere.

Hitler cannot now hope to reach the Caucasian oilfields within the next few weeks or months.

He may hope that the winter and the losses they have suffered will prevent the Russians from organising dangerous counter-attacks at any rate in the near future.

In that case there was no point in trying to persuade the Japanese to invade Siberia, the one territory from which serious air reprisals could be organised against Japanese cities.

DIVERTED SHIPPING

Winter would not hamper a campaign in Western Europe, and the Japanese destruction of units of the American Navy would very greatly facilitate it.

Mr. Churchill and others have emphasised the probability that some American shipping will have to be diverted from the Atlantic to the Pacific.

A shortage of shipping must lead to a shortage of supplies for Britain.

That, in turn, may lead Hitler to conclude that he will never again have so favourable an opportunity to isolate and to blockade the British Isles.

It was announced yesterday that the ex-Mufti from Jerusalem had been to see the German leader. The very fact that this was made public makes one sceptical about the rumours of impending German action in the Middle East.

Besides, there is reason to believe that the Germans will not be prepared to attack Turkey before the spring. Work on Bulgarian roads and railways, for example, is far from complete.

GOERING KNEW

It is, however, vitally important for the Germans to complicate communications between the British Isles, on the one hand, and the Middle and Far East, on the other.

Since the date and details of the Japanese attack must have been decided some weeks ago, it is legitimate to suppose that they were known to Goering before he summoned Petain to see him.

It is not known to what extent the veteran Frenchman agreed to German control over French ships and naval bases, but nobody expects him to have shown effective resistance to Goering's demands.

As for Spain, I understand that Senor Suner, the Foreign Minister, has returned from the Anti-Comintern Conference more enthusiastic than ever about the beauties of Hitler's New Europe.

LIBYA IS VITAL

Although the reluctance of the ordinary Spaniard to be dragged into the war has undoubtedly increased now that the United States is lined up with the British Empire, it is not generally expected that he will be allowed to express any opinion if Hitler now decides that, having failed to gain control of the Eastern Mediterranean, he must concentrate on the valuable and narrow stretch of sea between Gibraltar in the west and the French naval base of Bizerta in the east.

The political importance of the British campaign in Libya has therefore been very greatly increased by the Japanese attack on the United States.

Darlan May Go To Italy

The German radio last night broadcast what it described as a "rumour in Vichy political circles" that Admiral Darlan is on his way to Italy to meet Ciano, the Italian Foreign Minister.

"Official confirmation of this journey is not yet issued," the announcer added.

Tunisia is to be one of the main topics of discussions between Admiral Darlan and Mussolini and Ciano, it is reported in New York.

Nazi Warship Reported In South Atlantic

Montevideo, Tuesday. — The Montevideo newspaper "El Pais" today states that the Lutzow, one of Hitler's pocket battleships, is in the South Atlantic off the coast of Argentina.

Choppy

Straits last night: Overcast, low cloud; sea choppy.

LATEST NEWS OF OTHER CAMPAIGNS

Russians Retake Tikhvin, Rout 3 Nazi Divisions

Soviet troops have retaken Tikhvin, 110 miles south-east of Leningrad, the Soviet Information Bureau announced last night, according to Moscow radio.

Tikhvin, which fell to the Germans some weeks ago, is on the railway to Vologda, a highly important route for the transport of supplies to Leningrad.

Three German divisions were routed and 7.000 Germans killed.

Admission that the whole area east of Taganrog, on the Sea of Azov, is in Russian hands, was made by Berlin radio last night. It claimed that the Germans still held the town.

On the Moscow front the Russians are following up their successful attacks in the Tula sector, a vital point in the defence of the capital in the south.

Rommel Faces Encirclement

Pressure on the enemy in Libya is being maintained, and General Rommel is showing increasing reluctance to come to grips.

London's view is that he will have to put up a big fight for the important El Adem junction or else retire westward, and that quickly, if he is to avoid being surrounded.

Mobile columns of the Imperial Forces are extending their range of action, and it seems clear that they are now astride the Axis lines of communication in places both west and north of the enemy.

Meanwhile the R.A.F. are keeping up effective attacks on road transport well to the west.

No Cheap Trips to See Evacuees

There will be no cheap railway facilities for visits to evacuees from December 22 to 26 inclusive.

Vouchers already issued for outward journeys to reception areas during that period will not be valid.

Enemy Supply Ships Bombed

Hudson and Beaufort aircraft of Coastal Command yesterday afternoon attacked a large enemy supply ship escorted by patrol vessels off the Dutch coast. The ship was hit and left on fire, says the Air Ministry.

Off the Norwegian coast another supply ship was bombed by a Hudson aircraft.

Aircraft of Fighter Command, on offensive patrol over Northern France, attacked and severely damaged a factory. One aircraft of Coastal Command is missing from thes operations.

3 In 4 Asked For Fire Guard Exemption

Fire-guard registrations in September numbered 4,950,451. Of these, only 1,213,303 did not apply for exemption.

Staggering Loss of U.S. Battleships

—Vincent Sheehan

PHILADELPHIA, Tuesday.

The United States has lost more ships by Japan's attacks than Britain has lost in the whole of the war, Mr. Vincent Sheehan, the U.S. correspondent and author of "Personal History," asserted in a speech in Philadelphia today.

"The United States will have the greatest humiliation in its history when it learns of the staggering number of Pacific Fleet battleships lost during the first 36 hours of the Japanese attack," he declared.

"This is the greatest reverse of its kind in history. We have lost more ships since Japan attacked us than England has lost in the whole war.

"We have lost all our Pacific possessions except Hawaii and the Philippines."

Mr. Sheehan predicted that the eastern coast of the United States would be bombed in the near future, and said that responsible officials expected that eastern cities would be bombed last night.

He went on to paint a picture of total lack of preparations, saying that American warships lay side by side in Pearl Harbour, presenting an easy target. At Guam, he said that there were two golf courses but no aeroplanes.

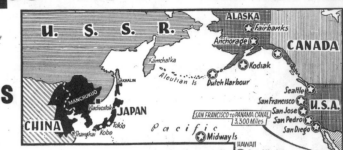

U.S. and Canadian warplanes patrol the Pacific coast from Alaska to Panama. Air and naval bases starred

NEW YORK HEARS THE SIRENS TWICE: Second Alarm Was False

From Our Own Correspondent

NEW YORK, Tuesday.

A "PHONY tip"—in the words of a War Department spokesman in Washington—resulted in an air-raid alarm being given in New York today.

Brooklyn, the New York borough on Long Island, also heard the sirens. In the city itself there were actually two warnings.

America's reaction showed striking determination not to leave anything to chance.

FIRE BEGAN IT

New York's second alarm resulted from an outbreak of fire at Mitchell Field, Long Island. In the confusion, the raid warning was sounded, as well as the fire gongs. "All Clear" came 37 minutes later.

New York wireless stations went off the air at noon, as a precaution, after a warning had been flashed to principal United States cities—in particular, New York, Washington and San Francisco—to be ready for air raids.

In the case of New York, a specific warning from Washington circulated at 12.24 p.m. to the effect that hostile aircraft were "two hours from the city."

The authorities, with eyes on the Nazi technique, were plainly acting on the assumption that a blow might be struck, without warning, from the Atlantic.

PURSUIT PLANES UP

At 1 p.m. U.S. Army pursuit planes could be seen from the News Chronicle office in the "New York Post" building — which fronts shipping piers downtown —circling in formation around the city.

Stevedores and men and women from offices roundabout stood in groups, watching them.

The New York stand-by warning appears to have originated at Governor's Island, military establishment 200yds. off the tip of Lower Manhattan, which is the headquarters of the First Army.

All planes at Mitchel Field, Long Island, biggest airport in the vicinity of New York, took to the air, and families were evacuated from the military reservation.

MRS. ROOSEVELT'S PLANE

Also as a precautionary measure, the aeroplane in which Mrs. Roosevelt and Mayor La Guardia were flying to Los Angeles, to supervise civil defence work, was ordered by the Fourth Civil Defence Command to land at Palm Springs, 100 miles inland, instead of flying on.

Later the War Department at Washington said all airfields were "on the alert." They added that there was no official information concerning a report that enemy bombers had been sighted off New York.

Preparations have been completed for blacking out the White House, Washington, if necessary.

After Brooklyn police broadcast: "Enemy aircraft expected over New York in ten minutes," all schoolchildren were ordered home.

Japanese planes flew over the Panama Coast in the morning, but no bombs were dropped, according to a Panama broadcast.

Nehru on India's Help in the War

Lucknow, Tuesday.—"I should like India to use her strength and resources in favour of possible good changes," said the Pandit Jawaharlal Nehru, at a Press conference here today.

"In the grouping of the Powers struggling for the mastery of the world there seem on either side to be dreams entertained by the Governments for world domination. . . . There is no doubt that the progressive forces of the world are aligned with the group represented by Russia, Britain, America and China."

He emphasised the need for India to take a wider view of things for, he said, there could be no doubt that national isolation was dead and there was hardly likely to be a large number of separate national entities in the future.

The immediate object before India must necessarily be to defend herself.

Mr. Gandhi declared that the Congress Working Committee and members of the All-India Congress Committee must not offer civil disobedience, nor should those interested in reversing the Bombay decision. Apart from these exceptions civil disobedience should continue.

German War Declaration On U.S. Soon?

A German declaration of war on the United States was last night expected at any moment.

Hitler may summons the Reichstag today.

It was stated by a Berlin spokesman: "Germany's position is expected to be clarified within the next 24 hours."

This came after an all-night session at which Hitler, Goering, Goebbels, Brauchitsch, Keitel and Raeder discussed what answer should be given to Tokio's call to Germany for a war declaration on America.

ALL AXIS SUBJECTS ENEMIES OF U.S.

WASHINGTON, Tuesday.— President Roosevelt has placed all Germans, Italian and Japanese in America in the category of "enemy aliens."

New York public safety officials revealed that series of alarms which electrified Eastern Seaboard were "dress rehearsal."

LONDON BLACK-OUT
5.21 p.m. — 8.25 a.m.
Moon rises 11.43 p.m.
Sets 1.15 p.m. tomorrow

No. 10,170 (E*) FRIDAY, DECEMBER 12, 1941 ONE PENNY

UNITED STATES GOES TO WAR WITH GERMANY AND ITALY

40,000,000 IN CALL-UP: 7-DAY WEEK ORDERED

From HESSELL TILTMAN, 'Daily Sketch' Special Correspondent Washington, Thursday

AMERICA IS IN—ALL THE WAY. TO-NIGHT, FOR THE SECOND TIME IN A QUARTER OF A CENTURY, THIS NATION IS FORMALLY AT WAR WITH GERMANY.

The news that Hitler had declared war and that Mussolini had obediently "goose-stepped" after him reached Washington around breakfast time.

It caused little or no excitement, for it changed nothing that counts.

In the words of President Roosevelt's message to Congress to-day: "The long-known and long-expected has taken place." America replied with calm, sure and fast action.

This afternoon Congress broke all records for speed. Within four hours of the news of the joint German-Italian declaration the President's message to Congress requesting recognition of a state of war with Germany and Italy had been passed unanimously by both Senate and House—and the war was officially on.

Overseas Expedition

New York's stock market became firmer on the news. So did the American people.

Then, moving with blitz speed, Congress unanimously voted the Bill authorising the President to send a second American Expeditionary Force anywhere in the world.

Voting in the House of Representatives on the war resolution was 393—0 against Germany and 399—0 against Italy. Senate figures were 88—0 against Germany and 90—0 against Italy.

The country's man-power was to-day estimated at 40,000,000 by Brig.-Gen. Lewis Hershey, Selective Service Director, who said it might be desirable eventually to register all men and women between 18 and 65.

Army of 10,000,000

Ten million could be used "in a military way, leaving 30,000,000 to do everything else."

All American men between 21 and 35 are registered now, and the director said: "We are undoubtedly soon going to consider registration of women."

Car production is to be cut still further so that war supplies can be speeded up. The passenger automobile production quota for December is to be six per cent. below the December output of last year, and the January quota 75 per cent. less than in January, 1941.

The American Federation of Labour and the Congress of Industrial Organisations have been asked by the Office of Production Management to introduce immediately the seven-day, 168-hour week in Defence industries.

Call was also made for 10,000 recruits for its corps of nurses, to fill existing and anticipated vacancies.

Mr. Churchill's War Statement; How the Prince of Wales was Sunk —Page 4; Hitler and Mussolini Speeches—Page 5.

The V.C. has been awarded to Lt.-Commander M. D. Wanklyn, of the submarine Upholder, for a daring attack on an enemy troop convoy. Story on Page Three.

FLEEING NAZIS BLOCK ROADS, SAYS MOSCOW

GERMAN reverses on the Moscow front are increasing. Soviet troops continue their advance, stated last night's Russian communiqué, and have "occupied a number of populated points."

Moscow radio said that the retreating Germans in the direction of Volokolamsk were being dealt ruthless and systematic blows by the troops of General Rokossovsky.

The Germans were attempting to make a stand on certain lines, but the persistent pressure of the Red Army was driving them back relentlessly.

Soviet reconnaissance planes had reported that one of the roads on the route of the German retreat was completely blocked by the fleeing Nazis.

27 Tanks Captured

A special Russian communiqué last night on the prizes captured at Tikhvin mentions, among other booty, 42 guns, 66 trench mortars, 190 machine-guns, 27 tanks.

According to observers in London, our Allies' latest successes at Tikhvin and Yelets have deprived the Germans of two important strategical positions.

The Red Army has recaptured 100 villages in its two days offensive around Yelets, which is 200 miles south of Moscow, according to a front line dispatch to *Izvestia.*

Continued on Back Page, Col. 5

HITLER PEACE HINT TO SOVIET

HITLER is putting out peace feelers to the Soviet Union, said *Pravda's* chief editorial writer, David Zaslavsky, yesterday.

"But the only peace with Germany would be made by the joint agreement of the Soviet Union, Britain and the United States," he added.

After seeing Mr. Cordell Hull, U.S. Secretary of State, yesterday M. Litvinov, Soviet Ambassador, said: "We are fighting in the common cause. We are fighting Hitler more than anyone else."

Lease-Lend Unchanged

He declined to make any comment on Russo-Japanese relations.

M. Litvinov later visited Lord Halifax.

Mr. Hull at his Press conference later said President Roosevelt had assured M. Litvinov that the United States intended to carry out its programme of aid to Russia.

DAYLIGHT RAID ON EMDEN AND HOLLAND

Aircraft of Bomber Command attacked a dock near Emden and an aerodrome in Holland in daylight yesterday states an Air Ministry communique. None of our aircraft is missing.

U.S. BOMBERS SINK BATTLESHIP, CRUISER, DESTROYER

UNITED STATES bombers have struck back in the Pacific by sinking three Japanese warships—a 29,000 ton battleship, a light cruiser and a destroyer—and two other naval units. Four Japanese air attacks on Wake Island in 48 hours have been repulsed by the marine garrison at this important base.

Last night's U.S. Navy communiqué stated that Japanese light naval units had also attacked the island, and added that further attacks and an attempted landing were expected.

"Despite the loss of part of the defending planes and damage to material and personnel," said the communiqué, "the defending garrison succeeded in sinking one light cruiser and one destroyer of the enemy forces by air action."

Seven Japanese planes were shot down over Wake Island, Chungking radio announced last night, according to Associated Press.

The U.S. War Department said last night that there was reason to believe the defence of Luzon Island, in the Philippines, against attempted landings was continuing successfully.

"Japanese planes subjected military and naval installations to occasional bombing throughout the day," said the communiqué.

"There is no change in the military situation in other areas."

Caught Fire

The battleship destroyed was the Haruna, protected by special armour-plate made by Krupps in Germany. Haruna was spotted by an American Army bomber ten miles off the north-east coast of Luzon Island, in the Philippines, where invasion attempts were being covered.

Diving to the attack the bomber scored three direct hits. Two bombs struck her very close together. The battleship caught fire and as the pilot returned to base to report she was blazing fiercely, states Reuter.

The news of this first great U.S. sea success in the Pacific battle was given in Washington yesterday by Mr. Stimson, the War Secretary, who said that he had received official confirmation of the sinking from American G.H.Q. in Manila.

Japs Retire

In Manila it is unofficially reported that the Philippine Army has recaptured the region around Appari, driving the Japs back to the sea coast.

According to Berlin radio the Japanese headquarters announces that units of the Japanese marines penetrated the U.S. island

Continued on Back Page, Col. 1

SINGAPORE SMASHES JAP RAIDS

JAP bombers yesterday tried several times to penetrate Singapore's air defences, but were unsuccessful, says the British United Press.

Penang was heavily bombed yesterday morning, last night's Singapore communiqué revealed.

"In Northern Malaya there has been little to report in the past 24 hours," the communiqué added.

"In the Kedah area our troops are in contact with the enemy near Thailand. At Kuantan our troops still hold original frontiers."

No New Landings

An earlier communiqué said there had been no further attempts to land at Kuantan, nor had air reconnaissance revealed any enemy ships in the area.

The Hong-Kong communiqué stated that there was nothing to report.

Australian bombers based on the Dutch island of Ambon have raided the Japanese air base on Pobra, between Celebes and the Japanese island of Palau.

How badly-hit Hudsons of the R.A.A.F., with bullet holes in the fuselage and even their tyres shot away, have been quickly patched up and returned to the fray was described in Singapore by troops and airmen from Northern Malaya.

These Hudsons have set on fire a Japanese liner, made direct hits on two merchant ships and chased off warships.

2,330 SAVED FROM SUNK WARSHIPS

THE Admiralty announced last night that 130 officers and 2,200 ratings had been saved from both ships. Of the 595 officers and ratings still missing some may be safe, but untraced yet.

It was announced in Singapore last night that Vice - Admiral Sir Geoffrey Layton had temporarily resumed command of the Eastern Fleet in place of Admiral Sir Tom Phillips, officially reported missing from the Prince of Wales. It was only recently that Admiral Phillips took over the Command from Admiral Layton, who had been appointed to a post in Britain.

Captain John Leach, Commander of the Prince of Wales, was also officially reported missing. Captain W. G. Tennant, commanding Repulse, and Captain H. L. Bell, Captain of the Fleet, were saved.

TIMELY WORDS OF FAITH AND WISDOM

Specially selected daily from the Bible for readers of the DAILY SKETCH by Lord Caldecote.

BEHOLD, THE TABERNACLE OF GOD IS WITH MEN, AND HE WILL DWELL WITH THEM, AND THEY SHALL BE HIS PEOPLE, AND GOD HIMSELF SHALL BE WITH THEM, AND BE THEIR GOD. Revelation xxi, 3

SUNDAY PICTORIAL, Dec 14 1941

Sunday Pictorial

No. 1,396 TWOPENCE

ALLIES FIGHTING BACK AT THE JAPANESE

KNOCKED OUT!

Half an hour before this picture was taken a German tank roared into action for the last time. It met its match in a British tank; and the crew found a desert grave.

NEWS from the Pacific was better last night. Successes are reported by Allied sea, air, and land forces.

In the air the R.A.F. over Penang brought down five Japanese planes during morning and afternoon raids on the city. Our own bombers blasted Japanese air bases in Thailand.

On land the Japanese attack is held, though our line has been straightened by a withdrawal on the western Malaya coast.

There are now estimated to be 50,000 Japanese troops in Malaya, and they have been able to bring south some mechanised forces.

Indian motorised detachments have carried out a successful raid on the enemy, inflicting heavy casualties and destroying an important position.

Bangkok reports that British and Chinese forces have invaded North Thailand at Chiengram and there is heavy fighting.

Four fully-laden Japanese transports carrying reinforcements to the invaders of Malaya have been torpedoed and sunk by Dutch submarines. They carried probably 4,000 troops.

Fall of Guam Feared

Colonel Knox, Secretary of the U.S. Navy, returned from Pearl Harbour by plane and left immediately for Washington. "I shall have no statements to release until after a conference with the President," he said.

The U.S. Navy Department announced last night that it was unable to communicate by radio or cable with Guam, the tiny isolated U.S. island base 4,000 miles west of San Francisco. The capture of the island by the Japanese is probable, they added.

It was defended by fewer than 400 sailors and 155 marines.

Japanese forces which had landed at three different points on Luzon Island (one of the Philippine group) have failed to make any new progress, and at Vigan and Lingayen Bay, on the west coast, have been beaten off.

Luzon Cleared of Japs

Another Manila report, quoting a U.S. Command communique, says the northern Luzon area has been entirely cleared of Japanese invaders.

The residential and native quarters of Manila and the nearby Nichols Airfield were heavily attacked by waves of Japanese planes. They were met by intense A.A. fire and U.S. fighters were in action. Several Japanese machines were shot down.

The raids followed a night of shooting in Manila as sentries, with orders to shoot to kill, battled with fifth columnists who fired rockets

Continued on Back Page

Libya Tanks Speeding Up

HARD-PRESSED by our tanks and armoured columns, the Germans and Italians are falling back on a forty-mile front in Libya.

Our advance to Gazala has thrown the enemy into confusion. Every hour more prisoners fall into our hands as we push on.

New Zealanders have encircled Axis troops at Gazala, while further back the last pockets of resistance at Bardia and Sollum are having a thin time.

The Italians are preparing their people for the worst by announcing attacks by an enemy "vastly superior in numbers and machines."

The new commander of our forces, Major-General Ritchie—44 years old—is thrilled by the quality of his men.

"I have never seen their equal," he said yesterday. "The armoured forces have fought on day after day without rest."

General Ritchie disclosed that when the German General von Ravenstein was captured, he declared: "I have never come up against such fighting in all my career."

Cairo messages last night suggested that his uncaptured friends agree with him. They spoke of "quickening enemy withdrawals that are growing more disorganised."

We Get a Telegram

LATE last night this telegram reached the "Sunday Pictorial":—

"Have sent the following telegram to the four Ministries concerned: Gratified to inform you of determined spirit of our workers. Immediately news regarding Prince of Wales and Repulse became known sections voluntarily approached the management and requested to be permitted to work additional overlapping week-end and shift hours for the next few weeks to assist in off-setting this loss. This request was willingly arranged and granted. Thought you would like to know there are some factories really getting down to it, both as regards work and management."

We would have liked to have been able to tell you the name of this managing director's firm, but to do so would merely tell the enemy the location of a factory that is really worth bombing.

Instead, on behalf of all readers, we'll send back this message:—

THANKS PALS!

Strike Hard Now!

Can we hit back at Japan? The answer is —yes. Read the views of the experts on pages 6 and 7.

Daily Express

No. 12,971 Saturday, December 20, 1941 One Penny

THE JAPS GO FORWARD ● BRITISH GARRISON ON INVADED HONGKONG ISLAND REPORTED TO BE MAKING LAST STAND AT VICTORIA PEAK, FORTIFIED PICNIC RESORT. PENANG ISLAND, MALAYA, EVACUATED; JAPS ADVANCE ON MAINLAND.

● RUSSIANS TAKE THREE MORE TOWNS ON MOSCOW FRONT, THREATEN GERMAN FLANK AT MOJAISK. ● BRITISH IN LIBYA TAKE DERNA AIRFIELD, CUT OFF AXIS FORCES IN PORT OF DERNA. **THE GERMANS GO BACK**

HONGKONG GARRISON FIGHT TO THE LAST

'Final stand' at picnic mountain turned into a Gibraltar

HONGKONG, FIGHTING TO THE DEATH WITH SWARMS OF JAPANESE WHO LANDED YESTERDAY AT MANY POINTS ON THE ISLAND, REJECTED WITH SCORN A THIRD OFFER OF SURRENDER TERMS, AND THEN CAME SILENCE.

Late last night it was officially announced in London :—

"The report from Japanese sources that Hongkong has been in Japanese hands since this morning cannot be confirmed or denied, as no communication has been received from the colony since early this morning."

Berlin, quoting Tokyo reports, said the Japanese flag had been hoisted in the port of Hongkong, and that points of final British resistance were being broken.

Tokyo announced last night that the remaining defenders of the colony had withdrawn to Victoria Peak, the 1,800 ft. "picnic mountain" at the western end of the island, where they were putting up a last stand.

PENANG EVACUATED

From Malaya came news that Penang, the island oil and rubber port on the west coast, had been completely evacuated.

British forces battling on the mainland south of Penang have withdrawn to a new defence line south of the River Krian.

The main battle ot the peninsula is now in Perak State, where a bold stand is possible from Bagan Serai (10 miles from the border of Wellesley Province) to Taiping, 20 miles southward. Taiping is about 320 miles north of Singapore.

JAPS CLAIM A CAPITAL CITY

IN messages from Kowloon, the Japanese claim to have "occupied Victoria, the capital of Hongkong, intact" . . . The city extends along the coast for about 5 miles . . . The harbour of Hongkong (Hongkong Roads) covers an area of 10 square miles.

Hand-to-hand fights on Hongkong shore

UNDER a pall of smoke, which the Japanese said came from blazing oil tanks, Hongkong Colony began an heroic fight to a finish for its 100-year-old British status yesterday under its "No surrender" Governor, Sir Mark Young.

PENANG
Georgetown
PENANG GARRISON EVACUATED
NEW BRITISH LINE
STRAITS OF MALAYA
AIRFIELD ATTACKED BY JAPS

Swarms of Japanese troops landed during Thursday night and yesterday. Streams of Japanese planes dive-bombed the defences.

Although Tokyo claimed that the island was in Japanese hands by 11 a.m., later messages poured in by cable and radio mentioning furious British resistance.

Last night, Domei, the Official Japanese Agency, said the invading forces were "keeping up a smashing offensive against the British defence forces under cover of artillery and air bombardment."

CANADIANS' FIRST

In a detailed account of the landings last night, a Japanese reporter cabled to Tokyo that the remaining British forces still in the fight had retired to the highest point in the island—Victoria Peak.

Hongkong's garrison consists of Canadians, who arrived in November, and the normal garrison of Indians, with technical and engineering units from Britain.

It is the first time the Canadians have been in battle in this war.

Victoria Peak is the Gibraltar of the colony. It has many natural caves which have been developed as vast air-raid shelters.

It dominates the western end of the island, overlooking the capital, Victoria, above which the Japanese claim that the Rising Sun flag is flying.

The mountain is 1,800 feet high, and is a picnic spot for all the races of the island in peacetime.

12-HOUR SHELLING

It is beautifully wooded, commands magnificent views, and is studded with magnificent bungalows, country clubs, and sanatoriums set in English-style gardens.

A tramway service runs up its slopes.

Here is the Japanese reporter's account of the battle for Hongkong :—

"While Japanese forces waited to embark our artillery kept up a 12-hour non-stop bombardment of the enemy batteries.

"The first detachments embarked at 9.35 p.m. last night as an artillery duel was in progress.

"They landed at three points—in the north-eastern part of

→ BACK PAGE, COL. SEVEN

Penang's women escape

SINGAPORE, Friday.

PENANG'S garrison, including volunteers and the police force, have been successfully taken off the island, it is announced in Singapore tonight.

The town and island of Penang rank next in importance to Singapore in the Straits Settlements, and are an export base for tin, rubber and oil.

Japanese occupation of part of the mainland coast opposite the island was announced yesterday.

Ninety British women and 118 British children who were evacuated from Penang arrived at Batavia, together with 19 Dutch women and children today. Other shiploads of evacuees reached Singapore.

The main battle in Malaya had now moved out of Wellesley Province into the State of Perak, further south.

Stronger line

Here the territory favours strong static defences. The withdrawal means that defences along the River Krian have been abandoned.

Reports from the front say that the Japanese are using infiltration methods in which groups of men are sent forward, and the Japanese commanders are apparently content if only 50 men out of 200 reach their objective.

Fighting under these conditions is savage guerrilla warfare.—B.U.P.

'Malay airfield blitzed'

German reports on the Malaya fighting said yesterday: "The Japanese, after crossing the Krian River, are pushing towards Ipoh, which has suffered a heavy air raid."

Chinese 10 miles from Kowloon

CHUNGKING, Friday.—Chinese forces attacking the Japanese flank along the Canton-Kowloon River have advanced to a point ten miles north-east of Shumchun, on the Kowloon border, and are pushing south-west.—Reuter.

The news is grave, says Duff Cooper

SINGAPORE, Friday.

MR. DUFF COOPER, who was today appointed Resident Minister in Singapore with Cabinet status, said tonight in a broadcast : "The news is grave.

"Our forces have been obliged to retreat in north-west Malaya and as this exposes Penang to attack and we have not sufficient troops to garrison it, it has been necessary to evacuate the majority of the civilian population.

"Let us not blind ourselves to the gravity of the situation or the seriousness of the task that awaits us.

"Let us frankly admit that so far the Japanese have been extremely successful."—Reuter.

FOOTNOTE by Express Military Reporter Morley Richards :—

Penang, unhappily, had never been fortified on an adequate scale. Its loss will mean this :

1—A first-class air base can be utilised by the Japanese to attack shipping in the Indian Ocean and gain some control over the Strait of Malacca, Singapore's best sea lane from India ;

2—Vital rubber and tin from Malaya can no longer be shipped by us from the port.

The considerable British withdrawal from the River Krian on the mainland means that our forces are now attempting to hold the main motor road from Bandar Serai to Taiping.

The enemy, with only a short pause, has evidently come on again in strength, barely giving us time to bring up much-needed reinforcements.

U.S. fighters break up Manila raiders

Express Correspondent

MANILA, Friday. — Japanese bombers attacking the Cavite naval base in two waves today were put to flight by swarms of American pursuit planes and heavy A.A. fire. Damage is believed to be slight.

NAZIS SENT TO BIZERTA

Express Correspondent

CAIRO, Friday.

DESPITE the undoubted toughening of the French attitude towards the Axis following the entry into the war of the United States, Hitler is insisting on using Bizerta as a naval base.

Reports received in Cairo from Vichy say that a number of German technicians have reached the Tunisian port in the last few weeks, some having come in an Italian submarine, to inspect the harbour facilities and establishments.

One or two Italians accompanied them, but Italy is taking a minor part in these activities, although there is a large Italian colony in Tunisia.

It is stated that the police had recently to break up a parade by students who were demonstrating in Bizerta's streets to shouts of "Tunis for the Tunisians."

Jap bombers kill children

Dutch town raided

BATAVIA, Friday.

Scores of people, a number of schoolchildren among them, were killed in a Japanese air raid on the town of Pontianak, Dutch West Borneo, it was officially announced today.

Many more people were injured. Dutch bombers have retaliated by attacking Japanese forces in British North Borneo, says a communiqué issued by the Dutch East Indies Government.—Reuter and B.U.P.

NO TRAINS

Eire warned

Withdrawal of all passenger trains, at least temporarily, was forecast yesterday by Eire's Great Southern Railway. The company is believed to have only one week's coal supply.

No bookings for Christmas travel will be accepted after today.

Roosevelt promotes Philippines general

WASHINGTON, Friday.—President Roosevelt today promoted Lieutenant-General Douglas MacArthur, commander of U.S. forces in the Philippines, to the rank of general.—Reuter.

Office milk cut

Milk cuts announced last night : Supplies to factories for workers by one-third; supplies for office tea, by one-half.

7,000,000 U.S. MEN TO MARCH

Express Staff Reporter

NEW YORK, Friday.

SEVEN million Americans will march to war during the next year.

That was the expectation in Washington tonight as Congress adopted a compromise Conscription Bill. The Senate and House of Representatives agreed to call men aged 20 to 44 inclusive into military service.

Before the Japanese attack on Hawaii the American Army had reached a figure somewhere near 1,500,000 men, according to the last published figures. At least 500,000 more were in the Navy.

As Congress acted today spokesmen for the Office of Civilian Defence declared that the registration of women for a land army to work on the farms next spring and summer was almost a certainty.

President Roosevelt revealed at his Press conference that day-by-day discussions between the Allies regarding the co-ordination of the various commands have been in progress for weeks.

The President will broadcast to the nation in a "fireside chat" on Christmas Eve.

5,000 Italians drowned

TUNIS, Friday.

TWO Italian cruisers, one destroyer and three transports were sunk in the Mediterranean with the loss of 5,000 men on December 12, it is learned in Tunis tonight.

About 1,000 Italians are reported to have been rescued on the Tunisian coast.

The cruisers were probably the Alberto de Giussano and the Aberico da Barbiano, of 5,000 tons. —A.P.

Admiralty communiqués have already reported an Italian cruiser sunk and a cruiser and a torpedo boat damaged by British destroyers on December 13.

ONE BURST—

Two Junkers

A pilot flying an old-type Hurricane over the North Sea yesterday saw two Junkers 88's.

He fired a burst at one, and hit it. It cannoned into the other and both crashed into the sea.

Lt-Com. resigns Navy job—'Call me mister'

Express Naval Reporter

LIEUTENANT-COMMANDER REGINALD FLETCHER, R.N., Socialist M.P. for Nuneaton, made the surprising announcement last night that he had resigned his position as Parliamentary Private Secretary to the First Lord of the Admiralty. He also said that he wished to be known in future as Mr. R. Fletcher.

Mr. Fletcher was named on Thursday as one of three Socialist M.P.s expected to go to the House of Lords soon.

But, says Express Political Correspondent, it has been noticed in the House this week that Mr. Fletcher had rejoined the rank and file of the Labour Party, on the Opposition side of the House.

There is no indication, however, concerning Mr. Fletcher's attitude to the controversy surrounding the Navy since the opening of hostilities in the Pacific, although it is understood he has been pressing for certain reforms in the work of the Admiralty.

Mr. Fletcher, who is 56, has been Socialist M.P. for Nuneaton since 1935. Before the war he had retired from the Navy, but returned to active service when war broke out. In May last year he joined Mr. Alexander.

Woman kills two German soldiers

STOCKHOLM, Friday.—A 33-year-old Russian woman, Maria Maroutaiev, confessed in Brussels today that she killed two German soldiers by stabbing them in a dark street.

Soon after her arrest a German N.C.O. was found stabbed in a wood. Reprisals are threatened.—B.U.P. and Exchange.

Spanish 'war goods' ship held in Cuba

HAVANA, Friday.—The 3,708-ton Spanish freighter Rita Garcia was today detained by Cuban authorities as she had "undeclared war materials" aboard.—Reuter.

Misty

Straits : Mist ; light north-westerly breeze.

Germans in Derna are cut off

Express Staff Reporter ALAN MOOREHEAD

OUTSIDE DERNA, Friday.

THE Germans are still on the run in Libya. By last night they had retreated over 70 miles in three days and were still falling back, pursued by the British in every sector.

Rommel's forces are split. The remains of his once powerful panzers—those he was able to extricate from the three-day battle at Alem Hamza—are retreating from Mekili westwards towards Apollonia and Benghazi.

Fifty miles north, on the coastal road, are the remnants of his defeated infantry divisions. Some of them are locked in Derna, where in last year's great Italian retreat from Libya the enemy made a ten-day stand.

Hurricane bombers

We are already in possession of the airfield on the escarpment 8½ miles from the town.

As they withdraw, the Germans and Italians, whether riding in tanks, armoured cars or trucks or trudging afoot, are taking a terrific beating from the R.A.F.

All day long Hurricane bombers, medium bombers and fighters swoop down on their long columns moving westward.

Yesterday the pilots counted dozens of trucks aflame, burnt-out or capsized their occupants scattered.

The retreat extends in depth. Our planes located and strafed troops as far back as west of Barce, on the other side of Jebel Akdar, and not 60 miles from Benghazi.

The roads which the retreating troops must take are pitted with bomb craters.

The Luftwaffe is fighting back with new planes received from Europe, but by now they can't have the fuel supplies necessary to keep them going long, and they have lost a number of valuable advanced airfields.

And meanwhile our infantry and guns are coming up. "Attack and pursue" was General Auchinleck's order to the Eighth Army, given in an Order of the Day at a time—November 25—when the battle was taking a turn for the better.

We attacked and won two great victories. Now we are pursuing.

The order said :—

"During three days at advanced

BACK PAGE, COL. FIVE

ROMMEL ESCAPES IN BOAT

Express Military Reporter

IT was unofficially reported to me in London last night that General Rommel has escaped from Bomba in a motor-boat after the defeat of his Libya army.

If this prove true, it is probable that the German commander would be landed further down the coast towards Benghazi.

He has fought so resolutely that it is not likely he will now abandon the remnant of his force.

RUSSIANS THREATEN MOJAISK

Express Staff Reporter

STOCKHOLM, Friday.

RECAPTURE of three towns on the Moscow front, and the wiping out of a whole German division with the death of the general commanding, are announced in tonight's Russian communiqué.

The captured towns are Ruza, Tarusa and Kanino.

Ruza is 12 miles north of Mojaisk, and 60 miles west of Moscow. Its capture gives the Russians easy command of the main highway from Moscow behind the advanced German forces in Mojaisk.

Tarusa is 70 miles south-west of Moscow, and Kanino is due west of Tula.

The communiqué adds: "Our troops have continued to advance.

"Units under Major-Gen. Gorodnyansky on the south-western front completely destroyed the 134th German Infantry Division.

"Not a single German escaped. The general in command was killed."

*** Russians smash on past dead Germans : Back Page.

WORLD WAR NEWS
3 A.M. LATEST

GERMANS LOSE 22,000 MEN IN SIX DAYS

MOSCOW, Friday.—Germans lost 22,000 men killed or wounded on Moscow Front between December 11 and 17, said Soviet Information Bureau tonight. In same period Germans lost 319 tanks, 48 armoured cars, 484 guns, 231 trench mortars, 659 machine guns, 1,093 automatic rifles, 3,783 lorries, and 440 motor-cycles.—Reuter.

New York World-Telegram

Copyright, 1942, by New York World-Telegram Corporation. All rights reserved.

Local Forecast: Cloudy this afternoon; cloudy with light snow tonight.

VOL. 74.—NO. 161.—IN TWO SECTIONS—SECTION ONE | NEW YORK, FRIDAY, JANUARY 9, 1942. | Entered as second class matter Post Office, New York, N. Y.

7TH SPORTS

Final Stock Tables

Latest Racing on Page 27.

PRICE THREE CENTS

JAPS PIERCE BRITISH LINE

Break Through in Malaya; Chinese Smash Into Canton

Dean Landis Named OCD Executive

Mayor to Remain Director; Harvard Aid to Have Charge of Personnel

By the United Press.

WASHINGTON, Jan. 9.—Administration of the Office of Civilian Defense was divided today between Mayor La Guardia of New York and Dean James M. Landis of Harvard University Law School. Mr. Landis will be the agency's $10,000-a-year executive, while Mayor La Guardia continues as the unpaid director.

The partial reorganization of the controversial OCD setup was announced by White House Secretary Stephen Early. He said it had been worked out by President Roosevelt, Mr. La Guardia and Mr. Landis. The latter will take leave of absence from Harvard.

Mayor Criticized.

Mayor La Guardia, who has been criticized in Congress and in his own city for seeking to attempt to run the OCD as director while retaining his post of mayor, said that the new arrangement would leave him free for organizational work throughout the country.

He added:

"Frankly, this plan meets the Washington situation because of the growth and the added activities of the Office of Civilian Defense, and will afford me more time in the field.

"Frankly, it does not meet the New York City situation because it will take more of my time. I must be realistic about this."

He declined to elaborate on this point, but previously had said he expects to continue as Mayor.

Warden Insurance Asked.

He continued:

"The matter of equipment is of the utmost importance. I must warn the country that we must have the fire equipment ordered and in production at once. There must be no delay.

"I also want to see the bill

(Continued on Page Two.)

George Sees 10 Billion In New Taxes Needed

But Sales Levy, He Asserts, Will Be Only a Final Resort

By the United Press.

WASHINGTON, Jan. 9.—Chairman George (D., Ga.) of the Senate Finance Committee said today that to meet President Roosevelt's budget plans it would be necessary to levy taxes that would bring in new revenue at a rate of $10,000,000,000 a year.

After a conference at the Treasury with Secretary Morgenthau and other Congressional leaders Mr. George said that additional taxes would be needed at the $10,000,000,000 annual rate, if $7,000,000,000 in new revenues is to be produced in the fiscal year which begins next July 1, as proposed by Mr. Roosevelt.

Problem a Big One.

The reason, he explained, is that some taxes will not begin to yield revenue immediately and that the increased national income subject to taxes contemplated under the war production program will not take full effect until late in the year.

"The problem," said Mr. George, "is even bigger than appears on the face."

Mr. George said that if Mr. Roosevelt's proposal for a $2,000,000,000 annual boost in social security collections is taken into consideration the annual rate of new revenue would have to be $12,000,000,000 instead of $10,000,000,000.

Today's Talks Preliminary.

He emphasized that he does not necessarily favor such great hikes in taxes, but that he was advancing the figures to make clear the problem now confronting the government in seeking ways of paying for all-out arms production.

He said today's conference was purely "preliminary." The Treasury, he said, did not present a program calling for any specific

(Continued on Page Eight.)

Cold Continues, Snow Tonight

Brooklyn Man Dies of Exposure

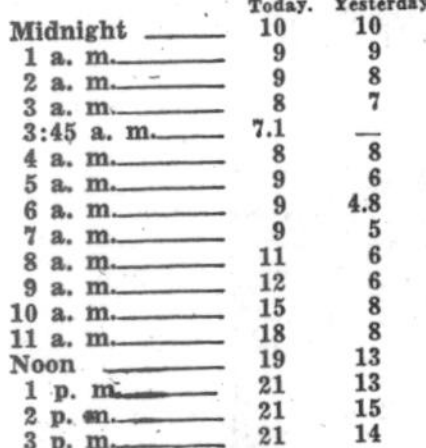

TEMPERATURES.

	Today.	Yesterday.
Midnight	10	10
1 a. m.	9	9
2 a. m.	9	8
3 a. m.	8	7
3:45 a. m.	7.1	—
4 a. m.	8	8
5 a. m.	9	6
6 a. m.	9	4.8
7 a. m.	9	5
8 a. m.	11	6
9 a. m.	12	6
10 a. m.	15	8
11 a. m.	18	8
Noon	19	13
1 p. m.	21	13
2 p. m.	21	15
3 p. m.	21	14

New York remained in the grip of the cold spell today for the fourth consecutive day as the mercury dipped at 3:45 a. m. to 7.1 degrees just 2.3 degrees higher than yesterday's low.

The Weather Bureau still held little hope of relief. The low expected tonight is 15 degrees. A

(Continued on Page Two.)

The Weather

(Official United States Forecast.)

New York and Metropolitan Area—Cloudy this afternoon; highest temperature about 20; cloudy with light snow tonight.

Lowest temperature expected tonight, 15 in city and suburbs.

New Jersey—Light snow and not so cold tonight.

Conne[illegible]—Cloudy with occasional [illegible] snow and warmer tonight, [illegible]ed by clearing, with falling temperatures toward morning.

Highest and lowest temperatures a year ago, 40-28.

Also Enter Nanchang, Lost in '38

By the Associated Press.

CHUNGKING, Jan. 9.—The Chinese reported today that their forces had penetrated the outer defenses of two of the most important Japanese-held cities of south China, Canton and Nanchang, capitals of Kwangtung and Kiangsi provinces.

The Chinese also claimed successes on a half-dozen other fronts of central China, and announced that while fresh expeditionary forces awaited only the word to enter British Burma troops already massed there were taking up "designated positions," mostly in northern Burma.

Drive Started Three Days Ago.

[A Chinese war communique said latest information from the north Hunan front indicated the Japanese Third and Sixth divisions, which led the attack on Changsha, have "almost completely been annihilated," according to a Chungking broadcast heard by the United Press in San Francisco.]

An army communique said that two Chinese columns had driven into the northern and northeastern suburbs of Canton in an assault that began three days ago.

Chinese dispatches said heavy casualties had been inflicted on the defenders of Nanchang.

Canton and Nanchang have been in Japanese hands since 1938.

[Nanchang is 190 miles northeast of Changsha, where the Chi-

(Continued on Page Eight.)

Recommends Army Take Jack Dempsey

Col. George H. Baird, Army recruiting officer for this area, today announced he had recommended to the War Department that Jack Dempsey, once heavyweight champion of the world, be accepted as a buck private even though 11 years beyond the age limit.

Mr. Dempsey volunteered earlier this week, passing the physical examination with flying colors.

The United States Marine Corps, meanwhile, disclosed that with the enlistment of 17-year-old Neil Clark of Rockville Center, L. I., five members of the Clark family are now engaged in war work. Two of Neil's brothers are with the Royal Canadian Air Force, a third is on duty at Pearl Harbor with the Navy, and their father is a civilian worker on a defense job in Greenland.

Only 11, Gives $428 To Help Win War

By the Associated Press.

ROYAL OAK, Mich., Jan. 9.—Teddy Burton, 11, wrote to the President:

"I am 11, and can't get in the Marines but am sending you $428.88 to help win the war."

The sum, his entire bank account, was withdrawn yesterday with the permission of his parents, turned into a cashier's check and mailed to the President.

Where Japs Broke British Line

World-Telegram Map.

Reds Break Siege At Leningrad

Recover All Lost In Nazi Drives

By the Associated Press.

Russia's armies were declared today to have virtually broken the long-drawn sieges of Leningrad and Sevastopol, and Soviet dispatches reported that "east of Leningrad the Germans have now lost everything they have been able to capture in the past three months."

This would indicate that the invaders had been thrown back from the eastern arc of their siege ring, with defenders of the old Czarist

(Continued on Page Seven.)

U-Boat Sinks British Cruiser

By the United Press.

LONDON, Jan. 9.—The Admiralty said tonight that the British cruiser Galatea had been torpedoed and sunk by a German submarine.

The Galatea was understood to have been sunk in the Mediterranean. She was of 5220 tons and carried a normal complement of 450 men. She was built in 1934.

Subway Stroller Gets Jail Term

Daniel Crane, 46, of 332 Pearl St., Brooklyn, who walked for five blocks along the Independent Subway tracks between Hoyt and Fulton Sts. stations in Brooklyn, was sentenced today in Flatbush Court to nine days in jail for trespassing.

Crane said he was looking for a silver dollar he had dropped through the street grating. He didn't find it.

Good News

Dutch East Indies oil center beats off Jap bombers, downs one.

Chinese penetrate outer Japanese defenses at Nanchang.

Japs suffer "incredible" losses in opening all-out attack on British lines in West Malaya.

Russians lift sieges of Leningrad and Sevastopol.

Allied submarines drive sea war to Japanese shores. Tokyo admits freighter torpedoed.

British navy blasts Axis positions in Halfaya Pass area, Libya.

United States volunteer fliers wreck seven Japanese planes in raid on Thailand airdrome.

Allied Sub in Action 100 Miles Off Tokyo

Torpedoes Freighter, Gives Japs Preview Taste of Dread Blockade

By the Associated Press.

Japan got a preview taste today of the thing she dreads most—a possible blockade of her densely populated island empire—as Imperial headquarters acknowledged an Allied submarine raid within 100 miles of Tokyo in which the 2225-ton freighter Unkai Maru No. 1 was torpedoed and damaged.

The nationality of the attacking craft was not given.

Previously, a U. S. Navy bulletin reported that submarines of the American Asiatic fleet had sunk a 10,000-ton Japanese transport and three 10,000-ton Japanese supply ships.

The navy's communique was the first report in many days from the sizable underseas force operating in Far East waters at the start of the war, a month ago, but naval officials emphasized that the dangerous missions of the submarines made prompt reports foolhardy while operations are proceeding.

Imperial Tokyo headquarters said the attack in Japanese waters occurred early yesterday morning off the Izu Shichito Islands, 100 miles south of Tokyo and Yokohama. The ship was severely damaged. The crew was reported saved.

Official acknowledgment that the war has been brought to Japan's own doorstep came as the victory-flushed Nipponese boasted

(Continued on Page Eight.)

The War Today

Japanese heavy tanks and dive bombers launch main Malaya offensive in Slim River area, 50 miles north of Kuala Lumpur, as endless waves of infantry charge slowly retiring Imperial line.

War Department reports lull in Luzon fighting, but adds Japanese are continuing movement of reinforcements into forward areas.

Japan admits freighter was sunk within 100 miles of Tokyo as United States Navy reports American submarine toll of one Jap transport and three supply ships.

Tokyo again claims United States aircraft tender Langley was sunk and press discusses Jap invasion of United States.

Russia, throwing new armies into action, reports virtual lifting of German sieges both at Leningrad in north, Sevastopol in south.

Chungking reports Chinese troops have penetrated outer defenses of Jap-held Canton and Nanchang.

British naval units join land artillery and air forces in unified effort to destroy Axis forces holding out at Halfaya Pass, eastern Libya.

American volunteer fliers destroy seven Jap bombers near Bangkok.

La Guardia and Landis to share responsibility as heads of OCD in new setup.

White House reveals United States fliers are dropping leaflets on occupied France.

Defenders Reported Circled in Kuala Lumpur—Enemy Loses Heavily

By HAROLD GUARD,
United Press Staff Correspondent.

WITH BRITISH ON WEST MALAYA FRONT, Jan. 9.—Japanese heavy tanks forced a break-through on the bitterly-contested front north of Kuala Lumpur, British military sources said today, and the battle front has assumed "a serious aspect."

The Japanese attacked in a general offensive with mechanized units heavier than the British defense and with great numbers of troops in support.

Japanese aerial reconnaissance planes flew low over the roads, apparently confident that they would not be attacked.

[The daring of Japanese aviators indicated lack of British air power on the Malayan front as the Japanese drove toward Singapore. Axis broadcasts reported from Tokyo that the British rear communications lines had been cut in the key sector of Kuala Lumpur, with only one road open for them to fall back to the west coast. These dispatches indicated that the Japanese had encircled the Kuala Limpur sector except for the one road.

[Tokyo radio claimed that the British lines were collapsing and that the British had fallen back to Negri Sembilan Province, less than 200 miles from Singapore, destroying bridges in a confused retreat.]

I returned southward after spending a day in Selangor positions in the vicinity of Kuala Kuba (north of Kuala Lumpur), where the British were greatly outnumbered but were inflicting tremendous casualties on huge enemy forces.

["The slaughter of Japanese in some areas in Malaya is unbelievable," the BBC reported today, quoting a British correspondent, and added that "British concentrated fire has mowed down wave after wave of them and whole detachments have been blown to pieces." The broadcast was heard by NBC.]

I was in an area of destroyed rubber and tin mining resources and blasted industries. Sun-baked, dishevelled and tired British and Indian troops were returning from advance outposts where they had been fighting against increasingly heavy odds.

There were amazing scenes along the roads of what onc ewas a peaceful, rich countryside. Lines of refugees fled southward on foot or in carts, carrying all they had bee nable to salvage from the battle zone.

Most of the refugees walked and carried bundles on their heads. Even the smallest child who could walk was burdened with a bundle. Many wounded also were en route southward.

On all side sthere were derelict tin mine dredges, burning rubber stocks and wrecked machinery.

Overhead were the enemy planes, watching every move.

The Japanese were using many dive-bombers along the front.

A brigadier who had reached the front line made his way 15 miles back to bring the news earlier that the Japanese had opened with their full striking force.

The attack was launched in the Slim River region, north of Tanjong Malim, or about 50 miles north of Kuala Lampur.

In the first assault the Empire troops capture done tank intact after killing its crew of five, including a lieutenant whose equipment included a valuable Japanese tactical handbook, maps, charts and a camera with negatives which were rushed to the general staff.

For days the Japanese had been sending bicycle troops in advance of their lines. Opening their gen-

(Continued on Page Thirteen.)

House Votes to Move Clocks Up One Hour

By the United Press.

WASHINGTON, Jan. 9.—The House today passed a bill providing for mandatory daylight saving time—advancing clocks one hour throughout the country—for the duration of the war.

The vote was announced as 67 to 20.

It provided that the "fast" time should begin 20 days after enactment and end six months after termination of the war.

The Senate has passed a bill to give President Roosevelt authority to move clocks forward or backward as much as two hours, it his discretion. The difference in the two bills now must be adjusted in a House-Senate conference.

Cop Nabs 4 Bandits And Gets a Wild Ride

At 3:30 a. m. today the sergeant at the Newtown station house in Queens looked up and saw four thugs march to his desk, their hands held high above their heads. Prodding the men along with his gun was Patrolman Robert McCarthy.

Patrolman McCarthy, who captured the four single-handed and then balked an attempt to escape as he was bringing them to the station house, told this story:

Half an hour before he had noticed the four men, all shabbily dressed, in a shiny new Packard parked at the corner of Roosevelt Ave. and Junction Blvd. in Queens. He ducked into a hallway to watch and listen.

One of the men got out of the

(Continued on Page Two.)

Fliers 'Bomb' Occupied France With U. S. Friendship Leaflets

By the United Press

WASHINGTON, Jan. 9.—The White House disclosed today that the United States, with the aid of the British Royal Air Force, has started a campaign of dropping leaflets on occupied portions of France stressing "the historic friendship" between the French and American people.

White House Secretary Early said more than 2,000,000 American pamphlets had been dropped on Nazi-occupied portions of France by the British.

Other leaflets probably will be distributed from the air throughout other occupied portions of Europe.

The pamphlet was designated as U. S. Leaflet No. 1 to the People of Occupied France.

The RAF dropped 1,380,000 copies of it in the area around Paris and more than 600,000 copies in the Lille area this week.

Mr. Early said the President had received a report from an RAF official in London saying:

"U. S. leaflet No. 1 was acclaimed everywhere in the RAF

(Continued on Page Eight.)

World-Telegram Index

Daily Mail

LATE WAR NEWS SPECIAL

NO. 14,270 ONE PENNY * * * FOR KING AND EMPIRE THURSDAY, JANUARY 22, 1942

DAY-LONG BATTLE IN MALAYA

Germans Ban Dancing 'at Army's Request'

BERLIN radio broadcast to the German people yesterday a comprehensive ban on all dancing—including even the teaching of dancing. This was done, it was stated, "at the express wish of members of the armed forces in view of the difficult operations on the Eastern Front." This is the first time that the Germans have banned dancing because of a German retreat. Always in the past the ban has preceded the launching of an offensive.

VAST NAZI LOSSES IN 6 WEEKS

300,000 Men; 4,800 Guns Lost

From RALPH HEWINS, Daily Mail Special Correspondent

STOCKHOLM, Wednesday.

THE German Army in Russia has lost 300,000 men killed since Stalin's great offensive was launched on December 6—just over six weeks ago.

Sherbakov, Secretary of the Moscow Communist Party, announced this to-day at the memorial meeting for the 18th anniversary of Lenin's death. Stalin was at the meeting.

Sherbakov gave immense figures of German losses of war material in the same period. Among them are:

4,801 guns, 15,000 automatic rifles, 2,760 tanks, 700 armoured-cars, 33,640 lorries, 6,000 motor-cycles, many thousands of bicycles, carts, and horses, and more than 1,100 planes.

The enormous German losses in men and equipment during the Mojaisk battle are not included in Sherbakov's figures.

Vast Withdrawal

The Germans had intended to blow up everything in Mojaisk, but the Russians were too quick for them. All public buildings were, however, wrecked.

General Govarov, the Russian field commander under General Zhukov, is already pushing on rapidly west of Mojaisk, harrying the fleeing Germans.

The capture of the town will probably be followed now by a wholesale German withdrawal towards Vyazma.

Berlin will not admit the fall of Mojaisk. Goebbels to-day announced: "In spite of continuous efforts, the Soviet troops have been unable to effect any change in the German eastern front, which stands firm from Leningrad to the Crimea."

The German communiqué, however, admitted a Soviet break-through on the upper part of the Donetz River.

Russian attacks on the northern and central fronts are also admitted.

German circles here say that fierce battles are raging in the vicinity of Kursk, one of the key towns on the Ukraine front.

Moscow Sweep

Incessant Russian attacks in the Valdai Hills area, south of Leningrad, where Moscow yesterday claimed the recapture of Ostashkov, are also admitted.

The Red Army Colonel Gurov reports that his troops are making a clean sweep of the Germans in the immediate vicinity of Leningrad.

German losses there in less than one month's fighting have been 18,000 killed, he says.

"The push from Leningrad gathered momentum after the recapture of the entire eastern bank of the Volkhov River and the establishment of a bridgehead at Novye Krisi," he adds.

MOTOR LOSSES WORRY HITLER

The vast destruction of German motor-lorries, cars, and motor-cycles announced last night by the Russians is reflected in Hitler's appointment yesterday of an "Inspector-General of Motorised Traffic."

Hitler's order says: "It has become necessary that I should be kept informed of all important questions of motorised traffic, as far as they concern the war, more quickly and thoroughly than before."

The inspector, Jakob Welin, will work directly under Hitler and take orders only from him. He is authorised to investigate motorised traffic is Greater Germany and the Occupied territories, including the war zones, whether in military, civil, party, or private hands.

German motor traffic has received special attention from the Red Army and Red Air Force. It is believed that the Russian High Command hope to cause such high losses as will bring about a transport crisis behind the German front.

Spain-Vichy Debt Agreement

From Daily Mail Correspondent

MADRID, Wednesday.—A financial agreement relating to the liquidation of non-commercial debts was signed here to-day by the Spanish Foreign Minister, Señor Suner and the Vichy Ambassador, M. Pietri.

Afterwards M. Pietri handed to Señor Suner a copy of Marshal Pétain's book "New France," which is dedicated to Señor Suner.

Keitel Sees Horthy

BERLIN, Wednesday. — Field-Marshal Keitel was received in audience by the Regent, Admiral Horthy, to-day, according to a Budapest telegram.

The Regent presented Keitel with his photograph and entertained him to luncheon.—*Reuter.*

The Ships Wait on Schedule E

Puzzled Workers Go Ca' Canny

By CHARLES SUTTON, Daily Mail Industrial Correspondent

SO urgent is the need for a certain ship now building on the Clyde that the workers have been asked to work overtime in order to get it launched by a certain date.

The ship is not likely to be launched on that date because some of the workers will not do overtime . . .

Freight trains in South Wales are often not able to leave to schedule because of the falling-off in coal production . .

Output in some aircraft and munition factories is falling. . . .

WHY IS THIS? The answer is simply, INCOME TAX.

★

SEVEN million manual workers are receiving their tax assessments on their earnings in the second half of 1941, and with the assessments they are receiving a shock.

Income tax is something that everyone talks about airily until the time comes to pay.

More than 6,000,000 who now have to pay the tax did not pay it before the war, and they do not like it because they do not understand it.

They take the simple view that overtime is a waste of time, because they think that out of every £1 they earn they must pay 10s. back in tax. That is not strictly true, of course, because a man has to earn a considerable sum before any part of his income is taxed at 10s. in the £1.

★

TRADE union leaders are disturbed by the ca' canny tactics of many workers when they get into the higher income-tax levels.

They have approached the Treasury, who simply say: "Everybody must make his or her contribution to the war effort. We cannot let any section of the community escape."

The staff of the Inland Revenue department, who have to assess the tax, have been so overwhelmed with work that it will be the middle of February before some workers begin paying, and their weekly deductions will be greater than if they had started on January 1, when they should have received their assessments.

What, then, should be done about this income-tax situation, which is reducing war output?

★

A CONFERENCE began in London yesterday of experts drawn together by the Inland Revenue Staff Federation and the Association of Inspectors of Taxes.

They are trying to work out a simple plan to take the war worker's tax from his current earnings.

One of the troubles at present is that men and women who earned overtime last summer are paying tax on it at a time when they cannot earn so much.

Take the case of Peter Drummond, a single man, who is working a 47-hours week in a Clyde shipyard. He now earns £4 10s. a week, and his tax deduction is £2 5s., because he earned £8 a week last summer on night shift and overtime.

Like most workers who have not previously paid this tax, he has not saved the money. Peter's lodgings and fares cost him £1 13s. 6d. a week, and when that is added to his income-tax demands, his insurance, and other charges, he has only a few shillings a week until the longer summer nights come to enable him to earn more money.

A deputation of shipyard workers

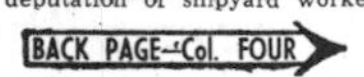
BACK PAGE—Col. FOUR

RUSSIAN DRIVE TO VYAZMA

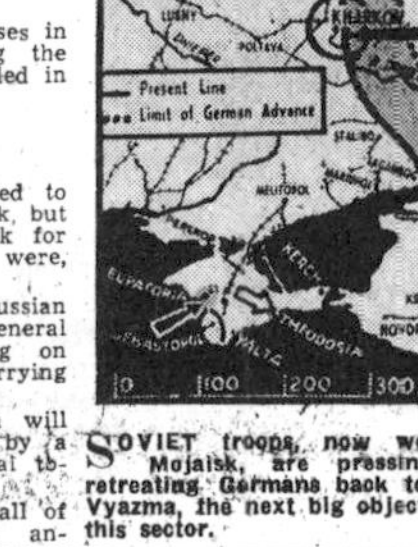

SOVIET troops, now west of Mojaisk, are pressing the retreating Germans back towards Vyazma, the next big objective in this sector.

Dr. Temple to Speak To-day

By Daily Mail Reporter

Dr. William Temple, Archbishop of York, who is mentioned as the likeliest successor to Dr. Lang as Archbishop of Canterbury, will address the Convocation of York today and pay his tribute to the work of the retiring primate.

"I cannot say anything now as to the future," he said to me yesterday. "That is in other hands."

Dr. Temple is 60 years old. He employs his spare time digging in the gardens at Bishopsthorpe, York. He lives in one wing of the palace once occupied by Cardinal Wolsey.

Dr. Lang's successor will be nominated by the Prime Minister for the approval of the King.

The Primate's income is £15,000 a year out of which he has to maintain Lambeth Palace, S.E., and the Old Palace, Canterbury, and pay large staffs, chaplains, and secretaries.

Did the Archbishop Miss Great Chances?—Page TWO; "I am Too Old"—BACK Page.

New Rank Created by RAF

'Flight Engineer' for Giant Planes

By COLIN BEDNALL, Daily Mail Air Correspondent

A NEW R.A.F. rank—that of flight engineer—will shortly be created.

The flight engineer will take his place as a designated member of air crews with the pilot, air-gunner, wireless operator, and observer.

I understand that he will be given the same privileges. The King's Commision will be open to men of outstanding ability.

At the same time, increasing numbers of engineer officers—mostly men with engineering degrees—are being posted to individual squadrons.

Bigger and better aircraft have made the flight engineer a necessity. He will supervise the engines in flight, seeing that they get their fuel and generally function properly.

Freedom for Pilot

His introduction means that, for the first time in the history of aviation, the pilot of multi-engined planes becomes wholly and solely a pilot, free to give his full attention to the primary controls of the aircraft.

In these big planes the pilot has already been relieved of observation, navigation, gunnery, photography, wireless-operation and in many cases, even the rôle of captain.

The flight engineer's job will be a very responsible one. It is my own opinion, formed as a result of an operational flight with a four-engined aircraft, that a means should be found to give the captain increased supervision over such details as the feeding of fuel.

For a long time Sunderland flying-boats have carried an engineer. But up to now he has been a fitter borrowed from the ground staff.

2 Killed by Home-Brewed Wine

One ounce of wood alcohol, or methyl, might be a fatal dose, it was stated at a Grays, Essex, inquest yesterday on two sailors who died after drinking home-brewed wine.

John Henry Cooper, of Sandown-road, Orsett, Essex, told the coroner that he brewed the wine in September from elderberries, to which he added molasses and alcohol. The coroner recorded a verdict of Accidental Death, and accepted Cooper's statement that he was ignorant of the danger of wood alcohol.

SHETLANDS BOMBED

An enemy aircraft dropped bombs on one of the Shetland Islands yesterday afternoon. One person was killed and a small number were injured.

AUK'S 'WELL DONE' TO HELLFIRE VICTORS

From Daily Mail Correspondent — CAIRO, Wednesday.

GENERAL AUCHINLECK, Commander-in-Chief Middle East, has congratulated the British commanders responsible for the successful and swift reduction of the Axis garrisons at Bardia, Halfaya, and Sollum.

In a message to General Ritchie, Commander of the Eighth Army, the Commander-in-Chief says: "Well done, and heartiest congratulations.

"The reduction of Bardia and Halfaya, including the capture of 14,000 prisoners and much material at a cost of less than 500 casualties, represents a fine feat of arms, for which all concerned, and particularly yourself and Generals Norrie and De Villiers, deserve the highest credit.

"Please tell them so from me."

I learned to-day that Major Bach, the German chaplain, was in command of all the Axis troops in the Halfaya area. General de Georgis, the Italian, commanded the whole area of Sollum and Halfaya.

Meanwhile the worst weather for ten years is holding up the Eighth Army on the Tripolitanian border, and is stopping, for almost the first time, the sorties of the Imperial Air Forces.

Severe sandstorms and torrential rains have not only converted the enemy's front at El Agheila, but have given Rommel's forces the necessary cover to mine the whole area.

To-day's communiqué from G.H.Q., which gave this news, also stated that the count of war material taken on the Egyptian frontier is continuing. So far 16 German and 44 Italian, field, medium, and heavy dual-purpose guns have been captured in first-class condition.

Axis prisoners from Halfaya total 5,526.

Berlin announces that Hitler has decorated General Rommel with the Oak Leaves with the Swords of the Knight's Cross of the Iron Cross for his "defensive victory" in Libya.

Cost of Living is Down a Point

The official cost-of-living index figure at January 1 was 100 points above the level of July 1914, as compared with 101 points at December 1, states the Ministry of Labour.

For food alone the index figure was 63 points above the level of July 1914, as compared with 65 points at December 1, the decline being due to the reduction of 1d. a pound in sugar on December 29.

AREAS marked black in this map of the Far East are those captured by the Japanese since they spread the war to the Pacific.

Japs Drive to Cut Communications

MALAYA FRONT

JUNGLE G.H.Q. GIVES 'SCORCH' ORDER

From Daily Mail Special Correspondent — SINGAPORE, Wednesday.

HEAVILY reinforced Japanese troops across the Muar river have turned south-east in an attempt to cut the railway and roads linking Singapore with our troops in North Central Johore. A major battle has been raging for 24 hours at Payong, where Australians holding hill positions are resisting an advance towards the important road junction of Yong Peng.

Both sides have thrown all arms into this struggle. Throughout yesterday dive-bombers and fighters roared over the front.

Some idea of the severity of the fighting is given by the official statement here that at one stage Australian guns were firing at short range over open sights.

During this phase the Japanese lost very heavily.

Enemy radio stations report that the battle area, which extends some ten miles inland, is being shelled by British warships.

At the same time the Japanese have for the first time appeared in strength on the borders of Eastern Johore at Endau.

Our outpost there has been withdrawn.

The enemy are steadily bombing and machine-gunning the areas behind our front in this sector, and a second dangerous thrust may well develop there

There is no doubting the gravity of the general situation or the grim reality with which it is being faced.

Here in Johore, at any rate, the scorched earth policy will be applied ruthlessly.

Last night I was privileged to be present at a meeting of three important generals held in a rubber

BACK PAGE—Col. FIVE

MAP of Malaya shows where Japanese forces are trying to seize the main railway through Johore to Singapore. Japanese radio last night claimed that their troops were within ten miles of Singapore Island itself.

Daily Mail Man in Jungle Ambush

From Daily Mail Special Correspondent

SINGAPORE, Tuesday (delayed).

ALL within the past 12 hours I have seen 10 Japanese tanks ambushed and destroyed, been cut off with the ambushing troops, and shared the joy of a besieged force which has been relieved.

With other war correspondents, I was making a rapid trip in the coastal area south of Muar, where Japanese infiltrations were reported.

There was nothing serious there, only intermittent skirmishing, so we turned northwards towards the Muar River and found Australian units on the point of clashing with the enemy.

Two anti-tank batteries were drawn up beside the road, one behind the other, covering a cutting.

Ten Japanese tanks were allowed to enter the cutting and six to pass the forward guns.

The rear guns allowed the first six tanks to come within 30 yards and then knocked out four of them.

In the centre two tanks were still undamaged, but a gunner ran along the banks of the cutting and lobbed Molotov cocktails under their tracks.

Encircled

By this time the whole cutting was in chaos, with the wrecked tanks ablaze and their crews endeavouring to escape, only to be cut down by tommy-guns and grenades.

All ten tanks were finally wiped out.

Meanwhile, Japanese infantry deployed round our position and we found ourselves cut off and compelled to dig in.

Japanese sharpshooters climbed trees, and, if you showed your head, "ping" went shot after shot, but after our troops had shot a few of them they became discouraged and quitted.

Late in the afternoon a burst of cheering heralded the arrival of several Bren carriers and infantry, thus raising the siege.

It was interesting to note the sangfroid of the troops during the day. They had dug a well and prepared to settle down for the night.

There is no doubt that our men are showing up magnificently at close-quarter fighting.

Escaped, Disguised

A good story comes from the Gemas front of an officer who was captured, disarmed, and locked in a shed. A few minutes later the bars of the window were levered open and a native's hand tossed in native clothing, in which the officer made his escape.

Returning from the Muar area we again ran into trouble, half a dozen bombs near a village sending us to cover among the rubber trees.

Four planes spent the next half-hour spraying our wood with machine-guns. I never found ant-hills so unsatisfactory as cover.

There is a rumour of air support coming. During the whole of the last two days we did not see any, though bombing of the Japanese rear was reported at divisional headquarters.

Personally, I share the feeling of the troops, who welcome ground-strafing or dog-fights near the front.

At another point we had experience of Japanese infiltrating tactics.

Small parties in native clothing, who had hidden all day, joined forces at night with a group of light tanks on the coastal road.

Heavy bombing, which caused us to stop to survey the situation, prevented us from falling into the hands of this particular force.

AUSTRALIA FEARS WAR 'AT DOOR'

From Daily Mail Correspondent

MELBOURNE, Wednesday.

THE Pacific war may be at Australia's door at any moment now.

With the appearance of fleets of Japanese aircraft over many parts of New Guinea, it is feared here that a major onslaught is about to be made on this great sprawling island, possibly as a preliminary to the invasion of Australia.

The south coast of New Guinea is less than 150 miles from the northern tip of Australia.

"Anybody in Australia who fails to perceive the immediate menace which these attacks constitute must be lost to all reality," said Mr. Curtin, the Prime Minister, to-day.

"The peril is nearer, clearer, and deadlier than before."

The raids were described in the following R.A.A.F. communiqué:

"A strong force of Japanese were sighted early this morning at a number of points in the Bismarck Archipelago and the northern coast of New Guinea.

Fighter Escorts

"Twenty fighters and 40 bombers early to-day attacked Kavieng. Three aircraft attacked Madang at noon, and more than 50 fighters and bombers were later seen flying in the direction of Salamaua, Lae, and Bulolo.

"A small force of Japanese fighters attacked Salamaua Aerodrome shortly after noon. The extent of the damage and the casualties have not yet been reported.

"The enemy displayed very considerable strength in aircraft in the operations over the Archipelago and the New Guinea coast, and major attacks in this area can be expected."

Madang, Salamaua, and Lae are on the coast of north-east New Guinea.

Another communiqué revealed that the Japanese used 100 flying-boats and both shore-based and carrier-borne aircraft in yesterday's attack on Rabaul.

Three raiders were shot down

Several Australian aircraft were lost, but the crew of one were saved.

Burma Outposts Withdrawing

RANGOON, Wednesday. — British outposts in Tenasserim Province, in Lower Burma, are withdrawing now to achieve a greater measure of concentration. This was stated by an official commentator in Rangoon today.

He said that the Japanese were superior in numbers.—*B.U.P.*

Japs Press On.—BACK Page.

STRAIT—'ARCTIC'

The Strait last night: Arctic-like weather, with severe frost. Sea choppy and misty. Sky overcast.

U.S. Builds 1,700 'Little Ships'

WASHINGTON, Wednesday.—A Bill authorising the expenditure of £825,000,000 to build 1,700 minor auxiliary combatant and patrol naval vessels was passed by the House of Representatives to-day.—*Reuter.*

LATEST

DEMPSEY JOINS HOME GUARD

New York, Wednesday.—Jack Dempsey, former heavy-weight champion of the world, being too old for the Army, has been sworn in as a lieutenant in the New York State Guard (equivalent to the Home Guard).—B.U.P.

NAZIS SEIZE 400 FISHING BOATS

The Germans are short of patrol vessels to guard the Norwegian coast, and have confiscated 400 boats of the Norwegian fishing fleet, says the Norwegian Telegraph Agency.

WEATHER
Light rain this afternoon and early tonight, followed by temperatures falling to near freezing, with diminishing winds

New York Post

BLUE FINAL
LATE SPORTS RESULTS ON PAGE 13

Founded 1801, Volume 141, No. 58
Copyright 1942, New York Post, Inc.

NEW YORK MONDAY JANUARY 26 1942 THREE CENTS

NEW AEF LANDS IN N. IRELAND

29 Jap Ships Sunk or Hit in 4 Days

GENERAL MacARTHUR IS 62 YEARS OLD TODAY

WASHINGTON, Jan. 26 (AP).—President Roosevelt cabled birthday greetings today to Gen. Douglas MacArthur, 62-year-old commander on Luzon Island. He praised the "magnificent stand" being made.

The text:

"Congratulations on the magnificent stand that you and your men are making. We are watching with pride and understanding and are thinking of you on your birthday."

The general's wife and his young son, Arthur, were believed to be on the island of Corregidor. Although the wives and families of most service personnel were evacuated from the Philippines before the outbreak of war, Mrs. MacArthur stayed behind.

In a tribute to MacArthur, Sen. Thomas (D-Utah) told the Senate: "Seldom in all history has a military leader faced such insuperable odds. Never has a commander met such a situation with greater and cooler courage; never with more resourcefulness or brilliant action."

Rep. McCormack (D-Mass.) called MacArthur "a great military leader and a brilliant strategist," and Rep. Fish (R-N. Y.) said his leadership was "an inspiration to the American people."

By the Associated Press

United States and Dutch sea and air forces, in a great, running battle with a Japanese invasion armada in the Straits of Macassar, have sunk or damaged as many as 33 transports and warships in four days, and may have shattered an attempt to invade Java, heart of the United Nations' defense in the southwest Pacific.

[The Allies' successes have been announced in a series of communiques from three different commands, so there may be some duplication of reports. A compilation of the communiques for four days shows eleven Japanese warships and transports sunk and 18 damaged, 29 in all—Ed.]

The next few days will tell in what strength, if any, the Japanese armada was able to negotiate the narrow shortcut to the inner arc of The Netherlands East Indies.

The Japanese, however, won at least one foothold on this sea road to Java—the Dutch oil port of Balik Papan, on the east coast of Borneo, but the size of the invasion fleet indicated that Tokio was shooting for higher stakes to the south.

The most direct route between Japanese concentration points in the Philippines and the rich island of Java, on which the United Nations have centered their supreme command and much of their armed strength, lies through the Straits of Macassar.

Soerabya, the great Dutch naval base, in eastern Java, is 350 miles southwest of the mouth of the straits.

Attack Continued

The latest successes in the battle of annihilation being waged against the Japanese sea forces in the Straits were announced in simultaneous communiques from the United Nations' command headquarters, "somewhere on the island of Java," and the Netherlands East Indies High Command, in Batavia.

The United Nations' communique said:

"On Jan. 25, action by Allied air forces against an enemy convoy off the Macassar Straits was continued.

"American Flying Fortresses

Continued on Page 8, Col. 6

SUMMARY OF JAP SEA LOSS

Allied sea and air forces have reported these successes in four days of combat with a Japanese armada in the Straits of Macassar:

	ATTACKING FORCE	JAP SHIPS SUNK	JAP SHIPS DAMAGED
Friday	Dutch planes	—	8
	U. S. destroyers	2	1*
Saturday	Dutch and U. S. planes	2	3
Sunday	U. S. cruisers and destroyers	5	1
Monday	U. S. planes	1	1
	Dutch planes	—	3
	Dutch submarine	1	1
	Totals	11	18+

*One "listing heavily, other vessels damaged."

U-Boats Sink 7th Ship; 23 Missing

Enemy submarines have sunk their seventh ship off the U. S. coast since Jan. 14, the Navy announced today.

The ship was the 8,016-ton ore carrier Venore, and she was hit by at least two torpedoes off the North Carolina coast at midnight Friday. She sank in a few hours. Twenty-one of her crew of 44 were rescued; the others are unaccounted for.

The Navy, some hours after announcing the sinking, revealed that the Venore had been lured into close range by an Axis submarine posing as a lightship, according to the Associated Press.

Members of the Venore crew were quoted as saying that they "fooled us completely" by blinking a code message that she was a lightship and requesting the vessel to draw near.

"We started toward her still thinking she was the lightship when a shell hit us in the bow," Allen Harte, an able seaman from Baltimore, said.

The Navy's announcement followed that covering the Norwegian tanker Veranger, sunk almost within sight of the New Jersey shore more than 24 hours fater the Venore attack. The Varanger's crew of 42 was saved.

The U-boat pack ranging the Atlantic from Canada to the Carolina capes has taken a toll of 75 known dead and at least 23 missing in U. S. waters.

The Venore was shelled first, survivors said, and then the U-boat pumped the torpedoes into her hull. The submarine circled the doomed ship in the darkness, according to Chief Mate Anfinn J. Krokeite, at times approaching to within 100 yards.

Hubert Clarke, of Boston, said he was below decks when the first shell struck the ship. He rushed above and —

"I saw the sub's lights about a half mile away. A minute later she sent a torpedo into the port side.

"If we had had a gun, I would have taken charge of it myself and blasted the sub out of the water."

Meanwhile, Canadian officials announced the arrival ot an undisclosed port of still another group of survivors from a U-boat victim, an unnamed Norwegian tanker.

Helen Keller Visits F. D. R., Touches His Face

WASHINGTON, Jan. 26 (AP).—Helen Keller, who was born deaf and blind, called on President Roosevelt today, was permitted to touch his face, and pronounced it "one of the great moments of my life."

"How very graciously he received me and how at home I felt with him," she said. "I also felt the magnificent courage in his hands and the smile that helps to sustain him throughout the hardest period of his life."

'Swimming Soon'

Special to The Post

NORFOLK, Jan. 26.—The radio operator of the torpedoed Venore told succinctly of the ship's plight, in messages received early Saturday morning.

"Two crashes so far. Will keep informed. Think swimming soon," he reported at 12:47 a. m.

Two minutes later he flashed: "Torpedoed twice. Ship still afloat but listing badly. Captain requests assistance immediately."

And at 1:22: "Can not stay afloat much longer."

The operator, Vernon W. Minzey, is missing.

Alien Property Lacks a Chief

By S. F. PORTER

EXCLUSIVE

After seven weeks of war, the U. S. still is without an Alien Property Custodian to administer the nearly $7,000,000,000 of foreign assets here and to help wipe out the Nazi influence in the Pan-American countries.

Leo T. Crowley, head of the Federal Deposit Insurance Corp., was designated by President Roosevelt as custodian Dec. 18, but, it was learned today, he has not yet accepted the appointment.

Contary to public impression, no bureau has been set up to take care of such vital—and potentially dangerous — matters as the cleaning up of General Aniline & Film Corp., Sterling Products and their

Continued on Page 11, Col. 1

100,000 Auto Stamps Sold

The sale of federal motor vehicle use stamps at Post-offices in Manhattan, The Bronx and Pelham passed the 100,000 mark on Saturday, Postmaster Goldman announced today.

Thousands Cheered; Band Plays

A PORT IN NORTHERN IRELAND, Jan. 26 (AP).—The second AEF has reached Northern Ireland, less than two months after the U. S. went to war with Germany and Italy.

Maj. Gen. Russel P. Hartle, the commanding officer of the disembarking troops, stepped ashore first and was warmly welcomed by British and United States army officers.

A band broke into the strains of "America' 'as he reached the end of the gangplank.

The British Press Association's account of the landing, as passed by the British censor, said:

"Several thousand men of an American infantry division landed at a northern Ireland port recently. They are combat troops with the usual components of field artillery."

A speech of welcome was delivered by British Air Minister Sinclair after the troops had formed ranks in front of the flag-draped shed.

The ships steamed slowly into the port as a large group of American and British army officers and journalists stood waiting.

The soldiers were eager for a glimpse of their new area of operations and were sticking their heads out of every opening.

Just before they reached the docks, the band struck up "The Star Spangled Banner" and a waiting throng gave three cheers,

Mixed emotions were apparent on the faces of the troops, who wore steel campaign helmets and full campaign packs.

Some of them flipped hesitant handwaves as the convoy neared the docks.

Several men quickly saluted the American flag which flew from a staff on the docks. The British Union Jack flew a similar staff a few feet away.

There was no announcement fo plans for the troops, but it was understood that they were being taken to an encampment somewhere in northern Ireland.

Immediately after announcing the arrival of the troops, the BBC noted tonight that there had been "slight enemy air activity" over northern Ireland but that there had been no damage or casualties.

WASHINGTON, Jan. 26 (AP).—Arrival of American Army forces in northern Ireland was announced today by Secretary Stimson. Maj. Gen. Russell P. Hartle is in command, it was announced, but the size of the force and other details were withheld.

Japs 'R' in Season for MacArthur Boys

Disguised as Americans, But Can't Get by Lollapalooza

By CLARK LEE

WITH GEN, MacARTHUR'S ARMIES IN BATAN, Jan. 21 (Delayed).—The Japanese are still trying to pass American sentries by wearing American or Filipino uniforms.

But the Americans have discovered an infallible way to detect them. The Japanese can't pronounce the letter L, which they say as R. The Americans simply pick a password with numerous L's, such as Lollapalooza.

Sentries challenge approaching figures, and if the first syllables of Lollapalooza come back as "Rorra" they open fire without waiting to hear the rest.

Love Finds a Way Out of the Barracks

And if Somebody Did Have Chickenpox, It Was Just Too Bad

FORT DIX, Jan. 26 (AP).—The soldier and the blonde, in love and engaged two years, had intended to be married Christmas Day but he was unable to obtain a furlough.

Transferred to this camp, near the home of his girl, the soldier sought the aid and advice of Mrs. Peggy Harris, principal hostess at Fort Dix's Service Club No. 1.

On Jan. 12, twenty-four hours later, Ruth Naoma Bell, 19, of Swarthmore, Pa., became the bride of Pvt. Durant Lee Pace, 23, of Chester, Pa., in the fort's flower-filled chapel.

Shortly afterwards Mrs. Harris, back at the service club, hunting baby bottles for visitors' babies, noted the newlyweds, in a crowd, holding hands.

"What kind of honeymoon is this?" she demanded.

The soldier explained. He was on the "alert," and couldn't leave the post. He was due back at his barracks at 11 p. m.

Mrs. Harris hastened to the morale officer who had helped arrange the wedding. They tried to reach the soldier's commanding officer, but were unsuccessful.

At 11 p. m. the bride started home and her bridegroom headed for his barracks. A large sign confronted him.

"Contagious disease — keep out!"

With his barracks barred to him, he was granted permission to leave camp for the night. And every night for a week the soldier has obtained permission to be absent from the post.

The quarantine? It was lifted the next morning. Somebody must have had a slight case of chickenpox.

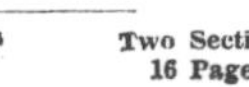

Two Sections 16 Pages

INDEX

Daily Sketch

No. 10,222 (E**) FRIDAY, FEBRUARY 13, 1942 ONE PENNY

GREAT SEA-AIR BATTLE IN STRAITS OF DOVER

SCHARNHORST, GNEISENAU OUT

ENEMY DASH TO HELIGOLAND

SCHARNHORST and Gneisenau, the German battle-cruisers, and the cruiser Prinz Eugen—survivor of the Bismarck encounter—which have been bombed more than 100 times in their hiding place at Brest, escaped yesterday in misty weather and a fierce naval battle raged in the Channel.

British long-range guns fired at extreme range. German big guns replied.

British destroyers, torpedo-boats, Fleet Air Arm and R.A.F. planes attacked the big enemy flotilla, which was heavily escorted by fighters.

Gneisenau and Prinz Eugen are believed to have escaped to Heligoland Bight.

This is the official communiqué:

"About 11 a.m. yesterday R.A.F. aircraft reported an enemy squadron consisting of the Scharnhorst, Gneisenau and Prinz Eugen, accompanied by destroyers, torpedo boats, E-boats and minesweepers, was approaching the Dover Straits.

"The enemy squadron was also heavily escorted by fighter aircraft.

"Visibility varied from three to five miles with low clouds and the enemy ships were never visible from the English coast.

"On receipt of the report coastal craft of the Dover Naval Command were immediately sent out to the attack, together with Swordfish aircraft of the Fleet Air Arm, strongly escorted by R.A.F. fighters.

"The attacks both by Swordfish and by the coastal craft were pressed close home in face of intense fire from all enemy surface vessels and opposition by the enemy.

"Reports indicate that the Swordfish scored at least one hit on one of the enemy heavy ships, and one of the motor torpedo boats also claims a possible hit, but owing to the intense barrage and a heavy smoke screen put up by the enemy it was impossible to see the results of the attacks.

"Six Swordfish aircraft are missing, but some of the crews have been saved. There were no casualties in the Coastal craft.

"During this time the Dover defences opened fire at extreme range, which was replied to by the enemy's shore batteries in the French coast.

"The enemy force was repeatedly attacked by aircraft of the R.A.F., strongly escorted by fighters.

"The attacks were pressed home with the greatest determination in the face of heavy anti-aircraft fire and strong fighter opposition, which resulted in the loss of 20 of our bombers (including five aircraft of Coastal Command) and 16 fighters.

"Fifteen enemy fighters were destroyed by our fighter escort and at least three more by the bombers themselves.

Continued on Back Page, Col. 4

THERE WERE THREE GERMANS—and radio pictures from Moscow show them (above) before being sent to the Eastern Front and (below) what happened to them there.

They've lost their martial bearing, these three Germans—Alfred Franke, Herbert Blum and Rudolf Pankratz by name. Ragged, footsore and frost-bitten, they are prisoners, captured by the Russians in the Donetz Basin.

SINGAPORE STILL FIGHTING ON

SINGAPORE is holding on. Singapore is fighting back. Counter-attacks on the Japanese left flank have been successful.

The Singapore radio station which yesterday radioed to the world: "We are not only going to fight . . . we are going to win," and then faded out, broadcast this official communiqué early this morning after a silence of some hours:

"Counter-attacks by our troops have been successful on the left flank of the Japanese.

"At 7.30 this morning Japanese military bombers with fighter escort fought an unsuccessful engagement against our air force over Malaya.

"Heavy fighting continues in the western and northern sectors. In the north of the island enemy activity has been intensified.

"Enemy air activity ceased during the night but was resumed early this morning. The enemy attack was supported by dive-bombing and machine-gunning as well as by medium tanks.

"The British line extends from the Naval Base in the north through the centre of the island to Tanglin in the south. From Sungei Sunya the line runs north."

Tanglin is the district to the north-west of Singapore City near the racecourse.

Tokyo, through the official Domei Agency, admits the ferocity of the British resistance in these words:

"British forces are still offering fierce resistance in the neighbourhood of Singapore Racecourse, some two miles north-west of the town, and in the region of the reservoirs, which lie more than four miles north of the town.

[In the reservoir region British artillery is powerful, and is fighting bitter big gun duels with the attackers.]

"Heavy fighting has been going on since yesterday around the city of Singapore.

"Two fortresses have turned their guns towards the interior of the island and have replied to the fire of Japanese artillery.

"Aerial reconnaissance shows Singapore is completely covered by clouds of black smoke from burning oil tanks. It is therefore impossible to reconnoitre the position in Singapore city."

Yet Berlin radio last night claimed street fighting in Singapore City had ended and that the defenders had been overcome.

'Warships in Action'

Before that Tokyo claimed that the racecourse was used by their troops as a rest base the previous night, while advanced Japanese forces had penetrated into Singapore itself and were engaged in hand-to-hand fighting in the streets.

Not a single British defender could be seen in the north-west suburbs, it was said.

British naval guns are in action shelling Japs in the northern area—say British reports.

Continued on Back Page, Col. 3

'Daily Sketch' Man With U.S. Army

WILLIAM (BILL) COURTENAY, "Daily Sketch" Air correspondent, is now our accredited war correspondent with the American forces.

Mr. William Courtenay

He is already with American forces on active service.

When the success of his lectures in America became known, the proprietors of the "Daily Sketch" readily agreed that his tour be extended from the original three months to six. He travelled 30,000 miles and spoke to 171 audiences in Canada and the United States.

NAZIS SAY 45 DIE UNLESS—

THE Germans have ordered the execution of 45 Frenchmen held as hostages unless the authors of two recent attacks against Germans in Occupied France are discovered within a few days, said an A.P. message last night.

Twenty of the men are to be executed at Tours unless the person who attacked a German sentry is found by to-morrow. The 25 others will be executed at Rouen unless the people who threw bombs at Germans there are arrested before Sunday.

The Germans last year shot several Frenchmen held as hostages for the killing of two German officers at Bordeaux and Nantes.

MRS. F.D.R. WILL RESIGN A.R.P. JOB

Mrs. Roosevelt, wife of the president, announced yesterday that she would resign "very soon" as assistant director of the Office of Civilian Defence, because she had "always intended to resign when the organisation was completed."

She has been accused in Congress and in the U.S. Press of granting appointments in the O.C.D. to Hollywood and stage friends—an accusation she denied.—A.P.

MYSTERY DEATH OF JAP ENVOY

THERE are two versions of the mysterious death in Paris yesterday of Kato, Japanese Ambassador to Vichy.

First report said that he became giddy and fell from the balcony of the Embassy into the street.

The other version, given later by the Japanese Embassy, said that Kato died of a heart attack. He was Counsellor to the Embassy in London from 1932 to 1935.

CHINESE TAKE 3 KEY TOWNS

CHINESE forces have recaptured three key towns, it was announced in Chungking yesterday.

They are Nanchang, important road junction and capital of Kiangsi Province; Mengcheng, in the Ko river valley of Anhwei Province; and Koyang, 60 miles north-west of Mengcheng.

The Chinese, said the communiqué, drove back three Japanese columns which launched an offensive in North Anhwei Province last week.

TIMELY WORDS OF FAITH AND WISDOM

Specially selected daily from the Bible for readers of the DAILY SKETCH by Lord Caldecote.

FEAR NOT: FOR THEY THAT BE WITH US ARE MORE THAN THEY THAT BE WITH THEM. II Kings vi, 16.

No. 8112 * * MONDAY, FEBRUARY 16, 1942 One Penny

SINGAPORE, SURROUNDED, FALLS TO JAPS

Penang
R MUDA
Butterworth
MALAYA
Pekan
SUMATRA
SINGAPORE
0 100 200 300 400
SCALE OF MILES
PALEMBANG

THE IMPERIAL FORCES IN SINGAPORE SURRENDERED UNCONDITIONALLY TO THE JAPANESE AT 7 p.m. (12.30 p.m. BRITISH SUMMER TIME) YESTERDAY.

This was announced by Japanese Imperial Headquarters.

Mr. Churchill, broadcasting last night, confirmed the fall of the island.

A Domei war correspondent in Singapore supplemented the Japanese High Command statement with the report that fighting ceased along the entire Malayan Front at 10 p.m. local time (3.30 B.S.T.).

"The British," he said, "sued for peace at 2.30 p.m., when they found themselves surrounded in Singapore City and in the central section of the island, helpless to defend themselves against bombs and shells.

"The British and Japanese Commanders-in-Chief, Lieutenant-General Percival and Lieutenant-General Yamashita, met in the Ford motor plant at the foot of Bukit Timah Hill in the centre of the island and signed the surrender documents.

"Thus, the most formidable of the Allies' three great bases in the Far East, has fallen.

"Ragged Tommies and Anzacs, stumbling with fatigue after being driven before the relentless Japanese Juggernaut, enjoyed their first real rest in the month and a-half that has elapsed since the Japanese machine got into its stride down the highway from Ipoh on December 31.

After a week

"A peace mission of four British officers, headed by Major Wilde, attached to the British Army Staff, approached Japanese army headquarters bearing a white flag of truce," Domei's correspondent proceeds.

"They were handed Japan's peace terms.

"They left the headquarters at 4.15 p.m., after arranging a time for a meeting between the leaders of the victorious and vanquished armies for the formal British surrender.

"The surrender of Singapore came one week after the Japanese stormed the island and effected a landing and brings to a climax the drive begun 70 days before at the opening of hostilities.

"It was on February 4 that orders were given for a general assault on the island after Singapore had turned down a demand for unconditional surrender.

"A four-days barrage by artillery and bombardment by warplanes preceded the night landing last Sunday.

"At 16 minutes past midnight on

BACK PAGE—Col. 3

SINGAPORE from the air.

RED ARMY MOVES ON

MOSCOW, Sunday.

WHILE the Soviet advance continues on all fronts, an article in "Red Star" finally confirms what has been clear for some days past—the Red Army is now encountering stiffer resistance.

The Russians, it would appear, are entering zones where the Nazis have had time to establish a definite system of defence and where reserves have had to be thrown in.

From all available sources it is clear that the Soviet troops are rapidly acquiring the tactics to meet these new conditions.

Their continued advance against increased opposition tends still further to build up the Soviet position against whatever Hitler may attempt in the spring.

An important "centre of resistance" was seized by the Soviet troops yesterday on the central front. At the same time a number of support points were rushed and the whole area swiftly consolidated.

Hope slipping

Summing-up the present position on the Eastern Front in more definite language than it has used for several weeks, "Red Star" says:—

"Hitler's generals feel that a base for a spring offensive, on which has been placed such hopes, is slipping from their hands.

"Therefore, they are striving by every means to maintain the will for battle among their troops.

"By destroying the support points of the German line we are destroying the German dreams of holding out behind their fortifications until the spring and escaping a crippling blow from the Soviet offensive."

"Red Star" explains that it is only by overcoming the chains of Nazi support points that the Soviet troops can break through to the enemy's defence in depth.

Stronger now

They are now stronger, "Red Star" says, and can fester like sores in the rear of the Soviet forward units. Thus, they must be either liquidated at the time of the advance or properly isolated and cleaned up by second line troops.

The Moscow front correspondent of the Swedish newspaper "Allehanda" says that Russian advanced forces now stand only 72 miles from the old Polish frontier and the Vilna district.—Reuter.

NAZIS FORTIFY NORWAY

STOCKHOLM, Sunday.

HITLER has entrusted his new Arms and Munitions Minister, Professor Albert Speer—who succeeds the late Major-General Todt—with the task of building a west wall along the Norwegian coast, according to the Berlin correspondent of Stockholm's "Tidningen."

This system of fortifications, he says, will be strongest at those points where landings are most probable.

Construction will begin immediately, and will be completed with "the greatest rapidity."

This may, perhaps, be taken as an indication that the Germans expect the British to make an invasion of Norway "when and if they attempt to regain a footing on the continent," the correspondent adds.

"Svenska Dagbladet's" Berlin correspondent says that all the usable material from the Maginot Line has now been taken by the Germans for fortifications on the Atlantic coast.—Reuter.

REPORT SHOWS UP WASTE

DISCLOSURES of waste and mismanagement of skilled man-power, particularly in the Army, are contained in an official Government report to be published to-day.

This is the report of the committee under Sir William Beveridge, which recently completed an inquiry into the whole man-power problem, writes Maurice Webb.

Publication of their final conclusions has been held up for some weeks because of resistance by some of the Departments concerned.

The War Office and other Departments are expected to issue simultaneously "explanatory comments" on the Beveridge findings.

BIG COAST BATTLE EXPECTED

RANGOON, Sunday.

THE battle for the control of the east coast of the Gulf of Martaban is approaching.

Japanese forces are attacking towards Thaton, from the sea-coast landing points, as well as on a deep salient on the road between Paan and Thaton.

A Japanese camp, river craft and motor vehicles at Martaban were bombed and machine-gunned late on Saturday by Blenheims, two of which were piloted by Canadians, it was unofficially reported.

Flying under a protecting screen of R.A.F. and American Volunteer Group fighters the Blenheims pressed home the second big attack of the day.

All the Allied aircraft returned.

Fighting has died down in the Paan area in the last few days, and observers believe that if the British forces continue to halt the Japanese advance west of the Salween River the most difficult phase of the defence of Burma will have been passed.

Details of our casualties are not yet available, but it is known that the Japanese have suffered considerable losses.

Meanwhile Rangoon has become semi-deserted.

Civilian evacuation up-country moves apace, but two English daily newspapers are still being published.

To keep Rangoon functioning as a base port for the Burma Road requires only a few thousand dock labourers, together with motor-car maintenance crews. General Chiang Kai-Shek has already provided a proportion of the dock labour.

The presence of frightened civilians in the city would hamper the Allied military effort, and the departure of those not essential to the war effort bolsters, rather than weakens, Allied arms.—Associated Press.

WHY Singapore was lost

BECAUSE we had not a big enough fighter force to hold the Malayan airfields, win the air battle of Malaya and keep the Japanese pinned down in the North.

Because our diplomats were blind to the Japanese threat to Thailand.

Because our military commanders misjudged the time of the Japanese attack, thinking they would choose the period from spring to early summer of the south-west monsoon, when weather conditions to the east are calm and stable.

Because reinforcements for that reason were not sent early enough. (Fighter aircraft were on the way when, or soon after, the attack began, so we had them to spare.)

*

BECAUSE

in spite of months, even years, of warning, an attack from the north down the Malayan Isthmus was not thought likely.

Because too few emergency airfields were made in Malaya.

Because other defences north of Singapore were neglected.

Because the defences of Singapore Island itself were planned to meet an attack from the south and not from the north.

Because we underestimated the Japanese Air Force and sent what the air-marshals call "second eleven" machines to fight a first-eleven war.

*

BECAUSE

a fighter force more than double the size of that which won the Battle of Britain was kept at home to face a Luftwaffe much weaker and much more preoccupied than that which lost the Battle of Britain.

Because we are too defence-minded, and yet forget that this island can be lost just as surely, though more slowly, by cutting its lifelines and stopping its supplies in places thousands of miles away.

Because we are still thinking of this war as a series of unrelated battles.

Because only a bomb in our own backyard ever makes us really fighting mad and then only when we hear the next one coming.

(A. B. AUSTIN, Air Correspondent.)

JAPS SWARM ON SUMATRA

From RONALD MATTHEWS

BATAVIA, Java, Sunday.

TRANSPORTS, powerfully escorted by warships and planes, to-day landed a huge Japanese force on the south-east coast of Sumatra.

The troops have marched inland and are attacking Palembang, second largest town in the Dutch East Indies outside Java, and one of the world's most important oil centres.

The invasion fleet is believed to have sailed from Pontianak, capital of Dutch Borneo, where the Japanese had been concentrating forces for nearly a fortnight.

Dutch and Allied planes engaged it.

It is now known that at least 700 paratroops were dropped around Palembang yesterday.

Swaying white mushrooms of dozens of parachutes broke from the bellies of the planes and drifted like aimless cobwebs down to earth.

By far the most dangerous attack on the Allied citadel of resistance in the South-West Pacific had begun.

Paratroops got short shrift

The paratroops were armed with tommy-guns, light mortars and other weapons, and the attack was clearly directed against the oil refineries.

"Our troops," said the Batavia communiqué to-day, "did a good job and made short work of the invader.

"Towards the evening two of the points of attack were completely cleared of the enemy, while on the third point we had the situation fully in hand with only a few dozen of the paratroops still alive.

"Anticipating a large-scale landing action this morning, we proceeded to carry out the thorough destruction of all vital points in the vicinity of Palembang."

It was the greatest act of deliberate destruction in the world's history. Beside it the Russians' destruction of the Dnieper dam looks small.

The refineries and surface works alone were valued at £8,775,000, and the output of the fields exceeded the entire output of Rumania.

They produced nearly 4,250,000 tons of oil a year—55 per cent. of the entire output of the Indies.

Must find new oil sources

Large supplies of fuel are stored in Java.

When these are exhausted production will be insufficient to maintain the Allied war machine here without bringing oil from the United States or the Persian Gulf.

Only reports of the battle now raging come from Japanese sources.

These claim the capture of Palembang aerodrome and the railway station.

"Formations of the Japanese air force, which assisted the paratroops, are now making use of the aerodrome," said a Tokyo communiqué.

They are said to have bombed the Pakan Baru aerodrome in Central Sumatra.

Batavia radio, calling on the Dutch to-night to stand firm, said:

"When your papers tell you that Japan's might is enormous, and that only a miracle can save you, that is perhaps true. But the days of miracles are not yet over. Look at England in 1940. Look at Moscow in 1941."

HEAVY BLOW, SAYS PREMIER

BROADCASTING to the nation last night Mr. Churchill said that he spoke under the shadow of a heavy and far-reaching military defeat.

"It is a British and Imperial defeat. Singapore has fallen.

"All the Malay Peninsula has been overrun.

"Other dangers gather about us out there, and none of the dangers we have hitherto faced successfully at home and in the East are in any way diminished.

"This is, therefore, one of those moments when the British nation can show its quality and its genius. This is one of those moments when it can draw from the heart of misfortune the vital impulse of victory.

"Not alone"

"Here is the moment to display that calm and poise, combined with grim determination, which not so long ago brought us out of the very jaws of death.

"We must remember that we are no longer alone. We are in the midst of a great company.

"Three-quarters of the human race are now moving with us. The whole future of mankind may depend upon our action and upon our conduct.

"So far we have not failed.

"To-night the Japanese are triumphant. They shout their exultation round the world. We suffer. We are hard pressed.

"But I am sure, even in this dark hour, that criminal madness will be the verdict that history will pronounce upon the authors of Japanese aggression after the events of 1942 and 1943 have been inscribed on its sombre pages.

Small margin

"We have only just been able to keep our heads above water at home," went on the Prime Minister.

"Only by a narrow margin have we brought in the food which keeps us alive and the supplies without which we cannot wage war. Only by so little have we held our own in the Nile Valley and the Middle East.

"We are struggling hard in the Libyan desert, where perhaps another serious battle will soon be fought."

Speech in full, Page Two

STOP PRESS

JAPS IN JAVA AND SUMATRA—*Nazi claim*

Occupation of Palembang, Sumatra, and neighbouring airfields is claimed in a Tokyo despatch received by the official German news agency.

Japanese troops have landed in Java, says German radio, uoting a Tokyo report.

Italian reports, the announcer said, state that the operations were supported by warships.—Reuter.

20 years' sentences

TWELVE "Communists" have been sentenced to periods of hard labour varying from three to 20 years by the special navy tribunal in Bizerta (Tunis), according to a Vichy dispatch to the official German News Agency.

The majority of the accused are stated to be employees of the State dockyards at Sidi Acdallan and of the Tunisian Railway Company.

They were arrested on charges of forming illegal Communist cells and of distributing Communist propaganda, the dispatch adds.

Death penalty

A decree imposing the death penalty on anyone giving help in any form to escaped prisoners of war, who are nationals of countries at war with Germany, has been issued by the German military authorities in Paris, according to the Paris correspondent of the Swiss News Agency.

The order has been issued, says the correspondent, to "prevent sabotage."

Previously, says Reuter, the death penalty applied only to those actually hiding escaped prisoners of war.

ACCUSES POLICE OF 'CRASHING' FUNERAL

According to the Roman Catholic Bishop of Down and Connor, the Most Rev. Daniel Mageean, a large number of police a fortnight ago "crashed in" on a funeral.

He protested strongly against such action.

"They invaded the cemetery," he said, "and as soon as the last prayers had been said, and while clay was still falling on the coffin, they arrested one of the mourners."

Neither the sacredness of the place nor the solemnity of the occasion was considered, he added.

"Claims made under Regulation 18B are ominous; the manner in which arrests are sometimes made causes still greater indignation."

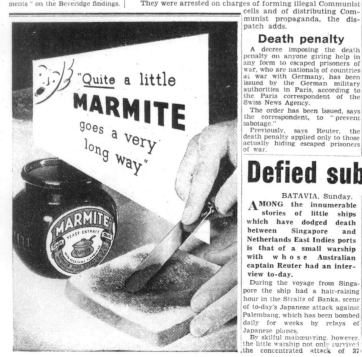

Defied submarine, 27 bombers

BATAVIA, Sunday.

AMONG the innumerable stories of little ships which have dodged death between Singapore and Netherlands East Indies ports is that of a small warship with whose Australian captain Reuter had an interview to-day.

During the voyage from Singapore the ship had a hair-raising hour in the Straits of Banka, scene of to-day's Japanese attack against Palembang, which has been bombed daily for weeks by relays of Japanese planes.

By skilful manœuvring, however, the little warship not only survived the concentrated attack of 27 bombers, but dodged a one-man Japanese submarine, whose torpedo passed within five yards of the vessel.

In dodging the torpedo the ship just grazed a sandbank in a narrow navigational channel.

"I reckon that was enough for one day," said the captain, "but a little while later more Japanese bombers dived on us.

"However, we managed to get clear again without injury."

Troopship rescue

The rescue of 1,500 Allied troops and the crew of an Allied troopship by an Australian warship was described by Australian radio, says an Associated Press message.

The broadcast said 40 Japanese bombers attacked the transport 10 miles from Singapore.

Bombs rained down for hours, a young Australian officer said, but despite the fierce attack from the air the men of the troopship still wheeled ammunition from below to feed the vessel's guns.

The entire super-structure of the troopship was a solid sheet of flames when the rescuing warship pulled alongside into the terrific heat.

The warship took 1,300 men aboard. There was no room for more than 200 others who had jumped overboard, but they were rescued by whaleboats.

Gunners on the warship, veterans of battles with the Germans and Italians, shot down three Japanese bombers.

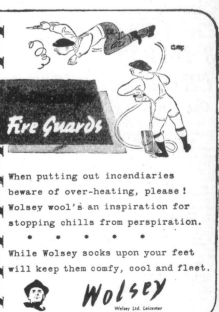

"FATHER AND SON" DRAFT

New York, Sunday.—Thousands of men between the ages of 20 and 44 began registering to-day in the nation's "father and son" services draft, which is expected to add 9 000.000 men to the strength of the United States armed forces.

Some of the new conscripts were expected to be with their units early in the spring, though those already registered would be the first to be called up.—Press Association.

PLANE OVER DUBLIN

An unidentified aircraft flew over Dublin and coastal districts yesterday afternoon between two and three o'clock, according to an Eire Government official statement. Ground defences were in action.

BLACK-OUT ZERO HOUR TO-NIGHT UNTIL 7.34 A.M.
MOON 10.21 RISES A.M. MOON 12.17 SETS A.M.

Daily Express

No. 13,022 Friday, February 20, 1942 One Penny

War Cabinet reduced to seven : Beaverbrook, Kingsley Wood, Greenwood go

CHURCHILL CALLS IN CRIPPS

Beaverbrook going to U.S.

Oliver Lyttelton coming back to take over production

PREMIER CUTTING DOWN SPEECHES

Express Political Correspondent GUY EDEN

MR. CHURCHILL HAS RECONSTRUCTED THE WAR CABINET AND REDUCED IT FROM NINE MEMBERS TO SEVEN.

The new War Cabinet, as announced from No. 10, Downing-street this morning, is to consist of:—

Prime Minister, First Lord of the Treasury and Minister of Defence, **Winston Churchill** (age 67);

Dominions Secretary, **Clement Attlee** (59);

Lord Privy Seal and Leader of the House of Commons, **Sir Stafford Cripps** (53);

Lord President of the Council, **Sir John Anderson** (59);

Foreign Secretary, **Anthony Eden** (44);

Minister of State, **Oliver Lyttelton** (48);

Minister of Labour, **Ernest Bevin** (60).

Lord Beaverbrook was invited to join the new War Cabinet, but declined on grounds of health. He will shortly go to the United States, where he will carry on the work which he has already begun in regard to the pooling of resources between the United Nations, together with such other special duties as may be entrusted to him from time to time by the War Cabinet.

He has, however, left the Government and is no longer a Minister.

PRODUCTION POST

Mr. Attlee will act as Deputy Prime Minister, and will give the Dominions the direct representation in the War Cabinet for which they have often asked.

Mr. Lyttelton is to exercise general supervision over production, and will co-ordinate the work of the various departments concerned with this. I understand he is likely to become Minister of Production when the precise scope of that office has been worked out.

Mr. Lyttelton, now in Cairo as Resident War Cabinet Minister, is returning home immediately.

Sir Kingsley Wood, Chancellor of the Exchequer, and Mr. Arthur Greenwood, Minister without Portfolio, are now no longer members of the War Cabinet. But both will retain their offices and will hold Cabinet—but not War Cabinet—rank.

A considerable number of changes in the more junior offices are involved.

TO LEAD THE LORDS

Lord Cranborne, Dominions Secretary until this morning, is likely to become Colonial Secretary, and to lead the House of Lords. Lord Moyne, the present Colonial Secretary, will give up that office.

Under the new arrangement Mr. Attlee will deputise for the Prime Minister in executive matters and in presiding at Cabinet committees and similar meetings.

Sir Stafford Cripps, however, will be his deputy in the House of Commons. He will answer the Prime Minister's questions for him and generally conduct the business of the House on behalf of the Government.

Mr. Churchill, who said only this week that he was feeling the strain of his parliamentary duties superimposed on those of conducting the war effort, will be seen in Parliament much less frequently in future.

It is expected he will select one day of the week on which to attend the House, to maintain personal contact with members and deal with matters which he alone can dispose of.

Sir Stafford Cripps is probably the first man in history to be

BACK PAGE, COL. TWO

This is Oliver LYTTELTON:

Conservative business - man Captain Oliver Lyttelton, P.C., D.S.O., M.C., became M.P. for Aldershot 1940, and six weeks later President of Board of Trade. Cut red tape, devised clothes rationing, introduced Concentration of Industry plan.

Appointed Minister of State last July, sent to the Middle East to represent War Cabinet.

An old Etonian, played golf for Cambridge University 1913, married, has three sons and one daughter.

This is a comment by Wm. Barkley:

He is tall with immense broad, rounded shoulders and a noble head. Only Eden rivals him for dressing with distinguished discretion. His voice is pleasant and cultured, and he conveys an air of intelligence and mastery of his subject. In style he has nothing of the public orator, but is quick and graceful as he might be in the board room of an important but not too old established company.

CRIPPS, man without a party

Sir Stafford Cripps (here pictured on return from Russia) is Socialist son of Lord Parmoor, was educated at Winchester and University College, London.

Lives at Filkins, Gloucestershire; was once dubbed "The Red Squire of Filkins."

Specialised in patent and ecclesiastical law, built up practice worth £25,000 a year, then gave it up at beginning of the war for national work. Socialist M.P. for East Bristol since 1931, but his pre-war advocacy of a Popular Front brought him into conflict with official Socialist Party. Is not member of any party now.

Appointed Ambassador to Moscow in June 1940; relinquished his post last month.

Married, has one son and three daughters.

Comments by William Barkley:

In manner at least, Cripps is the most restrained speaker in public life. He stands like a pillar, with never a gesture. Only his lips move, and even then his upper lip is drawn and tight. He has dark, piercing eyes behind magnifying lenses, and he fixes his gaze on his audience. His figure is tall and spare, his complexion grey, his features generally unsmiling. His health keeps him permanently on a vegetarian diet.

ATTLEE Bald and dapper, with quick, bird-like movements. Speaks rapidly in clear but not too strong a voice without emphasis or exaggerations. Conversational; argumentative; least pretentious.

EDEN Still handsomest man in Cabinet with readiest flow of language. Voice is high pitched, accent neat and clipped like his moustache, precise like the crease of his trousers.

ANDERSON Not a pillar but a tower, square set, built of solid masonry. Slow, formal dignity in every movement. Enunciates with gravity and verbosity of ancient Rome. Interruptions bounce off him.

BEVIN Vast bulk in a baggy suit. Voice deep and pitched for open-air work. Has little use for syntax as generally understood, but makes himself mighty clear.

3 PARTIES HOLD CRISIS MEETINGS

Opposition vote by Socialists?

Express Political Correspondent

POLITICAL parties have been very active at Westminster all this week, and they will hold further meetings before they decide their action in the coming war debate.

The Conservatives discussed the possibility of forcing a vote against the Government if Mr. Churchill refused to make concessions to his critics.

This proposal did not receive unanimous support, and no final decision will be taken until the debate has started and Mr. Churchill's views have been heard.

It seems certain that the Conservatives, although critical of some aspects of Government policy, will not vote against it.

The Socialists have had stormy meetings, in which some M.P.s urged the withdrawal of their Ministers from the Government, and a mass vote in opposition when the debate takes place.

MEET AGAIN

Today's changes in the Government will not overcome all criticism. Socialist M.P.s are determined to make outspoken attacks on the work of Ministers.

Before a vote takes place the Socialists will meet again.

Liberals met yesterday, and were addressed by Sir Archibald Sinclair, the Air Minister, their leader. The party was asked to hear Mr. Churchill in the debate before deciding.

The debate is likely to be frank, and there will be demands for vigorous future action.

Farm price row over

Express Agricultural Reporter KENNETH PIPE

THE dispute over the prices which farmers are to be paid for their produce this year was settled yesterday. The new schedule will be officially announced tomorrow.

Settlement of the dispute followed ten hours of secret conferences between the Minister of Agriculture, Mr. Robert Hudson, and leaders of the National Farmers' Union.

The Treasury would admit only one part of the farmers' claim, covering the £20,000,000 which they have to pay in increased wages. Subsidies for ploughing up land to increase national food production were held to be unnecessary

Prices which Mr. Hudson will announce tomorrow will be far below the proposals he submitted originally to the Cabinet, and below the original demands of farmers.

The settlement has been made possible by the farmers' leaders accepting a temporary compromise. They have agreed that in the national interest they must get on with planning the rest of this year's harvest.

The prices are not necessarily final.

BRIGADIER IN AIR CRASH

Brigadier F. Morris, an engineering expert of the Royal Army Ordnance Corps, who was returning to report on a secret mission, is believed to be one of the passengers killed in the South Coast air-liner crash announced on Wednesday.

He returned from service in India to the War Office for ordnance duty in 1939. An inquiry will be held into the crash, in which nine lives were lost.

No one hurt

A single raider dropped bombs in East Anglia last night. No casualties.

Fine but chilly

Straits: Fine and cold.

Gurkha the Second lost

Express Naval Reporter

THE destroyer Gurkha has been sunk.—Admiralty announcement last night.

The destroyer Gurkha has been sunk.—Admiralty announcement in April 1940.

Explanation: When the first Gurkha was lost, after a five-hour bombing attack off Norway, the name was given to a new destroyer at the request of the Gurkha Brigade, whose officers and men contributed to her cost.

Next of kin of Gurkha casualties have been informed. She was captained by Commander C. N. Lentaigne, who won the D.S.O. last month for action against submarines.

Ships torpedoed in harbour

PORT OF SPAIN, Thursday.—A U-boat at midnight damaged two ships in Port of Spain harbour, in the British West Indian island of Trinidad where the United States have a naval and air base.

Off the Dutch oil island of Aruba, which was shelled on Monday, a Panama tanker was sunk.—Express News Service.

Dillon ('fight for America') quits

Mr. J. M. Dillon, deputy-leader of Eire's Cosgrave Party, resigned yesterday following disagreement with his colleagues over Eire neutrality. Ten days ago he said in a speech that America's enemies were his enemies.

Roosevelt—a cold

WASHINGTON, Thursday.—President Roosevelt is confined to his White House apartments with a cold.—Express News Service.

New chief for Bombers

Air Marshal Arthur Travers Harris—nicknamed Ginger from the colour of his hair—has been appointed Commander-in-Chief Bomber Command, it is announced today.—*See Page Four.*

PRIORITY

For war-work canteens

War workers' canteens are put on the priority list for unrationed foods from March 19. The foods include: Biscuits, cakes, chocolate and sweets.

NEW ARMS ROAD TO CHINA FIXED

'Rangoon mined: supplies diverted'

Express Military Reporter MORLEY RICHARDS

A WAY has been found, according to messages flashed from Chungking last night, to send far greater supplies of war materials from India to China without using the port of Rangoon.

General Chiang Kai-shek, according to Reuter and Associated Press quoting an official Chinese statement, has solved the problem of transport with the Indian leaders.

Steps have been agreed by which a much larger quantity of goods than was carried over the Burma Road will be transported to China, with goods being sent direct from Indian ports.

Chinese officials stated that British ships have mined the approaches to Rangoon, which had been abandoned as a port of entry for goods consigned for China through Burma.

This news of a new route is very important, if rather puzzling. The question will at once be asked: How is it going to be done, and when?

If it is the case that Rangoon has been abandoned as a port of entry—there is no confirmation from any other source—the only other way by sea into Burma is Bassein. From there goods can be carried up to the Irrawaddy, the river which is already used to carry heavy materials to the Burma Road.

Rail and road

To supply the Chinese armies by land routes from India is difficult.

This is what is happening: a railway roughly following the route of the Burma Road is under construction. On the Chinese section the work is three parts completed. Progress on the Burma part is a military secret.

An alternative road is also being built. It will run from Chungking through Chengtu, south of Tibet, and link up with the Indian railway system in north-east Assam.

The route runs through some of the most inaccessible country in the world.

Chiang Kai-shek, with his remarkable vision, started work on it many months ago. Tens of thousands of Chinese labourers are giving their services.

Since then, I understand, American, British and Indian engineers have been sent to help.

It was originally estimated that the new road would take three years to build, but a year may be knocked off that building time.

If the Burma Road is cut it means that the Chinese will have to stand on the defensive for a long time until this alternative supply line can function.

See map—Back Page.

4 A.M. LATEST

32 PLANES RAID JAVA TOWN

BATAVIA, Friday.—Bandoen, on Java's north coast, was attacked yesterday by 12 enemy bombers and 20 fighters. Some damage was inflicted. Dutch fighters shot down one bomber. Two Dutch fighters lost, but one pilot parachuted to safety.—A.P.

Japs driven into Bilin River

Express War Reporter O. D. GALLAGHER

RANGOON, Thursday.

THE fate of Rangoon is expected to be decided within the next few days. Indications are that the Japanese are preparing their forces for a big-scale attack—one considerably heavier than those already met by the British Army in Burma.

Sittang (BRIDGE) · R. Bilin · R. Donthami · R. Salween · KYAIKTO · DANYENGON · Shwegun · BILIN · R. Sittang · Duyinzaik · THATON · PAAN · Pagat · GULF OF MARTABAN · Kado · MARTABAN · MOULMEIN · 0 25 MILES

There are also indications that the Japanese are massing their air forces.

Along the Bilin River, 40 miles east of the Rangoon railway, the British and Indian troops are already engaged in severe fighting.

Rangoon G.H.Q. announced tonight that new Japanese forces which tried to cross the Bilin were driven back into the river.

CUT FLANK

The communiqué said: "Since the withdrawal behind the Bilin River took place operations have developed.

"The enemy at first succeeded in cutting our flank north of the town of Bilin.

"Our troops were subjected to a heavy attack, and a counter-attack had to be launched.

"The enemy tried to engage our left flank, but by means of a counter-attack our positions were kept intact.

"The enemy tried to cross the Bilin River, but our troops drove them into the river.

"Fighting was extremely fierce and casualties were heavy on both sides."

British bombers and fighters are attacking the enemy over a wide area. More stores and lorries have been destroyed at the Moulmein base. Severe attacks have been made on other positions east of the Bilin.

SPEEDING UP

In Rangoon itself the tempo of life is speeding up.

During the first days when the threat against the capital appeared not as a possibility but as a fact there followed a rush of civilians to the countryside. It was the same old column of poor, dusty, foot-slogging men, women and children that I first saw in Abyssinia, then Spain, then China, and then France.

Immediately after their departure there fell a strange quietness on the city—the silence of waiting

BACK PAGE, COL. THREE

Step-by-step invasion

CHUNGKING, Thursday.—A Chungking army spokesman said today that the Chinese forces in Burma were determined to wrest the initiative from the Japanese by invading Siam "step by step."

He added that in a minor action on the Burma-Siam frontier Chinese vanguards drove the Japanese across the border. Chinese troops have moved up their positions "for a further gradual penetration."—Express News Service.

TOKYO goes off the air

Tokyo radio went off the air last night after broadcasting to Europe for five minutes in German.

U.S. sub. scores

WASHINGTON, Thursday.—A United States submarine has sunk a 5,000-ton cargo ship in the East China Sea.—Reuter.

BRITISH HOLD OUT IN SUMATRA

Express Special Correspondent MERRILL MUELLER

BATAVIA, Thursday.

NEWS of British troops in action against the Japanese in Southern Sumatra reached Batavia today. This is the first time they have fought in the Dutch East Indies.

Wounded soldiers who arrived here described the British artillery crews as battling "heroically" against wave after wave of Japanese planes. They stuck to their guns despite the severest attacks.

Refugees from Sumatra estimate that the Dutch "scorched earth" policy of destroying the oilfields there has caused them a loss of about £75,000,000.

Many rubber plantations have also been fired.

British and Australian units, plus small forces of American troops, have arrived in Java to reinforce the hard-hitting Netherlands East Indies army.

NOT ENOUGH

Dutch authorities welcome their arrival, but say their numbers are by no means large enough.

The United Nations are beginning to overcome the most difficult supply problem of the war.

I have seen some of the world's crack liners and long lines of freighters quietly convoyed into the battle zone with supplies that will mean eventual Allied victory.

The Javanese people, expecting blitzes relatively as bad as London's, are as confident and calm as Londoners.

War drums to sound air alerts—Back Page.

"Wavell wounded" is Tokyo's latest

Tokyo radio stated last night that General Wavell has been wounded and is receiving medical treatment in Sourabaya.—B.U.P.

Two days ago Tokyo radio reported that Admiral Hart had been killed in a U.S. cruiser—a report promptly denied by Washington.

No. 13,038 Wednesday, March 11, 1942 One Penny

REMEMBER HONGKONG!

JAP ATROCITIES HORRIFY WORLD

MR. EDEN'S disclosures in the House of Commons yesterday of Japanese atrocities in Hongkong have shocked and horrified the entire democratic world.

These were two of the worst revelations he made:—

Fifty British officers and men were bound hand and foot and then bayoneted to death.

Women, both European and Asiatic, were raped and murdered. One entire Chinese district was declared a brothel, regardless of the status of its inhabitants.

Even as his disclosures were being released, the Jap Domei radio mockingly proclaimed: "Peace and order are being rapidly restored in all the occupied areas."

Then (says A.P.) German radio quoted a denial of the atrocities by a Jap spokesman, who said:—

"These accusations are infamous. They are against the honour and traditional Bushido spirit of the Japanese Army, which can be considered *the best disciplined force in the world.*"

A group of Midland M.P.s met to appeal to Mr. Churchill to rouse the country by directing an intensive campaign on the peril which now confronts civilisation.

They want it brought home to people that such atrocities may be the fate of the citizens of all parts of the British Commonwealth unless everyone concentrates on the war effort.

Mr. M. F. Hepburn, Ontario Premier, said in Toronto: "I have warned the Canadians that we are menaced by a new class of society. The Germans and the Japanese have been taught to ravage, to torture and destroy. I am not surprised by the revelations."

William Barkley reports Mr. Eden on Page Three.

THE WAR this morning

Express Military Reporter
MORLEY RICHARDS

THREE pieces of news last night from the Far East give point to the belief that the Allies' purely defensive fight in the Pacific can soon be replaced by attack.

Most significant is the Washington report that convoys of shock troops, dive-bombers, fighter planes, and guns have reached the South-West Pacific, and that they are bigger than "even the greatest optimist thought possible."

Couple with that statement Lieut.-General Joseph Stilwell's appointment as Chief of Staff to Generalissimo Chiang Kai-shek. He is looked on as one of the United States' best offensive strategists. It is fair to expect that lively action against the Japanese is being planned between the Americans and the Chinese, with all available British support.

Thirdly, there is the success of the defensive attack which British troops with tanks made against the Japanese at Hmawbi, 25 miles north of Rangoon. The enemy had established themselves across the road leading to the north. Our withdrawal was cut off.

Can smash Japs

First attack made by General Alexander's infantry failed to move the Japanese, who were heavily supported by fighters and dive-bombers. Our men came back again, and after ferocious fighting the enemy were routed.

Importance of this is to show that even without adequate air support troops in good heart and leaders prepared to fight can smash the Japs.

It may well be that American reinforcements will be used in the defence of Australia. New York radio said last night it was believed that Japan, holding a large portion of the Indies, was concentrating against Australia strength surpassing anything she had yet used at any one point.

The commentator added: "Washington does not say where the American forces are going, but it is almost certain that they

→ BACK PAGE, COL. FIVE

BUT A VISCOUNT IS UNMOVED

Japanese, lives in a London flat, does not believe Mr. Eden

Express Staff Reporter MARY SEATON

TWO diminutive enemy feet paced the carpet of a six-roomed flat in London last night. They belonged to a Japanese, Viscount Kano, 55-year-old ex-manager of the London branch of the Yokohama Specie Bank.

This is the man who says it—

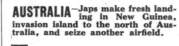

. . . But Viscount, look at this—

This, Viscount Kano, is a section from a photograph of the Nanking atrocities of 1937, showing Japanese soldiers at bayonet practice on live Chinese. The picture is too horrible for the Daily Express to print more than a part of it.

He is still at liberty and living an almost normal life.

He had heard Mr. Eden's terrible indictment of his army. But it did not move Viscount Kano.

"Eden's statement about Japanese atrocities is so much propaganda," he said. "I don't believe it."

(On December 4, 1940, Viscount Kano said in an interview: "The Japanese are your friends. I know Great Britain must win.")

The viscount (his Christian name is Hisao) looked round at the expensive furnishings of his flat, and his almond eyes gleamed.

"Soon I hope to be repatriated to my country," he said. "That will indeed be happy.

"I am glad my country is doing well. But all war is foolish, and this one was forced on us by economic measures.

"When I return I shall work for the peace. I am now writing a book, to be published after the war, giving the story of the economic reasons for war."

(On July 28, 1941, Viscount Kano said in an interview: "I do not believe Japan will be involved in war with Britain or America. We shall never attack either.")

The viscount turned back to his army.

"Atrocities? Japanese do not behave like that. It is not in us. Probably the report was inspired by Chinese propagandists—they have told dreadful untruths about us."

As he spoke he glanced at a large doll opposite, dressed in A.T.S. uniform. It belongs to his wife.

"When I visited my country early in 1940 there were no plans whatever to attack Britain. The highest in the land were innocent of such designs."

He described his emperor as a gentle biologist who spent his time peering through a microscope and collecting shell-fish.

(On July 29, 1941, Viscount Kano said in an interview: "Japan is ready to fight, but she doesn't want war. Japan enters Indo-China merely to bring an early end to the war in China.")

He leaned back, tapping his tiny hand on the table. "This war is a worrying business. Already I have some white hairs."

He said he took a stroll every day alone. But he avoided crowded places.

"I have had to hand over all my bank's funds—a nice present to your Government. But we have had our own back in Tokyo."

Then the viscount showed me out cordially. "You must visit Japan when the war is over," he pressed.

I left, wondering whether there could be a war on at all.

(.* Question: Why is Viscount Kano not interned? Answer: He is awaiting repatriation to Japan under an exchange scheme now under negotiation by the Foreign Office.)*

The way of a military gentleman

Express Foreign Expert

FROM the day they opened war in the Pacific, the Japanese have been plugging propaganda featuring Bushido, chivalrous code of the knightly Samurai of ancient Japan.

This is what Mr. Eden in Parliament yesterday called "nauseating hypocrisy."

Last century books and plays built up a Bushido myth around the Japanese as a noble and courteous people.

Seeking to exploit this, Japanese commanders have repeatedly tried to persuade those fighting against them that if they would surrender they would receive honourable treatment.

They have used the same appeal in broadcasts to native populations.

Bushido, dating back 12 centuries, is made up of two words—

Bushi = a military gentleman.
Do. = a way or doctrine.

Its maxims, governing the lives of the military class of the Samurai, the fighting noblemen, are handed down from father to son by word of mouth, with much traditional etiquette. They include the Seven Virtues of the Soldier:—

1, Loyalty; 2, Valour; 3, Patriotism; 4, Obedience; 5, Humility; 6, Morality; 7, Honour.

Followers of Bushido are commanded to show "a compassionate regard for the honour of the enemy."

Two men "bound" by this code are the officer commanding the Japanese troops at Hongkong—

LT.-GEN. SAKAI TAKASHI

and the Japanese Vice-Governor General at Hongkong—

LT.-GEN. ISOGAI RENSUKE.

The name Bushido originally came from China where these two exponents now hold office.

Rubbing it in

Moscow radio announced last night that programmes in German will be broadcast 17 times a day.—Express Radio Station.

Ghost voice calls

A ghost-voice interrupted the German short-wave programme yesterday with the cry: "Soldiers, refuse to go to the front."

AUSTRALIA—Japs make fresh landing in New Guinea, invasion island to the north of Australia, and seize another airfield.

INDIA—Viceroy calls all Indians to join in war front as country awaits statement on India policy by Mr. Churchill.

FRANCE—U.S. stops all shipments to French North Africa until "satisfactory arrangements" are made with Vichy.

Japs make new landing on invasion island

AUSTRALIA—AS THE JAPS SEE IT

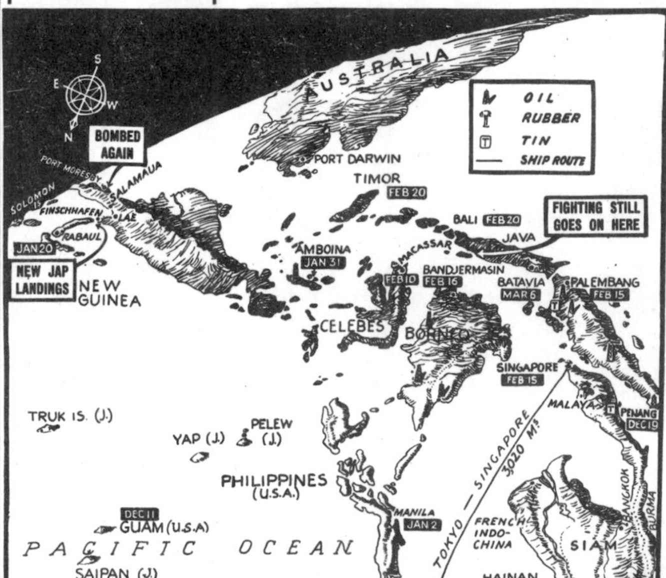

HERE is a Japanese-eye view of Australia. Looking south-east—the general direction of the Japanese drive—this perspective map gives dates on which the rich prizes of the Indies have been invaded or fallen.

Australia hits back with bombing of enemy bases

Express Correspondent ALAN BURBURY

MELBOURNE, Wednesday Morning.

JAPAN has won another foothold on the vast jumping-off ground of the Indies by occupying Finschhafen, in New Guinea. Invasion grows nearer to Australia every hour.

This third landing in New Guinea was made yesterday when a force of unknown strength got ashore at the one-time German mission station of Finschhafen, on the north coast, 60 miles east of Lae.

The harbour is of little importance, but the town has a small airfield which will help in the expected full-scale air attack against Port Moresby, on the south coast.

Port Moresby suffered its sixth daylight raid yesterday. It is the town's tenth raid since the occupation of Rabaul.

FIGHTERS, TOO

Growing frequency and severity of the raids support the Federal Government's conviction that the Japanese plan the swift conquest of New Guinea as a prelude to the attempted invasion of Australia.

Japanese bombers were previously hampered by the distance from New Britain, but the seizure of the airfield at Salamaua, New Guinea, brings Moresby within 175 miles.

Thus heavier bomb loads can be carried and fighter escorts provided.

There is a strong opinion in Australia that Port Moresby should be made quickly into a Tobruk for Australia.

The R.A.A.F. meanwhile is giving effect to the pronouncement of Mr. Drakeford, Australian Air Minister, that "whatever the odds, Australian airmen will continue to hammer the enemy to the utmost with whatever available strength can be provided."

A number of daring low-level raids were made yesterday on

BACK PAGE, COL. FOUR

3 A.M. LATEST

MYSTERY PLANE OVER GIB.

MADRID, Tuesday.—An unidentified plane which flew over Gibraltar this afternoon flew off apparently undamaged by A.A. fire from the Rock.—A.P.

Japs claim Tharrawaddy and Bassein

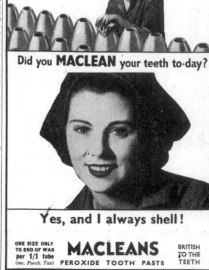

THE German radio yesterday quoted Tokyo reports that Japanese forces have occupied Tharrawaddy, on the River Irrawaddy, 60 miles north of Rangoon, and the port of Bassein, west of Rangoon.

The Tharrawaddy area was the centre of the Burma Rebellion of 1931.—*Gallagher's despatch from Mandalay is on the Back Page.*

BOMB THROWN IN BRUSSELS

Berlin radio, quoting a Brussels report, stated last night that a bomb was thrown in the Boulevard Anspach, which links the main stations of Midi and du Nord, after a ceremony to mark the departure of Belgian volunteers to Russia.

Some civilians were injured.

'Something in belly of the Hun'

Express Staff Reporter
NEW YORK, Tuesday.

BRITAIN is watching for a chance to launch a Continental offensive "when the time is ripe," stated the commander of the Canadian Forces in Britain, Lieut.-General McNaughton, this afternoon. He said:—

"No opportunity will be let slip. There is a steady flow of highly mobile, mechanised Canadian forces across the Atlantic.

"Canada is building up forces in Britain for a chance to put something in the belly of the Hun.

THE OFFENSIVE

"My discussions here with President Roosevelt and military leaders have been principally on the question of offensive action."

Then he gave warning that a German invasion of England may be attempted this spring, which would be "one of the most dangerous things that could happen to us." It must be a great temptation to Hitler to try to knock England out of the war, he said.

Still they come

More Canadians—infantry, ordnance, engineers, artillery, forestry corps, medical corps, and armoured corps—have arrived in Britain.

U.S. output can be doubled

WASHINGTON, Tuesday. — Mr. Donald Nelson, Chairman of the War Production Board, said in a radio speech tonight that America's output of military supplies could be doubled if all existing machinery were used 24 hours a day—seven days a week.

Unless production was brought to victorious levels neither management nor labour "could survive public wrath."—A.P.

U.S. STOPS FOOD SHIPS TO VICHY

Many replies: no satisfaction

Express Staff Reporter WASHINGTON, Tuesday.

PRESIDENT ROOSEVELT has stopped the sailing of food and other supply ships to French North Africa.

Reply after reply has come from Vichy to U.S. questions about collaboration with Germany. None of them is satisfactory.

So the last shipment was allowed to leave America early last month, and there will be no more until Marshal Petain is able to clear up the position to Mr. Roosevelt's satisfaction.

The supplies consisted mainly of food, cottonwool and low-grade oil.

Mr. Sumner Welles, Acting Secretary of State, announced the decision today. At the same time he said that the American Government has no confirmation of Russian reports that Vichy has turned over 40 warships to Germany.

To investigate

He did not mean to imply that the report was incorrect, but explained that there was no information in Washington about it.

It is probable that Admiral William D. Leahy, American Ambassador in Vichy, will be asked to investigate the report.

FOOTNOTE: Free French radio at Brazzaville (Africa) said last night that Vichy had replied to the United States request to be kept informed of French fleet movements with the statement that because America had stopped sending food Vichy was no longer bound by its undertaking.

Paris and Berlin off the air

Paris radio suddenly went off the air twice last night—between 7 and 8, and just after 9. Berlin also went off soon after 9. One bomb was dropped on Britain—in north Scotland. No one was hurt.

U.S. tanker sunk

New York radio announced last night that the 6,776-ton oil tanker Gulf Trade had been torpedoed off the Atlantic coast. Sixteen of the crew of 35 were rescued.

RUSSIA No. 1 ON U.S. GOODS LIST

WASHINGTON, Tuesday.

RUSSIA is to get goods before any other nation being supplied under Lease-Lend by the United States.

All agencies concerned with the supply of these goods have been instructed to place Russia at the top of all priority lists.

This applies to finished goods, semi-finished goods and raw materials.

Some manufacturers working on goods for Russia have already been receiving preferential treatment in supply of raw materials, and it is understood that there has been an appreciable increase in the deliveries to Russia from the United States.—B.U.P.

KINGSBURY SMITH CABLES FROM WASHINGTON:

The United States and China are nearing the conclusion of a mutual aid and economic pact, similar to the one recently signed with Britain.

Under its terms China will agree to co-operate with the United States in post-war economic reconstruction; both countries will pledge mutual aid until final victory is won; and the agreement will be effective even after the war.

'DON'T WED JAPS'

Order to Mexicans

MEXICO CITY, Tuesday.—The Government of Sinaloa, a strategic Mexican Pacific Coast State, refuses to legalise marriages of Mexicans to Germans, Italians or Japanese. This is part of a plan to clear all Axis nationals from the Pacific zone.—Exchange.

Straits guns fire for half an hour

German long-range guns at Cap Grisnez fired a number of salvoes across the Straits last night. Firing continued for about half an hour.

'INDIA! BE STEADY!'

Viceroy calls nation to action

NEW DELHI, Tuesday.

A "STAND STEADY" call to the people of India was made today by the Viceroy, Lord Linlithgow. His message said:—

"During the next few weeks you will be invited to enrol yourselves in the national war-front. The land we live in is threatened with danger.

"This call to action is for every one of us. Close your ranks and stand shoulder to shoulder against an aggressor whose conduct in the peaceful countries which he has outraged brands him as barbarous and pitiless.

"Stand steady. Encourage the brave. Strengthen the faint-hearted. Rebuke the babbler. Root out the hidden traitor.

"We are members of a worthy company—China, Russia, America, Britain, and a score of others. Let each one of us in India be worthy of our own country and our comrades. Thus shall we make our victory swift and sure."—Reuter.

Premier's speech awaited

BOMBAY, Tuesday.— Congress leaders are discussing the policy to be announced by Mr. Churchill on India at the next sitting of the House of Commons.

It is suggested that he will announce further expansion of the Viceroy's Cabinet, leading to the transfer of all offices, except defence, to Indian members, and a definite promise of self-government three years after the war.—Express News Service.

Hongkong relief ships held up

An official of the British Red Cross Prisoners of War section said last night:—

"For some weeks two special relief ships had been waiting to leave Calcutta and Sydney for Hongkong and Singapore.

"They are loaded with food and medical supplies, but they cannot sail until the International Red Cross in Geneva is notified of Japanese agreement and receives a guarantee of safe passage."

Chilly

Straits: Misty; chilly, raw easterly wind.

DAILY NEWS

Copr. 1942 by News Syndicate Co. Inc. NEW YORK'S PICTURE NEWSPAPER Trade Mark Reg. U. S. Pat. Off.

Vol. 23. No. 228 | New York, Wednesday, March 18, 1942★ | 68 Pages | 2 Cents IN CITY LIMITS | 3 CENTS Elsewhere

MacARTHUR'S COMMAND: ALL PACIFIC

Story on Page 3

The Chief

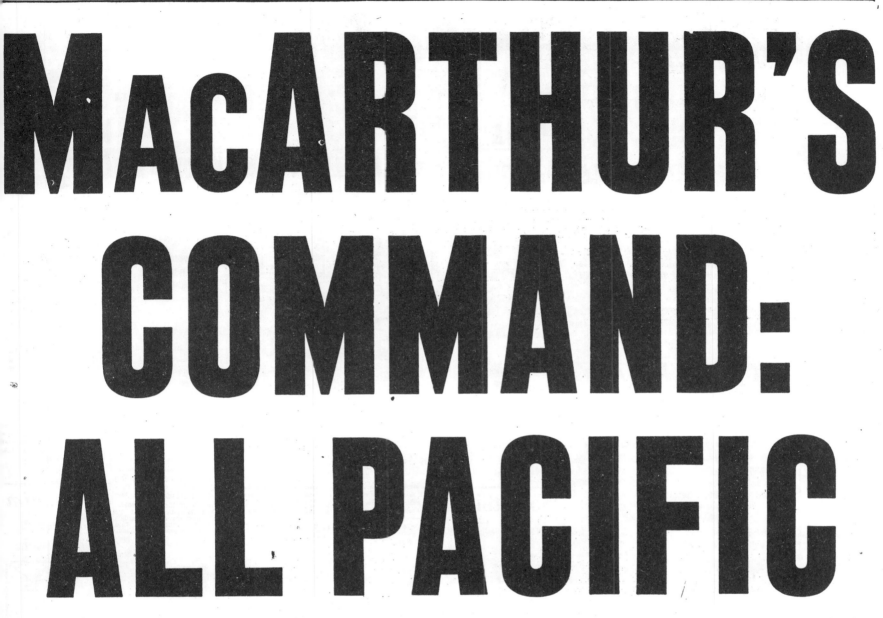

Trim, dapper Gen. Douglas MacArthur, hero of Bataan and America's foremost combat commander, becomes leader of all United Nations forces in the Pacific, according to a dramatic announcement yesterday by War Department. MacArthur, his wife and son, and members of his staff braved Jap pursuit planes and flew 2,000 miles from Corregidor to Australia to assume his new command.

MacArthur's Career In Pictures

—See Centerfold

News Chronicle

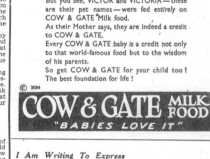

No. 29,918 • • • • • MONDAY, MARCH 30, 1942 RADIO PAGE 2 ONE PENNY

INDIA: DOMINION STATUS AFTER WAR

CRIPPS EXPLAINS THE PLAN

SIR STAFFORD CRIPPS, revealing the Government's proposals at his Press conference in New Delhi yesterday, said :

"In handing you a copy of the conclusions arrived at by the War Cabinet, I want to explain and make clear to you the form in which the document is drafted.

"It is in the form of a declaration by His Majesty's Government as to the future of India and as to the immediate problem of Indian government and defence.

NOT A DECLARATION

"I am giving it to you for publication today as a proposal which has been submitted to the leaders of Indian opinion by the War Cabinet, and its publication is not the publication of a declaration by His Majesty's Government, but only of a declaration they would be prepared to make if it met with a sufficiently general and favourable acceptance from the various sections of Indian opinion.

"I rely upon you all to make that position abundantly clear.

"Secondly, I am sure I can rely upon every paper in India and throughout the world to deal with this document with the deep seriousness and responsibility which it deserves

"You have a very great opportunity and a great responsibility in the way in which you deal with the matter.

"It is difficult to imagine a more weighty issue than this one, upon which the future, the happiness and freedom of 350,000,000 people may well depend.

"I CAN TRUST YOU"

"Whatever you say as to it, I know I can trust you to say it with a full sense of its importance and with a full realisation that you, too, may play a part in the solution of this difficult problem, by the way you treat the document and by the manner of your publicity

"I have waited to make the document public until I had had the opportunity of submitting it personally to the leaders of main interests in India and until they had been able to submit it to their colleagues

"Now it is to be given a wider publicity and I commit it to your hands in confidence that whatever your views may be you will seek to help to bring all Indian opinion together and not to divide or exacerbate differences.

"I shall myself be broadcasting an explanation tomorrow night to the Indian peoples, and in view of that fact I do not now propose to answer any questions except upon the meaning of the document itself, in case there are any passages which are not wholly clear to any of you."

R.A.F. Cross Channel Again

Formations of R.A.F. fighters, flying at a considerable height, crossed the South Coast yesterday afternoon and headed in the direction of the French coast. The Straits were hazy at the time.

Young Miners Released

Martin Urwin (19), and Edmond Cairns (18), two South Shields youths who were sentenced on March 4 to a month's imprisonment for refusing to obey a direction to work underground at Whitburn Colliery have been released from Durham Prison.

Durham Miners Association intervened on their behalf.

New Constitution If British Proposals Are Accepted Now

THE GOVERNMENT'S PROPOSALS FOR INDIAN CONSTITUTIONAL REFORM WERE MADE LAST NIGHT. THEY ARE :

(1) IMMEDIATELY AFTER THE WAR AN ELECTED BODY WILL BE SET UP TO FRAME A NEW CONSTITUTION WHICH WILL GIVE INDIA DOMINION STATUS.

(2) THIS WILL BE IMPLEMENTED FORTHWITH BY THE BRITISH GOVERNMENT, SUBJECT TO THE RIGHT OF ANY PROVINCE OF BRITISH INDIA TO RETAIN ITS PRESENT POSITION, BUT WITH THE RIGHT TO SUBSEQUENT ACCESSION.

THESE NON-ACCEDING PROVINCES CAN FRAME A NEW CONSTITUTION GIVING THE SAME STATUS AS THE INDIAN UNION.

(3) THE BODY THAT WILL FRAME THE CONSTITUTION WILL NUMBER ABOUT ONE-TENTH OF AN ELECTORAL COLLEGE FORMED BY THE ENTIRE MEMBERSHIP OF THE LOWER HOUSES OF THE PROVINCIAL LEGISLATURES. INDIAN STATES WILL ALSO SEND REPRESENTATIVES.

(4) A TREATY WILL BE NEGOTIATED BETWEEN THE BRITISH GOVERNMENT AND THE CONSTITUTION - MAKING BODY. THIS WILL PROVIDE FOR THE PROTECTION OF RACIAL AND RELIGIOUS MINORITIES, BUT WILL NOT RESTRICT THE RIGHT OF THE INDIAN UNION TO DECIDE ITS FUTURE RELATIONS WITH OTHER MEMBERS OF THE BRITISH COMMONWEALTH.

(5) UNTIL THE NEW CONSTITUTION IS FRAMED THE BRITISH GOVERNMENT MUST RETAIN CONTROL OF THE DEFENCE OF INDIA ; BUT THE INDIAN LEADERS ARE INVITED NOW TO CO-OPERATE WITH THE VICEROY'S COUNCIL.

SIR STAFFORD CRIPPS YESTERDAY MORNING AGAIN SAW MR. GANDHI, PANDIT NEHRU AND MAULANA AZAD, PRESIDENT OF THE ALL-INDIA CONGRESS.

IN THE AFTERNOON PANDIT NEHRU AND MAULANA AZAD HAD ANOTHER MEETING WITH SIR STAFFORD.

AT THE SAME TIME THE CONGRESS WORKING COMMITTEE WAS BUSY DISCUSSING THE BRITISH PROPOSALS. THE COMMITTEE ADJOURNED AND WILL MEET AGAIN TODAY.

"A POST-DATED CHEQUE"—GANDHI

New Delhi, Sunday.—"If the Congress President asks my advice I will say that the British proposals form a post-dated cheque Accept them or not.'"

It is stated, according to a current story in New Delhi, that Gandhi made this remark to Sir Stafford Cripps when pressed for his reactions to the British plan.

Gandhi's meeting with Sir Stafford today lasted for an hour and a half, and was preceded by conversations between the British Minister, Pandit Jawaharlarl Nehru and members of the Congress Working Committee.

Mr. Azad, Congress President, is meeting Sir Stafford again tomorrow afternoon, and it is believed that Congress representatives will state their reactions to the proposals by Tuesday at the latest.—B.U.P.

Full Text Of Cabinet Plan For Reform

THIS statement on the Indian problem was issued last night in London :

The conclusions of the British War Cabinet, as set out below, are those which Sir Stafford Cripps has taken with him for discussion with the Indian leaders, and the question as to whether they will be implemented will depend upon the outcome of those discussions which are now taking place :

His Majesty's Government, having considered the anxieties expressed in this country and in India as to the fulfilment of the promises made in regard to the future of India, have decided to lay down in precise and clear terms the steps which they propose shall be taken for the earliest possible realisation of self-government in India.

The object is the creation of a new Indian union which shall constitute a Dominion associated with the United Kingdom and the other Dominions by a common allegiance to the Crown, but equal to them in every respect, in no way subordinate in any aspect of its domestic or external affairs.

WHEN WAR IS OVER

His Majesty's Government, therefore, make the following declaration :

(a) Immediately upon the cessation of hostilities steps shall be taken to set up in India in the manner described hereafter an elected body charged with the task of framing a new constitution for India.

(b) Provision shall be made, as set out below, for the participation of the India States in the constitution-making body.

(c) His Majesty's Government undertake to accept and implement forthwith the constitution so framed subject only to—

(1) The right of any province of British India that is not prepared to accept the new constitution to retain its present constitutional position, provision being made for its subsequent accession if it so decides.

With such non-acceding provinces should they so desire, his Majesty's Government will be prepared to agree upon a new

Turn to Back Page, Col. Three

Russians Smash Five-Days Nazi Thrust

LATEST news from the war fronts last night was—

RUSSIA.—On the Kalinin front the Red Army has driven back a five-days German attack—the biggest operation the Nazis have undertaken since their last offensive against Moscow. In the South fierce battles are reported in the Kharkov sector.

BURMA.—Chinese troops have broken through the Japanese encirclement at Toungoo, where fighting is going on in the eastern suburbs. Japanese troops and Burmese traitors are now reported to be on the west bank of the Irrawaddy.

AUSTRALIA.—Four out of seven Japanese planes which raided Darwin were shot down by the R.A.A.F. Five enemy fighters were destroyed over Port Moresby, New Guinea.

Full Reports : Back Page

Petain Appeals To Peasants

Marshal Petain in a broadcast last night appealed to the peasants of France to collect all possible stocks of corn by April 21 to guarantee the daily ration of bread to the French public.

"I realise all the difficulties—the shortage of fertilisers, fuel, horses and means of haulage, the shortage of labour, and the fact that you are anxiously awaiting the return of the war prisoners," he said.

"You are to be pitied, but you are not the only ones. Help me once again to ensure that every Frenchmen gets his daily bread."

HITLER'S PLAN IS TO MAKE BULGARS FIGHT SOMEBODY

By VERNON BARTLETT

The categorical announcement by the German radio that Bulgaria was in a state of war with Russia betrayed a certain anxiety on the part of Dr. Goebbels to claim a new, if unimpressive, ally.

As reported in London, M. Filov, the Bulgarian Foreign Minister, made two statements in his Parliament.

One was to the effect that "Bolshevism" must be destroyed, a claim frequently trotted out by Hitler's minions without involving them in any action.

The other was that Bulgaria is in "a state of war," as indeed she has been against Great Britain for many months past, owing to her actions last year in attacking our allies.

The Germans may have been premature in linking these two statements together.

RELUCTANT SOLDIERS

It is, however, probable that Hitler has made King Boris promise the active co-operation of his few reluctant divisions, since there is a great deal of evidence that he has to find more cannon fodder at all costs.

Should these troops be sent to the Russian front, Hitler will have achieved his most remarkable success in making a people do what it does not want to do, for no other Slav country has had such close linguistic and other links with the Soviet Union.

AT TURKEY'S EXPENSE ?

Part of the bribe to Bulgaria is believed to be the promise of "territorial adjustments" at Turkey's expense.

Turkey, by way of compensation, is being told that she can take back her former territories in Syria, Iraq and Persia.

Herr von Papen, who went to Berlin at the same time as the King of Bulgaria, has the job of convincing the Turks that a bird in the hand is worth less than three in the bush.

If he fails, then the Bulgars, who will certainly not fight the Russians with the least enthusiasm, might be persuaded to co-operate against the Turks.

Commandos Sailed Into St. Nazaire Dock On Ramming Destroyer

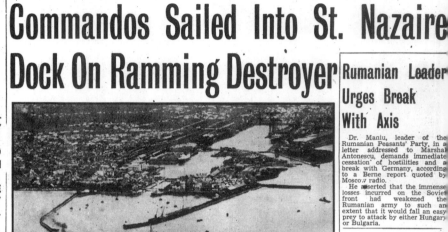

Aerial view of harbour and docks of St. Nazaire. At the mouth of the Loire, St. Nazaire possesses one of the finest harbours on the continent, giving egress to the Atlantic. It is only about 300 miles by air from London. The Germans have made the harbour one of their chief bases for the Battle of the Atlantic.

THE SMASHING OF THE MAIN GATE OF THE GREAT ST. NAZAIRE DRY DOCK—ROBBING HITLER OF THE ONLY ONE ON THE ATLANTIC COAST WHERE HE CAN LODGE A BATTLESHIP—WAS confirmed last night.

A second communique from Combined Operations H.Q. disposes of the German claim to have exploded the ramming destroyer before it struck the main gate at 1.34 a.m. on Saturday morning.

It says: "The raid, which was carried out by light forces of the Royal Navy, special service troops and aircraft of the R.A.F., was primarily directed against the large dry dock and the harbour installations at St. Nazaire.

"H.M.S Campbeltown, an ex-American destroyer (U.S. ship Buchanan), with bows specially stiffened and filled with five tons of delayed-action high explosive, forced her way through the double torpedo baffle protecting the entrance to the lock and rammed the centre of the main lock gate.

"The force of the impact was such that the destroyer came to a standstill only when her bridge was abreast of the gate itself

Pumping Station And Dock Gear Wrecked

"As soon as the bows of the Campbeltown were firmly wedged, special service troops landed as arranged and set about the work of demolition.

"The pumping station and dock operating gear were destroyed and other demolition work was carried out according to plan

"Meanwhile, a motor torpedo boat had fired two delayed-action torpedoes at the entrance to the U-boat basin and a motor launch had taken off the crew of the Campbeltown.

"A large explosion, followed by a smaller one, was seen and heard by our returning forces at 4 a.m., which was the time the delayed action fuses were due to go off.

"The raid caused panic among the enemy, who fired indiscriminately at friend and foe. The enemy's six-inch gun sunk one of their own flak ships at the time she was engaging our returning forces.

Some Troops Could Not Get Back

"Only a small proportion of the diversionary bombing could be carried out on account of low cloud, for fear of inflicting casualties on the French civilian population.

"Their task accomplished, our troops commenced to withdraw in motor launches detailed for the purpose, to rejoin the covering force of destroyers. Enemy machine-guns appeared to have prevented the full withdrawal of some of our forces

"Five German torpedo boats came into sight and opened fire on our motor launches. The escorting destroyers drove them off and forced them to retire. Although classed by the Germans as torpedo-boats, these vessels are similar to our S class destroyers

Air Battles Over The Sea

"Beaufighters, Hudsons and Blenheims of Coastal Command provided air protection to our returning forces

"There were several air combats, in which one Junkers 88 was destroyed and a number of enemy aircraft damaged. Two Coastal Command aircraft are missing

"The naval forces were under the command of Commander R. E. D. Ryder, R.N. Special service troops were led by Lieut.-Colonel A. C. Newman, of the Essex Regiment."

The first communique reported the reception of a signal from the

Turn to Back Page, Col. Four

Commander R. E. D. Ryder
Led Naval Forces

THESE MEN LED THE RAID

Commander Robert Edward Dudley Ryder, R.N., naval commandant of the St. Nazaire exploit, is only 34, but he has already sailed most of the world's oceans.

And the man who led the Commandos — Lieut.-Colonel A. C Newman—was a Territorial before the war, in the Essex Regiment

Until June last year he was a major.

Going straight into the Navy from school at Cheltenham, Commander Ryder in 1931 organised an expedition with four other officers on the China station and sailed a 54-ton ketch from Hong Kong to Britain.

ANTARTIC EXPLORER

Then he joined the British Grahamland expedition in a three-master auxiliary schooner and was two years exploring in the Antarctic.

In the Navy he has served in the battleship Ramillies, the submarine Olympus, the battleship Warspite and the corvette Fleetwood.

Eleven months ago he married Constance Hilary Myfanwy, third daughter of the Rev Lumley and Mrs. Green Wilkinson, of Windsor Forest

"I did not know my husband had taken part in the raid until he telephoned me saying that he was safe and well," said his wife last night.

Bataan Defenders Repulse Heavy Attack

Washington, Sunday. — The repulse of a heavy Japanese attack on the American and Filipino lines in the Bataan Peninsula, Luzon Island, was reported today by the U.S. War Department, which said the enemy was "driven back with heavy losses."

The fortified island of Corregidor was under frequent air bombardments the department's communique said, and the big guns of the Manila Bay defences destroyed many small boats of a Japanese invasion fleet on the south shore of the bay.

Rumanian Leader Urges Break With Axis

Dr. Maniu, leader of the Rumanian Peasants' Party, in a letter addressed to Marshal Antonescu, demands immediate cessation of hostilities and a break with Germany, according to a Berne report quoted by Moscow radio.

He asserted that the immense losses incurred on the Soviet front had weakened the Rumanian army to such an extent that it would fall an easy prey to attack by either Hungary or Bulgaria.

LAVAL GOES TO PARIS

New York, Sunday.—German radio announced that Laval had left for Paris where he would stay for a short while.

It has been suggested that Laval after his stay in Paris would go to Berlin to discuss the possibility of increased Franco - German collaboration.

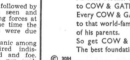

BLACK-OUT TIMES

	p.m.	a.m.
Birmingham	8. 7	6.16
Carlisle	8.13	6.19
Grimsby	8. 1	6. 8
Hull	8. 2	6. 9
Leeds	8. 7	6.14
Liverpool	8.12	6.20
Manchester	8. 9	6.17
Newcastle	8. 8	6.14
Nottingham	8. 4	6.12

Moon rises 5.7 p.m., sets 6.21 a.m. tomorrow. Full moon on Wednesday

Fair Play for the Army, by Gerald Barry, Page 2,

THE HOME PAPER
A Newspaper For the Rural Communities of the Miami Valley

The Middletown News-Signal

THE WEATHER
Continued Cold Weather Wednesday.

Entered as Second Class Matter In Middletown, Ohio, Post Office

MIDDLETOWN, OHIO, WEDNESDAY MORNING, APRIL 1, 1942

14 PAGES TODAY

Japs' Drive For Oil And India Near Prome

Jap Bombs Fire Philippine Church

Flames from Japanese incendiary bombs destroy famed Santo Domingo, one of Manila's oldest churches, after enemy blasted undefended city. Smoke rolls over the old walled city portion of Manila. (Passed by censor.) (NEA Telephoto)

Puzzling Ailment Affects 400 Persons At St. Marys; Water Supply Checked; School And Industrial Service Halted

ST. MARYS, O., March 31—(AP)—City Service Director W. R. Cook, today ordered water cut off from all manufacturing plants and schools in an attempt to isolate the cause of a mysterious ailment which had stricken at least 400 persons.

City Health Commissioner J. E. Heat said at least 400 persons were affected and ordered all drinking water boiled. Boy Scouts were used to distribute the warning from door to door.

ANALYSES IS ORDERED

Cook said he was "not at all certain" the blame was in the water supply, but had ordered analyses.

The city's entire system of mains was drained last night, Cook said, and water shut off from factories and schools, and supplied only to residential sections.

At Columbus, State Health Director H. R. Markwith said he had not been advised fully of the situation, but was dispatching men to St. Marys. The ailment affected the intestinal tract, Dr. Markwith said.

One plant affected by the water shutdown was the St. Marys Manufacturing Company, a subsidiary of the Goodyear Tire and Rubber Company of Akron. It was engaged entirely on defense orders.

Cook said he understood a similar ailment had been prevalent in areas outside the city limits.

The sweep of the epidemic, which first became evident Sunday night, was reflected in the absence of about 180 students and several teachers from schools today.

Supt. C. C. McBroom said use of water had been discontinued temporarily in the schools.

ARMY BASE PAY RAISE PROPOSED

Senate Passes Bill; Delay Seen In House

WASHINGTON, March 31—(AP) Hey, soldier, things are looking up on that idea of boosting your pay to $42 a month.

The Senate voted yesterday to double the $21-a-month basic pay of Army buck privates but at least a fortnight and possibly much longer will elapse before the House begins action on the legislation.

The House is in what virtually amounts to an Easter recess and there appeared little likelihood today that the military affairs committee would start hearings on the pay increase bill before April 13.

As passed in the Senate by a vote of 73 to 0, the measure would make the first basic change in the Army pay scale in 20 years.

The bill proposes increases all along the line for enlisted men in both the Army and Navy. In the Army a master sergeant, the highest non-commissioned classification would receive $138 a month instead of $126. Chief petty officers in the Navy would receive similar increases.

The Senate also passed and sent to the House a bill increasing the pay of the Philippine Commonweath army and the Philippine scouts to the same level as the United States Army troops, with whom they are now fighting shoulder to shoulder on Bataan.

Two-Year-Old Boy Slain, Dad Hunted

ALLENTOWN, Pa., March 31—Police Chief Arthuh V. Yohe asked police in three states today to search for the father of a two-year-old boy whose hacked body was found hanging from a water pipe in the cellar of his home.

Yohe said Mrs. Ralph Gavornik found the body of her son Edward, last night when she returned from a hairdresser's.

Coroner Alexander M. Peters of Lehigh County said he found this note tied on the body: "All I could bring is hell to anybody. My wife is the best in the world and the boys.

Another son, Bobby, 10, was at the movies.

"Little" Things Cause Much Ado

THOMASTON, Ga., March 31 (AP)—J. D. Hayes called on John Meier of Gainesville, Ga., and found him nursing cut hands and feet and ablack eye.

Meier explained he was getting ready for bed and turned the electric bulb to cut off the light but the bulb fell from the socket, and broke against the bedpost, cutting his hands.

Grouping for a match he stepped on the broken glass. Then he stooped to remove the glass from his feet, and struck his eye on a chair post.

LIBEL SUIT THREAT FACES SENATOR DIES

WASHINGTON(March 31—(AP) The threat of a libel suit faced Chairman Dies (D-Tex.) of the House Committee of un-American Activities today as a result of his charges that "at least 35 high officials" of the board of economic warfare had been affiliated with Communist-front organizations.

David B. Vaughan, chief of the board's administrative management division, said in a statement:

"I am making inquiries through my attorney to see whether Mr. Dies' statement is privileged. If instituted against Mr. Dies for it is not, I will ask that action be libel."

Dies made public his charges Sunday. Vice President Wallace, Chairman of the economic warfare board, to whom Dies wrote demanding removal of the officials immediately defended those charged and contended Dies' statement was worthy of having been made by a German propagandist.

Last night Dies announced he would recommend the committee invite Wallace to appear before it and also that it supply him with all data available to it to support the charges.

No Razor Blade Scarcity; Other Items Limited

WASHINGTON, March 31—(AP) Take it easy men. The Office of Price Administration says there won't be a razor blade shortage, after all, and it is unnecessary to stock up with them.

People who do that are hoarders, said Dan A. West director of OPA's consumer division, and besides, "in this case there isn't even a shortage."

West clarified matters today, however when he reassured shavers that the curtailment order would permit a "completely adequate supply," because it will mean manufacture of at least 2,400,000,000 blades this year. This compares with 2,000,000,000 in 1939.

WASHINGTON, March 31—(AP) The War Production Board has forbidden the manufacture of such familiar electrical ,household articles as toasters and flatirons after May 31.

In an order designed to speed the conversion of small utensil factories to war production, WPB yesterday forbade the making of a long list of electrical devices, including waffle irons, percolators, portable heaters, dry shavers and roasters, after the end of May.

In other orders, the board forbade the use of slide fasteners made of copper, steel or zinc; prohibited use of metals other than gold and silver in caskets and burial vaults (except for hardware fittings and metal linings) after July 1; limited the amount of critical materials which may be used in the manufacture of printing inks and banned the use of crude rubber and latex in a score of additional products, including wringer rolls.

ENGINE BLAST FATAL TO TRIO

All Dead Men Were Residents Of Lima, O.

REDKEY, Ind., March 31—(AP) The engineer, fireman and brakeman of a west-bound Nickel Plate Railroad freight train were killed today by the explosion of the locomotive boiler east of here.

The dead, all from Lima, O., were identified by Coroner Donald Spahr as E. L. Benner engineer; Fireman Herschberger whose first name was not available; and J. E. Schletter, the brakeman.

The coroner said he had reports the water level in the boiler was low.

The engineer was blown 100 feet from the locomotive. The fireman's body was found in the locomotive cab and the brakeman's body was found four cars back of the engine.

Bishop Is "Grave"

CLEVELAND, March 31—(AP)—Archbishop Joseph Schrembs was in a very grave condition today, the Chancellery said.

The 76-year-old prelate was stricken with pneumonia last Thursday.

Submit Question To El Haren

El Haren, noted astrologer who is offering advice to residents of this area through the Middletown Journal, is being called upon daily by hundreds of readers for solution to their problems.

Each day, letters sent to El Haren are answered through The Journal, and in this issue appear many questions and answers. Whether or not you are a subscriber to The Journal, you are invited to seek El Haren's advice.

Accompanying his column in this issue is a coupon, published for your convenience in submitting your questions. In no case will your name be used, and each question will carry only the initials of the writer.

INCREASED SUB RAIDS AWAITED

Favorable Weather To Aid Defenders, Foe

WASHINGTON, March 31—(AP) German U-boats, which have averaged a ship a day in American waters this month, can be expected to intensify their raiding in the weeks ahead as the weather becomes more facorable.

But better weather will work both ways naval experts said, explaining that it would be equally favorable for air and surface anti-submarine operations, with a resultant heavier destruction of raiders.

The experts asserted that the Nazis apparently had not reached the full power of their long distance undersea offensive and that an increased number of submarines probably would appear in American waters soon.

To offset this admittedly gloomy prospect, however, these authorities cited increasingly effective anti-submarine measures including:

1. Assignment of more and more patrol planes and blimps to the eastern sea frontier command of Rear Admiral Adolphus Andrews, who only last week was given unified control of Army as well as Navy aircraft engaged in sub hunting.

2. More general adherence by merchant ship skippers to the Navy regulations that vessels traveling in costal waters at night should run without lights and in patrolled lanes.

3. Partial blackouts of the heretofore brightly lighted sections of the coast which are believed to have aided the U-boats by silhouetting their targets.

Republic Steel Tax Figure Is Appealed

CLEVELAND March 31—(AP)—Republic Steel Corporation contends its strip mill machinery and equipment are personal property and not realty in a claim for a $7,321,900 reduction on tax valuation of its properties in Cleveland and Cuyahoga Heights.

The corporation told Tax Revision Board headed by County Treasurer John J. Boyle that in 1938 County Auditor John A. Zangerle fixed a valuation of $10,283,940 on its properties when it should have been only $3,082,980, resulting in a $62,000 increase in taxes.

The board continued the case two weeks to permit filing of further exhibits by the company.

30 Hurt In Crash

NORWALK, C., March 31—(AP)—Thirty passengers were injured today as a westbound Greyhound Bus crashed into the side of a bridge 12 miles east of here after colliding with a truck.

HOSPITAL ON BATAAN BOMBED; REDS BATTER NAZIS ON ALL FRONTS

ENEMY CLAIMS AIR GAINS, 183 RUSSIAN TANKS

Growing Battle Seen Along Allies Supply Line In North

By The Associated Press

Russia's armies, pressing a relentless Spring offensive amid the thawing snows of winter, were reported battering heavily at key German bases along the entire front today while the Nazi high command claimed aerial successes and the destruction of 183 Soviet tanks between March 23 and 30.

German field headquarters acknowledged severe Russian pressure in the Ukraine on the central (Moscow) front and in the far north, but asserted Nazi dive-bombers had "frustrated" a tank-led Soviet attack in the critical battle around Lake Ilmen.

DIE BOMBING RAID

The high command described the dive-bombing assault as taking place "northeast of Lake Ilmen," presumably referring to the Staraya Russa sector where the German 16th army has been trapped for many weeks.

Soviet front-line dispatches said Red army cavalrymen attacking in the same region northwest of Moscow, beat off a stiff German attack, forced the Nazis to retreat and seized an important populated place.

A bulletin from Adolf Hitler's headquarters said German bombers again attacked the Soviet Arctic supply port of Murmansk, and claimed three British bombers were shot down "in an attempt to fly by night into occupied Norwegian territory."

BATTLE IN NORTH

Other dispatches indicated a steadily growing battle along the United Nation's far north supply route to Russia.

The Berlin correspondent of the Swiss newspaper, La Suisse, said that the German fleet and air force were facing serious problems in Norway and Finland, and that a United States-British convoy had

Continued on Page 2, Col. 4

Ship Survivor Saved By Sub, Taken To Boat

MIAMI, Fla., March 31—(UP)—The crew of a German submarine which took one survivor aboard was credited today with sinking two Allied merchantmen.

The torpedoing of a small American vessel and a medium-sized British ship were announced yesterday in Washington. The American merchantman was sunk without warning off the Atlantic coast of Cuba March 12 and the British ship was torpedoed and shelled indiscriminately 'in the Atlantic" three days later. It was believed the same submarine made both attacks.

Thirty-one survivors of the American ship were brought here from Cuba. Forty-five British crewmen were taken to Fort Lauderdale from Nassau.

Per H. Janssen, 50, of Newport News, Va., fireman aboard the American vessel, was pulled from the water by the U-boat's crew and rode on the craft's deck for about five minutes until he was transferred to one of his ship's life-boats.

Ex-Governor Cox, 72, Hopes For Real Peace

DAYTON, O., March 31—(AP)—James M. Cox, publisher and former Ohio governor, took occasion of his 72nd birthday today to express hope for a constructive, enduring peace after the war.

Concerning the conflict, he said in a birthday statement issued from Miami to the Cleveland Plain Dealer:

"Our strength in thought and deed must be given to the task in hand. The hot breath of barbarism is close to our shores and its hideous portent must be plain even to our isolationists."

Cox advocated United States membership in the League of Nations during his 1920 presidential campaign on the Democratic ticket. His vice presidential running mate was Franklin D. Roosevelt, now President.

Number Of Casualties Listed; Plainly Marked Building Previously Avoided

WASHINGTON, March 31—(AP)—The War Department reported today that a base hospital in Bataan was bombed by the Japanese at noon yesterday, causing a number of casualties.

Plainly marked, the hospital had been avoided carefully by enemy bombers until yesterday, the department said.

Heavy aerial bombardment of the Manila Bay harbor defenses, accompanied by fire from enemy shore batteries, continued day and night, a communique said, but little damage has been inflicted, and a battery firing from Fort Hughes hit and destroyed an enemy launch in Manila Bay.

40-HOUR WORK WEEK LIFTING PLAN OPPOSED

Administration Will Battle To Last Ditch For Measure

WASHINGTON, March 31—(AP)—The Administration gave clear indication today that it would fight to the last ditch against any moves to suspend the 40-hour week law or to curb war profits except through taxation.

Senate Democratic Leader Barkley told reporters prior to a scheduled White House conference today on the legislative program that he was opposed to enactment now of any restrictive labor measures.

TAXATION FAVORED

Moreover Barkley said he favored attempting to recapture excessive war profits by high taxation such as the Treasury has suggested war profits by high taxation such as the Treasury has suggested rather than through a flat limitation of 6 per cent, a method the House approved when it amended a pending $18,000,000,000 military appropriation bill.

Barkley said suspension of the 40-hour week law was likely to cause "chaos" in war industries.

MORE THAN 40 HOURS

Contending most war industries were operating far in excess of 40 hours a week, Barkley said the only question involved was whether employes were to receive time and a half for work over that period.

This time and a half, he said, represented about a 10 per cent increase in pay over normal wages. He added that there had been an approximate increase of 15 per cent in the cost of living.

He said further that war contracts had been made by the government on the basis of overtime payments to obtain needed production speed. If labor loses its overtime pay contractors are likely to profit that much more, Barkley said.

FLOGGING CASE PAIR CONVICTED

Jail Term And Fine Facing Pupil's Parents

LAFAYETTE, Ind., March 31—(AP)—The jury that convicted Mr. and Mrs Arthur H. Leslie of assault and battery said they ought to be locked up for whipping a school teacher who scolded their son.

The verdict recommended each be fined $200 and improsioned 30 days for the beating given pretty Constance M. Davis, 33, in her fifth-grade room at Longlois School February 27.

Circuit Judge W. Lynn Parkinson will pass sentence Saturday. Meantime they are free on bond.

Danny Leslie, bright-eyed 11-year-old cause of the whole case, was not in court when the verdict was read.

FARISH DENIES STANDARD HELD RUBBER OUTPUT

Company Head Says Cartel Aided U. S. Gasoline, Explosives

WASHINGTON, March 31—(AP)—W. S. Farish, president of the Standard Oil Company of New Jersey, described today as without "a shadow of foundation" testimony that the company had prevented or delayed development of synthetic rubber in the United States.

"The facts and the record," he told the senate defense investigating committee, "are exactly to the contrary."

REPLIES TO ARNOLD

Farish appeared before the committee to reply to testimony by Thurman Arnold, assistant attorney general in charge of anti-trust enforcement, that the company had frustrated development of synthetic rubber in the United States as a result of cartel agreements made with I. G. Farben of Germany before the United States entered the war.

"Any charges the Standard Oil Company or any of its officers has been in the slightest respect disloyal to the United States are unwarranted and untrue," Farish asserted, reading from a statement.

"I repel all such insinuations with all the vigor at my command. I do so with indignation and resentment.

AID TO AMERICA

"Moreover, I wish to assert with conviction that whether the several contracts made with the I. G. did or did not fall within the borders set by the patent statutes or the Sherman Act, they did inure greatly to the advance of American industry and more than any other one thing have made possible our present war activities in aviation gasoline, toluol and exposives and in synthetic rubber itself."

Arnold had testified that the cartel agreements had "frustrated the creation of an American synthetic rubber industry."

Because of the agreement, he said, Stndard turned over to the Germans before United States entry into the war patents of synthetic rubber processes that were better and cheaper than any the Nazis had, while at the same time refusing to make the patents available to American manufacturers.

The anti-trust chief also testified that the company, through a German subsidiary, aided the Naxis in development of a synthetic aviation gasoline industry.

Arnold's testimony followed immediately the filing of consent decree and payment of fines by the company in settlement of anti-trust charges brought by the government.

Under the consent decree the company agreed to make all of its chemical patents as well as those obtained from I. G. Farben available to everyone during the war without royalty charge.

SPEEDY ACTION TO AID SMALL BUSINESS URGED

WASHINGTON, March 31—(AP) Sen. Murray (D-Mont.) asked the Senate today for prompt enactment of pending legislation to help small businesses obtain capital and war contracts, asserting that "the small businessman is the forgotten man of this critical hour."

Murray chairman of the Senate Small Business Committee, took the floor when the chamber began consideration of the measure, which was introduced by the committee after a special study.

The bill would provide for a special deputy to the chairman of the War Production Board to guard the interests of small business and would create a $100,000,000 smaller war plants corporation within the WPB.

This corporation would be empowered to act as a prime defense contractor and to let sub-contracts to small plants. It also could make loans of money and facilities to small plants for conversion to war production.

DANGER GROWS WHILE BRITAIN AWAITS REPLY

Toungoo Believed Lost As Enemy Increases New Offensive

By ROGER D. GREENE
Associated Press War Editor

Japan's drive toward the oil fields of northwest Burma and the gateway to India took a menacing turn today as British headquarters acknowledged Japanese troops supported by traitorous Burmese natives had advanced within 10 miles of Prome.

Prome is the British-held anchor on the right wing of the Allied defense line in Cental Burma.

BARRIER TO OIL

The city is strategically important as a barrier to the rich Yenangyaung oil fields. It also guards the Irrawaddy River route to Mandalay.

A British communique said the Japanese penetrated to Shwedaung, 10 miles below Prome, with frontier troops inflicting 300 casualties and capturing 70 prisoners.

The communique said British forces launched an attack to clear enemy roadblocks in Shwedaung. No information on the outcome was available.

CHINESE IN TROUBLE

Equally dark news came from the Chinese-held left flank on the Toungoo front. "A communique said Chinese troops "joined with other forces to north and east of Toungoo and readjusted their positions in that area."

This indicated the Chinese forces, commanded by Lt. Gen. Joseph W. Stilwell, U. S. A., apparently had withdrawn from Toungoo.

Later Chinese dispatches, however, said Chinese reinforcements moving south to aid Gen. Stilwell's hard-pressed forces had occupied a railroad station 10 miles north of Toungoo and had made contact with Chinese troops still holding out in the eastern part of Toungoo.

OUTNUMBERED BY FOE

A Chinese army spokesman said 10000 Chinese soldiers were holding the eastern part of Toungoo against 18,000 Japanese in the western section.

The spokesman said that Toungoo was important only as an outpost below the potential main battle area and that the mountains north of Toungoo could be more easily defended than the plains below the town.

Simultaneously Axis reports said the Japanese had carried out heavy aerial raids on Mandalay and attacked other key points on the Toungoo-Mandalay road evidently seeking to prevent reinforcement.

SERIOUS PROBLEMS

India—British negotiations to mobilize India's 390,000,000 as a fighting force on the side of the Allies met serious new difficulties. Dispatches from New Delhi said it appeared the dominant Indian party might reject the British plan for self-rule.

Japan—The Rome radio quoted Imperial Tokyo heaquarters as saying a Japanese submarine operating in the Indian Ocean attacked a British convoy east of Ceylon.

The blows were inflicted in the battles of the Dutch East Indies and Philippines.

BRIGHTER REPORT

A bright report of performance and skill—backgrounded on the fact fresh Allied air units are still massing for the battles of Burma and Australia—was presented in an interview at U. S. Army headquarters in Australia by Col. Eugene L. Eubank, head of the U. S. bomber command which struck at invasion forces from Luzon to Java.

Col. Eubank smashed Japanese claims to superior flying ability with a declaration his men had shot down half a hundred pursuit

(Continued on Page 13, Column 5)

CLOSING PRICES EVENING STANDARD. April 2. 1942 FINAL NIGHT EXTRA

Evening Standard

Amusements 6
Radio 6

BLACK-OUT 8.4 pm—6.3 am.
MOON rises 8.57 pm; sets 7.47 am.

No. 36,682 LONDON, THURSDAY, APRIL 2, 1942 ONE PENNY

JAPS LAND BEHIND US IN BURMA

Flank and Rear Threat Follows Capture of Port

Japanese forces have landed at Akyab, the port on the west coast of Burma, about 200 miles north-west of Prome.

THIS NEWS IS GIVEN BY THE CHINESE SPOKESMAN IN CHUNGKING TO-DAY, SAYS REUTER.

The landing was covered by cruisers and destroyers, the spokesman added.

It represents a new threat from the flank and the rear to the British defenders of Prome, whose position is now critical.

Lieut.-gen Alexander, the British G.O.C. Burma, is personally directing operations on the Prome front. it is reported in Chungking. says British United Press

United States Lieut.-gen. Stilwell, who commands the Chinese armies in Burma under General Alexander, is reported to be directing operations in the Toungoo sector

An earlier message from Associated Press said the Allied situation in Burma seemed to have taken a grave turn.

CHINESE RETREAT

This was in spite of heroic fighting by Chinese troops, who are now in positions north-east of Toungoo.

The Japanese still have complete control of the air, and are

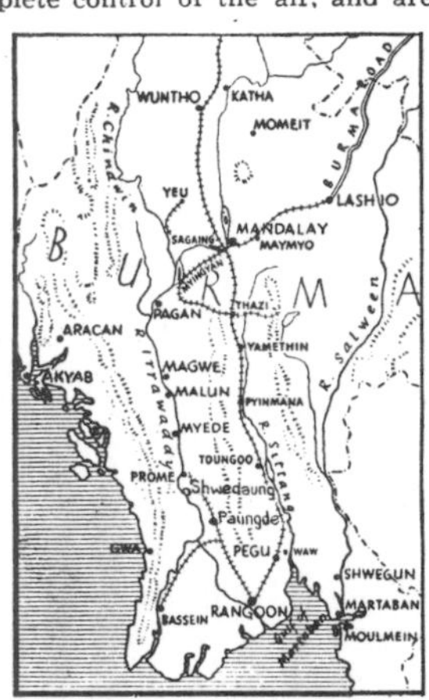

reported to be in force in Shwedaung and on the western bank of the Irrawaddy, as well as astride the railway to the east, north of Paungde.

A Burma communiqué from New Delhi says that an airfield in Northern Burma was raided yesterday.

A Tokyo report, quoted by the German-controlled Paris radio, claims that Japanese bombers have again cut the Burma Road in China beyond Lashio at several points with heavy heavy calibre bombs

Paris radio, quoted by Associated Press, said to-day that according to the latest Tokyo reports, the Japanese had landed strong reinforcements from the river at Yedashe. 20 miles north of Toungoo.

Colombo Alert

An Alert was sounded in the Colombo, Ceylon, area to-day. The All Clear came soon afterwards, says Reuter. No incidents were reported.

BOGUS FOOD INSPECTORS

Rob the Larders

Two householders in Lewisham are the victims of a new Black Market dodge.

Men who posed as Ministry of Food officials called and requisitioned part of their store of food. saying they had more than one month's supply allowed under the new order.

The local Food Committee are asking the Ministry of Food to issue identification badges to their inspectors

He Drank the Whisky at Windsor Castle

Whisky bottles in a Windsor Castle cellar were found to contain only coloured water . . . a butler had drunk the whisky.

This story was told at Windsor to-day when the butler, Digby Smith, 54, was sent to gaol for three months.

He pleaded guilty to stealing a gold cigarette case, a diamond and turquoise tiepin and a pair of diamond cuff links, worth in all £100, from Sir John Hanbury-Williams, of Henry III Tower Windsor Castle

It was stated that Smith was formerly employed by Sir John, and in 1940 he disappeared.

He was eventually traced. and was found to be working as a butler to Lord Carnarvon at Highclere Castle, Newbury

Some time after he disappeared it was found that a large number of whisky bottles in the cellar were filled with coloured water. and Smith admitted having drunk the whisky

"Rather Sad Ending to a Very Fine Life"

"A rather sad ending to a very fine life" remarked Mr G. Wills Taylor, coroner, giving a verdict of accidental death at Reigate to-day on Thomas Secrett, 66, of Observatory-road, Redhil, batman and manservant to the late Lord Haig.

Secrett died in the East Surrey Hospital last Sunday after a fall at a N.A.A.F.I. stores where he was employed.

Submarine Sinks Italian Patrol Ship

One of our light patrol vessels was unk by an enemy submarine in the Central Mediterranean" says to-day's Italian communiqué, quoted by Associated Press.

Donald Duck Called Up

Evening Standard Correspondent

MONTREAL Thursday

Donald Duck, a farmer. who lives near London. Ontario, called up for training, has been granted deferment He intends to join the R.C.A.F.

SIR WARREN FISHER'S STATEMENT

Sir Warren Fisher, who has been dismissed by the Home Secretary. Mr. Morrison, from his post as Special Commissioner for the London Civil Defence Region, made a further statement to-day.

The dismissal will be raised in the Commons on reassembly If a sufficient demand is made for a debate the. Government will arrange for one.

To-day Sir Warren said:

"Some weeks ago at a conference held under the chairmanship of Mr Mabane, Parliamentary Secretary to Mr. Morrison, and attended by the Deputy Regional Commissioners and Chief Fire Officers throughout the country. Mr. Mabane stated that the existing practice of using fire service vehicles for authorised sporting events could go on until and unless it was revoked

"The use of fire vehicles for the journey from Lancashire to Scotland was admittedly an error of judgment. but to sack the Deputy

(Continued on Back Page, Col. Three)

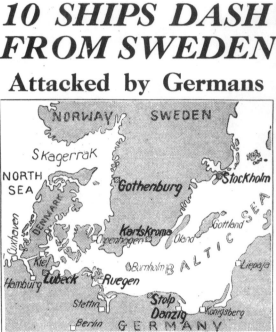

To-day's picture of Sir Warren Fisher.

BABY BORN IN LIFEBOAT

Mother Attended by Injured Doctor

The 28-year-old wife of a Jugoslav Consul Attache in New York gave birth to a baby boy in a crowded lifeboat pitched about by 15-feet waves.

She is Mrs Desanka Mohorovicic, and she was attended by a ship's doctor who was in agony because of two broken ribs

Their ship had been torpedoed and sunk off the Atlantic coast on Sunday

This news follows the story told in the Evening Standard yesterday of a mother and new born baby being saved after three days in an open lifeboat.

A Brave Woman

The doctor was L. H Conly of Brooklyn, New York

He worked in difficult conditions, with only the lifeboat's medical kit at his disposal

"Mrs. Mohorovicic," he said, "was a very brave woman."

Of 122 people on board the ship 30 are missing.

(Messages from Associated Press and British United Press.)

10 SHIPS DASH FROM SWEDEN

Attacked by Germans

From ***BERNARD VALERY***

STOCKHOLM, Thursday.

Ten Norwegian ships, which, since the invasion of Norway, had sought asylum in Sweden, escaped from Gothenburg a few days ago.

At least three of them have been sunk while trying to reach Britain.

Swedish coastguards have discovered the wreckage of three tankers.

Two were the Skytteren (12,358-ton floating whale oil factory) and the Buccaneer (6222 tons)

Scuttled

One report states that the crews scuttled these ships after being attacked off the Swedish coast by German armed trawlers They did this to prevent the Nazis from obtaining the cargoes

Another ship was seen drifting ablaze in the Skagerrak. German warships were near her.

It is believed that two large merchantment reached the open sea and that other ships have returned to Gothenburg.

Fishermen are convinced that explosions caused considerable loss of life. and that some of the crews were taken prisoner

The ships, in their dash from Gothenburg Harbour, would have to pass through the minefields of the Skagerrak

German airfields in Norway and Denmark lie on either side of this narrow stretch of water.

The ships. which included merchantmen, tankers and floating whale oil factories. were requisitioned by the Norwegian Government after the invasion of Norway. and were since chartered to the British Government

A writ was served on the British Government to show reason why they should not be returned to the ship owners in Norway. but the Government refused to answer the writ

Quisling Control

"The so-called Ship Owners Association in Oslo is completely under Quisling control," an official of the Norwegian Government said to-day.

The original leaders were arrested and sent to Germany and two or three Quislings were put in charge. The moves to obtain these ships were directed by the Germans hiding behind the facade of the Ship Owners' Association

The names of the ships concerned were the Charente, Buccaneer. Lind. Gudvang. Skytteren. Dicto. Storsten Lionel Rigmor. B.P. Newton and Rapid.

No Newspapers To-morrow

No newspapers will be published to-morrow either in London or the provinces. This is in accordance with the Government's wish that workers should have one day's holiday at Easter.

£146,063,225

London's Final Figure for Warship Week

The final figure of London Warship Week was announced to-day as £146,063,225.

To this total the County of London, including the City contributed £129,163,000, the County of Middlesex £12,676,000. the Essex boroughs of Barking, Ilford. East Ham, West Ham, Leyton and Walthamstow £3,226,000 The City of Westminster raised over £11,500,000.

Libya: "No Boil Up"

In Libya patrol activity continues but there is no indication of a possible "boil up," it was authoritatively stated in London to-day

To-day's Cairo communique says our fighting patrols went out during the night of Wednesday-Thursday, reaching enemy outpost positions about Aleima and Aggara south of Tmimi.

Cripps, Hopeful, Stays On

Sir Stafford Cripps, who should have been leaving India next Monday, announced in New Delhi to-day that he is postponing his departure as he thinks he can do something useful next week.

He told his Press conference: "The points of difficulty are coming down to fairly narrow limits, and with common goodwill we may be able to solve the difficulties"

Sir Stafford gave "an absolutely flat denial" of reports that he had been faced with the resignation of three great soldiers if he came to a settlement which involved the appointment of an Indian defence member.

He also emphatically contraidcted a report that the Viceroy is creating difficulties

NO OTHER PLAN

In answer to a question whether he had referred to London any proposal for the appointment of an Indian Defence Minister, Sir Stafford replied: "I have kept his Majesty's Government informed, but I have not got any alternative scheme on which to consult them."

Another answer was: "I have not yet received the official document from Congress which I understand from the Press I am going to receive.

"Mr. Jinnah has not yet given me any communication on the Muslim League's reaction."

All-India radio, quoted by Associated Press from New York, reported that Maulana Azad and Mr. Nehru this afternoon handed Sir Stafford the Congress resolution.

As they were leaving Sir Stafford told journalists, "I hope there will be many more meetings."

Struck Gold as He Dug A.R.P. Trench

When digging an air-raid trench for his family, a man in a remote town in New South Wales struck gold in sufficient quantity to pay for the construction of the trench, says Reuter.

The story of his good fortune has stimulated great trench-digging activity by the other residents.

Riom Trial Resumed

The Riom trial was resumed this afternoon, says Reuter.

Paris Works Bombed In Full Moon Raids

Aircraft of both Bomber Command and Fighter Command made attacks by the light of the full moon during the night.

"Bomber Command bombed industrial objectives and communications in West and North-west Germany," says an Air Ministry communiqué.

"In Occupied Territory bombing attacks were made on the Matford works at Poissy and on the docks and shipping at Le Havre.

"Mines were also laid in enemy waters

"Fighter Command aircraft attacked objectives in Belgium and Northern France. During these attacks an enemy bomber was destroyed

"Fifteen of our bombers are missing from the night's operations"

4—5.30 a.m. Paris Alert

The Matford works at Poissy are 10 miles north-west of Paris.

"The western and north-western outskirts of Paris had an Alert from 4 to 5.30 a.m.," says the Vichy news agency, quoted by Reuter

"The R.A.F. dropped bombs at a number of points, particularly at

(Continued on Back Page, Col. Four)

HONGKONG

Argentina Sends for Jap Ambassador

Swiss radio reported from Buenos Aires to-day that the Japanese Ambassador had been summoned for a conference with the Argentine authorities concernin Argentina's demarche on behalf of British prisoners in Hongkong, says Associated Press.

Argentina proposed to despatch a neutral commission to visit the prisoner of war camps. The Ambassador said he would forward the proposal to his Government.

Only a Worm

Husband at Tottenham.—I was a man when I married, but now I am no more than a worm.

No. 10,277 (E*) Monday, April 20, 1942 One Penny

PETAIN HANDS FRANCE OVER TO PIERRE LAVAL

French Told News In Ninety Second Speech

'DAILY SKETCH' DIPLOMATIC CORRESPONDENT

LAVAL is now in control of the internal and external affairs of France—under the authority of Marshal Pétain.

Marshal Pétain, in a ninety-second radio speech last night, announced this fact to France and to the world, ranging himself solidly behind Laval and his pro-Nazi policies. Here is the text of his speech:

"Frenchmen, a new Government has been formed.

Admiral Darlan, who remains my successor-designate, will take over the defence of our territory and our Empire.

M. Pierre Laval will, under my authority, direct the home and foreign policy of the country.

It was with him that, at the most tragic moment of disaster, I founded the New Order, which was to assure the rise of France.

To-day, at a moment as decisive as June, 1940, I find myself associated with him once more, to continue the task of national reconstruction and European reorganisation.

Frenchmen, your wisdom, your patience, your patriotism will help us to triumph over our trials and our sorrows.

With one heart, unite behind the new Government, which will give you new causes for belief and hope."

"Frenchmen, help us to triumph over our trials and our sorrows."—Marshal Pétain.

Laval for Paris?

Pétain's speech, made under stress of obvious emotion, marks what is probably one of the final stages in the complete Nazification of France.

Although Laval has set up office in the Hotel du Parc, Vichy, he will shortly move to Paris, according to de Brinon, now one of his personal Secretaries of State.

Laval has now become virtual dictator of France—with Germany—and the next few days will reveal how far he plans to go in his undoubted intentions of collaboration with Germany. He is to broadcast to-night.

One of Laval's first acts has been to sack Georges Mondanel, head of the political section of the French secret service, who arrested him in December, 1940. Mondanel, says a Vichy message, will be assigned to new duties, not in Vichy.

I DID IT FOR PETAIN

—SAYS LAVAL

"I BECAME chief of the Government on the order of Marshal Pétain," Laval said in Vichy last night, according to the German radio.

Laval started his new job yesterday morning, says the Vichy news agency. He has installed himself at the Hotel Du Parc.

Pierre Laval

His first visitor was Marshal Pétain, with whom he had a "long and cordial talk," according to the agency. He also had a long talk with Admiral Darlan and established "complete community of views."

To newspaper men Laval said:

"I am very touched by the welcome that the Marshal has given me during all these days of crisis. Many difficulties have been smoothed out.

'Easing My Task'

"I have a feeling that my task, which is heavy, will be eased by the clear understanding that the Chief of the State has of our present situation.

"It is not correct to say that he has relinquished his powers. I am the head of the Government in virtue of the powers which the Marshal has delegated to me.

"The authority of the Marshal is indispensable for the accomplishment of my mission."

'NAZIS TAKING OVER IN TOULON'

INSISTENT rumours in Toulon and Marseilles say that the battleships Strasbourg and Dunkerque and the cruisers Colbert and Dupleix will soon be handed over to the Germans.

It is reported that naval experts from Berlin have already arrived in Toulon and Marseilles and are only awaiting orders to take over the ships, according to a Tass message quoted by Moscow radio last night.

"Recently French sailors from the light cruiser Avanturier appealed to the men to resist any attempt to hand the French navy over to the Germans," says the report.

"Strong detachments of naval pickets are patrolling the streets of Toulon."

HEAVY DAMAGE IN TOKYO—AXIS REPORTS ON AIR RAIDS

WHILE U.S. official sources are still silent on Saturday's daylight raids on Tokyo and other Japanese cities, Axis reports indicate damage was considerable.

A Tokyo report quoted by Berlin radio yesterday said that factories, a cinema and houses had been burned down in the capital, while similar damage was done in other towns.

The Swiss radio last night said that alerts were sounded yesterday in five areas, including Tokyo and Yukosuka, an east coast naval base.

Land Or Sea?

IN the absence of official news the number of planes in the raids on Japan and their source is still a mystery.

A New York message says the raiders are believed to have come from U.S. aircraft-carriers.

On the other hand, a Calcutta message says the planes may have been land-based and operated from China.

The Japanese claim to have shot down nine planes.

According to this report "American planes—MA40 bombers—were recognised among the craft flying over the areas."

The plane referred to is probably the American N.A.40, a single-engined monoplane with a range of 1,725 miles.

Tokyo radio reported yesterday the cancellation of three sporting events "owing to the circumstances."

An alert in Tokyo on Sunday lasted from 2 a.m. till 4 a.m. All Japanese cities are now blacked out.

'Vast Offensive'

In Washington last night, says A.P. War and Navy Department officials were wearing broad smiles but saying nothing.

Congressmen and the Press see the raids as the "forerunner of a vast offensive that will ultimately crush Japan."

Mr. Forde, Australia's War Minister, said in Brisbane yesterday:

"At this moment many great movements are taking place in and around Australia. These are closely co-ordinated with Allied strategic movement throughout the Empire, the Pacific and the Indian Ocean area."

New 'Lawrence' Wins Us Burma Ally

From ALFRED WAGG, 'Daily Sketch' Special Correspondent

CALCUTTA, Sunday Night.

AN unnamed British officer—Burma's Lawrence of Arabia—has won for us a new ally against the Japanese invaders.

Living with the natives, moving through the Shan States, talking with village chiefs and headmen, this officer has succeeded in rallying the wild mountain tribes to the flags of the United Nations.

Now he is organising the tribes along the malaria-ridden border of Siam, and soon bows and arrows may be matched against the enemy in the battle of Burma.

The poison-tipped arrows which the natives use can be a deadly weapon in jungle warfare and the little brown men are adepts at guerilla fighting.

R.A.F. Hit Back

R.A.F. planes are now actively supporting our troops on the Irrawaddy front in Burma, says yesterday's air communiqué from New Delhi. Enemy aircraft, however, are still attacking heavily.

Blenheims have bombed and machine-gunned enemy troops and motor transport at Yinpaungwe and Sainggya.

Other planes hit enemy flying-boats at Port Blair, in the Andaman Islands, on Saturday, destroying two and badly damaging three more. One of our aircraft is missing.

Chinese forces in southern Burma have withdrawn from Ela, 160 miles south of Mandalay and 50 miles north of Toungoo, but British armoured forces have successfully cleared the road block across the highway from Yenangyaung to Kyaukpadaung.

FINE

Straits weather last night: Fine; light S.W. breeze; cool; low mist.

FOUR MYSTERY MEN FLY TO U.S. WITH MARSHALL AND HOPKINS

GENERAL GEORGE C. MARSHALL, Chief of the U.S. General Staff, and Mr. Harry Hopkins, America's Lease-Lend envoy, arrived back in the United States by air from Britain yesterday, it was announced in New York last night.

Four people, whose identity has not been disclosed, travelled with them to America.

General Marshall and Mr. Hopkins attended a parade of U.S. troops in Northern Ireland only on Saturday. Last week they conferred with Mr. Churchill and Allied leaders in London on strategy and war production.

R.A.F. SWEEPING THE CHANNEL

SECOND week of the R.A.F.'s non-stop offensive began yesterday with two sweeps across the Channel.

A large force of bombers and fighters took part in the afternoon attack. They crossed over Deal about four o'clock heading for Dunkirk and Calais.

Soon after a formation of fighters had crossed the coast in the morning raid distant explosions were heard.

Three Big Attacks On Malta

Malta had three heavy raids yesterday. Three bombers have been shot down, one probably destroyed and three others damaged in the past 24 hours.

Each of yesterday's raids was made by Junkers 88s and 87s, escorted by Me. 109s. There were civilian casualties and damage to property.

The harbour and an aerodrome were attacked.

TIMELY WORDS OF FAITH AND WISDOM

Specially selected from the Bible for readers of the DAILY SKETCH by Lord Caldecote.

THE THINGS WHICH ARE IMPOSSIBLE WITH MEN ARE POSSIBLE WITH GOD.

Luke xviii, 27.

SCRIPPS-HOWARD

New York World-Telegram

Local Forecast: Continued unseasonably warm today and early tonight.

VOL. 74—NO. 257—IN TWO SECTIONS—SECTION ONE. NEW YORK, FRIDAY, MAY 1, 1942. Entered as second class matter Post Office, New York, N. Y.

HOME

Opening Wall St. Prices

PRICE THREE CENTS

HITLER AND MUSSOLINI MEET

Strike Hits 800 Buildings

Service Halted In Apartments On West Side

War Activities Not Affected—Spread Of Tieup Feared

BULLETIN.

Mayor La Guardia said today that the strike of the building service men was "premature" and "not in keeping with agreements."

Eight thousand elevator operators and other service employees ni apartment buildings through a large section of the residential upper West Side were called out on strike at 6 a. m. today, grounding elevators and disrupting other services in 800 buildings.

The affected district, as announced by Local 32-B of the Building Service Employees International Union, is bounded by Central Park and the Hudson River, from 59th St. to 110th St.—but does not include any office buildings where war industries might be located.

Gave Pledge to Mayor.

A union spokesman explained that the union had pledged the Mayor some time ago there'd be no disruption of the war effort.

However, there was still the vague threat of a city-wide walkout, but union leaders admitted a strike in any building taken over by the government would be "suicidal." The spokesman, explaining away the possibilities of a spread into buildings engaged in defense activities, said:

"Everything reasonable will be done to prevent any disruption of the war effort."

While thousand of apartment dwellers, executives, stenographers housewives, school children, huffed and puffed down 10 or 15 flights—with the prospect of walking mack UP again tonight—the union announced "-00 per cent" effectiveness in the struck area.

At 5:30 a. m., Daniel Sullivan, president of the local, sent out the strike call, to be effective half an hour later. Day men reporting to work were called off, pickets set up and service stopped. In some and lucky early morning risers got service till almost 8 a. m.

Porters Walk Out.

Porters and maintenance crew men went out with the elevator men.

The strike came less than 24 hours after collapse of mediation efforts by Mrs. Ethel Epstein, the

(Continued on Page Nine.)

Japs Seen Set to Attack U. S. Pacific Supply Line

Warships and Troop Transports Assembled Among Marshall I slands

By the Associated Press.

WASHINGTON, May 1.—Reports of a concentration of Japanese warships and troop transports among the Marshall Islands in the South Central Pacific gave rise to speculation in informed quarters today that a major thrust against the American supply line to Australia was imminent.

The Island of Jaluit, center of the area, is 1500 miles north of New Caledonia, where American troops landed recently to join forces with the Free French. An equal distance to the southeast lies American Samoa, and 2100 miles to the northeast is Hawaii.

Could Try Feints.

Because of this location, experts said, the Japs could move in any of three main directions, or they could try feints to test American strength, then strike with full force if conditions appeared favorable.

Dispatches from Australia said the enemy was gathering ships and men in the mandated islands area. These reports were linked here with the disappearance of powerful Japanese naval units from the Bay of Bengal, off India, about a week ago.

Informed quarters suggested that those units, having carried out a purely raiding and reconnaissance mission against the British there, had been withdrawn eastward in preparation for an attempt to sever the sea route between Australia and this country.

Australia, rather than India, as these authorities see the situation, is Japan's primary military problem at this time, and since the rapid increase of American forces in Australia probably would make a frontal assault too costly even for the Japanese to contemplate, their logical move would be to attempt a blockade.

By the Associated Press.

PEARL HARBOR, May 1.—Japanese fighting ships that have been sunk by American sky, sur-

(Continued on Page Seventeen.)

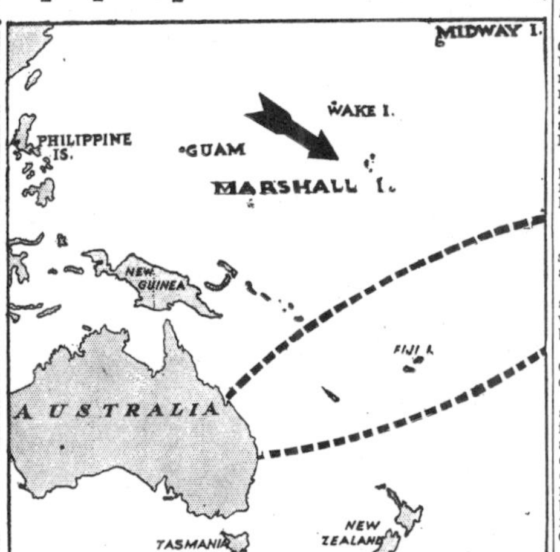

Japanese warships and troop transports were reported among the Marshall Islands (arrow) today, indicating a possible effort against American supply lines, shown by the curves ending in Australia. —World-Telegram Map by Goebel.

30 Jap Planes Smashed In Raid on Lae

Hangars Set Afire; Decisive Stage in Air War Held Near

By the United Press.

GEN. MacARTHUR'S HEADQUARTERS, Australia, May 1.—United States and Australian airmen smashed 30 grounded Japanese planes at Lae, New Guinea, and destroyed ground installations at the nearby Salamau base, Gen. MacArthur announced today.

Three enemy Navy-O fighter planes were shot down in a dog fight over Salamaua and light Allied losses were light, he said.

Set Airdromes Afire.

American pilots saw their bombs smash grounded Japanese planes at Lae and left the airdrome afire.

Direct hits were scored again and again on the planes and all were heavily damaged, if not blown to pieces.

They brought to a two-day total of 50 the Japanese planes smashed or destroyed.

Japanese planes, extending their attack zone in the northeastern invasion area, raided the Allied airdrome on Horn Island, 15 miles off Cape York, at the northeastern tip of the Australian continent. They used eight heavy bombers, escorted by fighters, but inflicted only negligible damage, Gen. MacArthur said.

Decisive Stage Near.

Both the Lae attack and the abortive Japanese raid on Horn Island, emphasized the belief at

(Continued on Page Seventeen.)

Ignore Japs In Salzburg Statement

Announce 'Perfect Accord'; Allies Believe Offensive May Have Been Topic

By the Associated Press.

Hitler and Mussolini, whose meetings in the past frequently have signaled the approach of momentous events, met in a two-day conference ending yesterday at Salzburg, Austria, it was announced officially today.

In the usual stereotyped form, a German communique said the Axis dictators met "in a spirit of close friendship and the indissoluble brotherhood-in-arms of their nations."

OFFENSIVE BELIEVED DISCUSSED.

Allied conjecture, however, centered on the possibility that these points were discussed:

1. Last-minute decisions on the heralded German grand offensive against Russia.

2. Reports of smouldering revolt and war-weariness in Italy.

3. A possible joint German-Italian "final offer" of peace on Axis terms.

BRITISH SEE 'PEP TALK' TO DUCE.

Informed British quarters declared the purpose of the Salzburg conference obviously was to keep Mussolini in line.

"Hitler must keep both ends of the Axis moving in the same direction," these quarters said, "and to do this he must give Mussolini a 'pep' talk."

It was the first meeting of the Fuehrer and Il Duce since their countries went to war against the United States last December.

The official announcement said: "The meeting resulted in a perfect acord of views on the situation created by the overwhelming victories of the Tripartite Powers and on the further conduct of the war by the two nations in both political and military spheres."

Japan Not Mentioned.

There was no mention that Japan, the third member of the Rome-Berlin-Tokyo bloc, had been represented at the meeting.

[The Japanese Radio reported that the Japanese military attache at Berlin, Lieut. Gen. Kazuyoshi Sakanishi, had departed for Rome, where he was expected to confer with Mussolini. The Japanese Ambassador to Berlin, Lieut. Gen. Hiroshi Oshima, was reported in Munich Thursday, but there was no word that he had participated in the conversations at nearby Salzburg.]

A curious sidelight of the Axis conference was that it was no longer held at the "half-way point" at Brenner Pass, where

(Continued on Page Seventeen.)

Revelers at Blackout Rebuked by Mayor

Million Out in Times Square Brings Warning Streets Must Be Cleared

In future blackouts New Yorkers must stay off the streets if they want to stay out of jail.

That was Mayor La Guardia's plain warning after a crowd comparable to those that fill the streets on election night or New Year's Eve had jammed Times Square and other centers last night to watch the brilliant heart of the world's greatest city go dark in one of New York's most successful blackouts to date.

Disagreeing flatly with Police Commissioner Valentine, who murmured happily that there were 1,000,000 persons out to see the "greatest show on earth," the Mayor said last night's performance was an air raid drill as well as a blackout and pointed out that more than 600 persons had been killed in London's first raid by falling fragments of their own antiaircraft shells through the operation of the old rule that what goes up must come down.

Praises Harlem's Behavior.

"As far as Times Square is concerned, I repeat emphatically that people must stay off the streets," the Mayor said. "I went to the other end of the area, in lower Harlem, where you might expect people to stay outside, and found up there that there wasn't even a child out.

"For the good of the people, for their own protection, they must stay off the streets and away from windows. If they don't obey us

(Continued on Page Two.)

Army to Induct Group in Class 1-B

By the United Press.

WASHINGTON, May 1.—The army soon will induct a small experimental group of selective service registrants now deferred in class 1-B for minor physical defects, it was disclosed today.

House Gets Bill To Hike Army Pay

By the Associated Press.

WASHINGTON, May 1.—Viewed by many as a forerunner to the induction into the armed services of men with dependents and government payments to their families, a bill hiking the pay of lower-paid service men was sent to the House today by its military committee.

As approved by the committee late yesterday, the measure would double the pay of buck privates and apprentice seamen, give service nurses substantial increases, and boost the base pay of officers and noncoms from corporals up to and including second lieutenants and ensigns. A buck private would get $42 a month, and a second lieutenant's base pay would be boosted from $1500 to $1800 a year.

GOP Club Backs Dewey

A resolution calling upon Thomas E. Dewey to "accept" the Republican party nomination for Governor of New York was adopted last night by the Washington Heights Republican Club of the 23rd Assembly District at a meeting in its headquarters, 1422 St. Nicholas Ave. This is the first Manhattan organization to indorse Mr. Dewey.

Woman Beaten Up During Blackout

At 6:30 a. m. today a woman staggered into a restaurant at 38 Lexington Ave. and collapsed into a booth. Her eyes were blackened, her face crusted with dried blood and her clothes shredded.

Doctors in Bellevue believe her skull was fractured.

Talkink incoherrently, she told Detective Joseph Gilmartin she was Mary Wheeler and lived at the Gramercy Hotel, 137 E. 24th St., but no one by that name is known at the hotel. A dry cleaner's receipt in her purse, which contained no money, gave the name Garrity.

The women said she received her injuries during last night's blackout, but could not remember where or how. She wore a brown dress and shoes and no hat. Her hair is light brown, her age indeterminate.

Spain Expects Big News

By the Associated Press.

LONDON, May 1.—Reuters reported from Madrid today that Spanish correspondents in Berlin were predicting "sensational news" may be published in the next few days, and the correspondent of the newspaper Madrid added, "the event does not refer directly to the Eastern offensive."

Liquor Is Frozen Out Double in Alaskan Town

By the Associated Press.

FAIRBANKS, Alaska, May 1. Nulato put the big freeze on John Barleycorn. And how.

Last fall the town of 11 whites, 200 natives and 200 dogs put in its order for its winter stock of booze. But the down boat on the Yukon got caught in an early freeze. And now, says Frank Alba, a Yukon trader:

"The church is full on Sunday. It used to be that the minister would have nobody in church but himself. The jail was empty this winter for the first time in years. And, when it came time to renew liquor licenses, a majority of the natives petitioned for continued prohibition."

Explosion Destroys Nazis' Belgian Plant

250 Killed, About 1000 Injured; Anti-German Group Active There

By the Associated Press.

LONDON, May 1.—A chemical factory at Tessenderloo, in the new industrial district of northern Belgium—a particular zone of activity for the anti-German White Brigade of the conquered Belgians—has been destroyed in an explosion which, according to the German radio, killed 250 persons and injured about 1000.

Berlin belatedly relayed an announcement today of the Nazi-dominated Belgian government that not only the plant but a technical school and a number of nearby houses were destroyed or severely damaged by the blast two days ago. No cause was given.

Belgians Differ.

The announcement emphasized that the factory produced "artificial fertilizers of various kinds and washing preparations for the Belgian market only."

The Free Belgian news agency, identifying the factory as a unit of La Societe Anonyme des Produits Chimiques, asserted, contrary to Berlin, that the factory turned out sulphuric acid, synthetic ammonia and nitric acid for explosives and gas. It was reported equipped with modern machinery, at which about 1000 persons worked when Belgium was free.

Production increased.

Since the coming of the Germans, the Belgian agency said, production has been increased under German direction. Tessenderloo is 30 miles northeast of Antwerp, in Limbourg province.

Much sabotage have been reported in this region, mostly credited to the secret armed organization, the White Brigade, seven of whose members were sentenced to death a week ago.

The War Today

SOUTH PACIFIC—Japanese reported concentrating fleet and transports in Marshall Islands for thrust against U. S.-Australia lines.

BURMA—British withdraw to line 25 miles south of Mandalay to escape entrapment.

PHILIPPINES—Corregidor downs three Japanese planes, shells enemy batteries and supply dumps.

AUSTRALIA — Allied fliers smash 3o grounded Japanese planes at Lae; pound ground installations and down three Zero planes at Saiamaua.

WESTERN EUROPE—Weather slows RAF offensive; eight Nazi planes downed over Britain; chemical factory at Tessenderloo, Belgium, working for Nazis, is blown up; 250 killed.

Smoker Is Suffocated

Walter Ruffles, 44, of 1152 Prospect Ave., Brooklyn, was suffocated last night by a fire believed caused when he fell asleep while smoking.

$543,000 Xmas Seals

Special to the World-Telegram.

ALBANY, May 1.—The 1941 sale of Christmas Seals in the state outside New York City was $543,000, it was announced today.

Swiss Say Nazis Want Air Truce

By the Associated Press.

LONDON, May 1.—The Daily Mail quoted the Geneva Journal today as saying Germany was willing to effect an "aerial truce" with Britain in the bombing of cities in the two countries.

The Journal's Berlin correspondent was quoted as writing:

"It is semiofficially stated here (in Berlin) that Germany will call off the bombing of English towns if the RAF will change its methods of bombing German cities."

The correspondent added that "the present bombing duel is highly unpopular with the German people."

Hanged in Murder

By the Associated Press.

OXFORD, England, May 1.—Harold Hill, 26-year-old soldier, was hanged at Oxford today for the murder of Doreen Joyce Hearne, 8, who was found strangled.

Indian Troops Smash Japanese at Mandalay

Tank Drive Inflicts Casualties; British Unti Falls Back 80 Miles

BULLETIN.

By the United Press.

NEW DELHI, India, May 1.—A British brigade of Indian Gurkhas with tanks smashed into Japanese forces on the Mandalay front in Burma and inflicted up to 500 casualties in a most successful action against the enemy, a Burma communique said today.

By the Associated Press.

LONDON, May 1.—British troops guarding the right flank of the Allied line in Burma have been forced to withdraw 80 miles to a triangle marked by Mandalay, Kyaukse and Myingyan by the Japanese penetration to Lashio, a military commentator disclosed today.

Kyaukse is less than 30 miles south of Mandalay; Myingyan is 50 miles west of Kyaukse on the Irrawaddy River.

The main bulk of the British forces in this area, it was stated, is protecting the approaches to Mandalay from the northeast and teh overland roads to India.

However, there are also considerable British forces across the Irrawaddy River around Pakookku, the commentator said. This is about 20 miles west of the westernmost point of the Mandalay-Myingyan-Kyaukse triangle on teh east side of the river.

A British armored brigade, including the Seventh Hussars, still is in action in Burma, this source reported.

Plane Ran Amok And Killed George

By the Associated Press.

ALLIED HEADQUARTERS, May 1.—Brig. Gen. Harold H. George, of the United States Army Corps, and Melville Jacoby, Time and Life Magazine correspondent, were killed at an advanced airdrome when struck by a fighter plane which got beyond control as it was taking off, allied headquarters disclosed today.

Their deaths were announced yesterday when it was stated the accident occurred Monday.

General George and Jacoby were about to board another plane when the fighter craft crashed into their party, the official announcement said.

Funeral services for Jacoby will be held today at a Melbourne crematorium. More than 30 news correspondents and a group of United States Army officers were present.

A military funeral was planned Saturday for General George.

8th of Skilled Men Here

By the Associated Press.

WASHINGTON, May 1.—Nearly an eighth of the nation's 4,949,132 skilled male workers are in New York. The last week of March, 1940, New York had 590,280.

War Stores Destroyed; Supply Lines Shifted

By the United Press.

CHUNGKING, China, May 1.—Japan won, in flaming Lashio, an

(Continued on Page Nine.)

The Weather

New York and metropolitan area: Continued unseasonably warm today and early tonight.

New Jersey: continued warm.

TODAY'S READINGS.

	Temp.	Hum.		Temp.	Hum.
Midnight	76	..	5 a. m.	75	..
1 a. m.	76	..	6 a. m.	75	37
2 a. m.	76	..	7 a. m.	73	42
3 a. m.	76	..	8 a. m.	75	42
4 a. m.	75	..	9 a. m.	75	40
			10 a. m.	76	38

Dutch Ship Is Sunk Off Atlantic Coast

By the United Press.

WASHINGTON, May 1.—A small Dutch merchant ship has been torpedoed and sunk off the Atlantic coast, the navy announced today.

Survivors have been landed at an East coast port.

World-Telegram Index

Rauschning Gets First Papers

Dr. Hermann Raushning, former Hitler aid and one time Premier of Danzig, yesterday received his first papers as a citizen of the United States.

After receiving his papers, he pointed to his picture and chuckled. It showed a broad face with regular features. "You know," he remarked, "I live in the city, but I'm really just a farmer. My boy works on a farm now in Oregon. I should like very much to go there too, but the war—it complicates a great many things."

He Buys a Cafe, Then It Blows Away

By the Associated Press.

PRYOR, Okla., May 1.—Eugene Booth, Tulsa printing pressman, thinks he may have established a speed record for going into and out of business.

Monday morning Mr. Booth invested $1600—his entire savings—in a cafe. Monday afternoon a tornado demolished the cafe.

There was a $1000 insurance policy on the place—but it covered fire loss only.

U. S. Expected to Recover Billion By Revision of Arms Contracts

By MARSHALL McNEIL,
Scripps-Howard Staff Writer.

WASHINGTON, May 1.—A billion dollars and more probably will be recovered from munitions makers as a result of renegotiation of arms contracts, officials estimated today. Already $150,000,000 has been recovered from three companies.

Thousands of contracts will be studied, the biggest ones first, and where excessive profits are discovered, or seem likely, renegotiation will be undertaken.

The machinery for the work coordinates the facilities of the Army, Navy, Maritime Commission and War Production Board. Each of these agencies has created a cost analysis section. In addition, the War and Navy Departments and the Maritime Commission have created price adjustment boards. The work of all seven units mesh.

A key man in correlating their activities is Dr. T. H. Sanders, chief of WPB's cost analysis section and a member of all three price adjustment boards.

The government has authority to audit the books of all war contractors. But voluntary offers by contractors to cut profits have already been received.

The renegotiation of contracts had started before the House passed a 6 per cent profit ceiling. Donald Nelson and the War and

(Continued on Page Nine.)

2 CENTS PAY NO MORE!

Chicago Daily Tribune

THE WORLD'S GREATEST NEWSPAPER

FINAL ★ ★ ★

VOLUME CI.—NO. C (REG. U. S. PAT. OFFICE. COPYRIGHT 1942 BY THE CHICAGO TRIBUNE.) WEDNESDAY, MAY 6, 1942.—42 PAGES THIS PAPER CONSISTS OF TWO SECTIONS—SECTION ONE * PRICE TWO CENTS IN CHICAGO AND SUBURBS ELSEWHERE THREE CENTS

CORREGIDOR FALLS!

CURTAIL CHARGE ACCOUNTS AND BUYING ON TIME

Anti-Inflation Drive Hits Consumers.

BY JOHN FISHER.
[Chicago Tribune Press Service.]

Washington, D. C., May 5.—As another drastic step in the anti-inflation program, the Federal Reserve board tonight clamped tighter restrictions on instalment buying and imposed new curbs on charge accounts.

The action, in the form of one amendment to a prior regulation, became effective at midnight tonight. The one order issued covered the various phases of the credit restrictions.

In expanding the scope of its regulation of consumer credit the board added many new items to the list of goods covered by its credit restrictions, increased required down payments, reduced the elapsed time for payment on instalment sales, and imposed time limits on payment of charge accounts and single payment loans.

Follows Roosevelt Talk.

This action was taken, the board explained, in conformity with President Roosevelt's special message to congress on inflation on April 27, in which he said: "To keep the cost of living from spiraling upward we must discourage credit and instalment buying and encourage the paying off of debts, mortgages, and other obligations." Reserve board officials estimated that the order would curb some two to three billion dollars in purchasing power in the coming year.

"As amended," said the board, "the regulation [as applying to instalment purchases] is extended to cover a comprehensive list of durable and semi-durable goods for civilian consumption and contemplates that the volume of outstanding consumer credit, already substantially diminished, will be further contracted in keeping with the government's purpose to prevent the rapid bidding up of prices."

Scope of Regulation.

Specifically the board's action curbs the nation's credit stream, the basis on which most business has been transacted, as follows:

1. The maximum period for payment of instalment purchases has been reduced to 12 months. It has been 15 months and under the board's original regulation was 18 months. The required down payment for virtually all articles on the list issued today has been raised to one-third of the purchase price. Down payments in the past have been allowed to range between one-fifth and one-third of the price.

The few exceptions to the above rule include instalment sales of automobiles and motorcycles, for which the down payment must be one-third and the maximum maturity 15 month the same as before; and furniture and pianos, where the required down payment is increased from 10 to 20 per cent, and the maximum time for payment is reduced from 15 to 12 months in the case of new furniture, and from 18 to 12 months in the purchase of pianos.

One-third Down Payments.

2. Hereafter, for the first time, mandatory down payments of one-third and a maximum payment period of 12 months are imposed on these commodities: automobile batteries and accessories, tires and tubes, bedding, draperies, binoculars, additional household electrical appliances, used furniture, jewelry, luggage, athletic equipment, table and kitchen ware, pottery, glassware, yard goods, and nonmilitary clothing and furs, including shoes, hats, and other haberdashery.

3. The new limitations on charge accounts provide that unless payment is made by the 10th day of the second calendar month following the date of purchase no further credit may be extended to purchase any article in today's list until the items in default have been paid for in full or have been placed on an instalment basis for payment within six months. No down payments are required on purchases under charge accounts.

4. Loans of $1,500 or less which a

[Continued on page 4, column 3.]

DIGEST OF WAR NEWS FROM ALL MAJOR SECTORS

Latest war developments:

Aided by new British and American equipment, a huge Red army struck at three German bases where Hitler is believed planning his "spring drive," attacking Kharkov, Kursk, and Taganrog under command of Russia's premier general, Marshal Semeon Timoshenko.

The British air ministry announced RAF attacks on Stuttgart and other industrial targets in southern Germany, for the second night in succession, and on the docks of Nantes and airdromes in the low countries and northern France.

General in Bomb Raid.

On the Australian front it was announced that Brig. Gen. Martin F. Scanlon had taken part in a United States bombing raid on Rabaul, New Britain. Planes of his command wrecked three Japanese planes at the Rabaul airdrome.

The fall of Corregidor, the last American stronghold in the Philippines, was announced in Washington. The famous fort, along with others in Manila bay, was forced to yield after a prolonged aerial siege and finally a landing attack by the Japanese. President Roosevelt revealed the defenders were short of food and ammunition.

Withdraw in Burma.

In Burma a general withdrawal by the British and Chinese armies was reported under way with the Japanese advancing over the Burmese border into China at Wanting. A second Jap column was driving to encircle and outflank the British along the Indian border in preparation for a march into India.

In Madagascar, where the British landed Monday, fighting was taking place between the French troops and the invaders. The Vichy government said a submarine and sloop operating against the British had been lost.

[Stories on pages 1, 3, 11, and 14.]

NAVY WILL TRAIN NEGRO RECRUITS AT GREAT LAKES

The navy department in Washington and the 9th naval district announced yesterday that Negroes volunteering for naval service will be given training at the Great Lakes Naval Training station. First contingents of the volunteers are expected to start their courses about June 15, when new barracks are put in commission. Recruiting of the Negroes will be started as soon as the facilities are available.

"These recruits who have recently been welcomed into the naval forces will be given every opportunity to learn the fundamentals of seamanship and military life required before being sent to specialist schools or for service at sea," the naval station announcement said.

About a month ago the navy began accepting Negroes for general service in the navy, coast guard, and marine corps.

THE WEATHER

WEDNESDAY, MAY 6, 1942.

Sunrise, 5:39. Sunset, 7:54. Moonrise, 1:46 a. m. Venus is the morning star. Mercury, Saturn, Jupiter, and Mars are the evening stars.

CHICAGO AND VICINITY: Intermittent rain ending by noon today; continued cool today and tonight; moderate to occasionally fresh winds.

For 24 hours ended 2 a. m. May 6:

3 a.m...46	9 a.m...47	3 p.m...49	9 p.m...48
4 a.m...46	10 a.m...50	4 p.m...48	10 p.m...46
5 a.m...46	11 a.m...50	5 p.m...47	11 p.m...46
6 a.m...46	Noon...50	6 p.m...46	Midn't...44
7 a.m...46	1 p.m. *51	7 p.m...48	1 a.m...46
8 a.m...45	2 p.m...50	8 p.m. †46	2 a.m...46

*Highest. †Lowest. ‡Unofficial. 8 p.m.-2 a.m.

For 24 hours ended 7:30 a. m. May 6:

Mean temperature, 48 degrees; normal, 54 degrees.

Precipitation, none.

Relative humidity at 7:30 a. m., 79 per cent; at 1:30 p. m., 56; at 7:30 p. m., 57.

[Official weather report on page 22.]

PERTAINING TO SUGAR

Uncle Sam is now doubling in his new role of "Sugar Uncle."

The whole nation will be completely registered for sugar ration cards in four days—showing how simple it would have been for the administration to poll the country on intervention or nonintervention during the debatable stage before Dec. 7.

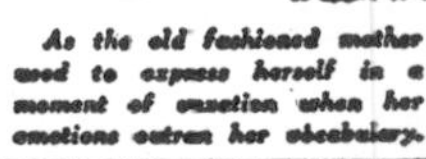

As the old fashioned mother used to express herself in a moment of emotion when her emotions outran her vocabulary.

Look out for him! He looks like a nonconformist.

Our first venture in romance had flowers and sugar intertwined in it.

WAR STILLS SONG OF 'SINGING LADY'

Pleads That Children Be Taught Why Men Die.

Columbus, O., May 5 [Special].—Her voice choking and tears misting her eyes, Ireene Wicker, the original "singing lady" of radio fame who used to sing to boys and girls across the land from station W-G-N in Chicago, today urged that radio stop giving American children soft lullabies.

Ireene Wicker.

Sharing part of her stardom in entertaining millions of young radio listeners a few years ago were her children—Nancy, now 17 years old, and Walter Charles, 19—who were in the "Nancy and Charlie" travel series. Last October, Walter went overseas as a flight sergeant in the royal Canadian air force.

Audience Enthralled as Children.

As spellbound as the children who once listened to her singing "Painted Dreams" and other radio make believe, her audience of men and women listened today as she spoke quietly at the convention of the Institute for Education by Radio.

Previous speakers had stressed that radio broadcasting must emphasize the implacability of war. The delegates wondered what attitude would be taken by the slender, attractive woman who had sung and laughed for so many young folks.

"Children, too," she began quietly, her eyes glistening, "must know for what men are dying and for what they also must be asked to lay down their lives.

Children Future Defenders.

"Children are to be our future defenders. They will have to die as our men are dying today to save the democratic way of life."

Her voice broke and she struggled to regain her composure. Then she went on:

"You men are writers; you know what you are talking about. Write . . . write . . . write for the children as well as the grownups."

Sobbing, she turned away and walked quietly from the hotel ballroom where the meeting was being held. The mystified audience sat speechless for a few moments. Then a man rose and explained quietly:

"Ireene Wicker received word last night that her son was killed in action with the royal Canadian air force."

35,000 Lilac Bouquets Bring Spring to Shut-Ins; More Today

BY GAIL COMPTON.

Great rivers of color and fragrance flowed into Chicago from all sides yesterday to open the 14th annual "Share Your Lilacs" campaign.

While the blooms were being distributed among the sick and shut-ins of the city's hospitals and institutions, hundreds of persons were at work in the suburbs cutting and wrapping more lilacs in preparation for today's distribution. Workers promised an even greater supply of flowers for today.

The work of gathering and delivering the lilacs is under the supervision of the Chicago Plant, Flower, and Fruit guild, which coöperates with THE CHICAGO TRIBUNE in sponsoring the lilac campaign.

Work Begins Early.

The first of the two lilac days began early when huge boxes and cartons of fresh flowers were delivered to railroad stations in suburban areas. At each station members of garden clubs affiliated with the guild supervised the placement of the blooms aboard the trains. Eight railroads placed more than 65 trains at the disposal of the lilac workers and brought the flowers freight free into city terminals.

At the terminals the fragrant bouquets were loaded into trucks and sped to orphanages, old people's homes, hospitals and other institutions, most of which were on the south and west sides. Nurses, interns, truck drivers, and passers-by carried great armfuls of the delicate blossoms into the wards and placed them at the bedsides of the patients.

As the fresh and fragrant perfume swept thru the rooms and wards, eyes opened everywhere, expressions of gratitude were heard, and in many cases heads were turned aside so that sudden tears of joy would go unseen.

35,000 Bouquets Distributed.

More than 90 hospitals and institutions were visited and almost 35,000 bouquets distributed.

Among the most grateful recipients of the lilacs were the veterans at the Edward Hines Jr. hospital. A huge truckload of the fresh blooms was taken directly to the hospital from the Tribune farm near Wheaton.

Several other truckloads were taken to Tribune Square before they were delivered and were piled in a colorful mass about the statue of Nathan Hale in the court between Tribune Tower and the W-G-N building. A soldier, sailor and marine posed beside the mountain of blooms for photographs. Assisting at the ceremony were T. V. Purcell, president of the guild, and Mrs. Warner R. Nelson, general chairman.

After the ceremony the flowers were loaded into the trucks and taken to Fort Sheridan and Great Lakes Naval station, where they were distributed among soldiers and sailors who are ill.

Today lilacs will be distributed to hospitals, homes, and settlements on the north side. If there are more than enough blooms to go around second visits will be made to other institutions.

Guild officials predict that this year's lilac campaign will rival last year's when a new record was set with the delivery of more than 100,000 bouquets to 25,000 patients in 158 hospitals and institutions.

LILAC PICTURES.
A full page of Lilac day pictures will be found on the back page.

Total average net paid circulation
MARCH, 1942
DAILY in excess of 1,000,000
THE CHICAGO TRIBUNE

FRENCH REJECT F. D. R. DEMAND; BATTLE BRITISH

Madagascar Forces Told to Resist.

BULLETIN.

VICHY, France, May 6 (Wednesday)—(AP).—A Madagascar communique declared today the island's air force had been hurled into action against British bombers. The French defense forces lost two of three light naval units which sailed out of the Diego Suarez naval base yesterday. The 1,379 ton submarine Beveziers and the 2,156 ton sloop Bougainville were sunk by British naval forces as they attempted to close in for a torpedo attack. A small auxiliary cruiser was reported damaged. Most of the crews of the submarine and sloop were able to reach shore.

BY DAVID DARRAH.
[Chicago Tribune Press Service.]

(Map on page 3.)

VICHY, France, May 5.—French troops tonight fought the British for possession of the island of Madagascar in the Indian ocean.

The military engagement came on the heels of the Vichy government's rejection of President Roosevelt's warning against putting up a fight for the big French island and the issuance of an order to the Madagascar garrison to resist "aggression" to the death "for the honor of France."

The fateful decisions were announced by Pierre Laval, new chief of government. He said that despite Mr. Roosevelt's note, "forbidding the French to defend their possessions, no definite gesture in breaking relations with the United States will be made by France."

British Occupy Cape.

At a late hour tonight the British were reported to be in possession of the Cape Amber peninsula, north of Diego Suarez naval base on Madagascar. Other advices said the British forces had reached Andrakaka, four miles from the naval base.

[The British said they were moving on the naval base. In Washington Secretary of State Hull disclosed that the United States was keeping an alert watch on the French island of Martinique in the Caribbean. Details on pages 7 and 8.]

The assault on Madagascar was made public by Laval, who said the British force consisted of about 20,000 men, assisted by seven units of the British fleet—two or three cruisers, two troop transports, and two destroyers.

The British approached Diego Suarez on the northern tip of the island and sent an ultimatum to the French to surrender the island unconditionally and at once.

Rejects Ultimatum.

Gov. Gen. Armand Annet of Madagascar rejected the ultimatum, replying that he would defend the island to the end.

The attack began immediately, the British making landings and using parachute troops to seize strategic points. Two British planes were reported to have been shot down.

The day's fast moving developments began with issuance of Laval's note rejecting Mr. Roosevelt's warning. The note said:

"In reply to the note handed in today by the chargé d'affaires of the United States of America, the French government raises the most energetic protest against the aggression of which Madagascar has just been the object on the part of British forces.

"It notes the assurance given that

[Continued on page 8, column 3.]

Map of Madagascar

In all issues of tomorrow's Tribune will appear a large scale color map of Vichy France's great island of Madagascar in the Indian ocean, which has been occupied by British forces with the full approval of the United States. The British move is seen as an effort to forestall possible attempts by the Japanese to seize the island in order to sever the supply routes around the southern tip of Africa to ports in the middle east.

Japs Drive Into China; Fight to Flank British

BULLETIN.

TOKIO, May 6 (Wednesday)—(From Japanese broadcasts)—(AP).—Imperial headquarters announced today the capture last Monday of Akyab airfield 60 miles south of the Burma-India border and slightly more than 300 miles airline from Calcutta. Akyab was the last Burma port in British hands. The Japanese air force earlier had raided Akyab heavily.

(Map on page 3.)

CHUNGKING, China, May 5 (AP).—The Japanese armies stormed onto Chinese soil thru the Burma back door today and began a movement of envelopment designed to entrap and destroy the British who stand between the invader and India.

The vanguard of the Japanese columns crossed the shallow Wanting river into China's Yunnan province at the end of a 500 mile advance up Burma.

The advance to Wanting represented a 90 mile drive along the Burma supply road from Lashio.

Meager military advices told of fierce fighting in the mountainous area on both sides of the border; official reports indicated the Chinese still held the Chinese customs station of Wanting and had, for the time at least, halted Japanese reinforcements at Chukok, on the Burma side.

British Face Flanking.

Another arm of the Japanese advance, based on Kutkai, inside Burma, appeared to be trying to forge northwest toward Bhamo, head of navigation on the river Irrawaddy, 170 miles north of fallen Mandalay.

This force will try to flank and cut off the British who are withdrawing up the Chindwin river valley toward the Indian frontier.

[A British communique said today the RAF had bombed and machine-gunned another convoy of laden Japanese barges in the Chindwin river hitting three of the barges.]

Japanese bombers heavily raided Yungchang, 100 miles inside Yunnan province at the intersection of the Burma road and the upper reaches of the great Mekong river.

Chiang Kai-shek's military spokesman indicated, however, that the defenders were prepared to tear up even the Chinese end of the Burma road above Wanting if necessary to bar the path to the heart of free China.

American volunteer flyers shot down eight Japanese planes in air battles today over Paoshan on the Burma road, it was officially announced in Kunming.

Rapid Withdrawal On.

NEW DELHI, India, May 5 (AP).—Officers returning from the Burma frontier said tonight that a rapid allied withdrawal was in progress in Burma. A spokesman here said it appeared likely a considerable number of both British and Chinese troops would be captured by the Japanese.

United States and British operated air lines were doing a "last ditch" job of evacuating as many troops and refugee civilians as possible. Those being brought out were mostly women and children.

[For the second successive day heavy United States bombers made a successful attack today on the Japanese-held airdrome of Mingaladon, just north of Rangoon, Burma, United States air headquarters announced.]

Seven planes of Pan-American airways were diverted from the China transport to the evacuation service and hauled out 1,200 persons before the Japanese virtually surrounded the air field several miles north of Mandalay.

British Are Flown Out.

The Chinese 6th army on the eastern side of the Irrawaddy river was scattered in small pockets for a hundred miles south of Lashio as well as to the north and east of this junction of the railroad connecting with the now severed Burma road.

British soldiers, who were flown out, had been fighting four months without relief.

Chinese Guerrillas Invade Capital.

CHUNGKING, China, May 6 [Wednesday]—(AP).—In a further report on the big scale guerrilla raids started April 20, the Chinese central news agency said today that on that date Chinese shock troops invaded Nanchang, capital of Kiangsi province.

While they were killing 30 Japanese and Chinese puppet soldiers in the streets, other raiders destroyed a section of the Nanchang-Kiukiang railway and blew up roads around Nanchang, the agency said. Telegraph lines and four bridges were reported destroyed.

ALL MANILA BAY FORTS TAKEN BY JAP INVADERS

Troops Exhausted, Short of Food.

(Map on page 7.)

Washington, D. C., May 6 (Wednesday) (AP).—Corregidor has fallen after 28 days of siege.

The doughty American-Filipino troops, who held the island fortress after the loss of Bataan despite sustained air bombardment and a shattering cross fire of heavy shore batteries from both sides of Manila bay, finally were forced to yield to an overwhelming Japanese landing attack.

Surrender of the battered rock was announced in a laconic communique from the war department which said that terms were being arranged.

"Resistance of our troops has been overcome," said the announcement, issued at 3:15 a. m., Chicago war time.

"Fighting has ceased and terms are being arranged covering the capitulation of the island forts in Manila bay."

Other Forts Given Up.

In addition to Fort Mills on Corregidor, a determined, last ditch fight to prevent the Japanese from making use of Manila bay had been waged from American forts on three smaller islands—Forts Drum, Hughes, and Frank.

It was assumed from the communique that colors finally had been struck on all four islands.

Hunger, fatigue, and lack of ammunition were believed to have worn down the defenders in the closing days of their heroic stand.

The victory which the Japanese won at great cost gave them control of the best harbor in the orient and strengthened the long communications lines they have thrust toward Australia and India.

American-Filipino troops continued to plague the enemy with guerrilla warfare in various parts of Cebu, Mindanao, and Panay islands.

Believe General Remains.

It was believed here, altho there was no official word, that Lieut. Gen. Wainwright remained with his troops to the end.

He signaled the beginning of the final battle in a message yesterday reporting that about midnight, Tuesday, Manila time (11 a. m. Monday, Chicago war time), the Japanese had assaulted Corregidor and that "a landing attack was in progress."

Hours of official silence passed before first word of the outcome was flashed from allied headquarters in Australia. At 1 a. m. Chicago war time a spokesman for Gen. Douglas MacArthur, who entrusted his command to Gen. Wainwright after leading the brilliant defense of Bataan, made this announcement:

"Gen. Wainwright has surrendered Corregidor and the other fortified islands in Manila harbor."

Just how many survived the weeks' long ordeal of air raids and artillery bombardments was not known, but it was generally

[Continued on page 7, column 3.]

Report AEF in S. Africa

EXTRA

In Two Sections—Section One

NIGHT EDITION 2

No. 19,855—DAILY THURSDAY, MAY 7, 1942 DAILY 3 Cents | SATURDAY 5 Cents | SUNDAY 10 Cents

MADAGASCAR FALLS; BRITISH LOSE 1,000

By LEO V. DOLAN, International News Service Staff Correspondent.

LONDON, May 7.---Great Britain scored her first major victory in the Far Eastern theatre of war today. Her forces smashed all organized resistance and captured the naval base of Diego Suarez at Madagascar. The huge Indian Ocean island now is under British and Free French sovereignty. Prime Minister Churchill himself announced that the naval and military commanders at Antsirane who control the island's defenses had capitulated after less than 48 hours of bitter fighting.

Negotiations are proceeding for the terms of surrender.

A huge British fleet which participated in Britain's first offensive action against a potential Japanese base of aggression will steam into Diego Suarez Bay this afternoon, victory emblems flying.

Churchill Tells of Victory

"Very strong forces" of all British arms were used in the operation, planned over a period of three months, Churchill said.

"Our first assault against one of the French positions was repulsed with losses which might exceed 1,000 men," he said.

"But Major General Sturges attacked again last night and captured the position.

"French naval and military commanders surrendered and the town of Diego Suarez was captured.

"We trust the French nation in time to come will regard the episode as a recognizable step in liberation of their country, including Alsace and Lorraine—from the German yoke."

The capture of Antsirane was effected through a diversionary drive on Diego Suarez, a joint Admiralty and War Office communique disclosed.

British units which landed at Courier Bay to the west began a march on Diego Suarez, it was revealed. Other forces disembarked a few miles south in the vicinity of Ambarata and gaine drapid headway toward Antsirane, six miles south of Diego Suarez, while the attention of the French defenders was diverted to the northern column.

Antsirane Taken in 2 Days

Antsirane was taken less than two days after British troops, including light armored units and a contingent of the famed Commandos, landed from transports under protection of British warships.

"Antsirane, chief town in the harbor of Diego Suarez was captured by a night attack last night," the joint communique said.

"The main British attack was launched from the south, but the landing of Royal Marines from the north created a valuable diversion.

"The French naval and military commanders at Antsirane surrendered, but there still are some pockets of resistance to be cleared up.

"One Vichy submarine and one sloop which were in Diego Suarez harbor were sunk.

"British landings were made at Courier Bay, and also at a bay a few miles south of Ambarata. The Courier Bay landing dealt with Diego Suarez and the other with Antsirane.

The latter was held up Wednesday a mile or two south of the town, where the French were holding a position strongly defended by .75-millimeter guns and machine-guns.

"Pockets of resistance still are holding out, probably on the Oronjia Peninsula east of Antsirane forming the south side of the harbor entrance where there are a number of coastal defense batteries.

"As the troops landed on the beach they were unable to carry heavy equipment nor was it possible to land a large number of guns.

"Close aerial support, therefore, was of great importance and worked out extremely well.

"It can now be assumed that all organized resistance has been stopped."

(Other Details on Page 2)

MADAGASCAR — 0 4 8 MILES

1—Organized resistance in the upper end of Madagascar was reported ended today with the capture of Antsirane, chief town in the island defense.

2—Surrender came after naval base at Diego Suarez was bombarded heavily from surrounding hills. Meanwhile British fleet was reported steaming to scene.

Yanks Landed In S. Africa, Vichy Says

LONDON, May 7 (INS).—The London Evening Standard today picked up a Vichy radio broadcast asserting that an American expeditionary force has arrived in Natal, British colony on the southeast coast of Africa.

Natal is an important British possession in the Union of South Africa lying north of the Cape of Good Hope Colony and southwest of the Island of Madagascar. Its chief city and port is Durban.

By LEE VAN ATTA,
International News Service Staff Correspondent.

UNITED NATIONS HEADQUARTERS IN AUSTRALIA, May 7.—American and Australian bombers dealt a smashing blow to Japanese naval units based north of Australia in a successful engagement in the Solomon Islands, Gen. Douglas MacArthur revealed today.

[According to the United Press American airmen have opened a heavy attack on a powerful Japanese fleet massing in the north-eastern invasion zone apparently for an imminent major offensive.]

At the same time it was revealed enemy naval activity in the vicin-

Continued on Page 2, Column 5.

Wanting Seized, Japs 25 Miles Inside China

(Map on Page 2.)

CHUNGKING, May 7 (INS).—Japanese forces have occupied Wanting in Yunnan Province and now have reached Chefang, 25 miles inside the Chinese border, a Chungking government spokesman said today. Bitter fighting now is raging at Chefang, he said.

By G. D. KARKARE
International News Service Staff Correspondent.

NEW DELHI, May 7.—Generalissimo Chiang Kai-Shek has arrived on the Burma fighting front to join American Lieut. Gen. Joseph W. Stilwell in planning a counter-offensive against Japan, reports reaching New Delhi said today.

Chinese reinforcements reportedly accompanied Chiang. Other reserves were believed to have been rushed into Yunnan Province to battle Japanese units pushing northeastward from Wanting.

It was believed in New Delhi that any Chinese counter-offensive aimed at salvaging something from the hiterto disastrous Burma campaign probably would be launched from Yunnan.

Average Autoist To Get 2 to 6 Gals.

With the nation warned it must "eliminate every non-essential use of petroleum products," average motorists in New York and other Eastern States today faced a ration of two to six gallons of gasoline weekly.

The two-to-six gallon range was indicated by the Office of Price Administration tc aid registrars in deciding the type of ration cards to be given individual motorists during registration, which begins here Tuesday.

OPA orders, however, emphasized that the limits may be changed before rationing becomes effective, May 16.

The final decision, it was pointed out, will "depend entirely upon the supply of gasoline that is available.

Just how limited that supply will be was indicated by Petroleum Coordinator Ickes, who said in New Orleans last night that tankers supplying the East Coast fuel needs are probably "out" for the duration.

"The soundest national policy," Ickes declared, "now dictates we should operate on the theory there will be no tankers available for East Coast service because the Army and Navy need those tankers elsewhere."

Consequently, he added, "driving as usual" will not be possible

Continued on Page 7, Column 4.

Attack on Island Fails, Italy Says

LONDON, May 7 (UP).—Radio Rome, in a broadcast recorded here, today said British forces had "attempted" a landing on Kupho Island south of Crete but had been repulsed by the Italian garrison.

Journal-American Expose:

Harlem Vice Pay-off 'Boss' Unmasked

This, the third of a series of articles on vice and crime conditions in New York, reveals how New York Journal-American reporters discovered "Big Joe," the man who alleged he could obtain "protection"—for a price.

His unmasking has drawn the applause of Harlem civic and social leaders who are anxious to drive out the small criminal element from their community so that it can no longer be called a spawning ground for crime.

At the same time these Negro leaders are hopeful that the expose of this newspaper will re-vitalize a dormant campaign to improve their living conditions—a status to which city officials have been too long indifferent.

By JAMES D. HORAN and LEON RACHT.

Until the sweeping police raids of Monday, "Big Joe" Richards was the man you had to see if you wanted to launch a shady enterprise in Harlem.

North of 110th st., Richards is called The Big Boss.

"Big Joe" has—or had—many rackets.

Not the least important of them was his sale of "protection." You either paid off, or else.

"Big Joe" set the price and verbally guaranteed protection against raids by police, except for those "by inspectors' men."

His racket extended to legitimate bars and grills as well, according to allegations contained in an official report in the hands of authorities.

Raided 'Unprotected' Places

"It is common knowledge in Harlem that all bars and grills, houses of prostitution, marihuana joints, etc., must pay off to 'Big Joe' if they wish to remain open," the report reads.

"Big Joe" had an alternative for the legitimate places which didn't pay off. He would send his hoodlums in to wreck them.

Two New York Journal-American reporters obtained an affidavit from a man who paid "Big Joe" $25 for the privilege of opening an "after-hours club" on W. 115th st.

The $25 was part payment for the first week's "protection." The price set by Big Joe was $35.

The "club" was duly opened and ran full blast with no trouble from anyone except an occasional "mugger" lurking in the hallway.

The writers chanced to meet the hapless club proprietor in an Eighth ave. bar one night—hapless because his place was one of those raided shortly after "Big Joe" was arrested.

They heard him outlining his plans for opening his place to

Continued on Page 6, Column 1.

THE WEATHER

Mild.

Sun rises 5:48 a. m., sun sets 7:58 p. m. High tide Governors Island 2:37 a. m. and 3:26 p. m.

HOURLY TEMPERATURES

9 p. m.	54	2 a. m.	53
10 p. m.	54	3 a. m.	53
11 p. m.	54	4 a. m.	52
Midnight	54	5 a. m.	52
1 a. m.	54	6 a. m.	53

Complete Weather Report on Page 20

TODAY'S INDEX

IN THE NEWS

Very many thanks to the readers of this column for the patience and forbearance they have shown in the past several months.

But they can relax now and cheer up.

Relief is at hand.

The writer purposes taking a vacation.

And if he has not earned it, you, dear readers, have.

WILLIAM RANDOLPH HEARST.

By CHARLES S. RYCKMAN

THE FALL of Corregidor brings to a close one of the most remarkable military holding actions in world history.

There have been few actions of comparable brilliance and tenacity in legendary annals, and fewer in authentic historical account.

Corregidor will stand with these amazing few as long as human records are kept.

A successful defense of Corregidor, especially after the loss of Bataan, was not expected and was not possible.

There was not enough men on the island fortress to hold it.

There was not enough food.

There were not enough guns or munitions.

There were not any planes.

There was no relief.

So the Japanese merely had to wait around until the scant food and munitions were gone and until the few men on the island were either dead or exhausted and starved.

But it took four long months to shell and starve Corregidor into submission.

It is to be wondered if the Japanese account that a victory.

Military experts say the interval of preparation afforded the United States by the holding action in the Philippines may provide the difference between our once possible defeat and our now assured victory.

It possibly cost Japan the only opportunity that ever existed for successful invasion and conquest of Australia.

It very likely saved Hawaii and Alaska.

It bought the precious time which, if it has been adequately utilized has sealed the security of the American West Coast.

Of course the Japanese have now won Corregidor itself, and that is a severe American loss.

The loss of many thousands of brave American and Filipino soldiers is much more severe.

But in terms of time gained, and defenses erected, and opportunities created for massing offensive forces, the real victory is ours.

Naturally we cannot expect to win the war with such victories.

At some point in this war, if we expect to win it, we must start taking ground and captives from the Japanese, instead of yielding our own ground and valiant men to them.

It is to be hoped that point is reached now.

There is no longer any vital area under our flag where it can be said the elements of preparation and surprise give the Japanese insurmountable advantage.

We have had the same time to get guns and men, ships and planes, to our remaining possessions that the Japanese have to accomplish these things.

We cannot plead other

Continued on Page 2, Column 7.

Daily Sketch

No. 10,293 (E*) Friday, May 8, 1942 One Penny

MORNING FLASH FROM WASHINGTON:—'EXCELLENT NEWS'

SEVEN JAP WARSHIPS SUNK

U.S. Naval Action Off Solomons

"DAILY SKETCH" NAVAL REPORTER

EIGHT Japanese ships—seven of them warships—have been sunk in a naval engagement off the Solomon Islands, which are about 1,000 miles north-east of Australia in the South-West Pacific.

Announcing this "very excellent news" early this morning, Washington said:

"A naval engagement between U.S. and Japanese forces on Monday resulted in the following damage to the enemy:

One light cruiser, two destroyers, four gunboats and one supply vessel sunk.
One 9,000-ton seaplane tender, one light cruiser, one cargo vessel, one transport badly damaged. Six planes destroyed.

Only Three Of Our Planes Lost

"This highly successful action took place in the vicinity of the Solomon Islands and was accomplished with the loss of only three planes."

The communiqué added that the U.S. submarines on patrol in the Far East had also sunk a medium-sized vessel and a tanker, and also one small cargo vessel.

There is little news beyond the communiqué, but the use of the term "naval engagement" leaves little doubt that American surface craft were in action as well as aircraft.

The battle, the only one of any considerable scale since the Battle of the Java Sea, took place, according to the latest information in London, about 500 miles off the coast of Queensland.

It is significant that a few hours before the news of this naval action, reports had been received in this country of Japanese warships massing in the northern approaches to Australia.

General MacArthur's headquarters had reported "increasing naval enemy activity" in the Kabane area in New Guinea.

Concentrations of Japanese naval units in the Solomon Islands were also indicated by the communiqué, which added that they had been "successfully engaged" by Allied bombers near Bougainville, one of the Solomon Islands group.

Whether this action and the U.S. naval action are related is not yet known, but it is quite likely they are.

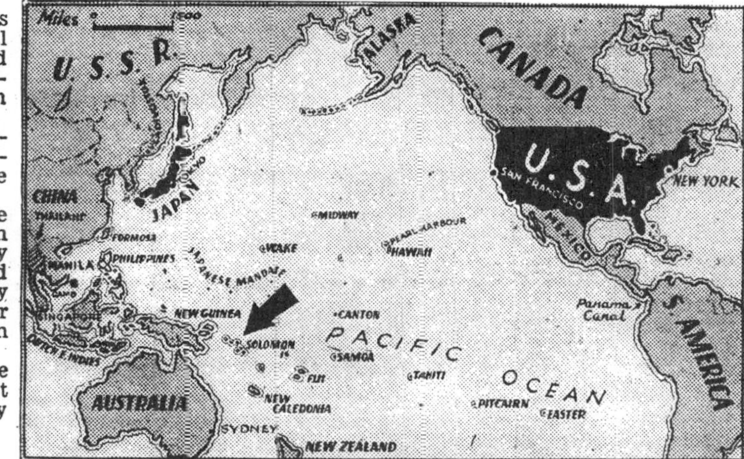

Map shows the position of Solomon Islands, north-east of Australia.

Japs' Big Losses

News of this naval victory has given a great lift both to America and Australia—and although it has not involved the loss of any major unit of the Japanese Navy, it is taken as an indication that the United Nations can and will hit back in the South-West Pacific with ever-increasing strength.

The Japanese losses in this action bring to 231 the total number of ships known to have been lost by the Japanese since the attack on Pearl Harbour.

This comprises 176 warships of all types and 55 commercial vessels—transports, cargo ships and tankers—figures based on official announcements by the United Nations and on Japanese admissions.

WEINGARTNER DEAD

Felix Weingartner, the conductor, died yesterday in a hospital in Switzerland, where he had been under treatment.

WOUNDED — BUT HE FLEW HOME

U.S. airman M. Kuykendall, who in a fight with two Japanese planes was wounded, but brought his damaged Tomahawk safely back.

Another scoop for INSIDE INFORMATION, Page 2.

British Fleet Steams Into Diego Suarez

THE British Fleet steamed into the harbour of Diego Suarez, the big Madagascar naval base, at 3.30 p.m. yesterday.

This practically marked the end of organised resistance in the island after an action lasting little more than two days, although Vichy reported last night that fighting was still going on.

Confirming the surrender of Diego Suarez, Vichy said that Colonel Claerebout and the commander of French naval forces were prisoners.

Meantime, the Governor of Madagascar, Annet, has dispatched this message to Vichy:

"All other parts of Madagascar will be defended with the same determination. Our troops continue to be loyal."

Mr. Churchill announced the surrender of Antsirane, principal town in the north of the island, and Diego Suarez, in the House of Commons yesterday.

The Prime Minister referred to the "episode" as a recognisable step in the liberation of France.

It was stated in London last night that British casualties were not heavy.

NAVY ON TIME

IN Parliament yesterday Mr. Churchill said the Navy was expected to enter Diego Suarez harbour "at about 3 p.m."

Berlin radio said last night: "British naval units entered Diego Suarez at 3.30 p.m."

Lord Gort New Governor And C.-in-C. Of Malta

GENERAL DOBBIE, Governor and Commander-in-Chief of Malta, who has been there throughout the war, has resigned, and is coming home for a rest. His place will be taken by Lord Gort, Governor and C.-in-C. of Gibraltar.

It is expected that Lord Gort will take with him to Malta the George Cross which was recently conferred on the island. The Cross is likely to be placed in Malta Cathedral.

General Dobbie   Lord Gort

There is no difference of opinion between the Government and General Dobbie. On the contrary, his inspired leadership in Malta is regarded as magnificent, and it is anticipated that he will receive a national welcome when he reaches England.

Viscount Gort, V.C., was the man who directed the evacuation of the B.E.F. from Dunkirk.

Russia Convoy Beat Nazi Sea-Air Blitz

THE convoy got through. Once again the Navy, fighting an attack by destroyers, U-boats and dive-bombers, that went on incessantly in the stormy wastes of the Arctic, has taken a convoy of merchantmen, heavily laden with vital supplies, to Russia.

And they brought home another convoy which had already delivered the goods, said an Admiralty communiqué, issued last night.

Of the outward-bound convoy we lost three ships—but 90 per cent. of the convoy got through.

On the homeward-bound convoy we lost one ship.

And, after valiant attempts to tow her home after she had been torpedoed—the 10,000-ton cruiser Edinburgh was again torpedoed and had to be sunk by our own forces.

One German destroyer was sunk and another was hit and severely damaged. Three dive-bombers were shot down and many others damaged.

Here is the Admiralty communiqué:

"Over a period of several days

Turn to Back Page, Col. 4

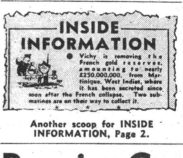

TIMELY WORDS OF FAITH AND WISDOM

Specially selected from the Bible for readers of the DAILY SKETCH by Lord Caldecote.

HE TALKED WITH THEM, AND SAITH UNTO THEM, BE OF GOOD CHEER: IT IS I; BE NOT AFRAID.

Mark vi, 50.

CHURCHILL WARNS HITLER NOT TO USE POISON GAS

NEW YORK ENQUIRER

FINAL EDITION

VOL. X. NO. 535  NEW YORK, MONDAY, MAY 11, 1942 ★ PRICE: FIVE CENTS

Will Retaliate In Event of Use Against Allies

"Britain Firmly Resolved Not to Use Odious Weapon, But Knowing the Hun, Has Not Neglected to Make Preparations on a Formidable Scale," Is British Premier's Blast at Axis Chiefs in Anniversary Address

(By United Press)

LONDON, May 10. (Sunday afternoon)—Prime Minister Churchill speaking to the empire, tonight warned Germany that any use of poison gas by the Nazi military machine would result in the RAF carrying gas war-fare "on the largest possible scale far and wide against military objectives in Germany."

"We ourselves are firmly resolved not to use this odious weapon unless it is first used by the Germans," Churchill said. "Knowing our Hun, however, we have not neglected to make preparations on a formidable scale."

Speaking on the second anniversary of his ministry, Churchill said that his tenure had been marked by "many misfortunes."

To Launch Air Offensive

He said that a British and presently American bombing offensive

Winston Churchill

against Germany would be one of the principal features of this year's world war.

Losses Costly to Japs

Referring to the Japanese, he said they could ill afford such losses as they sustained in the naval action of the Coral Sea.

"So far we have no detailed accounts but it is obvious from the lies of the Japanese that a most vigorous and successful battle has been fought by United States and Australian forces."

Intentions Secret

Regarding a possible second front, Churchill said that the "militant spirit" demanded one but "naturally I shall not disclose what our intentions are."

Reviewing the whole world scale of the war, Churchill said that already more Germans had been killed in Russia than died throughout the World War.

U. S. Strength

In the Far East, the pent-up forces of Japan were bound to prevail at the start, but "the strength of the United States, expressed in units of modern manpower, actual and potential, is alone many times greater than the power of Japan."

Will Lay Them Low

"I have no doubt tonight that British and American sea power will grip and hold the Japanese, and that overwhelming air power will lay them low. This would come to pass very much sooner should anything happen to Hitler and Europe.

"Therefore tonight I give you a message of good cheer. You deserve it, and the facts endorse it. But be it good cheer or be bad cheer it will make no difference to us. We shall drive on to the end and do our duty, win or die. God helping us, we can do no other."

At the beginning of his speech Churchill recalled Britain's plight when he became Prime Minister, when invasion was threatened at any hour, and said:

"Where are we now?

No Longer Alone

"We are no longer unarmed. We are no longer alone.

"There can be but one end. When or how it will come I cannot tell you/ But when some day our resources are marshalled and developed, we may stride forward into the unknown with growing confidence."

Dictators Blunder

He said the dictators, with all their preparations, had made more mistakes than the democracies.

Without provocation, he said, Germany last June invaded Russia which "like us will never give in."

That was Hitler's first great mistake and the second was to forget about the Russian winter "and I have never made as bad a mistake as that," Churchill said.

Russia Stronger

"Certain it is that the Russian armies are stronger than they were last year—that they have learned by hard experience how to fight the Germans in the field."

He said that "Herr Hitler himself" had not taken kindly to the RAF's "treatment" of Germany and called the Germans' own air force a thing of the past.

"Now the boot is on the other leg . . . he massacred in Warsaw, in Rotterdam . . . in those days he used to boast that for every ton of bombs we dropped on Germany, he would drop 10 times, a 100 times greater weight on England."

Suffered at Start

Then Britain had to suffer from Germany's superior strength, Churchill said but now it is the other way around and "this proportion will continue all the summer, all the spring, all the winter—the accuracy of our bombing will improve."

"The civilian population of Germany have an easy way to escape . . . all they have to do is leave the cities where the munitions are being made . . . abandon their homes . . . and watch the home fires burning."

Carefully Planned

He said the occupation of Madagascar was planned three months ago and the expedition force left England two months ago.

"While our troops were on the sea, I shivered every time I saw Madagascar in the papers . . . All these diagrams and maps . . . all this advice telling me to take Madagascar.

"We hold this island in trust. Madagascar rests under the safeguard of the United Nations."

Hold In Trust

He said the usual signs of a German offensive had not been observed on the Russian front, and referred to reported German use of poison gas in that theater in promising to bomb with gas if it is used by the Germans against Britain.

Four War Phases

He said the war, as it had unfolded, resolved into four phases:

1. The overrunning of Europe.
2. The invasion of Russia.
3. The Russian resistance—"long may it continue."
4. Pearl Harbor.

Thus the struggle has come world wide, he said, and the fates of all nations are at stake.

Weight In Our Favor

"Is there any sensible person who cannot see how decisively the weight has turned in our favor?

"The Japanees will find resistance on a widely spread front . . . they will lose more, such as the losses they sustained in the Battle of the Coral Sea . . . it is obvious from the lies the Japanese have been forced to tell that a most vigorous success was won by us."

He said that the Vichy Government under the grip of the Axis, has been made to bluster, but France "one day will rise in indescribable fury against the Nazis."

RAF Planes Blast Benghazi

(By United Press)

CAIRO, May 10.—Royal Air Force planes are continuing to carry the offensive burden in the Battle of Libya, bombing enemy bases and shooting down two planes in their latest raids, it was announced.

Sandstorms continue to delay the action on the ground front.

Raid Benghazi

The British airmen on Wednesday night raided the harbor of Benghazi, on the western side of the "hump" of Libya and battered an Axis airdrome at Martuba, near Derna, an RAF communique said.

"Fighter planes were active in the forward area, Thursday and Friday," it said. "An army cooperation squadron shot down two Macchi (Italian) 200's without loss to themselves on Thursday."

STILLWELL'S CHINESE ARMY IN MANDALAY

Decision Wins Acclaim

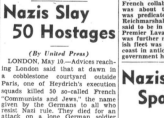

Justice Aaron J. Levy

Saving of Widow's Home By Justice Levy Recalls Jurist's Texas Charities

The action of Judge Aaron J. Levy of the Supreme Court in the Bronx in halting the proceedings brought to foreclose the mortgage on the home of a city fireman's widow, Mrs. Gertrude McMahon, by ordering the complainant's attorney to "work this matter out equitably," recalled to thousands of minds the many philanthropic endeavors throughout the last decade which have endeared him to countless citizens of New York City.

Notable among these was his speed in raising $10,000 from his friends for the construction of a Catholic church at Corpus Christi, Tex., in 1935,

From that city in the fall of that year Father John F. Donnelly, formerly a New Yorker, who was holding services in a tent there, came to this city to try to raise funds with which to erect a church building.

Met With Disappointment

It was in the midst of an exceedingly dull period, when things were just starting to pick up, following an exceptionally drab year, and he found, in addition to poor economic conditions, that so many personal commitments had been made to various local church and charitable drives for New York's need by those who could afford to give, that it was almost futile to expect them to contribute anything to his worthy cause on the Gulf. At the end of two months he had received only $100.

Someone mentioned his discouragement to Judge Levy, who invited Father Donnelly to call upon him. When he learned of the clergyman's struggles here and in Texas he promised his immediate aid. He telephoned a number of close acquaintances and within an hour had raised the full amount of $10.000.

Happy Father Donnelly returned to Corpus Christi and erected his church, which bears a plaque con-

(Please Turn to Page Two)

EDITORIAL

Corregidor Increases Our Incentive To Win

"Corregidor needs no comment from me. It has sounded its own story at the mouth of its guns. It has scrolled its own epitaph on enemy tablets.

"But through the bloody haze of its last reverberating shot I shall always seem to see the vision of its grim, gaunt and ghostly men still unafraid."—General Douglas MacArthur, May 7, 1942.

The worst has happened.

Old Glory has been hauled down from the flag-staffs on Corregidor and its adjunct forts in Manila Bay, to make way for the banner of Japanese aggression.

The American people are not indifferent to this development. Neither is the American people's Government.

THE PEOPLE OF THIS LAND, AS WELL AS THEIR GOVERNMENT, DEPLORE THE FACT THAT CORREGIDOR IS AT LAST IN THE POSSESSION OF THE ASIATIC PARTNER OF THE AXIS.

But displeasing and deplorable as is the loss of this stronghold, neither the American people nor their Government can experience any feeling of disgrace. Nor has their determination to carry on their fight with the Tokio war lords, and the war lords of Berlin and Rome, been dampened in the least.

On the contrary, the fall of Corregidor has strengthened their resolve to prosecute the war against the Axis until the Axis abjectly capitulates; until the cause of

(PLEASE TURN TO PAGE TWO)

Jap Fleet Driven Into Hiding by U. S. Forces

By BRYDON C. TAVES
(United Press Staff Correspondent)

GEN. MAC ARTHUR'S HEADQUARTERS, Australia, May 10.—Japan's battered invasion fleet, smashed and scattered by United States warships in a five-day battle in the Coral Sea, was believed today to have limped northward to shelter in the network of Japanese bases in the Solomon Islands and Bismarck Archipelago.

United Nations planes, increasingly active, weer believed to be sweeping wide areas of the Pacific, hoping to harass the fleeing enemy and add to the huge toll of damage, which was estimated to have cost the enemy up to 100.000 tons of costly battle craft difficult to replace.

Gen. Douglas MacArthur, who denounced Japanese claims of huge Allied losses as obvious propaganda, announced that there had been no

(Please Turn to Page 3)

Nazis Slay 50 Hostages

(By United Press)

LONDON, May 10.—Advices reaching London said that at dawn in a cobblestone courtyard outside Paris, one of Heydrich's execution squads killed 50 so-called French "Communists and Jews," the name given by the Germans to all who resist Nazi rule. They died for an attack on a lone German soldier a week ago.

Jap Burma Army Retreats, 4,500 Dead; Flight Cut

CHUNGKING, May 10.—Chinese forces, in a stunning turn of the tide in Burma, have smashed back into Mandalay and threaten to annihilate the Japanese forces which invaded China's Yunnan Province and now are in headlong retreat back to Burma after losing 4,500 killed, war advices said tonight.

A military spokesman said that U. S. Lieut.-Gen. Joseph W. Stillwell's "lost" Chinese Army, apparently surrounded last week when the Japanese overran northern Burma, had penetrated into Mandalay from the east and west. There was no indication, however, that the city had been recaptured.

Other units of Stillwell's force were reported driving north from recaptured Maymyo, important communications point 30 miles east of Mandalay, to intercept the Yunnan invaders who had taken a bad pummelfng from American Volunteer Group planes and lost 3.000 killed in further fighting around Chefang, 24 miles inside China.

These casualties were in addition to 1,500 killed when the Japanese attempted to flank the Chinese at Chefang last week and were in turn pocketed in the dizzy gorges flanking the Burma Road in that area.

The Yunnan invasion force—what little was left of it—was reported fleeing in trucks toward the Burma border, with China's Yunnan army in hot pursuit. They were said to face certain annihilation since their way of retreat was cut by the recapture of Maymyo and the presence of other Chinese forces ready to waylay them on the Burma Road north of there.

A British communique said that RAF bombers yesterday raided the Japanese - occupied airdrome at Magwe, 150 miles southwest of Mandalay, destroying at least two and probably four of 18 parked bombers and setting a petrol dump afire. No British planes were lost.

Nazis Charge Sweden's Maneuvers "Realistic"

Radio broadcasts from Stockholm, Sweden, recorded on local stations this Sunday morning reported that all telephonic communications between Sweden and Nazi Germany were broken off at 3 p. m. yesterday. The announcement stated that such moves have always been preliminary to actions of "prime importance" on the part of the Axis.

There was speculation, in Sweden, the radio states that "complete French collaboration with the Axis was about to take place." This was predicated on the report that Reichmarshal Herman Goering is said to be in Vichy conferring with Premier Laval and his cabinet. It was further reported that the British fleet was massed off the French coast in anticipation that the Laval government has or will turn over the French fleet to the Axis.

The German radio recorded here today declared that "the Swedes are busy wtih realistic military maneuvers in the vicinity of Stockholm."

GERMANS MAKE CHARGES

(By United Press)

The German Transoceanic News Agency today broadcast a curiously worded report that Stockholm, capital of Sweden, had a "bombing raid" last night as the first phase of maneuvers simulating a surprise attack on the city.

The broadcts said that this morning the presence of "enemy parachute troops" was reported from several dstricts outside Stockholm.

The maneuvers, which will include a "fight for the coastal regions outside Stockholm" will last until May 20, the German report said.

Nazis to Use Canary Isles, Spanish Morocco as Bases

(By United Press)

Germany is developing plans to use the Spanish Canary Islands for air raids on South America and the United States, Radio Moscow said Saturday in a broadcast recorded by Columbia Broadcast System.

It said a special delegation of the German Air Ministry and the Nazi civil air fleet already had arrived in Madrid, presumably to complete plans for using the Spanish bases. Plans also are being formulated for developing new bases on Spanish territory in the Mediterranean and the Atlantic, the Moscow broadcast added.

"A number of bases are also to be established in Mallorca and along the coast of Spanish Morocco," it said.

CHINESE IN COMEBACK, PENETRATE MANDALAY

LONDON, May 10 (Sunday noon)—Chinese troops on the comeback in Burma have penetrated Mandalay from the west and from the east, the New Delphi radio said today, quoting a Chinese military spokesman in Chungking.

TEXAN IN RCAF DOWNS NAZI FOCKWULF PLANE

LONDON, May 10.—Brady Oscar Parker, Royal Canadian Air Force pilot from Lyford, Tex., shot down a German Fockwulf 190 while escorting American - made Boston bombers during a British air attack on Bruges last night, ti was revealed today.

Dutch Will Fight On, States Premier

(By United Press)

LONDON, May 10.—Premier Pieter S. Gerbrandy, speaking on the second anniversary of the German invasion of the Netherlands, said today that the sufferings of the population of Holland under the Nazi occupation regime guaranteed "ultimate victory."

Speaking among the ruins of a bombed Dutch church at Austin Friars, he urged Dutchmen to adopt as their watchword the message of Rear Admiral Karel Doorman, Dutch Naval Commander in the Java Sea battle: "I am going to attack—follow me."

"We are filled with hope,' he told units of the Netherlands land, sea and air forces. "The hardships which we—the Netherlands and the East Indies—are suffering together bind us together more closely. They will cement, as nothing else can, the future unity of the Empire."

He referred to Nazi persecution of the occupied territory, and mentioned 72 executions recently ordered by the Germans in the Netherlands.

"We remember the morning of May 10, 1940, whose brightness was clouded by the black treachery of those who, contrary to all justice and their solemnly pledged word, fell upon our peaceful country," the Netherlands Indies News Agency quoted Gerbrandy. "We remember those who gave their lives in battle against the invader. We remember our Middelburg and Rotterdam. We remember the innocents who fell, and how fresh is the memory of the 72 victims of the latest legalized murder.

"The memory of the invasion, the battle on the soil of our fatherland, is branded on us. Our generation will be marked by its scar for life. We remember the suffering of those who groan under the heel of the oppressor. We know how many have been led away captive; how many have died in prisons and concentration camps; how many have paid dearly for their loyalty to the royal house of the fatherland.

"The vision of those sufferings is ever in our eyes. It accompanies us wherever we go. But the thought that even these sufferings are a guarantee of our ultimate triumph strengthens us . .

"The invader is one of those who is unaccustomed to victories. That is the reason for his brutality. But he is learning that the spirit of William the Silent lives in the Netherlands, that this nation refuses to be destroyed . . .

"Over the waters of the Java Sea . . . glitters forever that signal of brave Karel Doorman, Netherlands Rear Admiral commanding the United Nations fleet in the Battle of the Java Sea: 'I am going to attack—follow me.'

"Let that be our watchword. Let us go from here not only with the memory of what has been but with the hope of all that which will assuredly come—victory."

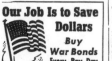

REYNOLDS NEWS, May 17, 1942.

REYNOLDS NEWS

GOVERNMENT OF THE PEOPLE, BY THE PEOPLE, FOR THE PEOPLE

No. 4785 Black-out: 10.32 p.m. to 5.19 a.m. Moon Rises: 7.45 a.m. LONDON: SUNDAY, MAY 17, 1942 RADIO: PAGE 2 PRICE 2d.

RED ARMY IS IN KHARKOV OUTSKIRTS

70 Nazi Tanks Smashed: 'Land-Battleships' Crash Through

NEW type land-battleship tanks are leading the Red Army advance into the outskirts of Kharkov in one of the greatest battles of the war.

Marshal Timoshenko's offensive, Moscow said last night, has now developed into a pitched battle, and latest dispatches describe the roads east from Kharkov to the front as 'a sea of burning tanks and lorries.'

The midnight communique said that during the day "our troops on the Kerch Peninsula waged intense battles in the region of the city of Kerch.

"On the Kharkov sector of the Front our troops fought offensive battles and continued to advance successfully, capturing booty and prisoners. The enemy left some 70 tanks destroyed on the battlefield.

"Fifty-six German planes were shot down on Friday. Our losses were 13. Our aircraft destroyed or damaged some 60 tanks, four railway and three material dumps.

"Russian ships and planes in the Barents Sea sank an enemy transport of 8,000 tons and a minesweeper and severely damaged another minesweeper, which was probably sunk."

Earlier, Moscow Radio had made a triumphant pronouncement.

"The Red Army is stronger than ever, and the offensive drive of Marshal Timoshenko, on the Kharkov Front, which is continuing successfully, provides but one symbol of that strength.

"The Red Army is conscious that the coming months are the most crucial for all mankind, and it is facing the titanic battle which is in the making with an unshakeable resolve to achieve the complete defeat of Hitler in 1942."

Line on Hills

Vichy News Agency dropped a significant admission. "The fighting at Kharkov, on which depends the fate of the whole Ukrainian Front, has relegated the Kerch offensive to second place.

"The Kerch battle has only the limited object of consolidating the German hold on the Crimea."

The agency added that Kharkov is not defended by concentric rings, but by a fortified zone of great depth extending some 30 miles around the city.

"The German dispositions are very strong. The first line is based on a chain of hills on the left bank of the Donetz.

"Another line is formed by

★ BACK PAGE COL. 4

Max Werner on KERCH & KHARKOV

'Nazis are in blind alley'

NEW YORK, Saturday.

GERMAN offensives are always powerful at the beginning, designed for a quick final decision. This was so at Sedan in the West and in the great battle of the frontiers in June, 1941.

But the Kerch attacks are merely a local operation and a very small one at that.

Here there is action on the extreme flank—a peripheral blow totally isolated from the main front.

It would make sense only as the prelude to a great offensive in south-east Russia and the Caucasus; but the German front on the Sea of Azov and in the Don basin is not moving eastwards, and without a co-ordinated offensive from this direction the Kerch offensive seems like a blind alley.

If the Germans are seeking economic conquest in the south-east while avoiding a military decision on the decisive central front, they are engaging in hopelessly risky strategy.

The Southern Caucasus is impregnable.

☆ ☆ ☆

HOWEVER, the Kerch offensive could be a diversion designed to conceal plans for an offensive in another direction, perhaps on the central front; the picture will clarify within a fortnight.

Nevertheless, in one sense the Kerch offensive has failed, since it provided the spark that set the Red Army in motion along the whole front, and no more surprises are possible.

The Red Army has launched in the Kharkov sector a far more important offensive, compared with which the Kerch affair is only a local skirmish.

☆ ☆ ☆

KHARKOV sees the Russians attacking at one of the most vital points of the entire front, providing a great test of the efficacy of the Red Army's offensive weapons and its capacity for offensive manœuvre.

The battle for Kharkov can determine the situation on the entire Southern Front from Kursk to the Crimea and also influence the situation on the Central Front.

At the end of the first week's operations the initiative on the main front is still in Russian hands: and that was certainly not the German intention.

There Stands His Champagne . . .

SOME weeks ago, in New York, a very sober man, not given to celebration, bought his first bottle of champagne.

He and his friends, he said, would open it the day the Red Army recaptured Kharkov, his native city.

The man was Max Werner, who is recognised now as the world's foremost military commentator.

Though he has been consistently right in his analysis of the fighting, he makes no claim to be a "forecaster." He deals in fact, not speculation.

THIS WAS ONLY A 'PROBABLE'

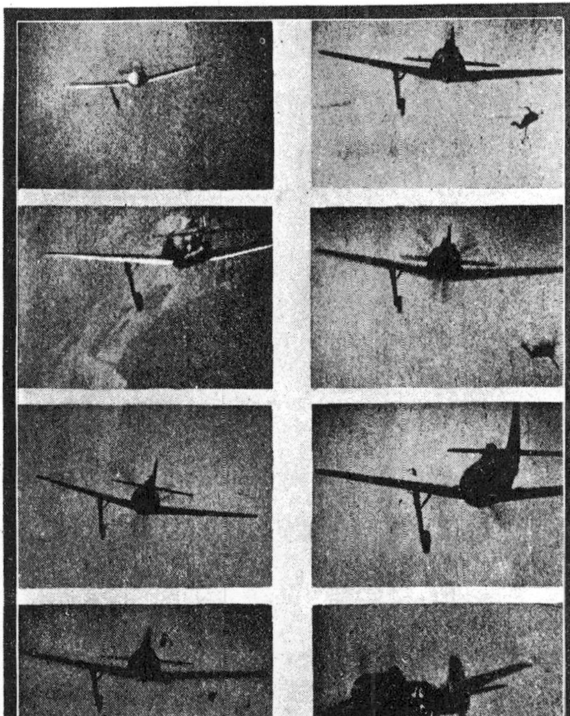

HOW CAREFUL the R.A.F. are to avoid over-statement in their compilation of losses inflicted upon the enemy is shown by the report made by Flight/Sgt. Robson, a New Zealander, whose gun-coupled camera took this series of pictures of his attack upon a FW 190 (Germany's latest and fastest fighter).

"When I last saw the aircraft," he reported, "it was flying at 2,000ft. with one wing down; but, as I then lost sight of it, I only claimed it as 'probably destroyed.'" The pilot was flying a Spitfire at 17,000ft. in the Cap Gris Nez area when he sighted the FW 190 and dived on it. Pictures show . . . "I dived on him and gave him two short bursts. . . ." "Then I followed him down and gave him the rest of my ammunition. I saw one of the wheels of the Jerry's undercarriage come down, the cockpit hood fly off (see it in the picture), and the pilot's helmet come out of the cockpit. . . ." "When I last saw the aircraft it was flying at 2,000ft. with one wing down."

Chinese Surprise Attacks Hit Japs

THE Japanese have suffered considerable losses in the last few days in a series of surprise raids by Chinese troops at Pailochi, north of Yochow (Northern Hunan), on the Yangtse River, according to Chinese field dispatches, quoted by Reuter from Chungking last night.

Large stores of oil and ammunition are said to have been concentrated by the Japanese at Pailochi recently, apparently in preparation for a renewed drive in that area.

In one of the raids the Chinese smashed their way into the town at night and showered hand Grenades on oil and ammunition depots.

A terrific fire resulted and explosions were heard for miles around.

CHINESE ATTACK

The Japanese yesterday opened an offensive in the Chinese coastal province of Chekiang, last night's Chinese communique stated. Many columns are driving south.

In the battle of the Burma Road a Chinese counter-offensive may be launched at any moment, it was stated in Chungking.

The capture by the Japanese of Tengyueh, 50 miles west of Paoshan, their immediate objective in Yunnan, was reported in a Chungking communique.

Paris Radio last night, quoted by A.P., broadcast Jap claims that fighting was going on in four Chinese provinces, in the south of Yunnan Province, in south-east Shansi.

R.A.F. Fighters Spare French

Two R.A.F. fighter pilots sweeping over France yesterday confined their attack on a passenger train to the engine, because, as one of them said later, "There may have been French people in the train as well as German."

Skimming over the waves and nipping in across the French coast, Spitfires of Fighter Command resumed their sweeps yesterday to harass the German defences in occupied territory.

Their targets included gasholders, dock gates and railways, states the Air Ministry News Service.

GASHOLDER FIRED

Two pilots on an earlier operation left a gasholder at Ostend with smoke and flames pouring from it; two others attacked targets at St. Valery-sur-Somme and saw their cannon shells strike home.

Others set a railway shed on fire, blew the roof off a signal-box, and shot the roof off a shed containing a locomotive.

One of a small number of aircraft which came over a place on the south-west coast of England, early yesterday afternoon, was destroyed, said last night's Air Ministry and Ministry of Home Security communique.

[Pilot's Death Dive, see page 5.]

Sir Walter Citrine is Better

Sir Walter Citrine, who has been confined to his hotel by illness, is recovering.

He told Reuter's correspondent that he had been compulsorily vaccinated at Lisbon because of the U.S. Government regulations for all those who enter the United States via that route.

"I succumbed against my will," he said. "I've had a very bad left arm indeed, and have been in bed for four days."

ROOSEVELT FREES BROWDER

EARL BROWDER, leader of the American Communist Party, was last night released from Atlanta Penitentiary, where he had served 14 months of a four-year sentence on a charge of holding a false passport.

This was the result of the special commuting of his sentence by President Roosevelt.

"NATIONAL UNITY"

A statement issued from the White House last night, quoted by the A.P., said that commutation of the sentence, coming before Browder was eligible for parole, would have "a tendency to promote national unity and allay any feeling that the unusually long sentence in Browder's case was by way of a penalty imposed upon him because of his political views."

"Now I will be able to take my place in the great war effort," were Browder's first words on his release.

British Fighters Busy in Libya

British fighter activity was on an increased scale in the forward area of Cyrenaica throughout yesterday, according to last night's Middle East communique.

Benghazi, Benina and Martuba were raided by our bomber aircraft during Friday night.

Coal Owners Bid for Lease and Lend Pit Deal

By a Staff Reporter

A PLAN to bring the coal industry under a form of control similar to that operating in railway transport is being considered by the Committee of seven Ministers charged with examining proposals to reorganise mining.

Under such a plan the Government would take out a lease on all coal pits for the duration of the war and pay the owners an annual rent equivalent to a guaranteed profit.

Control of the industry would come under a National Coal Board. Whether this would be composed of representatives of owners and men as well as nominees of the Government, or, as in the case of the railways, of nominees of the owners and the Government only, is not clear. Joint pit production committees would remain as now.

'Lesser Evil' for Owners

After the war, the lease would be terminated and the mines handed back to private ownership.

Although many owners are still opposed to any form of national control in the industry, the plan is being backed by coal-owning and Conservative interests.

They regard it as a lesser evil, from their point of view, than direct nationalisation or the imposition of a form of joint owners' and workers' control, which they fear would be difficult to retract after the war.

Miners' leaders, who have put forward their own proposals to the Committee for a Coal Board representative of both sides of the industry with powers to reorganise it, are distrustful of the new proposals.

Fear Effect on Miners

They feel that the Government, in dropping the Beveridge fuel rationing scheme, has shown an undue tenderness towards Conservative interests. If, in addition, it brings out a plan for the industry with guaranteed profits and the safeguarding of private ownership after the war as its leading features, the psychological effect on the miners will be, to put it mildly, detrimental to production.

(Government and Mines: See back page.)

'Bigger' Jap Fleet Nearing Australia?

Paris Radio last night quoted a "Shanghai report" that another Japanese fleet was on its way to northern Australia, and that this fleet was "more important" than the one which was involved in the Coral Sea battle, says A.P.

Laval Tells World of U.S. Pressure

NEGOTIATIONS between Vichy and U.S.A. seem near breaking point.

Scared by Washington's prolonged silence after his Note to U.S., sent on Thursday, Laval ran to Paris to consult "his collaborators."

Yesterday he rushed back to Vichy—on instructions—to release to the Press the text of his American Note.

The fact that he is still waiting for a reply suggests that Vichy's proposals have not pleased the U.S. Government.

Washington, says Vichy Radio, has threatened that unless U.S. demands are granted, the U.S. Government "will not guarantee the sovereignty of French possessions in America."

WARSHIPS

Laval, says A.P., disclosed that his Government's reply to the U.S. Government described the American conditions as a "grave blow to French sovereignty" over the French Antilles, and added that France would not "relinquish any of her rights over Martinique, no matter what happened."

The French warships at Martinique were, "in point of fact, already immobilised," Laval said, and Vichy had agreed to give Washington a guarantee on this matter so as not to aggravate the strain on Franco-American relations since the change of Government.

"Immobilisation of the ships will not, in any case, permit the handing over of them to any foreign Power, including the United States," he said.

He insisted on U.S. recognition of Admiral Robert as Vichy representative in Martinique.

Vichy reporters, hurriedly assembled to hear Laval's pronouncement, dutifully laughed when the "Chief of Government" remarked, "My presence in the French Government does not exactly inspire complete confidence on the part of the Washington Government."

AMERICAN NOTE

The American Note, delivered to Admiral Robert on May 9, stated:—

"The present head of the Vichy Government having declared that he would follow a policy of greater collaboration with Germany, it is no longer possible for the American Government to maintain the agreements concluded by Admirals Greenslade and Horne concerning French possessions in the Western Hemisphere, agreements which had hitherto been considered satisfactory.

"Under the provisions of these agreements, the French possessions might become bases for Axis aggression, either by the connivance of the High Commissioner or by the dispatch of a new High Commissioner.

"German pressure in this direction must be expected."

PREMIER CHEERED BY 25,000

Praise for Russians

MR. CHURCHILL yesterday paid tribute to "the noble manhood of Russia, now at full grips with the murderous enemy, striking blow for blow and repaying better ones for blows struck at them."

In a speech to a crowd of 25,000 from the steps of Leeds Town Hall, he praised the workers for their efforts in the common cause of the workers in many lands.

Russia, America, the Empire countries, and "all those in the human race who are not already gripped by tyranny or who had not already been seduced to its insidious vice," he said, were backing this common cause.

"NO FAVOURS"

"Here, in the 33rd month of the war," said Mr. Churchill, "none of us is weary of the struggle. None of us are calling for any favours from the enemy.

"If he plays rough we can play rough, too. Whatever we have got to take we will take: and we will give it back in even greater measure."

After reiterating that we had striven hard for peace, and had even gone into folly in our desire for peace, the Premier declared:—

"It is not now going to be brave men against men armed, but a fight of people not only with the resolve and cause but who also have the weapons.

"It would be premature to say that we had topped the ridge, but we see the ridge ahead now, and our perseverance will see us through these dark and dangerous valleys into the sunlight more lasting than mankind has ever known."

During the morning Mr. Churchill had made a triumphant tour of Leeds. With him was Dr. H. V. Evatt, Australian Minister for External Affairs.

Standing up in an open car, Mr. Churchill doffed his hat and waved at the cheering crowds that lined the route, giving them the Victory sign with his fingers. At some points he was within an ace of being mobbed in the enthusiastic reception.

(Picture on Page 3.)

SLAVS HIT AGAIN

A detachment of General Mihailovich's army threw back a new Italian attack in Bosnia, killing 150 and capturing machine-guns and other material. These reports, says A.P., reached authoritative Yugoslav circles in Jerusalem yesterday.

Salute to His People

King Haakon of Norway, in a personal message broadcast to his people in Norway on their Independence Day, said:—

"To-day it is our own generation which has taken up the fight for freedom and independence.

"You at home and we abroad share the same unshakeable faith that righteousness and justice must prevail in the end.

Forward to Victory

"Our national solidarity has never been more firmly welded than it is to-day, and we greet each other with the conviction that your May 17 spirit will give us the will power to fight on to the end.

"I look forward to the day when the youth of Norway can rejoice once more because our love for the constitution stands undefeated—because our heritage from the men of Eidsvold* has been regained."

**Norway's "Free Constitution" was framed at Eidsvold on May 17, 1814.*

'Italy Fed Up—Fears Invasion'

FEAR of invasion and hints of "great events" were expressed by a Rome Radio speaker last night.

The speaker declared: "Our Navy is fearlessly guarding our coast, and many preparations are taking place which we do not propose to disclose because, in the Mediterranean especially, silence is golden.

"All we can say is that we are on the eve of great military events."

WAR UNPOPULAR

Uneasiness in Italy is also revealed by a report yesterday by an American journalist who is being repatriated to the United States from Italy.

He states that the war, now that the United States and Japan are in it, is increasingly unpopular to the Italians, who remember that Mussolini used to speak about the "Yellow Peril."

A certain section of the people, says the journalist, are ready to revolt, but they are waiting for one thing—an Anglo-Saxon (which includes American) landing on the Continent. But until this is possible they are remaining quiet.

CLAIMS MAINTAINED

This commentator also declared that at the last Hitler-Mussolini meeting, Mussolini told Hitler that Italy maintained her claims against France (Djibuti, Tunis, Savoy, Nice and Corsica), and that any attempt to reduce these claims would hinder Italo-German collaboration.

In support of this opinion comes news from Istanbul, quoted by the Tass Agency in a Moscow broadcast last night, that Laval's failure to comply with the German demands presented by Goering would entail the immediate Italian occupation of Nice, Corsica, and Tunis.

Axis quarters in Istanbul said yesterday that negotiations were in progress between between the Vichy Government and Italy for a peace settlement, says A.P.

The Soviet News Agency, last night, quoting "an unconfirmed report from a Mediterranean centre," stated that two Italian destroyers had anchored at Bizerta, the French port in Tunis.

Labour M.P. Dies

Mr. William Lunn, M.P. for the Rothwell Division, West Riding, Yorks, died in Leeds last night. He was 69.

Starting work in the pit at the age of 12, Mr. Lunn became Labour Whip in 1922, and was a Junior Minister in both Labour Governments.

At the last General Election he had a majority of 14,000 over his Conservative opponent.

This will make the fifth pending by-election.

MALTA CENTURY

A British fighter squadron which arrived in Malta a year ago destroyed its 100th enemy plane yesterday, says B.U.P.

Yesterday's bag over the island consisted of one Italian and one German fighter destroyed and six raiders damaged.

R A F BOMBERS BLAST JAP INDIA INVASION AIR BASE

R.A.F. bombers struck yesterday to destroy Jap planes massed at Akyab aerodrome on the Burma coast.

The blow at Jap air power, the spearhead of any invasion of India, was delivered as our armies were falling back slowly to the Burma-India borders.

Messages from New Delhi, quoted by Reuter yesterday, revealed that the British have finally defeated the Japanese attempt to interpose a force between them and the Indian border and have fought their way to a more secure area.

Smashing Chinese counter attacks, in which the Japs were hurled out of the town of Mongling, Eastern Burma, with heavy casualties and the loss of prisoners, rifles and munitions, were reported in last night's Chungking High Command communique, quoted by the A. P.

1,000 CASUALTIES

The town had been occupied by a reinforced Jap column 10,000 strong, with heavy tanks and 20 guns, and the invaders suffered 1,000 casualties.

The communique added that once on May 12 and twice on May 13 the Japanese attempted to force a crossing of the Salween at Kongkum, under cover of artillery and air protection. They were repulsed.

General Alexander's forces, which, it was officially announced last, are still in Burma, have made no contact with the Japanese during the past 24 hours, a military spokesman at New Delhi stated yesterday.

It is now clear that the British fighting retreat has stopped short of the Indian frontier.

Mr. Forde, Australian Army Minister, disclosed yesterday that 395 letters from Australian prisoners of war in Japanese hands in New Guinea were dropped by Japanese aeroplanes over Port Moresby on April 28.

Average net paid circulation for April exceeded
Daily---2,000,000
Sunday-3,800,000

DAILY NEWS

Copr. 1942 by News Syndicate Co. Inc. NEW YORK'S PICTURE NEWSPAPER Trade Mark Reg. U. S. Pat. Off.

Vol. 23. No. 292 New York, Monday, June 1, 1942★ 40 Pages 2 Cents IN CITY LIMITS | 3 CENTS Elsewhere

1250 PLANES RAID COLOGNE; CITY IN RUINS

Story on Page 3

(Associated Press Radiofotos FLASHED HERE YESTERDAY from London)

Tea and TNT. Canadian crewmen of a Halifax bomber, one of the more than 1,250 planes that hamburgered Cologne, Germany, enjoy a cup of tea from a U. S.-donated canteen, after returning to Britain. *—Story on page 3; other pictures on page 21*

Back from Cologne

Pilot Officer W. H. Baldwin (left) of Ottawa and Flight Sergt. R. J. Campbell of Pawling, N. Y., have just returned from the attack on Cologne, history's greatest air raid. More than six million pounds of bombs were dropped on Germany's fifth largest city. Nazis retaliated early today with raids on a historic British town.

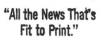

"All the News That's Fit to Print."

The New York Times.

LATE CITY EDITION
Scattered showers and somewhat warmer today.
Temperatures Yesterday—Max., 64; Min., 59

Copyright, 1942, by The New York Times Company.

VOL. XCI....No. 30,813. Entered as Second-Class Matter, Postoffice, New York, N. Y. NEW YORK, FRIDAY, JUNE 5, 1942. THREE CENTS NEW YORK CITY and Vicinity

JAPANESE PLANES RAID MIDWAY; BIG R. A. F. FORCES SWEEP FRANCE AFTER NIGHT BOMBING OF BREMEN

TWO 'GAS' ORDERS TIGHTEN RATIONING FOR NATIONAL PLAN

OPA Bids Local Boards Re-examine All Cards, Require Proof of Car Pool Pleas

SYSTEM SPLITS SENATORS

Revenue Depletion, Bootleg Peril Argued—House Group Seeks Delay for Inquiry

By FREDERICK R. BARKLEY
Special to THE NEW YORK TIMES.

WASHINGTON, June 4—Two indications were given today that the government is going to "get tough" in the administration of gasoline rationing, both under the present temporary plan and the permanent one going into effect on July 1.

First, the Office of Price Administration gave specific authority to local rationing boards to call in holders of all rationing cards to determine whether they had obtained the cards by mistake or fraud.

Under an amendment to the regulations, the boards may also require the surrender of unlimited "X" cards if found to have been wrongfully obtained or to be now used illegally for purposes other than the use for which they were issued.

Secondly, the OPA directed that Atlantic Seaboard motorists applying for supplemental gasoline rations under the permanent plan be required to prove statements that they are members of car-sharing or pooling groups.

End of Privilege as Penalty

The first OPA order of the day gave power to local boards to prohibit the obtaining of any gasoline rationing card or book, under any plan in effect now or later, by persons who refuse to appear for questioning when summoned, unless with good cause, or who refuse to surrender any cards now held.

Such action by a board, it was explained, could be appealed to the OPA State director, who has authority to reverse a local decision.

The new punitive procedure, it was stated, would be additional to any other actions which might be taken against violators of the rationing regulations. It also permits any board to review a card which it believes was improperly issued by a board in another area.

The inquiring board is required to give written notice to the card holder of the time and place fixed for his appearance, the notice to be mailed to the address shown on the application.

Strict Rules for Driving Pools

Regarding the second order, Joel Dean, chief of the OPA fuel rationing branch, said that "it will not be sufficient for motorists applying for more than the basic ration (under the permanent plan) merely to state that they transport other people to work."

Every applicant also would have to show that he has made every effort to form a club of at least four members, including himself, he said, and would have to supply their signatures together with their occupations.

He urged motorists contemplating such pools to form the clubs at once so as to have them in effect when the new rationing system goes into effect on July 1.

Each member of a pool must state the number of days a month he expects to be transported, specify his place of occupation and the miles between it and his home. Each car applicant must apply if

Continued on Page Fourteen

'Neutral' Japanese Want Soviet Beaten

By The Associated Press.

TOKYO, June 4 (From Japanese broadcast)—The Diplomatic Review, closely connected with the Foreign Office, said today that Japan was conforming to the spirit of her neutrality pact with Soviet Russia and yet, as Germany's ally, "desires the complete success of German forces against Russia."

ROOSEVELT BACKING TO BAR FISH SOUGHT

Entering Coalition Candidate in His Home District to Be Asked at Week-End Parley

By JAMES C. HAGERTY

Friends of President Roosevelt, faced with the possibility that Representative Hamilton Fish Jr. might be successful in his fight for re-election in the President's home Congressional district, will confer over the week-end with the Chief Executive in an attempt to gain his support in a move to align the Democratic county organizations in the district behind a single "coalition" anti-Fish candidate, it was learned here yesterday.

These friends of the President at present regard Mr. Fish as an almost certain winner in the coming Republican primaries in August, despite the open opposition to his candidacy by Thomas E. Dewey, probable Republican nominee for Governor, and Wendell L. Willkie. They point to the recent 190-26 endorsement of Mr. Fish by the Orange County Republican Committee and the 41-to-2 support given by the Putnam County organization as an indication of Mr. Fish's strength.

Political Aspects Weighed

While the President's friends admit that the Republican nomination of Mr. Fish could be used for political advantage both in the State and throughout the country in Congressional campaigns, they contend that the defeat of the Representative, whose Congressional record has been widely assailed as "isolationist," should transcend the political advantages.

And they hold, and will tell the President so, that should Mr. Fish be re-elected his victory would be construed both here and abroad as a repudiation of the President's war policies by his home district.

Continued on Page Fifteen

FIGHT TO DROP CCC WIDENS INTO MOVE TO KILL NYA ALSO

House Votes Scheduled Today on Abolishing Two Agencies, Following Sharp Attacks

NYA DECLARED NEEDLESS

Duplicates Work of Office of Education, Says Dirksen—CCC's Friends Cite Fire Peril

By C. P. TRUSSELL
Special to THE NEW YORK TIMES.

WASHINGTON, June 4—The House fight over the Appropriation Committee's decision to abolish the Civilian Conservation Corps broadened today into a movement to deny further operating funds to the National Youth Administration also and force the transfer of its war-worker training program, virtually its only remaining activity under present plans, to the Office of Education.

A showdown by vote on the future of the CCC, created by Presidential executive order in 1933, and the NYA, established two years later, was scheduled for tomorrow. The House was called in an hour earlier than the usual meeting time in anticipation of a long struggle.

To continue the NYA, Representative Dirksen of Illinois, a member of the Appropriations body, told the House today, would be to finance the duplication of work now being done on a larger scale by the Office of Education. Both the NYA and the Office of Education function under the Federal Security Agency, he pointed out.

Dirksen Sees Aid to War Drive

The abolition of the NYA and the transfer of its war functions, Mr. Dirksen held, would carry out further the purposes of the Reorganization Act to effect consolidations in the interest of efficiency and economy and at the same time expedite the war effort.

"The Office of Education," Mr. Dirksen said as the House resumed consideration of the $1,058,451,660 Labor Department-Federal Security Agency supply bill for the approaching fiscal year, "already carries on such a program under which 1,064,732 persons have been enrolled in the pre-employment training classes and 1,127,723 in the

Continued on Page Thirty-eight

War News Summarized

FRIDAY, JUNE 5, 1942

Japanese bombers, on the heels of the "feeler" raid on Dutch Harbor, Alaska, carried their assault 1,900 miles to the southwest yesterday with an attack on Midway Island, farthermost outpost of the United States in the Northern Pacific.

The Navy Department, reporting no details as yet on the Midway raid, declared that the bombing of Dutch Harbor appeared designed to test American defenses. A Navy communiqué revealed that the Japanese, apparently engaged in reconnaissance, dropped no bombs on their second flight over Dutch Harbor. [All the foregoing, 1:8; maps, P. 2 and 3.]

The underscored threat of Japanese air raids spurred a redoubling of civilian defense vigilance along the Pacific Coast, where a precautionary radio silence lasted more than eight hours last night. [3:4.]

From the Southwest Pacific theatre of war General MacArthur's headquarters reported the sinking of a Japanese transport and two supply ships and heavy damage to a third supply vessel in attacks by a lone submarine along enemy shipping lanes. The transport carried possibly 12,000 Japanese troops. [1:7.]

In China's coastal Chekiang Province, the defenders gained in a three-sided drive against Japanese-occupied Kinhwa and held a firm grip on Chuhsien, strategic railway city and air base about 700 miles from Japan. [4:1.]

Generalissimo Chiang Kai-shek, in the Chinese capital, held war councils with the ranking American commanders in Southeast Asia—Lieut. Gen. Stilwell, Major Gen. Brereton and Brig. Gen. Chennault. The capital buzzed with talk of a Japanese drive on Siberia. [4:5.]

Whatever the threat to their Far Eastern flank, the Russians were still striking at the German invaders. Although the lull in the ground fighting continued, Soviet planes bombed and machine-gunned Axis troops and supplies behind the lines in various sectors. [7:1.]

Amid furious sandstorms on the Libyan battlefront, the British recaptured Tamar, the point of easternmost Axis penetration through the nine-mile gap in their lines. They failed to narrow that gap, but brisk R. A. F. attacks and a mechanized assault against the Axis rear in the Bir Hacheim area frustrated Field Marshal Rommel's efforts to advance. [1:6-7; map, P. 8.]

In Western Europe, the R. A. F. kept up a round-the-clock tempo of attack with night raids centering on the German port of Bremen and daylight sweeps in which more than 1,000 fighters were reported to have given Northern French targets their heaviest battering. [1:4; map, P. 6.]

Britain's Commando raid between Boulogne and Le Touquet, which gained valuable information and rattled the German defenders, was followed by a French assault on a German post at Hazebrouck, according to Vichy dispatches. The French patriots blew up a munitions depot and fled. [1:5-6.]

Reinhard Heydrich, "the hangman" of the Gestapo, died painfully in Prague eight days after the Czech patriot attack on him. The Germans shot twenty-four more Czechs in their campaign of reprisal, bringing the official death toll to 176. [1:5.]

In Washington, the Senate voted unanimously to complete Congressional action on the declaration of war against Hungary, Rumania and Bulgaria. [12:1.]

Another Axis satellite nation, Finland—still at peace with the United States—received a state visit from Adolf Hitler, who presented a medal to Field Marshal Mannerheim. [7:2-4.]

CHANNEL BASES HIT

1,000 British Fighters Strike at Nazis in All-Day Attack

GERMAN PORT IS SEARED

Fires Hide Bremen Shipyards and Factories—Dieppe and Other Centers Targets

By JAMES MacDONALD
Wireless to THE NEW YORK TIMES.

LONDON, Friday, June 5—Flying right around the clock, the Royal Air Force kept up an almost incessant attack against the Nazis Wednesday night and all day yesterday.

British planes subjected Bremen to a heavy bombing raid, blasted the docks at Dieppe, attacked hostile air bases in occupied France and the Low Countries and laid mines in enemy waters. Other bombers and many squadrons of R. A. F. fighters swept over Northern France again throughout daylight and during last evening.

[More than 1,000 British fighter planes went across the Channel yesterday in what observers reported was the largest force yet used in daylight attacks, according to a United Press dispatch from London.]

The day offensive was directed chiefly against the Cherbourg region in the morning, against Boulogne and the Pas de Calais in the afternoon and against the port of Dunkerque last evening, the Air Ministry said.

Nazis Report Raid on Poole

The Germans sent what British officials said was a "small number" of planes over Britain during Wednesday night. The Nazi raiders made a sharp attack on one English South Coast district, causing some casualties and property damage. [The Berlin radio said "the British naval base of Poole" was attacked.]

In all the Wednesday night operations, British officials said, the R. A. F. lost ten bombers and two fighters. They reported two Nazi bombers destroyed over Britain and four other German planes shot down in fights over the Nazis airfields.

The Air Ministry reported three R. A. F. fighters lost in daylight yesterday and one German fighter destroyed on the sweeps.

The size of the R. A. F. raid on Bremen was not anywhere near that of the raids on Cologne and Essen on Saturday and Monday nights. But the British loss of ten bombers Wednesday night would seem to indicate that the "strong force" mentioned in yesterday's communiqué covered—on the ratio of losses of less than 4 per cent that the week's raids have cost the R. A. F.—more than 200 bombers dispatched over that second largest port of Germany.

Nearly 3,000 British bombers, it is estimated, have pounded various points in Germany since Saturday night, when more than 1,000 planes attacked Cologne.

Weather Aids Bremen Bombing

The Bremen attack was the ninety-fourth time the R. A. F. has raided that city, where there are shipyards for building U-boats, factories producing Nazi dive bombers and long-range Focke-Wulf and Kondor planes, a big oil-refining plant and important railroad terminals and freight yards. All these were targets of the British bombers.

Aided by a clear sky the raiders found no difficulty in reaching Bremen. A slight ground haze obscured the factories and shipyards, but the fliers met this obstacle by dropping many flares, by the glaring light of which they dropped their loads of explosives.

The attack lasted only about half an hour, in accordance with the R. A. F.'s latest technique of delivering its blows in lightning fashion.

In that short time, despite intense opposition by German night

Continued on Page Six

COMMANDOS RETURN AFTER RAID ON BOULOGNE

Wading ashore after surprise visit to the French coast

New York Times Radiophoto, passed yesterday by British censor

Commandos Rattle Nazis; French Blow Up Munitions

By RAYMOND DANIELL
Wireless to THE NEW YORK TIMES.

LONDON, June 4—The British made another jab early today at German defenses on the French coast. A small party of Commandos, supported by the Royal Air Force and the Royal Navy, landed on a beach between Boulogne and Le Touquet, tossed grenades at and exchanged rifle fire with the defenders, and retreated under a smoke screen with light casualties.

It was purely a reconnaissance raid, and the British are saying that "valuable information" was gained and that they are well satisfied.

While the British Special Service troops, commanded by Major K. R. S. Trevor, were ashore, light naval forces under Lieut. Comdr. T. N. Cartwright engaged two enemy patrol boats, sank one and damaged the other. The British craft suffered neither damage nor casualties.

[Vichy dispatches said French patriots stormed a strong German military guard at Hazebrouck, forty-two miles east of Boulogne, and exploded a German Army munitions depot, according to a London United Press report.]

Make Stand on Beach

Wearing shorts, stockings and soft woolen hats and with blackened faces a party of Britain's rough and tumble troops slipped ashore at 3 A. M. today and established themselves behind their own guns on the beach before Nazi troops opened fire. According to a newspaper correspondent who was permitted to accompany them, the defenders were so badly rattled that part of the time they were firing at each other.

Some of the raiders, it was said, managed to cut through the barbed-wire defenses and penetrate some distance inland. One pillbox at the edge of the dunes opened heavy fire upon the hit-and-run invaders, but the anti-tank guns and the Bren guns that the Com-

Continued on Page Six

HEYDRICH IS DEAD; CZECH TOLL AT 176

Gestapo Official Succumbs in Prague—Fatality Laid to Attack by Parachutists

By DANIEL T. BRIGHAM
By Telephone to THE NEW YORK TIMES.

BERNE, Switzerland, June 4—Reinhard Heydrich, deputy Gestapo chief and former Reich Deputy Protector of Bohemia-Moravia, died early this morning in Prague Hospital one week and one day after the attack on his automobile by two Czech patriots at Rokitzan last Wednesday afternoon.

A fourth blood transfusion, attempted shortly after 4 o'clock this morning, failed to rally the Gestapo official, who succumbed "in considerable pain," according to a Berlin radio report this afternoon. No date has been set for the funeral.

A blackout of information over the Czech and German radios concerning what was going on inside Czechoslovakia was not lifted until late this evening, when the executions of twenty-four more persons were listed. Six of them were women.

Slaying in Prague and Bruenn

Thirteen were condemned in Prague and eleven in Bruenn. Five in Prague and three in Bruenn were charged with "approving the attack on the Gestapo chief and encouraging by their utterances the protection of the two culprits." Four others in each group were executed for "lying to the police or not telling all they knew." The remainder were executed for "harboring persons guilty of anti-German acts or utterances and possessing arms."

While the total of executed persons reached the official figure of 176 for a crime they were in the main guilty only of "approving," the Prague radio set another precedent early this afternoon, between broadcasts repeating Deputy Reich Protector of Bohemia-Moravia Kurt Daluege's proclamation of martial law, by announcing in one bulletin that forty-six persons had been executed during the day yesterday instead of twenty-five as announced shortly before midnight last night. No explanation was given for the new figure.

Neutral reports from Berlin, where commentary tonight was scarcely encouraged, managed to speculate on the imminence of the "execution of the Fuehrer's orders" announced by Herr Daluege on assuming power last week. It was recalled by one authoritative news commentator that on the eve of his being wounded "slightly"

Continued on Page Thirteen

SUBMARINE SINKS 3 JAPANESE SHIPS

Transport Carrying Possibly 12,000 Troops and 2 Supply Vessels Are Victims

By The Associated Press.

AT UNITED NATIONS HEADQUARTERS, Australia, June 4—A United Nations submarine, presumably American, on cruise somewhere in the Japanese ship lanes, was credited officially tonight with the destruction or damaging of four enemy ships totaling 29,000 tons—one of them an overloaded troopship that went down with possibly as many as 12,000 Japanese soldiers.

[General Douglas MacArthur's headquarters reported this morning that United Nations bombers yesterday rained explosives on the Japanese-held airdrome at Koepang, Timor, and the docks at Rabaul, New Britain, The Associated Press reports.]

An armed transport of 6,000 tons and two jammed supply ships of 10,000 tons and 6,000 tons, respectively, were torpedoed and sunk, and a 7,000-ton supply ship was badly damaged.

Implying that the better part of a division might have perished aboard the transport, United Nations headquarters said all aboard probably were lost, and added:

"The Japanese are notorious for overloading troop transports. It is known that they put more than 12,000 soldiers on some 6,000-ton ships."

Attacks in Japanese Seas

It was indicated that the submarine had made its attacks well beyond Australian waters, somewhere on the seas between Japan's numerous Southwestern Pacific bases.

The news had a tonic effect on Australians, who had been sobered earlier today by Japanese submarine attacks on southeastern coastal shipping, hard on the heels of the

Continued on Page Two

Planes Pound Axis Units in Libya; British Recapture a Strong Point

By JOSEPH M. LEVY
Special Cable to THE NEW YORK TIMES.

CAIRO, Egypt, June 4—Sandstorms so terrific that they choked men's throats and buried vehicles hub-deep forced a comparative lull yesterday in the great Libyan tank battle that has been raging with only brief let-ups for more than a week, but whenever there was even a slight easing in the blow Royal Air Force planes continued their attacks on the enemy fighting forces and supply columns.

Italian troops, with a slight stiffening of German tanks, made a half-hearted attack on British positions around Bir Hacheim, but the combination of bad weather and fierce bombing and machine-gunning attacks by low-flying British planes apparently helped to discourage the Axis force. Meeting firm resistance, it did not press home the attack, and meanwhile British forces in the vicinity attacked from the rear.

Apparently to support the Axis assault, a force of enemy dive-bombers attempted to raid British troops in this area, but were driven off by an R. A. F. squadron, which shot down seven Stukas.

It is now reported that British armored forces late Tuesday drove a Nazi armored column out of Tamar, a strong point about six miles west of Knightsbridge, and destroyed at least fourteen Axis tanks. However, sporadic fighting continued yesterday in the Knightsbridge area whenever the weather permitted.

Although still closely pressed, the Germans east of the mine-field gap were able to protect their flanks, and British drives from the north and south did not

Continued on Page Eight

U. S. ISLE ATTACKED

Raid Follows Bombing and Scouting Flight at Dutch Harbor

STIMSON RENEWS WARNING

Secretary Says We Must Look for More Assaults Like That on Alaska Base

By CHARLES HURD
Special to THE NEW YORK TIMES.

WASHINGTON, June 4—Japanese bombers today struck at Midway Island, lying northwest of Hawaii on the route to Japan, within twenty-four hours after the foray against Dutch Harbor, in the Aleutian Islands, and a later reconnaissance flight over that base.

The report of the new attack on Midway was given out coincident with a positive denial by a Navy spokesman of reports, emanating from Canada, that there had been a third flight over Dutch Harbor.

The Navy announcement said Midway was bombed at 9 A. M., local time [2:30 P. M., E. W. T.]. It added only that "no further details are yet available." This communiqué was timed as of 4:30 P. M., E. W. T., and was issued at 5:10 P. M.

No Attempt to Take Midway

Midway Island lies 1,300 statute miles northwest of Hawaii. It is 1,900 miles southwest of Dutch Harbor. The island was shelled by Japanese ships early in the war, but no serious attempt ever was made to capture it such as brought the loss of Guam and Wake Islands farther to the south and west.

There was no indication in official advices—and necessarily none of any other type was available—as to the seriousness of this latest sally against Midway Island. Aside from possible protection by units of the United States Pacific Fleet in that region, Midway is isolated. It has relatively few inhabitants. It was developed only in recent years as a base of operations for Pan American Airways clippers. It is now fortified, but to what degree is not publicly known.

While officials maintained extreme reticence concerning the new attacks by the Japanese on American bases, the view was generally held that these bombings were "feelers" to test the strength of our outposts. Also it has long been expected that the Japanese would attempt offensive operations against American objectives as a reply to the April 18 attacks on Tokyo and other Japanese cities by the wave of bombers led by Brig. Gen. James H. Doolittle.

Secretary of War Henry L. Stimson, who predicted a week ago that the Japanese would not rest until they had made "face-saving" raids on American objectives, said today at a press conference that this country must expect further raids.

Declines to Speculate

He declined to discuss the Dutch Harbor attack specifically, referring questioners to the Navy Department's communiqués, but he said, "I warn you this is not the only and last raid we must expect."

When a reporter asked where he thought the Japanese would strike next—word had not yet been received of the Midway attack—the War Secretary smiled and said that he could not "place geographical boundaries on where the enemy might strike."

The only Navy statement about Dutch Harbor up to a late hour today was a communiqué issued at noon, stating that "the situation at Dutch Harbor is at present quiet."

Yesterday's first raid by the Japanese, the Navy commented, apparently was primarily to test our defenses. High explosives and incendiary bombs were dropped but casualties were light and damage not extensive. A few fires were started but were quickly extinguished.

The second enemy incursion six hours later appeared to have been solely for reconnaissance, the Navy said.

It has not been definitely determined where the planes came from

Continued on Page Two

If in Doubt, Put It Out

Windows in private homes must be shaded or screened in conformity with the Army's new dimout regulations, it was emphasized yesterday at the headquarters of the Second Corps Area. It was explained that some citizens were under the misapprehension that the new regulations applied only to offices, business establishments and factories.

Steps to prevent direct rays of light escaping from windows and skylights throughout the metropolitan area and along the New Jersey and Delaware shores are necessary to prevent building up the sky glow that has proved of assistance to enemy submarines by silhouetting our shipping for attack. Army officers attached to the Second Corps Area headquarters call upon the public to remember the slogan: "If in doubt, put it out."

No. 13,116 Thursday, June 11, 1942 One Penny

PACIFIC victory grows: Admiral Nimitz gives America the "Best News Yet"

HALF JAP FLEET OF 30 IS SMASHED

Thousands of invaders died in Midway battle

Express Staff Reporter C. V. R. THOMPSON

NEW YORK, Wednesday.

MORE than 15 Jap ships—half the main force—were "casualties" in the Battle of Midway, and thousands of Japanese perished, it is disclosed tonight in a new communiqué issued in Pearl Harbour by Admiral Chester Nimitz.

The Japanese fleet was closely clustered when the American bombers swept down on it, and the Japs were so hard pressed that they did not stop to pick up survivors.

Admiral Nimitz's report—which is incomplete—covers the first three days of the action. There may be more news of damage to the enemy yet to come.

Naval experts believe that some of the Jap ships attacked must have lost every man on board.

Admiral Nimitz's report and other news from the Pacific caused an air of suppressed elation among Washington higher-ups today.

Realists who earlier showed only cautious optimism wore the look of good news on their faces.

The cheerful spirit infected today's meeting of the Pacific War Council. New Zealand's Minister, Walter Nash, said as he left: "The President's report was full of good news—good news right through.

More news

"Perhaps the best we have had."

Usually phlegmatic Alexander Loudon, the Dutch Ambassador, said that the war in the Pacific may take a new slant.

Officials kept their cheerful looks while the Japs and their Axis partners were claiming landings on the Aleutian islands and "the occupation of important points."

Washington naval experts had been frank to warn Americans to put off celebrating the Midway victory until the situation was clear in the Aleutians, those strategic islands sweeping 1,000 miles from Alaska into the Pacific.

With the week's black-out of news from these northern outposts, the situation was anything but clear. There was even ominous-sounding talk that Dutch Harbour was not really a vital link in America's chain of Pacific bases.

"No visitors"

But today the news black-out was lifted with this statement by a Navy spokesman:—

"We have no information about any Japanese on Alaskan soil. Certainly none of our inhabited areas, islands or rocks are troubled with uninvited visitors up to this time."

The Japs, he suggested, put out their claims with the idea of fishing for information about U.S. naval dispositions.

So he gave the lie to Japanese trumpeting that American bases in Aleutians had been "reduced."

The German radio hurriedly enlarged this report by claiming that Japanese forces had landed in the Aleutians, and then the Japanese followed up with an announcement that "operations by Japanese navy and army forces against United States bases have led to occupation of important points in the Aleutian Islands."

Captain Hiraide, of Tokyo Imperial Headquarters, made this assertion, and in doing so gave an inkling, perhaps, of what Japan had hoped to do.

New slant

He said that American forces were unable to prevent occupation because they were "tied down by operations in the Midway Island area."

This was the first word about Alaska since the U.S. Navy Departments' announcement last Wednesday that Dutch Harbour had been raided by four Japanese bombers escorted by 15 fighters.

Whether the next word will record that the Japanese have withdrawn their naval task force, or have augmented it, is not yet known, but it is now argued in Washington that the final report on the battle of Midway may show that Japan's favourite striking weapon — carrier-based aircraft—has suffered such a severe blow during the past week that the major thrust everyone has been expecting may not come after all.

All the same, there is probably more to be heard of the Aleutians yet.

(Aleutian, pronounced Ahlooshian.)*

PACIFIC WAR MAP—PAGE FOUR.

VICTORY SMILE

YES, it's a Roosevelt smile—in London.

Lieutenant Franklin D. Roosevelt, Jr., of the U.S. Navy, son of the President of the United States, has arrived in Britain.

Last night he attended a reception to the visiting South American naval delegation—given by Rear-Admiral Allan G. Kirk, U.S. Naval Attaché in Britain and Chief of Staff to Admiral Stark.

U.S. COAST SAFE FOR 2 WEEKS

WASHINGTON, Wednesday.

COLONEL KNOX, Secretary of the Navy, announced today that not one ship had been sunk within 50 miles of America's coasts during the past two weeks.

Colonel Knox, who had given evidence before the Senate Committee investigating the sinking of merchant ships, told reporters that "every phase of the present situation" had been discussed.

The shipping situation would improve just as fast as shipbuilding output improved.—Reuter.

The Express Naval Reporter writes:—

Talks are going on with a view to a common policy being adopted by the British Admiralty and the United States Navy Department regarding news of shipping losses.

Last summer the Admiralty ceased making regular disclosures of shipping lost by enemy action.

But since America entered the war, disclosures, official and unofficial, have been made there, giving numbers of ships sunk.

Evatt: Japan is getting stronger

NEW YORK, Wednesday.—Dr. H. Evatt, Australian Minister for External Affairs, who was recently in London said in a broadcast tonight:—

"It is a dangerous doctrine for Americans to interpret the Battle of Midway as deciding the war against the Japanese.

"Japan is still in full enjoyment of its new empire and is making itself stronger every day. There is grave danger in trying to hold the Japanese at bay while we turn our attention elsewhere. The Japanese cannot be held at bay."—A.P.

Neutral hide-out?

STOCKHOLM, Wednesday. — Unconfirmed rumours say that Hitler has bought an estate at Sigtuna, summer resort 20 miles north of Stockholm.—Reuter.

Bostons attack Lannion again

Bostons, escorted by Spitfires, bombed dispersal huts and runways of the German airfield at Lannion, in Brittany, yesterday. This airfield was twice heavily attacked last Friday.

In mid-Channel 10 FW 190s dived on the bombers. Two FWs were shot down; others were badly damaged.

One Boston is missing, the first British daylight bomber to be lost in six weeks. In the morning Spitfires destroyed an enemy fighter and just before dark a fighter shot down an enemy bomber off the south-west coast.

THE PREMIER

Broadcast on Sunday?

Mr. Churchill is considering broadcasting to the world on Sunday, United Nations' Day, writes Guy Eden.

Duke of Gloucester

NEW DELHI, Wednesday.—The Duke of Gloucester arrived at Karachi, India, today, from the Middle East.—Reuter.

U.S. Fleet here

AND THE KING GOES ABOARD

AMERICAN warships, some of them big ships, are here.

They arrived in secret some time ago. Now they are serving with the Home Fleet.

They were met far out in the Atlantic by the British cruiser Edinburgh.

This historic duty was one of the Edinburgh's last tasks before she was sunk while protecting a convoy to Russia.

When the ships met Rear-Admiral S. S. Bonham Carter sent a signal to the U.S. admiral, Rear-Admiral Giffen, saying, "I have been sent here by the commander-in-chief to welcome you and to say how much he is looking forward to having you working with us."

Rear-Admiral Giffen replied:—"Thank you. We are happy to report for duty. Please set course for harbour."

Admiral Giffen said later that every member of the United States force was looking forward to "having a crack" at the Germans.

POWERFUL FORCE

Further details about the presence of U.S. warships were given last night in accounts of the King's visit to the Home Fleet in northern waters.

It was stated that the King went aboard an American *battleship* and a *cruiser*.

A war correspondent who was present reported:—

"Together with destroyers and other ships, the U.S. warships make up a powerful squadron—'task force,' in the American phrase—and the officers and men of the Home Fleet are delighted at their presence in the battle line."

U.S. sailors eat cafeteria style, and the King was interested in the way dinners are collected by the men on specially shaped metal trays. Soup, roast pork, apple sauce, vegetables and ice-cream were the menu for the day.

When the King returned to the British Fleet flagship, he sent a signal to Admiral Giffen saying:—

"I congratulate you and all those under your command upon the alert and cheerful spirit with which you are undertaking your duties in the common cause. . . . My best wishes for a safe return to your homes when victory is won."

Admiral Giffen replied and said afterwards:—

"The King talked to me as one sailor to another. He liked our ships, he liked the cut of our jibs, and he liked the way they are kept shipshape."

At the end of his visit the King honoured the Merchant Navy by sailing through the fleet in a merchant auxiliary vessel and reviewing the lines of warships from the bridge of a small steamer built for coastwise trade in Australia.

The King, with Admiral Harold R. Stark, inspects the crew of a U.S. battleship in British waters. Admiral Stark commands U.S. Naval Forces in European Waters.

Both the Verduns face final zero hour as Germans step up pressure and fling in waves of troops

HAKEIM: Fate in the balance

Seventh onslaught as Rommel orders 'wipe out all Frenchmen'

Express War Reporter ALARIC JACOB

CAIRO, Wednesday night.

GERMAN and Italian pressure on Bir Hakeim was even more intense today—the 14th of the battle—and tonight a seventh major Axis attack has been repulsed.

Thanks to German stiffening and support, the Italians might have had some justification today for making a sixth demand for the surrender of the Free French garrison, who, however, are fighting on magnificently against tremendous odds.

The five previous junkets with a white flag were, of course, mere Fascist braggadocio.

PITTED PLATEAU

The four square miles of desert plateau are now pitted with Stuka bomb craters like a Gruyere cheese.

Twisted, burned-out tanks dot the horizon. The air reeks of powder and petrol.

Today Bir Hakeim trembled in the balance.

More German tanks were brought down from the north to strengthen the already sinister accumulation of Axis armour ranged against the stronghold.

Against these squadrons of the R.A.F. hurled themselves with reckless bravery. A bloody battle raged all day long yesterday.

The fighting French showed their spirit by counter-attacking to the north after sustaining hours of dive-bombing and artillery pounding.

BEATEN BACK

They beat the enemy back from a threatening position they had occupied in that quarter.

At the same time, British tanks caught a body of Axis tanks and armoured vehicles in the act of concentrating and got in among them with killing effect.

British flying columns also fell on Axis supply convoys approaching Bir Hakeim from the west.

The enemy is believed to be regrouping great new forces for another attack on an even larger scale.

From statements made by prisoners it is known that stern orders were given to all ranks

BACK PAGE, COL. THREE

TOBRUK · GAZALA · Acroma · TAMAR · KNIGHTSBRIDGE · HARMAT · BIR HAKEIM · BRITISH AID FREE FRENCH · MILES 10

SEBASTOPOL is now in danger

500,000 Germans menace it

Express Staff Reporter E. D. MASTERMAN

STOCKHOLM, Wednesday.

SEBASTOPOL, "Verdun" of the Crimea, is in danger. Five hundred thousand Germans stand 15 miles from the besieged city; Stukas raid it incessantly, pouring explosives on every square mile.

The Germans outnumber the Sebastopol garrison by two to one. They have a greater weight of metal to throw into the fight.

The Russians, with few airfields in the area, cannot successfully interfere with German troop concentrations, which are well protected by fighter "umbrellas."

The Soviet midnight communiqué says no more of the situation than "In the Sebastopol sector fighting continued. Our troops repulsed enemy attacks and inflicted heavy losses."

But Russia admits the city's situation is becoming graver.

"The pressure is unrelenting," says Red Star, newspaper of the Soviet Army, "the enemy is advancing over the thousands of dead at the city's approaches."

The Germans claim to be using 2,000 planes on this narrow front—10 miles deep, 15 to 20 miles wide—in an effort to blast the belt of fortifications.

Tonight the German High Command announced: "All day long Soviet troops made counter-attacks, all of which failed. After extremely violent fighting German troops took more fortified positions."

Moscow radio emphatically denied tonight that any part of Sebastopol's defence ring had been broken.

Von Manstein's men are being killed at the rate of 2,500 a day, and the Germans, who used to claim advances in miles, now say they have to fight bloody hand-to-hand engagements to gain yards.

In one sector alone two entire German regiments were wiped out

BACK PAGE, COL. EIGHT

3 A.M. LATEST

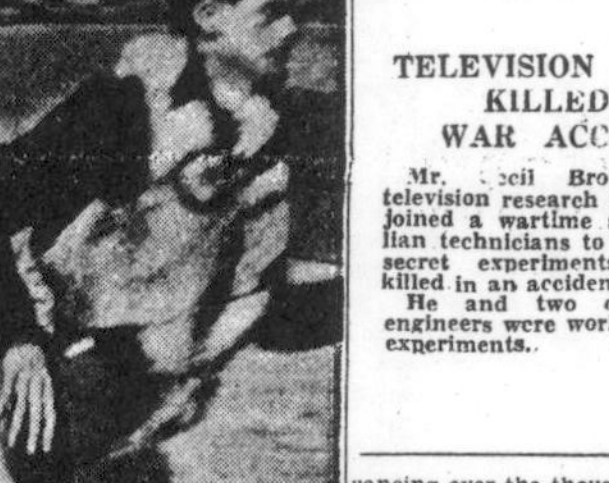

TELEVISION EXPERT KILLED IN WAR ACCIDENT

Mr. Cecil Browne, former television research engineer, who joined a wartime group of civilian technicians to do important secret experiments, has been killed in an accident—"on duty."

He and two other H.M.V. engineers were working on secret experiments.

LIDICE

Germans wipe it out

BUT ITS NAME LIVETH

Express Radio Station

HITLER'S No. 1 purge expert, General Kurt Daluege, who yesterday officially took over Heydrich's job as "Protector" of the Czechs, last night executed the entire male population of the village of Lidice.

Czech radio, announcing 31 more executions in Prague itself, broadcast the official German statement:—

"In the course of the search for the murderers of the S.S. Leader Heydrich it has been definitely proved that the inhabitants of the village of Lidice, near Kladno, in the Czech coal-mining district, have offered assistance and help to the perpetrators of the crime.

'ILLEGAL RADIO'

"Their hostility against the state has, furthermore, been established by the fact that pamphlets hostile to the state, as well as arms, and an illegal radio set, have been found

"Since, therefore, the inhabitants by their activities and the assistance rendered to the murderers have proved their hostility, all male adults of the village have been shot, and the female inhabitants have been taken to a concentration camp.

"The children have been sent to a more appropriate institution.

"All the buildings of the village have been razed to the ground and the name of the place has been abolished."

MORLEY RICHARDS weighs up chances

TWO ARMIES ARE POISED FOR BATTLE

Ritchie 'not inferior' in tanks

MORE than 100 German tanks have been sighted in battle formation during the last 24 hours in the neighbourhood of the Cauldron.

This is apart from the force used in almost ceaseless attacks on Bir Hakeim.

General Rommel, it is known, has brought up most of his panzer strength to the gap in the British minefields. It may be assumed that his total armour available for a new drive to Tobruk is up to 200 tanks.

If he could reduce Bir Hakeim and thus clear his right flank he has therefore enough strength to make a dangerous advance which might conceivably force General Ritchie to a decision to retire towards the Egyptian frontier.

To do that everything would have to go wrong for the Eighth Army.

Best position

Our tank strength cannot, of course, be stated. But there are grounds for believing that it is not inferior to the enemy's.

Tactically we are holding the best ground to meet any new thrust Rommel may try.

Signs are that, though Rommel is getting supplies through Benghazi, his tank strength has not been reinforced. It is possible that Hitler has no more to spare for him with his Russian commitments.

Battlefield this morning:—Both tank forces are poised for battle west of Knightsbridge. Rommel's renewed attacks on Bir Hakeim have not succeeded in drawing off enough armoured strength from this area to put us in inferiority.

Anticipation:—Rommel appears to have committed himself to assault on Bir Hakeim till he does get it. He has brought up 210mm. (8 in.) cannon to shell the fortress at long range.

If Koenig can hold out it may be Ritchie's chance to launch a new attack into the Gap.

Sober prospect, however, must be that Bir Hakeim may be overrun.

Berlin gets the jitters

From LAURENCE WILKINSON

LISBON, Wednesday.

BERLINERS are nightly awaiting a raid by 1,000 British bombers, as they believe their city to be an inevitable target in the near future.

A neutral just out of Berlin said to me today: "When I left it could be seen that official efforts to minimise the recent heavy raids on other German towns had failed.

"Anxiety in Berlin is heightened by a belief that the capital is being 'saved up' for a bigger raid than any yet seen, some night when flying conditions are perfect.

"Some people think that a huge raid on Berlin will open Anglo-American co-operation in bombing Germany."

Assassination plot discovered in Rome

FRENCH FRONTIER, Wednesday.—A plot to bomb the Fascist leaders meeting at the Piazza Venezia was discovered by Italian secret police.

The Fascists met to celebrate the second anniversary of Italy's entry into the war.—Reuter.

British double plane output

40,000 BIG GUNS A YEAR

WASHINGTON, Wednesday.

BRITAIN'S works manager, Mr. Oliver Lyttelton, submitted an interim report tonight to his partners in the war firm of Britain-America, Inc.

In a broadcast to the United States, Mr. Lyttelton, who is visiting Washington as Minister of Production, said:—

It is the most natural thing in the world for you in the United States to look us, the British, in the eye and ask: "What have you thrown into the battle? How much can you produce? What is the news from your battle front? What are you fighting for?"

These are some of the questions I hear, and I am going to answer them.

Britain's life depends on shipping. Until the shipbuilding of the United States can relieve the strain the British mercantile marine must remain the principal link which binds the United Nations together.

22,000,000

Britain's life depends on man-power. Out of a population of 33,000,000 between 14 and '65, 22,000,000 are working full time in industry, the armed forces or civil defence.

This is equivalent to the mobilisation of about 60,000,000 people in the United States.

Britain's life depends on woman-power. We have mustered five and a half million women in industry, and of this number one and a half million did not work in peace-time.

They work up to 55 hours a week, and do jobs which two years ago would have been described as impossible.

Britain's life depends on boys and girls. We have had to reach down into schools and playing fields and shift them to farms and factories. Today 77½ per cent. of the boys and 67½ per cent. of the girls between 14 and 17 are on war work.

Britain's life depends on self denial When John Bull wakes up in the morning he finds that the Minister of Labour has called him up for work in factories, if he isn't fit for military duties.

Food, too

The Minister of Food has taken all variety and spice and most of the volume of his breakfast, lunch and dinner.

The President of the Board of Trade has given him so much and no more clothing. His wife is working in a factory, and the Treasury is taxing him to the hilt.

Much more than 50 per cent. of the ships that used to bring food to us have been diverted to supplying Allied armies.

We are producing tanks, jeeps and other mechanical vehicles at the rate of 257,000 a year.

We are producing 40,000 big guns a year and supplying them with 25,000,000 rounds of ammunition.

We have increased aircraft production 100 per cent. above the last quarter of 1940, and merchant ships by 57 per cent.

There is no "Business as usual" There is no "Profit as usual."

We have thrown everything we have into this war and we will never quit.—Reuter.

MAN IN A BIG HURRY

What's the hurry? —See Page Three

Suner to see Ciano

BERLIN, Wednesday. — Spain's Foreign Minister, Senor Suner, left for Italy today to be a personal guest of Count Ciano, Italian Foreign Minister.—Reuter.

British, air-laid mines stop ships

STOCKHOLM, Wednesday. — British mines dropped in the narrow entrance to the Baltic by planes last night stopped ferries and vital German steamer routes today.—Reuter.

We take two more Madagascar towns

Small British columns have reached Vohemar, a port 105 miles south-east of Diego Suarez, and Ambilobe, 60 miles south of the same town.—*Vichy Despatch to the German News Agency.*

KEYNES A BARON, KORDA A KNIGHT

Birthday Honours: Page Three

Tanks fight 'hull-down':

Moorehead cable on Page 4

Demand Churchill Shakeup

Read the New York Journal-American for complete, accurate war coverage. It is the only New York evening newspaper possessing the three great wire services—ASSOCIATED PRESS, INTERNATIONAL NEWS SERVICE, UNITED PRESS.

Journal NEW YORK American
AN AMERICAN PAPER FOR THE AMERICAN PEOPLE

In Two Sections—Section One

No. 19,902—DAILY WEDNESDAY, JUNE 24, 1942 DAILY 3 Cents | SATURDAY 5 Cents | SUNDAY 10 Cents

LATEST NEWS

400,000 NAZIS ATTACK

Red Armies Driven Back At Kharkov, Sevastopol

MOSCOW, June 24 (INS).—The Nazi drive on the Kharkov front developed into a major offensive today as German Field Marshal Fedor von Bock thre win 400,000 men in a supreme effort to gain control of a portion of the vital Kharkov-Rostov railway.

Von Bock's immediate objective appeared to be seizure of a vital stretch of the rail line near Kupyansk, 65 miles southeast of Kharkov, industrial capital of the UKraine.

The situation of Sevastopol grew more serious by the hour.

[The United Press reported German assaults, ever mounting in fury, forced Russian withdrawals on both the Sevastopol and Kharkov fronts today.]

The entire front surrounding the beleaguered Black Sea naval base raged with intense fighting as German siege forces intensified their attacks.

OMINOUS NOTE.

As the Germans tightened their ring of steel around Sevastopol Russian fighters fell back to the inner defenses on the southern sector of the fortress where they were prepared to make a final stand.

The newspaper Red Star, organ of the Soviet Army, sounded an ominous note when it said that "nearly all" of the Nazi attacks on Sevastopol had been repulsed.

Subsequent dispatches said the Nazis, hurling in fresh reserves of tank forces had pushed back the defenders from two directions.

In some places, it was reported, the Germans broke through the Soviet forward positions, but were unable to penetrate deeply into Savastopol's defenses.

GAINS AT KHARKOV.

Nazi armies continued to gain some headway on the Kharkov front in the Ukraine.

[A Vichy radio broadcast heard by the Exchange Telegraph Co. in London reported Russian forces attempted to land troops on the coast of the Sea of Azov near Mariupol, in the southern Ukraine, but that German shore batteries drove them off. This attempt apparently was made to relieve pressure of the Nazi drive to the north.]

The noon communique of the

Continued on Page 2, Column 6.

319 Sinkings Axis Sub Toll Since January

Disclosure that Axis submarine attacks had blasted 15 more United Nations ships to the bottom today swelled to at least 319 the toll of vessels taken in waters of the Western Hemisphere since the middle of January.

In the darkest dispatch since the U-boats launched their ruthless assault against Allied shipping, the Navy Department revealed that 13 vessels had been sunk in the Caribbean in the 12-day period between June 3 and 14.

In addition, two more ships were torpedoed off the Atlantic coast, one of them with the heaviest loss of life in American coastal waters since the United States entered the war.

Casualties ran high, with 48 known dead and 87 missing in the Caribbean sinkings three dead and 85 missing in the June 15 sinking of a medium-sized U. S. merchant vessel off the New England coast; and five dead in the torpedoeing of a British freighter on the same day.

BELIEF IN NAVY.

In the wake of the Navy's announcement, high-ranking naval spokesmen assured the Senate Naval Affairs Committee that the anti-submarine campaign is being rapidly expanded.

The Caribbean victims were five U. S. ships, two medium-sized and three small; five British merchantmen, four medium and one small; and one Honduran, one Norwegian and one Dutch vessel, all small.

Tales of suffering and heroism

Continued on Page 2, Column 3.

U. S. Troops Rush Defense Work Of Australia

MELBOURNE, June 24 (UP).—At least 100 military airdromes have been built in Australia, thousands of miles of strategic roads have been built or improved and 11,500 separate projects are now under way. These are part of a gigantic program of construction by the Allied Works Council and the United States Army Engineer Corps.

Negro troops of the Engineer Corps have proved stars in an urgent task which requires mastery of doing much with little. One giant airdrome, costing nearly $10,000,000, was built in 71 days.

Brig. Gen. Hugh Casey of the Engineer Corps revealed the vast program today.

Gen. Casey said the work was well in hand despite shortage of labor, plants and machinery.

Lists Leaders In Congress 'Purge Plot'

By GEORGE R, BROWN,
Special to the New York Journal-American.

WASHINGTON, June 24.—The Dies Committee, in a lengthy special report to the House, today charged that the attempted purge of Congress, launched by the Union for Democratic Action, is part of a movement by a radical group, using the war emergency to advance its plans for a social revolution within the United States.

The report, released by Rep. Joe Starnes (D.-Ala.), acting chairman of the special House Committee on Un-American Activities, further alleges that many of the principal leaders of the union are Communists, or are or have been active in the Communist Party or in Communist-Front organizations.

The names of 50 of these leaders, with their radical records, are given in the report. Twenty-seven of the 50, the report said, "were national officers of the American League Against War and Fascism (later the American League for Peace and Democracy), or wrote for the league's magazine 'fight.'

Continued on Page 18, Column 5.

Incendiary Balloons Loosed in Hungary

ANKARA, June 24 (UP). — Newspapers arriving from Budapest revealed today that hundreds of balloons, carrying chemical incendiary bombs which ignite on contact, have been loosed over Hungary. Belief was expressed the bombs were intended to set fire to crops in addition to causing other damage.

Capital Draft Airing Looms

By WILLIAM S. NEAL,
International News Service Staff Correspondent

WASHINGTON, June 24.—A public investigation of deferment of young Government employes loomed today as the Tydings committee studying government fiscal affairs compiled evidence of draft evasion.

The committee's survey has disclosed over 6,000 deferments of Government workers and has revealed apparent cliques in some agencies to assure that employes can fight the war in Washington.

The inquiry shows:

Deferments made in many instances by draft boards outside of Washington of employes who have taken Government jobs since they registered. Letters to local draft boards are frequently exaggerated in importance because a high official probably has signed them without looking at them.

CONCERT EFFORT CITED.

More than one-fourth of the employes of one unit, many of them small salaried workers with little experience, were deferred on the ground that their services were essential. Investigators regard this as a concerted effort to avoid the draft.

While heads of many agencies refuse to request occupational deferment, if the draftee does so they will back him up.

(Other details on Page 7.)

Bullitt Aide to Knox

WASHINGTON, June 24 (UP). —William C. Bullitt, first United States Ambassador to Soviet Russia and later Ambassador to France, undertook unspecified duties today as special assistant to Secretary of Navy Knox.

Ask Churchill Shakeup in Commons

BULLETIN

LONDON, June 24 (UP). — A motion was introduced in the House of Commons today charging the Government with direct responsibility for the "disaster of Tobruk."

Laid down by W. J. Brown, Independent, and Alec S. Cunningham-Reid, conservative, the motion urged complete reorganization of Prime Minister Churchill's government.

It cited the Prime Minister's own policy, in defending his cabinet ministers from attack, that the Government as a whole is responsible for prosecution of the war, as justification for putting the blame for the Libya defeat on the cabinet.

Political quarters reported that cabinet leaders, alarmed over the storm which Churchill must face when he returns from his visit with President Roosevelt, had telephoned him warning him of the temper of the House of Commons.

Today's motion followed one which declared the House had no confidence in the central direction of war strategy.

So serious was the political situation that Labor members of Parliament held a secret session this morning to discuss it.

Deputy Prime Minister Clement Attlee, leader of the party, made a short statement amplifying his Commons speech yesterday and emphasizing that the full facts on Libya were not yet know.

It was decided to continue the discussion tomorrow.

British in Battle With Axis Army on Egypt Border

By GEORGE LAIT
International News Service Staff Correspondent.

CAIRO, June 24.—Engagements with Axis mechanized forces west of Solum, on the Libyan-Egyptian frontier, were reported today by the British Middle East High Command, as Imperial units and German and Italian forces assembled along the border in preparation for the forthcoming battle for Egypt.

British mobile columns carried out considerable activity west of the main positions held by the Eighth Army, to observe movements of Axis forces and conduct harassing tactics against the advancing Germans and Italians.

The Axis forces were observed by British patrols to be engaged in large-scale movements south of Gambut, midway between fallen Tobr uaknd the Egyptian frontier.

NAZIS REPORT FIGHTING.

(The official German news agency DNB reported that fighting between British and Axis forces was developing along the Egyptian frontier.)

"Our mobile columns were active to the west of our positions throughout yesterday," a communique of the British High Command said.

"Much enemy movement was observed southward from Gambut.

"Small parties of the enemy were engaged by our forces on the northern section of the front, westward from Solum, throughout the day."

ROMMEL MOVES EAST.

While British Lieut. Gen. Neil Methuen Ritchie was receiving land and air reinforcements for his Imperial Eighth Army, forced at the point of exhaustion to retire from Lobya. German Field Marshal Erwin Rommel moved strong mechanized columns eastward from Tobruk.

Rommel appeared to be massing his main forces opposite Fort Capuzzo, just inside Libya across the Egyptian border.

(Full page of pictures and map in Pictorial Review.)

Man Shot, Wife Claims Accident

Mrs. Anna Harrington, who is only 20 but has four children, found a revolver in the incinerator of her apartment house at 1155 Evergreen ave., The Bronx.

Today her husband, Alman, was in Lincoln Hospital with a bullet wound in his spine while Mrs. Harrington hysterically explained that the gun went off accidentally.

She said her husband insisted the revolver be turned over to police but that she demurred they might get into trouble. During the argument the gun went off.

Protest Tax Bill's Postwar Refunds

WASHINGTON, June 24 (AP).—The House Ways and Means Committee put minor finishing touches on its $6,640,100,000 tax bill today as protests piled up against its decision to grant certain corporations postwar refunds and to impose a 5 per cent tax on transportation of freight and express.

Members said they should take the final votes on the record-breaking bill by nightfall. Debate on the floor probably will begin about July 6.

The postwar credit was inserted late yesterday by a vote reported to have been 11 to 10. Several members were prepared to fight it on the theory it would nullify the committee's decision to boost corporate excess profits taxes to a flat 94 per cent.

The refund contemplates issuance of bonds to corporations, after they pay their excess profits taxes, which would be redeemable after the war in three installments.

Submarine Launched In Night Ceremony

PORTSMOUTH, N. H., June 24 (AP).—The submarine U. S. S. Sawfish cut dark water last night in the first night launching of World War II at the Navy Yard here.

Film Comedian Gets Year for Non-Support

BEVERLY HILLS, June 23 (AP). — Wally Vernon, screen, stage and night club comedian, surrendered today on a charge of non - support and was sentenced to a year in the county road camp.

70,000 'X' Names To Tax 3 Voices

WANTED: Three lusty-voiced volunteers to read the names of 70,000 New Yorkers who obtained X cards for gasoline.

APPLY: State Office of Price Administration, 535 Fifth ave., where the names will be read to newspapermen in acordance with the decision to disclose those who applied for unlimited amounts of fuel.

The names will be read all day today, with each of the trio of civilian defense volunteers intoning in turn for 20-minute periods each.

The names are being read instead of published to save the expense of printing lists.

THE WEATHER

Moderately warm.

Sun rises, 5:25 a. m.; sun sets, 8:31 p. m. High tide Governors Island, 4:40 a. m.; 5:36 p. m.

HOURLY TEMPERATURES

Midnight	67	5 A. M.	60
1 A. M.	65	6 A. M.	61
2 A. M.	64	7 A. M.	62
3 A. M.	63	8 A. M.	64
4 A. M.	61		

(Complete Weather Report on Page 19)

TODAY'S INDEX

The New York Journal-American has the largest circulation of any evening newspaper in America.

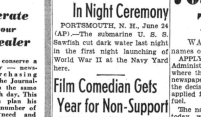

Three Pages of Pictures and Text

What Doolittle Hit—And What He Saw!

Next Sunday in the JOURNAL-AMERICAN

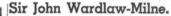

Read the New York Journal-American for complete, accurate war coverage. It is the only New York evening newspaper possessing the three great wire services—ASSOCIATED PRESS, INTERNATIONAL NEWS SERVICE, UNITED PRESS.

NEW YORK Journal-American

AN AMERICAN PAPER FOR THE AMERICAN PEOPLE

In Two Sections—Section One

No. 19,910—DAILY | THURSDAY, JULY 2, 1942 | DAILY 3 Cents | SATURDAY 5 Cents | SUNDAY 10 Cents

7TH SPORTS WALL ST. SPECIAL

Churchill Warns Empire IN 'MORTAL PERIL'

Defeats Ouster, 475 to 25

Army Board To Try Eight Saboteurs

BULLETIN

WASHINGTON, July 2 (INS).—President Roosevelt today created a military commission to try the eight Nazi saboteurs recently apprehended by the FBI after they were landed in the U. S. by Nazi submarines.

The commission will begin proceedings in Washington on July 8.

The President's order specifically denies the right of civil trial to any of the eight men landed on American shores by the submarines for the avowed purpose of sabotaging vital defense industries and communication facilities.

By SYD BOEHM.

Information obtained from eight captured Nazi saboteurs today sent G-men on a widespread series of raids designed to smash sabotage plans of the German-American Bund.

The raids were concentrated on the homes of Bundists in metropolitan New York and the vital war plant areas of Pittsburgh, Altoona, Pa. and Philadelphia.

Working on a time schedule, the Federal agents arrested suspects in and around New York, while other agents raided 225 homes in the Pennsylvania areas.

THE HORSESHOE CURVE.

The Altoona and Pittsburgh arrests, FBI officials revealed were designed to smash a plot to destroy the famous Horseshoe Curve on the Pennsylvania Railroad near Gallitzin, not far from Altoona.

Destruction of the Horseshoe Curve was one of the primary aims of the saboteurs, who had brought with them from the U-boat enough explosives to accomplish all their assignments of destruction.

Wrecking the Horseshoe Curve would have seriously hampered the national war effort, according

Continued on Page 5, Column 3.

Furious Battle Raging in City Of Sevastopol

MOSCOW, July 2 (AP). — The Red Army reported at noon today that bitter fighting was continuing in the Sevastopol area and dispatches telegraphed yesterday to the Army newspaper Red Star said German assault troops had carried the battle into the city itself.

Red Star's accounts pictured heavily superior numbers of Nazi forces rolling slowly forward against staunch defenders of the Crimean base.

While fighting was carried into the ruined city, the Russians were believed still to hold strong positions on rocky Cape Fiolent, to the south, between Sevastopol and Balaklava.

[The Germans have announced capture of Sevastopol and Balaklava but have acknowledged that fighting still is in progress on the Chersonese peninsula, of which Cape Fiolent is a part.]

Even without Sevastopol, the Red Navy's Black Sea fleet, including the modern cruisers Red Crimea and Red Caucasus, could find bases at a number of good ports on the Caucasian coast, including Novorossisk, Tuapse, Sukhum anad Batum.

7,000 NAZIS SLAIN.

On the Kursk front, 50 miles to the North, the Red Army amassed a toll of about 7,000 German dead in repulsing attacks over a 49-hour period, the Soviet Government reported.

A guerrilla detachment in the region of German-occupied Orel was declared to have slain nearly 1,000 invaders in two months.

The situation at Sevastopol was described as "extremely tense and difficult."

With hand-to-hand fighting going on and the Germans numerically 10 to 15 times superior, at some points Red Army troops and Black Sea Fleet sailors were reported to be refusing to surrender.

Germany 'Hears' Wasp 'Sunk'

BERLIN, July 2 (German Radio Recorded by UP)—A report received here "from the United States" today said the American aircraft carrier Wasp had been sunk.

It was the aircraft carrier Wasp that took planes to Malta.

This is the customary Axis technique for attempting to extract informaiton regarding the whereabouts of United Nations warships. Any official statement on such "reports" would be of great help to the Axis.

Private advices in New York said the Germans got their alleged Wasp report from Lisbon.

Lisbon quoted reports from Washington that the Wasp was "not sunk," and Germany took out the "not."

2 Big Oil Groups Blame Ickes for Rations, Famine

WASHINGTON, July 2 (INS).—Blame for gasoline rationing in the East and future heating oil shortages in homes throughout the country today was placed squarely on Secretary of the Interior Ickes by two petroleum producer groups.

Allan K. Swann, of Chicago, counsel for the Tri-State Petroleum Association, said an order issued by Ickes as Petroleum Co-Ordinator, so limited the drilling of wells that Illinois and Indiana fields could not meet production figures, also laid down by Ickes.

The second charge was made by an East Texas producer association in a letter to Sen. Pepper (D.-Fla.). Pepper has been advocating construction of a fleet of barges to carry oil and other cargo eastward to Philadelphia over improved inland waterways.

26,000 WELLS CURBED.

In the letter the association told Pepper that 26,000 East Texas wells were allowed to operate only 12 days in April and would be limited to 17 days in July.

Swann, testifying before a Senate Commerce Subcommittee investigating the barge plan, said:

"The fact is, the Department of the Interior does not want to release Illinois oil production. We have tried every means to get relief, and we can't get it.

"They want us to find new pools of oil before drilling new wells. All I can say is that you can't find pools unless you drill wells.

"Last year one independent contractor drilled 72 new wells in Indiana and Illinois, but this year has drilled only two."

He Buys War Stamps —But Tears Them Up

ST. JOSEPH, Mo., July 2 (AP).—Gregory Lagos, Grecian-born restaurant worker, walked into the post office, bought $50 of war stamps and tore them to bits.

"I want to give my $50 to the Government and it won't have to pay me back," he said. "I'll be back when I get some more saved up."

British Check Nazi Drive In Egypt

By GEORGE LAIT.
International News Service Staff Correspondent.

CAIRO, July 2.—The eastward drive through Egypt by Axis mechanized forces was halted today 70 miles west of Alexandria.

The British High Command announced, its forces based on El Alamein had smashed back heavy attacks by Italian and German units.

[Axis communiques claimed the capture of El Alamein yesterday.]

The Axis forces during the course of day-long battling yesterday, made a temporary break in the defense line of the British Eighth Army, but subsequently were driven back.

FIERCE BATTLE RAGES.

The British communique said fierce battles continued throughout yesterday, and that the results of the combat were "not unfavorable" to the defending forces.

Fighting raged all along the 35-mile front, extending from El Alamein, on the Mediterranean coast, southward to the salt marshes of the Qattara Depression.

Gen. Field Marshal Erwin Rommel sent his Axis legions smashing head-on into the defending British Eighth Army after an eastward sweep of 340 miles from fallen Tobruk in Libya in less than 11 days.

REVITALIZED BRITISH.

They were met by a determined and revitalized British Eighth Army, encouraged by a declaration of its commander, Gen. Sir Claude Auchinleck, that the battle of

Continued on Page 2, Column 4.

Auto Tax Delinquents Face Fine, Jail, or Both

Preparing to crack down with fines or jail sentences soon on motorists who failed to buy the $5 Federal auto tax stamp, police and Treasury agents today began handing out warnings as a prelude.

The stamps were required to be on cars by yesterday, and delinuents face a penalty of a $25 fine or 30 days in jail, or both. However, Treasury officials decided on the warning, and arrests will not be made until offenders have had a chance to buy the stamps.

Cuba Draft to Enroll Estimated 1,197,000

HAVANA, July 2 (INS).—Registration of Cuba's manpower for military service, which will begin Aug. 1, will enroll 1,197,000 from 18 to 50, it was estimated today. It was expected 574,000 would be available for active service.

By LEO V. DOLAN, International News Service Staff Correspondent.

LONDON, July 2.—Prime Minister Churchill won an overwhelming vote of confidence in the House of Commons today at a moment when he himself admitted the British Empire is in 'mortal peril.'

By the resounding tally of 475 votes to 25, the House threw out a motion of non-confidence in his conduct of the war, introduced by Sir John Wardlaw-Milne.

Thus Parliament and the nation once again entrusted their future to the Prime Minister, accepting his disheartening disclosure that 50,000 men have been lost in Libya, and his grave warning that instead of ending in 1942, as many wishful thinkers hope, the war will be a long one.

Declaring that the present situation is the most critical since the fall of France, Churchill told the House that "at any moment we may receive news of grave importance."

Says Egypt Battle Isn't Over

However, he asserted that the Battle of Egypt was not yet decided and declared that brilliant offensive activities by the United States Navy and Air Force had definitely swung the balance of power in the Pacific from Japan to the United Nations.

To the "blood, toil, sweat and tears," which were all he could promise at the outset of his regime, Churchill frankly admitted he had added "muddle and mismanagement."

He offered to take full responsibility and in heartfelt tribute to the "prodigious" war effort of the United States he held out hopes that better times will come.

The House celebrated Churchill's victory with one of those astonishing demonstrations characteristic of Britain's Parliament.

Wild Cheers for Churchill

For more than a week the House had been in a veritable lather of criticism and abuse—all of it, without exception, directed against the Prime Minister himself.

But when the tellers made known that he had so well survived the first non-confidence motion directed against him since he took office, there were thunderous cheers, a snowstorm of papers flying through the air and laughter and smiles.

Churchill's only promise of a turn for the better in Egypt was his calm observation that the battle now being waged by the British Eighth Army under Gen. Sir Claude J. E. Auchinleck "is not in any way decided."

Considerable reinforcements have reached and "are approaching" Auchinleck's forces, he said.

The main points of Churchill's long and frequently heavily pessimistic defense of his war stewardship follow:

1—At any moment, news of "grave importance" may come from Egypt.

2—Britain's hopes and prospects at the moment are blacker than at any time since the fall of France.

3—The night before Tobruk fell, Gen. Auchinleck advised London that the town was adequately garrisoned and supplied for a 90-day siege.

4—In the course of a single day,

Continued on Page 2, Column 2.

Prime Minister Winston Churchill, who in a grimly realistic speech before the House of Commons declared the British Empire is in "mortal peril."

TODAY *On All War Fronts*

BRITAIN—"British Empire in mortal peril; 50,000 men lost in Africa in two weeks," Churchill reveals, calling situation worst since the fall of France. Commons votes confidence in him, 475 to 25.

EGYPT—British army stops Axis forces in Egypt, smashing back heavy attacks at El Alamein, 70 miles from Alexandria.

RUSSIA—Battle at Sevastopol still rages, Moscow reports, saying enemy forces have penetrated into city.

PACIFIC—United Nations Air Force raids on six Jap bases in 2,500-mile arc north of Australia.

CHINA—Chinese bombers, escorted by AVG fighters, blast 110-mile stretch of Yangtze River at Hankow.

THE WEATHER

Warm; probably showers.

Sun rises, 5:28 a. m.; sun sets, 8:31 p. m. High tide Governors Island, 12:02 a. m., 12.42 p. m.

HOURLY TEMPERATURES

6 a. m.	69	10 a. m.	68
7 a. m.	69	11 a. m.	68
8 a. m.	69	12 Noon	67
9 a. m.	68	1 p. m.	65

Complete Weather Report on Page 16.

TODAY'S INDEX

NIGHT EDITION
★★★★★
MARKET PRICES
SCHOOL NEWS ON PAGE 21

The Sun

LATE NEWS
SCHOOLS — PICTURES

Moderate temperatures and less humid early this afternoon; early tonight scattered thundershowers.
Temperatures—Minimum, 72; Maximum, 72.
(Detailed weather report on page 22.)

VOL. 109—NO. 295. Entered as Second Class Matter Post Office, New York, N. Y. NEW YORK, MONDAY, AUGUST 17, 1942. THREE CENTS

CHURCHILL AND STALIN MEET

Farley to Warn Mead Forces Not to Risk Roosevelt Defeat

Will Call for Senator's Withdrawal at Convention Eve Meeting—Tammany Conclave Today Is Watched.

By GEORGE VAN SLYKE.

James A. Farley is preparing today to warn Senator Mead and his New Deal supporters that they must take the responsibility for defeat in the Democratic State Convention this week, which will reflect on President Roosevelt's party leadership, if they insist on going to a ballot on the nomination for Governor.

Such is the purpose of Mr. Farley and Attorney-General Bennett's backers as they made known today that they will demonstrate in the party conclave of State leaders tomorrow night, on the night before the convention meets in Brooklyn, that Mr. Bennett has an undisputed majority of the 1,014 delegates. They will urge Mr. Mead to withdraw after seeking to convince him that he cannot be nominated.

Delegates began arriving today for the convention and the State headquarters at the Biltmore Hotel took on the appearance of an old-time political assemblage.

There was a check and double check up and down the whole line, with the Mead leaders refusing to concede defeat and declaring that Mr. Farley's boast was a gesture showing weakness rather than strength.

Delegates and leaders in both camps are watching with deep interest and some concern the meeting this afternoon of the New York County Democratic Committee in Tammany Hall, which may supply the first real test of voting strength of the opposing forces.

Kennedy's First Test as Leader.

Michael J. Kennedy, the new Tammany chief, also is facing his first real test as county leader. He is one of Senator Mead's strongest backers with the banner delegation of 155. Five district leaders have deserted Mead and declared for Bennett. Three others are prepared to do so but are waiting the outcome of the session today. At least thirty Manhattan delegates are now counted in the Bennett column.

Mr. Kennedy is expected to call for a full and free expression of the views of the governing body in Tammany. The test will turn on a resolution to be offered by Mr. Kennedy pledging support to Mead and binding all delegates. The unit rule cannot be made to apply.

The Bennett backers will insist that they be released from the commitment taken some time ago by the executive committee pledging Tammany's delegation to Mead. If there is a substantial negative vote on the Kennedy resolution, it will split the Tammany delegation and may put Mr. Kennedy's leadership on the spot.

The bad breaks in the Mead forces in several quarters markedly advanced Mr. Bennett's position today.

Situation Reported to Roosevelt.

It is known that word was carried to the White House that Mr. Roosevelt can not hope to defeat Bennett and make good the purge of Mr. Farley. The President has been told he should ease Mead out some way. Some sensational development may come at any moment and would not surprise the politicians, whatever it may be.

Split in the labor ranks removed to a considerable extent the threat to Bennett from that quarter. The State American Federation of Labor bluntly re-

Continued on Page 3.

MAN-POWER BOARD MOVES TO ABOLISH HOARDING OF LABOR

Official Says That 35,000 Workers Are in Reserve in West Coast Plants.

Washington, Aug. 17 (A. P.).—A high-placed Government official said today that the War Manpower Commission would ask the War and Navy departments and the Maritime Commission to place inspectors in cost-plus war production plants to break what he called a growing practice of labor hoarding.

The official, who requested that his name not be used, disclosed that he had received an informal report, not yet checked by a detailed study, that 35,000 workmen could be taken out of West Coast airplane and shipbuilding plants without affecting the volume and quality of production.

Cost-plus plants were reported to be putting on their pay rolls thousands of workmen for whom they have no immediate, essential jobs, he said, and he explained that the plants were doing this to make certain they would have adequate workmen in the event that an increase in their operations created additional labor needs.

This hoarding was described as a serious interference to the rhythm of war production, with valuable workers held in virtual unproductivity in some plants while others were handicapped by actual shortages.

Hoarding could be stopped, he said, by putting inspectors in the plants to determine the number of unneeded workmen, whereup-

Continued on Page 11.

AMERICAN DECORATED

Sergeant Wins Medal After Shooting Down 5 Nazis.

London, Aug. 17 (A. P.).—Sergt. Claude Weaver, 20-year-old Royal Canadian Air Force pilot from Oklahoma City, was awarded the Distinguished Flying Medal today for shooting down five German fighters and assisting in the destruction of one bomber over Malta in a single week. Sergt. Weaver, who was born in Oklahoma City, was a student when he enlisted with the R. C. A. F. last year.

His citation said that he set a courageous and inspiring example.

In The Sun Today

STATE LABOR HEARS MEAD AND BENNETT

Rival Candidates Praise Workers in Address to Federation.

SENATOR MINIMIZES STRIKES

Attorney-General Cites Record He Has Made Enforcing Compensation Laws.

Rochester, N. Y., Aug. 17.—Speaking from the same platform to delegates of the seventy-ninth convention of the New York State Federation of Labor here, James M. Mead and John J. Bennett Jr., aspirants to the Democratic nomination for Governor, praised the effort organized labor was making in the war program and predicted defeat for the Axis.

"Labor," Mr. Bennett asserted, "is proving that democracy can survive any peril and its contribution to the war effort constitutes an incontrovertible repudiation of the canard that democratic government cannot operate in war time."

At the start of his first administration as Attorney-General, Mr. Bennett said, he had stated his labor credo, which included a living wage for workmen, but beyond this he wanted to obtain for the skilled and unskilled workmen of New York State a wage which would enable them not only to live, "but to secure those niceties and luxuries of life to which I believe every American is entitled."

Cites Labor Law Enforcement.

As examples of his record of labor law enforcement during the eleven years he has served as Attorney-General, Mr. Bennett said:

"Under the workmen's compensation law I have recovered for injured workers the sum of $2,594,419.46. Under the labor law I have recovered wage claims for unpaid workers the sum of $345,445.65. In fines and penalties for violation of the labor laws and workmen's compensation law, I have recovered $428,883.75 and convicted 91 per cent of those charged with violations of the labor law. In the same period of eleven years my office has recovered for victims of fraud in securities cases $13,094,521.09."

New York State, he continued, had benefited to the extent of $20,044,861.73, recovered after legal battles while the cost of maintaining the legal department had cost the taxpayers only $12,379,470.57.

When he took over the Attorney-General's office in 1931, Mr. Bennett said, the depression was deepening, and in an effort to halt the downward plunge the

Continued on Page 3.

FLYERS BAR JAP AID IN SOLOMONS; LONDON HEARS OF GREAT U. S. VICTORY

Sydney Correspondent Says Official Silence Is to Keep Enemy From Measuring Extent of His Worst Disaster.

Gen. MacArthur's Headquarters, Australia, Aug. 17 (A. P.).—Gen. Douglas MacArthur's airmen maintained ceaseless vigil over the waters northeast of Australia to prevent Japanese reinforcements from reaching the Solomon Islands as the battle for control of vital bases there entered its eleventh day today.

While United States Marines were believed to be extending beachheads already won in hard fighting in the Solomons, actual developments in that theater were hidden by official silence both here and in Washington.

[The Australian correspondent of the London Star said today that despite the caution of official announcements it seemed clear that the Allies had already won in land, sea and air operations in the Solomons the greatest victory yet achieved against the Japanese.]

No reference to the situation was contained in the daily communique from Gen. MacArthur's headquarters, which was devoted to a brief report of a new Allied bombing attack on Japanese-occupied Timor and to continued patrol skirmishes in the Kokoda area of southeastern New Guinea, sixty miles from the Allied base at Port Moresby. There was evidence, however, of quiet confidence in Australian circles, whose attitude was reflected by William H. Hughes, a member of the Pacific War Council, in a speech at Sydney yesterday in which he acclaimed the Solomon Islands offensive as "a revelation of the strength of our ally America."

"It has been shown," he said, "that, man for man, the Japanese are not equal to the United States Marines." The Japanese radio continued to broadcast sweeping claims of victory in the Solomons, which it failed to reconcile with the admission that "the battle is continuing between our forces and American Marines who have succeeded in landing."

Tokio Broadcasts Claims.

Relegating this fact to the background, a Tokio broadcast this morning made much of an imperial headquarters communique reporting that Japanese sub-

Continued on Page 2.

DOOLITTLE VISITS LONDON ON MISSION

General Won't Stay There Permanently, However.

London, Aug. 17 (A. P.).—The presence here of Brig.-Gen. James H. Doolittle, who led the United Army Air Force bombers in the attack on Japan last April 18, was disclosed for publication today. Gen. Doolittle, it was indicated authoritatively, will not be attached permanently to the American air command in the European theater.

This was his second special wartime mission to Britain. He came here in 1941, before the United States entered the war, as a member of a mission headed by Lieut.-Gen. George Brett, Gen. Douglas MacArthur's air chief in the southwestern Pacific.

Gen. Doolittle's arrival was a tightly guarded secret until after he had conferred with Major-Gen. Carl Spaatz, Commander in Chief of the United States Air Forces in the European theater, and his second in command, Brig.-Gen. Ira C. Eaker. He also made a three-day tour of American air bases in Britain.

He has been here ten days and is expected to return to the United States soon.

German Patrol Boat Sunk Off Dover

London, Aug. 17 (A. P.).—A light German patrol boat was sunk and three others were severely damaged in a spirited clash with British light coastal craft in Dover Strait last night, the Admiralty announced today.

British and German long-range guns also exchanged salvos across the English Channel and light naval guns were heard in Dover Strait half an hour before dawn. The firing during the night was sporadic.

The German High Command said that its heaviest coast artillery shelled "military targets in the area of Dover."

DUTCH FLAG AT HALF STAFF

Associated Press Photo.

An American soldier looks at the flag flying from the Netherlands embassy in Washington in honor of five Dutch hostages shot to death by a Nazi firing squad because a troop train was wrecked by others.

R. A. F. SQUADRONS ROAR OVER CHANNEL

Daylight Attack Is Begun—Raider Bombs England.

London, Aug. 17 (A. P.).—Fighters and bombers of the Royal Air Force, flying at such altitudes that they could not be seen through the haze, roared out over the Channel today, persumably to make another foray over the occupied coast.

On the south coast a lone-wolf German raider dropped a few bombs which caused some property damage and a few casualties.

Except for a few inconsequential German scattered blows, the channel air front was quiet in the hours before dawn today. Some enemy raiders stabbed inland as far as the north Midlands and bombs fell at one point on the east coast, but the British said that damage was slight and there were no casualties reported.

A moderate-sized Royal Air Force bomber force struck at western Germany on Saturday night and despite thick clouds, the Air Ministry said, some crews found their targets. The British listed five bombers as missing.

United States Army fighters flew with a Canadian squadron in one long sweep over France during the week end, but the operation was described as routine and a terse United States headquarters communique gave no details. Spitfires continued the aerial assault on occupied France yesterday with a tree-top run over a railroad, with Belgian pilots participating. A freight train was damaged.

A South Coast English Town, Aug. 17 (A. P.).—Property damage and some casualties were caused here today by a German raider which bombed the city in a hit-skip daylight attack.

NAVY SEEKS CLEW TO BLIMP MYSTERY

Searches for Men After the Craft Falls Into Street.

San Francisco, Aug. 17 (A. P.).—Two naval officers, missing when their crewless and broken blimp floated in from the ocean and descended on a street in suburban Daly City, were hunted at sea off the Golden Gate today.

The blimp had been on anti-submarine patrol. Two lifebelts were missing from the craft when it landed, but all of the parachutes and the rubber life raft were found in the gondola.

The blimp, torn and sagging in the middle, drifted in from the Pacific yesterday, five hours after it had taken off.

The craft floated along at tree top height and then left one of its depth charges on a golf course when it scraped the ground. Hundreds of persons followed it by automobile and street car until it settled to earth. It struck one house and two autos, but caused little damage.

The depth charges, one under the gondola and the other on the golf course, offered no hazard, inasmuch as it would explode only under water at considerable depth, naval men said.

CRETAN PATRIOTS SHOT

Mistook Nazi Parachute Test for British Invasion.

London, Aug. 17 (A. P.).—Greek patriots in Crete who mistook German parachute practice for a British invasion and tried to help by seizing Candia airdrome have paid with their lives, according to reports reaching the Greek Government in exile here today. Three hundred were said to have been arrested and an undisclosed number shot.

These reports said that fishermen's stories of large ship movements off Crete prompted rumors that a British invasion flotilla was approaching the island.

NAZI TROOP TRAIN REPORTED IN CRASH

Wreck at Dutch Station Called Serious.

London, Aug. 17 (A. P.).—Aneta, Netherlands news agency, quoted a Soviet information bureau report from Moscow today saying that a heavily laden German troop train collided with another train at a station near Groningen in the northern Netherlands, causing serious damage and suspending traffic.

Five prominent Netherlanders were executed by a Nazi firing squad Saturday as hostages after saboteurs whom the Germans blamed for a similar troop train wreck on August 7 were not captured.

The Germans previously had said the lives of 1,600 hostages would be taken if the saboteurs were not given up by their countrymen, and there was a possibility that other executions might follow the first five.

TEST PLANE FALLS IN FARMINGDALE

An experimental airplane on a test flight for the Grumman Aircraft Engineering Corporation made a forced landing on its belly about 10:30 A. M. today in a vacant field just off Main street, in Farmingdale, L. I., and burst into flames.

Witnesses of the crash dragged the injured pilot, Robert Hall, one of Grumman's veteran test pilots, from the burning wreckage and took him to the Meadowbrook Hospital. His condition is serious, doctors who gave him emergency treatment reported.

Fire apparatus of the village and of an aircraft plant a mile distant from the crash quickly responded to an alarm sent in by some one who saw the plane burst into flames and subdued the blaze.

Hall's home is on Bay avenue, Huntington, L. I.

Rains Cause Wide Damage

Heavy Showers Lash City on High Wind—Storm Lasts Twelve Hours.

Lightning struck seven buildings, cellars were flooded, automobiles stalled, small river craft capsized, and trees and advertising signs blown down in a series of rainstorms in the metropolitan area which continued until an early hour today

Police emergency squads were called out fifteen times in New York city to repair minor damage caused by the storm or to remove obstructions to traffic.

Rainfall thus far in August, including today's showers, totals 5.62 inches, the Weather Bureau reported. The normal total for the entire month is 4.33 inches.

The police continued a search today for the bodies of Patrick O'Grady, 40 years old, of 1249 Amsterdam avenue, and his children, John, 11, and Virginia, 9, who drowned in the Hudson River off Dyckman street when an outboard motor boat capsized.

J. A. Jaffee of 2535 Holland avenue, the Bronx, and a companion swam to Hart's Island when the Jaffee sloop overturned between Hart's Island and City Island.

Falls Into Furnace Room.

Miss Pauline Adelman, 39, of 1911 University avenue, the Bronx, fell into the furnace room of an apartment building at 325 Riverside Drive while seeking

Continued on Page 7.

Dave Boone Says:

I see where, at that public auction of furnishings and art belonging to a big estate, the ten tons of pea coal was knocked down for $5 a ton. Of course, it had to be moved out of the cellar and carted away, but it still looks to me like the bargain of the year.

But tapestries, rugs and old masters brought much bigger prices, so I guess that at these upper set auctions even a lump of coal ain't considered much good unless it's been in one family a long time and is signed by a Frenchman.

Maybe the experts looked the coal over and wouldn't okay it as authentic.

Say, that idea of using only three cylinders in a six-cylinder car to save gas is causing a lot of arguing. If it's true that I can run my jalopy with only half the cylinders working, then the service station has been gypping me all my life. Every time I took it in I had to pay a big bill because just one wasn't quite up to snuff.

Did you ever try to start a car on a cold morning with only three cylinders in commission? Before I swallow that idea, I want to see some fellow run a car up a hill on half an engine.

The reason gas ain't being saved is that the authorities who could stop fast driving in this country are only operating on half determination. You can drive by any cop in America in defiance of the gas conservation limits and he won't even look up.

HARRIMAN TOO ATTENDS TALKS ON WAR PLANS

British Prime Minister Is Revealed to Have Been Four Days in Moscow.

NAZIS SMASH ON IN SOUTH

Launch Powerful New Drive for Stalingrad and Push for Grozny Oil Fields.

Moscow, Aug. 17 (A. P.).—Prime Minister Churchill was in Moscow from August 12 to 15 with Premier Joseph Stalin, arrived at a number of decisions on the conduct of the war, and reaffirmed the alliance of their nations against the Axis, it was announced today.

W. Averell Harriman attended the conferences as President Roosevelt's personal representative.

A communique issued after Mr. Churchill had left Russia said that unspecified decisions had been arrived at and emphasized that an "atmosphere of cordiality and complete sincerity" prevailed.

The four days of dramatic negotiation, from Wednesday until Saturday, brought Mr. Churchill and Stalin together for the first time. Last winter the British Foreign Secretary, Anthony Eden, paid a visit to Russia and Foreign Commissar Vyacheslav Molotov repaid the visit in May, when he signed the Anglo-Russian alliance pact on May 26.

German Troops Smash Forward.

Meanwhile today the German offensive in the Great Bend of the Don flared to full force in a powerful new drive toward Stalingrad, while in the Caucasus the Russians fell back from the ruins of the Maikop oil fields toward their next petroleum producing area at Grozny.

An official communique reported a terrific toll of new Nazi manpower and material thrown into the assault southeast of Kletskaya and northeast of Kotelnikovski against the flanks of the fortified line guarding Stalingrad, and battlefront dispatches said that the Germans rolled forward at tremendous cost in the Kletskaya salient, seventy-five miles northwest of Stalingrad, but were held firmly at the Kotelnikovski flank, ninety-five miles southwest of that important strategic and industrial center of the Volga.

The Russian position at Voronezh, on the Don some 300 miles southeast of Moscow, took a turn for the worse as large German forces launched an attack and broke into a village on the west bank of the river. Street fighting was reported in progress there.

New and savage German attacks in another sector of the Voronezh front forced the Russians to evacuate a large wooded area, but the Russians regrouped and wrested the wood from the Germans in a counter-

Continued on Page 2.

Molotov Becomes Stalin's Vice-Premier

Moscow, Aug. 17 (A. P.).—Vyacheslav Molotov became Premier Stalin's chief aid for administration purposes today by appointment to the new position of First Vice-Chairman of the Council of People's Commissars, a post equivalent to that of Vice-Premier.

Molotov, who is Foreign Commissar, served as chairman of the Council until just before the war, when Stalin succeeded him. A dozen other Vice-Chairmen are already serving in special fields.

Acetylene Blast Rocks Eight-mile Area

Glasgow, Del., Aug. 17 (A. P.).—A parked truck trailer loaded with acetylene gas was blown to bits near here early today in a series of explosions that shattered windows and shook homes over an eight-mile radius.

The State police said that no one was injured. The trailer caught fire while moving. The driver tried to stop the blaze with extinguishers, the police said, then detached the truck and drove 100 yards away to await the explosions.

DAILY MIRROR, Thursday, August 20, 1942.

Daily Mirror

AUG. 20

No. 12,070 ONE PENNY

Registered at the G.P.O. as a Newspaper.

THEY ARE BACK

BIG HUN LOSSES IN 9-HR. DIEPPE BATTLE

AFTER the nine-hour battle around Dieppe yesterday, in the biggest Commando landing yet made on occupied territory, Canadian, American, British and French troops were last night returning to England.

The Allied forces re-embarked only six minutes late on scheduled time after fierce fighting in which they destroyed a radio-location station and flak battery, as well as a six-gun battery and ammunition dump.

Some indication of the size of the engagement may be gained from the Nazi report that 400 landing barges were used in one wave, and from the fact that about 300 planes—Nazi and British—were destroyed or damaged in the greatest air fighting since the Battle of Britain.

Heavy casualties on both sides were forecast in this communique issued by Combined Operations Headquarters last night:

"Despite the clear statement issued in our first communique at six o'clock this morning and broadcast to the French at 6.15 a.m. about the raid on Dieppe, German propaganda, unable to make other capital out of the turn the operation has taken, is claiming that the raid was an invasion attempt which they have frustrated.

"In point of fact the re-embarkation of the main forces engaged was begun six minutes after the time scheduled, and it has been completed nine hours after the initial landing as planned.

"Some tanks have been lost during the action ashore, and reports show that fighting has been very fierce, and that casualties are likely to have been heavy on both sides.

"Full reports will not be available until our forces are back in England.

"In addition to the destruction of the six-gun battery and an ammunition dump reported in our earlier communique, a radio-location station and flak battery were destroyed.

"Apart from the losses inflicted on the enemy, vital experience has been gained in the employment of substantial numbers of troops in an assault and in the transport and use of heavy equipment during combined operations.

"Our new tank-landing craft were in action today for the first time.

"There was intense activity by aircraft of all operational commands of the RAF in support of the landing of our troops against the heavy enemy defences, and air fighting on the most intense scale also developed. From reports so far received eighty-two enemy aircraft are known to have been destroyed, in addition to a number shot down by naval vessels.

"More than 100 enemy aircraft were also probably destroyed or damaged.

"Ninety-five of our aircraft of all commands are missing, but twenty-one fighter pilots are known to be safe, and it is thought that others will prove to have been rescued."

Throughout the operations this Union Jack fluttered from the cliffs of Dieppe.

It was planted there by one of the first parties of British troops to land. They took it out with them from England for this purpose, a gesture, but not only that. The flag was the beacon to guide the parties of raiders which followed to the landing stage, and to guide all the troops in their return to the waiting ships.

The men who planted it were not willing to leave it behind.

Amid the fire of Nazi guns and cannon they delayed their journey to the ships to pluck up the flag and bring it back to England.

When they landed back home last night they still had the flag, dirty and ragged, but it still blew when unfurled.

Nazi version

THIS was the German version of the raid issued last night in a special announcement from Hitler's headquarters:

"A large-scale landing made by British, U.S.A., Canadian and De Gaulle troops, about one division strong, in the early hours of today on the French Channel coast near Dieppe—under protection of strong naval and air forces and including tanks—was repelled by the German coastal defence troops with heavy losses to the enemy.

"300 to 400 Landing Barges in One Wave"

"The first wave of landing troops was transferred on the high seas from transports to 300-400 landing barges and reached the coast at 6.05 a.m., protected by thirteen-fifteen cruisers, destroyers and strong fighter formations.

"Behind them was a floating reserve of six transports and three freighters, and further to the north was a group of twenty-six transports as an operational reserve, probably the bulk of the landing forces.

"These were to go into action as soon as the first wave had established a bridgehead near Dieppe.

"But this did not take place. The enemy forces which had landed were wiped out everywhere in hand-to-hand fighting and forced back into the sea.

"So far twenty-eight tanks have been counted which had been landed and destroyed.

"More than 1,500 prisoners are in German hands, including sixty Canadian officers. The enemy's casualties are very high.

"Three destroyers, two torpedo-boats and two transports were sunk by artillery fire.

"The Luftwaffe shot down eighty-three enemy planes, sank two special troop transports and one motor-torpedo-boat, and damaged five cruisers or large destroyers and two transports.

German radio had earlier stated that several hundred British dead had been counted.

Marines Crush Jap Attack

16 Pages of Comics + 16 Page Color Magazine

WALL ST. SPECIAL

NEW YORK Journal-American

AN AMERICAN PAPER FOR THE AMERICAN PEOPLE

IN THREE SECTIONS—SECTION ONE

No. 19,960—DAILY | SATURDAY, AUGUST 22, 1942 | DAILY 3 Cents in City Limits, 4 cents Elsewhere | SATURDAY 5 Cents | SUNDAY 10 Cents

5¢

800,000 NAZIS MASSED AT STALINGRAD!

Jimmy Roosevelt In Thick of Fight At Solomon Base

MAJOR JAMES ROOSEVELT
Led Marines in Gilbert Raid.
Associated Press Photo.

Turns Down Desk Job 8 Days After Sneak Attack on Pearl Harbor for Active Duty

By HUGO SPECK,
International News Service Staff Correspondent.

WASHINGTON, Aug. 22.—"Jimmy" Roosevelt got to the fighting front in the Mid-Pacific as second in command of a hard-hitting bunch of Marines to raid little Makin Island because he chose that kind of a career for the duration instead of a swivel-chair job.

Eight days after the Japanese sneak attack on Pearl Harbor, the then Captain James Roosevelt, 37, eldest son of President and Mrs. Roosevelt, turned down an offer of promotion, if he would stay in Washington, and requested active duty, friends recalled today.

He got his wish—and earned his promotion the hard way, at the fighting front with the Marines, on the Pacific battle front.

PRESIDENT PROUD.

White House Secretary William D. Hassett today said President Roosevelt no doubt was proud, "as any father whose son is doing his part."

He added that it is doubtful if the President knew his son was in the action at Makin Island.

The promotion to rank of Major came May 20, and it was only a short time later, in June, that he took part in the Battle at Midway Island, when Marines and Army and Navy fliers turned back, with heavy losses, a huge Japanese invasion armada.

That wasn't "Jimmy's" baptism of fire, however. He experienced that in Iraq in May, 1941, while he was visiting the fighting fronts on a military mission. He and his party were machine-gunned by a Messerschmitt fighting plane as they rolled across the Iraq desert in an observation automobile.

The promotion to Major wasn't up to the highest rank the President's eldest son has held in the Marine Corps. In 1936, he was promoted to the rank of Lieutenant Colonel when he went to South America, as aide to his father, to attend a Pan-American conference. But when the war clouds broke over Europe three years later, he resigned that rank, and asked to be reappointed as a captain.

The rank of Lieutenant Colonel, he told friends, was too high for one of his "age and experience."

Smash Attack By Japs on Solomons

By RICHARD HALLER,
International News Service Staff Correspondent

PEARL HARBOR, Aug. 22.—A force of 700 Japanese who landed from speed boats in an attempt to dislodge American Marines from positions in the Solomon Islands was torn to shreds in hand-to-hand combat in which 670 of the enemy troops were slain and the remainder captured, it was disclosed today by Admiral Chester W. Nimitz.

The overwhelming defeat of the Jap counter-assault was announced by Admiral Nimitz in Communique No. 8 issued from his headquarters here as commander-in-chief of the U. S. Pacific Fleet shortly after he had reparted in Communique No. 7 destruction of a Jap base on Makin Island in the Gilbert group.

VANDERGRIFT LEADS.

Admiral Nimitz revealed for the first time that the marines in the Solomons were under command of Maj. Gen. Alexander A. Vandergrift of the U. S. Marine Corp

The task force assault on Makin Island, 1,100 miles northeast of the Solomons, was under command of

Continued on Page 2, Column 3.

Still Hot--If You Didn't Know

Our melting pot city will continue to stew in its own juice, the Weather Bureau announced today.

The forecast for this afternoon is warm and humid, with a few widely scattered thundershowers (surprise!. in the interior. Tonight (there must be a parrot in the house) will be warm and humid. There will be moderate winds, none of which will be discernible—in the subway.

At 10 a. m. the temperature was 76, four degrees above normal.

But who is?

Will Marry Norma For Love, Not Money

HOLLYWOOD, Aug. 22 (AP).—The Los Angeles Examiner said today a pre-nuptial financial agreement will be made by Norma Shearer and her ski instructor-fiance, Martin Arronge, which will give him no share in her community property. They will be marriel tomorrow.

"I love her," the story quoted the 28-year-old Arrouge as saying, **"and I don't want any of her money. I am marrying her for herself. I expect to go into the Army Air Force very soon."**

Own Story—Typical Life Of Criminal

[What makes a criminal? When does the urge to swindle, fleece and cheat show itself?

[The New York Journal-American, which in this series is revealing the trail of death left by gambling, today gives you a startling, X-ray picture of a typical criminal, to show you how he thinks, what makes him tick. The subject is the late, unlamented Isidore Juffe, king of Brooklyn swindlers, whose cry, "I paid plenty!" set off the John Harlan Amen investigation.

[Juffe left behind him an astonishing document, his own story of his life and how he bribed, fixed and cheated his way through a fantastic criminal career of 43 years.

[Here is this chronicle of crime, augmented by other data obtained by New York Journal-American investigators.]

By GEROLD FRANK.

There is nothing prepossessing about this Isidore Juffe. He is short, fat, with shrewd eyes in a fat face which never loses its yellow pallor. He has a pendant lower lip, a double chin. He looks like a dim-witted plug-ugly. But he's not.

He's Izzy Juffe, swindler par excellance, fur racketeer, unofficial referee of the underworld, a shifty, completely unscrupulous man in whom all the mean little tricks of the cheat rose to full flower. But he's telling his story . . .

"They tell me I was born March 15, 1890, in a little Polish village . . . you couldn't find it on the map today—Tarnopole, Galicia, in Lemburg. My father was a carpenter and do you know my first memory?

His Career in Crime Begins

"I steal 15 rubbles from him. I guess I was about eight. I had to steal. I wish to treat my friends in school, show them I am a big shot. I must have money.

"I took it from a small box in which my father keeps the money he gets from making shelves, fixing cabinets—whatever a carpenter in a little Polish village could do.

"But the money did the trick. The boys elected me their leader I got into a fight and I came home one day all black and blue, with blood over my clothes. My father took up a leather strap when he saw me, and set after me. 'You will fight like a peasant dog?' he shouted in a terrible voice. 'I will make a man out of you if it kills you!'

"Then he took me up into the hot little garret of our house—there was only one window, the size of your hand—

Continued on Page 4, Column 1.

Michel Fokine, 64, Dies; Ballet Artist

Michel Fokine, 64, famed Russian ballet choreographer who won his greatest fame with his creations for the Diaghileff ballet, died here early today.

At his bedside, in West Side Hospital, were his wife, Vera, and son, Vitale. Fokine succumbed to an attack of double pneumonia, incurred a week ago while returning from a Mexican tour.

One-time head of the Russian Imperial Ballet for the late Czar Nicholas, Fokine made his first trip to the United States to direct the dances for "Aphrodite," a spectacle staged by the late Morris Gest.

(For further details, see Obituary Page.)

ALP to Name Third Party Ticket Today

By SANFORD E. STANTON

Promising to name a candidate of "national stature" as a third entry in the Gubernatorial race this Fall, the American Labor Party today opened its State Convention at the Capitol Hotel.

Leaders kept the identity of their nominee a secret until the he was an 'up-State man" who last moment. But it was reported had been approved at least tacitly by persons high in the White House cortorie of New Dealers.

Unless there is a last-minute change of plans, the Laborite delegates will endorse the Democratic candidates, with the exception of Attorney General Bennett, who won the Gubernatorial nomination over the protests of President Roosevelt.

BENNETT REJECTED.

Rejection of Bennett was made final by the ALP State Committee last night although many conservatives questioned the wisdom of a third party move.

Democratic nomination of Bennett and the anticipated Republican nomination of Thomas E. Dewey at Saratoga next Tuesday "left the progressives of the State

Continued on Page 4, Column 7.

14 Danish Vessels Captured by British

LONDON, Aug. 22 (UP).— It was announced today that British warships and planes have captured 14 Danish vessels which disregarded a warning that ships of enemy-occupied countries, especially fishing vessels, must keep within coastal waters.

Soviets Crush Enemy Force At Don River

MOSCOW, Aug. 22 (UP).—Dispatches from the front today said the Germans have massed 58 divisions—possibly 800,000 men—on a 60-mile front at the Don river elbow in an attempt to crash through to Stalingrad.

The bloodiest fighting of the war was reported going on along the west bank of the Don and at points on the eastern shore where Nazi automatic riflemen managed to cross the stream.

Two parties of German storm troops, which reached the east bank, were said to have been destroyed.

The battle was raging throughout the entire Don elbow. It was admitted Nazi pressure slowly was forcing the Russian defenders back at some points.

In the Caucasus, front reports said, Nazi reinforcements are arriving to swell the already large German troop concentrations.

The Germans were pressing hard south of Krasnodar, reports said, despite constant counter-attacks by Soviet forces. In at least one sector the Russians were again forced to retreat.

However, Cossack troops were holding firmly at most points against Nazi tank assaults.

TANKS BEATEN OFF.

In one sector two German divisions and 40 tanks attempted to overwhelm the Soviet defense lines but were beaten off.

In the loop of the Don river, southeast of Kletskaya and 40 miles west of Stalingrad and the Volga river line, the Germans were doing their utmost to mop up the west bank and establish a foothold on the east bank, from which they could launch a final assault across the steppes.

The Germans already had forced the Don twice. The first crossing was wiped out; the second, more than 48 hours ago, was all but destroyed and its remnants driven back to the very edge of the east bank of the river.

FLANK IN PERIL.

The southern flank, northeast of Kotelnikovski, which is 90 miles southwest of Stalingrad, also was in peril. There the Germans had driven a wedge of tanks into Russian defenses.

Although last midnight's communique said there were only a few tanks, and they were being wiped out, front-line dispatches indicated the situation had not greatly improved.

On both flanks, German losses were heavy.

'In the Kletskaya area, Soviet units during the night inflicted a sudden blow to the enemy," the Soviet noon communique said. "After fierce hand-to-hand fighting, the enemy retreated and left on the battlefield 200 dead, two guns, eight machine guns, 13 trucks of war material and a radio transmitter.

THE WEATHER

Continued warm and humid with moderate winds.

Sun rises, 6:12 a. m.; sun sets, 7:45 p. m. High tide Governors Island, 5:26 a. m. and 6:04 p. m.

HOURLY TEMPERATURES

9 p. m.	82	2 a. m.	77
10 p. m.	81	3 a. m.	76
11 p. m.	80	4 a. m.	77
Midnight	79	5 a. m.	78
1 a. m.	78	6 a. m.	79

TODAY'S INDEX

Complete Weather Report on Page 14.

The New York Journal-American has the largest circulation of any evening newspaper in America.

ALLIED PRINTING TRADES UNION LABEL COUNCIL NEW YORK 230

It is the only New York evening newspaper possessing the three great wire services—ASSOCIATED PRESS—INTERNATIONAL NEWS SERVICE—UNITED PRESS.

DAILY MIRROR, Wednesday, August 26, 1942.

Daily Mirror

AUG. 26

No. 12,075 ONE PENNY

Registered at the G.P.O. as a Newspaper.

DUKE OF KENT DIES IN CRASH FLYING TO ICELAND

The Air Ministry regrets to announce that Air Commodore the Duke of Kent was killed on active service yesterday afternoon when a Sunderland flying-boat crashed in the North of Scotland.

His Royal Highness, who was attached to the staff of the Inspector-General of the Royal Air Force was proceeding to Iceland on duty.

All the crew of the flying-boat also lost their lives.

This tragic news was announced by the Air Ministry shortly before midnight.

The youngest brother of the King, the Duke, who was in his fortieth year, had been closely associated with the RAF since early in the war.

He was probably the most air-minded member of the Royal Family and its first member to fly the Atlantic. He had flown thousands of miles under war conditions in a plane equipped for battle with enemy aircraft.

For some time he had been making extensive but little-publicised air trips as a means of speedy transit.

The Duke relinquished the honorary rank of Air Vice-Marshal in 1940 when he joined the RAF, so that he should not be senior to experienced officers with whom he had to work in his capacity of welfare officer.

It was in July last year that he made a secret flight to Canada in a Liberator bomber to inspect the Empire air training schools. The crossing took eight hours.

He first landed at Montreal and then flew on to Ottawa in another plane.

Previous Mishap

During the flight the Duke, who held a pilot's licence, spent part of the time in the cockpit.

The Duke learned to pilot a machine in 1930, and lost none of his enthusiasm for flying when he was involved in a plane mishap at Dyce Aerodrome, Aberdeen, in July, 1939.

Wing-Commander Fielden was taxi-ing the machine across the field and increasing speed before lifting when one of the wheels became bogged.

The plane spun round, seemed likely to capsize, then suddenly stopped. The Duke stepped out of the plane, lit a cigarette, and smiled at the adventure.

Since that experience he had flown to various RAF stations and training fields all over the country.

The Duke's last public

Continued on Back Page

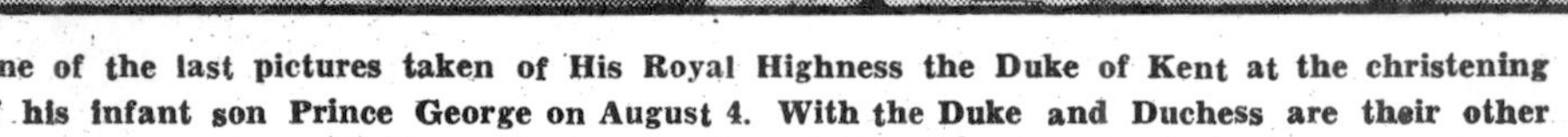

One of the last pictures taken of His Royal Highness the Duke of Kent at the christening of his infant son Prince George on August 4. With the Duke and Duchess are their other two children Prince Edward and Princess Alexandra.

Great Pacific sea-air battle

FROM JOHN WALTERS

NEW YORK, Tuesday.

THE power of the United States and Japanese naval and air forces are tonight locked in a great battle off the Solomon Islands.

Japanese warships, including aircraft carriers, appeared from their bases last Sunday in a desperate attempt to drive the victorious American Marines from the islands.

The Americans met the challenge head-on and so far more than eight of Japan's warships have been damaged, and at least twenty-one of her planes shot down.

But tonight the Japanese are still fighting violently, apparently hoping to crash through the American sea barriers and attack from the rear the U.S. Marines who are now mopping up Japanese garrisons.

In First Phase

The future of the entire Solomons campaign depends on this battle.

Among the Japanese vessels already bombed by Flying Fortresses and planes from American aircraft-carriers are:

One battleship;
Two aircraft-carriers;
Three (at least) fair-sized cruisers;
One transport; and
Several smaller cruisers.

American losses are so far described as "minor ones."

In the first phase of the attack on Sunday, Japanese carriers sent an air fleet to blitz the island of Guadalcanal.

American fighter planes were ready and quickly routed the Japanese, bringing down 21 of their planes.

Then Japanese destroyers shelled Guadalcanal, apparently without doing severe damage.

Following this the enemy fleet approached from the North-East. American land-based Flying Fortresses as well as aircraft-carrier planes went to attack it.

"Great Risks"

The Japanese aircraft-carriers damaged were a big one, disabled by four hits, and the 7,100-ton Ryuzyo, carrying 24 planes, which was severely battered.

A U.S. Navy spokesman in Washington said tonight that the Japanese were taking great risks to regain a foothold in the important Tulagi area—the main Solomons base. He was confident they would be frustrated.

A previous attempt to dislodge the Americans from the Solomons was made last Thursday when 700 Japanese tried to land near the U.S. Marines' positions from speedboats.

"Daily Herald," Tuesday, Sept. 22, 1942

LONDON BLACKOUT
From 7.30 p.m. to 6.16 a.m. Moon Rises 6.16 p.m. Moon Sets 5.04 a.m. to-morrow.
Lighting-up Time 8.00 p.m.

Daily Herald

No. 8298 TUESDAY, SEPTEMBER 22, 1942 ONE PENNY

STOP PRESS

SOVIET SUB'S FEAT

A Soviet submarine in the Baltic has destroyed 42,000 tons of shipping. The largest ship sunk was of 15,000 tons. For two hours the submarine was hunted by the convoying ships and 38 depth charges were dropped.—British United Press.

EVERY FIT MAN IN STALINGRAD IS NOW FIGHTING IN THE STREETS

RUSSIANS ATTACK, THROW ENEMY BACK IN NORTH-WEST SUBURBS

From WALLACE KING STOCKHOLM, Monday.

LATE TO-NIGHT CAME THE NEWS THAT STALINGRAD'S DEFENDERS HAVE BEGUN TO LAUNCH STRONG COUNTER-ATTACKS IN MANY SECTORS.

As a result, the German troops which penetrated into the north-western suburbs are being thrown back street by street.

During the past 24 hours the Germans have made no appreciable advance, despite their terrible losses and the fact that they constantly brought up reinforcements.

To-night's Soviet communiqué announced that several strong German attacks, supported by large tank forces, were repulsed.

For some days heavy rain has been falling. This had added to von Bock's difficulties in bringing up his tanks over roads and fields deep in mud.

Soviet troops, using grenades and bayonets, faced the German tommy-gunners from every corner.

Hand-to-hand fighting went on for every yard and house, and even for floors and rooms.

Sometimes the carnage was so great that staircases were blocked with bodies.

At the approaches to the city the Germans are hurling in a hundred tanks at a time, trying to widen salients and encircle groups of defenders.

Many Soviet units threatened with encirclement have held out for as long as five days before being relieved or reinforced.

Women Evacuated

While the desperate battle is going on amid Stalingrad's ruins, the city is being pounded afresh by long-range siege guns.

Every few seconds a shell explosion tears a fresh gap in the streets.

All children, and all women except doctors and nurses, have been moved to safety across the Volga.

Every able-bodied man is now under arms and fighting. Each house is a strong point. The whole long-spread-out town is a front line.

Don Struggle

Exceptionally heavy fighting has flared up on the Voronezh front on the Upper Don.

At one point south of the town the Germans counter-attacked eight times yesterday in an attempt to drive the Red Army back.

The Nazis are sending up big re-

(CONTINUED BACK PAGE)

"NEW BOYS" take their places in the Desert Army. They are just about to go into action for the first time on the Egypt front. Here you see them getting last-minute instructions from their lieutenant. In the distance guns are rumbling and transport lorries and trucks trundle across the featureless sand.

5,000 Jailed In Paris

FIVE THOUSAND Frenchmen were arrested in Paris over the week-end.

This news is received from the French frontier.

Some of the arrests were made for violation of the 36-hour "keep indoors" order the Nazis imposed when they shot 116 Frenchmen following repeated attacks on Nazi soldiers.

Official Protests

Other arrests were of people suspected of having been involved in the bomb-throwing at a cinema, when one Nazi soldier was killed and 30 wounded.

Another report from the French frontier is that Jean Terray, the official in charge of French labour for Germany, had resigned as a protest against Laval's conscription of labour.

Vichy messages said that Laval held an important conference yesterday on measures to increase the flow of labour to Germany.

Bomb At Police H.Q.

One of three bombs thrown at Nice, on the French Riviera, hit the headquarters of the "Riot Squad of the Legion"—Laval's recently organised terrorist police—in the Rue Trachel.

Another struck the propaganda office of the Revolution Nationale in the Avenue de la Victoire. The third exploded near the harbour.

A statement issued by the inter-Allied Information Committee gives the total number of persons executed by the Nazis in occupied countries to date as 207,373.

ONE TANK FOUGHT TWENTY

"Daily Herald" Special Correspondent

CAIRO, Monday.

A LANCASHIRE newsagent who fought 20 enemy tanks from a disabled British tank, and then crouched in a slit trench as tanks rumbled overhead, has just been given an immediate award of the D.C.M. in the field.

He is 21-year-old Trooper Richard S. Barton, of the 5th Royal Tank Regiment, whose home is in Watling-street, Preston.

On leaving school when he was 17 he joined the Tank Corps, was in the Dunkirk evacuation, and was reported missing in Tobruk.

Here is the story that has brought him the award:—

His tank was left in front of guns to await recovery, and he stayed in it with a gunner.

The 20 enemy approached to engage the guns. Barton and the gunner manned their gun and fired, claiming one hit.

Then their tank was hit by a shell, which set it on fire and badly wounded the gunner. Barton dragged him, under heavy machine-gun fire, into the slit trench.

The enemy tanks passed over them. Barton stayed until the gunner died and then rejoined his regiment.

Wiped Out 280

Sergeant Frederick Enderlein, of Somerset-road, New Barnet, has also been given the D.C.M. on the field.

He took out his tank with another one to investigate a collection of 60 enemy transport vehicles.

Though his tank came under heavy fire, and was hit several times, he managed to cut off and halt 21 enemy vehicles.

From the shield of these he dashed out and overran two anti-tank guns, whose crews surrendered. The enemy casualties were 280 killed, wounded or captured.

Used Four Tanks

A master lighterman, Captain Kenward Philp, of Sanderlands, East Croydon, has been awarded the D.S.O. on the field.

During a battle he "baled out" four times from wrecked tanks.

Tank No. 1 was disabled by a direct hit. Tank No. 2 was damaged by a mine. No. 3 was disabled and both guns wrecked. In No. 4 he found another officer wounded, sent him back, took over and fought on until the vehicle was disabled.

"He then baled out with the crew," says the citation, "and under heavy fire brought them back safely to our lines."

TARGET FOR 7 NIGHTS IN 8

TOBRUK, Rommel's main supply base in North Africa, was attacked again by Allied planes on Sunday night—for the seventh time in eight days.

The raid was made by RAF medium bombers.

South African Air Force light bombers attacked Axis aircraft dispersed on landing grounds in the El Daba area. One large fire and three small ones were observed. They were followed by two explosions.

FIRED ON BATHERS

German frontier guards have opened fire without warning on Swiss bathers in the Rhine near Basle, their usual bathing place.

The centre of the river forms the frontier between Switzerland and Germany. Nobody was hit—British United Press.

Within 37 Miles Of Madagascar Capital

"BRITISH troops are now less than 37 miles away," said the announcer at the radio station in Antananarivo, capital of Madagascar, yesterday.

He was referring to the column advancing down the road from Matunga, on the north-west coast, which has covered 200 miles in ten days.

General Platt, commander of the British and Dominion forces, announced that the column took Ankazobe, 50 miles from the capital, on Saturday and was advancing south of it.

The fact that this important position fell "after a short engagement" indicates that resistance is on a light scale.

One hundred miles to the east of the capital, Brickaville, a rail and road junction, has been captured by the force which landed at Tamatave last week.

The French have blown up a bridge on the railway running to the capital.

Through Storms

Heavy rain is impeding the progress of the column striking southward from Maromandia, in the north-west.

But it has occupied Befotaka, and is moving on towards Antsohihy—nearly 60 miles from its starting point.

The column moving down the north-east coast entered Sahambava, 140 miles south of Diego Suarez, at noon on Sunday.

Yet another column is advancing from Morondava, on the south-west coast, but there is no news of its progress.

BOY PILOT SHOT BEFORE WEDDING

A FEW hours before he was to have been married at Trull, Somerset, Pilot Officer John Weldon Butt, aged 19, was found shot dead in a field.

He was to have married Miss Penelope Mary Evans, to whom he became engaged only four days earlier.

It was stated at the inquest yesterday that since crashing in a Spitfire Butt had periodic "black-outs" in which he lost his sight for a few seconds, and the Coroner, holding that Butt took his life while the balance of his mind was disturbed, said the excitement of his sudden engagement was too much for him.

U.S. AIR CHIEF PROMOTED

Brigadier-General Eaker, head of the United States Army Bomber Command in England, has been nominated by President Roosevelt to be a major-general.

He is among 81 nominated for promotion in the Army.—Associated Press.

MALTA WORKERS SEE GEORGE CROSS

Malta's George Cross was displayed at the Royal dockyard yesterday, and workmen filed past to see it.—"Daily Herald" Correspondent.

IN CASUALTY LIST—

In the latest Air Ministry casualty list, between the names of Flight Sergeants Jones and Lewis, is that of Air Commodore the Duke of Kent, "killed on active service."

Two Shy People—

"Daily Herald" Reporter

TWO shy young people, holding hands, stepped in front of a microphone in London yesterday.

The girl, Dientje (Dinah), said softly: "Hello, Mother. Hello, Father. I have just got married. Here is my husband."

The boy, Hans, said haltingly: "Hello, parents. Well, here I am . . ."

And somewhere in German-occupied Holland a mother and father listened to their daughter introducing her husband they had never seen. . .

They were listening to Radio Orange.

Dientje could not tell her parents her husband's name—for the Germans listen to Radio Orange, too.

The broadcast over, some day Hans, too, will introduce his wife to *his* parents.

The Eyes Of Lieut. Lloyd

THE Eyes of the Navy are proverbially keen, and none are keener than the eyes of the men in the little ships that go out on night patrols.

But of all the eyes in all the ships that make up one of our light coastal forces that operate in the southern North Sea none are so keen as those of the commander, Lieut. H. L. Lloyd, D.S.C.

The motor torpedo-boats and motor gun-boats of the force were out on an offensive night patrol off Flushing when Lieut. Lloyd's eyes saw what appeared to be a ship about four miles away.

No one else could see anything and a motor gunboat sent to make a search failed to locate the enemy.

Lieutenant ("I saw them first") Lloyd, convinced he was right, persisted, and presently those eyes spotted the enemy again, this time picking out three ships.

By now the personnel in all the light craft were sweeping the horizon intently, and at midnight they saw what the eyes of Lieutenant Lloyd had seen minutes before. The patrol moved to the attack.

The enemy force, which consisted of four flak ships, was engaged by the motor gunboats, and a brisk action began.

The motor gunboats made six runs up and down the line of the enemy, scoring many hits. During this time one of our boats received one hit, causing no casualties.

Two Ships Hit

Then, under heavy enemy fire, the motor torpedo boats attacked. Two of the flak ships were torpedoed, one being almost certainly destroyed and the other left in a cloud of smoke.

Lieut. Lloyd brought all his little ships back without a casualty.

The eyes of Lieut. Lloyd are 24 years old and have been serving their owner in command of motor torpedo boats since July, 1939. Before that they were keenest of all among the officers of the watch in a cruiser squadron.

Nazi Dead Too Many To Bury

From RONALD MATTHEWS

MOSCOW, Monday

GERMAN veterans of the Stalingrad campaign, however it turns out, are going to remember it for the rest of their lives as an inferno as terrible as Verdun or Passchendaele.

Fighting is so intense and continuous, casualties so huge, that enemy burial squads and first-aid parties are being completely overwhelmed.

There is no question of interring more than a tiny proportion of the mounds of Nazi dead, even when the tide of battle has not rolled back to put the place where they lie behind the Russian lines.

The walking wounded are the lucky ones. They may manage to get back through the storm of fire to dressing stations.

But the German Red Cross is being obliged to leave a big percentage of heavily wounded simply lying on the battlefield amid the dust and rubble of the pounded houses.

First Aid Only

A hasty application of field dressings is the most that can be done for the horribly lacerated victims.

Hardly comforting are the surroundings which the dying Germans have around them. The ground is perpetually quivering with bombardment, which continues non-stop night and day.

The suburbs where fighting is going on are perpetually billowing new clouds of acrid smoke.

"Net" Defence

The Russian defence lines consist of scores of knots of resistance, each well linked with others like a fishing net, and each so sited and protected that even a comparatively tiny holding force can make it a formidable obstacle.

The defenders have to keep sharp eyes open, for the terrain in the outskirts of Stalingrad is seamed with miniature ravines which, though they may provide good defence positions, also form admirable channels for enemy infiltration.

NO EASY WIN, BERLIN ADMITS

"DECISIONS against the Russians cannot be achieved quickly."

This admission was made over Berlin Radio last night by General Dietmar, military expert and High Command spokesman.

"Every victory we have won has been the result of a hard struggle, often with critical moments.

"The easiest and most complete victories are achieved when the moral resistance of the enemy—the will to fight—is hit quickly.

"Against Soviet soldiers there is no chance of achieving such a victory.

"The Russians are unusually capable of both 'taking it' and 'giving it.'

"The war against the Soviet Union is a fight against the most powerful military organisation in the world. To bring it to its knees is a difficult task."—Reuter.

LEGLESS, TO FLY FIGHTER

Lieut. Colin Hodgkinson

"Daily Herald" Reporter

SUB-LIEUT. COLIN HODGKINSON, 21-year-old legless Fleet Air Arm pilot, who won his wings recently, has realised his greatest ambition.

He is being posted to an RAF Spitfire squadron.

Hodgkinson, a great friend of Wing Commander Bader—legless Spitfire pilot who is now a prisoner of war—hopes to fly into battle with Bader's old squadron.

The Admiralty has arranged the transfer to the RAF.

Hodgkinson is now spending a few weeks at an operational training unit before he joins his squadron.

He lost his legs in a flying accident before the war, but, as his friends say, "he just refused to leave the Service."

He resumed flying shortly after being fitted with special steel legs at Queen Mary's Hospital, Roehampton.

REVOLVER BY HER BED

Shortly after 29-year-old Mrs. Juanita Pagella, an American ambulance driver, returned to the American Women's Ambulance Driving Hostel, at Dingley Dell, Tunbridge Wells, she was found suffering from a bullet wound.

A revolver was on the floor beside her bed.

She was taken to hospital, where last night she was reported to be making a good recovery.

NEW SHIPS: WAR NEEDS FIRST

The Government's policy in all matters concerning the design and production of merchant ships is based solely on war-time requirements.

The Admiralty gives this assurance to Jarrow Town Council following a council resolution that war and not post-war needs should come first.

At a meeting of the Council's Parliamentary Committee last night, when the Admiralty's reply was read, the chairman, Mr. John Richardson, said it had been suggested that ships should be smaller.

In some vessels they were putting in trimmings the same as before the war, and cabins were taking two months to fit out.

It was decided not to discuss the matter farther.

WILLKIE SEES MOLOTOV

Wendell Willkie, President Roosevelt's special envoy, was received in Moscow yesterday by M. Molotov, Soviet Foreign Commissar.

ITALY IS UPSET BY VICHY

Describing Vichy's co-operation with Germany as "only a manoeuvre to gain a free hand against Italy," the official Italian review, "Relazioni Internazionali," says:

"Franco-Italian co-operation is a dead letter, while French public opinion remains outspokenly hostile to Italy.

"No attempt is made in Government circles to counteract this hatred of Italy, as it is fully shared by responsible members of the Government.

"One of Vichy's main aims is the frustration of Italian aspirations."—Reuter.

CANADIAN DESTROYER IS SUNK BY U-BOAT

The Canadian destroyer Ottawa has been torpedoed and sunk while escorting an Atlantic convoy, it was officially announced yesterday.

Its commanding officer, Lieut.-Commander C. A. Rutherford, was killed in action, one rating died of wounds, and four officers and 107 ratings are missing.

Formerly the Crusader, the Ottawa was launched at Portsmouth in 1931, and was of 1,375 tons, with four 4.7 inch guns.

FLAK SHIP FIRED

In offensive patrols yesterday our fighters set a flak ship on fire off the Dutch coast.

One of our fighters is missing.

THEY CALL HIM THE U-BOAT MAGNET

COASTAL COMMAND now has more aeroplanes than the entire RAF possessed at the beginning of the war—and that means hundreds of air crews, most of them employed in the war against U-boats.

But one pilot differs from most of the rest in his phenomenal luck on his patrols. He sights U-boats so much more often than the others that his colleagues now call him "the U-boat Magnet."

He is Flt.-Lieut. H. G. Pockley, of Randwick, New South Wales, the captain of "R for Robert," a Sunderland flying-boat that hunts the U-boats as they cross the Bay of Biscay on their trips to and from the Atlantic shipping lanes.

Pockley recently caught an Italian U-boat on the surface, and despite the weight of the giant four-engined flying-boat he attacked in a dive so steep that a Stuka would not have been disgraced by its angle.

Gun Battle

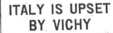

The bombs must have damaged the submarine, for the Italians remained on the surface and fought a gun battle with the Sunderland, which scored many hits on the conning tower and deck.

The Italian guns ceased firing. Another Sunderland and a Wellington came along, and after their bombs had fallen a number of Italians wearing only red and yellow bathing trunks, dived overboard. The U-boat slid under at an angle which clearly showed it was not under control.

A few days later "Magnet" Pockley surprised a German submarine on the surface and scored bomb hits which sent it under amid masses of air bubbles.

These are but two of his attacks In a few weeks he has made several.

BOMB HITS BLOCK OF FLATS

A block of service flats received a direct hit when two raiders made a tip-and-run attack on a south-east coast town yesterday.

Houses and shops were damaged by blast. Only one slight casualty was reported.

Two German planes which crossed the south-east coast last night turned back when ground defences went into action.

SATURDAY, SEPTEMBER 26, 1942

BLACK OUT 7.21 to 6.23 | MOON RISES 8 p.m. New Moon Oct. 10. | RADIO Page Seven

LATE NIGHT

THE STAR

No. 16,936 ★ ONE PENNY

R.A.F. HIT OSLO GESTAPO H.Q.

Quisling Cries "Murder Planes"

NEW RUSSIAN ADVANCES

'Still Grave' In Stalingrad

"NORTH-WEST OF STALINGRAD SEVERAL GERMAN ATTACKS WERE REPELLED WITH GREAT LOSSES TO THE ENEMY," SAYS TODAY'S COMMUNIQUE FROM MOSCOW.

"In another sector, our troops repulsed a counter-attack, pressed forward, and occupied more advantageous positions. Six hundred Germans were killed."

Dealing with the situation in the city of Stalingrad itself, the communique stated:

"In stubborn street fighting ten tanks were destroyed and 285 of the enemy killed."

Larry Lesueur, Columbia Broadcasting Corporation correspondent, in a Moscow broadcast quoted by Reuter this afternoon, said that the situation was still grave, as the Germans were bringing in fresh troops because they knew they must again try to take the city before the winter.

Harold King, Reuter's special correspondent, cabled from Moscow this afternoon: "Though manifestly getting near the point of exhaustion, the Germans at Stalingrad are making what may prove to be the last effort to reach their objective."

A B.U.P. cable this afternoon stated that one German prisoner taken in Stalingrad told his captors: "My regiment has lost seven men out of every ten in the last four days' fighting."

Volga River crossings are being constantly bombed by German planes in an effort to halt the stream of supplies going across to Stalingrad.

Resistance in the city during the past 48 hours has shown greater strength, and the Germans have been thrown out from a number of streets and many houses.

They have again failed to make any new advance, and in twelve hours (since the period covered in the communique) lost 1,500 men, 20 tanks, and twelve big guns.

Marshal Timoshenko's forces are today pushing farther into the Ger-

CONTINUED ON BACK PAGE, Col. TWO

She Was In Nazi Prison Camps

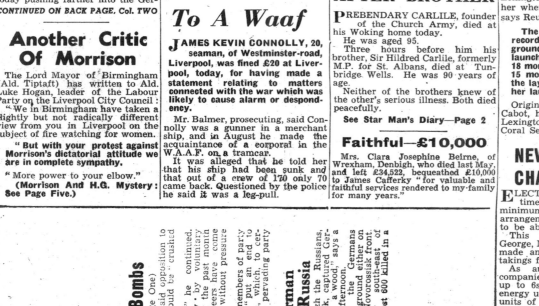

Miss Ruth Mitchell, who was a prisoner of war in several Nazi internment camps because of the aid she gave to Yugo-Slav guerillas, leaving the White House, Washington, after delivering a basket, made by British war prisoners in Germany, to President Roosevelt.

Another Critic Of Morrison

The Lord Mayor of Birmingham (Ald. Tiptaft) has written to Ald. Luke Hogan, leader of the Labour Party on the Liverpool City Council:

"We in Birmingham have taken a slightly but not radically different view from you in Liverpool on the subject of fire watching for women.

"But with your protest against Morrison's dictatorial attitude we are in complete sympathy.

"More power to your elbow."

(Morrison And H.G. Mystery: See Page Five.)

He Talked To A Waaf

JAMES KEVIN CONNOLLY, 20, seaman, of Westminster-road, Liverpool, was fined £20 at Liverpool, today, for having made a statement relating to matters connected with the war which was likely to cause alarm or despondency.

Mr. Balmer, prosecuting, said Connolly was a gunner in a merchant ship, and in August he made the acquaintance of a corporal in the W.A.A.F. on a tramcar.

It was alleged that he told her that his ship had been sunk and that out of a crew of 170 only 70 came back. Questioned by the police he said it was a leg-pull.

"DURING the rally of the Quisling Party in Oslo yesterday afternoon a flight of four R.A.F. bombers attacked the Nazi headquarters in the city," said the Air Ministry today.

"At the time of the attack a meeting of the party leaders was being held nearby.

"Bombs were dropped from about 100ft. and hits were seen on the Gestapo buildings.

"One of our aircraft is missing. The others returned safely.

"The German allegation that three of the attacking bombers were shot down confirms the effect of the attack."

Agency messages today said that Quisling was in the middle of a speech when the R.A.F. dropped their bombs. He, his bodyguard and his followers raced to the cellars.

Sirens were sounded twice again in Oslo during the night.

The meeting which was broken up by the bombs was held again this afternoon, and Quisling then said:

"There were four murder-planes over Oslo yesterday.

"Britain has sunk far down and we in Norway who have had such close contact with the real British people regret this very much.

"But the man whom the Norwegian people elected as the ruler of their country and the gang of ex-Norwegians with whom he surrounds himself have sunk still deeper than Britain.

"Now they are sending murderous planes to Oslo.

"It is the Nasjonal Samling (Quisling party) which is rebuilding Norway that they are trying to hit."

Quisling then asked the approval of the Assembly to order the victims of the raid, which he gave as four dead and 40 injured, to be buried at the expense of the State and Oslo.

PREB. CARLILE DIES 3 HOURS AFTER BROTHER

PREBENDARY CARLILE, founder of the Church Army, died at his Woking home today.

He was aged 95.

Three hours before him his brother, Sir Hildred Carlile, formerly M.P. for St. Albans, died at Tunbridge Wells. He was 90 years of age.

Neither of the brothers knew of the other's serious illness. Both died peacefully.

See Star Man's Diary—Page 2

Faithful—£10,000

Mrs. Clara Josephine Beirne, of Wrexham, Denbigh, who died last May, and left £34,522, bequeathed £10,000 to James Cafferky "for valuable and faithful services rendered to my family for many years."

General De Gaulle Back In London

General de Gaulle arriving at his headquarters in London today on returning from a tour of inspection of Fighting French units at Brazzaville, French Equatorial Africa.

SUBMARINES WRECK 8 AXIS SHIPS

"OUR submarines in the Mediterranean have inflicted further heavy losses on enemy sea communications," said an Admiralty communique this evening.

"Five, enemy supply ships have been sunk, two probably sunk, and one hit by torpedo and seriously damaged.

"One of the vessels sunk and one of those probably sunk were large ships. All the others were supply ships of medium tonnage.

"These recent successes have been achieved by submarines under the command of Lieutenant S. L. C. Maydon, R.N., Lieutenant-Comdr. L. W. Napier, R.N., Lieutenant H. S. MacKenzie, D.S.O., R.N., Lieutenant J. S. Stephens, D.S.C., R.N., and Lieutenant M. B. St. John, R.N."

£100 Legacy For Dog

Mr. John Boon Tutt, F.R.C.V.S., of Dounstead, Twyford, near Winchester, left £100 to his trustees for the upkeep and care of his dog "Sporan" during its life. His estate has been valued at £9,215 for probate.

LEXINGTON No. 2 READY YEAR BEFORE SCHEDULE

AMERICA'S latest and most formidable aircraft carrier, the new Lexington, was launched at Quincy (Mass.), today, a year ahead of schedule.

Several Naval Air Arm heroes who took off from the decks of the old Lexington, sunk in the Coral Sea battle in June, were present.

Rear-Admiral Frederick Shearman, who commanded the first Lexington and was the last to leave her when she sank, was also there, says Reuter.

The carrier has beaten all records for quick building. The ground from which she was launched was a waste space only 18 months ago, and not more than 15 months have elapsed between the laying of Lexington's keel and her launching today.

Originally intended to be called Cabot, her name was changed to Lexington after the battle of the Coral Sea.

NEW ELECTRICITY CHARGES ORDER

ELECTRICITY companies' peace-time practice of making a minimum quarterly charge, by arrangement with the consumer, is to be abolished.

This afternoon, Major Lloyd George, Minister of Fuel and Power, made an order prohibiting undertakings from making these charges.

As an alternative, electricity companies will be allowed to charge up to 6s. 3d. a quarter, including energy used up to that value. Extra units of electricity will have to be paid for.

Consumers at present on an all-in or two-part tariff are unaffected unless they feel that it is not to their advantage to remain on these tariffs because of reduced consumption.

(Dampness Will Beat Fuel Ban: See Page Three.)

H.G. COLONEL SHOT: MAJOR CASHIERED

MAJOR C. E. W. HOLDSWORTH, of the Green Howards, officer commanding a technical school, is to be cashiered by sentences of a general court-martial promulgated in Northern Ireland today.

He was found guilty of the manslaughter of Lieut.-Col. M. F. Hammond-Smith during a battle practice, and of negligently handling a Bren gun on the same occasion and causing injuries to an officer and n.c.o.

Lieut.-Col. Hammond-Smith was County Commandant of the Tyrone Home Guard, and while attending a course of instruction was shot during the firing of some live ammunition on July 27.

Lieut. R. A. Sheddon, of the Pioneer Corps, who was found guilty in Northern Ireland of altering a medical certificate with intent to deceive his superior officer has been sentenced to be dismissed the service.

Woolton's Hint

Lord Woolton, making a whirlwind tour of Glasgow docks today, said to dockers:

"You keep turning round the ships as quickly as you are doing, and maybe you'll get more meat in your sausages."

Examining a cargo of dried milk—one of the first consignments to reach this country dehydrated by a new process—he said: "That's for you in Scotland. You're short of milk here."

Oslo Bombs

(See Page One)

Later Quisling said opposition to Quisling regime would be "crushed by every means."

"It is our duty," he continued, "to help Germany by voluntary enlistment. During the past month a thousand volunteers have come forward, and this without pressure from Germany."

He appealed to members of party to help him to "put an end to internal dissension, which, to certain extent, is also pervading party itself."

More German Losses In Russia

North of Voronezh the Russians, in a surprise attack, captured German positions near "a wood," says a Reuter cable this afternoon.

In the Caucasus the Germans failed to gain any ground either on Mozdok or on the Novorossisk front.

In one sector south-east of Novorossisk they lost 600 killed in a day.

Daily  Mail

LATE WAR NEWS SPECIAL

No. 14,485 ONE PENNY FOR KING AND EMPIRE THURSDAY, OCTOBER 1, 1942

WAR OF EXHAUSTION NOW, SAYS HITLER

Germans Promised Food from a New Russia

STALINGRAD HIS AIM: 'WE WILL TAKE IT'

GERMANY will answer the British bombing, Hitler assured his countrymen last night when he delivered his delayed speech for the Winter Relief Fund in the Sports Palace in Berlin.

Hitler entered the hall with the Gestapo chief, Himmler, recently rumoured dead and, as the Nazi crowd roared their "Sieg Heil," paused to shake hands with General Rommel, who appeared in the uniform of the Africa Corps.

Hitler admitted that last winter had been a dreadful one for the German people, promised that the captured provinces of Russia were being organised into a great food-producing territory, and revealed the objectives of the advance into Russia.

These, he said, are the conquest of the area between the Don Valley and the Volga and the city of Stalingrad—"which will certainly fall into our hands."

Hitler began at once with an attack on Churchill and Roosevelt. After apologising for not having spoken in that hall for a year, he said :—

"Of course, those who have time to travel for weeks round the world with a sombrero on their heads and wearing white silk shirts, they, of course, can give more time to talk, while I, in recent months, have even more time to act.

"But what should I say? What should be said to-day is being said by our soldiers, although the subject has become more difficult for me than the subject of a fireside chat which my opponents send out over the world from their fireside.

The subject is more difficult because I think we should not talk to-day about the future. We should give our minds to-day to what time requests of us.

"To concoct an Atlantic Charter is simple, but it is also nonsense. But this nonsense will only last a very few years. It will be wiped out by hard facts.

"It is very witty for President Roosevelt to promise that in future everybody had the right not to suffer need. I can only ask why the President has not put the half power of his country to a useful purpose and seen to it that his people should have proper means instead of 10,000,000 unemployed.

"What we believe in we have also done, and now we believe that we must strike against the enemy to final victory. That we believe and shall also achieve.

'STALINGRAD OURS'

"Of course, it is difficult to argue with people who think, for instance, that Namsos was a victory, that Dunkirk was the greatest victory in history, and that an expeditionary force which lands for nine hours is a success with which our successes cannot compare.

"When we have advanced 600 miles, that is nothing. If in the course of the past few months we have penetrated to the Don and to the Volga, and if we besiege Stalingrad and shall also take it—you can rely on that—that is nothing at all.

"If we advance to the Caucasus, and occupy the Ukraine, the Donetz Basin, with their corn and iron ore and oil—that is nothing.

"But if a troop of Canadians with a small appendix of Englishmen come to Dieppe and remain for nine hours only to be wiped out finally, then this is a sure sign of the eternal power of the British Empire.

"What, against this, is our Air Force? What of our U-boats? They are nothing.

"In 1939 Mr. Churchill proclaimed that they had sunk more U-boats than Germany possessed.

"No, it was not Churchill, but Duff-Cooper. It doesn't matter whether it was one blackguard or the other.

"We chased them out of the Balkans, Greece, Crete, and North Africa. All that was nothing.

"But they have now promises for the future. They speak of a second front. They tell us a second front is coming. They tell us to be careful and turn round. We have not been careful, and we have not turned round. We have gone steadily on.

"I say to Mr. Churchill 'You have never frightened me.'

"It is true we must give some attention to this. If we had an opponent of some military size one could guess where he could start a second front, but if you have to deal with military idiots you cannot know where they will attack.

THESE DRUNKARDS

"But wherever those madmen, those eternal drunkards, may attack, I can tell them they won't stay longer than nine hours.

"Behind us lie the winters of 1941 and 1942, in which the German people have been tried by providence. Nothing worse than that trial can happen again.

"That we should have beaten this General Winter, that we could resume our attacks in the early summer is proof that Providence means well by the German people.

"When we resumed our offensive we did not do it according to our opponents' plan. We always choose our aims boldly, but carefully, and in this case we set ourselves the simple aim to hold on at all costs where we had to hold and let others attack, and attack where attack was absolutely necessary.

"Our aim is clear. It is the destruction of the right arm of the international bloc of capitalists with plutocracy and Bolshevism—the worst danger which ever threatened the German people."

Hitler surveyed the battles in Russia from the time of the fighting in the Crimea to the attack on Stalingrad.

The aim of the German offensive, he said, was first to deprive the Russians of their remaining grain areas, take from them their coal mines, and get as near as possible to their oil wells, and finally cut their main transport lines, especially the Volga.

"The occupation of Stalingrad, which will also be completed, will still further increase the cutting-off process, and you can be sure nobody

BACK PAGE—Col. FOUR

US Rebukes Its India Agitators

'How Not to Win'

From Daily Mail Correspondent

NEW YORK, Wednesday.

A SHARP rebuke to "agitators for American intervention" in the Indian problem was made by the New York 'Herald-Tribune" to-day in an editorial entitled "How Not to Win the War."

The newspaper's slap at American critics of British policy came at a time when a number of Liberal Press columnists and authors are trying to provoke public pressure on the Administration to make a move in India to force Britain's hand and guarantee the nation's complete independence.

The *Herald-Tribune* editorial said: "The motives of those who are still agitating for some form of American intervention in the Indian problem—what form is very vaguely defined—are beyond question, but it becomes increasingly difficult to respect their practical wisdom.

"Naturally, if President Roosevelt by a wave of some magic wand, could obliterate two or three hundred years of history, resolve all the complex conflicts of Indian politics, and convert the Indian masses into singleminded and determined front line fighters for the United Nations it would be most fortunate.

★

"BUT that kind of magic is rare in the actual world, and the efforts of those who still seem devoutly to believe in it can take on reckless forms."

After admonishing an American journalist, Louis Fischer, for recent articles charging the British with bad faith in India as "hardly contributing to the victory," the newspaper says:—

"The more one studies reports of India one begins to get a better grasp of the true difficulties of this problem, for which miraculous solutions simply don't exist, and a better understanding of the uselessness of American intervention into issues with which this people is totally unequipped to deal and for which it would never assume the necessary responsibility."

Gandhi men fight on—BACK Page.

NEW LANDING IN MADAGASCAR

British troops have landed and occupied Port Dauphin, on the south-west coast of Madagascar, a Vichy communiqué stated last night.

The garrison "was fairly quickly overwhelmed in spite of tenacious resistance."

The landing at Tullear, announced by Mr. Churchill on Tuesday, was also admitted.

It was claimed that the British advance from Antananarivo had been held by defensive positions 13 miles south of Ambatolampy (a large native village about 50 miles south of the capital) "in spite of incessant air attacks."—*Reuter.*

4,000 Indian Mob Attacks Police

CUTTACK (Orissa), Wednesday.—Eight people were killed and three others injured when the police fired on a mob of about 4,000 rioters attacking a police party at Katashi village, in Orissa, an official announcement by the Orissa Government said to-day. The police had gone to stop the mob extorting paddy from cultivators. A sub-inspector and some constables were injured before the police fired. The mob leader was arrested.

Two people were injured to-day in a bomb explosion in the Lambi area of Jamalpur, says a report from Ahmedabad.—*Reuter* and *B.U.P.*

Black Sea Pilots' Bag

The Soviet Fleet Air Arm in the Black Sea has in the past fortnight sunk 14 enemy merchantmen and seven gunboats, damaged 10 merchantmen, and destroyed 16 'planes.—*Reuter.*

Dakar Economy Talk

An important economic conference is taking place at Dakar under the presidency of General Boisson, stated Paris radio last night.—*B.U.P.*

Convoy Battle

A VIVID picture taken at the height of the four days' attack by torpedo 'planes and U-boats—the worst of the war—on the great convoy which battled its way to Russia. Smoke from stricken ships drifts over the sea. Other units of the convoy sail on. Losses were suffered, but in a great fighting defence by the naval escort the enemy lost 40 'planes and two U-boats for certain. This and another picture in Page Three were taken by a British Newsreel cameraman.

REVENGE, REBUILD

Plan for Burma

NEW DELHI, Wednesday.

GREAT armies are in training to put an end for all time to Japanese aggression, said Sir Reginald Dorman-Smith, Governor of Burma, in a broadcast from New Delhi to Burma to-night.

Plans for the rebuilding of Burma had been discussed by the British War Cabinet and were being elaborated by the Burma Government.

The invaders who had destroyed Burmese cities, defiled their women, and desecrated their sacred buildings would be punished with the utmost severity.

"I want you never for one moment to forget," said Sir Reginald, "that the Japanese occupation of Burma is only a temporary one.

'Keep Away'

"In the meantime, keep away from towns where soldiers are stationed and from railway and road junctions.

"We are going to attack the Japanese wherever we can find them. Air bombardment is one method we shall use, and as our air strength grows so will the weight of our bombing.

"You are friends we naturally do not want to hurt—the Japanese have hurt you all too much."—*Reuter.*

R.A.F. 'Kill' 3 Day Raiders

Three raiders were brought down over this country in daylight yesterday, when bombs were dropped in hit-and-run raids on five districts of East Anglia and the South Coast.

The raiders took advantage of low clouds to swoop on towns, some of which were machine-gunned. No fatal casualty has been reported.

Five people, including a Land Girl, were injured when a single raider swooped low over a South-East country town shortly before noon, dropped four H.E. bombs, and machine-gunned the area in the face of heavy A.-A. fire.

It made off, hedge-hopping, with a cloud of black smoke pouring from its tail.

Strike Holds Up Vital Work

A strike involving about 250 boilermakers occurred yesterday at a ship-repairing yard in the North-East. The men objected to other workmen on a vessel which had come from the shipyard to the repair yard. The management, however, stated that there had been no departure from the usual procedure.

About 40 boilermakers later returned to work, but other men in another department of the firm came out in sympathy.

Important work, it is stated, has been affected.

6,000 Doctors Defy Petain

VICHY, Wednesday.—More than 6,000 physicians from Paris and Nantes are included in the recent mass resignations from the Council of the National Order of Doctors founded by Marshal Pétain.

They protest against the disciplining of practitioners and contend that the council is not representative of the profession.—*B.U.P.*

Hungary 'Quake

VICHY, Wednesday.—Slight damage was caused in various parts of Hungary by an earth tremor recorded in Budapest at 4.29 a.m. (local time) and lasting three minutes.—*Reuter.*

BOCK HELD AT THE CROSS-ROADS

2,000 Nazi Guns Blaze in Battle of Streets

From Daily Mail Special Correspondent. STOCKHOLM, Wednesday.

THE defenders of Stalingrad were to-day still stubbornly holding the greatest attack yet launched against them by the Germans. More than 2,000 guns are concentrated against the city. Groups of 50 or 60 tanks are striving to break down the street-by-street resistance of the defenders.

Behind the tanks are the Tommy-gun men, shock troops pitting themselves against the expert street fighters of the Red Army.

For the last 24 hours a street crossing in the north-west suburbs has been the chief centre of the fighting. Tanks, supported by powerful infantry forces, were flung against the Russian positions, but every attack was held. Finally the Russians counter-attacked and improved their positions.

One house here was the centre of particularly fierce struggles.

When it finally fell into Russian hands 100 German dead were found in and around it.

A height held by the Russians dominates the battle in these suburbs at the moment. The Germans have launched attack after attack, but so far not a single tank has penetrated the Russian defence.

Marshal Timoshenko still holds the initiative north-west of Stalingrad where he is striking from the north in an effort to relieve pressure on the city.

Fresh German reserves have reached the battle area and are now ceaselessly counter-attacking.

30 Divisions

The German Command now has nearly 30 divisions drawn up in depth to halt at all costs Timoshenko's drive to the Don.

The Germans, fighting for their communications, have fired the dry steppes, putting a sea of fire several miles wide between them and the attacking Russians.

This has not deterred the Red Army, some of whose tanks drove through one of the fire "lines" and stormed a plateau held by the Germans.

At one point the Russians destroyed 50 German guns and cut up two infantry battalions. In another sector Rumanian troops who captured a height were driven back again by a Russian counter-attack with the loss of 1,000 men killed.

Meanwhile, south-east of Novorossisk, the Russians have again advanced in one sector, capturing a hill and a village despite a big counter-attack by a German-Rumanian force.

Commando Raid

Novorossisk itself has been raided by Soviet Commandos, who shot down the crews of two batteries in the town.

The weather is deteriorating in the Caucasus and threatens to bog the enemy.

Yesterday's German High Command communiqué said :—

"In the North-West Caucasus and south of the Terek German and allied troops advanced further after hard fighting.

"In Stalingrad more sectors in the northern part of the city were taken by storm. The enemy lost 34 tanks during unsuccessful relief attacks.

"On the Don front German and Italian troops repelled several Russian attempts to cross the river."

Bock's Flank is Menaced

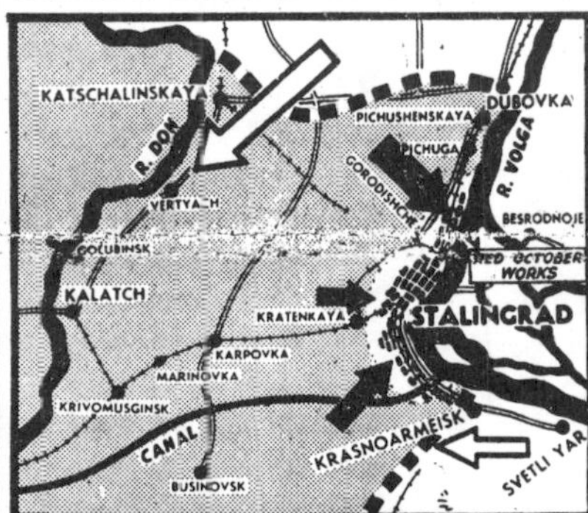

BETWEEN the Don and the Volga Timoshenko is thrusting down on the German left flank to cut Von Bock's vital line of communications between Katchalinskaya and Dubovka.

Thirty enemy divisions have been brought up to halt the Soviet advance. The Germans claim to have taken new sectors in the northern part of Stalingrad by storm.

SHIPS FROM BATTLE SAIL PAST THE KING

SHIPS of the Royal Navy were reviewed by the King at Portsmouth yesterday. Standing on a dais on the quay-side of the dockyard, he took the salute as the ships, many of which have been in action, passed slowly in line ahead.

Wheeling round, the ships formed into quarter-line three abreast to pass the King again. He stepped down from the daïs and leaned over the dock rails to get a closer view.

At the King's side was Admiral Sir William James, Commander-in-Chief Portsmouth, who struck his flag last night.

It was to bid farewell to the admiral on the last day of his command, which to-day is taken over by Admiral Sir Charles Little, that the King went to Portsmouth.

The King had lunch aboard H.M.S. Victory, Nelson's flagship. On the poop he inspected Navy League sea cadets.

Marine ratings and officers who fought at Madagascar, Crete, and in the Malta convoy battle were presented, and the King had a few words with each.

As he passed through the dockyard the King inspected the ship's company of a warship which has recently been in action. Men and women workers from the shops cheered him.

In the afternoon the King visited aircraft factories.

Japs May Free More Britons

New Talks Soon

NEGOTIATIONS are to be opened with the Japanese Government for the removal of more British subjects from the Far East.

This was stated by Mr. Anthony Eden, Foreign Secretary yesterday in a written reply about conditions in the Japanese internment camps.

While conditions in the Hongkong camps have to some extent improved since the early days, Mr. Eden said the general health of the internees has seriously suffered for lack of proper food and medicines.

The Japanese had refused to allow special relief ships to be sent, but agreed that food, clothing, and medical comforts might be sent on the return voyage of the ships in which British and Japanese officials are being exchanged.

Full advantage was taken of the exchange ships, and the total amount of supplies shipped in them was about 4,000 tons.

Arrangements had been made for an equitable proportion of these supplies to be landed in Hongkong, and the first ship is due to reach there within the next few days.

Mr. Attlee Flies Back Home

Mr. C. R. Attlee, Secretary of State for the Dominions and Deputy Premier, returned by air to London yesterday after his visit to Newfoundland and Canada.

More N. Africa Troops

MOSCOW, Wednesday.—Hitler has agreed to France adding to her "permitted" forces in Tunisia and Algiers two infantry divisions, two artillery regiments, a tank regiment and an air group, says a Geneva despatch to the Soviet News Agency.—*Reuter.*

Shots Fired at Antonescu

MOSCOW, Wednesday.—An attempt was made on the life of Antonescu, Rumanian Deputy Premier, shortly after his return to Bucarest last week from Hitler's headquarters, says a Cairo message to the Soviet News Agency.

Shots were fired as Antonescu was driving from the royal palace after a conference with the Prime Minister, but he was unhurt, apart from scratches caused by broken glass. An official and an officer were wounded. About 15 suspects have been arrested.

Alois Gruber, a high-ranking Gestapo official, was killed in Prague when "fighting the Reich's enemies in the Protectorate," says a Prague message.—*Reuter.*

Captives : Talks Go On

Mr. Anthony Eden, Foreign Secretary, told the Commons yesterday conversations regarding the repatriation of permanently disabled war prisoners had been proceeding for some time.

He was not yet in a position to make any further statement.

4 U-BOATS SUNK

By Canada's Navy

OTTAWA, Wednesday.

THE sinking of four U-boats and the probable sinking of two others was announced to-day by Mr. Angus Macdonald, Canadian Navy Minister.

He said ships of the Royal Canadian Navy "this summer" have also taken part in "many other promising attacks" on other enemy submarines.

There was no confirmation, he declared, of rumours that submarine parties made a landing anywhere on the Canadian coast.

He disclosed that the recent sinkings of the Canadian patrol ship Raccoon and the corvette Charlottetown by enemy action occurred in the Gulf of St. Lawrence.—*Reuter* and *A.P.*

New G2 Chief Here

Brigadier-General Robert A. McClure, General Staff Corps, United States Army, European Theatre, has been appointed Assistant Chief of Staff G 2 (Military Intelligence Division). Colonel Dwight Hughes jun., Cavalry, has been appointed Acting United States Military Attaché in London.

More Trades Controlled

Further tightening of trade activities on the home front were announced last night.

The cleaning and dyeing industry is controlled from to-day because of the increasing demands of the Forces, shortage of labour, and civilian needs "to make clothes do."

Boot and shoe menders, from the one-man kind to the big footwear retailers who carry out repairs on their own premises, will be unable to continue their business after November 1 unless registered with the Board of Trade. An order has been made so that every district in the country can be sure of adequate facilities for the repair of boots and shoes.

'WOMEN DO NOT TAKE LIFE'

LONDON (Ontario), Wednesday.—Major-General Jean Knox, 35-years-old Director of the British A.T.S., said to-day : "Women have won a merited place in the active army, but they cannot be trained to kill.

"I don't believe women can take life as men can. I know nothing of Russia, but I know women. Women give life. They are not designed to take life, even in total war."—*Reuter.*

Gestapo Gaols Henlein

From Daily Mail Correspondent

NEW YORK, Wednesday.—Konrad Henlein, used as a puppet by Hitler for the Sudetenland coup, has become a victim of one of the Gestapo's purges, and is now in gaol on the orders of Himmler, according to an announcement by the Czechoslovakia National Council of America to-day.

Henlein was said to be sharing a cell with Doctor Walter Darre, one-time German Minister of Agriculture.

Plenty of Tobacco

Despite Budget increases two thousand million cigarettes weekly are smoked in Britain, Mr. A. H. Maxwell, the Tobacco Controller, said yesterday on returning from the United States in quest of tobacco. There was no question of a shortage in 1943, he added, provided we had the ships.

SENATE ALTERS ITS MIND

Roosevelt Wins

WASHINGTON, Wednesday.

WITH less than 12 hours to go before President Roosevelt's threat of executive action might have come into effect, the United States Senate to-night passed the Administration's amendment to the Anti-Inflation Bill.

This last-minute change of mind came after the Senate had, late last night, adopted by 48 votes to 43 the farm bloc's amendment to the Bill that would have meant its vetoing by President Roosevelt and his executive action to control prices.

The farm bloc amendment had already been passed by the United States House of Representatives.

Price Parity

Farming interests have formed the main weight of the opposition to the Anti-inflation Bill.

Their main point of difference with the Administration was that they wanted production costs plus profits to form the basis of the prices on which the Bill would base its price ceilings on agricultural products and wages.

The Roosevelt plan, however, was to maintain parity prices which are designed to give the farmer roughly the same return for his produce as he received during the years from 1909 to 1914.

A plan for fixing a price ceiling for agricultural products at these levels was prevented by the farm bloc in Congress earlier in the year.—*B.U.P.*

LAVAL SEES U.S. ENVOY

Laval saw Mr. Pinkney Tuck, United States Charge d'Affaires in Vichy, says British United Press. Other callers were German Consul-General and Swiss Ambassador.

Admiral Gouton appointed C.-in-C. French Naval Forces, according to Vichy radio.

Daily Mail
LATE WAR NEWS SPECIAL
NO. 14,515 ONE PENNY * * FOR KING AND EMPIRE THURSDAY, NOVEMBER 5, 1942

ROMMEL RETREATS IN DISORDER

His Deputy Killed, Africa Corps Commander One of 9,000 Prisoners

RELENTLESS PURSUIT OF BROKEN ARMY

ROMMEL'S Africa Corps—pride of the German Army—and their Italian allies are in full and disorderly retreat. His second-in-command has been killed, the commander of the Africa Corps (General von Thoma) is in our hands with other high officers and 9,000 prisoners; and 260 of his tanks and 270 of his guns have been captured or destroyed.

Every available Allied aircraft has been flung against the fleeing Axis columns in day and night attacks. The Eighth Army is racing forward in relentless pursuit.

This tremendous news was given to an eagerly awaiting world late last night in a special communiqué from British Middle East Headquarters. Here is the text. It was broadcast to Germany and Italy again and again with all the resources available to the United Nations:

"The Axis forces in the Western Desert, after 12 days and nights of ceaseless attacks by our land and air forces, are now in full retreat. Their disordered columns are being relentlessly pursued by our land forces and by the Allied air forces by day and night.

"General von Stumme, a senior general who is said to have been in command during Rommel's absence in Germany, is known to have been killed.

"So far we have captured over 9,000 prisoners, including General Ritter von Thoma, Commander of the German Africa Corps, and a number of other senior German and Italian officers.

HEAVY AXIS CASUALTIES

"It is known that the enemy's losses in killed and wounded have been exceptionally high. Up to date we have destroyed more than 260 German and Italian tanks and captured or destroyed at least 270 guns.

"The full toll of the booty cannot be assessed at this stage of the operations. In the course of the operations our air forces, whose losses have been light, have destroyed or damaged in air combat over 300 aircraft, and destroyed or put out of action a like number on the ground.

"At sea our naval and light forces have sunk 50,000 tons and damaged as much again Axis shipping carrying supplies to North Africa. The Eighth Army continues to advance."

Dramatic 24 Hours Turn the Scales

This message from Paul Bewsher, Daily Mail Special Correspondent in Egypt, received shortly before the special communiqué was issued, shows how the battle in the desert suddenly changed from heavy fighting to rout.

CAIRO, Wednesday.

AFTER 11 days of relentless pounding and battering by the Eighth Army and Allied Air Forces, Rommel is withdrawing a portion of his vehicles westwards along the coastal road and has ordered his forces to fall back along 16 miles of front on his southern flank.

The whole situation has changed with lightning rapidity in the past 24 hours, and new developments follow each other hourly in Montgomery's great push. Here are the vital facts:

1. Columns of enemy transport of every kind are streaming back westwards along the coastal road pounded and blasted by a devastating concentration of aircraft of all kinds.

2. In the northern plain between the coast and the Ruweisat Ridge the enemy have fallen back everywhere to a line west of Sidi Abd el Rahman—except just near the coast—and there are no reports that tank battles are continuing to-day.

3. The enemy have withdrawn all along a front of 16 miles in the south—from the depression of Deil el Angar to the edge of the deep Qattara Depression.

STILL IN POCKET

4. The position of the German and Italian force in the pocket near the coast just west of Tel el Eisa has become so precarious that it will probably be dealt with at our leisure.

The position in the immediate area of the village of Sidi Abd el Rahman a few miles to the west of the pocket, is not clear, but in view of the westward movement of enemy transport columns it does not look as if it is likely to figure much in the news.

The entire weight of the Allied air striking force is being thrown against the retreating enemy transport moving along the coastal road.

Great formations of bombers are meeting with no opposition. Our fighters are also joining in, strafing the road and doing their best to turn retreat into panic.

Our troops are following up the enemy forces which withdrew from Himeimat and other tactical positions in the southern sector.

Considerable fighting has taken place since the offensive began in

BACK PAGE—Col. FIVE

AXIS GET 35 VICHY SHIPS

By Daily Mail Naval Correspondent

FURTHER evidence of the enemy's growing shortage of merchant shipping was forthcoming yesterday when it became known in London that Vichy is handing over to the Axis 35 ex-Allied merchantmen now in the Mediterranean.

Pressure by the Axis on Vichy to relieve the shipping situation has been mounting as the weight of our attacks, both by sea and air, on the enemy's coastal routes has been increasingly felt.

A "gift" of these 35 ships, however, useful as it may be in an emergency, does not amount to much more than a token. Their total tonnage is 120,000, one fiftieth of the total Axis merchant shipping losses up to the end of June.

Since June 30 our attacks on enemy shipping in the North Sea, the English Channel and, above all, on Rommel's supply routes in the Mediterranean, have been continued relentlessly and with success.

Between October 1 and October 25 in the Mediterranean alone 24 supply ships were sunk or damaged by British submarines. Fourteen of these were seen to sink.

The 120,000 tons represents about one-twelfth of the total Vichy-controlled tonnage in all waters, including French and ex-Allied ships, whether operating or laid up.

Australia Air Hustle

From Daily Mail Correspondent

MELBOURNE, Wednesday.—Australia's production of Beaufort bombers during October was three times the total production of the last six months of 1941. Senator Cameron, Aircraft Production Minister, revealed to-day.

Flight to the West

MAP illustrates Rommel's sensational flight to the west, recorded by Cairo G.H.Q. last night. His line has been broken on both flanks, and his columns are being bombed as they go.

RAF Race for Axis Airfields

By **COLIN BEDNALL**, Daily Mail Air Correspondent

NOW that the Egyptian battle has switched from static to mobile warfare, we are likely to see very shortly a grim and dramatic struggle for the chain of airfields, now in Rommel's hands, stretching across the face of Libya.

It may take the form of a race—a race in which Rommel will strive to get his transport as far back as possible before the R.A.F. can get hold of his present forward airfields to strafe him.

If Rommel should lose the race he risks finding himself at the wrong end of the greatest bombing strafe the desert has yet seen.

Position Changes

Rommel succeeded earlier in the year in advancing without air superiority. He will find it a very different proposition to retreat without it.

Already, now that the Germans have begun to move westward, the Allied Air Forces are taking heavy toll of his transport. With luck, we may now see the full and terrible meaning of air superiority operating this time from the British side.

He will probably strive to hold the aerodromes with strong rearguards while his main forces get beyond the radius of attack which these aerodromes would give to our short-range, as well as our long-range, aircraft.

One Within Range

The first of these aerodromes—El Daba—appears to be almost within reach of our forces now. Ahead of that, as the map above shows, are Fuka, Maaten Bagush, Sidi Hameish, and Mersa Matruh.

Then comes a wide gap to Sollum, which—probably because it formed a sort of No Man's Land for so long in earlier fighting—is not known to possess any well-established aerodromes.

It is probably cluttered, however, with landing-grounds such as exist at Sidi Barrani. Some of these may have been brought to a fairly high state of development by now.

In the area around Sollum, which has seen so much action in the past, there are clusters of both aerodromes and landing-grounds.

If Rommel is forced to make a real retreat, he may well make another stand in this area.

Excellent Targets

That he is already making withdrawals on some scale is shown by the reference in yesterday's Cairo communiqué to the fact that the "full force" of the Allied air-striking power had been concentrated on enemy units moving back along the coastal road.

Slow-moving transport, it was added, provided "excellent targets."

A study of official communiqués during recent months shows that statements of this kind are not made without a great deal to back them.

In addition to extending the reach of our own Air Forces, the capture of successive aerodromes would also have the effect of chopping miles off the air arm which the enemy struggles to keep stretched above his now hard-pressed land forces.

Transport processioning along a road offers a concentrated, elongated target which is ideal.

'They're Running' —Pilot Radios

From **PAUL BEWSHER**, Daily Mail Special Correspondent

CAIRO, Wednesday.

ABOUT one o'clock yesterday afternoon a British airman, peering down on the smoking battlefield near Sidi Abd el Rahman, saw a very remarkable sight.

He gazed down with tense, drawn eyes to make sure he was right—for it was a sight which has not been seen in the Libyan campaign for 11 long months. Sure enough on the dark blue coast road running between the white sand dunes and brown desert was a big stream of enemy transport.

And it was moving westward—moving westward away from the front at the height of battle.

A long column of soft-skinned transport moving back to safety, or what it hoped was safety—from the area of the tank fighting.

The moment the news was flashed back to Air Headquarters in the field the call went out to the squadrons to "send in every available bomber and every available fighter."

The whole dreadful might of the Allied bombing force, including huge four-engined Liberators, Wellingtons, Halifaxes, Baltimores, and Bostons, was launched against this vital and vulnerable target.

ROUTE OF CHAOS

Though every available bomber has been working in wave after wave since dawn in what was to prove the heaviest day's bombing ever known in North Africa, they were at once sent out to smash at this unexpected target.

Squadron after squadron roared up from the desert aerodromes, raced westwards, and in a few minutes turned the enemy's road into a route of chaos and disaster.

Hundreds of bombs shrieked down on to the long column of lorries, petrol cars, trucks, trailers, and staff cars moving in a drab yellow stream on the blue highway.

Cars blew up, caught fire, collided, overturned. Soon there was a long string of fires burning along the road among the snake of transport stretching out farther and farther westwards, right towards El Fuka.

Again and again the road got jammed by damaged cars. At one place the jam lasted 20 minutes when two trucks received direct hits at a stretch of the road where traffic could not pass by to the right or the left.

FIGHTERS IN

Then fighters and fighter-bombers whined down with terrific speed.

Tracers, cannon-shells, and bullets ripped down into the convoys as the terrified drivers and occupants leapt down and dashed into the desert on either side.

For the specialists who had been "beating up" the enemy road for many weeks all this was almost too good to be true.

A vivid glimpse of the scene was given by General A. C. Strickland, of the United States Army Air Force, who flew in the leading bomber of one American formation.

"We swept over the road and saw it packed with transport," he said. "Every vehicle was stopped, and everywhere were tiny trails of dust where the crews were running into the desert.

"Every bomber of our formation turned and sailed down the road, spilling their bombs on vehicles and men. I never saw such a scene of destruction."

A fighter pilot just returned from a strafing sortie remarked: "There is very little future in being a German this afternoon."

STUKAS SMASHED

As the swift desert twilight fell, the bombers still pounded at the convoys, guided by the trail of flickering red fires. And when darkness came, fresh squadrons of night bombers continued the attack.

Little resistance was offered by the enemy to our attack and enemy air activity was generally slight during the day.

Two attempts to carry out Stuka raids on our troops were roughly handled.

The first formation was forced to jettison its bombs before reaching the target, and eight Stukas of the second formation were shot down and two escorting Messerschmitts.

PANZERS SMASHED AND SET ABLAZE

From **EDWIN TETLOW**, Daily Mail Special Correspondent

WITH THE EIGHTH ARMY, Tuesday (delayed).

OUR casualties to date in the Battle of the Breach are comparatively light, and are believed to be many times less than the enemy's. Prisoner-of-war cages—a very reliable barometer of how the enemy is suffering—have been more crowded in the last two days than at any time since our offensive began nearly a fortnight ago.

To-day our tanks are smashing hard at Rommel's tanks and infantry, and latest reports indicate good progress. Many enemy tanks are burning.

The 15th and 21st Panzer Divisions and the 90th Light Division came down from the north and the Italian Ariete Division up from the south-west.

After many hours of confused fighting we have tightened our grip upon positions at the westerly side of the breach forced during Sunday-Monday night.

We now occupy an important position at Tel el Aqqaqir, together with an adjoining sector of the track linking Sidi Abd el Rahman, on the coast, with Qattara, in the south.

Italians Surrender

Last night we also made two successful attacks to the south-west of the breach and extended its width from approximately 4,000 yards to 5,000 yards.

One of these attacks was made by infantry and supporting tanks with such speed and dash that the enemy had little time to resist. The defenders were chiefly Italians, and believing they were surrounded they surrendered.

An artillery barrage we had planned had to be called off because it was not needed.

A big share of the credit for keeping our hold on the bridgehead during the critical hours of yesterday, when the enemy made counter-attacks, must be given to some of our tanks.

The men nad been trained to fight defensively as well as to carry out their customary rôle of attack; and in yesterday's test they did splendidly when the enemy came at them.

While the position in the breach steadily improves, the situation of the enemy force trapped in a pocket near the sea becomes more pre-

BACK PAGE—Col. FOUR

This Was the Only News

B.B.C. Tell World

At 11 o'clock last night B.B.C. announcer Bruce Belfrage broke into both Home and Forces programmes saying: "Here is some excellent news from Cairo."

Then in a special announcement he gave the first story of Rommel's retreat.

From 10.30 onwards the broadcast went out to the world—especially to America—in all languages, and was repeated throughout the night at frequent intervals.

On the Italian service it was repeated four times in 15 minutes.

Every works canteen during the midnight break drank "The toast is the Eighth Army." And in mines, factories, everywhere they "went to it" with new vigour spurred by the knowledge that their weapons had helped to dip the scale towards victory.

What Germans Said

At first, German and Italian radio kept silent. Then an hour after the Cairo communiqué was issued, the English-speaking announcer on the German radio said:

"There is little to report about the battle. The British are continually attacking with a superiority in artillery and tank forces, supported by aircraft.

"There is fierce fighting going on and the German-Italian troops threw back the British onslaught."

Earlier in the evening a German military spokesman, quoted by the German News Agency, had said: "Field-Marshal Rommel has the position well in hand. He is well able to take the initiative now as before, should he consider it necessary.

DAILY MAIL map shows the string of known German airfields stretching from El Alamein to Tobruk. It makes clear the danger Rommel runs should he lose control of the forward group at a time when his crowded transport is moving back along the coast road.

THE KING TO 8th ARMY

'—Well Done'

It was announced late last night that the King has sent the following message to General Alexander:

THE Eighth Army, magnificently supported by the R.A.F. and units of the Royal Navy, has dealt the Axis a blow of which the importance cannot be exaggerated.

For the last fortnight we have all been following with anxious interest the progress of the hard-fought battle, and I can assure all three Services, embracing as they do the many representatives of the British Commonwealth and our Allies, of the admiration and pride of the whole Empire in their brilliant victory.

In the name of your fellow countrymen all the world over I express to you, to Air Marshal Tedder, to General Montgomery, to Air Vice-Marshal Coningham, and to the Commander and all ranks of the three Services, my thanks for the far-reaching success which, by your untiring co-operation, you have so decisively achieved.—George R.I.

BRITISH MASS IN GIB.—BERLIN

BRITAIN is massing a great concentration of warships and transports in the harbour of Gibraltar, the German official News Agency said last night.

"Among other ships the aircraft-carriers Furious and Argus and another aircraft-carrier of unknown type have arrived

"In addition, there are six cruisers, one auxiliary cruiser, 26 destroyers, four submarines,

"This remarkable concentration of naval vessels is further strengthened by two transports of considerable capacity, as well as by 26 freighters and 12 tankers."

FISHING BOATS IDLE IN PORT

Fishing trawlers are laid up in a British port because the crews have refused to sail.

This stoppage follows the Food Ministry's order that some of the ships must be diverted from the port where they have landed catches for two years and go to other ports.

Yesterday owners of the boats expressed agreement with the men's attitude. Consequently the trawlers remain idle.

Three Trains in Crash

A driver, Percy Mason, of Battersea, was killed and a number of passengers were injured when a West Croydon to Sutton Southern electric train crashed into a stationary train and damaged another at Waddon early yesterday. The lines were blocked until late afternoon.

ITALIANS IN EGYPT ASK FOR TRUCE

The Italians have asked for an armistice to enable them to bury their dead.

A Reuter flash from Cairo early this morning gave this news. The message does not state whether the request applies to the whole of the Italian forces on the Mediterranean-Qattara front.

B.B.C. commentator, Godfrey Talbot, broadcasting from Cairo, said the pocket on the coast had been wiped out, and that "the thumb of the fist now rests on the coast."

It showed the severity of

A2

the punishment which the Axis troops are suffering, he said, that in one sector a group of Italians had asked for an armistice to enable them to bury their dead.

'NO PAUSE IN ATTACKS'

Daily Mail Radio Station

Still concealing the news of Rommel's defeat from the German people, a military spokesman on Berlin radio said at midnight: "The bitter fighting in Egypt is continuing.

"Thanks to the strategic skill of Field Marshal Rommel the enemy has not yet been able to break through decisively. The enemy is continuing his attacks in spite of heavy losses without a pause."

B2

SUNDAY NEWS
Copr. 1942 by News Syndicate Co. Inc. NEW YORK'S PICTURE NEWSPAPER Trade Mark Reg. U. S. Pat. Off.
5 CENTS PAY NO MORE
Vol. 22. No. 28 New York, Sunday, November 8, 1942★ 104 Main+48 Brooklyn+12 Queens+16 Comic+16 Coloroto Pages

U.S. INVADES FRENCH NO. AFRICA

F. D. R. CALLS ATTACK OUR SECOND FRONT

EXTRA

(Special to The News)

Washington, D. C., Nov. 7.—American forces have invaded French Colonies in North Africa, it was announced offically tonight.

In a special announcement made by the White House at 9 P. M., it was said that "powerful American forces" were landing at all French colonies on the Mediterranean and Atlantic coasts in order to "forestall an invasion" of Africa by Germany and Italy.

The announcement said the American landings, assisted by the British navy and air forces, were at that moment in progress. President Roosevelt described the landings as providing "an effective second front assistance to our heroic allies in Russia."

The announcement said the American force was under the command of Lieut. Gen. Dwight D. Eisenhower, chief of America's European land forces, and was equipped with "adequate weapons of modern warfare."

The points of landing were believed to be at Dakar, closest point on the African continent to the Americas, and Algiers on the Mediterranean, as well as other points. The landing in North Africa would constitute a threat to the rear of Marshal Erwin Rommel's battered divisions retreating after his defeat in Egypt.

Roosevelt himself made a shortwave broadcast in French to

(Continued on Page 3 col. 4)

DAILY MIRROR, Monday, November 9, 1942.

No. 12,139 ✦ ✦ ✦ ONE PENNY

Registered at the G.P.O. as a Newspaper.

Daily Mirror

NOV 9

OUR NEW FRONT IS OPENED IN N. AFRICA

GENERAL EISENHOWER

CARRYING scores of thousands of American troops, the greatest Armada the world has ever seen, yesterday launched a second front in North Africa.

Landings were made at several points on the Mediterranean and Atlantic coasts of French North Africa—Algiers and Oran being apparently the main points of attack.

The original landings were made by American troops, assisted by the British Navy and the Royal Air Force.

It has been announced, however, that several British divisions will follow.

Vichy sources reported that both the French Army and Navy were in action, but there was no confirmation of this from either London or Washington.

Fighting included a revolt by pro-Allied French in Casablanca.

The purpose of the landing is described in an Allied statement from London as helping the French to liberate themselves from Axis aggression.

Roughly the plan of campaign has been for rangers—U.S. equivalent of the commandos—to land in separate parties at strategic points with airborne troops brought up in support of the landing parties.

"INCREDIBLE SUCCESS" OF THE CONVOY

"There is some hope that the attitude of the civil population may be at least not unhelpful in this cause, so eloquently explained to them in the U.S. President's appeal," says the announcement.

First news of the invasion came in a dramatic Washington statement announcing the landings.

Then, at 10.30 a.m., Vichy radio declared

Continued on back page

Genoa counting its dead

GENOA, Rommel's supply port in Italy, had its heaviest raid of the war on Saturday night.

Crews of the strong force of RAF heavy bombers report great destruction to the port.

The raid was the second on the city on successive nights.

And the Italian communique yesterday said that the city is still counting its dead.

Many 4,000lb. bombs were dropped on the city.

Four Bombers Lost

When the bombing became heavy, the gunners ceased to fire and, in the words of a Lancaster pilot, "the attack became the same old piece of cake, only softer."

A wireless operator said it was the most successful attack yet made on Genoa.

"I counted many big fires and numberless small fires all over the port," he said. "Buildings just vanished in a series of violent explosions."

Four of our bombers are missing.

8th Army take Mersa Matruh

MERSA MATRUH is in our hands again. Rommel has less than 20,000 men of his once-proud Afrika Korps left.

We have captured or destroyed 500 tanks, taken between 900 and 1,000 guns, between 30,000 and 40,000 prisoners, the Italian Pavia Division and probably all the Italian Generals in Egypt.

The bulk of what once was the German panzer army has reached or passed the Libyan frontier in its non-stop flight from Egypt.

How badly the Germans panicked and left their Italian allies in the lurch is revealed in yesterday's Cairo communique and in a cable from Reuter's correspondent.

Up to Daba, halfway between Alamein and Mersa Matruh, the German withdrawal was more or less organised and co-ordinated. From there it became a debacle. The panic-stricken Germans

Continued on Back Page

IRON BLOWS MAN N. AFRICAN C-in-C

LIEUT.-GENERAL DWIGHT D. EISENHOWER is the man in supreme command of the land, sea and air forces, both British and American, engaged in the Allied Nations' operations to liberate North Africa.

General Eisenhower—known as Ike—is 51. His name is a German one meaning "The man who strikes iron blows."

A Washington War Department Communique states that some months ago Allied Force Headquarters were set up in London by the direction of the combined Chiefs of Staff in Washington.

United Staff

General Eisenhower was designated commander-in-chief of the Allied Force, and staff of British and American officers was selected.

When the threat of Axis invasion of North Africa became imminent General Eisenhower and his staff began making plans for the operation that is now under way.

General Eisenhower has concurrently been in command of all the American troops in the European theatre of operations.

ITALY'S BACK DOOR

AS this second front develops it should engulf the whole of North Africa except Spanish Morocco.

Vichy will no doubt do its utmost to urge resistance but the hold of Vichy on the loyalty and discipline of the troops in North Africa is not very strong.

Successful landings in Algeria will shorten the route to Tripoli by more than two-thirds and enable the Allies to cut off Rommel's supplies at their main port of entry.

The chances of Germany or Italy getting important reinforcements across to North Africa is slender.

Reconquest of the Mediterranean is the first vital step in the Allies' European strategy.

With secure bases on the North African coast for the Allied Naval and Air Forces the door is open to the invasion of Hitler's Europe through his back door—Italy.

The threatened coast would extend from Genoa to Salonika.

It means that they must immediately begin withdrawing their forces from Russia

Stalin's wish for the diversion of about 60 divisions from the Eastern Front may soon be gratified.—Reuter.

WEDNESDAY, NOVEMBER 11, 1942

BLACK OUT 5.48 to 7.41 | MOON SETS 8.2 p.m. Full Moon Nov. 22 | RADIO Page Six

LATE EXTRA

No. 16,974. ONE PENNY.

NAZIS OCCUPY VICHY FRANCE

Hitler Sends His Army In At Dawn

Resistance In N. Africa Ending

CASABLANCA FALL EXPECTED

RESISTANCE to the occupation by Allied Forces of the remaining areas in French North Africa was not expected today to last much longer on any appreciable scale.

With the fall of Oran and the wiping out of the French naval forces off Casablanca by the U.S. Fleet yesterday, it was believed that it would be only a matter of time before the Allies would subdue Casablanca, now the main centre of fighting.

The 35,000-ton battleship, Jean Bart, which was used as one of the principal defences of Casablanca, was still ablaze in the port today.

In Algeria the general situation is stationary. There is, as yet, no information that U.S. troops have entered Tunisia, but movements of trops across Algeria to the Tuniscan border have been reported. Most of the U.S. and British ships have left Algiers port.

Vichy radio said today that there was intense activity over Algiers during the night by U.S. air formation. There were two short raid warnings early today caused by Axis planes. The first was given at 4.20 a.m., and last half an hour. Bomb explosions were heard in the distance. The second was at 7.15, but no aircraft were sighted.

American assault forces captured the great French naval base at Oran at 1 p.m. yesterday after a whirlwind, well ahead of schedule.

Gen. Eisenhower, the Allied C.-in-C., announced the fall of the base to a combined land, sea and air assault, after an American tank column had broken into the city.

"2It was no child's play, and I am mighty proud of our boys, who have not had any sleep since Friday."

"But I don't want to make this appear as a great military victory. The French are our friends, and we want to keep them as our friends. We only fought because we had to."

General Fredenall launched the final assault at 7.30 a.m. yesterday, while the British Navy bombarded the harbour, and the Air Force, directed by General Doolittle, provided cover.

After the tank column broke into the city he French asked for an armistice, and Brigadier-General Oliver crossed the lines and arranged the capitulation.

Isolated French posts in the interior, now cut off, must surrender, giving to the Allies after a 60-hour fighting campaign nearly 1,000 miles of sea coast from Algiers to Gibraltar.

PETAIN IN AFRICA, SAY REPORTS

REPORTS are circulating on the French frontier that Marshal Petain has flown to North Africa to take command of the Vichy forces, states a B.U.P. message, which adds that there is no confirmation.

"Frenchmen of the metropolis and of the Empire, keep your confidence in your marshal, who is thinking of nothing but France," said Marshal Petain in a broadcast appeal shortly after he assumed the post of C.-in-C. of the French armed forces, says A.P.

Marshal Petain said he thought he had left the darkest days of his life, but the present situation reminded him of the bad memories of 1940.

He appealed to Frenchmen to face events with calm.

Armistice Day Ban In Vichy

ALL Armistice Day demonstrations have been forbidden by the Vichy Government, and special police measures will be enforced.

Demonstrations against the Government have already taken place in Marseilles, Toulon and other French towns, including some in the occupied zone, according to a Geneva message, quoted by Moscow radio.

Allied landings in North Africa were applauded, and there were shouts of "Down with Vichy!" adds an A.P. message.

More "Breaks" With Vichy

CUBA and Haiti are the latest countries to break off diplomatic relations with Vichy. A further "break" by Uruguay is imminent, says Reuter.

M. Paul Boncour, son of the French statesman, has resigned his post as commercial attache to the French Legation in Bogota, in protest against Petain's order to French troops to fire on the Allied forces in North Africa, says A.P.

CURFEW PROTEST

The decision of the South-Eastern Commissioner of Transport, Col. F. Gordon Tuckes, to impose a 9 p.m. curfew on buses, has aroused considerable feeling among the entertainment and catering industries of Brighton.

The Brighton and Hove Entertainment Managers' Association have sent a resolution suggesting that transport and fuel economy could be spread over the whole day, with less inconvenience, and urging that the curfew should be extended to 10 p.m.

GAYDA IS GRIM

"The world war has entered a new phase which has its centre in the Mediterranean and the Italian people are called upon to face new trials," said Gayda, Mussolini's mouth-piece today.

The situation was hard but islands barred the way to any invasion of Italy, he said, according to A.P.

Greeks Jubilant

Reports received in Istanbul state there is great enthusiasm and excitement in Athens over the North African landings.

Students walk the streets singing the Greek national anthem, and the police have had to use fire engines to disperse them.

Another Raid-Free Night

There was no enemy air activity over this country last night.

Buses Collide

Two buses met in head-on collision in Eastcote-avenue, Harrow, today.

"I HAD TO ACT BEFORE BRITISH AND AMERICAN TROOPS INVADED CORSICA AND SOUTHERN FRANCE"

GERMAN TROOPS MARCHED INTO UNOCCUPIED FRANCE AT DAWN TODAY TO TAKE OVER THE WHOLE OF THE COUNTRY. THE NEWS WAS ANNOUNCED TO THE FRENCH PEOPLE BY PARIS RADIO, WHICH QUOTED LETTERS FROM HITLER TO THE FRENCH PEOPLE AND TO PETAIN, GIVING HIS "REASONS" FOR THE DECISION TO MARCH IN.

In Vichy the decision was communicated to the Petain Government in a demarche by the German Consul-General Krugg von Nidda. The Petain Cabinet met immediately and sat for an hour. The Government, according to Paris radio, will return to Versailles.

According to a Lyons report the first German troops crossed the demarcation line by road and rail in the Lyons region and headed towards Chalons-sur-Saone.

In his message to the French people, Hitler said:

Frenchmen, officers and men of the French Army, on September 3, 1939, the British Government declared war upon Germany.

Those responsible for this war succeeded at that time in instigating the French Government to join in the declaration.

For Germany this constituted an unbearable provocation. The German Government has never made any claims on her which might have caused her offence.

The German people which then had to face this aggression, while sacrificing the blood of its sons, never felt any hatred for France.

After the crumbling of the Anglo-French front which, after the flight of the British to Dunkirk, developed into a catastrophe, France asked Germany for an armistice.

Under the armistice Germany asked nothing which might be incompatible with the honour of the French Army.

Precautions, however, had to be taken—in order to prevent the fight from being started again in the interests of the British war-mongers by means of paid agents.

Germany had no intention whatsoever of humiliating France, or of infringing the integrity of the French Empire. She hoped, by a subsequent reasonable peace, to achieve an atmosphere of mutual understanding in Europe

Since that time, Britain, and now also the U.S.A., have sought to set foot again on French soil in order to continue the war, as suits their interests, on French territory. After several attempts had come to a lamentable end, the Anglo-American attack was launched against the colonies of North and West Africa.

"CORSICA WAS NEXT"

Having regard to the weakness of the French forces in those parts, the enemy would find it an easier ground for operations than in the west, where the country is protected by Germany.

The German Government has known for 24 hours that the plans of these operations provide that the next attack will be made against Corsica in order to occupy that island and against the south coast of France.

In these circumstances I felt compelled to order the German Army immediately to march through the Unoccupied Zone—and this is now being done—and to march to points aimed at by the Anglo-American landing troops.

The German Army does not come as an enemy of the French people nor of its soldiers, nor does it intend to govern these territories. It has one sole aim: to repel, together with its allies, any landing attempt by the Anglo-American Forces.

Marshal Petain and his Government are entirely free and are in a position to fulfil their duty as in the past. From now on nothing stands in the way of the realisation of their requests, made earlier, to come to Versailles, to govern France from there.

The German forces have been ordered to see to it that the French people are inconvenienced as little as possible. The French people must, however, bear in mind that, by the attitude of its Government in 1939, the German people were thrown into a grievous war, which threw hundreds of thousands of families into peril and grief.

Only where blind fanaticism, or agents in the pay of Britain, oppose the advance of our troops will the decision be left to the force of arms.

In his letter to Petain Hitler said:

Since the day when the State called upon me to direct the destinies of my people, I have ceaselessly striven to improve our relations with France, even at the price of heavy sacrifices to Germany.

All my efforts proved futile. That was not my fault. The

CONTINUED ON BACK PAGE, Col. TWO

LAVAL DEAL WITH AXIS IS EXPECTED

MORE reports from Berlin of a meeting between Hitler and Mussolini in Munich are circulating on the French frontier, says B.U.P.

Other reports state that the meeting is to be held in Rome, with Laval participating.

The general belief is that Hitler will ask Mussolini to relinquish his territorial claims against France in return for full French collaboration and permission to land Axis forces at Bizerta immediately.

According to reports in well-informed quarters close to the Axis, both the Grand Hotel, Rome, and the Villa Madama, on the slopes of Monte Mario, Rome, where Hitler stayed in 1938, are being closely guarded.

"Daily Herald," Thursday, Nov. 12, 1942.

LONDON BLACKOUT
5.46 p.m. to 7.43 a.m.
Moon Rises 12.15 p.m.
Moon Sets 9.04 p.m.
Lighting-up Time 5.46 p.m.

Daily Herald

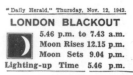

No. 8342 — THURSDAY, NOVEMBER 12, 1942 — ONE PENNY

STOP PRESS

GLIDERS FLY SOUTH

LISBON.—Large force of transport planes and bombers towing gliders sighted off Portuguese coast early this afternoon, flying from the north.—Associated Press.

ALLIES RACE TO MEET TUNIS NAZIS

HITLER'S INVASION HELPED BY LAVAL

WHILE German and Italian troops were racing through Unoccupied France yesterday to seize the Mediterranean coast, Laval returned to Vichy from his secret mission.

That was at 2 p.m.

Shortly before 9 p.m. an official communiqué was issued in Vichy revealing that he was deeply implicated in the second invasion of his country since May, 1940.

It stated:

"The events of the last few days caused a number of discussions to take place between the French and German Governments.

"In view of the seriousness of the circumstances, Laval left Vichy on Monday for Munich.

"He had several interviews with Hitler and von Ribbentrop, was kept informed hourly by telephone of developments in North Africa, and maintained contact with Marshal Pétain.

"At one of his interviews with Hitler, Count Ciano, the Italian Foreign Minister, was present.

Handed A Copy

"As Laval was leaving Munich he received a copy of Hitler's letter to Marshal Pétain *(reported on the Back Page)*.

"Certain events which occurred during the night had determined the decision of the German High Command.

"M. Laval took the plane from Munich, and arrived in Vichy at 2 p.m. to-day with Otto Abetz, German Ambassador to Paris.

"Later Otto Abetz was received by Marshal Petain. In the course of a Cabinet meeting at 5 p.m. M. Laval gave a comprehensive survey of the situation."

In spite of Laval's foreknowledge of German moves, Marshal Pétain protested against Germany's action.

Berlin announced last night that German and Italian troops had reached all their objectives and were taking up positions on the French Mediterranean coast.

It did not state the fate of the French Fleet, which was reported by Vichy, at 4 p.m., to be lying off Toulon.

The invasion of Unoccupied France was carried out at Panzer speed.

Marseilles, the great port on the Mediterranean, was warned to expect occupation before the end of the day.

Triple Drive

Italian troops timed their invasion to coincide with a double German drive from the demarcation line in the north and the strip of occupied territory down the western coast.

Nice was entered at 3 p.m. by an Italian force moving westward from the Alps of Savoy.

Reinforcements for the German garrison already stationed on the Franco-Spanish frontier arrived early in the day, presumably to prevent escapes.

The Franco-Swiss frontier was similarly reinforced.

BRITISH FIRST ARMY ADVANCES AGAINST GERMAN INVADERS

Darlan Gives Cease Fire Command

A COMBINED BRITISH AND AMERICAN ARMY IS DRIVING EASTWARD AT TOP SPEED FROM ALGIERS TO MEET AXIS AIRBORNE FORCES WHO HAVE LANDED IN TUNISIA.

This news came from General Eisenhower's Allied headquarters in North Africa last night at the same time as the official announcement that Darlan had ordered all French resistance in North Africa to end.

The "Cease Fire" came at 8 a.m. and seems to have been obeyed in all the chief coast towns, including Casablanca, which is occupied by American troops. The situation in the interior, however, remains obscure.

The Allied troops racing eastwards towards Tunisia include the British First Army, under Lieut.-General K. A. N. Anderson. They reached Bougie, on the coast, 110 miles east of Algiers, and 300 miles west of Tunis, early yesterday.

Bougie, Mr. Churchill disclosed, was occupied by an amphibious expedition. It is just over 500 miles in a direct line from Tripoli and has a good harbour.

New York reports last night said American troops were only 100 miles from the Tunisian border.

The announcement of the German landing in Tunisia was made by Allied H.Q. in London. The landing consisted of fighter planes and dive-bombers, ground crews and aerodrome defence units carried by air transports from Sicily and Sardinia.

LT.-GEN. K. A. N. ANDERSON commands the British First Army, revealed last night to be engaged in French North Africa.

He is a Scot, 50 years old, who has risen during the war from command of a brigade (writes Major E. W. Sheppard). He had a division at Dunkirk, and last April took over the Eastern Command in Britain.

Normally a British Army consists of two or more corps, each with two, three or more divisions, and of armoured motorised divisions. An army thus may number anything from 150,000 men upwards.

Our original First Army formed part of the B.E.F. in France in 1939, but has been entirely re-formed and re-equipped since.

Landings At Airports

It was estimated late last night that between 500 and 600 men had been landed by the Axis at El Alunia airport, outside Tunis, and probably at Sidi Armed, the airport for Bizerta, the French naval base.

As a parallel move to the German landing in Tunisia, Rome officially announced last night that Italian troops have landed at Bastia, in Napoleon's island of Corsica.

At the same time German and Italian troops were racing through Unoccupied France to seize the Mediterranean coast, with its vital bases of Toulon and Marseilles.

Nothing definite is known of what has happened to the French Fleet, beyond a Vichy report that it was still at Toulon yesterday afternoon.

It was revealed last night that Laval has been at Munich with Hitler helping to plan the new invasion of France.

'SURRENDER ARMS,' FRENCH ORDERED

ADMIRAL DARLAN, who has been secretly negotiating with Major-General Mark W. Clark, deputy to General Eisenhower, for the past few days, ordered all forces, naval and land, in North Africa to surrender arms and return to barracks at 8 a.m. yesterday.

This was the news last night from Allied H.Q. in North Africa.

"The position of Admiral Darlan remains obscure, although he signed himself as Commander of the French Forces in North Africa, a position which is also claimed by General Giraud, who has General Eisenhower's support," it was stated by correspondents at Allied Headquarters.

The last place of resistance was in Morocco, where Major-General G. S. Patton gave the "cease fire" order after a conference with Admiral Michelier, the French commander in that area.

In Petain's Name

Last night American troops were pouring into Casablanca.

It can be assumed that Admiral Darlan's order, issued after his conference with Major-General M. W. Clark, has put an end to all hostilities in Casablanca, says British United Press.

"Our engagements having been fulfilled," his order ran, "and bloody battle becoming useless, I order all land, sea and air forces in North Africa to cease the fight against the power of America and their Allies and, as from the receipt of this order, to return to their barracks and bases, and observe the strictest neutrality."

"In Algeria and Morocco," Darlan's order continued, "the commanders-in-chief will put themselves in liaison with local commanders on the subject of terms for the suspension of hostilities.

"I assume command over North Africa in the name of Marshal Pétain. The present senior officers will retain their commands, and the political administrative organ-

(CONTINUED BACK PAGE)

Hitler Had To Act In Hurry

By W. N. EWER

HITLER has acted very rapidly—and has done exactly what we expected him to do.

But this time his speed of movement is not a lightning stroke following careful preparation. It is the hurried action of a man taken by surprise.

The very method shows that. There was no time to fix things up with Pétain, though the whole tone of Hitler's announcement betrays his anxiety to keep on good terms with him.

He had to order his troops to move, and chance unpleasant reaction from Vichy. He has had it.

What Hitler wanted was that Pétain should not only accept but even welcome the German move, and agree that French troops should join with the Germans in "defending the frontiers of France side by side."

Alarmed

A little diplomacy, a little pressure, might have secured that before the move was made. But there was no time. The Nazi staff was alarmed by the thought that at any moment it might be faced by an Allied landing on the French Mediterranean coast.

So, without any sort of preparation, it has rushed divisions at top speed to the threatened area. Now it has to face the problem of replacing them in the north.

Similarly it has rushed airborne troops from Sicily to Tunisia. Note that it has not sent them to help Rommel.

That looks as though the Nazi staff has just written him off as a total loss.

The purpose of this Tunis move is not very plain. It hardly seems likely that sufficient forces can be transported to put up a really serious resistance to the Americans.

It may be that the Tunis expedition is just a gesture. It may be that it consists mostly of demolition parties out to wreck the Bizerta base before we reach it.

Hitler and his staff knew that something was cooking. But they expected Dakar rather than Algiers. And they completely under-estimated the strength of any possible expedition.

Tunisia occupies a strategic position on the southern shore of the Mediterranean equal in importance to that of Italy, on the northern shore.

It juts out to within 150 miles of both Sicily and Sardinia and commands the narrow waist of water through which all shipping must pass from East to West.

It has a score of first-class airfields, from which any part of Italy can easily be reached, and most of North Africa can be covered.

There are 2,000 miles of railways, excellent military roads.

Bizerta is a naval base of first importance. In the hands of the Allies, without naval power, it would be of tremendous strategic value.

Bizerta is 700 miles from Gibraltar, 1,100 from Alexandria, 240 from Malta and 450 from Marseilles.

The town stands on a narrow channel which opens out into a circular inland lake of about 50 square miles. Here is safe anchorage for the largest warships—and the channel entrance gives them protection against submarines.

Besides the large general naval base at Bizerta there is a special submarine base and a seaplane base.

If German airborne troops do establish a footing in Tunisia, it is through Bizerta Hitler will try to give them some formidable help. W. M. TOWLER.

Troops Flew 1,500 Miles To Attack Oran

THE American parachute troops who helped to attack Oran at dawn on Sunday had flown 1,500 miles non-stop from England.

This was disclosed from Allied H.Q. in North Africa early this morning.

Boarding the planes early on Saturday evening, they flew for eight hours across Europe and the Mediterranean.

It was the longest airborne invasion in military history.

When they started, the only man who knew where they were going was their leader, Colonel Raff.

He asked that his own battalion should do the job and that he should lead it.—Associated Press.

'EMPIRE' TALK CONDEMNED

Mr. Churchill's statement on Monday about the Empire was criticised by Senator Pepper at the convention of the Congress of Industrial Organisation, in Boston yesterday.

Senator Pepper said the Prime Minister had indicated that considerations of Empire had not been eliminated from the objectives of the war.

Senator Pepper added: "I wonder if he would have had the temerity to speak that sentence into the ear of a dying soldier or sailor."—Associated Press.

[Mr. Churchill said that he had not become the King's First Minister in order to preside over the liquidation of the British Empire. "We mean to hold our own," he declared.]

JOIN FIGHTING FRENCH

The French Consul-General in London, M. Etienne Jalenques, who continued his duties when France fell, stated yesterday that he was on the side of the United Nations and was ready to serve under a pro-Ally French authority set up in French territory.

EIGHTH ARMY LEAPS OVER THE FRONTIER

"DAILY HERALD" SPECIAL CORRESPONDENT

CAIRO, Wednesday.

NOW that our forces are across the frontier at several points, the Battle of Libya has begun.

Because Army headquarters are on the move westward, little hard news is coming back except that small enemy pockets of resistance are being cleared systematically just on the Egyptian side of the frontier, in the triangle of desert between the Sollum escarpment and the sea.

Actually our forces are on the move at a greater pace than in any previous advance, and single-engine fighters have been in action over Tobruk, 70 miles beyond the frontier.

Our air forces between dawn and early afternoon to-day destroyed 22 enemy planes, including 11 Ju 87s.

Eight planes were shot down when South African fighter pilots intercepted 15 Stukas over the Bardia-Gambut road.

Rescuing Italians

Allied airmen are also busy on an unusual job—rescue of thousands of Italian soldiers in peril of dying in the desert through lack of water and food.

In this work men of the Air Sea Rescue Service squadrons are taking a prominent part.

These crews are specially trained in the difficult task of finding airmen in distress far out at sea or on the equally vast ocean of desert.

When possible large machines actually land so that the Italians can be given water, and serious cases flown back for treatment.

In other cases water containers are dropped beside the exhausted men on parachutes, and the exact position is signalled to scouting parties on the ground who go out and rescue the miserable Italians.

BELLS AGAIN ON SUNDAY

CHURCH bells should be rung throughout the land next Sunday to celebrate the victory of the Empire and our Allies in the Battle of Egypt and as a call to thanksgiving and renewed prayer.

This announcement was made from 10, Downing-street, last night.

After consultation with the leaders of the Churches, it says, the Government asks that all clergy and ministers will, so far as possible, arrange for the bells in their churches to be rung before the mid-morning service.

The Government ban imposed in June, 1940, on the ringing of church bells, except as a warning of enemy attack, is waived for this purpose to cover any period between the hours of 9 a.m. and 12 noon.

AIR GENERAL HIT CRUISER

Major-General Brereton, Commander of the United States Air Forces in the Middle East, has been awarded the D.F.C. for an "extraordinary achievement."

While leading an attack on Port Blair, in the Andaman Islands, after a flight of 780 miles, he scored direct hits on an enemy cruiser, says Reuter from Cairo.

STRAITS GUNS AGAIN

Long-range guns on the French coast opened fire late last night for the third successive night. Shelling lasted about half an hour.

DOOLITTLE'S ESCAPE IN AIR FIGHT

GENERAL DOOLITTLE, Chief of the 12th American Air Force in North Africa, had a narrow escape when a Flying Fortress, in which he and a number of staff officers were travelling, was attacked by four enemy planes.

The co-pilot of the Fortress was hit by a bullet and General Doolittle took his place at the controls.

Four enemy planes were sighted when the Fortress was flying a few feet above the water.

As the pilot turned the enemy gave chase.

The leading German plane dived and was met by a burst from the Fortress top guns.

It wobbled and staggered off badly hit.

Almost simultaneously the second and third Nazi planes attacked, and machine-gun bullets smashed into the Fortress.

Another of the German planes was believed to have been badly damaged.—Associated Press.

H.M.S. ARGUS HIT, SAYS BERLIN

Berlin claimed last night that the British aircraft carrier Argus had been twice hit by a Junkers 88 off Algeria, and said the ship was being towed towards Gibraltar.

Argus, 14,000 tons, is Britain's oldest aircraft carrier.

HITLER WAS FOXED BY SECOND FRONT TALK:

Churchill Speech in full on Pages 2 and 3

Bigger Pension Early In 1943

By MAURICE WEBB

INCREASES in the weekly payments to old age pensioners and widows will be made in the early weeks of the New Year.

The statement in the King's Speech yesterday that "renewed consideration" will be given to the position of old-age and widows' pensions and further measures will be laid before you" is a specfic Government pledge to make further improvements.

But the Cabinet has not yet decided on the precise form and value of the intended concessions.

It is waiting for the Beveridge Report on the social services, which contains a comprehensive scheme of social insurance in return for a single weekly payment.

Ending Defects

As it may take some time to implement the Beveridge proposals, the Cabinet may introduce temporary legislation to meet the problems of pensioners.

It is impossible to say yet whether the basic pension will be increased. So far the Government has always refused to do this on the ground that it would require increased contributions from workers and employers to a pensions insurance fund.

What is certain is that some of the remaining defects in the supplementary scheme will be removed and adjustments made to the existing supplementary scales.

An important new measure containing agreed proposals for reforming the educational system will also be introduced early next year. Considerable progress has been made with the consultations between Ministers and the various bodies concerned in education.

Improvements in the scales of workmen's compensation are also on the way.

DOUBLE U.S. ATTACK IN SOLOMONS

AMERICAN troops in the Solomons continued offensive operations against the Japanese on the eastern and western flanks on Guadalcanal Island, said a United States communiqué yesterday.

Five enemy destroyers east of New Georgia were attacked by air.

Two Grumman Wildcats dived through a formation of 15 Zeros at an altitude of 27,000 feet near Guadalcanal. One Zero was shot down.

Army bombers in the Aleutians damaged two Japanese cargo vessels at Kisga.

Seven float planes were destroyed.

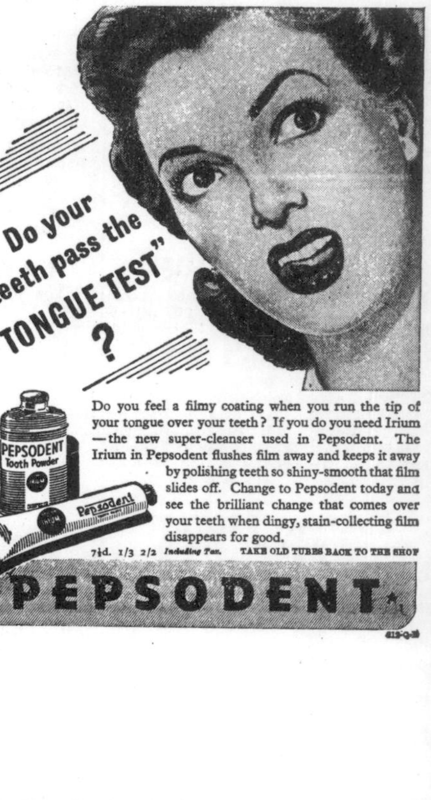

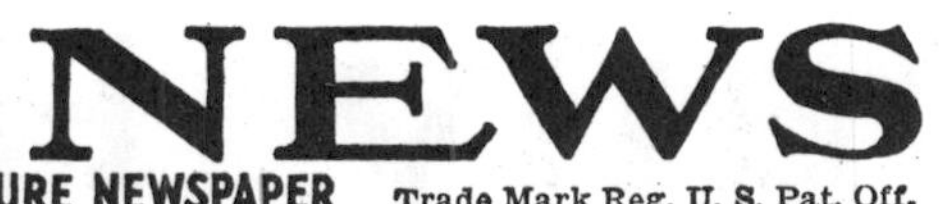

Copr. 1942 by News Syndicate Co. Inc. NEW YORK'S PICTURE NEWSPAPER Trade Mark Reg. U. S. Pat. Off.

Vol. 24. No. 120 New York, Thursday, November 12, 1942★ 60 Main+16 Brooklyn+4 Queens Pages 2 Cents IN CITY LIMITS | 3 CENTS Elsewhere

ALGERIA AND MOROCCO SURRENDER

End of Campaign Frees Yanks For Drive on Axis in Tunisia

NAZI OCCUPATION OF FRANCE COMPLETED

Stories on Page 3

"Daily Herald," Tuesday, Nov. 17, 1942.

LONDON BLACKOUT
5.39 p.m. to 7.52 a.m.
Moon Rises 3.18 p.m.
Moon Sets 1.53 a.m.
Lighting-up Time 5.39 p.m.

Daily Herald

No. 8346 TUESDAY, NOVEMBER 17, 1942 ONE PENNY

STOP PRESS

VICHY SHIPS AT ORAN

French steamers Diridon and Jamaique, which left Dakar and Marseilles at time of North African landings, have arrived safely at Oran, according to Vichy reports.—Reuter.

11 JAP WARSHIPS, 12 TRANSPORTS, SUNK IN BATTLE OF SOLOMONS

The desert skyline is broken by the smoke of burning lorries as the Eighth Army sweeps forward.

From ARTHUR WEBB WASHINGTON, Monday.

ELEVEN JAPANESE WARSHIPS, INCLUDING A BATTLESHIP, HAVE BEEN SUNK AND 12 TRANSPORTS DESTROYED IN A TERRIFIC THREE-DAY SEA AND AIR BATTLE OFF THE SOLOMONS.

Seven other enemy warships were damaged. American losses were two light cruisers and six destroyers.

Japanese losses, given in a Washington communiqué to-night were:

SUNK: One battleship, three heavy cruisers, two light cruisers, five destroyers, eight transports.

DAMAGED: One battleship, six destroyers.

DESTROYED: Four transports.

Washington naval circles said to-night that at least 24,000 Japanese must have died in the eight transports sunk.

And Admiral Nimitz, in a communiqué issued at Pearl Harbour, said this attempt to recapture Guadalcanal had been completely frustrated.

Moving On Guadalcanal

Air reconnaissance early this month, states the communiqué, revealed a heavy concentration of Japanese transports, cargo vessels and combatant units in the New Britain-N.W. Solomons region.

An attempt by the enemy to recapture our positions in the Guadalcanal-Tulagi area was indicated, and on November 10 it became evident that an expedition was being launched in force.

Japanese naval forces approached the S.E. Solomons from the north as other detachments, including many transports, moved south-eastward towards Guadalcanal from Rabaul and Buin, where the expeditionary forces had been assembling.

General MacArthur's aircraft were of great assistance to our naval forces both before and during the naval actions.

Jap Spearhead

Army bombers made repeated and successful attacks on units of the Japanese invasion fleet at Rabaul and Buin.

[These attacks were announced by United Nations headquarters in Australia.]

The spearhead of the Japanese attack was a force composed of two battleships of the Kongo class and

(CONTINUED BACK PAGE)

FIGHTING FRENCH ARE ALARMED AT RECOGNITION OF VICHY MEN IN NORTH AFRICA

DARLAN IS REPUDIATED BY GENERAL DE GAULLE

By W. N. EWER

STEPS are being taken to unravel the political tangle which Admiral Darlan's activities have created in North Africa.

Yesterday General de Gaulle saw Mr. Churchill.

Action will need to be rapid. For, whatever the immediate consequences of the Admiral's decision to change sides, the apparent recognition of him as a sort of Governor-General of North Africa has staggered and dismayed the Fighting French all over the world.

Their uneasiness has been further increased by reports that M. Flandin, the notoriously pro-German ex-Premier of France, is also in Algeria.

No Responsibility

Last night General de Gaulle's headquarters in London issued this statement:

General de Gaulle and the French National Committee announce that they are taking no part whatsoever in and assuming no responsibility for the negotiations in progress in North Africa with the representatives of Vichy.

Should these negotiations result in arrangements which would in effect confirm the Vichy regime in North Africa, such decisions could obviously not be accepted by Fighting France.

Impenitent

That is plain enough. It means that the Fighting French, who are delighted to co-operate with General Giraud, refuse flatly to co-operate with Admiral Darlan.

It is not just a question of Admiral Darlan's political past. That might, if he showed any sign of contrition, be forgiven.

More important is the Admiral's present conduct.

Caught in Algiers, he decided to join up: but in his own way and on his own terms.

He seems to have persuaded our soldiers that he and he alone could ensure quiet and order in North Africa, and enable them to give their whole attention to the task of fighting the enemy.

They gave him access to the radio, and he has used it to boost his own claims to authority.

Fiction

He has told the world that *he* has appointed General Giraud commander-in-chief of the French forces in North Africa.

But Giraud—as everyone remembers—had already spoken as commander-in-chief on the morning of the landing, long before Darlan had even decided to change sides.

He has told the world that it is he who ordered and secured the cessation of hostilities—which is a distortion of the facts.

How far Darlan is an asset in establishing a quiet and orderly administration in North Africa is doubtful.

Liability

Equally certainly he is a heavy liability in other ways. The belief that he is our preferred and favoured collaborator will have the most demoralising effect on the Fighting French outside and on the resistance movement inside France.

General de Gaulle repudiates him, and Darlan seems equally determined to repudiate Fighting France.

For the de Gaullists who were imprisoned by the Vichy administration in Algiers are apparently still kept in prison by Darlan.

It has all been done by the United Nations' military authorities with the best intentions, but with insufficient knowledge of politics and politicians.

The situation, if it develops further, may become not merely embarrassing, but very dangerous.

French Guards Beat Nazis Back In Tunis Clash

FRENCH TROOPS HAVE BEATEN BACK A GERMAN FORCE IN TUNISIA.

Allied headquarters in North Africa describing the clash in a communiqué last night said that on Sunday afternoon a German reconnaissance unit composed of motor-cyclists and armoured vehicles, proceeding from Tunis to Djedeida (a railway junction half way to Bizerta), met a French battalion of Guards.

The French troops opened fire on the Germans, who were forced to retreat.

A later communiqué announced:—

"Small French military units have begun to co-operate with the Eastern and Central Task forces.

"At Oran a French force has joined United States troops at their stations. The clearance and maintenance of ports and harbours proceeds.

Small Naval Losses

"On the east, the British First Army has been reinforced by mobile United States units.

"The Royal Navy maintains control of the Western Mediterranean and its approaches.

"This naval force has sustained losses, but they have been small in proportion to the size of the operations, and the casualties on the whole have been light.

"To-day we took into custody the officer and crew of a U-boat which had been sunk off the North African coast."

German claims to have sunk 89 Allied ships around the North African coast were authoritatively described as "vastly exaggerated—even beyond the usual German naval claims."

Allied headquarters admitted that the concentration of vast numbers of Axis submarines in the Mediterranean and off the entrance of Gibraltar was a major hazard.

"But," it added, "such concentration is resulting in a great number of kills by the British and American navies."

More Air Raids

British and American troops were reported yesterday to be fighting Germans near Tunis and other points in the Protectorate.

General Nehring, a former chief of Rommel's Afrika Korps, is commanding the Axis forces in Tunisia, it was revealed last night.

He has appealed to French troops to fight side by side with Germans "as comrades defending the cause of France."

Maintaining its attacks on the important aerodrome of El Aquina, Tunis, the RAF made three separate raids on Saturday night, adding considerably to the heavy damage and confusion already caused.

The first attack was carried out

(CONTINUED BACK PAGE)

THE man behind the German descent on Tunisia is 50-year-old General Wilhelm Student, chief of Hitler's paratroop and airborne forces.

He is a go-ahead officer of the Nazi school—in fact, a Rommel of the air.

He organised and directed the Nazi forces which turned us out of Crete.

In the paratroop attack on Holland—the first campaign of its kind the world had ever seen—he himself descended on Rotterdam aerodrome with a red parachute.

There has been no indication yet that he has actually landed in Tunisia, but there is no doubt his brain is behind this latest effort.

Early this year he was in Libya helping Rommel with supplies and reinforcements.

He returned to Germany with Rommel after the drive which took the Axis forces to Alamein.

Both men met Hitler and were feted. Then Rommel returned to Africa—and defeat.

Now Student has been called on again to make a desperate effort to get Rommel out of his difficulties.

C. de Garde
BONE
La Calle
C. Serrat
C. Blanc
BIZERTA
DJEDEIDA
ALLIED ADVANCE
TUNIS
Korba
Hammamet
Ain Beida
Maktar
Kairouan
Thala
Tebessa
Djilma
El Djem
Mahdia
ALGERIA
TUNISIA
Gafsa
Sfax
Tozeur
Gabes
DJERBA I.
LAKE DJERID
Medenine
LIBYA
Miles
0 20 40 60

BIZERTA
C. Guardia
C. Blanc
SIGNAL STATION
FORT SIDI SALEM
TO SICILY 150 MIS.
HARBOUR ENTRANCE (500 FT WIDE)
RD. TO ALGIERS
STATION
RESERVOIR
MENZEL DJEMIL
BIZERTA LAKE (NAVAL HARBOUR)
ROAD TO TUNIS
ARSENAL
Miles
0 1 2 3 4 5

DARLAN SETS UP NEW COUNCIL

Admiral Darlan, "In the name of Marshal Petain," last night instituted a legislative council to assist him as High Commissioner for French North Africa.

Members of the council will be required to give their views on "general questions of the legislative, administrative or legal kind on which they are consulted by the High Commissioner."—Reuter.

Petain Picks Successor

PETAIN has already appointed a new successor to himself in place of Darlan, according to German sources last night.

They said the decision was made at the Vichy Cabinet meeting on Sunday, but gave no name.

Earlier yesterday Petain issued a message in which he declared Darlan "bereft of all public office and military command." It said:

Darlan desires to affirm that I am not able to make my thoughts known to the French people, and claims to be acting on my behalf.

Several times I have confirmed my order to him to defend Africa.

He disregarded it under the pretext of preventing the chief rebel and felon, General Giraud, from usurping command of the troops.

Now he endorses his appointment.

The Admiral has put himself outside the national community.—Reuter.

G.C.B. FOR GEN. BROOKE

The King has approved the promotion of General Sir Alan F. Brooke, Chief of the Imperial General Staff, to be Knight Grand Cross, Order of the Bath.

General Brooke, who is 59, accompanied Mr. Churchill on his visit to the Eighth Army—following which changes were made in the commands—and to Moscow. He also went to America with the Premier in June.

GERMANS STILL KEPT IN DARK

GERMANS are still being kept in ignorance of the full extent of the Axis defeat in Egypt and Libya, and are even given the impression that the tide is turning.

They were told yesterday that Rommel's forces had reached the limit of their retirement, and were taking up long-prepared defensive positions on what might become a fixed line of resistance.

Considerable reinforcements, said a Berlin spokesman, had reached Rommel, in addition to large forces landed in Tunisia.

The whole African battle was described as a struggle for transport routes, and it was claimed that Allied shipping resources could not last much longer in face of the losses inflicted on them.

COLD IN STRAITS

Straits: Moonlit, cold; sea choppy off French coast.

8th ARMY RACING TO BENGHAZI

From CLIFFORD WEBB CAIRO, Monday.

NEWS travels fast—but not so fast as the Eighth Army in its pursuit of the Afrika Korps. That is why there is little news from G.H.Q. to-day.

The communiqué says that we have occupied the landing grounds at Martuba, 75 miles beyond Tobruk, and 20 miles south-east of Derna. That was yesterday.

As I write the Eighth Army is bowling merrily along towards Tripoli. It has probably reached and passed Derna, and may be in the Jebel Akdar region.

There are as yet no recorded signs of the enemy pulling his battered runaways together and trying to make some sort of stand.

Tripoli Last Hope

Rommel can only show fight if reserves of armour and weapons are available from Tripoli.

The speed of our pursuit and the pressure of our air attack have been such that it has been impossible for him to rush supplies through Benghazi by sea.

Allied pilots and observers already report that enemy traffic is beating it as hard as possible west of Benghazi right up to El Agheila.

There is much talk here about the eventual meeting of the Eighth Army with the First Army and the American Expeditionary Force in North Africa.

It is well to remember that apart altogether from other considerations, there are still well over 1,000 miles between the two forces.

One of yesterday's most successful air attacks was a surprise swoop on enemy transport 60 miles south of the Jalo Oasis.

Cannot Escape

Jalo is the junction of several inland tracks, the majority of which lead up to the coast between Benghazi and Tripoli.

It does not seem to matter which, or how many routes, the fleeing enemy uses. It is impossible for him to escape the attention of the Allied Air Force.

All the time it is occupying aerodromes deserted by the Luftwaffe only a day or two previously.

HE LEFT OUT AFRICA

Lieut.-General Dietmar completely ignored Libya and North Africa when he gave his weekly review over the German radio last night.

"The battle for Stalingrad," he said, "continues with undiminished violence, but our strategic aim has been reached."

"TRUCKS WERE AIRBORNE"

"TRUCKS airborne and goods locomotives thoroughly machine-gunned," was the report of one Hurricane bomber pilot who took part yesterday in a goods train wrecking attack near Le Treport.

Bombs hurled 15 wagons into the air.

The formation skimmed the harbour and machine-gunned barges before heading for home.

Both United States and British fighters carried out other small raids over Europe.

A low level attack by American fighter planes was made on trucks loaded with German soldiers.

Two Hurricanes bombed barges which were being loaded on the Bruges-Ostend canal.

A German transport aircraft was intercepted and destroyed.

Mosquitos of Bomber Command attacked objectives in Western Germany.

None of our aircraft is missing from these operations.

TOWNS SEIZED BY GUERILLAS

Resistance to the Nazis is spreading in the Balkans, says a Reuter message from the German frontier.

In Western Croatia a big-scale revolt has broken out.

Between 10,000 and 15,000 guerillas, operating independently of General Mihailovitch's forces, have seized two towns.

Montenegrin irregulars which landed at the naval base of Tivat destroyed important harbour works and were back in their boats before they could be captured.

250 AIR CASUALTIES

Of a total of 250 names in an Air Ministry casualty list issued to-day 117 officers and other ranks have lost their lives and 109 are missing.

RUSSIANS ADVANCE AT STALINGRAD

From WALLACE KING STOCKHOLM, Monday.

RUSSIAN troops have regained some more ground in the Nalchik sector in the Caucasus, while at Stalingrad Timoshenko has dislodged the Germans from positions they gained two days ago.

"In the course of the day," adds to-night's communiqué, "the enemy lost in killed and wounded up to 1,500 officers and men. Our troops destroyed two German tanks, six guns, 17 trench mortars, 11 machine-guns, and demolished ten pillboxes and firing points.

"Three German planes were brought down by A.A. fire.

"North-west of Stalingrad our units strengthened their positions."

The advance made south-east of Nalchik is described as slight.

But it shows that the Reds are successfully staving off the Nazi attempt to break through to the Georgian military road.

Heavy Nazi Losses

During the last few hours the Russians have destroyed in this area another 26 tanks and wiped out 800 more Germans.

According to Axis-inspired reports a great battle is also going on in the Alagir sector 58 miles north of Mozdok, in the Terek bend.

Both in this area and in the Western Caucasus, north-east of the Black Sea port of Tuapse, the Russians seem to have brought in large reserves of men and planes.

In 21 days' fighting in the Tuapse sector, the Russians are reported to have killed about 15,000.

Berlin claims that German troops in the Caucasus have encircled and annihilated two groups and in another sector drove off Soviet attacks with heavy casualties.

It gives no indication, however, where these alleged successes occurred.

(Stalingrad fights on and Russians like us better.—Page Two.)

SUBMARINE SINKS FOUR TRANSPORTS

Moscow Radio stated last night that a Soviet submarine of the Black Sea fleet, during a cruise of several days, penetrated an enemy minefield and sank four enemy transports.

An Istanbul cable says that the German tanker Ossag was struck by a torpedo in the Black Sea yesterday morning while bound for Burgas, in Bulgaria, and had to return to Istanbul with a large hole in her stern.

It is believed the tanker was attacked by a Soviet submarine.

An 8,000-ton German tanker has been sunk in the Barents Sea.

CLOSING IN ON BUNA

From RICHARD ODGERS SYDNEY, Monday.

THE final Allied assault on the Jap beachhead at Buna, in New Guinea, is expected very soon.

Australian and American columns covering the enemy's southern and eastern flanks have now joined up and are advancing on a wide front.

The Japanese still have considerable forces in this area.

They are under the command of Lieut.-General Horii, a specialist in landing operations.

Enemy troops, gun positions, barges, supply dumps, and motor transport are being constantly blasted from the air.

The Australian advance has increased in speed now that the Wairopi bridge has been repaired.

Forward advanced elements which have crossed the Kumusi river and are scouting the trails and roads to Buna have been "absolutely unopposed," said a spokesman at General MacArthur's headquarters to-day.

The main body is now crossing the river with supplies and equipment on improvised bridges.

U.S. TO FLOAT RECORD LOAN

The United States Treasury is about to float the biggest War Loan of all time.

It is hoped to raise between now and June 30 next £10,000,000,000 from the public.

The nearest approach to this is the British Government's 1914-18 5 per cent. War Loan (now 3½ per cent.), which totals something like £2,000,000,000.

Daily Mirror

NOV 18

No. 12,147 ONE PENNY

Registered at the G.P.O. as a Newspaper.

Ships race across the ocean as far as the eye can see. It is Britannia ruling the waves—the greatest convoy in the history of the world carrying an army to Africa and defying the whole might of the Axis to stop it.

This historic picture of some of the British naval and merchant ships forming the great armada was taken by an aircraft of Coastal Command from the "umbrella" that saw the fleet to safety.

You cannot see the Sunderland flying boats, the Whitleys, the Liberators, the Wellingtons and the Hudsons that patrolled overhead, pinning the U-boats in their Bay of Biscay bases, or the Beaufighters that beat off the German air attack. But you know the result when land, sea and air forces act like one.

SKY ARMY RAID TUNIS

BRITISH PARACHUTE TROOPS DROPPED FROM U.S. TRANSPORT PLANES ARE REPORTED FROM ALLIED HEADQUARTERS IN NORTH AFRICA TO BE SEIZING EVERY AERODROME POSSIBLE IN TUNISIA.

A large force of them—who, according to Axis reports, may have been flown direct from England—were dropped close to an important key town.

They were met and protected by fighter planes while they were dropping.

Most of the men in one air armada were Londoners formed into a unit after Dunkirk.

They spent most of the time on the flight singing or reading.

"Skylark"

One 21-year-old sergeant from Tottenham called out as he was about to jump: "Any more for the Skylark?"

When they landed they quickly got to work. Last night they were reported to be striking eastwards. They were counting on joining up with local French forces.

According to New York radio paratroops are fighting for the military aerodrome of Tunis itself, the chief base at which the Germans are landing their airborne troops and material.

Official statements from the Allied headquarters said that

Continued on Back Page

THE BEVERIDGE REPORT READY

BY OUR POLITICAL CORRESPONDENT

Sir William Beveridge has completed his report on Social Security and Pensions, and has handed it to the Government.

It is now being circulated to members of the Cabinet, and it is hoped that it will have been printed and in the hands of members of the House of Commons before the end of the next series of sittings. The public will learn the contents, if all goes well, within the next ten days.

There will be a request for a debate immediately the report is tabled, and there is no doubt that it will be granted.

8th Army's tanks ready to break 'last stand'

THE Eighth Army's tank units are gathering for what may be the final battle in Libya if the Germans decide to make a last stand along the El Agheila line, Reuter's special correspondent with an armoured column cabled early today.

This time there will be no "bounce back" from Benghazi.

Rommel's battered forces are careering along in the direction of Agedabia, east of El Agheila, harassed by our mobile columns, but the main body of our forces keeps together.

With the capture of Derna and Mekili the chase of the Afrika Korps develops into a two-pronged thrust for Benghazi.

With these two places in our hands, British forces are now in possession of all the vital road junctions leading to Benghazi.

General Montgomery may strike straight across to Benghazi inland, while other forces of the Eighth Army pursue the remnants of Rommel's forces along the coast road.

Amazing admissions of the German defeat were made by Major-General Ramcke, of the German Afrika Korps, in a recorded broadcast over Berlin radio last night.

Speaking in a tired and crocked voice, Ramcke, who was in charge of a brigade near the Qattara Depression, said:

"When the British broke through at El Alamein I received orders to retire northwest.

"My Worst Night"

"We were not motorised; the only vehicles we had were for heavy equipment and ammunition.

"We marched through the night under great difficulties. Next day the English renewed their attack and it became clear that they had not only torn right through the German lines to the west, but had also encircled us from the north and south.

"All the next night we went on and then came the third night's march—the worst I have ever experienced in my life.

"Just before dawn we saw the enemy coming—columns of Tommies from the left and the right.

"Our men were terribly hungry, having had no regular food for two days, and they were dead tired . . . but fortunately we then found food and water."

Here Ramcke almost broke down in his broadcast.

Eventually Ramcke and his men made a getaway during a thunderstorm.

DAKAR PACT NOW?

A military mission from Dakar is on its way to North Africa, said Monrovia, Liberia, radio last night. The report added that British officials believe negotiations for the peaceful capitulation of Dakar are in progress.

They had vast air umbrella

A VAST air umbrella played a vital part in the safe passage of the great Allied armada to North Africa—but it was invisible to the men in the ships and those in the sky knew nothing about the convoy.

It was put up over the Bay of Biscay as an anti-U-boat "screen" as the convoy steamed by further west, the Air Ministry revealed last night.

The men in the ships were too far out to see the planes. The pilots knew they were on the greatest U-boat hunt of the war—but they did not know why.

Unbroken Stream

It was another "best kept secret."

Sunderlands, Liberators, Halifaxes, Wellingtons, Whitleys and Hudsons in an unbroken stream made attack after attack on U-boats as the ships sailed safely on.

Long-range twin-engined Beaufighters completed the umbrella by intercepting German fighters that attempted to attack our U-boat hunting planes.

To provide this escort meant weeks of intensive organisation in advance. New aerodromes had to be made in quick time.

In one instance the runways and buildings were complete, but that was all. There was no petrol, lights, water, rations, sleeping quarters or kitchens.

In sixty hours the aerodrome was completely equipped.

LONDON BLACKOUT
5.34 p.m. to 7.58 a.m.
Moon Rises 4.56 p.m.
Moon Sets 7.37 a.m.
Lighting-up Time 5.34 p.m.

Daily Herald

No. 8350 SATURDAY, NOVEMBER 21, 1942 ONE PENNY

4 A.M. NEWS

BIG BATTLE FOR BUNA

New Guinea communiqué reported heavy fighting near Japanese coastal bases, Buna and Gona. Enemy planes thrown into battle. (Japanese Hedged In: Back Page.)

ADVANCE

RUSSIA

IN the Caucasus the Germans, outmanoeuvred and outfought by the Russians defending Ordzhonikidze, are in full retreat. They are abandoning tanks and guns as they flee to the forests.

Last night's Soviet communique reported that the Russians have captured a height south of Stalingrad and consolidated their positions. Four hundred Germans were killed.

TUNISIA

LATEST reports last night from this front were:

Occupation of Sfax and Gabes by the Allies is likely soon.

British columns are advancing from Beja and Kalaats:

General Giraud, with 30,000 French troops and tanks, is advancing on the Allied right flank:

Americans and French are moving on Gafsa and Feriana, which are occupied by Allied paratroops.

LIBYA

IT was believed in Cairo last night that the British have occupied Benghazi. There was no official confirmation of this, although the Germans admitted evacuating the town "according to plan."

As the Eighth Army chased the enemy towards the Agheila bottleneck a German military spokesman said that Rommel had retreated to positions "fairly far to the rear."

Axis Leaves Benghazi: We Cut Off Bulge

From F. G. H. SALUSBURY *8th ARMY H.Q., Friday.*

THE enemy "sideguard" on the Sceleidima-Antelat escarpment protecting the vital coast road running south from Benghazi to El Agheila has disappeared.

Our advanced forces which drove westward right across the desert south of the big Benghazi bulge have reached the sea in the Gulf of Sirte.

Any enemy forces remaining in that big bulge of coastline must fight their way out or surrender.

But it looks as if there is little left behind to do either.

In fact, the phase of Rommel's retreat is ending: the battle of the North Africa bridgehead is about to begin.

Rounding Up Remnants

Although most of the broken Panzer army still remaining has fled from the Benghazi area for the neighbourhood of El Agheila or farther west towards Tripoli, there are on the roads that lead from Barce some elements that are in the process of being collected.

They are, however, merely the dregs of the flow westward.

The enemy's strategy now would seem to be to delay us as long as possible in our advance on Tripoli in order to land fresh troops between us and the Allied forces moving eastward through Tunisia.

But he is short not only of troops.

His chief embarrassment at the moment is a lack of fuel, and it is likely that the Axis aircraft which were intercepted off Appolonia yesterday coming from the direction of Crete were carrying petrol.

A Junkers 88 and a Messerschmitt 110 were shot down.

At Bottleneck

The number of tanks at Rommel's disposal are whatever you like, according to your pessimistic or optimistic disposition.

It is highly probable, however, that those he succeeded in salvaging from the battlefield can be in no great shape after their long and rapid journey.

The next stage will almost certainly be a rearguard action at the narrow 15-mile-wide bottleneck at El Agheila, between the sea and the salt marshes to the south.

It looks, however, as if he will get most of his remnants away beyond the temporary protection of this bottleneck.

The Eighth Army's advance is now very fast in spite of atrocious weather.

Abandoned Tanks

Roads are quagmires, transport gets bogged and has to be eased out with stones and brushwood under the wheels, but so determined—and so ingenious—have been the efforts of all ranks that the pace has been scarcely slackened by the downpour and the mud.

Out of the 28 enemy tanks, 250 motor vehicles and 24 guns captured between Martuba and Slonta, on the middle road to Benghazi, more than half the tanks were German—and many of them were abandoned owing to lack of petrol.

IN 1915

An English mother heard the news that her 22-year-old son, Second Lieut. Alexander Buller Turner, had won the V.C. Below Mea Allan tells of an achievement recorded only twice in 85 years — the story of how—

IN 1942 SECOND SON GETS V.C.

THE eyes of Mrs. Charles Turner rested a moment on an engraving when they brought her the news yesterday.

For a quarter of a century the picture had hung on a wall of her home—the time it had taken to bridge two wars.

The picture was that of her first V.C. son, a second lieutenant, dead from German bullets in the Battle of Loos these many years.

Now another of her sons—Lt.-Col. Victor Buller Turner, of the Rifle Brigade—had gained the same award for valour against the same foe.

But it was a happier story.

To the quiet house at Thatcham, in Berkshire, there had just come a telegram that Colonel Turner was off the danger list.

He had been taken to a Middle East military hospital with head wounds.

"Grand News"

"It's grand news," said the V.Cs' sister, Millicent.

"We were worried about Victor's wounds and now not only have our minds been put at rest about that, but we have the wonderful news that he has got the V.C."

Only once before—during the Indian Mutiny 85 years ago—have two brothers won the Cross. They were Hugh and Charles Gough, who both later became generals.

The official citation of the second brother's deed states:

On October 27 Lieut.-Col. Turner led a battalion of the Rifle Brigade at night for 4,000 yards, through difficult country to its objective, where 40 German prisoners were captured.

He then organised the captured position for all-round defence; in this position he and his battalion were continuously attacked from 5.30 a.m. to 7 p.m., unsupported and so isolated that replenishment of ammunition was impossible owing to the concentration and accuracy of the enemy fire.

During this time the battalion was attacked by no fewer than 90 German tanks, which advanced in successive waves.

All of these were repulsed with a loss to the enemy of 35 tanks, which were in flames, and not fewer than 20 more which were immobilised.

(CONTINUED BACK PAGE)

PANZERS DRIVEN OFF CLOSE TO BIZERTA

"Daily Herald" Special Correspondent *ALLIED H.Q., N. Africa, Friday.*

SPEARHEADS OF THE ALLIED ARMIES, CLOSING IN ON TUNIS AND BIZERTA, HAVE MADE CONTACT WITH THE ENEMY AND HURLED HITLER'S CRACK INVASION TROOPS BACK IN THE FIRST REAL CLASHES OF THE BATTLE FOR TUNISIA.

A pitched battle was fought yesterday, less than 40 miles from Bizerta, between British tanks and infantry and a column of 30 German medium tanks.

Both columns were pushing along near the coast, in opposite directions. They met head on.

Four Assaults

German dive-bombers roared down on the British column as the German tanks attacked.

But our troops stood fast, and the enemy ran into a curtain of fire from the latest British quick-firing anti-tank guns and salvoes from heavy artillery.

One-third of the enemy tanks were destroyed, and heavy casualties inflicted on their supporting troops. The others retreated. British losses were light.

There was another clash 20 miles farther south, where a British and French column, reinforced by United States field artillery and A.A. and anti-tank guns, clashed with an advanced German motorised column.

The Germans launched four assaults, and dive-bombers and low-flying fighters strafed our positions.

Again we stood firm, and the accurate fire of the American gunners helped to drive every attack off with heavy losses. This enemy column also retreated.

Driven Back

To-night's Allied Force communiqué, reporting these clashes, says:

"There were engagements between enemy mechanised columns and Allied advance elements, as a result of which the enemy was driven back.

"The United States and French units have participated with the British First Army in these preliminary actions."

Two other Allied columns have driven far into Tunisia to harass the enemy.

One is reported to have repelled a German attack 30 miles south-east of Tunis, near the Gulf of Syrtis.

The other, more than 150 miles farther south, is working northwards in the area west of Gabes.

An increasing number of Allied parachutists are being dropped at many key positions. At one point they ambushed a German column, destroyed six armoured vehicles and took several prisoners.

"It appears that almost all Tunisia, except the Bizerta and Tunis sector, is either occupied by the Allies or controlled by pro-Allied garrisons," a spokesman at General Eisenhower's headquarters said to-day.

(CONTINUED BACK PAGE)

"THIS VICTORY IS THE SIGNAL FOR FURTHER ACTION AGAINST THE ENEMY," SAYS THE MOSCOW "IZVESTIA"

Germans Running In Caucasus

From WALLACE KING *STOCKHOLM, Friday.*

AS the Russians pursue the retreating enemy in the Central Caucasus, Berlin said to-night that heavy attacks have been launched against the Rumanians in the Don bend.

The Red Army's victory in the Caucasus is more important than earlier messages showed.

Moscow reports that the Germans are in full retreat south-east of Nalchik, after their failure to capture the key-town of Ordzhonikidze.

In their rush to gain cover of the forests they are abandoning tanks and guns.

Feeble Rearguards

General Lvov's victorious troops are having difficulty in maintaining contact with the enemy's rearguards as they yield one position after another.

To-night's Soviet communiqué reported that four rearguard attacks were repulsed, the Nazis losing 11 tanks.

A diversionary attack in the Mozdok area was also crushed after several days of bitter fighting in snowstorms.

Berlin radio said to-night that the Russian attack in the Don bend was "probably an attempt to loosen the grip on the Volga."

Earlier the German High Command reported "strong attacks" by infantry and tanks.

Stalingrad Success

At Stalingrad the Russians have repulsed more attacks, and have again improved their positions.

On the Volkhov front, east of Leningrad, the Russians carried out a large-scale raid.

Penetrating far into the Germans' positions, the Red troops played havoc with their supplies and communications.

Before returning to their lines the Russians killed 5,000 of the enemy.

(Caucasus Nazis Trapped—Back Page.)

ORDZHONIKIDZE, scene of this week's Russian victory, is a town of great strategic importance at the northern end of the Georgian military road that winds over the Caucasus Mountains to Tiflis, 100 miles to the south.

It has been named after Sergo Ordzhonikidze, Stalin's friend and fellow Georgian, who died five years ago.

As Commissar for Heavy Industries for six years, he was largely responsible for building up the factories on which Russia's war effort is founded to-day.

The town named after him was formerly known as Vladikavkaz, which means

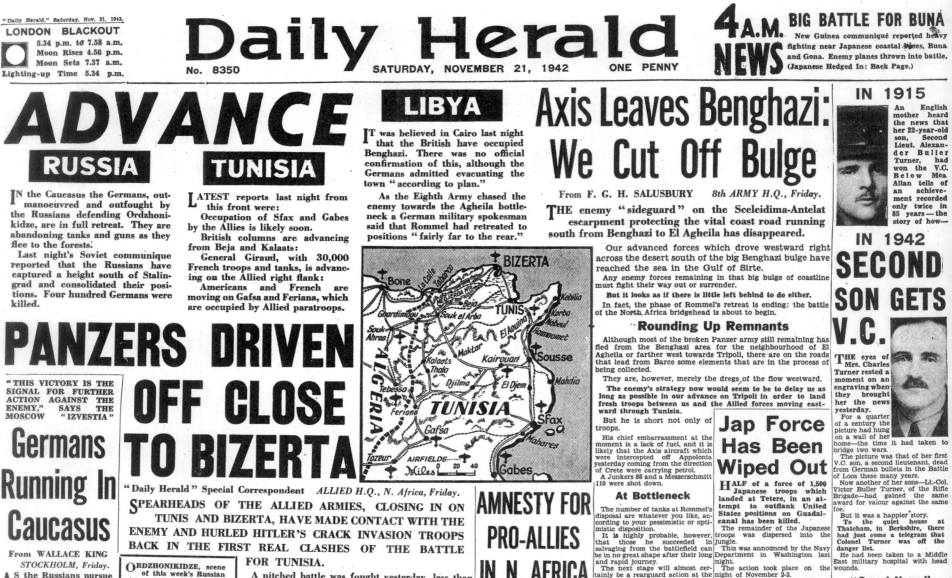

PRIDE OF CAUCASUS

Ordzhonikidze was noted as the fat and jolly Commissar, but his record of revolutionary activity, exile and imprisonment was as vivid as that of most Russian leaders.

Like some other towns named after the old Bolshevik leaders—Stalingrad and Leningrad — Ordzhonikidze has brought a new triumph to the Red Army.

The Germans wanted and needed it very much to provide good winter quarters for a considerable force.

★

In their possession the town would have sealed the Georgian road and prevented any Russian counter-attacks from the mountains.

It would have given the Germans a good starting point for an offensive up the road into the mountains when time and weather became suitable.

It would have helped them, too, to break the deadlock that has so long blocked their eastward drive towards the Grosny oilfield.

In their thrust towards Ordzhonikidze the Germans used two armoured divisions and one motorised division and a fortnight ago they reached the outskirts of the town.

But they could get no farther. Now the Russian counter-attack has set them in retreat.

W. M. TOWLER.

AMNESTY FOR PRO-ALLIES IN N. AFRICA

IT was officially announced last night that the French North African Commission has granted a full amnesty to all persons favouring the Allied action in Africa.

This order answers the request made by President Roosevelt last Tuesday.

Admiral Darlan went to the microphone at Algiers radio station yesterday to praise Marshal Petain and excuse his policy.

"Petain is the living embodiment of France," he said. "We have sworn allegiance to him, but not to Laval.

"His Instructions"

"By signing the Armistice, Petain made the survival of France possible and prevented Africa from being occupied.

"If this policy had not been followed, the Allies would probably have found it more difficult to help us to regain our liberty.

"I cannot imagine the victor of Verdun going hand-in-glove with the usurpers who want to rob us of Alsace-Lorraine, Savoy, Nice, Corsica and North Africa.

"I am sure I am the true interpreter of the Marshal's thoughts. I am following his earlier instructions in accepting the aid of the Americans and their Allies."

About the same time German-controlled Paris Radio was urging all Frenchmen to obey Laval.—Reuter.

'BRITAIN GIVING U.S. EXTRA LIFT'

"IT will be written in history that it was Montgomery's magnificent ability in the Battle of El Alamein early in October which made possible everything America is doing in North Africa to-day."

Mr. Wendell Willkie said this to the British War Relief Society in New York yesterday.

The British, he added, were deliberately playing down their own contribution to the North African operations so as to give an extra lift to America.—Reuter.

FRENCH LEGION TO FIGHT ALLIES

Pierre Laval, dictator of France under the Nazis, said in a broadcast last night that a legion of French volunteers is going to North Africa to fight the Allies.

"The volunteers will give the answer to the insult inflicted on France," he declared.

"Britain and the United States are tearing France to bits.

"By attacking North Africa, Mr. Roosevelt has done something irreparable, but the day will come when the French flag alone will fly over Algeria."

Jap Force Has Been Wiped Out

HALF of a force of 1,500 Japanese troops which landed at Tetere, in an attempt to outflank United States positions on Guadalcanal has been killed.

The remainder of the Japanese troops was dispersed into the jungle.

This was announced by the Navy Department in Washington last night.

The action took place on the night of November 2-3.

Colonel Knox, United States Navy Secretary, said yesterday that the American hold on Guadalcanal was now "very secure."

Last Wednesday a group of United States Army Flying Fortresses attacked Japanese cargo vessels in the Buin area at the south-eastern end of Bougainville Island.

Two hits were scored and 10 enemy Zero fighters and two seaplanes were shot down.

JAPS LOST 28 SHIPS

Colonel Knox, United States Navy Secretary, announced last night that the sinkings of Japanese ships in the Solomons battle reported on Thursday are all additional to those given earlier.

Known Japanese losses in the three-day naval action last week are thus 28 warships and merchant vessels sunk and ten damaged.

Saw Rommel In Rout

From "Daily Herald" Special Correspondent *CAIRO, Friday.*

MARSHAL ROMMEL, standing up in an open car—"a red-faced man with a jutting jaw with a look of sheer arrogance, almost truculence"—directed in person the headlong rout of his once proud Panzer army.

This was told to me by the first eye-witness who has been able to describe the historic retreat from the German side—a young South African fighter pilot who for four days actually took part in it as a prisoner, then escaped.

It is a grim story of rapidly dwindling transport columns sometimes hurrying westwards three abreast on or off the road in a desperate attempt to escape from the ever-advancing Eighth Army.

Trucks In Tow

"Rommel," the South African said, "was standing in an open car driving up and down the road near Derna, threading his way through the procession scurrying westwards.

"Four times he drove up and down, and Germans by the roadside sprang to attention as he passed.

"Most of the German transport was in very poor condition.

"Whenever a truck broke down completely its driver at once set it on fire.

"Then its occupants started the weary task of trying to get lifts, but most lorries refused to take any more aboard. So finally the stranded men joined the stream of stragglers walking along the road to the West."

RAF OVER ITALY

Air raid alarms in Geneva and Basle last night indicated that the RAF was over Italy again.

A steady stream of planes passed overhead from North-West to South-East, reported British United Press from Geneva.

U.S. TROOPS ARE IN FIJI

American forces, comprising all arms, have arrived in the Fiji Islands, the Governor, Sir Philip Mitchell, disclosed yesterday in the Legislative Council.

The Fiji Islands are about 1,000 miles north of New Zealand and a similar distance south-east of the Solomons.

PREMIER'S SON FIGHTS AS COMMANDO

Captain Randolph Churchill, 31-year-old son of the Prime Minister, is with one of the Commando units fighting in North Africa, says Reuter.

It was disclosed on October 27 that Captain Churchill had returned to his unit after being invalided home in July with injuries received in a motor smash in Egypt.

FIRST ARMY WON RACE TO MOUNTAINS

By Maj. E. W. SHEPPARD

WE have started our advance into Tunisia, and the first clash of forward troops on the northern route has ended in our favour.

This clash took place about 40 miles from Bizerta, on the high road hither from Bone.

The fact that we are past Tabarca is important, because it means that we have got across the first and, in some ways, the most difficult barrier to our further advance by this route.

A high spur from the Medjerda mountains runs almost down to the coast between La Calle and Tabarco. It is so high that the railway makes no attempt to cross it, and there is a break in the line here some 15 miles wide. A good but steeply graded motor road crosses the spur to fill the gap.

It would obviously have been advantageous for the Axis forces to reach and hold this spur before we could anticipate it.

And the fact that their forward troops continued attacks seems to show that they intended to do so. If they could not do this they no doubt hoped to be able to meet and counter-attack us as we descended the spur.

They have failed in both these plans, as our advanced troops got there first and a hostile counter-attack was repulsed with the loss of several tanks.

There was also another encounter farther south, presumably in the valley of the Medjerda river, where our central column is advancing. Here, too, the enemy lost some tanks.

We should not augur too much from these actions. The main battle for Tunisia is still to come, but we have made a valuable step forward.

Daily Sketch

No. 10,468 (E**) SATURDAY, NOVEMBER 28, 1942 ONE PENNY

FRENCH SCUTTLE FLEET AS NAZIS SEIZE TOULON

The 26,000-ton battleship Dunkerque, one of the French ships scuttled at Toulon, was completed shortly before the war. At Oran in 1940 she was shelled by British warships and beached. A year ago she was reported repaired and ready for action.

Arsenal And All Harbour Works Blown Up

CAPTAINS GO DOWN WITH THEIR SHIPS | GESTAPO MEN RUSHED INTO THE PORT

HITLER has lost the French Mediterranean Fleet. Every battleship, cruiser, seaplane-carrier, destroyer and submarine—except two which Vichy said escaped—in Toulon has been scuttled. Among them were the great battleships Dunkerque and Strasbourg.

As dawn broke yesterday over Toulon, fortress and key arsenal in the South of France, the Germans made a lightning descent on the port.

Tanks, bombs, magnetic mines and armoured cars were used to take the town—and to try to take the Fleet.

But the French Navy were too quick for them. Explosion after explosion came from the warships—the sailors had defied the Germans.

TRICOLOURS FLEW AS SHIPS SANK

Tricolours blazed at the mastheads as the ships went down—as France secured her greatest naval victory of the war.

It is not known, says a Marseilles report, how many ships escaped—Vichy said two submarines got away—but at 10 a.m. Admiral de Laborde, who gave the order to scuttle, reported to Marshal Pétain that the entire fleet "no longer existed."

The following units of the French Fleet were recently reported to be at Toulon:

BATTLESHIPS: Strasbourg 26,000 tons; Provence, 22,000 tons; Dunkerque, 26,000 tons.

HEAVY CRUISERS: Colbert, Algérie, Foch and Dupleix—all of 10,000 tons.

LIGHT CRUISERS: La Galissonnière, Jean de Vienne and La Marseillaise—all of 7,600 tons.

SEAPLANE - CARRIER Commandant Teste (10,000 tons), 25 destroyers and 26 submarines and sloops.

First indication that the Germans intended to seize the fleet came at 3 a.m.

A great wave of bombers flew over the port, dropping flares to find out where the ships were lying.

Other planes flew over the outer harbours, dropping magnetic mines, while bombers rained high explosives on the fort's defences.

A.A. DEFENCES IN ACTION

Toulon's A.A. guns immediately went into action, while many of the ships began to steam towards the port exits.

Meanwhile German columns poured into the town, occupying the harbour itself.

The French Naval Headquarters was stormed by the Germans, who entered the upper windows of the building by scaling-ladders.

Other German units entered the arsenal by the Port Castigneau, which was wrecked by explosions, while troops were posted with machine-guns in the Vauban Basin, one of the great inner quays where the Dunkerque was lying under repair.

More Germans rushed to the pier-head, where the Strasbourg was at anchor.

Suddenly a series of explosions were heard. It was the Strasbourg scuttling itself. A few minutes' silence, then—more explosions as the valiant fleet went down.

At certain points where the arrangements for scuttling had failed sailors opened fire while their ships were destroyed by explosions.

Many casualties were caused as real fighting developed, casualties to which must be added the scuttling crews who sacrificed themselves so that their ships should not be taken.

In addition there are the ships' captains, most of whom died on the bridges of their commands.

Turn to Back Page, Col. 5

Admiral de Laborde gave order to scuttle.

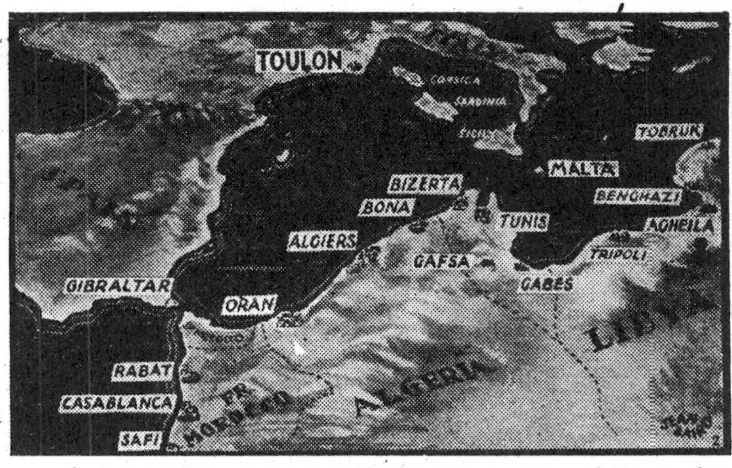

Toulon, Mediterranean base of the French Fleet, and its relation to the French African and Libyan battlefields.

RAF AND 1st ARMY STRIKE IN TUNISIA

ALLIED air forces, aided by an armoured column, yesterday destroyed or shot down 51 Axis aircraft in Tunisia—for the loss of two of our planes. Both pilots are safe.

This fact, reported in an Allied communiqué early this morning, indicates that, after careful and thorough preparation, the Allied forces have swung into the definite offensive in Tunisia.

The communiqué said:

Successive attacks by planes and an armoured column yesterday destroyed forty enemy planes at one of his advanced airfields.

Allied air forces successfully bombed enemy communications in North-East Tunisia, and fighter and bomber patrols attacked enemy reconnaissance units.

Planes operating in forward areas shot down 11 enemy aircraft against the loss of two of ours. Both of our pilots were saved.

It had earlier been reported from New York that Allied troops in Tunisia, including considerable detachments of French troops, supported by a large number of tanks and with a powerful air umbrella, had overcome enemy resistance and were now only 10 miles from Tunis.

Algiers radio said last night that the British First Army had launched its big attack against the German and Italian defences guarding Bizerta and Tunis—the period of patrol activity had finished.

At the other end of the pincer drive, in Libya, there is a comparative lull in the land war as General Montgomery masses men and material for his assault on Rommel's defence lines at El Agheila.

But the R.A.F., although handicapped by bad weather in the desert, went out to smash Rommel's ships and planes

TIMELY WORDS OF FAITH

The ships were broken, that they were not able to go to Tarshish.

2 *Chronicles*, 20, 37.

V for Victory In The New Year

NEW YORK Journal American

AN AMERICAN PAPER FOR THE AMERICAN PEOPLE

In Two Sections—Section One

No. 20,088—DAILY | THURSDAY, DECEMBER 31, 1942 | DAILY 3 Cents in City Limits, 4 cents Elsewhere | SATURDAY 5 Cents | SUNDAY 10 Cents

AFTERNOON EDITION

GERMANS ADMIT DON SETBACKS

Soviets Report Entire Front Near Collapse

LONDON, Dec. 31 (INS).—The Nazis admitted in a radio broadcast today that their forces south of the Don River have been forced to retreat in the face of severe Russian assaults.

The broadcast by the Nazis, recorded by Reuters, claimed the withdrawal was made "according to plan."

"In the Steppe region south of the Don it has been necessary to withdraw from some far advance bases according to plan," the Nazi announcer said.

REDS DRIVE WEDGE.

"South of the Don, the enemy succeeded in driving wedges of varying breadths and depths into the Steppe region in which we occupy a number of places."

Nazis Face Collapse South of Stalingrad

By NATALIA RENE

International News Service Staff Correspondent.

MOSCOW, Dec. 31.—German armies south of Stalingrad, shattered by relentless westward assaults across the North Caucasus by the Red Army, began a general retreat from most sectors today in the face of severe Russian attacks.

(According to UP, the Nazis'

Continued on Page 2, Column 2.

Liberty Light Burns Tonight

(Full page of pictures in today's Pictorial Review.)

By CHARLES ROLAND

The Light of Victory flames tonight for all the world to behold!

Five minutes after the advent of the New Year, the torch of the Statue of Liberty will flash its globe-encircling message to war-stricken mankind:

"V for Victory — a victory that will restore liberty throughout the world."

Augur of triumph for America in 1943, the electric flash of three dots and a dash of light, in the illuminated Morse code, will span the far horizons with word of unflinching courage and determination.

Thus from tiny Bedloes Island, its ten acres so microscopic they do not appear on any world atlas,

For details of tonight's city wide New Year's Eve celebrations see Page 3.

Miss Liberty symbolizes once more the justice and power of America's cause.

Paul Muni, Lawrence Tibbett and Marjorie Lawrence, in dramatic recitation and in song, will give physical expression to the far corners of the earth, of the historic ceremonies arranged at the request of the New York Journal-American in furtherance of the war effort.

An estimated 30,000,000 persons, most of whom will be too far from the Statue of Liberty to see the visible light, but all of whom share

Continued on Page 18, Column 4.

Smoke Fells 10 Firemen

Ten firemen were overcome by smoke, two affected so badly they had to be rushed to Gouverneur Hospital, during a fire in the basemen plant of the Roumanian State Bottling Works at 124 Attorney st. today.

The entire crew of Engine 17, one of the first companies to respond, was overcome.

The blaze started when boxes in the cellar of the one-story building were ignited by an overheated stove, according to Assistant Chief McCarthy.

Taken to the hospital in serious condition were:

LIEUT. FRANCIS McCALL, 37, commanding Engine Co. 11.

FIREMAN JOHN MEEHAN, 38, chauffeur for Battalion Chief Emil Schoeck.

Treated in an emergency first aid station set up at 116 Attorney st. were:

CAPT. HARRY HERTEL, 42, Hook and Ladder 18.

ACTING LIEUT. JAMES A. FITZSIMMONS, 34, of Engine 17.

FIREMAN LEO WRIGHT, 32, Engine 11.

WALTER KUHLMAN, 28, Engine 11.

FIREMAN LAWRENCE LIBRONATE, Engine 17.

STEPHEN SKORSKI, Engine 17.

ARNOLD JOELL, 45, Engine 17.

EDWARD SCHAEFFER, 34, Engine 17.

New Cut In Gas Ration Feared

Another major crisis in the critical gasoline situation—equal to the emergency that caused suspension of sales two weeks ago—threatened motorists along the Eastern seaboard today.

With supplies dipping to the low level that brought an OPA order cutting the value of B and C ration coupons from four to three gallons, the metropolitan area seemed destined for its second crippling shortage within a fortnight.

The Atlantic Refining Co., revealing its quota for A and B drivers had been exhausted, ordered its bulk plants through the 17-State Eastern area to halt sales except to preferred users.

EXPECT FURTHER CUT.

So critical was the situation that it was believed gasoline ration coupons would be cut further in value and a statement from the OPA and PAW was expected today.

Some city gasoline stations with supplies on hand planned to sell only to trucks and taxicabs. New Year's Eve is traditionally the biggest business night for the taxi industry and lack of gasoline would put a damper on the celebration.

SUPPLIES VERY THIN.

The Brick Service Stations, operators of 8 stations in the downtown and midtown area, reported their supplies "are very thin. We are not selling except to trucks and taxicabs."

Harry Shaikowitz, manager of a station at 6th ave. and 17th st., said he had had no deliveries since Tuesday. He is rationing sales to trucks and cabs.

However, Phil Black, at Canal and Watt sts., said his tanks were full and he will "sell to all comers."

Dewey Goes To Take Oath As Governor

By SANFORD E. STANTON

Thomas E. Dewey left for Albany at 9:20 a. m. today to become, at 40, the Governor of New York.

His departure on the "Mohawk" from Grand Central Terminal was accompanied by no bands or celebration. A small crowd gathered as the dark-coated, black-mustached man walking with a few friends was recognized.

There were cries of "Good luck Governor" and "Happy New Year." He answered with a smile and replied to those he recognized.

HOPES FOR UNITY.

He was to take the oath of office about 4 p. m. in the Executive Mansion at Albany, although he will not actually become Governor until midnight. He will repeat it with more formality in the inaugural ceremony around noon tomorrow in the Assembly Chamber.

Dewey made only a brief statement as he was about to board the train, saying:

"One cannot undertake the Governorship of New York with-

Continued on Page 3, Column 2.

Trains in Crash On West Shore

The New York Central Railroad here reported that a passenger train on its West Shore Division smashed into a stalled freight train south of Ravena, N. Y., early today, setting fire to the caboose and derailing an empty stock car. Ravena is seven miles south of Albany.

Both tracks were blocked temporarily.

No one was injured in the crash.

Curtin Assails Delay in Pacific

CANBERRA, Dec. 31 (AP).—Prime Minister Curtin today said that the United Nations in the Pacific area were being denied aid for their total war effort while Japan was building up its strength.

"There is no doubt that Japan is consolidating the gains she has made," Curtin said.

"Delaying an offensive against her makes it certain that the offensive when undertaken will experience greater resistance.

JAPAN PREPARING.

"Meanwhile, the United Nations in the Pacific area are being denied resources for their total war effort which is invaluable to them, and resources are being reserved by Japan for building up her capacity not only to wage war but to resist an offensive."

He said he agreed with statements, which he asserted had been published in the United States press, that the "Hitler first" policy was being overdone and that the United States should send more land, naval and air strength to the Pacific.

Those, he said, were "views which the Australian Government has repeatedly put to leaders of the United Nations."

Hatfield and McCoy In Same Army Unit

CAMP UPTON, Dec. 31 (UP).—Pvt. Clarence F. Hatfield and Pvt. Thorton McCoy are not feudin' mountain boys, and they're going to fight this war side by side. The two 19-year-old Negro soldiers left Camp Upton this week on the same train headed for the same outfit. Hatfield lives in Yonkers, N. Y.. and McCoy in Mount Vernon, N. Y.

Rommel Flank Threatened, Nazis Admit

LONDON, Dec. 31 (UP).—The German official news agency admitted today that armored patrols from the British Eighth Army were operating south of Tripoli, indicating that Lieut. Gen. Montgomery may be planning to outflank the shredded Afrika Korps and annihilate it in Tripolitania.

The agency claimed the majority of the force was destroyed and its comander, Maj. Street, captured by Italian units.

"The remaining few cars so far have successfully eluded the Italians, but will shortly be rounded up," the dispatch said. "Italian planes are aiding in the hunt."

Most of Rommel's forces apparently were still somewhere west of the Wadi Bei el Chebir, 185 miles from Tripoli. He was still in the greatest danger of being trapped before he reaches Tripoli, one of the last remaining Axis strongholds in Africa.

FACES U. S. THREAT.

Rommel was presumed to hope that eventually he would join forces with Lieut. Gen. Nehring in Tunisia for a last ditch stand. To prevent such a juncture an American tank and motorized infantry force was driving toward Gabes, in lower Tunisia.

These forces, speeding toward Gabes, were said to be 50 miles nearer Tripoli than Lieut. Gen. Montgomery's British Eighth Army on the east. The Americans were reported yesterday to be within 40 miles of Gabes.

'Nice Work', Mother

BUFFALO, Dec. 31 (AP).—Mrs. Agatha M. Warfield, 40, of Bradford, Pa., mother of four children and grandmother of four others, enlisted in the Women's Army Auxiliary Corps yesterday.

Giraud Balks Plot To Assassinate U. S. Diplomat

By JOHN W. JARRELL

International News Service Staff Correspondent.

ALGIERS, Dec. 31.—A new plot to assassinate high personages in North Africa, including U. S. Minister Robert D. Murphy and probably Gen. Giraud, High Commissioner who succeeded the murdered Admiral Darlan, was frustrated today with the arrests of 12 persons.

The arrests were revealed by Gen. Giraud, who disclosed that those seized included both Allied and Axis sympathizers and four policemen who had had prioor knowledge that an attempt would be made on Darlan's life.

"Some of my best friends are among those arrested," Giraud said.

TWO HELPED ALLIES LAND.

Two of those held were known to have lent valuable assistance to the Allied troop landings in North Africa.

The four policemen were arrested because of their failure to warn their superiors when they learned a youthful Frenchman with an

Continued on Page 2, Column 7.

Don't ... Drive ... With ... DEATH!

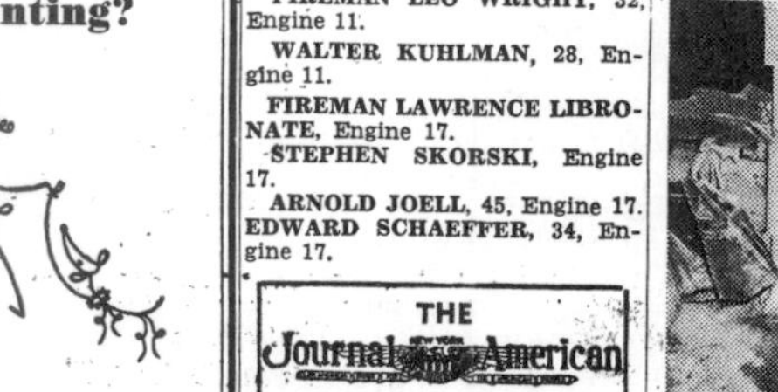

To those who are planning to drive to New Year's Eve celebrations tonight, remember that drink, driving, dimout and death are a macabre foursome that can turn your celebration into a night or a lifetime of horror. If you drive, don't drink. If you drink, don't drive. Then you'll have no regrets.

THE Journal-American Will Not Be Published Tomorrow, Jan. 1 *(New Year's Day)*

THE WEATHER

Snow fluurries, colder and windy.

Sun rises, 8:20 a. m.; sun sets, 5:38 p. m. High tide at Governors Island, 3:04 a. m. and 3:02 p. m.

HOURLY TEMPERATURES

2 a. m.	36	7 a. m.	37
3 a. m.	36	8 a. m.	37
4 a. m.	35	9 a. m.	37
5 a. m.	36	10 a. m.	37
6 a. m.	36	11 a. m.	38

Complete Weather Table on Page 19

TODAY'S INDEX

The New York Journal-American has the largest circulation of any evening newspaper in America. ALLIED PRINTING TRADES UNION LABEL COUNCIL NEW YORK 230

It is the only New York evening newspaper possessing the three great wire services—ASSOCIATED PRESS—INTERNATIONAL NEWS SERVICE—UNITED PRESS.

Complete Radio Programs for Today and New Year's Day **Will Be Found on Page 24**

DAILY MIRROR, Saturday January 23, 1943.

Daily Mirror

JAN 23

No. 12,202
ONE PENNY
Registered at the G.P.O. as a Newspaper.

TRIPOLI FALLS
HUNS FLED AS CITY BURNED

TRIPOLI HAS FALLEN. CAIRO RADIO FLASHED THAT REPORT TO THE WORLD AT MIDNIGHT LAST NIGHT.

The broadcaster added that he could give no official confirmation of the report.

Earlier, American-controlled Morocco radio announced that the Eighth Army was regrouping its forces for the final assault on the bomb-blasted port.

Eighth Army guns were then shelling the city from the plateau above it.

At that time, too, most of the city's fortifications had already been captured as the enemy retreated towards Tunisia in haste, pursued by the RAF and leaving behind small parties of resistance.

During the day, Allied airmen spotted the enemy demolishing installations likely to be of use to the Eighth Army.

Rommel's retreat is gaining speed. RAF attacks on his columns, moving along the coast road without air protection, are spreading panic.

Capture of Tripoli was the final Axis humiliation in an almost uninterrupted chase that has pushed them back about 1,200 miles in less than three months.

The fleeing enemy is being hammered in a three-prong air attack based on Malta, Tunisia and Tripolitania.

Castel Benito, main Axis airfield in the province, just outside Tripoli, is probably in our hands by now.

The greater part of the much-vaunted Afrika Korps has already crossed the border into Tunisia.

The German rearguard used tanks south of Tripoli in an attack which delayed the Eighth Army a bit, but could not stop it.

The majority of Montgomery's forces are reported to be skirting south of Tripoli, anxious to cut the road and railway along which the stricken and disorganised enemy is fleeing.

The Navy's There

The land and air attack on Tripoli was aided by British naval light forces which made a night raid on the harbour.

They destroyed a U-boat being towed on the surface by three tugs. One tug was fired and the others were hit.

Then our ships attacked the harbour works successfully under heavy but ineffectual fire from the defences.

Meanwhile, French troops, reinforced by British, have made an advance of several miles in Central Tunisia.

This success was scored in the valley of Oued Kebir, where the enemy had previously made a considerable advance.

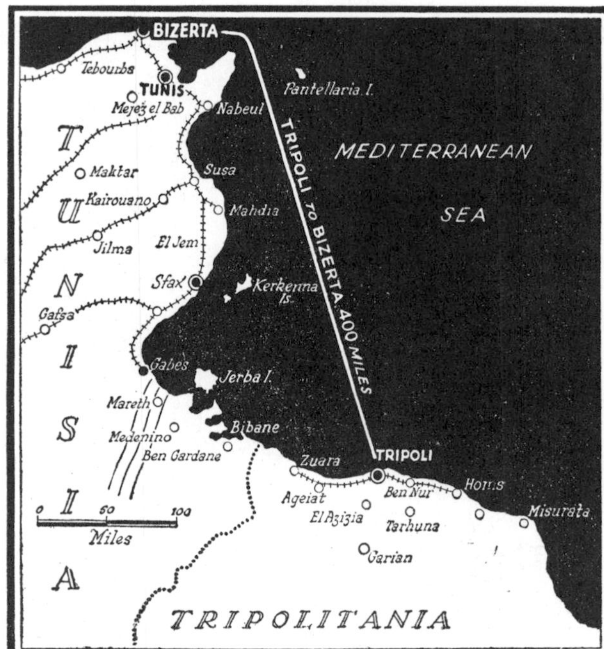

As Tripoli was falling to the Eighth Army other British Forces swept south in an attempt to cut off at least part of Rommel's army as it fled without fight along the main coast road. Real resistance to our advance is not expected until Rommel can make a stand behind the Mareth Line.

V.C. Hannah is out of RAF

Flight-Sergeant John Hannah, V.C., who received his award in 1940 at the age of eighteen for putting out a fire in a bomber which had been hit during a raid on enemy barges, has been invalided out of the RAF on pension.

Sergeant Hannah, who is living near Leicester with his wife and year-old baby Jennifer, told the "Daily Mirror" last night that he had been granted a pension of £3 7s. 3d. a week for himself, wife and child.

"I thought they would have given me a pension for life," he added, "but it is only for a year, and will be reviewed at the end of that time."

RAF POUND AIRFIELDS IN DAY SWEEPS

SEVEN German fighters were destroyed, and three German-occupied aerodromes and an enemy oil plant bombed in a series of great cross-Channel daylight raids yesterday by RAF bombers and fighters.

In addition a Hampden torpedo-bomber went into action in a snowstorm against two Nazi supply ships off Stavanger, Norway, and smashed a torpedo into one of them.

These were the targets battered in the bombing onslaughts: Oil installation at Terneuzen, near Ghent in Belgium; Maupertus airfield in the Cherbourg Peninsula, buildings, hangars and huts blown sky-high.

Abbeville and St Omer airfields bombed. Five F.W.s and one Me. destroyed in dog-fights.

Four bombers and six of our fighters are missing.

NAZI RADIO OFF

Berlin, Koenigsberg, Leipzig, Stuttgart and Luxembourg radios went off the air at 7.15 last night.

'Stop the gossip' pleads mother as twins search is called off

SEARCH for the 3½-year-old twins, Neil and Jacqueline Coleby, missing since Tuesday from their farmhouse home at Dwygyfylch, in the wild Penmaenmawr mountains, Wales, was called off yesterday.

Detectives questioned their mother, Mrs. Coleby, for several hours.

After they had left the farm Mrs. Coleby said to the *Daily Mirror*:

"It Is Cruel"

"I know what people are thinking and saying. It is cruel and unjust of them. I want this gossip stopped."

Pale and hollow-eyed after a three-day and night continuous vigil, the frail mother said:

"I don't blame the police for questioning me. I don't blame them for searching the place. It is their duty and I admire them for it. I have had a candid talk with the detectives and they believe me. All I want is my babies back."

Mrs Coleby has refused to

Continued on Back Page

Russians take Salsk in drive for Rostov

THE RED ARMY HAS CAPTURED SALSK, KEY RAILWAY CENTRES AND ONE OF THE VITAL POINTS IN THE ENEMY'S RING OF DEFENCES AROUND ITS PIVOT AT ROSTOV.

Its fall was announced in a special Russian communique which stated:

"Our troops on the Southern Front on January 22, as a result of determined fighting, captured the town and large railway station of Salsk.

"Troops on the Caucasus Front captured the town of Mikoyan-Shakvar," the communique also announced.

Salsk is 100 miles south-east of Rostov, and is the terminal point of the railway which runs down to it from Rostov by way of Zernovoi and Gigant.

Spearheads of the Soviet Army are reported to be thrusting irresistibly forward past points within sixty miles of Rostov itself.

The situation is that two gigantic Soviet pincers are closing relentlessly upon the Don city.

Strong Point Broken

To the north-west of Rostov other Soviet columns converging on the large Donbas industrial city of Voroshilovgrad constitute a third menace to the whole Axis position in the Lower Don.

A supplement to the communique said: "Our troops on the south-western front captured the railway junction of Kondrashevskaya, another railway station and a district centre.

The trapped enemy troops at Stalingrad have received another great blow.

One of their strong points in a big market square on the western outskirts of Stalingrad has been broken and another 2,000 of them killed.

The German High Command was forced to admit this disaster in its communique.

Soviet may cut across Finland to N. Norway

FROM JOHN WALTERS

NEW YORK, Friday.

SOVIET High Command may be contemplating a drive across extreme North Finland with the object of pushing into Northern Norway, taking Narvik and cleaning out Nazi raiders based there, according to reports in Washington says the *New York Sun.*

"If such an attack were launched it is believed the Germans would want to move troops through Sweden."

Some believe this is why the Swedish Premier warned the nation that their neutrality was imperilled.

KENYA MURDER TRIAL WIDOW OF 2 MONTHS MARRIES A RANCHER

LESS than two months after the suicide of her husband—acquitted in 1941 of murdering Lord Erroll because of a love affair between her and the peer—Lady Diana Broughton was married by special licence at Nakuru, Kenya, yesterday.

The 29-year-old Mayfair beauty's second husband is 55-year-old cattle rancher Gilbert de Previle Colvile, formerly in the Grenadier Guards, eldest son of the late Major-General Sir Henry Edward Colvile.

Sir Delves Broughton took an overdose of drugs in a Liverpool hotel last month. Encased in plaster of paris he arrived there by ambulance for treatment for a spinal injury.

His twenty-seven-day trial rocked Kenya society. He was accused of shooting Lord Erroll, 39-year-old High Constable of Scotland, a few months after his marriage to Lady Diana, then Miss Diana Caldwell.

Sir Delves denied all knowledge of Lord Erroll's death in a car. There were applause and congratulations in court when he was acquitted.

5 DEAD IN RAID ON S. COAST TOWN

Five persons were killed when bombs were dropped on a small south coast town yesterday.

They were Mrs. Moran and her three small daughters—Gabrielle, Norma and Pauline—and a little boy named Brian Holloway. The boy's mother has been taken to hospital in a serious condition with multiple injuries.

An enemy bomber was destroyed in a north-east coastal area last night.

Raiders were also over the south-west.

DAILY MIRROR, Wednesday, January 27, 1943.

Daily Mirror

No. 12,205
ONE PENNY
Registered at the G.P.O. as a Newspaper.

ROOSEVELT AND CHURCHILL IN NORTH AFRICA TEN-DAY TALK MEET DE GAULLE AND GIRAUD

MR. CHURCHILL and President Roosevelt have met near Casablanca in North Africa, and, during ten days of non-stop conference, have planned a more intensive war drive in all spheres.

Stalin was invited, but could not attend because he is personally directing the Russian offensives.

De Gaulle and Giraud met at the conference and attended many of the talks.

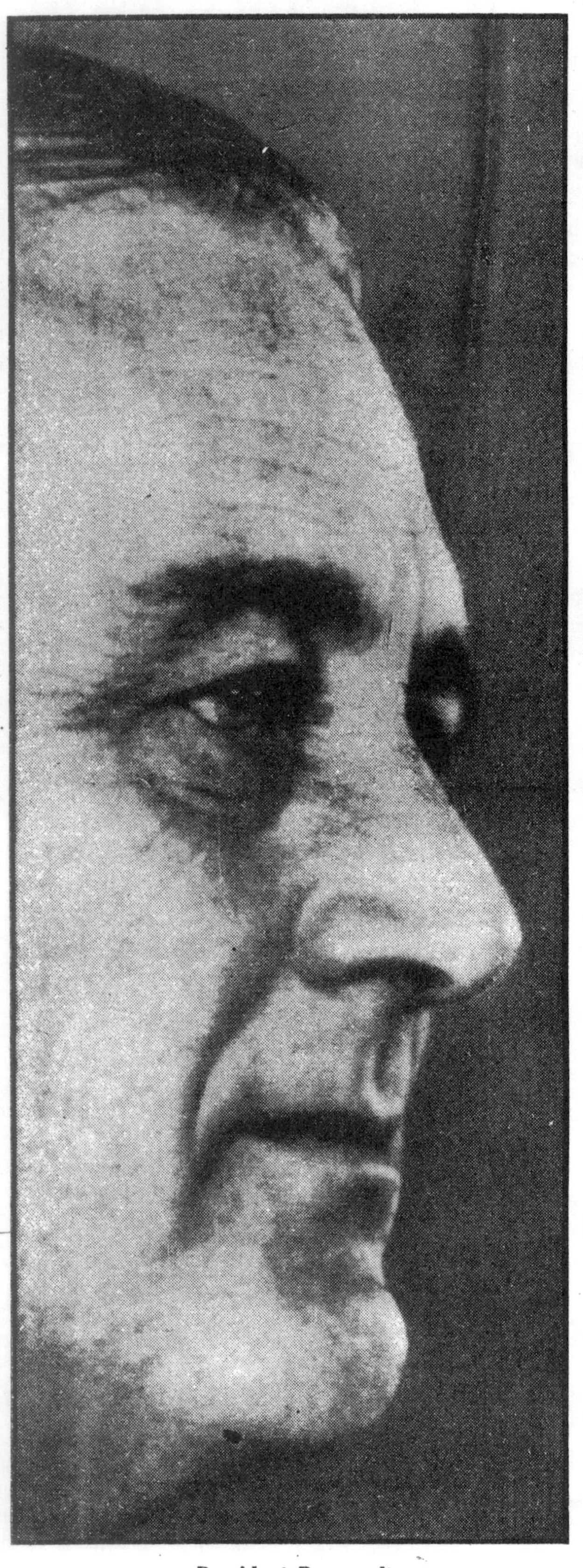

President Roosevelt.

Stalin was invited but was too busy directing Red Army offensive

By Archer Brooks

"DAILY MIRROR" SPECIAL CORRESPONDENT IN NORTH AFRICA

CASABLANCA, Tuesday.

IN day and night talks extending to ten days, Mr. Churchill and President Roosevelt have—in collaboration with chiefs of staffs—surveyed the field of war theatre by theatre throughout the world, and marshalled all resources for more intense prosecution of the war by land, sea and air.

The conference is unprecedented in history, as it has taken in the whole global picture. Combined staffs have been in constant session, meeting two or three times a day and reporting progress at intervals to the President and Prime Minister.

General Alexander, British Commander-in-Chief, Middle East, and General Eisenhower, Allied Commander-in-Chief, North Africa, were present.

To Keep Initiative

Talks have proceeded on the principle of pooling all resources of the United Nations and they have reaffirmed the Allies' determination to maintain the initiative against the Axis in every part of the world.

Plans decided upon include combined operations in different areas of the world and sending all possible material aid to the Russian offensive, with the double object of cutting down the man power of Germany and satellite Powers and continuing the very great attrition of German materials.

At the same time staffs agreed in giving all possible aid to China, now in the sixth year of her heroic struggle, and eliminating Jap domination in the Far East.

IT CAN BE CALLED THE UNCONDITIONAL SURRENDER CONFERENCE—THAT WAS PRESIDENT ROOSEVELT'S NAME FOR IT AT THE PRESS CONFERENCE.

He indicated that peace could come to the world only by the total elimination of Axis war power which means unconditional surrender by Germany, Italy, Japan.

In Full Agreement

Only that will mean reasonable assurance of real world peace. It does not mean, he emphasised, destruction of the Axis population, but destruction of philosophies in those countries based on conquest and through fear and hate the subjugation of other people.

While the conference had not included representatives of all Allied nations, he declared he and Churchill are in agreement, in fact both had great confidence that the same purpose and objective were in the minds of all the other United Nations.

It was a meeting of unity regarding all military operations, and therefore the war was going to be prosecuted against the Axis Powers according to schedule with every indication that

Continued on Back Page

Mr. Churchill.

General de Gaulle.

Daily Mail
NO. 14,588 ONE PENNY FOR KING AND EMPIRE MONDAY, FEBRUARY 1, 1943
LATE WAR NEWS SPECIAL

STALINGRAD ARMY WIPED OUT

16 Axis Generals Among the 46,000 Captured

MARSHAL PAULUS IS A PRISONER

FIELD-MARSHAL VON PAULUS, Commander-in-Chief of the German Sixth Army and Fourth Tank Army at Stalingrad, was captured yesterday a few hours after he had been promoted to the highest rank by special proclamation made in an announcement from Hitler's headquarters.

He was seized with his staff when the Russians stormed the Ogpu headquarters in the heart of the city and completed the greatest disaster that has befallen Germany in this war.

It is now revealed as a disaster of unsuspected proportions. Instead of 220,000 men, the trapped army, it was announced by Moscow in a special communiqué last night, consisted of 330,000 troops.

In addition to the Sixth Army, the Fourth Panzer Army has been trapped and destroyed. Twelve German and five Rumanian generals have been captured.

Booty taken between January 10 and 30 includes 744 aircraft, 1,517 tanks, and 6,523 guns.

THE FULL STORY

HERE is the full story as told in the special communiqué:

"Our forces on the Don front between January 27 and 31 completed the annihilation of the German troops surrounded west of the central part of Stalingrad.

"In the course of the fighting, and from the depositions of enemy generals now prisoners in our hands, it was ascertained that by November 23 the German forces there numbered at least 330,000 if the auxiliary engineering and police units are taken into account, and not 220,000 as had been reported previously.

"As is known, the German forces encircled before Stalingrad between November 23 and January 10 had lost up to 140,000 from the action of our artillery, bombing from the air, the action of our land troops, sickness, frost, and exhaustion.

"In this way, by the time of the general offensive which our forces began about January 10, the German forces, including the reinforcing units, engineering units, police units, and army rear organisations, numbered about 190,000 officers and men.

"The calculation has been confirmed by the acting Quarter-Master-General of the German Sixth Army, Colonel von Kobrvsky, who is a prisoner in our hands.

"He stated that on January 10 the effective of the German forces encircled before Stalingrad numbered, including non-combatant organisations, 195,000 men.

46,000 CAPTIVES

"In view of this data the victory of the Soviet forces before Stalingrad assumes even greater importance. The number of prisoners between January 27 and 31 increased by 18,000 officers and men.

"In the course of the general offensive against the encircled enemy forces our troops captured 46,000 officers and men in all.

"To-day, our forces captured General Field-Marshal von Paulus, commanding the group of German forces before Stalingrad, consisting of the Sixth Army and the Fourth Tank Army, his Chief of Staff, Lieut.-General Schmidt, and the whole of his staff.

"The following generals were also taken prisoner.

Lt.-Gen. Schlener, commanding 14th Tank Corps;
Lt.-Gen. Seidlitz, 51st Army Corps;
Lt.-Gen. of Artillery Vetter, 4th Army Corps;
Lt.-Gen. Pappe, 4th Light Infantry Division;
Lt.-Gen. Leider, 29th Motorised Division;
Lt.-Gen. Portes, 295th Infantry Division;
Maj.-Gen. von Bretberg, 297th Infantry Division;
Lt.-Gen. von Daniel-Edder, 376th Infantry Division;
Lt.-Gen. Dubois, 44th Infantry Division;
Maj.-Gen. Holz, Chief of Artillery of the 4th Army Corps;
Maj.-Gen. Ullrich, Chief of Artillery, 51st Army Corps;
Gen. Dimitriu, Commander of the 20th Rumanian Infantry Division;
Gen. Bratescu, 1st Rumanian Cavalry Division;
Lt.-Gen. Otto Rinoldi, Chief of Medical Services of the 6th Army; and
Col. von Kobovski, Deputy Quartermaster-General.

[The communiqué also named seven colonels of regiments.]

"In addition, our troops have captured the staffs of the 14th Tank Corps, 3rd Motorised Division, 297th and 376th German and 20th Rumanian Infantry Divisions, 44th, 83rd, 132nd, 297th, 523rd, 524th, 534th, 535th, and the 536th Infantry Regi-

BACK PAGE—Col. EIGHT

Casablanca: The First Pictures

FIRST pictures of the historic meeting at Casablanca between Mr. Churchill, President Roosevelt, General Giraud (extreme left), and General de Gaulle have now been released. For ten days Premier and President and their staffs planned the next blows at the Axis—and promised that they could have peace only with unconditional surrender. General Giraud and General de Gaulle had talks which it is hoped will lead to the two French forces being brought closer together. More pictures in BACK Page.

Russia Front, 1941-2-3.

THE progress of the Russian offensives compared with the limit of the German advance in 1941 and 1942 are shown here.

Twin Soviet Attacks Near Their Climax

From Daily Mail Special Correspondent

STOCKHOLM, Sunday.

TWO great offensives are approaching their climax in Russia to-night. West of Voronezh the defeated Germans are retreating at full speed on Kursk with the Russians pressing hard on their heels. Hitler must hold Kursk if he is to retain the link between his central and southern armies.

And in the Caucasus some 20 enemy divisions are threatened with envelopment and annihilation following the capture of Tikhoretsk and Maikop.

The German News Agency, which has been reflecting the war situation with some accuracy since the High Command decided to admit its seriousness, said to-night:

"Between Voronezh and the Donetz Estuary the enemy continued his attacks with increased pressure. Between the Kuban and the Lower Don the enemy attempted to break through the German lines."

Flying Columns

From Moscow came reports of Russian troops under General Reiter driving hard towards the great German base at Kursk. The retreating Germans are under continuous attack from Stomovik dive-bombers. Leading the pursuit are flying columns of tanks carrying tommy-gunners.

Behind them, east of Kastornaya, the destruction of the remnants of seven German infantry divisions continues.

In the Caucasus the Russians are overrunning the great Kuban plain in all directions and pushing rapidly towards the Black Sea coast.

One column is moving forward with great speed down the railway from Kropotkin towards Krasnodar, 65 miles from the naval base of Novorossisk.

Advancing 35 miles in 48 hours, Soviet troops yesterday reached Ladozhskaya, 50 miles north-east of Krasnodar. On the way they captured Tbilisskaya, about 20 miles from Kropotkin.

Soviet armies now stand in an arc around Rostov. On the Lower Donetz Front they are once more on the move towards the city. They have captured several more points, including a big town which has not yet been named.

A new Russian attack south of Rzhev with powerful tank and artillery forces was reported by the German News Agency last night.

3-day Gale on Strait Coast

A THREE-DAYS gale in the Strait of Dover reached its greatest force—70 m.p.h.—yesterday.

The gale blew from the south-west and was accompanied by heavy rainstorms at times, but a feature of the weather was the mildness of the temperature, which was more than 50 degrees during the whole of the day.

The wind began to increase in intensity late on Saturday night, when there was also lightning and thunder.

Mountainous seas were running, and the waves broke high over promenades and breakwaters along the whole of the coast.

Late last night the gale was reported to be moderating.

NEW PLAN 'SILENCED' HITLER

Peace Offer to Russia

By WILSON BROADBENT, Daily Mail Diplomatic Correspondent

HITLER'S failure to speak to his people on the tenth anniversary of his seizure of power must remain a mystery for the time being.

In the opinion of the people in London best able to judge of the situation in Germany, it is a mystery which we should not forget or underrate.

President Roosevelt and Mr. Churchill will very soon tell the world what they think of this development and the conclusions of the Casablanca Conference.

This is significant. They have little to hide save those technical details which might help the enemy.

Satisfactory

I am assured by those who have just returned from the Casablanca Conference that the conversations were most successful. For the first time the "planners" were in session at the same time as the President and the Premier.

All worked harmoniously and hopefully. There was no friction. All had the same end in view.

To this extent, the results must be judged as satisfactory. President Roosevelt and Mr. Churchill were in complete agreement.

As one of those present said to me last night: "I never thought that we could get so close. In my opinion, the conference was a great success."

These words must spell action, and soon.

I gather that the Casablanca Conference examined every aspect of strategy, much of which had been laid down months before, and therefore the talks were only confirmatory.

But the conference also decided on some big things to happen in the near future.

The Reason

The main strategy cannot be fulfilled all at once. Mr. Churchill has told us that time is the most important thing in military strategy.

The Libyan campaign has proved this, but following the Casablanca Conference we are assured things are now certain to happen.

Hitler has declared in the past that he prefers action to talking. It serves as a good excuse when you cannot justify your past boasts. This may be the reason why he did not speak on Saturday.

Instead, he allowed Göring to say that it was the Führer's intuition that led the German Army into the disastrous Russian campaign, and Goebbels to demand greater sacrifices from the German people.

Both these points are significant. Hitler is planning some move, and

BACK PAGE—Col. THREE

KNOX TELLS TOKIO 'GET READY FOR RAIDS'

NEW YORK, Sunday.

TOKIO was warned by Col. Knox, U.S. Secretary of the Navy, to-day that "they had better get ready" for an air attack.

The warning was conveyed in a message received from Pearl Harbour which revealed that during a 20,000-miles Pacific air tour in the past fortnight Col. Knox has twice been under Japanese air attack.

The first attack was a short one at Espiritu Santo, in the New Hebrides. The second, at Guadalcanal, was much heavier and lasted for seven hours. No casualties were reported from either attack.

Discussing the attack on Espiritu Santo, where Admiral Halsey met him, Col. Knox said: "It was the first attack there. How the Japanese got the information we don't know, but they didn't do us any harm except to keep us awake."

He said that a survey of Pearl Harbour and Oahu showed that they had been transformed into a fortress and Oahu was now adequately defended. Midway Island was also now satisfactorily defended.

"On Guadalcanal," he said, "I think we have dissipated the threat of the Japanese ground forces. In my judgment the Japanese have abandoned any idea of reinforcing their troops there, and within the next 30 days all organised resistance on Guadalcanal will disappear."—*Reuter.*

Gen. Giraud Talks Frankly to 'Daily Mail'

Differences with Gen. de Gaulle

Their Armies

The frankest statement yet made on the position between General de Gaulle and General Giraud was given to G. Ward Price, Daily Mail *Special Correspondent in North Africa, yesterday by General Giraud himself.*

His comments on the political situation follow; the rest of the interview appears in Page TWO.

I ASKED General Giraud (cables Ward Price) how far arrangements had gone for collaboration between himself and General de Gaulle.

He answered: "We agreed on our aims. Our only differences are about the means to attain them.

"My own view is that it is only natural that the much smaller forces controlled by General de Gaulle, amounting to some 15,000-20,000 men, should be amalgamated with the larger army under my command.

"As regards the political administration of the various parts of the French Empire respectively under his authority and mine, I am content that each of us should continue in charge of the territories he now controls.

"The problems of governing Syria, for instance, are quite different from those that confront me in North Africa.

PERSONALITIES

"There are also questions of personalities on which General de Gaulle and myself do not see eye to eye. He objects to the presence of certain people in my administration. I maintain that these are quite secondary matters, which time will solve.

"One thing is sure: It will be neither General de Gaulle nor myself who will determine the future government of a liberated France. That is to be settled by 40,000,000 French people—now so brutally oppressed that hundreds of innocent men have been shot in revenge for attacks on members of the German Army committed far from the places where the victims lived.

"I feel confident that General de Gaulle and I will gradually reach a basis of co-operation. He was delayed in arriving at Casablanca, but we were there together from Friday till Sunday. We shall doubtless meet again, though no time has been fixed."

I asked: "Will you go to London for that or any other purpose?"

General Giraud replied: "I am much too busy with the operations my troops are carrying on in Tunisia. I shall shortly be paying them a visit at the front."

DARLAN ARRESTS

This brought me to the question of the arrests carried out by the French Administration in North Africa of some people here who are said to have worked for the Allied cause and to have helped to prepare our landing.

I mentioned to the General that in Britain and America these arrests had aroused much comment and had been interpreted as a sign that the spirit of the Vichy Government was still strongly represented in his Administration.

He replied with energy and emphasis:

"This matter is one which concerns me alone as head of this Government. When there is reason to suspect that any persons have been party to an assassination like that of Darlan I am determined that they shall be brought under the proper process of common law.

"It matters nothing to me whether such persons are partisans of General de Gaulle or my own supporters. As a matter of fact, some of both are in custody for the examination of their cases.

"Some will shortly be liberated, and you can take it from me that I should be the last of all French men to try—or to wish—to impose a Vichy-minded Administration on either North Africa or France.

"My own record is sufficient evidence for that.

LAW AND ORDER

"The young man who shot Admiral Darlan acted probably on his own impulse. But he had been mixed up with some excitable elements among the population here, and if it transpires that any of these instigated, even indirectly, the murder of my predecessor, it is a matter of ordinary justice for such criminal conduct to be brought home to them.

"My action in setting these inquiries on foot was inspired by no political consideration whatever.

"I regret that it has been so widely misinterpreted abroad by people ignorant of conditions existing here, but my sense of duty and justice left me no choice. Murder is not a crime that can go unpunished for fear of arousing political criticism."

EIGHTH ARMY ATTACK—AXIS

Tanks Follow Big Barrage

GENERAL MONTGOMERY has launched a large-scale attack on Rommel's rearguard near Zuara, between Tripoli and the Mareth Line, according to an announcement by the German Official News Agency last night.

The attack, the Germans say, was launched on Saturday. General Montgomery prepared the way with an intense artillery barrage, and then began the assault with what the Axis describe as "far superior tank formations."

MAP shows where the Germans have broken through the French lines in Tunisia.

According to the Germans the Axis line held all along the front, and it is claimed that guns and planes accounted for 18 British tanks.

Beyond the phrase "near Zuara" the Germans give no indication of the scene of the attack, but Morocco radio reports that a second column of British troops yesterday crossed the Tunisian border by the coast road after bypassing Zuara.

This column is said to be advancing parallel with the column which crossed the frontier farther inland on Saturday.

Late last night an American correspondent, broadcasting on Algiers radio, quoted unconfirmed reports that some Eighth Army men had reached the Mareth Line.

Bad weather prevented air operations over the battlefront on Saturday, but R.A.F. and United States bombers attacked targets in the port of Messina and the important power station of Avola, Sicily.

The R.A.F. scored direct hits on the station, which was also machine-gunned.

TUNISIA ATTACK

MEANWHILE, in Tunisia, a German force of all arms—tanks, infantry, and artillery—has broken through the French lines 60 miles west of Sfax, occupied Faid Pass, and advanced six miles towards the important road junction of Sidi Bouzid.

This blow at the Allies' centre

BACK PAGE—Col. TWO

Envoy Eludes Nazis, Lands in Britain

ONE of France's leading diplomats, M. Rene Massigli, has escaped to London and has joined General de Gaulle.

He was French Ambassador to Turkey until July 1940, when he was dismissed by the Vichy Government on orders from Berlin.

On the Germans' entry into Unoccupied France last November a warrant was issued within 24 hours for his arrest. He eluded the police and had been in hiding until his escape from the south of France.

M. Massigli, who is 53, holds the British K.B.E. He was French delegate to the Franco-Soviet Conference in 1926, the London Naval Conference in 1930, and the Disarmament Conference in 1932.

SEAMEN: GIVE FAST SHIPS OWN CONVOYS

THE grouping of fast ships in special convoys and the immediate construction of high-speed merchant vessels for war purposes were among the suggestions for beating the U-boat made at the International Seamen's Conference in London yesterday.

The conference passed a resolution saying that the building of high-speed ships had been prevented by "considerations relating to post-war speculations and interests."

At an earlier sitting on Saturday, Mr. Jarman, general secretary, British National Union of Seamen, said that in a confidential talk with Mr. A. V. Alexander (First Lord of the Admiralty) he had urged that convoys should have better air protection.

Chief Praises the Mosquito Men

Air Marshal Sir Arthur Harris, Commander-in-Chief, Bomber Command, has sent a message to the Mosquito crews who bombed Berlin on Saturday, congratulating them on their "magnificent" attack.

"Their bombs," says the Air Marshal, "coincided with an attempt by Göring to broadcast to the German people on the tenth anniversary of Hitler's usurpation of power and cannot have failed to cause consternation in Germany and encouragement to the oppressed peoples of Europe."

Story of Raid—Page THREE.

British Submarine is Lost

The Admiralty announce that H.M. Submarine P 222 (Lieut.-Comdr. A. J. Mackenzie, R.N.) is overdue, and must be presumed lost.

Next of kin have been informed.

As no reference to the P222 is to be found in "Jane's Fighting Ships," it is assumed that she is of recent construction.

Three submarines bearing the same letter have previously been announced as overdue and presumed lost—the P38 on March 22, 1941, and the P32 and the P33 on dates in September 1941.

'1943—Year of Blood'

Mario Appelius, Rome radio commentator, told Italians last night: "The one who loses 1943 will lose the war: 1943 will be a year of blood and sweat."

Duce Sacks His Chief of Staff

Army Reshuffle

MUSSOLINI has sacked his Chief of the General Staff and Under-Secretary for War, Marshal Ugo Cavallero — the "man who lost the Italian Empire."

Rome radio, putting it the official way, stated last night that he had been "relieved of his post at his own request."

Gen. Vittorio Ambrosio, Chief of Staff of the Italian Army, takes his place, and Gen Ezio Rossi, commanding the 6th Army Corps, replaces Ambrosio.

A reshuffle was fully expected following the Italian débâcle in Libya and the heavy defeats suffered by Italian divisions on the Don and Donetz.

Cavallero, the "business man soldier," divided his time between the Army and big steel interests. In 1929 he resigned the under-secretaryship to become a director of the Ansaldo ironworks.

In 1933 he returned to the Army and commanded the Italian Legionaries in the Spanish Civil War. His units suffered the heavy defeat of Guadalahara.

He also took part in campaigns in East Africa and Albania. In March, 1941, after Badoglio's resignation, he was appointed Chief of the General Staff.

LATEST

TIGHTER ITALIAN BLACK-OUT

New black-out regulations will come into force in Italy as from to-day, says Rome radio. The black-out of all Italian towns will be from 6.30 p.m. until 8.30 a.m.

BIG SPANISH FIRE

Seville, Sunday.—A big fire broke out this afternoon at a Seville cork factory owned by an industrial concern whose manager is a German named Ludvig Bodoheimer. Half the stocks of cork and machinery, valued at a total of £100,000, were destroyed.—Reuter.

2

SCRIPPS—HOWARD

New York World-Telegram

Local Forecast: Tonight somewhat colder than last night. Sunset 6:23 p. m. Dimout 6:53 p. m.

7TH SPORTS
Final Stock Tables
THREE CENTS IN CITY
Elsewhere Four Cents

VOL. 75—NO. 187—IN TWO SECTIONS—SECTION ONE   NEW YORK, TUESDAY, FEBRUARY 9, 1943.   Entered as second class matter, Post Office, New York, N. Y.

JAPS DESERT GUADALCANAL

Reds Pierce Rostov Line From East

By M. S. HANDLER,
United Press Staff Correspondent.

MOSCOW, Feb. 9.—Soviet forces have pierced a fortified line east of Rostov and forced the Germans to retreat toward the city for the second time within 24 hours, front dispatches and communiques disclosed today.

Meanwhile new gains were reported north, east and southeast of threatened Kharkov, where the Soviet forces of Col. Gen. Nikolai F. Vatutin and Col. Gen. Philip Golikov registered steady advances.

[In London military authorities believed disaster threatened the Germans from both ends of the Russian offensive line and discussed the possibility that they might have to fall back to the Dnieper River, 250 miles west of Kharkov, before arrival of the spring thaw. A Radio Ankara broadcast said long columns of German troops already were retreating along the coast from Rostov.]

Nazi Attack Repulsed.

The noon communique said the Red army had repulsed a strong counterattack near Rostov and had occupied a series of fortified positions.

[A BBC broadcast recorded by the United Press said Russian dive bombers were incessantly bombing and machine gunning enemy troops retreating from Rostov toward Taganrog, 30 miles west of the gateway city.]

Red Letter Day for Russia.

[It said the Russian advance on Rostov was making steady progress, although German tank units were attempting delaying actions "in Rostov itself."]

Yesterday was one of the most glorious days of the winter campaign. The fall of Kursk, 125 miles north of Kharkov, endangered the entire German anchor line based on Kharkov, and at Rostov the Russians cleaned out the Yeisk Peninsula, to the southwest, and made important gains east of the city.

Today General Golikov continued to press westward after

(Continued on Page Twelve.)

Father Explains All In Naming Boy Hitler

Joseph Mittel, 37, a rather paunchy son of an Austrian soldier, somewhat of a vegetarian and the bearer of a little black toothbrush mustache, insisted today that children should not be taught hatred, and said that the name of his seventh child really is Adolf Hitler Mittel, and that the name will stick.

"It's a name, and that's all," he said with mild-mannered finality. "A rose by any other name. We'll leave it lay.

"Any person has a right to name its child what it likes. It's a constitutional right. I heard there's a doctor in Long Island City who's named Adolf Hitler."

Consternation Spreads.

While babies have been christened Franklin Roosevelt McDermott and Winston Churchill Swenson with scarcely more to-do than the passing out of cigars, two-weeks-old Adolf Hitler Mittel has convulsed a good part of Queens, where he was born last month, and the consternation is spreading.

Sees No Handicap.

St. John's Hospital refused to accept Mrs. Mittel's choice of the name, and the Health Department sent her another blank to fill in. When she remained steadfast, a department representative called upon her to warn her about kidding with the city records. He went away considerably upset.

Today, in the Mittels' poorly-furnished four-room flat at 27-37 First St., Astoria, for which they

(Continued on Page Two.)

OPA Denies Plan To Ration Clothing

Rationing of clothing is not being planned as a follow-up to shoe rationing, the local OPA office emphasized today. Local clothes buying, it reported, has remained at normal since the shoe order went into effect Sunday.

"The belief that clothing rationing will follow in the wake of shoe rationing at this time is unfounded," an OPA spokesman said. "No rationing of clothing is contemplated at this time."

Many stores throughout the country reported extremely heavy "scare" buying of men's heavy coats and suits and women's apparel.

In Columbus, Ohio, where unprecedented clothes buying was reported, one store official said a week of such business would exhaust his stock, and a Bond clothing official reported:

"We never have seen anything like it. The people didn't pay any attention to color or pattern. They just wanted clothes—any kind of clothes."

In Cleveland George H. Richman, president of Richman Bros., one of the largest retail men's clothing store chains, said he was rather upset by the rush buying, which he termed ridiculous.

Similar panic buying occurred in Chicago, where six leading men's stores said purchases had topped the all-time business following last year's announcement of the ban on trousers cuffs. In Baltimore a run on socks, shirts, underwear and ties, as well as suits and overcoats, was attributed to the shoe rationing.

Florida Divorce Snags On Issue of Residence

Though drug magnate Robert Schnabel's chances of getting out of alimony jail had brightened visibly today, the state of New York still maintained a "back turned" attitude toward the validity of a Florida divorce obtained by him three years ago.

Regardless of the recent decision of the Supreme Court of the United States holding that each state must recognize the validity of a divorce secured legally in any other state, Supreme Court Justice Ferdinand Pecora replied:

"If the defendant was not domiciled in Florida, and there is no evidence before me that he was, then this court, even under the Williams (U. S. Supreme Court) decision, is not bound to give full faith and credit to that decree."

Counsel for Schnabel's wife, Ro-

(Continued on Page Twelve.)

They're Really Mad

By the United Press.

LONDON, Feb. 9.—Alexei Tolstoy, Russian novelist, warned the Germans on the Moscow radio today that "the Red army is now really angry."

All Maryland Race Tracks Face Closing

Operation Would Hurt War Effort, U. S. Official Says

By the United Press.

BALTIMORE, Feb. 9.—Plans for a spring racing season in Maryland hit a snag today when state and local war manpower authorities inferentially asked that all tracks be closed to hold down absenteeism in war factories.

The Maryland Racing Commission had announced plans to hold Bowie, Havre de Grace and Pimlico spring meetings at Baltimore's Pimlico track. The commission was at work ironing out details for the meetings when the new development arose.

Official Explains.

A spokesman in the office of Lawrence B. Fenneman, War Manpower Commission director for Maryland, expressed the belief that racing would "interfere materially with local war production."

"We feel," he added, "that all horse racing should be banned for the duration as a way of fighting war plant absenteeism."

Mr. Fenneman and the Area Manpower Committee, composed of four representatives each of management and labor, sent telegrams to the Racing Commission and Gov. Herbert R. O'Conor warning that races this year would have a serious effect on war industry.

Commission Meeting Is Called Off

The telegram said that the Manpower Committee had adopted a resolution expressing the opinion that "horse racing in Maryland will tend to increase absenteeism in war industries, with the result of loss of manpower, curtailing production."

Upon receipt of the telegram, Frank Small, Jr., chairman of the Racing Commission, called off a commission meeting scheduled for this afternoon. He said he would get in touch with Mr. O'Conor to get his views and with Mr.

(Continued on Page Twenty.)

Hands Mate Suicide Note And Goes Out

It was shortly after midnight and Joseph Guittieriez, 29, was asleep in his bedroom at 844 Columbus Ave., when his wife, Julia, 29, tiptoed in and placed a slip of paper in his hand. The movement only half awakaned him and he lay there several minutes before unfolding the paper to see what it was.

When he did see, it brought him to with a start. "Dear Joe," the note read. "Can't stand the pain any longer. Going out to commit suicide. Will make it look like an accident."

Mr. Guttieriez dressed quickly and hurried out to look for his wife. When he found no trace of her he reported the note to the W. 100th St. police station. The police today searched for the woman—described as 5 feet 6, weight about 120 pounds, with brown hair and eyes—in an effort to prevent her from taking her life.

Remember '34? Brrr!

A gamble, at best, this weather business.

Nine years ago today New York City experienced its coldest day in history—14.3 degrees below zero at 7:25 a. m.

Forecast today; rising temperature, moderate winds.

Come seven! Baby needs a new pair of non-rationed, soft-soled shoes.

The Weather

(Official United States Forecast.)

New York and Metropolitan Area: This afternoon moderate temperatures with diminishing winds; tonight somewhat colder than last night with winds increasing moderately.

New Jersey: This afternoon moderate temperature; tonight about as cold as last night.

TODAY'S READINGS.

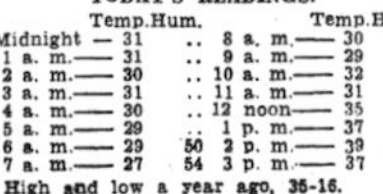

	Temp.	Hum.		Temp.	Hum.
Midnight	31	..	8 a. m.	30	57
1 a. m.	31	..	9 a. m.	29	62
2 a. m.	30	..	10 a. m.	32	47
3 a. m.	31	..	11 a. m.	31	48
4 a. m.	30	..	12 noon	35	49
5 a. m.	29	..	1 p. m.	37	41
6 a. m.	29	50	2 p. m.	39	43
7 a. m.	27	54	3 p. m.	37	40

High and low a year ago, 35-16.

U. S. Now Able to Strike Other Bases, Knox Asserts

Now We Have a Springboard

The American victory over the Japs on Guadalcanal (1) will enable our troops to strike important enemy bases, Secretary of the Navy Knox said today. These bases include New Georgia Islands (2), Shortland Islands (3) and Bougainville Island (4). A. P. Map.

Air and Sea Fighting Continues Sporadically In Solomon Islands

By SANDOR S. KLEIN,
United Press Staff Correspondent.

WASHINGTON, Feb. 9.—Secretary of the Navy Knox said today that United States forces finally had smashed all organized Japanese resistance on Guadalcanal and were now in position to strike the enemy's "most important bases" in that part of the world.

"All resistance on Guadalcanal apparently has ceased," except for a few isolated enemy troops trapped in jungle defiles and valleys, Mr. Knox said.

The Secretary held a press conference soon after the Tokyo and Berlin radios broadcast a Japanese Imperial Headquarters communique announcing withdrawal of Japanese forces from Guadalcanal "after their mission had been fulfilled."

Mr. Knox said information from Guadalcanal, where American forces landed for the first time last Aug. 7, supported the Japanese reports.

AIR ENGAGEMENTS CONTINUE.

The Secretary indicated, however, that surface and air engagements which started more than a week ago were continuing sporadically.

In bringing the Guadalcanal phase of the Solomons campaign to a successful conclusion American forces in control of the most strategically important island are now in position to launch assaults at remaining enemy bases in the island group.

These include the New Georgia Islands, important because of the Japanese air base at Munda, 180 nautical miles northwest of Guadalcanal; the Shortland Islands 295 miles northwest, and Bougainville Island with its important base of Buin, about 307 miles northwest of Guadalcanal.

"The South Pacific story might have been vastly different for the last three or four months had we not established ourselves in the Solomons successfully," Mr. Knox observed.

ESTIMATE OF JAP RESISTANCE.

He recalled that when he returned from his recent tour of the southwest Pacific he had made an estimate that significant Japanese resistance on Guadalcanal had collapsed. Then he quoted from the Axis broadcast on the Japanese communique.

"I don't think there's any doubt about the truth of that," Mr. Knox said. "What we thought were attempts to reinforce may have been attempts to evacuate. But that is speculative and we will have to await confirmation."

"Did the enemy have much to withdraw?"

"No, they didn't. The number of Japanese on the island when we were down there—on Jan. 21-22—was estimated to be between 4000 and 6000.

"We are satisfied by our air and ground reconnaissance that there is no large number of Japanese in any

(Continued on Page Six.)

Murray Attacks Mayor on Transit

Mayor La Guardia's attitude toward the Transport Workers Union relegates its members "to the status of Grade B citizens" and 'admittedly" is impairing efficiency of the city's transit lines, Philip Murray, president of the CIO, declared here today.

"Desperation," he added, is compelling thousands of transit workers to leave the city's employ for other industries which offer "higher pay and the other tradi-

(Continued on Page Twelve.)

WLB Denies Pay Rise To 'Big 4' Packers

By the United Press.

WASHINGTON, Feb. 9.—The War Labor Board, refusing to relax its "Little Steel" wage stabilization formula, today denied a general wage increase to 180,000 employees of the "Big Four" meat packing companies.

8 'Chute Spies Shot

By the United Press.

LONDON, Feb. 9.—Radio Morocco said today that eight spies who parachuted from an Italian transport plane over North Africa had been shot. One was French.

Traces Queens Killing To a Woman's Remark

A talkative woman started the events which ended in the killing of tousel-haired Mrs. Carol Tuttle, mother of two children.

The man who had been going out with Mrs. Tuttle, James J. Mallon, 32, a soda dispenser, told about the other women when he took the stand today in county court Long Island City, to defend himself against a charge of murder.

He said he and Mrs. Tuttle had been having some beers in a tavern the night of last Nov. 4. He said he had "about 20," and "Carol had a few more than I did." Then the other woman, the talker, walked in.

"She asked Carol how her husband was," Mallon told Judge Thomas Downs and the jury. "And then Carol said to me: 'I think this will be all over town.' "

A few hours later Mrs. Tuttle was found lying dead, her throat

(Continued on Page Six.)

7 Army Fliers Killed in Iowa

By the United Press.

SIOUX CITY, Ia., Feb. 9.—Seven men were killed and three others injured, one seriously, when a heavy bomber plane crashed southeast of the Sioux City air base last night, Capt. Francis Hettinger, Public Relations officer, announced today.

War Today

SOLOMONS—Jap resistance on Guadalcanal apparently has ceased, says Secretary Knox as Tokyo and Berlin radios tell of withdrawls both from Guadalcanal and Buna, New Guinea.

AFRICA—U. S. air forces strike hard at Rommel and Von Arnim, battering troops, artillery positions, supply and communication lines; Axis reports big scale Eighth Army attack to cut Rommel off from the sea; Allied bombers attack train-ferry at Messina, Sicily.

RUSSIA—Reds pierce Nazi lines at Rostov from the East; capture of Kursk and new advances endanger entire Nazi anchor line based on Kharkov.

LONDON—London has brief raid alarm; silent radios on Continent hint new Allied air offensive; heavy guns duel across Dover Strait.

World-Telegram Index

Pop Won't Believe Son Lost; UP Finds He Isn't

By the United Press.

BIRMINGHAM, Ala., Feb. 9.—William J. Parson, a mine forman, came into the United Press bureau here last week. He had in his hand a message from the War Department which said, "We are sorry to inform you that your son, Staff Sgt. Nolan F. Parson, is reported missing in action."

What hope the elder Parson had centered around a dispatch from Walter Logan, United Press staff correspondent at Allied Air Force headquarters, North Africa, dated Jan. 28.

Logan had told how six Americans, crewmen of a B-26 Marauder bomber, shot down behind Axis lines, threw the Germans who captured them out of the automobile in which they were being taken to a prison camp. The six fled in the car, three finally reaching the bomber base. The other three haven't turned up yet.

Among the three who came back was Sergeant Parson, waist gunner.

"Could you find out if Nolan is all right now?" the mine foreman asked. "Maybe the message is about something that has happened since Nolan came back."

Last night the answer came in. C. R. Cunningham, United Press correspondent in Algiers, sent a cablegram which was relayed to the Parsons in Brookside.

It read: "Sgt. Nolan Parson from Brookside, Ala., said 'I am very much alive and I am all rested up now and ready to go again.' "

The sergeant's father went to work as usual in the mine today.

"My heart was almost too heavy to work after I got that telegram from Washington, but I felt I just had to. Now it'll be different," he said.

Pyle Depicts Realism Of Deaths in Africa

This is the last of two articles describing the battle for Ousseltia by American forces.

By ERNIE PYLE,
Scripps-Howard Staff Writer.

AT THE FRONT LINE IN TUNISIA (By Wireless).—The afternoon sun went over the hill and the evening chill began to come down. We were sitting on a bushy hillside—just a small bunch of American officers forming what is called a forward command post.

Officers who had been in battle for Ousseltia Pass all day began wandering in through the brush to report. They were dirty and tired. But the day had gone well and they were cheerful in a quiet and unexpressed way.

Ernie Pyle.

A Medical Corps major came up the hill and said:

"Those blankety-blanks! They've knocked out two of my ambulances that were trying to get the wounded back. A hell of a lot a red cross means to them!"

Nobody said anything. He went back down the hill as mad as a hornet.

The officers kept talking about three fellow officers who had been killed during the day and a fourth who was missing. One of the dead men apparently had been a special favorite. An officer who had been beside him when it happened came up with blood on his clothes.

Death Described.

"We hit the ground together," he said. "But when I got up he couldn't. It took him right in the head. He felt no pain."

"Raise up that tent and pack his stuff," an officer told an enlisted man.

Another man said: "The hell of it is his wife's due to have a baby any time now."

Just then a sergeant walked up. He had left the post that morn-

(Continued on Page Twelve.)

No. 10,556 SATURDAY, MARCH 13, 1943 ONE PENNY (2d. in Eire)

Russians Kill 9,000 Nazis in Capturing Vyazma

GERMANS CLAIM KHARKOV

"CITY CENTRE REACHED" REPORT UNCONFIRMED

SMOLENSK, Hitler's main base in Central Russia, is now directly threatened. Two great Soviet armies are converging towards it after the capture of the last "hedgehog" stronghold of Vyazma, announced officially from Moscow last night.

Meanwhile the situation at Kharkov, key to the whole of the southern front, has become extremely grave.

The German News Agency last night claimed that German troops had reached the Red Square, in the centre of the city, adding: "After three weeks of Soviet occupation Kharkov is now in German hands."

There is no confirmation of this report, but latest dispatches make it clear that the Soviet defenders, fighting as tenaciously as ever, have been hard pressed at every point.

900 Tanks Used in Assault

Several infantry divisions, supported by 900 tanks and strong Luftwaffe forces, have been hurled against Kharkov from the south and the west.

Under the mass onslaught, launched on a very narrow front, Soviet troops may have retired to new lines, Reuter's Special Correspondent says.

The German attempt to pulverise the Soviet artillery by a powerful barrage did not succeed in knocking out enough of them to create gun superiority.

When groups of German tanks tried to force their way across the Donetz River there were still sufficient Soviet guns left to beat them back.

Main danger to the city has come from the heavy German attacks from the west, where the broad Ukrainian plain rolls down to the city from a range of hills.

Fluctuating Battles

Hard, fluctuating battles are at present being fought for many forward positions north of the Kharkov area, in the Sudzha and Syevsk areas.

This represents roughly a 100-mile front, stretching north and south across the Kursk-Kiev railway about 50 miles west of Kursk and Orel.

The strength of the German counter-attacks, in which big tank forces are being used, shows that the German High Command is now making a large-scale attempt to stop the Soviet offensive once and for all.

The whole front from Leningrad to Kharkov is in a state of flux at the moment, and it is too early to say where the new "line" will harden, if it ever does.

Continued on Back Page

BOMBER "RUIN" FOR ROUEN

AMERICAN heavy bombers attacked railway yards at Rouen in daylight yesterday.

The bombers were Flying Fortresses, and the R.A.F., U.S.A.A.F. and Allied Spitfire squadrons escorted and covered them. None was attacked by enemy aircraft and none is missing, but three enemy fighters were destroyed by the Spitfires.

Hitler's desperate counter-attacks on the Kharkov front, pressed regardless of losses, may be the result of his fears that the Red Army were getting within bombing distance of the Rumanian oilfields, Germany's main source of supply.

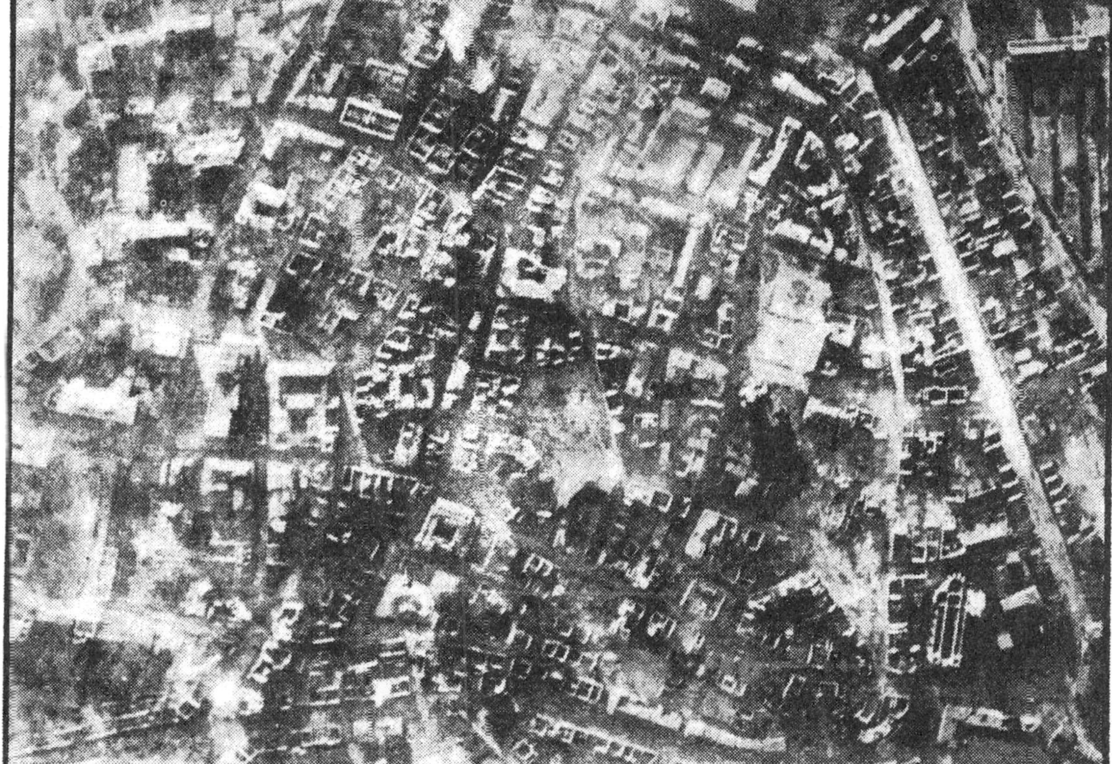

Thirty thousand Krupp's workers at Essen have been made homeless by R.A.F. raids, said Sir Archibald Sinclair, in the House of Commons. This R.A.F. picture shows about 140 acres of devastation among workers' houses and commercial buildings adjoining Krupp's works. Other pictures on Page Five.

13 HIT-AND-RUN RAIDERS DOWN IN 24 HOURS

GERMANY, stepping-up sneak raids over Britain, in the 24 hours ending at dusk last night made four attacks on this country with 74 bombers and lost 13 of them—the highest proportion of "kills" for months.

The four attacks included a night raid on the North-East (the Germans claimed that Newcastle-on-Tyne was their target), a dawn raid on the London outskirts and an afternoon attack in the South-West.

Hospital Machine-gunned

Some of the bombers reached the Greater London area and machine-gunned streets, a hospital and a railway station. Twelve people were killed.

Three trains in East Anglia, one crowded with London workers, were machine-gunned—but there were no casualties.

The total destroyed is more likely 15, as there were two "probables" and several more damaged.

The raids during the 24-hour period were:—

Thursday. — South-East Coast Town: About 30 'planes, four destroyed, one "probable," more damaged. North-Eastern Area: Scattered raids of about 20 bombers, four were destroyed.

Yesterday at Dawn. — London Outskirts Area: About 24 raiders, five destroyed, one "probable," at least four damaged. Afternoon: South-West Coast Town: Five raiders.

Pilots of a Norwegian fighter squadron shot down the five aircraft destroyed over the Thames.

The raiders—all single-engine fighters or fighter-bombers—took advantage of bad visibility and ground haze to cross the Essex coast.

After dropping their bombs they recrossed the coast with our fighters in close pursuit, and made out to sea, where other enemy fighter formations were waiting to cover their withdrawal.

LEAPFROGGING THE CHIMNEYS

By A DAILY SKETCH REPORTER IN THE LONDON RAID

I STOOD in my garden on the outskirts of London and watched four Nazi fighter-bombers swoop over with machine-guns blazing early yesterday morning. They flew at roof-top height and made straight for the railway station.

Out of a cloudless sky a Spitfire swooped on the tail of the leading Focke-Wulf, raking it with fire. Spent clips from the machine-guns fell around me. Other Spitfires joined the first and the amazing air circus swept over the station, scattering passengers waiting for a train.

A few hundred yards further on

Continued on Back Page

HITLER Complete Breakdown —Sumner Welles

A REPORT has been received by the U.S. State Department that Hitler is suffering from a complete breakdown, says a Reuter message from Washington yesterday.

Mr. Sumner Welles, Under-Secretary of State, in revealing this, did not imply that the State Department was attaching much importance to these reports, but merely asserted that the Department had received unconfirmed reports similar to those published recently in newspapers of various countries.

There have been reports from neutral sources that a mental specialist had been called from Sweden to Berchtesgaden.

Germany's "Heroes' Day," which was to have been held next Sunday, March 14, has been postponed until March 21, says Reuter. Hitler usually speaks on this day.

If the Fuehrer fails to make a speech on this occasion it will give support to rumours of a mental or physical disability which prevents a public appearance.

Adolf Hitler's death has been hinted at in various dispatches since January 30, the tenth anniversary of the Fuehrer's accession to power.

TIMELY WORDS OF FAITH

STAND FAST IN ONE SPIRIT, WITH ONE MIND STRIVING TOGETHER FOR THE FAITH.
Philippians 1, 27.

THE STARS AND STRIPES
AFRICA

Vol. 1 - No. 16 - Friday, March 26, 1943 — U. S. Army Newspaper — Two Francs

British Open Mareth Line Attack As Americans Begin Drive Eastward

Churchill Sees Long War, Plans Future Course

LONDON—In his first speech since his recent illness, Prime Minister Winston Churchill outlined a future possible organization of United Nations to prevent further aggression and chartered a four-year plan for post-war Great Britain to follow.

Speaking in sober and confident tones, Mr. Churchill made it clear at the start that he did not share the belief of a good many others that the war would soon be over.

THEN FOR JAPAN

"I can imagine that sometime next year—but it may be the year after—we might beat Hitler and his powers of evil into death, dust and ashes," he declared. "Then we shall immediately transport all the necessary additional forces and apparatus to the other side of the world to punish the greedy and cruel Empire of Japan."

Mr. Churchill expressed the hope that the United Nations, headed by the three great victorious powers—the British Commonwealth of Nations, the United States and Soviet Russia—would begin to confer upon the future world organization which would be the safeguard against war. He visualized the time when all nations would come into a council of Europe and a council of Asia.

For Great Britain, the Prime Minister offered a vigorous five-point program covering national insurance, agriculture, education, public health and employment.

SECURITY PLANNED

"The best way to insure against unemployment," he said, "is to have no unemployment. Unemployables, rich or poor, will have to be toned up. Idlers at the top make idlers at the bottom. No one must stand aside in his working prime to pursue a life of selfish pleasure."

With his characteristic flair for the dramatic, Mr. Churchill concluded with the following announcement to the world: "I have just received a message from Gen. Montgomery that the 8th Army is on the move and that he is satisfied with their progress."

YANKS ON THE WAY back to Gafsa halt for a brief and cautious inspection of a road block, where the Germans have planted a land mine.
—*Stars and Stripes Photo by Pete Paris*

Gafsa Quiet, Empty As Yanks Return

By RALPH G. MARTIN
(*Stars and Stripes Staff Writer*)

WITH THE AMERICAN FORCES IN GAFSA—When American troops walked into Gafsa last week, they found it as quiet and empty as a graveyard and as full of ghosts.

The Germans and Italians were gone but there was plenty to remember them by. Doors throughout Gafsa were bolted with booby traps, land mines were carefully planted in bombed rubble and the scared people of the town were hiding in the hills and in cellars and caves.

Two weeks before, Gafsa had been alive with crowds of jabbering Arabs selling tangerines and eggs to Yank soldiers. Kids were yelling all over the place for "chawklit and shoonrum" and camels and cows walked the streets. It was a living town then, with noise and smell to it. Last week, when we entered the place, Gafsa was different.

The taking of Gafsa was one of those affairs in which the enemy was merely check-mated, knew it and pulled out without a fight. Jerry took everything he couldn't burn with him.

The movement toward the town began when the medium and light bombers went over, followed by low-level strafing fighter planes.

(*Continued on Page 8*)

Tommies Outflank Line In Long Desert March; Maknassy Is Captured

The push for Tunisia is on.

With the smashing of the Mareth Line and the capture of Gabes as the first objective, Allied Forces have launched a concerted, coordinated air and ground attack against Axis positions in southern Tunisia.

A bitter struggle has been raging since Saturday when the 8th Army struck along a six-mile line from the sea to the coastal highway. The British here used much the same tactics as had been used when they broke through the Afrika Korps' prepared positions at El Alamein early last November.

With the aid of a heavy artillery barrage and continuous aerial bombing and strafing, infantry units forced a breach in one sector of the first defense line of the Mareth zone. Fierce counter-attacks soon, however, forced them back. As this edition went to press heavy artillery duels were taking place.

Meanwhile, a second British armored column was executing a brilliant flanking movement around the Mareth Line. After a forced march of more than 100 miles over the desert beyond the Matmata Mountains, this column arrived at the edge of the great salt lakes west of Gabes, a good 35 miles this side of the Mareth outposts.

For Rommel this was an extremely dangerous but not unexpected, development and he met this outflanking movement in force. A strong German force gave battle to this column about 10 miles southeast of El Hamma at the entrance of what is known as the Gabes Gap, only 20 miles from Gabes itself.

As if these threats were not serious enough for Rommel, a French force was also moving around the fringes of the salt lake.

Farther north, the American forces, having taken Gafsa the week before, branched out in two directions.

To the northeast American armored units rumbled through Sened, twice before captured, and then advanced half a dozen miles past Maknassy. This force now occupies the high ground surrounding Jebel Bou Dou Aou. It is with-

(*Continued on Page 3*)

Bags 26 Jap Planes For New Ace Record

NEW YORK—According to delayed dispatches from Guadalcanal, Capt. Joe Foss, of Sioux Falls, S. D., has displaced Capt. Eddie Rickenbacker as America's all-time air ace.

Capt. Foss has downed 26 Jap planes—one more than Rickenbacker's World War I record take.

A-T Gun Crews Score Bullseyes

IN TUNISIA—Certain members of Co. B of one engineer outfit, serving on 37 mm. anti-tank guns, are now proudly displaying one of those papers from the colonel referring to "skill and courage under fire." The boys, led by Sgt. Ed. W. Lewis, faced three Axis frontal attacks in one day, knocked out, among other vehicles, a German armored car, a couple of reconnaissance cars, a truck loaded with German soldiers. They also took seven Italian prisoners and eight Jerries, all members of the Afrika Korps.

In each case, the crews, knowing very well that their weapons were not for long range work, held fire until the vehicles were well within range and then let loose. Hits were scored on every occasion.

Atebrin Enlists In Malaria War

The Allied Forces in North Africa are about to open up a second front, this time against the mosquito and malaria. Beginning April 22, every last soldier in North Africa, from Gen. "Ike" Eisenhower down to the lowliest buck private, will begin taking twice weekly a new malaria killer called atebrin.

A synthetic substitute for quinine, atebrin comes in the form of little golden-brown pills. So strong is this new drug that a dose of only two-tenths of a gram every three or four days is considered, in most cases, sufficient to ward off the disease. Along with taking of atebrin, U. S. Army units have been instructed to take every other possible protective measure against mosquitos, such as the use of mosquito bars at night and the wearing of head nets and gloves.

The malaria season will be in full swing in North Africa in late April and will continue until November. The disease itself is so common that in some areas from 90 to 100 percent of the population is chronically infected. Few sections are free of it.

It is literally true that malaria, with its periodic rises of fever, has disabled or killed more men than all Hitler's Panzer divisions could ever hope to do. The order announcing the atebrin plan warns:

"Military operations in the North African Theater during the summer months will be seriously jeopardized by malaria unless malaria control measures are strictly enforced."

The atebrin pills will be taken Mondays and Thursdays after supper. They must be taken with liquids—with plenty of water, tea, or coffee. On a small number of men, nausea may result, in which case unit commanders, on the advice of the surgeon, may modify the dose. In areas where malaria is especially prevalent, the dosage may also be increased.

Mosquito repellent will also be issued to all men at the rate of one bottle a man every 28 days. The use of flit guns and good old

(*Continued on Page 8*)

Hitler Ends Long Silence, Would Bolster Germans

LONDON—The German people finally heard from Adolf Hitler last Sunday.

Der Fuehrer, breaking the long silence which began with the Russian offensive early last fall, also made his first public appearance in well over four months. He appeared at the tomb of the German Unknown Soldier.

Unlike his usual flights of emotional and frenzied oratory, Hitler talked for only 11 minutes in a high pitched and monotonous voice as if he were reading from a script. Some listeners here who are familiar with Hitler's delivery said the speech and the breaks in transmitting sounded suspiciously like a recording.

RETURNS COMMAND

The broadcast disclosed the possibility that Hitler had turned the command of the German armies back to the generals. Hitler assumed supreme command of the Wehrmacht last year; yet the German announcement last Sunday mentioned Marshal Wilhelm Keitel as now having that job.

The Fuehrer, in his speech, appeared to be answering a popular demand when he announced that leaves from the eastern front, cancelled when the Russians launched

(*Continued on Page 8*)

It's Bock Time In Springy U. S.

SOMEWHERE IN U. S. A.—Spring has came to the States.

The poet has tossed his winter coal bill into the waste basket and fared forth to the woodland glade.

Red-bellied, saucy robins have returned from the South to drag worms from the new, green grass.

Bock beer signs pervade the land, and Pop stands at his favorite bar with his schnozzle deeply buried in a glass of suds.

Mom has dragged out her dust mops, vacuum cleaner and bucket: she's not ready for spring cleaning.

Business booms at the zoo. Lured by sunshine and gentle zephyrs, survivors of one of the severest winters on record again gaze upon their favorite monkeys and smile. What the monkeys think is something else again.

As is their custom, the famous cherry trees around the Washington Tidal Basin have burst into bloom. But being Japanese they probably haven't got their hearts in it, even though they've been renamed "Oriental Cherry Trees" by some of our better patriots.

Spring not only came to Camp Edwards, Mass., but it delivered a paralyzing blow to a young lieutenant. Dizzied by dulcet breezes, this ardent swain sent an astonishing missive to the idol of his dreams. Instead of "Free" he wrote "Love" in the right-hand corner of the envelope.

Softened by warmth, Americans abound in brotherly love and good cheer.

This was particularly evident in New York, where a husky 19-year-old truckman's assistant named John Cammarota toted a keg of best bock into Times Square and offered free beer to one and all. He said he'd just been inducted and wanted to show how much he loved everybody.

A wise night-court magistrate, in fine humor after putting away his snow shovel, sent John back into the fresh spring air a free man. "What a commando he'll make!" commented the admiring judge.

Yes, gentlemen, spring has certainly came to these United States!

DAILY MIRROR, Thursday, May 13, 1943.

Daily Mirror

MAY 13

No. 12,295
ONE PENNY
Registered at the G.P.O. as a Newspaper.

Von Arnim captured

Von Arnim, the man who hates Britain.

IT'S ALL OVER IN TUNISIA

THE Axis bid to seize an African empire, which has cost them 600,000 Germans, Italians and natives in killed, wounded and prisoners, has come to an inglorious end.

All armed resistance in Tunisia ended officially at 8.15 last night.

Von Arnim, the English-hating Axis commander, is our prisoner.

He fell into our hands yesterday in Cape Bon, the Nazis' last tiny foothold in Africa, and he shared the fate of 150,000 of his troops who have poured into captivity since May 5.

With most of his staff he was seized by British armoured forces at his camp.

The official announcement from Allied H.Q. that resistance had ended and Von Arnim was a prisoner came late last night as the climax to a swift succession of sensational news flashes.

These were the events which led to the final collapse:

Occupation of the Cape Bon peninsula after a brilliant dash by the British 4th Division.

The mopping-up by the Eighth Army and French Forces of 30,000 Germans and Italians trapped in a pocket at the base of the peninsula, north of Enfidaville.

The unconditional surrender to the French of 25,000 Axis troops outflanked west of the Enfidaville line.

Of the 150,000 prisoners in the final stage of the campaign 110,000 are Germans. The conquest of Tunisia by the Allies has been accomplished in fifty-three days.

He Hates Us

Twelve Axis generals have been captured.

The Axis has lost 200 'planes in its attempt to evacuate troops by air.

It was a bitter moment for Von Arnim when he surrendered to us, for he hates the British, though he is said to have an English mother.

The Axis had put out various reports of his whereabouts. Following a statement that he had flown to Rome, Paris radio said just before the news of his capture that he was in Africa.

He took over supreme command in Tunisia shortly after Rommel's unsuccessful attack on March 6.

In a recent letter to his officers he commanded them to teach their troops a "cold hate" for anything English.

Describing the final mass-surrender of the Axis forces, correspondents say German and Italian soldiers, crowded into every kind of vehicle except tanks, drove in an endless stream along the almost unguarded roads, asking their way to the British prison camps.

For some fifty miles between Cape Bon and Tunis, the beaten Axis survivors drove without any sort of British escort along a route where military police were ten or more miles apart.

Some of the prisoners played accordions and mandolins, but most of these lorry-loads of defeated men preserved a tired silence.

Some did not even know that Tunis and Bizerta had fallen

Ten U-boats down in 8-day battle

TEN U-boats were probably destroyed—out of a total force of twenty-five—in the great eight days and nights battle in which, as already announced, Britain's secret weapon was used.

Four were destroyed for certain, four "very probably destroyed" and two probably destroyed, it was officially announced last night.

The U-boats began to congregate at the end of April, and after a gale had blown up on May 1 the battle started in earnest on May 4.

The enemy pressed home his assaults by day and by night in a series of thirty attacks

Two U-boats were rammed, one by the destroyer H.M.S. Oribi (Lieutenant-Commander J. C. A. Ingram, R.N.), and the other by the corvette H.M.S. Sunflower

Heavy Explosion

Another corvette, H.M.S. Snowflake (Lieutenant H. G. Chesterman, RNR), destroyed a third with depth charges. A fourth was sunk by the destroyer Vidette

Planes of the RCAF joined in the battle and carried out many attacks on the U-boats.

The corvette Loosestrife (Lieutenant H. A. Stonehouse, RNR) attacked another U-boat with depth charges, forcing her to the surface.

The sound of a heavy explosion was heard shortly afterwards

The frigate H.M.S. Spey (Commander G. H. Boys-Smith) scored two hits with gunfire on the conning tower of a U-boat

The gale was blowing for three days of the struggle. The U-boats eventually withdrew after spirited counter-attacks.

Two frigates—the larger and more heavily armed type of corvette—a sloop, a cutter, destroyers, and four corvettes were among the escorting vessels to score successes either by ramming, depth charges or gunfire.

Premier to broadcast

The Prime Minister will broadcast at 9 p.m. tomorrow, on the occasion of the Home Guards' third anniversary.

The broadcast will be made from America.

It will be heard on the B.B.C.'s Home and Forces programmes, and will be carried on all the other B.B.C. transmissions.

Manslaughter verdict at detention camp inquest

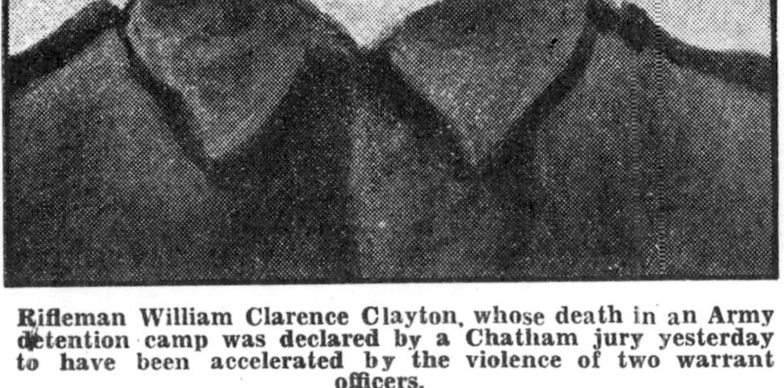

Rifleman William Clarence Clayton, whose death in an Army detention camp was declared by a Chatham jury yesterday to have been accelerated by the violence of two warrant officers.

Two W.O.s are sent for trial

AMID cries of "Lynch them" and "Shoot them to death," the coroner at the Chatham detention camp inquest yesterday committed R.S.M. Culliney and Quarter-Master Sergeant L. F. Salter to Maidstone Assizes charged with the manslaughter of Rifleman William Clayton, who died at the camp.

The inquest hearing ended last night when, after an absence of half an hour the jury had returned a verdict that death was caused by tuberculosis accelerated by violence by R.S.M. Culliney and Q.M.S. Salter.

They exonerated Staff Sergeant Webber, who yesterday gave evidence on what he saw, from all blame

The foreman added: "The jury express great dissatisfaction with the camp medical officer (Captain Joseph Bailley), and recommend that a thoroughly efficient staff should be at the camp, with one officer on duty to examine all prisoners arriving, they to have a thorough examination, and that prisoners' history sheets should arrive before or with them."

When the verdict was announced, men and women relatives of Clayton shouted in court "Lynch them" and "Shoot them to death."

There was also a burst of cheering from the corner where the relatives were sitting.

The coroner committed Culliney and Salter to Maidstone Assizes to stand their trial for manslaughter. They were allowed bail in their recognisances of £20.

The Assizes open on June 22. Culliney and Salter left the building where the inquest was held with a detective-sergeant and another police officer.

Explanation of Law

They were taken to Gillingham Police Station in a police car and formally charged with manslaughter and released on bail.

They will appear at Chatham police court at a date to be fixed.

The coroner summed up for nearly two hours.

"My first duty," he said, "is to give you some direction as to the law of both murder and manslaughter. I don't think I need dwell on murder. A general definition is, killing with malice aforethought, either express or implied and, of course, premeditation comes into it.

"In this case there has been no evidence of malice, and certainly no evidence of premeditation

"With regard to the lesser one of manslaughter, a general definition there is, the felonious killing of another without any malice, either express or implied. But death may be brought about not only by the actual violence done, but death may be accelerated.

"A man may be in a dying condition but have some prospect of living—maybe only an hour, a week, a month, or even more—and he is entitled to that, and if anybody accelerated his death by even a few hours that amounts to manslaughter

"Now, another point is this—that it may be the doing of more than one person—and in that case it is not necessary that you should have to find who struck the actual blow. If it is a case of a blow, which killed him or accelerated his death

"If somebody else is there and in any way assists, he also is liable to be charged with manslaughter.

"Then the other point is that in some cases, of course, force which may bring about death is justified. I need not dwell on that because obviously in this case it was justified neither from a civil nor a military point of view."

Questions for Jury

It was for the jury to decide these questions:—

When were Clayton's injuries inflicted? By whom were they inflicted? Was the force used justified?

"We have had evidence," he said, "that this man was in an advanced state of tuberculosis, and you will have to come to your own conclusions as to whether he died from T.B."

As soon as the verdict was made known, Staff-Sergeant Webber hurried across the court-room to grey-haired Mr. Clayton, father of the dead rifleman, and clasping his hand said: "I am deeply sorry about your son's death, and I would like you to know that I had nothing to do with it."

Full inquest story on Page 2, picture on Back Page.

New York World-Telegram

Local Forecast: Tonight intermittent light rains ending tomorrow morning; not much change in temperature. Sunset 8:11 p. m. Dimout 9:11 p. m.

SCRIPPS—HOWARD

VOL. 75—NO. 274— IN TWO SECTIONS—SECTION ONE. NEW YORK, FRIDAY, MAY 21, 1943. Entered as second class matter Post Office, New York, N. Y. A

7TH SPORTS FINAL
BASEBALL—RACING
3 CENTS IN NEW YORK CITY
4c in Suburbs—5c Elsewhere

'BATTLE OF GERMANY' IS ON; NONSTOP AIR WAR PLEDGED

Pacific Zone Is Reinforced Heavily, Roosevelt Declares

American Planes Raid Europe from Two Sides, Destroy 113 Axis Craft

By WALTER CRONKITE,
United Press Staff Correspondent.

LONDON, May 21.—The great Allied air offensive, now described as the Battle of Germany, gathered momentum today as American air power heavily raided the Nazi U-boat installations at Wilhelmshaven and Emden, destroyed 113 Axis planes off southern Italy and bombed a huge dam in Sardinia.

The RAF also hit hard at Fascist Europe. Speedy Mosquito bombers of the Royal Air Force last night raided Berlin for the second successive night, while other planes struck at Nazi communications and industrial targets on a broad front in northern France and northwestern Germany.

As Allied aerial armadas pounded Europe from both sides, Archibald Sinclair, British Air Minister, declared that the pile-driver blows now being delivered can be called the "Battle of Germany" and would be continued day and night without respite for the rest of the war.

Referring to the effects of the recent Allied attacks, Mr. Sinclair said they were "more than raids—they were battles."

Ties Down Huge Army.

He said the Nazis were making desperate attempts to fend off the deadly blows against their war power, constantly strengthening their defenses at a rate never before achieved.

The Allied offensive now is tieing down on the western front a huge, concentrated Nazi army exceeded in size only by their army struggling against the Russians, Sir Archibald said.

Twelve Boeing Flying Fortresses were lost in today's attacks on Emden and Wilhelmshaven.

An American communique revealed that, in addition to the 12 bombers lost, three United States fighters were missing in diversionary sweeps and "many" German fighters were destroyed.

113 Planes Wrecked In Southern Italy

By C. R. CUNNINGHAM,
United Press Staff Correspondent.

ALLIED HEADQUARTERS, North Africa, May 21.—American air power struck another paralyzing blow at the Luftwaffe Thursday by destroying 113 Axis planes on the invasion route to southern Italy, it was disclosed today, while U. S. Lightnings bombed a dam in northwestern Sardinia.

The Italian dam 10 miles east of the town of Sassari was hit by three bombs during another phase of the fierce and growing Allied bid for complete aerial supremacy over the Fascist stepping stone invasion islands.

Not Identified.

The dam was not identified nor was damage reported, but it recalled the recent RAF bombing of three Ruhr Valley dams which loosed floods in the industrial heart of Germany.

(There are two artificial lakes in Sardinia, both providing huge hydroelectric power. One collects the waters of the Tirso River in the center of the island and the dam backs up some 450,000,000 cubic meters of water. The dam is about twice the size of the quarter-mile long Eder dam. The other in the north part of the island has a capacity of 342,000,000 cubic meters. Both generate about 24,000 horsepower.

(The Tirso is the only big river on Sardinia. It has a course of 94 miles.)

Total of 186 Planes.

[In addition to bombing the dam east of Sassari, Lightnings attacked the railway yards and barracks at Sassari and shot up five army trucks and three trains, according to the Associated Press. The locomotive of one train blew up.]

In Thursday's blow at southern Europe American bombers, fighter-bombers and fighters shot down 22 Axis aircraft and destroyed 91 others aground for a two-day total of 186 enemy planes knocked out.

Only one Allied plane was lost in the operations extending 80 miles northwest of Rome on Thursday, making a total of five missing for the two days—a ratio of about 37 Axis planes destroyed for each Allied craft lost.

Many 'Probables.'

The destroyed enemy planes included seven giant ME-323 transport planes that carry from 120 to 140 fully equipped soldiers.

Many other enemy planes were believed destroyed in addition to the 113 reported at headquarters, although pilots were not permitted to score "probables" as destroyed planes. The operations were described as one of the greatest days of air attack on the enemy air forces since the start of the Tunisian campaign.

The Allied raids were directed against Sardinian bases and against Grossetto, 80 miles northwest of Rome, where American Flying Fortresses flew on a 400-mile thrust into Italy.

Headquarters announced that between June 10, 1940, when Italy entered the war, and May 12, 1943, at the close of the Tunisian campaign, a total of 5172 Axis aircraft had been destroyed in air combats alone in the Mediterranean area.

The Middle East Command, including Malta, destroyed 3415 and the Northwest African air forces destroyed 1757.

Japan's No 1 Admiral Is Killed

Attu Campaign Virtually Over, Knox Declares

EXTRA

BULLETIN.

By the United Press.

WASHINGTON, May 21.—Secretary of the Navy Frank Knox said today that to all intents and purposes the Attu campaign is over, and that only mopping up work remains to be done by the American forces.

By SANDOR S. KLEIN,
United Press Staff Correspondent.

WASHINGTON, May 21. — The battered remnants of Japan's Attu Island garrison, trapped in a 15-square-mile area, have dug in for their last stand on high ground east of Attu village, the Navy announced today.

Attu village is at the head of Chichagof Harbor. The area where the Japanese are penned by our troops is between Chicagof Harbor and Sarana Bay.

Planes Blast Trenches.

"On May 19 operations on Attu continued," the Navy reported. "Japanese forces have established positions on the high ground east of Attu village. U. S. Army bombers attacked Japanese entrenchments in the area north of Sarana Bay."

These entrenchments were believed to be part of the enemy's last remaining defense line.

Kiska Threatened.

[The Associated Press said the Jap base on Kiska Island was threatened with complete blockade today as the result of the imminent collapse of resistance on Attu. It said authorities believed the fall of Attu to be a matter of hours and was expected within a day or two, at the latest.

[The Vichy radio, in a broadcast recorded by Reuters, announced "the Japanese have begun to evacuate Attu." The broadcast did not explain how an evacuation could be accomplished against the American naval and aerial blockade.]

Belmont Park Results

(Charts and Other Race Results in Sports Section.)

Race	Horse	Win	Place	Show
FIRST RACE	1—Appeal Agent	5.80	3.10	2.40
	2—More Wine	—	3.20	2.60
	3—Robert T.	—	—	3.30
SECOND RACE	1—Esterita	10.10	4.80	3.60
	2—Orange Leaves	—	6.00	3.80
	3—Flying Son	—	—	4.20
	Daily double paid $28.10.			
THIRD RACE	1—Naruna	8.90	3.80	2.80
	2—Rougemont	—	3.00	2.20
	3—Cupid	—	—	2.90
FOURTH RACE	1—Everget	8.90	5.00	3.30
	2—Estate	—	16.50	7.30
	3—Blenette	—	—	3.50
FIFTH RACE	1—Eye for Eye	13.50	5.80	4.40
	2—Eurasian	—	4.10	2.60
	3—New Moon	—	—	3.10
SIXTH RACE	1—Tola Rose	4.60	3.20	2.30
	2—Bolingbroke	—	6.40	3.50
	3—Corydon	—	—	2.50
SEVENTH RACE	1—Free Air	16.50	10.10	6.80
	2—Happy Guess	—	6.70	4.50
	3—Guerryton	—	—	17.10
EIGHTH RACE	1—Spoon Bread	9.00	5.10	3.60
	2—Five o' Eight	—	10.50	4.60
	3—Skirmish	—	—	4.90

Kin of Mayor's Aid Put in Line for Job

Because the Municipal Civil Service Commission refused to certify the No. 1 candidate on the ground that she is a woman, Norman M. Stone, brother of Mayor La Guardia's $10,000-a-year executive secretary, Lester B. Stone, has moved from fourth to third place on the civil service list for the job of director of education in the Department of Correction, it was learned today.

Headed List.

Under the rules of the commission appointments for any competitive job are restricted to the top three eligibles on the civil service list.

When the list was published last Aug. 19 Mr. Stone, the department's choice for the job and the acting director of education by provisional (noncompetitive) appointment, came out No. 4.

First place was won by Miss Ruth Lentz, a correction officer in the Women's House of Detention.

Shortly afterward the commission announced that women were disqualified for the job, despite the fact that the examination had been open to men and women alike.

Harry M. Marsh, president of the Civil Service Commission, declared today that the commission had acted at the request of Commissioner of Correction Peter F. Amoroso. He said that department heads have the right to choose between men and women.

Commissioner Amoroso later declared that Norman Stone is "qualified in every respect" for the job

(Continued on Page Eleven.)

Sailors Break Up Rally Led by CIO Organizer

By the Associated Press.

GROTON, Conn., May 21.—Submarine sailors tossed a public address system microphone over a fence yesterday at the Electric Boat Co. plant, tore down union signs, stamped on union buttons and smashed a table during a CIO organizer's attempt to speak to a luncheon crowd at the submarine building plant.

Police Called.

H. T. Perry of the Groton police said the sailors charged that Maurice Miller, the organizer, had referred to them during his remarks as "$50-a-month-punks," but that Miller had denied using the phrase.

[Miller, according to the United Press, was making a speech urging the workers to join the CIO when the disturbance began. The Electric Boat Co. has a company union. The CIO began efforts to organize the workers about two weeks ago.]

Perry said police were called to the scene four times, and that finally they escorted Miller to the Groton end of the Thames River Bridge, whence he headed for New York.

Police Capt. Bernard Chapman said that "35 or 40" sailors, whose submarines were fitted out at the plant, interrupted the organizer.

Chapman said that "what trouble there was had quieted down when we got there and all we did was to break up the crowd."

Quotes Sailors.

Gavin MacPherson directing a CIO organizational drive at the plant, said he was unable to explain the sailors' action, but asserted the sailors said something about "union activities while submarines are urgently needed in the Pacific."

He said the Electric Boat Co. was building the submarines, not the CIO.

Yamamoto Dies in Plane During Action

Head of Fleet Planned Strategy Of Pearl Harbor

By the United Press.

Admiral Isoroku Yamamoto, who boasted he would dictate peace terms in the White House, died in aerial combat, Radio Tokyo disclosed today in broadcasts suggesting that the foremost naval commander was killed, possibly by Americans, while directing a South Pacific battle.

The broadcasts did not fix specifically how the 59-year-old commander in chief of Japan's fleet was killed except that it was on a "foremost front" and that Yamamoto, a flier, had gone up to lead the fight himself.

(Robert T. Bellaire, former United Press bureau head at Tokyo, says that Yamamoto may have committed hari kiri. The admiral, he writes, had said he would kill himself if Japan ever lost any of her territory. The hari kari theory was accepted by many in Washington, many naval men, according to the Associated Press, expressing doubt that Yamamoto had been killed in battle. Some suggested he might have killed himself because of the many recent Jap reverses.)

Leading Strategist.

A Tokyo report heard in Chungking fixed the approximate place of Yamamoto's death and said the time was mid-April. The South Pacific might mean anywhere along the broad front where American fliers, with the aid of Australians, are holding Allied outposts.

One of Japan's top air leaders and probably the greatest war strategist in Jap history, Yamamoto was chief of the Japanese fleet from which the fliers embarked to pull the attack on Pearl Harbor that sent Japan and the United States into war.

Heard in London.

[The Associated Press pointed out that Yamamoto plotted the Pearl Harbor blow and directed the successful aerial attack which resulted in the sinking of the battleship Prince of Wales and the battle cruiser Repulse.]

Yamamoto was "personally directing the operations in an air-

(Continued on Page Ten.)

Jan. 24, 1941—"I am looking forward to dictating peace to the United States in the White House . . ."

Admiral Isoroku Yamamoto.

A. P. Photo.

May 21, 1943—Killed . . . "while directing the operations in an airplane against the enemy."

Chinese Bombers Rip Jap Yangtze Base

By the Associated Press.

CHUNGKING, May 21.—A large number of Chinese bombers attacked the Yangtze River port of Ichang, one of the bases for the Japanese drive against the Chinese rice bowl west of Lake Tung Ting, today and started large fires among the Japanese installations there, a Chinese communique said today.

The Chinese bombers unloaded huge quantities of bombs on the enemy military headquarters, military depots and important installations in the suburbs, it was announced. All the Chinese planes returned safely.

World-Telegram Index

Censorship in Bolivia

By the United Press.

LA PAZ, Bolivia, May 21.—The government has decreed general censorship on all communications effective today.

Kaiser Plans to Build Postwar Trains

By the United Press.

OAKLAND, Cal., May 21.—Henry J. Kaiser announced today that he plans to enter the railroad business after the war and build fast, lightweight trains.

He disclosed he is negotiating with some of the nation's biggest railroads to develop new passenger cars made of steel alloys, aluminum and magnesium.

His plans envisage large-scale production not only of passenger cars, but of engines and freight cars that could speed cargo from the Pacific to the Atlantic coast in half the present time at half the cost.

The Weather

(Official United States Forecast)

New York and Metropolitan Area—This afternoon and tonight intermittent moderate rains, ending tomorrow morning; fresh winds on and offshore, not much change in temperature.

Connecticut—Intermittent rains and continued cool this afternoon and tonight; fresh winds along the coast.

TODAY'S READINGS.

	Temp.	Hum.		Temp.	Hum.
Midnight	55	..	9 a. m.	51	92
1 a. m.	55	..	10 a. m.	55	99
2 a. m.	55	..	11 a. m.	52	87
3 a. m.	56	..	12 noon	55	89
4 a. m.	55	..	1 p. m.	53	93
5 a. m.	54	..	2 p. m.	54	89
6 a. m.	54	87	3 p. m.	54	90
7 a. m.	53	87	4 p. m.	53	90
8 a. m.	52	85			

High and low a year ago, 69-62.

Budget Slash Proposal Would Lease WNYC

With a blistering attack on Mayor La Guardia's 1943-44 city budget, the Democratic-controlled City Council finance committee today submitted a report slashing $10,864,905.68 from the budget. One of the proposed savings would result from the dropping of radio station WNYC as a municipally-operated enterprise.

The report, containing the greatest budget cuts ever to be considered by the council since its inception, would bring about a tax rate seven points under that estimated by the Mayor, the committee declared. This would leave the figure at $2.87 or $2.88 per $100 assessed valuation.

In a statement issued before the council meeting at which the report is expected to be approved, Councilman Joseph E. Kinsley (D., the Bronx) said the reductions

(Continued on Page Eleven.)

Allied Chiefs Will Submit War Program

Churchill to Study Plans with President Over Week End

By the Associated Press.

WASHINGTON, May 21.—President Roosevelt disclosed today that the British-American chiefs of staff would submit some preliminary recommendations tonight to him and Prime Minister Churchill, and he said probably final decisions on them would be made next week.

At the same time the Chief Executive told a press conference it is absolutely true that a large majority of American forces outside the United States are in the Pacific.

Mentioned by Churchill.

The British Prime Minister had mentioned that in a speech to Congress Wednesday, and the President said it is particularly true of the army and navy. About half of our air force is in the Pacific, he asserted.

Asked if he could give a progress report on his conferences with the Prime Minister, the President replied that so far most of the work has been done by the combined chiefs of staffs—the top military, naval and air advisers who flank the two consultants.

Tentative recommendations are expected to be made at a meeting tonight, he said, and these will

(Continued on Page Eleven.)

The War Today

May 21, 1943.

EUROPE — RAF raids Berlin for third straight night and hammers inland rail transport and shipping in France and northwestern Germany.

RUSSIA—Russians widen bridgehead along 110-mile stretch of Donets River after smashing German attacks; Red artillery smashes 12 German strong points in Kuban area as heavy guns and planes sink six troop-laden barges in Black Sea.

U. S. FORCES IN ACTION.

EUROPE—American air power smashes at Europe from north and south, raiding Emden and Wilhelmshaven, destroying 113 Axis planes off Southern Italy, and bombing a dam in Sardinia.

ALEUTIANS — Japs dig in on Attu as army bombers blast enemy lines.

BURMA—Tenth U. S. Air Force drops more than 100 tons of bombs on Jap positions in third successive day of heavy raids.

Yamamoto Death Just Brings 'Gosh'

By the United Press.

WASHINGTON, May 21.—President Roosevelt was informed at his press conference today about the death of Admiral Isoroku Yamamoto, the Japanese naval leader who had promised to write the final terms of American surrender in the White House.

Mr. Roosevelt's comment: "Gosh."

Story of Company K Is Thrilling Pyle Tale

By ERNIE PYLE.
World-Telegram War Correspondent.

NORTHERN TUNISIA (By Wireless).—This column has three heroes, if you want to call them that. They are the three men who commanded, one after the other, the same infantry company—all within five hours of battle.

For lack of a better name we'll simply call it Company K.

It was daytime. The whole company was pinned down on a green wheat field that led up onto the slope of a hill. We were trying to take the Germans on the back slope of the hill, but from the ridge they could butcher our men below with their machine guns if they stirred.

Ernie Pyle.

Lt. Richard Cole of Worcester, Mass., was commander of Company K. In mid-afternoon a German shell found him as he lay in hiding with his men in the wheat. One leg got only a slight wound, but the other was shattered.

Lieutenant Cole saved his life by using his head. He made a tourniquet of his handkerchief, and, using a fountain pen for a lever, he twisted the tourniquet and held it, and at the same time began slowly crawling to the rear. For he knew the medics didn't dare to venture onto the

(Continued on Page Two.)

New York World-Telegram

Local Forecast: Temperature tonight abcut the same as last night, with scattered showers; tomorrow morning warm. Sunset 8:29 p. m. Dimout 9:29 p. m.

VOL. 76—NO. 6—IN TWO SECTIONS—SECTION ONE | NEW YORK, THURSDAY, JULY 8, 1943. | Entered as second class matter Post Office, New York, N. Y.

CLOSING WALL ST.
SEVENTH SPORTS
3 CENTS IN NEW YORK CITY
4c in Suburbs—5c Elsewhere

HOW U. S. WON SEA VICTORY

U. S. Forces Within Six Miles of Munda

Marines Hurled Japs Off High Cliff to Take Viru

By the Associated Press.

WITH AMERICAN INVASION FORCES IN NEW GEORGIA, July 5 (Delayed).—United States Marines borrowed a page from the bloody Japanese notebook marked "Singapore" to capture strategic Viru Harbor.

The marines sprang a rear attack on Jap troops around the harbor area after four days of a circuitous, slogging march through the jungles to reach their objective.

Then screaming Leathernecks drove undetermined numbers of the enemy off a 130-foot cliff into the sea and sent others fleeing into the jungle.

That's how they made the harbor safe for the New Georgia invasion.

In many respects, Uncle Sam's fighters wrote perhaps the most spectacular page in the history of the South Pacific theater.

The captain leading the Marine force admitted that had he known the difficulties he never would have attempted the coup. He also disclosed the Marines spearheaded the direct invasion of New Georgia by landing at Segi June 20 and remained inactive until the full central Solomons offensive got under way a week later.

They were charged with the responsibility of the attack on Viru Harbor from the rear and by this move surprised the defending Japanese, who were prepared for a frontal attack.

The surprise attack—copying the method by which the Japs overwhelmed Singapore—came after the Marines had made a heartbreaking jungle trip.

During the 30-mile trek the Leathernecks were harassed by snipers and occasionally ran into machine gun nests, which they wiped out in short order.

But the Americans, prepared by rigorous training, lived on their "D" ration of solid chocolate, much of the time without water. And they ate roots and licked the dew-covered leaves of bushes to get water.

Sgt. Howard Biggerstaff, combat correspondent from Cincinnati, described the tortuous trip.

"Our two companies left the night of June 27 in rubber boats for a native village north of our landing point and we reached there four and a half hours later.

"Early the next morning the hike began. During the first day, a group of from 20 to 40 Japs began hitting our rear and we dispatched a detachment to take care of them. We killed 18.

"The last platoon of our column charged up a hill in the face of machine gun fire, throwing grenades.

"One kid was shot in the right knee during the fracas. He stumbled, fell sideways, breaking his right ankle. But in spite of intense pain, he insisted on continuing. We bandaged his knee

(Continued on Page Nine.)

Japs Stranded By American Island Drive

9-1 Sea Victory For MacArthur in New Georgia Push

By BRYDON C. TAVES,
United Press Staff Correspondent.

ALLIED HQ., Southwest Pacific, July 8.—American assault troops drove inland from new bridgeheads less than six miles from the Jap air base of Munda on New Georgia Island today following a shattering nine-to-one United States naval victory in the Kula Gulf.

Munda and the Jap supply port of Bairoko Harbor, 10 miles to the north, were the twin objectives of the Americans following surprise landings on both sides of bomb-shattered Munda. The enemy forces on New Georgia apparently were isolated from supplies or reinforcements and were being engaged by the Americans along the Barike River east of Munda.

Nine and perhaps 11 Jap cruisers and destroyers were destroyed by American warships in a little more than 20 minutes of actual fighting early Tuesday, a communique from General MacArthur, supreme commander of co-ordinated South and Southwest Pacific offensives, announced.

Another Jap warship was

(Continued on Page Six.)

Every Enemy Ship in Sight Sunk or Hit

By FRANK TREMAINE,
United Press Staff Correspondent.

UNITED STATES NAVAL HEADQUARTERS, South Pacific, July 8.—Every Japanese warship sighted by American naval forces in the battle of Kula Gulf was either damaged or destroyed, the first available description of the engagement disclosed today.

Advices reaching headquarters of Adm. William F. Halsey said that during one phase of the battle five Japanese ships were seen exploding, burning or sinking within a few minutes after the American onslaught began.

Conservative estimates were that the Japanese lost eight ships definitely destroyed and two others damaged. The damaged ships may have escaped. American forces lost the cruiser Helena. (A communique from the headquarters of Gen. Douglas MacArthur said nine Japanese ships were sunk and two more were possibly sunk.)

The numerically inferior American naval force, which was later aided by navy and army airplanes, carried out the operation against the enemy warships in three phases. In the opening phase on July 6 the Americans surprised the enemy in a night attack. The whole operation lasted about two hours.

FORCE INTERCEPTED.

The American light cruisers and destroyers intercepted a larger force of Jap light cruisers and destroyers about 3 a. m. on Tuesday as the enemy steamed from Kula Gulf at the northwestern end of New Georgia in the Solomon Islands.

The enemy was engaged immediately and within "a very few minutes" five Jap ships, apparently all destroyers, were sunk or burning, it was stated here.

In the second phase of fighting the Americans made contact a short time later with three or four Jap light cruisers or large destroyers. It was stated that all the enemy ships were believed destroyed or crippled within "a short period."

Later two American destroyers intercepted an enemy light cruiser and two destroyers attempting to sneak out of Kula Gulf. The big guns cut loose again and one light cruiser and one destroyer were definitely sunk, while a second enemy destroyer was damaged.

Later in the morning navy dive bombers and army Mitchell bombers found two crippled Jap destroyers stranded near Kolombangara, and scored several hits. One pilot said the ships were seen burning and exploding and were believed a total loss.

On the basis of available reports, it was impossible to determine definitely whether some Jap ships were involved in more than one phase of the fighting but the estimate of eight enemy warships definitely destroyed was regarded as conservative.

Authorities said the Kula Gulf battle was not considered a major naval engagement, but that it was one of the most successful ever fought by the U. S. Navy in view of the destruction or damaging of the entire enemy force. The Japanese presumably were supplying or reinforcing the enemy at Vila or Munda, on New Georgia Island, when surprised by the American warships.

A large percentage of the crews of the Helena and the destroyer Strong, which was lost in another action, were rescued and still others may have reached shore and returned to American positions.

American forces suffered no other damage than loss of the Helena in the Kula action, it was stated, although the fighting was at close to medium ranges.

Food and Drink Prices in Cafes Will Be Frozen

All restaurant food and drink prices are expected to be frozen shortly throughout New York, Pennsylvania, Maryland, Delaware, New Jersey and the District of Columbia, a spokesman for the price division of the regional OPA announced today.

The disclosure came in the wake of published reports that restaurant prices in the Baltimore area were rising steadily. In response to a question about this situation, the OPA spokesman said:

"An order regarding restaurant prices is in process. The entire situation is under study with the co-operation of the trade and, when issued, a regulation will come from this regional office. Action is expected shortly.

"The regulation will include the Baltimore district as well as the entire region. It is expected the order will freeze prices of all food and drink at the levels charged between April 4 and 10, 1943, by individual sellers."

The OPA spokesman explained that this period covered the time when all restaurants throughout the region filed their menus with thet OPA. He indicated that restaurant prices in many cases had risen sharply.

Veronica Mother Of 3-Pound Baby

By the Associated Press.

HOLLYWOOD, July 8.—Screen actress Veronica Lake gave birth today to a three-pound boy, two months prematurely. The child was placed in an incubator and her physician, Dr. Raymond D. McBurney, said both apparently were doing well.

Half an hour later Miss Lake's sister-in-law, Mrs. Stanley Detlie, became the mother of a nine-pound girl at the same hospital, with the same physician attending.

Miss Lake went to the hospital last Thursday after she tripped and fell on a motion picture set.

Suspend Legion License

Special to the World-Telegram.

NEWARK, July 8.—After agents of the Alcoholic Beverage Control Board had found a slot machine hidden in a cabinet at Fairview Post No. 1, American Legion, the board today suspended the post's club license for five days.

Jamaica Results

By the United Press.

FIRST—5½ furlongs; purse $1500; claiming; maiden colts and geldings; 2-year-olds.

Knight's Armor	9.50	4.90	3.10
Town Gallant	—	5.40	3.20
Hayal Tinty	—	—	2.80

Off at 1:52.

SECOND—6 furlongs; purse $1500; claiming; 4-year-olds and up.

Freeland's Lad	57.90	17.70	6.60
Scotch Trap	—	5.00	3.20
Bleneed	—	—	2.80

Daily double paid $338.40.

WACs Don't Tell Military Secrets

Second of a Series
By ERNIE PYLE,
World-Telegram War Correspondent.

NORTH AFRICA (By Wireless).—The fond mothers of WACS in Africa may have visions of their poor little girls all alone over here in this big bad world fighting off olive-skinned rogues with one hand and snakes with the other.

Ernie Pyle.

They needn't worry. The girls are perfectly safe. The city they are in is as modern, though in a European way, as cities back home. Thousands of French women and girls, dressed just as Americans dress, crowd the streets at all hours. There are American Army nurses and British nurses, WAAFs, WRENs and ATS girls, and five different kinds of French service girls in uniform.

There is the thrill of being in the midst of vital things here, without the drawbacks of either physical danger or spiritual peril.

Our WACS do about a dozen kinds of work here. It takes a couple of dozen to run their own barracks, their three messes and their headquarters. They are proud of being a self-contained unit, requiring no help from anybody. They even repair their own stoves.

Five of the others are car drivers, and the rest work in offices. They serve as secretaries, typists, draughtsmen, phone operators and mail sorters. They get up and "go to the office" just as though they were on civilian jobs back home.

There are six WACS in General Eisenhower's office. There are 30 in the Adjutant General's office, 11 in the Judge Advocate's office, 14 in Civil Affairs. The Signal Corps has 50 running switchboards and teletypes and deciphering code messages. And since there are no WAVES over here yet, two WACS are working for the navy!

When a WAC takes over a telephone switchboard from a soldier efficiency goes up about a thousand per cent. If there is one single thing the male species does

(Continued on Page Five.)

Capt. Frances Marquis.

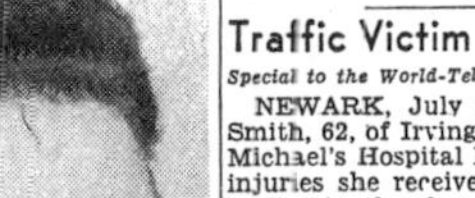

Maj. Margaret M. Janeway.

Laundry Men Hail Extortion Probe

Allan Steckel, business manager of the Brooklyn Hand Laundrymen's Assn., Inc., said today that his organization was highly gratified that State Attorney General Nathaniel L. Goldstein exposed the alleged $100,000 yearly extortion from independent drivers and operators of small hand laundries.

"Independent operators have been victims of this racket, which, under the guise of a labor union, has been exacting a heavy toll from small businessmen for the past five years," Mr. Steckel said. "We have always co-operated with the attorney general's office in an effort to stamp out this unjust situation and we shall continue to do so."

World-Telegram Index

Snite Treated For New Ailment

By the Associated Press.

CHICAGO, July 8.—Fred Snite, Jr., infantile paralysis patient who has been encased in iron lungs since 1936, was being treated for a stomach ailment today.

His father reported that young Snite had been ill for several days and had been given oxygen to aid his breathing and offset the effects of nausea. The elder Snite said his son had shown slight improvement during the day.

Voice of Doom For Axis Seen In Arms Output

By the Associated Press.

TORONTO, July 8.—The North American continent alone will outproduce the Axis in munitions this year by nearly two to one, Chairman Nelson of the U. S. War Production Board reported today to the Canadian people.

Before the year's end Canada and the United States will be producing a plane every 4 2-3 minutes around the clock, Mr. Nelson told the Canadian Club, and already they have turned out enough small arms ammunition to fire 1500 bullets at every soldier in the Axis armies.

Asks Output Boost.

All the United Nations this year will make three times the Axis output of arms, and next year four times, the United States production chief declared.

"These figures speak to the world in a big voice," Mr. Nelson said. "And if the Nazi and the Jap warlords are not completely insane, they will recognize that the voice is the voice of doom."

For the second time this week Mr. Nelson spoke guardedly of impending vast military developments, to underscore a plea for renewed production effort "to defeat the enemy so crushingly that his spirit will be broken and the day of his unconditional surrender hastened."

Cites Strike Effects.

"You will shortly see gigantic battles in which unheard-of quantities of war materials will be consumed," he said. Mr. Nelson added he would warn the enemy "not to take too much comfort from the so-called sagging of the home front in the United States in recent days."

"I would be the last to attempt

(Continued on Page Twenty-one.)

Traffic Victim Dies

Special to the World-Telegram.

NEWARK, July 8.—Mrs. Anna Smith, 62, of Irvington, died at St. Michael's Hospital last night from injuries she received when struck earlier in the day by a truck.

The War Today

July 8, 1943.

RUSSIA — Germans throw nearly 500,000 men into pincers attack on Red Army's Kursk salient; Russians acknowledge slight Nazi gains in Belgorod sector, report enemy losses as 30,000 men killed and 1539 tanks and 649 planes destroyed.

EUROPE — British Parliament told that about 1,000,000 tons of Axis shipping has been sunk or badly damaged since the Allied invasion of North Africa, cutting Germany's tonnage to a bare minimum.

MEDITERRANEAN — American and British air forces carry intense offensive against Italy's inland outposts through fifth straight day as hour for assault against Europe approaches.

U. S. FORCES IN ACTION.

PACIFIC—Americans close against Munda after establishing nearby bridgeheads on New Georgia Island in Central Solomons; U. S. naval victory in Kula Gulf enhanced with disclosure that nine and possibly 11 Japanese warships were destroyed.

AFRICA—Flying Fortresses, Marauders and Mitchells of Northwest African air forces concentrate on Sicily in smashing Allied attacks on Italian islands.

Nazi Admiral Admits U-Boats' Sting Lost

By the United Press.

Admiral Luetzow, the German naval expert, broadcasting to the German people tonight "frankly told them that the U-boat war is now going in favor of the Allies and offered no consolation," the London radio reported in a broadcast recorded by CBS.

Reds' Backing of Hague Flusters New Dealers

By THOMAS L. STOKES,
Scripps-Howard Staff Writer.

WASHINGTON, July 8.—New Dealers here are being put in a highly embarrassing position through the recently announced support by the Communists of Mayor Frank Hague of Jersey City, a few years ago the most highly publicized foe of the Reds.

The New Deal Democrats are not pleased because the latest Communist wrinkle as solemnly recorded in the party organ, The Daily Worker, gives publicity to administration support for Boss Hague, who is needed for the fourth-term campaign.

Also it emphasizes for them again, for their own consciences, the way they let down Governor Edison in his fight to stamp out boss rule in New Jersey.

Capital Amused.

Outside of these New Deal circles, Washington generally has found amusement in the fact that the Communist party has jumped into bed with Boss Hague whose thugs used to chase labor union organizers out of his baliwick, whose policemen roughly escorted Norman Thomas out of town when he tried to make a speech in Journal Sq., who even frightened away a couple of Congressmen there to speak against his suppression of civil liberties.

Not to speak of the corruption of the ballot and the persecution of any citizen who dared raise his voice against the Jersey City dictator.

This Is a "New Day."

This is a new day, it seems, according to William Norman, secretary of the New Jersey Communist party, in his indorsement of Boss Hague in the Daily Worker, and people must not follow "outworn conceptions," because Mayor Hague is supporting President Roosevelt and the war 100 per cent. That washes his sins away. Mr. Norman said:

"Labor in New Jersey has the

(Continued on Page Five.)

Late News Bulletin

By the Associated Press.

WASHINGTON, July 8.—Bowing to threats of a veto, the Senate abandoned by a 34 to 33 vote today a legislative prohibition against the payment of food price subsidies.

(Earlier details on page 2.)

Lot of Beef on Way From Western Plains

By the Associated Press.

COTTONWOOD FALLS, Kan., July 8.—Don't throw away that steak pan yet, pardner! Thar's a lot of beef coming in from the hills and the plains.

The thundering herd is on the march again; millions of pounds of beef from the great grass ranges of the Southwest is ready for market.

The ranges are beginning to dry up—a little later this year because of the heavy rains during the grazing season. Now the ranchers face the choice of selling their big herds or holding them and feeding expensive and scarce grains.

Some associated with the cattle industry believe the beef famine will be broken with a rush of grass-fed beef in the next two weeks.

The Weather

(Official United States Forecast.)

New York and Metropolitan Area—This afternoon and early tonight moderately warm with light winds. Cool on beaches. Later tonight and tomorrow forenoon scattered light showers. Temperatures tonight about the same as last night, except cooler in the suburbs. Moderately warm with moderate winds tomorrow forenoon.

New Jersey—Moderately warm this afternoon. About as cool tonight as last night with showers and gentle winds continuing. Lowest temperature tonight between 55 and 65 degrees.

Connecticut—Moderately warm this afternoon; moderately cool tonight with moderate winds.

TODAY'S READINGS.

	Temp.	Hum.		Temp.	Hum.
Midnight	67	..	8 a. m.	66	79
1 a. m.	66	..	9 a. m.	67	76
2 a. m.	66	..	10 a. m.	68	71
3 a. m.	65	..	11 a. m.	70	70
4 a. m.	66	..	12 noon	73	68
5 a. m.	66	..	1 p. m.	75	66
6 a. m.	64	87	2 p. m.	73	75
7 a. m.	66	79			

High and low a year ago, 78-63.

Nazis Sacrifice Men In Belgorod Drive

By HENRY SHAPIRO,
United Press Staff Correspondent.

MOSCOW, July 8.—The Germans, hurling nearly half a million men and thousands of tanks and planes against Soviet defenses in a do-or-die bid for a breakthrough, inched eastward in the Belgorod sector today as the blazing battle of the southern front went into its fourth day on a

[A DNB dispatch broadcast from Berlin and recorded by the Associated Press declared that the Germans had destroyed 862 Soviet tanks and 847 aircraft in the last three days. Fortifications of the Belgorod area were "overcome in great depth" and the Russians southeast of Orel were "thrown back on their own mine fields," the propaganda agency said.]

Front dispatches said the Nazi High Command was rushing fresh reserves into battle without pause to replace the 30,000 men, 1539 tanks and 649 planes lost in the first 72 hours of assault along a 165-mile stretch of the front between Belgorod and Orel.

[While the German losses in

(Continued on Page Nine.)

Report Yanks Bomb Canton

By the United Press.

The Berlin radio today quoted a Tokyo report that about 20 American bombers attacked Canton yesterday. It said most of the bombs dropped in the raid on the South China port fell into the water and Japanese fighters shot down two bombers.

SATURDAY, JULY 10, 1943

BLACK OUT	Moon Sets 1.53 a.m.	RADIO
11.1 to 5.10	Full Moon July 17	Page Four

LATE NIGHT

THE STAR

No. 17,178 ★ ONE PENNY

SICILY INVADED
Paratroops In Action

BRITISH OFFICIAL

Allied forces under the command of General Eisenhower began landing operations on Sicily early this morning. The landings were preceded by Allied air attack. Allied naval forces escorted the assault forces and bombarded the defences during the assault.

ITALIAN OFFICIAL

The enemy last night, with the support of very powerful naval and air formations and with parachutist detachments, began his attack against Sicily. Axis forces are decisively countering the attack. Fighting is in progress along the S.E. coastal sector.

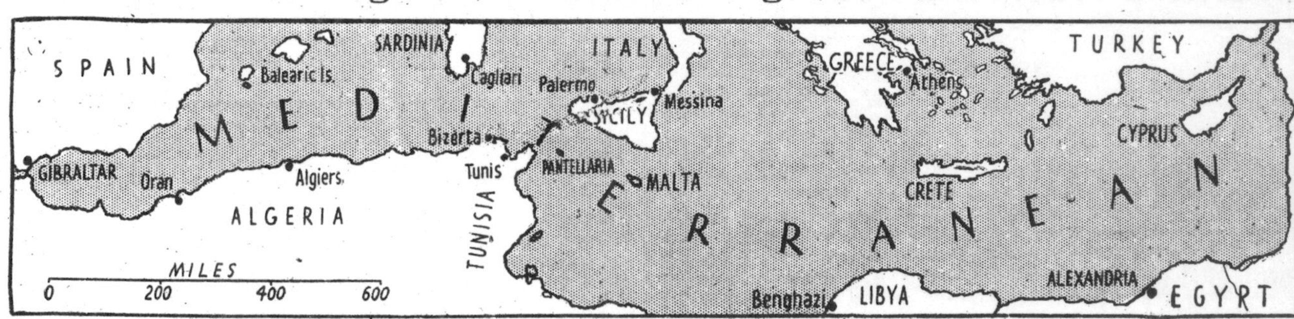

From BUP War Correspondent, ALLIED H.Q., Saturday.

ALLIED PILOTS RETURNING FROM FLIGHTS OVER THE SICILIAN BATTLEFIELD TODAY TOLD MOST GRAPHIC STORIES OF HOW THE INVASION OF THE ISLAND LOOKED FROM THE AIR. "A CHAIN OF SMOKE AND FLAME TEN MILES INLAND FROM THE COAST COULD BE SEEN FROM THE AIR," ONE PILOT SAID TO ME.

"Allied warships shelling without interruption as our forces landed sometimes dashed in close to the shore, fired salvoes and then swooped out again. I have never seen so many ships in my life.

"Landing barges seemed to be everywhere—waves of them dashing towards the island in relays and others piling in on the beaches."

It was about 6.30 a.m. when this pilot was over the island. But even then, he said, there was a tremendous battle raging down below. He had not met any enemy air opposition whatever over Sicily.—BUP.

The above dramatic cable reached London tonight after reports to Allied headquarters had said: "Everything is going according to plan." Morocco radio stated: "The Allies are rapidly consolidating their positions."

The invasion began about 3 a.m., according to Algiers radio, in good weather. It was preceded by scientific round-the-clock bombing. Then troopships and landing craft and escorting warships, including British and American battleships and cruisers, ploughed their way through minefields.

Gen. Guzzoni

The invading troops—British, Canadian, and American—went ashore under a great barrage from our warships, and covered by an air canopy provided by practically every type of Allied plane, including the new fighter-bomber Mustangs. The United Kingdom troops are believed to consist mainly of First Army units. It is presumed in Washington that the bulk of the American Fifth Army is also engaged.

Berlin was the first end of the Axis to give any news about the invasion. After broadcasting that the Allies had met strong opposition, this further statement was made: "Immediately after they had landed, contact was made with the invasion troops. Very heavy fighting followed, in which they suffered many losses. Parachutist units who were dropped were encircled and rendered harmless. Coastal batteries and Axis bombers sank a number of landing barges and transports laden with troops and material."

The broadcasts were made after several hours' silence. Italian people were first given the news from Mussolini in his communique. Later Rome radio said: "The whole of the Axis forces have been hurled against the enemy, and enemy action is being efficiently checked." The German communique also referred to the landings and added: "The attack at once met with violent resistance on the ground and in the air. Battles are in progress." The only news of paratroops being in action is from enemy sources.

There is no indication, says Reuter, about how many points landings were made at, but the number is likely to be large. While the invasion might have been no surprise to the enemy the methods employed by the Allies possibly were. There is plenty of scope for new ruses and deceptions.

The Italian forces on Sicily consist of the 6th Army, commanded by General Guzzoni, writes a military correspondent. Including

CONTINUED ON BACK PAGE, Col. TWO

BOMBERS DEMOLISH AXIS DEFENCE H.Q.

"IMPORTANT Axis targets in Sicily, during daylight on Friday, felt the crushing weight of nearly 100 Liberator heavy bombers of the Ninth U.S. Air Force, said a U.S. communique from Cairo this afternoon.

"The bombers smashed suddenly at the nerve centre of the Axis Sicilian defence forces Command Headquarters, at the resort town of Taormina, on the east coast

"The San Dominica Hotel, in which the GHQ were housed, and the General Post Office building, in which were concentrated all telephone, telegraph, and other communication facilities, were completely demolished by a concentration of direct hits.

"Wreckage and debris were thrown high into the air and huge fires broke out.

"Bursts were also seen on railway tracks. In general, the target area was reduced to rubble and left in smoke and flames.

"On Friday Middle East based Liberators of the Ninth U.S. Air Force attacked Comiso airfield, dropping approximately 120 tons of high explosives. Hits were observed in the southern hangar area followed by fires. The north-west and south-west dispersal areas were well covered with bursts.

"An uncounted number of enemy aircraft were seen burning on the ground. An explosion near one hangar was followed by black smoke.

"At Malame airfield, the largest in Crete, dispersal areas were hit and severe damage was done to repair sheds. Bombs fell among a number of enemy aircraft on the ground, and, although results were obscured by smoke clouds, they are believed to have been destroyed.

"Our bombers were met with heavy fighter opposition, five enemy aircraft being destroyed with five others listed as damaged. From all these operations one of our aircraft did not return."

Today's North African Allied communique stated:—

"The North-West African air forces continued their heavy attack on Sicilian airfields and vital points in the enemy's defence system during yesterday and the previous night.

"Despite indifferent visibility, good results were reported.

"Enemy resistance was on a slightly increased scale, and during air battles we shot down 15 Axis aircraft.

"Ten of our aircraft failed to return."

According to a spokesman at Ninth U.S. Air Force headquarters in Cairo, quoted by Reuter, the Axis GHQ in Sicily was "completely wiped out" by the Liberators' raid. The buildings were flattened by the very accurate bombing. The telephone "nerve centre" in the GPO building was "completely obliterated."

RUSSIA: GOOD NEWS

Moscow reports today that Russian counter-attacks on the Bielgorod front have wiped out the German gains and thrown the enemy back to his original positions.—See Page 5.

Allies' Chances in Sicily, by Sir R. Gordon Finlayson.—See Page 3.

Map of Sicily.—Page 2.

VERY HEAVY RUHR RAID: GREAT DAY ONSLAUGHT

OUR bombers last night made a very heavy attack on the Central Ruhr, including Gelsenkirchen.

Ten planes are missing, said an Air Ministry communique this afternoon.

Last evening an aircraft of Coastal Command destroyed a Ju88 off the Coast of Norway.

Today hundreds of Allied planes both bombers and fighters—roared over the Channel to keep up the great offensive against German-occupied territory.

As they swept seawards, with a terrific roar, some only just cleared the housetops of south-east coast towns, but as soon as they had cleared the coastline they dived almost to sea level and sped towards the French coast, some steering south-east and the others direct towards Dunkirk.

There were so many that people who rushed into the streets could not count them.

Operations seemed to be on a rising scale as the day advanced.

More Than 100 Kept Secret

More than 100 British and American war correspondents in North Africa had kept the secret of the Allied plan to invade Sicily since the middle of June.

They were attending a Press conference at which General Eisenhower was speaking of the situation generally.

Suddenly he said overseas operations would be undertaken within a month, and the attack would be aimed at Sicily.

The Allies might be riding for a "bloody nose," but he thought the job could be done.

Before the conference ended he warned his listeners not to talk.

A few days ago a British colonel attached to the Press Relations Branch, said: "I would advise all of you to telephone me every night at midnight from now on."

Last night he told everybody to be in the conference room at 4.45 a.m. today. At 4.45 British and American press officers pushed their way through the jam in the packed room with the brief communique.

Turco-Syria Border Closed

The Turko-Syrian border was closed again today, presumably on account of troop movements and the need for keeping them secret, according to reliable reports in Ankara.—BUP.

MOSCOW EXCITED

THE Russian people joyously welcomed the Allied landing in Sicily.

It is still too early for newspaper comment, says A.P., but people in the streets were excited.

"It is not the second front, of course," they said, "but it is another important blow to the Axis."

"Panic In Sofia"

'Phone communication between Turkey and Bulgaria has been interrupted since yesterday morning, says BUP.

Strong rumours of Allied landings are stated to have caused panic in Sofia.

All reserve officers and most Bulgarian and German troops are stated to have been called up and sent to Salonika, which Axis circles estimate will be the first major objective. They say that airborne troops will be used on a big scale.

Union Jack Evening Paper

No. 35
MONDAY JULY 26 1943
Price : 1 franc

TUNIS TELEGRAPH

All the Local News

MUSSO. GOES

King and Badoglio take over but say Italy Fights on

BENITO MUSSOLINI, Dictator of Italy for almost 21 years, has resigned in the face of the Allied advances in Sicily.

King Victor Emmanuel, who announced Mussolini's resignation, said that he was appointing Marshal Pietro Badoglio, former commander of the Italian armies in Abyssinia, as his successor.

The war goes on. Both the King and Badoglio make this clear.

Rome Radio last night gave the first news of this sensational collapse of the man who has led Italy into so much sorrow. Then, six and a half hours later, the German radio gave the bare announcement.

There is no news as to what has happened to Mussolini and the members of his Cabinet.

The news caused the greatest excitement in London and New-York. Mounted police had to be called out to control the crowds in Times Square, New York.

Washington is optimistic, but British newspapers to-day, accept the news cautiously, and point out that the war against Italy is not yet over.

KING IS IN COMMAND

The statement of King Emmanuel was as follows:—

The King-Emperor has accepted the resignation from office of the Head of the Government, the Prime Minister, and Secretary of State, presented by His Excellency, Benito Mussolini, and has named as the Head of the Government, the Prime Minister, and Secretary of State, His Excellency, Cavaliere Marshal Pietro Badoglio.

His Majesty the King-Emperor has made the following proclamation to the Italian people:

Italians! From today onwards I assume command of all armed forces. In this solemn hour which weighs upon the destiny of the Fatherland, let everyone take his position of duty, of faith, and of combat. No deviations must be tolerated, no recrimination can be permitted. Let every Italian bow before the deep wounds which have torn the sacred soil of our Fatherland, Italy, through the valour of its armed forces and through the determined will of all its citizens, will discover the path to recovery in respect for the institutions which have always permitted her to rise up.

Italians! Today I am united with you more indissolubly than ever in unshaken faith in the immortality of the Fatherland.

Signed, Victor Emmanuel,
Counter-signed, Pietro Badoglio.
Rome: July 25th, 1943.

THE WAR GOES ON

Marshal Badoglio, has made the following proclamation to the Italian people:

Italians! By order of His Majesty the King-Emperor, I today assume the military government of the country with full powers. The war goes on. Italy, hard hit in her invaded provinces, in her destroyed cities, maintains her given word, a jealous guardian of her thousand-year old traditions. Let the ranks be serried around his Majesty the King-Emperor, a living image of the Fatherland, an example for all. The order I have received is clear and precise and it will be carried out scrupulously and whoever cherishes illusions of being able to disrupt normal developments, or of trying to disturb public order, will be inexorably punished.

Long live Italy, Long live the King.

Signed, Marshal of Italy, Pietro Badoglio.
Rome: June 25th, 1943.

This official and authorised comment on the resignation of Benito Mussolini was given by the B.B.C.:

This is the beginning of the end for Fascism and Nazism everywhere. It has fallen before a combination of irresistable forces.

The British and American forces which have swept through Sicily, are now preparing to carry the war against the Italian mainland, unless the government in Rome capitulates.

(Continued on back page)

STORY OF A WOULD-BE CAESAR

BENITO MUSSOLINI, the man whom Mr. Churchill has described as «the bloated bullfrog of the Pontine Marshes», «Hitler's tattered lackey», and «the pocket Caesar with feet of clay», is the son of a blacksmith and was born at Predapio, in the province of Forli. His resignation almost coincides with his 60th birthday, for he was born on July 29th, 1883.

In his youth he was a Socialist but in 1914 he turned nationalist, and when he favoured the intervention of Italy in the war, he was expelled from the Socialist party.

When Italy entered the war in May, 1915, he joined the Army, as a private. Like his friend, Adolph Hitler, he reached the rank of corporal before being wounded, and discharged from the Army in February 1917.

On October 28th, 1922, after a congress at Naples, Mussolini led 40,000 Fascists in a march on Rome. Historians have since said that Mussolini followed the marchers later by train, fearing to risk his neck in any fighting.

Mussolini made himself dictator of Italy in 1925.

On Good Friday, 1939, he ordered the siezure of Albania. In May, 1939, a formal military alliance was concluded with Germany and on June 10th, 1940, he brought off his famous «stab in the back» act by declaring war on France.

This is worth remembering

THE paper «Schwarze Korps» official organ of the Nazi S. S.—says that if the war is lost by Germany, a new world war must be envisaged in 1963.

In another issue, the same newspaper says that young Germans should marry as soon as possible, «for prudent people must know that life goes on and that our grandchildren must accomplish the task if our children are not able to do so.»

BITTER FIGHT FOR TIP OF SICILY

THE ALLIES hold every important town in Sicily to-day, except Catania, the port on the east coast and Messina, the island end of the ferry to the mainland.

German and Italian resistance is, if anything, hardening. They seem determined to hold at all costs to a line from Catania, sweeping round Mount Etna to the northern coast of the island.

The Italians also are said to be fighting harder than they have done anywhere else. Italian parachute troops have been dropped behind our lines on sabotage missions, but were all rounded up before they could do anything.

Despite heavy losses, the enemy is still sending reinforcements across the straits to Messina.

Correspondents say that much will depend on the speed with which the American and Canadian forces, who cut up the middle of the island, can turn east to harass the north-western flank of the Axis line.

100,000 PRISONERS

There was no official news yesterday of the American force which has taken Marsala and Trapani, but the Italian radio said that there had been bitter attacks on their northern flank. The Canadians who turned east after passing through Enna are meeting bitter opposition from the reformed 15 Panzer division.

The southern part of the Axis line is apparently being held by Germans and the north-western part by Italians. This north-western part is still apparently very fluid as the Allies continue to harass the enemy.

It was stated last night that the American force had taken 50,000 prisoners and more thousands had still to come in. In all, it is estimated that about 100,000 prisoners have been taken.

General Bernard Montgomery met war correspondents near Mount Etna. He told them that he was very pleased with the way things are going, and he thought the Sicilians were glad to see the last of the Germans and Italians.

They were now coming out to greet the Allied troops and in return we were feeding them. The Axis soldiers had taken everything they could

In the air, the enemy is still taking a terrific hammering.

Ten landing barges have been sunk off the Sicilian coast by our aircraft. One merchant ship was sunk and an escorting destroyer was left on fire off the Italian coast.

BOLOGNA RAID

Flying Fortresses from North Africa made a heavy raid on Bologna, their farthest north target in Italy. Bologna is Italy's most important railway centre, as all the traffic from Germany which must come through the Brenner Pass must also go through the town. The Flying Fortresses found the railway marshalling yards full of traffic. Great damage was done and an ammunition train was blown up.

The Allies have also made their heaviest air raid yet on the island of Crete. Well over 100 planes took part and ammunition dumps were blown up and factories wrecked.

MONDAY, JULY 26, 1943

Closing Prices

BLACK OUT 10.44 to 5.29 | Moon Rises 2.38 a.m. New Moon Aug. 1 | RADIO Page Six.

LATE NIGHT

THE STAR

No. 17,191 ★ ONE PENNY

ITALY UNDER MARTIAL LAW

"Mussolini And Cabinet Arrested"

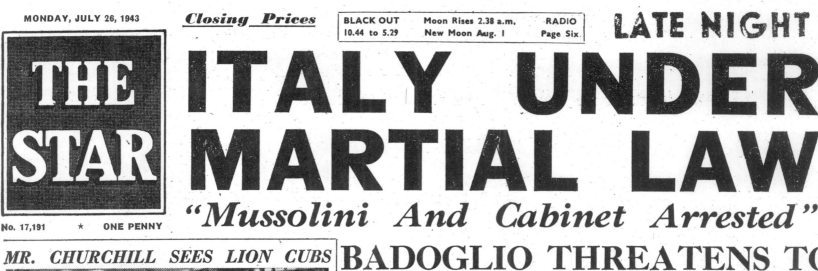

MR. CHURCHILL SEES LION CUBS

Mr. and Mrs. Churchill at the Zoo today, with one of the cubs of his lion, Rota, which was presented to him by Mr. George Thomson, of Pinner. (Story on Page Three, Column Five.)

CATANIA THRUST IS CONTINUING

10 Generals & An Admiral Taken

"VIOLENT fighting is taking place at the approaches to Catania, and the Allies are still steadily advancing," said Algiers radio this afternoon."

This afternoon's Allied communique said: "Pressure on the enemy was maintained in all sectors. Canadian troops continued to advance, but their progress was slow in the face of bitter resistance.

"The Seventh (American) Army has captured over 7,000 prisoners, including many generals.

"Medium bombers yesterday attacked centres of communications in north-eastern Sicily.

"The port of Milazzo (on the north coast, 25 miles due west of Messina) was attacked during Saturday night, and many fires were started. Our fighters maintained their sweeps and patrols during the day. Three enemy aircraft were shot down by our night fighters.

"One of our aircraft is missing from these operations."

"Ten generals and one admiral have been captured by the U.S. Army in West Sicily," said an American broadcaster from Algiers this afternoon.

"A total of 56,000 prisoners have now been captured by Americans. The Axis has 6½ divisions left on the island."

Milazzo has railway sidings which were last attacked early in June by Malta-based aircraft. On Saturday a merchant vessel was hit off Milazzo by fighter bombers.

Termini and Cefalu, respectively 25 and 50 miles east of Palermo, on the Northern coastal road, were reported by Algiers today to have been captured by American troops advancing towards the Messina tip.

German-controlled Vichy radio said today: "The final assault on Catania seems imminent. Five-sixths of Sicily is in Allied hands, and it is not certain if Axis forces in the centre of the island will reach the east coast in time."

Discontent and unrest in the rem-

CONTINUED ON BACK PAGE, Col. Three

"Surrender" Call

New York radio broadcast to Italy in Italian today, making a new call for unconditional surrender and offering the Italian people a free choice of "Whatever Government they wish as long as it is not Fascist."

Very Heavy Raid On Essen

AIRCRAFT of Bomber Command made a very heavy attack on Essen last night, stated an Air Ministry communique this afternoon. It added:

"The weather over the target was good, and preliminary reports indicate that the bombing was concentrated and effective.

"Mosquitos of Bomber Command attacked objectives in Hamburg and Cologne. Two enemy aircraft were destroyed by our bombers.

"Twenty-five aircraft of Bomber Command and one of Fighter Command are missing from the night's operations."

Mosquito bomber crews, who went to Hamburg last night, were guided to the city by fires.

After the 2,300-tons raid on Saturday night and yesterday's daylight attack by U.S. bombers, the fires had apparently become so much out of control that they could be seen from 70 miles away.

There was a violent explosion before the Mosquitos had dropped their loads.

A fighter pilot reported missing from yesterday's offensive operation is now known to be safe, making two pilots safe during the day.

Out Again Today

A large force of bombers and fighters crossed the South-East Coast near Dungeness today, but haze prevented a big proportion of the planes being seen, although a number of bombers flying lower than the others were observed.

Heavy anti-aircraft gunfire from the French coast was heard shortly afterwards, and subsequently aircraft returned over the coast, having apparently come from the vicinity of Calais.

BADOGLIO THREATENS TO SHOOT DEMONSTRATORS

ROME RADIO THIS AFTERNOON ANNOUNCED MARTIAL LAW THROUGHOUT ITALY. BEFORE PHONE COMMUNICATIONS BETWEEN ITALY AND SWITZERLAND WERE CUT, FIGHTING BETWEEN ITALIANS AND GERMANS AND GREAT DEMONSTRATIONS THROUGHOUT THE COUNTRY WERE REPORTED.

Mussolini is under house arrest, and Scorza, Fascist Party secretary, and the entire Italian Cabinet are detained under a strong guard at a place outside Rome, according to Berne reports.

The martial law order was contained in a proclamation by Mussolini's successor, Marshal Badoglio, which:

Imposed a dusk to dawn curfew, during which all places of entertainment must close;
Banned all demonstrations and assemblies of more than three persons;
Stopped the use of cars, motor-boats or planes; and
Forbade the carrying of ammunition and firearms.

Berlin today quoted the Italian news agency as saying the change of Government in Italy was believed to have been due to the state of Mussolini's health. He was said to have been ill for some time.

A recent portrait of Marshal Badoglio.

Rome radio this afternoon announced that Dr. Raffaele Guariglia is to be Foreign Minister. He is the Italian Minister in Ankara, and was reported to be on his way to Rome by plane.

It had previously announced that Field-Marshal Kesselring, the German commander in the Mediterranean area, and von Mackensen, the German Ambassador to Italy, were negotiating in Rome with Badoglio.

The line being taken by Goebbels in treating the resignation of Mussolini soon became apparent.

A German overseas broadcaster said: "The stiffening of the German-Italian positions in Sicily and the continuous influx of reinforcements across the Straits of Messina, as well as the conversations between Marshal Badoglio and the Commander-in-Chief of the German forces, are considered a sign of the Axis decision to defend Sicily to the last."

Reports from Rome reaching Berne, say that the crisis began on Sunday morning at a Cabinet meeting of defence Ministers, who heard Mussolini outline the proposals Hitler made to him at their recent meeting.

These proposals called for such great Italian sacrifices that the Under-Secretaries for War, Air and the Navy refused to accept the responsibility for their execution without consulting the entire Cabinet.

The Cabinet, after a lively debate, decided to submit the entire problem to the King, whose refusal to accept the conditions was emphatic.

"Hitler's principal proposition to Mussolini," the Berne correspondent of the "New York Times" adds, "is said to have been immediate withdrawal from Sicily with sufficient rearguards on the Catania front to enable the Hermann Goering division to withdraw first.

"The Italian troops would then be called on to fight a resisting rearguard action the entire length of the mainland from Naples, Calabria and Puglia to a line running east-west through the southern limits of Tuscany while defence preparations were completed in the Appenines.

"Rome would be abandoned, with several large shipments of war material which have just arrived from Germany being destroyed."

For weeks past Italy has been withdrawing her troops in the occupied territories.

Italian garrisons were withdrawn a week ago from the Savoie and the Haute Savoie districts of France. Italian divisions were earlier reported moving out of Greece and the Balkans.

Most significant of all—Italy has been recalling troops from Yugo-Slavia despite increased guerilla activity there involving heavy fighting for the Axis troops. And Italian workers in Germany have also been trying to get back to Italy.

Taken altogether, all these recent reports take on a new significance when read in conjunction with news of Mussolini's downfall.

These two reports on the Mussolini affair were given in the Stockholm "Allehanda," quoting a German underground radio:

1.—Mussolini has been taken prisoner by Italian army officers, who intend to hand him over to the Allies as soon as peace is concluded.

2.—Mussolini's resignation preceded a conference between Badoglio and the Pope. Badoglio asked the Pope to join in the proclamation issued by Badoglio and King Victor Emmanuel, but the Pope refused, declaring that he was only working for peace, and did not want to become mixed up in politics.

Many observers believe that Mussolini has sought sanctuary in the Vatican, says Reuter. Others think that his ultimate refuge will be Switzerland, whence he came as a journalist to Milan.

Badoglio, whose moderate tendencies have been known for a long time, is regarded here as interim manager for Italian destinies.

Badoglio's Proclamation.—See Back Page, Col. Two.

POPE'S APPEAL FOR ROME

The Pope has made another appeal to the King of Italy to declare Rome an open city, according to reports from Vichy political circles reaching Madrid.

An interest in the suggestion that Italy should make peace before an Allied invasion of the Italian mainland has also been expressed by the Pope, according to these reports.

Lemons Ten A Penny

Lemons are being sold at ten a penny in Sicily. The Allied troops are able to buy cheaply as many peaches or oranges as they can eat, cabled BUP today. Almonds are also abundant, and the men eat them wherever they go.

FINAL
No. 26301 (Established 1864) TUESDAY, JULY 27, 1943 THREE-HALFPENCE

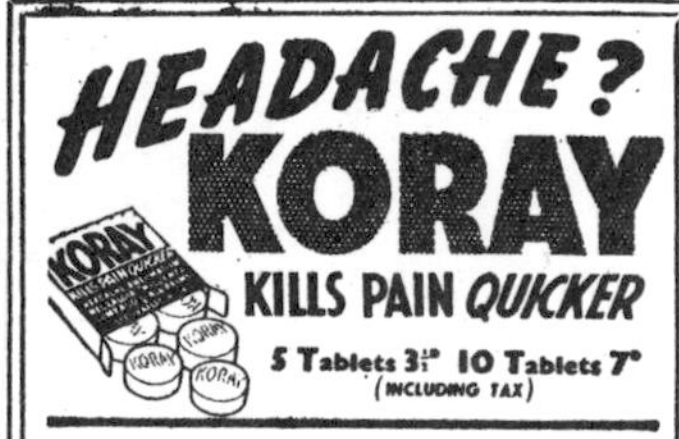

Premier Says Keystone of Fascist Arch Has Crumbled: Entire Edifice Doomed

ITALIANS TO STEW IN THEIR OWN JUICE FOR A BIT, WHILE WE HOT UP THE FIRE

No Approaches Yet By Their Government

UNCONDITIONAL SURRENDER SHOULD BE WHOLESALE

MR. CHURCHILL TOLD THE HOUSE OF COMMONS TODAY THAT SO FAR WE HAVE HAD NO APPROACHES FROM THE ITALIAN GOVERNMENT.

The Premier said "We should allow the Italians, to use a homely phrase, to stew in their own juice for a bit, and hot up the fire to the utmost, in order to accelerate the process, until we obtain from their government, or whoever possesses the necessary authority, all the indispensable requirements we demand for carrying on war against our prime and capital foe, which is not Italy but Germany.

It was to the interests of Italy, and also the interest of the Allies, that the unconditional surrender of Italy should be brought about wholesale and not piecemeal.

"The keystone of the Fascist arch has crumbled," said Mr. Churchill, "and, without attempting to prophesy, it does not seem unlikely that the entire Fascist edifice will fall to the ground in ruin, if it has not already so fallen."

He warned the Italians of the grim consequences if they let the Germans have their own way in making Italy a preliminary battleground.

MR CHURCHILL

Close Of An Epoch

MR Churchill began amid loud cheers, "The House will have heard with satisfaction of the downfall of one of the principal criminals of this desolating war. The end of Mussolini's long and severe reign over the Italian people undoubtedly marks the close of an epoch in the life of Italy.

"The keystone of the Fascist arch has crumbled, and, without attempting to prophesy, it does not seem unlikely that the entire Fascist edifice will fall to the ground in ruins, if it has not already so fallen.

"The Totalitarian system of a single party, armed with the secret police, engrossing to itself practically all the offices, even the humblest, in the Government, and with magistrates and courts under the control of the executive, with its whole network of domestic spies and neighbourly informants—such a system when applied over a long period of time, leaves the broad masses without any pendent figures apart from the influence upon their country's destinies, and without any independent figures apart from the official classes.

"That, I think, is a defence for the people of Italy— one defence, although there can be no really valid defence for any people which allows its freedom and inherent rights to pass out of its own hands..

"Now the external shock of war has broken the spell which, in Italy, held all those masses for so long—in fact, for more than 20 years, and held them for all this period in physical, and even more in moral subjection.

"We may therefore reasonably expect that very great changes will take place in Italy. What their form will be, or how the will impinge upon the forces of German occupation, it is too early to forecast.

It Looked So Safe

"Sir, the guilt and folly of Mussolini have cost the Italian dear. It looked so safe and easy in May, 1940, to stab a falling France in the back and advance to appropriate the Mediterranean. Interests and possessions of what Mussolini no doubt doubt sincerely believed was a decadent and ruined Britain.

"It look so safe and easy to fall upon the much smaller State of Greece, but, however, there have been undceptions. Events have taken a different course.

"By many hazardous turns of fortune and by the long marches of destiny, the British and United States Armies, having occupied the Italian African Empire, the North of Africa, and the great bulk of Sicily now stand at the portals of the Italian mainland, armed with the powers of the sea and the air, and with very large land and amphibious forces equipped with every modern weapon and device.

"What is it, Mr Speaker, these masterful forces bring to Italy?

"Sir, they bring, if the Italian people so decide, relief from war, freedom from servitude and, after an interval, a respectable place in the new and rescued Europe.

The Main Wish

"When I learned of the scenes enacted in the streets of the fine city of Palermo on the entry of the United States' Armies, and reviewed the mass of detailed information with which I have been furnished, I cannot doubt that the main wish of the Italian people is to be quit of the German taskmasters, to be spared the further and perfectly futile ordeal of destruction, and to revive their former democratic and parliamentary institutions.

"These they can have.

"The choice is in their hands, and what is the alternative? The Germans naturally desire that Italy shall become the battleground, the preliminary battleground, and that, by Italian sufferings, the ravages of war shall be kept as far away as possible for as long as possible from the German Fatherland.

Seared and Scarred

"If the Italian Government and people choose that the Germans are to have their way, no choice is left open to us. We shall continue to make war

(Continued on Back Page, Col. 5)

Italian Peace Demonstrations Reported

PROCLAMATION BY ANTI-FASCISTS

REPORTS of peace demonstrations in Italy are reaching neutral countries. According to a message from Switzerland, the Turin newspaper Stampa di Sera printed a proclamation from long-dormant anti-Fascist parties declaring that the men responsible for dragging Italy into war must be punished.

The proclamation was signed by the Italian parties which went underground when the Fascists seized power.

First disclosure of how Mussolini was sacked came today from the official Italian News Agency. Count Dino Grandi, Fascism's first diplomat and a protege of Mussolini, proposed the sensational step at a meeting of the Fascist Grand Council on Saturday.

After a debate of ten hours Grandi's resolution was carried by 19 votes to seven.

DEMANDS FOR PEACE

Eyewitnesses from Turin reaching Switzerland say that students in the city have started demonsrations demanding that a commission be sent immediately to Lugano to negotiate peace, reports Reginald Langford, Reuter's special correspondent on the Italo-Swiss frontier.

There is still no official news of what has become of Mussolini but the rumour is persistent that he and his Ministers are under house arrest.

Rome has issued a communique denying that disorders have broken out.

It is thought in Istanbul that Count Guariglia, now Marshal Badoglio's Foreign Minister, received instructions from his Government about a week ago to throw out peace feelers.

BERLIN SHOCK

Bernard Valery, Reuter's special correspondent, cables from Stockholm, the German Nazis there are convinced that Italy will be out of the war in two or three weeks, and that the Allies will use Italy as a base for operations against Germany.

Swedish correspondents in Berlin do not conceal that the news of Mussolini's resignation came as the greatest shock there since the beginning of the war, and might have the "gravest consequences for Germany."

The Italian Army has received orders to arrest leading Fascists as a measure of precaution and to avoid disorder, according to information from the frontier quoted by Swiss radio.

RED FLAGS IN MILAN

Associated Press says that a wave of anti-Fascist enthusiasm is sweeping through Italy, according to reports received from the German frontier. Crowds paraded in Milan carrying red flags and shouting, "Long Live Socialism."

New York, Tuesday. — King Victor Emmanuel and Marshal Badoglio have been branded as "Fascists" in short wave broadcasts beamed to Italy in the Italian language by the Office of War Information—Associated Press.

FRENCH VIEW

Denis Martin, Reuter's correspondent, cables from Algiers this extract from a statement from official French circles: "Could one maintain the theory of the 'Good Italy' after a conditional surrender?

"The French have seen the downfall of the first Dictator of modern times, and feel the breaking of their bonds. But they remember June 10, 1940, and the cries of 'Tunisia, Corsica and Sayor' that went up for years. We do not want to negotiate, we want to fight.

Madrid, Tuesday.—The Berlin correspondent of the Spanish newspaper Informaciones quotes the German Foreign Office spokesman as saying: "What has happened is not related in any way to the last meeting between Hitler and Mussolini."

From this the correspondent assumed that "things have taken place without the complete knowledge of the German Government."

MOSCOW ON AXIS BANKRUPTCY

Moscow radio's political commentator, Sermashov, comments: "Mussolini's resignation is not just a change of leadership in the Italian Government. This is the bankruptcy of the policy and strategy of the Axis Powers.

"A few more such blows as those delivered to the Fascist bloc at Stalingrad and now at Kursk, and Hitler's bloody machine will collapse as well."

Istanbul, Tuesday.—"Italy is now being sacrificed, but tomorrow it will be the turn of Hungary and Bulgaria," says the Turkish newspaper Vatan, quoted by Reuter.

"A wind of pessimism and panic is blowing in the Balkans. This is not surprising. Germany's vital positions begin on the German frontier. The dark

(Continued on Back Page—Col. 2)

Canadians Progress In Sicily After Heavy Fighting

THE North Africa communique, quoted by Reuter, says: "In the eastern sector patrol activity continues. Canadian forces have made further limited progress after heavy fighting. Operations of the Seventh Army are proceeding according to plan.

"During offensive sweeps over the Messina area on Sunday our fighters encountered a large formation of JU 52 transport aircraft; in the ensuing combat 21 of the JU 52s and five of their escorting fighters were shot down.

"Later in the day three more enemy aircraft were destroyed by our fighters.

Railways Attacked

Railway communications at Marina Dipoala in Southern Italy were attacked yesterday. Our light bombers and fighter-bombers continued their attacks on shipping in Sicilian harbours and road communications on the island.

"Fighters carried out offensive sweeps over Sardinia and maintained their patrols over Allied shipping and ground forces.

"On Sunday night the port of Milazzo was attacked by our medium bombers. Torpedo-carrying aircraft damaged and sank an enemy merchant vessel in the Tyrrhenian Sea. During these operations eleven enemy aircraft were shot down. Three of ours are missing."

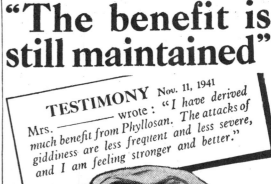

LATE EXTRA

Evening Chronicle

No. 21,009 [Est. 1885] NEWCASTLE, Friday, September 3, 1943 Threehalfpence Radio: Page 3

British Troops Again Fighting On European Continent

8th ARMY INVADES MAINLAND 'TOE' OF ITALY

LAND, AIR, SEA SUPPORT FOR PRE-DAWN LANDING

AXIS BATTERIES SILENCED

From CYRIL BEWLEY (Evening Chronicle" War Correspondent)

Allied H.Q., North Africa, Friday.

To-day, four years after Britain entered the war, British troops are again fighting on the mainland of Europe—in Italy itself.

TWO hours before dawn this morning British and Canadian units of the Eighth Army, protected by the most powerful naval and air bombardment of the Mediterranean campaign, crossed the Straits of Messina and landed on the beaches around Reggio on the toe of Italy.

Before the landing, guns from ship and shore thundered out against the batteries on the Italian slopes that rise from the narrow coastal strip opposite Messina and were in an excellent position to oppose landing attempts. Our guns sought out these batteries and silenced them. A hail of bombs from our planes gave further cover.

The Eighth Army has travelled 2,050 miles from Alamein to be the first to set foot on the European mainland.

Coincident with the invasion, heavy air attacks were made on communications in North, Central, and Southern Italy. The railway bridge carrying the line from the Brenner Pass was hit and broken at Bolzano, while this line was again cut at Trento, and a road bridge broken. Bologna and Naples outskirts were other targets.

German reports say that the 8th Army landings took place each side of Reggio.

The invasion was announced in a special communique from Allied Headquarters this morning. It stated:

Allied forces under the command of General Eisenhower have continued their advance.

British and Canadian troops of the 8th Army, supported by Allied sea and air power, attacked across the Straits of Messina early to-day and landed on the mainland of Italy.

An Allied Navy communique stated:

British and Canadian troops landed on Italian mainland were moved to the assault in landing craft of the Royal Navy, escorted and supported by a force of cruisers, monitors and destroyers, gunboats and other small craft.

General Eisenhower, Allied Commander-in-Chief, went to Sicily by air to join Generals Alexander and Montgomery in a last-minute conference.

Though the invasion preparations must have been apparent to enemy reconnaissance, there was very little preliminary opposition — restricted to desultory artillery shots.

Press correspondents at Allied H.Q., North Africa, reported that the landing took place on the shores opposite Messina in darkness at 4.30 a.m.

Continued on BACK P.

Russia Rolls On

Russia is rolling up the Nazi lines "like a carpet. Page Eight.

This is the Toe of Italy.—Page Two.

It is reported that many leading Fascists have been arrested in Italy.—Page Five.

FATEFUL HOUR OF 11

From Our Air Correspondent

At exactly 11 o'clock this morning — anniversary of the beginning of the war and the hour of Prayer to-day—Londoners lining the streets were thrilled to see scores of U.S. Flying Fortresses silhouetted against the sky pass over the capital.

Flying in perfect battle formation, the drone of the bombers' engines could be heard above the roar of the street traffic.

After circling around, the Fortresses headed in a south-easterly direction, probably in continuation of their offensive against Hitler's European "fortress."

Britain prays as troops invade Italy.—Page Four.

Seven specials carry parcels

(From Our Own Correspondent, London).

What is believed to be a record dispatch of prisoners-of-war parcels, involving seven special trains, has been completed at St. Pancras Station, London.

They numbered 424,000, filled 286 vans. Loading on which the depleted station staff was augmented by women, occupied six days.

Some of the women have relatives in enemy hands.

HEART OF PARIS BOMBED TO-DAY

Huge Anglo-American Air Armada Strikes In Daylight

The centre of Paris suffered its first raid by Allied aircraft to-day, according to Paris Radio.

"Anglo-American air forces carried out a new terror raid on the region of Paris to-day," said the broadcast, quoted by British Uniteds Pres. "For the first time in these raids the centre of the capital has been hit, particularly districts on the left bank of the Seine.

"South-western districts also received bomb hits," proceeded the radio, which added: "Damage and casualties appedr to be very great...

A.R.P. and welfare services went into action immediately, and the first conribution of 700,000 france has already been distributed among the victims."

BOMBERS AND FIGHTERS

It was revealed in London that American Eighth Air Force Flying Fortresses and Marauders attacked targets in Northern France this morning, with U.S. Thunderbolts and R.A.F. Dominion and Allied fighters supporting and covering the operations.

Within a few hours of the opening of the fifth anniversary of the war what seemed to be the biggest air-armada that has yet set out from this country in daylight crossed the English Channel.

Swarms of bombers, escorted by fighters, could be heard and seen crossing the coast. The continuous hum of engines filled the sky for well over an hour, and it is calculated that in numbers the aircraft engaged in these vast operations were comparable to some of the recent large-scale night raids on Hamburg and Berlin.

Paris "alert" lasted two hours

The "alert" in Paris lasted almost two hours—an hour and 55 minutes, to be exact—reports Reuter which, quoting Vichy Radio, adds that further air attacks took place in France during the morning.

The most recent raid on a target in the Paris area was by Flying Fortresses, escorted by Thunderbolts, which smashed the German airfield at Villacoublay, eight miles south of Paris, on August 24.

To-day's big Continental attacks by Allied aircraft followed yesterday's biggest single day operation of the year, when Bostons, Marauders, Mitchells, Venturas and Fortresses, with Spitfire and Thunderbolt escorts, pounded targets in France and the Low Countries.

YESTERDAY'S TARGETS

The Cie de Bethune lowee station at Mazingarbe was severely damaged, also the Serquex marshaling yards and a junction between the Paris-Dieppe and Amiens-Rouen ines, the three ocks at the south end of the Hansweert Canal, which carries shipping to Antwerp, and enemy shipping in the neighbourhood.

Meanwhile Fortresses, escorted by Thunderbolts of the U.S. Eighth Fighter Command, pounded aerodromes at Mardyck and Denain.

R.A.F mine-laying last night

An Air Ministry communique issued to-day stated:—

"Last night mines were laid in enemy waters. Airfields and other targets in Northern France and in the Low Countries were also attacked.

"One of our bombers is missing."

Anothers of the German Navy's light coastal craft was sunk outside Boulogne harbour during the night by a Fleet Air Arm Albacore, operating with Fighter Command states Air Ministry News Service.

The German boat was spotted just before midnight making for Boulogne harbour. The Albacore came up astern of the vessel and a stick of six bombs was dropped, as the pilot said this morning, "right on top of it." The boat disappeared.

Berlin radio stated that the R.A.F. made "nuisance raids" over Western Germany during the night, "single bombs causing only insignificant damage."

R.A.F. attack transport

Middle East air communique, issued to-day, states:

"In the course of operations along the west coast of Greece yesterday R.A.F. Beaufighters attacked and damaged enemy transport vehicles on the road south of Preveza, causing an explosion and a number of fires.

"An enemy merchant vessel found at anchor near Preveza received a direct hit amidships. From these and other operations one of our aircraft is missing."

Gateshead girl missing

Gateshead Police state that Audrey Beatrice Forsyth (15) has been missing from her home since Wednesday morning. She was wearing a grey cloth coat, flannel pin-stripe skirt, no stockings or hat.

She has four vaccination marks on the left leg below the knee, looks older than her age, is well built, and about 5ft. 4 or 5 ins. in height, being fair-haired and fresh-complexioned.

Anyone who knows anything of this girl's whereabouts is asked to communicate with Gateshead Police.

Heavy Air Attacks On Northern Italy

The main line between Germany and Italy through the Brenner Pass has been cut in two places by Allied attacks at Bolzano and Trento.

To-day's Allied air communique from North-West Africa states:—

The North-West African Air Forces made heavy attacks on enemy communications on Northern, Central and Southern Italy.

Unescorted heavy bombers, one of which is missing, attacked the railway yards at Bolzano, Trento and Bologna in strength. At Bolzano, the railway bridge carrying the line from the Brenner Pass was hit and broken. Hits were also made on the yards and adjacent tracks.

RAILWAY BLOCKED

At Trento, also on the route from the Brenner Pass, the railway was blocked and the road bridge broken.

At Bologna, the yards and warehouses were hit and explosions and fires were seen.

Medium bombers escorted by long-range fighters made a heavy attack on the railway yards at Cancello. Many hits were made and lines radiating from the yards were blocked.

Strong fighter opposition was encountered during these attacks and 27 enemy fighters were destroyed, 23 of them in the attack on Cancello, from which 10 escorting fighters are missing.

Medium and light bombers and fighter-bombers made intensive attacks on railway communications and enemy positions at many points in Southern Italy. An ammunition dump was blown up and barges off the cost were attacked, one being left on fire.

Intruder aircraft attacked enemy airfields in Southern Italy on the night of September 1-2.

From all these operations and from fighter patrols and reconnaissance missions a total of 34 enemy aircraft were destroyed.

A total of 15 of our aircraft are missing.

ITALIANS ADMIT DAMAGE

To-day's Italian communique states: "Bolzano, Trento and Bologna and the outskirts of Naples were bombed by enemy planes which dropped numerous bombs, causing damage, especially heavy at Bologna."

Airmen smash Brenner Pass line

The 80-mile single line track through the Brenner Pass, which is being smashed by Allied airmen, is Europe's most overworked railway, writes an air correspondent.

It carried the major part of Germany's military traffic through into Italy and is open all the year round.

Lowest of all the defiles through the Alps—less than 5,000 feet high—it rises in Northern Italy and connects Bolanza with Innsbruck.

The only remaining passes of value to the Germans are the Simplon and the St. Gothard, both belonging to Switzerland, who has hitherto not permitted the passage of military materials

(Reuter and British United Press messages.)

SUNDAY EXPRESS

SEPTEMBER 5 1943 | BLACK-OUT (London) 8.10 p.m. to 5.49 a.m. | Founded by LORD BEAVERBROOK | Moon: Rises 12.10 p.m. Sets 10.17 p.m. | TWOPENCE

BRIDGEHEADS 3 MILES DEEP, WE NOW HOLD 55 MILES OF ITALIAN COAST

Vichy says Germans abandon the whole Cape Spartivento area

Axis radio reports 'Huge numbers of tanks'

EXCELLENT NEWS ABOUT OUR INVASION OF ITALY REACHED LONDON LATE LAST NIGHT. VICHY, WHICH USUALLY RELAYS REPORTS DIRECT FROM BERLIN, SAID THAT THE WHOLE OF THE CAPE SPARTIVENTO AREA, IN THE SOUTH-EASTERN TIP OF THE ITALIAN TOE, HAD BEEN EVACUATED BY GERMAN AND ITALIAN TROOPS.

This admission, following the official Italian statement earlier in the day that Melito, a few miles west of Cape Spartivento, had been evacuated, means that some 55 miles of the curving Italian coastline is now in our hands.

This front apparently stretches from Scilla, in the north-west (which earlier Axis reports said we had reached and which Vichy said we left subsequently after the loss of several landing barges), through San Giovanni and Reggio de Calabria to Melito and Cape Spartivento in the south-east.

The Algiers radio last night added the information that in the last 24 hours the Allied bridgehead had been extended to the depth of three miles. This means that the mountainous interior of "the toe" is now falling into British and Canadian hands.

Algiers added that massive reinforcements are reaching Calabria without interruption, with powerful airplane and tank support, and that the Italians are surrendering in groups, just as they did in Sicily. At Reggio, the Italians called to our troops as they entered the town: 'We have been waiting for you a long time.'

Oslo radio, which is, of course, German-controlled, described the landings as an operation carried out in great strength with the employment of huge numbers of tanks.

Two chief ferry ports

Reggio di Calabria and San Giovanni, the two chief ferry ports on the mainland side of the Strait of Messina, fell into British hands in the first 24 hours of the invasion, it was officially announced yesterday.

Reggio, population 119,000, is the terminus of the coast railway from Naples, 248 miles to the north.

Berlin radio yesterday named the British Sixth Armoured Division as one of the leading units in the invasion. This division landed in Tunisia early last December and fought at Pichon, Fondouk and Kairouan, and in the final assault on Tunis.

Berlin yesterday admitting the evacuation of the Cape Spartivento-Melito area said, "After putting up a gallant fight against a far superior enemy, the Italian screen retreated towards the north."

FROM GENERAL EISENHOWER'S H.Q. LAST NIGHT CAME THE NEWS: "THE ADVANCE IS CONTINUING. A LARGE NUMBER OF PRISONERS HAVE BEEN TAKEN."

After several hours on the Italian mainland there was not one casualty among the Canadian troops, who met with hardly any resistance. But Vichy declared last night that extremely violent fighting is now going on at the rear of the original bridgehead.

Sea, air command complete

Allied command of the air and sea is complete, broadcast John Daly, the C.B.S. correspondent at Algiers.

"Sortie after sortie of our fighters and fighter bombers not only found no enemy planes willing to give battle," he said, "but had to return to their bases with cannon and machine-gun ammunition unused and bombs in the racks because there were just not any enemy targets on the ground to attack.

David Brown, Reuters correspondent at H.Q., said the invasion moved like well-oiled clockwork.

Whether German troops have been entirely withdrawn from the toe of Italy still remains a matter of conjecture, but it appears very improbable, he said; that any were contacted during the first 24 hours of the invasion.

The swift capture of the airfield at Reggio gave the Allies a valuable airfield immediately usable by fighter planes. Its runway is nearly a mile long.

A broadcast from Algiers last night stated that the opening barrage which preceded the invasion of Italy was the greatest artillery concentration to date, even exceeding the bombardments before the attacks on the El Alamein and Mareth positions.

Wallace Reyburn, war reporter with the Canadians, says in two hours something like 150,000 shells were fired.

So many guns, so many ships, no trouble

By JAMES WELLARD,
Sunday Express Correspondent at Allied H.Q.

COVERED by an intense artillery barrage, which included new machine guns firing bullets right across the Strait of Messina, and protected by a powerful flotilla of warships, which included two battleships, our landings and advance were made with minimum difficulty and with little opposition. Our casualties are negligible—our prisoners many.

The whole operation has gone with chronometric precision. We had so many guns massed on Sicily and on the sea, and such supremacy in the air that even the firmest Axis resistance must have crumbled under the weight of metal poured on to the ten-mile stretch of beaches where the Canadians and British were scheduled to land. But opposition was not offered.

Of all the coastal guns the Italians had mounted on the Calabrian side of the Strait only one is

BACK PAGE, COL. THREE

'ROME COLLAPSE AT ANY MINUTE'

WASHINGTON confidently expects the unconditional surrender of Italy in a matter of weeks, or even days, cabled Harold Hutchinson, B.U.P. correspondent in the American capital, last night.

Mr. Churchill and President Roosevelt are receiving reports a most hourly from the battle zone—and both are said to be "very cheerful." Both men sat up talking in the President's study until the early hours yesterday.

There is a growing feeling in Washington that something big and new is coming.

Military officials, questioned on the role the other Anglo-American armies in the Mediterranean area would play, said: "There are going to be a lot of surprises, and they will probably come soon."

The Washington expectations were backed up by this comment over Rome radio by the diplomatic correspondent of the Italian News Agency: "The internal situation of Italy is critical. But we still have resources at our disposal which the enemy would do well not to forget."

Earlier yesterday reliable reports said that peace demonstrations on a great scale were going on all over Italy and that "sit-down" strikes had started in many industrial areas.

In Rome, Milan, Turin, Genoa and Florence processions through the streets demanded peace. Except in Milan, neither the police nor troops attempted to disperse the demonstrators.

'Any demands'

In Milan, however, German troops broke up a procession.

Once a clear demonstration is given of the ability of the United Nations to shake the German mastery over Italy, collapse is certain.

Rome radio, in a broadcast to Britain yesterday, said: "Italy will accept any demands from the Allies that could possibly sound just and practicable.

"The British and Americans have asked for our unconditional surrender. If we were given half a chance we could really do things in a serious way."

Germans clash with Italians

GERMAN troops have clashed with Italian civilians in the Calabrian towns of Castrovillari and Corenza, which the Germans are said to be evacuating, according to reports reaching the Italian frontier late last night.

Similar disturbances between Germans and Italians are going on in Bologna after the Allied bombings, the report added.

Peace demonstrations occurred in Bologna after Friday's raids. University students crowded the streets, demanding an immediate peace.

Demonstrations are also going on in Milan, Turin and Genoa. Many arrests have been made by troops and military-police.—B.U.P.

Nazis send Herriot to a mental home

M. Herriot, the former French Prime Minister, had been confined in a mental home as the doctors state he is suffering from incurable mental disease, German overseas radio said last night.

M. Herriot was interned by the German authorities for trying to contact the Allies in North Africa. His guards reported that he showed signs of mental disturbance and hallucinations.

The landings on "The Toe" and the progress of British and Canadian invasion troops are shown in this Sunday Express map. Facing the Eighth Army is bleak country—of granite rocks or forested with pine and beech. For a few miles beyond the beaches there is a strip of rich land—and then the great granite massif. There are few roads—and all of them bad.

BIG SOVIET ADVANCES, 400 PLACES CAPTURED

ALL along the present 600-mile-long offensive front in Russia the German armies were in full retreat last night. From the Sea of Azov, in the south, to the Smolensk area, west of Moscow, Russian advances were reported by Moscow.

The capture by the Russians of two vitally important towns was announced. They are Gorlovka, in the Donetz Basin, only 25 miles from the steel centre of Stalino, and Merefa, the important railway junction 19 miles south-west of Kharkov, the only town of any consequence in the Kharkov area that the Germans still held.

Altogether 400 places were announced by Moscow as having been liberated, while advances ranged all along the front from four to 15 miles.

Key rail town

Here are the advances reported in Moscow's official communiqué:—

Donetz Basin.—Soviet troops successfully developed their offensive and advanced from seven to 15 miles, occupying more than 90 inhabited localities. These included the town and large railway station of Bedantsev, the town of Zolatieva, the town and railway station of Gorlovka, the town and large railway junction of Nikitovka, the town and large railway junction of Yenomais, the town of Kalinin, the district centre of Stalinsk, the province of Yama, and the following inhabited localities: Perebryanka, Troiskaya, Luzhanskaya, Alkhabatskaya, and the following large railway stations: Pshenichnaya, Natalyebka and Almaznaya.

THE VOROSHILOVGRAD PROVINCE HAS BEEN COMPLETELY LIBERATED FROM THE GERMAN INVADERS.

Konotop (on the hinge between the southern and central fronts)—Soviet troops successfully continued to develop their offensive and advanced on different sectors from seven to eight miles, and occupied more than 150 localities, including the district centre of Chernigobsk province, the town of Korop and Ulyanovka and Shtepovka.

West and south-west of Kharkov.—Soviet troops advanced and occupied several localities, including the town and railway junction of Merefa.

South of Bryansk.—Soviet troops moved forward from four to seven miles and occupied 50 localities.

Smolensk.—Soviet troops continued to advance and occupied several inhabited localities.

Stalino threat

During the day, the communiqué added, 90 German tanks were put out of action and 31 enemy planes were shot down by A.A. fire and in air combats.

The most spectacular Russian advances are on the Donetz Basin, the rich industrial area, where earlier reports yesterday said the Germans had been routed and were in full retreat to the west.

Stalino, capital of the Donetz is being rapidly encircled.

The capture of Debaltsevo, an important railway junction, brings the Russians to within 37 miles of Stalino from the north-east, while in the south-east they are only 22 miles from the city following the capture of Ilovaisk.

The crumbling of the Donetz front, says a B.U.P. cable from Moscow, is due not only to the new advances in the Kharkov area, which threaten to cut off the whole Donetz, but also to local encircling movements by the Russians in the Donetz area itself, and the heavy toll which Russian Cossacks are taking of the German forces.

Reuter cables from Moscow said the whole German "east wall" in Russia was cracking, with the Germans falling back before ever-stronger Soviet blows.

Day attack on Boulogne

Ships bombed

R.A.F. bombers, continuing their non-stop daylight offensive against Axis-held territory, switched yesterday from airfields to railway marshalling yards and shipping. They attacked Rouen, Amiens and Abbeville—all of them important junctions—and ships in Boulogne harbour.

The bombers were escorted by fighters.

'Pleasure trip'

A New Zealand wing commander, who led Mitchells on the Rouen raid, said: "It was a pleasure trip. There were no enemy fighters and practically no flak."

Spitfire pilots from this section reported hits on yards, warehouses and railway bridges.

"Looking from Rouen to the east, I could see extremely large fires and smoke about 30 miles away," one pilot said.

Bostons carried out the raid at Amiens, where railway workshops were hit. There was some fighter opposition here and the leader of a Norwegian squadron destroyed one Me.109 and damaged another.

Soon after the aircraft had landed from the morning operations more Mitchells, Venturas and Bostons went out for the attack on Boulogne Harbour.

Pilots of the Alsace (Fighting French), Mysore and Natal fighter squadrons gave high cover to the Bostons. An F.W.190 was shot down when six enemy fighters were chased over the forest of Crecy.

French patriots blow up strategic frontier railway

ALL occupied Western Europe was astir last night as news of the British landing in Italy spread swiftly across the Continent.

In France and Denmark patriots were in action against the Germans and their quisling supporters.

The railway line running from Thonon, on the French shore of Lake Geneva, to Annemasse, a distance of 17 miles, has been blown up at several points, according to Algiers radio.

Oil dumps fired

"German oil dumps have also been destroyed by patriots," said the announcer.

From German controlled sources come the report that General de Lattre de Tassigny (the first French officer to lead an armed revolt against the Germans in France) had escaped from Riom prison.

Messages from the Franco-Swiss border yesterday stated that the police station of St. Etienne, near Lyons, was attacked by patriots armed with machine guns.

Meanwhile, the German-controlled Paris radio yesterday continued to warn the French people of an imminent Allied invasion.

Invasion prelude

Robert de Beauplan, political commentator, said that Friday's air raids on Paris were a prelude to this attack.

Three further reports from inside Europe reached London last night to prove that France expects Anglo-American forces to invade France. They were:—

(1) A "pre-alarm" zone has been proclaimed along 150 miles of the south coast, from the Italian frontier to Marseilles;

(2) In the Haute-Savoie—the region at the Swiss-Italian corner of France—German troops are taking over, and the Italians are being pulled south;

(3) A "plan for repression" has been completed to purge the French patriots the day the Allies land.

The German Overseas Agency announced last night that "a number of British agents involved in acts of sabotage had been arrested in Denmark."

The agency again warns that everybody must hand over all rifles and pistols to the Germans tomorrow—on penalty of death.

Last night reports reaching Stockholm state that a bridge was blown up over the canal at Christianshaven, while Roskilde railway station has been put out of action by saboteurs.

A series of explosions occurred as a long train laden with German war material was leaving Roskilde station. The track was blown up over a long stretch and the train derailed.

Blow at Naples expected

RESPONSIBLE Italian officials have told journalists in Rome that the Italian Command expect the Allies to land near Naples to cut off Southern Italy, which would then be occupied by the landing forces from Sicily, says B.U.P.

The Italians are interpreting the landings as the Allied intention not to occupy the entire Italian peninsula, although they believed the Allies would advance as far as Naples, after which they would consolidate their southern positions for use as a springboard against the Balkans.

BEAT 100 FIGHTERS

Bombers hit railway

ONE hundred enemy fighters, adopting a new "formation technique," rose to intercept U.S. Liberator bombers from the Middle East which raided Sulmona, vital railway junction 75 miles east of Rome.

Fierce battles followed above the target area, but the fighters failed to stop the Liberators from carrying out their mission.

After shooting down 27 of the fighters and probably destroying another six, the Liberators went on to bomb railway installations and an explosives factory.

Direct hits

The raid is officially described as being "highly successful."

A concentration of bombs struck the main railway station, warehouses, locomotive repair shops and intersection railroad yards. Other direct hits were scored on an administration building.

Hits on the explosives plant and storage sheds resulted in great explosions.

Six Liberators are missing from the raid.

CIANO IS ARRESTED

Edda also seized

CIANO, Mussolini's son-in-law and Italy's ex-Foreign Minister, has been arrested, according to the Turin newspaper Stampa, quoted in an A.P. message from the Italian frontier last night.

Stampa said it was believed that Ciano's wife, Edda, had also been arrested.

Ciano had "taken refuge in the house of a foreign personality from across the ocean," it was added.

This, it is considered, may have been the home of the Argentine representative to the Holy See.

RADIO—PAGE 6

War latest

RUSSIA ON NEW COMMISSION

A Joint Mediterranean Commission is being established by the United Nations for the purpose of handling political matters arising from the war.

Russia will be represented on the commission.

Russia has also definitely agreed to join in a tripartite meeting of the Foreign Ministers of U.S., Britain and Russia.

BRITISH IN FAR EAST WAR

Active participation by British forces in the Pacific war against Japan was discussed yesterday in a conference in Washington between Mr. Churchill and Sir Owen Dixon, Australian Minister in Washington.

Nazis protect Mussolini: Plan 'quisling' Italy

The newspaper Stampa, of Turin, reported yesterday that Mussolini was still on the island of Ponza, but under "protection" of a German garrison.

Other reports say that possession of the ex-Duce caused conflict between the Badoglio Government and the Nazis, the latter holding Mussolini with a threat to restore him to power.

It is believed in some quarters that Mussolini will soon be moved to Germany, where Farinacci—now spoken of as an Italian quisling—escaped disguised in S.S. uniform, and where, according to some reports, Count Ciano has also arrived.—A.P.

DAILY MIRROR, Thursday, September 9, 1943.

Daily Mirror

SEPT 9

No. 12,397
ONE PENNY
Registered at the G.P.O. as a Newspaper.

First of the final victories

ITALY IS OUT

Announcement of defeat

This is how General Eisenhower announced the surrender over Algiers radio at 5.30 last night:

"This is General Dwight Eisenhower, Commander-in-Chief Allied Forces: The Italian Government has surrendered its armed forces unconditionally.

"As Allied C.-in-C. I have granted a military armistice. The terms of this have been approved by the Governments of the United Kingdom, the United States and the Union of the Soviet Socialist Republics. I am thus acting in the interests of the United Nations.

"The Italian Government has bound itself to abide by these terms without reservation.

"The Armistice was signed by my representative and representatives of Marshal Badoglio and it becomes effective at this instant.

"Hostilities between the armed forces of the United Nations and those of Italy terminate at once.

"All Italians who now act to help eject the German aggressors from Italian soil will have the assistance and support of the United Nations."

Fleet and Army of 7,000,000 lost to Axis

80,000 British prisoners will come home

ITALY has laid down her arms in unconditional surrender to the United Nations—utterly defeated on lan[d] and sea and in the air. The birthplace of Fascism is th[e] first of the Axis pillars to fall; the fate of the other[s] is now beyond all doubt.

SEVEN MILLION ITALIAN SOLDIERS HAVE CEASED TO FIGHT THE ALLIES, AND LAST NIGHT MARSHAL BADOGLIO HIMSELF BROADCAST A SURRENDER PROCLAMATION, WHICH WARNED THE GERMANS:

"We will oppose attacks from any other quarter."

As he was speaking Allied planes were dropping "battle orders" leaflets all over Italy.

These declared:—

"Backed by the might of the Allies, Italy now has the chance of taking vengeance on the German oppressors and of aiding in the expulsion of the eternal enemy from Italian soil."

The Italians were told to give the Allied armies every assistance and obey their orders in this phase of the "liberation of Europe."

Railway, dock and road workers were ordered to see to it that no German troops or materials are permitted to move.

"Workers, the war in Italy is your battle of transport.

Continued on Back Page

V SIGNS

GERMAN Home Service radio was broadcasting a musical programme under the heading, "Let us go on dreaming," as Eisenhower made his announcement of armistice.

CANADIAN Prime Minister, Mr. Mackenzie King, proclaimed today a National Thanksgiving Day

DEMONSTRATIONS of rejoicing at the signing of the Armistice are taking place all over Italy, according to reports reaching Madrid

IN New York's Italian quarter bars and saloons offered free drinks to all-comers

ON the New York Stock Exchange yesterday, war stocks were unloaded and so-called "peace shares" moved upward sharply

GERMAN overseas radio announced last night that all telephone communication between Berlin and Italy had been severed.

BADOGLIO'S daughter-in-law—Countess Anna Badoglio—and daughter, Maria, have arrived at a large hotel in Lausanne, in Switzerland, where they will remain for about ten days, according to Berlin radio last night

ITALIAN NAVY TOLD: GO TO ALLIED PORTS

ADMIRAL CUNNINGHAM, Allied Naval C.-in-C. in the Mediterranean, last night called to the Italian Fleet and Merchant Navy to make for Allied ports and protect themselves against the Germans.

He appealed to them not to scuttle except as a last resort, for their ships would be needed to carry supplies to Italy.

Here is Admiral Cunningham's message as broadcast by Algiers radio in Italian:—

"Sailors of the Italian Fleet and of the Italian Merchant Marine, your country has ceased hostilities against the Allied Nations.

"The German armed forces are now openly hostile to the Italian people, whom they have so often betrayed, and intend to seize your ships.

"Your ships are urgently needed to assist in the work of carrying supplies into Italy, and your warships to protect them from the Germans.

"Take heed, therefore, and do not scuttle your ships or allow them to be captured.

"The forces of the United Nations are watching out to receive you and protect you. Sail your ships and follow the directions given you by the United Nations.

"Ships in the Mediterranean, sail to a place safe from the interference of the German armed forces. Sail, if you can, to North Africa or Gibraltar, into Tripoli or Malta, to Haifa or Alexandria or to Sicily, and there await the outcome of events.

"Ships in the Black Sea, sail to Russian ports. If you have

Continued on Back Page

Booked for "Blighty"

IMMEDIATE release of roughly 80,000 British prisoners in Italian hands will unquestionably be one of the prior conditions imposed.

Recent reports, says Reuter, indicate that probably no more than 2,000 British prisoners were smuggled out of Italy into Germany, and that any German plans to speed up this smuggling were frustrated by congestion of Italian railways following the bombing of key rail targets.

Altogether there are about fifty camps housing British prisoners. There were two camps in Sicily, but it is assumed by the Red Cross that these were merely transit camps.

Some of the camps are within or near the line of the River Po, an area in which the Germans have recently been concentrating several divisions of troops.

There are roughly 400,000 Italian prisoners, 300,000 of whom surrendered up to the fall of Tunisia.

A few hundred have been exchanged between the two countries, but not enough to affect the totals materially.

'TREACHERY'—HUNS

THE news has hit the Huns in a tender spot. Broadcasts by German radio last night contained at least a dozen references to "betrayal" and "treachery." Here are some extracts:—

In English:—

"The German Government has been prepared for this open betrayal by the present Italian Government and has therefore taken all the necessary military measures.

"That it was treachery there can be no doubt—treachery not only against an ally who has remained unflinchingly loyal in spite of the greatest difficulties, but treachery against the interests of the Italian people

Another commentator described it as "one of the most despicable acts of treachery ever committed against an ally."

In German:—

"The veil is lifted from Badoglio's treacherous game.

"A clique of Jews and elements alien to the Italian nation have brought about the treachery against the Italian nation.

"Germany and Europe are strong enough to punish the originators of that crime, and German arms will carry out that punishment."

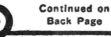

THURSDAY, SEPTEMBER 16, 1943

Closing Prices

BLACK OUT 7.45 to 6.6 | Moon Rises 8.43 p.m. New Moon Sept. 29 | RADIO Page Six

LATE NIGHT

THE STAR

No. 17,236 ★ ONE PENNY

Reinforcements Pour In To 5th

BRIDGEHEAD IS STRENGTHENED

WITH REINFORCEMENTS POURING IN, ALLIED TROOPS HAVE TIGHTENED THEIR HOLD ON THE SALERNO BRIDGEHEAD. COMMUNIQUES FROM GENERAL EISENHOWER'S HEADQUARTERS GAVE THIS NEWS TODAY. THEY ALSO REVEALED THAT EIGHTH ARMY TROOPS HAD ADVANCED ANOTHER 12 MILES TO SCALEA

"On the Fifth Army front our troops have strengthened their hold on the beach-head," said the communique dealing with land operations. "Reinforcements continue to arrive. Naval and air support are playing a great part in asssisting consolidation. In the Taranto area there is nothing to report. Eighth Army troops have reached Scalea and are pushing north."

The naval communique stated: "Unloading on the Salerno beaches continues satisfactorily. Destroyers working inshore are bombarding enemy

positions and troop concentrations. Yesterday targets in the Salerno area were also bombarded by battleships."

The air communique announced: "Attacks on the enemy around the Salerno area were continued by the North-West African Air Forces during Tuesday night and throughout yesterday. Heavy, medium, and light bombers, fighter bombers, and fighters attacked the roads, enemy transport, troop concentrations and positions, mainly in the Eboli area.

"Fighters maintained patrols over the area and destroyed five enemy aircraft.

"Last night roads in the Terra Annunciata (Pompeii) area were attacked by our night bombers. From these operations and from patrols and reconnaissances four of our aircraft are missing."

A military spokesman at Allied headquarters this afternoon stressed that General Clark's Fifth Army was composed equally of British and American troops, and there "should be no attempt to make this an exclusive American or British show."

The American and British troops were using some of the most daring tactics of the war and accepting "suicide" assignments as a matter of course.

General Clark was personally on the field with the troops, declaring that there must be no withdrawals and that every soldier must fight to the last.

At General Spaatz's headquarters it was stated that the daily bomb tonnage deluging the Germans in the Salerno area was "vastly greater than any previous effort in the Mediterranean." This included

CONTINUED ON BACK PAGE, Col. Three

RAF BOMB FRENCH FACTORY

Berlin Targets Also Attacked

AIRCRAFT of Bomber Command made a heavy attack on the rubber factory at Montlucon, some 40 miles north-west of Vichy, last night.

An Air Ministry communique added: "Cloud over the target made it difficult to see the full results of the bombing, but first reports indicate that the attack was effective.

"Targets in North-west Germany and in Berlin were also attacked.

"Fighter Command aircraft on intruder operations over France attacked a number of enemy airfields and transport targets.

"Eight aircraft of Bomber Command and two of Fighter Command are missing."

FIRST VISIT

This was the first time the RAF have visited Montlucon.

The rubber factory there is one of the two biggest tyre factories in France, receiving a large allocation of raw material, Buna, from Germany. Before the war it employed 3,500 workers.

The factory may have been producing fewer tyres than the pre-war output, but they have been of a much heavier type, such as those required by German army vehicles.

Most of the output has gone direct to Germany.

AIRFIELDS BOMBED

Within an hour of the return of Spitfires and Typhoons from the dusk operation with American bombers, the first of several Fighter Command intruder aircraft took off for widespread attacks on enemy airfields, marshalling yards and locomotives in occupied territory, states the Air Ministry News Service.

Airfields at Evreux, Coulommiers, St. Andre and Abbeville were among the targets.

The last-named received a successful concentrated attack from Typhoons and Hurricanes which dived through flak to bomb by moonlight.

Hits were scored on dispersals, causing "huge flashes," to quote one pilot.

Other pilots reported seeing several small fires and heavy black smoke as they went in to release their bombs.

Paris Targets Bombed In Dusk Raid.—Page Five, Col. One.

Montgomery: "We Hit Germany Soon"

Algiers radio today quoted this order of the day issued to men of the Eighth Army by General Montgomery:

"The war will not be over until we can strike at Germany directly. But we will do so soon."

3 Killed In Lisbon Crash

One of nine British planes about to land at Sintra airfield, 15 miles from Lisbon, struck a wireless-aerial tower and crashed, three members of the crew being killed, cabled Exchange today.

Italian Duke Escapes

Dutch radio, quoting reports from Berne, said that the Duke of Turin, a member of the Royal House of Italy, has arrived in Switzerland.

London Raid: 4 Out Of 15 Nazis Down

FOUR aircraft were shot down during raids on Britain in the night.

Three of the raiders, according to the Ministry of Home Security, were destroyed over this country; the fourth was shot down over Melun airfield, France, by Flying-Officer K. F. Dacre, a Mosquito pilot, said the Air Ministry today.

Fifteen bombers crossed the coast; two or three reached London, where there was a warning lasting an hour.

When a bomb fell on a recreation ground in one London area a good deal of blast damage was done to adjoining houses. One man was injured.

A factory was also damaged, but a fire which began was promptly put out. Two shops were burned out.

Major A. Thorp, aged 60, a bomb expert, was killed when a bomb fell in front of his home in a South-East village. He had just opened the door to look out.

Four other people who were trapped were quickly rescued.

Bombs at another village caused no casualties and only slight damage.

In another town a bomb which fell on allotments damaged about 30 houses, some seriously.

WOMAN KILLED BY A.A. SHELL

When two A.A. shells fell at Chadwell Heath during the night, Mrs. Susan Sammons, of Burlington-avenue, Chadwell Heath, was killed by splinters. She was on her way home from a cinema. Her husband was fire watching at Woolwich.

Another shell fell on a paint factory, which was set alight. Considerable damage was done. A NFS company officer received burns and other injuries while fighting the fire.

100-Mile Drive Ahead Of 8th

A party of British war correspondents, including Eric Lloyd Williams, of Reuters, has driven nearly 100 miles across no man's land in front of the advancing Eighth Army to a point only a few miles south of the Fifth Army positions on the right flank of the Salerno bridgehead.

Williams cabled this afternoon: "We didn't hear a single shot fired or see a single German. We found ourselves on a grand motoring run along the Corniche road.

"At Policastro, about 25 miles from the Fifth Army's right flank, the people told us that Italian soldiers were sniping at German sappers trying to blow up a nearby bridge. Italian soldiers cleared the mines as soon as the Germans planted them.

"Today we continued our 100-mile dash between the Eighth and Fifth Armies and linked up with an American patrol about ten miles south of the main American positions around the Gulf of Salerno."

Overcast

Straits of Dover weather today: Dull and overcast, with strong south-westerly breeze; sea choppy and many white-capped breakers in Channel; fairly high ceiling of cloud; good visibility; moderate temperature.

Italian Ex-Army Chief's "Suicide"

Former Chief of the Italian General Staff, Marshal Ugo Cavallero, who was stated to have been freed from captivity by the Germans, was reported today, in a broadcast message from the Nazi-controlled Italian News Agency, to have committed suicide, being unable, it was said, "to bear the burden of dishonour and the shameful treachery of his country."

Gen. Cavallero, who was 63, was known in Italy as the "businessman-soldier," dividing his time between the Army and big steel interests. He resigned last January from his post as Chief of Staff.

He was Chief of the Italian Operations Bureau in the last war, and gained a reputation as an able organiser. He was president of Italy's military delegation at the Peace Conference, and served on the Allied Military Committee at Versailles in 1919-20.

From 1937 to 1940 he was Commander-in-Chief in East Africa, and afterwards Commander-in-Chief in Albania until January, 1941.

After the arrest of Mussolini, Cavallero was said to be imprisoned with Mussolini.

"Save The Pope"

An underground Italian radio station calling itself Free Milan, stated today:

"The Pope is a prisoner. We must save him. We know that German parachutists descended on Vatican City and are guarding the entrance. Germans are in control of Vatican radio.

"Not more than 50,000 German troops are in Rome. All Romans and all Italians living in the provinces around Rome, all officers at the head of their units, must march against the Germans. Churchbells should ring and call the people to chase the Germans out of the capital."

Trapped By Letter

Felix Cassidy Mathieson, aged 47, a postman, of Churchbury-road, Eltham, was sentenced to three months' imprisonment at Woolwich today for stealing a £1 note from a letter in course of transmission at Catford, and stealing a postal packet containing cigars.

It was said that a test letter containing £4 was posted in a pillar-box and £1 was missing from it when he handed it in although it was apparently intact.

Ship Missed Convoy

When Joseph Frances Roland Keeble, aged 38, a ship's fireman, of Burrell-road, Ipswich, was charged at Ipswich today with disobeying orders to go to sea, it was said that a ship was delayed in New York because of his action and missed a convoy. He was fined £5.

BIG RAIDS EAST OF SALERNO

"Liberators of the Ninth USAAF bombed the marshalling yards at Potenza, 60 miles east of Salerno, yesterday, scoring direct hits on a railway bridge. Severe damage was caused in the area of the yards," said this afternoon's Middle East communique.

"RAF Liberators and Halifaxes bombed a road junction at Potenza during Tuesday night.

"Wellington bombers attacked sidings and the main railway line at Khalkis, in Southern Greece, on Tuesday night and shot up a goods train an engine, and railway sheds.

"A Junkers 88 was intercepted and destroyed by Spitfires in the Benghazi area.

"From these and other operations, none of our aircraft is missing."

MTBs ATTACK NAZI CONVOY

The German News Agency, quoted by Reuter, today said: "British MTB's repeatedly attacked a German convoy off the Norwegian coast yesterday morning. Thanks to the accurate fire of the German escort craft the attacks could not be developed. The enemy boats retired under cover of a smokescreen after they had been hit several times."

Dearer Dates

The maximum retail price of dates is to be increased from 7d. to 9d. per lb. under a new control and maximum prices order for dried fruit which comes into force on Sunday.

EIGHTH ARMY NEWS

Thursday, 23 SEPTEMBER, 1943 | No 58 : Vol. 2 | SICILY

OFFENSIVE TAKES SHAPE AS

EIGHTH ARMY CAPTURE VITAL RAIL CENTRE

The 8th Army from the south have driven up to take Potenza, almost due east of Salerno in the centre of southern Italy. Rail lines from Foggia, Taranto and Naples converge at Potenza, making it the most important communications centre in Southern Italy.

It is just two weeks since the Fifth Army first landed at Salerno. Today the whole of the Salerno valley has been cleared of the Germans and the enemy is being chased into the hills. At some places our troops have pushed about 20 miles inland.

North of Salerno the Germans are falling back more reluctantly and are making use of the good rearguard country.

A report from Algiers says the extent of German demolitions in Naples indicates that the enemy has given up all hope of holding the city.

The Germans are still clinging stubbornly in the rough country north of Salerno. The terrain, which one reporter describes as more difficult than any in Tunisia or Sicily, greatly favours the defenders, and the Germans are fighting back hard with machine-guns, artillery and mortars.

5th Army troops have forged ahead, unhampered by enemy air action, and have captured San Cipriano, 16 miles northeast of Salerno. All of the Salerno valley is now in our hands, and reinforcements are landing steadily.

The sandy beaches have been converted by our engineers into the makings of a fine port and Allied aircraft control the skies.

100 SHOT FOR ONE GERMAN

Refugees escaping from Naples say the German governor of Naples has decreed that 100 Italians will be shot for every German soldier that is injured.

Flying Fortresses and medium bombers from Northwest Africa have made more devastating attacks on communications lines by which the Germans will retreat from Naples.

Tactical Air Force planes have made continuous attacks on roads, railroads and gun positions a dozen miles ahead of our forces. No enemy air opposition was met and all our planes returned safely.

Marshal Badoglio attacked Mussolini's policy last night in a broadcast to the Italian people.

He said: « The Germans have always treated us as an inferior race and the Italian people will not forget that Italian soldiers had been sent to France, Greece, Russia and the Balkans with the sole object of fighting for Germany. »

He went on to say that the armistice conditions were hard but reminded the Italian people that they had been defeated.

POST CHIEF ON MAIL DELAY

As a result of a letter published in « Eighth Army News » in which a L/Cpl complained that the delay in mail was caused because Air Mail was taking too long to reach Eighth Army, the Army Post Chief has written to « Eighth Army News. »

He reveals that the Army Postal Authorities are already investigating the cause of the delay.

Lt-Col. W. Scott, the Assistant Director of Army Postal Services, says: « The Army Postal Authorities also think that the Air Mail is taking too long to get to the Central Mediterranean Forces and they are already trying to track down the cause of the delay.

« The reason when we do get at the cause of the trouble may, of course, be one which we are not at liberty to publish, but if we do get results they will speak for themselves.

« As you remark, the service has been worse in the past, and in the case of the forward troops it will be a long trek by road for the mail until we can get air transport forward. »

CORSICAN PATRIOTS SLAUGHTER GERMANS

Corsican patriots, 15,000 of them have been armed, are helping to throw the Germans out of their island.

Operating with the regular soldiers they are using their knowledge of the country to its best effect. Over one thousand Germans have been killed and some hundreds taken prisoner despite the speed of their retreat.

8th Air Force Liberators, operating from bases in Northwest Africa, struck two heavy blows on the Germans' escape route from Corsica. One formation attacked the port of Legnan on Italy's northwest coast.

The harbor was crowded with ships and many hits were reported. Another formation dropped a pattern of bombs on the harbour at Bastia in Corsica. Wellingtons returned at night to give Bastia another pounding.

On the other side of Italy in the Mediterranean there are more reports of trouble for the Germans in Yugoslavia. Yugoslavs, fighting with Italians, were reported to have occupied the Adriatic port of Split a few days ago. Latest reports say the Germans have been cleared out of a peninsula south of Split.

Also the Yugoslavs are reported to be driving along the railroad in the Trieste region at the northern end of the Adriatic and have considerably disorganized German traffic through this region. One unconfirmed report says they have captured Gorizia, north of Trieste and well inside the Italian border.

CHILDREN BURIED ALIVE

Moscow radio says that the Soviet Atrocity Commission reported more than [illegible]0,000 Soviet citizens and war prisoners died in concentration camps set up by the Germans in the Orel town prison.

Graves containing several thousand bodies each were found in the forests outside the city. Children had been buried alive. Special squads of dynamiters set up by the German command destroyed towns villages and areas.

RUSSIANS IN SIGHT OF KIEV

Smolensk Outflanked ?

Kiev, 24 miles from the Russians closing in on the city along a 100 mile front, is now within sight of our Allies, though the Dnieper river presents a formidable barrier to its capture. Down in the Ukraine the Soviets are now 15 miles northeast of Dnyepropetrovsk, and still farther south are within shelling distance of Melitopol.

The Russians are still pressing rapidly ahead. Yesterday 880 more towns were liberated, making a total of well over 5000 in 5 days.

Smolensk is being slowly but steadily outflanked. In a drive towards Vitebsk north of Smolensk, the town of Demidof, 40 miles northwest of Smolensk, was announced as captured in an Order of the Day describing it as « One of the strongest defence positions ». The Russian drive in this sector has covered 30 miles in 2 days.

18 Mile Gains

South of Smolensk the Red Armies have driven closer to Roslavl, and 18 mile gains are reported in the drive from the Desna toward Gomel.

Down in the Kuban, where the Germans had at one time hopes of reaching the Caucasian oil fields, the Moscow communique announces the capture of Anapa, midway between the Kerch straits and Novorosissk. The Germans have apparently given up hopes of maintaining the bridgehead, and they didn't gain a single barrel of oil.

The roads into the Ukraine are reported to be crowded with refugees pouring back into the rich farmlands in the wake of the Russian armies. Farm animals are among the goods the Russians are taking with them to put the large collective farms back into operation.

NEW ALLIED LANDING

As dawn broke over a small, sandy beach six miles north of Finchhaven, Jap base in New Guinea, Allied troops poured ashore.

Fighters swept the skies and U.S. warships trained their guns on known Japanese strongpoints.

There was little opposition.

Finchaven is 60 miles North of Lae, recently captured by Australian and American troops, and brings the Allies much closer to the main Japanese base of Rabaul in New Britain.

EDEN WARNS FRANCO

Britain's Foreign Secretary has warned the Fascist General Franco about the pro-Nazi attitude.

Mr. Eden, addressing the House of Commons, revealed that His Majesty's Government had warned Franco about his Axis activities, including the Blue Division fighting against our Russian Allies.

The Spanish policy in Tangiers, where German agents enjoy a wide degree of freedom, was also among the protests.

Mr. Eden said that **the Spanish Government had promised to investigate the complaints.**

MONDAY, OCTOBER 11, 1943

FINAL NIGHT EXTRA

Evening Standard

37,155 BLACK-OUT 6.48 p.m. to 6.47 a.m. MOON rises 5.51 p.m., sets 5.26 a.m. ONE PENNY

"Devastating Defeat" for Kesselring at Termoli

EIGHTH WIN BIG VICTORY

Now Driving Across the Italian Peninsula

Kesselring has suffered a devastating defeat at the hands of General Montgomery, said Cairo radio this afternoon. The battle of Termoli has been won.

THE EIGHTH ARMY ARE NOW THRUSTING ACROSS THE ITALIAN PENINSULA FROM LARINO. THEY HAVE CAPTURED THE VILLAGES OF LUCERA AND SAN MARCO, ON THE ROAD TO VINCHIATURO.

Vinchiaturo is 62 miles by rail from Termoli, and is the junction for Benevento, already captured by the Fifth Army.

"The Allied occupation of Vinchiaturo will force the Germans to carry out a general retreat towards the north," added Cairo radio.

To-day's communiqué records the capture of Ponte Andolfo, 12 miles north of Benevento, and adds:

"Eighth Army patrols pushed vigorously westward

"On the Fifth Army front patrol activity continues

"In the central and the northern sectors limited advances have been made

"The enemy continues to fight hard, and is using the broken and difficult country to assist his defence. Demolitions are still being met on a heavy scale."

Ponte Andolfo is north of Ponte (whose capture was reported yesterday) on the central Italian front. This new advance by the Fifth Army straightens out the bulge in the Allied line of advance across Italy

VOLTURNO DUEL

The Fifth Army are now 40 miles beyond Naples, and, according to Algiers radio, there has been a violent exchange of gunfire along the River Volturno.

The Allied air communiqué says: "Medium and light bombers attacked enemy road and rail communications in the Italian battle areas.

"Gun positions and troop concentrations were attacked by medium bombers, fighters and fighter-bombers.

"Last night the coast road at Terracina was attacked by night bombers."

HEAVY FIGHTING

Earlier reports from Algiers radio to-day said American troops of the Fifth Army were engaged in heavy fighting north-east of Capua

The reports coincided with Berlin messages that "powerful Allied drives" were being made on the Volturno positions

Winston Burdett, broadcasting from Algiers to-day, quoted a military spokesman as saying: "German resistance is toughening all along the line.

"There will be hard slogging ahead, especially along the Volturno."

Naples Has Its Biggest Explosion

The worst explosion since the Allied occupation of Naples occurred in the heart of the city yesterday, said a despatch reaching London to-day quoted by Reuter.

A time bomb went off in the artillery barracks formerly used by the Germans. Many were buried under the debris. Already 25 dead and 35 wounded have been taken out.

General Mark Clark, Fifth Army commander, visited the scene and ordered the neighbouring buildings to be evacuated.

Before leaving the Naples area the Germans blew up the great Ilva steel works and chemical factory, one of Italy's largest, employing 4000 men. They spent 15 days systematically laying cordite charges.

The Toughest Job at Cos

FELL TO SQUADRON OF R.A.F. REGT.

A squadron of the R.A.F. Regiment, transported by air, complete with guns, played a great part in the defence of the island of Cos, said George Crawley, Reuter's special correspondent, in a cable from Cairo to-day.

An Army major who has returned from the island said to-day:

"These boys had the toughest job on Cos. Although some of them were having their baptism of fire they stood like veterans under the blazing guns of the Junkers 88s and Messerschmitt 109s."

The squadron was landed on the first day of the Allied entry into the Dodecanese.

During one week of almost incessant air attacks the R.A.F. Regiment shot down five enemy aircraft, with three others probables.

In low-flying attacks on aircraft and R.A.F. gun positions on the island the enemy swept in almost at zero feet, giving the R.A.F. men only a few seconds in which to focus their gun sights.

That the enemy later kept at a more respectful height was a testimony to the accuracy of their fire.

Fire-Watcher's Death Mystery

Police inquiring into the death of George Eaton, 57, a firewatcher of Lund-lane, Lundwood, Barnsley are trying to get in touch with his son, Frederick Eaton, a 19-year-old colliery worker, who may be able to help them.

They have issued a description of the son.

George Eaton was found on Friday at his home with head injuries.

Italian Legation Interned

The Italian Minister in Copenhagen and the entire Legation staff have been interned after refusing to recognise Mussolini as head of the new Italian Government, according to the Danish Press Service in Stockholm, says British United Press.

AIRFIELDS OF GREECE HIT AGAIN

Pounding of the Greek airfields goes on. Those at Athens and Araxos were hit by heavy bombers of the North-west African Air Force yesterday.

On Saturday heavy bombers attacked the airfields at Maritza and Calata on Rhodes and Heraklion in Crete, says the Allied air communiqué

FRIENDS MEET ON VESUVIUS

After 13 Years

Two friends who had not seen each other for 13 years have met on Vesuvius

They are Captain Geoffrey Mason, a schoolmaster at Chippenham, and Corporal "Bill Bailey," from Shepton Mallet, Somerset

The story, as told to-day by Basil Gingell, Exchange Telegraph correspondent, who says Mason and Bailey last met each other on a botany course in England in 1930.

U-Boat Claims

The Germans to-day claimed that in the North Atlantic, the Mediterranean and other areas, U-boats had sunk eight merchant ships totalling 40,200 tons, three destroyers and one patrol boat.

Actress Sues for Breach

Evening Standard picture of Miss Marjorie Murray, of Boreham Wood, Herts, musical comedy actress, who brought an action for breach of promise of marriage in the King's Bench to-day. — *See PAGE EIGHT.*

MISSING Winant's Son

First-lieutenant John Winant, junior, son of the U.S. Ambassador in Great Britain, is missing from yesterday's U.S. raid on Munster.

It was his thirteenth raid. He took part in the Regensburg attack earlier this year, and his Fortress was the only one which successfully followed its group leader all the way to Africa.

Lieutenant Winant is 21. His father was an airman in the last war.

Three Killed in Car-Train Crash

Three people were killed and two injured at March, Cambs, to-day when a car in which they were travelling to work on a farm was in collision with an Edinburgh to Colchester passenger train at a railway crossing.

The dead were Mr. William Kisby, of Ramsey House, Dartford-road, March, the driver of the car; Mrs. S. P. Chambers, of Wisbech-road, March; and Mrs. King, of Wisbech-road

The two people injured were taken to Peterborough Hospital They are Mrs. Anker and Mrs Wright, both of Wisbech-road.

The train was delayed for 35 minutes and four coaches were detached owing to slight damage.

ARMY TEAM IN CRASH

Six soldiers were killed and 12 others seriously injured in a road collision in the Cotswolds early yesterday

They were returning in an Army lorry from a football match in which their regimental team had taken part.

Only one of the party escaped injury. The lorry crashed into a civilian lorry from Newport, Mon., which was drawn up at the side of the road.

CUNNINGHAM: MAN OF ACTION

Admiral Alfred Saalwachter, naval commentator over German overseas radio, to-day expressed these opinions of:

Admiral Sir Dudley Pound.—"He worked so hard he finally collapsed under the strain. He certainly did his duty as well as he could, and no more can be expected of any man."

Admiral Sir Andrew Cunningham.—"He scored his successes exclusively against Italian naval forces, though sometimes under rather difficult conditions. He displayed considerable initiative on some occasions. He is regarded as an advocate of action."

"Closed Areas"

Stuttgart, Friedrickshafen and Chemnitz have been declared closed areas, according to a German report reaching Reuter via Stockholm to-day.

Stuttgart was raided by the R.A.F. on Thursday.

KIEV: GERMAN LINE PIERCED

New Dnieper Bridgeheads

RUSSIAN TROOPS HAVE PIERCED IN DEPTH THE SEMI-CIRCULAR OUTER DEFENCES OF KIEV, SAYS BRITISH UNITED PRESS FROM MOSCOW.

Tremendous battles, as fierce as any fought in Russia, are now going on along the west bank of the Dnieper, as the Russians attempt to widen their bridgeheads around Kiev and south-east of Kremenchug.

The breach north of Kiev is so bad that two entire infantry formations, probably divisions, with anti-tank guns and mortars, have gone through the gap, Henry Cassidy, American broadcaster, reported from Moscow to-day.

"The Germans are still hitting back hard with infantry and tank counter-attacks and heavy air raids, but there no longer seems to be any question of their throwing the Russians back across the river," added Cassidy.

"The battle is now not so much for the Dnieper as for the high hills and important positions well west of the river."

Fresh bridgeheads have been established across the Dnieper north of Kiev and near Kremenchug.

Already, with Kiev in danger of being surrounded, the Germans are beginning to evacuate civilians from the city, and carry away loot, says Reuter.

Out of Range

The Luftwaffe are making as many as 2000 sorties a day in a vain attempt to check the stream of Russian troops pouring across the river. Red Army sappers

working under fire, are keeping the pontoon bridges in constant repair.

At some points, especially in the bridgehead south-west of Pereyeslavl, the river crossings are now out of range even of the enemy's heavy guns.

Heavy fighting is going on at the outer approaches to Vitebsk, where the Soviet spearhead has driven to within 15 miles of the city. The Germans are making very determined efforts to save this bastion.

Gomel is also gravely threatened by the broad Soviet wedge pushing from the north-east and the east.

Quiet Night Here

During darkness there has been nothing to report, says to-day's communique from the Ministry of Home Security.

PORTUGAL: STATEMENT BY SALAZAR

Dr. Salazar, the Portuguese Prime Minister, may make an important declaration to-day, according to reports reaching Madrid, says British United Press.

Diplomatic quarters in Madrid believe that Portugal may declare war on Japan unless the partly Portuguese-owned island of Timor, north of Australia, is evacuated immediately by the Japanese troops.

Other reports say that Dr. Salazar will announce that Portugal intends to take up an attitude of non-belligerency.

Anxious crowds are stated to be filling the Lisbon streets The city has experienced its first black-out. The Naval Brigade of the Portuguese Legion have been ordered to report to their barracks with full uniform and equipment

BRITISH CROSS INTO BURMA

British troops entered Burma, crossing a river, on the frontier, Tokyo radio said to-day.

About 250 British troops crossed the river in ten barges and engaged the Japanese forces a little more than half a mile over the frontier, said Tokyo.

The German overseas news agency said to-day that in Tokyo the Chindwin River move is expected to be followed by further operations.

"The enemy," the agency said, "will at least try to establish a link between India and the Chinese province of Yunnan by way of Northern Burma.

"At the same time enemy landing attempts on the Nicobar and Andaman Islands in the Bay of Bengal are considered likely as those islands could serve as bases for air attack on Burma, Malaya and the East Indies."

The same message reported a raid on the suburbs of Rangoon on Saturday night

CURTIN PUTS OFF VISIT

Evening Standard Correspondent
CAIRO, Monday.

The Australian Prime Minister, Mr. Curtin, has postponed his proposed visit to the United States and London.

He planned this visit—which would have been his first trip abroad as Prime Minister—after his sweeping election victory. He had intended making the trip this month, but now "finds it impossible to leave Australia at the present moment."

TURKS' SEA DEFENCES

The German overseas news agency, quoted by Reuter, to-day said:

"The Turkish Government have declared certain areas of the Turkish Black Sea coast military defence zones.

"This measure follows earlier orders declaring certain parts banned to all but military personnel."

Senators Vote Postwar Plan

3 Full Pages
Of Interesting Pictures in
Today's Pictorial Review

NEW YORK Journal-American

AN AMERICAN PAPER FOR THE AMERICAN PEOPLE

DAILY 5 Cents | SUNDAY, 10 Cents in New York City and 50-mile Zone. 15 Cents Elsewhere

No. 20,370—DAILY WEDNESDAY, OCTOBER 13, 1943 In Two Sections —Section One

B

7TH SPORTS
WALL ST.
SPECIAL

ITALY DECLARES WAR ON HITLER

WASHINGTON, Oct. 12 (AP).—President Roosevelt, Prime Minister Churchill and Premier Stalin today announced that Italy had declared war against Germany. The White House said Marshal Badoglio had communicated Italy's declaration against her former Axis partner to Gen. Eisenhower, Allied commander in the Mediterranean theater.

In his message to the General, Badoglio said that "by this act all ties with the dreadful past are broken and my government will be proud to be able to march with you on to the inevitable victory."

In a joint statement released by the White House, Roosevelt, Churchill and Stalin accepted "the active co-operation of the Italian nation and armed forces as co-belligerent in the war against Germany."

Italy thus turned against her former partner a little more than a month after her armistice with the Allied powers.

In a proclamation to the Italian people, Badoglio said that "shoulder to shoulder, we must march forward with our friends of the United States, of Great Britain, of Russia, and of all the other United Nations."

Badoglio said an Italian government headed by himself would be completed shortly and that representatives of every political party would be invited to participate so that it may constitute a true expression of democratic government.

PEOPLE ARE TO CHOOSE.

"The present arrangement will in no way impair the untrammeled right of the people of Italy to choose their own form of democratic government when peace is restored," the Marshal said.

"Italians! I inform you that His Majesty the King has given me the task of announcing today, the 13th day of October, the declaration of war against Germany."

The British, Soviet and American governments acknowledged the Italian pledge to submit to the will of the Italian people after the Nazis have been driven from their homeland.

Roosevelt, Churchill and Stalin said it was understood that "nothing can detract from the absolute

Continued on Page 4, Column 5.

Grill Queens Gardener in Sex Murder

A sullen, 51-year-old Queens gardener was seized today by Jamaica police as a suspect in the brutal sex murder of Mrs. Marie Pearson, mother of four, who was slain in a vacant lot Sunday night near her home at 144-08 Liberty ave.

The man was taken into custody at his home after a wild chase by two detectives who observed him following a woman only two blocks from the murder scene.

A powerful individual who came here from Italy in 1910, the suspect maintained through all-night questioning that he had nothing to do with the crime, continuing his denials this morning when taken to view the woman's body at the Queens morgue.

TAKEN TO MORGUE.

After his visit to the morgue, as well as to the weed-grown lot at Brisbin st. and Liberty ave., Jamaica, he was returned to Jamaica Police Headquarters where it was said he would be booked on homicide charges later.

The dramatic excursions with the suspect were ordered by Queens District Attorney Charles P. Sullivan, who accompanied detectives.

Confronted with the body of

Continued on Page 3, Column 3.

Epitaph by Japs

In marked contrast to the usual attitude of the Japanese to their enemies is this marker over the grave of an American pilot who was shot down during a raid on Kiska before the Nipponese evacuated that strategic island. The sign reads: *"Sleeping here, a brave air-hero who lost youth and happiness for his mother land."*

International News Photo.

2d Front Put 1st on Agenda By Soviets

MOSCOW, Oct. 13 (UP).—The first public Soviet pronouncement on American-British-Russian conference said emphatically today that primary consideration must be given to immediate joint Allied military action—in other words, the second front.

The Communist party organ Pravda published the comment on the forthcoming meeting of Secretary of State Hull, Foreign Secretary Eden and Foreign Commissar Molotov.

Discussion of such problems as postwar settlements and politico-economic co-operation can be achieved only as a result of recognition by the conferees of the immediate military action, Pravda said.

PART OF SOVIET UNION.

The editorial further made clear the Soviet Union's uncompromising position regarding the Baltic states and the Russian frontiers generally. The Baltics are considered an integral part of the Union, comparable to the relation of California to the United States, it said.

Pravda at the same time de-

Continued on Page 6, Column 4.

Senators Vote Postwar Plan

WASHINGTON, Oct. 13. (INS)—A Senate Foreign Relations Subcommittee, by a vote of seven to one, today approved a broad resolution pledging the United States to join in establishment of international authority to preserve future peace.

The resolution was described by members as a compromise between conflicting views on the best means of preventing future wars and suppressing aggressor nations.

The resolution reads:

"Resolved by the Senate of the United States;

"That the war against all our enemies be waged until complete victory is achieved;

"That the United States cooperate with its comrades-in-arms in securing a just and honorable peace;

"That the United States, acting through its Constitutional processes, join with free and sovereign nations in the establishment and maintenance of international authority with power to prevent aggression and to preserve the peace of the world."

The sub-committee scrapped the Fulbright resolution on America's post-war attitude, which was adopted by the House, and proposed instead a simple Senate resolution. This was done, members said, because the Senate alone has the duty of advising the President on foreign affairs.

Senators approving the resolution were Connally (Dem., Tex.); George (Dem., Ga.); Thomas (Dem., Utah.); Barclay (Dem., Ky.); Gillette (Dem., Ia.); Vandenberg (Rep., Mich.), and White (Rep., Me.).

Sen. LaFollette (P.-Wisc.), who is ill at his home, sent word requesting that he be recorded against any resolution, Connally announced.

The resolution probably will be placed before the full committee next Tuesday and Senate leaders indicated it would be brought up for Senate action about Nov. 10.

Bus Rams Trailer; 17 Hurt

Seventeen passengers, many of them war workers, were injured today in the collision of a bus and a truck-trailer at Route 1 and Broadway, Jersey City. Ten required treatment at the Jersey City Medical Center.

The bus, filled with workers of the Federal Shipbuilding and Dry Dock Co. plant at Port Newark, was bound for Journal Square, and was coming off the Pulaski Skyway at Broadway when the accident occurred. Police said the bus struck thetrailer, directly in the rear of the truck cab.

Strikes Today

ENGINES—Chysler plane plant crippled as 40 moulders walk-out in Chicago.

TRUCKS—Army, union and U. S. officials ask 10,000 southern drivers to return to jobs.

SHIPS—Leaders act to avoid outlaw strike at Kearny shipyard.

Assail Newsprint Export Secrecy

By DAVID CAMELON,
N. Y. Journal-American Washington Bureau.

WASHINGTON, Oct. 13.—"If this be espionage, let them make the most of it."

Rep. Boren (D.-Okla), paraphrased the words of Patrick Henry today to smash through what he called an unwarranted veil of bureaucratic secrecy.

Boren, chairman of the Boren-Halleck Special House Committee investigating the curtailment of newsprint, handed to the press, and placed in the record of his committee, a forbidden table showing that the United States had exported nearly 18,000 tons of newsprint in the first six months of this year.

The table had been furnished to his committee last week, but it bore the words:

"Confidential; disclosure punishable under the Espionage Act."

Committee members were incensed. Chairman Boren called upon the OWI for an explanation

Continued on Page 9, Column 3.

TODAY On All War Fronts

ITALY—5th Army advances nine miles in flanking threat to Volturno line. 4 towns seized.

RUSSIA—Nazis virtually out of Kiev after burning city. Gomel also evacuated.

PACIFIC—Further Jap evacuations in Solomons hinted in announcement of Allied air raid on barges off Choiseul.

Costello Before Probers Today

Frank Costello, ex-convict, will appear later today before the Grand Jury investigating charges he influenced the nomination of former Magistrate Aurelio for Supreme Court Justice, Costello's counsel said this morning.

King George Bestows Knighthood on Eaker

LONDON, Oct. 13 (UP).—Maj. Gen. Ira C. Eaker, commander of the 8th U. S. Air Force, was received today by King George, who invested him as a Knight of the British Empire.

Call Japanese Diet

The Japanese Diet will hold a three-day session beginning Oct. 25, a Tokio broadcast said today.

CYO Aids 100,000 City Boys, Girls

(New York Public Library has a constructive influence on the social adjustment of children. Pictures and story in Pictorial Review.)

By CHARLES ROLAND.

For sheer size and range of activities, the youth work of the Archdiocese of New York must be reckoned overwhelming.

Its leisure-time program embraces more than 100,000 boys and girls in 257 parishes, through the Catholic Youth Organization.

All-inclusive in scope, that program spans spiritual, athletic, social and cultural activities, with this proviso:

"Every parish and every boy and girl residing in the parish are eligible for participation in the CYO."

Archbishop Francis J. Spellman is honorary president of the organization, founded here under the late Cardinal Hayes.

Citizens of national eminence closely cooperate, among them Joseph P. Grace, head of the shipping lines, as chairman of the board, and Daniel P. Higgins of the Board of Education, president.

The Postmaster General of the

Continued on Page 7, Column 1.

Please Patronize the Same Newsdealer Each Day!

The Journal-American, due to the newsprint shortage and Government restrictions, regrets its inability to print enough papers to meet the demand.

Because newsdealers, in most cases, are not receiving a sufficient supply of papers, many readers find it difficult to obtain a copy of the Journal-American.

By patronizing the same newsdealers, you will help ease the situation and be best assured of obtaining your copy of the paper.

★

Again today, 57 columns of paid advertising were omitted from the Journal-American in order that readers may continue to receive full news coverage.

THE WEATHER

Fair and warmer today. Warmer and fresh winds Thursday.

Sun rises, 7:04 a. m.; sun sets, 6:20 p. m. High tide at Governors Island, 8:49 a. m. and 9:11 p. m.

HOURLY TEMPERATURES

4 a. m.	49	9 a. m.	51
5 a. m.	49	10 a. m.	55
6 a. m.	49	11 a. m.	60
7 a. m.	48	12 Noon	65
8 a. m.	49	1 p. m.	66

TODAY'S INDEX

Complete Weather Report on Page 14

The New York Journal-American has the largest circulation of any evening newspaper in America.

ALLIED PRINTING TRADES UNION LABEL COUNCIL NEW YORK 230

It is the only New York evening newspaper possessing the three great wire services—ASSOCIATED PRESS—INTERNATIONAL NEWS SERVICE—UNITED PRESS

—(PHONE YOUR NEWS TIPS TO CORTLANDT 7-1212)—

FRIDAY, OCTOBER 22, 1943

Latest Prices

BLACK OUT 6.24 to 7.6 | Moon Rises 1.4 a.m. New Moon Oct. 29 | RADIO Page Seven

LATE NIGHT

THE STAR

No. 17,267 ONE PENNY

DNIEPER: FULL RETREAT

"The German War Machine Is Tottering"—Moscow Radio

GERMAN FORCES IN THE DNIEPER BEND ARE IN FULL RETREAT, ACCORDING TO DUNCAN HOOPER, REUTER'S MOSCOW CORRESPONDENT. IN A CABLE THIS AFTERNOON HE SAID THE ENEMY POSITIONS HAVE LOST ALL SEMBLANCE OF A LINE.

The Germans are apparently withdrawing in a frenzied bid to avoid encirclement by the Russian troops, who broke through south-east of Kremenchug, and are now less than 20 miles north of Krivoi Rog.

This means that the Nazis' escape route, west from Dnepropetrovsk, has been almost cut by half, as Krivoi Rog is in the centre of the Dnieper "loop," halfway to Nikolaev, on the coast.

Moscow radio declared this afternoon: "The German war machine is tottering and daily growing weaker, following the enormous losses suffered in the battles over the Dnieper."

The Russian sweep into the bend is pushing the Germans back with unchecked momentum. Soviet armoured spearheads are hammering the retreating enemy, and inflicting huge losses.

The Germans are fighting hastily improvised actions from one fortified point to another.

According to Swiss radio Dnepropetrovsk is now completely encircled.

Moscow radio said that a

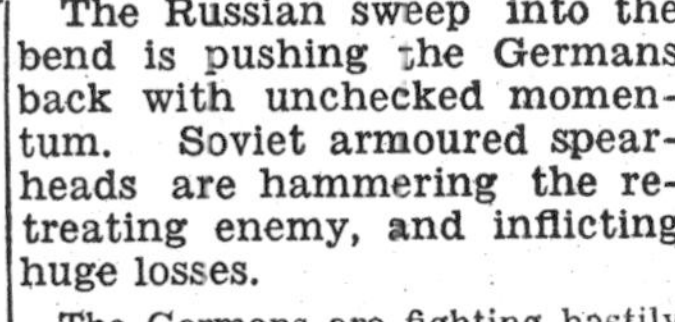

"titanic" battle for Kiev is in progress. "The cannonade thunders ceaselessly over the Dnieper," it was stated.

A "Pravda" correspondent reported that east of Kiev Soviet troops are entrenched before the city, but the real battles are raging north and south of the town on the western bank of the Dnieper.

Soviet troops are gradually pressing the enemy back, and the front is steadily receding westwards.

To the south only the northern part of Melitopol is now held by the Germans, and there they were being steadily dislodged from the streets.

Knowing what the evacuation of what they have described as the "Gate to the Crimea" will mean, the Germans are clinging desperately to the city, said Moscow.

The German news agency quoted by Reuter stated this afternoon reported a landing attempt by the Russians on the east coast of the Crimea.

Earier a Soviet war correspondent had said that "feeling of expectancy" was sweeping the population of the Crimea as the thunder of the Red Army's Azov offensive could already be heard in Yalta and in the Bay of Sebastopol.

German radio said that the Russians have launched a new attack west of Smolensk on both sides of the arterial road.

"Back 300 Miles"

The Germans are planning a 300-400-mile withdrawal in Russia to a line from Memel (Lithuania), through Lwow (Poland) to the Carpathians south of Stanislawow, according to Frederick Kuh, London correspondent of the New York paper "P.M.," quoting Allied intelligence sources.

A reduction of the present 1,200-mile line to 650 miles would result from such a withdrawal, he says, adding that his source is "that which learned of the German plan to invade Russia, two months before it took place."

FIFTH ARMY THRUST IN HILLS

2 Towns Taken

MORE places of strategic importance have been won from the Germans by troops advancing through the hills on the right flank of the Fifth Army, General Eisenhower's communique reported this afternoon.

"In the Eighth Army sector positions gained are being consolidated and patrols continue to be active against varying enemy resistance," the communique stated.

"The Fifth Army continue to push northward, in spite of enemy counter-attacks, which were repelled.

"Piedimonte d'Alife and Alife have been captured.

"Enemy rearguards are active and demolitions are being extensively encountered."

Alife is nearly 20 miles north-east of Capua, and Piedimonte d'Alife about six miles farther north.

Alife, in the Volturno valley on the southern slopes of the Matese mountains, is on the railway line from Naples, and on the road from Capua to Isernia.

Don Hollenbeck, U.S. commentator, broadcasting from Algiers this afternoon, said:

"The enemy yesterday threw in two heavy counter-attacks on the east and west flanks of the Fifth Army front. They were calculated to gain time and prevent our offensive plans from maturing while the Germans strengthened their line.

"Alife, which was captured by the Americans, is important because it stands on the road leading to Venafro, which is the left pivot of the new German defence line."

John Daly, another U.S. broadcaster, said that the Germans counter-attacked at Alife after we had captured it. They were beaten off. The

CONTINUED ON BACK PAGE, Col. FIVE

Nazi Reinforcements

"Fresh German contingents, including armoured columns, are streaming through Northern Italy towards Rome," said a New York radio broadcast today.

"The number of German planes thrown into the battle further south has also been greatly increased, but the Allied advance goes on slowly and methodically."

LION AT LARGE IN LONDON

The lion after it was cornered.

"STAR" REPORTER

A LION escaped today from a box car attached to a train which pulled up at Clapham Junction station.

The lion was in transit between St. Pancras and Petersfield, travelling in a wooden crate inside a railway box car. It broke out of the crate, went to the window of the car, and when the train stopped, jumped out of the window on to the platform.

After strolling down the line, it went into a sunken garden in Plough-road, where railwaymen barricaded it with sleepers and ropes.

The lion seemed fairly comfortable, but Home Guards who were called out took no chances, and Major Ford, in command of the Clapham Junction Company, stood with an automatic rifle at the ready.

Mr. Hubert Watts, a shunter, said, "Three or four of us were working on the line when we saw the lion coming. We drove it gently along, away from the station. It seemed as seared of us as we were of it. Our chief concern was that it should not get on the electric line."

Mr. R. Goddard, of Chessington Zoo, and Mr. Frank Foster, his ringmaster, were called in, and decided to get a travelling den, and lure "Leo" into it with a meat bait.

In the roads around the station there was great excitement, especially among schoolchildren going home to lunch. Many parents went to meet their children, and rushed them past the enclosure containing "Leo," who, however, remained quite unconcerned.

Don't Resent My Death —RAF Father

WHEN the two sons of the late Sergt. Pilot Eric Victor Durham, RAF, of Liverpool, become young men they will read a letter written by their father to the eldest son, John.

Sergt. Pilot Durham died in action over Germany in 1941, when John was one year old. His second son was born after his death.

"Respect all women," says Sergt. Durham in the letter. "If ever a woman is found to go wrong, or get into trouble, the cause can usually be traced to a man.

"You were born while the guns were firing at enemy planes, an enemy which took your Daddy from you. Live a clean life, help the weak, despise the bully, be proud of your ideals, don't feel resentful because your Daddy was taken from you.

"He felt it his duty to fight for the right. You can be proud your Daddy belonged to the RAF. I am proud to have belonged to a great Service."

Sergt. Pilot Durham's father is the Rev. G. E. Durham, known on Merseyside as the "Fighting Parson." He was a sergeant-major in the Royal Marines and was ordained after the last war.

At one time he was a curate at St. Martin-in-the-Fields. Now he is serving as a chaplain with the Pioneer Corps.

Mrs. Durham told "The Star" today: "My son was 27. He was a great sportsman. His widow is doing a grand job of work at a Windermere war nursery, and she has the two boys there with her.

"I feel that they must reach years of discretion before they read their father's letter. Fourteen would, I think, be a suitable age."

Thetis Widows Win Claim

Mr. Justice Wrottesley, in the King's Bench Division, today, gave judgment for plaintiffs against Cammell Laird and Co., Ltd., of New Chester-road, Birkenhead, for an amount to be ascertained in the consolidated test actions arising out of the Thetis disaster in Liverpool Bay on June 1, 1939, when the submarine was undergoing trials.

Stay of execution was granted pending consideration of an appeal.

The action was brought by the widows of two civilian workmen who were among the 99 persons who lost their lives in the Thetis.

The judge found that claims against a number of others named as defendants failed.

At the conclusion of his judgment he said, "The behaviour of the officers and ratings trapped in this submarine was in accordance with the highest traditions of the Royal Navy. The civilian members of the ship's company appear not to have fallen short of these high standards."

Paint caused Thetis defects.—Page Four.

GREEKS TOLD "STOP INTERNAL FIGHTING"

THE Allied C.-in-C. Middle East, Gen. Sir Henry Maitland Wilson, today warned the Greeks against "internal quarrels," ordered "fratricidal strife" in Greece to cease, and said that the United Nations were looking to the Greeks to "fight on, shoulder to shoulder, to speed up the coming day of freedom."

"This last year has been full of victories for the United Nations," he said. "These victories have been due to united strategy, where all worked together, regardless of those differnces which must be sunk in the stress of war.

"British and American troops served under an American general in Italy. American naval and air units served under British commanders in the Mediterranean. Greek, Norwegian and Dutch ships sailed together with ships of all the United Nations to carry the sinews of war to every port.

"As a result of this vast sommunal

CONTINUED ON BACK PAGE, Col. Four

Big RAF & U.S. Day Sweep Over France

STRONG forces of RAF bombers and fighters kept up the offensive against Northern France today. Bombers went out over the Channel while fighter sweeps on a large scale were in progress.

U.S. Eighth Air Force Marauders escorted and supported by RAF, Dominion, and Allied fighters, attacked the Evreux-Fauville air field (France) today, the U.S. headquarters in England announced this afternoon.

"Last night Mosquitos of Bomber Command, without loss, attacked objectives in Western Germany," said this afternoon's Air Ministry communique.

Unidentified foreign planes flew over Switzerland last night, according to an official Swiss report today. Flares were dropped in several places.

A German plane which flew over Swiss territory near Lugano, having apparently lost its way, came down at Dubendorf, near Zurich. The crew of four was interned, the report added.

Flares shot out in London raid—See Page Five.

HOARE GOES TO BARCELONA

Sir Samual Hoare, British Ambassador in Spain, is travelling to Barcelona to be present at the exchange of prisoners there, says Reuter.

He is accompanied by Lady Maud Hoare and by Mrs. Yencken, wife of Mr. A. S. Yencken, Minister at the British Embassy, who, as an Australian, will welcome the Australian prisoners.

The German Ambassador in Madrid will leave for Barcelona during the week-end.

No. 30,439 • • • THURSDAY, DECEMBER 2, 1943 ONE PENNY

CHURCHILL, ROOSEVELT, CHIANG HAVE MET, AGREED ON PLAN TO BEAT JAPS

To be stripped of all territory taken since 1895

PLANS FOR THE DEFEAT OF JAPAN AND THE STRIPPING FROM THAT COUNTRY OF THE TERRITORY IT HAS GAINED BY AGGRESSION HAVE BEEN DECIDED AT AN HISTORIC CONFERENCE IN NORTH AFRICA BETWEEN MR. CHURCHILL, PRESIDENT ROOSEVELT AND GENERALISSIMO CHIANG KAI-SHEK.

There are four main points in the communique issued this morning:

1—Military operations have been agreed upon; unrelenting pressure will be brought against "a brutal enemy" by sea, land and air;

2—Japan will be stripped of all islands in the Pacific seized or occupied since Aug., 1914;

3—Manchuria, Formosa and the Pescadores will be returned to China;

4—Korea will "in due course" obtain its independence.

The Conference lasted five days. It opened on Monday, Nov. 22, and by the Thursday afternoon complete agreement had been reached on all points. In the remaining two days minor points were straightened out.

In addition to the leaders, the Chiefs of Staff of the three Powers were present.

Mr. Eden, Foreign Secretary, was also there. So, too, were Lord Louis Mountbatten, C.-in-C. South-East Asia, and Major-Gen. Laycock, Chief of Combined Operations.

The Mediterranean war chiefs joined in the Conference on Friday after the Far Eastern situation had in the main been settled.

The Allied leaders have now left for an undisclosed destination.

From PHILIP JORDAN, News Chronicle Special Correspondent
CAIRO, Wednesday.

GUARDED by miles of bristling barbed wire and hemmed in by security measures without parallel, Mr. Churchill, President Roosevelt and Generalissimo Chiang Kai-shek have now completed a five-days conference and have all left for undisclosed destinations.

Thus the first part of the greatest international conference ever known or imagined has come to a close. It was a conference at which there were no empty chairs.

Although the conference officially began on Monday, Nov. 22, it was heralded in at seven o'clock on Sunday morning when Generalissimo Chiang's great U.S. aircraft landed at the aerodrome set apart for the flood of delegates due to arrive during the next 24 hours.

With the Generalissimo was his wife, whose arrival here was unexpected, and about 20 members of the Chinese staff.

Mr. Churchill flew in at five o'clock on the same evening, thus ending a voyage begun in a British ship.

The Premier's party arrives

The Prime Minister's party included his daughter, Mrs. Sarah Oliver; Mr. Winant, U.S. Ambassador in London; Admiral Sir Andrew Cunningham, First Sea Lord; and Major-General Sir Hastings Ismay, Chief of Staff to Mr. Churchill.

It was joined later by Air Marshal Sir Charles Portal and General Sir Alan Brooke, C.I.G.S.

On his way Mr. Churchill met General Eisenhower, General Alexander, Air Chief Marshal Tedder (Air Commander Middle East), and Admiral Sir John Cunningham, all of whom came on to the conference later.

With the exception of one rough day at sea the whole journey was made through days of sunshine and was without incident of any kind. Lest it should have proved necessary for the Premier to hurry his voyage and advance the time of his arrival an alternative plan for air travel was arranged.

Mr. Roosevelt made the last part of his journey by plane also, and arrived at 9.25 on Monday morning. He drove in a curtained motor-car to the villa reserved for him through streets lined by United States soldiers with their backs turned to him.

Two jeeps and a command car preceded the President's limousine in which he travelled with some of his personal staff, including Mr. Harry Hopkins and his Chief of Staff, Admiral Leahy.

Met Generalissimo for first time

Half an hour later the conference began with a call on the President by the Premier, followed an hour later by one from Generalissimo Chiang and his wife.

Thus, for the first time, Mr. Churchill met the Chinese twin heads of State, and the President for the first time met the Generalissimo.

In addition to the Chiefs of Staff of the three Allied countries, all of whom conferred regularly during the Conference, political and military advisers poured in from the four quarters of the earth.

Lord Louis Mountbatten, C.-in-C. South-East Asia, came with 12 of his staff. Mr. Eden and Sir Alexander Cadogan, permanent under-secretary, Foreign Office, flew in on Wednesday, as did Mr. Macmillan from Italy, Minister Resident North Africa.

Lord Leathers, Minister of War Transport, came with nine officials of Combined Operations, Major-Gen. Laycock, new Chief of Combined Operations, brought six and

Continued Back Page A

The muddle

All the world knew except Britain

BRITAIN, said B.U.P last night, was practically the only country which was not told of the historic conference.

Axis Press and radios, neutral newspapers, and papers in the United States and in the Dominions have told their readers what was going on.

Newspapers in the United States on Wednesday morning carried big headlines on a story from Lisbon which gave all the facts about the meeting which were not allowed to be published here.

In Madrid one news agency, quoting a Lisbon message, gave the details of the meeting and included a number of other details which are still banned here.

In Ankara the news of the conference has been known for some time, and has been published and cabled abroad.

South American newspapers yesterday published full dispatches from Lisbon, telling more or less the whole story and also including details still secret here.

* * *

The reason for this premature announcement is the procedure by which British censorship allows news from a foreign point to be transmitted through this country to any other point but does not allow it to be published here.

Instructions were given that the news was not to be released in this country and the U.S. before the morning, but apparently the U.S. censorship could not prevent the newspapers from giving the full story from a Lisbon dateline, as sent by a British news agency. [This was Reuter's.]

* * *

Elmer Davies, head of the U.S. Office of War Information, hit at that agency yesterday. He said: "If Churchill, Roosevelt and Chiang Kai-shek conferred as reported it may be assumed that arrangements were made for simultaneous announcement in all the capitals. If that were the case this agency broke the release date.

"If there were no conference the story would be pure invention, which is equally reprehensible."

And Philip Jordan says . . .

I have never yet attended an international conference at which the Press arrangements were so incompetently handled.

When the full story is published the name of the British Minister of Information is going to stink from one end to the other of the U.S.

We were not only begged to make bricks without straw and to act as "stooges" for policies which were not explained to us and to which British opinion might take exception, but we have been daily treated to a flood of vulgar trivialities concerned mainly with what X ate or Y wore.

The general impression given us was not so much that this was a conference of high strategical import, but that it was a sort of international beanfeast, marred only by the hideous skeleton in the cupboard called war.

Time alone and the sorting out of perspectives will correct that impression

For all practical purposes world correspondents were under orders here, although "travellers" were allowed to move freely and to speak freely, with no restraint on their tongues.

Security's motto seems to have been "Look after the pennies and the pounds will look after themselves."

It was a motto that has let them down badly.

Muddle about pictures, too

THE Ministry of Information in London were last night sitting on the pictures of the meetings.

It awaited New York to give the order for their release.

This further muddle, it was stated, was caused by an agreement "between the higher-ups," for the photographs to be issued simultaneously in Britain and the States. The pictures had not yet arrived in America.

The News Chronicle picture editor advised the British M.O.I. to radio the prints to New York. He was told this would not do. The U.S. authorities insisted on original "surface" pictures.

PACIFIC EMPIRE THAT JAPAN WILL LOSE

MEETING WITH STALIN IS NOT FAR OFF

By E. P. MONTGOMERY, The Diplomatic Correspondent

HAVING been led by the statements of Mr. Churchill and others to expect a meeting between Mr. Churchill, President Roosevelt and Marshal Stalin before the end of the year, it may come as something of a surprise to the general public that the communique from Cairo should announce it is Generalissimo Chiang Kai-shek who has met the President and the Prime Minister.

There is no reason, however, to suppose from this that the promised meeting of the British and American leaders with Marshal Stalin has been either postponed or long delayed.

It will be noticed that the messages from Cairo speak of the Allied chiefs having "left for unknown destinations." The reports do not say that they are returning home, as would be natural if the purposes for which they have journeyed abroad have been entirely completed.

TWO WAR THEATRES

The war must still be regarded as being separated into two distinct theatres, the European and the Asiatic. The meeting between Mr. Roosevelt, Mr. Churchill and the Generalissimo has been concerned with the Asiatic theatre, and the declaration they have issued makes it clear that they discussed the political as well as the purely military aspects of the war against Japan.

So far as Britain is concerned, the first point to be noted about the declaration is that it re-emphasises the assurances so frequently given by Mr. Churchill that Britain is in the fight against Japan to the finish with all her resources.

What will certainly arouse worldwide interest is that, in their statement, for the first time the United Nations leaders have declared their minds in clear and explicit geographical terms on some of the thorny questions of post-war territorial restitution and revision.

THE MANDATED ISLANDS

The declaration does not, however, go into the question of what is to be the final disposition of the mandated islands—whether they are to be distributed among the nations with interests in the Pacific or are to come under some form of international control as safeguards against any renewal of Japanese aggression.

"Japan will also be expelled from all the other territories which

Continued Back Page B

Hadji Ali refused Premier's baksheesh

From Our Special Correspondent
CAIRO, Wednesday.

ONE of the proudest men in Egypt today is Hadji Ali Rubushy, number one dragoman at the Pyramids.

During the conference Mr. Churchill and President Roosevelt took a respite from official business to see the Pyramids and the Sphinx.

When their car stopped Hadji Ali planted his foot firmly on the running board and for an hour without a pause treated the Prime Minister and the President to a running commentary on their wonders.

The two statesmen listened with interest, but all their attempts to interpose questions and comments were firmly brushed aside by Hadji Ali.

When he had exhausted his commentary — and with it almost his entire command of English—Hadji Ali salaamed deeply and departed, refusing with dignity Mr. Churchill's offer of baksheesh.

Hadji Ali — the title Hadji signifying he had been to Mecca—who wore red robes and a blue Algerian fez, has been a guide at the Pyramids for 35 years.

His only comment on his conversation was a masterpiece of statesmanlike brevity — "I was most glad to see them here."

France wants voice in Germany's future

Algiers, Wednesday. — France refuses to be bound by German settlements unless she participates in the decisions, authoritative Frenchmen asserted here today.

London alert

An alert sounded in London last night—the first since Sunday.

As the sirens sounded A.A. guns opened fire. The alert was brief.

No bombs fell in the London area.

Minesweeper lost

Minesweeper Hythe (Lieut.-Cmdr. L. B. Miller, R.N.) has been lost.

BERLIN CHAIN LETTER CALLS FOR PEACE

A chain letter, urging Berliners to demand peace immediately, is circulating throughout Berlin, according to a report reaching Stockholm from a neutral correspondent in Berlin.

The letter said that a secret meeting had been held in Berlin by workers and representatives of the middle classes who formed a committee to contact opposition elements from other parts of the capital

The chain letter demanded peace to prevent the complete devastation of Berlin by the R.A.F.

A report reaching Zurich said that when everybody in Vienna had to register their spare rooms for accommodating bombed-out Germans there were huge demonstrations, and crowds shouted, "Stop this war."—Reuter.

FACTS

KOREA (Japanese name "Tyosen") —Area 85,246 square miles, population (1938) 22,633,851, of which 633,320 were Japanese. Korea was formally annexed by Japan by a treaty concluded between Korea and Japan signed Aug. 22, 1910. Up to 1895 Korea had been a semi-independent kingdom under Chinese suzerainty, but after that fell more and more under Japanese influence.

MANCHURIA (Japanese name "Manchukuo") — Area 522,653 square miles, population (1939) 39,454,026, of which 642,356 were Japanese. Formerly provinces of China, Japan invaded Manchuria in 1931 after the so-called "Mukden incident." In 1932 Japan set up the puppet state of "Manchukuo" and set Henry Pu-Yi on the throne as emperor in 1934.

FORMOSA (Japanese name "Taiwan"). — Area 13,890 square miles population (1935) 5,212,426 of which 299,280 were Japanese. It was ceded by China to Japan under a treaty signed on May 8, 1895.

PESCADORES ISLANDS. — Area 85 square miles, population 70,000, are a group of 48 small islands, 21 of which are inhabited, lying 30 miles west of Formosa, between it and the Chinese mainland. They were ceded to Japan by China in 1895 at the same time as Formosa.

MANDATED ISLANDS. — Three groups of islands in the Western Pacific, the Marianas (or Ladrone) group, the Caroline group, and the Marshall group. Formerly German possessions, they were mandated to Japan by the Treaty of Versailles.

Japs driven from Changteh

Chungking, Wednesday.— Japanese forces have been driven from Changteh, key-point of the Chinese defences in eastern China, after 40 hours of hand-to-hand fighting.

This is announced in a Chinese communique issued in Chungking tonight.

The Chinese pursued the enemy from the town. Meanwhile two Chinese columns are converging on Changteh from north and east and are pinning the Japanese into a narrow pocket of land.

Vichy Government may move to Paris

Barcelona Wednesday.—Various departments of the Vichy Government have received orders to prepare to move to Paris, according to reports reaching here from the Franco-Spanish frontier.

"8th have broken through Adriatic Axis"—Montgomery

'I AM PROUDER THAN EVER OF THEM'

From S. L. SOLON, News Chronicle War Correspondent
ALLIED FORCE H.Q., Wednesday.

GENERAL MONTGOMERY, from his car in the battle area, said to a Reuter correspondent: "It was a good show. We have broken into and through the German defence line and Adriatic axis."

With a smile, he added, "I am prouder than ever of the Eighth Army soldiers."

In the fiercest infantry fighting the Eighth Army has seen in Italy they have sent the German troops of the 68th Division reeling from the high ground which dominates the tangle of roads north of the Sangro.

The main enemy defence link—on the five-miles ridge overlooking the Sangro Valley—is shattered, and the Eighth has advanced three miles on a 25-miles front in the last 24 hours.

[German Overseas News Agency last night admitted an Allied "dent" of 2½ to 3 miles in the German line.]

Small pockets of Germans are being mopped up and our main force is pushing ahead.

German resistance was savage. They launched counter-attack after counter-attack in an effort to retain their chief defences.

FEW PRISONERS

For a brief time at Mozzagrogna the enemy succeeded in cutting off our troops in that town. We launched an attack which forced the Germans back and relieved situation.

Eighty German prisoners were taken in Santa Maria and 50 in what was momentarily a dangerous Fossacesia. The small number captured is more an indication of the bitterness of the fighting than of the scale of the battle.

The day went to our infantry and to the brilliant air support they received through every fighting hour.

GREAT AIR EFFORT

The Tactical Air Force is making the heaviest and most sustained air effort ever seen in the Mediterranean theatre. In the number of offensive sorties flown, and in bomb load dropped, it exceeds anything in the whole African campaign.

Yesterday nine waves of light bombers swept into battle in support of Eighth Army troops.

At the same time 50 formations of fighters and fighter bombers worked with the forward fighting men, attacking gun positions, fortifications, trenches, troops and transport.

There were times when our bombers were attacking only 500 yards ahead of our troops.

Of nearly 50 enemy planes five were destroyed and others damaged.

While the Tactical Air Force was busy over the battle area the bombers of the Strategic Air Force were active deep in the heart of German-occupied Italy.

American heavies, escorted by Lightnings, hit the Adriatic seaport of Fiume, while Marauders attacked railways in Tuscany and along the West Coast of Italy.

In all the day's operations three Allied aircraft were lost.

Five enemy planes were destroyed.

49 Labour M.P.s rebel in Mosley debate

By The Political Correspondent

A FEW hours after Mr. Attlee, Deputy Prime Minister, had warned a private meeting of Labour M.P.s that the amendment protesting against the release of Mosley amounted to a vote of censure on the Government, 49 of them voted for the amendment.

In all 62 M.P.s supported the amendment and 327 voted against.

At the next meeting of the Parliamentary Labour Party Mr. Attlee will reprimand the Labour "rebels."

The private party meeting before the debate revealed a serious split among Labour M.P.s.

A demand that Labour M.P.s should be free to vote as they pleased was narrowly defeated by 55 votes to 47.

In the end the meeting decided by 58 to 38 to support the Government.

The A.E.U. executive council has asked the general council to convene a special meeting of union executives to discuss the Mosley situation.

Debate Page Three.

Berlin's "secret weapons" terms

Madrid, Wednesday.—A suggestion that if the Allies cease bombing Germany the Germans would agree not to use their "too terrible secret weapons for reprisal," has reached here from Berlin in the form of a personal opinion of Spanish newspaper correspondents.

Fighters' 9-7 score

Nine enemy aircraft were destroyed by our fighters during offensive operations from Britain yesterday. We lost seven of our aircraft, but the pilot of one is safe.

Four Mosquitoes, on offensive patrol, encountered six Ju 88's over the sea south of Land's End and shot down three for the loss of one Mosquito.

R.A.F. Typhoon fighters, with squadrons of Spitfires, supporting American heavy bombers on their withdrawal from Western Germany, were attacked by German fighters yesterday afternoon.

They destroyed two of the enemy and damaged others for the loss of one Typhoon.

Enemy ships hit

Many hits on two heavily laden merchant vessels were scored by a force of Coastal Command Beaufighters from an R.C.A.F. squadron when they attacked an enemy convoy off the Norwegian coast on Tuesday.

The supply ships were strongly protected by escort vessels, but despite fierce anti-aircraft fire the Beaufighters pressed home their attacks. All returned safely.

200,000 FRENCH TO WORK FOR NAZI ARMY

News has just been received from France by the French Delegation in London (writes Henry Stone) that Laval has agreed to allow the Germans to take control of French youth organisations and to use these young men in auxiliary services in the German forces.

They include about 200,000 men of the 1943 class who, as there is now no army in France, have been "mobilised" in the youth organisations. Over 21,000 will work in the Todt organisation, 5,000 in the air force, 2,000 in the army, 3,000 in powder factories, and the rest in unspecified jobs connected with "German national defence."

Alarm clocks for early risers

Workers who can fulfil three conditions will be granted an alarm clock buying permit, the Board of Trade announced last night.

They are those who have to get up between midnight and five a.m. because their work makes it necessary, who do not already possess an alarm clock, and who have no other means of being called.

Papen refuses

Stockholm, Wednesday. — Von Papen, German Ambassador to Turkey, has refused an offer to take over Ribbentrop's job of Foreign Minister, according to Aftontidningen today.

Baron von Neurath has also declined the offer.

SOVIETS TAKE TOWN ON PRIPET

SOVIET forces, continuing to attack between the Rivers Sozh and Dnieper, north-west of Gomel, advanced and captured several localities, the Moscow communique announced last night.

Narovlya, 68 miles north of Korosten, was taken in an advance along the lower Pripet.

Operations to extend the bridgehead on the Dnieper right bank continued in the Cherkasy area, and south-west of Kremenchug several strongly fortified defence points were captured after stubborn battles.

From PAUL WINTERTON News Chronicle Special Correspondent
MOSCOW, Wednesday.

LARGE sections of the Eastern battlefront are now dominated by erratic and unseasonable weather conditions.

Over great areas there are heavy falls of snow, mainly at night, which thaw or partially thaw in daytime, leaving the ground soaking wet and ready to be churned up into deep mud by the first passing vehicles.

There is no doubt that the battle west of Kiev is still of outstanding importance.

It is clear that the main German reason for throwing in what amounts to a substantial proportion of Nazi armoured strength in Russia on this one sector was the urgent necessity of blunting the Russian spearhead and trying to prevent a new Soviet drive which would threaten communications to the 300-miles salient ending in the eastern Dnieper bend.

A temporary blunting has certainly been achieved, at the cost of hundreds of Nazi tanks, and a counter-drive has won back for the moment the Korosten and Zhitomir positions.

The Russian aim during the 18-day battle—a struggle as grim and significant as anything which has taken place on the front this year—has been to exhaust the enemy's armoured units at minimum cost, without bothering about holding any particular piece of ground.

LATE NEWS

INVASION OF INDIA "OUT OF QUESTION"

Madras, Wednesday.—Sir Arthur Hope, Governor of Madras, speaking of rumours of invasion, said that beyond attempts to carry out nuisance raids, there was no question of any Japanese invasion of India.

BLACK-OUT TIMES

	p.m.	a.m.
Birmingham	5.28	8.28
Carlisle	5.20	8.43
Hull	5.16	8.26
Newcastle	5.14	8.38
Grimsby	5.15	8.24
Leeds	5.20	8.31
Liverpool	5.28	8.36
Manchester	5.25	8.32

Moon rises 12.58 p.m., sets 10.17 p.m.

News Chronicle
No. 30,443 • • • TUESDAY, DECEMBER 7, 1943 ONE PENNY

Churchill, Roosevelt, Stalin declare: We have agreed on plans and timing for the destruction of Nazi armed power

ATTACKS TO BE MADE EAST, WEST AND SOUTH

United Nations are determined to make a peace which will banish scourge and terror of war for generations

The whole world could hear news at once

THIS is how the world was told of the Teheran talks.

On the stroke of six the radio network of the United Nations broadcast to listeners all over the world the first joint communique of the three Powers.

The B.B.C. told its Home and Forces programme listeners in this country, while at the same time the B.B.C. overseas services transmitted it round the globe.

Moscow Radio broadcast the news in Russian.

New York Radio was heard in English and in French at the same time. Algiers gave the news in German.—Reuter.

DECISIONS REACHED BY CHURCHILL, ROOSEVELT AND STALIN DURING THEIR FOUR-DAYS CONFERENCE IN TEHERAN WERE ANNOUNCED LAST NIGHT IN THIS COMMUNIQUE:

"We, the President of the United States, the Prime Minister of Great Britain, and the Premier of the Soviet Union, have met these four days past in this, the capital of our ally, Iran, and have shaped and confirmed our common policy.

"We expressed our determination that our nations shall work together in war, and in the peace that will follow.

"As to the war—our military staffs have joined in our round table discussions, and we have concerted our plans for the destruction of the German forces. We have reached complete agreement as to the scope and timing of operations which will be undertaken from East, West and South.

UNDERSTANDING GUARANTEES VICTORY

"The common understanding which we have reached guarantees that victory will be ours.

"And as to peace we are sure that our concord will make it an enduring peace. We recognise fully the supreme responsibility resting upon us and all the United Nations to make a peace which will command the good will of the overwhelming mass of peoples of the world, and banish the scourge and terror of war for many generations.

"With our diplomatic advisers we have surveyed the problems of the future. We shall seek the co-operation and active participation of all nations, large and small, whose peoples, in heart and mind, are dedicated, as are our peoples, to the elimination of tyranny and slavery, oppression and intolerance.

FAMILY OF DEMOCRATIC NATIONS

"We will welcome them as they may choose to come into a world family of democratic nations.

"No power on earth can prevent our destroying the German armies by land, their U-boats by sea, and their war plants from the air.

"Our attack will be relentless and increasing.

"From these friendly conferences we look with confidence to the day when all the peoples of the world may live free lives, untouched by tyranny, and according to their varying desires and their own consciences.

"We came here with hope and determination. We leave here friends in fact, in spirit, and in purpose.

THE Teheran conference began on Friday, Nov. 26, when Marshal Stalin, Mr. Molotov and Marshal Voroshilov arrived.

On the next day President Roosevelt and Mr. Churchill arrived. And on Sunday, Nov. 28, the talks proper began. They lasted four days.

On the Thursday the roar of departing planes signalled the end of the Teheran conference, but not of the Allied talks.

For, after Teheran, Mr. Churchill, President Roosevelt and a number of Chiefs of Staff left for a place in North Africa where further discussions were to be held.

Mr. Churchill, immediately on his return to North Africa, consulted with General Sir Henry Maitland Wilson, Commander-in-Chief, Middle East, Air Chief Marshal Sir Sholto Douglas, Air Officer Commanding, Middle East, and Major-Gen. Laycock, Head of Combined Operations.

Broadcasting from Cairo yesterday Grant Parr, of the N.B.C., stated that "As early as Friday morning General Marshall, Admiral King, and General Arnold conferred with Sir Alan Brooke, Admiral Sir Andrew Cunningham and Air Chief Marshal Sir Charles Portal.

"The military decisions taken at the present conference, together with details perhaps related to the sessions at Teheran, have posed a planning problem which has kept the American and British chiefs of staff busy ever since.

"Last night the combined military chiefs held a really tough session. They worked without interruption until three a.m. today.

And now the world knows the news, and this is what the world thinks:

HOW RUSSIAN PEOPLE FEEL

THE conference has ended in splendid success (cables Paul Winterton, News Chronicle Moscow Correspondent). Of that there can be no doubt whatever. The fertile ground, well-tilled during the Moscow conference, has yielded fine fruit, and Anglo-Soviet-American relations pass into a new stage of triumphant co-operative endeavour and cordial friendship. The decisions of the Big Three will undoubtedly be given an enthusiastic reception throughout the Soviet Union, both in the Press and by the public.

The supreme confidence of the declaration—"no power on earth can prevent our destroying the German forces"—and the evidence of real amity will meet the dsires of the whole Soviet people.

The key phrase of the declaration, on which they will certainly concentrate, is the one saying that the three leaders have reached complete agreement as to scope and timing of operations which will be undertaken from East, West and South.

The Russians will now feel for the first time that the plans of the Western Allies have not merely been integrated with the Russian at the highest level, but that in every respect they have been approved by their own leader, Stalin, in whose direction of the war they have implicit faith.

Though the Russians are naturally more immediately concerned with questions of speeding victory than with questions after the war, they have seen enough of what war means on their own territory to approve the determination of the three leaders to lay the foundations for enduring peace through the post-war concord of the three nations.

What makes the conference particularly noteworthy in the minds of the Russian people is that for the first time since he attained a position of authority in the councils of State, Stalin has been outside Soviet territory, and that the journey to Teheran, though it was comparatively short, was symbolic of the total abandonment of isolation by the Soviet Union and of her readiness and, indeed, eagerness to play a full and equal part in the rebuilding of the world when the war is won.

Once again, no subject was taboo in the four-day talks. The President and Marshal Stalin, meeting for the first time, got on extremely well together.

One of the most eloquent indications of the really good feeling between the leaders was the very appropriate declaration about the future status of Iran, showing the attitude of all three towards the smaller nations.

It is difficult to exaggerate the satisfaction of all concerned at the way this conference has gone. The three top men have probed deep into many questions and the beneficient results of their conference will be felt for a very long time.

The fullest hopes have been realised.

AMERICANS ARE WELL SATISFIED

AMERICANS, who look upon the declaration as the prelude to the greatest offensive in the history of warfare, are well

Continued Back Page (A)

THE PLANNERS OF VICTORY GIVE US A SMILE

FIRST pictures of the meeting in Teheran of the leaders of Britain, the U.S. and the Soviet Union were received in London last night by special aeroplane.

It was the first time Marshal Stalin, President Roosevelt and Mr. Churchill had met together, and the first personal meeting of Stalin and the President.

This picture was taken at the Soviet Legation in Teheran. Stalin, wearing his Marshal's uniform, and the President are in specially good humour. Mr. Churchill, whose smile is more restrained, is in the uniform of a Commodore of the R.A.F.

Other pictures of the leaders with their staffs, and a 69th birthday party for Mr. Churchill, are on the Back Page.

Inonu meets Premier and President

By The Diplomatic Correspondent

CONFIRMATION of reports from Axis sources, which have been circulating throughout the world for the past three days, that President Roosevelt and Mr. Churchill were having discussions in North Africa with President Inonu of Turkey, reached London last night.

Up to a late hour official circles in London had received no information whatever to throw any light upon the reasons for or objects of the meeting.

It will be recalled that about a month ago, on his return journey from the Moscow conference, Mr. Anthony Eden met the Turkish Foreign Minister, M. Menemencioglu, in Cairo, and had conversations with him which lasted for two days.

TURKEY'S ATTITUDE

At the time, that meeting aroused widespread spectulation, and it was freely suggested in some quarters that it heralded Turkey's immediate entrance into the war on the side of the Allies, or at least the granting to the Allies by Turkey of air bases and other facilities.

So far, all of these spectulations have been falsified by events.

The only indications of the Turkish attitude have come from the Turkish Press, which has consistently in recent weeks stressed these points: (1) Turkey's loyalty to the Anglo-Turkish alliance; (2) Turkish independence of action; (3) Turkey's neutrality.

It is "more than a friendly visit"

The following comment on the new conference, purported to have been made by M. Yalchin in his newspaper Tanin, was quoted by the German News Agency.

"This was not only a friendly visit, but talks were held which concerned the most important questions of the present as well as of the post-war period and touched upon the fate of the world and Turkey.

"The Turkish nation is convinced that it would not be plunged into an adventure as long as vital Turkish interests are not imperilled.

"The Turkish army is ready for battle. It would, however, be ridiculous to assert that Turkey's entry into the war has been decided in North Africa."

GERMAN COMMENT

"The Wilhelmstrasse does not think fit to consider this Turkish-Allied meeting as just a routine trip of the Turkish President," was the comment at the German Foreign Office Press conference yesterday. "After all, it has come in the wake of the Anglo-Saxon leaders' trip to Russia.

"What is more, Anglo-American sources hint at the possibility that a Balkans campaign was discussed in Teheran, and if that was the case it was imperative to know what Turkey's attitude would be.

"If one analyses the present military position in Russia, the defeats the Russian Army have suffered in their attempt at laying hands on the Crimea, one may say that Roosevelt and Churchill will have demanded from Inonu the cession of air bases in Western Anatolia and the opening of the Dardanelles.'

The Cairo Arabic afternoon newspaper Mokattam said yesterday: "Turkey has several times recently expressed her sympathy with the democratic cause and it is therefore not improbable that she should be inclined to grant what is expected of her."

NAZI TROOP MOVEMENTS

According to reports reaching Hungarian circles in Stockholm, German troops have been moving towards the Turkish frontier all the week-end.

Troop concentrations have been made in the Chaskovo area of Bulgaria, say these reports.

On Sunday a German motorised detachment with two waggon-loads of officers moved towards the River Tunsha.

GOEBBELS WAS WRONG ABOUT THAT "PEACE OFFENSIVE"

By VERNON BARTLETT

THE "Declaration of the Three Powers" is a remarkable and unexpected document. Nowhere will it cause greater surprise than in Berlin.

Indeed, the most encouraging feature about it is the way in which a fourth Power, Germany, has become an involuntary ally in dropping "propagandist block busters on the German people," to quote from the German Official News Agency.

Ever since Dr. Goebbels first got wind of the Roosevelt-Stalin-Churchill meeting he and his scribes have been explaining what sort of an appeal these Allied leaders were going to make to the German people.

On no previous occasion have such efforts been made to discredit a document in advance. And instead of a "peace offensive" the "Declaration of the Three Powers" is a cold, calm and confident statement of intention. Thus the most devastating "block buster" comes from Dr. Goebbels himself.

NO COMFORT

There is no comfort for the Germans in the statement that "*We have concerted our plans for the destruction of the German forces.*"

There is less than no comfort in the statement that "we have reached complete agreement as to the scope and timing of the operations which will be undertaken from the East West and South."

If words mean anything these words mean that the possibility of discord between the Allies because the Soviet Union has suffered such losses while the British Commonwealth and the U.S. were mustering their forces for the final blow has been removed.

Stalin, Roosevelt and Churchill have deepened the understanding reached by Molotov, Cordell Hull and Eden, and it is significant that the document appears to attach equal importance to the destruction of "*the German armies by land, their U-boats by sea, and their war plants from the air.*"

ENDURING PEACE

On the political side the document is no less definite and confident.

"As to peace, we are sure that our concord will make it an enduring peace."

The further possibility of discord between these three Powers and

Continued Back Page (B)

HISTORY WAS MADE AT TEHERAN

The first meeting between Marshal Stalin and President Roosevelt took place on Sunday, Nov. 28, in Teheran.

When this meeting had ended Mr. Churchill drove over from the British Legation, and history was made.

For the first time in the war the three Allied leaders had at last been brought together.

They toasted each other during the conference; Marshal Stalin was handed the Stalingrad Sword.

But, far beyond these things, they decided the fate of Nazi Germany.

The whole colourful story is told by

PHILIP JORDAN
on Page Two.

Soviet advance in Dnieper bend

A further advance in the Dnieper bend was announced in last night's Soviet communique.

"South-west of Kremenchug," it stated, "our troops overcame enemy resistance and captured Alexandriya, also 18 heavily fortified German strong-points and four railway stations."

The communique said that north-west of Gomel offensive operations continued and several inhabited localities were occupied.

In the Chernyakhova area (Kiev salient) Soviet troops repelled attacks by strong forces of enemy infantry and tanks.

As the result of a swift blow, the railway line Smela-Znamenka was cut.

Paul Winterton's cable: Back Page.

FIFTH TAKES 3 MORE MOUNTAIN BASTIONS

From S. L. SOLON, News Chronicle War Correspondent
ALLIED H.Q., Monday.

THE battering ram attack of the Fifth Army against the German mountain strongholds is slowly but surely breaking down the defences.

Three more high points, fortified in concrete and sheltered deep in the rock, have been taken on the mountain masses of Magiore and Camino.

The Fifth Army now holds five positions dominating the southern end of the Liri Valley.

Local gains are also reported on other portions of the line, but the effect of German reinforcements is beginning to be felt.

West of Venafro the Germans threw a large force into a bloody counter-attack. It was beaten back after fierce close-up fighting. German casualties were severe.

On the Eighth Army front our troops have cleared the way to the Moro River and now face reinforced defences on the opposite bank.

HEAVY RAIN AGAIN

In pouring rain a fierce battle is going on in the Casone area, six miles inland and three miles north of Lanciano. Tanks and infantry are mixed in a type of close fighting which is becoming a characteristic of the Italian campaign.

It is reported that we have captured a flame-throwing tank.

Air activity is on a reduced scale because of the bad weather, but on the Fifth Army front, where conditions are somewhat better, fighter-bombers carried out successful missions.

American Invaders and Warhawks bombed gun positions just ahead of the forward troops, and ranged north into the Rome area to shoot up transport.

Our aircraft dropped emergency rations to American troops on Mount Maggiore

So difficult is the terrain in this mountainous region west of Mignano that even mule trains have difficulty in getting supplies to our troops.

On the Eighth Army front our fighter-bombers attacked gun positions 20 miles south of Chieti, in high mountain country.

Naval support to our ground forces fighting on the east coast continued.

HARBOURS BOMBED

Although all operations of the North-West African Air Forces were limited by the weather on Sunday, the harbour of Split was attacked by medium bombers, a ship was hit in Paludi harbour, near Split, and the floating dock at Orbetello, on the west coast of Italy, was hit and left burning.

The Middle East communique states that R.A.F. heavy bombers attacked the railway station at Salonika on Sunday night.

LATE NEWS

"DAWN OF NEW WORLD"
—Canadian Premier

Washington, Monday.—Mr. Mackenzie King, Canadian Premier, travelling through Washington on holiday, said: "The conference statements mark the dawn of a new world. The good will demonstrated at Teheran can itself be the medium for solving all war and post-war problems."

BLACK-OUT TIMES

	p.m.		a.m.
Birmingham	5.26	—	8.34
Carlisle	5.15	—	8.51
Hull	5.12	—	8.34
Newcastle	5.10	—	8.46

Moon rises 3.12 p.m., sets 4.42 a.m. tomorrow. Full moon Saturday.

H.M. KING GEORGE VI
AWARDED TO MALTA
The "GEORGE CROSS"
ON THE 956th. DAY
OF THE WAR
APRIL 15th., 1942.

TIMES OF MALTA

No. 2,588 Price 2d. SATURDAY DECEMBER 11 1943 1,560 DAY OF WAR AGAINST NAZISM

ROOSEVELT VISITS MALTA

America's Tribute to Island's People and Defenders

HISTORIC CEREMONY AT LUQA AERODROME

LUQA aerodrome was the scene of an historic occasion in the annals of Malta when last Wednesday President Roosevelt arrived there in a C. 54 Douglas Transport plane escorted by twenty Lightnings and Spitfires.

It was a perfect December morning with a blue sky lightly flecked with white clouds and brilliant sunshine. All was peace on the aerodrome on which in the past hordes of Junkers and Stukas had for months concentrated their efforts making it the most bombed airfield in the world. On the 8th. December 1943 the once crater-pocked airfield stretched without a ripple to the sky-line.

FRANKLIN D. ROOSEVELT
PRESIDENT OF THE UNITED STATES OF AMERICA

AT THE AERODROME

Awaiting the President's arrival were H.E. Field Marshal Viscount Gort V.C. Governor and Commander-in-Chief, attended by Major Gordon Duff, Military Secretary, Lieutenant Colonel V. Micallef, A.D.C., Captain Holland, Major Geddes, and Major Woodford. There were also His Lordship Mgr. Gonzi attended by his chaplain, the Rev. John Vella Galea, B.A.; the Lieutenant Governor Mr. D. C. Campbell, the three Service Chiefs, Vice Admiral Hamilton, Major General Oxley and Air Vice Marshal Sir Keith Park, along with Lieutenant Templeton R.N.V.R., Lt. H. A. F. Radley A.D.C. and Fl/Lt. H.C.C. Carver in attendance. Together with the Service Chiefs were Sir George Borg Chief Justice of Malta, and the members of the Executive Council including Lt. Colonel Strickland leader of the elected majority and Mr. E. Valenzia L.P.

PRESIDENT'S ARRIVAL

A Guard of Honour drawn up in a hollow square, three deep was formed by detachments from the Royal Navy and Marines, the Army and R.A.F. The Army detachment comprised men from infantry units of the United Kingdom and Malta. The band of the Royal Malta Artillery was in attendance.

At 0930 the President's 'plane and its escort were to be seen circling over the aerodrome. Then the great moment arrived as the President's 'plane piloted by Major Otis Bryant of the U.S.A.A.F. touched ground and made a perfect landing ten minutes later.

HIS EXCELLENCY'S GREETING

The 'plane taxied to its allotted position as the escort 'planes hovered over the aerodrome and then landed, taking up alignment while His Excellency Lord Gort was welcoming the President of the United States and Mr. Roosevelt's distinguished companions.

They were General Eisenhower, Supreme Allied C-in-C Mediterranean; Admiral Leahy; Mr. Harry Hopkins, General Spaatz; Major General Bedell Smith, Chief of Staff to General Eisenhower; Rear Admiral Wilson Brown, Naval A.D.C. to the President; Rear Admiral Ross Macintire, the President's personal physician; Major General Edwin Wilson, Secretary and Military A.D.C. to the President; Major John Boettiger, the President's son-in-law. While Lord Gort remained by the 'plane with President Roosevelt the other distinguished visitors moved forward to greet the Service Chiefs and their companions. General Eisenhower was heard to say "Delighted to see you all again."

INSPECTION OF GUARD OF HONOUR

Meanwhile President Roosevelt had entered the waiting jeep. It was one of the American jeeps presented last July by General Eisenhower at the time of the invasion of Sicily to the Governor and that had been allotted by him to Air Vice Marshal Sir Keith Park. It had been newly painted. "Husky" as the A.O.C's jeep is known throughout Malta came to a standstill facing the Guard of Honour where the President took the salute as the Band of the R.M.A. played the Star Spangled Banner and the Stars and Stripes broke at the mast-head. History was made without precedent—the flag of the United States of America waved over Luqa aerodrome and the President of that great country proceeded to inspect the Guard of Honour together with Field Marshal Lord Gort.

PRESENTATION TO THE PRESIDENT

At the conclusion of the inspection His Excellency presented the following to President Roosevelt:—His Hon. the Lieutenant Governor Mr. D. C. Campbell; His Lordship Mgr. Michael Gonzi, Bishop of Urbe, Administrator of Gozo and Coadjutor of His Grace the Archbishop of Malta; the Air Officer Commanding Mediterranean Air Vice Marshal Sir Keith Park, the Vice Admiral Malta, Vice Admiral Hamilton; General Officer Commanding the Troops Major General Oxley; His Honour the Chief Justice Sir George Borg; the Attorney General the Hon. Mr. L. Galea LL.D.; the Hon. Mr. G.N.N. Nunn and the Hon. Mr. T. V. Scrivenor Assistants to His Honour the Lieutenant Governor; the Treasurer to the Government, the Hon. Mr. E. Cuschieri; the Hon. Mr. P. Bell, Legal Secretary; the Hon. Mr. R. Castillo, Secretary to the Government; the Hon. Lieutenant Colonel R. Strickland leader of the Elected Majority and the Hon. Mr. E. Valenzia, L.P.

As President Roosevelt shook hands with Air Vice Marshal Park he was heard to say: "I have heard about you from my boys."

PRESIDENT DELIVERS CITATION

After the presentation Lord Gort attended by Major Gordon Duff and Lieutenant Colonel Micallef took up a position in the centre of the square formed by the Guard of Honour facing President Roosevelt. Behind Lord Gort, were Bishop Gonzi, the Service Chiefs the Chief Justice and members of the Executive Council. President Roosevelt, a powerful and commanding figure, remained seated in the jeep and standing alongside were two members of his staff. At a distance of a few yards in a line were the distinguished visitors who had accompanied President Roosevelt; and behind them again were their personal staff and the aides-de-camp of the Service chiefs.

In the firm resonant tone which the radio has made familiar to all freedom-loving peoples, President Roosevelt addressed the assembled gathering:

"Lord Gort, Officers and Men, good People of Malta.

"Nearly a year ago the Prime Minister and I were in Casablanca shortly after the landings by British and American troops in North Africa, and at that time I told the Prime Minister some day we would control once more the whole of the Mediterranean and that then I would go to Malta.

For many many months I have wanted on behalf of the American people to pay some little tribute to this Island and to all the people civil and military, who, during these years have contributed so much to democracy, not just here, but all over the civilized world and so at last we have been able to come. At last I have been able to see something of the historic land and I wish I could stay but I have many things to do. May I tell you though that during these past three weeks the Prime Minister and I feel that we two have struck strong blows for the future of the human race and so in this simple way I am taking opportunity to do what all the American people would join with me in doing. I have here a little token a scroll, a citation from the President of the United States speaking on behalf of all the people and may I read it to you:—

"In the name of the people of the United States of America I salute the Island of Malta, its People and defenders who in the cause of freedom and justice and decency throughout the world have rendered valourous service far above and beyond the call of duty.

Under repeated fire from the skies, Malta stood alone but unafraid in the centre of the sea, one tiny bright flame in the darkness, a beacon of hope for the clearer days which have come.

Malta's bright story of human fortitude and courage will be read by posterity with wonder and gratitude throughout all the ages.

What was done in this Island maintains all highest traditions of gallant men and women who from the beginning of time have lived and died to preserve civilization for all mankind."

FRANKLIN D. ROOSEVELT
President.

DECEMBER 7, 1943.

"I have signed it at the bottom and I wrote on it not today, but yesterday, December 7, because that was the second anniversary of the entry into the war of the American people. We will proceed until that war is won but more than that we will stand shoulder to shoulder with the British Empire and our other Allies in making it a victory worth while."

Concluding, President Roosevelt handed the case containing the scroll to Major Boettiger who placed it in the hands of His Excellency.

The citation is written in illuminated letters on a scroll of parchment. The scroll reposes on a velvet backing in a beautiful leather case, the cover of which is embossed with the national white and red shield of Malta edged with gold. At the top of the scroll are the Malta arms backed by the crossed flags of Britain and the United States. The whole is contained in a mahogany case which Lord Gort handed to Major Gordon Duff.

LORD GORT'S THANKS

His Excellency in thanking the President, said:—

"Mr. President,

"We are very sensible of the greatness of this occasion and of the important place which December 7, 1943 will occupy in our history. It is a day which Malta will never forget and I can assure you Sir, that this Citation, presented in person by the President of the United States of America, has moved us very deeply. May I be permitted, on behalf of the Armed Forces and Peoples of Malta to thank you, Mr. President, most respectfully, most sincerely and most gratefully for the sentiments it expresses and for the great gesture of friendship which inspired you to undertake this special journey.

Malta is, perhaps not unjustifiably proud that she has been able to play her part in the Mediterranean war, but the language in which the Citation is couched and, if I may be permitted to say so, Mr. President, the moving phrases which you have so generously used in making this presentation impress upon us how highly you rate such services as our Island Fortress has been able to

(*Continued on Page 4*).

H.E. THE VISCOUNT GORT, V.C., RECEIVES FROM MAJOR JOHN BOETTIGER, MR. ROOSEVELT'S SON-IN-LAW, THE MAHOGANY CASE CONTAINING THE ILLUMINATED SCROLL, IMMEDIATELY AFTER THE PRESIDENT HAD DELIVERED THE CITATION.

BROOKLYN QUEENS LONG ISLAND

DAILY NEWS

Copr. 1943 by News Syndicate Co. Inc. NEW YORK'S PICTURE NEWSPAPER Trade Mark Reg. U. S. Pat. Off.

Vol. 25. No. 158 New York, Monday, December 27, 1943★ 36 Pages 2 Cents IN CITY LIMITS | 3 CENTS Elsewhere

BRITISH SINK SCHARNHORST

Nazi Battleship Destroyed In Sea Fight Off Norway

Story on Page 3

(By Acme)

Her Raiding Days Are Over

Adolf Hitler suffered his biggest naval defeat since losing the Bismarck in 1941, when units of the British Home Fleet caught the 26,000-ton Nazi battleship Scharnhorst and sank her in a battle off North Cape, Norway. The sister ship of the Gneisenau was trapped when it tried to intercept a Russian-bound convoy. The battleship was armed with a main battery of nine 11-inch guns and normally carried a crew of 1,461 officers and men. Recently, the Scharnhorst spent weeks in a Norwegian fjord, licking wounds inflicted by Allied bombers.

—Story on page 3

Daily Mail
LATE WAR NEWS
NO. 14,874 ONE PENNY ** FOR KING AND EMPIRE TUESDAY, JANUARY 4, 1944

UTILITY FOOTWEAR
George Webb
FOOTWEAR FOR MEN
MADE BY CRAFTSMEN IN NORTHAMPTON

RED ARMY ON THE POLISH BORDERS

70-Mile Wide Advance—and Gathering Speed

RAF Wreck Hitler's HQ in Berlin

Chancellery Down: Hundreds Buried

'Major Blow'

From RALPH HEWINS, Daily Mail Special Correspondent

STOCKHOLM, Monday.

GERMAN pioneers are to-night reported to be digging frantically to rescue hundreds of people trapped in the shelters under Hitler's Chancellery in Berlin.

Three-quarters of this mighty building—centre of Government and symbol of the Nazi Party's rise to power—were laid in ruins by last night's R.A.F attack.

Travellers reaching Stockholm from Germany to-day report that "block-busters" smashed down on the fortress-like pile, reducing most of it to rubble.

They describe the blow as a major disaster. Hitler was not in the building, but many important officials are believed to be buried under its ruins.

Huge, three-storied shelters were constructed under the Chancellery, and by Hitler's order most of them were reserved for women and children.

The safety of those under his personal protection became a point of honour for the Führer. Hence the arrival of mobile cranes and bulldozers and thousands of men at the Chancellery at dawn.

But their task is well-nigh impossible. When Hitler completed the Chancellery early in 1939 he thought that its roof of 9ft. of concrete and massive walls would be proof against any bombs.

ROOF CRASHED IN

He failed to foresee the block-buster, and last night the great roof was brought crashing down to trap the shelterers deep under ground.

The new Reich Chancellery had a frontage of a quarter of a mile from the Wilhelmstrasse to the Hermann Göringstrasse.

The finest marbles and stones that Germany could produce were brought to Berlin to make it the show place of Nazi power.

Huge bronze double doors gave entrance to a "court of honour" which in turn gave way to marble halls, tapestried galleries, and beautiful gardens.

In the very heart was Hitler's huge workroom. Now all this is reported to have been swept away.

Last night's tenth mighty blow against the German capital appears to have been one of the most devastating since the Battle of Berlin began seven weeks ago.

Although the tonnage of bombs was less than in some attacks the destruction is reported to be at least as great as on the worst previous night.

A report quoted by the Swedish newspaper *Aftontidningen* says that so far 2,760 people are known to have been killed and 140,000 made homeless.

CITY EMPTIES

The German detector apparatus registered 730 planes attacking the city.

Non-stop evacuation is reported to have reduced the population from 4,000,000 to about 1,000,000.

Three Regular divisions of the German Army have been tied down in Berlin by the R.A.F., according to a Swedish engineer, G. P. Cedergren, chief of Stockholm's A.R.P.

Back from a tour of inspection in the German capital, he confirmed earlier reports that troops are being rushed to fires which the civilian authorities could not cope with.

Another duty of the soldiers is to prevent riots, demonstrations, or mutinies by the hundreds of thousands of foreign workers and prisoners camped in and around Berlin.

Cedergren told a Stockholm audience how Berliners were often kept in their cellars 12 hours after the "All Clear" for fear of time-bombs; how fires suddenly broke out a whole day after a raid owing to undetected fires started by incendiaries.

He was full of awe for the R.A.F.'s ingenuity in dropping a few explosive bombs from time to time along with incendiaries dropped by the Pathfinders.

This tactic had the effect of driving A.R.P. workers under cover at the beginning of a raid, and thereby giving illuminating fires a better chance of getting going before the main attacking force reached the target.

Absence of corridors connecting basements of individual buildings had resulted in thousands being trapped.

AREA BY AREA

STOCKHOLM, Monday.—Sven Hansson, correspondent of the Swedish newspaper *Svenska Dagbladet*, who returned from Berlin to-day, said: "Last night's raid was extremely heavy in the centre, as well as the outer districts.

"The attack on the centre of the city was concentrated on the Potsdamerplatz and its surroundings, which were badly hit.

"It is obvious that the British are systematically bombing and destroying one district after another. The west was first to be attacked, followed by the Stettiner Bahnhof district, then the south and south-east, but the east has not yet been smashed.

"So many buildings with sirens attached have been destroyed that the alarm is now much weaker than it used to be.

"Evacuation from both districts is proceeding at a rapid pace."—Reuter.

—Every Enemy Fighter Up to Meet R.A.F.—BACK Page.

BROKEN ARMIES IN FULL RETREAT

GERMANY PROPER — GERMAN OCCUPIED POLAND 1939 — SOVIET OCCUPIED POLAND 1939 — SOVIET UNION
BERLIN — WARSAW — PRESENT LINE — JULY 1943 LINE — STALINGRAD
0 MILES 200 400 600 800 1,000 1,200 1,400

SCALE diagram illustrates in vivid form the course of events since Stalingrad. Note distances between Stalingrad and the front to-day and between the present front and Berlin.

From Daily Mail Special Correspondent

STOCKHOLM, Monday.

THE Red Army to-night stands on the old Polish frontier—at the climax of a breathtaking advance of 90 miles in eleven days.

Novograd Volinski, last big town east of the border and held by the Germans since July 19, 1941, was stormed by three infantry divisions supported by tanks and mobile artillery, said Stalin to-night in a Special Order of the Day.

Some 45 miles to the north another column has captured **Olevsk,** ten miles from the frontier on the railway from Korosten.

Advance patrols are far beyond these towns, the most important of the 170 localities captured in to-day's great westward surge which has widened the Zhitomir front to at least 70 miles.

Between the two rail bases a score or more of small towns and villages have fallen, keeping the line almost straight from the north to the south.

South of Novograd Volinski more towns, including **Baranovka** and **Dzyerjinsk** have been taken.

The Ukrainian front now runs to the south-east from the Kiev-Warsaw road, loops round Berdichev, which is practically surrounded, and probably under shell fire, and south and east for another 80 miles.

On this sector—big enough almost to be a separate front—more gains were recorded to-day.

They were chiefly south of the great base of Byelaya Tserkov. By the fall of **Pyatigori,** 18 miles farther south of Byelaya Tserkov, the Russians appear to have begun a distant encirclement of the town and to be heading for the deep rear of the German garrisons in the Dnieper Bend.

BLIZZARDS RAGE

On this sector, as on the Zhitomir front, the advance is maintaining a steady average of about 10 miles a day, an incredible performance in the face of winter blizzards such as Berlin says are now raging all over the Eastern Front.

Indeed, the progress made by Gen. Vatutin's armies lends colour to the belief (openly expressed in Moscow) that Manstein's men are in full retreat.

Evidence is also accumulating that the German High Command has largely lost control of the battles in the Ukraine and that many formations and units are fighting hopeless local rearguard actions against the encircling Russians.

The loss of almost all their major rail connections with the west cannot fail to be reflected very quickly in the toughness of the German defences.

Modern automatic weapons use up ammunition so swiftly that supply is always a major problem—and it is an insoluble one for many of the German commanders in the Ukraine.

Berlin reports to-night indicate that General Rokossovsky has launched a new offensive along the Zhlobin-Rogachev front. Breaches were admitted.

SINGLE TRACKS

In the approaches to Vitebsk the battle is raging more fiercely than ever as the Red Army seeks to storm the great fortress.

And nearly 400 miles to the south the sweep to Jmerinka and the Bug goes steadily on in the face of fierce blizzards and across country studded with small villages and farmhouses which the Germans are hastily converting into strong-points.

It is believed that Manstein has some 60 divisions, approximately 800,000 men, in the enormous area east of Jmerinka into the Dnieper Bend.

Once Jmerinka falls these troops must rely for supplies on the single-tracked Rumanian railways across the Carpathians. Expert opinion holds this to be a physical impossibility.

Sertorius says that this is the "neuralgic point" and that a Russian success would put the Germans in a most perilous situation.

The only hope held out by Berlin commentators to-day was that the blizzards may check the Russian tide.

DAWN ATTACK

North of Nevel the advance continued with the capture of 70 inhabited areas.

A German Overseas News Agency commentator said that so strong were the Soviet forces now fighting in the Zhitomir sector "that it was almost surprising that they have not yet achieved a break-through on a large scale.

"The strength of the German forces fighting under rather unfavourable weather conditions has been extremely heavily tested. As conditions are the Germans have had to surrender ground and have not been capable of launching any counter-attack.

"For the time being it cannot be yet gauged what the strategic repercussions of Vatutin's advance on the position in the large Dnieper Bend will be."

Col. Hammer reported a dawn offensive yesterday by Rokossovsky which achieved a considerable local penetration. He claimed it was liquidated later and that heavy counter-attacks are in progress.

Hammer admitted heavy casualties in the "swaying battle" be-

BACK PAGE—Col SEVEN

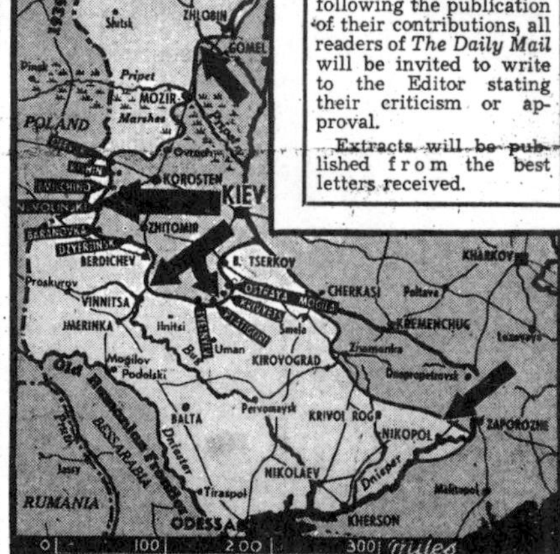

THE Red Army is now practically on the old Polish frontier on a 70-miles front west of Kiev. | Another striking advance has been made south of Byelaya Tserkov, which is almost cut off.

Front Moving Out of Russia

THE Russian battlefront, as this map shows, is moving steadily towards Continental Europe. It is now closer to Berlin than it is to Stalingrad. The time is now in sight when the Russian front will become the Polish and Rumanian fronts, and then the German front.

Daily Mail — How would YOU deal with Germany?

A PLAN for dealing with Germany at the end of the war will be published in *The Daily Mail* to-morrow.

It is the subject of an article written by an expert political observer, and although *The Daily Mail* does not associate itself necessarily with the opinions expressed, it takes pleasure in publishing the first concise and constructive plan to be put forward.

★

We have asked a number of eminent men and women to give their views on the plan, and, following the publication of their contributions, all readers of *The Daily Mail* will be invited to write to the Editor stating their criticism or approval.

Extracts will be published from the best letters received.

THE MANY SEND THEIR MITES FOR THE FEW

By Daily Mail Reporter

TWO thousand letters marked "Battle of Britain Memorial Fund" were delivered to the Bank of England yesterday. They came from the Many for the memorial to the Few, and brought cheques and postal orders ranging from 1s. to £1.

Last night bank officials told me. "We have not been able to open them all yet, but they appear to be from people all over the country and mostly the amounts are small—tributes from ordinary people who cannot afford large sums and just the sort of contributions the organisers of the fund wish to have."

To-night fund officials hope to cast an approximate total to take advantage of the offer made by Mr. Vivian Van Damm, theatrical producer, who has promised £100 for every £1,000 subscribed by mid-night.

"Despite the contributions which have come in since *The Daily Mail* drew attention to the flagging interest," I was told last night, "it is unlikely that we shall have more than £10,000 in hand yet."

The fund needs £20,000, and contributions can still be sent to the Bank of England, Threadneedle-street, London, or handed in to any bank. If there is a surplus, it will go to the R.A.F. Benevolent Fund

Duce's Plane Flies With RAF

Daily Mail Special Correspondent

ALLIED H.Q., N. Africa, Monday.—An Italian Cant flying boat, which was built specially for Mussolini and which he used to fly on official and private visits, is now being used by the North-West African Coastal Air Force.

This aircraft is fast and has a most luxuriously-equipped cabin.

'Tell All' is German Radio Line

Russian Horrors Given in Full

ALL reports and comments from Berlin on the Eastern Front battles yesterday were couched in the grimmest terms. There was not a word of comfort or hope anywhere.

Neutral correspondents were allowed by the censors to send out messages indicating that the position of the Germans is one of extreme gravity.

And broadcasts for home consumption touched the horrific in their recital of the "impossible conditions" facing the troops.

It may be that this particular brand of propaganda was especially put out to counter the effects of the recent R.A.F. bombardments of Berlin.

One example of the dispatches passed by the Berlin censor was that published in the *Social Demokraten.* It said:—

"The entire German line from Vitebsk to the Black Sea appears to be wavering."

'Shoot Like Madmen'

A panzer officer, broadcasting from Berlin, said:

"The Russians are attacking us at a terrific speed. They are marksmen—and hit their target again and again.

"Our comrades are getting very disquieted and we are shooting like madmen, but the enemy have so many guns that we are unable to achieve anything.

"Now our troops are retreating and our lines of communication with the rear are interrupted."

And this is what a war correspondent broadcast:

"Though all I am going to tell you seems impossible, yet it really is so.

"Fighting and even our very existence on the Eastern Front are on the borderline of impossibility.

"Mud and rain alternates with snow and icy cold winds, against which our warm clothing cannot stand. Hot food does not reach our lines—it is the same story all along the front.

"A cigarette is a great thing . . . delicious . . . when you can get one. It is so terrible that you cannot think—you can only act. Many soldiers are ill and there is a lot of gastric trouble. We all have a bitter lot to bear. Those of you who think they are near to despair should think of us in Russia, for life on the Eastern Front cannot be compared with anything."

F. D. R. ESTATE FOR U.S.

President's Gift

HYDE PARK, Monday.—The President and Mrs. Roosevelt have deeded their family home and estate of 33 acres at Hyde Park to the United States Government as a "national historic site," it is revealed to-day.

The President and Mrs. Roosevelt signed the deeds on Thursday in Washington, and Mr. Harold L. Ickes, Secretary of the Interior, accepted the gift on Friday.

The President and his immediate family will have the use of the home during their lifetimes. They will pay all taxes.—*A.P.*

Roosevelt Much Better

WASHINGTON, Monday.—The condition of President Roosevelt, who has been suffering from a cold, has definitely improved, but he is remaining in bed to-day.

This was stated to-day by Mr. Stephen Early the White House secretary, who added that it is uncertain whether the President's condition will permit him to deliver in person next week his message to Congress.—*Reuter.*

Argentina Greets Bolivian Govt.

BUENOS AIRES, Monday.—The Argentine Government, it is announced here, has formally recognised the Bolivian Government of Major Villaroel, formed after last month's coup d'état

The Inter-American Committee for Political Defence recommended South American States not to be in a hurry to recognise the Bolivian Government.—*Reuter* and *A.P.*

Duff Cooper Flies to Algiers

ALGIERS, Monday.—Mr. Duff Cooper, accompanied by Lady Diana Cooper, arrived in Algiers to-day to take up his post as Ambassador to the French Committee of National Liberation.

He was greeted on alighting at the airfield by representatives of General de Gaulle and M. René Massigli, Commissioner for Foreign Affairs.—*Reuter.*

Turkey-Bulgaria Phones Cut

NEW YORK, Monday.—All telephone and telegraph communications between Turkey and Bulgaria were broken off yesterday, according to an *Associated Press* report from Istanbul.

The report adds that there are rumours in Istanbul that the Bulgarian Government led by M. Bojilov has fallen.—*Reuter.*

INVASION 'COUNCIL' MAY MEET SOON

HOME

Chiefs are Arriving

GENERAL MONTGOMERY pictured in London yesterday after it had been announced that he had arrived home from Italy to take up his post as commander of the British invasion forces.

An "Invasion War Council" in London is probably imminent. It would be attended by such Second Front leaders as Air Chief Marshal Sir Trafford Leigh-Mallory, General Sir Bernard Montgomery and General Spaatz, who are already here. Others are due shortly.

General Montgomery, whose arrival was officially announced yesterday, told people who recognised him: "I don't expect to be here long. I am always on the move these days."

From ALEXANDER CLIFFORD, Daily Mail Special Correspondent

EIGHTH ARMY FRONT, Thursday (delayed).

GENERAL Montgomery said his good-bye to his Eighth Army men to-day.

There was no big formal parade—there could not be with the divisions scattered along 50 miles of snowy, hilly front line. But thousands of Eighth Army soldiers saw their leader driving along the muddy roads for the last time.

And all read the farewell message which he composed for them.

He gave one last talk to the officers of his staff, and as many other ranks as could crowd into a little provincial theatre. He made it as informal as he could.

He strolled casually on to the stage scratching his ear while the men in the audience were still shuffling and chatting.

But as soon as he got in front of the microphone he began to wonder whether he could possibly go through with it.

He was very deeply moved indeed. He told us that he might falter a little because it was no easy thing to say good-bye to the Eighth Army.

He asked our help in getting

BACK PAGE—Col. THREE

'WHY WAS I BORN A GERMAN?'

Nazi's Heart-cry

Daily Mail Special Correspondent

ALLIED H.Q., North Africa, Monday.

ONE of the most illuminating documents taken from a captured German in this war is a diary kept by an ex-Hitler Youth Storm-troop leader who was made prisoner by the British in Italy.

The writer is a very young man. His entries begin on a note of high pride and end in horrified disillusion.

His first entry is made on January 23, 1943, when he joined the German Army proper. It reads:

"Fitted out in uniform. Feel and look fine, if a little odd." A month later he writes: "Gradually I am beginning to feel myself a real soldier." He arrives in Italy on September 10, 1943, and records his feelings of "pride and honour because I am fighting for our great and well-loved Führer."

This entry, clearly written in a state of high Teutonic emotion, concludes with this verse from the Song of the Panzer Grenadiers:

"We have battled and fought;
No pain laid us low.
For death cared we nought,
We triumphed o'er the foe;
For always we lead, and when danger nears
It's—Forward the Panzer Grenadiers!"

The change comes towards the end of November. By this time the diarist has had his fill of fighting on a British sector of the front.

'Old Values Gone'

Early in December he writes bitterly: "I wish I was an Englishman! All this retreating does not agree with me."

The last entry in the diary is dated December 22, the day before the writer was captured:

"Yesterday night during the retreat I finally broke with my old life. Gone are the old values, all that was precious to me. In my soul only one thing remains—a hatred of the bestiality of the German Army.

"At the least one is a human being. Everyone curses the Nazi Government, but few have the courage to turn against it. The brutality of oppression is still so strong

"I would like to help strengthen the thousands who long for final collapse. Why was I born a German? I feel myself always a slave."

British Army 'Best Ever'—Berlin

The British Army was highly praised last night on the Berlin radio.

The German News Agency, quoting the Spanish weekly *El Espanol,* says: "Britain has never had a better Army than that which will invade the Continent.

"This is true not only of its training but also of its equipment. Moreover, the British Command is fully alive to the greatness of the task ahead."—*Reuter.*

U.S. Accuses 30 of Treason

WASHINGTON, Monday.—Two women and 28 men were indicted to-day by a Federal grand jury on charges of conspiracy to aid in the establishment of a Nazi form of Government in the United States

All defendants are alleged to have conspired with German Government officials and Nazi leaders to encourage mutiny in the American armed forces.—*Reuter.*

Balkans 'Ready to Break Away'

Daily Mail Special Correspondent

MADRID, Monday.—Diplomatic travellers reaching Vichy and Paris say that the situation in Hungary and Bulgaria resembles closely that prevailing in Italy last July. A break can be expected at any moment.

M. Massigli for U.S.

ALGIERS, Monday.—Political quarters here believe that M. Massigli, Commissar for Foreign Affairs, may before long leave for an extended mission abroad, which may take him to the United States.—*Reuter.*

'Hitler Must Die'—War Trials Chief

NEW YORK, Monday.

GENERAL MARCEL DE BAER, chairman of the Inter-Allied Commission for the Prosecution of War Criminals, was asked to-day the correct punishment for Hitler. He replied: "Death."

He added that only the assurance to the peoples of the occupied countries that justice will be done to war criminals can avoid chaos.

The commission's plan calls for trials by national courts, or by an international court in respect of leaders such as Hitler, Mussolini, and possibly Tojo, and for crimes such as those against British prisoners of war in Germany.—*Reuter.*

PHONE CALLS TO MOSCOW

London Link Again

Direct telephone contact between London and Moscow, severed since 1939, is to be re-established on February 1. The new service will be available at the London end—for outgoing calls—for three hours daily, from 10 a.m. to 1 p.m. (B.S.T.).

All calls will be made from the Ministry of Information, and must be booked through a language censor. Scripts will have to be submitted and from half an hour's to an hour's notice will be necessary for a fixed-time call.

Incoming calls will come into the International Telephone Exchange, be routed to the Ministry switchboard, and then to the subscriber.

A telephone link between New York and Moscow was established last September at a cost of about £5 for three minutes.

RAIN IN STRAIT

Strait of Dover last night: Rain; sea choppy; barometer falling.

THREE KILLED IN INDIA CLASH

Peshawar, Monday.—Three people were killed and some property damaged following a clash between Moslems and Sikhs at Haripur to-day.—Reuter.

PISTOIA RAIDED

Allied planes have again attacked Pistoia, north-west of Florence, says Rome radio. High losses are feared.—Reuter.

LUFTWAFFE CHIEF IN SERBIA

German radio reveals that German military forces in Serbia are under the command of Air-Marshal Fe[illegible]r.—Reuter.

2

The Daily Sketch

o. 10,818 ★★★ MONDAY, JANUARY 17, 1944 ONE PENNY

NAZIS LOSE 100,000 IN 3 WEEKS

INVASION CHIEF HERE

By 'Daily Sketch' Correspondent

GENERAL EISENHOWER, Supreme C.-in-C. of the Allied invasion forces, may ay his broad invasion plan efore his leaders to-day at heir first meeting in Britain.

His arrival here to take over ommand was announced from Vashington last night.

General Eisenhower had important talks with President Roosevelt and Mr. Churchill on is journey from the Mediteranean.

If the War Council meet to-day t will probably be in the newly-prepared and secret H.Q. of the Supreme Command of the Allied Expeditionary Force.

The C.-in-C. is expected to eveal his plan in general terms, and, at an early date, to call a eries of "war councils" to thrash out, with the chiefs concerned, he exact part which each arm vill play.

General Eisenhower.

New Breach On Front Of Nine Miles

IN less than three weeks in Russia — between December 24 and January 13—the Germans lost 100,000 officers and men killed, 7,000 prisoners and more than 2,500 tanks.

This news was given in Moscow last night simultaneously with the Russian communiqué announcing that the Red Army, after a three days' offensive, yesterday had broken the enemy line on a nine-mile front to a depth of five miles west of Veliki Luki.

Costly Losses of Men

Brigadier E. C. Anstey, D.S.O., THE DAILY SKETCH Military Correspondent, analysing the Russian communiqué, writes:

"There are three items of importance in the Russian news—the opening of a minor offensive near Novosokolniki, the repulse of German counter-attacks near Vinnitsa, and the heavy losses inflicted on the enemy during the last three weeks on the First Ukrainian front.

"Of these, the last item is the most important. The Germans can afford to lose ground, but they cannot afford to lose men.

"The failure of their counter-attacks has been very costly and offers the best promise we have, by the losses incurred, of a shortening of the war."

Novosokolniki (19 miles west of Veliki Luki), theatre of the new Russian breakthrough, is 200 miles south of the Leningrad area where, for the past three days, the Germans have reported heavy Red Army attacks aimed strategically at the Baltic States.

More than 40 places have been taken by the Russians in their

Turn to Back Page, Col. 2

'Across The Bug'

Advance Russian troops of a powerful tank unit have crossed the river Bug at Vinnitsa, says the Stockholm newspaper "Dagens Nyheter," this morning, quoting a Berlin military spokesman.

The spokesman claimed that German reserves had trapped the Russians, who were doomed unless they could get reinforcements.—Associated Press.

Map shows position of new Soviet break-through at Novosokolniki, north of Nevel.

Premier, Fit Again, Meets Gen. De Gaulle

From JAMES McDOWALL, 'Daily Sketch' War Correspondent, Algiers, Sunday

MR. CHURCHILL, who has been convalescing at Marrakesh, capital of French Morocco, after his recent illness, has been in conference there with General de Gaulle, it was revealed to-day.

The Prime Minister, completely restored to health, was in excellent spirits.

The talk took place last Wednesday and was the first meeting between the two leaders since they lunched at Algiers in June.

Among the matters discussed were: Recognition of the French Committee of National Liberation and its authority on French soil after the liberation of France; participation of French forces in freeing France; immediate sending of arms to the members of the French underground resistance movement.

'Cordial Atmosphere'

The official statement issued to-day on the meeting says: "The conversation was pursued in a most cordial atmosphere."

It took place after a luncheon given by the Prime Minister and Mrs. Churchill at the villa which was requisitioned for them.

Also present were Lord Beaverbrook, Mr. Duff Cooper, and M. Gaston Palewski, General de Gaulle's Director of Cabinet.

After lunch the party sat around the swimming pool, where they talked for several hours.

The conversation was not confined to politics and the war. The General asked the Premier if he still painted. Mr. Churchill replied: "No; I am too weak for that sort of thing nowadays—but I am still strong enough to wage war."

The conversation lasted until five o'clock. The following morning Mr. Churchill, wearing R.A.F. uniform, attended a parade of French troops in Marrakesh, standing beside the General.

WE HAVE BEEN TRAMPING

—Mrs. Churchill

MRS. CHURCHILL told General de Gaulle, at Marrakesh, that the Prime Minister's health had been completely restored, and added:

"We have been for many long tramps on the mountain sides in the sunshine."

Mr. Churchill gave de Gaulle two cigars, and they smoked as they strolled in the gardens together after lunch.

Lady Diana Duff Cooper and the Prime Minister's daughter, Sarah Churchill, were also at Marrakesh.

TIMELY WORDS OF FAITH

Thus saith the Lord, Even the captives of the mighty shall be taken away, and the prey of the terrible shall be delivered.

Isaiah, 49, 25.

15 Killed, 30 Injured In London Train Crash

By 'Daily Sketch' Correspondent

FIFTEEN people were killed and 30 injured when a train from Norwich to Liverpool-street, London, crashed into the back of one from Yarmouth, also bound for Liverpool-street, at Ilford station last night.

It was the most serious accident on British railways for two years.

Most of the casualties were passengers in the rear coach of the Yarmouth train.

The coach was lifted into the air and remained perched on the engine of the second train, which at the time was moving comparatively slowly.

Three of the coaches of the Norwich train were telescoped and at least two of those of the front train wrecked. The platform was strewn with wreckage, and a dining-car saloon had been flung across the opposite track and rested against the platform.

Railway first aid parties tended the injured, and a fleet of ambulances was rushed to the station, while Civil Defence rescue squads, working by the light of flares, strove to rescue trapped passengers, helped by British and American soldiers.

Thought It Was Bomb

The L.N.E.R. in a statement said the seriously injured were taken to the King George V. Hospital, Ilford, where many emergency operations were performed.

John Duffield, a passenger in the Norwich train, said: "I was in the corridor when there was a crash. We thought it was a bomb. Everyone in my carriage clambered on to the track."

A sailor in the Yarmouth train said: "I was in the corridor with my wife. There were two bumps and we all fell on the floor. I came back and joined in the rescue work. I think we got out about eight injured."

People Under Wreckage

Mr. I. Bagfee, of Craven-gardens, Ilford, who helped in the rescue work, said there were at least two dead in one telescoped carriage.

Constable Yardley said when he got into one of the coaches all the seats were piled up, with people underneath the wreckage.

Some in one carriage were pinned underneath the buffers of the following coach, which had crashed through. We had to jack the buffers to get the people out. An American soldier in this coach was badly injured and said to the men trying to release him: "I will get to Berlin yet."

Turn to Back Page, Col. 3

U.S. Rocket Gun Helps Russia

Washington, Sunday.—The United States gave Russia the secret Bazooka (rocket) gun to help the Red Army fight Nazi tank attacks, a U.S. Army ordnance expert, Colonel Miller, revealed to-day.

It was used by the Russians in stopping the Nazi attempt to break through at Kursk and Orel in June last.

Another new weapon, the United States bomber B29, is described as the super-Fortress.

The Joint Aircraft Committee, composed of British and American Army and Navy representatives, have made this statement. They add that in their new policy for naming warplanes, names will be designed to ensure uniformity, simplicity and meaning.—Associated Press.

5th CAPTURE HILL BLOCK TO CASSINO

From JAMES McDOWALL, 'Daily Sketch' War Correspondent, Allied G.H.Q., Sunday

MONTE TROCCHIO, last mountain bastion blocking the way to Cassino, has been captured by American forces of the Fifth Army.

They completed the task by nightfall yesterday, after facing fierce shelling from German artillery posted on the top of the ridge and along the slopes.

French and American troops in the mountain sector north of the Rome road have taken two more villages and an important mountain peak.

The combined assault is going on unchecked along the whole Cassino front.

Main assault on Monte Trocchio, 1,475-ft. ridge two miles along wedged in between the Rome road and the railway, three miles south-east of Cassino, was launched at dawn.

Artillery 'Carpet'

One column of American forces attacked from the north-east, crossing the Rome road from Cervaro. Another column approached the ridge from the south-east.

The Allied infantry were covered by an artillery "carpet."

The attackers first had to overcome the main defences, consisting of gun emplacements and concrete strong-points. Having got to the base of the mountain they pressed home their initial gains to occupy the whole ridge.

Continuing to move towards the Rapido, French and American troops under the command of General Juin have occupied the 3,600ft. high Monte Croce, where the river has its source.

A pincer movement, in which French forces advanced from the newly-captured heights of Ferro and Pagano, led to the taking of the village of Valle Rotonda.

The "Bazooka," the U.S. Army's anti-tank rocket gun.

Daily Mail

NO. 14,890 ONE PENNY ** FOR KING AND EMPIRE SATURDAY, JANUARY 22, 1944

LATE WAR NEWS

BERLIN'S WORST NIGHT OF TERROR

THE CZARS' SUMMER PALACES SACKED

THE Germans sacked Peterhof, the most brilliant and elaborate summer residence of the once Russian Court, where two centuries of architectural taste were reflected, *Red Star* revealed to-day. The Great Palace and Mon Plaisir Palace, where Peter the Great lived as he was building St. Petersburg, were burned. The Germans had made public rest rooms and a comfort station out of Peterhof Cathedral. Great damage is also reported from the ancient city of Novgorod, of which hardly a building has been left intact.—*A.P.*

Fourth Offensive Opens Below Leningrad

BIG RAIL BASE OF MGA TAKEN

From Daily Mail Special Correspondent

STOCKHOLM, Friday.

STALIN to-night announced the opening of the fourth offensive on the Northern Front in six days. It has been launched by the combined armies of the Leningrad and the Volkhov sectors and has captured the railway junction of Mga.

This new attack, announced in a Special Order of the Day, is clearly synchronised with the offensives already in progress south-west of Leningrad and west of Novgorod. It is aimed at driving the Germans from their great defences.

It is the beginning of the final phase of the Winter War and means that the 150 miles of the Northern Front from Lake Ilmen to the Gulf of Finland is ablaze.

Mga controls the railway south-east from Leningrad to the interior, and the advance westward will aid in freeing the close network of railways around Leningrad.

Its fall has also cut the main supply line to the garrisons of the German defences along the line to Kirishi and Chudovo, which lies north of Novgorod.

A hundred miles to the south of the new front the victors of Novgorod are now ten miles west of the city on the main road and railway through Batetskaya to Luga, less than 50 miles away.

The capture of Batetskaya, 20 miles west of the new Russian line, will cut the railway running north to Leningrad and complete the encirclement of all the Germans still manning the Volkhov River defences.

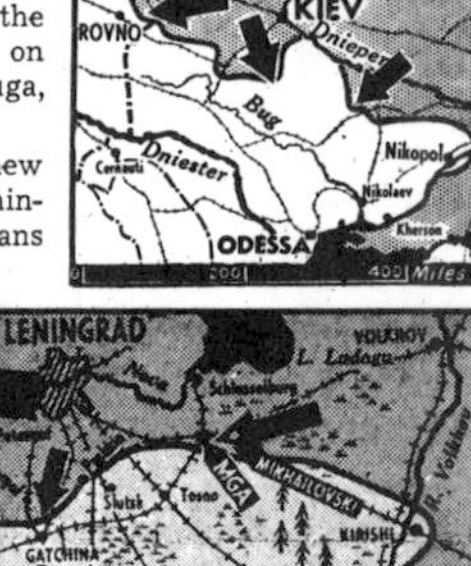

THE Russians have now started a third offensive on the northern front—this time against the north-eastern part of the German salient.

First success has been the capture of Mga, an important junction which had been blocking the direct rail route S.E. from Leningrad.

A considerable advance south-west of Leningrad was reported in the routine communiqué.

The town of Vitino, 36 miles from the city, has fallen. It cuts the main line to Leningrad along the Baltic coast.

Moscow added that the Germans encircled in this area have now been "liquidated." Remnants of the Novgorod garrison are being steadily mopped up in the woods west of the city

Berlin to-night admitted a withdrawal "south of Ropha," which agrees with the Russian report.

Many miles ahead of the troops advancing beyond Novgorod large numbers of ski battalions are carrying out their now classical tactics of harassing German supply lines and cutting up supply columns.

They are being actively assisted by thousands of Russian guerillas, who are also reported to have created very considerable confusion on the supply route from the west which runs to the Leningrad front along the Baltic coastline.

'DEFENSIVE BATTLE'

Heavy fighting is now spreading along the whole of the front north of the Pripet Marshes.

Reports from Moscow to-day said that battles are raging along the line south from Leningrad along the Moscow railway, near Chudovo junction, and down the River Volkhov.

These attacks are obviously aimed at holding the Germans in their defences until the great pincer movement has been completed behind them.

Berlin reports fresh attacks north of Nevel and the German communiqué to-day gave great prominence to what it described as the "Vitebsk defensive battle."

The battle, said the Germans, began on December 13 and by January 18 had cost the Russians 40,000 dead, 1,203 tanks, and 349 guns.

The Red Army had attacked with 50 rifle divisions and the Germans, under a major-general, had held their positions, added the High Command

The reference to the commander suggests that the city is besieged A major-general would hardly direct a defensive battle against 50 enemy divisions (probably more than 500,000 men) unless his troops were surrounded.

NEW ADVANCE

A fresh series of attacks is also reported by Berlin from the Mozyr area where yesterday the withdrawal from a strongpoint was admitted.

The Moscow communiqué reported advances north-west of Kalinkovichi, with the capture of several places.

Although there is no news from Moscow about the progress of the great battle for the River Bug crossings near Vinnitsa on the Dnieper front, there is some indication that General Vatutin has begun to counter-attack.

Colonel Hammer said that a Russian tank attack north of Uman was repelled and ground gained.

In a further comment on the northern battle Hammer said:

"The enemy has not been able to make the break-through which he is striving to achieve, despite the constant arrival of fresh forces and an array of technical weapons remarkable even for the Eastern Front.

"No slackening of the fighting is, however, discernible. It rages day and night with extreme bitterness on both sides. Every inch of ground is hotly contested with the numerically superior attacker."

The Vichy radio also reported that the Germans "are now regrouping and carrying out a general shortening of their lines around Leningrad.

COLDER IN STRAIT

Strait of Dover last night: Fine and cool; some low cloud banks; temperature nearing freezing point.

No Divorce Cases for the Magistrates

By **WILSON BROADBENT,** Political Correspondent

THE suggestion that divorce cases should be tried by magistrates has been rejected by the authorities. The highest legal opinion is opposed to the idea. The strongest reason advanced is that divorce is a serious social problem, and demands close scrutiny of individual cases. But three new judges are likely to be appointed immediately.

Divorce cannot be placed on the same level as the minor problems which are dealt with by local magistrates.

Nor are there sufficient stipendiary magistrates in the country to undertake the additional burden of divorce actions in their localities. They are already fully employed, as are county court judges.

It would mean appointing a large number of additional stipendiary magistrates or county court judges if divorce actions—even undefended cases—were allotted to them instead of coming before High Court judges.

Expense Reduced

But the authorities fully appreciate the advantages of allowing more divorce actions to be heard in the provinces, if only for the reason that the congestion of the Law Courts in London would be relieved, and in many cases the expenses to the parties concerned would be reduced.

In the past it has been the custom to hear the majority of divorce actions in London because of the shortage of High Court judges, but there is no legal compulsion about this.

The Lord Chancellor has drafted a Bill, which will be debated in Parliament shortly for raising the maximum number of High Court judges in all the divisions from 25 to 32.

Under this Bill it will be left to the Lord Chancellor to determine when extra judges shall be appointed, up to the new maximum of 32, and also in which division they shall adjudicate.

It is understood that immediately the new Bill becomes law, the Lord Chancellor will appoint three new judges especially to deal with arrears of divorce courts, and that two of these will go on circuit to try divorce actions in the provinces.

WE MAY HAVE LESS BUTTER

SOS for Supplies

The Ministry of Food has sent out an S O S to all butter-producing countries for more supplies, otherwise the ration of 2oz. a week may have to be cut.

Australia, where the ration of butter is half a pound weekly, has promised to do everything possible to increase her exports to this country. Everything depends on the available shipping

The Hon. D. L. Campbell, Minister of Agriculture, Manitoba, said yesterday that the liberal allowance of bacon in Canada should be reduced so that more could be sent to Britain.

Air Command for U.S. General

ALLIED H.Q., North Africa, Friday.—General Eaker announced to-day the appointment of General John K. Cannon as commander of the U.S. 12th Air Force.

General Cannon will also serve as commander of the Tactical Air Force, composed of British and American units, which acts in close support of the Fifth and Eighth Armies.—*A.P.*

India RAF Get 6

CALCUTTA, Friday.—R.A.F. Spitfires shot down six Japanese aircraft and damaged a number of others in a sharp air battle yesterday in Burma.—*Reuter.*

U.S. 'Subs' Sink 12

WASHINGTON, Friday.—American submarines have sunk 12 more Japanese vessels in the Pacific and Far East, according to a Navy communiqué issued here.—*Reuter.*

Daily Mail TRANSATLANTIC EDITION

U.S. PRESS QUOTE VOICE OF BRITAIN

On Germany's Fate

From DON IDDON

NEW YORK, Friday.

IT is becoming plain that extracts from the *Transatlantic Daily Mail* are to become a weekly feature of many American newspapers.

The Associated Press Agency sent out to-day to hundreds of newspapers throughout the country a 600-words story quoting passages from a special feature in the *Transatlantic Daily Mail's* second issue on the future of Germany.

Extracts from the views of George Bernard Shaw, Mr. Shinwell, M.P., and Lord Vansittart were given great prominence.

Then came inquiries from editors from Cleveland, from Baltimore, and nearer at hand.

Cleveland asked permission to quote articles from the *Transatlantic Daily Mail* in full each week. Others wished for shorter extracts.

Letters Pour in

American newspapers gave the *Transatlantic Daily Mail* full credit. To-day's *New York Post* ran a front-page headline: "Shaw, Shinwell, and Vansittart on What to Do with Germany," while the *New York Sun* ran a similar story under the headline: "Three British Thinkers at Odds on Germany's Disarmament."

A number of radio commentators also quoted extracts from the second issue.

Meanwhile, letters continue to pour in. General of the Armies of the United States John J. Pershing, who rarely writes letters and never sees newspapermen, wrote to me:

"Thank you very much for the first issue of the Transatlantic edition of The Daily Mail, *London, which I have found very interesting indeed.*

"I appreciate your courtesy in introducing it to me, and am, of course, in entire sympathy with its one purpose—to contribute towards a closer understanding between the British and American people."

Federal Chief

Mr. J. Edgar Hoover, head of the Federal Bureau of Investigation, has also written. Lord Halifax has expressed his appreciation. So has British Minister Harold Butler.

Former head of the United States Supreme Court Justice Charles Evans Hughes sent a charming note. Presidential candidate Alf Landon has been in touch with us.

And President Roosevelt's secretary, Stephen Early, writes:

"The President greatly appreciates your thoughtfulness in sending him a copy of this unique publication."

Governors of almost every State have written, together with mayors, business men, college professors, and leaders in every walk of American life. The *Transatlantic Daily Mail* strides forward to new success.

NAZIS ATTACK IN ITALY

Big Gains Claimed

The Germans have launched a full-scale counter-attack against the Fifth Army on the Garigliano.

Their attack appears to be concentrated along the line of our new advance and they claimed last night to have forced the British back to the "mountain fringe of the Garigliano plain."

Allied Forces were said to be cut off north of Minturno, and to have been "dislodged" from Castelforte, a town which has so far not been claimed by the Allies.

Gustav Line Threatened.—BACK Page.

Poland: No Soviet Reply to U.S.

From Daily Mail Correspondent

WASHINGTON, Friday. — Mr. Cordell Hull, Secretary of State, said to-day that the United States was keeping in close touch with the United States Ambassador in Moscow on the Polish situation, but that the Soviet Government had not yet accepted the American friendly offer of good offices.

Mr. Hull's phraseology "has not yet accepted" was regarded as an indication that he is still hopeful of Soviet acceptance.

All-day Blitz on France

Hundreds of Allied planes kept up a dawn-to-dusk battering of the Pas de Calais area yesterday. Eight types of bombers took a hand, from U.S. Forts to R.A.F. fighter-bombers.

Mosquitoes bombed at such low level that they were able to use their cannon. Six enemy planes—including a flying-boat shot down off the Norwegian coast—were destroyed during the day for the loss of two Mosquitoes.

8 Down Last Night

London Barrage in Full Action

Eight German raiders were destroyed last night, it was officially announced early to-day.

By Daily Mail Raid Reporter

FIERCEST barrage Londoners have heard for many months met German planes which last night penetrated the ring of defences.

The crash of shell fire increased as the raiders, coming in high from the South Coast, flew nearer, until at times the full force of the A.A. guns appeared to be in action against the small number of planes which twisted and circled in the mesh of searchlight beams.

British and German planes were in the sky at the same time. The drone of the R.A.F. bombers was heard just before the general Alert.

The raiders dropped flares in great numbers. One group, which fell some distance away, silhouetted St. Paul's against their glare. Others were shot out by the ground gunners.

NFS in Action

High - explosive bombs were dropped in some districts. Houses were damaged and people were trapped at one place. Fires started by incendiaries in one residential area were quickly dealt with.

The Duchess of Kent was one of many thousands of theatre-goers who were caught by the Alert. She was in the stalls at the Palace Theatre, W.

West End crowds gathered in doorways to watch the flak and searchlights. Raiders climbed, circled, and zoomed down almost to roof-top height to escape the shells and the network of light.

Many people believed the raid to be an attempt at reprisal for the devastation of Berlin.

Shells Mark Course

From a point 20 miles out the flashes of bursting shells could be seen over London as planes were "handed" from one searchlight beam to another.

As the raiders sped away home bursting shells marked their course.

A big aerial battle was fought over a south-east town, when enemy planes were attacked by night fighters and ground defences.

A few bombs were dropped in the district causing some damage.

'NAZI FEELERS SPURNED'

U.S. on Peace Moves

NEW YORK, Friday.—The American Press to-day published reports from Washington that Germany has made several peace overtures to Britain in the past, but that all have been turned down.

"Parties representing Germany have been advised that the only terms on which Britain would make peace with Germany are unconditional surrender to the United Nations as a whole," said Kingsbury Smith, International News Service correspondent, in a dispatch to the *Journal-American*.

John M. Hightower, Washington diplomatic correspondent of the *Associated Press*, said: "The British Government, in full agreement with the U.S., Russia, and the other United Nations, has taken, and will take, none of the proposals seriously until the Germans get ready for unconditional surrender."—*Reuter.*

'Conscription Will Stay after War'

Mr. A. T. Lennox Boyd, Parliamentary Secretary to the Ministry of Aircraft Production, said at Oxford last night: "I take it that universal military service as we have got it now would be accepted after the war by all political parties."

'Sixth Sense' Filled Shelters Before Raid

CITY 'DIVE-BOMBED' BY LANCASTERS

For the second time in 24 hours a great force of R.A.F. heavy bombers streamed out to the Continent last night over the east coast. Another force passed over the south-east coast. Shortly afterwards Berlin and Paris long-wave stations went off.

From WALTER FARR

STOCKHOLM, Friday.

BERLINERS are to-day convinced that last night's 2,300-ton attack on the German capital was more terrifying than all the assaults that have gone before, Swedes who experienced the raid and who have reached Malmö, reported late to-night.

The raid, they say, was paralysing despite the fact that a "sixth sense" had warned many Berliners that it was "just the right night for an attack."

People queued at the entrances to the capital's deep shelters long before these were opened at five o'clock, and most of them stayed underground until the early hours of this morning—though Berlin's final "All clear" had sounded about midnight.

All eye-witnesses stress that the British squadrons bombed from a lower level than previously. One of them told me: "It seemed as if thousands and thousands of planes were diving straight for our shelters."

It is clear now that a great deal more than half Berlin has been laid waste. Casualties in last night's raid alone are believed to be in the region of 3,000 dead.

Here is the story of the "super attack" told to me by a Swede whose name I cannot give because he expects that in the future he will be compelled to return to Berlin.

"Last night seemed to come very near to the November vintage. Somehow Berliners sensed that there would be a raid.

"There was nothing really to go on. It was a night much like any of the other nights since January 2 (the date of the previous big raid), but Berliners now claim they have a 'sixth sense' about raids.

"People rushed home from theatres, which all finish about 5 o'clock, and there were very long queues outside the deep shelters all afternoon.

FEINTS

"No one may go into them until five, but people were sure 'they' were coming and decided to make certain of a place down below.

"The R.A.F. tactical feints have played heavily on Berliners' nerves.

"When news comes out that a great fleet is heading for the capital and is then switched somewhere else it shakes people up.

"In the shelters last night the people were saying 'Perhaps they won't come after all, but somehow it seems to be the right sort of night, and they have not been over now for nearly three weeks.'

"That was just before 7 o'clock.

"Some people brought tiny bottles of precious liquor down with

BACK PAGE—Col. FIVE

'Oust Hitler' Army Plot

Gauleiter's Warning

From Daily Mail Correspondent

GENEVA, Friday.

A WARNING to Nazi Party leaders that the German Army is planning a putsch to overthrow Hitler and make peace has been circularised by Gauleiter Erich Koch, one of the party's chiefs.

This is stated by the Gazette de Lausanne, which quotes the circular letter sent out by Koch.

★

THE letter says: "The Führer is in danger. Parties of reaction are trying to displace him and establish a military dictatorship under which Germany would immediately start peace negotiations against the will of the people."

The Few Fund Has Passed the £20,000

By Daily Mail Air Reporter

ANNOUNCING last night that the Battle of Britain Memorial Fund has passed the £20,000 mark, the committee revealed that the heroes' shrine with which the memory of The Few will be commemorated in Westminster Abbey is to be named "The Royal Air Force Chapel."

It was hoped that the fund would be largely subscribed in small sums by the many. That hope has been fully realised since *The Daily Mail* drew attention to the fact that donations were not coming in as quickly as was expected.

Many thousands of subscriptions of £1 or less have been sent from all parts of the country.

The King and Queen are among the subscribers. Queen Mary also sent a donation.

The fund will be closed on January 31, except for subscriptions from overseas. A new committee has been set up to administer the fund and plan the memorial.

It consists of Lord Trenchard (chairman), Lord Dowding, Colonel E. Gore Browne, Professor A. E. Richardson, and Air Vice-Marshal D Harries.

Messrs. E. H. Keeling, M.P., and N. P. W. Viner-Brady are honorary secretary and treasurer respectively. Their office is at 20, Wilton-street, S.W. 1.—**C. E.**

Pathfinders Work all through Raid

By Daily Mail Air Reporter

THE largest force of Lancasters and Halifaxes yet sent to the German capital by Bomber Command finished their task—from a comparatively low level—in half an hour, which means that the city was plastered at the rate of nearly 80 tons a minute.

The tonnage unloaded in the latest attack was probably a good deal larger than in the previous heaviest raid—on the night of November 22.

As on that occasion, our raiders bombed through cloud with the aid of sky markers—flares which hang on parachutes to mark the target.

Last night the Air Ministry let out another secret about the Pathfinders technique. They disclosed that their job is not completed, as is commonly supposed, by the time the bomb-aimers of the main force start pressing their buttons.

"A great cluster of sky markers," the Air Ministry said last night, "was continuously maintained over the target from 7.30 p.m. until 8 o'clock."

Fighters gathered over the target in large numbers as the attack developed, and the crews of one bomber group reported 40 sightings "all over the target area." Thirty-five aircraft are missing.—**C. E.**

GERMANS HELD IN ITALY

Haig Nicholson, Reuter Special Correspondent with the Fifth Army, cabled late last night: The critical stage of the Garigliano battle has safely passed. The Germans have thrown in every man they had, but have failed to push the British back across the river. Despite determined counter - attacks, British have held their positions and in some cases improved them. German casualties run into thousands.

BEVIN'S PLEDGE ENDS PIT BOYS' STRIKE

By **CHARLES SUTTON,** Industrial Correspondent

THE 140 Bevin Boys who struck at Askern Colliery, near Doncaster, on Thursday for more money went back to their training centre yesterday after receiving a promise from a Ministry of Labour official that their claim would receive an answer to-day.

They wanted to know why they could not have an answer then and there, as they had been led to believe they would.

The official had to explain that there had been a slight delay, but he gave them a promise that they would receive an advance on their first week's wages to-day, as well as a definite reply to their demands.

The hitch occurred when Mr. Bevin submitted his solution to the Treasury, which has to foot the bill. The Treasury was not satisfied that the wording of the solution was in the correct form.

So much hangs on Mr. Bevin's concession. It must be worded in such a way that no other workers in war industries can claim the same consideration.

Mr. Bevin himself was busy all day yesterday trying to find the correct form of words. He wrote and discarded many formulæ, but he has made up his mind that the problem of these boys must be settled before Sunday.

The whole scheme is in the melting pot, and if it is to be a success a quick decision must be made. Mr. Bevin knows that, and that is why he worked so hard yesterday to find a solution.

3 BOMBS HIT DESTROYER

Enemy on Fire

Two enemy destroyers lying in the same Channel estuary were attacked by Coastal Command Albacores early yesterday morning.

Three bombs hit the stern of one destroyer, and large explosions were followed by a fierce fire. One Albacore is missing.

A pilot, Flying Officer D. C. Thomson, a Canadian, said: "The destroyer's gunners opened with everything they had, but I got away without being hit."

U.S. Strikers Go Back

DETROIT, Friday.—Some 1,100 foremen involved in a series of strikes at the eight Chrysler plants here returned to work to-day after voting to end the stoppage in compliance with the request of the War Labour Board.—*Reuter.*

Daily Mail
NO. 14,892 ONE PENNY ✱ ✱ FOR KING AND EMPIRE TUESDAY, JANUARY 25, 1944

LATE WAR NEWS

LITTORIA FALLS: APPIAN WAY CUT

Beach Armies Dig In After a 14-miles Advance

'BIG BATTLE IN THE NEXT 48 HOURS'

LITTORIA town and airport, the Croydon of Rome, have been captured by Allied troops fanning out from the Nettuno bridgehead, according to a Rome broadcast last night.

Littoria lies off the Appian Way 30 miles from Rome, and its capture supports other Axis reports that the Allies have reached this highway and are digging in.

This represents a 14-miles advance, and presumably embraces the town of Aprilia, reported by the Germans to have been reached by American troops yesterday.

These Axis admissions, and a German report that a new landing has been made between Nettuno and Rome, have so far not been confirmed by the Allies, but it is known that up to the present the Germans have been able to deploy only small forces in the path of our advance.

What clashes have taken place are in the nature of patrol actions, but these have become more frequent and may be the prelude to bigger operations.

Behind the Allied patrols now probing the German lines lies the double bridgehead of Nettuno and Anzio, where our main assault forces, the bulk of which are now ashore, are preparing for the next move.

According to General Sir Henry Maitland Wilson, Commander-in-Chief in the Mediterranean, who is now in Italy, the next 48 hours will see the first major battle in the bridgehead area.

Signs of this impending battle came late on Sunday, when the landing force at Anzio Point beat off German counter-attacks and took prisoners.

WIRE ROADS

New roads are already beginning to radiate from the Allied bridgehead—wire roads laid across the sands and marshes so that heavy equipment may be moved up to the inland Italian highways.

Nettuno and Anzio were largely empty towns when the Allies entered—for two months their civilians had been evacuated to an area four or five miles away. Yesterday some of these civilians began drifting back; by last night 300 of the area's 11,000 inhabitants were seeking their old homes.

Last night the Germans claimed a big offensive had been started in the main mid-Italy battle zone in an effort to prevent the German forces there from disengaging.

Allied sources are silent about this offensive, but it is known that the Germans have suffered severe casualties in their counter-attacks against the Southern Italy line—losses which may make an immediate counter-offensive by our forces probable.

Cairo radio last night reported that on the Garigliano front alone hundreds of German prisoners had been taken during the enemy counter-attacks.

SURPRISE COMPLETE

Front-line reporters last night began to send the first full picture of the Nettuno landing and the later development of our bridgehead.

A 15-minute naval bombardment preceded the landing, the selected beaches receiving an average of 200 shells a minute.

The assault troops found the coast was held by only one battalion of Germans; one company of these was captured almost complete.

The only resistance encountered was in the British sector, and our casualties are described as "fantastically light."

So complete was the surprise that Germans fled from some posts in their underclothes, leaving uniforms and arms behind. One British force surprised an armoured car crew in a house 100 yards from the beach. One German was captured—in pyjamas. The others, also in pyjamas, escaped in their armoured car.

One British party "captured" a large group of men in enemy uniform. They came up crying "Russki Russki!" They were Russian prisoners, captured by the Germans in the Ukraine.

After landing our troops began to seek out the Germans inland. One Allied patrol encountered 10 Germans. In three minutes five were dead, three wounded, and two prisoners.

Close-up

CLOSE-UP of the Allied bridgehead area in Italy. The Germans say Allied troops are only four miles from the Appian Way.

Pope Says 'I Stay'

German Plea Rejected

Daily Mail Special Correspondent

Stockholm, Monday.

FIELD-MARSHAL Kesselring, with the climax to the battle of Rome now imminent, is reported to have sent an envoy to the Pope urging him to leave the Vatican for a Catholic area of Germany.

The Pope, according to these reports in Stockholm to-night, has flatly refused.

Kesselring's emissaries are stated to have been a high officer of the German Army and a political envoy.

They are said to have explained that the situation near Rome is now such that the Germans may be forced not only to defend every house in the city but to occupy an area of the Vatican itself.

The reply was: "No, not in any circumstances. The Vatican State is neutral. As its head, I stay here."

NETTUNO: THE FIRST PRISONERS

THE first prisoners taken by Allied troops which landed at Nettuno. German troops in the area were taken by surprise and were captives almost before they knew what was happening.

Russians Slam Gate to West

LENINGRAD LINE CUT

From Daily Mail Special Correspondent

STOCKHOLM, Monday.

GENERAL GOVOROV'S troops, driving south-west from Leningrad, have shut the German gate to the west by cutting the railway leading to Estonia, east of Gatchina.

All the garrisons still holding the northern and eastern sides of the "Leningrad Box"—which runs from Gatchina to Tosno, then south to Chudovo and south-west along the Volkhov River—are practically trapped.

There is a railway from Gatchina to Pskov, the great enemy base at the foot of Lake Peipus.

But Gatchina has already been reported under shell fire from the Russian guns.

To the east there is another line to the south, reaching Pskov via Batatskaya and Dno. But the Red Army sweeping forward from Novgorod is no more than 25 miles from Batatskaya—and the Germans must travel 85 miles from Tosno to Batatskaya, and nearly 150 miles from their Volkhov River positions below Chudovo.

The menace is greatly increased by to-day's successes south of Leningrad.

A Special Order of the Day from Stalin announced the storming of the railway "fortresses" of Pushkin and Slutsk, 17 and 21 miles from the city.

DESPERATE PLIGHT

Later it was announced in the routine communiqué that other places on the railway network around Tosno had been captured.

These successes bring the Russians almost to within gunshot range of the vital Tosno-Gatchina link. When this line is cut, the plight of the Germans will be desperate indeed.

Tosno itself is closely threatened from the north and the east—the Red Army being respectively six and three miles away.

An intensification of the threat from the southern corner of the "Box" is shown by the capture of Zapolye, 15 miles north-west of Novgorod.

An advance here is in the rear of the remnants of the German line, and with no east-west railway the Germans appear to be trapped.

The fortified junction of Chudovo is also closely menaced with Russian troops four miles to the east and ten miles to the north.

A NEW RETREAT

Berlin reports of the northern battles are uniformly gloomy. They estimate that the Russians are using 40 infantry divisions and 20 tank formations, and say the object is to drive up from Novgorod to Kronstadt Bay "and smash the entire German front."

A new retreat west of Novgorod was admitted, and the German-controlled news agency here said that at Nevel the Russians had a 5-1 superiority.

Further progress has been made in the Pripet Marshes, and one report says that Rokossovsky's men have burst through the swamps into open country.

Colonel Hammer, the German military analyst, said the Russians have made a new landing near Kerch, in the Crimea, and admitted fighting in the "harbour area."

He also reported a great new offensive on the Novgorod sector and the Dnieper Bend Front.

A great number of tanks and men were flung into action, he added, and it was possible that the Russians "are trying to build up an offensive which would represent the equivalent of the attack on the Northern Front."

Footnote.—The German radio to-night complained bitterly of the unusually mild weather in Russia, which "makes it extraordinarily difficult to move heavy equipment."

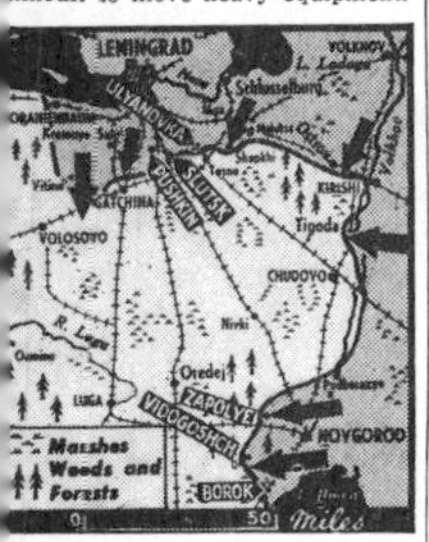

All Germany Off the Air

There was another European radio black-out last night. Berlin and Paris long-wave stations and all stations relaying their programmes went off at just after 8 o'clock. German medium stations reduced power, and the Northern German radio network closed down. Budapest and Sofia were off at intervals during the evening.

Reuter reported that an Alert had been sounded at Bâle, Switzerland.

Southerly Gale Sweeps Strait

A southerly gale blowing off the Continent lashed the Strait of Dover at dusk yesterday. Big seas broke along the English shore, with rain and cloud down to sea level.

The gale was still blowing strongly up to late last night, but there were finer intervals. The barometer fell steadily.

NETTUNO TEST FOR 2nd FRONT

To Stem Reserves

By COLIN BEDNALL, Air Correspondent

THE Allied "left hook" landing at Nettuno has all the appearances of being a test of air power which has particular relation to Second Front calculations.

So far the test has produced remarkably successful results. It now remains to be seen whether the avalanche of bombers and fighters turned upon the area can prevent the enemy from counter-attacking against our bridgehead.

The enemy has now had time to recover from the initial surprise of the landing and to begin moving his strong reserves up against the Fifth Army.

The Nettuno landing differed from Salerno for this reason: in the latter action, the Allies deliberately struck at an established enemy strong-point.

But at Nettuno our forces—just as must happen on the Second Front—chose a point most likely to suit them strategically. Apparently they had no precise knowledge of the opposition which would be encountered.

The much-vaunted German "defence wall" was in position, but, as has now been proved, it depended for successful resistance against a large, determined attack on an important factor.

This was the ability of troops held in the rear to move up quickly upon the point of invasion. They failed to do so because of a preliminary aerial bombardment closing all roads leading to the area.

Bridgehead Army is Ready to Strike

AT ADVANCE H.Q., Italy, Monday.

GENERAL SIR HENRY MAITLAND WILSON, Commander-in-Chief, Mediterranean, told war correspondents to-day that the British and American Forces were building up their bridgehead below Rome with a view to striking as soon as possible. It was expected that the Germans would counter-attack the beachhead at the earliest possible moment.

The next 48 hours, he said, would see a battle in the area of the landing.

General Wilson said that "there is a possibility of Salerno over again, but we have this advantage—we are not so far from our main land and air forces.

"This landing has been thought of for some time to overcome two handicaps—the weather and terrain. Given reasonable weather we hope to make full use of our superiority in weapons and material.

"The enemy will possibly attack to prevent a junction of the two Allied forces.

"He will possibly attack the bridgehead and, farther south, delay the advance of the Fifth Army by the employment of strong hedgehog positions.

"If he attempts to send reinforcements from the north of Rome we hope to delay their progress by air attacks on roads and communications.

Complete Surprise

General Wilson stressed the surprise of the whole landing operation. "In spite of the fact that the whole armada left Naples and proceeded up the coast," he said, "we have no news that the enemy was aware of it.

"That was due almost entirely to the Allied airmen who, by their attacks on enemy aerodromes in the Rome area, disrupted his means of reconnaissance.

"It is largely due to the magnificent efforts of the Allied airmen and the Allied navies for landing the troops on time that the landing forces established the perimeter of their beachhead in a few hours."

The beaches were not so good as in places where previous landings had been made. There was a sandbar which made it necessary for landing-craft to stand farther offshore than in the cases of Sicily and Salerno.

The port of Nettuno was now in operation. Two air attacks by the enemy had not so far seriously interfered with getting equipment ashore.

Referring to the Fifth Army front, General Wilson said there had been heavy fighting for ten days.

The German intention was to prevent the Fifth Army making a break-through. The British were across the Garigliano and the Americans, who had been heavily counter-attacked in the Rapido region, were in a position to take a renewed offensive across the river.—*Reuter.*

GOEBBELS SAYS 'LONDON WAS IN PANIC'

Daily Mail Radio Station

Paris radio last night broadcast a fantastic account of aerial torpedoes falling on panic-stricken Londoners last Friday night.

This is the latest German propaganda attempt to make the two raids—when actually only 30 planes reached the London area—look like a full-scale retaliation for Berlin. The account alleged that London's A.A. guns were kept firing on successive waves of bombers from 8 p.m. until 5 a.m.

On the same night, said Paris, R.A.F. bombers failed in their attempt to reach Berlin.

13 Down Last Friday

Another enemy plane was yesterday confirmed as having been brought down during Friday night's raids on this country. This brings the Luftwaffe's losses for the night to 13—out of 90. Thirty reached London.

'UNKNOWN' GENERAL IS C-IN-C FOR JAP WAR

By Daily Mail Reporter

AN "unknown" general, expert in the training of native troops, is announced to-day as the new Army chief in the war against Japan. He is 57-years-old General Sir George J. Giffard, D.S.O., who is to be Commander-in-Chief Army Group, South-East Asia.

His job in relation to Admiral Lord Louis Mountbatten, Supreme Allied Commander in South-East Asia, will be similar to that held by Alexander under Eisenhower in North Africa.

Another appointment in the Far East battle zone is that of Lieut.-General W. J. Slim, D.S.O., M.C., who becomes Commander of the 14th Army on the Burma frontier—built round the units who fought the Japanese in Burma.

General Giffard (the "G" is soft as in "general") has had over 30 years' service in Africa. He has made few public speeches, but he is the man who mobilised West Africa—he has been G.O.C.-in-C. there since July 1941.

Over 6ft tall, he served for a few months as Military Secretary to Mr. Hore-Belisha when he was War Minister. He was formerly G.S.O.I. to General Wavell.

Lieut.-General "Bill" Slim, Indian Army, who is 52, has been on continuous active service in East Africa, Iraq, Syria, Persia, and Burma since July 1940.

A jungle warfare expert, he won the D.S.O. for the way he brought a corps out of Burma in the fighting retreat.

PM WILL NOT SEE FARMERS

Mr. Churchill has declined to receive a deputation of the National Farmers' Union before the debate on agriculture in the House of Commons, it was announced last night.

In his telegram he said the full case for the Government would be stated in the debate.

He hoped the debate would clear away misunderstandings and enable the particular issues in dispute to be considered within the framework of the Government's general policy towards agriculture.

Montagu Norman Ill

Mr. Montagu Norman, Governor of the Bank of England since 1920, is suffering from a slight infection of the lung following influenza. He had a relapse during the week-end and yesterday his illness was causing anxiety.

Last night his condition was said to be unchanged. He is 72.

See Page TWO

Swiss to Call Up 19's

BERNE, Monday.—A communiqué issued to-day said that the greater part of the 19-years-old men in Switzerland will be called up to begin military training this year in addition to the regular contingents, because of "the necessity of the hour." Military training normally starts at 20.—*A.P.*

GERMANS TRY TO SMASH '5th'

Daily Mail Special Correspondent

ALGIERS, Monday.

ONLY comparatively light enemy resistance has so far been offered to the British and American troops which made the surprise landing on the beaches immediately to the south of Rome.

What has happened is this, according to reports from advanced Allied Headquarters in Italy:

Marshal Kesselring was caught so badly off his balance by the tactics of General Alexander that he is carrying on more fiercely than ever his organised attack on the Fifth Army on the Lower Garigliano, and on the Rapido River is throwing in his full strength.

It would seem that his plan is to break the pressure of the Fifth Army offensive so that he will have breathing space in which to withdraw sufficient troops under his own conditions to deal with the peril of the new landing in his rear.

Kesselring may even have the

BACK PAGE—Col. TWO

Mr. Eagle of RAF Took on 12 Germans

Shot Down 3: The Rest Ran

By Daily Mail Reporter

FLYING OFFICER EAGLE, of the R.A.F., yesterday attacked single handed a force of 12 enemy fighters, destroyed three of them, and routed the rest.

He had gone out with a Typhoon wing on an offensive patrol to the Dutch coast.

When flying alone he spotted the 12, all Me. 109's, close to the water, well out to sea.

He did not turn back but went in on his own to attack just as they saw him.

"They were about 50ft. above the water when I saw them," he said afterwards. "With my first burst I got their wing leader, and he blew up.

"Then, when I hit a second one near the cockpit with my cannon shell he half rolled into a third Me. flying by his side. Both crashed into the sea.

Feint Attack

"Four of the other enemy fighters immediately made for home as fast as they could, while the rest of the formation made a feint attack on me. They failed. I last saw them, too, making for land."

Flying Officer Eagle—William G. Eagle—who is 24, started flying Typhoons only five months ago. Before that he flew a Hurricane in North Africa and while there shot down four enemy aircraft and damaged others. He was wounded in combat there, but was able to fly his aircraft back to base.

Flying Officer Eagle was formerly an engineer in Birmingham. His home is at Hall Green, Birmingham.

'FORTS' SHOOT DOWN 21

W. Germany Raided

American heavy bombers with American fighter escort and R.A.F. withdrawal cover shot down 21 enemy planes when they attacked targets in Western Germany yesterday.

Marauders and R.A.F. medium bombers, also with fighter support, raided objectives in the Pas de Calais area. Vichy radio said ten localities in Normandy were attacked.

Excellent results were reported from this raid, in which nearly 200 Marauders took part. Flak was negligible. From all operations two heavy bombers, one fighter-bomber, and 10 fighters are missing.

Nazi Press Chief Arrested

From Daily Mail Correspondent

GENEVA, Monday.—Dr. Frauweiler, German Foreign Press Director, has been arrested, according to reports from Berlin.

His predecessor, Karl Boehmer, was arrested in 1941 and sent to the Russian front, where he was killed.

RAF Sink Three in Ægean

Three sailing ships have been sunk and many others damaged by the R.A.F. in operations over the Ægean Sea, said a Middle East air communiqué yesterday.

Heavy bombers started fires in Piræus harbour on Saturday night. Two of our aircraft are missing. The crew of one is safe.

Crashed Air Crew Save Village

Two airmen were killed when a bomber crashed in the village of Shelfanger, Norfolk yesterday. The plane carried a big bomb load, but the crew, though dazed and shaken, quickly made it harmless and so cleared all danger to the villagers.

The Navy is Ready

The Navy has everything ready for the Second Front, said Admiral Sir William James, Director of Naval Information, at Leeds yesterday, "and whatever is required of it will be done."

HALIFAX TELLS CANADIANS:

'The Empire Must Act As One Big Power'

BRITAIN can play her full part in the preservation of peace only as a member of an armed, united Commonwealth, following one foreign policy—the fourth Great Power of the post-war world.

This forecast was made by Lord Halifax in Toronto last night, when he said that the post-war United Kingdom alone could hardly claim equality with the U.S., Russia, and China.

Drained of men and money, Great Britain must yet possess comparable strength with the three Great Powers to exercise any real influence—and that could be found only in a united Empire following one common policy.

Lord Halifax said that while the Statute of Westminster provided each Dominion with complete self-government it "left unsolved the more obstinate problems arising in the fields of foreign policy and defence."

He amplified this by pointing out that in 1939 the Dominions went to war in pursuance of the foreign policy of a Minister whom they had not appointed and who was responsible to a Parliament in which they were not represented.

"They were themselves in no danger of direct attack," he went on.

STOUT BULWARK

"They had influenced but had not been responsible for the foreign policy of Great Britain.

"In fact, as well as in theory, they were entirely uncommitted.

"The best proof of this reality is that Eire pursued, and still pursues to-day, a policy of abstention and neutrality.

"Yet not only did the great Dominions enter the war without hesitation, they showed at once that theirs was no formal acquiescence in a situation which, though disagreeable in the extreme, could by no means be avoided; they realised that Great Britain was the first line of their own defence.

"They immediately threw all that they had in men, money, and material into the struggle. They held nothing back, and in the summer of 1940, when Britain faced the probability of invasion and the possibility of conquest, they were unflinching in their support.

"When the history of those fateful days is written I do not doubt that the unshaken staunchness of

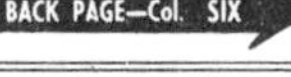
BACK PAGE—Col. SIX

2 Escaped Generals to Get New Posts

Air Marshal, Too

By Daily Mail Reporter

THREE British war-leaders—Lieut.-General Sir Richard O'Connor, Lieut.-General Philip Neame, V.C., and Air Marshal O. T. Boyd—who have escaped from Italy and are now safe home are expected to be given important commands again very soon.

Air Marshal Boyd was captured by the Italians in November 1940, after a forced landing while on his way to become deputy to the Air Officer Commanding-in-Chief, Middle East.

The two generals were captured in April 1941 by German motorcycle patrols in the desert near Derna.

Added strength is given to the British senior ranks by the fact that these experienced commanders are now at liberty.

Air Marshal Boyd had been singled out for high responsibility when his career was temporarily stopped by a sheer accident. The man sent out in his place was the

LATEST

SOFIA BOMBED AGAIN

Berlin raido said early this morning that Sofia was raided again yesterday by U.S. bombers with fighter escort.

GOERING IN BULGARIA

Zurich, Monday.—Göring is in Bulgaria, according to reports from the Balkans reaching here to-night.—Reuter.

2

brilliantly successful Air Chief Marshal Sir Arthur Tedder.

It is understood that Air Marshal Boyd will spend some time studying the latest advances in air technique before he takes up a new post.

General O'Connor, who was called "Wavell's right-hand man," was one of the most brilliant tank generals produced in the earlier stages of the war.

Rommel is reputed to have said of him: "He is the only British general who really makes me nervous." At that time Rommel had still to make the acquaintanceship of General Alexander and General Montgomery.

Wavell Visits Bombay

BOMBAY, Monday.—The Viceroy, Lord Wavell, to-day concluded a three-days visit to Bombay. He spent the day mainly studying the working of food rationing.—*Reuter.*

Daily Mail

NO. 14,956 ONE PENNY ** FOR KING AND EMPIRE MONDAY, APRIL 10, 1944

LATE WAR NEWS

UTILITY FOOTWEAR
A98 with CC41 signifies
George Webb
FOOTWEAR FOR MEN
MADE BY CRAFTSMEN IN NORTHAMPTON

GERMANS SEIZE PLOESTI OILFIELDS

Rumanian Intruders 'Shot at Sight'

NEW THRUST DEEP BEHIND JASSY

THE Germans have taken over the entire Ploesti oilfields region, according to reports from Moscow late last night, and have posted guards with "shoot-at-sight" orders at all vital points. Even Rumanians are barred from the area.

The Ploesti oilfields, bombed by the Allies and vital to the German war effort, are to-day less than 170 miles from the advancing Russians.

The battle for Rumania was the main point of last night's Soviet communiqué.

This reported that more than 200 places have been captured between the rivers Pruth and Sereth, that Jassy, main German stronghold on this front, was outflanked, and that the railway linking Jassy with Pascani had been cut.

Jassy, once the German H.Q. and now the pivot of their defences before the Galatz Gap, is now to all intents and purposes encircled—and the spearhead of the Red Army is now less than seven miles from it, an advance of over 20 miles in a day.

Odessa, encircled by land, now has Soviet troops less than three miles away—and inside the city Russian guerillas are in action, fighting from the catacombs under the city streets.

The city's marshalling yards are already in Soviet hands.

German resistance to the Russians appears to have increased, for the Soviet communiqué reported that 104 German tanks and 71 planes were destroyed in one day's fighting—the highest total for some time.

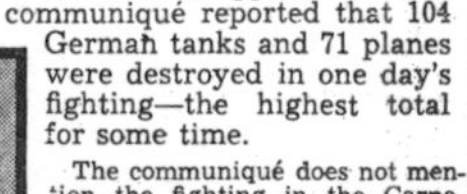

The communiqué does not mention the fighting in the Carpathians, where it is known that Red Army troops, in face of heavy blizzards, are driving into Czecho-Slovakia against fierce German resistance.

As yet, Moscow has not announced that the frontier has actually been crossed, but unofficial reports make it clear that the Red Army is fighting on Czech soil.

PASSES BATTLE

London Czechs report that the Jablomica (Tartar) Pass has been forced, and they believe that the spearhead of Marshal Zhukov's men has reached Jasena, 10 miles inside Czecho-Slovakia.

A Czech guerilla army, organised and controlled from London, has got into action to aid the advancing Russians, who themselves have the support of a Czecho-Slovak brigade.

Last night's reports from Moscow painted a grim picture of this mountain battle.

The roads, heavily mined by the Germans, are under heavy snowdrifts, and horses dragging up supplies are struggling stomach-deep in snow.

All around the valleys Soviet artillery is in action, raking the German positions in a non-stop cannonade.

East of the Carpathians the forces of Zhukov and Koniev have linked up in Rumania and are now moving south on a broad front.

Their aim is to clear the whole of the foothill country stretching from the Pruth at Jassy up to the mountains and then to drive for the Galatz Gap and the Ploesti oilfields along the line of the Rivers Pruth and Sereth.

Between the Pruth and the Sereth several columns are on the move, thrusting deep into the enemy lines to prevent any concentration of the German and Rumanian forces.

These troops are in difficult country—country broken by valleys, forests and streams, and deeply cut by ravines.

The Germans are having difficulty in coping with these tactics, and are abandoning much heavy material as they fall back.

'TRAP' BATTLE

In the far south General Malinovsky's men are now in the outskirts of Odessa.

The city, says *Reuter*, is heavy with the dust and smoke of German demolitions. It is almost empty of civilians, and those who are left are half-starved, without fresh water, and in dread of epidemics.

Behind the battle-line Koniev's men are steadily destroying the German forces trapped near Skala.

The Germans are now herded into a narrow strip of land between two rivers, and are reported to have assembled all their armour at one point in readiness for yet another attempt to break out to the west.

Axis radios last night admitted that the Russians had reached the Czecho-Slovak border and had crossed the Sereth.

One Berlin commentator described the Southern Russian front as a "most moving and terrible picture," adding that the Red Army "had now reached the real walls of the European fortress."

Col von Hammer, military correspondent of the German News Agency, said of the fighting:

"Fresh Soviet attacks north of Jassy against German and Rumanian positions have failed.

"North-west of Jassy, where strong Russian forces are seeking to drive south-west across the Pruth and extend their bridgehead. Rumanian covering forces are fighting violently.

"In the Kovel area Soviet attacks from the south-east and north-east were repelled before reaching the new German line."

Moscow, Sunday.—According to *Izvestia*, the Germans have established army headquarters at Bucarest.

The paper adds that Jassy is the most short-lived headquarters ever taken up by the German High Command.—*Exchange*.

LVOV TARNOPOL PROSKUROV JMERINKA RUMANIA HUNGARY JASSY KOLOMYJA ODESSA PLOESTI MILES

THE Red Army yesterday made another 20-mile bound forward between the Rivers Pruth and Sereth and cut the Jassy-Pascani railway (shown in map below). At the same time, Czech partizan reports said the Russians had crossed the Tartar Pass through the Carpathians and had reached Jasina, 10 miles inside Czecho-Slovakia. At Odessa, the Russians closed in further and are now only three miles from the city. Above is key map showing the relation of the three fronts.

LVOV TARNOPOL DROHOBYCZ PROSKUROV STRYJ JMERINKA STANISLAVOV SKALA K. PODOLSK KOLOMYJA M. PODOLSK HOTIN CZECHO-SLOVAKIA JASINA Tartar Pass CERNAUTI ZABIE VYJNITSA DOROHOI SERETH SIGHET BOTOSANI BALTI CARPATHIANS SUCEAVA HUNGARY CAMPULUNG RUMANIA PASCANI JASSY 50 100 150 MILES

The Secret Army Has London HQ

Guerillas Rise in Czech Mountains To Aid Soviets

M. Jan Sramek, Czecho-Slovak Prime Minister, has sent a message to Stalin declaring that his people and Government "will never forget" the arrival of the Red Army on Czecho-Slovak territory.

M. Sramek adds: "It is with profound emotion that we are following the further development of events, when the Czecho-Slovak people and the Czecho-Slovak Brigade are side by side with the victorious Red Army fighting for the complete liberation of their country.

"The sacrifices made in this struggle still further strengthen the old friendship between the nations of our States."

By Daily Mail Reporter

NOW that the flag of Czecho-Slovakia is flying from the peaks of the Carpathian Mountains, I can tell the story of how military experts in London have organised an army of guerillas to aid the advancing Russians on the frontier of the country which was Hitler's first victim.

One of the London organisers of the Czech guerilla forces told me last night: "At 11.30 this morning we in London heard that Soviet troops are actually fighting on our territory proper.

"Their advance continues, and they are being helped by bands of guerillas organised by us in London during the past few days."

Ten days ago people living in small towns and villages in the easternmost part of Czecho-Slovakia received a secret message from the London military headquarters of the Czecho-Slovak Government. They acted on it at once.

Farmers left their ploughs, tradesmen walked quietly from their shops, village wives said farewell to husbands.

Walking casually past German guards, small groups of Czechs made leisurely for the hills, giving satisfactory excuses to all who questioned them.

★

BUT on reaching the hills which they know so well these harmless looking civilians lost their casualness

Farmers and tradesmen, clerks, labourers, blacksmiths, and butchers became soldiers, ready for immediate action in the field, vital links in the new rebel army now growing as every hour passes.

With all speed they made for secret ravines and creeks among the mountains which ring this part of the Czecho-Slovak border, where they sought out their leaders and reported for duty.

No disorder awaited them. Thanks to the constant communication which London has kept for weeks past now, they were able at once to receive their orders, their arms, and their food.

So this week-end the Germans did not meet with ill-organised bands of desperadoes, but with courageous groups of guerilla fighters who placed every possible obstacle in their path.

In the last seven days these warriors have contacted the Red Air Force and have informed Russian Military Headquarters of enemy plans, positions, and strength.

The Russian Air Force and Red Army were quick to seize this proffered help from behind the lines and eagerly made the most of it.

★

AT the London headquarters of this rebel army I was told:

"We are anxiously awaiting further reports of their progress.

"They are obviously doing a fine job of work, and are accepting orders from London like a well-organised military machine.

"They have aided the Russian armies, we believe, in climbing the saddle of the Jablomica Pass. We now believe the Russians to be well past Jasina [ten miles inside Czecho-Slovakia].

"We also believe that our guerillas are active in the area of the Ushok Pass.

"Commanding these forces from London is General Miroslav, who, by another name, is well known to the Czech nation. He is in touch with the guerilla leaders all the time."

I was also told: "There is great enthusiasm that this happened for our country on Easter Saturday, which we call White Saturday.

"But we are having no celebrations. This is no time for celebration in London when we know that our comrades, our relations, are fighting and dying out there, and that our women and children may be victims of the retreating Nazis.

"We are glad, very glad, but we are not celebrating."

★

I TOURED three London clubs where Czecho-Slovakian soldiers, airmen, and civilians were thirsting for more news of the advance.

These men were quiet, but obviously this was the most cheering news to them for months.

"But how we wish we were back home fighting with them," one Czech soldier told me. "All of us envy our comrades who are fighting back home, and hope that the day won't be long before we are with them."

All yesterday, London, Moscow.

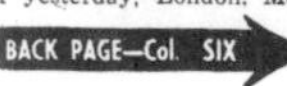

BACK PAGE—Col. SIX

U-war Fiercer on Sea Route to Russia

THE weight of the U-war has shifted from the Atlantic to more distant waters. That is the main point made in the March joint statement issued last night under the authority of President Roosevelt and Mr. Churchill.

The focus of attack is now concentrated on the northern route to Russia. That is made plain by the statement that—

"The enemy has persevered vainly in strenuous endeavours to disrupt our flow of supplies to Russia by the northern route."

March was an active month in the U-war, said the statement. The U-boats operated in widely dispersed areas from the Barents Sea to the Indian Ocean.

Still Low

"Our merchant shipping losses were mainly incurred in far distant seas; though a little higher than in February, they were still low, and the rate of sinking U-boats was fully maintained.

"The Allied Merchant Fleet continues to improve both in quantity and quality, but the strength of the U-boat force remains considerable, and calls for powerful efforts by surface and air forces."

February's losses were the lowest since the U.S. entered the war, and the second lowest month since hostilities began. U-boat losses were described as higher than the number of Allied merchant ship losses.

The reference to the "quality of the Allied merchant fleet may mean bigger ships or faster ships, or both. It is evident that the vast shipbuilding programmes of Britain and the U.S. are coming to fruition, and that vital supplies are reaching the battle-fronts.

Larger White Flags

Commander Robert Norden, of the U.S. Navy, broadcasting from New York to the German people yesterday, said all U-boats should carry a white flag measuring at least two by three yards.

When his destroyer attacked a U-boat, he said, the crew poured out on deck frantically waving white handkerchiefs, while the U-boat captain rushed madly to the top of the conning-tower and fired revolvers. "Had a white flag been hoisted I would have gone to the rescue," he added.

SAVINGS BALM FOR GERMANS

'Gains to Come'

By Daily Mail Radio Station

Germany hopes to offset her huge war debt by her territorial gains in the West. That is what the Reich Finance Minister, Count Von Krossinck, told the German people when he appealed to them in a broadcast yesterday not to be alarmed by inflation, but to go on saving.

He admitted that the trebling of the bank-note circulation since the war was worrying the people.

"We have not been able to prevent Black Market prices altogether," he said, "but these artificial prices will burst again after the war." He then forecast further "taxation measures."

Illness No Excuse to Visit Coast

Would-be visitors to the closed coastal areas are asking to be allowed in because they are ill. And people already there are asking to be allowed to stay and present medical certificates.

The rule is firm: Only patients of hospitals or those on their way to a hospital, nursing home, or a sanatorium are permitted to break the ban.

'Sack Antonescu' Michael Told

WASHINGTON, Sunday.—King Michael of Rumania must dismiss Antonescu's pro-Nazi Government or the monarchy will be repudiated, declared M. Davila, exiled Rumanian leader, to-day.

Only by a resurgence of democracy, he said, could his nation hope to regain respect at the Allied peace conference.—*Reuter*.

Dutch Introduce Death Penalty

From Daily Mail Correspondent

NEW YORK, Sunday.—Capital punishment, unknown in Holland before the war, is to be introduced by the Netherlands Government in exile to deal with Dutch Nazis and quislings.

'Three Raids on Rome'

Rome radio claimed last night that Rome was raided three times yesterday, says *B.U.P.*

Truk Now Being 'Softened Up'

From Daily Mail Correspondent

WASHINGTON, Sunday.—Softening-up operations against Truk, Jap base in the Carolines, are continuing, a Navy Department communiqué stated to-night.

Liberators and medium bombers took part in assaults on Moen and Dublon isles in the Truk atoll.

CLEARING IN STRAIT

Strait of Dover: Barometer rising and sky clearing after day showers and sunshine.

Nazi Mission to Turks

ANKARA, Sunday.—It is believed that a German trade delegation will arrive here shortly, and economic negotiations may be resumed at the beginning of next month.—*Exchange*.

Second Air Invasion in Burma

New Glider Force Links with Old

AIR COMMANDO H.Q., Burma (delayed).

BRITISH airborne troops have made a second landing by glider train far behind the Japanese lines in Burma.

They were put down to meet one of the columns of the first force—which was led by the late Major-General Wingate—marching out from the original landing points.

The second unit landed between the Chindwin and Irrawaddy rivers, due east of Imphal [the British base in Manipur State now threatened by Japanese advances].

Early on March 22 the glider train crossed the rugged frontier hills with jeeps, bulldozers, and masses of other kit for building airfields.

As soon as the Allied column on the ground heard the aero engines they lit two lanes of lights and landing flares.

Bombers' Haven

The gliders cut loose and swept down on to a stretch of relatively level ground. By nightfall it was already looking like a landing strip, and by the night of March 23 the ground was ready for the heavy transports to come in.

An hour after dark twin-engined Douglas transports came in with British and Indian troops.

Supplies were also brought in to the ground column, marking a new development in the process of building supply points behind enemy lines.

The same night bad weather came down while Allied bombers were raiding targets deep in Burma. They flew to the landing strips built after the initial airborne landing early in March, and came down there.

This is believed to be the first time that Allied bombers have actually landed behind enemy lines and spent the night in safety after raiding enemy positions.—*B.U.P.*

The first airborne landing was made 150 miles inside Burma in the heart of Japanese-occupied territory. Location has not yet been officially revealed, but it is estimated to be in the region of Katha, in the bend of the Irrawaddy.

The new force is apparently under the control of Colonel Cochran, Wingate's "disciple" and chief of the Air Commando Unit.

Their landing point is due west of the original force, whose task was to disrupt enemy communications.

The Japanese forces which attacked **Kohima**, Allied base on the road from Imphal to the Bengal-Assam railway, have been forced from the outskirts of the town.

Japs Repulsed

The enemy, who claimed during the week-end to have captured the base, which is 40 miles inside India, are now being driven back.

An impromptu Home Guard has been organised among the British in the area. Young men have rallied to the Commissioner's office in a village east of the town and been armed with whatever weapons could be found.

Stiff clashes are taking place only eight miles from **Imphal**, says *Reuter*, as Japanese troops slowly edge their way into the plain north of the town.

Every day the Japanese delay attempting to capture Kohima and Imphal their chances lessen. While the Imphal and Tamu roads remain in our hands the enemy is prevented from bringing in his motorised vehicles.

Imphal is the greatest tactical prize in the area. There are enormous supplies of rice there, sufficient to maintain an army over a long period.

Our troops have retired to strong-points on the Tamu-Imphal road, about 50 miles from the base, and are beating off Japanese attempts to penetrate farther in this sector.

WHERE the new British airborne force has landed between the Chindwin and Irrawaddy rivers in Burma.

AIR WORKS POUNDED AGAIN

Forts Hit Poland: 1,600-mile Flight

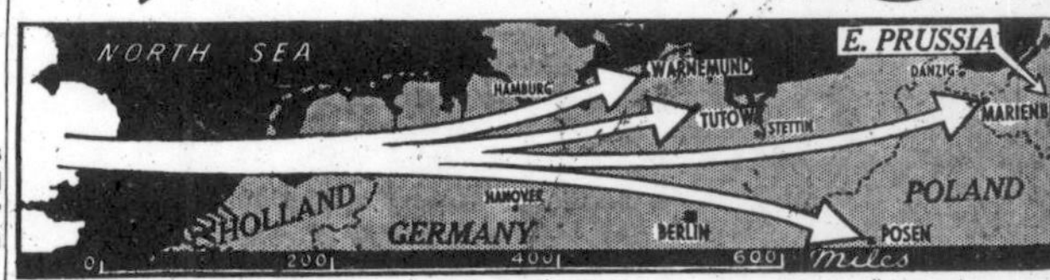

ARROWS show the lines of flight of the great armada of Flying Fortresses and Liberators in its long trip across Germany into Poland and East Prussia yesterday—200 miles beyond Berlin.

By Daily Mail Air Reporter

AMERICAN heavy bombers flew one of their longest missions from Britain yesterday, to bomb aircraft factories at Marienburg, in East Prussia, and Posen, in Poland.

About 1,500 warplanes went out to launch this second great blow in two days after the two-weeks lull imposed by the weather. There were between 500 and 750 Fortresses and Liberators and they were escorted by relays of nearly 1,000 fighters.

Blows fell on two other targets—aircraft plants at Warnemunde and Tutow, near the Baltic port of Rostock.

The raids on the F.W. 190 fighter assembly plant at Marienburg—previously bombed by Fortresses exactly six months ago—and on aircraft factories at Posen took the U.S. "heavies" farther over enemy territory than on any mission since long-range Mustangs, Thunderbolts, and Lightnings began giving fighter cover all the way to distant targets.

Marienburg meant a round trip of at least 1,600 miles.

The bombers raiding Posen travelled nearly as far, the big Polish industrial and rail centre being 160 miles beyond Berlin, and only 180 miles west of Warsaw.

This two-pronged thrust deep into enemy territory brought the Western air war to within about 300 miles of the Eastern Front.

The Reminder

As bombs crashed among the German workshops, they gave the enemy a reminder that war plants set up in Poland and East Prussia, hundreds of miles from British bomber bases, are no longer beyond the reach of our day bombers.

It brought home forcibly to the Germans that they cannot rely on factories in Eastern Europe to make up for the lost production of aircraft and other war materials caused by the destruction of factories in Western Germany.

It was Posen's first raid. The R.A.F. went there in March 1940, but only on reconnaissance. Warnemunde, which has a Heinkel aircraft factory and a seaplane base, was attacked by the Americans in July last year and by the R.A.F. in May 1942. Tutow is about 50 miles south-east of Warnemunde.

Yesterday's bombing was done visually in good weather and fierce battles raged over Northern Germany almost all day.

Within a few hours of Germany's

BACK PAGE—Col. FOUR

Hull: U.S. will Aid French Committee

MR. CORDELL HULL, United States Secretary of State, in a broadcast on foreign policy last night, said that although America could not recognise the French Committee of Liberation as the Government of France, she would aid the Committee in administering France until the French people could choose their own Government.

The speech outlined America's foreign policy in some detail.

Mr. Hull told the neutrals that America could no longer allow them to aid the enemy while at the same time they drew on Allied resources.

"We will not coerce," he said, "but we ask them with insistence to cease aiding our enemies."

On the problem of boundary disputes, Mr. Hull said it was difficult to settle these while the war was on, but he repeated that America was still willing to aid Russia and Poland to reach agreement.

Speech in full—BACK Page.

GIRAUD: 'NO TO DE GAULLE'

Algiers Report

ALGIERS, Sunday Night.—General Giraud is believed to have replied in the negative to his nomination as Inspector-General of the French Forces.

He was formally appointed to the post to-day in place of his former office of C.-in-C.—*Reuter*.

'Stay-in' Tribute for 2 Nations

Daily Mail Special Correspondent

STOCKHOLM, Sunday.—Norwegians and Danes, responding to requests broadcast by the B.B.C. from their free representatives in Britain, stayed indoors as an act of mourning to-day—the fourth anniversary of the German occupation of Norway and Denmark.

The streets of Copenhagen and Oslo were deserted, except for a small number of timid-looking quislings and German troops, who held parades.

Fuel Cut Need Not Shorten Hours

Some firms may have to reduce overtime because of cuts in gas and electricity for industry, but the Ministry of Production have not made a rule that they should do so.

An official of the Ministry said yesterday: "We have informed about 75,000 managements that while the cuts have been forced on the country by the shortage of coal, we look to them to apply the cuts in such a way as to cause the minimum loss in production."

Fish: Plenty To-day

Plenty of fish should be available to-day in London, the Midlands and the north. Big catches were landed at Grimsby and Fleetwood yesterday, mainly cod, haddock, coal fish, and plaice.

Dockers worked through yesterday getting away train loads. Many at Grimsby earned £9 for their day's work.

PIT STRIKE IS BROKEN: 100,000 GO BACK

THE Yorkshire miners' strike is over. Of the 100,000 men who were idle last week, 75,000 are back at work, a further 20,000 are ready to start on Wednesday, and of the remaining 5,000 only a few will stay out.

Maintenance men were busy during the holidays preparing for a restart, and while they were busy, agitators were leaving the coalfield, admitting their defeat.

Some who tried to distribute strike pamphlets had a warm reception from miners on their way to work.

In some pits good production figures have already been recorded, and it is expected that the men will try to make up for the tonnage lost in the dispute.

How feeling has veered round is shown by the fact that in the Wombwell area, where three days ago an official plea to restart was rejected, a ten-minutes discussion yesterday ended in a unanimous decision to resume work.

Thirty-five thousand Belfast shipyard and aircraft workers who have been on strike, some of them for six weeks, will return to work to-morrow and Wednesday.

The shipyard fitters, who stopped work on February 26 for a flat rate of 3s. per hour, accepted by a 3 to 1 majority on Saturday a wage agreement reached between trade union officials and representatives of Harland and Wolff's Belfast shipyard.

Miners' Leader Talks Frankly to Men.—BACK Page.

Germans say: 'New Italy Landings'

NEW Allied landings on the north Italian coasts, both in the Gulf of Genoa and the head of the Adriatic, are expected hourly by the German Command as part of an all-out drive for Rome.

This was stated by one of Kesselring's staff officers, quoted last night by Gunther Weber, German war correspondent.

Defence positions and troop concentrations have been directed to the northern flanks of both coasts, the staff officer reported.

"The calm reigning for the last few days on the Italian front may be the calm before the storm," he said.

"Fighting will shortly flare up again. Major battles may then have to be fought.

"The German Command do not worry about the location of this expected Allied drive. They are prepared for all eventualities, including new landings."—*Reuter*.

German Beetle Tanks Fall—BACK Page.

NIGHT RAF OUT

Formations of bombers crossed the east coast of England last night, flying towards the Continent. U.S. headquarters said that in the Forts day raids fighters shot down 2[illegible] enemy planes and destroyed others on airfields in Germany. Thirty-one U.S. bombers and [illegible] fighters missing.

GREEK UNITY TALKS

Cairo, Sunday.—E.A.M., the Greek national liberation front, has accepted a proposal to send a representative to Cairo to discuss proposals for Greek unity.—Reuter.

2

More Algiers Trials

Twelve Moslems will be tried for treason when the French military tribunal resumes its sessions on Wednesday, announced Algiers radio yesterday. At the end of the month several officers will face the court.—*Exchange*.

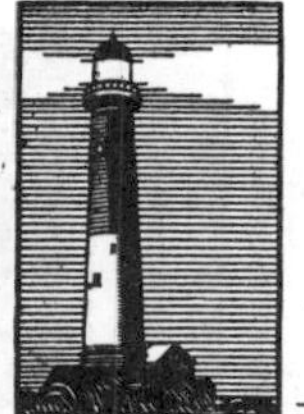

New York World-Telegram

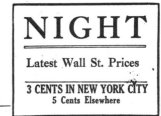

NIGHT
Latest Wall St. Prices
3 CENTS IN NEW YORK CITY
5 Cents Elsewhere

Local Forecast: This afternoon, cloudy, occasional showers; gentle to moderate winds.

VOL. 76—NO. 237—IN TWO SECTIONS—SECTION ONE. NEW YORK, MONDAY, APRIL 10, 1944 Entered as second class matter Post Office, New York, N. Y.

NAZIS ABANDON ODESSA

Ex-Official Tells How Smearers Tap the Mails

Censors Intercept Letters as in the Kellems Episode

By ROGER W. STUART,
World-Telegram Staff Writer.
First of two articles.

As plans were under way in Washington today for a Senate inquiry into means by which a House member and a columnist gained access to purported correspondence of a Connecticut businesswoman William J. LaVarre, former chief of the American Republics division of the Department of Commerce, revealed how information obtained by the government's interception of foreign-bound mail had, "in countless instances," found its way into the hands of "hatchetmen and smearers."

The system of "intercepts" originally developed by the Office of Censorship for official use as a wartime method of running down suspicions of espionage, Mr. LaVarre told the World-Telegram, had been "perverted" into a "scandalous and vicious means" by which even correspondence "having no relation whatever to the war" is made available to unauthorized persons.

Doubts Price Knows.

In his detailed explanation of the system the former Commerce Department official said he doubted that Byron Price, Director of the Office of Censorship, knew of the use to which the "intercepts" was put. He blamed employees of other government departments who, he said, gained possession of the intercepted matter.

Upon learning of demands by Senator Reed (R., Kan.) that the Senate Postal Committee, of which he is ranking minority member, trace the official source which allowed excerpts from letters allegedly written by Miss Vivien Kellems to get into the hands of Drew Pearson, columnist, and Representative Coffee (D., Wash.), Mr. Price said in Washington he would be glad "to co-operate in any

(Continued on Page Five.)

Davis Builds Big Propaganda Mill

Taxpayers Foot Bill for Lavish World Operations

By CHARLES T. LUCEY,
World-Telegram Staff Writer.

Elmer Davis is a world evangelist who lacks a sturdy gospel, but in two years he has taken three or four foundering government information agencies and parlayed them into the biggest propaganda machine America has ever seen.

It is costing nearly three million dollars a month—66 millions since the war began—to run the global effort of the Office of War Information to win friends and influence people.

Elmer Davis.

That looks pretty big beside the two and one-quarter millions a year George Creel spent to tell the American story in 1917-18. The 5561 OWI employees Mr. Davis has strung around the world are more than 10 times the number on the propaganda pay roll of the earlier war.

You may not know what an immense proposition this OWI is——

It is, OWI officials say, the country's biggest radio network; its 350 daily programs are twice the number sent out by the National Broadcasting Co. and the Columbia Broadcasting System combined.

It is, they say, the largest single enterprise disseminating news, features and pictures abroad. Quite aside from a vast shortwave propaganda operation, it has a daily cable-wireless output of 100,000 words—several times the output of a major wire news bureau in such a world news center as Washington.

It is one of the world's largest pamphlet and magazine publishers.

It operates the first co-ordinated worldwide radiophoto system.

OWI makes the pictures that go into the pack-on-the-back projectors of itinerant peep-show men in remote China and into little news-sheets of Tahiti. It turns out leaflets telling Axis soldiers they'll be smart to lay down their arms and it feeds news surreptitiously to underground papers of Nazi-occupied Europe.

With the United States taxpayer picking up the check, of course.

Woodrow Wilson gave George Creel the Fourteen Points on which to build the American propaganda story in the other war and they were forged into a mighty weapon. Mr. Davis, by contrast, has the heavily generalized and now badly mauled Atlantic Charter which allows nothing like the positive and definite day-after-day hammering policy important to the most effective propagandizing.

The OWI is doing a lot of improvising and some of it resembles the made-work stuff of WPA days. It is spending an average of $7.77 apiece to make up to 3500 transcribed recordings monthly, some of them on such highly imaginative subjects as the dramatization of an American mail order catalogue. It can turn out a heroic-size picture 60 feet tall for exhibitions. It will produce a 14-part series on American women for a Swedish magazine or a million copies of an ABC book for children overseas.

What has it to do with winning a war?

Even some OWI people wonder. Dramatizing a mail order catalogue or a jeep so that Balkan peasants, say, who may hear it, will understand and like us better may seem as fantastic to them as to you. Many OWI projects are on

(Continued on Page Six.)

Berlin Admits Loss of Great Black Sea Port

Complete Liberation Of Ukraine Near as Russians Sweep On

By ROBERT MUSEL,
United Press Staff Correspondent.

LONDON, April 10.—The Germans announced today the loss of the great Black Sea stronghold of Odessa, biggest Soviet city that had been in their hands, bringing the Russians to the verge of complete liberation of the once overrun Ukraine.

German and Rumanian troops completed the evacuation of Odessa last night "in the course of large-scale detaching movements on the southern sector of the eastern front," the official DNB agency reported at noon (6 a. m. EWT).

"During the last few weeks

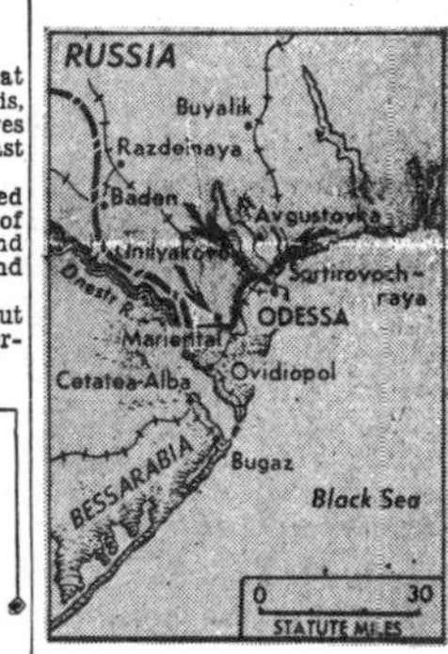

A. P Map.

Soviet troops, advancing from the north (upper arrows) have forced the Germans to evacuate Odessa, while Red forces driving toward the southwest have seized Mariental (lower left arrow), placing them within a few miles of Ovidiopol, the bottleneck ferry which is the enemy's only means of escape.

all installations which might have been of importance to the Soviets have been systematically destroyed and all war materiel in the city has been carted away," DNB said.

The evacuation of Odessa leaves only the isolated Crimea as the last major Nazi holding in southernmost Russia.

Thousands Believed Trapped.

Despite the DNB announcement, military observers were inclined to doubt that the Germans were able to extricate more than a portion of the beleaguered garrison of Odessa.

[Recent estimates placed the number of Germans and Rumanians in Odessa at 100,000 to 200,000, the Associated Press said.]

Premier Stalin was expected to confirm the fall of Odessa at the southern tip of the Ukraine in a special order of the day later today. A victory salute of Moscow's guns was certain. The port had been held by the Nazis for two and a half years.

With the fall of Odessa, the Red army completely cleared the Germans from the prewar Ukraine with the exception of a slender segment looping around Tiraspol

(Continued on Page Nine.)

Japs Driving To Cut Around Imphal Base

By the Associated Press.

NEW DELHI, April 10.—The Jap besiegers of the plain of Imphal have sent small parties west of Bishenpur, 18½ miles southwest of Imphal on the Tiddim Road, where they have been in contact with Allied forces and suffered casualties, the Southeast Asia Command announced today.

This was the first time that Japs had been reported west of the Tiddim-Imphal road. (It indicated a Jap effort to sweep around the Imphal defenses from the southwest.)

British forces stoutly defending Kohima, northern Imphal plain strong point, have wiped out Jap groups which penetrated the town's tight ring of defenses, killing at least 50 and taking others prisoners, the communique said.

(The Japanese have claimed capture of Kohima.)

Jap Pressure Steady.

The Japs were bringing steady pressure to win the Imphal plain, rich in food, before the monsoon next month halts most military activities, but Allied troops were said to have a firm hold at the moment at the edge of the plain.

Undeterred by losses, the Nipponese invaders continued their pressure in the whole Kohima area. Along the road from Tiddim to the south of Imphal the Japs increased their pressure and were in contact with Allied defenders.

Fighting also was reported in the foothills north of the plain

(Continued on Page Nine.)

Two Demand Tammany Oust Red 'Wreckers'

John L. Buckley and Dennis J. Mahon powerful Democratic leaders on the West Side, demanded today that Tammany Leader Edward V. Loughlin remove Bert Stand as the Wigwam's secretary and that its executive committee refuse to recognize Clarence H. Neal, Jr., and James Pemberton as committee members.

Renewing their charges of a Communist plot to wreck the Democratic party in New York County, the district chiefs warned Mr. Loughlin that "if you are unable or unwilling to undertake and at once to cleanse our organization of the un-Democraeic Communist-dominated influences now within it, we shall demand your resignation and seek to force it if not forthcoming."

This latest explsion in Tammany's turbulent affairs was precipitated by disclosures in the World-Telegram last week of a political deal between Messrs. Stand and Neal, on one hand, and Representative Vito Marcantonio, on the other, to have Pemberton appointed confidential clerk to the Supreme Court Board of Justices. Mr. Marcantonio is left wing leader of the American Labor party.

Point to Marcantonio.

Mr. Buckley, leader of the 7th A. D., and Mr. Mahon, leader of the 9th A. D., wrote Mr. Loughlin that "the Messrs. Stand, Neal, Pemberton and all their ilk in our organization openly and viciously traffic with Representative Marcantonio, whose voting record in Congress prior to Pearl Harbor was un-American."

They said there was "conclusive evidence in hand" that:

"1. The loyal Democratic supporters of Representative Martin J. Kennedy are to be betrayed by our organization to further the ambitions of Representative Marcantonio.

"2. This same Marcantonio has been permitted to dictate the designee for Congress on the Democratic ticket in the new Congressional district embracing Harlem, which holds its first election under reapportionment this fall.

Debt Settlement.

"3. An attempt is being made to debase both our organization and the Supreme Court by forcing Pemberton, servile tool of Marcantonio, on the justices of that court in payment of an alleged political debt."

The district leaders said there was "ample evidence" that Communists and Communist sympathizers "are already well, embarked on a campaign to despoil first and ultimately destroy the Democratic party in New York County."

They declared also that indorsement of President Roosevelt by Tammany's present hierarchy "would be a travesty and a liability," and that under the present setup Tammany could not hope for "any voice in the selection of candidates on the city-wide ticket next year."

Hull Demands Unity to Bar 3rd World War

By JOHN A. REICHMANN,
United Press Staff Correspondent.

WASHINGTON, April 10.—Secretary of State Cordell Hull's vigorous new defense of U. S. foreign policy was hailed enthusiastically in administration circles today, but some critics charged anew that the government was sidestepping a specific stand on many pressing problems awaiting settlement.

Mr. Hull's defense came last night in a 45-minute nationally broadcast address in which he touched upon the Atlantic Charter, postwar world organization, his handling of the French and Italian questions, the Soviet-Polish boundary dispute and other problems.

He appealed for national unity to prevent a third World War—"A tragedy to you and to your children and to the world for generations."

Policy Summed Up.

He said that:

The United States cannot recognize the French Committee of National Liberation as the government of France because Gen. Dwight D. Eisenhower must have absolute authority when he leads Allied armies into France; the Allies will adopt a firmer attitude in stopping neutrals from aiding the enemy; more democratic elements will be introduced into the

(Continued on Page Six.)

Yank Fliers Spread Havoc in Nazi Plants

By PHIL AULT,
United Press Staff Correspondent.

LONDON, April 10.—U. S. Air Forces switched the full weight of their pre-invasion offensive against Germany's waning air power to occupied France and Belgium today, smashing aircraft plants and airfields along a 300-mile front.

Strong forces of Flying Fortresses and Liberators made their third multipronged assault on the Nazi aircraft industry in as many days only a few hours after RAF heavy bombers dropped 1100 or more tons of bombs each last night on railway targets at Villeneuve-St.-Georges in the southeastern suburbs of Paris and Lille, controlling the supply lines to the French invasion coast.

Belgian Air Works Hit.

Upward of 700 American four-engined daylight raiders divided their cargoes of destruction among the Evere and Vilorder aircraft repair works and Melsbroek airdromes in the Brussels area of Belgium, aircraft factories at Bourges, 135 miles south of Paris, France, and military objectives along the French invasion coast and elsewhere.

The big bombers were escorted by equally strong forces of Thunderbolts, Mustangs and Lightnings of both the Eighth and Ninth air forces.

Today's attacks rounded out three days of concentrated Amer-

(Continued on Page Five.)

The War Today

Monday, April 10, 1944.

RUSSIA—Red army captures Odessa, last large Soviet city in German hands; breaks last German toehold in once completely overrun Ukraine.

AIR WAR—American air forces switch full weight of preinvasion offensive against Germany's waning war power with attacks on aircraft plants and airfields along 300 mile front in occupied France and Belgium.

PACIFIC—American airmen blast Truk again in attacks described officially as "softening-up" operations against large Jap naval supply base.

INDIA—Japs repulsed after breaking into British defenses before Kohima; suffer casualties in minor action southwest of Imphal.

ITALY—New Zealand troops attack two German strongpoints at Cassino; minor patrol clashes reported on other fronts.

Berle, Beaverbrook Fence on Aviation

By the Associated Press.

LONDON, April 10.—The American-British conferences between A. A. Berle and Lord Beaverbrook on post-war civil aviation were described by the Mirror's political writer today as "preliminary fencing" and "a poker game."

"Bath men took up a few cards and then tried to size up the other fellow's hand before leaving the game—unfinished," the Mirror said.

"Lord Beaverbrook's announcement that he had to make concessions is not taken seriously in political circles. It is taken as having been said with his tongue in his cheek."

James Roosevelt Going to Capital

By the United Press.

BURABANY, Cal., April 10.—Lt. Col. James Roosevelt, eldest son of the President, was en route to Washington today after a visit with his wife, the former Romelle Schneider, here.

Col. Roosevelt, who left last night after spending Easter week at his home, said he was traveling under Marine Corps orders and expected to be in Washington only briefly.

One Burst Downs 2 Messerschmitts

By the United Press.

EIGHTH AIR FORCE BOMBER BASE, England, April 10.—"Two for the price of one," Sgt. Stephen Z. Jones, 20, said, jokingly, pressing his triggers as two Messerschmitt 109 fighter planes flashed across his gunsights over Germany Saturday. To the amazement of the former farmboy, who comes from Hale, Mo., the first plane nosed down sharply and collided with the second as the tracer bullets struck. Both planes exploded.

Winant, Stettinius Talk with Churchill

By the Associated Press.

LONDON, April 10.—U. S. Ambassador John G. Winant and Undersecretary of State Edward R. Stettinius, Jr., had a long conference yesterday with Prime Minister Churchill, it was announced today.

World Freedom Marshall's Prayer

By the United Press.

ARLINGTON NATIONAL CEMETERY, Va., April 10.—While a host of military and civilian notables looked on, Gen. George C. Marshall, army chief of staff, prayed at an Easter sunrise service here yesterday that "we may have strength to secure the freedom of all peoples."

"May those who have given their lives rest in Thy care," he said. "Any may those who offer their lives in support of Thy divine cause to secure freedom for all peoples find strength. May it end with peace on earth and good will among men."

Allied M. D's Gain On Naples Typhus

By the Associated Press.

NAPLES, April 10.—Allied doctors apparently have won the Naples winter campaign against typhus-bearing lice and American troops have been readmitted to the city.

Naples was off limits to Allied troops on leave for several months while a typhus epidemic was threatened. An official announcement said marked improvement in the situation had allowed a partial lifting of the restriction.

Invasion Barges Built of Concrete

By the Associated Press.

LONDON, April 10. — Invasion barges of concrete are now being built on a mass-production basis along the English coast in a program designed to conserve steel. The 128-ton craft, which are 84 feet long and 22 wide, are poured right at the water's edge and are launched by crane as soon as dry. The record building time thus far is 74 hours.

Tito Holds Off Thrusts in Bosnia

By the Associated Press.

LONDON, April 10.—Yugoslav Partisans have smashed renewed German thrusts toward the stronghold of Mrkonjicgrad, recently seized by the Army of Liberation in the Jajce sector of western Bosnia, the headquarters of Marshal Tito announced today.

What's in a Name?

By the Associated Press.

SYRACUSE, N. Y., April 10.—Thomas J. Corcoran, area director of the War Manpower Commission, checked on the birth certificates of 10 of his 11 children at City Hall and found they contained eight mistakes, most of them omissions of first names. Discovery that his own certificate identified him only as a male child, without a first name, led to his quest.

Met Opera Gives 4 Scholarships

Three men and a woman won Metropolitan Opera contracts yesterday at the end of the ninth annual session of auditions of the air, bringing to 35 the total number of American singers acquired by the company in this manner.

The winners, each of whom also received $1000 and a silver plaque, are Morton Bowe, 39, tenor, 37-53 74th St., Jackson Heights, Queens; Regina Resnik, 21, soprano, 233 W. 77th St.; William Hargrave, 38, baritone, 98-50 67th Ave., Forest Hills, Queens, and Hugh Thompson, 28, baritone, 427½ E. 52nd St. In addition, Angelo Raffaelli of Chicago won a $500 scholarship.

English Mine Strikers Drifting Back to Pits

By the Associated Press.

LONDON, April 10.—Thousands of South Yorkshire miners returned to work today, virtually ending a week-long strike by nearly 100,000 men that cost an estimated 1,000,000 tons of coal.

A total of 75,000 men had returned this morning, with 20,000 more due back in the pits Wednesday. Thirty thousand miners resumed work in the Doncaster district alone after a vote last night. Hemsworth miners also agreed to return and voted confidence in J. A. Hall, Yorkshire Mine Workers' Assn. president, who termed the wildcat strike a "stab in the back" to him.

In Belfast 35,000 shipyard and aircraft workers will return to work Tuesday and Wednesday. Some have been on strike six weeks.

Her Pin-up Plaint

Police of the W. 54th St. station today were investigating a complaint by Mrs. Doris Hucko, 26, of 225 Dwight St., New Haven, Conn., who said that she sat on a seat in an IRT Broadway local in which three large pins had been affixed. Mrs. Hucko made her complaint soon after she sat down.

Berlin Reports Bombing of Rome

From Axis Prapaganda Sources.

By the Associated Press.

LONDON, April 10.—The Berlin radio declared today that Allied planes had bombed Rome yesterday just as Pope Pius XII was celebrating Easter mass in the hall of the Consistory.

The raid, at 11 a. m., was the last of three attacks made on the city, declared the broadcast. It said the first raid was carried out about 6 a. m. and the second an hour later. Allied headquarters in Naples said today railway communications in the Rome area had been attacked.

Jamaica Races Today Up to Striking Grooms

By FRANK ORTELL,
World-Telegram Staff Writer.

Whether the thoroughbreds would run as scheduled at Jamaica today, or the races be called off, depended upon the action of the stable grooms, who delayed for 20 minutes the start of the opening program last Saturday, much to the annoyance of a record turnout of 45,796, by calling a strike about an hour before scheduled races.

The dispute remained unsettled early today as the Metropolitan Jockey Club firmly refused to meet the demands of the grooms.

Track patrons were warned to retain the stubs of admission tickets today and if all the scheduled races are not in, the stubs will be honored for a full refund.

The grooms petitioned the Metropolitan Jockey Club for the payment of $5 for each horse led into the paddock, and $15 for each winner. Now the grooms received only $10 for each winner, but it comes out of the purse. In order to prevent confusion, and run off the inaugural program as scheduled, the association contributed to the various owners $5 for each starter in the card Saturday. This action was for that day only. Now

(Continued on Page Eighteen.)

Today's Scratches

At Jamaica.

No scratches on card.
Weather clear; track fast.

World-Telegram Index

Reds Follow Custom In Kravchenko Case

By IRVING JOHNSON,
World-Telegram Staff Writer.

The Soviet Embassy's attitude in the Victor A. Kravchenko case is strictly in line with the old Communist custom of always belittling former members of the party who dare to criticize its leadership or acts.

Kravchenko, former member of the Soviet Purchasing Commission, was called a liar and deserter by the Soviet Embassy after he had accused the Russian government of "double-faced" dealings with the Allies.

Earlier, the embassy had said he was unknown and then that he was a minor clerk in the commission. Finally, the embassy said he was an inspector of pipes and was due to report back to the Red army, hence was a deserter.

The Krivitsky Case.

A prior case was that of Gen. Walter G. Krivitsky, born Samuel Ginsberg, ex-Soviet military intelligence head in Western Europe, who came to the United States in 1939 and published four articles in the Saturday Evening Post beginning in April of that year.

The articles warned of the impending pact between Stalin and Hitler and were based on his orders from Moscow.

Immediately, the Daily Worker shouted "imposter," and the New

(Continued on Page Nine.)

Yanks Now 'Leap Frog' Islands, Tokyo Warns

By the Associated Press.

Declaring that the speed of the American advance in the Pacific has "become rapid by contrast with the days of the Solomons operations," the Tokyo domestic radio warned the Japanese people today that the war "is about to enter a real stage."

The broadcast, recorded by U. S. government monitors, said that the United States has full confidence in her military strength and that the American offensive has changed in character from island hopping to "leap frogging."

The Weather

New York and Metropolitan Area—This afternoon cloudy, occasional showers, highest temperature 70 degrees, gentle winds. Tonight rain, ending early, cooler, lowest temperature about 45 degrees.

New Jersey—Cloudy with mild temperature; showers in the afternoon.

TODAY'S READINGS.

	Temp.	Hum.		Temp.	Hum.
Midnight	50	..	5 a. m.	53	..
1 a. m.	54	..	6 a. m.	52	84
2 a. m.	54	..	7 a. m.	53	86
3 a. m.	52	..	8 a. m.	54	87
4 a. m.	53	..	9 a. m.	56	83
			10 a. m.	60	73

High and low a year ago, 49-30.

EIGHTH ARMY NEWS

Dominion Premiers' Declaration
(See Page Three)

No. 53, Vol. 4. FRIDAY, 19th MAY, 1944. ITALY

"The Enemy Has Been Completely Outmanoeuvred"

EIGHTH CAPTURE CASSINO

Battle For Hitler Line Due To Start—*Communiqué*

A SPECIAL communique announced yesterday that Cassino and the monastery have been captured by the Eighth Army.

The official report says: "The final assault on the town was carried out by British troops while Polish troops took the monastery.

"The enemy have been completely outmanoeuvred by the Allied armies in Italy, following the original breach of the Gustav Line by the Fifth Army on May 14, and the subsequent rapid advance of French and American troops through the mountains.

"The troops of the Eighth Army have fought their way forward in the Liri Valley, and during the last 24 hours have developed the decisive pincer movement which cut Highway Six, and so prevented the withdrawal of the enemy.

"A substantial proportion of the First German Parachute division has been destroyed in its efforts to escape.

"Both armies have contributed to this victory.

"The Gustav Line south of the Apennines has now ceased to exist."

An earlier communique said that the "Battle for the Hitler Line is about to commence."

At Last They Saw The Sun

By FRED REDMAN

CASSINO, Thursday.

The whitest men in the Eighth Army saw the sun to-day for the first time for a fortnight.

I met them in the rubble heap that was Cassino—men who had lived and fought underground in a town where it was death to move by day.

This morning, while the Poles raised a triumphant flag over the Monastery, British forces wiped up the rearguard of the withdrawing Germans in Cassino with a Piat attack against a house where in the crumbling ruins a few Germans could be heard running about like rabbits.

I walked into Cassino along a narrow dirt track where none could walk in daylight during the long siege.

It was worn hard by the path of many beas s, for this was the route by which supplies were brought under cover of darkness to the British forces entrenched in cellars and caves in the town. It was lined with shell holes.

Lieut. C. P. Muir, pale from his 14 days underground, showed me a crypt which had been his headquarters. In its ancient passages they had cooked, eaten, slept and kept guard.

I looked for the Hotel des Roses and the Continental, remembered by tourists as

(Continued on Page 4, Col. 1.)

BOSTONS DROP FOOD TO ADVANCE TROOPS

WITH the heavy bombers out again against German supply ports on both sides of Italy the M.A.A.F. flew more than 2,000 sorties compared with the single enemy plane seen over the battle area. We lost 15 planes and shot down one

Medium bombers blocked the main highway from Rome to the battlefront as fighter-bombers continued to pound objectives immediately behind the enemy line.

Mitchells and Marauders attacked the Frosinone road junction during the day, making the route impassable, and Wellingtons paid the same spot a night visit.

Mitchells also bombed one of the Viterbo landing grounds, potholing the runway. Thunderbolts added to the damage

A bridge at Poggibonsi was attacked by Mitchells, while Marauders hit bridges at Ceprano, Cesano, Pesaro and Fabriano

Bostons carried out a two-fold task. They dropped food to advanced Allied troops and bombed army targets near Valmontone.

Targets of Liberators were the causeway at Orbetello, and the docks at San Stefano, Piombino and Porto Ferrajo. Fortresses attacked Ancona on the east coast and troop concentrations in Yugoslavia.

Lightnings swept over northern Italy strafing airfields. They encountered about ten enemy planes and shot down one.

Tanks line up in San Giorgio waiting to attack their next objective in the drive against the German southern line

CARRIER PLANES BLITZ SHIPPING

LONDON, Thursday.

IN a daring sea-air operation, ships of the Royal Navy on Tuesday swept close in to the Norwegian coast to enable carrier-borne aircraft to make a sharp attack on shipping and shore installations, it was revealed here last night.

Taking the enemy by surprise Fleet Air Arm fighter-bomber swept in on a harbour, which in a moment was turned into a cauldron of smoke, escaping steam and flying wreckage.

Two medium-sized supply ships were left belching black smoke and three others were probably damaged.

Later German fighter-bombers attempted a retaliatory attack against our naval forces, but were forced to jettison their bombs before they could do any damage.

Striking again yesterday morning, this time 120 miles to the south, our bombers could only find armed trawlers as shipping targets.

In addition to shooting up two of these, our bombers flew as far as the enemy-held coast where they attacked a fish-oil factory working for the Germans.

BURMA TOWN BESEIGED BY ALLIED FORCE

A STRONG composite American-Chinese force has captured the aerodrome at Myitkyina, largest city in north Burma, which has been in Japanese hands for over two years and are directing mortar fire into the city.

The strong Chinese force, advancing on the Sino-Burma border, have only 75 miles to go to meet up with the forces of General Stilwell in north Burma

In New Guinea, Allied troops, in pursuit of Japanese remnants fleeing into the interior, have at last made real contact with the enemy 35 miles south-east of Aitape. Japanese troop concentrations are being heavily attacked from the air.

Bevan Appeases Party

The clash between the Parliamentary Labour Party leaders and Aneurin Bevan, Labour Member, over his recent "revolt" against Party policy has been smoothed over by a letter from Bevan to the Party leaders undertaking in future to accept the standing orders of the Party.—*Reuter.*

GERMAN PRISONERS, dispirited and in many cases lousy, behind barbed wire in Eighth Army prisoner-of-war cages.

REDS LEAVE HUGE FIRE

ATTACKS by Soviet bombers on German bases in White Russia are the main feature of the news from the Eastern front

The Red Air Force has again raided Polotsk 50 miles south-west of Nevel

Following a raid on the capital of White Russia, Minsk, seven large fires broke out at the railway junction, states the Russian communiqué

These fires spread into one huge area of flame and many heavy explosions were observed

North of Nevel, trains laden with enemy troops and equipment were smashed by direct hits at Baranovichi and Kholm junctions. Flames could be seen over 60 miles away.

In the Gulf of Finland, Russian aircraft sank three German trawlers and two escort vessels.

Cruisers Silence German Batteries

Allied warships off the west coast have continued to make things difficult for the Germans facing the Fifth Army.

They have registered many hits on enemy batteries and troop concentrations in the Itri-Formia sector and although in their latest bombardment there was increased and more active return fire our ships had no casualties or damage.

In the last six days Allied cruisers have fired nearly 3,000 rounds at enemy positions and minesweepers have been carrying on their work off the enemy coast under spasmodic shell fire.

It is reported that during last Saturday night naval patrols operating off the Anzio bridgehead sank one E-boat and damaged a second.

Marshal Petain yesterday received Marshal von Rundstedt, German anti-invasion chief, says Vichy radio. German radio earlier quoted Rundstedt as having said "Invasion will begin any moment now."

Limited Leave For Indian Army

MR. AMERY told Commons yesterday that arrangements on a limited scale had been made to grant home leave to certain officers and men in the Indian Army.

He had been asked by Viscount Suirdale "if in view of the fact that officers and men of the Indian Army are not covered by the scheme for repatriation of British Army personnel who have served continuously for long periods overseas, and in view of hardship imposed upon such officers and men who have served in the East for many years, he is making arrangements for granting leave at home for such personnel."

Amery replied: "Yes. Arrangements have already been made on a limited scale and I hope that in the present year it will be possible to increase considerably the numbers of British officers and men of the Indian Army to whom home leave can be granted."

Viscount Suirdale: "Is he aware that many relatives of British people are unhappy about this?"

No answer was given—*Reuter.*

Daily Mail

NO. 14,997 ONE PENNY * * FOR KING AND EMPIRE SATURDAY, MAY 27, 1944

LATE WAR NEWS

TWIN ARMIES DRIVE NORTH IN ITALY

Kesselring Orders Great Retreat: Ten Towns and Monte Cairo Taken

LAST night brought the best news yet from Italy — a statement by Berlin that Kesselring has been forced to order retreat at all the main points of General Alexander's attack. This news followed a day of sweeping successes for both the Fifth and Eighth Armies. Ten towns, including Cisterna, Cori, San Giovanni, and Fiedimonte, and the mountain mass of Monte Cairo have been captured. The Fifth Army is now attacking the last defence line before Rome, driving on the town of Velletri, 18 miles from Rome; the Eighth Army is pouring forward up the Liri Valley. The Beachhead Army, now eight miles beyond its starting point, has taken 2,500 prisoners out of a total of over 12,000.

Big Gains on Whole Front
Advance Speeds Up

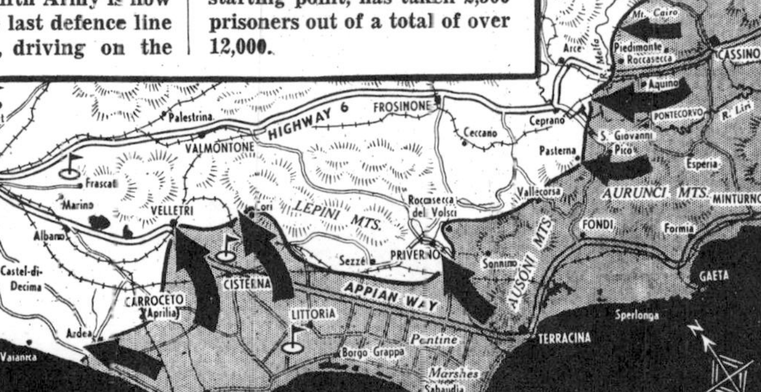

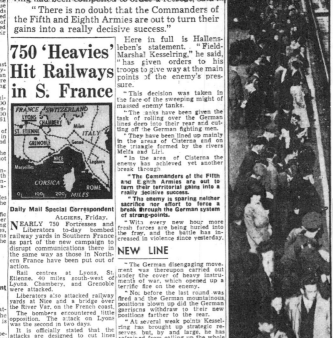

IMPORTANT gains by the Allied Armies in Italy were announced last night. The Fifth Army were stated by the Germans to be fighting in Velletri, vital stronghold on the last possible line of defence before Rome, having taken Cori, eight miles beyond the former perimeter of the Anzio beachhead. The capture of Cori has severed the last communications of any Germans struggling back from the Pontine Marshes. Meanwhile troops of the Eighth Army have stormed Monte Cairo, the height dominating Cassino from which the Germans were shelling Highway Six. Other troops pressed on to capture Roccasecca, on the Melfa River. Ten towns all told were taken.

Our Planes Bombing Non-stop
1,800 Kesselring Lorries Hit

From PAUL BEWSHER

ALGIERS, Friday.

THE German supply system in Italy to-day is reeling under the effects of a tremendous new blow just administered by the Allied air forces.

In two days alone nearly 1,000 road transport vehicles were completely wrecked or set on fire, while another 850 were damaged.

This means that over 1,800 urgently-needed lorries and other vehicles have been destroyed or put out of action.

Now that the whole Italian railway system has been completely disorganised by months of scientifically planned air attacks the Germans are compelled to rely almost entirely on road transport for bringing up men and material—or for withdrawing them from the battle area.

When the German front has been driven back so far and so rapidly as it has in the last fortnight this means that the headquarters repair and supply depots and countless other auxiliary services behind the modern army must be pulled back to a safe distance.

And in this case pulled back very quickly.

That is one reason why the Germans have been forced to use close columns of lorries along roads in broad daylight. These offered first-class targets to our fleets of fighter-bombers, who have worked tirelessly and methodically on their work of destruction.

ROADS BLOCKED

The results achieved in the past few days have far exceeded anything known in the whole African campaign, because the targets were bigger and probably our attacking force much greater.

Wednesday's record of 359 vehicles destroyed and nearly 300 damaged was left behind by yesterday's astonishing figure of 600 vehicles destroyed and 561 damaged.

Pilots made the work of destruction easier by bombing in front of the transport columns, and so blocking roads.

As vehicles piled up behind the blocks they were bombed and shot up.

"We made ten passes at one convoy and left every third or fourth vehicle burning," said one pilot engaged in transport blasting operations.

"At least half-a-dozen vehicles turned over trying to get off the road."

While attacks on the traffic columns are being made, other formations of aircraft are blocking the roads by bombing bridges, crossroads, and other key positions so as to further disorganise the transport system.

CONFUSION IS GROWING

Daily Mail Special Correspondent

IN THE LIRI VALLEY,
Thursday (delayed).

CONFUSION among the scattered remnants of the defenders of the Hitler Line is hourly growing more acute.

The enemy is obviously bewildered by the speed and power of the Canadian armoured thrust through the valley, and for once his genius for swift reorganisation seems to have deserted him.

Paratroops, split into disorganised groups, are making desperate efforts to sneak back through our lines and link up with the rest of the Tenth Army which is already over the Melfa.

Scores of them have already been rounded up by mopping up parties of infantry, and the total of prisoners is mounting rapidly.

FEW GUNS

All this morning more and more Canadian tanks have been streaming across the valley.

Apart from small delays, the general picture in the valley as I write is of a completely disrupted and badly worried enemy.

The paratroops, for instance, have been out of communication with their artillery for many hours, and advancing tanks repeatedly report parties of unarmed stragglers making their way back through waist-high fields of barley and vineyards towards our lines.

The Germans have pulled out of many positions so hastily that they have left guns and other weapons intact and a considerable amount of booty is already in our hands.

They have abandoned so many anti-tank guns in the Hitler Line that they now have very few to fight with

Paris Evacuees

Paris radio said last night that 1,500 women and children from Paris had arrived at Vesoul. Evacuation is proceeding.—*A.P.*

ALLIES 'ALL-OUT FOR DECISIVE WIN'

AS the Allies pour forward on all the Italian fighting fronts, Berlin last night issued its most sensational account yet of the defeat suffered by Kesselring's army.

The speaker was Marten Hallensleben, Military Correspondent of the official German News Agency, who, after disclosing that Kesselring had been compelled to order a retreat, said:

"There is no doubt that the Commanders of the Fifth and Eighth Armies are out to turn their gains into a really decisive success."

Here in full is Hallensleben's statement. "Field-Marshal Kesselring," he said, "has given orders to his troops to give way at the main points of the enemy's pressure.

"This decision was taken in the face of the sweeping might of massed enemy tanks.

"The tanks have been given the task of rolling over the German lines deep into their rear and cutting off the German fighting men.

"They have been lined up mainly in the areas of Cisterna and on the triangle formed by the rivers Melfa and Liri.

"In the area of Cisterna the enemy has achieved yet another break through

"The Commanders of the Fifth and Eighth Armies are out to turn their territorial gains into a really decisive success.

"The enemy is sparing neither sacrifice nor effort to force a break through the German system of strong-points.

"With every new hour more fresh forces are being hurled into the fray, and the battle has increased in violence since yesterday.

NEW LINE

"The German disengaging movement was thereupon carried out under the cover of heavy instruments of war, which opened up a terrific fire on the enemy.

"Not before the last round was fired and the German mountainous positions blown up did the German garrisons withdraw to their new positions farther to the rear.

"At several weak points Kesselring has brought up strategic reserves, but, by and large, he has refrained from calling up the whole main body of his reserves.

"The present front line now runs from the north of Anzio and through Velletri, and thence, via Cisterna-Sezzo-Priverno, to the area north of Vallecorsa, and here to Pastena, towards the estuary of the Melfa and the Liri, and then up to the area of Roccasecca and Piedimonte, where it joins the old mountainous front from north of Cassino to the Adriatic."

CORI FALLS

But even as Hallensleben was speaking, reports pouring in from Allied war correspondents showed that already the new defence line he names is gravely threatened.

Cori, defence bastion south-east of Velletri, has fallen: Velletri itself is under attack: the Beachhead Army is at least eight miles beyond its starting point.

In the Liri valley, San Giovanni was captured as the Germans, dis-

BACK PAGE—Col. FIVE

750 'Heavies' Hit Railways in S. France

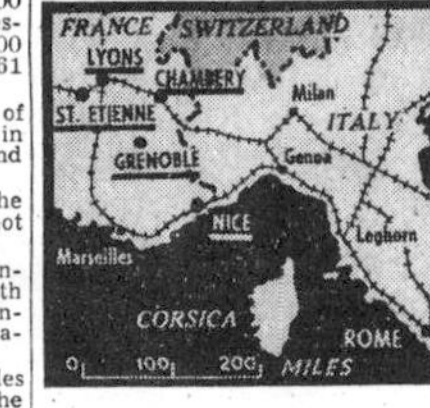

Daily Mail Special Correspondent

ALGIERS, Friday.

NEARLY 750 Fortresses and Liberators to-day bombed railway yards in Southern France as part of the new campaign to disrupt communications there in the same way as those in Northern France have been put out of action.

Rail centres at Lyons, St. Etienne, 40 miles south-west of Lyons, Chambery, and Grenoble were attacked.

Liberators also attacked railway yards at Nice and a bridge over the River Var, on the French coast.

The bombers encountered little opposition. The attack on Lyons was the second in two days.

It is officially stated that the attacks are designed to cut lines over which the Germans have been moving armour and supplies to the Italian front.

What's It Like in the Strait?

State of the Sea.—Moderating.

Weather.—General improvement and promising outlook: sunny since 3 p.m. Temperature: Highest, 66deg.; 49deg. at 10.30 p.m. Visibility: Fair. Sky clear. Wind: West.

Barometer.—Slight rise.

High Tide Across the Water.—4.01 p.m. and 4.14 a.m.

SUN SETS 10-2 P.M. MOON SETS 2-25 A.M. SUN RISES 5-52 A.M.
MOONLIGHT HOURS OF DARKNESS

DEFIANT JOURNEY

HERE is a section of the big holiday crowd waiting at Paddington last night for a train to the West Country—1½ hours before the train was due to depart. Other Daily Mail pictures in Page THREE.

Himmler Tells Judges

Daily Mail Radio Station

Himmler, S.S. chief, has lectured the highest German judges and public prosecutors on justice and party principles, states Berlin radio.

FDR CALLS WORLD MONEY TALKS

WASHINGTON, Friday.

PRESIDENT ROOSEVELT has called an international monetary conference to be held on July 1, it was announced in the White House to-day.

The conference will be held at Bretton Woods, New Hampshire, and will be known as the United Nations Monetary and Financial Conference.

Invitations have been sent to all the United Nations and the nations associated with them in the war, asking them to send official representatives.

The French Committee of National Liberation is included in the 42 nations to which invitations have been sent.

The conference is expected to last several weeks. All the agreements worked out will be later submitted to the respective Governments for their approval.

Mr. Henry Morgenthau, Secretary of the Treasury will head the United States delegation.

Argentina and Bolivia are not included in the list of Governments and authorities invited to take part in the conference.

Mr. Stephen Early, the White House secretary, said that apart from Mr. Morgenthau the American delegates have not yet been named.—*Reuter*

WHITSUN CROWDS DEFIANT
The 'Wanderbugs'

By Daily Mail Reporter

WHITSUN holiday crowds in thousands, disregarding warnings not to travel, and the possibility of trains being cancelled at a moment's notice, besieged the main London railway stations yesterday.

Every long-distance train from Paddington left with people standing in compartments and corridors. Passengers were left behind from more than half a dozen trains during the day.

Officials at Paddington arranged for a number of "heavy" trains, which normally leave the open platform No. 1, to start from one of the platforms with a barrier, so that the crowds could be controlled

Hundreds Left

Among the trains from which passengers were turned away was the 1.15 p.m. to Bristol and the West of England, as well as the 1.55 p.m to South Wales. Bristol passengers who could not leave by the 1.15 waited for the 4.15 p.m., but again about 500 passengers were left.

Two or three hundred people left behind the closed barriers of the 1.55 p.m. to Bristol and South Wales had also to wait for the 4.15 p.m.

One of the biggest queues of the day was for the 5.55 p.m. for South Wales. Women fainted after queueing up several hours.

Queueing for the 9.50 Swindon-Exeter-Plymouth express began at 7.45.

Conditions at Waterloo were comparatively quiet.

Queueing six-deep for trains to Blackpool, hundreds of "wanderbugs" made a start at Manchester yesterday on the "riskiest" Whitsun holiday they have ever spent.

AIR OFFENSIVE ON AGAIN
Bridges Hit

The air offensive was resumed last evening when large forces of bombers and fighters crossed the south-east coast, flying high towards Northern France.

Later, it was announced that Ninth Air Force Marauders attacked bridges in Northern France and an airfield at Chartres, while Havocs bombed an airfield at Beaumont-sur-Oise. All were escorted by Thunderbolts.

Mosquito bombers attacked German military targets in Northern France without loss during the day, when, apart from routine fighter patrols, operations were on a reduced scale.

WOOLTON'S PLAN

War Declared on Depression
WORK 'GENERAL STAFF'

By WILSON BROADBENT, Political Correspondent

SKILLED economists are to be recruited by the Government to form a "general headquarters staff" in Whitehall to organise the maintenance of full employment throughout the nation and to fight the forces of depression after this second world war has been won.

The task of this general staff will be to keep a constant watch on all economic trends and to warn the Government when and where a trade slump is threatened.

Man-power experts will, at the same time, have under ceaseless review the ebb and flow of all sources of employment and the means by which they can be satisfied.

By this method, it is argued that the battle for national prosperity can be won in the post-war years.

With information supplied by the Economic General Staff the Government and Parliament can agree on a general strategy for maintaining employment, and, where necessary, speedy practical decisions can be taken by the Cabinet for defeating depression wherever it shows itself.

This is the foremost practical proposal put forward by the Government in a White Paper, issued yesterday, in which is reviewed Britain's post-war prospects.

EXPANSION

Never before has there been such a frank and detailed Government survey of the economic problems facing us and the plans by which they may be overcome.

The White Paper has taken more than two years to prepare and represents principles which have the unanimous support of all parties in the Government.

For instance, the principle of economic expansion to solve the problems which must arise after the war is accepted with greater official alacrity than ever before.

The hopes of the Government and the justification of the many theories advanced—for they are, as yet, mostly theories and not legislative proposals—are contained in the last paragraph of the White Paper, which reads:

"The Government believe that, once the war has been won, we can make a fresh approach, with better chances of success than ever before, to the task of maintaining a high and stable level of employment without sacrificing the essential liberties of a free society."

The proclaimed object is to secure for the nation the most effective use of its man-power and its material resources. But it is pointed out that this can only be achieved if the whole productive power of the nation is employed efficiently.

PURCHASE POWER

It cannot be sufficient for this productive power merely to be employed.

"The Government, therefore seek to achieve both work for all and a progressive increase in the economic efficiency of the nation as joint elements in a growing national power to produce, to earn, and to enjoy the fruits of increased well-being."

In this connection it was pointed out yesterday that the White Paper must be regarded as only a part—albeit a vital part—and not the whole programme of the Government's post-war policy.

One reason for the long period occupied in its preparation has been the necessity of initiating international trade and currency talks with other countries.

The Government make it clear that, while they will spare no effort to create favourable conditions for expanding our export trade, final responsibility and, above all, initiative must rest with industry to make the most of opportunities.

Indicative of the Government's ideas for assisting purchasing power within this country in times of fluctuation are two suggestions.

(1) A system of deferred tax

BACK PAGE—Col. TWO

MP's CHARGES AGAINST U.S. MEN 'RECKLESS'

CHARGES made in the House of Commons by Mr. W. D. Kendall, Ind. M.P. for Grantham, concerning the conduct of U.S. troops in the district were condemned yesterday as "grave but reckless" by Lord Brownlow, Lord Lieutenant of Lincolnshire, Councillor A. Barnett, Mayor of Grantham, and Alderman Rothwell Lee, chairman of the Watch Committee.

They issued a statement that they have no evidence whatsoever of any incident which in any way supports Mr. Kendall's charges.

"Mr. Kendall, it seems, did not take the elementary and obvious course of consulting the local police authority as to the facts before asking his question," they say.

"The Chief Constable of Grantham has categorically stated that he is entirely satisfied with the conduct of the American troops and has no knowledge of complaints of molestation or bad manners.

"We feel that the people of this district owe a wide debt of gratitude to the American Forces for their presence here, their hospitality, and their friendship, and we deplore any public statements which carry the implications referred to."

Footnote: In a Commons question on Thursday Mr. Kendall declared that it was "unsafe for a woman to walk unescorted, day or night" in Grantham and many other towns, and referred to "unconcealed immorality" and to "alcoholic excesses."

'Wembley' Plan for Hyde Park

An Empire exhibition, like that at Wembley in 1924-25, should be held in England immediately after the war, said Capt. Somerset de Chair, Parliamentary Private Secretary to the Ministry of Production, at Manchester last night. He suggested the site be Hyde Park, so that visitors could see London's battle scars.

Capt. de Chair said that Lord Woolton, Minister of Reconstruction, thought it an interesting suggestion which should not be overlooked.

Partisans Attacked

An all-out offensive against the Partisans in Northern and Central Italy began yesterday, according to a German News Agency dispatch.

"Midnight was zero hour for the amnesty granted to the Partisans," said the agency.—*Reuter.*

Army's Cars Were Sold for Salvage

By Daily Mail Reporter

A WIDESPREAD conspiracy to dispose of Army motor vehicles — even ambulances — at salvage prices is being investigated by Scotland Yard officers at the request of the War Office.

The vehicles are said to have been falsely condemned as unfit within a few weeks of their being taken into service.

Already Chief Detective Inspector Thorp and his staff have visited many parts of the country making inquiries. I understand they have collected a considerable amount of evidence.

They have taken detailed statements from traders who are said to have purchased vehicles at ridiculous prices.

Yesterday the War Office and the Ministry of Supply were given an interim report of the progress of the investigations.

The full report is expected to be in the hands of the Director of Public Prosecutions next week.

The aid of Scotland Yard was sought after a conference between senior officials of the Ministry of Supply and the War Office.

OUR AIRMEN 'OUTLAWS'
Goebbels' Threat

Goebbels, in an article quoted last night by the German News Agency, again made threats against Allied airmen who are taken prisoner by the Germans.

"Allied airmen have begun to attack civilians openly," he said.

"Only by means of armed guards is it now possible to protect from the fury of the people enemy airmen who have been shot down during such attacks. It would be asking too much of us to demand that we employ German soldiers to protect the murderers of children."—*Reuter.*

WE USE ROCKET PLANES
'Secret Weapon' is Disclosed

ROCKET-FIRING aircraft are now being used in attacks against the Germans on land and at sea.

U-boats, shipping, and land targets, such as bridges, gun emplacements, radio stations, and military buildings, have all been attacked with success.

The R.A.F., Coastal Command, and the Fleet Air Arm are equipped with these new-weapon planes, which have been in action since June last year. Four types of aircraft — Beaufighters, Hurricanes, Typhoons, and Swordfish—are fitted with the projectiles.

Each aircraft carries eight rockets, four under each wing. They are fired along guide rails, either in pairs or as a salvo—eight projectiles at once.

First Coastal Command pilot to use rockets was Wing Commander Roderick Hugh McConnell, D.F.C., of Mayfield, Sussex, in an attack on a stranded German merchant ship in a Norwegian fiord east of North Christiansund in June 1943. He commanded the first R.P. Beaufighter Squadron.

The rocket case consists of a shell tube filled with cordite which is ignited by a small platinum fuse wire. The consequent flow of gas

RAF 'HEAVIES' OUT AGAIN

As darkness fell last night a stream of R.A.F. heavy bombers was heard crossing the east coast.

KURILES AGAIN BOMBED

New York, Friday.—A Pacific Fleet announcement from Pearl Harbour states that Ventura search planes bombed Shumushu, in the Kuriles, on Wednesday. Started several fires, and encountered moderately heavy A.A. fire. All the planes returned safely.—Exchange.

2

from the tail propels the rocket, complete with its head, along the rails in the sighted direction. Four fins are fitted to the trailing end for stabilisation in flight.

A favourable feature of this new weapon is that there is no recoil, and the aircraft flies steadily on its course during the firing of successive rounds.

Rockets are used as primary weapons to sink shipping or as secondary weapons to keep down fire from the flak ships and damage the vessels themselves.

Picture in BACK Page.

Roosevelt's 'Medical'

WASHINGTON, Friday. — President Roosevelt visited Bethesda naval hospital here to-day for a medical examination. The President's physical condition was thoroughly checked. Later he held a Cabinet meeting.—*Reuter.*

DAILY MIRROR, Monday, June 5, 1944.

Daily Mirror

JUNE 5

No. 12,625 ONE PENNY Registered at the G.P.O. as a Newspaper.

ROME FALLS

ALLIED TROOPS IN CITY'S CENTRE

Rain of bombs on 200 miles of France

A 200-MILE stretch of the coast of Northern France was yesterday the battlefront for great Allied air fleets.

It is estimated that more than 8,000 tons of bombs swamped targets in Northern France and Belgium since the RAF opened the week-end onslaught just before midnight on Saturday.

Allied bombers, streaming over the coast in an unending parade yesterday, gave the enemy coast the most sustained pounding of the war.

Boulogne was the main single target in a week-end of raids which must have involved about 7,500 sorties.

None Missing

Rocket-armed RAF planes joined with more than 150 Marauders and Havocs in pouring a withering concentration of H.E.s on military installations. More links in the enemy's radio chain along the Atlantic Wall were smashed, and another road bridge over the Seine was wrecked.

The Luftwaffe, which lost 280 planes over Europe last week, didn't come up to fight, and no Allied planes are missing.

In the evening, according to Paris radio, our bombers attacked the suburbs of Paris.

Between 500 and 750 Allied heavy bombers, escorted by fighters, yesterday bombed railway targets on both sides of the Franco-Italian frontier.

THE WEDDING WENT ON

THREADING its way between lines of waiting dust-laden soldiers, tanks and guns in outer suburbs of Rome yesterday morning, there came a strange procession.

Two by two they marched, the men on the right, the girls on the left. And in front was a young girl in something better than her Sunday best, with a young man conspicuously uncomfortable in a hot dark blue serge suit, and a stiff collar.

What could it be, the soldiers asked themselves. Could it be a wedding?

Men leaped from their tanks and their guns and trucks and gathered around the leading couple. "Is it a wedding?" they asked. "Marriage?"

The girl nodded her head. Yes, it was her wedding day.

And her little wedding was filmed and photographed and finally, to cheers of soldiers, the bridal party walked on past guns, tanks and troops. Some of the soldiers threw the bride a kiss. Others offered gratuitious advice.

Air blitz on Hun forces retreating from capital

THE Fifth Army reached the heart of Rome at dusk last night after a resistance in the outer suburbs by the German rearguard.

And so—ROME, SUNDAY NIGHT—was the proud date line on the war correspondents' cables as they flashed their stories across the world.

The German main army is apparently retreating fast north of the city.

Highways fifty miles beyond Rome are jammed with Germans and transport, indicating that the enemy is making a big withdrawal to far behind the capital.

Allied fighter bombers are hammering at these congested roads and attacking troop concentrations and gunposts with great success. Already over 300 vehicles have been smashed and another 300 damaged.

Kesselring made a last-ditch stand before the city yesterday morning, aimed at holding off the Fifth Army long enough to enable his main forces to get away.

The Fifth Army, uncertain as to whether the Huns intended to fight in Rome itself or evacuate, held off the start of the final assault several hours

Then they began to shell the German position at 11 o'clock

The last lap: how Fifth Army's spearhead came to the capital's gates

FOLLOWING the savage artillery duel, our armoured units rushed on into the Eternal City yesterday afternoon, fighting it out with the German rearguard.

In a delirium of joy, the Italians walked beside our tanks, shouting through the shell bursts. Some were killed by flying fragments.

Fifth Army tanks and infantry fought German rearguards to the edge of the ancient Forum.

Then a column of the force from the old beachhead completed the mopping up of the heart of the city at 9.15 p.m.

First news of the events which proved to be the prelude to the fall of Rome came to me at Corps Headquarters, cables T. E. Healy.

"Kesselring Line pierced everywhere," shouted an excited colonel.

"We have got at least three columns pushing into the hills behind it. Way things are going we may be well on way to Rome tonight.

"We could even be in Rome!"

I raced to my jeep and turned it towards Valmontone, last town reported in our hands. At every command post where I stopped for news the colonel's jubilant predictions were supported.

At the headquarters of a famous infantry division there was a dramatic meeting between the French Commander, General Juin, whose Algerian troops had fought their way through the hills to link up with the Fifth Army forces from the Beachhead, and the American General commanding the division marching on from Valmontone along Highway Six.

General Juin brought good news that already his great fighting Goums had fanned out protectively along the right flank of the hard pushing Fifth Army, ensuring

Continued on Back Page

Germans wreck city works

AN American radio correspondent broadcast last night:

"Amid the crack of machine-gun fire in the outskirts of Rome we heard some heavy explosions and saw great clouds of smoke rising above the roof-tops.

A civilian told Allied troops that the city's gas, water and electricity works had been blown up by the Germans on Saturday.

AFTER 4 YEARS

Children he had not seen for four years dash across the station platform at Torre, Devon, to greet their daddy, Corporal Phillips, a repatriated prisoner-of-war, on his arrival home.

First was Clifford, 12, closely followed by Bernard, 15, and Beryl, 9. Margaret aged 4½ was shy at first, but decided later: "I like my daddy, he's a nice man."

WEATHER

Party Cloudy and Cooler on Tuesday

Sun rises at 5:57 and sets at 9:04

DETROIT TEMPERATURES

7 a. m. 72	8 a. m. 73	9 a. m. 75
10 a. m. 77	11 a. m. 80	12 Noon 83
1 p. m. 85	2 p. m. 86	3 p. m. 88
4 p. m. 88	5 p. m. 87	6 p. m. 88
7 p. m. [illegible]	8 p. m. 79	9 p. m. 81
10 p. m. 81	11 p. m. 80	12 p. m. 73

The Detroit Free Press

EXTRA

TUESDAY, JUNE 6, 1944 — On Guard for Over a Century — Vol. 114—No. 33 — Five Cents

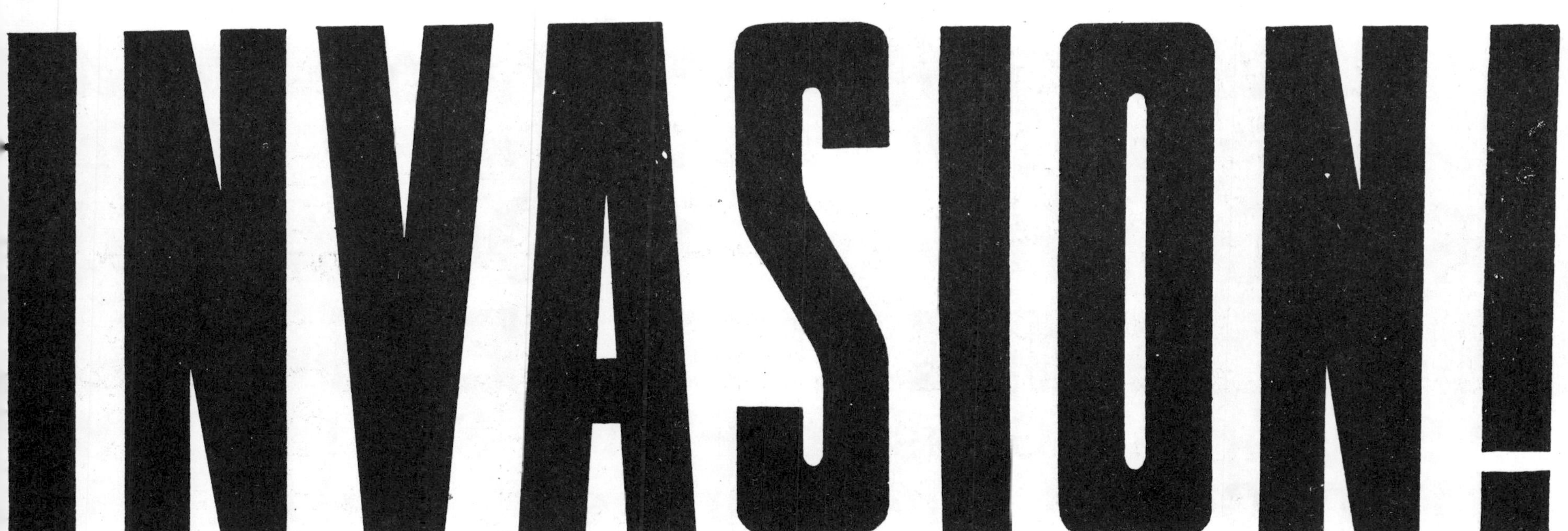

SUPREME HEADQUARTERS, Allied Expeditionary Force—(AP)—Gen. Dwight D. Eisenhower's headquarters announced Tuesday that Allied troops began landing on the northern coast of France Tuesday morning strongly supported by naval and air forces

Under the command of Gen. Eisenhower Allied naval forces supported by strong air forces began landing Allied armies this morning on the northern coast of France.

The Germans said the landings extended between Le Havre and Cherbourg along the south side of the bay of the Seine and along the Northern Normandy coast.

Parachute troops descended in Normandy, Berlin said.

Berlin first announced the landings in a series of flashes that began about 6:30 a. m. (12:30 a. m. Eastern War Time).

The Allied communique was read over a trans-Atlantic hookup direct from General Eisenhower's headquarters at 3:32 E. W. T., designated "Communique No. 1."

A second announcement by Shaef said that "it is announced that Gen. B. L. Montgomery is in command of the army group carrying out the assault. This army group includes British, Canadian and U. S. forces.

Berlin Says Landing Is at Seine River

LONDON—(AP)—Three German news agencies early Tuesday flashed word to the world that an Allied invasion of Western France had begun with Allied parachute troops spilling out of the dawn skies over the Normandy peninsula and sea-borne forces landing in the Le Havre area.

The Germans also said that Allied warships were furiously bombarding the big German-held French port of Le Havre at the mouth of the Seine River, 100 miles west of Paris.

German shock troops also were hurled against Allied troops rushing ashore from landing barges, the broadcasts said.

Le Havre lies 80 miles across the Channel from the British coast.

Dunkerque and Calais, just across the Channel Coast from Britain, were under attack by strong formations of bombers, DNB said.

"The long-expected invasion by the British and Americans was begun in the first hours of the morning of June 6 by the landing of parachute troops in the area of the mouth of the Seine," declared the Transocean broadcast.

Allied headquarters remained silent.

The German DNB agency said Le Havre was being "violently bombarded at the present moment" (7 A. M. German time, or A. M Detroit time).

"German naval forces are engaged in fighting with enemy landing craft off the coast."

Calais and Dunkerque important French ports along the invasion coast 150 miles northeast of Le Havre.

DNB added that "no enemy landings were made yet" at Calais and Dunkerque, obviously an indication that the Germans were expecting Allied assaults all along the intervening 150 miles separating Dunkerque and Le Havre.

Murphy Says He Will Return Bribe Money

BY KENNETH McCORMICK
Free Press Staff Writer

LANSING—Resting following a heart attack, Francis (Frank) Murpkhy said Monday that he would ask the court's permission to return $2,500 in graft Wednesday, when he will plead guilty to grand jury graft dharges before Circuit Judge Leland W. Carr.

The former lieutenant governor confessed to this writer in an exclusive interview Sunday that he had taken the money for his part in obtaining the passage of an amendment which reduced the annual license fee of distilleries from $5,000 to $1,000.

"Judge Carr and Kim Sigler (special grand jury prosecutor) have been square with me," he said Monday. "I will go in and help them all I can. There is only one request I want to make. I will make it Wednesday when I go to Lansing. That is that I be permitted to return the money.

"I'm a sick man. I don't know.

Turn to Page [illegible], Column 2

F.D.R. Hails Fall of Rome

WASHINGTON—(AP)—Hailing the capture of Rome with the jubilant phrase "one up and two to go," President Roosevelt declared Monday night that the aim now is to drive Germany "to the point where she will be unable to recommence world conquest a generation hence."

Mr. Roosevelt, in a nationwide radio broadcast, cautioned that this struggle with the Nazis would be tough and costly and that the day of Germany's surrender "lies some distance ahead."

Whether his reaffirmation that the fight would be pressed until Germany surrenders was a reply to the recent speech of Pope Pius XII was not stated. The Pope had asserted last week that the idea that the war must end either in complete victory or complete destruction was a stimulant toward prolonging the conflict and expressed hope for an early peace.

Speaking of Rome as the great symbol of Christianity, the President declared: "It will be a source of deep satisfaction that the freedom of the Pope and of Vatican City is assured by the armies of the United Nations."

"The allied generals maneuvered so skillfully," he said,

Turn to Page 5, Column 1

Allies Cross Tiber; Chase Routed Foe

BY ROBERT VERMILLION

ALLIED HEADQUARTERS, Naples — (UP) — Allied troops swept across the Tiber in force Monday to the tumultous cheers of liberated Romans, pursuing two shattered German armies whose disordered retreat was so precipitate that they had entirely disengaged themselves except for the merciless hawking of Allied fliers.

(Madrid dispatches said the Allies had driven three miles beyond Rome. In London it was estimated that German Field Marshal Albert Kesselring's forces had suffered 70,000 casualties and lost 75 per cent of their combat effectiveness. In another month, it was predicted, the Germans will have withdrawn to the Leghorn-Florence-Rimini line, 160 miles north of Rome.

BRITISH CHASE NAZIS

Smashing northward on the right flank of the Rome occupation forces, the main body of the British Eighth Army scrambled over endless German demolitions in pursuit of enemy units who were fleeing through Subiaco to the Pescara trunk highway leading from Rome to the east. The Pescara road already has been cut just east of Rome, but the Germans can get out over a number of connecting roads to the north through the Appenines.

British troops on the left flank drove within six miles of the Tiber

Turn to Page 7, Column 5

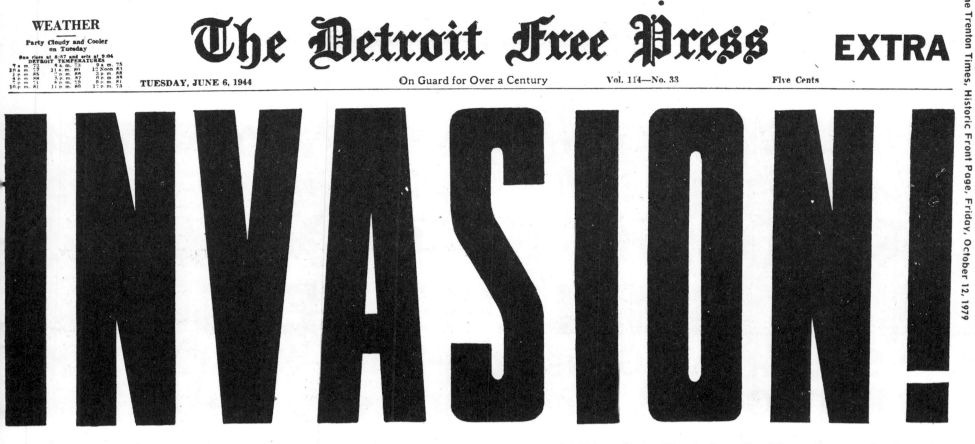

Report from Dover

LONDON — (UP) — Invasion weather over the Dover Straits Monday: Cloudy and cool, but the wind dropped a little and the sea became less choppy. Visibility was variable, but at nightfall the outlook was more favorable, with the cloud cover rising higher and the barometer showing no further loss.

All Warned to Quit Belt 20-Mi. Deep

LONDON (AP)—A spokesman for Gen. Dwight D. Eisenhower, in a London broadcast told the people living on Europe's invasion coast Tuesday that "a new phase of the Allied air offensive has started" and warned them to move inland to a depth of about 20 miles.

In a special broadcast over the BBC ,directed to France and other coastal countries, the spokesman said:

"A new phase of the air offensive has started. It will affect the entire coastal zone situated not less than 35 kilometers inland from the French coast. People will be advised by special announcements dropped from Allied planes.

"The attack will take place less than one hour later. As soon as the warning has been given, the following orders are to be followed:

"First, leave the town at once."

"Second, choose such a route out of town as to avoid the main road.

"Third, leave on foot only carrying essentials.

"Fourth, go to the country at least two kilometers from town.

"Do not assemble in groups which might appear to be troop concentrations."

The broadcast advised the people to keep as far as possible away from roads and railroad lines and to take nothing with them they cannot carry personally.

The spokesman concluded with the advice that those able to leave the 20-mile-deep coastal belt should do so at once, adding that those who cannot leave now must do so when the Allies give warning.

Victor Quits as Ruler; Umberto to Control Italy

NAPLES—(AP)—King Victor Emmanuel II stepped aside as monarch of Italy Monday as he previously had said he would do upon the liberation of Rome and handed to his thirty-nine-year-old son, Crown Prince Umberto, all 'royal prerogatives."

Italian political pressure had been brought to bear against him since the conquest of Naples.

In a decree signed by himself and countersigned by Premier Marshal Pietro Badoglio, head of the Italian Liberation Government, the King named his son Lieutenant General of the realm.

RETAINS HIS TITLE

The monarch, however, retained his title as head of the House of Savoy and remains as King without power.

King Victor, who became ruler July 29, 1900, had announced last April 12 his "irrevocable" decision to withdraw from public life "on the day on which Allied troops enter Rome," and to turn his powers over to the Crown Prince.

Little more than a figurehead since Mussolini assumed the dictatorship of Italy, Victor had won a reputation the first years of his reign as a sympathetic monarch.

Turn to Page 7, Column 4

Let Moon Mullins, Free Press comic, erase your frown today.

Rome Hails Liberators in Wild Joy

BY HERBERT L. MATTHEWS
New York Times Foreign Service

ROME—Never has there been such a Roman triumph as this day. Jeeps on Campidoglio, tanks rolling past St. Peter's Cathedral almost under the windows of the Pope's office, GIs buying flowers for Roman lasses and excitement everywhere.

Romans have seen conquerors galore in 2,500 years of history, but others had come to devastate. The Fifth Army was welcomed as deliverers and June 5 will go down in history as a joyous Roman holiday.

MONUMENTS UNHARMED

Best of all, this city is unharmed by war except in those unfortunate residential districts around railway yards. Nearly all of its glorious churches and monuments are intact. So far as is known, nothing in the museums has been harmed, although it remains to be seen how much the Germans have taken away.

But the Nazis, after all, did not fight for Rome proper. Technically they did defend Rome inside the city, but it was only a screen and when it broke Sunday evening, the whole city was ours for the taking.

Patrols and journalists roamed around at will, stopping at the Grand Hotel for a drink, looking at the Forum, answering excited happy people, thousands of whom had waited up all night.

ALL OUT TO CHEER

All Rome came out with the dawn, laborers and patricians, young and old, to cheer the army which had entered and swarmed all over its streets.

The Roman citizens did not rise at the end as the Neapolitans did. It is not in their temperament to do so. There has been much va-

Turn to Page 12, Column 1

LONDON — (AP) — The German-controlled Calais radio came on the air Tuesday with the following announcement in English:

"This is D-Day. We shall now bring music for the (Allied) invasion forces."

TUESDAY, JUNE 6, 1944

FINAL NIGHT EXTRA

Evening Standard

37,357 BLACK-OUT 10.57 pm to 5.0 am MOON Rises 9.50 pm; Sets 6.29 am. ONE PENNY

Churchill Announces Successful Massed Air Landings Behind Enemy in France

4000 SHIPS, THOUSANDS OF SMALLER VESSELS

"So Far All Goes to Plan"—11,000 First Line Airplanes

An immense armada of more than 4000 ships, with several thousand smaller craft, has crossed the Channel, said Mr. Churchill to-day, announcing the invasion.

"MASSED AIRBORNE LANDINGS HAVE BEEN SUCCESSFULLY EFFECTED BEHIND THE ENEMY'S LINES," HE SAID.

MR. CHURCHILL DESCRIBED THE LANDINGS AS THE "FIRST OF A SERIES IN FORCE ON THE EUROPEAN CONTINENT."

"The landings on the beaches are proceeding at various points at the present time. The fire of the shore batteries has been largely quelled, said Mr. Churchill.

"The obstacles which were constructed in the sea have not proved so difficult as was apprehended.

"The Anglo-American Allies are sustained by about 11,000 first line aircraft, which can be drawn upon as may be needed for the purposes of the battle.

"I cannot, of course, commit myself to any particular details, as reports are coming in in rapid succession. So far, the commanders who are engaged report that everything is proceeding according to plan—and what a plan!

"This vast operation is undoubtedly the most complicated and difficult that has ever occurred.

SURPRISE

"There are already hopes that actual tactical surprise has been attained," said the Premier, "and we hope to furnish the enemy with a succession of surprises during the course of the fighting.

"The battle which is now beginning will grow constantly in scale and in intensity for many weeks to come, and I shall not attempt to speculate upon its course.

"Complete unity prevails throughout the Allied Armies. (Cheers.)

"There is a brotherhood in arms between us and our friends in the United States.

"There is complete confidence in the Supreme Commander, General Eisenhower, and in his lieutenants, and also in the Commander of the Expeditionary Force, General Montgomery.

"The ardour and spirit of the troops as I saw them myself embarking in these last few days was splendid.

"Nothing that equipment, science and forethought can do has been neglected, and the whole process of opening this great new front will be pursued with the utmost resolution both by the commanders and by the U.S. and British Governments whom they serve.

WHAT A PLAN!

Replying to Mr. Greenwood, Mr. Churchill said that certainly in the early part of the battle he

(Continued on Back Page, Col. Four)

No. 1

At 9.30 a.m. to-day the following communiqué was issued from General Eisenhower's Supreme Headquarters:

"Under the command of General Eisenhower, Allied naval forces, supported by strong air forces, began landing Allied armies this morning on the Northern coast of France."

The statement was marked "Communiqué No. 1." At the same time it was revealed that General Montgomery is in command of the Army Group carrying out the assault. This Army Group includes British, Canadian and U.S. forces.

The King on the Radio To-night

It was officially announced from Buckingham Palace to-day that the King will broadcast at 9 o'clock to-night.

HITLER IN COMMAND

Hitler is taking personal command of all the anti-invasion operations, according to news reaching London from underground sources.

His four marshals are Rundstedt, titular commander-in-chief; Rommel, Inspector-General; Sperrle, in charge of air forces; and Blaskowitz, acting deputy to Rommel.

Thousands Of Fighters Strafe The Nazi Guns

Since the invasion began, Allied fighter-bombers have been dive-bombing, glide-bombing and strafing German defences and communications.

They fly literally into the mouths of guns and dive within feet of the spans which hold bridges together.

A gun is silenced, a truck carrying ammunition for a company of German soldiers is blown up, a bridge is shattered, making German supply convoys detour 20 or 30 miles, a gun crew is wiped out—multiplied by thousands, the fighter-bomber attacks will help the surface forces in 1000 ways, and will have an enormous effect on the battles below.

Bomber Command last night made their heaviest attack to date on the German batteries along the French coast.

In all, Bomber Command despatched more than 1300 aircraft.

'LANDINGS ON JERSEY, GUERNSEY'

German Overseas News Agency said this afternoon that landings have been made on the Channel Islands—Jersey and Guernsey—by Allied parachute troops.

Quoting the German High Command spokesman, the agency said: "Early to-day Allied airborne formations landed on Guernsey and Jersey.

"They were at once engaged in extremely costly battles."

SHELLED BY 640 GUNS

The Supreme Headquarters of the Allied Expeditionary Force state that over 640 naval guns, from 16in. to 4in., are bombarding the beaches and enemy strong points in support of the armies.

About 200 Allied minesweepers, with 10,000 officers and men, are engaged in the operations.

The weight of minesweeping material used amounts to 2800 tons, and the amount of sweep wire in use would reach almost exactly from London to the Isle of Wight.

The Press Association learns that enemy destroyers and E-boats are reported coming into the operational area.

'Tanks Ashore on Normandy Coast'

—SAYS BERLIN

The Allies have established beach-heads in Northern France and are driving inland, according to pilots who have flown over the battle.

This afternoon the Germans announced that landings were continuing in the Seine Bay—the stretch of the Normandy coast between the two ports of Cherbourg and Le Havre.

They reported parachute landings on Guernsey and Jersey, the two principal Channel Islands, and said that Allied troops were ashore at these points on the coast of Normandy:

ST. VAAST LE HOUGE (on the Cherbourg Peninsula): "Mass landing" supported by considerable naval forces, while strong American airborne forces jumped near Barfleur, a few miles to the north.

OUISTREHAM (at the mouth of the River Orne): "Landing barges under strong air umbrella are making landings," said the Germans.

Earlier the Germans had mentioned that Caen, a few miles inland up the Orne, was "the first focal point," where sharp fighting was taking place. The Germans also reported fighting 10 miles inland.

ARROMANCHES (in the middle of the Seine Bay): Tanks have been landed there, says Berlin.

ST. MARCOUF ISLANDS (just off the coast south of Cherbourg): "New landings made before noon particularly in this area."

VIRE ESTUARY

Another focal point mentioned by the Germans was the estuary of the Vire, another river running north into the Seine Bay.

Parachute landings were reported in several areas besides Barfleur—

(Continued on Back Page, Col. Two)

Stories of The Men Who Watched

Here are the stories told by men who watched the landings.

Fighter pilots returning from over the landing areas report that Allied infantry scrambled ashore at 7 a.m. in two areas of the French coast, apparently without heavy opposition, says Robert Richards, British United Press war correspondent at a U.S. Fighter Base.

One of the pilots, an American Colonel, William Curry, told me:

"I saw the first troops wading ashore about 7 a.m., from light landing craft. From the height at which I was flying they did not appear to be meeting heavy opposition and were covered by extensive and heavy naval bombardment from our warships.

"Flying Fortresses were also bombing the beach which appeared to be marshy instead of sandy.

Major John Locke, of Texas, who led a squadron of Thunderbolts, said:

"I have never seen so many ships in all my life. Flying over the harbour at one port I counted great numbers of cruisers, destroyers, corvettes and other craft. The constant flashes from their guns indicated that the beach was getting a heavy pounding.

"Behind this advance brigade, stretching in a never-ending stream across the Channel, came line after line of L.C.T.s (landing craft, tanks) escorted by corvettes and P.T. boats.

"We were never attacked by enemy airplanes although the flak was terrific."

Second Lieut. Benson, from Iowa, said: "The Channel waters were fairly calm and the boats bounced along smoothly. They were constantly patrolled by warships and many were towing barrage balloons."

Colonel William Schwartz added: "When I arrived over the beach our battleships brought all their fire to bear on the shore."

DAILY MIRROR, Wednesday, June 7, 1944.

Daily Mirror

JUNE 7

No. 12,627
ONE PENNY
Registered at the G.P.O. as a Newspaper.

Midnight news: Landings are successful

Naval losses "regarded as very light"

INVADERS THRUSTING INLAND

What the Germans are saying

GERMAN radio last night reported new Allied landings at Calais and Boulogne.

Powerful paratroop formations dropped behind Boulogne and north of Rouen were said to be engaged in "vicious" fighting. Other paratroops had a firm grip on a nineteen mile stretch of the Cherbourg-Caen road.

Sertorius, military commentator, said the offensive had extended to the entire Normandy peninsula.

Paris claimed a German counter-attack in the Cherbourg region was "still developing" late last night.

Our bridgehead, said to be fifteen miles long and several miles deep, was first reported to be between Villers-sur-Mer and Trouville.

Later broadcasts corrected this to further west on both sides of the River Orne and north-west of Bayeux, between Caen and Isigny.

A British-American group, with light tanks and tank reconnaissance cars, was operating on dunes north-east of Bayeux "trying to link up with the larger bridgehead," said Berlin.

Other enemy radio reports were:

Allied reinforcements "pouring in."

Except for the beachhead at Caen, all invasion troops landed from the sea thrown back. This beachhead narrowed down in some places.

"Navy Off Dunkirk"

Strong Allied naval forces seen off Dunkirk and Calais.

Fifteen cruisers with fifty to sixty destroyers operating off Le Havre last night, with landing craft, apparently waiting to attack.

Allied airborne troops on the Cherbourg peninsula "wiped out to a man" at Barfleur and La Pernelle, but more airborne troops pressing against Caen.

Allied landings on Channel Islands. Troops from 280 ships attacking Arromanches and Ouistrehem between Cherbourg and Le Havre. Cliffs scaled by ladder and tanks landed.

Allied landing craft penetrated Orne and Vire Estuaries; main centres of the big landing between St. Vaast de la Hogue and the Cherbourg peninsula tip.

In heavy artillery duel with coastal batteries off St. Vaast, a cruiser and troop-carrying landing craft were sunk.

Paratroops made twelve landings in all from Cherbourg to Boulogne. First and Sixth British and 28th and 101st American airborne divisions engaged.

Allied troops tried to break into Carentan, west of Isigny.

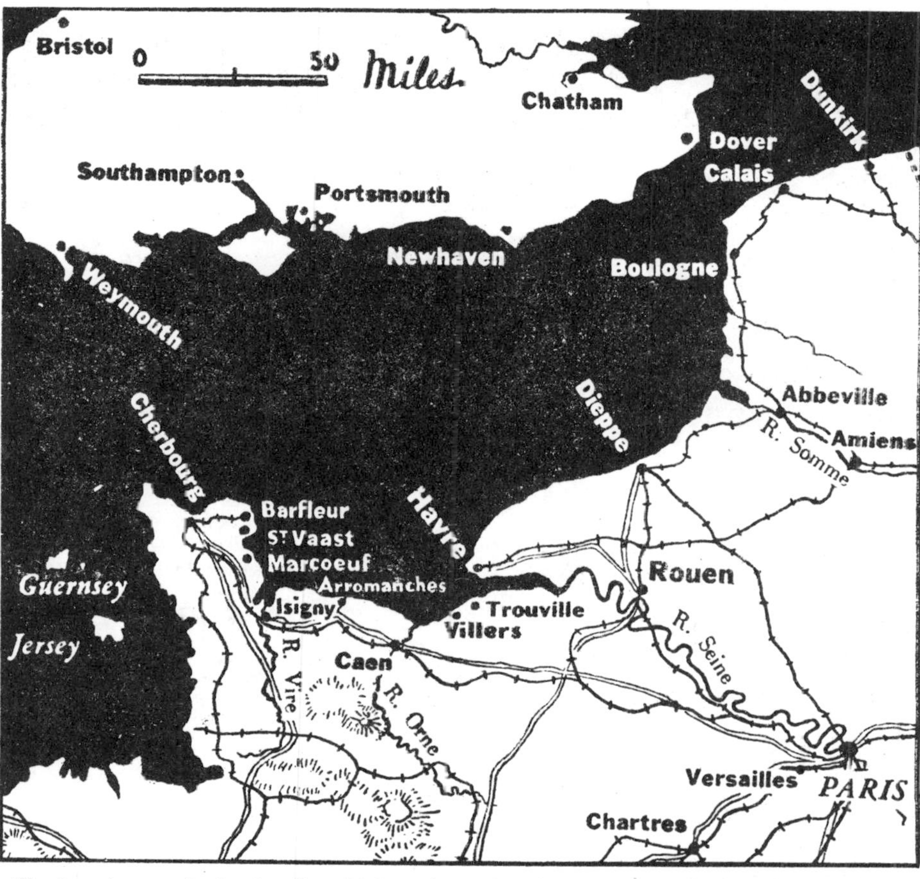

The invasion coast, showing the chief centres of activity between Cherbourg and Havre. Latest German radio reports suggest new Allied landings further north near Boulogne and Calais

MIDNIGHT COMMUNIQUE FROM SUPREME ALLIED H.Q. ANNOUNCED: "REPORTS OF OPERATIONS SO FAR SHOW THAT OUR FORCES SUCCEEDED IN THEIR INITIAL LANDINGS. FIGHTING CONTINUES.

"Our aircraft met with little enemy fighter opposition or AA gunfire. Naval casualties are regarded as being very light, especially when the magnitude of the operation is taken into account."

In Washington, Mr. Henry Stimson, U.S. War Secretary, said the invasion was "going very nicely." President Roosevelt said it was "running to schedule." Up to noon, U.S. naval losses were two destroyers and a landing vessel. Air losses were about one per cent.

Allied airmen returning from attacks on North France last evening reported that our troops were moving inland. There was no longer any opposition on the beaches now guarded by balloons. One pilot saw the Stars and Stripes flying over a French town.

According to earlier reports, British, Canadian and American spearhead troops of the Allied Armies have gained footholds along the Normandy coast, and in some places have thrust several miles inland.

Fighting is going on inside the town of Caen, seven miles from the coast, and several intact bridges have been captured.

BATTLING STILL FURTHER INLAND, AND WELL ESTABLISHED, IS THE GREATEST AIRBORNE ARMY EVER FLOWN INTO ACTION. THESE TROOPS WERE LANDED WITH GREAT ACCURACY AND VERY LITTLE LOSS.

The airborne fleet consisted of 1,000 troop-carrying planes, including gliders.

But though several vital obstacles have been overcome with much less loss than expected, the Germans will concentrate their reserves. Heavy battles are looming.

This was the situation outlined in the Commons last night by Mr. Churchill.

(Continued on Back Page)

I saw them leap to beach

ABOARD A BRITISH DESTROYER, OFF NORTH FRANCE, Tuesday.

GUNS are belching flame from more than 600 Allied warships. Thousands of bombers are roaring overhead, and fighters are weaving in and out of the clouds.

The invasion of Western Europe has begun.

Rolling clouds of dense black and grey smoke cover the beaches south-west of Le Havre, writes Desmond Tighe, of Reuter.

We are standing some 8,000 yards off the beaches of Berniere-sur-Mer, seven miles east of Arromanches, and from the bridge of this destroyer I can see vast numbers of naval craft.

In ten minutes more than 2,000 tons of H.E. shells have gone down on the beach-head.

It is now exactly 7.25 a.m., and through my glasses I can see the first wave of assault troops touching down on the water's edge and fan up the beach.

Under the supreme command of Admiral Sir Bertram Ramsay, Allied Naval Commander, Expeditionary Force, two great forces are taking part.

An eastern task force, mostly British and Canadian warships, is led by Rear-Admiral Sir Phillip Vian, of Cossack fame.

A western task force, mainly of American warships, is commanded by U.S. Rear-Admiral Alan G. Kirk.

The weather for the landings was not perfect, but despite high running seas and a strong north-westerly wind a bold decision was taken to go ahead.

The plans allowed for four phases:

1. *—Landings by airborne paratroops in the rear.*
2. *—A tremendous night bombing by the RAF on the landing beaches themselves.*
3. *—A bombardment by more than 600 Allied warships from battleships, cruisers, monitors and destroyers.*
4. *—A daybreak bombing attack by the full force of the U.S. Air Force just after dawn and before the first troops went in.*

Events moved rapidly after 4 a.m., and I will put on record the diary kept on the bridge:

5.7 a.m.—Lying eight miles from the lowering position for invasion craft.

5.20.—Dawn. Innumerable assault ships appear smudgily.

5.27.—Night bombing has ceased, and the great naval bombardment begins.

5.33.—We move in slowly.

5.36.—Cruisers open fire. We

Continued on Back Page

FIRST WOUNDED ARE BACK IN ENGLAND

The first Allied wounded were landed back in England yesterday. Some were taken to an East Anglian hospital.

Despite their wounds, many were smiling cheerfully.

Officially recorded next-of-kin of a wounded soldier on the danger list in a hospital at home will be sent a telegram, production of which at a police station will secure travel warrants for two persons.

MONDAY D-DAY HELD UP BY WEATHER

The invasion was delayed twenty-four hours, it was revealed at S.H.A.E.F. last night.

With his D-Day fixed for Monday morning, General Eisenhower was told by weather experts that conditions would be too bad.

But they forecast that by Tuesday there would be an improvement.

Eisenhower had to make a decision knowing that, once launched, the invasion could not be called off.

He took the decision to go in on Tuesday—and though the weather was not kind, the experts' forecast was largely fulfilled.

The landing craft, except for four, were able to battle on to the other side.

Rain fell in the Straits last night and the outlook was unsettled. The sea was smooth.

DAILY MIRROR, Friday, June 9, 1944.

Daily Mirror

JUNE 9

No. 12,629 ONE PENNY Registered at the G.P.O. as a Newspaper.

Midnight Communique:

BRITISH GO FORWARD

German reserves in action all along line

BRITISH and Canadian troops are continuing to make progress, against Rommel, whose reserves are now in action along the whole front in Normandy.

This was announced in the midnight communique from Supreme H.Q. This said also:—

"Repeated enemy attacks against the 6th Airborne Division have been held. The American bridgeheads are being gradually enlarged.

"THE ENEMY IS FIGHTING FIERCELY. HIS RESERVES HAVE NOW BEEN IN ACTION ALONG THE WHOLE FRONT.

"WITH THE SAFE AND TIMELY ARRIVAL OF MERCHANT CONVOYS AND IMPROVEMENT IN THE WEATHER, UNLOADING OF SUPPLIES IS PROCEEDING AT A SATISFACTORY RATE. DEVELOPMENT OF THE ALLIED BEACHHEADS CONTINUES.

The supply by air of arms to our airborne troops early this morning was completely successful.

"Last night enemy E-boats operating in four groups entered the assault area and attempted to interfere with our lines of communication. A series of running fights ensued and the attacks were beaten off.

"Three of the enemy were seen to be repeatedly hit before they escaped.

"During the early hours of today, E-boats were attacked off the French and Belgian coasts by coastal aircraft.

"One E-boat was sunk and three others sunk or severely damaged.

"OUR AIR ASSAULT IN SUPPORT OF THE LAND AND NAVAL FORCES AGAINST A WIDE VARIETY OF TACTICAL TARGETS HAS CONTINUED UNINTERRUPTEDLY AND IN VERY GREAT STRENGTH.

"THE ENEMY AIR EFFORT IS AS YET ON A LIMITED SCALE, BUT SOME OPPOSITION FROM FLAK HAS BEEN ENCOUNTERED.

"Ceaseless patrols were maintained over the immediate battle positions by our fighters and fighter bombers.

"ROCKET-FIRING PLANES ATTACKED A TANK CONCENTRATION WEST OF CAEN.

"OUR AIRCRAFT HAVE FLOWN APPROXIMATELY 27,000 INDIVIDUAL MISSIONS FROM DAWN, JUNE 6, TO MIDDAY TODAY; 176 ENEMY AIRCRAFT HAVE BEEN DESTROYED IN THE AIR. OUR LOSSES WERE 289 AIRCRAFT."

★

LATER it was learned that the air losses given in the midnight communique include all types of planes, except gliders.

One Allied division claims over 1,000 prisoners. "Beetle" and Hornet tanks have been captured. The Hornets are reported to have 88 m.m. guns on a Mark IV chassis.

Ten enemy divisions have been identified. German troops and transports are known to be concentrated twelve miles south of the assault area.

The 27,000 Allied air sorties announced is regarded by Supreme H.Q. as "terrific."

18—wounded

Home from the invasion battle, 18-year-old Geoffrey Smith, Beverley, Yorks, an Army volunteer at 17, is telling a comrade how he was wounded:—

"Yesterday was my big moment. I got clear of the assault craft, waded through the water, and rushed up the beach at Caen with my rifle at the ready.

"Then I saw a group of Germans behind a machine-gun. It was pointing at me. I saw the smoke round the muzzle, then there was a terrible pain in my arm and I fell down."

Geoffrey says he saw concrete pillboxes, pit timbers sticking up from the beach—everywhere signs of determined fortifications, but very few Germans.

50th Northumbrians led the invaders

The British 50th Northumbrian Division and the American 1st Infantry Division, which fought in North Africa and Sicily, spearheaded the invasion, it was announced late last night.

IT is likely that Allied planes will soon be operating from landing strips in Normandy.

Supplies to the battle front will be speeded up and planes will be able to operate virtually in the assault area.

Meanwhile the Allies are blasting the twenty-five first-line German airfields within a 150-mile arc of Bayeux and Caen.

Fortresses and medium bombers attacked at least six of them yesterday, and fighter bombers and fighters bombed and shot up others.

The Germans had seven airfields in a fifty-mile radius of the assault zone, three more in a 100-mile radius and fifteen more in a 150-mile radius.

Details of our airborne successes were revealed last night by 48-year-old U.S. Colonel Ralph B. Bagby, the first paratroop to return to England from Normandy.

"Casualties among our boys

Continued on Back Page

What the Germans are saying

HERE is the picture Axis reports drew of the Normandy battlefield last night:

LANDINGS.—Large-scale airborne landings being made on the eastern side of the Cherbourg Peninsula, south of Azeville, five miles from St. Mere Eglise.

Centre of Wednesday night's landings was the sector between Houlgate and Arromanches. These Allied forces pushed seven miles inland.

Hundreds of transport planes and gliders landed near Granville, on the west side of the peninsula

"LANDING BIDS."—New "attempt" at Barfleur, north-east point of the Cherbourg Peninsula and twenty-five miles from Cherbourg itself repulsed.

Coastal batteries drove off seaborne forces approaching St. Martin's Bay and Cap de la

Continued on Back Page

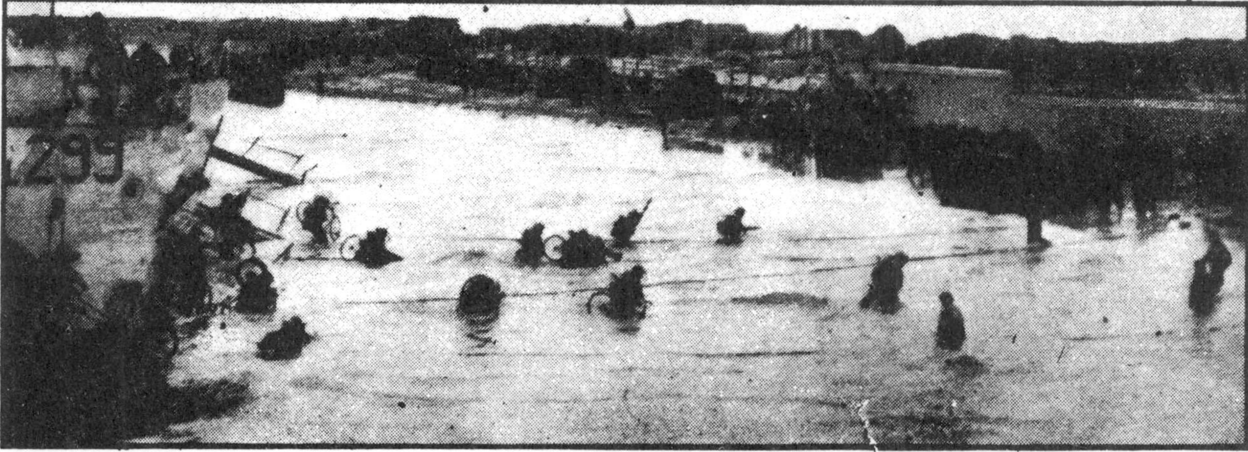

MIND MY BIKE! The quickest way to the beach is being taken by these infantrymen who are equipped with bicycles.

Daily Mail

LATE WAR NEWS

NO. 15,015 ONE PENNY * FOR KING AND EMPIRE SATURDAY, JUNE 17, 1944

'PILOTLESS' ATTACK MAY NOT LAST

Midgets Too Costly to German Material

DAY OF RAIDS THEN 2 NIGHT ATTACKS

At least three people were killed and several badly injured by a pilotless plane which crashed on some houses in Southern England during the first of two attacks last night. Houses were wrecked and an adjoining shopping centre was considerably damaged. Before it crashed the plane was seen streaking across the sky with A.A. shells bursting around. Then it dived and there was a terrific explosion.

By COLIN BEDNALL, Daily Mail Air Correspondent

IN their mad quest for both a military novelty and a substitute for the Luftwaffe, it is believed, from the nature of the pilotless planes used against this country, that the Germans have prejudiced other forms of vital war production to produce these weapons.

They are extremely costly devices, and have absorbed many thousands of man-hours, both in their production and in their launching.

It would appear certain that they contain many intricate and elaborate devices.

The red light seen on the flying bombs as they approach their target may have been placed there to enable ground controllers to place them on their course after they become airborne.

It might be feasible for the Germans to employ the radio beam principle, best known under the name of the Lorenzo Beam in peace-time, to direct the flying bombs towards their objective across the Channel.

But in their tremendous respect for gadgets the Germans may also have installed automatic devices.

This being the case, it may take the enemy a little while to prepare for another prolonged attack.

Each individual launching would take some time to prepare, apart from the fact that the enemy would have found it no easier to move up pilotless planes to the coastal areas of France than he has found it to move tanks.

It is believed that the Allied bombing forced him to establish assembly depots beside each launching installation.

The flying bombs have probably arrived in parts, and must therefore be assembled before being put into action.

A point has arisen as to who is responsible for dealing with the German novelty.

It combines characteristics for which both the War Office and the Air Ministry might be concerned, but perhaps its true grading is indicated by the fact that it was the Minister of Home Security who handled the matter in the House of Commons yesterday.

BBC ANNOUNCE RADIO 'BAFFLE'

MILLIONS of people in Britain, after a day of robot raids on southern England, heard the B.B.C. announce last night that programmes may be liable to interruption or cancellation.

They took that to mean action against the pilotless planes now being used by the Germans.

The announcement also led people to think that the planes are controlled by radio beams from the ground.

To cancel the route of these craft and to prevent the powerful transmitters acting as magnets, the B.B.C. will switch off their programmes.

When I put these conjectures to the B.B.C. last night they would not go beyond the official announcement:

"That in order to avoid giving information to the enemy, programmes for the time being are liable to interruption or cancellation at short notice."

MORE EXPECTED

Big Ben will not be heard direct from Westminster in future, but records of the chimes will be played to synchronise with the exact time.

The first official news of the new weapon was given in Parliament yesterday by Mr. Herbert Morrison, Minister of Home Security, following a night during which the robot machines were sent at intervals over parts of southern England.

More came over in daylight yesterday, and Mr. Morrison says more are expected.

He described them as "nuisance" raids and said that they should not be exaggerated. Counter-measures are being applied with full vigour.

Mr. Morrison says that when a

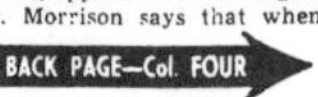

THESE three views of the German pilotless plane — (1) Head-on; (2) Plan; (3) Side view —were issued by the Ministry of Home Security last night. The wing span, it was officially stated, is 16ft., the length of the plane 25ft. 4½in. The section marked x in the third drawing is the propulsion unit.

GERMAN RADIO HAS GLOATING NIGHT

'Vengeance for RAF Has Begun'

THE entire German radio system at short notice last night changed its programme, after announcing several times that a special broadcast would be made by Hans Fritsche, Director-General of the German radio information service.

He spoke on the pilotless plane raids, saying:

"The German nation follows with deep interest the development of an action for which we have prepared for some years.

"Repeatedly Dr. Goebbels declared that retaliation for the attacks on German towns is no mere propaganda bluff.

"However, many a man in Germany may have doubted whether this would be so. And yet the German leadership has always acted according to laws of opportunity.

"Such was also the case this time. And this time, at least, the German leadership has found the right moment for first employing a product of German genius.

"Reports on the further development of this strictly military action will be issued by the German High Command. We do not wish to make forecasts. We rather wish to wait and see how this action will go on.

"The British people will be surprised to realise that we can also hit back."

★

HITLER gave the order for the use of the "flying bomb" against Britain, said the German-controlled Oslo radio last night. In defending its use the announcer said:

"When the fundamentally good hearted and morally inspired Führer gave orders to the Luftwaffe to attack only military objectives, he was up against a world-wide unbelief.

"Now when this new powerful weapon comes into its own the air gangsters will reap the storm they have sown.

"It is not our Führer's fault that in the present deadly crisis he has no other choice but to resort to this weapon.

"It may well be that our enemies did not believe that superior justice will ever reach them, but tens of thousands of German civilian dead cry for revenge from their graves."

★

BERLIN gloated over the new German weapon being used against London. The keynote of Goebbels' propaganda was that this was a reprisal for Allied raids on German cities.

"The feeling of hatred and glowing wish for revenge inspiring the German people was lit by our enemies by their mean terror crimes,' said the German Overseas News Agency.

German radio said last night that dense smoke clouds cover wide stretches of Southern England.

This, it was stated, was reported by German reconnaissance planes.

"Kingston and Bromley seem to have been particularly hit," the radio claimed.

"Large fires were observed at Sevenoaks and Sutton.

"Daventry station was heavily

Damage is Small—Morrison

THE Minister of Home Security makes this announcement:

"The enemy has begun to use his secret weapon—the pilotless aircraft. The damage it has caused has been relatively small, and the new weapon will not interfere with our war effort and our sure and steady march to victory.

"The enemy's aim is clearly, in view of the difficulty of his military situation, to try to upset our morale and interfere with our work

"It is essential that there should be the least possible interruption in all work vital to the country's needs at this time, and the Government's counsel is that everyone should get on with his or her job in the ordinary way and only take cover when danger is imminent.

"There is no reason to think that raids by this weapon will be worse than, or indeed as heavy as, the raids with which the people of this country are already familiar and have borne so bravely."

The Pilotless Plane

THE pilotless plane, photographed in flight by a Daily Mail cameraman in southern England yesterday. It is like a half-size Spitfire of beautifully clean lines, says Colin Bednall.

'SUPER FORTS' COULD POLICE THE WORLD

From Daily Mail Correspondent

WASHINGTON, Friday.

THE raid on Japan by the giant American Super-Fortresses (B-29s) gives some idea of the kind of striking force which may be used in keeping the peace in the high-speed world after the war.

The disclosure that the new bombers can form an independent force which will be able to strike anywhere on earth has caused a considerable stir in diplomatic circles here.

A super Air Force with such a wide striking range, it is pointed out here, would be a powerful weapon in maintaining peace. With such a weapon it would be possible for the United Nations to make a demonstration of force over a threatening territory in a matter of hours, something never possible before in world history.

Speed in such undertakings is regarded as important, because American post-war planners hope that a mere show of force will be enough to discourage a potential war-maker.

The War Department disclosed to-day that the target of the Super-Fortresses which bombed Japan was the great Yawata steelworks on Kyushu Island.

Four aircraft were lost, two by accident, one over the target, and one is missing.

The bases in China from which the Super-Forts took off were only recently completed in secrecy by a labour force of Chinese which totalled nearly 500,000 men.

Germans Shot 3 More Officers

Three more officers of the R.A.F. and Allied Air Forces were shot by the Germans, in addition to the 47 previously reported, after the escape from Stalag Luft III in March.

This information, received from the Protecting Power, Switzerland, was issued by the Air Ministry last night.

The officers now reported shot were: Flying Officer James L. R. Long, R.A.F.; Flying Officer Stanislaw Krol, and Flying Officer Pawel Tobolski, both of the Polish Air Force.

BATTLE BEGUN FOR VIBORG

In Finns' Last Line

Swift new thrusts by the Red Army have won them over 100 more places in the Karelian Isthmus and brought them to the outposts of the original Mannerheim line last Finnish barrier before Viborg.

Latest successes, announced in last night's Soviet communiqué, bring one spearhead within 28 miles of the great Finnish port, with the capture of the railway station of Lounatjoki—a six-miles advance in one day.

Now both sides are rushing up reserves for the decisive Mannerheim-line action. Victory for General Govorov would give him command of the main land approaches to Helsinki, which is already being cleared of women and children.—*Reuter* and *B.U.P.*

New Vice-Admiral

The Admiralty announce that Rear Admiral Frederick Hew George Dalrymple-Hamilton, who commanded Rodney when she sank the Bismarck, is promoted vice-admiral, to date from Thursday. He is 54.

AMERICANS RETAKE MONTEBOURG, DRIVE WEST

8 Miles Will Decide the Fate of Cherbourg

From HENRY GORRELL

WITH U.S. FORCES, Friday.

THE next few hours are likely to decide the fate of thousands of Germans defending the Cherbourg area.

Allied assault troops have stormed into St. Sauveur le Vicomte, control point on Rommel's main communications with Cherbourg.

At the same time other forces have recaptured Montebourg, 12 miles north-east of St. Sauveur and barely six miles from Valognes, the last big town before Cherbourg itself.

Seizure and consolidation of St. Sauveur would leave the Germans with only roundabout roads running south through La Haye du Puits, seven miles away.

American forces directly threatening La Haye in a drive west from Carentan are driving a wedge across the base of the Cherbourg Peninsula.

The Germans began pulling out of St. Sauveur at 2 a.m., and within two hours all but the German suicide squads and snipers had left the town, which had been shelled heavily by our batteries.

This evening the town is under German mortar fire.

American artillery is shelling the only coastal road available to the Germans, and our infantry are advancing fast towards the west coast. —B.U.P.

G. Ward Price, in a message from Supreme Headquarters, said:

BEST news at the end of a day of hard fighting all along the front is that American troops have entered the vital village of St. Sauveur le Vicomte, which commands the last road running north up the Cherbourg Peninsula.

It may not yet be firmly in our possession, for it is dominated by high ground to the north, and until that has been cleared we shall not have real control of the road.

Behind the advanced elements of the Allied advance, strong supporting detachments of our troops have almost cleared the flooded areas across the base of the peninsula.

They are getting on to rising ground that is free from inundations.

Along the rest of the front the position is stationary, with hard fighting going on almost everywhere, especially between Caumont, Tilly and Caen.

Tilly is still held by the enemy.

BACK PAGE—Col. EIGHT

THE KING is welcomed by General Montgomery on his arrival in France yesterday. The King came ashore from the cruiser Arethusa in a "duck."

The King's Day in France

Montgomery Gave HQ Luncheon

From **LOUIS WULFF**, Reuter's Special Correspondent

ABOARD H.M.S. ARETHUSA, Friday.

THE KING to-day visited the battle areas in Normandy, and lunched with General Montgomery at his Advanced H.Q.

He afterwards held an open-air Investiture less than six miles from the front line.

He made his historic journey to France and back in the cruiser Arethusa, which led the line of bombarding ships on D-Day.

He landed at a beach just west of Courselles, where the Canadians stormed ashore, and while we were in the motor-launch transferring from Arethusa to the duck, six-inch shells from the cruiser Hawkins, which we had seen firing on our way in, tore high over the King's head, engaging a land target at a range of 10 miles.

His 'Mae West'

The range flash of her salvos were the first shots the King has seen actually fired at the enemy in this war.

Bo'suns piped the King on board Arethusa early this morning and ten minutes later we were under way for France. Two destroyers, H.M.S. Scourge and Urania escorted the King's ship, and flights of Spitfires circled overhead, providing a continuous air cover from the moment the King sailed till he returned home at night.

At once, the King, with Admiral of the Fleet Sir Andrew Cunningham, the First Sea Lord, Admiral Ramsay, Allied Naval C.-in-C., Air Chief Marshal Sir Charles Portal, Chief of the Air Staff, Major-General Laycock, Chief of Combined Operations, and Major-General Ismay, went up on to the bridge.

With a "Mae West" yellow life-jacket over his tunic, the King stayed on the bridge all the way over, watching through his glasses the endless stream of convoys and craft of every kind going to and from the beachhead.

He had a cup of soup on the bridge before he had his first glimpse of the French coast, and a moment later the Royal Standard was broken from the peak, announcing to all that the King was on board.

Complete Secret

The visit had been kept completely secret in advance.

Wearing naval uniform as an Admiral of the Fleet, the King drove straight inland with General Montgomery towards the battle zone.

With an escort of British and American military police, armed with tommy-guns, the King's car passed along the straight Normandy road through the little villages of Graves-sur-Mer and Banville, which were in enemy hands only a few days ago.

After lunch, the King held an open-air investiture in the château grounds. He decorated seven officers and men, headed by Major-General Keller, commander of the Canadian Third Division, who received the C.B.E.

Three or four hundred troops, including many green-bereted Commandos and some Canadians, watched the ceremony formed up in three sides of a square.

"Monty" called for three cheers, and then took the King into one of his three famous caravans and spent a full half-hour explaining with his maps the whole course of the battles so far.

'Vive le Roi!'

By this time news of the visit had spread, and as the King drove back towards the beaches again in the open car with Gen. Montgomery there were many more troops on the roadside to cheer him.

In Tierceville and Courselles several little groups of French men and women and children who have found their way back to their homes again gathered at the corners to wave and cheer

An elderly woman in black stood at the door waving her handkerchief, with tears running down her cheeks, and cried, "Vive le Roi! Vive l'Angleterre!" The King acknowledged her greeting with a salute.

The last time the King was in France was in 1939, when he toured the Maginot Line and did not see any fighting.

The Weather Last Night

State of Sea.—Smoother after slight disturbance.

Weather.—Cool, but clearing and sky ceiling improving; no rain. Temperature Highest, 6?deg., 57deg. at 10.30 p.m. Visibility: Good during day, fair towards evening. Wind West-north-west, light.

Barometer. — Steady since noon.

High Tide Across the Water. —10.17 p.m. and 10.36 a.m.

Luftwaffe Told 'Die Fighting'

GORING has issued an appeal to the Luftwaffe to go all out to smash the invasion which, if it succeeds, "will mean the death of the German people."

He warns his men that the Allied air challenge must be accepted.

"If, at the end, our Luftwaffe be smashed to pieces to gain our victory, our sacrifices will have been worth while," he says.

"Once more I beg you, comrades, pilots, paratroopers, ground forces and signal personnel of the Luftwaffe, do not forget that all and everything depends now on your sacrifices and your courage.

"We have learned how strong the enemy is. His pursuit planes reach the very heart of Germany. His bombers are in the air from six to eight hours daily.

"Four to six hours are spent over our territory. You yourselves know what it means to fly four or five hours over enemy territory."

Front Page News in the U.S.

From Daily Mail Correspondent

NEW YORK, Friday.—The pilotless plane raids on England were the main news in most U.S. papers and radio broadcasts to-day, despite nation-wide jubilation over the latest "super-Fort" attacks on Japan.

Many American observers are puzzled because Hitler did not use the weapon against the invading forces. Some believe that the Germans decided that the first landing would be in the Calais area, and when the Allies landed in Normandy decided to use the weapon against England.

Vichy Calls Us 'Enemy'

The French Press has been ordered to call Britain and America "enemies," Berlin radio announced last night.

RAF Out in Force

A large force of R.A.F. heavy bombers crossed the east coast last night flying south. They took an hour to pass.

NEXT LINE IN ITALY 60 MILES

'Gothic' Defences

ALLIED H.Q., Friday.

FIFTH Army troops to-day captured Grosseto, last important German stronghold before Pisa, 60 miles away, it was announced to-night.

Pisa is the western hinge of the Pisa-Rimini line, which, according to captured documents, the Germans call "the Gothic Line."

Allied officers are convinced that Kesselring will not attempt organised resistance until he gets to this line.

But the Allied advance is so rapid that the next big battle may not be far off

Most spectacular advance was made by Eighth Army troops, who gained 25 miles in a day to take Todi in the drive from Terni.

They are now well on the way to Perugia.

Other Eighth Army forces are now pressing on beyond Orvieto, the important road junction which was taken yesterday. British tanks have reached Ficulle, ten miles north of Orvieto. So fast is the

RAF BOMB BERLIN

British nuisance raiders attacked districts in the Berlin area during the night, the official German news agency announced early to-day.—B.U.P.

ICELAND BREAKS WITH DENMARK

Reykjavik, Friday. — The Danish-Icelandic treaty was formally abrogated to-day when the Icelandic Parliament unanimously ratified the nation's desire to break the constitutional link with Denmark.—A.P.

3

enemy retreating in the Adriatic sector that our troops are having difficulty in keeping up with him.

Allied reconnaissance elements have reached the Vomano river, some 22 miles north of the Pescara river, without meeting any resistance.

Farther west, fighting is going on in Aquila.

German remnants in this sector are in danger of being outflanked by the capture of Terni.—*B.U.P. and Reuter.*

Map in BACK Page.

Germans Conceal Guns

ANKARA, Friday.—The Turkish police have found guns under a cargo of coal in a German boat detained in the Bosphorus, it is stated here. A Turkish protest to Germany will probably follow.—*Exchange.*

The Daily Sketch

2 Pages of Pictures

No. 10,949 ★★★ MONDAY, JUNE 19, 1944 ONE PENNY

Rommel's Last Bid to Break Out Ends in 'Massacre'

30,000 GERMANS CAUGHT IN PENINSULA

THIRTY thousand German troops are to-day trapped in the Cherbourg peninsula. A desperate two-hour counter-attack, led by the 77th Division with a spearhead of tanks, failed to break through the Allied cordon thrown across the peninsula.

The slicing of the peninsula, which ends the first phase of the Allied invasion, was completed just before midnight on Saturday—eve of the anniversary of the Battle of Waterloo—after less than a 48-hour offensive across the enemy mid-section.

Driving along a corridor from six to seven miles wide, the U.S. Ninth Division reached the west coast of the peninsula in the vicinity of Cap de Carteret and Barneville.

Germans Taken By Surprise

The Germans at Barneville were taken by surprise and were resisting only very weakly. Apart from two burning tanks in the main street, the town was practically untouched.

Last night the citizens were feting the Allied troops, while hundreds of crestfallen Germans were sitting glumly in barbed wire enclosures awaiting transport across the Channel.

The German assault yesterday was launched along a front about two miles wide. It was Rommel's latest throw to get an escape gap for his troops.

American infantry and artillery met the attack and, says Associated Press war correspondent, it was "literally a massacre—the massacre of St. Jacques de Nehou.

The Americans mowed down the Germans in what was one of the bloodiest encounters of the invasion.

St. Jacques de Nehou lies almost directly north of the crossroads where the Americans first slashed across the peninsula to cut off the escape route.

The enemy's 77th Division bid was met with a wall of steel.

Artillery and infantry received orders to hold out at all costs. They did, and as the last salvoes

Turn to Back Page, Col. 4

We Did This In 12½ Days

ALLIED forces in Normandy now hold a beachhead of 52 miles which has a perimeter of approximately 116 miles.

The greatest area of penetration to the west—in the Peninsula — is 23 miles and the greatest to the south is 18 miles towards St. Lo.

Transposed on to the South Coast of England, a tracing of the area covers practically half of Sussex, from Rye to Hayling Island.

More than 15,000 prisoners have been counted through the cages. All this has been achieved in 12½ days of fighting.

Airborne Division Fights 11 Days

From MAURICE WATTS, 'Daily Sketch' War Correspondent at SHAEF

THE Cherbourg peninsula is cut. That is magnificent news and a great triumph for the U.S. 9th and 82nd Airborne Divisions—particularly the latter.

The 82nd dropped in Normandy on the night before D-Day, and had been in continuous action for 11 days when they captured St. Sauveur le Vicomte.

Once he saw that the American drive across the Peninsula could not be checked Rommel did his best to get his troops out southward. Violently harassed from the air, their resistance slackened as the Americans neared the coast.

No official estimate was given here of the number of Germans remaining in the north, but there are many thousands of garrison and specialised troops in the Cherbourg area.

The task now facing the Americans will be to widen the wedge southwards from the area of St. Sauveur and thus nullify any attempt by Rommel to split the U.S. forces and so get back to the aid of his garrison troops cut off in Cherbourg.

The cutting of the Peninsula naturally overshadows the news from other parts of the Normandy front—but there is news, very good news, from other points.

A drive by the American forces south of Isigny area has taken them to a point which is only six miles from St. Lo.

Heavy German Losses

The Germans yesterday launched a very strong attack three miles east of Caumont before which our troops, with some losses, had to withdraw. By evening we counter-attacked and the situation was restored.

Fighting in the Tilly sector—where Rommel has four Panzer divisions tied down to hold the British and Canadian troops facing him, Panzer divisions which he badly needed to throw against the Americans—has brought us limited gains and the Germans heavy losses.

King Peter And Tito Agree

MARSHAL TITO and Dr. Subasic, Minister of the Royal Yugoslav Government, held discussions in Yugoslavia from June 14 to 17, it was announced at Allied G.H.Q., Italy, last night.

An official communiqué said: "Mutual effort for the continuation of the struggle of Yugoslavia with the goal of unifying to the broadest extent possible the national forces was the spirit which led to the negotiations.

"The participating parties reached agreement and mutual accord on many problems.

"Yugoslav-Allied relations will undoubtedly be strengthened even more and the Yugoslav peoples aided in the fight to free as rapidly as possible their country."

ULTIMATUM BY MAQUIS

GREATER co-ordination between French patriots is definitely beginning to harass German movements and the maintenance of order by Laval's puppet administration, cabled W. T. Stuttard, "Daily Sketch" correspondent, from Madrid last night.

The German and Darnand authorities have been clearly warned that if any of the Maquis are caught and summarily punished as franc-tireurs, the patriots will deal out similar treatment to hostages they now hold.

The wedge driven across the Cherbourg peninsula in the latest Allied advance.

MANNERHEIM LINE BROKEN

THE Red Army has broken through the Mannerheim Line, last Finnish defence wall on the Karelian Isthmus, and was last night within 16 miles of Viborg, gateway to Finland.

Last night's Soviet communiqué said that Koivisto, western anchor of the Line on the Gulf of Finland coast, was captured and 120 places taken in an "impetuous advance by infantry and tanks, supported by powerful blows by artillery and air force."

General Govorov, the man who smashed the Mannerheim Line in 1940 and has now broken through it again, has been made a Marshal of the Soviet Union.

The complete evacuation of Viborg was ordered yesterday by the Finnish Government, according to a Swedish radio report.

A Russian attack on a German convoy off Kirkenes, the Norwegian Arctic port near the Finnish border, was followed by a mass raid by 150 Bostons and Stormoviks on Kirkenes itself on Saturday night.

The Soviet Air Force on Saturday night dealt massed blows on German aerodromes in the area of Baranovichi, Pinsk and Minsk.

Forces' Chiefs Watch Shelling

Admiral of the Fleet Sir Andrew Cunningham (left), First Sea Lord, and Marshal of the Royal Air Force Sir Charles Portal watching from the bridge of a motor launch the bombardment of the invasion coast by ships of the Royal Navy.

Another Raid Near Japan

AMERICAN carrier-borne planes, for the second time in a week, have attacked Iwojima Island, in the Bonin Group, 550 miles from Tokyo, according to Berlin and Tokyo reports yesterday.

The attack was made on Friday by 100 bombers and fighters, the reports said, and the Japanese claimed that eleven of the aircraft were destroyed.

Meantime, in their advance across the shell-torn cane fields of Saipan Island, American assault troops have driven half-way across this heavily-fortified island of Japan's Mariana chain, it was announced in Pearl Harbour yesterday.

In China the High Command fear that the Japanese advance may neutralise Allied air bases, the most serious threat comes from the enemy advance on the Peiping-Hankow and Canton-Hankow railways.

TIMELY WORDS OF FAITH

Wait on the Lord, and keep his way, and he shall exalt thee . . . when the wicked are cut off, thou shalt see it.

Psalms, 37, 34.

SUNDAY EXPRESS

JULY 2 1944 | BLACK-OUT MANCHESTER 11.26 p.m. to 5.0 a.m. | Founded by LORD BEAVERBROOK | Moon rises 6.16 p.m. Sets 3.48 a.m. | TWOPENCE

ROMMEL TAKES OVER AT CAEN

British troops prepare for a mass attack by tanks

Men from Russia among 7 panzer divisions

FIELD-MARSHAL ROMMEL, IT WAS STATED AT SUPREME HEADQUARTERS LAST NIGHT, HAS NOW ASSUMED PERSONAL COMMAND OF THE GERMAN ARMIES IN THE NORMANDY CAMPAIGN.

He will therefore be responsible for directing the seven panzer divisions engaged in the Caen-Tilly area against the British Second Army.

It is believed he will mass his panzers and throw in large formations.

Our forces in the salient are being regrouped, and tanks are standing by in hull-down positions to meet this new threat.

German units which infiltrated into the shoulders of our Odon bridgehead early yesterday have been thrown out, and the position is firm.

North of the River Odon we are mopping up isolated pockets of German tanks and infantry which are still holding out in our salient between the road and the river.

German troops which were fighting in Russia as recently as March have been identified in the Caen area.

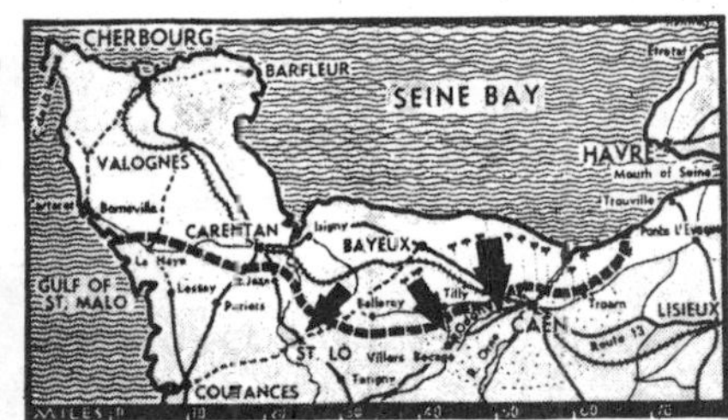

Dempsey's men hold all attacks

FROM the British Tilly-Caen front in Normandy yesterday it was reported that Rundstedt is quickening the tempo and intensity of his small-scale counter-attacks against our bridgehead despite extravagant and mounting losses.

But non-stop attacks by crack panzer formations—tanks and infantry—against General Dempsey's salient around Evrecy have failed to shift the strong British forces there, says Reuter's special correspondent at Supreme Headquarters of the Allied Expeditionary Force.

Beaten down and then thrown back, cut off after infiltration and destroyed, the Germans have gained no ground at all from this thrust into our territory, which has reached to and still holds the now legendary Hill 112 dominating the immediate area.

MONTY CALLS THE TUNE

Among new arrivals bolstering Rundstedt's defence are German troops who may have come from Russia.

The battle is in true Montgomery style, and is being played to his tune. It is a grinding-down process, in which Rommel is meeting a steady drain on his infantry and tanks. The British Second Army alone has destroyed 142 tanks since it landed.

Latest news received is that the Second Army forces over the River Odon are consolidating the newly-won positions while finally liquidating in the rear the strong pockets of resistance which were originally by-passed.

Until this phase has been completed there is little likelihood of any big-scale advance, and in any case Evrecy is as good a place to destroy Rommel's armour as anywhere else.

On no part of the front is there any movement of size at the moment.

North of Caen, where at one time British forces were within two miles of the city, the battle appears to have quietened down after shifting back to near Breville, four miles north-east of the town and on the bank of the Orne Canal.

THE GERMAN FORCES CORNERED IN CAP DE LA HAGUE IN THE CHERBOURG PENINSULA, HAVE NOW SURRENDERED, AND FOR ALL PRACTICAL PURPOSES ALL RESISTANCE IN THE PENINSULA HAS ENDED. AMERICAN PATROLS ARE NOW SEEKING OUT STRAGGLERS IN THE WOODED COUNTRY NEAR THE SHORE LINE.

Larry Lesueur, an American radio commentator, said early yesterday: "Only about 1,500 men out of the four

HOW THE 'CAB-RANK' WORKS

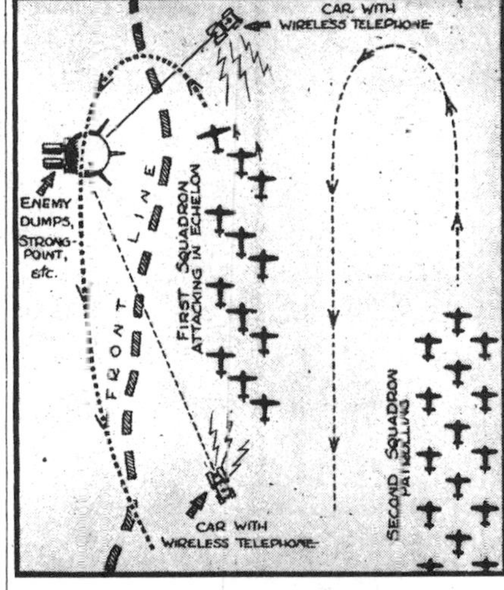

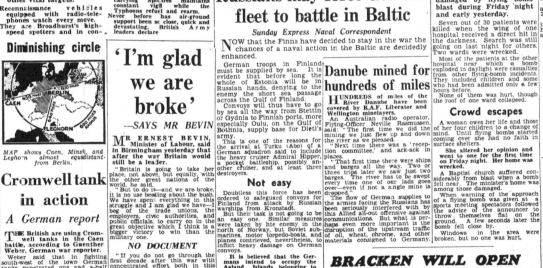

THIS front-line sketch by a Sunday Express artist shows how Air Vice-Marshal Harry Broadhurst's miniature air force in Normandy uses this "cab-rank" or "merry-go-round" technique in advanced areas against enemy tanks, parks, convoys, troop concentrations, gun positions, fuel and ammo dumps, and other vital targets.

Reconnaissance vehicles equipped with radio-telephones watch every move.

They are Broadhurst's high-speed spotters and in constant touch with his advance echelon of the Second Tactical Air Force.

One of them has just located an enemy strongpost and signalled its map reference. Response to the call is immediate—a matter of split seconds.

One by one the patrolling Typhoons swoop down from the "rank" with bombs, rockets and blazing automatic guns. Then with a fast climbing turn they resume their places on the rank ready for the next summons.

A squadron of Broadhurst's bomb-carrying Spitfires maintains constant vigil while the Typhoons refuel and rearm.

Never before has air-ground support been so close, quick and devastating, British Army leaders declare

Diminishing circle

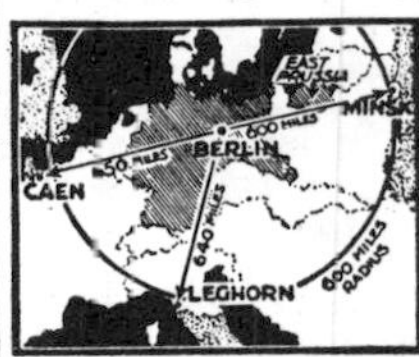

MAP shows Caen, Minsk, and Leghorn almost equidistant from Berlin.

Cromwell tank in action

A German report

THE British are using Cromwell tanks in the Caen battle, according to Guenther Weber, German war reporter.

Weber said that in fighting south-west of the town German tanks penetrated one and a-half miles into the British line and shot up 12 Cromwells.

DE GAULLE WILL CONTROL NEWS

The French Provisional Government have made plans to take control of all newspapers as France is liberated, said Morocco radio yesterday.

Radio and cinemas are also covered by a series of measures adopted by the Provisional Government.

20 Mustangs rout 60 Hun fighters

When a force of 20 Mustangs, led by the Polish pilot, Wing-Commander Skaliski, D.F.C. and two bars, was returning from operations in northern France last week 60 German fighters were seen over the Channel.

Wing-Commander Skaliski ordered his force to attack. A series of dog-fights followed, in which the Germans lost six planes down and four probables.

The attackers lost only one plane.

Leningrad took this

During the siege of Leningrad the city was hit by 150,000 heavy German shells and more than 100,000 large bombs. Two and a-half million square yards of housing space was demolished, but it is expected that 950,000 will be restored this year.

More Beauforts

Ten thousand Australians now make Bristol Beaufort torpedo bombers.

First time in, but they fought like veterans

THE British troops who smashed back Rommel's big counter-attack in a four-hour battle between the Odon and Orne had never been under enemy fire before.

They were the untried product of Britain's battle schools, but they showed they were equal to the best Rommel could put against them.

Split into little groups under junior officers when German tanks and infantry bit into their positions, they fought back determinedly, smashed the attack, and retook the lost ground.

'OFTEN DO BETTER'

It was a feat worthy of a famous division, yet their division is new, and so far has not been officially identified.

Its newness may have something to do with its success. A brigadier said: "There is a tendency for divisions with great reputations rather to rest on their laurels, so that new divisions eager to earn fame often do better."

Already the Canadian Third Division and the U.S. 29th—both unseasoned formations—have distinguished themselves in the bridgehead.

Another senior officer commented: "These new divisions fight just as well as seasoned troops, and are perhaps a little quicker off the mark. But they pay a heavier price in casualties—they have not yet learned all the tricks of how not to get hurt."

In the stiff fighting in the woods north of Caen, too, the new boys are doing well. A tank officer there said: "Most of my lads are under 21, and new to fighting like this. They have put up a grand show."

SPECIAL SCHOOLS

All this is giving great satisfaction in those military circles where the battle school was evolved. In Britain, the United States, and Canada the toughening process is much the same—after initial training the troops are sent to special schools where they fight mock actions in realistic—sometimes fatally realistic—conditions

They use live ammunition, and live ammunition is used against them. Machine-gunners fire over their heads as they advance.

Artillery and mortars lay a barrage around them. Hand-grenades, are tossed on their flanks, and land-mines are exploded in their path.

It is hard on the nerves, but prepares them for the real thing.

RUSSIA'S OFFER TO HER POLES

RUSSIANS who have served in the Polish Army in Russia or have helped this army have the right to adopt Polish citizenship under a decree published in Moscow yesterday.

The decree applies to "inhabitants of the western regions of the Ukrainian and White Russian Soviet Socialist Republics, and to Soviet citizens of Polish nationality of other regions of the U.S.S.R."

The decree covers Poles who have taken Soviet citizenship since 1939, and the ancient Polish colonies in Siberia who have maintained their national language and customs for generations.

People of Polish descent who went to Russia from foreign countries may also adopt Polish citizenship.—Reuter.

Train-buster-in-chief takes over

Wing-Commander Gordon Panitz, of Southport, Queensland, train-buster with 17 trains to his score, has taken over command of a second Australian Mosquito fighter-bomber squadron.

He successfully attacked six goods trains in about ten minutes on his first daylight expedition. Another time he shot up the slipways and hangars of a German seaplane base, strafed a launch, fired a small ship, and destroyed a Junkers 88.

'I'm glad we are broke'

—SAYS MR BEVIN

MR ERNEST BEVIN, Minister of Labour, said in Birmingham yesterday that after the war Britain would still be a leader.

"Britain is going to take her place, not above, but equally, with the other great nations of the world, he said.

"But to do it—and we are broke, it is no use beating about the bush. We have spent everything in this struggle and I am glad we have—I beg of the trade unions, the employers, civic authorities, and public officials, to carry on in the great objective which I think is a bigger victory to win than the military one.

NO DOCUMENT

"If you do not go through the first decade after this war with concentrated effort both in this country and with the United Nations I defy any living statesman to build a peace that will not lead to a recurrence of this trouble.

"At the Teheran Conference, Marshal Stalin, President Roosevelt, and Mr Churchill arranged the vital dates for victory, but there was no document, no elaborate signed agreement.

"I hope that those three great nations will always be able to work with the same degree of confidence."

Montgomery to Harris: 'Thanks'

General Montgomery sent this message last night to Air Chief Marshal Sir Arthur Harris, Air Officer Commanding-in-Chief R.A.F. Bomber Command:—

"My grateful thanks to Bomber Command and to you personally, for your contribution to the tactical battle in Normandy last night.

"It was a most inspiring sight for the Allied soldiers in France to see the might of Bomber Command arrive to join in the battle. Your action will not be forgotten by us or the enemy. Please thank all your pilots for me."

'Attack on Guam repelled'—Tokyo

Tokyo said last night: "The Jap garrison of Guam (former U.S. base in the central Pacific) yesterday repelled three enemy cruisers or large destroyers attempting to shell our airfield from the sea."—Reuter.

Germans loot radios

About 100,000 of the radio sets confiscated by the Germans in Norway just after the occupation have been exported to Germany.

GERMANS FACING BIG MINSK TRAP

Tanks speed through the gaps

RED ARMY divisions last night were advancing steadily towards north Poland and Lithuania after pouring through the three gaps which have been torn in the German line at Vitebsk, Mogilev, and Zhlobin.

Marshal Rokossovsky's tanks and shock troops are driving along the high road to Warsaw after storming the German stronghold at Slutsk. Other units are pushing to the north-west in a deepening and outflanking movement on Minsk, the last big German-held base before Vilna.

Another great encirclement plan is taking shape through the marshes and forests of White Russia as Red Army units close in on Minsk from the north, east, and south.

Fierce battles are developing on the approaches to Minsk, but the Germans are being pushed back on both flanks, and the whole enemy grouping before the city is being herded into a huge salient running from Borisov in the west to Slutsk in the north.

There is no exact information on the distance the Russian spearheads are from the city, but latest reports reaching Moscow put them only 25 miles away.

Many surrender

Soviet correspondents have reported that hundreds of Germans are surrendering before they can reach Minsk. The Red Army troops are having some difficulty in moving up for a direct blow at the city because the roads are clogged with prisoners.

On the northern sector of the offensive the Russians are over the old Polish border west of Polotsk, the German base about 16 miles from the old Polish frontier, which guards the approaches to the Baltic States.

The Russian forces have flowed round it in a great flood and its garrison appears to be doomed.

The Germans lost all hope of holding their White Russian line when the Russians burst through the defences based on the Beresina River.

General Chernakhovsky's forces north of Borisov smashed across the river almost unopposed, thanks to the assistance they received from partisans who controlled the great forest stretching from Borisov to Lepel and held an important bridge which the Germans were unable to destroy.—Reuter and B.U.P.

Russians may force German fleet to battle in Baltic

Sunday Express Naval Correspondent

NOW that the Finns have decided to stay in the war the chances of a naval action in the Baltic are decidedly enhanced.

German troops in Finland must be supplied by sea. It is evident that before long the whole of Estonia will be in Russian hands, denying to the enemy the short sea passage across the Gulf of Finland.

Convoys will thus have to go by sea all the way from Stettin or Gydnia to Finnish ports, more especially Oulu, on the Gulf of Bothnia, supply base for Dietl's army.

This is one of the reasons for the arrival at Turku (Abo) of a German squadron said to include the heavy cruiser Admiral Hipper, a pocket battleship, possibly another cruiser, and at least three destroyers.

Not easy

Doubtless this force has been ordered to safeguard convoys for Finland from attack by Russian warships from Kronstadt.

But their task is not going to be an easy one. Similar measures were taken by hte enemy in the north of Norway, but Soviet submarines, motor torpedo-boats, and planes contrieved, nevertheless, to inflict heavy damage on German convoys.

It is believed that the Germans intend to occupy the Aaland Islands, belonging to Finland. The strategic position of this group is highly im- approaches to both the Bothnian and Finnish Gulfs.

German forces in the Baltic comprise two pocket battleships, two heavy and four light cruisers, two old coast defence ships, and some destroyers, motor torpedo-boats, and submarines.

Air Arm, too

Against this the Russians can muster two old battleships of 23,000 tons and three or four cruisers, with an equal or greater number of destroyers, motor torpedo-boats and submarines.

In addition there is the Soviet Fleet Air Arm, which has distinguished itself on many occasions against the German Navy in Estonian waters.

B.U.P.'s Stockholm correspondent also reports that the occupation of the Aaland Islands by the Germans is likely.

A high German officer, he says, is expected to set up his headquarters at Mariehamn, capital of the islands.

Vichy quislings closely guarded

Rigorous security measures are being taken to protect Deat, Darnand, and other Vichy quisling Ministers, even against their own wishes German radio stated yesterday.

The decision follows the assassination of Henriot, Vichy Propaganda Minister.

Formosa bombed

American Liberators bombed Takao, a port on the island of Formosa, on June 29 and damaged dock installations, it was announced in Chungking yesterday.—Reuter.

Danube mined for hundreds of miles

HUNDREDS of miles of the River Danube have been covered by R.A.F. Liberator and Wellington minelayers.

An Australian radio operator, Flying-Officer Neville Rasmussen, said: "The first time we did the mining we just flew up and down the river as we pleased.

"Next time there was a 'reception committee,' and ack-ack in places.

"That first time there were ships and barges all the way. Two or three trips later we saw just two barges. The river has to be swept every time one of our lads goes over—even if not a single mine is dropped."

The flow of German supplies to the armies facing the Russians has been seriously interfered with by this Allied all-out offensive against communications. But what is perhaps even more important is the disruption of the upstream traffic of oil, wheat, chrome, and other materials consigned to Germany.

Bombs hit two more hospitals

TWO more hospitals in southern England were among buildings hit or damaged by flying bomb blast during Friday night and early yesterday.

Seven out of 30 patients were killed when the wing of one hospital received a direct hit in the darkness. Search was still going on last night for others. Two wards were wrecked.

Most of the patients at the other hospital near which a bomb exploded in daylight were casualties from other flying-bomb incidents. They included children and some who had been admitted only a few hours before.

None of them was hurt, though the roof of one ward collapsed.

Crowd escapes

A woman owes her life and those of her four children to a change of mind. Until flying bombs started coming over she had no faith in surface shelters.

She altered her opinion and went to one for the first time on Friday night. Her home was wrecked.

A Baptist church suffered considerably from blast when a bomb fell near. The minister's home was among those damaged.

When warning of the approach of a flying bomb was given at a sports meeting spectators followed the advice of the announcer to throw themselves flat on the ground. A few seconds later the bomb fell close by.

Windows in the area were broken, but no one was hurt.

BRACKEN WILL OPEN FLYING BOMB SHOW

VERGELTUNGSWAFFE—otherwise Hitler's "revenge weapon No. 1," known to southern England more familiarly as the flying bomb and other names — is on view in London.

A full-scale model based on latest information from the Air Ministry occupies pride of place in the Daily Express exhibition, the Battle of France, to be opened tomorrow by Mr Brendan Bracken, Minister of Information, at Dorland Hall, Lower Regent-street, London, S.W.1.

Cleverly reconstructed, the model measures 25ft in length with wing spread of 16ft, and has sections which open to show parts of the interior mechanism.

Life-size pictures

Round the walls are life-size photographs telling the story of the Battle of France from D Day onwards. They will be added to as the latest pictures arrive from the battle front.

General von Schlieben and Rear-Admiral Hennecke, captured in the fall of Cherbourg, stand outside the hall—as over life size cut-out silhouettes.

And inside are two more models, this time of the men who are helping to beat the other Germans still there — a Commando complete down to knuckledusters, and a paratrooper.

Samples of some of the weapons and equipment our men are using are there, too—from mortars and machine-guns to odd-looking motor scooters and folding bicycles—just some of the things that are among our surprises for the Germans.

The exhibition opens tomorrow at 11.30 a.m. and afterwards from 10 a.m. to 7 p.m. daily, including Saturdays. Sunday hours are 2 p.m. to 7 p.m.

Admission: — Civilians, 1/- (children half price). Forces in uniform, 6d. All proceeds go to Service charities.

Florence an 'open city'

Hitler's order as Allies near it

A SWIFT advance by the Allies all along the front brought the Fifth Army last night to within 16 miles of Leghorn and 35 of Florence.

As they pushed on towards the Gothic Line, on which these two cities stand, the German radio announced that Hitler had declared Florence an open city.

Florence, capital of Tuscany, is rich in works of artistic and historic interest, with libraries, galleries, and museums—"irreplaceable treasures," said Berlin—but as it stands at present it is within the German fortification system stretching from Leghorn across the peninsula to Rimini.

Latest battle reports say:—

General Clark's Fifth Army, making Leghorn its next big objective, has passed through Cecina and pushed on across the river three miles north-east of the town.

Over on the Adriatic coast, Allied forces are again pressing forward hard on the heels of the Germans, who are withdrawing from their Chienti River line to a new line along the Musone River, only ten miles south of the port of Ancona.

They control it

In the inland sector, General Juin's French troops, after taking two more towns, now dominate the whole area south of Highway 73. They have pushed a two-prong drive to within four miles of Siena, the nearest point reached in the direct advance towards Florence.

A combat team composed of American soldiers of Japanese origin is fighting with the Fifth Army.

Medium bombers yesterday continued to attack communications in northern Italy, particularly along the important Pisa-Rimini railway lines.

Ten heavily-laden barges, believed to be loaded with fuel and explosives, were set on fire by coastal Beaufighters east of Novi-Sad, on the Danube.

Fighters and fighter-bombers gave the battle-weary Germans no rest, spraying the retreating army with bombs and bullets.

Hungary bombed

ALLIED H.Q., ITALY, Saturday.—Up to 500 heavy bombers took part in yesterday's attacks on communications in Hungary, and airfields and a harbour in Yugoslavia.

Good bombing was reported on Banjaluka airfield and Split harbour, on the Adriatic, and on the Barc railway bridge and the Kapsovar railway yards in Hungary.

Cloud obscured the results of attacks on military targets in the Zagreb and Budapest areas.

Enemy fighters in some strength intercepted the fighter-escorted heavies, which fought them off after shooting down 11.—Reuter.

World war news

GERMANS LOSE 11 PANTHERS IN NEW 'JAB'

Eleven Panther tanks knocked out in new German "jab" against point of British salient.

Many German dead are lying in poppy fields round small towns. More prisoners taken.

RADIO Page Seven

Average net paid circulation for June exceeded
Daily---2,075,000
Sunday-3,700,000

Vol. 26. No. 21 New York, Wednesday, July 19, 1944★ 44 Main + 4 Manhattan Pages 2 Cents IN CITY LIMITS | 3 CENTS Elsewhere

BRITISH SPLIT CAEN LINE

Reds Cross Bug River, Roll Toward Lwow, Brest Litovsk

Stories on Page 3

(Official U. S. Navy foto via A. P. Wirefoto)

Hundreds Die in Munitions Blast. Two bits of twisted metal (arrows) jutting from Suisun Bay are all that remain of two munition ships whose explosion spread devastation at Port Chicago, Calif. In foreground is wreckage of Navy pier. More than 300 are believed dead. *—Story p. 2; other pics center fold.*

BLACKOUT TIMES
Manchester ...... 11.08 p.m. to 5.23 a.m.
Liverpool .... 11.11 p.m. to 5.26 a.m.
Moon Rises .... 7.09 a.m.
Moon Sets .... 10.57 p.m.

Daily Herald
No. 8865 * * FRIDAY, JULY 21, 1944 ONE PENNY

STOP PRESS

SHANGHAI BOMBED

American bombers flying from China have made a heavy attack on Shanghai, says Berlin radio, quoting a Tokyo report.

Army Plot Suspected Against Fuehrer And "Intuition" Brains Trust

BOMB PLANTED ON HITLER

Thirteen Men Who Opposed Sacked Generals Are Blown Up

WITHIN HOURS OF DISMISSING THE LATEST OF THE GENERALS WHOM HE SUSPECTS OF TRYING TO THROW HIM OVER, HITLER LAST NIGHT ANNOUNCED AN ATTEMPT ON HIS LIFE.

He himself, said the announcement from his headquarters, received slight burns and concussion, but no serious injury.

Thirteen others were hurt—three seriously, ten less seriously. All were members of his personal staff, the men who provide the material for his military "intuition" in opposition to the regular military leaders.

Nothing was said as to where the attempt took place. All indications—from the names of the injured, which range downward from General Jodl, chief of Hitler's own staff—are that it was at the H.Q. from which the news was issued.

The armoured train which Hitler normally uses is guarded by the most reliable S.S. Black Guard formation in all Germany.

None but accredited army representatives could hope to pass the ring of steel, machine-guns, bayonets and Gestapo agents around it.

It is only a few weeks since Admiral Canaris, chief of the German Intelligence, for 30 years the Wehrmacht's master spy, was sacked.

Only One Revealed

The radio announcement which broke the news to the German people last night spoke of attempts against Hitler on "several occasions before in the last few years." Only one has ever been officially revealed—the Munich beer cellar bomb in November 1939.

Maximum advantage was taken of that attempt to rally German feeling behind Hitler.

Hitler's own official announcement said: "Hitler at once began to work again. He then received Mussolini for a long meeting, which had been previously arranged."

Goering was again absent at the critical moment—just as he was during the beer cellar attempt. Once again he was officially reported to have hurried at once to Hitler.

Goering reputedly is playing with both sides—with Hitler and with the generals. Last night the German Overseas News Agency went out of its way to mention that one of the injured men, General Bodenschatz, is one of Goering's closest collaborators.

NO WONDER THIS WAS CANCELLED!

AFTER the German home radio had announced the attempt to kill Hitler solemn music was broadcast instead of the arranged programme.

The first cancelled item was a talk on "*The Extermination of Rats.*"

First announcement of the attempt was made on the German overseas radio.

Nearly an hour later the home service announcer went on the air with an "Achtung" call followed by headlines.

"Achtung, Achtung," he said.

"We are broadcasting an important announcement. Attempt to murder the Fuehrer. The Fuehrer not hurt."

"Hand Of Providence"

After reading the official statement the announcer went on:—

"The German people will learn with deep gratitude and satisfaction that the life of our Fuehrer has not been harmed by this criminal attempt.

"Providence has protected the Fuehrer from an attack made by an enemy who has so often made use of murder, and who thought he could obtain by murder that which he could never attain through honest fighting.

"As on several occasions before in the last few years the German nation can see the protecting hand of Providence, under which the Fuehrer is fulfilling the great task with which he has been charged by fate.

"For every German this abortive attempt must be a warning to intensify our war effort."

Afterwards radio war reports were introduced by a spokesman of the German armed forces, who said:—

"This unsuccessful deed has brought every German soldier closer to the Fuehrer, and it will drive every member of the German armed forces to fight harder than ever."

It Shook Them

The news was too much for the staff of the official German News Agency.

Everybody seemed to lose their heads (says British United Press).

The usual methodical flow of news over the agency's printer suddenly stopped in the middle of a Stock Exchange report.

Then came interval signals and without number or headline the first two sentences of the report.

Back went the printer to the Stock Exchange prices again to be cut in the middle of a sentence. A continuation of the names of wounded followed.

The German Overseas Agency operator was so shaken when sending out the report that he had to cancel his first sentence and start all over again.

HEADQUARTERS scene, with Hitler and Jodl together studying the battle-map. And below, Lieut.-General Schmundt, also injured in the attempt to kill Hitler.

Gestapo Start Hunt: More News Soon

A GESTAPO hunt of suspects is on, and revelations were promised in a few days on the German radio last night.

George Schroeder, editor in chief of the Overseas News Agency, said:—

Official quarters have cast an impenetrable curtain of secrecy over the details of the attempt on Hitler's life.

The report of it is datelined "Fuehrer's H.Q.," but this gives no clue as to the place where Hitler was at that time.

Every place where the Fuehrer is working with his staff is known as the Fuehrer's H.Q.

It was 13 days after the attempt on Hitler's life in Munich in 1939 before detailed revelations were made.

Police measures and investigations against the assassins and their accomplices would be seriously hampered if all known facts were now released to the public.

It is believed, however, that this silence will last only for a few days.

MORE CHILDREN URGED TO GO

A new campaign to persuade parents to evacuate children from flying-bomb areas is to be launched this week-end by the Government.

Posters will be put up in certain districts stating that the Government wish all schoolchildren in the area to be evacuated.

There has been a big falling off recently in the number of evacuees.

Since the peak of 41,000 reached on July 8 the daily average has fallen to a few thousand. On Wednesday the total was 3,802.

More flying-bombs were over Southern England, including London, yesterday, after a night in which the attack was not quite so heavy.

The night robots met the biggest A.A. barrage yet. During a prolonged burst of fire three bombs blew up in a minute or so.

WATCHDOG M.P.s QUERY AN ORDER

The committee recently set up to scrutinise Ministerial orders and regulations has referred to Parliament a recent order on utility apparel and cloth.

This order, which was presented to Parliament on July 5, in the view of the committee, "makes some unusual or unexpected use of the powers confirmed by Statute, and its form calls for elucidation."

As the order has been brought to the attention of the House it will now be necessary to debate its terms with a view to proposing appropriate amendments.—M.W.

R.O.C. HELPED A LOT ON D-DAY

"The seaborne volunteers have more than fulfilled their duties and have undoubtedly saved many of our aircraft from being engaged by ships' guns."

This is how Sir Trafford Leigh-Mallory, C.-in-C. Allied Expeditionary Air Force, in a message to Air Commodore Crerar, Commandant, Royal Observer Corps, pays tribute to the 700 men of the R.O.C. who played their part in the invasion of Europe.

Another Award For "Mad Jack"

"Mad Jack" Churchill of the Commandos has won a bar to his D.S.O.

To give him his full title and honours he is now Lieut.-Colonel John Malcolm Thorpe Churchill, D.S.O. and bar, M.C.

He won the M.C. with the Manchester Regiment at Dunkirk. His D.S.O. was the result of a landing in the Gulf of Salerno, when he led the storming of a German battery, and was under constant fire for 36 hours. One of his most famous escapades was the Vaagso raid, when he piped his troops ashore on the bagpipes with which he used to brighten up West End parties before the war.

10,000-Tons Arms Dump Blown Up

Authoritative French sources in London state that at Orugey, between June 19 and June 22, a munitions dump supplying all aerodromes in the south-east of France was completely destroyed.

It contained some 10,000 tons of munitions in 700 to 1,000 railway trucks.

U.S. Heavies' Greatest Bombing Week

By WING-COMMANDER CHARLES BRAY

THIS has been the greatest bombing week in the history of the United States heavy bombers.

It surpasses even the famous week, February 20 to 26, which was the decisive factor in the war on the Luftwaffe.

Then, by a series of terrific attacks on the German aircraft factories and attacks on aero engine factories, on assembly depots and on airfields, German aircraft production was disorganised and damaged to such an extent that production dropped far below the demand for replacements.

The Luftwaffe has never recovered from that week.

Since last Sunday up to yesterday over 5,000 heavy United States bombers have attacked targets in Germany and Austria. It was a co-ordinated attack by the heavies based in this country and in Italy.

An army of more than 50,000 trained officers and men, all air-crew, have fought over Germany.

And the blow has been struck at German oil, aircraft factories, repair factories, aero-engine plants, and chemical plants, including Peenemunde, the main experimental station of the Reich, at which the flying bomb was developed and perfected.

In the week of February it was necessary to send 4,700 long-range fighters with the 4,300 bombers. This week only 3,500 fighters have been used to protect over 5,000 bombers.

It should also be pointed out that in addition to the attack on the German aircraft industry, the United States heavies have also taken part in close support of our troops in Normandy.

There have been 1,500 sorties by the heavy bombers, escorted by 750 fighters, on this work.

Yesterday morning the 8th United States Air Force sent out over 1,200 heavy bombers.

BRITISH FIGHT WAY INTO TROARN, PUSHING ON IN SOUTH

From RONALD MATTHEWS, "Herald" War Reporter WITH THE BRITISH FORCES OVER THE ORNE, Thursday.

FIGHTING under a brassy sky and in a countryside stifling with heavy dun-coloured dust, British troops to-day fought their way well over the Caen-Vimont-Paris main road and railway and tanks stormed into Troarn.

In the centre of the line, the Germans have been forced to withdraw the screen of anti-tank guns which they had established north of Bourguebus, and there has been brisk scrapping in the streets of that little town.

Over on the left, the Canadians have pushed down the east bank of the Orne from Vaucelles to take the little village of Fleury and Hill 67, more than a mile farther on.

The Germans are still resisting grimly at Troarn, where they have been laying down fierce mortar fire to stem our attacks.

Regular salvos of fire from our medium artillery are screaming over my head towards the enemy mortars.

So far, there has been no sign of a major enemy counter-attack and he is using his tanks largely defensively.

Camouflaged Panzers

He established them in little packets of half-a-dozen or so in village strongpoints.

They are superbly camouflaged with concrete smeared on the front, so that they merge into the background of a ruined house or roughly loopholed wall through which they fire.

They continue firing until they feel it is time to pull back or they are knocked out.

The flat, rolling wheatland, with its occasional copses, which forms the base of the bottleneck, is ideal tank-country. But the impression which dominates everything else is the all-pervading dust. After an hour or two driving through it your face is covered with a thick, clinging mask.

Rommel Rushing Up Tanks

From STANLEY BISHOP, "Herald" War Reporter at SHAEF, Thursday midnight.

A GERMAN army of five and a-half divisions is wedged in the plain of Caen, between Troarn, on the east and the Falaise road, on the south, bitterly contesting the advance of Montgomery's armour and infantry.

We now hold firmly a front running in an arc within a radius of about five miles from Caen.

The most southerly point we have reached is Bourguebus, where we have cut the rail to Falaise.

The most difficult obstacle so far has been the anti-tank screen of mines, guns and traps running diagonally for two miles between Frenouville and Emieville across the Paris road and railway.

This afternoon we forced our way into Emieville, and turned the flank of the screen.

More panzers are being sent up to aid Rommel.

Two train loads of them were caught to-day by our bombers as they were passing through Amiens, and some panzers were seen toppling out of the trucks into the waters of the Somme.

It is doubtful if either of those two trains of extra panzers will ever reach the battle area.

WORLD MONEY VOTES

Votes distributed to members of the proposed international exchange stabilisation fund total 99,000, says a Bretton Woods message.

The United States has 27,750, Russia 12,250, the United Kingdom 13,250, and other members of the British Commonwealth 11,250.

Russians Reach Lvov

30-MILES DRIVE TO REACH BUG

DRIVING on in battles of unimagined fury, Russian armies were last night fighting in the suburbs of Lvov, the Germans' biggest base in Southern Poland, and closing in on Brest-Litovsk.

Other Soviet forces were by German admission only eight miles from the pre-war frontier of East Prussia.

And last night an Order of the Day from Marshal Stalin revealed that troops of the First White Russian Front, advancing from Kovel, broke the strong enemy defence system, and during fighting which lasted three days penetrated to a depth of 31 miles, enlarging the breach to 93 miles.

During their offensive they occupied over 400 inhabited localities, and reached the Western Bug.

Among the places captured were Lyumboml, 30 miles west of Kovel; Maloryta, 23 miles south-south-east of Brest-Litovsk; Opalin, 44 miles west of Kovel, and Ratno, 46 miles south-east of Brest-Litovsk.

Defensive Battles

"Great defensive battles are raging from Lvov to the area south of Pskov," declared Colonel Hammer, the German commentator.

The battle for Lvov is at its height.

Great columns of Koniev's tanks are thrusting forward attacking the solid stone houses on the suburban roads which the Germans are using as defence points.

The Germans have thrown in the biggest panzer forces they can muster to stave off the Russian advance.

Soviet troops may already be fighting inside the city, according to an N.B.C. broadcast from Moscow.

Fighting at Augustovo, only eight miles east of the real East Prussian frontier, was admitted by the German Overseas News Agency yesterday.

Bitter Fighting

Moscow has been quiet about this sector for some days. Such silence is often a prelude to an announcement of outstanding success.

Bitter fighting was also reported on the Kaunas front in Lithuania, and along the Latvian border.

Hammer declared a concentration of German forces in the north was being carried out according to plan, despite determined Soviet attempts to frustrate it.

A characteristic feature of the present Soviet mammoth offensive is that whenever German resistance thickens in one sector, as has evidently happened now on the western bank of the Niemen on the immediate approaches to East Prussia, the Russians reply by a new attack in a different sector.

Waning Forces

Consequently no sooner have the distraught German generals frantically tried to plug one hole in their leaky lines than other holes appear far faster than the Wehrmachts waning forces and overworked communication lines can cope with them.

This Russian tactic is similar to that employed in last winter's offensive, with this distinction that pressure is maintained simultaneously along virtually the entire length of the front.

So far there has been no repetition of the local counter-offensives which last winter either succeeded in regaining some ground temporarily, or at least halting the Red Army's advance.

And now the Germans are being pushed to where every additional yard they yield is an amputation.

HELPING LONDON

More than 60 W.V.S. members from all parts of Scotland are now in London helping in the management of hostels, canteens and other war services in which they have experience. They are working in three teams.

DEARER CLOTHES FOR BABY

BABIES' clothes and girls' school outfits are to be dearer.

The Board of Trade yesterday issued "Schedule I.G.2," which fixes higher ceiling prices for the following:—

Infants' and girls' blazers, girls' gym tunics, gym blouses and other blouses, infants' robes.

Infants' and girls' overcoats not of stock size will also be dearer

But there is one concession for parents catering for their families' clothing needs—babies' coats up to 14in. in length will require fewer coupons. A wool coat with a lining now takes seven coupons. The new coupon rating will be announced soon.

The Board of Trade also announces that girls' utility cloth hats to match coats up to 28 inches in length—fitting girls in their early teens—may now be made. They will, of course, be coupon-free.

OIL MISSION ON WAY TO U.S.

A British Ministerial mission, led by Lord Beaverbrook, will shortly arrive in Washington to discuss post-war oil supplies with the United States Government.

Ministerial meetings have been held in London to define the British attitude and provide the necessary instructions to the mission.

Lord Beaverbrook will be accompanied by Mr. Geoffrey Lloyd, Petroleum Minister, Mr. Ralph Assheton, Financial Secretary to the Treasury, and Sir William B. Brown, a leading Civil Servant.

Mr. R. K. Law, who is already in America, will join the mission on its arrival to represent the Foreign Office point of view.—M.W.

JAVA ISLE BOMBED

Five American flying-boats have bombed Madura Island, off the north-east coast of Java, says Tokyo.

COMPLETE NEWS—MAGAZINE SECTION—COMIC FEATURES

New York Post

FOUNDED 1801, VOLUME 143, NO. 212. COPYRIGHT, 1944, NEW YORK POST.

TWO SECTIONS NEW YORK, THURSDAY, JULY 27, 1944 40 PAGES

Americans:

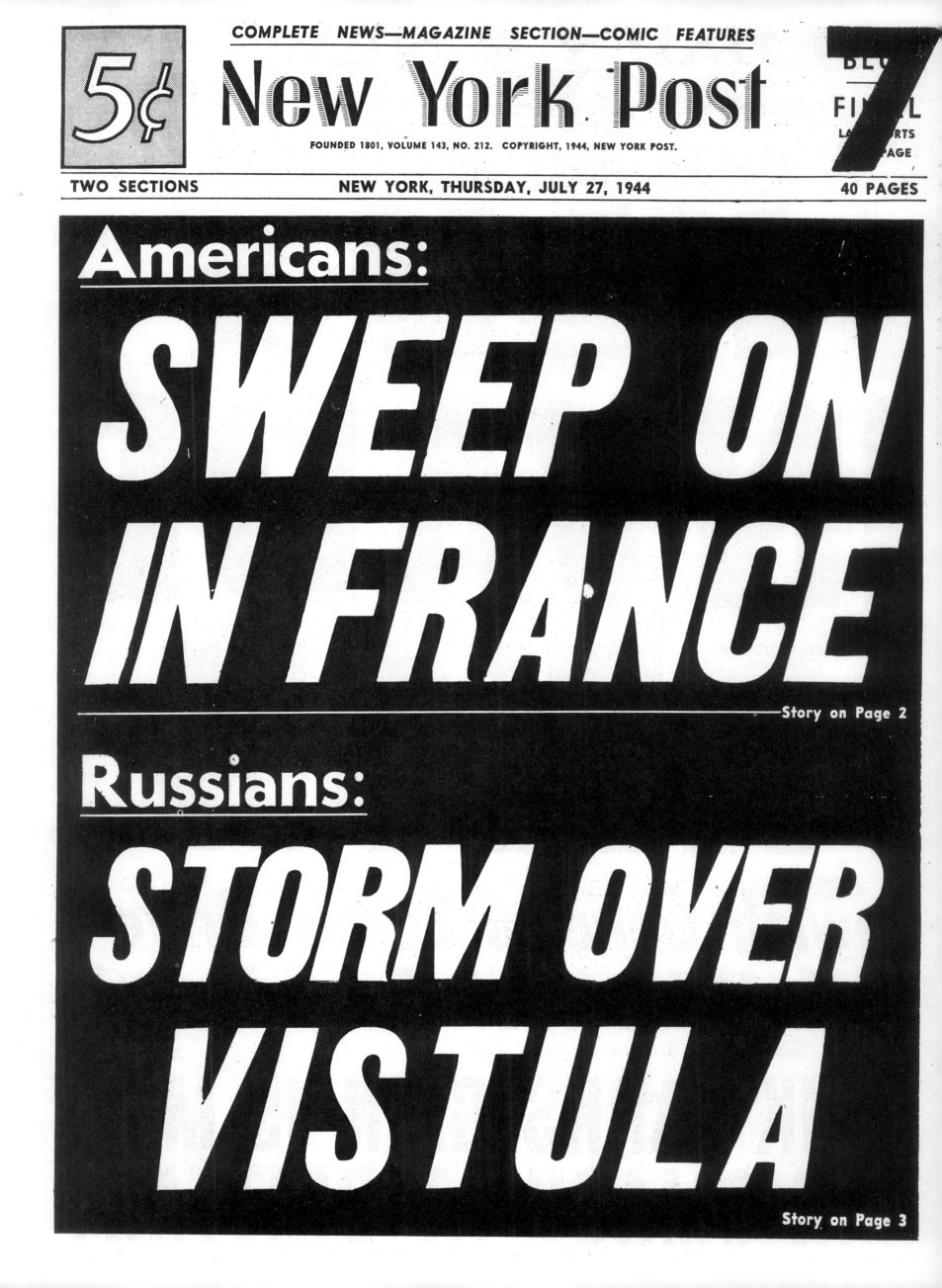

SWEEP ON IN FRANCE

Story on Page 2

Russians:

STORM OVER VISTULA

Story on Page 3

Average net paid circulation for June exceeded
Daily---2,075,000
Sunday-3,700,000

DAILY NEWS

Copr. 1944 by News Syndicate Co. Inc. NEW YORK'S PICTURE NEWSPAPER Trade Mark Reg. U. S. Pat. Off.

FINAL ★★★

Vol. 26. No. 31 New York, Monday, July 31, 1944★ 28 Main + 4 Manhattan Pages 2 Cents IN CITY LIMITS | 3 CENTS Elsewhere

REDS INVADE REICH

Jewish General Leads Drive 7 Miles Into East Prussia

Story on Page 2

YANK TANKS GAIN 15 MI. IN SMASH AT BRITTANY

Story on Page 3

Daily Mail

LATE WAR NEWS

No. 15,055 ONE PENNY FOR KING AND EMPIRE THURSDAY, AUGUST 3, 1944

GERMAN FRONT COLLAPSES

Allies Win Greatest Victory Since Invasion Day

TANKS NEAR RENNES IN BRITTANY DRIVE

THE German front west of Caen has collapsed. Allied tanks rolling into the interior of France are meeting virtually no opposition. American armour, fanning out in strength from the north-east corner of Brittany, is well on the way to Rennes, key to all communications to the Brittany Peninsula, and St. Malo.

British troops have broken through the German positions 15 miles south of Caumont, and an official spokesman describes the British attack as a "major success."

The outskirts of Vire have been reached and the Vire-Vassy road cut, but so speedy has been the Allied advance that the exact whereabouts of many of the forward units are not known.

Hour after hour last night reports poured in of the greatest victory since D-Day. Scores of French towns and villages have been captured, and the extent of the advance may be judged from the fact that Rennes lies about 45 miles south of Avranches, captured on Monday.

While American troops captured Villedieu British forces closed in from the east, thus placing the Germans still in the Tessy pocket in a precarious position. The British have already taken 1,500 prisoners.

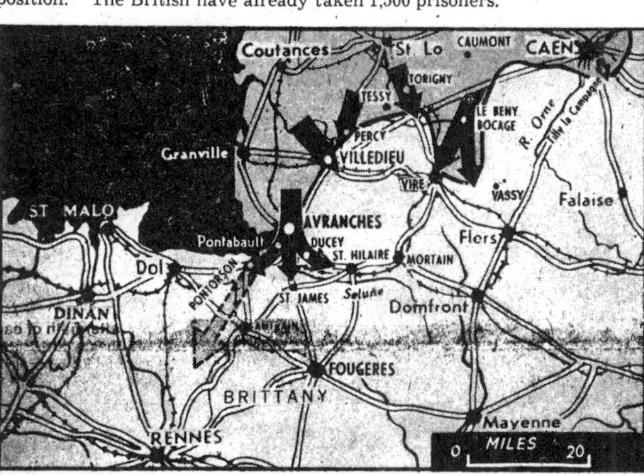

Everything Moving-and Moving Fast

Clifford's Story of the Battle

'Our Chance'

From **ALEXANDER CLIFFORD**

LE BENY BOCAGE, Wednesday.

THE spirit of advance was as clearly in the air to-day as the yellow dust itself.

The whole Second Army seemed to be on the move forward. You could feel the excitement in its veins. You could feel it as plainly as we used to feel it in those mad desert advances.

The situation geographically is still so untidy as to be indescribable.

But we are on beyond Le Beny Bocage, through a whole cluster of vilages to the south-east. We are on beyond Jurques. We are going ahead everywhere.

Just here and there the Germans are holding and resisting.

The line of advance runs like a great hook round the west and south of the area between St. Martin des Besaces and Le Beny Bocage, and there are Germans still in it.

In woods here and there and along the bushy banks of streams, little enemy battle groups are fighting, but it is no longer an organised front.

★

I COULD list you the name of a hundred villages but they are only confusing. The important thing is this instinct of movement and sucess which has seized the Army. There is a feeling that a chance is being afforded to us and we are taking it.

Our mileage is admittedly not spectacular. We have made 12 or 13 miles in four days, which is not impressive beside those whirlwind advances in Africa. But this is not a country where you can overrun empty square miles.

Where each field and each lane and each farm may be an enemy [illegible] you cannot expect a [illegible]. You must measure our mileage against the quality of this close-grained country. Then you will see why these 13 miles have bred this mood of success to-day.

Everything was moving, and moving fast, to-day.

The roads that were no-man's-land last week are peaceful and empty again now. But the roads ahead are endless tunnels of choking dust.

But you could leave these main arteries of traffic and drive sideways into a quiet, manless country. Unmilked cows grazed in the vegetable plots and chickens hopped in and out of parlour windows. The inhabitants had fled or been driven out by the Germans. The main tentacles of war had passed it by.

Along the wayside you saw all the signs of a recent rapid advance. French peasants—men, women, and children — gathered jubilantly to watch German prisoners being searched. Rommel had swept through this district a week before with an S.S. bodyguard, who had left bitter memories behind.

★

IN the next place the people were trying to shave the heads of three women who had been too friendly with the enemy. The women hid in a shop, but village tempers were roused and the crowd hunted them down.

In the end they simply had their hair clipped off, not shaved. They sneaked off home in a disgrace that will never be forgotten.

Prisoners are still straggling in from the thick, by-passed country round about.

Just beyond here to-day I saw a puzzled despatch rider trying to cope with two Germans who had surrendered to him. He was shepherding them along on his motor-bike, looking for someone to give them to.

Some way farther on a little action was in progress—one of the thousands of tiny engagements which together compose the present battle.

Some Germans had dug-in a couple of anti-tank guns beside a stream and were lying in wait there. A squadron of British tanks went clattering off down the road to see to it. Some dived left into the woods and the others went straight ahead "The old princer movement," said someone.

The armoured car patrols took no notice. They carried on with their exploration programme while the tanks mopped up.

★

THAT is how this advance is being done. The men who are doing it down here are members of a division that is earning a great name for itself in Normandy—though for some inscrutable reason its name cannot yet be mentioned.

There had been fascinating doings at these cross-roads the evening before. First the woman who was emptying her washtub was waiting on her doorstep to warn the armoured cars about the mines the Germans had just laid outside her house.

Then two Germans came from another house and surrendered. Then two Frenchmen said they supposed they had better surrender, too, because the Germans had forcibly conscripted them.

Then a whole German patrol with armoured cars was seen approaching down the road.

A British N.C.O. with an empty pistol held them up. He got two motor-cyclists and six other Germans in a truck. The armoured cars turned off on another road and ran head on into a British tank. The tank fired its Brownings and the armoured car crews all took to the woods.

When things like that happen you can be quite sure that the battle is going well.

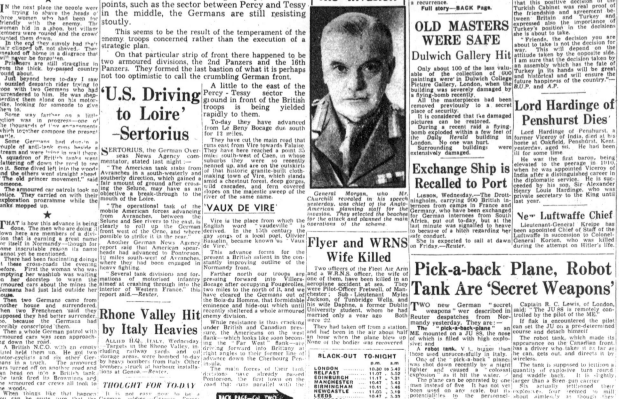

British Drive Reaches Vire

From **G. WARD PRICE** SHAEF, Wednesday Evening.

LIKE the break-up of a log jam on a Canadian river, the front in Normandy has to-day been a scene of jostling, confused movement —all in one direction. Everywhere on both the British and American sectors the whole line is advancing, with armoured cars and tanks swooping about in front.

Along part of what was till lately a most stubbornly contested battle line, our troops have lost touch with the retreating enemy. At other points, such as the sector between Percy and Tessy in the middle, the Germans are still resisting stoutly.

This seems to be the result of the temperament of the enemy troops concerned rather than the execution of a strategic plan.

On that particular strip of front there happened to be two armoured divisions, the 2nd Panzers and the 16th Panzers. They formed the last bastion of what it is perhaps not too optimistic to call the crumbling German front.

A little to the east of the Percy - Tessy sector the ground in front of the British troops is being yielded rapidly to them.

To-day they have advanced from Le Beny Bocage due south for 12 miles.

They have cut the main road that runs east from Vire towards Falaise. They have here reached a point 35 miles south-west of Caen, in whose suburbs they were so recently penned up, and are on the outskirts of that historic granite-built cloth-making town of Vire, which stands amid a chestnut forest, deep gorges, wild cascades, and fern covered slopes on the majestic sweep of the river of the same name.

'VAUX DE VIRE'

Vire is the place from which the English word "vaudeville" is derived. In the 15th century the gay songs of a local poet, Olivier Basselin, became known as "Vaux de Vire."

This advance forms for the present a British salient in the constantly improving outline of the Normandy front.

Farther north our troops are pressing forward into Villers-Bocage after occupying Fougèrolles, two miles to the north of it, and we have cleared the Germans out of the Bois-du Homme, that formidable eminence and hide-out which until recently sheltered a whole armoured enemy division.

While resistance is thus cracking under British and Canadian pressure, the Americans on the west flank—which looks like soon becoming the "Far West" flank—are driving forward into Brittany at right angles to their former line of advance down the Cherbourg Peninsula.

The main forces of their tank divisions have already passed Pontorson, the first town on the road that runs parallel with the

BACK PAGE—Col. TWO

'U.S. Driving to Loire' –Sertorius

SERTORIUS, the German Overseas News Agency commentator, stated last night:—

"The American tank stabs from Avranches in a south-westerly and southerly direction, which gained a fair amount of ground after crossing the Selune, may have as an objective a break-through to the mouth of the Loire.

"The operational task of the mobile American forces advancing from Avranches, between the Selune and See rivers to the east, is clearly to roll up the German front west of the Orne, and where possible to strike it in the rear."

Another German News Agency report said that American spearheads had advanced to Pontorson, 12 miles south-west of Avranches, where they had been engaged in heavy fighting.

"Several tank divisions and formations of motorised infantry aimed at crashing through into the interior of Western France," this report said.—*Reuter.*

Rhone Valley Hit by Italy Heavies

ALLIED H.Q., ITALY, Wednesday —Targets in the Rhone Valley, including railway yards and oil storage areas, were bombed to-day by heavy bombers from Italy. Other bombers struck at harbour installations at Genoa.—*Reuter.*

THOUGHT FOR TO-DAY

It is not easy now to be a German soldier.—*German Forces radio last night.*

He Planned the Invasion

General Morgan, who Mr. Churchill revealed in his speech yesterday, was chief of the Anglo-American planning staff for the invasion. They selected the beaches for the attack and planned the main operations of the scheme.

Flyer and WRNS Wife Killed

Two officers of the Fleet Air Arm and a W.R.N.S. officer, the wife of one of them, have been killed in an aeroplane accident at sea. They were Pilot-Officer Fretwell, of Manchester; Sub-Lieutenant Myles Jackson, of Tunbridge Wells, and his wife Daphne, a former Dublin University student, whom he had married only a year ago. Both were 22.

They had taken off from a station, and had been in the air about half an hour when the plane blew up. None of the bodies was recovered.

BLACK-OUT TO-NIGHT

	p.m.		a.m.
LONDON	10.30	to	5.42
BELFAST	11.07	„	5.52
EDINBURGH	11.17	„	5.21
MANCHESTER	10.47	„	5.43
BIRMINGHAM	10.41	„	5.46
NEWCASTLE	11.05	„	5.19
LEEDS	10.47	„	5.39
LIVERPOOL	10.50	„	5.46

R.A.F. Did Knock Out Rommel

'Injured in a Car Crash'—Berlin

BERLIN has at last admitted that Rommel has been injured and that for the time being he is "out of the war."

The German News Agency announced last night:—

"Field-Marshal Rommel met with a car accident as the result of an air raid in France on July 17

"He suffered injuries and concussion. His condition is satisfactory, and his life is not in danger."

Rommel was first reported wounded last Saturday. Prisoners captured on the American sector said he was hurt when Allied planes strafed his car in the Lisieux area.

On the same day a French woman was quoted by front-line correspondents as saying that she nursed him after the attack and actually saw him die.

Flood of Rumours

On Monday the German News Agency issued an ambiguous message intended by implication to mean that the German field commander was fit and well.

This did not serve to halt the flood of rumours about Rommel's fate, and messages from the United States Army front quoted reports so circumstantial that they make sense, that he died after receiving serious chest injuries from the strafing plane.

19 Canadians Murdered

By S.S. Captors

MR EDEN announced with regret in the Commons last night that an officer and 18 men of the Canadian forces, taken prisoner in Normandy, had been murdered while in custody by the 12th S.S. Reconnaissance Battalion of the 12th S.S. Panzer Division, under the direction of certain of their officers.

The Swiss Government had been asked to lodge a strong protest with the German Government demanding an immediate searching investigation, the punishment of those responsible, and an assurance that orders would be issued to prevent a recurrence.

Full story—BACK Page.

OLD MASTERS WERE SAFE

Dulwich Gallery Hit

Only about 100 of the less valuable of the collection of 600 paintings were in Dulwich College Picture Gallery, London, when the building was severely damaged by a flying-bomb recently.

All the masterpieces had been removed previously to a secret place of security.

It is considered that the damaged pictures can be restored.

During a recent raid a flying-bomb exploded within a few feet of the *Daily Herald* building in London. No one was hurt.

Surrounding buildings were extensively damaged.

Exchange Ship is Recalled to Port

LISBON, Wednesday.—The Drottningholm, carrying 900 British internees from camps in France and Germany, who have been exchanged for German internees from South Africa, put out to-day, but at the last minute was signalled to heave to because of a hitch regarding her safe conduct.

She is expected to sail at dawn on Friday.—*Reuter.*

Berlin is Angry With the Turks

'Broke Their Pact of Friendship'

AN angry communiqué announcing Turkey's decision to break with Germany as from midnight last night was broadcast from Berlin last night.

It stated: "The Turkish Government has to-day communicated to the Turkish National Assembly its decision to break off diplomatic and economic relations with Germany.

"After violent discussion at a secret session of the Turkish People's Party yesterday, the Turkish National Assembly has to-day accepted the Government's decision.

"By this act Turkey has abandoned her traditional policy of friendship with Germany and of neutrality as a condition of her independence, thereby breaking her treaty of friendship with Germany.

'Despite Warning'

"Despite the warning of the Reich Government, the Turkish Government has yielded to pressure by England, America, and Russia and has chosen a way which deprives it of free and independent action.

"The Foreign Office has informed the Turkish Chargé d'Affaires this afternoon that his mission in Germany has ended, and has requested him to leave Reich territory forthwith."

The break, writes the Diplomatic Correspondent of B.U.P., was described in diplomatic circles yesterday as "a diplomatic defeat of the first order for Hitler and his arch-conniver Von Papen," who have spent the entire war trying to keep the Turks in line with the interests and solidarity of Hitler's Balkan coalition.

That Turkey has now made the plunge after months of wavering indecision is a tribute to the Allied military position as it stands at present.

Turkey, on her side, is now obviously qualified for participation in the Lend-Lease agreement.

Turkish Statement

"The friendship that unites Turkey with Britain induces her to present to the Grand National Assembly the British and American proposal to break off economic and political relations with Germany," said M. Sarajoglu, quoted by the German News Agency.

"In order to meet the difficulties which would arise from this decision, economic and financial help were asked for," continued M Sarajoglu.

"Following a positive answer to this request given by our British allies, our Government informed the British Ambassador that the Government would pass to the National Assembly the decision taken by the Cabinet to break off diplomatic and economic relations with Germany as from the night of Wednesday to Thursday.

London Satisfaction

"This positive answer was received with great satisfaction in London. Two days later, the British Ambassador in a signed letter to the Foreign Office stated that this positive decision of the Turkish Cabinet was real proof of the friendship and agreement between Britain and Turkey and expressed also the importance of Turkey's position in the decisions she is about to take.

"Friends, the decision you are about to take is not the decision for war. This will depend on the attitude taken by the opposite side. I am sure that the decision taken by an assembly which has the fate of Turkey in its hands will be great and historical and will ensure the future happiness of the country."—*B.U.P.* and *A.P.*

Lord Hardinge of Penshurst Dies

Lord Hardinge of Penshurst, a former Viceroy of India, died at his home at Oakfield, Penshurst, Kent, yesterday, aged 86. He had been ill for some time.

He was the first baron, being elevated to the peerage in 1910, when he was appointed Viceroy of India after a distinguished career in the diplomatic service. He is succeeded by his son, Sir Alexander Henry Louis Hardinge, who was private secretary to the King until last year.

New Luftwaffe Chief

Lieutenant-General Kreipe has been appointed Chief of Staff of the Luftwaffe in succession to Colonel-General Korten, who was killed during the attempt on Hitler's life.

Pick-a-back Plane, Robot Tank Are 'Secret Weapons'

TWO new German "secret weapons" wer described in Reuter despatches from Normandy yesterday. They are:—

The "pick-a-back-plane" an ME. mounted on a JU 88, the nose of which is filled with high explosive; and

A **robot tank,** V 1., bigger than those used unsuccessfully in Italy.

One of the "pick-a-back" planes was shot down recently by a night fighter and caused a "colossal explosion" as it hit the water.

The plane can be operated by one man instead of five. It has not yet been used on any scale, but its potentialities to the personnel-starved Luftwaffe are most attractive.

Captain R. C. Lewis, of London, said: "The JU 88 is remotely controlled by the pilot of the ME."

If flak is encountered the pilot can set the JU on a pre-determined course and detach himself.

The robot tank, which made its appearance on the Canadian front, has a driver who takes it as far as he can, gets out, and directs it by wireless.

The tank is supposed to jettison a quantity of explosive turn round and waddle back. It is slightly larger than a Bren-gun carrier.

Six actually jettisoned their explosives, four seemed to mill about aimlessly as though they were out of control, and two were knocked out by mortars.

Partisans Join Warsaw Battle

20,000 ATTACK NAZIS

AS the Russians develop their flanking movements around Warsaw the German defenders face a grave threat in the capital itself by the sudden appearance of 20,000 Polish Partisan troops who have engaged the enemy in street battles in four parts of the city.

The Partisans are led by General Bor, who is in contact with the Russians in the suburb of Praga on the north-east side of the capital.

The Polish Forces Press Bureau in London says the four main areas where fighting is raging are Kercelak, Belvedere - square, Pulawska, and the Avenue of Polish Forces—all in the western part of Warsaw.

Strong Russian forces have crossed the Vistula south-east of the city and established a second bridgehead, according to a German High Command broadcast last night.

Moscow claims that the Germans have lost about 570,000 men in the last month—equal to their losses between August and November 1918.

The Red Army is now building up its strength in readiness for the onslaught on East Prussia.

The Germans are being forced back to their border fortifications.

Yesterday's German High Command communiqué admitted that in heavy fighting between the forest of Ugustow and Memel they had lost the localities of Kalvarija and Vilkaviskis.

The latter place is only 12 miles

BACK PAGE—Col. FOUR

'Break With Germany'

Next Finn Move

MARSHAL MANNERHEIM, newly appointed President of Finland, is to take the oath of office on Friday. His first step towards peace, according to a National Broadcasting Company report from Stockholm yesterday, is likely to be a break with Germany.

M. Eero Vuori, head of the Finnish trades unions, was named in the same report as likely to become the new Premier, as he is believed to have been a powerful factor in crystallising the activity of the "peace opposition" and is known to be acceptable to the Soviet Union.

The Swedish *Aftonbladet* reported yesterday that the Russians had offered the Finns substantially the same peace terms as those of last February.

Meanwhile, the paper said, the Germans have now concentrated a third of all their forces in Finland round Aabo (Turku), on the west coast, and it is believed that they will occupy the Aaland Islands (between Finland and Sweden) if Finland tries to make peace.

Optimism is the keynote of Finnish Press comments on Ryti's resignation. Most of them hope Finland will be able to retain her independence.—*Reuter* and *B.U.P.*

LATEST

WARSAW DRIVE: RUSSIANS TAKE 200 PLACES

Russian communique announces capture of 200 places north and west of Siedlce in drive on Warsaw.

More than 100 places taken north of Kovno. Town of Vilkaviskis, near East Prussian border, captured.

Sunday Pictorial

August 6, 1944
TWOPENCE
No. 1,534

BIG NEWS!

Russians Are Fighting On German Soil—Montgomery Bursts Through

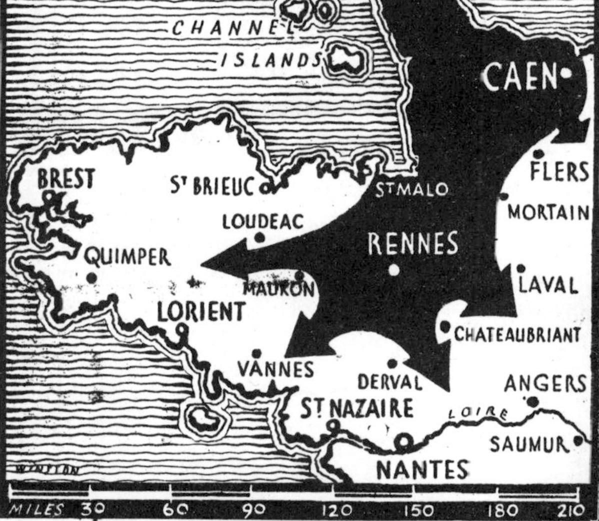

THIS MORNING WE BRING YOU NEWS OF TWO EVENTS THAT WILL RANK AMONG THE MOST IMPORTANT IN THE HISTORY OF THE WHOLE WAR. THEY MARK THE FINAL TURNING OF THE TIDE AFTER NEARLY FIVE YEARS OF WAR.

In the west Montgomery's two-fisted blows have struck home. American tanks have not only reached the outskirts of Brest, at the tip of the Brittany peninsula, but have reached the River Loire and cut the peninsula in two.

That is not the only news of great importance. In the East the Russians have smashed across the frontier of East Prussia—and for the first time the Allies are fighting on German soil. The whole story is told on the back page.

Montgomery has burst through the German defences. Our whole line is on the move, and the road into France becomes clear. And in Italy, Florence has fallen.

The beachhead fight in Normandy has become the Battle of France.

Reeling under Montgomery's attack, the Germans, while attempting to hold a hinge in the Caen area, are swinging back their whole front.

For the moment there is no settled front.

In the Caen sector, held by British and Canadian troops, our tanks are rolling eastward. The enemy in twenty-four hours have abandoned fifty square miles even in this vital area.

But even more spectacular is the way American tanks are sweeping through Brittany. The great peninsula, with its vitally important ports of Brest, Lorient and St. Nazaire—all U-boat bases—is cut off.

Pushing along the Channel coast the Americans are in St. Malo, though the town is not yet entirely captured. Fall of St. Malo means the cutting-off of the Channel Islands.

Berlin admits that the Americans have got six armoured and motorised divisions out into open country in Brittany.

Berlin also says that fifty-four Allied divisions are now in France. If this figure is correct it means we must have something like 650,000 men

"This settles the matter," commented Berlin. "Normandy is of decisive importance."

AS THE MAP SHOWS THE GERMANS FACE DISASTER

Fuller Says—

IT WILL NEED A MIRACLE TO SAVE ROMMEL NOW

The Germans in France are facing disaster, says Major-General J. F. C. Fuller, one of the world's leading tank experts and "Sunday Pictorial" Military Correspondent. Here, in his last night's commentary on the news, he explains that for Rommel to retrieve the position it is necessary for him to perform one of the most remarkable withdrawals in the whole history of war.

HISTORY I think will decide that the supreme event of the last few days is the collapse of the German front in Normandy. Because in strategic importance it exceeds all the great happenings in Eastern Europe—the assault on Warsaw, the occupation of the Gulf of Riga and the invasion of East Prussia. For tactically it has opened the long sought Second Front in the West.

Since the initial landing and until a few days ago, the Allied forces in Normandy occupied no more than a bridgehead. Now that bridgehead has vanished, and in its place we see a true base established from which operations are in full swing.

The Normandy door—the door to the whole of Western France—has been burst in at its lock—Avranches. Its centre, south of Gaumont, has been smashed, and what now remains of it is precariously swinging on its hinge—the Caen area.

Yet, even more important than this bursting, smashing and swinging, is that a gap has been created in the German strategic front in the West—a gap extending from the Gulf of St. Malo to the Mediterranean.

This is no exaggeration. For if, as has been proved, the Germans have not force enough to hold a front of a hundred miles, it certainly may be assumed that they have not force enough to hold one of greater length unless they can place between them and their enemy an obstacle of such strength that it will lend power to their waning numbers.

Only one such obstacle exists within reach. It is the river Seine—the magnet which all but certainly will draw them eastwards. And the more it does so, the wider grows the gap.

Can the Germans withdraw to it? Or can they be prevented from doing so? These, so it seems to me, are the two vital questions which must be answered by the Allied Command before they commit their forces to the next step.

As regards the first: Should Rommel, or whoever is now directing the German forces in Normandy, successfully carry out this retirement, then, indeed, it will be one of the most remarkable retreats in history.

Can this withdrawal be prevented? Here we touch on future operations and the answer must therefore be left to the future. Yet one thing may be mentioned. It is this:

Should the answer be that we can stop the retreat and do so, then the decisive moment in the Battle of France is approaching. Because the final overthrow of Rommel will follow, and that will knock the foundations from under the feet of every other German army corps, division and brigade now in France.

That is why I have stressed the importance of the winning of the strategic gap. For once Rommel and his army are annihilated that gap becomes France.

Begins Today

No woman in this war has had an adventure to equal that of Alice Leone Moats, young American authoress, noted for her daring and audacity. Unknown to anyone she made her way through Spain to the Pyrenees and then got the French to smuggle her to Paris.

For five weeks she moved among the Gestapo—to bring out an astonishing story of life under the German heel. She has written it all down and the "Sunday Pictorial" has secured the exclusive rights in Britain to tell it—the story of a girl the whole German Army could not stop. Miss Moats' narrative—

ON PAGE 4

AND CHEERS FOR THE BOYS DOING IT!

Daily Mail

NO. 15,062 ONE PENNY ** FOR KING AND EMPIRE FRIDAY, AUGUST 11, 1944

PARIS: ONLY FIFTY MILES TO GO

Rommel's Entire Army Now in Deadly Peril

TANKS AT THE GATES OF CHARTRES

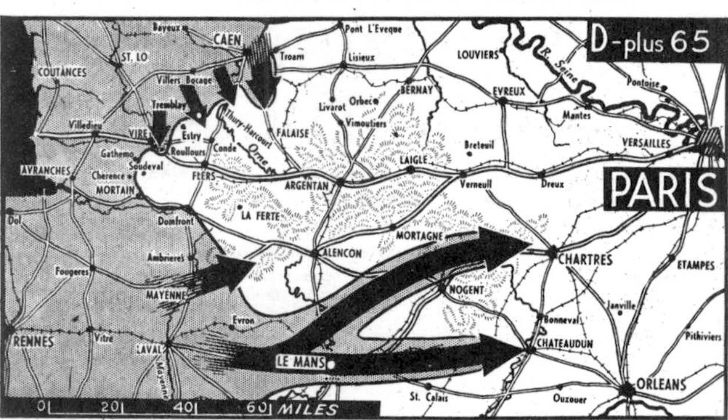

A SENSATIONAL American thrust from Le Mans to the gates of Chartres, some 50 miles from Paris, last night threatened to envelop von Kluge's entire Normandy army, leaving it with only the bridgeless Seine as an escape route.

A secondary column of General Bradley's tanks has reached Chateaudun, 22 miles south-west of Chartres, in an astonishing race to the east, which, like the dash towards Chartres, has been carried out in the deepest secrecy to prevent the Germans knowing the hour-by-hour position of the speeding tanks.

Behind these spearheads the entire left flank of the American forces yesterday began a general offensive. The scope of this attack, which probably covers the Vire-Mortain sector, has not been officially indicated, but it is known that by last night gains of up to one and a half miles had been registered.

North of these thrusts British and Canadian troops are deeply engaged in a series of desperate battles with von Kluge's reeling armies. German resistance on this front stiffened suddenly yesterday. But by last night a new assault south-east of Caen, striking down the main road to Vimont, had progressed some three miles and overwhelmed Vimont itself, one of the key hedgehogs of the German defences and a vital strong-point in the event of a retreat to the Seine.

At nearby Falaise Canadian and British troops yesterday launched a powerful attack against the anti-tank screen of 88mm. guns with which Rommel had tried to stop the Allied drive south. An S.S. panzer division is stationed behind the massed 88's—Rommel's guns are bunched together in groups of 24. Up to early to-day there was no news of the progress of this attack.

Behind these two battles British, Canadian, and American troops, waging a series of isolated actions, are steadily breaking down the German salients that bite into the Allied lines. In Brittany the Americans are meeting fierce resistance in their efforts to subdue Lorient and Brest.

French Boy Gave Us the Bridge

Le Mans 'Saved'

From PIERRE HUSS

LE MANS, Wednesday. (Delayed.)

THE welcome Le Mans gave to its American liberators was so enthusiastic that it slowed their pursuit of the retreating Germans.

The population of 100,000 apparently turned out en masse to greet the U.S. troops, but they had little time to pay attention to the cheering crowds who lined the route of their advance three-deep.

Though the bulk of the enemy had fled, some of them had run for cover in the side streets, and they began sniping at us from behind barricades or the windows of reinforced houses.

So our entry became a manhunt. German rifles were crackling when the Americans began mopping-up.

A hundred Germans barricaded themselves in the police headquarters in the southern section of the city. They resisted for a while with machine-guns and grenades. Then they surrendered.

Snipers Busy

As I jeeped past one cross-road I saw U.S. soldiers, applauded by hundreds of French civilians, peppering cornered snipers halfway down a street.

One German was leaping across a roof when a sharpshooter caught him in mid-air. His body hit the cobblestones close to where I watched.

The enemy were caught by surprise through the speed of our advance. They were able to blow up only a few bridges leading into the city.

The central bridge was saved by an alert 14-years-old French boy who cut the fuse after the last rearguard had set it.

Consequently, the American authorities are sending the lad a reward for his courageous feat.

The speed of our progress also saved Le Mans from destruction.

Coming into Le Mans was like an arrival in a normal city. In the great central square, hundreds of Frenchmen sat at café tables on the pavement having lunch or sipping cognac.

Britain Invited to Shipping Talk

From Daily Mail Correspondent

NEW YORK, Thursday.—An invitation to British shipping leaders to join in a "conference of the seven seas" was extended to-day by Mr. Basil Harris, president of the United States Lines, one of the biggest shipping companies in this country.

Mr. Harris wants to hold round-table talks on shipping problems in the post-war world, and suggests that these talks should be extended later to include all the United Nations.

Luftwaffe Warns Warsaw

Luftwaffe planes flew over Warsaw while street battles were still raging between Germans and Poles yesterday to deliver an ultimatum demanding that the city be abandoned by the entire population.

The ultimatum, which sets a time limit calls on the people of Warsaw to march from the city towards the west carrying handkerchiefs in their hands.

Sky Clears in the Strait

State of Sea.—Moderate.

Weather.—Clear, with some mist patches, after day of much cloud. Maximum temperature 80 deg.: 61 deg. at 10.30 p.m. Visibility good. Wind, S.W.

Barometer.—Slight rise.

Rommel Still Striking for the Coast

From ALEXANDER CLIFFORD

BRITISH FRONT, Thursday.

THE Germans are on the point of taking their major decision in Normandy: whether to fight it out to the bitter end here or whether to retreat. They must take it very soon or it will be too late.

HINGE BATTLE

Their front line is being forced into an impossible shape.

Now at last the exhilarating alarms and excursions of the American advance are settling into a solid pattern. And it is being revealed that Rommel is threatened with the old-fashioned pincer movement.

This only became a reality to-day. The top arm of the pincer is our drive on Falaise. And now the Americans have taken Le Mans and are attacking Chateaudun [22 miles south-west of Chartres]. From there to north of Falaise the line forms, as it were, the mouth of a bag. And the whole of Rommel's army is in that bag.

Of course it cannot all be caught there. The Germans still have enough grip on the situation for that. And the Allied southern flank is still not solid enough to be absolutely watertight.

But it is the moment for the big decision.

The Germans to-day have regained some control of the situation round Falaise. They have pulled themselves together now and are offering us real opposition.

DESPERATION

They have made a temporary flank against us on the eastern side of our salient.

And they are collecting their best available troops to check us.

Further west, on either side of the Orne, they are relaxing their hold. They have even given up some villages without being threatened. Others they have yielded easily to us.

But, farther west still, right at the very extremity of the bag, is the most astonishing situation of all. Here, in the Mortain sector, it seems Rommel has not given up his mad, spectacular attempt to get back to the sea at Avranches.

He has collected what tanks were left him after the Typhoons had finished with them. He has bribed the Luftwaffe into giving him a strong fighter cover. And he is still trying to dig his way deeper into the bag.

It seems a counsel of complete desperation. He can only hope that

BACK PAGE—Col. THREE

VC INVALID WINS DFC

Determined to Fly

Acting Wing Commander James Briddley Nicholson won the V.C. in the Battle of Britain in August 1940 for shooting down a German plane when his was afire and he had been wounded and burned.

He became known as "the man determined to fly." Now, after two illness bouts, through which he flew on, the *London Gazette* tells of his D.F.C. for leading hazardous sorties.

"He was so badly burned in August 1940, when he won the Victoria Cross that every day I thought he would die," his wife Muriel said last night.

Penicillin Controlled

Under regulations, made by the Minister of Health as a safeguard against the sale of inferior and possibly dangerous preparations, penicillin preparations may be manufactured only under licence.

Men Shoot German Officers

They Wanted to Surrender

From HAL BOYLE

WITH THE AMERICANS AT ST. MALO, Wednesday (delayed).

GERMAN troops to-day began shooting their own officers to make surrender easier as the Americans in flaming hand-to-hand battles occupied all of St. Malo except parts around the Citadel.

Inside the battered granite fortress the enemy still held out at 6 o'clock last night under the command of the fanatical leader—Colonel von Auloch, who was carrying to the bitter end his threat to make St. Malo a "new Stalingrad."

He is described as tall and grey-haired, about 55, a native of Wiesbaden, and well mannered, although seemingly obsessed on the subject of Stalingrad, and his determination to turn St. Malo into a similar siege, even if it cost the lives of all his men and his own life.

Stalingrad Wound

French refugees and German prisoners said the colonel suffered from delusions as a result of a head wound received at Stalingrad, and was embittered by the death of his wife and children in a Berlin bombing raid.—*A.P.*

U.S. CHIEF FOR AIR TROOPS

Browning is Deputy

The combined airborne forces of Supreme Headquarters have been consolidated in one command, approximating to an army in size and importance, under Lieut.-General Lewis H. Brereton, U.S. Army, it was announced last night.

General Brereton formerly commanded the Ninth U.S. Air Force. Lieut.-General Frederick A. M. Browning, D.S.O., of the British Army, is his deputy.

The new organisation will "integrate and make more effective the large airborne forces at the disposal of the Supreme Commander," it is stated.

Trek to Freedom Takes 7 Months

It will take seven months after the war ends to repatriate all the Allied nationals now in Germany—that is, if 35,000 people can be moved every day.

This period could be reduced if many of the nationals walked home. It is estimated by U.N.R.R.A. that about 13,000,000 Allied nationals have been uprooted, of whom 9,000,000 are in Germany and Austria.

Ploesti Hit by Night and Day

ALLIED H.Q., Italy, Thursday.—The Ploesti area got its 13th daylight attack to-day from Italy-based Flying Fortresses and Liberators, bombing with instruments through a smoke-screen to set fires blazing in military installations.

R.A.F. medium and heavy bombers had bombed Ploesti last night. There was intense flak and some brushes with fighter planes.—*Reuter.*

Istanbul Alert: 'Plane Down'

An air-raid alarm was sounded in Istanbul early yesterday morning and A.A. guns went into action, Ankara radio reported last night.

A plane, later identified as British, crashed, but the pilot baled out. The only casualties were caused by an A.A. shell falling near a factory and injuring workers.

Sosnkowski Loses Polish Post

M. Tomass Arcianzewski, who has for years "worked underground" in Poland and who arrived in London a fortnight ago, has been appointed President-Designate of Poland.

General Sosnkowski, who has been relieved of the functions, remains C.-in-C.

Another General Has Oak Leaves

Colonel-General Sepp Dietrich, one of Hitler's closest friends and Commander of the Panzer Corps "Bodyguard of Adolf Hitler," now in Normandy, has been "personally decorated" by the Führer with the Oak Leaves with Swords and Diamonds of the Knight's Cross of the Iron Cross.

Wavell Tours Assam

NEW DELHI, Thursday.—Lord Wavell, the Viceroy, has just completed a three-days tour of the Assam territory—including Impnal and Kohima—recently freed from the Japanese. He decorated 14th Army men who have won awards.—*Reuter.*

Report on the Men Who Crack

Doctors Contrast 1940 with 1944

Somewhere in England 100 British soldiers from the battlefields of France are patients in an Army neurosis centre.

Army doctors have been studying them. They have made some striking discoveries about the psychological factors which lead to brave men breaking down in battle.

Here are extracts from their report as given in the current issue of "Lancet."

MOST remarkable of the doctors' findings concerns the contrast between this type of case to-day and the similar cases that came out of the retreat from Dunkirk.

To-day the morale of the men is high. They want to get fit and they want to get back into the fighting.

But this is what the doctors reported of the Dunkirk men:

"For the neurotics who were evacuated from France four years ago there was no security anywhere, save in the love of their wives or mothers.

"Their army had retreated. Their ships were bombed. Their country itself was threatened. They wanted to isolate themselves in small domestic units.

"But when they did return to these, their neurotic demands could never be gratified. They were dependent children who could not forget the injury done to them.

"They said: 'I am ill and weak and so I cannot serve,' but what they meant was: 'I can find security only at home, and even there no one will protect me from myself.'"

★

AND then, by contrast, the men from Normandy:

"The men who broke down in the invasion had complete confidence and security in their Army, ships, and country and gave way only when they felt—because of inner insecurity and external stress—that they could not overpower their enemy as they had in their fantasies."

The ages of the men reported on ranged from 18 to 32. The average was 28.4—"not particularly young in a military sense." Four out of five were new to battle. The rest had fought with the Desert Army in North Africa Sicily, and Italy. A few fought in France four years ago.

All broke down in the first ten days from D-Day. All were fighting soldiers in the vanguard of the invasion.

Describing the treatment, the doctors say: "All our patients were encouraged to discuss and go through their battle experience and their battle dreams, and readily grasped what these meant to them in fantasy.

"After two days in bed most of our patients were up and busy with physical training and diversional and occupational therapy."

★

"THE whine and explosions of accurate mortar fire profoundly shook these men," says the report.

"Some gave way gradually, others suddenly. One soldier was calmly fighting side by side with his brother who flung himself upon him to save him from the explosion of a mortar.

"The brother was killed, and the man collapsed immediately from grief, rage and fear.

"Another, who kept his poor sight to himself, and always went into battle wearing spectacles he had hidden, gave way only after he had lost his glasses. For then he could see neither the enemy nor his missiles."

The doctors found that only 5 per cent. could be said to have suffered from pure physical exhaustion. A few had mild headaches and 70 per cent. were disturbed by battle dreams which dwindled after a few nights.

"Within two days most men became calm and equable and wanted to rejoin their comrades in France."

The changed neurotic attitude of the men from Normandy, say the doctors, contrasting the circumstances of evacuation and invasion, arose from high-group morale, confidence in leadership and equipment, and from prompt and effective treatment by unit medical officers.

Patients had a high degree of insight into the origin of their symptoms. They did not have to deny their acute fear. It was accepted by themselves and their comrades as a temporary phenomenon that dwindled with rest and sleep.

FDR—'Enemy Peoples Need Not Fear'

HOME!

HOME after years of internment in Germany, Mr. Newman, one of the repatriates who arrived in London yesterday, is given a welcoming hug by his sister. Story in Page THREE.

BUT THEY MUST SURRENDER

Daily Mail Special Correspondent

NEW YORK, Thursday.

PRESIDENT Roosevelt, who, it was disclosed to-day, has been to Pearl Harbour, there gave the clearest definition yet of what the Allies mean by unconditional surrender.

"The victorious United Nations," he said, "have no intention of starving the peoples of Germany or Japan.

"The populations of these two nations need not fear for their own lives after they have been defeated."

But he made this clear: "Unconditional surrender means that no terms will be given to the enemy war machines which would permit them to remain partially intact as future war-makers."

The President—missing from the American scene for 21 days—went to Honolulu to hold his first Pacific War Council, aimed at the early defeat of Japan.

His definition of surrender—the first offered by himself or Mr. Churchill since Casablanca—was given at a Press conference close to the spot where the first Jap bomb dropped on U.S. soil.

Roosevelt, who travelled to Pearl Harbour in a cruiser, talked for three days with General MacArthur, Supreme Commander, South-West Pacific, and with many more admirals and generals who are relentlessly driving the Japanese back to their island homeland.

They all endorsed his definition.

The President added that neither

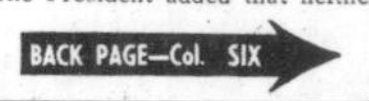

CHARTRES REPORTED CAPTURED

Unconfirmed reports state that Chartres has been captured by Americans. Nantes and Angers have been occupied against slight resistance.

ALL YOUTH TO FIGHT FOR REICH

Goebbels Call-Up

EVERY boy and girl in the Hitler Youth was last night mobilised for Germany's war factories and the battle lines.

This decree, announced by Berlin radio, came at the end of a day of "last-ditch" call-up orders for the defence of the Reich, to fill the need for "hundreds of thousands" more workers and soldiers.

All German film and stage actors except the aged have been given notice that they are to be transferred en bloc to the arms industry. The "rather unfortunate star system" will be abolished.

Whole age groups of Germany's exempt found themselves with their exemptions cancelled and under orders for front-line service.

Domestic servants are due for the factories or to be sent to "priority" households. Every foreign maid or cook will be drafted into armament works.

The new decrees were issued by Goebbels as "Trustee for Total Mobilisation" in what he called "scraping the bottom of the barrel."—*Reuter.*

'Free' Italians to Work as Slaves

The last of several hundred thousand Italian soldiers interned in Germany after the Italian armistice will be released by the end of the month, the German Overseas News Agency reports.

They will be transferred to German factories as "free" workers or to the auxiliary services of the German armed forces, under an agreement signed by Hitler and Mussolini on July 20.

LITTLE SHIPS GET 3 MORE

In Channel Fights

Light coastal forces of the Royal Navy under Lieut.-Commander S. D. Marshall, R.N.V.R., caught an enemy force of four escort ships and four R-boats off Cap d'Antifer, 13 miles north of Havre, early yesterday.

They attacked with torpedoes and the flashes of two large explosions were seen as the enemy withdrew in the direction of Fécamp. During the action several of the enemy vessels were seen firing at each other.

Later two enemy vessels and four R-boats were engaged a mile from Fécamp by gunboats under the command of Lieut.-Commander F. P. Baker D.S.C., R.N. Although shore batteries joined in the action, our ships pressed home their attack and a torpedo hit was scored on one of the vessels, which was left in flames.

Goebbels Closes Famous Paper

From Daily Mail Correspondent

STOCKHOLM, Thursday. — Goebbels to-day ordered the shut-down of Germany's most influential financial paper, *Berliner Börsen Zeitung*, founded in 1855.

This is ostensibly part of the new German general mobilisation, but actually is a reprisal for the part that officers from the nobility played in the attempt against Hitler. Other well-known papers are expected to be stopped.

Super-Forts Hit Japan Again

WASHINGTON, Thursday.

AMERICAN Super-Fortresses, in medium strength, have struck again at Nagasaki, big industrial city on Japan's home island, Kyushu, it is officially announced to-night.

A second force of the great bombers attacked an oil refinery at Palembang, in Sumatra.

The announcement said the attack against Sumatra was carried out from bases of the South-East Asia Command. The attack against Nagasaki was delivered from bases in China.

Nagasaki is one of Japan's most important shipbuilding and repair centres, and a major military port.

The highly industrialised area has already been twice hit by the China-based Super-Fortresses.

Palembang is the site of the Pladjoe oil refinery, the largest in the Orient, and the principal source of aviation petrol for the enemy.—*Reuter and A.P.*

Submarines Sink 16 Jap Ships

WASHINGTON, Thursday.—Sixteen more Japanese vessels have been sunk in the Pacific, says a U.S. Navy Department communiqué.

All the vessels, which included one warship, were sunk by U.S. submarines operating in Japanese waters.—*Reuter.*

MOSQUITOES LAY MINES FROM 50ft. UP

MOSQUITOES of Bomber Command swept down to within 50ft. of the water to mine the vital Dortmund-Ems Canal on Wednesday night.

The Air Ministry describes the operation as "one of the most important and daring" of the war.

Mosquito fighters flew with the Mosquito bombers to cover their attack. They engaged the packed ground defences along the canal, and had almost silenced them when the bombers arrived.

The Dortmund-Ems Canal is one of the most important of the enemy's inland waterways. It connects the Ruhr with the River Ems, which flows into the sea at Emden, and with many important towns farther inland.

DAILY EXPRESS

No. 13,795 | Black-out 9.47 pm to 6.21 am | FRIDAY AUGUST 18 1944 | Moon rises 7.9 am (Sat) sets 9.51 pm | One Penny

Hitler 'liquidates the front' and gives up the battle: Now a desperate retreat to the Seine begins—and Chartres, Dreux, Orleans fall

RUSSIANS REACH BORDER OF EAST PRUSSIA—Back Page

GERMAN ARMY WITHDRAWING FROM NORMANDY—*BERLIN*

Only 23 miles from Paris: New British attack

GERMANY'S News Agency late last night made the sensational announcement that the Germans have given up the Battle of Normandy as lost. Now, on their own admission, they are trying only to save their remnants from the gigantic attacks of the Allies.

The statement was made in these words by the agency's military correspondent, Max Krull: **"The Normandy front has been liquidated by the German High Command. German forces are withdrawing in an easterly direction.**

"The cards now are being dealt for a new game. Fast Allied troops, meanwhile, are trying to overrun the German forces on their march back and if possible to encircle them again. An attempt of this sort is being made at Dreux where thrusts in several directions, including Paris, are being made.

"The lines everywhere are dented and interwoven to an extraordinary degree."

SECRET ATTACK

The German announcement came after news of mighty Allied blows in all directions.

American patrols are approaching Paris, after capturing Chartres, Dreux, and Orleans. To the north, the British and Canadians are bursting through towards the Seine. For two days this attack has been going on in secret. Now the Germans are in retreat over a 30-mile front from around Falaise to the sea.

A late German High Command report says that "grim and costly" fighting is going on at St. Arnoult, 23 miles south-west of Paris and about the same distance east of Chartres. It is on one of the two main Chartres-Paris roads.

Battles are also reported by Berlin at Epernon, on the other road, 30 miles south-west of Paris.

BRITISH FRONT.—Storming units of British, Canadians and Poles have made big advances in a spectacular 48-hour swing to the east. For weeks the front had faced south. Now, dramatically, it has turned towards the Seine.

Canadian and British tanks, armoured cars and infantry have crossed the River Dives at several points, capturing St. Pierre, Mezidon and dozens of other places. The advance is now going well to the east.

RETREAT ROAD CUT

The Falaise-Lisieux retreat road has been cut at a many points. Stubbornly defended Troarn, east of Caen, has fallen too.

Another lunging column has driven eight miles south-east of Falaise and has reduced the Falaise-Argentan gap to four miles.

A senior staff officer said: "There is no doubt about it, the Germans are in an awful mess—a chaotic mess." Another declared: "There is no front any more."

The German defensive line appears to have been broken completely.

Von Kluge's men are fleeing across the marshes to high ground further east of the Dives, and the Allied troops have not been meeting heavy resistance since breaking the crust.

Some German pockets, which have been by-passed, are holding out, although they are hopelessly cut off.

PARIS FRONT. — Field despatches reveal that Chartres, Dreux and Orleans fell on Wednesday. The Americans, "only an hour's car ride from Paris," sped eastwards from Chartres and joined another armoured column driving down from Dreux.

Orleans was captured with only slight resistance.

The Air Force reported the strongest opposition for weeks from the Lufewaffe in the Paris area. Eleven German planes were destroyed; two American fighters were lost.

General Patton's Third Army, which is making these lightning drives, has knocked out about 100,000 Germans—11,000 killed, 41,800 captured and 47,000 wounded.

DAMP SQUIB

THE POCKET. — As the Falaise gap was narrowed to four miles, brilliantly swift attacks reduced the pocket at the western end also to a width of four miles. This was achieved by the British capture of St. Honorine-la-Chardonne, after a bridgehead had been forced across the Noireau river, east of Conde.

The rapidly shrinking pocket is now only 12 miles long, so that the total area of it is about 50 square miles.

Leading tank formations are four miles east of Flers

A counter-attack by German armoured units ranged along the southern American flank near Argentan was launched. It was a "damp squib" and was soon squashed.

Rocket Typhoons, says a front despatch, played a notable part in reducing the enemy's "swan-song" counter-blow to nothing.

Then the Germans turned on their guns to try to stop the Americans.

An estimate at First U.S. Army H.Q. is that only one panzer division managed to escape from the pocket.

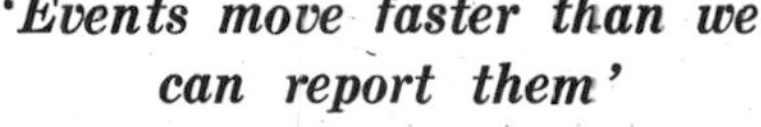

'Events move faster than we can report them'

20 DIVISIONS WORTH NOTHING

The Seine barges wait

From ALAN MOOREHEAD: Falaise Thursday

EVERYTHING now is in movement, and events are racing on more rapidly than we can report them, faster than the censors can get permission to censor. Tomorrow perhaps we shall be able to write of one or two things that are secret at the moment.

The Falaise-Argentan pocket is fast dwindling into nothing. Some of the Germans inside have been killed, some taken prisoner, and several thousands are still there.

Those who have filtered out in small broken columns to the east are withdrawing towards the Seine.

Hastily mustered barges are said to be waiting to ferry them across to the northern bank of the river, where the German 15th Army is deployed from Le Havre to Paris to defend the flying-bomb sites.

Only a battered portion of von Kluge's Seventh Army is retiring to the east. It retreats as the German armies have retreated in Russia and in Africa—leaving the landscape scattered with the burned-out hulks of tanks and lorries and guns, and a trail of smashed towns all the way across Normandy.

CONFUSION

It leaves behind many little graveyards in the quiet angles of the woods, many broken bridges, and piles of empty shell cases in the dust.

It travels in every available French or German vehicle that can be got on the roads, but for the most part it walks and bicycles It goes by side lanes and at night

It turns and fights for a little at every other bend along the roads, and yet in general one has the impression of immense confusion in the German ranks, of no proper central direction and no fixed policy beyond a planned and stubborn retreat.

Of all the divisions which Rommel committed so confidently to Normandy—and we have contacted about 40 since D Day—at least half of them are worth nothing at all now, and indeed some of them have either lost their identity or have been wiped out almost entirely

The Seventh Army falls back without even its general, who is either critically wounded or dead. One headquarters after another has

BACK PAGE. COL. FIVE

'Allies land in Albania'

Say the Turks

ALLIED forces have landed at Durazzo, Albania, according to the Turkish radio.

The radio said it was quoting an Allied Mediterranean news bulletin.

Durazzo, principal port of Albania (population, 85,000) is about 20 miles west of Tirana, the capital It lies across the Adriatic, 85 miles from the nearest Italian port, Bari.

Fifty miles to the north, in Montenegro, new attacks have been launched this week by Marshal Tito's forces.

From Durazzo, where Mussolini struck in Albania on Good Friday, 1939, the Allies would be in a position to give great aid to the Balkan Partisans

They could push east into Greece, north into Yugoslavia, or north-east towards Bulgaria and Rumania

Daily Express

ITALY INVADES ALBANIA

King Zog resists: 50,000 troops landed at dawn on Good Friday: All day battles

—*From the Daily Express, April 8, 1939.*

'Wails from the Hun'

MEDITERRANEAN H.Q., Thursday. — General Eisenhower has sent this message to General Sir Henry Maitland Wilson:—

"All the indications are that you have got off with a flying start. Every step of your progress will bring a wail of dismay from the Hun and a cheer from all of us here.

"Congratulations to you all, your commanders and their troops. Best of luck."

16 spies executed

ROME, Thursday.—Sixteen Italians spying for the Germans in Italy have been executed.—Reuter.

This was the day the pilots waited for

A rout—and it's blitzed

From NORMAN SMART

NORMANDY, Thursday.—Hundreds and hundreds of Germans fleeing from the Falaise gap in a fantastic collection of vehicles are being slaughtered from the air tonight by bombs and cannon fire.

The German Army in the steel bag formed by British and American troops further east may be retiring in orderly fashion, but this is a rout.

In their hurry to get away the Germans are ignoring all military rules of spacing their vehicles on the roads. They are wheel to wheel, riding on horse-drawn guns, on limbers, on farm carts, in trucks, and on cycles.

Our pilots since early evening have been carrying loads of bombs and rockets to throw into this confusion.

Immovably stuck

When they have exhausted their rockets or bombs they empty their cannon and then go back for more. Every side turning is reported by pilots to be a scene of hopeless confusion, where German vehicles, trying to go westwards on urgent errands, are immovably stuck in the face of this great stream of traffic.

These are the people who managed to escape through the Falaise gap during the night, and trundled eastwards under low clouds this morning, when few of our aircraft could operate.

Then they were spotted by reconnaissance aircraft, and a general alarm call went out to all airfields for every available aircraft.

A sweating air liaison officer came out of an operations truck on one airfield I visited this evening, threw his hands in the air, and said: "We are getting so many targets now that it is almost impossible to pin-point them on the map."

Chaotic scene

There are twin columns of smoke and dust rising from the area of this destruction tonight. One comes from the fire of our advancing troops, and the other—streaked with flame and black smoke, where vehicles are burning—comes from the German columns.

There was no flak.

Pilots who dived to drop their bombs and streaked low along the roads to strafe with cannon, could see our own troops advancing on to this chaotic scene.

They are having the time of their lives, giving the Germans a taste of what they have often done to other people.

It has been an astonishing day. Despite reports that many of the Germans had escaped, reconnaissance pilots brought back photographs which showed the roads leading from the gap just cluttered up with transport.

Wave white flags

One pilot said he saw nearly a thousand on all the side roads in the gap in one short flight They were all trying to go eastwards, and again there were tremendous traffic jams as they came up against scores of German ambulances going in the opposite direction trying to evacuate wounded.

Flying Officer Richard Garside, of Leeds, saw hundreds of Germans waving white flags at him as they stood beside their tightly packed lorries near a railway bridge midway between Argentan and Falaise

SOUTH: FOUR MILES FROM TOULON

ALLIED troops driving along the main Riviera road in South France are within four miles of the great naval base at Toulon, reports Algiers radio.

Another force is storming into Hyeres, on the coastal road, nine miles east of Toulon, says a report from Allied H.Q., Mediterranean.

Berlin last night said Allied paratroops who dropped north of Cannes have broken into the town and are battling through the streets.

Strong Allied reinforcements are pouring into the beachhead under cover of two battleships, an aircraft carrier, three cruisers and 18 destroyers, according to the Germans.

Unconfirmed reports from the Italo-Swiss frontier say Allied forces have occupied the Italian Riviera towns of Ventimiglia, Bordighera, Ospedaletti and San Remo.

First despatch from WALTER LUCAS, in Southern France with the French Commandos

Madame Lieutenant fights

RIVIERA, Thursday.—One of the first soldiers to reach the beaches here was a woman—a famous "pistol-packing momma" of the French Commandos.

With a full pack on her back and the ribbon of the Croix de Guerre on her breast, a long, ugly-looking knife hanging at her side, and a revolver in her hand, she went ashore from a landing craft a little before midnight on Monday.

I cannot give her name as she is a wife and mother who has relatives still in occupied France.

She fought in Tunisia and at landings at Elba, was decorated for bravery and twice mentioned in despatches.

She is tall and has clear-cut features and a pleasant soft voice.

Her rank is first lieutenant and her fellow officers make no difference between her and them. She drinks with them, joins in their poker games and smokes unceasingly.

Her main job with the Commandos is the welfare of the men who regard her as a sort of universal mother. But at the same time she goes into action with them and, so I was told, is generally in front of the fighting.

British girls, too

IN contrast to this fighting mother were two British girls who are also with the French Commandos—Rachel Howard Evans from Wimborne, Dorset and Joan Pryke, from Barnes.

Both these girls have been nursing with a French ambulance and have been through the Italian campaign with French troops since last February. Today they followed the first Commando waves on to the beaches with their team of seven French surgeons and 25 ambulance men

Three bursts

OUR Commandos had to cut road and rail links, and, with American Rangers, destroy batteries on the islands of Port Cros and Levant.

Surprise seems to have been complete. We hadn't been spotted during daylight, although we were within easy range of German reconnaissance planes.

Assault craft grounded ashore; their landing-ramps clattered on to the sand; and the Commandos fanned out over the beach and into the thick scrub that climbed up into the low hills.

Twenty minutes earlier a dozen tough men had gone in to polish off two German pill-boxes which guarded both flanks of the beach.

One post on the western side was as mute as the grave, and the other gave three wild machine-gun bursts and then went silent.

Veteran of 15

WE are a mixed lot. French from all parts of France and Algeria, Arabs and Berbers, British and U.S. liaison groups, a Georgian who is the butt of the Commandos—but retorts that it is the Georgian Stalin who won the war on the Eastern Front—a Corsican boy of 15 decorated with the Croix de Guerre.

With us also are men who organised coups in Algiers and Oran. We have boys who escaped from France, one barely two months ago. We have the grandson of a famous general of the last war. We have also a few men conscious that their conduct was not blameless in the years after 1940, and who are seeking honour in death.

Last week was a hectic round of exercises on the Italian coast.

Then the colonel in command gave his last orders, and the British and French wished each other good luck.

OVER 'THE HUMP'

Invaders carry slopes of Maures Mountains

From JAMES COOPER: Italy H.Q., Thursday

WE are over "The Hump." The significance of this afternoon's first official announcement of progress is that we have not only completed a continuous front along 50 miles of coast to an average depth of ten miles but we are over the first obstacle—the Maures Mountains.

These granite slopes rise to 2,500 feet in an arc from Toulon to the mouth of the River Argens.

What might have been a defence for the Germans is now a wall against which we can rest our backs, if need be. More than that, it means we are overlooking the main railway for most of its distance from Toulon to Nice and by capturing the inland towns of Le Luc and Le Muy have cut it into at least three parts.

Le Luc is the furthest announced penetration, because this town lies 15 miles from the nearest coast and is more than 30 miles from where the troops landed at St. Tropez.

And the capture of St. Tropez fortress and seaport, with St. Maxime across the harbour, gives us control of a sheltered bay.

This swift success of something more than 10 square miles an hour since the landings began may be taken as the triumph of perfection of airborne warfare.

BITING A CHUNK

Because some of these troops were flown up the valley of the River Argens to give us Frejus and Le Muy, along its banks, and were then able to turn and meet the ship-landed troops, it was possible to give us so quickly the breathing room of the Cavalaires Peninsula.

This biting of a whole chunk rather than nibbling at the edges of the coast has enabled us to pour French and American reinforcements ashore, together with their armour

It is as if we had used a gigantic airborne grab, swung it over this

BACK PAGE, COL. FOUR

Police of Paris told: 'HIDE'

THE people of Paris were told on the radio by the Allied Supreme Command last night that the day is imminent when they will be given orders to rise.

The spokesman also gave a warning to the Paris police force, who went on strike yesterday following the appointment of a [illegible] post.

They were told that Darlan, Vichy police chief, plans to move them to Nancy, and the spokesman added:—

"Refuse to obey. Hide in Paris. Do not leave the capital under any pretext. All policemen of Paris must be warned of the danger which threatens them."

Stockholm reports say the Paris Underground has stopped, and all Parisians are being fed by field kitchens, as the gasworks are closed. The food situation is serious.

Keitel goes to Finland

STOCKHOLM, Thursday — Field-Marshal Keitel, German Chief of Staff, has gone to Finland.

With General Rendulic, commanding the German troops in North Finland, he has had talks with Marshal Mannerheim, Finland's new President.—Reuter.

Churchill wanted to invade

RIVIERA, Thursday. — Mr. Churchill, it is reported today, was anxious to land on one of the Riviera beachheads when he watched the invasion from a destroyer, but it was thought unwise for him to go ashore at that stage.—Reuter.

Mrs. Askey saves her beer

Trapped in a third floor flat yesterday when a flying bomb damaged the staircase, Mrs. Betty Askey, aged 43, was helped to safety clasping a bottle of beer.

She took a drink and said: "I had to leave my dinner, but I'm dashed if I was going to leave my beer."

3 a.m. LATEST 'IN PARIS'

Moscow radio broadcast in German says Allies entered Paris. —B.U.P. (This report is unconfirmed.)

FIGHTING IN MARSEILLES

French patriots are fighting Germans in centre and suburbs of Marseilles, says Algiers radio. East of Allied beachhead Germans are retreating on Italian frontier.

Seventh Army troops have occupied Draguignan, 20 miles inland from Mediterranean, and five other towns in Var Province, Allied H.Q. announced.

BULGAR PREMIER TALKS OF PEACE

Bagrianov, Bulgarian Premier, said in Bulgarian Parliament yesterday: "Government is determined to remove all obstacles which stand in the way of the Bulgarian people's love of peace."

COMMENTARY—by Morley Richards

INTO OUR ARMS

THE German armies, west and south, in France are on the run.

Broken, in some places completely disorganised, they are fleeing before Allied arms with no attempt to stem the tide flowing beyond them other than with localised rearguard actions.

The news released after days of operational silence that General Patton's tank army was last night barely 20 miles from the Seine and in possession of the high ground between Dreux and Chartres means that there can be no sustained defence on the river before Paris.

Kluge's one aim now is to get out of Western France what is left of his Seventh Army. That remnant may total 60,000 men—less those killed under a steady hail of air bombardment.

It certainly does not include 1,000 tanks. The Germans do not have that number in the whole of France. One thousand tanks and armoured cars is a more accurate estimate.

15,000 captured

So far 15,000 prisoners have been collected in the pocket around Falaise. There are many more to come. The enemy has left behind most of his heavy weapons and his stores.

This may not be annihilation, but it has prevented the Seventh Army from being an offensive force again in France. Its casualties in dead are considerably larger than the number of prisoners.

Note that the British have now begun an attack in the Troarn sector, crossing the Dives River where the enemy might have attempted to keep a sea flank on the western side of the Seine.

What will happen? Driven away from the general Paris direction, the Seventh Army is being pushed both towards the estuary of the Seine and the sea itself into the arms of the British awaiting them.

The German admission last night that they cannot stand against the Allies west of the Seine is a preparation to their own people that France is lost.

A front—'in liquidation'

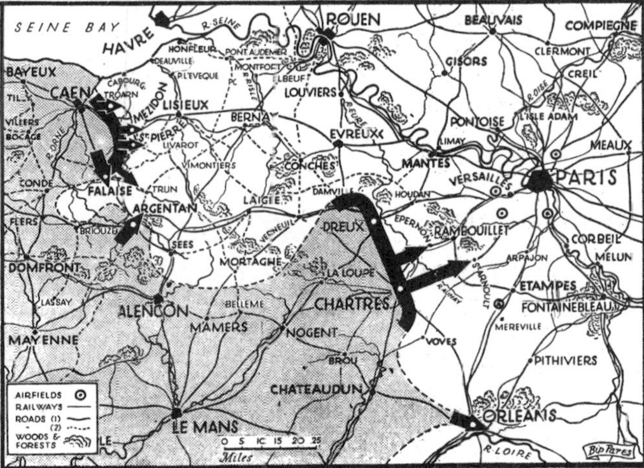

Daily Mail
NO. 15,069 ONE PENNY * * FOR KING AND EMPIRE SATURDAY, AUGUST 19, 1944

LATE WAR NEWS

FRANCE: WE HAVE WON DECISIVE VICTORY

Kluge's Beaten Army is Being Pursued—and Destroyed

From ALEXANDER CLIFFORD Normandy, Friday.

WE have won a decisive victory in Normandy. The German Seventh Army is now in full retreat. You can state this tremendous news as simply as that to-day. Overnight the situation has suddenly become sharp and clear and overwhelmingly important. The Germans here are defeated. Most of those enemy divisions, including crack S.S. formations, are, after all, still trapped in the pocket.

Only yesterday did the Germans themselves recognise the extent of their plight. The gap is now down to three or four doubtful miles. And the panzer divisions are trying to fight their way through it in a tremendous running battle.

You can call the victory decisive without hesitation. It does not mean that the Germans will immediately cease fighting.

It does not mean that this particular battle will not drag on for a few days yet. It does not even guarantee a big bag of prisoners in the end. But it does mean that the best German divisions are irretrievably disorganised.

It means that they can never again bring a really serious force against us in Western Europe. It means they will probably never again be able to organise any sort of a front in France.

All our thrust is north-east now. We on the left and the Americans on the right are heading straight for the Seine. Between our stretching arms the Germans who fight their way out of the little pocket find themselves being still embraced and funnelled towards the river.

THEN SOMETHING HAPPENED

The clue to to-day's situation is that the Germans never really knew they were trapped. They thought they could counter-attack against the Americans and shoulder off that whole southern flank.

They thought they could break the trap, instead of merely escaping from it. But something happened at midday yesterday. Someone suddenly got the true facts. A fantastic scramble to leave the pocket began. The German defeat was abruptly and glaringly revealed.

All yesterday afternoon German vehicles began to appear in the lanes and fields between Falaise and Argentan. They were all wildly striving to get east, every man for himself. And the Seine ferries started to operate in daylight for the first time.

The tanks began to shoot their way east. The news spread from unit to unit. Right in the middle of the pocket they began to hang out white flags and tablecloths to the air forces.

They couldn't really surrender because the units all round them were not surrendering. So the Air Force told them to keep right on waving or they would be bombed.

The adjutant of the Ninth Panzer Division went out to reconnoitre a route for a counter-attack. He found to his astonishment that his maps were marked utterly wrong. His route lay through Allied territory. Then he was rocketed by Typhoons. And in supreme bewilderment and discouragement he surrendered.

The air forces were out attacking the gap all yesterday afternoon and again to-day. But stubbornly and desperately the mobile German forces passed on. This, at last, is a disorganised retreat. It would be a rout if we allowed it to be.

To get the full flavour of this victory, to realise why the crisis has crystallised so suddenly, you must add up the three big blunders

BACK PAGE—Col. FOUR

Double Trap is Nearly Closed

British Overlap

THE Battle of the West in France falls now into two clearly defined parts.

In one, the city of Paris would appear to be the prize glittering before our armour, though it may yet prove that we intend to by-pass it to the south and drive on.

Of far greater importance is the battlefield which sprawls between the Seine (from Paris to the sea) back to the Falaise Gap area. If the Allied arm at Dreux can reach Mantes on the Seine—and consolidate—the entire German forces to the west are trapped.

Here is the situation front by front:

BATTLE OF TRAP

BRITISH and Canadian troops driving down from the north finally settled the fate of the German Seventh Army.

The great American encircling arm reached Argentan, but there the Germans threw in the panzer formation which they had been able to withdraw from Mortain.

It looked as if the mouth of the pocket would be kept open for the enemy to make an organised withdrawal.

Then Canadians and British struck south-east from Falaise to Trun and Chambois, and the panzer divisions at Argentan suddenly found they had been overlapped.

At that point panic set in, and it became every man for himself in a desperate effort to escape to the east.

To-day the pocket has become a double pocket, and promises to develop into a yet bigger pocket as the Americans drive for the Seine below Paris.

BATTLE OF PARIS

OUR forces have reached the area of Etampes and Dourdan (halfway between Chartres and Paris), where some resistance has been met.

The Germans are operating a fluid defence. On some roads American patrols have been able to reconnoitre into the vicinity of Paris without appreciable opposition. On nearby roads the Germans are positioned to fight every inch of the way.

We now have substantial infantry fighting just north of Chartres.

SEINE BRIDGES ALL SMASHED — PARIS — D-plus 73

BERLIN SAID LAST NIGHT

'We Must Prepare to Leave All France'

THE German War Ministry officially stated last night: "We must be prepared for a German withdrawal from France. We must expect the loss of places with world-famous names."

A military spokesman in Berlin added: "No fresh German divisions can be sent to France. Troops in the battle have been warned of this. They have been ordered to fight to the last man."

The "Volkischer Beobachter," Goebbels's newspaper, declared yesterday: "We must sacrifice territory to gain time. We must sacrifice places with world-famous names. People must understand why this is being done.

"The enemy is reaching the Loire's middle course; the enemy has gained a port in the South by seizing Cannes; the German High Command must, therefore, make new decisions.

"The German High Command cannot be expected to use its reserves to hold the present front line in France."

Spokesmen in Berlin were saying openly that Paris is likely to fall in a matter of hours.

The German armies are being told: "Hold out until October. That will give us all winter to prepare new secret weapons which will turn the tide in our favour in the spring."

—AND THE REASONS WHY

Pounded to Pieces, Hunted Like Rats

BATTLEFRONT messages poured in from France last night all telling of the destruction of the German Seventh Army. It is a story of an army which is being pounded to pieces by artillery, blasted off the roads by our air forces, and hunted like rats over the countryside.

Every fresh dispatch brought news of greater chaos in the enemy ranks.

German armour has broken off action near Argentan and joined the mass retreat to the north-east . . .

The enemy have discarded camouflage in a pell-mell race to escape . . .

Seven thousand vehicles have been caught in a four-miles triangle near Troarn and attacked by every available plane. Two thousand vehicles have been destroyed . . .

Other messages told of areas from which our troops had been held back to give the guns free play; of prisoners being taken in droves.

Reuter's correspondent, Doon Campbell, cabled:

'Killing Ground'

Hundreds of British, Canadian, and American guns are annihilating the remnants of the German Seventh Army in the Falaise pocket.

The "killing ground" of the mauled divisions huddled against the now virtually sealed exit of the pocket is south and south-east of Falaise.

The Germans in the valley are being pounded without a stop. Along the lateral roads they have come headlong for the exit which was below Falaise—but they did not come soon enough.

Richard McMillan, of the B.U.P., said:

Hunted like rats over a hundred miles of front both round and outside the double pocket, the German Army is fleeing through France.

"We are catching them in droves," said a company commander in the forward area. "They have lost all real cohesion because we are cutting their communications.

"Some very fierce fighting is going on in some isolated pockets, particularly where there are S.S. men. As for the others, they wander across the roads and surrender to us when the roar of battle goes past.

'Crazy to Fight'

"Those who are still fighting are simply madmen," the prisoners say. "They haven't the slightest hope, and they really know it, but they still fight because they are crazy."

"It looks as if the entire German Seventh Army is going to be wiped out, either before or on the Seine," I was told at forward headquarters.

"It is open warfare almost all along our front, and we are cutting up the retreating German columns. Some of our men have been fighting almost without a break for five days, but they carry on because they know they have won a great victory"

Roger Greene, A.P. Correspondent, watched the rain of shells falling:

A battle of annihilation on a grand Russian scale is blazing towards a climax to-night in the Normandy trap.

A British Headquarters officer said, "The Germans are being knocked to bits as they try to escape.

The next 48 hours, it is believed, will see the final destruction of von Kluge's doomed legions.

As I write on a hill-top overlooking the battleground, massed guns of the British, Canadian, and American armies are pouring steel into the ranks of the trapped enemy,

'DECISION' IS MADE

Eisenhower's Talk

ADVANCED SHAEF, Normandy, Friday.

GENERAL EISENHOWER and his field commanders conferred this afternoon as Allied patrols pushed towards the Seine, and momentous decisions are believed to have been made.

The Supreme Commander emerged from a long session at the field headquarters of Lt.-Gen. Omar Bradley looking determined. With him were Major-Gen. K. W. D. Strong and Major-Gen. R. R. Bull, officers of his staff in charge of intelligence and operations respectively.

This group conferred with Eisenhower's other field commanders by telephone during the afternoon.

What the Allied Command decided was not indicated, but the Germans themselves, when they feel the weight which the British, Canadians, and Americans have piled up behind the Seine, will probably be the first to know the answer.

An air of confidence and optimism attended the generals' meeting.—*A.P.*

'Forts' Blast Ploesti

ROME, Friday.—Strong forces of 15th Air Force Fortresses and Liberators again blasted the Ploesti oil installations to-day, and hit oil targets at Campina, 10 miles north-west of Ploesti in Rumania. Between 500 and 750 bombers participated.—*A.P.*

STAFF OFFICER SUMS UP THE BATTLE

Germans in France are Broken

No Strength Left to Resist

21ST GROUP H.Q., Friday.

A SENIOR Staff Officer at General Montgomery's H.Q. said to-night: "The Battle of Normandy has been won. The enemy's power to resist effectively again in France is gone.

"The Germans are no longer able to conduct anything beyond strong rearguard actions.

"There will now be a phase of pursuit battles.

"There is no sign of preparations to hold the Seine in strength, nor is it possible to see where the enemy has the manpower to do it. What strength is left in Germany is 'muck.'

"The enemy sent a reserve army over the Seine to try to stop the gaps, but owing to the lack of mobility they arrived not in bulk but in series, and they arrived too late.

"The Germans have been very slow to react to our encircling movements and their major movement to the east began only yesterday. A considerable bag of infantry is expected.

17 Divisions

"Twelve infantry divisions, one paratroop and four panzer divisions are still in the Falaise-Argentan area.

"Very large concentrations of motor transport, tanks, and artillery are still trying to get out.

"Yesterday there was a convulsive attempt to get out by S.S. troops and infantry as they realised the trap was closing. They have now only one route to withdraw north-east of the Seine. The Paris gap is not available to them.

"The pocket will be eliminated in the next few days and we expect quite a considerable crop.

"Not one of the generals opposing us, from Field-Marshal von Kluge down, is in a position to surrender. They are all on the Russian list because of the atrocities committed under their command. It would be suicide for them to surrender.

"We have achieved the military conditions of 1918, but not the political ones.

"The American conduct of the battle has been extremely far sighted. General Omar Bradley has refused to take his eye off the ball.

"He insisted on fighting the main battle instead of being diverted in Brittany. This has paid enormous dividends.

Lines Cut

"The American drive eastward caught the enemy off their balance and swiftly severed 60 per cent. of the lines of communication of the forces still operating in Normandy.

"Most of their dumps were overrun. They were left with only the Seine ferries as their main line of supply.

"We are after the German Army wherever it cares to go.

"The Germans have been giving the Russian front top priority in the last month, but now they must reconsider. We are hurting him now."

Asked if attacks on the flying-bomb sites were high on the Allied list of intentions, the Staff Officer said: "If the Germans like to defend them that will suit us very well."—*Reuter and B.U.P.*

24 HOURS—NO BOMB DEATH

But Some Injured

In the 24-hours period, Thursday night and yesterday, no fatal casualty was caused by flying bombs sent over Southern England, including the London area. People were injured, however, and there was damage to property.

The Lord Mayor of London, Sir Frank Newson Smith, who visited Manchester yesterday during a tour of the reception areas, said: "The number of deaths from flying bombs now is extraordinarily low."

With the object of blocking the entrance to an underground fly-bomb supply depot at L'Isle Adam, near Paris, Lancasters made an effective attack on it yesterday. Another depot in the same area was demolished on August 6.

Allies Driving On Toulon

Port is Isolated; Bombers Smash Warship Guns

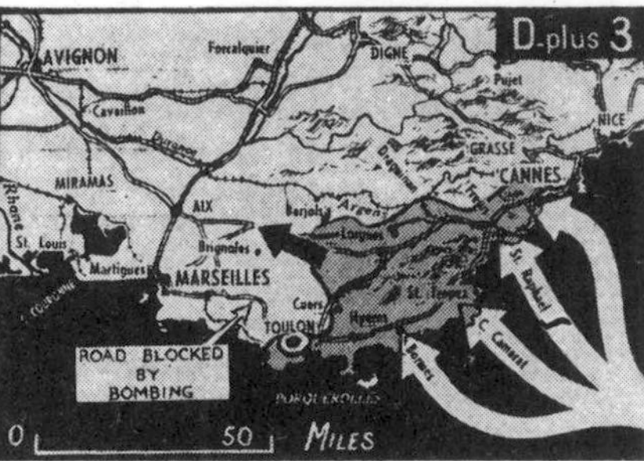

THE RIVIERA Army took a great leap forward yesterday. To the west of the beach-head the Allies reached Solliès Pont, seven miles north-east of Toulon, in a three-miles advance which has cut the port's communications to the north.

Seizure of Solliès Pont means that the naval base is now isolated, since its communications with the west and Marseilles have been cut by Allied bombing.

North of Solliès Pont, it is officially stated, the Allies have advanced to within five miles of Brignoles; still farther north there has been a three-miles advance around Draguinan.

The Germans tried to stop the advance on Toulon by manning the guns of the 26,000-tons French battleship Strasbourg and firing on the Allied spearhead from inside Toulon harbour.

Medium-bombers swept into action to stop the battleship's fire. They scored a number of direct hits that caused explosions and started fires.

In addition, the 7,600-tons cruiser La Galissonniere, a destroyer, and a submarine were also bombed.

On land, meanwhile, the Allied troops seized the second German general to be captured since D-Day.

The general was found in a slit trench, sheltering from Allied artillery fire. "Every second shell seemed to be aimed at me," he said—an unconscious tribute to the effectiveness of our fire.

The general knew nothing of the Allied advances in Northern France or of the Red Army's progress; Germans, he said, receive only such information as the High Command permits.

Riviera front-line reporters last night summed up Allied progress

BACK PAGE—Col. SIX

S.S. Sacrifice Wehrmacht: Army Split

From WILLIAM STEEN

SHAEF, Friday.—Clear indications of a split between the Wehrmacht and the S.S. were reported to-night as the crisis mounted hourly for Paris and the trapped German Seventh Army.

The fanatically pro-Hitler S.S. formations are said to be doing everything possible to keep themselves intact at the expense of the ordinary German Army. They are trying to get out of the trap, leaving the Wehrmacht behind.

In this latest crisis within the German Army another of Hitler's generals — Obergruppenführer Hausser, Commander of the Seventh Army—assumes a sinister rôle.

The fact that he, or his command, is apparently trying to sacrifice the ordinary German soldier to save the S.S. fanatics may have a very deep significance.—*Reuter.*

PARIS RADIO MYSTERY

Silent All Day

Daily Mail Radio Station

Paris radio was silent throughout yesterday.

No reason has been given for the shut-down, but the Allied advance—the Paris transmitters are at St. Rémy-l'Honoré, 20 miles south-west of Paris—may be responsible.

Named Chief of South France

ALGIERS, Friday.—Raymond Aubrac, delegate from the French Resistance Movement to the Consultative Assembly in Algiers, has been appointed Commissioner for liberated territories in Southern France, it is announced in Algiers.

M. Aubrac is accompanied by Lieut.-Colonel Pierre Tissier, one of General de Gaulle's first supporters and a Councillor of State, and Jean Escande.—*B.U.P.*

German Papers Late

From Daily Mail Correspondent

LISBON, Friday.—For the past two days no German newspapers have appeared on the Lisbon news stands. It was customary for the German newspapers, including *Das Reich*, Goebbels's paper, to arrive in Lisbon from Berlin punctually every day by air.

Dash to Free Italy

ROME, Friday.—Signor Giani Agnelli, 24-years-old grandson and heir of Signor Giovanni Agnelli, proprietor of the Fiat works in Turin and Italy's leading industrialist, has escaped to liberated Italy.—*Reuter.*

ROOSEVELT TO MEET CHURCHILL SOON

WASHINGTON, Friday.

PRESIDENT ROOSEVELT announced to-day that he is going to confer with Mr. Churchill soon.

He gave the news at his Press conference.

Asked whether the meeting would be this year, he merely replied that it was the same old story.

The meeting, when it takes place, will be the tenth between President Roosevelt and Mr. Churchill during the war.

The President also announced that a general understanding had been reached between Russia, Britain, and the United States regarding the occupation of Germany.

This understanding was arrived at regardless of how or at what date Germany capitulated.

The three Powers had entered into discussions and everything was proceeding satisfactorily.

A general understanding on details had not yet been reached. These included the sections of Germany to be occupied.

The President added that it would be just as easy to reach agreement with China regarding the occupation of Japan. He had discussed such an occupation.—*Reuter.*

Clear and Still in Strait

State of Sea.—Rippled.

Weather.—Still and clear after perfect day of sunshine. Maximum temperature 77 deg., 61 deg. at 10.30 p.m.; visibility good.

Barometer.—Half-point fall.

LATEST

GERMAN SUPER-TANK CAPTURED

Germans retreating from Normandy front left behind a "Royal Tiger," a cross between the Tiger and the Panther tanks. The "Royal Tiger" weighs 65 tons, has 6in. armour, and is 23ft. long. Early yesterday Red Army announced that "Royal Tigers" are being used on East Prussia front.

A2

KEITEL QUITS HELSINKI

Stockholm, Friday.—Field-Marshal Keitel, who has been conferring with Marshal Mannerheim in Helsinki, left the Finnish capital this afternoon.—Reuter.

JAP BASES HIT

Pearl Harbour, Friday.—Pressing the air attrition campaign against Jap bases north of American-held Guam, Tinian, and Saipan, Liberators have hit Iwo Jima, in the Bonins, Admiral Chester Nimitz reported to-night. Other planes raided Japanese positions in the Mariana and Caroline groups.—A.P.

B2

NEW HUNT FOR LINDEMANN

£40,000 Reward

The Germans yesterday announced a £40,000 reward for the capture of the "deserter Fritz Lindemann, lately resident in Hamburg, who participated in preparation for the attempt on Hitler's life."

This Lindemann may be the "General of Artillery Lindemann," earlier reported to have been involved in the plot, and to have deserted to the Russians

The Germans also report the arrest—with confiscation of his estates—of Baron Kraft von Palobini, on a charge of having sheltered Goerdeler, the former Mayor of Leipzig, for whom a £50,000 reward has been offered.

SATURDAY, AUGUST 19, 1944

BLACK OUT 9.45 to 6.22 | Moon Sets 9.51 p.m. Rises 8.14 a.m. | Full Moon Sept. 2 | Radio Page 7

LATE NIGHT

THE STAR

No. 17,523 ONE PENNY

HUGE BLITZ AS GERMANS FLEE

3,800 Vehicles Wrecked: Battle Now In The Last Stages

THE BATTLE OF NORMANDY HAS NOW DEFINITELY REACHED THE LAST STAGES, AND WHAT REMAINS IS PURSUIT, ANNIHILATION, AND BEATING-UP OF THE ENEMY, WROTE A "STAR" REPORTER AT SUPREME ALLIED HEADQUARTERS THIS AFTERNOON.

It is clear that there is a complete disorganisation of German elements trying to get away between the immediate battle area and the River Seine. This disorganisation is being intensified by Allied warplanes, which are waging an all-out blitz on the enemy.

In the biggest road blitz of the war our airmen destroyed 3,800 of Von Kluge's urgently needed motor lorries. They also smashed 720 railway cars, 47 oil tank cars, 38 locomotives, 71 planes—51 of them on the ground—and ten tanks actually engaged in attacks. At least 100 barges were sunk.

There is a great degree of confusion in the pocket, now roughly about 100 square miles in area.

We can now say that the German retreat is not a co-ordinated retirement from one prepared position to another, but an "each man for himself" scramble.

So far as the American forces under General Patton are concerned, it is known that from Dreux, Chartres, and Orleans armoured reconnaissance patrols have fannexd out in various directions. Often these patrols have afterwards been withdrawn. It is officially stated that to avoid giving useful information to the enemy, no reports giving the names of places reached or the location of forward elements in this area will be conrmed for the time being.

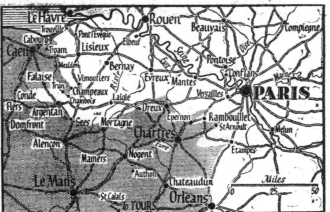

A senior officer at British headquarters in the field this afternoon described the plight of Kluge's army "as the greatest muddle ever, with thousands of Germans struggling chaotically to escape eastward, says A.P.

"We have killed a frightful lot of Huns. The enemy is in bad shape," he added.

Elements of eighteen German divisions were captured yesterday, and although the number of prisoners taken on this front dropped appreciably, the officer said that the enemy were suffering terrific losses in killed and wounded.

"As the situation now stands I do not think he can stop at the Seine," he said. "He must go flat out to a narrower front.

"In my opinion the business of delaying us on small rivers is finished. There will be one big jump back to the Seine, and I cannot see the Boche holding us there."

Only 400 enemy troops were checked through the forward prisoner cages on General Dempsey's front, but British gunners, sitting on high ground south of Falaise had a field day, shooting up German columns frantically attempting to run the gauntlet in the Ronai sector between Falaise and Argentan.

The Allied air forces flew 5,000 offensive sorties during the day. The Luftwaffe, getting sensitive about the approaches to the Fatherland, flew 300 sorties in the area between Paris and the German frontier.

Today's communique from Gen. Eisenhower is on the Back Page.

RIVIERA BRIDGEHEAD DOUBLED

CLOSING IN ON TOULON

Drive For Marseilles

OUR South of France bridgehead is now more than 1,000 square miles, today's Mediterranean Allied communique announced. This means that it has doubled in size in 36 hours.

Allied troops are within six miles of Toulon, the communique added. They have occupied Sollies Pont (six miles from the outskirts of the town on the road to Brignoles), La Roquebrussane (28 miles from Marseilles), Saint Gareoult, Brignoles, Vins and Salernes (30 miles inland on the road to Aix en Provence).

French troops have overcome the last enemy resistance in the Cap Benat area.

A force of German motor torpedo boats atempted to attack ships landing troops on Thursday night, the Navy announced.

Allied destroyers opened fire on the would-be attackers, sinking four of them and repulsing the others. Some survivors were rescued.

It was officially stated at H.Q. today, Reuter's correspondent cables, that strong opposition is being encountered in the approach to Toulon.

The advance, which is unopposed in some sectors, has been relatively small on this left coastal sector west of Bormes.

American spearheads have penetrated well into high ground west of La Roquebrussane, where a broad encircling drive has now headed in the direction of Marseilles along the main highways.

Forces of the FFI are fighting in the streets of Marseilles as well as in the suburbs, said Algiers radio today, quoting dispatches from inside France.

It stated that the Americans, coming from the Hyeres region, were about $4\frac{1}{2}$ miles north-east of Toulon, advancing along the coastal road.

Fighting in the suburbs of

CONTINUED ON BACK PAGE, Col. Three

MAQUIS STRIKE NORTH

THE great "battle behind the battlefront" continued in France today, with the Maquis striking at the Germans in 16 Departments.

One Department—Haute Savoie—is almost completely in their hands, says BUP. Annecy, the capital, is under siege.

Two railway towns near Bayonne have been liberated, and the German garrison in Bayonne is surrounded.

According to reports reaching Madrid, Maquis, 90 miles south-west of Chateauroux, are rushing up through the Limoges area to link with the Americans in the north in a great bid to cut France in two.

Junction of the two forces would cut off the south-western Atlantic coastline of France and the Franco-Spanish frontier, trapping the Germans still left in those regions.

Blowing Up On Spanish Frontier

The Germans today blew up dumps at the Pyrenean frontier post of Cerbere, and then evacuated it, said a Reuter cable from Barcelona.

Cerbere (2,000 inhabitants) is the last French town on the west coast of the Mediterranean. It is 25 miles south-east of Perpignon, on the Franco-Spanish border.

6ft. 9in. Bridegroom

The tallest member of the Metropolitan Police, Sub-Insp. Sidney Ireland, who has served in the special constabulary 18 years, was married today at Emanuel Church, Forest Gate, to Miss Grace Holmes, of Forest Gate.

Mr. Ireland, the youngest of three brothers all over six feet, is 6ft. $9\frac{1}{2}$in. tall.

£600 Clothes Stolen

Thieves broke into the premises of Mr. Albert Haffner, of Kingsbury-parade, Kingsbury, and stole coats, dresses, slacks and skirts worth £600.

New Plane At Ceylon

The latest type of aircraft to arrive in Ceylon is the Vickers Warwick, used mainly for air-sea rescue work, says Reuter.

Taking The Air

Wife at Tottenham: Since beer has become short my husband wants to live in a brewery town where he says he would at least get the scent of the brewing.

"FIGHTING ON SEINE"

German communique said: "Our security troops are fighting on the Seine at Mantes and Vernon with the foremost American reconnaissance troops."

10,000 Moved From London Hospitals

Ministry of Health statement this afternoon reveals 10,000 patients have been moved from London hospitals to safer areas by special ambulance trains.

1,000-PLANE RAIDS

Attack On Nazi Oil Plants Goes On

ALLIED bombers and fighters crossed the Channel in force today, after a night in which more than 1,000 aircraft of RAF Bomber Command were sent out with Bremen and the synthetic oil plant at Sterkrade-Holten as the main objectives.

Mosquitos attacked Berlin. Cologne and other objectives in North-West Germany were also bombed and mines were laid in enemy waters. From these operations four of our aircraft are missing.

It was announced today that yesterday afternoon and evening Lancasters and Halifaxes attacked a long-range weapon supply depot at L'Isle Adam, north of Paris, and several flying-bomb launching sites in northern France. Four planes are missing.

People on the South Coast heard heavy explosions at intervals during the night, and just before and after daybreak.

One report says that these may have been caused by demolition or the blowing up of ammunition dumps.

FLY-BOMBS DESTROYED

For a short time during the night flying-bombs came over the Southern Counties, including the London area, and damage and casualties were caused.

A siren sounded in the London area in daylight today.

One bomb fell near an isolation hospital and caused slight damage to the doctors' quarters and offices. The hospital itself was not affected and no one was hurt.

RAF fighters and A.A. gunners had a good "bag."

Expect Fireworks

One of Sweden's biggest firework firms is receiving many orders for firework-portraits of Marshal Stalin, Mr. Churchill, and Mr. Roosevelt, says the Stockholm "Tidningen," quoted by BUP.

"Missing" Son At The Door

The last person Mrs. Ellis, of Patteson-road, Norwich, expected to see when she answered a knock at the door was her son Thomas. He had been reported missing in Normandy some weeks ago. He explained that he had been captured, made his escape, and had been flown home before he could write.

PARIS RADIO FREED?

THERE was almost a complete "blackout" on the French radio system today.

According to a number of listeners in London the Paris station was making no broadcasts.

One observer, however, reported that the Fighting French call sign was heard from this station shortly before 7 a.m. Immediately after the eight-note call sign, which is given before every Fighting French broadcast to the partisans, had been heard, the radio went silent again.

Heat Haze

Straits today: No wind; sea calm; heat haze over the water.

Daily Mail
NO. 15,070 ONE PENNY ** FOR KING AND EMPIRE MONDAY, AUGUST 21, 1944

LATE WAR NEWS

ALLIED ARMOUR RACING TO ENCIRCLE PARIS

In Versailles and Fontainebleau: Spearheads Cross the Seine

ALL yesterday the Allied armies in France exploited the great Normandy victory at a furious pace. American tanks on the Seine both north and south of Paris brought the famous names of Versailles and Fontainebleau into the news as they began to throw out encircling arms to embrace Paris.

Patrols were reported to have reached both these former playgrounds of kings, while other advanced units pushed on to Corbeil, ten miles south of Paris; to the area of Melun, on the Seine, 21 miles south-east of the capital, and 20 miles beyond Orleans in the direction of Montargis.

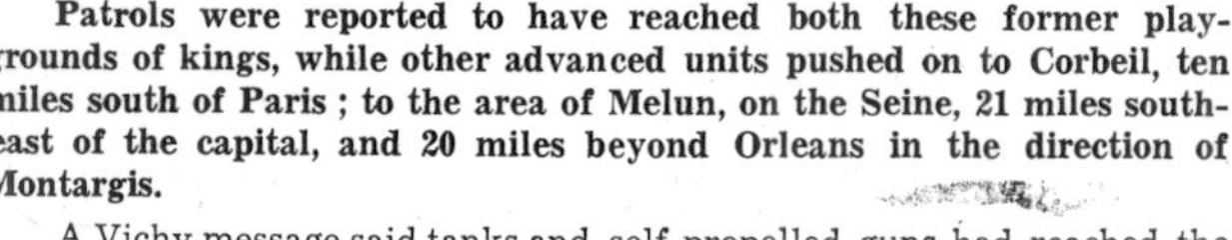

A Vichy message said tanks and self-propelled guns had reached the hills of St. Cloud and Meudon, directly overlooking Paris from the west, but were refraining from entering the capital so that the Germans would have no pretext for shelling it.

The German High Command confirmed an earlier Berlin report that Allied troops had crossed the Seine north of Paris, and announced that they had been reinforced and were fighting to widen their bridgehead.

Away to the west the British Second Army and Canadian First Army were cutting to pieces what remains of the Falaise pocket and threatening to overtake and overwhelm the retreat of the German divisions between Argentan and the Channel.

The Allied front now runs from the Channel coast near the mouth of the River Dives to the area of Argentan. It then swings eastwards to the Seine at Mantes.

18 DIVISIONS

From Mantes it runs in a big semicircle to Menun. Such has been the German defeat that the Americans have met only scattered resistance all along this semicircle.

Well behind the western half of the front lies the Falaise pocket, and the best part of 18 German divisions have been and are being destroyed there.

By last night the pocket had been reduced to a box barely three miles square south of Trun. In this tiny space, so crowded together that they are almost shoulder to shoulder, there are 40,000 men, it is estimated at British H.Q.

They are the remnants of the fighting troops of 14 divisions, and elements of four other divisions, who were originally trapped by the American and Canadian pincers.

The pincers finally closed on Saturday afternoon, and by yesterday morning the trap was sealed by a great mass of men and material.

The Germans made one last attempt to break out to the east. They collected about 70 tanks and 1,000 vehicles and struck across the Trun-Chambois road.

Massed artillery fire was brought down on the attacking force. Fighter-bombers were called in. And the attack was stopped dead.

The battle of the pocket has become only a major mopping-up operation, and one battlefield message predicted last night that it would be over within 24 hours.

First estimates are that it has cost the Germans 500 tanks. This represents the strength of three and a half panzer divisions out of a total of seven originally in the pocket. Final panzer losses may be between 700 and 1,000.

Both the Canadian First Army and the British Second Army have swung their main weight eastwards in pursuit of the remaining divisions of the German Seventh Army.

These divisions are fleeing through the woods in a desperate effort to escape over the Seine.

INVASION BARGES

"Between 12 and 20 crossings have been organised to speed their escape over the river. The crossings consist of pontoons and every kind of craft, including big barges each holding 500 men which the Germans originally built for the invasion of Britain.

As they pour pell-mell towards the Seine and over it the Germans are constantly threatened by the American northward thrust along the river bank.

British and Canadian troops pressing hard on their heels from the west have advanced rapidly in the past 24 hours.

On the Channel coast British troops driving east towards Le Havre captured Merville and Franceville, stormed into the streets of Cabourg, and threatened Houlgate from the south.

Farther south British and Canadians reached Livarot, about 15 miles east of Falaise, taking 2,900 prisoners.

Canadian troops advanced all along the line between Mezidon and Vimoutiers.

South again troops of the British Second Army advanced to Gace, about eight and a half miles east of Chambois on the main road from Alençon to Rouen.

One of the most important towns in the path of our advance is Lisieux. Last night leading troops were only four miles away.

So far the only news of the crossing of the Seine has come from German sources.

A German News Agency account of this achievement said:

"After reaching the Middle Seine between Vernon and Mantes the Allies made a first attempt to establish a bridgehead on the eastern bank of the river.

"This attempt having failed, the Allies then landed parachute and airborne troops east of the Seine, and Allied tanks subsequently crossed the river under the protection of these troops.

Then last night came the German High Command statement that fresh Allied forces had been brought up from the Dreux area to widen the crossing.

Messages from Daily Mail correspondents, Reuter, B.U.P., and A.P.

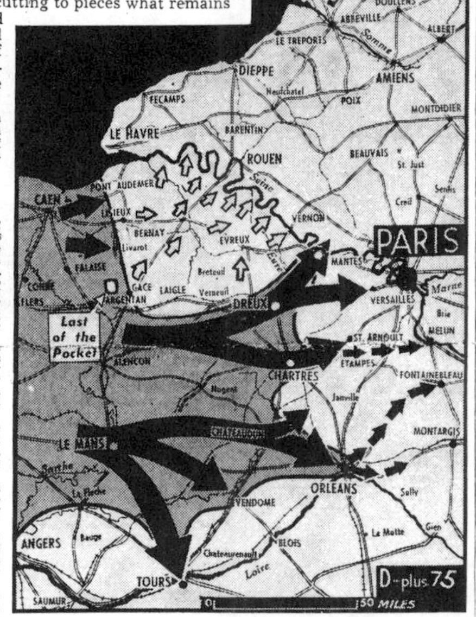

THE southern end of the flying-bomb coast comes into the battle map (above) for the first time with the reported Allied crossing of the Seine. Right: The narrowing gap between the two invasion forces—a gap already largely controlled by the F.F.I. Below: French tanks, by reaching Aix, have by-passed Toulon and Marseilles.

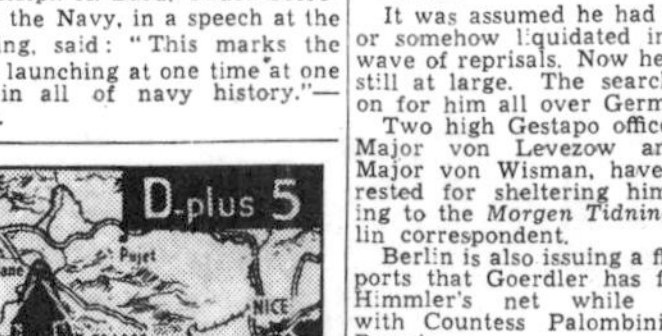

Midnight West Front Digest

THE SEINE: Allied armour is reported by Berlin across the Seine west of Paris. Advance, if continued, will menace the flying-bomb and rocket coast of the Pas de Calais, 80 miles to the north. West of this crossing a disorganised rabble of Germans are trying to escape across the river by ferry, barge, or swimming.

THE POCKET: A 5,000-yard-square compound of death is all that is left in this sector, where most of von Kluge's Seventh Army is being pounded into extinction by massed Allied guns.

PARIS: General Bradley's armoured spearheads are edging round the suburbs of the capital as if engaged in an encircling movement.

THE RIVIERA: French tanks, driving 30 miles in two days, have reached Aix, 16 miles north of Marseilles, which, with Toulon, is thus facing encirclement.

Nazis Fear Landing in Belgium

'Pre-Attack' Blitz

From WALTER FARR
STOCKHOLM, Sunday.

THE Germans now view the bombing of Belgium as "invasion bombing," the German-controlled Scandinavian Telegraph Agency reports.

They believe Allied landings will be made somewhere in this part of Europe in an effort to finish off Germany before winter. They expect these new landings to be timed to coincide with the new Russian thrust through East Prussia, now getting under way.

Highly placed persons who know the German strength in this part of Europe told me to-night that they expect Allied landings either in the Lowlands or in Scandinavia—probably Denmark—within the next few weeks.

They say that the German force in Denmark is now reduced from 200,000 men to 100,000, most of whom are very old or very young, and many of whom are Hungarians, Czechs, Poles and Russians.

One authority told me: "If even a fairly small British force, backed by good naval strength, appeared in the Skagerrak, the Germans in Jutland would scarcely have anything with which to keep the Allies from landing in Denmark and breaking into Germany from the side door."

PAY RISE FOR CD WORKERS

More for Observers

Increases in basic and service pay for War Police, C.D. workers, and the Observer Corps are announced to-day. They date back to June 1.

Civil Defence, N.F.S., and local authority fire guards get a 2s. increase in weekly base rates for men and 1s. 6d. for women. Service pay for basic grade men with three years' service will be 12s. instead of 7s., and 8s. instead of 5s. for women.

Whole-time observers of the Royal Observer Corps are to receive an increase in basic pay of 2s. a week for men and 1s 6d. for women, and also service pay increases which will not exceed 5s. a week for men and 3s. a week for women.

20,000 Casualties Flown Home

Since D-Day aircraft of R.A.F. Transport Command have flown more than 20,000 casualties from the battlefields of France to hospitals in Britain.

As Allied forces strike deeper into France so it will be possible to transport a high percentage of wounded by air.

Oak Leaves for Mannerheim

Marshal Mannerheim of Finland has received a special award from Hitler, Berlin announced yesterday. It was the ill-omened Oak Leaves to the Knight's Insignia of the Iron Cross.

Paris Rises Against the Germans

THIRD ARMY, Sunday.

THE people of Paris are rising against the Nazis.

The first definite news about what is happening inside the capital was given by a Frenchman to our advance reconnaissance units outside Versailles to-day.

He had left Paris only a few hours previously.

Dozens of armed clashes are taking place between French students and the Germans, he said.

He appealed to the Americans to help the French, who are rising throughout the city. The Germans are using machine-guns on the demonstrators.—*B.U.P.*

FRENCH RADIO RIDDLE

Network 'Black-out'

An almost complete silence descended on the French radio yesterday. Radio Paris has been off the air for the past four days, except for intermittent broadcasts and announcements in German.

Throughout yesterday the Vichy network failed to transmit on any of the medium-wave bands, but it is believed that some short-wave stations were transmitting in code.

It is thought possible that the Germans and their Vichy assistants have left Paris, and that the capital's electric supply has been cut off.

The Maquis may be in control of Vichy stations, or they may have cut electricity supplies.

Strait Clouds

State of Sea.—Moderate.

Weather.—Warm; considerable clouds, with sunny periods after slight rain in the morning. Maximum temperature, 76 deg.; 58 deg. at 10.30 p.m. Visibility good. Wind: W.S.W., light.

Barometer.—Going up again.

CLIFFORD, FROM THE 'POCKET,' CABLED:

This is Our Revenge for Europe

Death of an Army

From ALEXANDER CLIFFORD
ARGENTAN ROAD, Sunday.

I DROVE slap through the middle of the German pocket to-day with the Germans still in it, and I saw scenes of destruction which beggar all description.

This is the pay-off of the battle—not cages full of prisoners but this huge and terrible annihilation of an army from the air.

The pocket was finally hermetically sealed yesterday evening. A firm junction was welded together by Allied forces which met near Trun, which is south-east from Falaise and north-east from Argentan, and since then no Germans have battled their way through.

East and north-east of there the rest of the Seventh Army is in rout. Its remnants are dragging themselves in chaos to the Seine. But west of this junction there is still the frayed and tattered pocket.

Still a Front

It was already breaking up when I drove down from Falaise this morning. Columns of prisoners, in 80's and 100's, were emerging out of the side roads and making their way north.

There was no sound of guns, but there was that atmosphere of excitement, almost of holiday, which marks the final achievement of a victory.

We came, however, to a village where there was still a front line.

On one side of the road was a 17-pounder gun and on the other a Bren gun. The battalion commander was just putting up a notice saying "Enemy ahead."

The road stretched down to a valley and then up the other side, dead straight for three miles ahead, and this was still not conquered. It was a gap right in the middle of the pocket which still extended to right and left of it.

The pocket had, in fact, become like an hour-glass — two little pockets, connected by a corridor. The troops were calling the western half "the trap" and the eastern half "the killing area," and the Germans were being funnelled across from "the trap" into "the killing area."

Given Up

Now and again you could see them scuttle across on the road below. Sometimes the Bren gun would splutter at them, but they were across too quick.

Usually they went from west to east. But some this morning came back again in the other direction—sniping blindly from "the killing area."

A British motor-cyclist — Corporal Harold Wilby, who lived in Southampton until he was blitzed out of it—tore past the notice and down into the gap. We shouted to him, but his crash-helmet made him deaf. So we gave him up for lost.

But half an hour later he came back with a wonderful tale. He had gone on until a roadful of burning German tanks had made him suspicious.

So he turned into a farmhouse, where the French people welcomed him with kisses and wine.

They showed him the bed of a German officer who had lived there

BACK PAGE—Col. TWO

South: Racing for Rhone

TANKS REACH AIX, 40 MILES TO GO NOW

THE Riviera Army is sweeping inland at sensational speed. By last night its main spearhead of French tanks, with U.S. infantry support, had swept forward to the outskirts of Aix-en-Provence, little more than 40 miles from Avignon, gateway to the Rhone Valley.

This great thrust to the Rhone Valley has engulfed the towns of Peyrolles, Rians, Borjols, and St. Maximin, and has completely by-passed the great ports of Toulon and Marseilles—the Allies are actually north of Marseilles at points 16 miles or more inland.

The garrisons of these bases have now to decide whether to get out while a road to the west is still open or to stay and be besieged.

If they withdraw they will have to run the gauntlet of Allied bombing—and of the Maquis, ready everywhere to pounce on the enemy.

The Maquis have already struck in the bend of the River Durance—crossed by the French and Americans in their drive west—and have surrounded the German garrison of Pertuis.

Below the great Allied "fist" driving for Avignon, the troops striking for Toulon are engaged in fierce fighting.

Toulon Battle

The garrison of the port was heavily bombarded from sea and air yesterday, and the assault was followed up by a French land attack which is reported to have taken the Allies to Hyères, nine miles from the port itself.

To the north-east of Toulon American troops are now more than 50 miles inland, and have established contact with powerful forces of the Maquis deep in the mountains.

The last known positions of these forces was at Castellane, 25 miles north of Draguignan, and La Bastide.

This advance has cut Cannes main highway to the north-west. A closer threat to Cannes comes nearer the coast, where the Allies are closing in on Grasse.

The Cannes garrison is using heavy guns to try to hold off the Allies. The guns are mounted on islands south of the resort.

Prisoners are pouring into the Allied cages; more than 12,000 had been counted up to Saturday.

The beachhead, now 2,000 square miles in extent, was yesterday visited by Generals Devers, Eaker and Cannon.

General Didn't Know

By LARRY NEWMAN
SEVENTH ARMY, Sunday.

MAJOR-GENERAL Lucien K. Truscott, commanding the Sixth Corps, rode through a hail of bullets this afternoon and didn't know it.

It happened when Maquis and German snipers met, and I and two companions were with the Maquis when the firing started. We leaped

BACK PAGE—Col. FIVE

Petain

MARSHAL PETAIN is believed to be at the Pavillon de Sevigné, Vichy, where he called together his civil and military advisers and told them he was resolved to await the arrival of those "who would be called on to represent the new France."

"Maquis Win Battle with Gestapo."—BACK Page.

DE GAULLE LANDS IN FRANCE

Return to Paris

General de Gaulle has landed at Cherbourg, according to a radio report from Normandy late last night. He was met by Gen. Köenig, Gen. Juin, and Admiral d'Argenlieu.

From PAUL BEWSHER
ROME, Sunday.

MEMBERS of the French Provisional Government are ready to leave Algiers at short notice.

Within a comparatively short while a French Government will be established on French soil to administer the great areas recently liberated until elections can be held.

"Things have happened so quickly that the original plan of moving the French Provisional Government into Southern France as a preliminary step will almost certainly be abandoned," I was told to-day by an official who had just been recalled to Algiers from Rome.

It is expected that General de Gaulle will move his Government direct to Paris as soon as possible after the capital has been freed.

It is possible that there may be changes in the Government as leading French political figures become available to serve their country again, owing to the liberation of their homes.

The administrative officer made it clear that General Cochet, appointed by the French as Military Delegate in the Southern Zone, has had complete authority over French matters in all territory liberated during the past week.

11 KILLED BY FLY-BOMBS

Block of Flats Hit

Six people were killed and several injured when a block of flats in Southern England was hit by a flying bomb in daylight yesterday.

In a residential area elsewhere five people, including two Canadian soldiers, were killed.

The bombs were sent over at intervals. Many were destroyed by fighters, A.A. gunners and balloons.

Story on Page THREE.

HIMMLER MEN DESERT TO REBEL PARTY

Daily Mail Special Correspondent
STOCKHOLM, Sunday.

SUBSTANTIAL elements of the Waffen S.S. have deserted Himmler and are now hiding, having joined the underground anti-Hitler organisation headed by the ex-Mayor of Leipzig, Karl Goerdler, and General Fritz Lindemann.

The leader of the rebel S.S. men is Obergruppenführer Nebe, who was said to have "disappeared" immediately after the unsuccessful attempt on Hitler's life on July 20.

Long articles were published describing Nebe, and his photograph has been widely circulated by the German Press. But no mention was then made that he was "wanted."

It was assumed he had been shot or somehow liquidated in the first wave of reprisals. Now he is clearly still at large. The search is going on for him all over Germany.

Two high Gestapo officers, Police Major von Levezow and Police Major von Wisman, have been arrested for sheltering him, according to the *Morgen Tidningen*'s Berlin correspondent.

Berlin is also issuing a flood of reports that Goerdler has fallen into Himmler's net while sheltering with Countess Palombini in West Prussia

No pictures of him under arrest are available, nearly two days after his alleged seizure, and he has not yet been brought before the "People's Court."

All the evidence from Germany to-night indicates that the "shadow Chancellor" Goerdler, of whom the Nazi hierarchy is terrified, is still at large but in the situation whence his friends find it very difficult to extricate him.

Everything known here indicates that we are on the eve of a supreme internal crisis in the Nazi régime.

Carrier, Cruisers in One Launch

PHILADELPHIA, Sunday. — The 27,000-ton aircraft carrier Antietam and two powerful 13,000-ton cruisers were launched here to-day.

Mr. Ralph A. Bard, Under-Secretary of the Navy, in a speech at the launching, said: "This marks the largest launching at one time at one place in all of navy history."—*Reuter.*

LATEST

EISENHOWER, DE GAULLE MEET

Learned early this morning that General de Gaulle met General Eisenhower in France yesterday.

ALLIED FORCES ON SEINE IN STRENGTH

Near Versailles, Sunday.—Allied forces have reached the Seine in strength in the area of Mantes to form a solid wall moving on Paris.—A.P.

A

30,000 PARISIANS WAIT TO STRIKE

Algiers radio said last night that 30,000 Patriots in Paris were waiting for the Allied signal to strike. "The last German officials and Vichy collaborators are now packing their bags," said the radio.—Reuter.

NAZI DIPLOMATS 'REPRIEVED'

Ankara, Sunday.—German diplomats in Turkey who were scheduled to leave Ankara to-night on their return to Berlin have received permission to remain in the Turkish capital until next Saturday.—Exchange.

B
2

70,000 IN NAZI DEATH CAMP

Warsaw Fire Terror

The German terror in Warsaw is approaching its climax.

Reports from Warsaw reaching the Polish Telegraph Agency by radio yesterday state that a huge concentration camp has been formed at Pruszkow, where 70,000 men, women, and children have been interned. No food is given to the internees, who are dying in thousands.

The south-western part of the town is in flames. The Germans are systematically setting house after house, street after street, on fire.

Daily Mail
NO. 15,072 ONE PENNY ** FOR KING AND EMPIRE WEDNESDAY, AUGUST 23, 1944
LATE WAR NEWS

GERMANS FACE COMPLETE ROUT ON SEINE

Patton's Tanks Past Sens, in Great Drive to East

GREAT news came in from the battlefronts of France again last night. The German retreat to the Lower Seine was reported to have turned into a rout, with British and Canadian troops so closely in pursuit that our air forces are unable to operate.

And on the Allied right wing General Patton's tanks have made another great bound to beyond Sens, on the Seine 60 miles south-east of Paris.

This sensational thrust has carried the American Third Army nearly two-thirds of the way across France to the German frontier. They are on the direct road through Troyes and Nancy to Alsace-Lorraine.

On the Channel coast the left wing of the Canadian First Army is also advancing at amazing speed. Yesterday it pushed nine miles from Houlgate to Deauville and was last night reported to be only a few miles from the Seine Estuary.

WHOLE FRONT ON MOVE

Inland, British troops fought their way into Lisieux. Farther south still another column pushed six miles south-east of Gacé. The whole British front moved forward more than five miles into an area full of German dead and wrecked equipment.

At the same time, the Americans punched hard at the German southern flank. They have broadened their attack and are now driving northward in the region west of Drieux, as well as along the Seine.

The full weight of three armies has been turned against the new German pocket taking shape against the Seine. Vast forces released from containing the pocket south of Falaise are wheeling into line for the advance to the Seine and beyond.

West of Paris the Americans stand on an arc ten to 20 miles from the city. They have advanced beyond Rambouillet and broadened their bridgehead over the Seine in the Mantes-Gassicourt area.

A communiqué from General Koenig's headquarters announced that French forces fighting inside the capital were using light artillery.

They attacked German forces in the Place de la République and on the Boulevard des Bonnes-Nouvelles. There were losses on both sides.

Announcing the end of the Battle of the Pocket a spokesman of the British Second Army said: "The pocket is definitely liquidated and the general advance is continuing. We are advancing without much resistance."

The last flicker of life and resistance in the pocket was blown out yesterday by massed guns.

THE DISASTER

The total sum of the German disaster has still to be told, but this much was known last night:

Since D-Day the enemy have lost 300,000 men in dead, wounded, and prisoners—a figure comparable with Stalingrad and Tunisia.

They have lost 700 tanks destroyed and another 500 damaged—the equivalent of six full panzer divisions.

On Monday alone, when the last enemy concentrations were rapidly being mopped up, the Second Army took 3,800 prisoners and the Canadians 2,800.

Vast quantities of stores and equipment remain to be counted.

In a statement last night the German High Command announced that S.S. Senior Group Leader General of the Waffen S.S. Hausser, Commander-in-Chief of the German Seventh Army, was in personal command of the attempt to break out of the pocket.

These front-line dispatches filled in the background of the mighty new surge forward which has just begun:

Charles Lynch, Reuter's special correspondent with the Canadian Army, cabled:

Belgian troops, in a sudden dash along the coast, have reached Deauville while to the south British troops have fought their way into Lisieux.

The Belgians are fighting under the Canadian Army Command and

BACK PAGE—Col FOUR

CLIFFORD SEES THE GREAT PURSUIT

Villages are Full of Beaten Men

Tanks, Guns, Cars in One Big Jam

From ALEXANDER CLIFFORD
IN PURSUIT OF THE GERMANS, Tuesday.

THE chase is on now.

The sun returned to a sparkling, rain-washed world to-day. And through it in rising excitement our pursuit columns dug into the enemy rearguards.

There are a dozen thrusts going east simultaneously. But no list of the villages captured can convey the feel of the thing—the extraordinary exhilaration of success tempered with awestruck horror at some of the things we see.

You want a picture of it such as I found in a little village east of Argentan today. It was a place where some of this muddled fleeing German Seventh Army had got itself caught.

The scene was so stupendous that the mind hardly accepted it. The first thing you noticed were the helmets. The ditches and the sides of the road were black with German helmets.

Their smooth, round, black shapes stretched all through the village and overflowed into the front gardens. It looked as though someone had laid a trail of gigantic caviar through the place.

★

THE main street of the village—it was called St. Lambert—was choked with tanks. Every type the Germans have ever used was represented. They had lurched drunkenly to rest all over the place as the shells had hit them.

A blackened thing you could not bear to look at showed that the crew had not escaped from one Mark IV.

The streets and lanes and alleyways and barns were jammed with trucks and guns and wagons. Some were destroyed, but some were standing as their crews had fled from them. They had not even been looted yet.

At first it looked like another of those columns which the air forces have been so relentlessly attacking. It was bigger than anything I had ever seen before. But it didn't look different in quality.

The difference appeared when you looked beyond the village into the fields. There you got the full, tremendous impact of the sort of thing that is happening in Western France.

And you got that mad inconsequential feeling that I last remember on Cap Bon—when the enemy army has gone completely to pieces and you are prepared to accept anything as natural.

★

THE fields round this village were crammed to bursting-point, with what looked like the arms and equipment and vehicles of a division. The stuff was simply standing about there. And wandering among it all were Germans.

But they were so obviously not on the warpath. They clearly did not know what to do. I hadn't a moment's hesitation in standing on a wall and hailing them. And they obediently came to parley.

As a matter of fact most of them were Russians and Poles. The Germans had known what to do with themselves—surrender. Some 3,600 had already surrendered to one Canadian company in the village. But a few odd foreigners had been forgotten and were hanging around waiting to be told what to do.

You have to analyse what had happened before you could get the significance of the scene. And these prisoners filled in the details.

The German units who had reached these fields believed they were out of the pocket. They had parked just for the moment in the fields while their tanks scouted ahead for them.

Then the tanks had been shot to pieces in the villages and our artillery came down on the fields.

This whole series of fields was bordered by deep-lying streams fringed with willows, and there were only two possible exits. As the shelling started the vehicles had

BACK PAGE—Col. FIVE

Strait Sunny

State of Sea.—Calm.

Weather.—Sun broke through after morning drizzle and fog, and has continued clear except for few high clouds. Maximum temperature, 77 deg., 62 deg. at 10.30 p.m. Visibility restricted by haze. Wind, N., freshening.

Barometer.—Still rising.

EAST DRIVE: A column of General Patton's tanks whose movements had been secret since the capture of Orleans were last night reported past Sens, 60 miles S.E. of Paris and 170 miles from the German border.

PARIS: All news of General Patton's spearheads which have crossed the Seine west of the capital is still withheld. But his tanks were reported to be threatening Beauvais, big rail junction and fly-bomb store. In the streets of Paris, the F.F.I., with grenades, rifles, and light artillery, are attacking the German garrison.

SEINE AREA: The big crush-in on the remnants of the German Seventh Army is under way. On the west we have reached Deauville, 22 miles from the Seine mouth. Lisieux, farther south, is falling. United States troops west of Dreux have widened their attack and are pressing hard. The Falaise "pocket" has been wiped out.

RIVIERA: Toulon's German garrison are making a last stand near the waterfront. Marseilles is almost isolated. Hyères, Blue Coast holiday resort, has been entered. Allied troops stand 35 miles from the Rhone Valley.

City After City Falls to Maquis Armies

From HAROLD CARDOZO
MADRID, Tuesday.

FRENCH Forces of the Interior, the phantom army that became a real and mighty force in a day, are in full control of almost half of France. The Germans' depleted forces are either penned into cities or roaming the countryside.

Throughout South and South-West France thousands of Germans are wandering about the country in hopeless bands, with the only remaining idea of avoiding F.F.I. formations and reaching a neutral frontier.

Throughout all this area German garrisons have surrendered.

It is possible to-night to say that German military rule has collapsed in all France south of the Loire.

General Koenig, Chief of the F.F.I., to-day issued his first communiqué since his new appointment as Militray Governor of Paris.

Limoges is encircled and road blocks have been established at Tarbes, where the militia surrendered with their arms.

Battle for Belfort

Savage fighting with the Germans is taking place for possession of Belfort, the fortress town near the German frontier, where members of the Vichy Ministry have taken refuge. Belfort controls a gap through mountainous regions leading to the Rhine and Germany.

Fourteen freed departments were listed in the communiqué, and it was added: "In all these the last traces of enemy resistance are being cleared up."

Areas of France now completely under the control of the Maquis are on the Swiss border and on the Spanish border.

A force of 8,000 Frenchmen stormed and captured Fort Ecluse, in the Savoy, and Bellegarde, on the Rhone near Lake Geneva.

The Germans admitted to-night that Vichy and Grenoble are also in the hands of the Maquis.

On the French-Spanish border, following up the occupation of Hendaye, a Maquis force pushed along the coast and liberated Bayonne, the large town near Biarritz. No doubt the British naval bombardment of the town's fortifications at the week-end was in support of this operation.

Somerville Gets G C B

In recognition of service as C.-in-C., Eastern Fleet, Admiral Sir James F. Somerville has been awarded the G.C.B., states last night's *London Gazette*.

LEADS GUARDS IN FRANCE

The Taxi General

Major-General Allan Adair, D.S.C., M.C., the officer who took a taxi to the front line in Belgium in 1940 is in command of the Guards Armoured Division in Normandy, it was announced last night.

He was Chief Instructor at Sandhurst, with the rank of Lieut.-Colonel, when he "wangled" his way out of a job in England and taxied to the fighting zone across the Channel, where he took over command of his old battalion.

Now aged 47, Major-General Adair took over command of the Guards Armoured Division in September 1942.

Churchill May See the Pope

ROME, Tuesday — Mr. Churchill has arrived in Rome after his visit to Eighth Army troops.

It is thought that he might meet the Pope, Crown Prince Umberto, Badoglio, and Bonomi, the Italian Premier.

Before leaving the battle areas he saw Florence.—*B.U.P.*

All German Hopes on V2 Sites

Our Answer to Robots Nearer

Britain's answer to the flying bomb becomes more effective every day.

COLIN BEDNALL — who tells, in Page 3, the story of new developments—writes that General Sir F. Pile, the Ack-Ack chief, has taken his staff to the south coast to watch the successes of the gunners.

He has the help of outstanding American as well as British brains, and experts now crowd the battle area.

From JOHN HALL
AT U.S. ADVANCED H.Q., Tuesday.

HITLER is withdrawing troops from his precious "rocket coast."

He has been forced to pull out men from the Pas de Calais area to meet the new Allied threats which have developed with lightning speed from the closing of the Falaise trap.

The American Third Army already endangers the huge robot supply depots which Hitler is known to have assembled near the French capital.

They Admit It

I have been long convinced from conversations with German prisoners of all type, particularly during the last two weeks, that the rocket sites mean infinitely more to Hitler than the rest of France, including Paris.

The truth is that the morale in the German Army is now largely founded on rocket philosophy—on the dreadful things V 1 is supposed to be doing to London and on the much more terrible devastation promised for V 2.

Hitler has told his troops that if only they will fight on a little longer V 1 and V 2 will bring Britain to her knees.

To the millions of Britons who have never heard a rocket bomb this may sound incredible, but it is the truth. In the past few days I have heard, categorically, that "rocket" hopes alone are keeping the German army fighting.

Significant

German commanders we have captured say frankly they have nothing else to bolster morale. Since the breakthrough of July 25, the Germans in Normandy have been outmanœuvred, outgunned, outfought, whipped. And the German commanders know it.

The significance, therefore, of enemy troop movements from the Pas de Calais is apparent.

Militarily the Germans in France are beaten. The rocket coast is their last propaganda prop.

Footnote.—On the German radio last night "pep" talkers and front reporters told German troops in France and Russia: "We must hold out against the enemy assault; we must try to stop their tanks, never mind where, until the new weapons are ready. Then we shall have the upper hand again."

P-PLANE SITE CAPTURED

In Normandy

Men of a Home Counties regiment in their advance on Lisieux have captured a fly-bomb site, hidden in the grounds of a château.

It had a concrete runway 75 yards in length and nearby was the storage house built of the thickest concrete.

Although it had never been used, it appeared to be completed in every way. It was directed towards London on an almost due northerly bearing.—*Exchange.*

De Gaulle Tours Freed Areas

RENNES, Tuesday.—General de Gaulle, now travelling through France, was in Rennes last night. On the road from devastated Coutances and Avranches people stopped his car time after time and covered it with flowers.

He talked to 10,000 cheering Frenchmen in the driving rain in Rennes.

"Our immediate duty is to carry the war to a victorious end," he said. "But we must rebuild to bring France back to her rightful place among the nations."—*B.U.P.*

TOULON GARRISON BATTLING TO END

South Army Nears the Rhone

35 MILES TO AVIGNON

From Daily Mail Special Correspondent
SOUTHERN FRANCE, Tuesday.

EXCEPT for the desperate efforts of the Germans trapped along the Riviera coastline from Cannes to Marseilles, resistance in Southern France has folded up like an empty sack.

The story of this collapse is told in these words:

To-night Allied spearheads are three miles from Marseilles.

In Toulon they are three-quarters of a mile from the water front. This German base was described as "not yet completely captured."

North of these battles the Allies had advanced beyond Aix-en-Provence to positions which bring them within 35 miles of both Arles and Avignon, key towns controlling the Rhone Valley.

In Marseilles and Toulon fanatical "suicide" units are fighting like cornered rats, but the rest of the Germans in the bridgehead are more concerned with getting out than giving battle.

Now that he has the Huns on the run, General Patch is determined not to give them a moment's breathing space.

"Keep 'em going," is the keynote of his Order of the Day to the Seventh Army, in which he speaks of their "great initial victory."

"The enemy in our area are perplexed and stunned," he says. "Except for his coastal defence forces he is in full retreat. Opportunity for decisive results is in front of us and we must and will move with the utmost speed and effectiveness."

In Toulon the French in the northern and western suburbs are for the moment pinned down by intense artillery fire—the Germans

BACK PAGE—Col. SIX

Madman of St. Malo

MONOCLED, "Mad" Col. von Aulock marches out to ignoble surrender after swearing to Hitler that he would defend St. Malo to "the last drop of blood." The blood shed needlessly was not his—he lived in a comfortable office deep below ground—but that of his men. Then the day after Hitler gave him the Oak Leaves to the Iron Cross he wears so proudly, he gave in. More pictures in BACK Page.

GERMAN SCREEN BROKEN

With U.S. Army, Tuesday.—American columns attacking to west of the Seine cracked through German defensive screen to-day and captured St. André de l'Eure, 15 miles north of Dreux.—Reuter.

GERMANS' NEW APPEAL TO PARIS

Radio Lille broke a 12-hours silence last night to broadcast a German High Command appeal to Parisians to return to work and to maintain public services.

2

'News Too Grave to be Hidden'—Dietmar

GERMAN High Command spokesman Lieut.-General Dietmar went on the air last night to tell his country and the world: "The gravity of our situation cannot be disguised.

"Events in the west have taken a turn which places a burden of heavy anxiety on the German people."

Dietmar did not disguise the High Command's intention of putting the blame for the disaster on the weakness of the Luftwaffe.

"What has happened," he said, "is chiefly due to the tremendous superiority of the enemy in the air.

"There is no doubt that this superiority has been, and is, the principal cause of all our difficulties.

"Under the conditions in which we have to fight on the Western Front, where the enemy's aerial superiority makes our every movement a hard and ticklish business, the difficulty of the task is redoubled.

"The fighting spirit of the German ground troops has proved so good that up to now the enemy High Command has not been able to make a success of the trap which it set for our forces.

'Greater Feats'

"There is, however, no running away from the fact that our men will have to bring off still more extraordinary fighting feats and our Command will have to remain very cold-blooded indeed to tide the German forces over the grave period on which we are now entering.

"Already side by side with the more point-blank close quarters encirclement from the north and south a new and more formidable, far-flung pincers movement is taking palpable shape.

"The most important basis of our resistance remains the steadfast will of the German soldier to go on fighting.

"In the east we know that the worst is not yet over even there. It becomes plainly evident to us that considerable Russian forces have remained quite unaffected by the fighting of the present summer.

"Looking both east and west, we see the threat of what in 1940 we considered to be the fundamental pillars of our military strength.

"Perhaps also in the west we shall be compelled to fall back to a new and more narrowly confined base for our conduct of the war. Let us face this issue without flinching."

Nazi Envoy in Lisbon

From Daily Mail Correspondent

LISBON, Tuesday.—Colonel Eberhard Karl Kaulback, new German military attaché to Lisbon, and his wife arrived in the last aeroplane to leave Berlin. He replaces Colonel Esebeck.

TWO SOVIET ATTACKS, JASSY IS CAPTURED

THE Red Army has launched two new offensives against Rumania, and last night was pouring forward towards the Galatz Gap from the area of Jassy and along the coast from the Lower Dniester.

Offensive No. 1 has advanced 37 miles on a 75-miles front in three days, and has captured the key strong-points of Jassy, Targu-Frumos, and Unghen.

Offensive No. 2, from the Lower Dniester, has advanced 42 miles on an 80-miles front. Both advances outflank the great junction of Kishinev and the defences south of the town. Only 70 miles separates the Lower Dniester assault from the Galatz Gap.

The Germans, who have already lost 25,000 men killed in the new attacks, last night issued the warning that the offensive is likely to become wider and more powerful, and say that the Russians are superior in "men and material" to the defending Germans and Rumanians.

Battle Story and Map: BACK Page.

Daily Mail

LATE WAR NEWS

NO. 15,073 ONE PENNY ** FOR KING AND EMPIRE THURSDAY, AUGUST 24, 1944

RUMANIA ACCEPTS ALLIES' PEACE OFFER

Kluge's Army Massacred Along the Seine

HUNDREDS OF GUNS POUNDING NEW 20-MILE-LONG POCKET

From DOON CAMPBELL

ON THE BRITISH FRONT, Wednesday Night.

ANOTHER great massacre of routed German divisions has begun in the 20-miles-long killing-ground between the rivers Risle and Seine. Hundreds of guns are throwing an enormous weight of fire-power into a box bounded by Neubourg, Breteuil, the Forest of Laigle, and Bernay.

At forward Headquarters to-day I found maps marked "killing ground," with the boundaries drawn in blue pencil. The Americans lining the west bank of the Seine are behind the Germans, and British guns have already started the drumbeat of death.

They face the battered remnants of the German Seventh Army which escaped from the Falaise trap, and thousands of other Germans who crossed the Seine to help their hard-pressed comrades and walked straight into the new trap.

The front is moving at incredible speed. I went to look for a headquarters south of Argentan yesterday and found it had moved to a position more than 20 miles away.

Military police cannot keep up with all the latest locations. We are now driving eastwards so fast that there is much clearing up to be done in the rear areas.

British officers are driving in vehicles still bearing the German camouflage. The feeling of the complete disintegration of the German Army hangs over this fluid front.

We now seem to be in a position to get the enemy wherever we want him, then hammer him to death or submission. The abandoned German material is inferior.

We are now holding a solid and secure line several miles east of Touques and are across the Risle in strength at Laigle.

Thick woods behind the front still harbour Germans, but they are being picked up every hour. There is no fight left in them.

It is expected that the liberation of Paris will shatter German morale on this side of the Seine.

But between us and the river there are many thousands of still resisting enemy troops.

TOWN AFTER TOWN

Those who are resisting are being killed ruthlessly. More than ten German divisions have been destroyed and more are in a too decimated condition to fight again. We have got the Germans on the run.—*Reuter*.

Another Reuter correspondent cabled:

A whole string of towns between the rivers Dives and Touques have been liberated. For many liberation amounts to no more than armoured vehicles and troops racing through the streets where the Germans had been for four years.

A Canadian Army spokesman said: "Everybody is going great guns and the situation is changing every 15 minutes"

A 15-miles advance to Orbec was made by Canadian infantry sweeping across the countryside in lorries.

The Belgian, Dutch, and airborne troops on the coast are being shelled by the heavy coastal guns of Le Havre.

German rearguards tried to hold up the Allied troops at Lisieux until they saw the overwhelming force assaulting, when they collapsed.

PRISONERS ROLL IN

South of Orbec Gen. Dempsey's columns made the most spectacular advance of the day, storming east for more than 17 miles from Gace across the River Risle to capture Laigle

The Germans blew the bridge across the river, but the advance of the British troops was not affected

A senior Staff officer said: "Yesterday was a very bad day for the enemy. They had to retreat in force They tried to hold the river

BACK PAGE—Col. EIGHT

Midnight war digest

PARIS: There is still no full story of the capital's liberation, announced in General Koenig's dramatic communiqué yesterday, which is reproduced in the BACK Page. Allied troops are believed to be pouring into the city on their way northward.

SEINE AREA: The second 'pocket' has taken shape—20 miles long, 14 miles wide—and into it, having herded the wreck of the German Seventh Army, hundreds of Allied guns are pouring a deadly storm of fire. The river bridges are all destroyed, the ferries pounded from the air and the German retreat has become a major rout.

THE SOUTH: U.S. troops who drove 140 miles north from the Riviera beachhead to capture Grenoble have raced on and are 34 miles from Lyons. Far behind them, the Allies are in Marseilles and the net round Toulon is closing. Many more towns have been liberated in South and South-West France by the Maquis forces.

Marseilles Falls to the French

MARSEILLES, second city of France and the country's greatest port, has been captured by French troops. The city fell yesterday almost without a fight after French and American troops had encircled it and cut its escape routes.

Small pockets of resistance are still holding out inside this city of 914,000 people, but the few remaining Germans are unlikely to hold out for long.

Both United States and French troops played their parts in the final success, for when the French broke into the town American troops took a major part in cutting the city's escape routes.

Toulon Battle

In Toulon, now completely isolated, French troops are steadily driving forward against stiff resistance.

General Patch's flying columns were last night reported to be only 34 miles from Lyons, the great industrial city of Southern France, after sweeping through Grenoble in their secret dash north from the Riviera coast

This thrust threatens not only Lyons but also the entire Rhone Valley. It brings the Southern France front to within about 210 miles of the Allied armies in Northern France.

Two days ago the Maquis, who have greatly helped the U.S. drive north, were stated to control most of the Lyons area.

The American race to Grenoble, itself a centre of resistance, met only patchy opposition, although a stiff action was fought at Digne, when a German corps commander, Major-General Hans Schuberth, was captured.

North-west of Marseilles an American column, thrusting along the Durance Valley, reached Lauris, 27 miles from Avignon and the Rhone River.

Another column occupied the town of Salon, 18 miles west of Aix-en-Provence, and 25 miles from the Lower Rhone. Salon is the gateway to the Rhone Valley.

FRENCH SEIZE LYONS AREA

Perpignan Freed

All through yesterday news poured in of the French Forces of the Interior who continued to free vast areas from the Germans.

Most dramatic of these was the announcement from General Koenig's H.Q. that the whole Lyons area was in the hands of the Maquis, for the U.S. column whose occupation of Grenoble was disclosed yesterday, is only 30 miles away to the south

Another town liberated was Perpignan, close to the Spanish border on the Mediterranean coast

Evacuees in Plane Crash Disaster

At least 54 were killed when a Liberator crashed on an infants' school and other buildings in the Lancashire village of Freckleton yesterday.

Children evacuated from London were among the 11 in the infants' school, though most were from local homes. Thirty-five of the infants were killed.

Story in Page THREE.

RAF Go Out Again

Strong formations of the R.A.F. were heard passing out over the east coast last night.

Gen. Hausser Wounded in Seine Trap

Statements put out by Berlin suggest that the German High Command is uncertain about the fate of Colonel-General Hausser, the fanatical Nazi who leads their broken Seventh Army in France.

On Tuesday night the German News Agency announced that he was in personal command of the break-out attack from the Falaise pocket.

Last night the agency said he was in the trap west of the River Dives "with German formations which had been temporarily cut off from the main body, and was wounded in the course of the fighting for the break-through."

These reports suggest that Hausser may fall into Allied hands. He is 63 and was promoted Colonel-General of the S.S. on August 1.

He was made second-in-command to Rommel in France last month, after being in command of the S.S. in Italy, the Balkans, and Russia.

THE RETREAT VICTORIOUS

Berlin Has Alibi

Alibi for the German retreat in France and Russia, put out by German-controlled Brussels radio last night:

Since the Germans have developed an "astonishing series of new weapons," and since these will appear in "great masses very soon," the German General Staff has decided to retreat on all fronts in order to limit losses until the time for their use arrives.

Germany could launch most of these new weapons straight away, but she prefers to wait "until the war has reached the highest climax."

Paris Wins on the Boulevards

Rising Began in 'Good News' Street

THE first blows to liberate Paris were struck by French patriots on Friday, and in the very centre of the city, appropriately in the Boulevard des Bonnes Nouvelles (the Street of "Good News"), the first shots were exchanged.

Many Parisians were killed and more were wounded in the Rue Faubourg St. Denis when they were machine-gunned by S.S. troops, and in the Rue de Rivoli, which runs along the Tuileries Gardens and the Louvre.

The Germans used light field guns, but fired only a few rounds.

Maquis units along the stretch from the Place de la Concorde to the Bastille were machine-gunned.

Two days before the signal was given for the general insurrection, French railwaymen showed great courage by starting a general strike, and some of them lay on the rails to prevent trains from running.

Others unbolted sections of the line and carried the rails away, knowing that the penalty would be instant death.

★

AMONG the first buildings captured by the French Forces of the Interior were the Town Hall and the Ministry of the Interior.

The Town Hall is on the right bank of the River Seine and covers the approaches of the Ile de la Cité, which the police, also on strike, had turned into a fortress.

Then the rest of the public buildings in Paris fell one by one until all were again under French control.

News of the successful rising was received by French sources in London on Tuesday, but for security reasons it was kept secret.

The first hint of the Patriot uprising came last Sunday night, when the city's radio station broke a four-day silence to issue a proclamation from the German military commander which declared that the

BACK PAGE—Col. FOUR

King Michael Broadcasts: 'We Will Fight Germany'

'BOY KING' SPEAKS

KING MICHAEL, *Pledged his country.*

RUMANIA has quit the Axis and has joined the Allies. This was announced on Bucarest radio last night in a broadcast by King Michael. The proclamation disclosed that the terms accepted had been offered by Britain, the U.S., and Russia, whose armies were last night reported to be sweeping forward to the Galatz Gap, the gateway to Rumania proper.

The broadcast, repeated throughout the night, said that the dictatorship Government of Marshal Antonescu had resigned, and that a Liberal Government had taken its place.

King Michael's broadcast was received in bad conditions, but it made six points for the new Rumania. These were:

A National Government is to be formed in Rumania; Russia's peace terms would be accepted; Rumania will become an ally of the United Nations.

Rumania will "take its fate in its own hands and fight against its enemies." The broadcast then called upon citizens to rally round the Throne, and said that "the Vienna Award" (the agreement under which Hitler divided Rumania and gave part of Transylvania to Hungary) was rejected.

The broadcast was given without any warning—a fact which Allied observers suggest means the Rumanians intended to give the Germans as little warning as possible. A fair number of German troops are still in Rumania, and German Staff H.Q. is in Bucarest. In spite of this, the Germans apparently made no attempt to interfere with the Rumanian broadcast—or, if they did, the attempt failed.

ENEMY NOT WARNED

The broadcast said that the new Government would be headed by General Konstantin Senatescu. Its members include M. Maniu, veteran leader of the Peasant Party and a constant advocate of peace with the Allies. M. Bratianu, the Liberal leader, is also in the new Cabinet.

Here, in full, is King Michael's broadcast: "Rumanians! In this difficult hour of our country it has been decided for the salvation of the Fatherland that there shall be an immediate cessation of hostilities with the United Nations.

"I call upon the Government of National Union to fulfil the determined will of the country and conclude peace with the United Nations Rumania has accepted the armistice offered by the Soviet Union, Great Britain, and the United States. From this moment all hostilities against the Soviet armies and the state of war with Great Britain and the United States cease.

"I receive with confidence the appeal of these nations. The United Nations guarantee the independence of Rumania.

"They have recognised the injustice of the Diktat of Vienna under which Transylvania was torn from us.

"Anyone who opposes the decision we have taken and who takes justice in his own hands is an enemy of our nation.

"I order the Army and the whole nation to fight with all means and at the cost of any sacrifice against him.

"All Rumanians must rally round the Throne and the Government. He who does not assist the Government and resists the will of the nation is a traitor to the country.

CHURCHILL'S HINT

"At the side of the Allied armies and with their help (there was an indistinct phrase here) . . . we will cross the frontiers unjustly imposed upon us at Vienna"

There was no official confirmation in London last night on Rumania's decision, but in view of Mr. Churchill's statement in the House of Commons on August 2, it was considered that her action was likely.

Mr. Churchill then said:

"It seems to me that Rumania must primarily make its terms with Russia, whom they have so outrageously assaulted and at whose mercy they will soon lie.

"Russia has offered generous terms to Rumania, and I have no doubt they will be accepted with gratitude by the Rumanian people if only the Rumanian leaders do not get a Prussian automatic pistol pressed pretty closely against their breasts or at the nape of their necks."

STRONG MAN

At the same time the Premier said of Bulgaria, who in the past few days has been reported to be making peace overtures: "Three times in my lifetime has this wretched Bulgaria subjected her peasant population to all the pangs of war and chastisement of defeat. To them also the moment of repentance has not passed, but it is passing swiftly."

Dr. Julius Maniu, in the new Rumanian Cabinet, resigned the Premiership in 1930 At one time he was regarded as the strongest political figure in Rumania.

In 1941 he was interned: two years later huge crowds appealed to him with shouts of "Save Our Country."

The story of Rumania's decision begins in June, 1940, when the

BACK PAGE—Col. TWO

THE gap torn in Hitler's eastern front by Rumania's defection.

Front-line Deauville Wild About Paris

From ALEXANDER CLIFFORD

DEAUVILLE, Wednesday.

DEAUVILLE is sunny, undamaged, and half-deserted. But delirium is beginning to creep through it as the news from Paris spreads. They are beginning to take the shutters down from the windows and hang out every flag.

They are unearthing bottles of champagne hidden for more than four years and kept for this moment.

Every man in the place is huddled round a table at his regular café, or standing at the street corner, volubly shouting the news.

The front line is right here, but you would never know it. Not 50 yards away, across the river Touques, you can see the big Casino of Trouville, with its cream walls and black roof. There are supposed to be Germans in it.

But Paris is the thing. I don't suppose Deauville ever expected to have a firing-line running through it in the height of the season. But even more surprising is the fact that Deauville doesn't talk about it It talks about Paris.

Fly Bomb Bases

There was celebration in the air. As soon as our English uniforms were seen we were carried off to luncheon parties.

We had to go to other houses for coffee and liqueurs, so that no one should be offended. There was champagne for everyone.

From the windows of Deauville you can look across the mouth of the Seine to the great port of Le Havre.

It is 45 minutes away by ferry, and in the sun to-day it looked less. Somewhere just over there are the first operational flying-bomb bases. They can't be far away now

Loads of Prisoners

Gradually we are mopping up this German army which we have so decisively beaten. There were truckloads and truckloads of prisoners on the roads to-day.

There are very few even of the loneliest roads left where you are in danger from snipers And the total of captured material is swelling all the time.

But they have got into their rearguard rhythm against us It is the position we faced in the desert after Alamein

The Germans are totally incapable of meeting us in battle any more. But they are just strong enough to hold us off with endless mines and demolitions and the odd suicide rearguard detachment.

Of course, it doesn't matter. They are being outflanked and encircled on a gigantic scale. They have been told that if only they can hold a line round the flying-bomb sites they will win the war in a couple of months.

But that can't sound very plausible to-day.

GERMANS FIRE ON OUR SHIPS

Every Shell a Miss

By Daily Mail Reporter

Allied shipping in the Strait of Dover late yesterday afternoon caused German coast artillery suddenly to spring into action. The longest range guns were not used.

When the guns on the cliffs between Boulogne and Cap Gris Nez opened up, the small vessels immediately put out a smoke screen. The shells were seen exploding in the sea far from their target and outside the screen.

Heavy explosions behind Calais and Boulogne rocked towns in the Dover area, and it was thought the R.A.F. were dropping their heaviest bombs on flying bomb sites or that the enemy were demolishing fortifications.

Premier Sees Bonomi

ROME Wednesday.—Mr. Churchill received Signor Bonomi, the Italian Prime Minister, at the British Embassy in Rome yesterday morning, it was announced to-day. Afterwards Signor Bonomi and Marshal Badoglio lunched with Mr. Churchill at the Embassy.—*Reuter*.

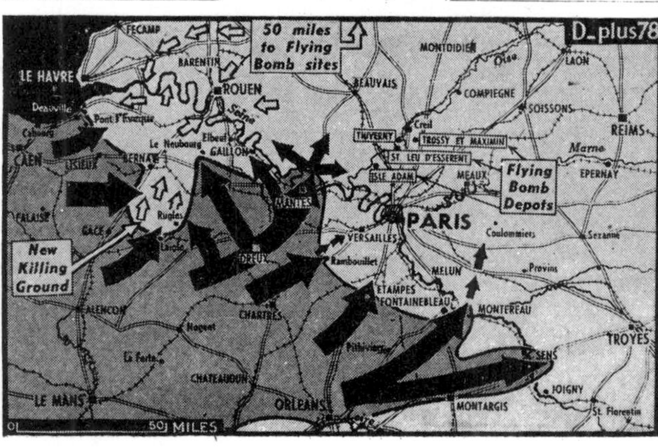

'Blow Lamp' is Latest RAF Bomb

By COLIN BEDNALL

A DEADLY new fire-bomb, it is revealed this morning, has been introduced in great numbers by R.A.F. Bomber Command for the "knock-out" bombing attacks on German cities.

The fire-bomb weighs 30lb., is

2

dropped by parachute, and shoots out a roasting jet of flame 15ft. long and 2ft. wide. The flame is fed by a solution of methane and petrol, forced out of the bomb under pressure.

An aerial "blow-torch" of terrifying power, the bomb drifts down to the roofs and into the streets of German cities in clouds.

By its use recently a force of less than 250 Lancasters caused as much damage to Munich as had previously been achieved by a force more than twice its size.

Twenty-four hours after the attack on Bremen last Friday night fires still raged unchecked from the dock area of the port right up to the centre of the town

It has been established for some time that incendiaries, properly employed, cause more damage in built-up areas than high explosives.

"Scientists in War Dance"—Page THREE.

155 MILES FROM GERMANY

SHAEF announces American reconnaissance forces advanced 15 miles east of Sens yesterday and reached a point 155 miles from the German frontier. Allied troops closing in on Seine pocket have liberated Evreux and reached Conches.

FLEEING GERMANS BOMBED

German troops withdrawing up the Rhone Valley were bombed last night, fires and explosions being caused. Events point to rapid junction of Allied forces in Northern and Southern France.

The Daily Sketch

NEWS AND PICTURES

No. 11,008 ★★ SATURDAY, AUGUST 26, 1944 ONE PENNY

FRENCH GO WILD AS GERMANS SURRENDER PARIS

This was the joyous scene in Clamart, only two miles from Paris, when an Allied column passed through with difficulty to the relief of the French fighting in the capital.

'Only Dead Nazis Are Left'

De Gaulle Is Back In Triumph

PARIS is clear of Germans—except dead ones. The German commander surrendered unconditionally yesterday.

Last night General de Gaulle, Fighting French leader, re-entered his capital, which went wild with joy.

A commentary by liberated Paris radio was made against a roaring background of shrieking crowds, the thumpings of a military band and bursts of gunfire.

The crowds roared a welcome first to General Leclerc and then to de Gaulle. When de Gaulle arrived the Marseillaise was played and the crowd burst into a deafening roar.

So terrific was the noise that the radio commentator had to scream at General de Gaulle when he asked him to say a word in the microphone.

"Just a word General," he cried. All General de Gaulle was able to say was: "I have only one word to say: "Vive Paris. Vive La France!"

All day long dishevelled Germans, their arms held high, many of them in civilian clothes, looking completely demoralised, had been routed out and herded together under the bitter taunts of the people.

Screams—And Kisses

An old lady, speaking in broken English, told Robert Reuben, Reuter's correspondent: "My stomach is empty but my heart is breaking with happiness to-day."

These scenes were the climax to the greatest day Paris can remember—to one of the most memorable spectacles in military history.

To Gen. Leclerc, Commander of the 2nd French Armoured Division, had been given the honour, by the Supreme Allied Commander, of first entering Paris in the morning. Later yesterday morning an American infantry column drove to Notre Dame.

As they fought their way towards the centre of the city people screamed wildly. Women kissed them and cried.

News of their arrival spread like wildfire. The bells of Notre Dame rang out, and the chorus was taken up by all the other churches in the

Turn to Back Page, Col. 4.

MASSACRE IN SEINE POCKET

THE Allied armies in France have had their greatest day. In the past 24 hours they have:

Fought their way into Paris;

Broken through the last defence line in the German "pocket" west of the Seine;

Penetrated to Troyes, 130 miles from the German frontier;

Extended the bridgehead in the Riviera, where 30,000 prisoners have now been captured.

It is probable that we are across the Seine south of Paris on a broad front.

We have liberated both Montereau and Montargis, and the enemy are in retreat north-east from Montargis. We are across the river in the area of Melun.

While world interest centred on the entry into Paris, General Patton's patrols in their "hush-hush" sweep south-east of the capital pushed on from Sens to the great road junction of Troyes, on the Seine.

This advance to 70 miles east of Paris is probably the most significant move of the day.

'Rheims Reached'

A German report that the Allies have reached Rheims, 80 miles north-east of Paris and 15 miles north of the Marne, is not confirmed at Supreme H.Q.

The report, if true, would appear to refer to the troops pushing on from Troyes.

This advance would rank as the speediest and most spectacular in military history—more than 100 miles in less than three days.

At the north-western end of the front, the first Canadian army has smashed across the River Risle at half a dozen places, shattering the last possible line on which the Germans might have tried to make a stand to cover their final escape moves.

This is the second river line the Canadians have forced in less than 24 hours—earlier yesterday it was announced that they had crossed the Touques, 20 miles to the west.

Turn to Back Page, Col. 2

Rumania Declares War On Germany

RUMANIA'S declaration of war against Germany yesterday has thrown the whole of the enemy forces in the country into a state of chaos.

Twelve German divisions are surrounded in a new Russian encirclement trap south-west of Kishinev.

More than 13,000 Germans have already surrendered, and the Moscow communiqué said that fighting was going on for the liquidation of the forces.

Bucharest Liberated

Yesterday the Russians occupied 550 towns and villages in their sweeping drive on to the Galatz approaches and the roads to Ploesti and Bucharest.

In five days' fighting on the Rumanian front the Russians have taken more than 105,000 prisoners and the enemy lost more than 100,000 men killed.

Within a few hours of Rumania's declaration of war Bucharest radio flashed the news that the capital had been liberated after fierce fighting. The remnants of the German garrison laid down their arms and surrendered.

Here is the text of the Rumanian Government's proclamation:

"On the basis of His Majesty's proclamation the new Government informed the German Legation and the German Army Command in Rumania that our country desired to liquidate in good understanding her relations with Germany, and that the Rumanian Army was determined to defend itself and would not undertake on its own initiative any hostile act against the German Army.

Machine-Gunned People

"The Rumanian Government announced at the same time that it would allow an orderly withdrawal of German troops which were ready voluntarily to leave our territory.

"After assurances, as solemn as they were perfidious, given by the commanders of the German army to the effect that no hostile action would be taken against our troops, German units attacked and tried to disarm Rumanian units. They even machine-gunned the peaceful populations of villages and the capital.

"At the same time the German Air Force in strength bombed the capital and other towns of the country, destroying non-military objectives and aiming particularly at the Royal Palace, and inflicting numerous casualties on the civilian population.

"By these acts of aggression, which occurred simultaneously in various parts of the country, Germany has placed herself in a state of war with Rumania.

"The Government therefore orders the Rumanian Army to begin the struggle against all German military forces on Rumanian territory for the liberation of the country from German usurpation."

The collapse of the German front in Rumania was admitted by von Olberg, Berlin radio commentator.

Tension is rising throughout the Balkans following Rumania's withdrawal. Here is a survey, according to reliable reports received in London from Cairo and Ankara:

BULGARIA: The Bulgarian Cabinet have been in almost continuous session, and observers in Sofia believe that the fast-moving situation throughout the Balkans will come to a head, possibly within 24 hours, with the collapse of the entire satellite system.

Hungary Tension

HUNGARY: General mobilisation has been ordered throughout Hungary and all leave for public employees in Budapest has been cancelled. The new Government appears to be in complete control and the only Germans to be seen in the capital are the guards outside the embassy.

Ribbentrop is said to be in Budapest negotiating with leading politicians, according to a Basle report.

Sea–Air Blitz Opens Brest Attack

BESIEGED German troops who for more than three weeks have been staging a "last ditch" battle for Brest, yesterday took the impact of a Ninth Bomber Command assault, co-ordinated with Allied sea and land bombardments.

More than 300 Marauders and Havocs hammered at enemy strong points.

Striking at closely-timed intervals, nine separate waves directed their attacks against the stubbornly defended arsenal, coastal guns, anti-aircraft batteries and other strong points delaying Allied occupation of the city. The attacks continued for nearly an hour.

The battering left the harbour area ringed by smoke and fire, and bomber crews also reported that Allied ground artillery, battleships and fighters synchronised their attacks with the bombing assault. Results were described as excellent.

Staff Sgt. George B. Judd, a Marauder gunner, reported: "Brest is completely hemmed in by huge fires."

While the air assault was in progress battleships outside the harbour entrance and artillery surrounding the city laid down heavy barrages on the port.

"Fire from our artillery was so terrific that smoke and flames all but obscured the target," said another Marauder pilot.

No enemy aircraft were encountered and flak was light. All our bombers returned.

A general land assault may now be in full swing against Brest, the occupation of which cannot be long delayed.

Gen. Ritchie Now In France

Commanders of three British corps in France were named yesterday:

They are: Lieut.-Gen. Neil M. Ritchie, Lieut.-Gen. Bryan Horrocks and Lieut.-Gen. Sir Richard O'Connor.

This means that there are now four British corps in France, as it was announced more than a month ago that Lieut.-Gen. J. T. Crocker was a corps commander there.

TIMELY WORDS OF FAITH

Whoso keepeth his mouth and his tongue keepeth his soul from troubles.

Proverbs 21, 23.

MONDAY, SEPTEMBER 4, 1944

Latest Prices

BLACK OUT 9.10 to 6.48 | Moon Rises 9.54 p.m. Sets 10.29 a.m. New Moon Sept 17 | Radio Page 5

LATE NIGHT

THE STAR

No. 17,536 ONE PENNY

"DUNKIRK AND CALAIS FREED"

(Unconfirmed Report By Algiers Radio)

BRITISH TANKS TAKE BRUSSELS: 30 MILES FROM HOLLAND

BRITISH TROOPS HAVE LIBERATED BRUSSELS, AND A FLYING COLUMN WHICH HAS THRUST ON BEYOND THE CAPITAL IS LESS THAN 30 MILES FROM HOLLAND, REPORTERS AT SUPREME HEADQUARTERS ANNOUNCED THIS AFTERNOON.

Unconfirmed reports quoted by Algiers radio this afternoon said Dunkirk, Boulogne, Calais and Le Touquet have all been liberated, and that Metz and Nancy have also been freed. It is known that General Patton's Army is operating in the area of Nancy.

The A.P. military correspondent at SHAEF this afternoon said that the American First and Third Army spearheads were reported by unofficial foreign sources to have stabbed into Germany at two points a hundred miles apart.

Reports from Stockholm said the Americans had broken through to Perl, just over the German border, and a Paris FFI broadcast said that another column had driven through 100 miles north to Aachen, 70 miles east of Brussels.

"Allied troops which crossed the Belgian frontier early yesterday morning rapidly freed Tournai and pushed on to the north and east to enter the capital in the late evening," said today's communique from General Eisenhower's H.Q.

"Further west other armoured forces drove north through Bethune and Lillers and reached the neighbourhood of Aire.

"In the Abbeville area the River Somme was crossed on both sides of the town, which is now in our hands, after some fighting. Our troops pushed on northward from the river. North and east of Le Havre, we closed in on the main defence of the port.

"Some 40 miles south-west of Brussels, the Belgian frontier has been crossed by other columns advancing north-east. Elements are in the area of Charleroi.

"Further south, the advance westwards has brought our troops to the vicinity of Nancy. Units following up this thrust have made other crossings of the Meuse River near Chalaines, 10 miles south-east of Commercy, and our troops are in St. Mihiel."

The "Star" reporter at SHAEF wrote this afternoon:

The Belgian border has been crossed in at least three distinct areas—by the force which freed Brussels, by other columns which drove on to the Mons area, and by others which crossed near Hirson yesterday.

Mons was reached by American troops, and, while fighting continued in some parts of the town, fast-moving columns fanned out and were last reported in the outskirts of Charleroi, 60 miles from Germany.

Troops which captured Bethune went on without pause to the Aire. Belgians are forging ahead alongside the British.

Abbeville was captured after we crossed the Somme on both sides of the town and closed in against strong resistance. This is the only place mentioned in today's news at which

CONTINUED ON BACK PAGE, Col. Three

Captured German Nurses

Two German nurses, captured during the advance into Brittany, resting in a prisoner of war compound before being removed to an internment camp.

'CEASE FIRE' ON FINNISH FRONT

HELSINKI announced officially today that the Finns and Russians had agreed to an armistice, on Finnish-held sectors of the front, from 10 a.m. today, says Reuter.

Field-Marshal Mannerheim, the Finnish President, issued the "Cease fire" order.

It was on June 28, 1941, that Finland declared war on the Soviet Union, the year after the disastrous "winter war" which ended with a Finnish defeat.

A BUP message from Stockholm said it was believed in Helsinki that a Finn peace delegation would leave for Moscow immediately, possibly today.

German radio this afternoon quoted the following official statement from the Finnish Office of Informaton. No comment was made.

"The Finnish Government have broken off relations with Germany and demanded the withdrawal of the German troops from Finland by September 15 at the latest. If the German troops fail to be withdrawn within the prescribed period, they will be disarmed and handed over to the Allies as prisoners of war."

Earlier Moscow had demanded the breaking off of relations and the withdrawal of the Nazi forces by September 15, before the Russians would begin peace talks.

The German Minister in the Finnish capital, Von Bluecher, has given an assurance that Germany will evacuate her troops, according to Swiss radio.

Other reports said the Nazis were already getting out. Lorries loaded with German troops are driving into Norway from Northern Finland, not far from the Swedish border.

Getting Out Of Norway?

An Oslo message, quoted by Reuter, said that the Nazi occupation authorities have ordered all hotels and boarding houses in Southern Norway to close. It was believed they were to be used to house the troops from Finland.

Indications that the Germans have already begun to move out of North Norway and that the RAF are hampering their evacuation came from German radio today.

The Nazis reported an attack by 50 Beaufighters on a German convoy off the north-western coast of Norway.

Patriots have already opened up heavy fighting with the Germans in Northern Norway, including the Narvik area, according to usually reliable sources quoted by Reuter's Stockholm correspondent.

Weapons are said to have been dropped to the patriots by Allied planes.

U.S. Haw-Haw 'Lost'

Berlin radio, in its English broadcast today, said: "Our North American listeners will now hear the daily commentary by Paul Revere."

After a five-minutes silence the announcer said: "I am sorry, but Paul Revere cannot be found."

Paul Revere is Douglas Chandler, the American Haw-haw, and is one of eight Americans indicted for treason in 1943, Reuter adds.

BLOWING HARD

Although clouds were breaking a little, a south-westerly wind was still blowing hard in the Straits today, and was whipping spray off the top of the big waves.

Conditions were generally unsettled, and there were slight showers at times.

Earlier the gale had reached a velocity of 60 mph.

PATCH 50 MILES N.E. OF LYONS

GENERAL PATCH'S troops, advancing from the south, were today reported 50 miles north-east of Lyons, which was liberated only yesterday.

BUP's correspondent at Allied H.Q. said that American troops were engaged in sharp fighting 12 miles north of Bourg, which is 38 miles north-east of Lyons and about 30 miles south of Chalons, the next big town.

This brings Patch's forces to within 110 miles of General Patton's army.

From Lyons, which was almost empty of Nazis when the Allies entered, the Germans continued fleeing north, and large numbers of

CONTINUED ON BACK PAGE, Col. TWO

All Quiet—Again

The flying-bomb lull continued today. London had not heard the sirens since Friday, and, by then, robot attacks had dwindled to a few widely-spaced-out efforts.

"Last Ditch Stand"

A last-ditch stand in Germany was foreshadowed by the German overseas radio today. "We have just to stick it through," it said. "We have, if necessary, to hold out in the last corner of Germany until it has become technically possible for the German command to launch its counter-measures."

Another German radio commentator offered his hearers the consolation that the German people were now geared up for total war, had faith in the V-1 and other German technical developments, and were certain that once the force of the Allied advance had spent itself, the tide would turn again in favour of Germany.

Peace Prizes This Year

The Nobel Peace Prizes are to be awarded this year for the first time since 1939, according to the Swedish newspaper "Dagens Nyheter," quoted today by German radio.

LATE FINAL

The Star

No. 18,039. Radio: Page 2. SHEFFIELD, MONDAY, SEPTEMBER 4, 1944 Threehalfpence

General of 37 Took Antwerp

Antwerp was captured by the 11th British Armoured Division, commanded by Major General George P. B. Roberts, D.S.O., M.C., it was disclosed at Shaef last night. The 53rd British Division later reinforced the 11th in Antwerp.

Major General Roberts, who is only 37, was a captain at the beginning of the war.

BRITISH OCCUPY BRUSSELS & ANTWERP

Germans Say Boulogne and Calais Evacuated

BRUSSELS has been liberated. Allied troops which crossed the Belgian frontier early yesterday morning rapidly freed Tournai and pushed on to the north and east to enter the capital in the late evening, says Shaef communique.

An Associated ress report to-day datelined "The French Frontier" said it was reliably reported that the Allies had entered Antwerp.

British troops have thus advanced 180 miles since they crossed the Seine at Verdun on August 26th, only eight days ago. Boulogne and Calais have been evacuated, according to German reports in Switzerland.

LILLE AND METZ FREE

Unconfirmed reports, quoted by Algiers radio to-day said Dunkirk, Boulogne, Calais, and Le Touquet have all been liberated.

United Nations (Algiers radio) quotes unconfirmed reports that Mettz and Nancy have been liberated. Lille, a town of 200,575 people, is also reported to have been freed.

The Canadians have advanced 20 miles north of Abbeville to the River Authie towards Boulogne and Calais.

The north to south line-up against the Siegfried Line has been practically completed by the British 21st Army Group column which has liberated Brussels (in a brilliant coup described on Page 3), and pushed on to within about 25 miles of the Dutch border.

It formed the spearhead of the whole Allied northward thrust and the latest advance has completely neutralised the flying bomb coast from the Somme to the Scheldt.

FLUID POSITION

Belgium is falling without a battle, and many Allied columns are racing on the heels of the routed Germans making for the Siegfried Line.

The situation is so fluid that any estimate of the distance to the Siegfried Line is out of date as soon as it is made or before.

On the whole of the front from Aachen, south to Switzerland, our average distance from the line is less than 50 miles, and at no point is it very much more than 50.

Nowhere are we any more distant than a modern army's day's march.

Holland has become untenable for the Germans and they are probably clearing out. The Dutch airfields are the last Hitler has apart from those in Germany itself in Western Europe.

Yesterday, when six of them were heavily bombed, there was no fighter opposition and only very light flak.

SCHELDT DRIVE

Brussels was reached yesterday evening. The liberating British troops, who probably had a Belgian contingent with them, swung south of Lille to take Tournai and then raced for the Belgian capital.

Already they are on their way beyond it in a drive for the Scheldt, which will complete the sealing off of the Channel coast.

The Belgian contingent were

Turn to Back Page Cols. 3 & 4

Unsettled in the Strait

CONDITIONS were generally unsettled in the Strait of Dover to-day following a stormy night.

Nazis Blow up More Big Coast Dumps

MORE explosions occurred in the Boulogne area during the night, as the Germans continued to blow up installations.

There was one very big explosion at Boulogne, followed later by another one, which was more distant and may have been nearer Abbeville.

People on the cliffs at Dover heard, above the roar of the wind, the roll of gunfire from the French coast.

Finns Quit After Four Years of Fighting

AFTER over four years of fighting the war between Finland and the Soviet Union came to an end to-day.

The cease fire—the first of this war—on the Finnish held sectors of the Eastern front was ordered by Field-Marshal Mannerheim, the Finnish President, at 8 a.m. to-day (10 a.m. London time), it was officially announced at Helsinki.

The German forces, estimated to number 160,000 men, have until September 15th, to get out of the country, failing which they will be disarmed and handed over to the Russians by the terms of the preliminary armistice conditions

It is believed in the Finnish capital that the peace delegation will leave for Moscow immediately, possibly to-day.

Germans Starting to Get Out?

Indications that the Germans have already begun to move out of Finland and that the R.A.F. has started to hamper their evacuation operations came from the Official German News Agency to-day.

The Agency reported a big attack by R.A.F. Beaufighters on a German convoy off the north-western coast of Norway. Three waves of planes swooped down on the German ships from a bank of low cloud. It is claimed the attack was warded off and three planes shot down.

The first detachment of General Lothar Rendulic's army has left Finland, said a Reuter Stockholm cable to-day. A steady stream of motorised vehicles loaded with troops has been observed moving across the Finnish-Norwegian border, said reports from Karesuando, over the Swedish side.

Other reports say that the German Legation in Helsinki is burning its papers, and that German ships in Finnish ports have been ordered to leave for unknown destinations.

Von Bluecher, the German Minister to Finland, with the entire German Legation in Helsinki and the German colony in Finland, will leave the country on Friday, says the Stockholm "Svenska Morgonbladet."

Minister Recalled From Berlin

Kivimaeki the Finnish Minister to Berlin, has been recalled to Helsinki, with his entire Legation.

Finland's move towards an armistice has been followed in Moscow with grim satisfaction, cables Duncan Hooper.

Moscow's insistence on the fulfilment of preliminary conditions is seen in the capital as a sign of Soviet determination that this time there shall be no fizzling out of Finland's peace enthusiasm at the eleventh hour.

Finland is the third German ally to desert the sinking Nazi ship. A fourth, Bulgaria, is tottering, says J. McDowall, "The Star" war correspondent.

If the preliminary reports of Russia's terms are correct, Finland is getting out easily.

She is being given a fortnight to get rid of the German troops, and there has been no mention of her being required to take arms alongside the Soviet Union.

Severe Blow to Nazi Morale

The Nazi leaders are probably rather relieved at getting leave in which to extricate their men, and try and get them back for the defence of the hard-pressed Reich.

The gain to the Allied cause is as much moral as material.

NAZI AIR FORCE RETIRING

The Luftwaffe is now drawing back into Germany for the defence of the Reich, says Major W. MacLauachan, "The Star's" Air Correspondent.

During extensive operations yesterday only a few enemy planes were encountered over Holland and Belgium, and two out of three were shot down in the neighbourhood of Louvain.

In a heavy raid on the synthetic oil plant at Ludwigshaven, however, a strong force attempted to attack some of the Fortresses that took part. The escorting Mustangs shot down seven.

Altogether 200 transport vehicles were destroyed. Two of our aircraft are missing.

AIRFIELDS HIT

Yesterday was a field day for many squadrons. Among other targets, the six main Dutch airfields were bombed by heavies, but no enemy fighters appeared.

The "Forts" at Brest were repeatedly bombed by large formations.

The enemy's withdrawing from Brussels in two long columns provided excellent targets for fighter-bombers of the 8th Air Force.

In the Pas de Calais area there was little movement, indicating that the Germans may already have evacuated the area except for a few garrison troops.

Words of Wisdom.

THOUGH hand join in hand, the wicked shall not be unpunished; but the seed of the righteous shall be delivered.—Prov. XI, 21.

The War—1829th Day

BLACK-OUT TIME:
9.19 p.m. to 6.51 a.m.
LIGHTING-UP TIME:
9.49 p.m. to 6.21 a.m.
Moon rises at 10.0 p.m. and sets at 10.36 a.m. (Tuesday).

THURSDAY, SEPTEMBER 7, 1944

Evening Standard

37,437 BLACK-OUT 9.3 p.m. to 6.53 a.m. MOON rises 11.10 p.m., sets 2.30 p.m. ONE PENNY
FINAL NIGHT EXTRA

LONDON'S 80 DAYS: THE FIRST FULL STORY

8000 Fly-Bombs Came Over: Only 9 p.c. Reached London in Last Days: Fighters Got 1900; Defences Had 2000 Balloons, 2800 Guns

"The Battle is Over," Says Duncan Sandys

THE FIRST FULL STORY OF BRITAIN'S BATTLE WITH THE FLYING BOMB, IN WHICH 92 PER CENT OF THE FATAL CASUALTIES WERE IN LONDON, IS REVEALED TO-DAY.

Mr. Duncan Sandys, M.P., Chairman of the Flying Bomb Counter-measures Committee, revealed that during 80 days' bombardment 8000 flying bombs were launched, of which 2300 reached the London area.

THE STORY TELLS OF A GUN BELT WHICH STRETCHED FROM MAIDSTONE TO EAST GRINSTEAD SO AS TO SCREEN LONDON, AND HOW IT WAS DECIDED LATER TO MOVE THE ENTIRE A.-A. BELT DOWN TO THE COAST SO THAT THE GUNS SHOULD HAVE AN UNINTERRUPTED FIELD OF VIEW.

In the first week 33 per cent were brought down and the same proportion reached London, whereas in the last week 70 per cent of the bombs were brought down by the defences and only nine per cent reached London, the others being inaccurate or erratic.

"Except possibly for a few last parting shots, what has come to be known as the Battle for London is over," said Mr. Sandys, who disclosed that bombs were also launched from aircraft, Heinkel 111 being specially adapted.

"As was noticed by many people, a small proportion of the bombs came in by night from a due easterly direction.

"This puzzled us a little at first; because so far as we knew there were no firing sites either in Belgium or Holland. However we very soon obtained information that these flying bombs were being launched not from the ground, but from aircraft.

"Specially adapted Heinkel bombers were carrying the bombs pick-a-back and launching them from the air over the North Sea. These bombs proved less accurate than those fired from the land.

OUR INTRUDERS

"To meet this new form of attack additional guns were rapidly sent to the Thames Estuary, and intruder squadrons were sent out each night to patrol over the Dutch and Belgian coasts.

"At the same time attacks were made on the airfields from which the launching airplanes were operating.

"These counter-measures have reduced the scale of airborne launchings to very small proportions.

"This form of attack can, of course, be carried on from airfields in the heart of Germany.

"We cannot, therefore, as yet assure the public that flying bomb attacks will cease altogether. We can, however, be reasonably confident that the scale of attack will be very small."

A RECORD BAG

The record bag was on August 28, when out of 101 bombs which approached the coast of England 97 were brought down by the defenders and only four reached London.

"More than 2000 flying bombs have been launched at an average of 100 a day. Of these 2300 got

(Continued on Back Page, Col. One).

AMERICANS ARE THRUSTING INTO THE ARDENNES

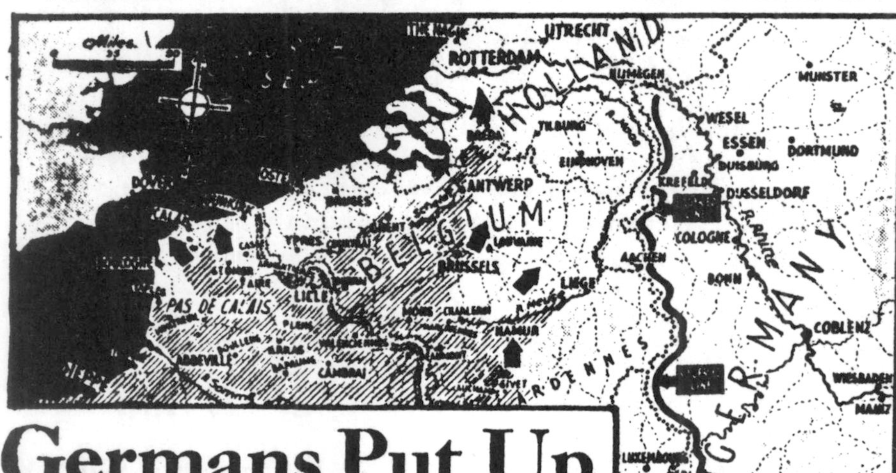

Germans Put Up Stiffer Fight

GERMAN RESISTANCE IS STIFFENING, AND THEY ARE PUTTING UP A DETERMINED FIGHT AROUND NANCY, METZ, CALAIS, BOULOGNE AND LE HAVRE.

Elsewhere the German withdrawal is continuing, say reporters at Supreme Headquarters to-day.

But there are increasing signs that a considerable force of German troops has still to be engaged and defeated either on or before the Siegfried Line.

A new threat to Germany is developing from a drive by the American First Army, who have pushed a column across the Meuse and through the Ardennes Forest beyond Auchamps, 11 miles north of Charleville.

Other columns of the First Army, who crossed the Meuse at Namur, are operating south-east of Namur and north-east of Givet.

This drive across the Meuse is developing well, but reports that our troops are at Liege and Aachen are premature.

"LITTLE CASSINO"

Indications are increasing that General Patton's forces thrusting on to Germany from the Verdun area will face their heaviest fighting within the next two weeks, adds Robert Richards British United Press war correspondent.

"Little Cassino" is the next objective before our assault troops. This is the German position in the hills overlooking the village of Pont à Mousson on the Moselle.

Troops are pouring across the Moselle to build up the bridgehead for the next step to Germany. Petrol armour and supplies have to be brought up before the commander can hit the Germans a real blow and follow up without halting.

PORTS BATTLE

The Germans are still fighting hard for the Channel ports.

Boulogne and Calais are now closely invested. We are in the outskirts of Boulogne, and reconnaissance elements have reached the outskirts of Calais all round the port but no direct assault has yet been launched against either place.

Charles Lynch, Reuter correspondent, says that advance Canadian spearheads are seven miles west of Dunkirk. Polish troops became the first units of the Canadian Army to cross the Belgian frontier, driving to Ypres and beyond.

The foulest weather since D-Day with cold rain and fog, failed to hold up the advance as troops by-passed Calais and raced east towards Dunkirk, Ostend and Zeebrugge.

Fanatical resistance continues at Brest and Le Havre.

Communiqué—PAGE THREE.

TERRIBLE CRISIS, SAYS GOEBBELS

"There is no need to be bowled over with astonishment that neutral countries and part of our camp following, too have begun to get wobbly in face of the dramatic sweep of events in the world war situation," says Goebbels in his weekly article in Das Reich, quoted by Reuter.

"A people which defends its freedom can rely only upon itself and its own strength in times of terrible crisis, and this strength suffices in most cases to safeguard the nation's liberty.

"Total Effort"

"That is why it is our duty to pursue the tasks of the people's total war effort with a gravity and zeal as if life itself were at stake. And indeed our national existence is in the balance and with it the personal existence of every single one of us.

"If our enemies now are racing against time, they are forced to do so by dire necessity.

"They see no other way out of the dilemma of a miscarried military policy, which sooner or later must bring about the gravest conflicts among them."

The V-Sign in the Sky

The last rays of the setting sun last night caused a large unmistakable V-sign to appear says Reuter from Wellington, New Zealand.

'NAZI LINE SHORTENED IN SOUTH'

The Germans this afternoon admitted that their troops in Southern and South-Western France "have been taken back to a shorter line."

They say the German air force have had to help their troops, "often evacuating their wounded by air and dropping arms and ammunition."

French troops moving due north up France have covered 75 miles since they were last checked at Lyons.

They are now well within 25 miles of Dijon.

Reuter's correspondent David Brown says General Patch's Seventh Army are rolling on unchecked towards the Doubs Valley and the Belfort Gap.

They have reached the town of Arbois on the road to Besancon after taking Poligy on the way.

Arbois, adds Reuter, is 25 miles north-east of Lons-le-Saunier, reported occupied by the Americans yesterday.

The French and Americans between them have liberated another large segment of Eastern France between the Saone River and the Swiss frontier.

PATTON AND PATCH LINK NEAR BORDER

An American commentator, broadcasting from Southern France this afternoon, quoted by Reuter, said: "General Patton's 'Will o' the Wisps' and the Seventh Army (General Patch's forces from Southern France) have joined forces very close to the German border.

"It is not permitted to name the exact point of the junction, but the battered German 19th Army are apt to be caught by it roughly in the region of Belfort."

Berlin asserted to-day, says Reuter, that the German armies in Southern France had got back and joined the main German armies in the north.

100 Times More Light In Streets

Evening Standard Reporter

The new "half lighting" which becomes legal on September 17 is 100 times stronger than the "star" lighting which has previously been allowed, it was learned to-day.

But there will be no "flash up" all over the country, or even all over London. Lamps which have fallen into disrepair, shortage of labour and shortage of materials will make the great light up a gradual affair.

One of the difficulties facing lighting authorities is that certain materials have to be bought from specialised firms and this is likely to take some time. Labour supplies, it is pointed out, are "an unknown quantity" depending on many priority factors.

London authorities quickly moved to "action stations," and while workmen overhauled installations many emergency conferences were held to perfect the capital's plans.

Westminster City Council and **Battersea** Borough Council have already given a lead. Westminster have already begun work on the new half-lighting, and Battersea, said Mr. H. F. J. Thompson, the chief engineer, to-day, has all the necessary equipment. Only the labour supply is needed.

A start has been made to light up Piccadilly Circus, but Westminster City Council, whose system is partly gas and partly electricity has no master switch plan. Piccadilly can therefore be expected to be lit like a side street.

At Armistice

A leading official in the gas industry said to-day that preparations for the re-establishment of full lighting at the conclusion of an Armistice are well advanced.

"There is no doubt that the streets in the West End of London will be pretty bright on armistice night."

Master Switches

Among the cities with a "master switch" are Leeds and Glasgow. They will benefit by having almost a pre-war standard of lighting.

Curtains

The Board of Trade have already arranged for mills making black-out material to switch to the production of ordinary curtaining.

The Board's officials are considering whether the material, already off the coupon, can be sold without coupons for other purposes.

Batteries

More radio high-tension batteries, now scarce, may be one result of the dim-out. Manufacturers, who expect to make far fewer torch

(Continued on Back Page, Col. Six)

The "Reply" Cost A Shilling

An ingenious range-finder, so simple that the whole device cost little more than one shilling, was the complete answer to fly-bomb night fighting, said Mr. Duncan Sandys, chairman of the Flying Bomb Counter-Measures Committee, to-day.

It was produced by 56-year-old Sir Thomas Merton.

(See Londoner's Diary.)

We Know Quite a Lot About V2

Mr. Duncan Sandys, asked about V2 to-day, said:

"I am a little chary of talking about V2," he replied. "We do know quite a lot about it.

"In a very few days' time I feel that the Press will be walking all over these places in France and will know a great deal more then than we do now."

A.A. DIARY

Here is the week by week toll taken by the A.-A. guns after the belt had been moved to the coast:

First week	**17 per cent**
Second week	**24 per cent**
Third week	**27 per cent**
Fourth week	**40 per cent**
Fifth week	**55 per cent**
Sixth week	**60 per cent**
The last week	**74 per cent**

"The people of London owe much to the men and women of the A.-A.," said Mr. Sandys. "And in particular to General Pile, to whose energy and personal leadership these achievements are in large measure due."

Daily Mail

NO. 15,086 ONE PENNY * * FOR KING AND EMPIRE FRIDAY, SEPTEMBER 8, 1944

LATE WAR NEWS

ARMIES DRIVE ON COLOGNE

Advance on Germany Starts Up Again

SEDAN FALLS TO 1st U.S. ARMY

ALLIED armies in France are on the move again. After a pause of a few days to bring up fresh masses of men and material, British and American forces have made big new advances in their drive to the Siegfried Line.

The British Second Army were last night reported to be only 70 miles, and the American First Army only 80 miles, from Cologne. Both these advances were made in a surge to the Albert Canal.

At some points American forces were stated to have advanced as much as 30 miles, and the Siegfried Line is soon likely to be shelled by Allied guns.

Farther to the west General Patton's Third Army, battling strongly against heavy resistance between Metz and Nancy, has now forced armour across the Moselle. The Americans are across the river at two points. American troops have also taken Sedan.

Here are details of the advances: **1.** General Dempsey's men smashed through stiff German resistance to reach the Albert Canal, about 30 miles north-east of Louvain. The Germans brought down troops from Holland in a desperate bid to hold up the advance. They failed.

PUSH TO LIEGE

On this front alone 7,912 prisoners were taken yesterday. Other troops of the British Second Army are driving towards the Dutch frontier.

2. American forces from Namur have pushed on to the north-east, have captured Huy, 18 miles from Namur, and were last night half-way to Liége.

3. The Moselle Front.—General Patton has got his armour across the Moselle after first losing his bridgehead at Pont-à-Mousson.

A powerful German force, throwing in everything to stem the advance, forced the Americans to withdraw.

The infantry, fighting in a wake of fallen comrades, got another foothold, and within an hour U.S. tanks splashed into the Moselle and a few moments later were out on the other side.

An officer commanding the troops said he was confident that this time they were over for good.

The Americans are closing on the two main defence points in this area—Metz and Nancy. Algiers radio reported last night that street fighting was raging in Nancy, with half the town captured.

Other U.S. forces are said to have driven into the outskirts of Metz. The Germans are fighting stubbornly along the west bank opposite the main part of the city.

Below the city a full-scale battle raged throughout yesterday as American tanks and ground troops charged repeatedly into concentrations of enemy artillery and machine-gun fire to fight their way across the Moselle.

SS MOVED BACK

Few S.S. units have been contacted by the Allied armies in front of the German frontier.

The enemy is probably hoping to withdraw his crack troops to the Siegfried defences while rearguard actions are fought by the ordinary Wehrmacht.

German resistance appears to be concentrated around three strongpoints—Metz, Toul, and Nancy.

A third general was listed yesterday as having been taken in the Mons pocket.

Meanwhile, to the south, General Patch's forces were last night reported to have linked up with Patton's troops.

The link is said to have taken place in the area of the Belfort Gap, one of the gateways to Germany in the south.

The radio commentator who reported the link-up said: "It is not permitted to name the exact point of the junction, but the battered German 19th Army is apt to be caught by it roughly in the region of Belfort."

The town of Belfort is in the gap between the mountain ranges astride the entrance to the industrial region of South-Western Germany.

General Patch's forces have captured a whole succession of towns and villages on their way towards the Belfort Gap and the German frontier.

Official reports said the fast-moving Americans from the south were closing in on Besançon, the last big highway town before the gap.

Their advance is rolling on unchecked towards the Doubs valley, which skirts the foot of the mountains forming the southern side of the gap.

On the left flank General de Lattre de Tassigny's French forces have reached within 25 miles of the great communications centre of Dijon. Since they were last checked at Lyons they have covered 75 miles.

On the other main zone of operations, the Channel coast, Allied troops are compressing the Germans into smaller space.

General Dempsey's forces have penetrated into Calais, and Canadians are fighting in Boulogne.

Resistance in this area continues strong.

Germans On Moselle Fight Back

Big Battle for Road to Reich

Daily Mail Special Correspondent

WITH U.S. THIRD ARMY ON THE MOSELLE, Thursday.

ARMOURED troops under General Patton went to the banks of the Moselle opposite Metz to-day as the initial outpost battle for Germany flared up in increasing violence along the heavily defended river.

This battle of the gap is flaring up along a 50-miles front from Thionville through Metz to Nancy.

Patton's attacks follow the exploratory thrusts 24 hours ago. Under his command he is reported to have the greatest armoured force ever assembled under one field command.

But the Germans have assembled plenty of men, artillery, and tanks, including some of their heavy armour, to counter the American assault. And they are fighting back.

Big Battles

The swift advance of Patton's pursuit of the retreating Germans actually gave some aid to Hitler in preparing Germany's defences, as a breathing spell has been required during the last few days to permit the Allies to bring up supplies and organise their great assault against the West Wall.

Aerial reconnaissance already has established that the German High Command made the most of this delay by rushing masses of troops, heavy guns, and large and medium tanks into the line behind the Moselle, foreshadowing severe battles to come.

Patton made a personal inspection of the Moselle line yesterday He moved along the front from point to point in an armoured car watching the battle, and saw the fighting for several villages where German fire was holding up the Allied advance.

It is familiar ground for General Patton: he fought over it in the last war as a colonel.

Small American advance units which crossed the Moselle have suffered considerable losses at the hands of the superior German forces.

But forces of Panzers and Grenadiers moving up to the battle south-east of Nancy were severely mauled.

One column is reported to have been completely destroyed.

Grim Fight

Senior officers at a forward post said to-day that they had received information that Metz is strongly held. The Germans there are reported to have been extending and improving the fortifications.

German infantry, tanks, and heavy guns were active on the west bank of the Moselle last night across from Metz and there were brisk encounters with American forces.

Flames from burning tanks and buildings destroyed in last night's fighting still marked the undulating countryside on the outskirts of Metz with lurid splotches of red.

These flames show how far the advance elements of Gen. Patton's thrust penetrated towards the German homeland. It also shows that the Germans, as expected, are putting up a grim fight for the road to the Reich

Headquarters information indicates that Field-Marshal Von Kluge, missing for some weeks and several times reported dead, is again in command of the German defences.

HE CAPTURED ST. VALERY

Once Prisoner There

When the Highland 51st Division recaptured St. Valery, 17 miles from Dieppe, on Sunday, their commander was Major-General T. G. Rennie, who was taken prisoner in the same town in June, 1940.

He could—if he would—tell one of the best escape stories of the war. He was a prisoner for only ten days.

He took over command of a battalion of the Black Watch in December, 1941, and led them at El Alamein, where he won the D.S.O. He has been twice wounded.

SINGLE FRONT UNDER EISENHOWER SOON

SHAEF, Thursday.

THE merger of the southern and western invasions into a single front for a co-ordinated assault on the Siegfried Line is expected to result from the link-up of Patch's Seventh Army and Patton's Third now converging on Dijon.

A recent Washington report indicated that the decision had already been reached by the combined chiefs of staff.

Eisenhower's appointment to the over-all command was likely to be announced soon.

There is no indication of how Patch would come into the new set-up.

The removal of his army from Wilson's Mediterranean command would represent only its transfer from one theatre of operations to another.—*A.P.*

VC FOR A DCM

First Award to be Substituted

The V.C. The D.C.M.

By Daily Mail Reporter

EIGHT months after the award of the Distinguished Conduct Medal to Company Sergt.-Major Peter Harold Wright, of the Coldstream Guards, it was announced last night that he has been awarded the V.C. for the same acts of gallantry.

The deeds which won C.S.M. Wright first the "cancelled" D.C.M. and then the V.C., took place in Italy on September 25 last year.

So far as is known this is the first occasion on which a soldier has been decorated with the D.C.M. and the award of the Victoria Cross substituted for it.

It was explained last night that General Alexander, in common with other Army commanders, had the power to make immediate awards for cases of great gallantry up to the D.S.O. and D.C.M.

New Steps

In view of C.S.M. Wright's exploits coming near to deciding a battle, General Alexander made the immediate award of the D.C.M.

At the same time, steps were set in motion with a view to the higher award being made. This recommendation, supported by the evidence of witnesses from the spot, was sent through various commands to General Alexander and thence to a committee of three high-ranking officers at the War Office.

This committee, having satisfied itself that C.S.M. Wright's deed came within the measure of heroism which made good a claim to the V.C., made its recommendation to the King for the award of the medal.

Two More V.C.s.—Page THREE.

The Enemy Said Last Night

Our Turn for Fate's Knock at the Door

Daily Mail Radio Station

IN moments of crisis, Dr. Goebbels is fond of holding up Britain as an example to the citizens of the Reich.

He repeats the dose in this week's *Das Reich*.

"This summer and autumn will see the military and political crisis of the war," he writes.

"In such a crisis we see a test of our character. When we captured the Atlantic coast in 1940, and Britain lay open to our air forces, the supreme test had come to the British people.

"In the autumn of 1941 the Soviet Union had to pull itself together for its final exertion.

"With the enemy attacking our fronts, fate is now knocking at our own door."

★

There were other voices in Germany last night. Ace reporter Schelkopf soliloquised over Berlin radio:

"The situation changes hourly, and at any moment our leadership is faced with new problems. Only too often this causes grave anxiety to the German Command.

"The enemy's all-out effort has to be met by weak and limited German forces only. Nothing can be done but to devise new methods of warfare."

The German Forces radio last night made an appeal to the S.S. troops:

"Every day gained now amounts to a reinforcement of our national strength for the defence of the Reich itself.

"It is therefore the duty of our soldiers in contact with the enemy to delay the enemy's movements to the utmost."

'Peace? Never,' says Berlin

Berlin radio, commenting on rumours of German capitulation, declared last night: "The Reich's attitude is characterised by the unflinching resolve not to surrender no matter what happens and no matter what the circumstances.

"Germany is thinking neither of peace feelers nor of peace, but only that in any event it must and will master the situation."—*Reuter*.

5,817 DIED IN BATTLE OF FLYING BOMBS

UNLESS there are any further incidents, the last "Alert" in the London area was sounded on Thursday, August 31, and the last "All Clear" ten minutes later.

During this interval the last recorded bomb on London fell on a county school playing field. There were no casualties.

From the beginning of the flying-bomb attacks total casualties were 5,817 killed and 17,086 seriously injured.

Of these, civilians killed and injured in London were 5,181 and 15,550 respectively; elsewhere in the country, 341 and 1,112: Service personnel in all districts, 295 and 424.

London's worst week of casualties was the first one, from June 14 to 21, when 720 people were killed and 2,191 injured in the metropolitan area.

The incident which cost most lives occurred at Lewisham High-street, when 51 were killed and 216 were injured.

In the whole country more than 870,000 houses have been damaged.

"How the Battle of the Flying Bomb was Won"—Page THREE.

VICTORY LIFTING MORE BANS

Evacuation Ends—But Stay Put

No Crowd Limits

By Daily Mail Reporter

THE official evacuation scheme is ended. No more mothers or children will be sent away from London or Southern England.

Facilities will still be given to expectant mothers and elderly people and to the blind and infirm whose homes are uninhabitable."

Since the beginning of the flying-bomb attacks 282,118 mothers and children have been officially evacuated from the London area and 23,396 from other places, a total of 305,514.

NO FREE TRIPS

There are, in addition, in the "safe" areas 160,000 people, of whom 120,000 are children, who were evacuated under the earlier scheme during the big London blitz.

Many of these have now been away for more than four years. Altogether there are now in the country 465,564 official evacuees, in addition to a probably much larger total of voluntary evacuees.

The problem of their return is difficult, and has not yet been solved. It involves extensive transport facilities which cannot at present be officially provided.

For that reason principally the Ministry of Health ask all evacuees to remain where they are for the present. Until a further announcement is made there will be no free journeys back.

Those who decide to return, or to bring their children home, will have to do so at their own expense. No special trains will be provided.

The housing problem in London seriously affects the question of return About 870,000 houses still await repair.

When official arrangements are made for this, priority must be given to people with habitable homes, either their own or those of friends ready to receive them.

For others with nowhere to go, full payments will be continued as long as necessary.

Many schools are also damaged.

CROWDS FREED

RESTRICTIONS on the size of crowds at football matches, boxing tournaments, greyhound racing, and other sports meetings are likely to be withdrawn almost immediately.

The Ministry of Home Security last night would not confirm this good news beyond stating that "war-time regulations will be relaxed as soon as conditions permit."

But I understand that local authorities who limit the attendance at these meetings may now permit grounds and halls to be filled to reasonable capacity.

At present the number of spectators permitted at football matches and other sports is decided by the local authority concerned. This is usually 85 per cent. of the ground or hall capacity.

It is unlikely that greyhound tracks will resume evening meetings because of fuel economy and restrictions on lighting. But it is probable that the number of meetings, now restricted to one a week, may be doubled.

There may also be more horse-racing. The season may be extended for a month from the present closing date, October 14. Steeplechasing, which stopped in 1942, will probably be resumed "in the new year."

A GENERAL parade of Home Guards throughout the country will be held for the return of kit and equipment. This follows the War Office instruction to "Stand easy."

Disciplinary measures or other action can be taken against those who are unable to produce equipment issued to them.

It is being suggested that articles of clothing, some of them already partially worn, should be sold at a reasonable price without coupons.

The date of a general parade for the return of equipment will be delayed as long as possible because it is felt that it is the universal wish of Home Guards to take part in a victory march in full uniform.

Hitler Summons Madrid Envoy

MADRID, Thursday.—Hans Dieckhoff, German Ambassador to Spain, has left for Berlin by air, it is reported here.

He is said to have received an urgent cable from Hitler to return for consultations.—*Reuter*.

Big Allied-Soviet Attack Begins in Balkans

20 ENEMY DIVISIONS ARE IN DANGER

ALLIED Headquarters in Rome announced last night that a major campaign has been launched to trap and destroy the 20 German divisions in Yugoslavia, Albania, Greece, and the Greek islands.

Allied land, sea and air forces are attacking in co-ordination with Russian armoured columns driving into Yugoslavia from Rumania.

The vital link between the two forces is being provided by the powerful partisan formations under Marshal Tito, whose operations have been closely co-ordinated with the offensive.

Already Russian tank spearheads driving over the Yugoslav frontier west of Craiova have made contact with the partisans. "Joy is sweeping the towns and villages at the news," said Cairo radio.

The Russians were last reported to be fighting at Orsava, beyond the "Iron Gate" gorge on the Danube and only 90 miles east of Belgrade.

DOOR TO HUNGARY

Capture of this capital city would not only cut nearly all German communications with troops to the south, but would open the back door into Hungary.

In a message to the Balkan countries last night General Wilson made it clear that he expects events to move fast in the new theatre.

"The armies of the United Nations are advancing on all fronts" he said. "The Germans are falling back everywhere. Very soon all countries in Europe, including the Balkan countries, will be free."

He then uttered this stern warning: "It is reported to me that some persons and some political organisations in the Balkans are assisting the Germans to escape.

"These persons and organisations

BACK PAGE—Col. FIVE

Jap Suicide Break at Prison Camp

900 Had Knives

A STATEMENT issued by the Prime Minister of Australia, Mr. John Curtin, last night disclosed an amazing "suicide break" from a prisoner of war camp by 900 Japanese.

The price they paid was 231 dead and 108 wounded, but only the steadiness of the Australian guards averted a massacre.

Mr. Curtin's statement, which pays a tribute to these men, ran:

In darkness at about 2 o'clock on the morning of August 5, more than 900 Japanese prisoners of war in a camp in Australia made an unprovoked mass attack upon their guards.

The Japanese had armed themselves with mess-knives, baseball clubs, and other improvised weapons. They first set their sleeping-huts alight and then rushed the fences of the camp.

The Japanese had provided themselves with extra clothing, gloves, and padding for surmounting, or passing through, the wire fences.

Steady Fire

Large numbers who escaped through the outer fences of the camp attacked and killed an Australian machine-gun crew and attempted to storm the garrison quarters.

These attacks were met by fire from the guards, who showed excellent discipline and restraint throughout the incident.

The prisoners who escaped after the attack had failed were subsequently recaptured, all but a small number, by nightfall on the day of the escape.

During the search for the escaped internees, an Australian officer was brutally murdered by a party of Japanese.

Many other prisoners committed suicide or were killed by their comrades inside and outside the camp.

The total casualties sustained by the prisoners of war were as follows: One officer killed, 230 other ranks killed or died of wounds or died by suicide; one officer wounded, 107 other ranks wounded.

Court of Inquiry

A military court of inquiry was immediately appointed to investigate the matter. The court's report can be summarised as follows:—

First, that conditions at the camp were fully in accordance with the provisions of the international convention.

Secondly, that no complaints as to treatment had been made by, or on behalf of, the Japanese prior to the mutiny.

Thirdly, that the action of the Australian garrison in the successful resistance of the attacks averted a greater loss of life.

Fourthly, of the 231 dead Japanese, it is found that 20 died by hanging and strangulation inflicted by the Japanese on themselves or on one another, nine by suicide from stabbing, two by suicide under a train, five from a combination of self-inflicted wounds and gunshot wounds, and 12 from causes unknown

The extensive preparations made by the Japanese prove beyond all doubt that the onus for the incident rests entirely on the prisoners, and that it was their intention to engage in suicidal combat with their guard.

Strait Fine after 12 Hours' Rain

Sea.—Rippled.

Weather. — Fine after 12 hours' heavy rain until mid-afternoon; about an inch fell Maximum temperature 62 deg.; 45 deg at 10.30 p.m.; visibility good; wind S.W.

Barometer. — Rising after fall.

Mass Murders at Legation

BUCAREST ENVOY WENT MAD

From **HAROLD CARDOZO,** Daily Mail Special Correspondent

MADRID, Thursday.

DIPLOMATIC circles in Madrid are telling the story of a dramatic tragedy which involved many deaths in the German Legation at Bucarest.

From this it appears that when the German Minister, Baron von Killinger, found Rumania had deserted the German cause, was making peace with Russia, and had turned on her former ally, he had a brain-storm and ordered all doors of the Legation to be closed. Then, with a machine-gun, Killinger stormed through the building, killing all he met.

Women clerks begged for their lives, but it is reported that Killinger, shouting "We must all die for the Führer," continued his executions.

Finally, he locked himself in his study and blew out his brains with a pistol.

It will be recalled that last week, according to the German Foreign Office spokesman, there arrrived in Berlin by car an attaché from the German Legation in Bucarest.

Later it was revealed that this attaché had brought in a car with him the bodies of his wife and daughter — allegedly slain by Rumanian partisans.

It is strongly suspected that the attaché's wife and daughter were in the Legation during Killinger's brain-storm, and were included in the wholesale shootings.

LATEST

BOULOGNE BATTLE STILL RAGES

Battle in the Boulogne and Calais areas continued during the night. Strait watchers saw gun flashes sometimes in the Boulogne dock area, but more frequently near Calais and inland. Two fires were burning between Boulogne and Calais.

DUFF COOPER IS GOING TO PARIS

Algiers radio reports that Mr. Duff Cooper, British Ambassador to the Provisional Government, is to leave Algiers next week for Paris.

2

The Daily Sketch

NEWS AND PICTURES

No. 11,019 ★★ FRIDAY, SEPTEMBER 8, 1944 ONE PENNY

General Patton Crushes German Bid To Stem Advance

U.S. TANKS OVER MOSELLE

British Are Only 70 Miles From Cologne

IMPORTANT new gains by the Allied armies in the great two-way advance on Germany were reported in the battlefront messages early to-day.

1. General Patton, meeting his first real opposition since he smashed across from Normandy, last night stormed over the Moselle at two points in the Toul area.

2. Swinging north-east across Belgium, General Dempsey's British Second Army have reached the Albert Canal on a 10-mile front and are piling up huge quantities of armour before moving forward.

The Allied line now runs on a great arc 225 miles long between Antwerp and Toul, the fortress town due west of Nancy.

We control five main crossings over the Meuse and hold 50 miles of the west bank of the Moselle, a tributary of the Rhine.

Eighteen miles north-east of Namur, an American column has captured Huy. The advance here is already driving on Liege.

Further south, Sedan has been liberated and Bievres, 18 miles to the south-east, occupied.

The two new bridgeheads across the 80ft.-wide Moselle were built up by U.S. Third Army infantry who crossed the river under the covering fire of tanks and artillery

Nazi Counter-attack

First big counter-attack by the Germans was launched against the Americans in this sector.

They succeeded in throwing back across the river some troops in the Pont-à-Mousson area, half-way between Metz and Nancy.

The establishment of the new bridgehead is regarded as of the highest importance. It means that the outer defence of Germany is pierced. It was achieved in the teeth of bitter German resistance by near perfect ground and air co-operation between the army and the 19th Tactical Air Command.

General Dempsey is moving his tanks and guns on to the south side of the Albert Canal, said a cable from Doon Campbell, Reuter's correspondent.

Here, again, there was fierce resistance and shell fire. The *Turn To Back Page, Col. 1.*

ALL-OUT BALKAN DRIVE

WITH the Russians sweeping across the Balkans—Berlin reported them last night as having reached Greece—Allied land, sea and air forces have begun a combined all-out assault against the German lines of communication in Yugoslavia.

The offensive is designed to smash the German escape routes in the Balkans, it was stated at Allied Mediterranean H.Q.

British warships in the Adriatic, Marshal Tito's armies, the Balkan Air Force, and the 15th U.S. Air Force are taking part.

Allied H.Q. added that the battle began a week ago, with "Land Forces Adriatic"—the official title of the Allied units in Yugoslavia — and Slovene patriots participating.

The Allied land forces are Commandos who have been staging raids lasting between one and four days, says B.U.P.

'Russians In Greece'

German sources said that the Russians, advancing 160 miles in two days through Bulgaria, reached the Turkish border and entered the Demotica area of Greek Thrace.

In London and Moscow it is believed that only a strong junction of Tito's men with Malinovsky's troops is required to spring the trap on these divisions.

Malinovsky has crossed the Danube with his main forces at Ruschuk and is driving along the good highway to Sofia, while Tolbukhin's men are in Bulgaria on the eastern flank and are driving towards Salonika.

The Battle For Prussia

In the mighty battle raging north-east of Warsaw Russian forces are trying, for the fifth day, to dig a decisive hole in German defences guarding East Prussia.

Col. von Olberg, Berlin war commentator, last night admitted that the Germans had withdrawn a mile or more—the first time since the offensive started that the Germans have admitted retreat.

"It was to avoid the danger of a Russian breakthrough on the southern border of East Prussia," he said.

The Russian communiqué last night referred only briefly to this fighting. It said: "To-day, south-west of Lomza, our troops fought their way into several inhabited localities."

'Truly Great Victory By Montgomery'

—U.S. TRIBUTE

A SPOKESMAN of the U.S. Third Army said in France yesterday that Field-Marshal Montgomery's victory was a truly great one which entirely upset the German plans for withdrawal and perhaps the course of the war.

"The two greatest events of the war to date," he went on, "were Gen. Omar Bradley's strike south of St. Lo and Montgomery's advance through Belgium, which was magnificent."

Montgomery drove into Brussels yesterday morning in pouring rain. The crowds in the cafés and restaurants did not recognise the grey-green touring car until it stopped in front of the town hall.

The Field-Marshal got a terrific reception, and people rushed up, cheering and shouting.

Later the Field-Marshal talked with Prince Bernhard of the Netherlands and the Commander of the armoured and infantry forces at the Albert Canal.

They Beat The Fly-Bombs

LEFT: Prof. Sir Thomas Merton, named yesterday as the inventor of a 1s. range-finder which enabled night-fighter pilots to destroy many flying bombs.

"The idea for this little gadget came to me suddenly," said Sir Thomas yesterday, "and within a matter of hours I had made one up from odd scraps of material."

RIGHT: Squadron-Leader Joseph Berry, D.F.C. (won over Italy) and Bar, named as the R.A.F. Tempest pilot who has destroyed more than 60 flying bombs—all but three at night.

Berry is 24, married, and his home is at Sunnydale-road, Nottingham. He was an income-tax collector till he joined the R.A.F.

Full Story and Pictures—Pages 3, 4 and 5

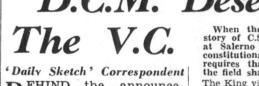

C.S.M. P. H. Wright, V.C., being congratulated by fellow members of the sergeants' mess at a southern England camp where a "Daily Sketch" photographer found a celebration party in full swing. It was nearly eight o'clock last night when his commanding officer gave him the news.

The King Decided D.C.M. Deserved The V.C.

'Daily Sketch' Correspondent

BEHIND the announcement this morning of the award of the V.C. to C.S.M. Peter Harold Wright, of the Coldstream Guards, lies a story of the personal intervention of the King, who, on his visit to the Italian battlefield, said to Gen. Alexander:

"If ever a man deserved the V.C. it is this man to whom I have awarded the D.C.M."

The King asked General Alexander to check all the facts of the story of the Sergeant-Major's gallantry and to report to him personally.

New Investiture

General Alexander did so. The sequel appeared in last night's *London Gazette* which stated briefly that the D.C.M. awarded to C.S.M. Wright and announced in the *Gazette* on January 27 had been cancelled.

Heading a special supplement to the *Gazette* was the announcement that the King had awarded the sergeant-major the Victoria Cross and giving the full story of the gallantry that had won the admiration of the King and led to his personal intervention.

Sergeant-Major Wright, whose home is Old Hall, Wenhaston, Suffolk, will return his Distinguished Conduct Medal and again attend an investiture to receive the V.C. from the King.

The King's personal intervention was thoroughly in accordance with military procedure, which covers such an eventuality.

When the King heard the full story of C.S.M. Wright's gallantry at Salerno he followed the full constitutional procedure which requires that the commander in the field shall be consulted.

The King visited his troops in Italy at the end of July and there, during his meeting with General Alexander, he had the opportunity of discussing the award, which he had waited for since he heard the full story.

General Alexander ordered a full investigation in the field. The reports from eye-witnesses he forwarded to Sir James Grigg, Secretary for War, who then made the recommendation to the King that the D.C.M. should be cancelled and the Victoria Cross awarded.

Immediate Award

It was pointed out in London last night that C.S.M. Wright was given the immediate award of the D.C.M., the highest award that a G.O.C. in the field could bestow on him on his own initiative.

It was in Italy, at Salerno, last September, that C.S.M. Wright, seeing his company held up, went forward and found there were no officers left.

He immediately took charge, crawled forward to see what the opposition was and returned with the information that three Spandau posts were holding them up.

Single-handed he attacked each post in turn with hand grenades and

Turn to Back Page, Col. 4.

TIMELY WORDS OF FAITH

They had devised devices . . . saying, Let us destroy . . . Therefore thus saith the Lord of hosts, Behold, I will punish them.

Jeremiah 11, 19-22.

COMPLETE NEWS—MAGAZINE SECTION—COMIC FEATURES

New York Post

FOUNDED 1801, VOLUME 143, NO. 250. COPYRIGHT, 1944, NEW YORK POST.

TWO SECTIONS NEW YORK, MONDAY, SEPTEMBER 11, 1944 40 PAGES

BRITISH INVADE HOLLAND!

Story on Page 3

F. D. R., CHURCHILL MEET AT QUEBEC

Story on Page 2

Lewis Plans Strikes in Stop-Roosevelt Drive: Riesel

Story on Page 36

The Daily Sketch

No. 11,022 ★★ TUESDAY, SEPTEMBER 12, 1944 ONE PENNY

ALLIED TROOPS FIGHTING IN GERMANY

ALLIED troops are fighting on German soil. General Hodges's U.S. Third Army, after a fierce artillery bombardment, yesterday smashed their way five miles into the Reich north of Trier.

The border was crossed from Luxemburg in "reasonable strength," Supreme Headquarters announced early to-day. Trier is in the heart of the Siegfried Line defences.

General Patton's U.S. Third Army, swiftly driving through Lorraine, captured intact many miles of the Maginot Line along the Luxemburg frontier.

Almost at the same time, General Patch's Riviera invasion army linked up with the "Third" at Cambernon, 16 miles west of Dijon, on the main road to Paris.

And yesterday Goering sent up the Luftwaffe to challenge the Allied Air Forces in a battle which raged all over Central Germany from Hanover to Leipzig—AND LOST 175 FIGHTERS.

Contrary to expectations the Germans did not oppose in any great strength the first invasion of the "sacred soil of Germany," as Hitler once put it.

General Hodges's men have not penetrated far into the Siegfried Line, which is set in depth round Trier, but they have made contact and are undoubtedly probing its strength.

Maginot Guns Intact

Trier is a town with a population of about 60,000. It lies on the river Moselle and does a busy trade in textiles, dyeing and iron production. It claims to be the oldest town in Germany.

Eric Downton, Reuter's correspondent with the U.S. Third Army, cabled to-day: "The Maginot Line guns are still in place, but ammunition and much equipment has been removed.

"Last night advanced units of the Third Army entering Crusnes discovered the entrance to the underground system of communications for the forts in this area."

General Patton yesterday launched an assault to force the Moselle. Everywhere along the 50-mile front stubborn resistance was met and several counter-attacks were reported.

South of the Metz sector an American bridgehead was lost.

Turn to Back Page, Column 2

Luftwaffe Joins Battle —Loses 175

Big Slice Of The Maginot Line Taken

British Slaughter Their Way Into Holland

BRITISH armour and infantry have entered the "inner porch" of the Dutch frontier, and, in the words of a fighting officer, "have got stuck into the Germans and fairly slaughtered them," says Doon Campbell, Reuter war correspondent with the British Second Army.

It has been General Dempsey's biggest and best 24 hours of the campaign in the west. More Germans were killed and more of their equipment destroyed yesterday than in the whole 200-mile run to Brussels.

★ ★ ★

In a fight for a vital road junction the British attacked with everything on hand, won the junction and moved on through 200 German corpses. They took 500 prisoners in this operation.

A bridge across the Escaut canal was badly needed—and strongly defended. The only thing to do was to take it by storm. A famous armoured unit roared into action and crashed the German line.

In two hours the bridge was in our hands, intact and firmly held. A German battalion of 800 men was wiped out in that sector.

★ ★ ★

"It was the hardest fighting since the Seine," said Captain Michael Constant, of Cobham, Surrey. "We have slashed through thousands of Germans who will try to get organised behind us. Now we must do some mopping up."

The taking of that bridge brought us within a mile and a half of the Dutch frontier. The Germans are being squashed by our advance.

They have thrown the weight of their fire power against the Gheel bridges, but British infantry, holding and extending their bridgehead there, had a day's bag of more than 750 prisoners.

With the Luftwaffe practically banished from the skies of Italy, British Ack-Ack guns now concentrate on ground targets. Here are some in action against the Gothic Line. An adjustable fuse in the nose of the 3.7 shell gives the guns a new and deadly punch.

'Crocodiles' Blazing Way Into Havre

From MATTHEW HALTON, Kemsley Newspapers Correspondent With the First Canadian Army

THE First Canadian Army, with its British, Canadian and Polish troops, is now fighting a stiff battle for the Channel ports.

As the American First and Third Armies approach the German frontier our vast supply organisation needs and must have the Channel ports—Le Havre, Boulogne, Calais, Dunkirk, Antwerp.

So once more our fighting men are in a roaring of guns and a moaning of mortars. Again the infantry, the tanks, the sappers, have to wade into powerful positions through the deepest of steel.

On the right wing of the First Canadian Army, Canadian troops now have a bridgehead across the Ghent Canal and should hold Bruges.

In the centre British and Canadians are attacking towards Dunkirk—we are reported within a mile of the town—Calais and Boulogne.

On the left British troops are fighting in the outskirts of Le Havre. A full-dress British attack to take Le Havre was launched on Sunday night. The first men took the high ground dominating the port. Other units then had to go through minefields.

Flails, "crocodile" flame-throwers and certain other strange engines went first to clear gaps. The attack ran into trouble. Some of the tanks were knocked out as they passed through and new gaps had to be made under murderous fire.

The battle continued yesterday, and British forces reached Fontaine le Mallet and the Mongeon Forest, just north of the town, which they now dominate. More than 400 prisoners were taken.

Numerically the German garrisons in the ports are not strong—about 35,000 in all. But the towns are powerfully defended with terrific minefields, many guns and picked troops.

Except for Dunkirk, the whole 55 miles of coast from Gravelines to Zeebrugge has now been cleared.

An unconfirmed report last night said the German commander of Brest had surrendered but that his troops were still fighting it out, house by house.

★ ★ ★

German long-range guns on the French coast yesterday put in three bursts of shelling, apparently against our shipping in the Channel.

STARRY STRAITS

After another sunny day a fresh and cool easterly breeze blew through the Straits of Dover last night. The sky was starlit and cloudless. The barometer has been steady and high for more than 24 hours.

TIMELY WORDS OF FAITH

I will cause them to walk by the rivers of waters in a straight way, wherein they shall not stumble.

Jeremiah, 31, 9.

Daily Mail

NO. 15,092 ONE PENNY ★★ FOR KING AND EMPIRE FRIDAY, SEPTEMBER 15, 1944

LATE WAR NEWS

SIEGFRIED LINE BREACHED

Model May Pull Back Army Behind the Rhine

8 MILES INTO REICH, FIRST FORTS FALL

AMERICAN attacks are tearing apart the Siegfried Line. As reports came in hour by hour last night telling of the success of General Hodges' newly launched assaults, it became obvious that the Germans are merely attempting a fierce and protracted delaying action. Their plan is to cover a general withdrawal of their whole remaining strength in Western Europe behind the Rhine.

There, with as many men and as great a concentration of armour as he can muster, Model will make his all-out stand in the great battle for Germany. But his plan may be upset. The rapidly developing American thrusts may carry the Allied troops to the Rhine before the German forces can mass.

Already yesterday, within hours of the opening of the American drives, tanks and infantry had breached the outer perimeter of the Siegfried Line at three points and were pushing on into the main defences.

South-east of Aachen the Americans smashed five miles into Germany through the first belt of the Siegfried defences. They were last reported one mile from Aachen, driving on to the second belt.

North-west of Trier troops and tanks drove two miles deep into the Siegfried positions, blasting them open bunker by bunker and pill-box by pill-box. Under the attacks Germans came pouring out of forts to surrender.

The biggest advance was made midway between these two penetrations—in the direction of Prüm, a road junction north-east of the border of Luxemburg. The Americans thrust forward eight miles and last night were fighting within two miles of Prüm.

In the Aachen area the American infantry have reached the villages of Forstbach, Kopschen, and Wurmhof. Enemy resistance everywhere is disjointed. Heavy artillery fire is being encountered at some places, but at others only fire from small arms is met.

The German Official News Agency admitted last night that the Americans had penetrated the Siegfried positions at two points south of Aachen.

"Very strong" Allied forces were said to be operating with "uninterrupted air support."

Allied troops were reported on the western approaches of Aachen.

The Agency added: "Extremely bitter fighting developed in the whole area between Maastricht and south-east of Aachen. The Americans succeeded in making several penetrations and the German forces had to be taken back to the Maastricht-Valkenburg line and the western approaches of Aachen."

NOON ATTACK

Reports from war correspondents all suggested that the Germans had hurriedly improvised the Siegfried defences.

Pierre Huss, *I.N.S.* correspondent, reported that the attack on the defences in the Trier area began at noon yesterday.

The German defenders attempted to hold the Americans with machine-gun fire, but the American tanks poured over their positions. The infantry followed.

Machine-gun fire persisted from pill-boxes, which were manned fairly fully, but there were no heavy guns.

Many prisoners surrendered from overrun pill-boxes. They were aged from 35 to over 45, and said they were non-combatant labour troops.

They had been recently evacuated from France and were returned to Trier on Monday last to be dumped into the Siegfried Line.

They had been given rifles and machine-gun ammunition only.

Before night the Americans were holding a strip of German territory north-west of Trier and were then threatening the town.

Mopping-up was proceeding fast, and stubbornly held pill-boxes were being attacked with fire and dynamite.

Huss adds: "I accompanied the American infantry into the Siegfried Line at 3 p.m. and stood on Hitler's Reich for the first time since November 1941, after entering without a passport or Gestapo supervision."

MOSELLE BREAK

To the south of General Hodges' attacks, General Patton has set his American Third Army in motion again.

His troops have captured two more towns south of Nancy on the main Epinal road south towards the Belfort Gap.

They are Charmes and Mirecourt, 25 miles south of Nancy.

The bridgeheads across the Moselle, it was officially stated, have been extended.

The German News Agency expanded this report of General Patton's move.

It reported a complete break-through by the Americans beyond the Moselle towards Chateau Salins, 16 miles north-west of Nancy.

This puts Patton some 20 miles forward from his last-known positions on the Moselle itself.

INTO HOLLAND

Meanwhile, to the north, the drive into Holland is still making good progress. Allied troops have crossed the Dutch border round Maastricht, and British Second Army men stand on Dutch soil somewhere north of De Groote.

British troops have gained more ground between the Albert and Escaut Canals, further extending what was a triangular bridgehead across the Albert Canal, some 17 miles broad and 15 miles deep.

The head of the bridgehead is well across the Escaut Canal, and forward patrols are in Holland.

The towns of Gheel, Mol, Neerpen, as well as Bourg-Leopold

BACK PAGE—Col. SIX

D-plus 100

THE VOICE OF THE ENEMY

Prepare for the Worst says Berlin

'Inner Line' Talk

Daily Mail Radio Station

GRADUALLY, through the voice of Goebbels and his henchmen of the German Propaganda Bureau, Germany is becoming familiarised with the prospect of defeat.

Penetration of German territory is being admitted frankly. Hints are being thrown out of the abandonment of big stretches of the Reich itself.

Walter Farr, *Daily Mail* Special Correspondent in Stockholm, cabled last night:

The whole German Press and battery of radio commentators indicate that the Nazis expect catastrophic news within the next few weeks.

In Berlin, according to travellers arriving here, people are asking: "Where is Hitler? What are our leaders doing?"

The plight of the bombed-out living in temporary houses already amounts to real suffering. Thousands of French, Belgian, and Dutch workers in German factories are asking Germans bluntly to be allowed to go home.

A neutral in touch with German military circles told me: "It is very unlikely that the German people will agree to carry out the 'scorched earth' policy which the Nazis demand as the Allies advance into Germany."

★

A NOTE nearing despair was echoed by Goebbels himself in *Das Reich*. He writes:

"Our path now leads through the vale of grief," and makes the rather damaging admission that:

"It was not so much the valour of our troops which allowed us to penetrate deeply into enemy territory during the first three years of this war. It was rather the luck of the draw—and it was only to be expected that it would not favour us for ever."

He tries, throughout the rest of his article, to reassure.

"We are not allowing ourselves to be mesmerised by the enemy's successes," he says. "We are not rabbits, waiting without a stir, without a move of resistance to be devoured by the serpents.

"Now we know where we stand. We are firmly resolved to make use of any means for the defence of our country and its life, and never, never, even in our most secret thoughts contemplate a cowardly capitulation."

★

THE new strategy of retreat seems to be evoking many awkward questions. Military commentator, Captain Hartmann told Berlin's radio audience last night:

"Germans are puzzled about the term 'Inner Line' which is increasingly emphasised now in German newspapers. They want an explanation.

"Our forces," he added, "now hold lines whose total length is only one-third of what they were towards the end of 1942.

"The 'Inner Line' allowing us to shift troops swiftly over short distances, helps us to tighten our resistance."

Ending as usual with an admission: "By disengaging ourselves from our enemies in the West, East, and South, and by yielding ground to them—almost all that ground which we conquered in the first few years of the war—the German forces become stronger for further defence."

★

POINT to the invasion threat was given in a broadcast by Berlin to the people of the "Siegfried" towns on their behaviour when invaded.

The main news bulletin last night began with a report on the attitude of the population of the Allied-conquered Eupen, "half-Nazi" city, formerly in Belgium.

"The British and American forces must realise what it means to carry the war into enemy territory," said the spokesman.

"The people living in front of the West Wall are greeting the enemy only with the deepest hatred."

To which the spokesman added, spoiling the effect slightly:

"All this is merely a sample of what the Allies will have to experience in the future should they be able to set foot on the soil of Germany proper."

Strongpoint Smashed

Precision bombing by R.A.F. Mitchells and Bostons yesterday eliminated an enemy strongpoint on the outskirts of Boulogne, which was important to the enemy in defence of the town, says 2nd T.A.F. headquarters.

Germans May Quit Norway

To Man West Wall

MR Henry L. Stimson, U.S. Secretary of War, said to-day that the Germans might abandon Norway and Denmark to strengthen the West Wall.

"The Germans are doing additional work on the Siegfried Line," Mr. Stimson said.

"Such parts of the Seventh and Fifteenth German Armies as escaped from Northern France and Belgium have partially recuperated and may be manning the West Wall.

"A good section of the Nineteenth Army got back to Germany, weary and suffering and bereft of most of its heavy equipment."

Mr. Stimson said reports indicated that civilians were being conscripted for a final crucial stand, regardless of their physical condition.—*B.U.P.*

First Allied Radio from Germany

To the roar of Allied and German guns the first Allied broadcast direct from Germany was made yesterday when James Cassidy, N.B.C. correspondent on the Western Front spoke from near the front line.

A C.B.S. correspondent said: "We have broken into the Siegfried Line. From here we can see how our aircraft are strafing German pill-boxes."—*Reuter.*

LIGHTS-UP AREAS TO BE ANNOUNCED

By Daily Mail Reporter

DETAILS of how different areas will be affected by the partial lifting of the black-out restrictions on Sunday are expected to be announced by Mr. Morrison, Minister of Home Security, within a couple of days.

In several coastal belts the black-out will continue without any modification whatever.

Although Mr. Morrison had announced that "half-lighting" would replace the black-out in all parts of the country, with the exception of a few coastal areas news of the continuance of the restrictions in some of these districts has caused disappointment to thousands of residents.

In Cornwall, a notice signed by the Chief Constable, Major E. Hare, states that, pending further directions from the Ministry, there will be no relaxation of the restrictions now in force.

In scores of houses black-out materials have already been taken down and in some cases destroyed.

THESE ARE THE GERMANS

They Thaw Now to U.S. Troops

Apples and V-sign

From RICHARD TREGASKIS
ROTGEN, Germany, Thursday.

THE Germans here are beginning to thaw and are telling the American troops of the terrific regimentation to which they were subjected under the Hitler régime.

For example, a farmer came to me to-day and asked if he could kill a pig. When I laughed he said it was a capital offence to slaughter pigs without permission.

Another man asked if he could go to a special Mass.

One officer said: "A woman told me they are freer now that the Americans have come than they have been during the last 11 years."

At first the people showed great fear and there was a good deal of sniping, but now the reception the Americans are getting has astonished them.

White Sheets

Many faces are wreathed in smiles, the people are bringing gifts of apples, and occasionally a German gives the V-sign.

Now that the people know us they are beginning to curse Hitler.

Most of the people were scared to death at first because propagandists had told them we were going to kill them, but one woman declared, "I knew you wouldn't bother us."

This woman disclosed that she had been listening to the British radio and had hung a white sheet out of her window to show willingness to surrender. The windows in practically every house in the town flew white sheets.

Many people had been living in underground caves for weeks.—*I.N.S.*

On another sector the Germans' reaction is similar. Henry Gorrell, *B.U.P.* correspondent, cabled last night:

As we go farther and farther into German territory there is less evidence of fear or anger on the part of the German population.

So far there has been no sign of resistance from civilians.

Some Germans told us that they had expected to be shot and were very relieved when they were permitted to go their own way.

But not all the Germans are welcoming the U.S. troops. Another *B.U.P.* correspondent cabled from the Aachen area:

Crowds of civilians—many of them German refugees from bomb-shattered Aachen—are lining the roads on the Belgian side of the frontier as the invasion troops stream over the frontier.

There are no smiles. There is no cheering, no hand-clapping. The refugees watch grimly. Many of these people were moved from Aachen into Belgium after heavy raids which, it is said, destroyed three-quarters of the town.

'Right of Asylum'

"Asylum is a right for the country which granted it, a favour for those who ask for it—and not everyone is worthy of this favour," said an official Swiss statement broadcast last night.

Eisenhower Going to the Far East

IF GERMANY COLLAPSES IN TIME

From W. F. HARTIN, Naval Correspondent

GENERAL EISENHOWER is likely to become Supreme Commander for all forces—British, Dominion, American, and Dutch—now converging for simultaneous attack on Japan and her conquests in the China Seas. His appointment is one of the decisions to be made by Mr. Churchill and President Roosevelt at Quebec.

General Eisenhower's position was put to me yesterday in these words: "His appointment would be a foregone conclusion but for the fact that operations against Japan, on the lines now being laid down at Quebec, may begin before his work in Europe is completed."

Against this one can set the fact that Eisenhower has already gone far towards breaking the back of German resistance, and it should not be difficult to find someone to follow him now.

The qualities which have made General Eisenhower such a conspicuous success in Europe are just the ones needed to co-ordinate the efforts of the various commanders in the scattered Eastern theatres of war.

Each, in the long and individual struggle against the advanced posts of Japan's conquests, has fought in a world largely of his own making.

For any one of them now to surrender authority to a headquarters already in the field would undoubtedly create a conflict of personalities.

At the moment nothing but the framework of the plans against Japan is visible in Far-Eastern operations.

Reinforcements of the Royal Navy and the R.A.F. are already finding their way to the SEAC area, but eventually we may expect a concentration there of the best that all three Services can supply.

Likewise, Admiral Chester Nimitz in the Pacific and General MacArthur in New Guinea are merely clearing the path for the liberation of the Philippines and the China coast.

Many new commanders of battle experience in Europe are likely to be brought in, and it is recognised that General Eisenhower is obviously the man who could get the best out of such a diverse gathering of lieutenants.

NO SUPER-COMMAND

QUEBEC, Thursday.—Mr. Stephen Early, President Roosevelt's secretary, stated to-day that the command for the forthcoming offensive against Japan was decided on before the Quebec Conference.

Speaking with great emphasis, he declared: "There has been no question at this conference of the creation of a so-called super-command for the Pacific.

"The commanders were decided upon before President Roosevelt and Mr. Churchill met."

Asked if London had been consulted on this big decision, he replied: "I cannot answer that. It is not within my province."

Mr. Early added that he did not know whether the approved commander for the Pacific included men now operating or whether it was a new command.—*Reuter.*

Lancaster Our First 'Air Liner'

Better Than York After All

By COLIN BEDNALL

THE famous Lancaster heavy bomber may, as the result of plans now being made, prove the salvation of British prestige in civil aviation for the first year or so after the war.

Tests have shown that the ordinary Lancaster, now flying over Germany by day and night, can be converted readily into an air transport of surprisingly high value.

It is believed to be better by a considerable margin than the York, into which the Lancaster had previously been converted at great cost.

In other words, the original is better for transport purposes than the improvement.

More important still, experts are convinced that the Lancaster, in the rôle of an air liner, will have a better performance, a longer range, and a considerably higher speed than any transport likely to be produced by foreign competitors before 1946.

I understand that Canadian enterprise is largely responsible for this face-saving development. The Canadians, furthermore, are already flying Lancasters across the Atlantic as air freighters.

Handed Over

It is expected the Government will shortly announce that a substantial number of British-built Lancaster liners are to be handed over almost immediately to the British Overseas Airways Corporation.

These will "show the flag" to the world immediately after hostilities cease, and may do so in a sensational manner.

Non-stop flights between London and New York are a certainty. The Lancasters will be primarily concerned with fast mail carriage, but it is possible that they will each have sleeping accommodation for about nine passengers.

I believe that behind this development there is a story also of considerable enterprise on the part of the British Overseas Airways Corporation.

Soviets Take Warsaw 'Key'

SOVIET troops yesterday stormed into Praga, eastern suburb of Warsaw and key to the Polish capital.

This was announced last night by Marshal Stalin in an Order of the Day. Praga was taken by troops under the command of Marshal Rokossovsky.

See BACK Page.

'GERMANS' KILL THEIR OFFICERS

Seventh Army Front, Thursday.—Wehrmacht infantry unit composed exclusively of Ukrainians pressed into service, have killed their German officers and come over to Allies.—A.P.

RED CROSS SHIP SUNK IN RAID

Lisbon, Thursday.—The Swiss ship Albula, which was chartered by the International Red Cross for carrying prisoners-of-war parcels, was sunk at Marseilles during an Allied air attack, it is learned here.—Reuter.

2

Cyclone Near New York

From Daily Mail Correspondent

NEW YORK, Thursday.—As New York prepared to weather the greatest Atlantic hurricane since 1926, all ships off the coast and in harbour were ordered to batten down, and squads of life-savers and ambulance men patrolled the beaches.

In the nation's weather bureau experts traced the course of the hurricane as it roared northward, and forecast that it would sweep across New York and south-eastern coastal sections of New England early to-morrow morning.

Story In Page THREE.

Ten-Hour Shelling of South-East Coast

TOWNS in the south-east coast area were still under shell warnings from the enemy's cross-Channel guns at dusk last night. The bombardment then had been in progress for nearly nine hours. Shelling went on hour by hour from midday, with an occasional lull of between 15 and 30 minutes.

The rate of fire was speeded up at times and twice three shells exploded in under five minutes. At dusk the enemy were firing still more. The shelling was again scattered.

The bombardment became more intense after nightfall, and once six shells were fired one after the other from the French coast. Others followed soon after. The shelling was still in progress after 10½ hours.

During the warning, bus services were stopped for some hours, and last night there were no cinema performances.

It is believed that the shelling is being directed from the Cape Gris-Nez and Calais areas.

The daylight bombardment came after ten hours' shelling during the night, which went on until 3 a.m. yesterday.

In the afternoon the English coast was repeatedly shaken by some of the heaviest and longest explosion rumbles yet heard.

It was believed that targets in the Boulogne area were heavily bombed by waves of Allied planes.

Holiday-makers in one town were advised yesterday to move out.

JOCK WHITNEY ESCAPES

Jump from Train

ALLIED H.Q., Mediterranean, Thursday.—Colonel John Hay ("Jock") Whitney, 40-years-old American millionaire racehorse owner, who was captured on August 21, has returned to his headquarters after escaping from a moving train.

The German units moving him from Southern France were dive-bombed, shelled by artillery, and attacked by the Maquis, Colonel Whitney said.

He jumped from a train about five miles north-east of Gray, north-west of Dijon, with another American colonel.—*Reuter.*

New Governor of Malta

The new Governor of Malta to succeed Lord Gort is Lieut.-General Sir Edmond C. A. Schreiber, D.S.O., who is 54.

He went overseas with the B.E.F. in April 1940 as a brigadier, and rose to the command of a division.

More Foot-and-Mouth

Foot-and-mouth disease among pigs has been confirmed at Gwersyllt, Denbighshire, and the usual stand-still order has been made.

Clear Sky in the Strait

Sea.—Calm.

Weather.—Summer-like day with haze clear after dark except near sea level. Maximum temperature 72deg.; 59deg. at 10 p.m.

Barometer.—Steady.

Average net paid circulation for August exceeded
Daily---2,050,000
Sunday-3,700,000

DAILY NEWS

Copr. 1944 by News Syndicate Co. Inc. NEW YORK'S PICTURE NEWSPAPER Trade Mark Reg. U. S. Pat. Off.

FINAL ★★★

Vol. 26. No. 73 New York, Monday, September 18, 1944★ 32 Pages 2 Cents IN CITY LIMITS | 3 CENTS Elsewhere

SKY ARMY IN HOLLAND, OVER RHINE

—Story on Page 3

PRELUDE TO THE DUTCH INVASION

Parachutes strapped to their backs, steel-helmeted Yanks stow battle-gear aboard a C-47 transport at base somewhere in England prior to take-off for Holland. An aerial caravan of 1,000 huge transports and troop carrying gliders carried out yesterday's airborne onslaught on Nazi-occupied Holland, coming down behind Germans opposing the British-Canadian land drives into the Netherlands near the northern end of Hitler's Westwall defenses.

—Story on page 3; other picture back page.

(A.P. Wirefoto from Signal Corps Radiofoto)

"Daily Herald," Monday, Sept. 18, 1944.

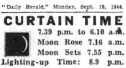

CURTAIN TIME
7.39 p.m. to 6.10 a.m.
Moon Rose 7.16 a.m.
Moon Sets 7.55 p.m.
Lighting-up Time: 8.9 p.m.

Daily Herald

No. 8915 MONDAY, SEPTEMBER 18, 1944 ONE PENNY

STOP PRESS

STOCKHOLM A.A. FIRE

Stockholm, Monday.—"Foreign" planes w over Stockholm last night. A.A. de-nces went into action.—Associated Press.

AIRBORNE ARMY CAPTURES DUTCH TOWNS NEAR REICH BORDER

Thousands Of Paratroops Landed Before AA Guns Opened Fire

From STANLEY WOODWARD, "Herald" War Reporter, Somewhere In Holland, Sunday

MEN of the First Allied Airborne Army, who landed behind the German front line in Holland to-day from a great sky-train of more than a thousand gliders, troop-carrying planes and towing planes, had cleared the enemy from several Dutch towns before nightfall.

Strong units swooped down near the German border, and by night English and American troops were established. The strong fighter and bomber support made the move a success. Losses from flak were small.

It is as yet too soon to assess the tactical situation, but the landing has definitely gone according to plan.

Mortar, machine-gun and artillery fire are going on around us.

We have seen the first prisoners. They looked fit, surly and bewildered. And some of them are unusually young.

The planes and gliders landed with their loads or dropped their paratroops right to time table.

I travelled with them in the fourth glider and landed with them in a turnip field near a house, outside of which a Dutch family greeted us in their Sunday best.

I am writing this from my half-dug foxhole in a little wood near that turnip field.

On the way over it seemed that all the gliders and aircraft in the world were gathered together.

BRITISH ADVANCE

AS the enemy began to rush troops to the areas of Holland menaced by the Allied air landing, General Dempsey's Second Army launched a big offensive from its main bridgehead on the Escaut Canal.

The attack was preceded by a barrage from hundreds of guns. When the barrage lifted, tanks lumbered across followed by British infantry.

Tommies rode on top of the tanks and in carriers. Ahead of them a creeping barrage swept forward 200 yards per minute, while more infantry stalked the woods and fields on both sides.

The landing in Holland was the greatest airborne invasion ever known—and it took the Germans by surprise.

Not a Nazi plane was in the sky when the aerial armada crossed the coast, and clouds of paratroops, followed by glider-borne units, were dropping on their objectives before the enemy's A.A. guns opened fire.

At first, German resistance on the ground was light, but later reports said that stiff opposition had developed in many places.

Jeeps, Tanks, Guns Landed

Supreme H.Q. is maintaining secrecy about the area where the assault from the air was made. But a broadcast to the people of Holland revealed that our troops were landed south of the Rivers Rhine and Lek.

Berlin said that a strong landing was made at noon on the north bank of the Rhine near Nimejen, and that other landings were near Tilburg and Eindhoven, and near the mouth of the Rhine. The German News Agency said later that landings were still taking place.

British, American, Polish and Dutch troops took part in the landing, which began at noon. Some of the gliders probably carried light guns, jeeps and light tanks.

"Everyone in Holland seemed to have been to church," said a fighter pilot.

"They had been walking home in their Sunday best, but everybody was standing in the streets. You could almost see their open mouths.

"The gliders went down as if they were parking. There they were parked together, wing-tip to wing-tip, in straight lines, just like cars in a garage.

"They were all bang in the right spot, and unloading was going on. In one place I got right down and saw the local people in their Sunday best lending a hand with the unloading.

"In another landing zone, the troops were already leaning over an orchard wall talking to a crowd of girls."

Weather conditions were ideal. Low clouds provided cover for the unarmed, unarmoured troop-carriers, but over the zones where paratroops were to drop and gliders to land the clouds lifted and gave perfect visibility.

Enemy Positions Pounded

The paratroops were in action with the enemy long before the last of the gliders had reached the target.

Fifteen hours before the landing the Allied air forces opened a terrific attack on enemy positions in Holland.

Late on Saturday afternoon, Marauders and Havocs bombed Dutch dykes, to impede German concentrations and reinforcements. At night, Lancasters and Mosquitos hit Dutch airfields.

Yesterday morning 850 Fortresses bombed gun positions over a wide area and Mosquitos strafed barracks. The Forts operated in sections with six to 12 bombers in each, and each section was allotted different gun-sites.

Just before the landings began, United States fighters, flying low to draw enemy fire, swarmed down on enemy gun positions in a day of "suicide" flying.

The fighters, carrying fragmentation bombs and extra ammunition, swooped down to roof-top height to draw the guns' fire and then silenced them with bombs.

At the same time, Spitfires, Mosquitos, Mitchells and Bostons attacked the barracks, bombing and strafing the soldiers' quarters, and rocket-carrying Typhoons attacked flak ships.

'GOING WELL' REPORTS ARE COMING IN

From STANLEY BISHOP

"Herald" War Reporter at SHAEF, Monday, 1 a.m.

GOOD radio contact was established last night between the Airborne Army in Holland and Supreme H.Q., and progress reports have begun to filter through.

But it must be, of necessity, some time yet before the first tactical picture of the initial successes can be given.

We must expect a delay of perhaps from twelve to twenty-four hours before the situation can be assessel.

So far everything has gone well and according to plan in the air and on the ground.

Until dusk last evening Allied fighter bombers and fighters were working ahead of the airborne advance, attacking enemy gun posts and defence positions, and breaking up transport columns wherever they were found.

At Heart Of Reich

The attack is being made in the area where the enemy hoped his flank was secure, anchored on the waterways of Holland and the North Sea.

As the operation develops, the right flank of the German armies will be turned.

The new invasion, linked with the advance of the British 2nd and the Canadian 1st Armies from Belgium, is an immediate thrust intended for the heart of the Reich.

CALL TO START RAIL STRIKE

THE Dutch Government, in a broadcast to Holland last night, called for a general strike of all the railway workers "to impede enemy transport and troop concentrations as much as possible."

"The Government," said the broadcast, "is fully aware of the great responsibility which it is taking, but after careful consultation with the High Command it is of the opinion that in the given circumstances this act is of such primary military importance it can no longer be delayed.

"It wishes all faithful and courageous patriots to ensure the carrying out of this action to the best of their abilities."

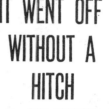

Rings show landings reported by the Germans.

IT WENT OFF WITHOUT A HITCH

From WAR REPORTERS

With First Allied Airborne Army, Sunday.

WAYFARERS in a certain part of Holland to-day saw the most tremendous sight of the war, tight, low formations of sky trains stretching for miles, all round them—above, below and at their sides—fighters forming an armoured aerial tunnel.

Then thousands of multi-coloured parachutes glittered in the bright noon-day sun, gliders, released from their tow planes, drifted gently to earth.

An Army of Liberation dropped from the skies; an army fully equipped, its own supplies dropping with it, to launch a new blow at the Reich and harass the retreating Germans in their rear.

More than a thousand British and American troop carriers took part in the operation.

Germans Caught Flatfooted

By the time the last of them and the last gliders reached the dropping zone hundreds of the earliest arrivals had set up their equipment and were ready for action.

It was aerial D-Day. It had been expected for some time.

Since this First Allied Airborne Army was formed other plans for its operation had had to be scrapped because our ground troops had advanced quicker than was expected or because the weather closed in.

But when it was eventually carried out—H-Hour was 1 p.m.—it caught the Germans flatfooted. The great sky armada was over the drop area before they could man their guns.

By the time the second and third formations of the C.47 Douglas transport planes began to drop their human loads light flak was shooting up.

Late arrivals saw some planes burning down below and others had crash-landed.

Suicide For Any Nazi Plane

But the fighter escort did a smashing job in snuffling out the German gun positions, and the percentage of troop-carrier losses was the lowest of any airborne operations.

Only a matter of minutes before the first troop-carrying planes arrived bombers hammered the area.

A building—believed to be the Luftwaffe H.Q. in Holland—was ablaze. One of our Mosquitos had scored a direct hit.

★ Continued on Back Page

700 TONS ON A GUN POSITION

In daylight last evening a strong force of Lancasters attacked an important gun position and the German garrison on Walcheren Island in the mouth of the Scheldt.

Nearly 700 tons of H.E. bombs were dropped in a highly concentrated attack.

A GUNNER in an escorting aircraft had a front-seat view of part of the huge Allied air fleet as it sped on its way for the airborne assault on Holland.

GERMANS THROW HOME GUARD INTO FRONT LINE

BATTALIONS of Germany's Home Guard, ranging from boys of 1? to men of 65, were flung into the line with paratroop units yesterday in a vain effort to stem another advance on the German frontier.

This attack was opened after American units had crossed the Meuse in force north of Maastricht.

United States officers said that extreme measures to take forts and pillboxes were mostly unnecessary.

"Our shells scared the daylight out of the German kids and the old men. They would scatter into the woods, and when we began shelling the woods they would run into the fields, only to be mown down or taken prisoner by our machine-gunners."

As Aachen's garrison fought pitched battles against Americans driving in from north and south, a Third Army spearhead struck past Stolberg, six miles east of the city to a point only 25 miles from Cologne and the Rhine.

The spearhead troops broke right through the second defence chain in the Siegfried Line.

Big guns, rolling up in support, were in position when the Germans launched a furious counter-attack—the most serious since the Normandy breakthrough.

Cottage Pillboxes

Salvo after salvo crashed on the enemy, silencing his guns and scattering his tank and infantry formations.

Despite Luftwaffe support—30 Messerschmitts strafed and bombed Allied units—the counter-attack was beaten off.

Fast-moving American motorised units pressed on to capture still more fortified zones.

A war reporter with them cabled:—

Just in front of us is a row of little concrete cottages which are catching the special core of the fire.

They look very homelike, pretty little places, and you almost look for vines around the doors until suddenly you see that the "windows" are machine-gun apertures. They are pillboxes, complete with friendly little gable roofs.

These pillboxes are the last fortified line in this area behind the main Siegfried Line—which we have already broken.

Like Madmen

The Nazis are struggling like demented men.

Three times they counter-attacked in broad shoulder-to-shoulder lines, screaming hoarsely as they came forward and falling in unbroken rows before our tanks and guns.

The drive into the Schnee Eifel forest, north-west of Prum, has met strong opposition.

In the Moselle Valley our troops are now across the river in strength.

Metz is reported to be almost completely encircled, and the units that took Chateau Salins and Luneville have now linked up on a 20-mile wide front east of Nancy.

Seventh Army troops are rapidly wiping out the pocket south of Epinal.

Clear And Cool

Straits weather last night: Clear and cool, light easterly breeze. Barometer steady and high.

20,000 Nazis Surrender Without Fight

TWENTY THOUSAND German troops, with their commander, General Elster, surrendered to a 24-year-old American officer on Saturday without firing a shot.

They had been cut off at Beaujency, near Orleans, by the junction of the Third and Seventh Armies.

Lieut. McGill, the American, said yesterday:—

While we were operating 50 miles south of the Loire, F.F.I. units told us that the enemy column was willing to surrender, but would like us to send out two bottalions for a token battle—"to make it look good."

That was impossible.

I drew up terms of surrender, and told two officers—one Belgian and one British, both of whom spoke German—to visit the German general.

Air Watch

I also called for air support to come immediately in case the whole thing proved to be a false alarm.

If our airmen saw a white panel on the ground, they were to know that surrender was making progress; if they saw a red colour they were to strafe the German column.

As it turned out, General Elster agreed to the terms sent over.

But he insisted on formal surrender to an Allied general, and this ceremony was carried out later.

He handed his revolver to General Robert Macon, commander of the 83rd Infantry Division, a unit of the new Ninth United States Army.

Our Heavy Guns In Action

British heavy guns fired across the Straits of Dover in the morning and in the late afternoon yesterday.

Just before dusk the enemy replied with fewer than a dozen shells, including a three-gun salvo.

Men In Charge

The man in command of the Allied Airborne Army is Lieut.-General Lewis H. Brereton.

His deputy-commander is Lieut.-General F. A. M. Browning, British Army.

The Two Men, by Stanley Bishop —Page 2

CANADIANS FIGHTING IN BOULOGNE

CANADIAN troops yesterday received the order: "Capture Boulogne!"

An all-out offensive was launched. By 6 p.m. the outer defences were breached, and by 9.30 p.m. the suburb of Wimereux was captured.

The attack went in with tremendous support from hundreds of Halifaxes and Lancasters which blanketed the outer defences with 3,500 tons of high explosives in little over four hours.

There was large-scale artillery support as flail tanks, flame-throwers and armoured troop carriers advanced against strong gun positions and pillboxes.

Infantry stormed the entire north-eastern defence line, and quickly secured positions dominating the whole town.

Coast Watchers

Many people lined the cliff tops along the South-Eeast Coast of England to watch the battle, which became fiercer after nightfall as R A F bombers went out again to blast enemy strongpoints.

Flares were dropped in and around the port.

The Germans seemed apprehensive of a sea attack as well, for they constantly swept the sea with powerful searchlights, the beams reaching well beyond mid-Channel.

At other times they threw their searchlights on to the cliffs farther to the east, apparently to spot any troops preparing for a flank attack.

Germans Raid Rome

German planes yesterday raided Rome for the first time in strength, and dropped bombs on the outskirts.

FORWARD INTO GERMANY—MONTY

THE triumphant cry now is: "Forward into Germany!"

This was Field-Marshal Montgomery's message to his men broadcast last night. He said:—

The Allies have removed the enemy from practically the whole of France and Belgium, except in a few places, and we stand at the door of Germany.

By the terrific energy of your advance northwards from the Seine you brought quick relief to our families and loved ones in England by occupying the launching sites of the flying bombs.

We have advanced a great way in a short time, and we have accomplished much.

The total of prisoners captured is now nearly 400,000, and there are many more to be collected from those ports in Brittany and in the Pas de Calais that are still holding out.

"Immense Losses"

The enemy has suffered immense losses in men and material. It is becoming problematical how much longer he can continue the struggle.

Such an historic march of events can seldom have taken place in such a short space of time.

You have every reason to be very proud of what you have done.

Let us say to each other "This was the Lord's doing and it is marvellous in our eyes."

And now the Allies are closing in on Nazi Germany from the East, from the South and from the West.

Their satellite Powers have thrown the towel into the ring and they now fight on our side.

Our American Allies are fighting on German soil in many places. Very soon we shall all be there.

Useless Order

The Nazi leaders have ordered the German people to defend their country to the last and dispute every inch of ground.

This is a very natural order, and we would do the same ourselves in a similar situation. But the mere issuing of orders is quite useless. You require good men and true to carry them out.

The great mass of the German people know that their situation is already hopeless and they will think more clearly on this subject as we advance deeper into their country.

They have little wish to continue the struggle.

But whatever orders are issued in Germany and whatever action is taken on them, no human endeavour can now prevent the complete and utter defeat of the armed forces in Germany.

Their fate is certain and their defeat will be absolute. Good luck to you all—and good hunting in Germany.

Fly–Bombs Over

Two flying bombs which crossed the East Coast last evening fell in Southern England.

The first damaged two cottages and smashed a considerable area of glass in a market garden.

Daily Mail
NO. 15,096 ONE PENNY ** FOR KING AND EMPIRE WEDNESDAY, SEPTEMBER 20, 1944
LATE WAR NEWS

BRITISH REACH THE RHINE AFTER 50-MILE RACE

Dempsey Deep in Holland: the Trapped Germans Hit Back

GENERAL DEMPSEY'S Second Army was last night engaged in heavy fighting on the southern bank of the Rhine close to the Dutch town of Nijmegen, three miles from the German border. Nijmegen, where Dempsey's tanks have linked up with the second of the three Air Army groups dropped in Holland on Sunday, was reached before midday yesterday—an advance of more than 50 miles in less than 48 hours. Thirty-seven miles were covered yesterday.

The Airborne Army is also fiercely engaged. Some of the 70,000 Germans trapped between the Dutch coast and the border by the Allied air swoop have joined up and are attempting to break through the Allied corridor. They have brought up heavy artillery to help them to smash through.

Their attack began with sporadic engagements by isolated units. Then the assault became more organised, and a definite onslaught developed against one of the original landing places of the sky-men.

This fighting is going on within gunshot range of the German border. British and Polish troops are believed to be engaged.

With this news came the report also that the Germans are massing for an attack aiming to cut off the spearhead of Dempsey's armour driving on Nijmegen. This concentration is apparently on the German border.

Latest reports indicate that the Germans still hold Nijmegen itself. Dempsey's tanks are on the outskirts of this city, and are helping the airborne men to smash its defences.

At Nijmegen, reached after crossing two of the great water barriers—the Maas and the Wilhelmina Canal—the Second Army is 330 miles from Berlin—10 miles nearer than the Russians at the Warsaw suburb of Praga.

Air reinforcements poured into Holland yesterday, and it is probable that many of these went to the Air Army's stronghold at Arnhem, 15 miles beyond Nijmegen and the Dutch Rhine on the northern bank of the River Lek. Berlin last night reported new landings in Gelderland, the province containing Arnhem, and also in the province of Utrecht, on the Zuider Zee.

When Dempsey's tanks cross the Rhine and link up with the skymen at Arnhem, Germany's last defence line will have been turned.

In front of Dempsey will be gentle, rolling country, ideal for tank warfare, stretching through the Ruhr to Berlin.

RACING ON

Below Doon Campbell, Reuter's Special Corespondent, describes Dempsey's advance. "The position is changing hourly," he says. "Nothing can stop us."

AT 11 o'clock this (Tuesday) morning General Dempsey's spearheads were on the outskirts of Nijmegen, through which the Rhine flows under its Dutch name of Waal.

Everything in this great cross-Holland sweep is going better than "according to plan."

The Second Army is going all out. Generals and Staff officers say: "The Army's swanning again."

The parachutists who landed on Sunday found formidable opposition, and they are now blasting the Germans from fortified positions.

It is a beautiful clear forenoon and the armour is still racing on.

General Dempsey's armoured columns broke the block before Eindhoven at 6.30 last night.

In the town I saw dozens of the Allied airborne troops who came down to win the areas making this great drive possible.

We have shattered the German crust and nothing can stop us. The position is now changing hourly.

The halt last night before Eindhoven was a momentary pause which paid good dividends.

The Second Army put in a set-piece attack and everything collapsed before it. Our main stab through Holland is being well protected on both flanks.

THE LANDING

On the left, British infantry is well across the border and racing on.

On the right, opposition has been more severe, but progress is satisfactory.

An Allied officer, Colonel R. H. Cartwright, who landed among the first paratroopers on Sunday afternoon, told me the story of the Airborne Army's fight.

"From the point of view of technique, the jump we put on was better than the one we put on for Mr. Churchill—but that was a parade ground effort," he said.

"We made a beautiful pattern. It was not our intention to drop on our objectives, but to form up near them.

"Most of the opposition during the landing came from flak. One field was heavily shelled, but we cleared it. So far as I could see, most of the flak was coming down in the Eindhoven area.

AMBUSHED

"At one place we found a lot of dead Germans when we attacked a bridge. We had had that bridge under small arms fire and then the Germans blew it up.

"The Germans at the best fought stiffly.

"Early yesterday morning I started with a convoy of seven jeeps from Son (five miles north of Eindhoven). It was dirty going.

"We were going along a quiet road when we were ambushed. The Germans were behind haystacks and house shutters and they poured a volley of mortar and machine-gun fire into us.

"We stopped and got out of the jeeps—one just ahead was set on

BACK PAGE—Col. SIX

AIM WAS DIRECTED FROM FRANCE

Dover Guns Open up on Germans

Two Batteries Hit

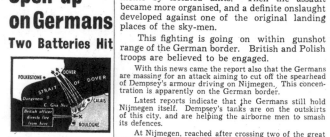

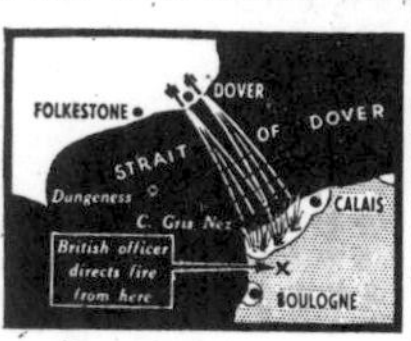

Daily Mail Special Correspondent
OUTSIDE BOULOGNE
Tuesday

DOVER'S long-range guns, directed by radio by a British naval officer on the French side of the Channel, joined in the battle of the French coastal ports and knocked out two enemy batteries. The range was 20 miles.

The guns were ordered to attack the German shore batteries in the Calais-Cap Gris Nez area at extreme range to prevent those batteries joining in the defence of Calais.

It was the first time the Dover guns had fired on a French land target. Previously they had been used only to attack enemy shipping attempting to sneak through the Channel.

Accurate Fire

They ranged first on the wrecks of ships they had sunk off the French coast.

Then, directed by an aircraft flying over the enemy batteries and by the British forward observation officer near Calais, they found their targets.

Their one-ton armour-piercing shells crashed on the enemy's concrete emplacements, putting their guns out of action.

The ground observation officer was Lieut.-Comdr. R. M. Prior, R.N., M.P. for the Aston Division of Birmingham, who is attached to the 1st Canadian Army.

He lay within mortar range of the German positions at Calais directing the shoot.

He said afterwards: "The shoot was a great success. The fire was very accurate for the extreme range.

"Each time the Dover guns fired I could hear two explosions: first the crash of the shell on the German positions, then the boom of the gun from the English coast."

Flames Help

The Dover guns are "Winnie" and "Pooh," each 14in. or 15in. When they are in action they fire alternately.

Meantime, in the battle for Boulogne, flame-throwing Crocodiles forced the surrender of Mont Lambert after knocking out 18 pill-boxes. The citadel inside Boulogne itself, fell about the same time.

Canadian troops hold the port facilities and the northern section of the town. They are advancing slowly towards the south-western defences, and are still mopping-up the main section of the town.

It is believed that 3,000 Germans are manning the south-western defences, and it is thought that they will surrender quickly as soon as the Canadian infantry get near them.

The German News Agency reported last night that General Ramcke, "with the remnants of his followers," has left Brest and is now on the peninsula of Crozon, south of the city.

Stop-Press News

Radio call (intercepted yesterday) from Berlin office of German Army newspaper *Front und Heimat* to its Amsterdam office:

"*Chief editor of 'Front und Heimat' calling Amsterdam branch: Heymer* (presumably the local editor at Amsterdam) *is to return to head office with all technical equipment.*"

The call was repeated throughout the day.

Cloud and Rain in Strait

Sea.—Calm.

Weather.—Overcast all day, with heavy rain in the evening. Maximum temperature 65deg.: 55deg. at 10.30 p.m. Visibility limited to about three miles. Wind, varying between S. and W., light.

Barometer.—Still falling.

Hitler Does Not Bite Carpets

Official—from Berlin

From EDWIN TETLOW

ITALY FRONT, Tuesday.

HITLER does not bite carpets, nor curtains. This is official now.

Eighth Army troops have captured a document addressed to the German 1st Parachute Division from the division's political education officer, saying so, in these humourless words:

"Officers must counteract, with all possible means and with conviction, assertions made by the enemy, as well as some of our own people, that the Führer goes mad with rage and when in that state tears down curtains, bites the carpet, and rolls in convulsions on the floor.

"In actual fact, there are witnesses who know that Hitler is well above such lack of control, though many a man in the street, if he were exposed to such disappointments and grief which the Führer has to bear, would have gone under long ago."

'It Will Be Over This Year,' Says Monty

By Daily Mail Reporter

The most up-to-date review of the war was given in a field in Belgium by a great expert—Field-Marshal Sir Bernard Montgomery, who presented medal ribbons to officers and men of the 15th Scottish Division for heroism on the Normandy beaches, and then told them:

"BEFORE we started this business I gave it as my opinion that if we did our stuff we could have the war against the Germans over this year.

"It is now the middle of September, and I will go so far as to say that that statement is absolutely right. There is no doubt about it.

"The Germans are in a very awkward position.

"No human power can stop the utter and complete defeat of the remnants of the German Army. If you defeat the German armies, everything else is yours for the asking.

"I would say that there is no point in rushing straight away to Berlin to-day or this week. If you first defeat the Germans or collect them in as prisoners you will make the job easy.

Big Blunder

The Germans had made many mistakes. Their first was on the day the Allies landed on the Normandy beaches.

The answer to invasion should be very quick — counter-attack—but the Germans waited. Then, instead of conserving their reserves and giving up ground if necessary to do it, they gathered reinforcements from all over Europe and flung them piecemeal into the battle.

This enabled the Allies to gain a great victory in Normandy, and from that moment everything was easy.

The second great German mistake was after the American break-through on July 25, when they assembled six panzer divisions in an attempt to break through to the coast.

"At that moment," he said, "our right flank had reached Le Mans, making for Paris. We immediately stopped our right wheel and turned the flank northwards to go in behind the Germans.

"And from that moment, I maintain, we had won the war.

LEOPOLD TO RETURN

Say the Belgians

BRUSSELS, Tuesday.—King Leopold is to return to the throne of Belgium. This was stated by M. Pierlot, the Belgian Prime Minister, speaking at the first meeting of the Belgian Parliament held in liberated Brussels.

As Chief of the State, Leopold will resume and exercise his constitutional prerogatives and the Monarchy will remain, said M. Pierlot. "For more than a century it has been an essential element of the unity and stability of the nation and the State," he added.—*B.U.P.*

Greek Officials Go to Greece

CAIRO, Tuesday.—Representatives of the Greek Government have left for Greece, it was officially announced in Cairo to-night. "Your hour has come," the Greek Prime Minister, M. George Papandreou, said in a message to the Greek population from Italy.

It is not stated that the Greek Government is going to Athens, but presumably to territory evacuated by the Germans.—*B.U.P.*

Three E-boats Sunk

The frigate Stayner (Lieut. A. V. Turner, R.N.V.R.) patrolling with light coastal forces off Dunkirk on Monday night sank one of a force of three E-boats and M.T.B.s sank the other two, states an Admiralty communiqué.

CLIFFORD CABLES FROM HOLLAND

Our Tanks Packed the Roads to Rhine

The Dutch Gaped

The following message, delayed in transmission, was received last night from Alexander Clifford, who is with the spearhead of the British Second Army in Holland. Clifford describes the early stages of General Dempsey's breathtaking thrust to the Rhine.

WITH BRITISH ARMOURED FORCES, HOLLAND,
Monday Night (delayed).

YOU never saw such a sight as the road into Holland.

For mile after mile beyond the frontier it was solid with British tanks. They overflowed into the fields and parked down among the heather and under the fir trees. And the stolid Dutch villagers gaped at them dumbfounded.

The strength and solidity of our thrust was the impressive thing. It has hammered through the tough crust of the German defence.

Paradoxically, the tip of the mighty spearhead, the front line, was an anti-climax. You realised what a little thing is sufficient to hold up a mighty column for an afternoon. And you sensed the atmosphere of an armoured thrust like this—an atmosphere very different from accepted ideas of a blitz.

The focal point of it all was a modern villa south of Eindhoven. It was painted white and its roof was thatched and it belonged to someone connected with the huge Phillips electrical works.

His children were playing on the lawn and sailing boats in the swimming-pool. In the drawing-room the colonel of the leading battalion was directing operations.

The trouble was the Germans had planted perhaps half a dozen anti-tank guns in the street of a little village.

★

THE stationmaster—whom we consulted by ordinary telephone—said there were three tanks as well. But whatever the Germans had was well dug-in and camouflaged, and waiting for us.

Just near the white villa which was headquarters we had already knocked out a German self-propelled gun mounted on a Mark III. tank chassis. But when we tried to get farther ahead we found these anti-tank guns firing slap down the road.

There were probably not more than a couple of hundred Germans there. But it was going to cost us a massacre of tanks if we set out to overrun the positions. There were probably minefields as well. And the guns were manned by resolute men with orders to defend to the end.

Reconnaissance parties were sent out right and left. They found every little road blocked in some way. The armoured cars careered away across country and wirelessed back that they had met parachutists.

But that still left this ring of German positions challenging our progress.

There it was.

We had started a tremendous armoured drive into Holland in conjunction with a fantastic airborne landing. And here we were, held up not by any stupendous battle, but by a handful of men who were doing a small-scale suicide act.

★

THE colonel paced the smooth lawn — dodging the bathing costumes which were laid out to dry—and then telephoned back to the artillery.

The shells started to whimper spasmodically overhead.

Sightseeing Dutch civilians cowered impulsively behind tanks and then pulled themselves together and continued their stroll. The shells landed near a windmill just ahead.

The Germans fired back with whatever they had. For a few minutes the smug garden city looked like a battlefield. Then the smoke cleared and everything went on as before.

Parties of infantry went forward, dodging from house to house and hedge to hedge.

The rhythms of the British and

BACK PAGE—Col. FIVE

'V1 Inventor' Charge

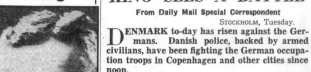

GEORGES CLAUDE, the French scientist, has been arrested at Nancy charged with being the inventor of the "V 1" flying bomb. Claude, who invented the Neon light, is an expert on the production of liquid air and artificial nitrates, and had long been engaged on experiments with rockets. A Royalist, he is alleged to have been one of the earliest and most enthusiatic collaborators.

German Bayonets Evict Germans

From RICHARD TREGASKIS

INSIDE GERMANY, Tuesday.

GERMAN documents captured by the First American Army include orders for the evacuation of all citizens, except males aged 16 to 60, in the Aachen-Cologne area of 2,000,000 people.

Thirty thousand people remained in their cellars despite efforts by Storm Troopers to rout them out at the point of the bayonet.

Until yesterday they had hidden in concrete fortifications, from which many of them were driven out.

Word was passed from strong-point to strong-point, and they escaped to their own shelters to await the arrival of the Americans.

Half a dozen Germans who fled from Aachen to the Allied lines say that people were driven from the bunkers by bayonets.

According to these people, Nazi Party officials began to leave last week, and 30,000 civilians went with them.

Democrats

When the 30,000 remaining Aachenites saw that the Nazis and the police were deserting them, they set up a "democratic" Government at the old German military H.Q.

The official evacuation order allows each person 33lbs. of luggage, and extra for baby carriages and bicycles. This order is being widely disobeyed in the towns of Brand, Kornelimunster, and Aachen.

Last Thursday Himmler was in Aachen, and after consultations with the local Nazis, the eviction of Germans from their homes began.—*I.N.S.*

Brownshirt formations have been sent to Western Germany for "special duties," said Berlin radio last night.

They were inspected by Chief of the S.A. Scheppmann, who told them that they must be an example to the civil population of the western provinces of the Reich.

DEWEY IN A RAIL CRASH

Train Hits Wreckage

CASTLE ROCK, Washington, Tuesday.—Mr. Thomas Dewey, Republican candidate for the U.S. Presidency, escaped injury but was severely shaken when a special train in which he was travelling crashed into the wreckage of a goods train at Castle Rock to-day.

Mrs. Dewey, who was travelling with her husland, was also severely shaken. Several passengers were injured.—*Reuter.*

FINNS TO LEASE BASE CLOSE TO HELSINKI

ERNST VON BORN, Acting Prime Minister, last night broadcast to the Finnish people the armistice terms to Finland signed with Britain and Russia earlier in the day in Moscow.

"To-day will be one of the hardest days in our history," he said. The principal terms he outlined were:

1. Porkkala Peninsula, south-west of Helsinki, and adjacent territory to be leased to Russia for 50 years. This will bring the Russians within 10 miles of the Finnish capital;

2. Return to the frontiers drawn up after the 1939-40 war. Thus Finland loses Viborg, and a large part of Karelia;

3.—Petsamo area (Finland's only outlet to the Arctic) to be ceded to Russia:

4.—Airfields in South and South-west Finland as well as the Finnish merchant fleet to be temporarily placed at the Allies' disposal:

5.—German troops in Finland to be disarmed and handed over to the Allies:

6.—Finnish Army to be placed on a peace footing; and

7.—£75,000,000 reparations to be paid over six years—only half what was proposed in the spring negotiations.

Revolt Sweeps Denmark

KING SEES A BATTLE

From Daily Mail Special Correspondent

STOCKHOLM, Tuesday.

DENMARK to-day has risen against the Germans. Danish police, backed by armed civilians, have been fighting the German occupation troops in Copenhagen and other cities since noon.

King Christian, the Queen, and the Crown Prince and Princess watched the battle in Copenhagen raging round the Royal Palace of Amalienborg.

A hundred and sixty of the palace police, backed by civilians, were to-night still holding out against attacks by detachments of German marines.

At one time in the afternoon the King and the Royal Family stood on the balcony while Danes and Germans were firing at each other's positions.

As the fighting developed, however, the Royal Family were forced to take shelter in the palace cellar.

The Germans have entirely surrounded the palace, and to-night are said to have brought up light artillery.

In the meantime, civilians are demonstrating in Copenhagen streets, making things more difficult for the German authorities.

The revolt broke out when the Germans throughout Denmark attempted to disarm the police everywhere.

It is thought that the Allied air invasion in Holland heartened the Danes to resist. They have believed for some time now that a landing of some sort is coming in Denmark.

The German-controlled radio reported that the fighting started in Copenhagen when Danish Royal Guards opened fire on German troops. Losses were suffered by both sides.

The radio accused the Danish

BACK PAGE—Col. THREE

Winter Milk Ration is Threatened

By Daily Mail Agricultural Correspondent

ANXIETY is growing over whether the winter milk supply will be sufficient to maintain the consumers' ration.

The ration from November 7 to April 16 last winter was two pints a week for each person.

Drought in the South and excessive rain in the North have seriously diminished the crops grown for cows and spoiled their quality, and the National Farmers' Union have placed the facts of a "grave outlook" before Mr. Hudson, Minister of Agriculture.

It is felt that only by an official grant of emergency supplies of feeding-stuffs in the areas chiefly affected can a serious decline in the winter output be prevented.

Footnote.—Although the milk ration may reach its lowest level yet, the weekly cheese ration will be increased from two to three ounces from Sunday, October 15.

'WAR OVER BY NOVEMBER 15'

Montreal, Tuesday.—Delegates to the U.N.R.R.A. Conference were told by military observers recently back from overseas that all indications were that the war in Europe would be over by November 15, according to to-day's "Montreal Star."—Reuter.

DUREN UNDER FIRE

American artillery is shelling German town of Duren, ten miles beyond Stolberg and 18 from Aachen.

2

Heavies Raid the Tirpitz

LANCASTERS with 12,000lb. earthquake bombs have attacked the 41,000-ton German battleship Tirpitz.

Though a smoke-screen prevented crews from judging results, one pilot saw a sudden red glow, too large even for the effect of a 12,000-pounder explosion.

Story in BACK Page.

DAILY MIRROR, Friday, September 22, 1944.

Daily Mirror

SEPT 22

No. 12,719
ONE PENNY
Registered at the G.P.O. as a Newspaper.

DEMOBBING—FULL PLANS

Pay rises for long service | New call-up of deferred men

By BILL GREIG

HERE is the news for which the country has been waiting . . . how the men and women will be demobbed, what will happen to the men now deferred, the new rates of pay for the Services. Main points are:

After the ending of the war with Germany and while that with Japan continues, young men now deferred will be called up and also men reaching military age, while at the same time demobilisation will begin.

Men and women from the Forces will replace those called up so that there will be no loss of output.

Demobilisation priority will be based on age and length of service. (See Key Chart on Back Page.) Neither overseas service, marriage, size of family, nor having a job waiting will count.

Certain skilled men will be released out of their turn to assist in restarting industry and building houses. They will not be allowed to go back to their old jobs but will work where directed.

No man will be forced to leave the Forces out of his turn and all will be able to volunteer for further Army service. Those leaving out of their turn will lose certain benefits.

Service pay rates are increased as from September 3 by 1s. for the first three years of service for privates with 6d. for each succeeding year up to five. N.C.O.s and officers receive proportionate increases.

Japanese campaign pay will range from 1s. a day increase for a private to 11s. for senior officers. This also applies to troops in India and naval men serving ashore.

The cost of these increases will be £100,000,000 a year.

DEMPSEY'S 2nd BRITISH ARMY REACHES THE LAST RHINE CROSSING—LINKS UP WITH PARATROOPS AT ARNHEM, SAY NAZIS

GENERAL DEMPSEY'S Second British Army, bursting across the southern arm of the Rhine delta over the captured Waal bridge at Nijmegen, have reached the northern arm—the Lek, last big water barrier to the outflanking of the Siegfried Line

This sensational admission was made by Berlin last night. Dempsey's men, it was stated, have linked up with the isolated British paratroops in heavy fighting at Arnhem, on the Lek.

This reported ten-mile thrust found no confirmation at SHAEF, where it was stated at midnight that there was still hard fighting at Nijmegen.

Air scouts have spotted German transports moving east out of Arnhem.

Allied front-line messages said the spectacular battle for the concrete bridge at Nijmegen ended in our favour soon after the harried Germans had loaded it with dynamite intending to destroy it.

But before they could do so they were surprised by American airborne troops who crossed the river to the west and closed in from behind while British tanks made a frontal attack.

More reinforcements, including Polish paratroops, and supplies were flown to the airborne army yesterday

Thunderbolt escorts destroyed twenty German planes in air fights. Four Thunderbolts are missing.

"RED ARMY IS INSIDE WARSAW"—ANNOUNCE HUNS

THE Red Army has entered the western suburbs of Warsaw, the German News Agency announced last night within twenty-four hours of their earlier admission that small parties of Russian troops had crossed the Vistula and are fighting in isolated pockets around the city area.

This unconfirmed statement followed a denial by Polish official circles in London that Polish commando paratroops had been dropped on the city, as reported in an earlier German broadcast.

On the Baltic front the Russians were yesterday rolling on another capital, Tallinn, pursuing the Huns through the Estonian countryside "like an avalanche."

One Estonian unit is in the forefront of the advance, passing their burning homesteads set on fire by the Germans.

The capture of the key railway town of Rakvere, fifty-five miles from Tallinn, was announced in last night's Soviet communique.

The Red Army drive through Western Rumania is now only twelve miles from the Hungarian frontier.

HUNS SWITCH TO HOLD DEFENCES IN GOTHIC LINE

KESSELRING was reported yesterday to be moving troops from the west coast of Italy to bolster up his defences in the central Gothic Line, after the Fifth Army had captured four more mountains guarding the route into the Lombardy Plain.

The Allied drive smashed a way toward the mountain village of Santa Lucia which forms part of the Futa Pass defences.

Eighth Army troops continue their hard-driving advance against most bitter resistance between the San Marino Republic and the Adriatic with Greek forces now within a mile of Rimini.

Bulldozers earth up Huns in pillboxes

BULLDOZERS are earthing up Siegfried Line pillboxes containing "No surrender" Germans, according to a Reuter war correspondent last night.

Deadly house-to-house fighting was raging last night in Stolberg, ten miles east of Aachen. The Allies have taken valuable high ground on the eastern edge of the town.

The Press liaison officer at Hitler's H.Q. broadcast: "North-west of Aachen, in the Maastricht salient, Allied columns forced their way forward but were halted west of Geilenkirchen, twelve miles north of Aachen."

Most of the port of Boulogne has been cleared. About 6,000 prisoners have been taken so far.

In Belgium, south of the Scheldt, progress in driving the trapped Germans back to the estuary is quickening.

Poles have closed up to the Scheldt mouth from north of Antwerp to Terneuzen and have taken 1,300 prisoners.

BELGIAN REGENT

The Belgian Parliament yesterday approved the decree appointing Prince Charles Regent in the absence of King Leopold.

DEMOBBING

Service and age the key: marriage does not count

GENERAL demobilisation does not start till Japan is beaten, but piecemeal demobbing starts when Germany is beaten.

Man (and woman) power will have to be re-arranged, between the Services and the factories as the military situation develops, and the call-up will continue, even while men are being released from the Forces to return to industry.

The Fifty and Overs will be out first, if they want to go.

Age and length of service will count together for the others. Two months service gives a man the credit of an extra year on his age.

Thus a man of twenty-four, with five years' service, a man of thirty, with four years' service, a man aged thirty-six, with three years' service, a man aged forty-two, with two years' service, and a man of forty-eight, with one year's service, will all be equal in the demobbing Age, plus service.

RARE EXCEPTIONS

to this will be certain specialists, such as some builders, wanted urgently for reconstruction. They will be demobbed out of turn, but some men now exempt as munition makers will be called up.

No man will be released from the Forces if the military situation is such that he ought to stay in, and, again,

(Continued on Page 2)

CALL-UP

Building to have any priority that is going

I UNDERSTAND that it is not intended to go high in the age limits in the new call-up of men for the war in Japan. In most cases they will be below 30, but the final decision will not be taken until it is clear how many men will be required, writes Your Political Correspondent.

As they leave the munitions factories and the office desks those workers will be replaced by men who have had Army service and are being released in their groups.

The call-up of boys for the mines will continue, and it is not anticipated that many miners will have to be released as specialists as most of them were called up in the early days of the war. They will therefore be among the first out, but their numbers may not give all the workers required.

Almost all the skilled men to be released under Class B—that is men essential to restarting the country's industry—will come from the building and allied trades.

They will not be allowed to pick and choose their jobs but will go where directed.

A few teachers may also be released, but most of them will have to wait until the builders have got the schools ready.

No employer will be allowed to ask for any particular man.

Mr. Bevin is determined that the system which operated after the last war when employers brought out relatives and friends first will not happen again.

This, of course, applies only to the men released as specialists out of their turn.

PAY

7 shillings a week extra for those below sergeant with three years' service

By Your Political Correspondent

NEW long-service-pay rates for the Forces come into operation as from September 3, Japanese campaign rates on November 1.

It will be impossible for the authorities to cope with the new rates at once, and men should not expect to receive new rates and back money immediately. Some weeks may elapse or even longer in certain theatres of war.

I understand that the Chancellor of the Exchequer has ruled that War Service increases are to be subject to income tax, but not the special pay for the Japanese campaign.

Women will receive two-thirds of the War Service increase and of the Japanese pay and full Far East allowance. This allowance takes the place for all ranks of additions now made because of service in certain areas.

Under the War Service increase a private soldier who was in the Army on September 3, 1939, and will, therefore, have completed five years' war service, will be entitled to three increments—the first 1s. for completing three years' service, the second and third 6d. each for completing his fourth and fifth years.

Thus he will be entitled to another 2s. a day on top of his present pay which is 4s. 9d. or 5s. a day.

For other ranks the rates are:—

7s. a week below Petty Officer and Sergeant, after three years' war service, with an additional 3s. 6d. a week for each subsequent year's war service.

10s. 6d. a week for Petty Officers and Chief Petty Officers, Sergeants and higher N.C.O.s and Warrant Officers of the Army and RAF after three years' war service, with an additional 3s. 6d. a week for each subsequent year's war service.

15s. 9d. a week for officers be-

(Continued on page 2)

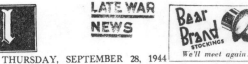

Daily Mail
NO. 15,103 PRICE 2 FR. 50
CONTINENTAL EDITION
THURSDAY, SEPTEMBER 28, 1944

LATE WAR NEWS

THE NEWSPAPER FOR THE ALLIED FORCES IN FRANCE

EPIC OF SKY MEN

THE AGONY OF ARNHEM

TO-DAY The Daily Mail is able to print pictures *taken from the inside* that show the Agony of Arnhem. The photograph above—radioed from a neutral source last night—is of exhausted and wounded parachutists captured after their great fight against odds.

PARATROOPS in action, firing on the nearby enemy with a 3-inch mortar, while themselves are under heavy fire. The Airborne men brought this picture back with them when the survivors were finally withdrawn. Other pictures on BACK Page.

ONE of the airborne photographers wrote: "We are completely surrounded. Our perimeter becomes smaller every hour. Now it is a matter not of taking pictures, but of fighting for our lives. If the land forces don't contact us soon, then we've had it."

230 HOURS OF HELL

From **RICHARD McMILLAN**, B.U.P. War Correspondent

WITH BRITISH ARMY BEFORE ARNHEM, Wednesday.

STRUGGLING through a hurricane barrage of fire from 88mm. guns, tank cannon, and machine-guns, the last survivors of the noble band of British Airborne troops who held the Arnhem bridgehead for nine days were ferried over to our lines during Monday night.

I saw the tragic but heroic cavalcade of bloody, mudstained, exhausted, hungry, and bearded men flood up from the river bank into our lines after going through 230 hours of hell.

Many were stretcher cases. Many were wrapped in blankets. Some hobbled with sticks. All were so completely exhausted that they could hardly keep their eyes open. They were beaten in body, but not in spirit. "Let us get back again; give us a few tanks and we will finish the job," they said.

Every one of them had a story to tell of terror by day and by night, of ceaseless enemy attacks with flame-throwers, tanks, and self-propelling guns firing high explosive and armour-piercing shells.

Captain Bethune Taylor, of Landsdowne-place, Cheltenham, wearing a beard like a French poilu's, told me his story of the tragic adventure as he struggled against sleep.

"Most of the division dropped on Sunday," he said. "I—a gunner—dropped on Monday. It was easy. A bit of flak hit our glider, but we landed west of Oesterbeek, and took up positions.

"There were odd snipers, but they did not cause much trouble, and we started moving towards the bridge. One brigade began to move down the railway lines.

"It ran into the first tough opposition. Eighty-eight millimetre guns were at the road and rail crossing and they forced this section back.

FIREWORKS BEGIN

"That was the beginning of the fireworks. The next day the situation began to deteriorate. We were forced to take up new positions.

"We scooped out some earth in a cabbage patch and got our guns going. We took a bit of a bashing that day—from 88mms., from tanks, and machine-guns.

"We were told to withdraw, and at nightfall we did so, with tanks following us up. We then got into a field in the middle of a wood. The German tactics were to send in tanks followed by infantry. The tanks fired then turned away, leaving the infantry.

"We usually managed to clean up the infantry, who were not too good. But then the Germans brought in flame-throwers and self-propelling guns. They gave us more than we gave them. They also sent over fierce fire from mortars.

"The weather was fine, with odd spots of rain. We had two days' food, with an extra day's food for the whole division. The resupply seemed to work well.

"We marvelled at the amazing

BACK PAGE—Col. FIVE

'Break-out' Order to Survivors

From **ALAN WOOD**, Representing the Combined Press

WITH ARNHEM AIRBORNE FORCE, Tuesday.

THIS is the end. The most tragic and glorious battle of the war is over, and the survivors of this British airborne force can sleep soundly for the first time in eight days and nights.

Orders came to us yesterday to break out from our forest citadel west of Arnhem, cross the Rhine, and join up with the Second Army on the south bank.

Our commander decided against a concerted assault on the Germans round us. Instead, the plan was to split up into little groups, 10 to 20 strong, and set out along different routes at two-minute intervals, which would simply walk through the German lines in the dark.

Cheeky patrols went out earlier tying bits of white parachute tape to trees to mark the way. To hinder the Germans waking up to what was happening, Second Army guns laid down a battering box barrage all afternoon.

The first party was to set off at 10 p.m.; our group was to leave at 10.1 p.m. They went round distributing little packets of sulphanilamide and morphia. We tore up blankets and wrapped them round our boots to muffle the sound of our feet in the trees.

Waited for Boats

We were told the password—"John Bull." If we became separated, each man was to make his way by compass due south until he reached the river.

Our major is an old hand. He led the way, and linked our party together by getting everyone to hold the tail of the parachutist's smock of the man in front of him, so our infiltrating column had an absurd resemblance to some children's game.

It was half-light, with the glow of fires from burning houses around, when we set out. We were lucky; we went through a reputed enemy pocket without hearing a shot except for a stray sniper's bullet.

Another group met a machine-gun with a fixed line of fire across their path. Another had to silence a bunch of Germans with a burst of Sten fire and hand grenades.

Another had to pause while a German finished his evening stroll

BACK PAGE—Col. FOUR

'Jet' Planes Beat the Fly-bombs

BRITISH jet-propelled aircraft fought "with success" against the flying bombs, it was announced last night.

This is the first statement about our jet-planes since January last.

Reports from the south-east coast areas during the heavy flying-bomb attacks stressed that the two fighters most successful against them were the newest Spitfire and the secret Tempest.

The statement last night was issued simultaneously in Britain and America.

It added: "Details of the jet-propelled aircraft and their engines must still remain secret, but research scientists, aircraft technicians and workers in both Britain and America may take pride in their work."

About Germany's jet-planes, the Ministries say: In spite of their high speed and rate of climb, they have shown themselves to possess poor manœuvrability.

'Hot Gospeller' Dies

OAKLAND, California, Wednesday.—Aimée Semple MacPherson, the "hot gospeller" evangelist, died at Oakland to-day of heart disease. She was 53.

She had a temple of her own and her services had stage settings and theatrical lighting. She visited England in 1926 and 1928.—*B.U.P.*

Arnhem Gave Us Nijmegen

2,000 Men Safe Out of 8,000

TWO thousand troops of the First British Airborne Division were evacuated from the Arnhem bridgehead out of 7,000 to 8,000 dropped in the area, according to an American broadcast from Paris last night.

The speaker said the figure may be higher. About 1,200 wounded were left behind in the care of the Germans and British doctors who stayed with them.

The Germans claimed that they held 6,450 prisoners, including 1,700 wounded, and that British killed numbered 1,500.

At SHAEF last night it was emphasised that the Arnhem operation must not be regarded as a failure.

Without it we could never have hoped to capture the even more vital Nijmegen bridge, where the Waal is twice as wide as the Lower Rhine at Arnhem.

The British troops prevented the Germans from moving south at speed to Nijmegen, and forced them to send their reinforcements by a roundabout route through Emmerich. When they reached Nijmegen they were too late.

Two to three days is regarded as the fighting span of airborne troops. The First Division held out for nine days.

Bad weather eventually made withdrawal necessary.

★

A correspondent with the British Second Army has given his reasons for the failure of General Dempsey's spearhead to relieve the airborne forces.

After the weather he blames the difficult, canal-intersected Dutch countryside, where our tanks had to keep to elevated roads and were consequently good targets for hidden German 88mm. guns.

The epic of the airborne invasion of Holland began on Sunday, September 17.

While American formations were securing the bridge at Nijmegen, British troops, dropped 10 miles deeper behind the German lines, fought their way into Arnhem and for a time controlled the bridge there.

But the Germans, acutely sensitive to this grave threat, rushed up some of their best units and finally the gallant little band controlling the bridge was overcome.

From then on the rest of the British force held out grimly on a stretch of wooded high ground about three miles to the west of Arnhem.

General Dempsey's men struck north from Nijmegen in a determined effort to relieve them, but only a few patrols and limited quantities of supplies got across the Rhine.

German troops lining the north bank in strength prevented an effective link-up.

Enemy Retreat in Holland Begins

BRITISH 2ND ARMY H.Q., Wednesday.

MORE than 100,000 Germans in West Holland are in process of organising a mass getaway. They are attempting to withdraw north and then eastward through the 25-miles gap between Arnhem and the Zuider Zee.

The gap is their only hope of escape.

The British corridor from Eindhoven to west of Arnhem bars all other west-east routes to the Reich.

The Luftwaffe yesterday made an all-out attempt to aid the withdrawal by an attack on the great Nijmegen span bridge, across which all Allied transport must pass to Arnhem.

From five o'clock onwards last night the German planes used everything, from bullets to a pick-a-back glider bomb, in the attack.

Allied traffic was halted for a short time while débris was cleared round a 20ft. hole near one of the approaches.

The British corridor continues to broaden. General Dempsey's forces are making steady progress in the two-flank advance west and east of it.

Canal Line

British and Canadian troops on the west hold a firm line along the Antwerp-Turnhout canal.

They have mopped-up a six-mile stretch of territory.

Farther north on this flank there is very stiff fighting in the woods to the west of Oedenrode—where 48 hours ago the Germans momentarily cut the corridor highway.

The Germans are fighting well to hold this flank to make possible the general withdrawal from West Holland.

East of the corridor two re-equipped German divisions, the 107th Panzers and the 10th S.S., have had 150 of their 200 new tanks smashed by the British armour, and opposition to our thrust is diminishing.

Meanwhile, in their offensive against Calais the Canadians have cleared the whole area west and south-west of the town.

The Germans have withdrawn into the town itself and, protected by water inundations, are offering heavy opposition.—*Reuter.*

Throughout the British south-east "hell-fire" area bills were posted yesterday carrying this message from Mr. Herbert Morrison to the townspeople: "Every sympathy with the gallant citizens in the concluding stages of their ordeal. Hold on! I am assured by the competent military authority that the end of your trial will not be long delayed."

Everybody In Insurance For Injuries

By Daily Mail Political Correspondent

EIGHTEEN million people are affected by the Government's revolutionary plan for reforming the laws on workmen's compensation which have been in existence in various forms for the past 50 years.

Complete details of the Government's proposals are issued as a White Paper to-day.

All who work for their living and receive wages or a salary are eligible for all benefits. They will be placed on the same footing as ex-Service men.

Disability will be assessed by medical boards, and compensation will be awarded on the basis of medical reports without recourse to the law courts.

Once an award has been made it will be permanent and will not be varied not even should the recipient earn extra money.

A new principle is introduced whereby compensation will not only be paid as in the past, to those who lose their earning power, but also in future to those who "lose their health, strength, and power to enjoy life."

Outline of Scheme: Page THREE.

Rainstorm in the Strait

Sea.—Little disturbance.

Weather.—Fine until 6 p.m., when there was a rainstorm. Maximum temperature, 66 deg., 52 deg. at 7.30 p.m. Visibility fairly good. Wind west, light; sky overcast.

Barometer.—Steady.

THE 'CARPET BAGGERS'

Commons Question

Mr. J. H. Wootton-Davies (Con., Heywood and Radcliffe), in a Parliamentary question to the War Secretary next Tuesday, will ask:

"What principles are being applied by the Supreme H.Q. of the Allied Expeditionary Force with regard to granting permission to business men of Allied nationality to go to France for the purpose of re-establishing their trade connections, and whether he can give an assurance that British business men will be given facilities in this respect not less favourable than those accorded to other Allied nationals."

'Civil Air' is to Have a Minister —But a Junior

By **COLIN BEDNALL**

THE Government, I am reliably informed, is more or less agreed on the appointment of an Under-Secretary for Air (Civil Aviation).

As the title implies, it is intended that this junior member of the Government should devote himself exclusively to the needs of the future Merchant Air Fleet—but still under the ægis of the Air Ministry.

The announcement is intended to convince the reassembled Parliament of the Government's good faith.

Parliament's reaction, it is expected, however, is more likely to follow the first thoughts of those already aware of the new proposal.

★

IT is thought, in fact, that only one of two reasons can really be responsible for the appointment now of an Under-Secretary for Air (Civil Aviation).

The first is that the Lord Privy Seal, Lord Beaverbrook, at any moment will show himself to be weary of the frustration involved in representing the present Government on Civil Aviation. Some sort of ready stop-gap for the exasperated Lord Beaverbrook may, therefore, be considered desirable.

The other more cynical explanation advanced is that the appointment is a convenient way of ensuring political suicide for some gentleman not held in very great affection by his colleagues.

Nowhere in aviation circles is it now expected that Parliament will tolerate the continued administration of Civil Aviation by the Air Ministry. Many reasons for this view are being advanced. Some of them are considered to be a little unfair to a Ministry which after all won the aerial Battle of Britain and the aerial Battle of Germany.

One fact, however, is not disputed. If the Air Ministry is to continue with its task of ensuring superiority in military aviation, it cannot, and will not, give a fully sympathetic attention to a serious rival. The rival, of course, is Civil Aviation.

★

THE Government's failure on Civil Aviation is known to be much more the result of high Cabinet policy than the inadequacy of any one of the confusing number of Departments now charged with responsibility for it.

To blame the Air Council, for instance, for the lack of the air-liners wanted for the peace or even for insufficient numbers of British military air transports is a waste of breath.

The Air Council — and this apparently may be something of a revelation—is not constituted to deal with Civil Aviation.

Aviation circles fear, in fact, that astute political organisers might be delighted to see Parliament launch itself once again into an endless discussion around such "red herrings."

The Government has an embarrassing list of *specific* charges to answer. They can be listed in their full array, if necessary.

ALBANIA FORCES PRESS ENEMY

Partisans Link

From **EDWIN TETLOW**, Daily Mail Special Correspondent

SOUTH EUROPEAN H.Q., Wednesday.

ALBANIA, pocket kingdom on the Adriatic, occupied by Mussolini five years ago, is the newest war front.

Picked Allied troops have landed secretly in a sea and air invasion, and are already fanning out on a wide stretch of country.

Partisans have linked with them and the joint forces are now engaging the Germans, prodding them on into a general withdrawal from the south-west Balkans.

The landing is the fruit of months of "cloak and dagger" stabs at enemy garrisons on the Adriatic seaboard.

British and Allied troops have been ashore for weeks, living in caves and in mountain hideouts, training Partisans and leading them in resistance and sabotage against the Germans.

The Allied invasion has come as the climax to their operations.

In addition to the landings on the Albanian mainland troops are ashore on the islands off Yugoslavia. No Allied mention is made of operations in Yugoslavia itself, but the Germans report landings along the whole Dalmation coast.

The Allied troops now in Albania can count on the help of some 20,000 Albanian guerillas. In addition, Yugoslav Partisans of Marshal Tito's command have been operating with the Albanians in recent weeks, and it is possible that these forces have been strengthened.

General Tolbukhin's Russian troops in Bulgaria are also only 165 miles from the northern Albanian coast, and an Allied drive inland might result in a link-up which would cut off the five German divisions in Greece.

Heavy fighting is already raging in Macedonia, west of the Belgrade-Salonika railway, the Germans' main escape route from Greece, and between Leskovac and Nigh, farther up the line, between Yugoslav Partisans and the enemy.

FRENCH GOVT. TAKE RENAULT WORKS

The French Government have decided to requisition the Renault works at Billancourt as part of the policy of purging firms which aided the Germans.—Reuter.

RIGA: NEW SOVIET ADVANCE

Soviet communique announces more progress in the drive on Riga. Over 200 places captured.

Daily Mail

4 A.M. EDITION

NO. 15,107 ONE PENNY FOR KING AND EMPIRE TUESDAY, OCTOBER 3, 1944

BIG U.S. THRUST FOR THE RHINE

Shock-troops Two Miles Through Pill-boxes

DEADLY DIVE-BOMBING BLASTED PATH

From **JOHN HALL**, Daily Mail Special Correspondent NEAR AACHEN, Monday.

TROOPS of the American First Army to-day crashed two miles through the Siegfried Line north of Aachen in their new offensive towards Cologne, on the Rhine 40 miles away. Shock units swept over the little River Wurm and crossed the Aachen-Düsseldorf railway.

By noon they had advanced about one and a quarter miles through the Siegfried Line pill-boxes, but this afternoon opposition was more stubborn and the advance was slower.

The Siegfried Line in this sector is three to four miles deep, with old coalmine workings linked to the defences by new tunnels deep below ground. Behind the pill-boxes are "Die for Germany" trenches, which are outsize V-shaped foxholes dug by the thousand in woodlands and open fields.

Bloody fighting is going on among pill-boxes and trenches to-night. When I left the battlefield reports were that progress was good for this type of fighting against fortified positions.

PILL-BOXES SMASHED

An air and artillery blitz softened the way for the infantry. For nearly two hours 400 American bombers pounded a sector of the Siegfried Line. More than 300 heavy guns, some of them of 10in. calibre, joined in. Hundreds of tons of explosives hit the Huns.

Then dive-bombers came in. They had specific targets chosen from the more formidable pill-boxes. They achieved what an artillery officer described as "one of the prettiest dive-bombing jobs of the war."

Using special bombs, they blasted open pill-box after pill-box. Their accuracy was uncanny. One extra large pill-box—it was really a small fort—had been assigned as a target for several aircraft. The leader swooped and attacked. There was a terrific burst of flame, followed by billowing columns of black smoke.

It looked as if an oil well had been fired. When the smoke cleared a voice came from the nearest observation point: "Don't put any more on that one." Not one Hun came out.

MORTAR FIRE

But they came scrambling out of some of the other pill-boxes, racing helter-skelter for shelter. As they ran artillery observers directed fire on them. Scores were blown to pieces.

Before noon the infantry moved. At first nothing but weak small-arms fire met them and shock units quickly crossed the Wurm, which varies from 10ft. to 15ft. in width.

Beyond that lay the double-track railway which runs from Aachen north-east to Düsseldorf.

Mortar and artillery fire was coming over by the time the first Americans had edged forward to the tracks, but they dashed over, slid down a bank into a coppice and crawled toward the outer pill-boxes.

By this time prisoners were coming back to battalion and regimental headquarters.

Many of them said the bombing was a heaven-sent opportunity for them to surrender, because it had scared away the S.S. men, whose main job just now is to see that other troops stay in their positions until they are killed.

It is obvious that we gained a tactical surprise. What helped to scare and confuse the enemy was that U.S. bombers on another mission used this sector as a sort of cross - roads. Whenever he peeped out the Hun saw planes, and so far as he knew each one had a bomb for him.

LINE IS THIN

I have seen a number of air strikes, but never one so well delivered and so highly successful as to-day's dive-bombing.

A significant fact for Hitler was that to-day's air mission was largely mounted from airfields in France.

Most of the dive-bombers carried heavy bombs, some of which burst with the effect of giant incendiaries, splitting the pill-boxes and throwing up columns of dense black smoke.

The tiny village of Palenberg, grouped round a large pill-box, was hit at 10.2 a.m.: when the smoke cleared at 10.7 Palenberg was not there.

We chose a "thin" part of the Siegfried Line for this new attack. The line here is hidden in wooded downland something like the Surrey countryside.

Pill-boxes are much overgrown with shrubbery and it took expert air photography to pinpoint them.

To complete the defence in depth behind the line the Germans have

BACK PAGE—Col. SIX

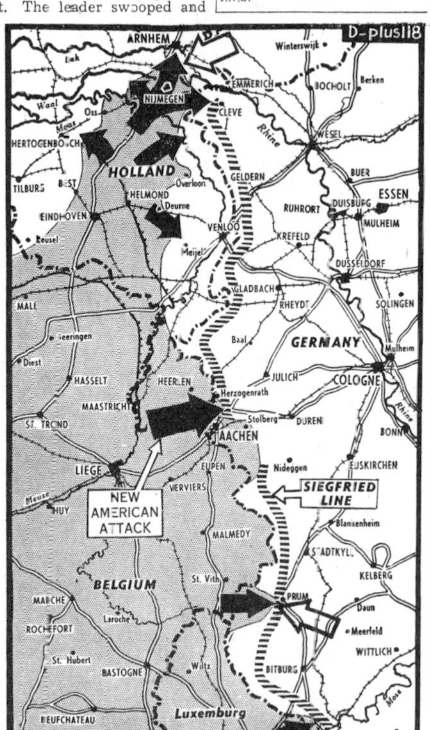

MAP shows the section of the Siegfried Line selected by the U.S. First Army for its blow.

DUNKIRK BOMBARDED DAY AND NIGHT

Dunkirk, last of the Channel ports in German hands, is being bombarded day and night, the German radio reported last night.

Brussels radio yesterday announced that the assault on Dunkirk started on Sunday night, but there was no news of its development last night.

The count of prisoners at Calais yesterday reached 7,130, including 130 officers.

So well was the garrison dug in that only 60 men were killed and 130 wounded in all the bombing and shelling. Civilian casualties were between 200 and 300.

The garrison had abundant ammunition and provisions—sufficient to have lasted them for another three weeks.

It appears that German Marines wanted to continue the fight but troops had no heart left for the battle.

Messages from Reuter and Exchange.

THESE ARE THE GERMANS

The People Who Do Not Smile

Their Need—Orders

Daily Mail Special Correspondent

KORNELIMUNSTER, Monday.

NINE THOUSAND Germans living in this occupied corner of the Reich have now been under Allied rule for two weeks—and their behaviour has been "exemplary," but utterly negative and blank.

That was the answer given to me to-day by officials of the first Allied Military Government team to take over in Germany when I came here asking: "How are the Herrenvolk responding to life as a conquered people?"

The officials explained: "They have been regimented so long that obeying orders has become natural to them. They expect us to do their thinking for them."

One of the officials is Captain John S. Roberts, former Burnley (Lancashire) police inspector, who told me:

"Our job here is much easier than it was in some parts of France, where people liked asking questions."

It sounds encouraging in a way, but I should explain that this is largely a rural area, where Nazism was never strong, and so far as we know all the Nazis fled before we arrived.

Those people who have remained are meek and docile.

If you see them in the streets—which is rare, because Allied orders are that for the present they must stay in or near their homes—they give you completely blank looks.

They do not appear relieved, afraid, apprehensive, or resentful—just blank.

★

A MIDDLE-AGED farmer, who looked good for another 30 years of life, gave me a lead clue to their thoughts when he asked me, "When I die how will you bury me?"

It is fixed in these people's minds that we are here for a lifetime at least and that everything will be arranged just so—births, marriages, and deaths included.

Biggest problem which has faced the A.M.G. officials this past fortnight has been the behaviour of the impressed workers: Poles and Russians, mostly women, who were taken from their homes and brought here literally as slaves.

Some were placed in factories and lived in barracks, others worked on farms and were made to sleep in outhouses.

They had their own ideas on how the Germans should be treated, and it was a pretty problem preventing them from exacting physical revenge, and items in kind for back pay.

Yesterday, however, most of the impressed workers were moved out of Germany.

One of the first things we did was to order complete disarmament. The Germans were ordered to surrender their arms.

The result is that A.M.G. has accumulated an amazing collection of shotguns, rifles, pistols, daggers, and duelling swords.

★

ALL the people remaining have been registered, and passes, which must be renewed daily, have been issued to doctors, midwives, and such people as key tradesmen, to enable them to move about more freely.

Everyone must observe a curfew which begins at 7 p.m. and ends at 6 a.m. Few Germans have shown any inclination to move about.

The exceptions have been, first, a few women who, bombed out, are living with friends and tried to sneak back home to get a few more clothes; and second, one or two farmers who had cattle in out-barns and were anxious to milk them.

In each town or village a new burgomaster has been appointed, and it is his job to see that A.M.G. orders are complied with and someone appointed to see to getting in what foodstuffs are available.

The Germans are having to live on themselves, but there is no privation because nearly every home is stocked as if for a siege.

However much the *hausfraus* here loved and trusted the Nazis, they believed in hoarding all they could.

From the civilians we also appointed a few police who help directing traffic.

I have asked everywhere in the occupied territory if there have been any cases of German civilians demonstrating against the Americans or making attacks.

Not one instance has been reported, and the A.M.G. officials are satisfied that a few cases of sniping which have occurred in newly-occupied areas have been the work of regular members of the German Army left behind for that purpose.

★

HOW eagerly the "subject" Germans carry out orders is exemplified by the action of a newly-appointed burgomaster who was told that if there were members of the Wehrmacht in hiding he must turn them in.

Off he went and soon returned with 16 soldiers who had been absent without leave.

Here in Kornelimunster the new burgomaster is a former school teacher, Herr Hupgen. He is

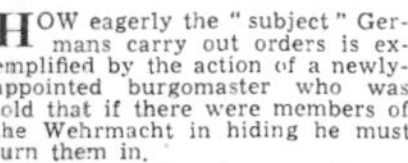

Strong Tank Forces Mass for Attack

'Plenty of Muscle'

From **RICHARD TREGASKIS**

OVERLOOKING SIEGFRIED LINE, Monday.

IT is 10.5 a.m. now and Lightning fire-bearers are applying the final touches to the hour-long drubbing which has been dealt out to the pill-boxes and dragons' teeth which form this sector of the Siegfried Line.

Guns are booming all around. Brown-clad G.I.s are filing over the rolling country and tanks are rumbling towards the weakened belt of fortifications.

From my vantage-point the fire-bombs seem to have set even the grass and trees aflame.

Buried in the woods in the distance are ten or a dozen concrete bunkers, and it is towards these that we are now advancing.

Jeeps full of serious-faced men are whizzing forward past this spot. They are mostly officers going to join their troops.

Columns of Sherman tanks are trundling into position behind the infantry. There is plenty of muscle in this attack,

First prisoners are of low calibre, hastily mobilised, but it is pointed out that they are probably being used as a screen while better troops are assembled farther back.

Aerial reconnaissance shows great clusters of foxholes being dug behind the Siegfried Line, probably by community digging.—*I.N.S.*

Urquhart of Arnhem Tells Story

Town Blown Down House by House

'Hectic Time'

By Daily Mail Reporter

MAJOR - GENERAL R. E. Urquhart, commander of the Men of Arnhem, sat in a room at SHAEF last night and told his story.

Stocky, dapper, in battle-dress, with not a hair out of place, he spoke of the epic in the traditional understatement of the British Regular officer.

These were some of his phrases:

"The whole episode was a rather hectic period of some ten days.

"One day was a repetition of the last—shelling and mortaring.

"We occupied a cellar . . . and it was darned hard to get out of it.

"The German tactics were to start at the end of a street and blow up each house in turn. That was all very well until there were no more streets left. Then it became really rather uncomfortable.

"It was just as well the withdrawal was ordered when it was. We couldn't have held out another 24 hours."

General Urquhart was introduced by the American Brigadier in charge of Public Relations as "that very great British soldier."

HEAVY FLAK

From the very beginning, said General Urquhart, the adventure was in peril. Flak was so heavy that the division was landed not in Arnhem but eight miles out of the town.

The division was the third in the list of priorities. First and second places had to be given to the American 101st and 82nd, dropped farther south, and, as a result, the complete First Division could not be put down in one "lift."

That had a very marked effect on the outcome.

The second "lift" was due on the morning of the second day, but for weather and other reasons it did not arrive until about 5 p.m.

The parachutists of the first "lift" moved off 95 per cent. strong—better than the average in practice. The gliders also came in extremely well, and there were few accidents.

General Urquhart went on: "But we bumped into opposition sooner than we expected. The early stages did not go at all 'according to plan.'

"It became quite obvious that our original aim to make a complete perimeter round the town had gone."

STREET BATTLES

From the first street - fighting developed "with an enemy a damned sight stronger than anticipated."

It was not long before the division was scattered, and not much longer before the various elements were out of communication.

One battalion got to the Arnhem bridge; the rest were on the outskirts of the town. One company of the battalion on the bridge was south of the bridge, the rest to the north, and the bridge was secure if anything had come up from the south.

The men succeeded in removing the enemy's demolition charges, "a remarkably fine achievement."

Improvising a plan, General Urquhart decided to hold the ferry three or four miles to the west of the town.

Engineers, R.E.M.E. units, and R.A.S.C. men were all thrown in to hold the perimeter.

The perimeter—a mixture of ribbon building and high, wooded ground occupied by the Germans—was 900 yards by 1,200 yards.

Against us the Germans launched tanks and self-propelled guns, usually in the strength of about a company.

NO RATIONS

"It was lucky they didn't put in anything big," said General Urquhart. "As it was, we 'bagged' about 25 tanks and guns."

Towards the end, the Germans got into a wood within the perimeter, and we were shelling them there—"a little bit awkward."

Men had no official rations for the last three days; there was food lying about in the houses, but no one had a cooked meal for four days.

The men were "absolutely magnificent. I had never a moment's doubt they'd do their damnedest."

Random incidents illuminated General Urquhart's talk.

Our field dressing-station was 200 yards outside our perimeter—because there was no house left inside it that could be used.

One end of it was used by the Germans—also as a hospital. Our own doctors worked in it and arrangements were made under the Red Cross flag to permit jeeps to take our wounded there . . . until we were so hard pressed that we

BACK PAGE—Col. FIVE

MTB Fought in Circles

With her steering gear jammed but with guns blazing, a motor torpedo boat swept in circles among a heavily escorted enemy convoy off the Dutch coast early on Sunday morning until she rammed a coaster and sank after being abandoned.

While speeding round her guns scored hits on one of several armed trawlers.

The torpedo boat was one of a light coastal force which, says an Admiralty communiqué, fought "fierce and spirited actions," during which torpedoes struck home on two of the convoy and two trawlers were left in flames.

A second torpedo boat caught fire and sank while disengaging.

Tirpitz Down by the Bows

Air photographs of the 41,000-ton German battleship Tirpitz, after the surprise attack by Lancasters with 12,000-pounders in Kaa Fiord, Norway, on September 15, show signs of serious damage.

Forward of the A turret is a large area of discoloration

Here also the hull appears to be rough and broken in outline. Other indications suggest that the battleship may be down by the bows.

Cool Breeze in Strait

Sea.—Little disturbance.

Weather.—Sky clear after day of sun, with a cool breeze. Maximum temperature, 61 deg.; 40 deg. at 10.30 p.m. Visibility good after mist. Wind N.W., light.

Barometer.—Steady.

FIRST MAN IN

SMILE belongs to Driver Cantrill, from Sherwood, Notts. He and the crew of a Sherwood Rangers' Recce car were the first British troops to cross the German frontier—from Beek, in Holland.

JET-PLANE BATTLES DUE SOON

Over the Reich

From **COURTENAY EDWARDS**, Air Correspondent

WELLSIAN air battles between British and German jet-propelled fighters at speeds of 500 m.p.h. are in prospect before the war ends.

Jet propulsion has been brought to a more advanced stage than is generally realised in both countries.

Recent new pointers to these developments are:

1. Fighters escorting Bomber Command Lancasters and Halifaxes raiding Ruhr targets saw two of the largest formations of jet-planes yet encountered. Sixteen were seen over Bocholt and 12 near Peddenberg; and

2. Official release for the Press of the big part played by R.A.F. jet-propelled aircraft in the Battle of the Flying Bombs.

The sighting of such large formations by our bomber escort supports the theory that the Luftwaffe now has ready for us a complete *gruppe* of jet-planes.

Neither of the two big German jet-plane formations made any attempt to interfere with our bombers or their escort. Nor were the types announced They may have been bomb-carrying Me. 262 "Swallows."

Another possible explanation is that Milch, the Luftwaffe commander-in-chief, is not prepared to use his jet-planes as interceptor fighters until his pilots have had more experience in handling them.

'NAZIS ESCAPE IN U-BOATS'

Crews Warned

U-boat crews were warned last night over Moscow radio that Nazi leaders are already making escape trips by submarine to Spain and South America.

The German National Committee, broadcasting in Russian, reported that cases were increasing of single passengers boarding the craft on alleged diplomatic or economic missions.

Crews were advised to take the fugitives to British or French ports. "It is your duty," they were told, "to prevent the escape of Nazi leaders and agents sent to pave the way."—*Reuter.*

Police Guard at Caruso's Grave

ROME, Monday. — A 24-hours police guard has been mounted over the grave of Pietro Caruso, the recently executed Fascist police chief of Rome, following an attempt to steal his body.

The body-snatchers stole spades from a gravedigger's hut in the Verano cemetery and began to try to dig the coffin out of the grave. They appear to have been disturbed by a night watchman and fled.—*Reuter.*

Cologne Mystery Shut-down

Daily Mail Radio Station

Cologne radio, after broadcasting intermittently throughout last evening, suddenly closed down during the 10 p.m. news bulletin.

No explanation was given, but the shut-down may have been due to shortage of power, as even while transmitting it could be only faintly heard.

Prisoners Broadcast

German prisoners of war last night spoke to their Fatherland in a new series of daily broadcasts begun by the B.B.C.

The first speaker was an N.C.O. captured in Normandy. "We shall show you how many of us have undergone a change of heart," he said.

Britain's Police to be Reorganised

REGIONS MAY ABSORB SMALLER 'FORCES'

By Daily Mail Reporter

REGIONAL police forces, run on the lines of the National Fire Service and involving the extinction as separate units of many of the 180 independent forces now operating in England and Wales, are proposed in a report which has been drawn up by Home Office experts.

The report suggests that, when the war ends, the war-time amalgamation into six county police forces of 26 county and borough forces in Southern England, carried through by Mr. Morrison at the end of 1942, should not only be continued but extended to other parts of the country.

Mr. Morrison carried out the compulsory amalgamations — which in counties like Sussex meant the absorption of the separate forces at Brighton, Hove, Eastbourne, and Hastings, as well as the West Sussex Constabulary and the East Sussex Constabulary, into one body—on the grounds of public interest and the efficient prosecution of the war.

Experience gained during the amalgamations in Sussex, Kent, and other Southern areas has strengthened the hand of the experts who before the war were urging the abolition of many of the smaller police forces and some form of unified service.

The report now under consideration claims that resultant simplified administration and improved efficiency far outweigh claims of some local authorities for the continuance of their own small forces.

Before the war some form of amalgamation was a declared policy of the Home Office.

Experts suggested that smaller counties should be grouped, and small boroughs merged, so that forces consisting only of 20 to 30 men under a separate chief constable next door to forces of over 1,000 men would cease to exist.

It is now suggested that each chief constable should have under his control approximately the same number of men.

Recruitment

Police chiefs throughout the country have also been requested to assist in a recruiting and training scheme designed to bring the police force up to strength when war ends. The report before them estimates that 14,000 men will be needed.

This number is made up of 4,000 young policemen who are now in the Services and will wish to return to police work, and 10,000 recruits who will replace a similar number now serving in the police force and who, when the war ends, will want to retire.

It is proposed to establish training centres in the principal police districts of the country.

Special attention is, I learn, paid to the problem of the young men who were just starting their careers in the police force when war broke out and have since reached high rank in the Services.

One proposal is that they should be given special courses at establishments similar to the Hendon Police College, and then appointed to suitably high rank in the reorganised police services.

Atom Bomb is Hitler's New V Weapon

From **RALPH HEWINS**, Daily Mail Special Correspondent

STOCKHOLM, Monday.

ATOM-BOMBS, whose explosion is likened to "frozen lightning," are the new secret weapons

4

which German scientists are rushing to produce before Germany is defeated.

Detailed reports reaching neutral scientists and Allied experts here all agree that they have already been made experimentally in considerable numbers.

Mysterious explosions which have been seen 80 miles away from the Danish island of Bornholm are now fairly conclusively established as being caused by atom-bombs.

The new V weapon—already nicknamed here the "atomb"—has an extremely delicate and complicated mechanism.

The general principle is that an electric shock splits the atom if and when the missile reaches its target.

Many reports indicate that "atomb" research is headquartered in a wide stretch of Northern Germany, consisting mainly of the coastal areas and the islands of Mecklenburg.

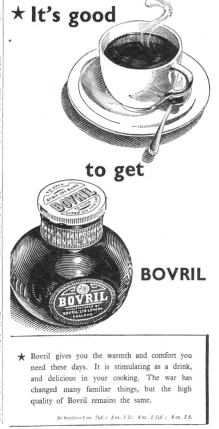

NEW BLOWS AT PHILIPPINES

General MacArthur's communiqué to-day said American air forces continued to deal blows against the Japanese in the Philippines and Celebes, sinking or damaging nine small cargo ships.

AMERICANS TAKE CHAMBREY

American troops have occupied Chambrey, 15 miles north-east of Nancy, says a Reuter message from Third Army H.Q.

THE STARS AND STRIPES
MEDITERRANEAN
Vol. 1, No. 291, Friday, October 20, 1944 ITALY EDITION TWO LIRE

Philippines Invaded, Japs Say

Red Army In Germany

Krauts Say Railhead Lost

LONDON, Oct. 19 — The Red Army is fighting tonight on German soil.

They have taken the town of Eydtkuhnen in East Prussia, Germany's easternmost province, according to the latest German Overseas News Agency broadcast, which has not yet been confirmed by any Allied source.

This is the first time in the war that Germany has officially admitted the loss of any wholly German town to the Soviets.

"Penetration at Eydtkuhnen is the deepest yet made in Reich territory," the Nazi broadcast added, "and the enemy, who keeps on bringing in fresh divisions, has gained further ground beyond the town."

Eydtkuhnen, also known as Eydkan, is a communications center of some importance through which main-line traffic between Germany and the Baltic republics used to pass.

Today the Russians' replies to Hitler's broadcast of yesterday are coming both in actions and in words.

The words came from Radio Moscow, which told the German people in a special beamed broadcast that the heart of Germany is going to be turned into a battleground.

The action came in many places along the vast Russo-German front, especially in Czechoslovakia —into which territory the Red Army is pouring in considerable

(Continued on Page 8)

START OF THE ROAD BACK

AMERICAN FORCES have landed on Suluan in the Philippines, according to Japanese reports, with strong U. S. naval forces said to be operating in the Leyte gulf.

Heavy Guns Batter Enemy At Aachen

SHAEF, Oct. 19—Strengthening German resistance was noticed today along the rainswept Western Front as both the American 1st and the British 2nd Armies continued to pound away without appreciable gains at the dents made in the Siegfried Line at Aachen and below Venraij on the eastern flank of the Dutch salient.

Aachen, now a mass of rubble, is proving a tough nut to crack. Yank infantry is pouring into the city and every position has to be taken by assault.

German efforts to break the ring of steel around the city have been thrown off, while 1st Army long-range heavy artillery continued to soften up the towns on the road to Cologne, some 45 miles to the east.

The British 2nd Army spearhead thrusting into the Siegfried Line was within four miles of the frontier town of Venlo which is less than 33 miles from the Ruhr-Rhine port of Duisberg. Fighting here was heavy and both sides suffered heavy casualties.

There were indications here that the Allies may launch a major attack against Venlo where the main crossing of the Meuse River is located. American tanks of the 1st Army were sloshing north through the mud for a possible junction with British armor, now reported only three miles away.

Strong counterattacks were reported in the American 3rd and 7th Army sectors. In the former sector, dispatches told of heavy shelling by the Germans who were said to be using railway guns of about 200 mm. caliber.

Back along the Belgium-Holland border, where the Germans are fighting fiercely to prevent Allied use of the port facilities of Antwerp, captured more than a month ago, Canadians and British troops were cleaning up the Scheldt Estuary.

While the Germans maintain their positions along the Scheldt, the port facilities at Antwerp cannot be used. Once the Allies clear the Scheldt, the employment of Antwerp's port, seized intact, would

(Continued on Page 8)

U.S. Navy Reported Inside Leyte Gulf

HONOLULU, Oct. 19 — In the midst of continued large-scale air and naval attacks on Japanese strongpoints, American forces have landed in the Philippines, according to a Japanese news broadcast.

The landings are on Suluan island in the Sulu archipelago, according to the enemy broadcast, which quotes Japanese sources in Manila.

The archipelago is a group of islands at the southwestern corner of the Philippines — and the Philippines themselves number more than 7,000 islands. The group is northeast of the large Malayan island of Borneo and about 200 miles south of Zamboanga.

A landing at this point would be the first such landing by United States forces since the Japs seized the Philippines in 1942.

The Japanese communique says that our naval units have penetrated the Leyte gulf as well, about 350 miles southeast of Manila, bringing warships and some troop transports into the heart of the Philippines.

American planes raided the north Philippine island of Luzon again yesterday, sinking or setting fire to seven Japanese ships and destroying 19 planes, according to Admiral Chester W. Nimitz's communique today. Our ground forces have now occupied the Mgulu atoll in the Caroline islands.

There were additional air raids over Cebu and Tacloban in the Philippines yesterday.

Today's communique from General Douglas MacArthur's headquarters says that 150 Allied planes attacked installations, shipping, and airdromes at Ceram and the Boeroe islands.

Today's victories are part of an accumulation of steady, relentless blows aimed to push the Japs back into their own corner for the knockout.

Despite the absence of details, either from enemy or Allied sources, the picture of Allied movements is becoming increasingly clear.

Terrific blows against Formosa, Palau, the Ryukyus and the Mariana islands were obviously to prevent the Japs from interferring effectively with Allied operations from bases closer to their homeland.

The air attacks appear to be enabling the legendary "Task Force 53," under Vice-Admiral Marc A. Mitscher, and the 3rd and 5th Fleets to bypass stronghold after stronghold in the drive westward

(Continued on Page 8)

Stars And Stripes Reporter Is Killed

ROME, Oct. 19—S-Sgt. Alfred M. Kohn, former managing editor of the Rome edition of The Stars and Stripes, has been killed in action while covering the 36th Division in Southern France, it was disclosed yesterday. He was 23 years old.

Details of his death were incomplete but correspondents returning from that front said it was reported that Sgt. Kohn had been cut down by a German machine gunner while traveling with one of the companies of the regiment he was covering.

Just about one year after he joined the staff in Algiers from the Air Corps, Kohn felt he had enough of desk work and asked for a frontline assignment.

He covered the 34th Division in their successful drive to Leghorn. He spent his first night at the front with Italian partisans who took him through the enemy lines to the outskirts of Leghorn. Later he was the first correspondent to enter southern Pisa despite the heavy shelling the Americans were receiving at that time.

Upon his return from the 5th Army front, he asked for and received a reportorial assignment for

(Continued on Page 2)

British Casualties

LONDON, Oct. 19 (ANS)—Deputy Prime Minister Clement Attlee told the Commons yesterday that British Imperial Forces, including those of the Dominions, suffered 103,842 casualties from D Day to the end of August.

Florida West Coast Struck By Hurricane

MIAMI, Oct. 19 (ANS) — A violent tropical hurricane struck the Florida mainland early today, and west coast residents from Fort Myers to Tampa rushed for shelter to escape death and destruction.

The Miami Weather Bureau said the Caribbean-born disturbance "is apparently entering the Florida west coast just south of Sarasota."

St. Petersburg reported winds of 70 mph, which left the city without electrical power. Tampa had 45-mile winds, and a 32-mile wind swept Orlando.

The hurricane gave the Florida Keys a severe lashing, but the city of Key West, which earlier expected to feel the full force of the storm, apparently suffered no serious damage.

Patton's Life Spared By German Dud Shell

FRANCE, Oct. 19 (ANS)—Lt. Gen George S. Patton, Jr., 3rd Army Commander, narrowly escaped death Wednesday when a 700-pound shell from a Nazi railway gun landed within eight feet of him. The shell proved a dud.

Nazi Manpower Barrel Empty

By Pvt. LYLE DOWLING
(Stars and Stripes Staff Writer)

NAPLES, Oct 19—Hitler's speech of Wednesday raised two questions, the "peace" question and the "second mobilization of Germany" question.

The gist of Hitler's "peace" statement was simply that he wanted a peace that would safeguard Germany and her allies.

The "second mobilization" statement boils down to a series of orders apparently aimed at scraping the bottom of the German manpower barrel.

In view of Hitler's reputation in the past, there is no ground to believe that his simple broadcast of orders to mobilize is the same thing as an actual mobilization.

Indeed, there are many grounds to believe that Germany some months ago reached for and struck the bottom of the manpower barrel.

Early in August, Hitler named one of his chief henchmen, Joseph Goebbels, as "Plenipotentiary for the Total War Effort" in a drive to squeeze out the last ounce of German and satellite manpower.

There followed decrees by Goebbels aimed to raise about a million additional German troops: government offices were combed for men, even high-ranking Nazi officials had to go into the army. Such enterprises as could possibly be dispensed with were closed down and their manpower was sent into the fighting end of the war.

A series of careful estimates published in May of this year—prior, of course, to the German crack-up in Rumania and prior to Allied operations opening and extending the Western Front—by the United States publication, "Foreign Affairs," puts the total German army strength at about 320 divisions of all types, plus corps and army troops to a total of about 5,426,-250 German soldiers and 1,308,750 non-German soldiers fighting, with various degrees of intensity, as part of the German army.

That makes a total of 6,700,000 soldiers fighting for Germany—and that was as estimated prior to May of this year.

Losses of Germany in all Western

(Continued on Page 8)

DAILY EXPRESS

No. 13,853 | Black-out 6.17 pm to 7.12 am | WEDNESDAY OCTOBER 25 1944 | Moon rises 3.24 pm sets 12.17 am (Thurs) | One Penny

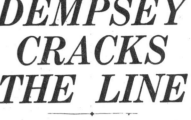

PACIFIC: Big sea-air battle starts near Philippines | **HOLLAND: Germans 'cave in' under blow on 12-mile front** | **EAST FRONT: Russians deeper into East Prussia**

JAP FLEET COMES OUT

Powerful force hit by carrier planes

ANTI-INVASION THREAT

Express Staff Reporter: New York, Tuesday night

THE Jap Fleet has come out. In a 42-word communiqué issued by Admiral Nimitz at Pearl Harbour tonight, it is announced that powerful enemy naval forces moving towards the Philippines invasion area have been attacked by U.S. planes. It may be the beginning of a Pacific show-down.

This is what the Pacific C.-in-C. released :—

"On October 23 (west longitude date) enemy forces, including battleships and cruisers, were sighted moving eastwards through the Sibuyan Sea and Sulu Sea in the Philippines and were attacked by carrier aircraft of the Third Fleet.

"Further details are not yet available."

The fact that Admiral Nimitz does not mention the presence of any Japanese aircraft-carriers might indicate that the Japanese are trying to slip heavily gunned surface ships close to the western side of Leyte Island to subject General MacArthur's ground forces to severe bombardment.

Sulu or Mindoror Sea is flanked on the east by the Philippines Islands, on the west by the island of Palawan and on the south by Borneo.

It is about 600 miles wide at its broadest point and the same distance in length. The Japanese are known to have had powerful forces based in this area.

FLED—THEN RETURNED

This is the first news of any Japanese naval attempt to interfere with the strongly established Philippine landing forces, and the first appearance of the enemy fleet since it turned and fled when confronted by U.S. naval forces before the invasion.

If another big Pacific battle is under way it will be the third of the war.

In the battles of the Coral Sea and the Midway Island—3,000 miles from the Philippines—the Japanese were completely routed and lost at least one battleship, five carriers—three of a new type—and three heavy cruisers.

The Japanese also lost a battleship, a cruiser and a destroyer in action off the Northern Philippines in the first month of the war.

CAR KING RENAULT DIES UNDER ARREST

PARIS, Tuesday.—Louis Renault, famous French car manufacturer, died of heart failure today in a hospital where he had been taken, a broken man, from Fresnes prison.

Renault, who was 67, was arrested last month on charges of collaboration with the enemy by making tanks and other war material.

Renault's defence was that his factories were taken over by the Germans while he was in America.

The huge Renault factory at Billancourt, one of the targets in Allied raids on the Paris area, has been taken over by the French Government.

It rose from a workshop started by Renault in his father's garden at Billancourt.—B.U.P.

Princess Beatrice

Grave anxiety

PRINCESS BEATRICE, youngest and last surviving child of Queen Victoria, is seriously ill. She is 87.

A bulletin issued last night said: "Her Royal Highness's health has been gradually failing for some time, and has shown a marked deterioration during the last week.

"Her condition is now causing grave anxiety."

The bulletin is signed by Dr. Charles Gordon Holland Moore, physician-in-ordinary to the Princess, and by Dr. Greville Tait, of Handcross, Sussex.

Princess Beatrice's daughter, ex-Queen Ena of Spain, arrived in London last night from Swit-

Eden stops the show

CAIRO, Tuesday.—Mr. Anthony Eden, British Foreign Secretary,

Mystery flashes in the night

In lit-up Cologne

From MONTAGUE LACEY

GERMANY, Tuesday.—Pilots patrolling over the Rhineland have seen mystery flashes at night in lit-up Cologne, Bonn, Dusseldorf and Duisburg.

They were first seen in the streets of Cologne on October 12, when these cities suddenly switched lights on after black-out time.

A special watch was kept, and the lights have been on again several nights since.

There may be something more behind the lighting-up than the German explanation that it is to stop looting.

It is possible that the mysterious flashes came from firearms. There is much uneasiness in the Rhineland following the evacuation of Aix-la-Chapelle, and there may have been trouble over this problem.

Information from several sources indicates that all is not well in the Rhineland towns

What was in the houses?

From LAURENCE WILKINSON

HOLLAND, Tuesday. — Two houses in a park at Dordrecht, Holland, today received the biggest air pounding ever given to any target of the size.

Five squadrons of R.A.F. fighter-bombers and rocket Typhoons dropped tons of bombs on the houses, and sent 63 rockets and thousands of cannon shells through the walls and roofs.

What was in the houses is not revealed. They were merely described as "an important military target." Now they are gone.

400 shoot up Germany

FOUR HUNDRED U.S. Thunderbolts and Mustangs swept between Hamburg and Kassel yesterday to give Germany its biggest shoot-up of the war.

They hit 150 locomotives and 400 rail trucks, set oil trucks blazing and shot down the only German plane they met.

Four Heinkel 111's—the plane used for launching flying bombs—were destroyed on the ground.

Mustangs found a ravine filled with German soldiers, and reported 50 killed.

4,500 tons—and off again

Express Air Reporter

WAVES of R.A.F. heavies again roared out over the East Coast just before dusk last night.

Achtung radio soon reported raiders approaching the Hanover-Brunswick area.

The R.A.F. were swiftly following up their Monday night blow at the Krupps city, Essen, which was blasted by 4,500 tons

Though every available gun round the city was put into action, R.A.F. losses were only eight out of 1,000 planes. In the last Essen raid on April 26 losses were 29 out of 1,000.

Less milk

The weekly milk allowance is to be cut from two and a half to two pints on Sunday week, November 5.

Supplies to catering establishments will be reduced from seven and a half to six pints per hundred hot drinks served

Recent stormy weather, with three months' rain in six weeks, has reduced output, and the

DEAD END KIDS—NAZI MODEL

ON October 9 the Daily Express published the extraordinary picture of the German women who fight the Allies.

Here, today, is a tougher example of German resistance.

An American unit, mopping-up near Aix-la-Chapelle, were met, at one point, with fire from two rifles.

The Etschenburg brothers—*pictured above*—were in action, with Hubert Heinrichs. Willy Etschenburg (aged 14, member of the Hitler Youth) is on the left, Heinrichs (aged 10) wears the braces, Bernhard and Victor Etschenburg are 10 and eight.

All four boy snipers—and their parents—are in custody.

—And this tough said he was 14

Here is another small German, in uniform this time, at the head of a column of prisoners marching out of Aix, after the surrender. He said he was 14—but looks considerably more.

RUSSIANS DRIVE INTO NORWAY

Berlin: Tanks near Kirkenes

Express Naval Reporter W. A. CRUMLEY

THE Russians have invaded Norway, says Berlin radio. Strong tank spearheads are closing on Kirkenes, Northern Norway, main supply base of the lost Austrian Alpine Legion, which retreated from Finland into Norway, and principal air base of the Luftwaffe's Fifth Air Fleet.

Russian forces are, according to the German reports, thrusting towards Kirkenes along the Arctic Highway from Petsamo and from the south.

Soviet planes and motor-torpedo-boats are also attacking the German supply and evacuation convoys along the Northern Norwegian coast.

Capture of Kirkenes would :—

1. Cut supplies to the 25,000 German soldiers who have been driven north out of Finland.
2. Restrict air attacks on Allied Arctic convoys to Russia.
3. Give the Russians a modern naval and air base that would threaten the German hold on Arctic Norway.
4. Compromise Alten Fiord and remove any last possibility that the damaged 45,000-ton German battleship Tirpitz could remain there during the winter.

Kirkenes is roughly 200 miles from Alten Fiord on the Arctic Highway completed by the Todt organisation last winter. It is 160 miles from Kirkenes to Alten as the bomber flies.

There is no reason to doubt the German report that the Russians have begun a new campaign in the Arctic darkness, lit for an hour or two each day by a brown, foggy twilight.

Thinly held

Weather conditions are already severe, but the Russians are equipped for the campaign. The country is in places mountainous and difficult, but it is thinly held by the enemy

In addition to the troops driven out of Finland, the Germans have no more than 30,000 men between Kirkenes and Tromso.

The Fifth Fleet of the Luftwaffe once totalled 300 first-line torpedo bomber and fighter aircraft to cover the whole of Northern Norway, defend the Tirpitz, and attack Allied convoys in passage or in port at Murmansk. Its strength is now thin.

Russia's powerful and effective Arctic fleet is now beginning to exert control over the coastal seas westward from the Barents Sea to the North Cape.

Further westward, recent Home Fleet strikes against the Norwegian coast showed how Germany's main winter lines of communication at seaborne can be disrupted

Modlin falls: Insterburg bombed

From E. D. MASTERMAN

STOCKHOLM, Tuesday.—Fierce fighting is going on tonight in Gumbinen, only 15 miles from the East Prussian city of Insterburg, on the direct road to Koenigsberg.

Soon after Moscow radio gave this news, Berlin reported a powerful new offensive on the south-east flank of East Prussia's defences.

Modlin, big German fortress 20 miles north-west of Warsaw, has fallen, according to Berlin. Further east, the Russians have reached Serock, 20 miles north of Warsaw

These reports show that the Russians are over the River Narev at many points along an 80-mile front from Modlin to Lomza, which is 20 miles from the East Prussian border.

East Prussia is now being squeezed on a 350-mile front from the Baltic, round its northern and eastern borders down to Modlin, 45 miles from the southern frontier.

12-MILE RETREAT

Marshal Stalin's communiqué tonight reported the capture of a number of strongpoints round Gumbinen and said the Germans are counter-attacking with tanks. Berlin claimed that the counter-attacks had halted the invasion in this area.

But the Germans admit a 12-mile retreat south of the Rominten Heath, Goering's former playground

Insterburg was bombed by the Red Air Force last night for the fourth successive night.

Air liner lost

MADRID, Tuesday.—The German air liner which should have arrived last week-end from Stuttgart is missing. It is reported shot down over France.—Reuter

Tory revolt dwindling

DEMPSEY CRACKS THE LINE

Germans retreat 5 miles

BRITISH troops were fighting into the fortified Dutch cathedral city of Hertogenbosch from three sides yesterday when General Dempsey opened yet another attack from the south and broke the German line on a 12-mile front.

Late last night it was announced that the enemy's line had caved in and that he was moving back, abandoning many towns and villages. Our advances have been from three to five miles.

The fall of Hertogenbosch, anchor of the whole German line south of the Maas, is expected at any hour. We are fighting in its streets.

Its loss may force the Germans to abandon their stand below the river.

Dempsey's new attack swept through the little town of Brest, which has been heavily defended, and linked up with another spearhead which was fighting towards Hertogenbosch south of Boxtel.

Bridges taken

Two bridges over the River Maler were taken intact, and the British are now only ten miles from Tilburg.

Over to the west the Canadians finally cut the narrow exit from South Beveland and isolated 11,000 Germans fighting there and on Walcheren Island.

At midnight Ronald Clark, B.U.P. war reporter, summed up :—

It appears that the German grasp in Western Holland is more seriously endangered than at any time since the start of the Arnhem attack. The inability of the enemy to fight for the line south of Hertogenbosch is most significant.

Scheldt truce refused

From JOHN REDFERN

SCHELDT POCKET, Tuesday.—Five miles west of Breskens Canadian soldiers are on the outskirts of Groede, where the enemy have a hospital.

Today a German officer on the Groede sector sent out an officer with a white flag to ask for a truce while about 200 German wounded and 14 of ours are evacuated to our lines.

The reply was given that we were fighting and intended to go on fighting, but if the wounded were moved out on the road under the Red Cross they would not be fired on.

In Breskens the situation is unchanged. The German-held fortress outside the town is isolated by our fire. Weather conditions today did not allow heavy air attacks there.

[NOTE: The report issued by Supreme Headquarters on Monday night that the Canadians had lost Breskens was officially denied yesterday and was stated to be due to "false official interpretation of front line reports."]

DEMPSEY IS HITTING HARDER EVERY DAY

From PAUL HOLT, near Hertogenbosch, Tuesday

HOW stimulating it is to fly direct from London to the battle, and how different the feeling is here.

The chair-borne people at home who gloom about the war going back to 1914-1918 style would do well to be silent, for the war is going well, and the fighting men are getting cocky again

The past 48 hours has given such a jolt to the German 15th Army of the Lowlands that hopes of a war of movement again in the immediate future are beginning to grow.

The resistance we are meeting now in this westward drive to the mouth of the Maas is nothing like so grim or stubborn as we had to the north of Nijmegen or to the east of Overloon

CLEARED OUT

It is not that the Germans are fighting badly. The 712th Infantry Division which took the brunt of our surprise on Sunday, is well known to us, and has done some good, plodding, journeyman fighting against us for some months

The Germans are not short of manpower but they seem to be badly under-gunned and completely without tanks, or anti-tank artillery, and our 3-pronged attack for Hertogenbosch had by dawn

Christmas leave

Plans for Monty's troops

Express Staff Reporter

NUMBERS of British troops serving in Western Europe, I learned last night, may have leave at home by Christmas.

For some weeks provisional plans for their transport and reception in England have been worked out by a sub-section of the War Office. Progress of the battles to come will affect the final arrangements, but the policy has been laid down that troops who have served longest and seen most fighting in France and Belgium—and now Holland—will be brought home as they can be spared.

The Y.M.C.A., one of the organisations approached by the War Office, has agreed to earmark beds for homecoming soldiers. It is probable that the Central Hall, Westminster and a restaurant near Victoria Station would be taken over.

Two Kensington hotels may also be used, and the list of hostels where men may spend the night at a reasonable charge—probably not more than 5s. for officers and 1s. for men—before going to their homes is likely to be extended.

3 a.m. LATEST

GERMANS FALL BACK ON TILBURG

German troops in south-west Holland are falling back on Tilburg before Dempsey's new drive and British are racing to catch up with them, says an N.B.C. broadcast from the front.

CANADA RELEASES FRENCH FUNDS

OTTAWA, Tuesday.—Canada is releasing $200,000,000 (about £42,000,000) in French funds. They have been frozen for two years since Canada broke with Vichy.—Exchange.

France left out of talks

WASHINGTON, Tuesday.—France will not be included in the post-war security talks, President Roosevelt said today.

It is unlikely there will be a full United Nations conference this year. Acting-Secretary of State Stettinius says problems left over from Dumbarton Oaks may be cleared up in time for a conference in the New Year.

A Churchill-Stalin meeting with Roosevelt might be necessary before some of the issues were ironed out.—Express News Service.

FRIDAY, NOVEMBER 10, 1944

FINAL NIGHT EXTRA

Evening Standard

37,492 DIM-OUT 5.49 pm to 7.40 am. MOON sets 3.51 pm ; rises 2.55 am ONE PENNY

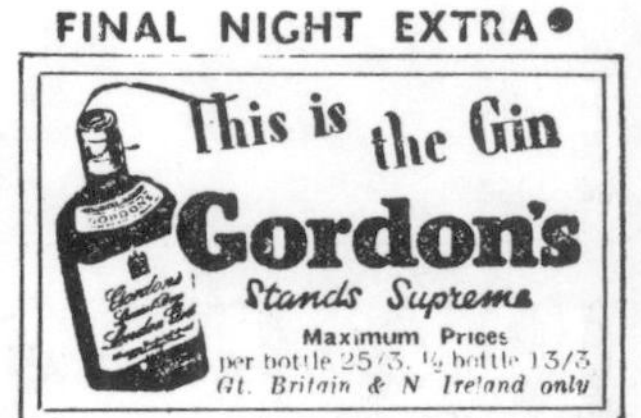

CHURCHILL SPEAKS ON V2

A Number Have Landed at Widely-scattered Points: Casualties and Damage Are Not Heavy: German Stories Highly Coloured

SOME WERE FIRED FROM WALCHEREN

Mr. Churchill made a statement in Parliament to-day about V.2. He said:

Last February I told Parliament the Germans were preparing to attack this country by means of long-range rockets, and I referred again to the possibility of this form of attack in my statement in this House on July 6.

FOR THE LAST FEW WEEKS THE ENEMY HAS BEEN USING HIS NEW WEAPON, THE LONG-RANGE ROCKET, AND A NUMBER HAVE LANDED AT WIDELY SCATTERED POINTS IN THIS COUNTRY.

In all, the casualties and damage have so far not been heavy, though I am sure the House will wish me to express our sympathy with the victims of these attacks.

OUR SILENCE

No official statement about the attack has hitherto been issued. The reason for this silence was that any announcement might have given information useful to the enemy and we were confirmed in this course by the fact that until two days ago the enemy had made no mention of this weapon in his communiqués.

Last Wednesday an official announcement, followed by a number of highly coloured accounts of attacks on this country, was issued by the German High Command.

I do not propose to comment upon it, except to say the statements in this announcement are a good reflection of what the German Government would wish their people to believe, and of their desperate need to afford them some encouragement.

May I mention a few facts. The rocket contains approximately the same quantity of high explosive as the flying bomb.

TO PENETRATE

However it is designed to penetrate rather deeper before explosion. This results in somewhat heavy damage in the immediate vicinity above the crater, with rather less extensive blast effect around it.

The rocket flies through the stratosphere, going up 60 to 70 miles, and outstrips sound Because

(Continued on Back Page, Col. Six)

Counter Attack

From HARRY ASHBROOK
Evening Standard Reporter

Counter-measures against V2 must for the time being remain secret. But this I can say. The same team of men who finally defeated the flying bomb are in constant consultation with a special defence committee under Mr. Duncan Sandys.

They include some of Britain's greatest scientists and most able defence experts.

As Mr. Churchill to-day revealed, the rocket travels at an enormous speed—some experts state more than 2000 m.p.h.—and no warning of its approach can be given.

Consequently the fighter pilots and South Coast gunners who broke the back of the V1 attacks on London in the summer cannot be effectively used in this new struggle.

For the time the two-way answer to the rocket shell is;

Bombing

1—An all-out bomber offensive against V2 launching sites, factories and experimental stations.

Throughout the summer concrete emplacements in the Pas de Calais area, believed to be connected with the launching of V2, were attacked several times. The damaged sites were overrun by Allied forces before they could be used.

Peenemunde, the German secret weapon experimental station on the Baltic, constantly pounded for months, became a No. One bomber target.

According to neutrals, the repeated raids on Friedrichshafen are part of the R.A.F.'s counter-moves against V2.

The same neutral reports state that following these raids production of V2 components at Friedrichshafen ceased.

On August 25 the German research station at Rechlin was badly damaged when attacked by Allied bombers.

Underground

According to Stockholm reports, the Allied bombers have driven the Nazi rocket factories underground.

Although these underground and cave factories are more difficult to locate and destroy the Germans are clearly finding it hard to maintain normal production rate.

To sum up: The Allied bomber offensive has already slowed down the tempo of V2 production. As the attacks develop, more and more installations will be put out of action. But as a single offensive arm it does not seem likely that air attacks can completely defeat V2.

2—As we thrust deeper into Holland and Western Germany more and more launching sites will fall into our hands.

The battle of V2 resolves itself into a race between German scientists and advancing Allied armies.

BOMBERS GO OUT FOR 3 HOURS

A three-hour procession of heavy bombers flew out over the East Coast to-day while Londoners saw part of a force which went out over the Channel across the South Coast.

German radio at various times reported bombers approaching North-West Germany, bombers over Western Germany and bombers heading for Thuringia and Franconia.

Later the "Achtung" radio issued a continuous series of coded air-raid warnings, says Reuter's radio station.

Bomber Command Mosquitoes attacked objectives in Western Germany last night.

THE GERMAN "FORTRESS"

The Soviet News Agency to-day (quoted by Reuter) stated:

According to Stockholm military circles a conference has been held at Hitler's H.Q. to discuss the reliability of Germany's frontier fortification.

These had been recently inspected by special commissions headed by Goebbels for Western Germany, Himmler for the eastern front, and Ley for the south.

The conference decided to build new fortifications in the border areas and to order an extra mobilisation of the population for the work.

'V2 Cannot Win War'—Berlin

"USED TO DENY ALLIES USE OF ANTWERP"

"It is true that V2 by itself would never decide the war in Germany's favour, but after all we never made such an assertion in the first place," said a Berlin radio commentator, Wilfrid Von Ofen, to-day.

"V2 is by no means the last secret weapon we have in store for Londoners and the people in Southern England," he added.

"What we do assert is that Germany, despite hardest air attacks, and in the face of all the ordeals of this last year of war, was still able to produce an entirely new weapon, and that she knew how to use it against the enemy.

"V2 is the result of our greatly increased war effort. More soldiers and more weapons—this watchword comes nearer to its realisation as each day goes by.

"To-day Churchill has had to admit the existence of V2.

"The weapon is a technical revelation. There are no warnings and no defences able to cope with it.

The German official news agency (quoted by British United Press) says: V1 and V2 have been in action against Paris and Antwerp for some weeks past.

"Should this bombardment increase," the agency added, "the harbour installations of Antwerp will hardly be usable for the unloading of troops and material to any extent."

To-day's German communiqué states: "In many weeks' fighting on the Breskens bridgehead, on South Beveland, and on the Island of Walcheren, our troops barred to the enemy free access to Antwerp.

"The German Command thus gained time to take measures for the elimination of the port. For weeks past the harbour area of Antwerp has now been under heavy fire of our 'V1' and 'V2.'

[Later the Germans issued a correction to this statement, saying attacks on Paris and Antwerp were made "in recent days," and not "for some weeks."]

"The bombardment of London by 'V-1' and 'V-2' is being continued," says the communiqué.

In preparation for the use of V-2, new robot sites were built behind the "West Wall," and the bombardment of the larger Belgian towns and Paris itself was begun, said Christian Jederlund, Berlin correspondent of Stockholm Tidningen, according to a German broadcast to-day.

A German military spokesman, referring to Mr. Churchill's statement that damage and casualties caused by V2 have not been heavy, said the Prime Minister would have to revise his statement "when larger salvos hit British targets in quicker succession."

PATTON'S MEN CAPTURE THE DELME RIDGE

From PHILIP GRUNE, Evening Standard War Reporter

WITH THE U.S. THIRD ARMY.

GENERAL PATTON'S THIRD ARMY, IN THEIR OFFENSIVE FOR FLANKING METZ, ARE ADVANCING ALL ALONG THE LINE AND PUSHING INTO WHAT THE GERMANS BELIEVED WOULD BE THEIR WINTER DEFENCES.

They made gains of one to three miles during the night and took several towns.

Their two most important gains were Chateau Salins—road junction 17 miles north-east of Nancy and about 27 miles from the German

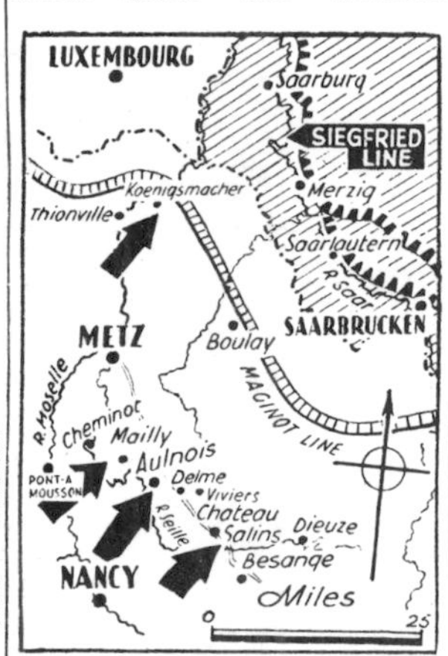

frontier—and the 1500ft Delme ridge, 16 miles north-east of Nancy.

Chateau Salins was found to be empty. It is the biggest town taken in the advance.

FRONTIER—6 MILES

Delme Ridge commands important strategic ground in the whole area behind Nancy and Metz.

The 35th division are now three miles beyond Delme.

Infantry occupied Louvigny, nine miles houth of Metz, after a night battle.

The Americans have also captured several towns in the Koenigsmacher area, 19 miles

(Continued on Back Page, Col. Two)

The Money Jugglers

HOW THE RACKET IS WORKED

Evening Standard Correspondent

Steps are likely to be taken soon to put a stop to a Continental currency racket—juggling with Belgian and French francs.

Some Servicemen, I am told, are making hundreds of pounds a day at this game.

An airman on leave in this country said to me to-day: "Give me £4 and I will bring you back £16."

He told me that in Belgium he can get 1000 Belgian francs for the £4. In turn these are exchanged for 3200 French francs. "The present rate of exchange over here is 200 French francs to the £," he explained, "and so I can bring back the francs and get £16 for them."

Inquiries in this country which I made to-day revealed a rather anomalous position. An airport official said: "Civilians are subjected to a strict currency check, but there is no check on Service men, British or Allied, who form the overwhelming bulk of the passenger traffic through sea and air ports at present." Maximum amount allowed to be taken out is £10, but inwards a passenger may bring in any amount of foreign currency, in addition to £10 sterling.

Americans in Paris and other parts of France, I am told, are being stopped in the streets and offered any amount of French francs for a few dollars.

DRIVE TO OUTFLANK BUDAPEST

The Red Army are to-day rolling forward in an out-flanking sweep on Budapest on a 90-mile sickle-shaped front from the Upper Tisza to points west and north-west of the railway junction of Szolnok, says Reuter.

The renewed Soviet drive, which is being pushed with full force across open country, appears to aim at forcing the Germans back to the Danube above Budapest, and to open the way for a pincer movement on the city.

The Russians are moving directly across the main German north-south communications, and have straddled the Miskolc-Budapest railway north-east of the Hungarian capital.

The remnants of more than 30 German divisions now find themselves pincered between the Baltic port of Libau and Tukhum, 35 miles west of Riga.

HERE IS THE NEWS OF—

The Lights Of London

Evening Standard Reporter

Not more than seven or eight authorities out of the 29 in the County of London, and probably only as many more among the 96 local authorities in the 714 square miles of the Greater London area, are able to introduce the improved street lighting now permitted in the London Civil Defence region.

Technical difficulties, shortage of materials, labour and counting the cost are the obstacles in the path of more light. L.C.C. Boroughs in which the public will begin to see the lights go up at varying intervals of time from this evening are:

Battersea, Bethnal Green, Fulham, Hammersmith, Poplar, St. Marylebone, St. Pancras, Stoke Newington, Woolwich.

Marylebone Moon

West End shoppers will be pleased to hear that Oxford-street from Marble Arch to Holborn, one side of Edgware-road and half of Regent-street will be "moon" lit by St. Marylebone.

"Our present system of star-lighting can easily be adapted within a fortnight or so by substituting reflectors of a type different from those in use now," the Borough Engineer, Mr. A. L. Downey, told me.

There is little hope for the other side of Edgware-road and the other half of Regent-street. The first belongs to Paddington, a completely gas-lit borough; the second belongs to one of the gas-lit areas of Westminster, and the City of Westminster wishes to take time to consider what to do with their electrically lit streets.

The City

The City of London is averse from the introduction of any modification of its present street lighting, but no final decision has yet been made.

Boroughs which are either negative or anticipate coming to a negative decision at their lighting committee meetings in a few days' time are: Finsbury, Bermondsey, Holborn, Hackney, Hornsey, Camberwell, Chelsea, Hampstead, Deptford, Islington, Lambeth, Lewisham, Paddington, Shoreditch, Stepney, Kensington, Wandsworth and Southwark.

There is little hope for all-gas boroughs, Chelsea and Paddington are in this position in the L.C.C. area. Further afield the number includes Harrow, Ruislip and Northwood, Wanstead and Woodford.

Motorists, subject to police approval, are likely to find the stretch of the Great West Road which is in the County of Middlesex, better illuminated. This piece of broad highway is about equally divided between the boroughs of Brentford and Chiswick and Heston and Isleworth.

36 GAS-WORKERS FINED £10 EACH

Thirty-six night-shift workers at Bradford-road Corporation gas works, Manchester, were summoned at Manchester to-day.

They were accused of failing to comply with a direction of the Ministry of Labour and National Service to return to work.

After the defence had agreed that the direction had not been complied with, each of the defendants was fined £10.

The men were given seven days to pay the fine, but some said they did not intend to pay.

Nazi Envoys Going

German envoys in Madrid and Lisbon are to be replaced, says the German official news agency, quoted by British United Press.

DAILY HERALD 4 A.M.

No. 8964 — TUESDAY NOVEMBER 14 1944 — ONE PENNY

RAF QUAKE BOMBS SINK TIRPITZ

WING-COMMANDER J. B. TAIT, D.S.O. (three times), D.F.C., of Abercynon, Glamorgan, led the attack by Lancasters to sink the Tirpitz.

Norway Force Is Back In Norway

"HERALD" REPORTER
Stockholm, Monday.

A SMALL Norwegian force has landed in Northern Norway.

A reliable but unconfirmed report to this effect was current here to-night.

The force, it is stated, came by sea from England.

Mr. Trygve Lie, Norwegian Foreign Minister, who arrived here from Moscow, to-night, said complete unity had been reached with Russia about waging war against the Germans in Northern Norway.

Agreement was also reached on political questions.

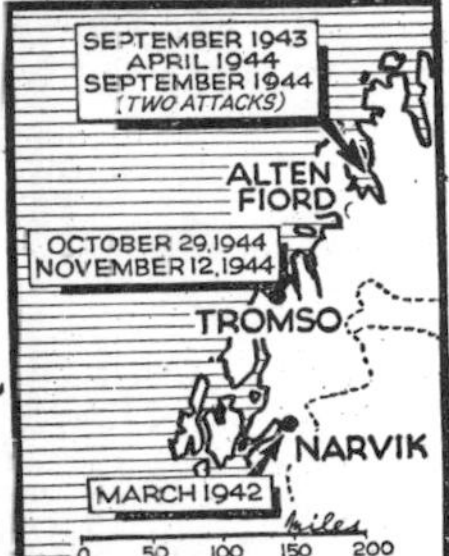

He Happened To Pass—

IT was lucky that Fireman Maskell was passing a cottage at Little Mount Sion, Tunbridge Wells, last evening.

The cottage was on fire and five children were inside.

Maskell, who is 57, dashed upstairs through flame and smoke and saved David and Raymond Maile, three-year-old twins, and their baby brother Michael, who were trapped in a bedroom.

Then from a downstairs room he saved Kathleen Hayward, aged 18 months, and her two-year-old brother, Willie. Maskell had just handed over the children to a neighbour when he collapsed.

Bulldozing Beach For Mines

Soldiers are using bulldozers on Brighton beach to locate land mines moved from their original settings by waves and shifting shingle.

The bulldozers are at work near the piers, where the usual mine detectors are upset by the magnetic influence exercised by the steel piles.

Hit 10.30, Ablaze 10.45, Capsized 11 a.m.

THE END—Tirpitz gets a direct hit. Another bomb lands on the shore. Smoke plumes up, and beneath it the ship, so often attacked, keels over and sinks.

TRIPLE D.S.O. LEADS 32 PLANES TO THE KILL

THE Tirpitz, Hitler's last big naval unit, has been sunk. The Royal Air Force did it.

Launched on All Fools' Day, 1939, the 45,000-ton battleship had been able to make only one operational sortie—the 1943 raid on Spitzbergen.

Now the crews of two RAF squadrons have put the finishing touch to the Allied plans for incapacitating the German surface Navy.

British Navy spokesmen said late last night that there was no longer any German surface naval menace.

Sinking of the Tirpitz means that we shall be able to set free two battleships of the Home Fleet and their myriad escorts—battleships that had always to be kept ready in case the Tirpitz "came to life."

This is the full story of the victory, told late last night by the Air Ministry:

Shortly before 10.30 a.m. on Sunday a force of 32 Lancasters arrived over Tromso Fiord, where the Tirpitz was lying.

They were led by Wing Commander J. B. Tait, triple D.S.O., D.F.C., of Abercynon, Glamorgan, and Squadron Leader A. G. Williams, of Cirencester.

At 10.30 the Tirpitz was hit. At 10.45 she was seen to be on fire.

As the last aircraft turned for home at 11 a.m. she was seen to be heeling over in the shallow water of the fiord.

Three Direct Hits

Reconnaissance after the attack showed that the battleship had by then completely capsized and settled on the bottom of the fiord, with about 700ft. of her keel sticking out of the water.

All around the wreck was a great pool of oil, through which could still be seen the booms protecting the battleship from attack by torpedoes.

This was the third attack on the Tirpitz with 12,000lb. bombs, but it was the first time that the attackers were able to see the ship properly.

In the first attack, when the Tirpitz was in Kaa Fiord, the Germans put up a smokescreen so rapidly that only one or two of the first air crews to arrive could see the ship.

The second attack, when the ship had moved westwards to Tromso Fiord—on her way for repair in a German dockyard, and because of the threat of the Russian advance into Norway—was made through cloud, and crews could obtain only an oblique view of the target from some distance.

But on Sunday the weather was clear and there was no smoke-screen.

One 12,000-pounder apparently hit the Tirpitz amidships, another in the bows and a third hit towards the stern.

There were also apparently two very near misses which must themselves have done serious under-water damage so violent is the explosive effect of these bombs when they burst in the water.

The ship heeled over rapidly. The last air crew to leave the scene said they saw that something was going to happen, and they turned hastily so that they might be over the ship to watch.

By the time the turn was completed the Tirpitz had capsized.

The rear gunner of this Lancaster—an aircraft from a RAAF squadron dispatched to make a film of the attack—said he saw the ship heel over when the aircraft was flying at a height of only 5,000 feet.

"We were just returning to make our run," he said. "when I

② Continued on Back Page.

Smoke and flames envelope the Tirpitz as she capsizes and sinks in the shallow water of Tromso Fiord.

Outflanking Budapest

AS the Russians tighten their grip on the south-eastern approaches to Budapest their right wing is threatening to outflank the Hungarian capital from the north-east.

Berlin military commentators last night stressed the power and danger of this wheeling of Marshal Malinovsky's army group.

"The great battle for Budapest has flared up again with extraordinary fury," said Colonel von Olberg, of the German Overseas News Agency.

"The Russians are trying to execute an encircling movement by driving from the Middle Tisza.

"An enemy army group consisting of at least ten infantry divisions (100,000 men) has emerged across the Tisza on the Eger-Alberti line, having thrust westward on a front of some 60 miles.

"The object is to overrun Budapest from here and simultaneously to outflank the German defence thrusts."

Berlin had earlier admitted that Soviet tanks had broken into Jaszbereny, a communications centre 34 miles due east of Budapest.

HITLER HAS SHUT HIMSELF AWAY

From WALLACE KING
"Herald" Reporter, Stockholm Monday.

OUT of a mass of rumours mostly planted by Goebbels I have sifted the latest reliable information about Hitler.

In the last weeks of October he was still alive, but was causing his immediate entourage the greatest anxiety.

Living in his armoured train he was so restless and apprehensive of Allied bombing that he hardly ever spent more than two days in one place. At night his train was run into the deepest convenient tunnel.

Dietrich, his Press chief, whose duty it is to give the Fuehrer a word-of-mouth report on world opinion each morning, was again and again sent away without seeing him.

During October Hitler paid only two brief visits to Berchtesgaden.

Heinrich Hoffmann, his personal photographer, has not been able to send out any photographs of him since the second week of September, when one showed Hitler receiving the Japanese Ambassador at his headquarters.

New indications of the uneasiness in Germany over Hitler's failure to make a public appearance were given in official statements to-day.

For consumption abroad the Overseas News Agency issued this statement:

"The Fuehrer is in excellent

① Continued on Back Page.

CLOTHES PROSPECTS BRIGHT FOR 1945

By ROY MARSHALL

A MASTER plan to give more clothes and better clothes for everyone in 1945 is being worked out by Mr. Dalton's advisers at the Board of Trade.

It will be at least six months before the public feels any all-round improvement.

But the outlook for 1945 is better than for any year of the war, both for the housewife and for every other member of the family.

Civilian clothes are now a Number One priority, and workers released by the Ministry of Aircraft Production and the Ministry of Supply are in many cases to be directed into the textile and clothing industries.

First extra supplies will reach the shops in small quantities in January.

Next year's clothes rationing books are already being printed, and provision has been made for an increase in the coupon allowance if Mr. Dalton finally decides to give one.

A "medium" price range will probably be introduced, bridging the gap between utility and "expensive" clothes.

RAF Shoots Up Nazi Ships

Low-flying Mosquitos and Beaufighters of Coastal Command attacked with cannon and machine-guns two small merchant vessels and a tug with an armed trawler and an R-boat as escort off the Norwegian coast yesterday.

MORE FLY BOMBS

After a long lull the Germans launched more flying bombs against Southern England last night. A bomb was hit by the guns in mid-air and blown up.

STILL CHILLY

Straits last night.—Chilly N.E. breeze. Barometer still falling.

Three Metz Forts Fall: Germans Getting Out

THE Germans, retreating in sleet and snow on the great fortified city of Metz, are abandoning the fortresses with which the town is ringed.

Midnight news from SHAEF announced the capture of three of these forts by General Patton's Third Army without opposition.

One of the captured strongholds was reported to be one of the nine great forts of the inner ring. The other two were described as lesser forts, probably of the outer ring.

The main fort may have been Fort Verny, five miles south of Metz, which was named in earlier reports as having been captured by the American 5th Infantry Division.

The surprising capture of these defences came as the Third Army plunged ahead all along a 40-mile front south and south-east of Metz, enveloping at least 15 more towns.

The German border is now only 13½ miles away, and the Americans hold a solid line forming a half-circle within a five-mile radius of Metz. The escape gap to the east has been narrowed to 14 miles.

Fifteen miles north of Metz the 95th Division fought its way into another fort at Thionville.

After a terrific 30-minute bombardment by American guns the garrison flew the white flag and surrendered.

Captain Sertorius, German military commentator, said last night that Patton is also attacking Fort Driant—most formidable fortress in Europe, five miles north-west of Metz.

It has hundreds of underground pillboxes, concrete casements and underground barracks, and the Americans tried in vain to capture it two months ago.

Why the Germans are giving up the Metz fortifications is mystifying.

Sunken Forts

Ronald Matthews, "Daily cabled last night:

The ring of forts around the town was completed by the Germans in 1911.

Nine of the forts are described as "fortified groups," each having a number of mutually-supporting defences, with a perimeter around them.

In addition to these nine miniature hedgehogs, there are other strongpoints called "forts" or "works."

The strongest side of the fortified ring looks to the west.

All the forts are sunk level with the ground, giving them greater protection against hostile fire.

In each there are from six to eight guns, mounted in pairs in turrets, heavily protected with armour and concrete and with the main walls six feet and more thick.

Underground Links

The range of the guns varies from five to twelve miles, and near each battery is an armoured observation tower.

Shelters for the fort garrisons are in two storeys, the lower being completely underground, and the strongpoints are linked by subterranean passages which up to 1940 were electrically lighted.

When the French evacuated Metz in 1940 they sabotaged many of these installations, but there is little doubt that the Germans must have got most, if not all, of them into working order in the last few months.

Last March Of Home Guard

By WESLEY CLAPTON

A LONG line of khaki will wind through London's West End on the afternoon of Sunday, December 3.

It will be the same line that stood between Britain and invasion after the dark days of Dunkirk.

The Home Guards will be marching for the last time. They will be honoured in the capital of the country they sprang to defend when the call went out in the hour of danger.

Every unit throughout the country will be represented. Many of the marchers will be veterans of two wars.

There is keen competition for the honour of representing the unit. Some units are deciding by ballot who shall go

arms, but will wear steel helmets and greatcoats.

The route will be Piccadilly, Regent-street, Oxford-street, and back to Hyde Park via Marble Arch.

Churchill At Front With De Gaulle

MR. CHURCHILL and General de Gaulle visited French units on the Belfort front yesterday.

They drove through heavy snow and thick mists to a divisional command post 12 miles from the front.

Later, Mr. Churchill reviewed troops at a French training camp.

In the party were Field-Marshal Sir Alan Brooke, Miss Mary Churchill, General Juin, and M. Diethelm, French War Minister.—B.U.P.

Of the 30 cars which set out with the Churchill party, only ten finished the journey, the others being either ditched or snowbound.

(Helping France and Belgium to Re-arm: Back Page.)

FRANCE TO PLAN HER INDUSTRY

A national planning council to work out a long-term scheme for French economy is to be set up shortly, said M. Mendes-France, the National Economy Minister, yesterday.

Private enterprise, labour and other interests will be represented on the council.

It was obvious, said M. Mendes-France, that France, like other big countries, was moving towards a greater degree of planning in her economic life.—Reuter.

"BLUE DIVISION CHIEF JAILED"

General Infantes, former Commander of the Spanish Blue Division, which fought in Russia, and his brother, Col. Infantes, have been imprisoned by order of General Franco, according to a frontier report last night.

Many Blue Division soldiers are in concentration camps charged with Communist propaganda, the report added.—British United Press.

WEST HAM LIT UP

West Ham switched on the lights last night.

The whole of the main road from the borough boundaries at Bow Bridge to the Thatched House at Leytonstone was fully illuminated.

SWEDES' TRADE "NO"

Formal trade relations between Sweden and Germany, it is learned in Stockholm, will end on January 1 next when the present trade treaty lapses.

FRENCH HUNT SHADOW 'KING'

"HERALD" CORRESPONDENT
PARIS, Monday

THE Comte de Paris, Pretender to the throne of France, has been wounded on French soil, and an order to arrest him was issued today by the Ministry of the Interior.

He is reported to be in hiding somewhere in the neighbourhood of Perpignan, near the Spanish frontier.

The Pretender is charged under a law which forbids the eldest descendant of a family that has ruled France to enter the country under pain of two to five years' imprisonment.

He is also accused under a law of 1940 of illegally crossing the frontier.

One report to-night unconfirmed by the Ministry of the Interior, says he has already been arrested and that he was wounded at the time of his capture.

The Comte is 37 and married to his cousin, Princess Isabelle of Orleans-Braganza.

In 1938 he flew in secret to a chateau near Paris. Since the war he has twice been to London—before and after the French disaster.

Recently he has lived in Spanish Morocco. De Gaulle issued an order to arrest him if he tried to go to Algeria.

It was reported last May that he went to Algiers in disguise.

So He Lived As A Nun

"Herald" Cable From Wellington last night:

TRAPPED in Marseilles when the enemy occupied the city, Capt. Osborne Willits, a New Zealand ex-officer, escaped capture by living in a nunnery disguised as a nun.

His sister, Mrs. Crawford, of Auckland, has received word that he recently introduced himself to a correspondent at Voiron, near Grenoble.

His hair was shoulder-length.

He said he lived dressed as a woman in a small cell, never setting foot outside it.

Illness prevented his escape from Marseilles, after which the nuns gave him sanctuary.

STOP PRESS

HUNGARIANS GIVE UP

Hungarian battalion, 520 strong, led by their commander, went over to Russians, says Moscow. Colonel said he did not wish to sacrifice Hungarian lives in German interest. On another sector 200 Hungarians surrendered.

CURTAIN TIME

5.43 p.m. to 7.47 a.m.
Moon Rose 6.14 a.m.
Moon Sets 5.3 p.m.
Light Lamps 5.43 p.m.

172 RAID DEATHS

During October 172 civilians were killed and 416 injured and detained in hospital as a result of air raids on this country.

DAILY EXPRESS

No. 13,899 | Dim-out 5.22 pm to 8.33 am | MONDAY DECEMBER 18 1944 | Moon rises 11.28 am sets 7.54 pm | One Penny

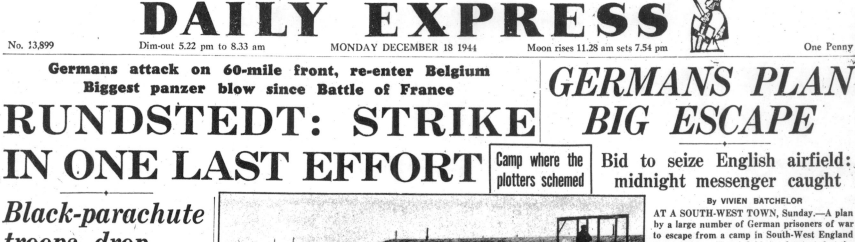

Germans attack on 60-mile front, re-enter Belgium
Biggest panzer blow since Battle of France

RUNDSTEDT: STRIKE IN ONE LAST EFFORT

Black-parachute troops drop behind Allies

From MONTAGUE LACEY: 1st U.S. Army, Sunday

GERMAN tanks since dawn have been thrusting into our lines at points over a 60-mile front from the River Roer to Luxemburg, and they have re-entered Belgium and Luxemburg.

It seems that the Germans have decided to launch a counter-offensive of some considerable strength. They are throwing in fresh divisions of infantry, and these men, with the tanks, have overrun a number of villages and made several wedges on the Belgian-German and Luxemburg-German borders.

ATTACK SINCE SUNRISE

Fierce fighting is raging around many towns and villages and long columns of German armour and troops have been attacked from the air since sunrise.

The Germans are pressing forward fanatically with an Order of the Day from von Rundstedt saying: "Now is the time for the German Army to strike. Give your all in one last effort. Everything is at stake."

We also captured a German divisional order—a sort of pep talk, whipping up the troops on behalf of the Fatherland.

German infantry began yesterday to probe for likely soft spots, and made some progress.

IN THE DARK

Then, in the blackness around four o'clock this morning, the Germans brought over formations of Ju.52 troop-carriers, loaded with paratroops, and escorted by fighters.

Scores of paratroops were dropped, with orders to cut our communications and hold the roads until the tanks and infantry came up.

The enemy used black silk parachutes, so that we should not see them in the dark.

Already we have rounded up many of these tough youths from woods and hiding places behind our front lines.

As I drove to the front this morning guards were out everywhere, still hunting them down. They are armed mainly with machine-gun pistols and grenades.

It was nearly daylight when crack German panzer troops were thrown into the offensive, one strong column of tanks.

TWO MILES IN

This was the heaviest concentration we have seen since the Battle of France. It was found pushing forward near Honsfeld, two miles inside Belgium, and eight miles from Malmedy.

As hundreds of Thunderbolts, Lightnings and Mustangs dive in to try to halt the panzers, news comes through to headquarters that the Germans have made penetrations around Honsfeld and into Luxemburg near the border towns of Vianden and Echternach.

One group of Thunderbolts found a column of 100 vehicles in the Honsfeld area. The trucks were parked bumper to bumper, many of them loaded with infantry.

The planes had their best field day for months as they went down and bombed the column and then poured machine-gun fire into the smoking ruins.

All through the morning and afternoon our armoured units, with their tank destroyers and anti-tank-guns, have been tearing into the panzers.

TANKS HIT

Several German tanks held up at road blocks were knocked out and left burning.

In the woods, American troops are standing and fighting back.

We may have to give some ground before this big battle is over. But with the arms at our disposal we shall be able to inflict heavy destruction on the attacking Germans.

Yesterday, for instance, we took more than 1,000 prisoners, the highest day's total for some weeks.

It seems likely that General Hodges had some idea that the Germans were massing for an attack, because on Friday night they shelled our positions along the Roer for hours. This was probably

BACK PAGE, COL. FOUR

The camp in South-West England from which Germans—many of them Luftwaffe and U-boat men—planned to escape. A crowd of prisoners can be seen on the left, behind the barbed wire. . . . The changing of the prison guard is taking place here. Troops are constantly on the watch from the towers surrounding the camp. At night, lights from these towers and other points are turned inwards.

H.Q. COMMENTARY

Nazis send in their best men

Express Staff Reporter

SHAEF, Sunday. — Rundstedt is obviously basing high hopes on the counter-offensive against the First U.S. Army. Some of his best men and material have been committed.

He clearly believes that if his attack goes well he may force us to divert men from other sectors, halt the slow progress to the Rhine and gain time.

No doubt the German war leaders calculate also on disappointment being caused among the public in Britain and America.

Yet, in using at last some of his good and fresh troops instead of continuing to fight a slow retreat with second-rate defensive forces, Rundstedt may bring the day of settlement nearer.

At General Eisenhower's headquarters there is no tendency either to conceal the full force of the German offensive or to greet it with more than due concern.

It is seen as yet another proof that the war has still to be fought bitterly to the finish.

'Last throw, like March 1918'

FIRST U.S. ARMY, Sunday.—It was said at forward H.Q. today that this counter-offensive is the Germans' last throw of the dice, an all-out break-through bid comparable to the big push of March 1918. By its means, Hitler hopes to force the Allies to terms.

The battle is likely to bring in its train the complete annihilation of the German armies.—Exchange.

LUFTWAFFE GOES UP: 110 SHOT DOWN

Express Staff Reporter

SHAEF, Sunday.—The Luftwaffe today lost 110 planes, from 450 sorties, in making its most determined challenge since D Day.

This activity was designed to create a diversion so that the counter-offensive south of the U.S. Ninth Army Zone should have the minimum of interference from the air.

The U.S. Ninth Air Force, which met this offensive, lost 35 planes.

The Germans attacked even when in a minority. This puts the whole show in line with Rundstedt's "Give your all" Order.

The Luftwaffe was also up in strength over and behind the battle front of General Montgomery's 21st Army Group

BY TEMPESTS

Tempests shot down eight Focke-Wulf 190s and destroyed a Messerschmitt 262—a jet-propelled plane—by forcing it to crash into a house.

At 2.40 p.m. today the Germans had 100 planes up in formations of from four to 20. They attacked for an hour.

Many of our formations which were attacking German troops had to break off to tackle the planes.

So we have had our planes giving ground support and engaging in dog fighting simultaneously. This is something new.

This daylight activity followed the biggest night-bombing effort the Germans have made in the U.S. Ninth Army area.

Ulm bombed last night

R.A.F. Lancasters last night made the first major attack on the industrial and railway town of Ulm, on the Danube, between Stuttgart and Munich.

Ulm—population 68,000—is a railway centre. The Magirus works there produce tanks and armoured vehicles and are also the enemy's chief source of supply for fire-fighting equipment.

The Ruhr fears knock-out

Goering's own newspaper, the Essener Nationalzeitung, says:—

"The enemy has now launched a new air offensive on the Western German towns with a series of the heaviest imaginable attacks.

"He wants to make life here so unbearable that the population will buckle up and cry for peace at any price.

"We shall be compelled to endure the enemy's air war, and must draw the necessary conclusions."

BULGARS CROSS GREEK BORDER

Athens shelling starts again

ATHENS, Sunday.—Shelling in Athens was resumed this evening after a 24-hour lull, and fighting continued around Omonia-square. Spitfires strafed the stadium area and rocket-firing Beaufighters attacked E.L.A.S. headquarters in northern Athens.

Reports that some hundreds of Bulgarians have crossed the frontier into Northern Greece are confirmed by British sources today. It is not known whether they are deserters or guerrillas.

It is feared that they may be taking advantage of Greek strife to seize Greek territory. Several Bulgarian officers have been seen in Salonika.—Reuter, B.U.P.

Archbishop says EAM must disarm

From ERIC GREY: Athens, Sunday

ARCHBISHOP DAMASKINOS, of Athens, whom I interviewed today, made it clear that he would serve as Regent—but not as a member of a Regency Council.

He said: "I am not one of those who seek office, but to whom it is offered. I am deeply moved by the faith the people of Athens have in me.

"The post is Calvary for me, but so many have asked me to take it that I will accept."

Discussing the future of Greece the archbishop said he believed E.A.M. was undoubtedly a force for good provided it was led peacefully.

He could not conceive it as an armed force now that the country is liberated from the Germans.

"Social and economical reforms there will have to be in Greece," he said, "but they must be achieved by peaceful democratic measures."

In the talks now going on with the Greek political leaders, we have, I understand, made it clear that we are not going to stand for the Right fighting the Left to the last British soldier—which is what the Left fears and undoubtedly what some of the Right would like to see us do.

NO REPRISALS

If a reasonable compromise can be reached we shall ensure that there will be no reprisals by the Right afterwards.

For this reason, the proposals from many quarters to appoint the Archbishop as Regent, are receiving strong British support.

General Plastiras, who recently returned to Greece, tonight appealed to E.L.A.S. to lay down their arms.

He said: "Do not forget that the war is in its last phase. It is the duty of the Greek nation to reconstitute the army to take part in the effort of our Allies, British, American and Russian.

"Greece dealt the first blow at Fascism. She should not be absent at the moment when the last blow is struck.

"Avoid coming into collision with the soldiers of Great Britain, a great friendly and Allied nation, thanks to whom Greece has been freed and for whom the gratitude of the Greek people will be eternal."

READY TO FIGHT

The Papandreou Government announces that it has received messages from most of the Ægean islands that the E.L.A.S. elements there have been arrested and disarmed, and that the people "reiterated their loyalty to the Government and their readiness to fight to suppress rebellion."

General Scobie's communiqué today said:—

"It is now confirmed that the Socialist Party and the Union of Popular Democracy (E.L.D.) have broken away from E.A.M. in the Salonika area. The leaders of both groups have been arrested by E.L.A.S."

In the freed parts of the Piræus the British Naval Command has begun to distribute hot meals to women and children.

GREEK KING MAY DECIDE TODAY—

'ABDICATE' ANNIVERSARY

Express Staff Reporter

KING GEORGE OF GREECE sat yesterday with his closest advisers in his suite at Claridge's Hotel, London, listening to Athens broadcasts and studying the latest diplomatic despatches on the Greek situation.

He knew that he had to face squarely the prospect of abdication, and today he may have to make a decision.

Today—December 18—is a date that has lived vividly in his memory for 21 years, for on this day in 1923, after a military coup d'etat, his abdication was demanded at the Royal Palace in Athens. When he refused, he was ordered to leave the country at once.

He had then been on the throne for only 15 months. He was given little time for consideration. A Republican officer marched into his study, pointed a pistol at him, and presented a deed of abdication.

'Sign, or—'

"Sign or be shot," he demanded.

The King, a great-grandson of Queen Victoria, replied: "I will not sign. I will never abdicate."

The officer was too astonished to shoot. King George left for Bucharest.

He was formally dethroned after a plebiscite in March 1924, and said: "The plebiscite was faked."

His Greek estates were taken from him, and his total remaining wealth was stated to be not more than £25,000. He came to London and lived quietly at Brown's Hotel, Dover-street.

He often travelled by bus, and visited country public houses and East End fish-and-chip shops.

In November 1935, after another military coup d'état, a plebiscite, held under military law, decided by 98 per cent. to ask him to return.

Now the latest plans to end the fighting in Athens involve the acceptance by all parties of Archbishop Damaskinos as Regent. It is believed in London they will not do this unless King George abdicates.

Last post today

Today is the last day for posting parcels, letters and cards for certain delivery by Christmas Day.

The public are asked to prepare their mail at home to prevent congestion by addressing letters and cards at Post Office counters.

35 hostages hanged

ROME, Sunday.—Thirty-five hostages have been hanged by the Germans in public in Bologna.

Patch drives to Siegfried Line

Seven German towns taken

From DOUGLAS WARTH

GERMANY, Sunday.—In a vast elm forest some seven miles east of Wissembourg the infantrymen and anti-tank gunners of General Patch's Seventh Army came slap up against the Siegfried Line this afternoon, and dug themselves in while 120 medium bombers swooped ahead to do some softening up.

The five bridgeheads across the German frontier are now resolved into two thrusts on either side of Wissembourg, with seven German townships in American hands.

This barrier will take some cracking. The defence system goes back in great depth.

The first obstacle our patrols ran into in the forest was an anti-tank ditch 20 feet across. It was flooded, and stretched for miles away through the trees.

In the mountains the front-line defence consists of row after row of dragons' teeth and concrete pyramids lined thickly. Then come the pillboxes and behind, at various intervals, the forts- square concrete underground gunsites.

The big guns have already started duelling.

Plane crash shakes town

THE whole of West Worthing, Sussex, was shaken recently, when an aircraft, one of a number heading for the Continent, crashed about 200 yards from the houses on Marine-parade, and its bombs exploded.

The explosions of cannon shells and machine-gun bullets followed.

The crew baled out with the exception of the pilot, who is thought to have remained at the controls to clear the town.

GERMANS PLAN BIG ESCAPE

Camp where the plotters schemed

Bid to seize English airfield: midnight messenger caught

By VIVIEN BATCHELOR

AT A SOUTH-WEST TOWN, Sunday.—A plan by a large number of German prisoners of war to escape from a camp in South-West England and seize a nearby airfield was frustrated at the last minute.

The Germans are known to have been prepared to lose half their numbers in a desperate attempt to get the rest back to Germany by air.

Plans prepared in the most minute detail for ruthlessly killing the guards, seizing the armoury, forming up at an assembly point outside the camp and rushing the airfield are in the hands of the authorities.

The scheme was probably hatched in Germany for use by any large body of prisoners who might be housed near an airfield.

Extra troops were rushed to the camp when suspicion was aroused and the ringleaders have been removed

U BOAT MEN

Many of the men are from Luftwaffe and U-boat crews—fanatical Nazis.

They are housed in what was formerly a tank training school on a main road connecting two important towns.

It was the keen watch of a British soldier guard which prevented the mass escape.

The guard, watching the prisoners from a raised pill-box overlooking the camp, first noticed groups of Nazis in furtive conversation.

Five or six of them were huddled together while one appeared to be keeping a look-out. Then the groups broke up and each prisoner spoke to five others.

In this camp the prisoners are allowed freedom to walk all over the enclosure. Every afternoon they had a football match and most of the non-playing prisoners gathered to watch.

EXTRA WATCH

When the guard reported his suspicions, all the camp guards were instructed to keep extra watch and those who understood German mixed with the prisoners.

Shortly before dawn a Nazi prisoner was seen to leave his nissen hut and creep to an out-building. There he met another prisoner from a second hut.

A piece of paper passed between them. It was confiscated and found to contain last-minute instructions for the escape.

This afternoon the prisoners were standing behind the barbed wire discussing the English people who were out for an afternoon walk along the country road. Only a small hawthorn hedge and the barbed wire separated them from the public.

Their washing was hanging on improvised lines and the prisoners who were not watching this afternoon's football match hung about aimlessly.

Latest for the troops—

Floating breweries and cinemas

By MORLEY RICHARDS

THERE will be floating breweries in three ships which the Admiralty have released to go to the Far East for the entertainment of our troops.

These liners are to be specially equipped with brewing apparatus and completely enclosed vessels for the beer—to allow for movement of the ships—and they will brew as they go.

This is partly because there are not enough bottles and casks to supply the needs of all the troops abroad. There will be plenty of mild-and-bitter for all visitors to the new-style Showboats.

Theatres, too

In each liner will be a large theatre and a cinema, reading and writing rooms, a cafeteria, a shopping centre—which will include a barber, a dry-cleaner, a library and a tailor—as well as "hard" and "soft" bars, and an ice-cream and soda fountain.

Before Parliament rises this week, Mr. Churchill, who has taken over personal direction of the amenities to be provided for our Far Eastern Forces, will make a statement about the new floating Servicemen's clubs.

Each will have permanent dance orchestras, and they may also have "resident" artists. Other entertainers organised by Ensa are to be flown out to give shows aboard.

Swiss turn back runaway Nazis

ZURICH, Sunday.—The Swiss have turned back two Messerschmitt works officials who said they were not anti-Nazi but wanted to leave Germany before the collapse, which they think is imminent.—B.U.P.

CHILDREN KILLED AS V-BOMB FALLS

Express Staff Reporter

FIVE children were killed by a V bomb falling in a narrow street of workmen's homes in Southern England recently.

Lorries in a garage were hurled into the houses opposite and C.D. workers used acetylene-flame cutters to get through tangled steel to reach trapped victims.

There were piles of rubble in the road, and by the light of searchlights A.R.P. workers and soldiers worked with cranes, clearing a passage for ambulances.

Houses in nearby streets were shattered. Mrs. Collins and her daughter Anne were brought out of their house, dead.

Hours after the bomb, rescue squads searched the debris of a house behind the garage for a widower and his three daughters, who lived there.

Damaged shops were used as temporary clearing stations.

When another V bomb landed hundreds of people queueing up for a local cinema a few hundred yards away escaped.

The bomb hit a small cardboard-box works. One person was killed in the street.

A passing bus was blasted, but there were only a few minor casualties.

Cortes to meet again

The seldom-summoned Spanish Cortes (National Legislature) has been called for a full session on December 29.—Madrid radio.

Germans dig potatoes

German prisoners are digging potatoes in Eastern England to help relieve a shortage in the London area.

Most of them are working without military escort, and farmers say that they are better workers than the Italians.

This week British troops will help to sort and load potatoes.

The Food Ministry said yesterday that the present shortage should be over by the end of this week. On Saturday 367 railway truckloads and hundreds of lorry loads arrived in the London area.

Three cadets die

Three officer-cadets died in a dormitory fire at an O.C.T.U. camp at Alton (Staffs) yesterday. Two others are in hospital with shock and burns.

The dead were Edward Foster, aged 19, of Myrtle-grove, Lowfields, Gateshead; Thomas Carl Malone, of a Canadian Irish regiment; and Walter G. Burwell, of Wilson-street, Darlington.

94 ITALIAN PRISONERS GET AWAY

BY TUNNEL

Express Staff Reporter

SEARCH was still being made last night for about 47 Italian Fascists who escaped from a prisoner-of-war camp in the West of Scotland on Saturday.

The Italians had dug a tunnel from well inside the camp to a considerable distance outside. In all 94 got away.

Nobody saw the break, and the absence of the 94 was discovered only on a check.

All the men wore chocolate-coloured battledress and arrived at the camp only recently.

When they got clear the men broke into groups and scattered over a wide area. Police forces in the area were told and they helped the military in cordoning the district.

Strategic points were patrolled and reports came frequently into headquarters of small parties of prisoners having been caught. Four were recaptured near the suburbs of Glasgow.

A Scottish Command officer said yesterday: "There are some 'difficult' men among the Italians who escaped. They are unarmed, but if they got a chance they might attempt sabotage."

3 a.m. LATEST

GERMAN SHIPS SUNK IN PORT

Soviet bombers have sunk a warship and three supply ships in Baltic port of Libau. Fighter planes attacked German airfields destroying 19 planes and preventing others from taking off.

Planes of Northern (Arctic) Fleet also sank a 3,000-ton transport in the Barents Sea.—Moscow official.

GERMAN ATTACK 'UNDER CONTROL'

Late despatch from First Army front says German attack seems "fairly well under control."—Reuter.

From arms to make clothes

Several thousand munition workers are being sent back to their old jobs in the clothing industry to enable the Board of Trade to honour the February issue of clothing coupons.

Mr. Dalton, President of the Board of Trade, told Mr. Bevin, Labour Minister, that only an immediate influx of clothing workers could prevent a serious cut or postponement of the February ration.

The switch will not seriously affect munitions output.

Front-line 500,000

A German radio war correspondent said yesterday that the four American armies on the Western Front now comprise 46 divisions, with 500,000 men actually in the front line.

Daily Mail
NO. 15,176 ONE PENNY ★ ★ FOR KING AND EMPIRE FRIDAY, DECEMBER 22, 1944

LATE WAR NEWS

35-MILE PUSH INTO BELGIUM

Rundstedt's Panzers Drive for Meuse

PARIS ALERT FOR 'INFILTRATORS'

GERMAN troops were last night officially stated to have driven 35 miles inside Belgium, west of Malmedy. A front-line dispatch said that Rundstedt appears to be aiming to reach the Meuse around Liége and drive northwards, into the rear of the Allied forces on the Roer.

On both flanks the German thrust is being checked. But in the centre, in the Ardennes Forest, the situation remains fluid. Sertorius, German military commentator, claimed last night that a breach 60 miles wide had been torn in the centre of the Allied lines.

He added that in the south General Patton's forces and in the north Allied troops from the Aachen area were striking at the German salient.

The Germans have cut the Liége-Bastogne road about 14 miles south of Liége, and have reached Habiemont, 30 miles west of the Belgian frontier. German armour has broken through another U.S. road block in the past 24 hours.

A bitter battle is raging for Malmedy. In Luxemburg the Germans have gained more ground, but have failed to retake Echternach.

Paris radio last night broadcast a warning that Germans disguised as Allied troops were infiltrating into France.

France Calls 'Mobilise'

ALLIED reverses on the Belgian-Luxemburg front have produced a nation-wide cry in France for general mobilisation. Posters appeared on the walls of Paris this afternoon headed: "We are still at war: a mobilisation order is essential," says Reuter.

The Radical-Socialist Party Congress to-day passed a resolution demanding "immediate mobilisation."

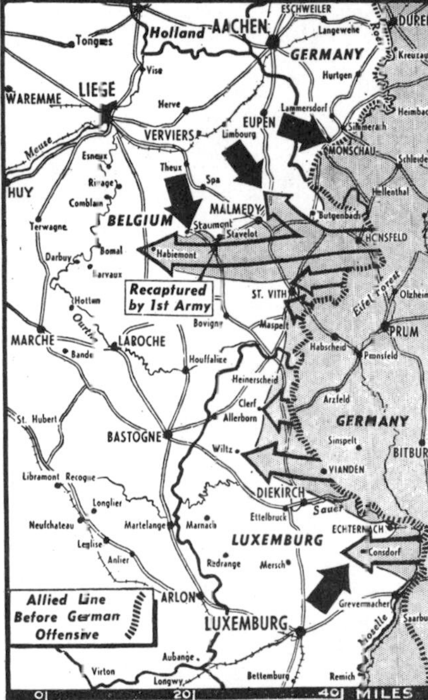

Hall Cables: Tension Less, Still Serious

From JOHN HALL, Daily Mail Special Correspondent
WITH THE ALLIED FORCES, Thursday.

SOME of the tenseness has gone out of the atmosphere to-day, but while I feel than von Rundstedt has not achieved as much as he hoped, the position is still serious. Most encouraging fact here is that our counter-measures have swung in steadily and are beginning to show results. Also, the nearer the fighting you get the more optimistic is the atmosphere.

The men who are in there grappling with the enemy feel they have his measure.

Their confidence has spread to the civilians close to the fighting areas. They are not nearly so apprehensive. On Sunday and Monday many of these people thought this was 1940 over again, and that we could not stop the Nazi "steamroller" once it got started.

Well, we have checked the first mad rush, and are steadying and building up against heavier pressure.

And that may come. Let no one get the idea that von Rundstedt staked all on one terrific thrust with nothing much behind. He is far too good a general for that.

My view is that, bloody and bitter as the fighting is now, bigger battles will be joined in the next day or so and that a gigantic tank battle is inevitable.

GERMAN HELPED

No one here shrinks from that battle, least of all the men who will fight it. Many of them have seen the tremendous weight of material that has been rushed forward to check the offensive—and is still rushing forward.

To-day, while the security silence still blankets current operations, I have tried to gauge the feelings of the Germans in towns and villages occupied by us.

Of course, the news that the Wehrmacht was attacking quickly flashed round, and from all manner of sources the German civilians have gained scraps of information.

It is a mystery to me how some of them seem to know so much. Only explanation must be that the few Germans who were in contact with the Nazi paratroops have passed the word round.

Reactions were mixed. In one village a German farmer actually gave the Americans their first warning that a German tank force was racing towards them.

At grave risk of being shot he ran along a road to a command post, waving his arms and crying: "Achtung! Achtung!" Breathlessly he explained that from a crest above the village he had seen the tanks.

DESTROYED

He was held, and the officer in charge gave orders for his story to be checked and defensive measures taken at the same time.

Three minutes later a German reconnaissance car nosed round the corner 300 yards away. It was destroyed first shot and all the crew killed.

The tank force behind halted, wheeled, and raced up another road. But the alarm had been given, and before nightfall the whole force had been destroyed.

I saw one of the tanks. It was

BACK PAGE—Col. FIVE

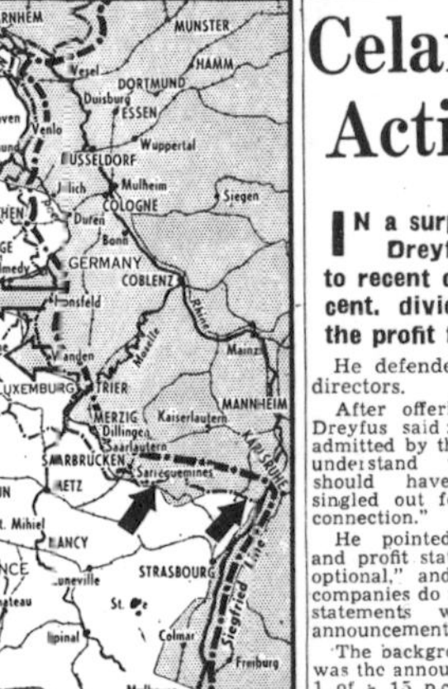

Enemy are Playing with Fire

In U.S. Uniforms

From ALEXANDER CLIFFORD, Daily Mail Special Correspondent
WESTERN FRONT, Thursday.

AMERICAN official circles stated definitely to-day that some of Rundstedt's troops attacked in the present offensive wearing Allied uniforms. The announcement has certainly been made only after careful investigation.

This is the first time in the war the Germans have taken such a step as a definite official policy. It is a tricky and dangerous policy. It carries an automatic death sentence for anyone taken prisoner. And it necessitates a very clever and unmistakable set of recognition signals to avoid getting fired on by your own side.

Using captured vehicles and weapons is an old trick and perfectly permissible. In some of the Western Desert mix-ups there were moments when the opposing armies seemed to have exchanged vehicles. But exchanging uniforms is another matter.

In this case it is said to have been ground troops and not parachutists who did it. One motive might be to try to encourage American troops to be suspicious of other American troops and perhaps even fight them.

But it is not a thing the Germans have ever thought worth doing before, and it is significant that they should have suddenly started now.

★

Other reports of infiltration by disguised Germans were received in London last night.

PARIS radio broadcast a warning that the masqueraders had infiltrated as far as into France.

The radio said: "Groups of Germans in American and British uniforms and in possession of British or American identity cards have infiltrated through the lines and have reached rear areas.

"These groups have American and British vehicles marked with Allied signs. The task of these groups is to sabotage and destroy installations most vital to the war effort."

A message from Paris said that three German soldiers were seen by French police in woods ten miles north-west of Paris. They fired several shots and then fled.

★

LEE CARSON, *Daily Mail Special Correspondent*, cabled that in one area behind the front 120 jeep-loads of masquerading Germans were reported.

Three Germans were discovered in an ordnance depot by a mechanic who "didn't like the way they looked at him."

"The Germans, in a medical corps jeep, pulled up at the ordnance depot, climbed nonchalantly out, and walked over to the mechanic. One did all the talking in perfect Americanese, complete with slang, the other two remained silent and watchful.

The mechanic acted quickly, and the Germans are now in a prison cage. The English-speaking German had 900 American dollars on him."—N.S.

U.S. GUNS SMASH UP TRAPPED PANZERS

OUTSIDE STAVELOT, Belgium, Thursday.

AMERICAN tank destroyers to-day smashed the attempts of German armour to break through and rescue elements of their forces, including 60 tanks, trapped near this embattled village.

Firing round after round through thick mist and fog, the anti-tank guns destroyed five captured American Sherman tanks, manned by German crews, which were spearheading the enemy drive to crash through the American positions between Stavelot and Malmedy. We have destroyed 30 to 60 German tanks.

The new German attack was launched about a mile and a quarter south-east of Malmedy. Unable to probe farther west, the Germans began trying to pull back through Stavelot across the Amblève river, but this route was closed two nights ago when the Americans blew up the only bridge.

The Germans were left helplessly trapped by the river on the south-east, by impassable hills, forests, and marshes to the north, and the Allied defences on the west.—A.P.

'1945 a Year of War'

Warns Arms Chief

WASHINGTON, Thursday.

ARMS production must be based on the possibility of heavy fighting against Germany through next year or longer, stated Mr. J. A. Krug, chairman of the War Production Board, to-night.

"If General Eisenhower had been able to break through the West Wall promptly, the equipment we had under procurement would have been sufficient," he said.

"We must get ready to fight the kind of war we have been fighting in the last two or three months for the next year, or as long as it takes."—Reuter.

Heavies Go Out Again

Heavy bombers were out again last night after the lull in night flying. A large force passed over the east coast for about an hour travelling towards Germany.

Celanese Reply: "Our Action was Justified"

By Daily Mail City Editor

IN a surprise statement issued last evening Dr. Henry Dreyfus, chairman of British Celanese Ltd., replied to recent criticisms of the board in announcing a 15 per cent. dividend—the first for 25 years—without giving the profit figures.

He defended the action of the directors.

After offering explanations, Dr. Dreyfus said: "No blame can be admitted by the board, and I fail to understand why our company should have been specifically singled out for criticism in this connection."

He pointed out that dividend and profit statements are "entirely optional," and that "many public companies do not publish such profit statements with their dividend announcements."

The background to this statement was the announcement on December 1 of a 15 p.c. dividend on British Celanese 10s. Ordinary shares. The shares then rocketed from 33s. to 41s. 3d.

Ten days later the report came out showing that the dividend had not been earned. This caused a slump, and the shares dropped 5s. in a few minutes.

Unusual Step

The Stock Exchange Committee then took the unusual step of issuing a statement in which they drew attention to the inadvertent omission on the part of the Celanese directors to publish the profit figures simultaneously with the dividend announcement.

Dr. Dreyfus immediately called a meeting of his co-directors.

Dr. Dreyfus last night said that he would be dealing with the subject at the general meeting of the company on January 16, and claimed that he would "provide full justification for the action of the directors."

His statement added:

"Had the secretary of the Stock Exchange 'phoned the company and asked for the profit statement when they received the dividend announcement on December 1, such statement would have been forthcoming at once, and all the trouble might have been avoided.

"Unfortunately, the company did not receive such a request from the Stock Exchange until a week later."

Steps were immediately taken, Dr. Dreyfus said, to give the profit statement to the Stock Exchange and the Press.

More Beer Soon on West Front

From Daily Mail Correspondent

WITH THE 21ST ARMY GROUP, Thursday.—British troops on the Western Front have been promised three large bottles of beer a week for 10½d. soon.

Three big Belgian breweries, with supplies of British malt and hops, will brew the beer. Our troops have already named it "Winston Ale."

CD Duty-free Smokes

Duty-free cigarettes, tobacco, and cigars in parcels weighing not less than four ounces may be sent by post to members of the Overseas Column, Civil Defence Reserve.

U.S. Facing Up to Reverses

The Hardest Blow Since Bataan

From DON IDDON, Daily Mail Special Correspondent
NEW YORK, Thursday.

THE gravity of the news from the Western Front has now been fully realised by the American people and is monopolising the Americans' thought and conversation.

The public here were not psychologically prepared for the sudden German counter-attack, and during the first few days Washington sources minimised the danger. It was described as "local," as "a flash in the pan," "nothing to get worried about."

Then the experts changed their tack. They said it was a last, desperate, all-out effort by the Nazis.

To-day, however, everyone faced up to the reality and agreed that the situation was bad. One of the most prominently featured dispatches here was the United Press story from Paris which said bluntly:

Headline Scare

"This is the pay-off. The U.S. Army has suffered, in Belgium and Luxemburg, its worst set-back since the loss of the Philippines in 1942."

Headlines on a thousand front pages, right across America, read: "Greatest Battle of the War," "Nazis Still Gain."

Commentators here are not attempting to analyse the situation, but many are expressing the hope, as Mr. Stimson did to-day, that if the Nazi attack fails, as it will fail, the war will be appreciably shortened.

In Washington to-day the War Production Vice-Chairman, Samuel W. Anderson, said that the Allied set-back in Europe "will hit us between the eyes," and that the German counter-offensive makes it impossible to predict the end of the civilian production freeze.

The present urgent demands for more shells, guns, trucks, and other vital material will certainly be followed by new armament problems, "as difficult as the ones we have now," Anderson told his Press conference.

'KEEP AT IT CALL' TO TUBE MEN

By Daily Mail Reporter

A THREATENED unofficial stoppage on Christmas Day by London's Underground railwaymen reached a further stage last night when the men's unions appealed to their members to remain at their posts.

Bus drivers and conductors have decided, it is stated, to cease work also if the Underground strike matures, and they are called upon to work after 4 p.m. on Christmas Day as a result.

The Underground men's grievance is over the London Transport Board's refusal of their demand for two days' holiday at Christmas.

In efforts to avert the strike the unions concerned—the N.U.R. and the Associated Society of Locomotive Engineers and Firemen—held meetings all day yesterday with representatives of the men.

Late last night the unions issued a statement dissociating themselves from the demands which have been made, and calling upon all members to ignore the unofficial action proposed, and to present themselves for duty on Christmas Day.

FORECASTS ON THE WAY

But Only Cold Snaps

Weather forecasts will be back again shortly—but they will be restricted to news of approaching cold spells, both in the papers and on the radio.

This partial lifting of the war-time ban on advance weather news will be initiated by the Ministry of Fuel and Power, so that people will be able to conserve heat in their homes when a cold snap is coming.

The forecasts will be based on international meterological information.

Your Ration is Safe

Great Stocks Here

BRITAIN'S rations are not in danger.

Reports from America yesterday that Lend-Lease food supplies to this country are likely to be reduced in the New Year owing to shipping shortage are regarded by the Ministry of Food as untrue.

Recent developments in the military situation in Europe may demand extra cargo space for munitions for a short time, but even so there are large reserves in this country of all the foodstuffs, mainly meat, cheese, bacon, and egg powder, which we have been receiving from America.

☆

These should be ample to maintain the basic rations for any period of temporarily restricted imports.

The *Daily Mail* New York Correspondent cables that a cut in British rations had been considered in light of shipping space, but been rejected as the British were "down to a minimum."

Abbey Bride is Home, Weds To-day

Midnight Meeting

SISTER EDWINA.
"No need for any delay."

By Daily Mail Reporter

SISTER EDWINA HOWARTH, who failed to appear at Westminster Abbey on Saturday to marry Lieut. Darrell Evans, of the R.A.M.C., is to be married at the Abbey this afternoon.

For last night Miss Howarth arrived at an east coast port after a four-days journey from her post as nursing sister in a British hospital in Holland.

Miss Howarth's first act was to telephone her fiancé, who is spending the last days of his embarkation leave at his parents' home in Harrow.

"My son answered the telephone," Mr. Elliott Evans, his father, told me later. "He was so surprised and overwhelmed at hearing his fiancée's voice that he fell in a faint on the stairs and we had to revive him with the aid of brandy."

'Rushed'

The wedding has had to be rushed, for Lieut Evans's leave expires on Boxing Day.

Within half an hour of hearing Miss Howarth's voice, Lieut. Evans was on his way to her home at Maidstone, where they met shortly before midnight.

There she explained that she failed to turn up at the Abbey for their wedding last Saturday only because her duties detained her in Holland.

"There will be no need for any further delay," she said. "I did my utmost to come across by plane, but eventually I had to come by boat. I have been on the way since Monday."

Miss Howarth will be married in her nurse's uniform.

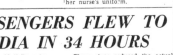

PASSENGERS FLEW TO INDIA IN 34 HOURS

By Daily Mail Reporter

THE journey from this country to Karachi, India, will be cut to less than a day and a half when the regular passenger air service starts.

In a test flight a Sunderland flying-boat, carrying seven passengers and freight, covered the 5,039 miles from Poole, Dorset, in 33 hours 52 minutes.

Three stops reduced the actual flying time to 28 hours. This is said to have been a record performance.

The present time to Karachi, on a longer route and flying by day only, is approximately four days.

The Sunderland had accommodation for 16 passengers, including sleeping quarters designed in the shops of British Overseas Airways Corporation.

'SAAR AND SILESIA FOR ALLIES'

France will Watch the Rhine

BIDAULT'S PLEDGES

From Daily Mail Special Correspondent
PARIS, Thursday.

M. BIDAULT, French Foreign Minister, to-day announced to the Consultative Assembly plans under which Germany would lose her two most important industrial regions—Silesia in the East and the Saar in the West.

Both M. Bidault and General de Gaulle spoke on the signing of the recent Franco-Soviet Pact in Moscow, and made it clear that French policy would be based on alliances with Britain and Russia.

"In the East," said M. Bidault, "Russia intends to give Poland Eastern Prussia, Pomerania, and the entire industrial basin of Silesia. To those boundary changes we agree.

"In the West we shall mount watch on the Rhine and make certain that the factories in the Rhine and Saar valleys will repair the devastation caused by Germany."

Both France and Russia, he said, wished to see a strong Poland, so that she may be able to stand up to German pressure—but until the Polish people have a chance to express themselves, the French diplomatic representation will undergo no change.

"The present treaty will put an end to the German danger which for more than 100 years threatened Russia and France," M. Bidault told the Assembly. "That is why our mutual aid will be quick and automatic.

"The Moscow Treaty is only the beginning of an entente in which the Government will follow."

Later on M. Bidault added: "We have declared clearly that we intend

BACK PAGE—Col. EIGHT

ATTACK BY BRITISH IN ATHENS

Tanks and Rockets Hit Rebels

ATHENS, Thursday.

GENERAL SCOBIE to-day launched his full-scale offensive against the E.L.A.S., using rocket-firing planes, tanks, and paratroops.

Tanks climbed high up the monastery-topped Likabettus mountain, strafed E.L.A.S. snipers, and scattered rebel concentrations in areas north of the British-held defence lines.

Rocket-firing planes were used concurrently with the tanks, which also found targets in and around the Averoff Prison area and the Military Academy to the north-west.

In Omonia-square, tank-supported paratroop patrols made a series of sorties, demolishing snipers' nests and taking a number of prisoners.

The Omonia-square billet of the Air Force Transport Command rocked with shell-blast as the buildings behind the requisitioned Cosmopolite Hotel were plastered.

Minister's Return

Mr. Harold Macmillan, British Resident Minister in the Mediterranean, returned here to-day following talks with Field-Marshal Sir Harold Alexander. The position in Greece was discussed, but Italian questions were the main subject.

By order of the Minister of War, the 1935-40 age groups in the liberated areas of Athens, the Piræus, Phaleron, Perama, and Clyphada, have been called up for military service. There is an enthusiastic response.

As part of the campaign to curtail the rumours flooding Athens, a Greek "Tim" has been installed. When Athens telephone subscribers dial to get the time they hear instead a recording made by the Allied Information Service about the Greek crisis.

Christmas fare for the British troops in Greece has been postponed as the present operations have delayed importation of N.A.A.F.I. supplies.—*A.P., Reuter, and Daily Mail Correspondent.*

PLANES PASS OVER SWEDEN

Swedish radio reported last night that "large numbers of foreign aircraft" had passed over Sweden from west to east.—Reuter.

U.S. FIGHTERS USE MINDORO BASES

American fighters are now operating from bases on Mindoro Island, in the Philippines, says General MacArthur's communiqué. There is still no Japanese ground resistance on the island.

MONTGOMERY. COMMANDS U. S. 1st AND 9th ARMIES.
British Official Photo from AP.

MONTY LEADING 2 YANK ARMIES

PARIS, Jan. 5 (UP).—Supreme Allied Headquarters announced officially this afternoon that Field Marshal Sir Bernard L. Montgomery has taken over command of all Allied forces on the northern side of the German salient, including the U. S. 1st and 9th Armies.

The decision was made for "tactical, geographical and supply" reasons, SHAEF said.

The remaining American forces of the 12th Army Group of Lt.-Gen. Omar N. Bradley, including the 3rd American Army and U. S. 1st Army elements on the south side of the salient remain under Bradley's command, SHAEF said.

For tactical purposes, the U. S. 1st and 9th Armies now are under Montgomery's control through 21st Army Group headquarters, SHAEF announced.

The official disclosure was made after war correspondents bitterly protested against not having been permitted to report the command change previously.

The official SHAEF announcement said:

"When German penetration through the Ardennes created two fronts—one substantially facing south and the other north—by instant agreement of all concerned, that portion of the front facing south was placed under command of Field Marshal

Continued on Page 10, Column 1.

British Battle in Belgium

NEW YORK Journal-American
AN AMERICAN PAPER FOR THE AMERICAN PEOPLE
Daily 5 Cents, Saturday 5 Cents in New York City; 10 Cents Elsewhere | SUNDAY, 10 Cents in New York City and 50-Mile Zone, 15 Cents Elsewhere
No. 20,809—DAILY FRIDAY, JANUARY 5, 1945 In Two Sections—Section One

B

7TH SPORTS WALL ST. SPECIAL

Parents to Join Hero Today for City's Welcome

SHOOTING THE SUN . . . Harvard Hodgkins, young Maine hero who helped trap two Nazi saboteurs, "shoots the sun" with a sextant aboard the Merchant Marine training vessel Cape Frio, one of his many thrills during his visit here. *(Full page of pictures of his activities for the day in the Pictorial Review.)* Journal-American Photo.

By EDWARD A. MAHAR

The Big Town's got a million thrills, sure, but 17-year-old Harvard Hodgkins called "Time Out" in his whirlwind tour here this afternoon for an even bigger thrill: welcoming his parents to the city to share the honors being heaped upon him for spotting the two Nazi saboteurs who landed in his Maine village.

Deputy Sheriff Dana M. Hodgkins, Mrs. Winifred R. Hodgkins and Harvard's beaming brother, Herbert, 10, donned their Sunday best this morning and journeyed to Bangor, Me. There they boarded a plane at 12:34 p. m., and arrived in Boston at 2:20 to board an Eastern Air Lines plane that will bring them into LaGuardia Field at 4:42 p. m.

Harvard, guest of the N. Y. Journal-American, will be at the field to meet them and tell them how the whole town, from the big names to the man and woman and boy in the street, has acclaimed him as a war hero.

The Hodgkins have never been here before. They will be guests of this paper, too.

GARDEN HONOR TONIGHT.

And they will be at Madison Square Garden tonight when Sgt. Joe Louis, the heavlweight champion, steps into the ring just be-

Continued on Page 7, Column 1

3 Women Die, 30 Injured in B'way Blaze

(Pictures in Pictorial Review)

Fire raged through the two upper floors of a seven-story apartment house at 231 W. 96th st., off Broadway, at 3 a. m. today, killing three aged women and injuring 30 persons.

The dead were:

Mrs. Etta Lesser, 72.
Zaide Ash, 82.
Mrs. Inez Brotchner, 74.

More than half the injured were firemen and police. Their heroic efforts, plunging through flames and lung-searing smoke to carry unconscious tenants to the street, saved many lives.

245 DRIVEN OUT.

The fire drove 125 other tenants of the 25-family structure into the freezing streets in their night attire, and 120 persons living at 230 W. 97th st., separated from the blazing building only by a five-foot areaway, also were routed.

Eight ambulances and emergency trucks were rushed to the scene to provide inhalator treatment for those overcome.

Most of the firemen were over-

Continued on Page 7, Column 6.

Delay Drafting Of Fathers

Non-fathers will be taken before fathers in calls for induction during this and next month, it was promised today by Col. Arthur V. McDermott, New York City Selective Service director.

At the same time Col. McDermott announced that "every consideration" will be given to fathers with families, it also was disclosed that the local draft quotas for this and next month will be stepped up at least 20 per cent.

Col. McDermott, who declined any specific comment on the statement of Maj.-Gen. Lewis B. Hershey, national director, that the war should no longer be regarded as "a young man's war," said that induction of fathers will be delayed as long as possible.

As for registrant fathers in the age group of 30 to 37, a spokesman at draft headquarters said they had little reason to fear being called away from their families for military service, because the emphasis is being laid on induction of younger men in all groups.

Currently there are 290,868 pre-Pearl Harbor fathers registered in New York City.

Soviet Accepts Lublin Regime

LONDON, Jan. 5 (AP).—Russia today announced recognition of the Polish provisional government of Lublin, making a clean break with the Polish government-in-exile in London, which still is recognized by the United States and Britain.

[The United States today reiterated in Washington its recognition of the Polish exile government despite Russian recognition of the new Polsih regime at Lublin. The State Department said it had received advance notice from Russia of the Soviet action.]

Bringing to a head one of the thorniest questions facing the impending Big Three parley, the broadcast announcement came within four days of the joint announcement by the United States and Britain that they stood by the London Polish Government.

Leaders of the Polish Peasant Party in London had sensed a possibility that Moscow would recognize the Lublin government before the Roosevelt-Churchill-Stalin meeting.

They charged that if Russia acted before that meeting it would be an attempt to present the other two powers wih a "fait accompli."

Russia broke relations with the London Polish government April 26, 1943, in a dispute over the reported discovery of graves of thousands of Polish officers in the Smolensk forests.

Russia accused the Germans of executing the Poles, but the London Polish government requested that the International Red Cross make an investigation.

Moscow's recognition of the Lublin group made no reference to the rival London government.

Tools in Strike Seized

PITTSBURGH, Jan. 5 (UP).—Because production of war-vital materials was hampered by a five-day strike, removal of tools and materials from two strike-bound plants of the Pittsburgh Equitable Meter Co. was begun today by Army officials.

U.S. Planes Again Nearing Tokyo

Tokyo radio reported enemy planes had been sighted again after dusk tonight (Jap time) over east central Honshu, following incursions by single B-29's in the vicinity of Nagoya, Hamamatsu and Osaka between dusk last night and noon today.

This area includes Tokyo and Yokohoma.

Earlier, the Jap domestic radio reported that a single B-29 had carried out a reconnoissance over the "Nara area" some 20 miles east of Asaka at 11:40 last night and two others were over the Nagoya and Hamamatsu areas this morning.

One plane, Tokyo said, "penetrated the Okazaki area" some 20 miles southeast of Nagoya, and "dropped a few bombs." The other flew over Nagoya and Hamamatsu some four hours later on reconnaissance.

Mercury to Touch 15 Degrees Tonight

It will be cold tonight, 15 degrees in town and 10 in the suburbs, the Weather Bureau forecast today. Slightly warmer tomorrow, the temperature will rise to a peak of 35, with diminishing winds and clouds forming.

Today's coldest was 21 at 8 a. m., rising to a maximum of 30.

Send for Free War Poster

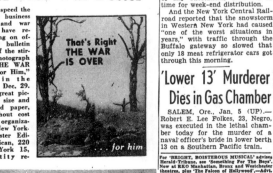

In an effort to speed the war effort, many business men, transport and war plant managers have requested for posting on office and factory bulletin boards, reprints of the stirring full page photograph "That's Right, THE WAR IS OVER . . . For Him," which appeared in the Journal-American, Dec. 29.

Copies of this great picture, in full page size and printed on coated paper, are available without cost to all firms and organizations in Greater New York.

Write War Poster Editor, Journal-American, 220 South St., New York 15, indicating quantity required.

That's Right THE WAR IS OVER
. . . for him

FDR Message On Foreign, WMC Policies

WASHINGTON, Jan. 5 (AP). — President Roosevelt will take to the air tomorrow night to summarize to the nation his State of the Union message to be delivered to Congress earlier in the day.

The Chief Executive message will deal with foreign policy and manpower, among other things, and will be about 8,000 words long.

His foreign policy discussion, he indicated, may touch on more materials for the French.

The broadcast hour has not yet been set, but a White House Secretary said sometime between 9:30 and 10:30 p. m., E.W.T, would be preferred.

MORE FOOD FOR ITALY.

The President said a new program for feeding Italy has been agreed upon and that more food is going in there. He could not estimate the increase in pounds but said there were more calories in the new shipments. Shipping still is a very great problem in feeding the Italians, he said.

Told that some people believe the Italian armistice terms should

Continued on Page 2, Column 5.

Sunday Meat Looks Skimpy

So little meat arrived in the city today that only the faintest hopes for weekend relief were held out.

Armour & Co. reported receipts of 105,000 pounds of beef, lamb, veal, pork, ham and bacon. This was described as 50 per cent of a normal shipment.

Offsetting that news, however, the Cudahy Packing Co. reported that its deliveries were still being delayed by snow, with little chance of any substantial deliveries in time for week-end distribution.

And the New York Central Railroad reported that the snowstorm in Western New York had caused "one of the worst situations in years," with traffic through the Buffalo gateway so slowed that only 18 meat refrigerator cars got through this morning.

'Lower 13' Murderer Dies in Gas Chamber

SALEM, Ore., Jan. 5 (UP).—Robert E. Lee Folkes, 23, Negro, was executed in the lethal chamber today for the murder of a naval officer's bride in lower berth 13 on a Southern Pacific train.

Allies Make Small Gain In Bulge

PARIS, Jan. 5 (AP).—British 2d Army infantry and armor—veterans of [illegible] sweep into Belgium and Holland—have [illegible] thrown into the battle of the Belgian bu[illegible] and have attacked, it was announced tod[illegible]

Field Marshal Montgomery's forces went into action yesterday in the Marche area [illegible] the northeastern tip of the von Rundstedt salient and have reached the village of Waha in a 1,500-yard advance that is continuing, a field dispatch said today. Waha is just south of Marche.

Other British units attacked the Germans on the outskirts of newly captured Bure and Wavreille, south of Rochefort at the western end of the salient.

A score of top priority targets behind a 150-mile stretch of the German lines between Cologne and Karlsruhe were attacked today by more than 1,000 U. S. Fortresses and Liberators in one phase of a full-scale assault.

Five hundred P-51 fighters escorted the American bombers from Britain.

Holland-based Mitchells and Bostons of Montgomery's airforce—the RAF 2d Tactical—raided a concentration of German material near St. Vith before noon.

The British troops were rushed to the front at the first sign of danger to Liege, when von Rundstedt launched his offensive, and backstopped American lines until yesterday, when they went on the offensive.

Six Allied and German armies thus were committed to the grinding battle being fought in drifting snow, fog and miserable terrain—some of the worst fighting conditions of the war—and the Allied assault on the German north flank was broadened to 35 miles.

Field reports also announced

Continued on Page 4, Column 3.

The Journal-American, only New York evening newspaper, to carry all three great news services, presents these latest developments on the Western Front:

UP says Marshal Montgomery has been given overall command of U. S. 1st and 9th Armies in assault on Nazi bulge in Belgium.

AP reports British 2d Army joins offensive of U. S. Armies in bulge. Allied front broadened to 35 miles.

INS says Allies make steady but slow progress.

THE WEATHER

Clear and cold, fresh winds.

Sun rises, 8:20 a. m.; sun sets, 5:43 p. m. High tide at Governors Island, 2:17 a. m. and 2:15 p. m.

HOURLY TEMPERATURES.

4 a. m.	26	9 a. m.	21
5 a. m.	24	10 a. m.	22
6 a. m.	24	11 a. m.	24
7 a. m.	23	12 Noon	26
8 a. m.	22	1 p. m.	25

(Complete Weather Report on Page 24)

TODAY'S INDEX

DAILY EXPRESS

No. 13,918 | Dim-out 5.44 pm to 8.32 am | THURSDAY JANUARY 11 1945 | Moon rises 6.14 am sets 2.55 pm | One Penny

'Arctic chase' after German troops withdrawing in the Salient

RUNDSTEDT PULLS BACK TO FORM NEW LINE

Allies, following up, take empty villages

From ALAN MOOREHEAD: With the British, Wednesday

RUNDSTEDT is withdrawing from the salient. It began on Monday, continued all through yesterday, and it is going on now. It looks as if he may be going back about 20 miles to a line running from Bastogne through Houffalize to Vielsalm, and after that it is anybody's guess.

Perhaps he will try to regroup and come on again, but for the moment the order is—retreat, get back before you get cut off.

Seen from this side of the line it is like some weird Arctic chase, a manhunt over the endless plains of foot-deep snow.

All through today the American and British reconnaissance units beyond Marche drove on into village after village and found them unoccupied.

WOMAN TANK-DRIVER

The Germans got out in the night. Where they had time they mined the roads, and now that fresh snow has fallen over the mines it is a courageous thing for the scouts to drive forward in pursuit.

Strange incidents occur along the line of the chase.

Once yesterday a German rearguard tank waited too long. It turned to fight and it was knocked out.

When our men went up to the wreck they found the gunner in the tank was a woman. She was dead like the rest of the crew, a girl of perhaps 23 or 24 with fair hair under her beret and dressed in an ordinary German uniform.

As far as I know it is the first time the Germans have put their women into the front line, let alone the tanks.

At another place, an American doctor called to a soldier across the road. The soldier approached and threw acid in the doctor's face.

When he was captured he was found to be a German paratrooper wearing American uniform, and that is the first time I have heard of the Germans arming their men with acid.

LOST CONTACT

But these are minor things in an immense and moving picture.

German armoured divisions are on the march backwards, their one concern to get their tanks away while they still have petrol and still have time.

It is an orderly retreat, a thing that has been carefully planned at least a week ago when it apparently became obvious to Rundstedt that his front was about to break and all hope of keeping the offensive was gone.

Indeed, at the first light this morning the British lost contact with the retiring enemy.

When I drove forward to one of the leading pursuit divisions, the scout cars were still going forward into an empty wilderness, and they hoped to make another four miles by nightfall.

The sunshine had given the battlefield a breathless and most simple kind of beauty. Everywhere the crisp virgin snow spreads out for mile after mile.

It gives the deserted villages a curious toy-like appearance. It turns the round and pointed haystacks into igloos.

Here and there the tracks of tanks, and cars with chains on wheels, lead off through the snowdrifts and past copses of firs and beeches.

Every mile or so you come to a tank that has slithered off the road and is threshing about wildly in a ditch.

AIR FLEETS

The tracks of the infantry lead off mysteriously over the horizon.

There is little sound of artillery in the sharp, clear air, but the Allied air fleets are a remarkable thing to see.

As they came streaming over from England they dragged their vapour trails right across Belgium from the Channel to the German border.

Even the bigger formations of Fortresses were too high to see clearly, and so these advancing and expanding vapour trails were all you could discern in an otherwise empty sky, and the bright light coloured them a brilliant silver.

It was rather like watching gnats buzzing about on the calm surface of a pond.

This was towards mid-day. Earlier, the visibility was down to a hundred yards. Vehicles had

→ BACK PAGE, COL. FIVE

Bastogne vital as Alamein

From Alan Moorehead's cable last night:—

ALL this news is so decisive and good that one can now put down something one hesitated to say before. It is this.

Everything at one moment depended on the Americans holding Bastogne. Had they lost it, there was a reasonable chance of the Germans sweeping through to the coast and taking Antwerp, which would have meant the encirclement of the British armies.

There would have been no escape route by sea this time.

But Bradley and his Americans hung on somehow.

Now that the full reports are coming in they were saying at this British headquarters that Bastogne compares in importance with Alamein in its effect on the war.

It was a bigger battle down there than we knew about, perhaps one of the greatest American efforts of the war.

100 panzers mass near Strasbourg

From GORDON YOUNG: Supreme H.Q., Wednesday

THE threat to Strasbourg continues. Allied airmen today sighted and attacked a total of a hundred German tanks assembling in the area of the Colmar pocket to the south of the city.

One tank park attacked was in a wood on the west side of the Rhine, about 12 miles north-east of Colmar, where 50 vehicles were bombed, four destroyed and a number damaged in two attacks.

The other group of 50 was in a wood on the eastern side of the Rhine, where five tanks were destroyed and seven damaged.

Northwards of this Colmar pocket there is still a confused swirling battle of little groups of tanks and infantry going on from village to village in the area about 12 to 17 miles south of Strasbourg.

Many villages are changing hands as small parties of Germans appear here and there among our troops, who in some parts are fairly thinly spread.

Main threat

Spots we have withdrawn from in the past 24 hours include Boofsheim, on the main Colmar-Strasbourg road and 17 miles south of the city, and Kraft about 12 miles from Strasbourg.

But simultaneously we have cleared the Germans from the outskirts of Herbsheim and Rossfeld on the western side of the Rhone-Rhine Canal.

The main threat to Strasbourg comes from the south, but the enemy is hanging on to his bridgehead only seven miles north of the city where American troops are now attacking on a big scale.

Further north the immediate danger seems to have lessened.

In the Bitche salient German artillery has been harassing our troops, but north of the Hagenau Forest the large force which attacked us has suffered considerable losses, with at least 14 out of about 20 of its tanks destroyed.

BRITISH GAIN 3 MILES

BRITISH and American troops advanced on a 25-mile arc along the north-western borders of the Belgian salient yesterday, and Field-Marshal Montgomery's spokesman said the enemy was making a general withdrawal in these sectors.

The British, after winning the bitter fight for the strategically important village of Bure—one of the hardest struggles since the battle of Tilly in Normandy—pressed on for 3½ miles and crossed the River Homme.

The whole of the diminishing bulge is now within range of Allied artillery fire.

FROM TWO SIDES

On the northern flank there was a battle for Laroche as two columns—British and American—struck at the road junction town from two sides.

The Americans won what is described as the biggest tank battle of the winter on the Western Front and captured the hilltop village of Samrée dominating Laroche from the east.

On the southern flank of the salient General Patton's infantry advanced another half mile beyond Bastogne and gained 1½ miles further east to reach high ground overlooking the town of Wiltz.

Jets strafe roads

From DOUGLAS WARTH

SAAR FRONT, Wednesday.—A new feature of this front today was the silent strafer—jet planes gliding along our roads and opening up at convoys.

You hear nothing of the engine and take off. All you hear is a quiet zoom-zoom.

The jet planes strafed the roads we were on three times this afternoon, but I did not see a single truck hit.

Peter speaks today

King Peter of Yugoslavia has reached a decision about the appointment of a Regency of three to rule his country.

At noon today he will meet the Press at his house in Upper Grosvenor-street, W. It is expected that he will review the consultations he has had with his "old guard" advisers in the last few days, and announce his policy.

Formation of the Regency, pending a plebiscite, has been agreed between King Peter's Government in London and Marshal Tito.

Canada prepared for V bombs

OTTAWA, Wednesday.—"German submarines have been more active in the Atlantic in recent weeks, but not nearly so active as in the early stages of the war," said Canada's Navy Minister, Mr. Angus MacDonald, today. He added: "Civil defence authorities at Halifax, Nova Scotia, are prepared for any emergency such as German robot bombs."—Exchange.

Mussolini bombed

LUGANO, Wednesday. — Mussolini's Lake Garda villa was destroyed by U.S. bombers last Thursday, but he was safe in his air-raid shelter, say reports reaching Switzerland.—Reuter.

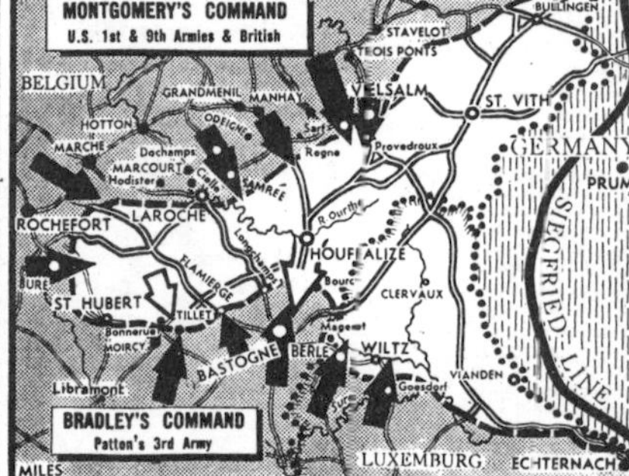

HOPES OF PEACE SOON IN GREECE

By GUY EDEN

MESSAGES reaching Whitehall last night suggested that the situation in Greece had taken a strong turn for the better, and that the fighting may cease soon.

E.A.M. representatives have been in conference for many hours with General Scobie, the British commander.

Peace terms are likely to include the surrender of arms by all who are not members of the Greek Army.

I understand that General Plastiras, the Greek Premier, is likely to announce a general amnesty for all except those guilty of "war crimes."

JOIN CABINET

If the amnesty is granted the end of the fighting is expected to follow quickly. Then representatives of E.A.M. will join the Government, which at present consists of only 10 Ministers.

The view of the Greek regent, however, is that extremists of the Right or Left—Communists and Royalists—should be excluded from the Government. This view has the support of Mr. Churchill and Mr. Eden, who have been consulted.

The British Government is, I learn, willing to send a mission to see that the election is held fairly.

A proposal that an international police force should take charge of the whole voting machinery is under consideration.

Mr. Churchill is to make a statement on the Greek situation and on war developments generally in the House of Commons next week and there will be a debate.

Scobie gives his terms

From ERIC GREY

ATHENS, Wednesday.—General Scobie's final terms are being presented to E.A.M. this afternoon.

The E.A.M. envoys are empowered to accept them if they see fit.

Today the Union of Popular Democrats, known as E.L.D., announced that it disassociates itself from the actions of the Communists.

This amounts to a withdrawal of E.L.D. from E.A.M., which is now reduced almost entirely to the Communist Party.

General Plastiras has issued a statement on Government policy with these four points:—

1. Reorganisation of the army and police. Britain has been asked to send a special police mission.
2. Collaborators will be punished.
3. Everything will be done to provide full employment. Workers' rights are guaranteed.
4. Elections for a National Assembly as soon as possible.

OWN POINTS

These are precisely the points for which E.A.M. have been fighting, and Plastiras declares: "If they are honest men, the insurgents will lay down their arms, cease fratricidal strife, and assist in rebuilding our country on these lines."

Plastiras means to raise a national, non-party army, and he therefore announced he cannot accept volunteers from various organisations.

The remnants of the E.D.E.S. forces, which had fled to Corfu island when the insurgents defeated them on the mainland, are accordingly disbanded.

Big pockets come back

ARMY and A.T.S. officers are to get back their "poachers' pockets"—large, pleated pockets which adorned the Service tunic before it went austere, on Board of Trade orders, in 1942.

At War Office request, restrictions on the style of Army uniform will be relaxed from February 12 and tailors may begin making the smarter pattern on Monday.

Cuffs will be allowed again and the two upper tunic pockets may be made with pleats.

The concessions are optional. Higher prices will be announced.

NOW THEY ARE POISED FOR THE BIG BLOW

Russian lull—here are the reasons

Express Staff Reporter

MOSCOW, Wednesday.—The Red Army is on the eve of its plunge towards the heart of Germany.

From the East Prussian frontier regions to the Carpathian foothills, the stage is being set for what is believed will be the final march to Berlin.

The complexity of the necessary preparations might be compared with the months in Britain before the opening of the Second Front.

This is the explanation of what the Russians frankly call the "lull" on the major sections of the Eastern Front (but no Russian would give it to you without pointing proudly to the Red Army's impressive series of successes in the Balkan theatre).

Ever since the Battle of Warsaw came to a standstill there has been a mounting rather than a slackening of the urgency in the Soviet attitude, as reflected in its Press, towards ending the war in the quickest possible period.

Improvise towns

Enormous supply problems such as re-tracking many hundreds of miles of permanent way with Russian broad gauge lines, and the restoration of scores of cunningly blown tunnels and bridges, confronted Red Army engineers when they were set the task of preparing a smooth-running base for the Red Army's full-scale invasion of the Reich.

Between the Dnieper and the Bug there is hardly any river bridge standing that is not either rebuilt or new.

In some places whole towns which are of vital importance as war bases have had to be "improvised" into existence again.

And this has been only the preparation for the actual job of moving up millions of troops, scores of thousands of guns, and thousands of tanks to the chosen battlelines.

Late autumn mud, stubbornly persisting over wide areas up to the last few weeks before Christmas, further complicated the task.

In considering why all this has been necessary, it is important to realise what the East Prussia-Warsaw line—the line the Red Army is going to break—means to Germany.

Last barrier

The Vistula, and the great chain of fortified zones based on that river, is virtually Berlin's last main barrier on the Eastern European Plain.

The northern flank, anchored deeply in concrete and steel in East Prussia, and the southern flank, backed against the Carpathians, are two equally vital bastions, for if either should crumble the effects would soon be felt in the centre.

To those abroad who are asking when the Russians are going to get moving on the main road to Berlin, the answer can be no more than "Very soon."

Budapest three-quarters in Russian hands

MOSCOW, Wednesday.—Hitler's severely mauled tank groups west and north-west of Budapest are tonight massing for a new and possibly final bid to break through to the capital.

In a number of sectors Marshal Tolbukhin's troops have already switched over to counter-attacks.

Tonight's Moscow communiqué says the Russians have smashed to within a mile of Komarno, springboard for the relief attempts.

Three-quarters of Budapest are now in Russian hands. Today the Red Army won more ground than on any day since the siege started and took the biggest bag of prisoners—3,000.—Reuter.

Negress envoy for Britain

NEW YORK, Wednesday.—Mrs. Maida Springer, first Negress to represent U.S. labour abroad, will arrive in England soon with three other women workers by invitation of the Ministry of Information. She is a dressmaker.

Won't play

BUENOS AIRES, Wednesday.—The Argentine announced today that it will not attend meetings of the Pan-American Union "until Argentine rights are recognised."—Express News Service.

Hanover last night

R.A.F. Mosquitos hit the German city of Hanover with 4,000lb. bombs last night.

THE GREAT BLACK WAY

NEW YORK, Wednesday.—The lights of Broadway are faced with extinction.

The U.S. Government has requested the elimination of all outdoor advertising throughout America.

This will mean a black-out along New York's Great White Way.

Another step to forestall what is described officially as "an impending coal shortage" is that heating in all American homes and public buildings will be limited to a maximum of 68 degrees.

These steps, says Mr. James Byrnes, Director of U.S. War Mobilisation, will save 16,000,000 tons of coal a year.

All special and excursion trains are to be cut out and increases in passenger traffic in holiday areas prevented.—Reuter and B.U.P.

Hitler guards old clo'

Hitler yesterday signed a decree establishing the death penalty for anyone sabotaging the old clothes collection just organised in Germany to equip the Volkssturm.

According to the German News Agency the decree states:—

The collection of clothing and equipment is a new sacrifice of the German people for its soldiers. Whoever, for his own purpose, uses articles which have been collected or have been set aside for collection, or withdraws such articles from their lawful purpose, will be sentenced to death.

U.S. PLANS BIG-5 ALLIANCE

And free hand for FDR

Express Staff Reporter

NEW YORK, Wednesday.—Congress did its best today to allay fears in Britain and Russia, and in America itself, that it is going to run out on post-war security. And the initiative was taken by the Republicans, always pictured as America's Isolationist Party.

Senator Arthur Vandenberg, who certainly was not an Interventionist before Pearl Harbour, proposed a hard and fast alliance between Britain, America, Russia, France and China to ensure peace.

He also proposed that Congress immediately vote the President power to use force to keep Germany and Japan demilitarised after the war, the power to be used without first consulting Congress.

This goes further than any proposal yet made by President Roosevelt or any other Democratic leader.

Many Republicans, generally regarded as representing the more Isolationist point of view, went out of their way to offer their warm congratulations to Senator Vandenberg after his speech.

NO EXCUSE

He said that the purpose of the speech was to remove the excuse which some of the Allies had used for the unilaterial actions they had taken to ensure their own security.

"Surely," he said, "we can agree that we do not want an instant's hesitation or doubt about our military co-operation in the peremptory use of force, if needed, to keep Germany and Japan demilitarised.

"It should be handled as the present war is being handled. There should be no need to refer such action to Congress any more than Congress would expect to pass on battle plans today. The Commander-in-Chief (the President) should insist on power to act, and he should act."

Senator Vandenberg added that he did not blame the Allies for their doubts about the United States. Russia's actions to ensure her post-war security were perfectly understandable.

"The alternative is collective security," he said, "but at that point Russia or others like her have a perfect right to reply: 'Where is there such an alternative until we know what the United States is going to do?'"

MOST IMPORTANT

Senator Austin, a Republican member of the Foreign Relations Committee, described Senator Vandenberg's speech as "one of the most important addresses ever," and Senator Tom Connally, chairman of the committee, said: "The greatest inducement and guarantee we can give our Allies would be the assurance that the United States is going to stand by the Dumbarton Oaks plan.

"It's either going back to the old order, with all its horrors, or else it's the creation of an international organisation in which we could take the leading part."

And then Senator Frederick Ferguson offered a resolution calling for American participation in a world security organisation prepared to use force to preserve peace, and re-emphasising this country's determination to stand by the Atlantic Charter.

To Russia via Dardanelles

WASHINGTON, Wednesday.—Mr. Edward Stettinius, U.S. Secretary of State, said today that the shipping of supplies to Russia via the Dardanelles was in accordance with the Montreux Convention, which allows merchant ships of all nationalities to pass through the Straits. The arming of merchant ships with A.A. guns might have created a technical difference with Turkey.—Reuter.

100,000 men start march on Manila

JAPS CRASH-DIVE BEACHES

From NEWELL ROGERS: New York, Wednesday

GENERAL MacARTHUR has driven his bridgehead on Luzon four miles inland, and already got 100,000 men ashore, in spite of suicide attempts by Japanese planes to combat the landings.

His communique tonight also reports the capture of Lingayen airfield, and of four towns.

Earlier the Japanese News Agency announced: "Our entire air force in the area has been turned into a special attack corps of crash planes."

"Even our reconnaissance planes, with specially installed bombs, are crashing into enemy ships."

A hint also came from Tokyo that the landings will draw the Japanese Navy out for another showdown.

Lieut.-General Masaharu Homma, former Japanese C.-in-C. in the Philippines, declared:—

"The American landing on Luzon is a threat to Japan's position in East Asia which cannot be ignored.

"Immediate counter-measures are essential, particularly as the enemy may make further landings which would expose Manila to fresh dangers.

"It may be taken for granted that the Japanese Navy will now go into action and deal blows in this theatre of operations."

The latest Japanese reports speak of "fierce battles" as the Americans strike out from Lingayen Gulf towards Manila, capital of the Philippines, 120 miles away.

But MacArthur's communiqué says the Japanese "are unable to mount serious resistance yet, and are now feverishly bringing up troops from positions in the south."

In fact, D Day and D-plus-One were ridiculously easy. Too easy, said some sunburned veterans of Lieut.-General Walter Krueger's Sixth Army—who knew how tough

BACK PAGE, COL. SEVEN

Springboard to Tokyo.

SEA TURNS LEAVE SHIP BACK

Express Staff Reporter

A THOUSAND British soldiers—fresh troops and compassionate leave men—sailing to the Continent were forced back to a British port by heavy seas and had to spend a night in pier sheds.

After one of the worst Channel crossings of the war, in which waves threatened to sweep crews and soldiers overboard, the boats found it impossible to ride into Continental harbours.

They returned for re-coaling and sea-sick men and officers were taken ashore on stretchers.

The men stayed the night in pier sheds because the boats had no sleeping accommodation.

Next day they re-embarked and arrived safely.

4 a.m. LATEST

MacA. IS IN 14 MILES

New York radio said early today that Americans were 106 miles from Manila, indicating an advance of 14 miles.

3 DESTROYERS LOST IN STORM

WASHINGTON, Wednesday.—Three destroyers have been lost in a typhoon in the West Pacific, the Navy Department announces.—Reuter.

5/- more for farm men recommended

Express Staff Reporter

FARM workers are satisfied that "a step in the right direction" was made yesterday when the Agricultural Wages Board in London recommended a 5s. rise in their weekly pay—making a minimum of £3 10s. for adult men workers.

They are also getting an increase of a penny an hour for their overtime.

Women's minimum wage remains at £2 8s. a week.

The Board's decision was carried by the independent members. Representatives of the farmers all objected to the increase.

'NOT ENOUGH'

The recommendation now goes for consideration to each of the 47 county farm wage committees—the majority of whom approved the suggestion when it was put to them previously—and back to the Board for final approval on February 21.

It is expected to come into force some time in March.

Mr. A. C. Dann, general secretary of the National Union of Agricultural Workers, said last night: "The new wage is not enough, but progress has been made. I will continue the fight until farm workers have a real living wage to compare with skilled workers in other industries."

The right spirit

WASHINGTON, Wednesday.—Guatemala, Central American State, has offered 10,000 men to fight abroad with the Allies.—A.P.

Daily Mail
NO. 15,198 ONE PENNY * * * FOR KING AND EMPIRE FRIDAY, JANUARY 19, 1945
N.A.A.F.I. FREE ISSUE Distributed by ARMY WELFARE SERVICES

RED ARMY ENTER GERMANY

Nazis Hurl in Volkssturm and Police

FIRST picture of the new "Stalin" tank, playing a big part in the great Russian drive. The Germans say it weighs 50 tons, has a 5in. gun and heavy armour. It fords rivers with ease.

HOUSE-TO-HOUSE SILESIA BATTLE

From Daily Mail Special Correspondent

STOCKHOLM, Thursday.

KONIEV'S tanks, driving west from the Czestochowa area, have smashed through to the German border and were to-night engaged in bitter fighting with German battle groups flung into the line in a desperate endeavour to stem the advance while a defence is organised farther back.

This break-through was disclosed by a German News Agency report which said that battle groups and infantry had been rushed to towns and villages along the Upper Silesian border to break the impetus of the Soviet onrush.

These army units have been reinforced by every man capable of firing a rifle. The Volkssturm (Home Guard) has been rushed into the line; police have been collected from town and village to reinforce the defence.

One German version of the battle to-night said: "Upper Silesia will defend itself to the last. Men of the Volkssturm—miners, peasants, shopkeepers—are going through bitter fighting. They are fighting from this home front line . . . 500,000 men are assailing us."

As the fighting raged from hamlet to hamlet, from house to house, along the border, Koniev's men farther north, and the armies of Zhukov and Rokossovsky swept on to success after success.

To **Koniev's** men fell the great communication centre of Piotrkow, 23 miles from Lodz.

to **Zhukov** went Lowicz, 48 miles west of Warsaw on the road to Kutno, and Skierniewice, 30 miles from Lodz;

to **Rokossovsky** went 1,000 towns and hamlets, including such large towns as Modlin and Zakroczym and Przasnysz.

German admissions took Rokossovsky even farther west, and spoke of fighting in the Mlawa region, which means that the Red Army is within a dozen miles of East Prussia's southern frontier.

Rokossovsky, according to Berlin, flung 20 fresh infantry divisions into the battle to secure these successes.

ENCIRCLED

Behind the spearheads of these assaults the German defence is in many sectors dissolving into chaos.

Units have been encircled and cut off; others have been split and split again.

Commanders can be heard frantically sending out radio calls for aid that their superiors cannot send.

The background to the battle was filled in to-night by Colonel von Oldberg, military correspondent of the German Overseas News Agency, in these ominous words:

"Places far to the west have been reached by Russian spearheads to-day. Behind them, no longer in a continuous line, German forces ringed in by attackers are fighting their way back to the west.

"The German High Command is faced with the difficult task of finding a strategic solution at this moment. Only if reserves can be brought up will the High Command be in a position to determine where and when to meet the onrush."

35-MILE THRUST

For home consumption the Germans are announcing that the Russians will "find things very different" on the Reich borders.

Reserves were being rushed into the line, particularly in the south; counter-attacks were smashing at the flank of the Silesian wedge; below Czestochowa "a new barrier line is taking shape."

This line is said to run south to Cracow, into which Berlin admits the Russians have penetrated.

Moscow has not yet confirmed Lublin's report that Cracow has fallen, and it is probable that heavy fighting is in progress either in or around the city.

Below Cracow the Germans report that a Red Army attack from the Jaslo area—so far unannounced by Moscow—is "pressing towards Nowy Sacz," which represents an advance of about 35 miles by men of General Petrov's army on Koniev's left flank.

This attack they claim to be "under control," but admit that the front will have to be "levelled out" to conform with the line farther north.

Lublin Poles Now Rule Warsaw

The Polish Provisional Government has taken over the administration of Warsaw, according to a statement last night by M. Osubka-Morawska, Premier of the Provisional Government, quoted by Lublin Radio.

Soviet Blow Was Timed With Allies

Washington, Thursday.

MR. HENRY STIMSON, Secretary of War, commenting on the Russian offensives, said to-day: "They reflect the constancy of the Russian effort, in co-operation with that the U.S., Britain, and the other Allies, to bring about the complete defeat of Germany.

"A powerful Russian offensive through Poland, aimed directly at the heart of Germany, is being linked with heavy pressure by Allied forces in France, Belgium, and Holland.

"The new Russian offensive comes at a time when American and British troops in the Ardennes have driven back the enemy with losses that must weaken his stand in the west."—Reuter.

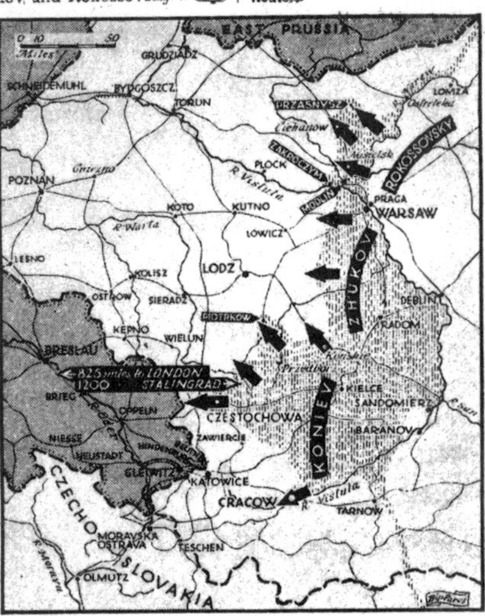

New Motor Fuel That Costs Nothing

TWO local authorities in the London area, Middlesex County Council and Croydon Corporation, are between them operating more than 100 motor vehicles on a fuel which costs practically nothing.

The vehicles are private cars, dust-carts, 4-ton lorries, and even vehicles with a laden weight of 11 tons. They are all running on methane—sludge gas.

Although experts had long been exploring the possibilities of methane as a motor fuel, no large-scale use was made of it in this country until Major W. H. Morgan, the Middlesex County engineer, was faced with the problem of burning sludge gas at the Mogden sewage works, Twickenham, during the black-out.

Sludge gas arises from the destruction of sewage waste and is 70 per cent. methane.

Major Morgan decided to collect the methane, and he told me yesterday that besides running vehicles on it it was used in heating the buildings and for the pumping and operation plant.

Croydon Corporation operates a fleet of 30 heavy lorries on methane Mr. C. E. Boast, the borough engineer, says it has proved "most satisfactory."

The vehicles run three or four times longer on methane before decarbonising than when petrol is used.

Local authorities in all parts of the country are experimenting with this war-time fuel. Before long the Man in the Street may be able to buy methane in liquid form at 3d. a gallon or less.

While the gas itself costs nothing, an elaborate compressor plant is needed to liquefy it.

80-MPH GALE IN STRAIT

Ship Calls for Doctor

Mountainous seas, lashed by an 80-m.p.h. south-westerly gale, swept through the Strait of Dover last night. There was also heavy rain at times.

Waves crashed over the piers at south-east coast towns. Visibility was down to a few yards.

Dr. James Hall the SOS sea surgeon, went out in the Walmer lifeboat to a steamer which had sent out a call for medical aid.

More Italy Ships Leave Spain

From Daily Mail Correspondent

MADRID, Thursday.—Three Italian landing barges and one trawler left Barcelona to-day to join the cruiser and four destroyers which were released by Spain on Sunday, despite German protests.

The nine vessels were manned exclusively by their original crews of 1,300 men, while less than a score declared themselves in favour of Mussolini's German-dominated Government.—*A.P.*

Shops are 'Rationing' Potatoes

Unofficial Move During Shortage

POTATO rationing has been unofficially introduced in many areas of Britain and will remain in force until the present shortage ends.

This follows a recommendation by the Retail Fruit Trade Federation to greengrocers, who in the worst areas of shortage have already been supplying regular customers only.

In some cases, little more than 3lb. a head is being sold a week. The normal potato consumption is about 6lb.

In Liverpool, one of the worst areas, potato supplies available in the shops were at one time only 15 per cent. of normal. Many shops had no potatoes at all.

Since last week-end 761 tons have been sent to Liverpool, and a further 400 tons were expected from Northern Ireland last night. Long-keeping stocks have also been released.

'Shop-crawling'

Manchester, Newcastle on Tyne, and Brighton, all areas of more than average shortage, have begun unofficial rationing.

"People are actually shop-crawling for potatoes," one Brighton greengrocer told me. "I have never seen such a shortage here since the last war.

"There are so many women in Brighton who have nothing else to do but go on a shop-crawl. I overheard one woman the other day say that she had managed to collect 36lb. of lemons by queueing and hadn't an idea what to do with them."

Rationing has not been introduced in some areas where stocks can be drawn on. But the situation in London and the densely populated industrial areas may not improve at once.

Bad weather and the lack of labour and transport are blamed for the shortage. A small part of the main potato crop, which has been a normal one, is still in the ground, although there are hopes that it may be lifted soon.

Reprieve for Big Factory

On Merseyside

MR. DALTON, President of the Board of Trade, stated yesterday that negotiations are in progress for letting the Rootes Securities factory, at Speke, Liverpool, where thousands of workers have been given notice that they are to be discharged as redundant.

Mr. Dalton told a deputation from Liverpool City Council that he was determined that a high and continuous level of employment would be maintained at the factory.

Several firms have applied for the factory, and as soon as the Board made a decision the name of the firm would be announced.

HALF V2's FAIL TO LEAVE

Says Dutch Report

Half the V2's fired from the vicinity of the Hague fall on Dutch soil, most on the Hague itself, according to a 21-years-old Dutchman who has crossed the German lines into liberated Holland.

The Dutchman, quoted by a Dutch war correspondent, said that the rockets were brought up in lorries and fired from mobile platforms firmly secured to the ground.

They were shot from mortars carefully aimed from a car fitted with special devices. When 150ft. up the rocket's own propulsion system started to work. The launching lorries could be moved.—*Reuter.*

Capetown Beats Back Huge Fire

From Daily Mail Correspondent

CAPETOWN, Thursday.—The greatest fire ever to sweep the face of Table Mountain roared down towards Capetown this morning and was only beaten back after it had penetrated the residential areas of the city.

Five thousand volunteers answered urgent radio calls for fire-beaters to tackle the solid five-miles blaze, advancing one mile every ten minutes. The fires are now under control, but not yet out.

Sir R. Campbell for Whitehall

Sir Ronald Ian Campbell, British Minister at Washington, has been appointed an Assistant Under-Secretary of State in the Foreign Office.

He will be succeeded by Mr. John Balfour, at present Minister in Moscow, states the Foreign Office.

Monty Bans Ice Cream

From Daily Mail Correspondent

BRUSSELS, Thursday.—A general Order of the Day from 21st Army Group H.Q. forbids all troops to buy ice-cream, owing to the danger of this product carrying typhoid germs.

Our Tanks Smashing Roer Line

Monty Widening His Attack

BRITISH tanks have smashed through Rundstedt's defences in the 15-miles bridgehead west of the Roer river, the German News Agency admitted last night.

Three British divisions are attacking, the agency added; and German motorised forces are in action.

No confirmation has yet come from the Allied side. But Field-Marshal Montgomery's H.Q. reported a widening of the attack on the Roer salient from the Dutch "corridor" between Germany and Belgium.

After an all-night barrage by massed guns, British troops swarmed forward in a new attack north-east of Sittard. They advanced more than a mile towards the German town of Hongen.

On a ten-miles front between Sittard and Echt, Dempsey's men cleared a number of Dutch villages, after advances of up to two miles, and are edging into Germany.

St. Vith—One Mile

Stretches of the road from Sittard to Roermond, northern shoulder of the salient, are in British hands.

Sertorius, Berlin military commentator, said last night: "It remains to be seen whether this attack means more than meets the eye or whether it is just an attempt to pin down German forces."

American **First Army** troops compressing Rundstedt's salient in Belgium and Luxemburg are reported within a mile of St. Vith, one of the last bastions held by the Germans.

To the south-west they have pushed a mile beyond Cherain, where the salient is being crushed in at its most westerly point.

... salient, Patton has flung two Third Army divisions over the River Sure near Diekirch. They have advanced up to two miles on a seven-miles front.

PANZERS HELD

From **COURTENAY EDWARDS**, Daily Mail Special Correspondent

SUSTEREN (Holland), Thursday.

MARKS in the trampled snow between the shattered shops and wrecked houses of this Dutch town bear witness to-day to the fierceness of the fighting yesterday before Susteren was cleared of the Germans.

British infantry have never fought more bravely than they did here when, armed only with Piats, Bren guns and rifles, they held at bay a whole "fleet" of German tanks.

I have borrowed the word "fleet" from an English officer who took part in the battle of Susteren. "They came charging through the streets just like warships going into action," he said.

"There were five or six small panzers forming a kind of protective screen round a King Tiger—just like destroyers circling round a battleship. I have never before seen the Hun use tactics quite like these."

Against this German armour our lightly armed troops held out until British tanks arrived. They sniped at the tank crews from upstairs windows and fired their Piats at the panzers from shop doorways.

One Piat crew knocked a tank right out.

Rattled by this unexpected opposition from a handful of infantrymen, the Germans lined up captured British troops and made them walk in front of the tanks as they rumbled along the main street.

Taking careful aim, our men kept firing. The tanks stopped. From out of one turret popped the head of an officer, who shouted in English: "If you shoot any more of my

BACK PAGE—Col. SIX

PM FLAYS OPPONENTS IN ONE OF WAR'S BEST SPEECHES

Only Extremists to Press Greece Division

EDEN TO END DEBATE

By **WILSON BROADBENT**, Political Correspondent

EXTREMISTS in the Labour Party, and a few Independents who have persistently criticised the Government's policy in Greece, are expected to force a division in the House of Commons to-day, when the debate on Foreign Policy and the war situation, opened by the Prime Minister, is brought to a close.

Not more than a handful of M.P.s are likely to vote against the Government unless there is some unforeseen development.

Mr. Churchill's exposition of the Government's policy, his exposure of happenings in Greece, and his denunciation of his critics was numbered among his most powerful orations by commentators in the Lobby last night.

They declared that they had not heard him make a more dynamic and dramatic speech in this war-time Parliament.

Supporters of the Government were overjoyed at the vigour Mr. Churchill displayed.

It remains to be seen what the Opposition can offer in reply, and particular attention will be focused on the speech of Mr. Aneurin Bevan, the brilliant, but fiercely critical Welsh debater, who so frequently has crossed swords with the Prime Minister.

Grave Warning

Mr Anthony Eden will wind up the debate for the Government this afternoon.

Apart from Greece, Mr. Churchill's speech was one of the most comprehensive and confident he has ever made, embracing as it did a fervent and eloquent appeal for national unity in this, the final stage of the war in Europe.

His warning to Germany to seek peace by unconditional surrender led to an elaboration of the conditions which will be demanded of her in defeat.

Equally, his assertion of the principles underlying the purpose and determination of Britain's war where the glory and responsibility was conveyed in a passage which reached a degree of nobility of phrase which caused even those members most used to Churchillian oratory to pause and then to applaud excitedly.

Report of speech begins in Page TWO.

SEA-AIR LEADERS

Vice-Admiral Burrough Takes on Ramsey's job

Major-General Gale Commands the 'Airborne'

New Invasion Names are Announced

Burrough to Lead Naval Forces

By Daily Mail Reporter

TWO new names came into the Allied Command in the west last night, when the appointments were announced of:

Vice-Admiral Sir Harold M. **Burrough** to be Allied Naval Commander, Expeditionary Forces, in succession to Admiral Sir Bertram Ramsay, killed on January 2 in a Paris air crash, and of

Maj.-General Richard Nelson **Gale**, to succeed Lt.-General F. A. M. Browning as Deputy Commander of the First Allied Airborne Army.

Admiral Burrough, who is 56, has been Flag Officer Commanding Gibraltar since September 1943.

He commanded one of the three main naval forces in the North Africa landings and was awarded his second D.S.O. He gained the first in command of the naval forces in the Vaagso raid in 1941. He was knighted for his command of the escort of a great Malta convoy.

Admiral Burrough led the first combined operation in this war of British and Soviet Navies—a joint raid on enemy shipping in the Arctic port of Vardo.

He is married and has two sons and three daughters.

The Spearhead

Maj.-General Gale raised and trained the British Airborne Division which afterwards became the spearhead of the Allies' invasion.

At the outbreak of war, General Gale became G.S.O. 11 of a planning staff which did brilliant work in moving the British Expeditionary Force to France.

Later he became Director of Air at the War Office—a guide, philosopher and friend to all the rapidly increasing airborne forces in Britain.

It was General Gale's audacious and brilliantly executed plan which enabled the division, within a few hours of jumping into Normandy, to report that all the tasks allotted by higher command had been accomplished.

After the initial airborne assault, General Gale and his men fought in Normandy for some months.

His Beret

His D.S.O. was won during the battle of the Breville Gap, soon after the invasion began. He was also awarded the American Legion of Merit.

"*His presence*," says the citation, "*still wearing his beret, combined with the utmost calmness and coolness, suggesting more an exercise than the middle of a very bloody battle, had such an amazing effect on the troops that wounded and attackers alike cheered and attacked with such élan as nothing could resist.*"

Both General Gale and General Browning are 48. General Browning was appointed Chief of Staff to Admiral Lord Louis Mountbatten, Supreme Commander South-East Asia, in November.

The Admiralty also announced last night that Rear-Admiral V. A. C. Crutchley, V.C., has been appointed Flag Officer, Gibraltar and Mediterranean Approaches, and Rear-Admiral J. H. Edelsten has been given a sea-going appointment.

Rear-Admiral Crutchley won his V.C. as a lieutenant in the Vindictive at Ostend in 1918.

Shelter Statement

Mr. Morrison, Home Secretary, told Mr. Chater (Lab., Bethnal Green), in the House of Commons yesterday that he hoped to make a statement to-day on the Bethnal Green shelter case.

Full Holidays Planned for This Year

NORMAL holidays, of peace-time duration, are in prospect this year for thousands of war workers. Industry, which has drawn up 1945 labour schedules assuming holidays will be on the same basis as last year, is expected to be recommended to follow the lead of the Civil Service, which has just been notified that holiday leave has been extended.

Personnel of Government Departments will get 24-days holiday, in addition to the usual Bank Holidays, compared with 18 days during 1944, and 16 in 1943.

Ministry of Labour officials said yesterday that they regarded the extension of Civil Service holidays as a first step towards a probable relaxation of Mr. Bevin's war-time regulations governing the number of "man-hours" which must be worked

"If the regulations are relaxed," they said, "the result will automatically be that employers will be able to grant longer holidays."

BRITISH ATTACK GAINS MOMENTUM'

German High Command reported late last night: "The British attack in the Roer salient is gaining momentum."

'BUILD OWN HOMES,' GERMANS TOLD

Dr. Robert Ley, German Labour Front leader, said last night: "Bombed-out people must not look for help to the authorities. They must build their temporary homes themselves."—Reuter.

'Big 3 Chief Has Spoken'

"Herr Churchill has spoken again," said a German commentator on Berlin radio last night. "We must not overlook that, whatever we think of him, he is the very mouthpiece of the 'Big Three.'"

[Mr. Churchill's call to the German people to surrender was plugged at Germany last night by Allied stations, while neutrals made the speech headline news.]

WEDNESDAY, FEBRUARY 14, 1945

Evening Standard

37,672 DIM-OUT: 6.42 pm to 7.45 am. MOON: Sets 8.36 pm; Rises 9.58 am. ONE PENNY

FINAL NIGHT EXTRA●

THE BLASTING OF DRESDEN

1350 Forts and Liberators Over Germany To-day After Night Attack by 1400 'Planes of R.A.F. Bomber Command

KONIEV INSIDE BERLIN PROVINCE

Marshal Koniev, crossing river barriers, to-day continued his advance towards Dresden and the heart of Germany as the gap between his forces and those of Marshal Zhukov narrowed to about 15 miles.

A link-up between the two forces for an outflanking drive south of Berlin is expected soon, says Reuter.

Koniev's men are to-day storming the Queis River, half-way between Breslau and Dresden, now less than 70 miles ahead.

The Germans are said to be showing increasing alarm over the possibility of a new Oder crossing by Zhukov's forces in the sector just beyond Koniev's right wing.

A Soviet blow here would split the remaining co-ordination between the German forces on the Berlin front and those in Silesia.

In Brandenburg

Berlin to-day named Cottbus and Guben, twin bastions guarding the south-eastern approaches to the capital, as the main objectives of Koniev's northern drive.

According to the German communiqué the Russians have reached Sorau, eight miles west of Sagan, and less than 30 miles from Guben.

This means that Marshal Koniev's forces have crossed the border into Brandenburg. Sorau is five miles inside the border and under 90 miles from the Reich capital.

To-day's German communiqué also admitted that the Russians have widened their penetration area north-west of Breslau.

"In the area south-west of Breslau," it stated, "the enemy hurled freshly brought up forces into the battle. Despite the stubborn resistance of our troops, who were backed by Volkssturm and alarm units, the enemy in Lower Silesia was able to gain ground to the west and north-west.

"Bunzlau was lost during bitter fighting. Many enemy attacks against the fortress of Glogau were beaten back.

"In Southern Pomerania the Russians launched vain attacks. Fighting stubbornly the defenders of Arnswalde, Schneidemuhl and Poznan held out.

Stettin Hears Guns

"In the southern part of West Prussia, the Russians continued their breakthrough attempt in the area of Konitz and Tuchel. Heavy fighting is in progress.

"Enemy attempts to push in our front on both sides of the Elbing-Koenigsberg autobahn from the west, and at Zinten from the east, failed, as did pinning-down attacks between Wormditt and Landsberg."

Massed formations of Koniev's tanks are attacking west of Breslau in the direction of the town.

A Moscow military commentator broadcast this afternoon that Stettin can now hear the rumble of the Soviet guns.

German radio reported this afternoon that the Red Army had established another bridgehead across the Oder in the Frankfurt sector facing Berlin.

Martial Law Ends In Greece

Martial law ended in Greece to-day. The decree lifting it also annulled all sentences passed by the military courts in their trials of E.L.A.S. supporters.

To-day's Official Gazette promulgated the amnesty signed by the Government last night for all political offences committed during the events of December.

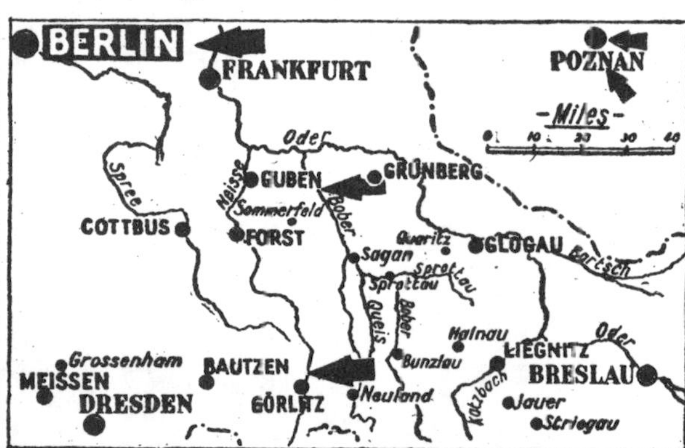

FIRES SEEN BY KONIEV'S MEN

More than 1350 Liberators and Fortresses of the U.S. Eighth Air Force to-day attacked transportation and industrial targets in Dresden, Chemnitz, and Magdeburg, and a road bridge across the Rhine at Wesel.

The bombers were escorted by more than 900 Mustangs and Thunderbolts of the same Command.

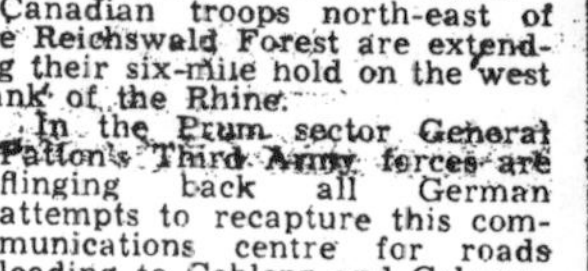

BURNING DRESDEN, POUNDED LAST NIGHT BY 800 BOMBERS OF R.A.F. BOMBER COMMAND, WAS AGAIN HIT TO-DAY BY AIRCRAFT OF THE U.S. EIGHTH AIR FORCE.

The raids were in support of Marshal Koniev's troops who are less than 70 miles away.

Russian troops may have seen the fires burning in the city last night after a double raid by our bombers. Crews of the bombers said that they could see the glow 200 miles away.

Two great blows were struck at Germany to-day. One 300-mile long stream of airplanes flew from the west, and other formations went from the south.

The Germans may be using Dresden—almost as large as Manchester—as their base against Koniev's left flank. Telephone services and other means of communication are almost as essential to the German Army as the railways and roads which meet in Dresden.

Its buildings are needed for troops and administrative services evacuated from other towns.

Dresden has large munition workshops in the old arsenal No major attack has been made before on the town.

Six hundred more bombers struck last night at the synthetic oil plant at Bohlen, south of Leipzig, and Magdeburg.

JAPS AND PEACE

Tokyo radio, which is rigidly controlled by the Government, broadcast to-day that the Japanese Foreign Minister's policy is "not to reject any hand which offers peace."

The spokesman of the Japanese Information Bureau, Iguchi, said: "The Yalta Conference was a masterpiece of power politics.

"The only way to re-establish peace in the world is by a just policy as outlined by Foreign Minister Shigemitsu, whose principle is not to reject any hand which offers peace."—Associated Press.

10,000 Tons of Bombs on Budapest

Allied and R.A.F. bombers of the Mediterranean Allied Air Force flew more than 4500 sorties over Budapest and dropped about 10,000 tons of bombs on it between April 1 and late in 1944, says Reuter.

SUNSHINE FOR SIX HOURS

By mid-afternoon the sun had been shining in the Straits for just on six hours. The temperature at 2 p.m. was 50, and the westerly breeze had backed a little to the south-south-west.

"Last Ditch Stand In Bavaria"

The Germans are hastily preparing Bavaria for a last ditch defence, said Moscow radio to-day.

Princess Elizabeth

Princess Elizabeth, who is suffering from mumps, is "progressing normally."

MONTGOMERY ADVANCING ON THIRD SIEGFRIED BELT

Hochwald Line Is 10 Miles Ahead

Montgomery's British and Canadian tank columns are now fighting their way forward towards Rundstedt's third and final Siegfried defence belt—the Hochwald Line—guarding the west bank of the Rhine and about ten miles beyond present Allied positions, said war reports reaching Reuter to-day.

Since the offensive began six days ago Allied troops of Montgomery's command have advanced up to 10 miles into the German lines along the front of 14 miles.

Canadian troops north-east of the Reichswald Forest are extending their six-mile hold on the west bank of the Rhine.

In the Prum sector General Patton's Third Army forces are flinging back all German attempts to recapture this communications centre for roads leading to Coblenz and Cologne.

Farther south, elements of three U.S. Third Army divisions are fighting through the Siegfried defences from the Our River bridgehead between Echternach and Wallendorf.

This is How Part of the "West Wall" Looked to the British

Sergeant-major Leonard Allington, of Birmingham, and Sergeant Gordon Dudgeon, of Glasgow, inspect a captured Siegfried Line strongpoint with ten-feet thick walls, while their comrades in a Scottish artillery regiment eat a quick meal before resuming the battle.

Double Onslaught Repulses Nazis

From RONALD MONSON

WITH THE FIRST CANADIAN ARMY, Wednesday.

Flame-throwers roaring on from the south-east fringe of the Reichswald Forest belched death into the ranks of the Germans trying to prevent the British advance beyond the forest late yesterday.

Behind them came men of the North Country regiment which had carried out the final clearing up of the forest.

The enemy who survived broke and fell back before the double onslaught.

Away on the north-east of this advance other troops, moving down after mopping up near Cleve, fought their way along roads leading south-east to Udem and to Calcar.

A British motor battalion after routing out Germans from the woods just south of Cleve, dashed on down the Udem road, 2000 yards beyond Bedburg.

Hasselt Captured

Reaching the Cleve State Forest, they found it full of Germans.

The Air Force and artillery were called in and the woods were plastered from end to end.

Few of the enemy were left in fighting condition when the guns ceased and the airplanes went home.

One pocket in a copse north-

(Continued on Back Page, Col. Two)

Spitfire Up With Waaf On its Tail

Evening Standard Reporter

A Waaf flight mechanic, 35-year-old Margaret Ida Horton, of Woodmansterne-lane, Banstead, Surrey, was working on the tail of a Spitfire when the aircraft suddenly took off.

She clung on for ten minutes until the extra weight on the tail was noticed by the pilot. By then the Spitfire had gained considerable height.

Throttling back carefully the pilot landed safely with Miss Horton still clinging on.

She was severely bruised and had to be taken to hospital suffering from shock. She is now recovering.

"The matter is now subject of an inquiry," an official of the Air Ministry told me.

Parachute Padre Is War Captive

News has been received at Beaumont College, Old Windsor, that the Rev. Bernard M. Egan, who was reported missing at Arnhem, is a prisoner of war in Germany.

Rev. B. M. Egan

Fr. Egan, who was the first padre to make a parachute descent from a glider, was wounded, and is now in hospital suffering from severe injuries to his legs. He was a master at Beaumont College.

His mother, Mrs. S. A. Egan, who lives at Buntingford, Herts, told the Evening Standard to-day: "I have received five letters from my son, who is in hospital at Stalag 9. In his last letter, which I got yesterday, he told me he is now able to walk about again with the aid of two sticks

M.P. ON YALTA FLIGHT DISASTER

"Wrong Type Of 'Plane Alleged"

Mr. Granville (Ind., Eye) asked the Air Minister in Parliament to-day if he had any statement to make on the recent accident in which 15 British Service people and officials lost their lives on their way to the conference between the Prime Minister, President Roosevelt and Marshal Stalin.

Sir Archibald Sinclair replied: "I deeply regret the loss of life caused by this accident. The aircraft was a York belonging to the R.A.F. It was of standard design, and fitted with standard equipment The R.A.F. pilot and crew were highly experienced. The aircraft was obliged to come down in the sea.

"A court of inquiry are now sitting.

Mr. Granville: "There is a good deal of serious concern in the public mind as to the repetition of these accidents.

"In view of the fact that this might have happened to any of the aircraft engaged on the flight, can you give an assurance that all machines engaged in the Prime Minister's flight were given adequate mechanical supervision and inspection right throughout the journey?"

Highly Efficient

Sir Archibald.—I cannot give an assurance about right throughout the journey, but I can give an assurance that the maintenance arrangements of Transport Command are highly efficient

Earl Winterton (Con., Horsham and Worthing).—Will you look into the allegations that have been

(Continued on Back Page, Col. Five)

"Every German Will Kill, Murder, Poison"

"Every enemy, no matter when or how he penetrates into Germany, will be met by fanatical men, women and children, who know what treatment is in store for them and therefore wish to kill, murder and poison all who attempt to oppress them."

This extract from the broadcast by Paul Schmidt, the German Foreign Office spokesman, in which he declared that the Yalta declaration released Germany "from all moral scruples," was quoted by the Swedish paper Svenska Dagbladet to-day, says Reuter.

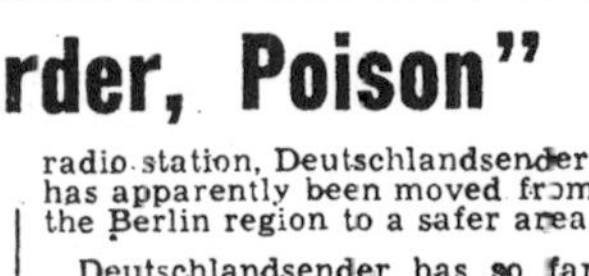

Large scale thefts of arms from Volkssturm barracks outside Berlin have sharpened German fears that a rising may be attempted once the military situation worsens, private Berlin reports to Stockholm said to-day, quoted by British United Press.

The main German long-wave radio station, Deutschlandsender, has apparently been moved from the Berlin region to a safer area.

Deutschlandsender has so far been broadcasting from Koenigswusterhausen, 15 miles south-east of Berlin. It went off the air after 1 a.m. because of approaching raiders; yet among the numerous warnings put out every few minutes by the German achtung stations there was none reporting raiders over the Berlin area.

Average net paid circulation for February exceeded
Daily---2,000,000
Sunday-3,700,000

DAILY NEWS

Copr. 1945 by News Syndicate Co. Inc. NEW YORK'S PICTURE NEWSPAPER Trade Mark Reg. U. S. Pat. Off.

★★★ FINAL

Vol. 26. No. 220 New York, Thursday, March 8, 1945★ 48 Main + 12 Brooklyn + 8 Kings Pages 2 Cents IN CITY LIMITS | 3 CENTS Elsewhere

PATTON'S MEN REACH RHINE

Story on Page 3

Reds 29 Miles From Berlin In Oder Drive, Nazis Say

Story on Page 2

Death Shrouds Cologne Victory

In the shadow of Cologne Cathedral (background), the camera records a moment of death and victory as the Yanks sweep into the Rhine metropolis. A wounded American struggles (arrow) free from his tank which has just been blasted by an enemy shell. While one Yank runs to the rescue another dashes off to summon aid. The rest of the crew, killed in blast, are in the smoking tank. The street clock marks the hour. -A few moments later . . . (see back page).

(Official Signal Corps foto via Associated Press Wirefoto).

News Chronicle
No. 30,845 MONDAY, MARCH 26, 1945 ONE PENNY
4 a.m. EDITION

Population of Frankfurt fleeing before advancing Third Army's armour

MONTY HOLDS 200 SQUARE MILES

Two bridges across and 8,000 prisoners taken

ENEMY RESISTANCE STIFFENS

From S. L. SOLON, News Chronicle War Correspondent

MONTGOMERY'S H.Q., Sunday.

THE bridgehead across the Rhine in the north now comprises over 200 square miles of the east bank.

The two armies—the British Second and the American Ninth—commanded by Field-Marshal Montgomery have today consolidated crucial gains necessary for the great build-up of men and material that is now in progress.

The area won in 36 hours of fighting extends for 30 miles along the river from north of Rees to south of Dinslaken [on the main motor road running north out of the Ruhr into the Wesel and Bocholt areas].

At its deepest the bridgehead has driven seven miles east of the Rhine.

The airborne forces—the British 6th Airborne Division and the U.S. 17th Airborne Division—are completely joined up with the ground forces which launched the assault across the river.

Casualties on the Allied side have been light Eight thousand prisoners have been counted—including 1,500 by the British Second Army and 3,500 by the airborne divisions. More are pouring in from every quarter.

WEEK OF TOUGH BATTLES AHEAD

German resistance is weak—yesterday, when flying over the bridgehead combat area, I found it difficult to pick out the points of heavy fighting—but it has gradually stiffened all through today.

As this is written tonight fighting in some parts of the bridgehead perimeter is becoming ferocious. German paratroops moved into the lines are fighting back with a desperation they have shown only in the hardest battles.

German reinforcements are moving up, and it can be expected that a week of tough battles is ahead of us.

While the rubble towns of Wesel and Bislich have been cleared, a number of German paratroops are still holding out in Rees.

Units of the 15th Panzer Grenadiers have been identified north of Rees, where the opposition is steadily growing stronger.

4,000 YARDS GAINED

As British and Canadian troops spread out in the area around Rees and Wesel they will very likely meet new German formations being brought in as reinforcements.

The American Ninth Army, which advanced 4,000 yards across the Wesel-Dinslaken road, are up against elements of the 84th German Infantry Division and Hamburg Division. Hard fighting is going on.

Once again the so-called "battalions of defectives" organised by the Germans are being encountered.

Bait

These are units made up of men who share a common disability — ear trouble, stomach ulcers and the like—and for whom special provisions are made.

These units are obviously being used as artillery bait while Kesselring deploys the regular forces with which he hopes to do the impossible—seal off this growing bridgehead.

Bridge-building is well ahead of schedule. The British Second Army and the American Ninth each has a bridge across the river, with more nearing completion.

The overall picture shows successes more rapidly achieved than had been expected. It is worth remembering, however, that the chief German defences in this area have not yet been engaged. No commander in Kesselring's position would hope to defend the river at its edge. His plan was to keep his mobile reserves farther in the rear—perhaps 30 or more miles—and rush them into the breach made by an Allied assault for the purpose of driving it back or sealing it off. His attempt to do this is now beginning, and the next seven days may see the decisive battle of the bridgehead develop.

MOST ROADS LEAD TO BERLIN

What will happen when Kesselring's last dispositions are beaten and overrun will be a matter for the Allied commanders. Loose on the great plain of the north, most roads, if not all, lead to Berlin.

The opportunity that Gen. Patton has seized so rapidly in the south will open before our northern armies now attacking.

9th Army breaks into open

The 30th ("Roosevelt's") Division of Gen. Simpson's Ninth Army have broken through the Rhine defences into open country north of the Ruhr, eight miles from their starting point on the east bank, states an A.P. front-line dispatch.

In this sector resistance appeared to be completely disintegrated.

From WILLIAM FORREST
News Chronicle War Correspondent

WITH THE NINTH ARMY, Sunday.

ONE more river—and by far the greatest. It is just over 24 hours since we came across—the trip by stormboat took exactly 55 seconds—and already on this army's front a substantial bridgehead 12 miles long and up to five miles deep has been won, and white flags are fluttering in half-a-dozen newly captured German towns.

In this same week-end two years ago I saw Montgomery and his men come up against the first of the many water barriers that have lain across their long, long road to victory. That was the flooded bed of the Wadi Zigzaou, in the Mareth Line.

On the banks of that distant stream and in defence of alien ground the Germans fought with far more spirit—and success—than they have so far shown on the banks of the German Rhine.

Ear battalion

But the Africa Corps was the pick of the Wehrmacht, when the Wehrmacht was at the peak of its strength.

Today Germany is compelled to throw in the dregs of her man-power to defend her last ditch.

One of the towns that fell to us yesterday was held by an "ear battalion"—that is, a battalion of deaf mutes. They were led by S.S. officers and made a game fight of it.

Perhaps because of their affliction they were less affected than they would otherwise have been by the deafening barrage from 1,250 guns which heralded the assault.

In 15 minutes

The barrage certainly stunned the enemy infantry manning the river dykes. Before they could recover the first wave of the assault was upon them and, still in a daze, they were soon being ferried back as prisoners to the western bank.

Only 15 minutes after zero hour prisoners were actually being brought in.

As villages and small towns began to fall—Gesterhof, Spellen, Lohnen. Gotters-Wickershamm, Vorde, Mollen, Overbruch and

Continued Back Page (A)

THE PRIME MINISTER GOES OVER THE RHINE

Mr. Churchill crossed the Rhine yesterday and spent 15 minutes in the U.S. Ninth Army sector. He came within 50 yards of being hit by a German shell. In this picture he is seen in a landing craft with Field-Marshal Montgomery, talking to Gen. Simpson, the Ninth Army commander, as they cross to the east bank

Patton captures Darmstadt and crosses Main

From NORMAN CLARK, News Chronicle War Correspondent

WITH THE THIRD ARMY, Sunday.

PATTON'S tanks plunged many miles from the bridgehead today, crossing the River Main at an unspecified point. It can be said that they reached a point 27 miles east of the Rhine, covering some 40 road miles in 18 hours.

Prisoners too numerous to handle are being taken, and told to march to the rear without escort after being disarmed. [Earlier reports said that Third Army men had taken 19,000 prisoners in a record day.]

New Third Army crossings of the Rhine were made during the night across the Coblenz-Boppard reach, against stiff opposition.

The enemy's lines, which have been straining to contain the bursting Mainz-Worms bridgehead, broke today.

This morning, as you jeeped many miles to the east—I myself reached a point more than 100 miles inside Germany—there was no sound of war.

But for the columns of tanks, guns and vehicles that march with you, you could have believed yourself back in England.

Where were the enemy—apart from those trudging back along the roads, capless heads bowed?

DESERTED TOWN

Certainly they had not disengaged or withdrawn. No, all the forces the enemy had been able to muster had been absorbed by the pressure of our bulging bridgehead.

This afternoon I left the infantry as they were about to enter Darmstadt. It would be purely a matter of occupying it.

Patrols reported not a single German soldier in the town. Civilians were awaiting our entry.

The enemy has abandoned a town bigger than Mainz.

Artificial fog from smoke-pots hiding the river crossings, and the heat haze of a brilliant day smudged out the skyline.

Everywhere there is a holiday spirit, but no one could believe that they were across the worst obstacle and were pushing on after three days.

The Rhine has been the easiest of all the many river crossings made by the Third Army. In one division the first 24 hours brought only six casualties.

In the first 36 hours 2,500 prisoners was the haul. I also saw more bodies than it has been my lot to see before.

Naval occasion

The first assault crossing of the Rhine in history was a naval occasion.

When the moon was bright, and with complete disdain of anything the enemy could do to defeat it, the assault craft were launched into the river.

Near here is the demolished landing stage where in other times river steamers tied up and trippers sipped hocks and Moselle wines on the canopied sun terrace.

The riverside hotel is still more or less intact; a few panes of glass have been smashed. Today they were moving bedsteads out of it, but two toddlers played unconcerned in the kitchen garden.

A good deal of what goes on nowadays is incongruous and out of place in a war scene.

Weeping woman

Take the sight that met our eyes as we fell into line in a convoy of lorries—there must have been 50 of them, the sides of each bulging with 60 or 70 prisoners.

Along the dusty roads German villagers, strolling from church or sunning themselves at the front door of a cottage, waved to the prisoners.

Many went indoors and reappeared to shower the lorries with loaves of bread and bottles of wine.

In other villages women smiled brazenly at the Americans, and German men doffed their hats in salute at a tank column.

In one village where we searched the signposts for our route a German sycophantically motioned us round the right corner.

A woman was weeping as other prisoners passed, as she sat on a doorstep while her toddler of a daughter clung to her neck to console her.

Frankfurt achtung gives warning of tanks

WHILE the civilians of Frankfurt-on-Main—city of over half a million people—were fleeing yesterday to escape the menace of Patton's Army, the radio station there was pouring out "Achtung" messages about tanks—and spies.

"The population of Frankfurt is streaming from the city," said an Order issued by the Gauleiter of Hesse-Nassau, quoted by the German radio.

"In order to assure medical attention for them, doctors, midwives and chemists in the rest centres of Gelnhausen, Bad Soden and Schluechtern are urgently requested not to join, for the time being, the marching columns of evacuees," the Order added.

The Frankfurt announcer warned listeners of Allied armoured car thrusts. Reconnaissance cars, he said, had crossed the town of Oberramstadt, near Darmstadt, and were moving on Grundernhausen, which is 20 miles from the Rhine.

Ten minutes later the radio said tank spearheads were approaching Dudenhoffen, 30 miles east of the Rhine and 15 miles south-east of Frankfurt.

An earlier "Achtung" had informed police, Volkssturm and defence posts of a grey Army lorry with four persons wearing German officers' uniforms, "presumably enemy agents." It must be stopped at all costs and its passengers arrested or, if they resisted, killed.

Their dire need

Berlin broadcast this appeal:

"A furious tornado of material powers is unleashed in the West and the East against our fronts.

"The enemy wants to shake our nerves, to wear us down into dumb resignation, reckless fear and helpless anxiety. Nothing, no military success of the enemy, no threat or horror must rob us of our steadfastness of which we now stand in such dire need."

German civilians in Darmstadt say Frankfurt will not be defended, but will be declared an open city.

ON OTHER PAGES

Monty is satisfied

Field-Marshal Montgomery, over the Rhine with the Premier, said: "I am well satisfied with the progress of the battle."

Rhine weather

On the Lower Rhine front the weather had deteriorated last night, a front line correspondent cabled. The change came late and had no effect on the success of the Rhine crossing.

NAVY TOOK FLEET BY LAND

By VERNON BROWN
The Naval Correspondent

FOR the first time it is possible today to tell the full story of how the great armada of landing craft in a naval operation which has no precedent was able to cross the Rhine 200 miles from the nearest ocean.

The story goes back many months to a time when a small group of experts left this country for Holland Their task was to report on the possibility of moving vast masses of landing craft overland to the assault are-

Streets widened

They toured hundreds of miles inspecting roads, bridges and canals and there were times when they worked under shell-fire.

The fact had long been realised that crossing the Rhine was child's play compared with getting the craft to the river The landing craft varied in weight from nine to 26 tons. One type on its carrier was 77ft. long, 15ft. wide and 20ft. high.

When the time for the assault approached engineers drove along the routes. Shellholes on the roads were filled in, some narrow village streets were widened, makeshift bridges were made secure.

While this work was in progress the first of the landing craft were being assembled along the southern coasts of England. Gradually—at night—they were taken across the Channel.

It was from Antwerp that most of the vast fleet set off for Germany. They assembled there and were brought along the network of canals more than 100 miles to a point where they were loaded on wheels for the remainder of the journey overland.

The sailors who were to man them sat in the craft as the boats were carried along the Dutch roads towards the assault area.

The river crossing proved to be a difficult task even for the powerful naval craft. The crews had to manœuvre their boats to and from pinpoint landing spots in a strong right-angled current, and to launch them from muddy river banks.

This had all been foreseen when the force was formed in Britain in February That was why exhaustive experiments were made on British rivers, and also on the Continent.

The sailors while carrying out these tests were bound to secrecy and lived and worked as soldiers, wearing Army uniform and insignia.

No leakage

It is a tribute to our security precautions that not an inkling of the special type of this unique naval operation leaked out.

Today, the White Ensign is fluttering over our naval camps and maintenance depots along the banks of the Rhine as the landing craft ferry service works round the clock rushing men, weapons, ammunition and supplies across the river.

Remagen: tanks 19 miles east of Rhine

Tanks of the U.S. First Army are 19 miles beyond the Rhine, state front-line cables to London this morning.

From Stanley Baron
News Chronicle War Correspondent

With the U.S. First Army, Sunday.

THE Remagen bridgehead has erupted. Columns abreast, in the greatest force, tankmen of an ace First Army division this morning broke out at six o'clock to scythe through an enemy who appears to have been caught completely unprepared.

The advance was prepared by an infantry attack at 4 a.m. The infantrymen went in riding on light tanks. Dead on time, they secured every position which might have endangered the armour. Then the armour came sweeping through.

It has been a bewildering day. What we know at the end of it is that the enemy crust has been cracked wide open.

On either side of the spearhead which has broken through, remnants of German divisions have been left to fight it out with American infantry without knowing what has happened to the rest of their units.

Enemy tanks, in groups of four and five, have been sent from the north only to come under wave after wave of fire-bombing by Thunderbolt pilots who, in the

Continued Back Page (B)

LATE NEWS

U.S. PARACHUTISTS LAND IN SWEDEN

Stockholm, Sunday.—Five U.S. parachutists, with explosives, were dropped from planes in Sweden near the Norwegian frontier today, it is officially announced in Stockholm. They thought they had landed in Norway.

LONDON DIM-OUT
7.52 p.m.—6.18 a.m.
Moon rises 4.53 a.m., sets 8.34 a.m. tomorrow. Full Moon Wednesday.

Premier may make statement to M.P.s

MR. CHURCHILL may make a statement in the Commons this week on his visit to the Rhine battlefields

I understand (writes the Political Correspondent) that but for his desire to be at Field-Marshal Montgomery's headquarters when the Rhine crossings were launched the Prime Minister would have spoken in last week's housing debate.

Earl Lloyd-George

There is no improvement in the condition of Earl Lloyd-George.

News Chronicle
No. 30,849 SATURDAY, MARCH 31, 1945 ONE PENNY
LATE LONDON EDITION

News Chronicle War Correspondents all report Victory near

S. L. SOLON — The master plan is succeeding

COLIN WILLS — Across Reich flows our quicksilver

NORMAN CLARK — Now for large-scale mopping-up

STANLEY BARON — Greatest turning movement in history

W. FORREST — Collapse finds workers leaderless

RONALD WALKER — No real life in Duisburg for six months

JAN YINDRICH — Volkssturm took first chance to go home

ANNIHILATION IS NOW AT HAND

Flood of Allied armour loose in Germany

From S. L. SOLON
News Chronicle War Correspondent

MONTGOMERY'S H.Q., Friday.

MORE than 20 armoured columns, pouring forth from the Allied armies in the greatest flood of armour yet used in this war, are loose in Germany.

The security silence regarding the decisive advances that are being made is still on—and so is the most remarkable co-ordinated operation yet known to military history.

For the rolling armour is following a master plan from the north to the south designed to grip all of Germany and strangle what is left of the German military machine.

FIVE ARMIES DRIVE ON

Here are the latest disclosed positions of the British and American forces in Germany:

BRITISH SECOND.—Forty miles beyond the Rhine and ten miles from Muenster,

U.S. NINTH. — Fritzlar reached — 15 miles south-west of Cassel on the Frankfurt-Berlin autobahn.

U.S. FIRST. — Gen. Hodges's tanks, striking north-east, reached a point 29 miles south-west of Cassel. Paderborn, 57 miles north-east of Dortmund, was reached.

U.S. THIRD.—Gen. Patton's tanks reached a point ten miles south-west of Fulda and cleared Lauterbach, 31 miles east of Giessen.

U.S. SEVENTH.—The ancient university town of Heidelberg has been occupied.

What is happening now is not a matter of improvisation. It is a planned exploitation of the break-through that has taken place over the whole front. It is intended to bring the war to an end before the enemy will have any opportunity to regain balance and form some sort of a front.

This much can be said: the plan is succeeding and the hour of the Wehrmacht's annihilation is near.

Large German formations, behind which our armour has advanced to cut their communications, are surrendering.

German commanders are out of touch with their forces, and soldiers are discarding their arms and surrendering.

Naturally this is not happening at the same tempo throughout the front—war is not fought in such neat patterns.

Before the Third Army front the disintegration of the German Army is probably most complete, with a number of German officers urging general surrender before Patton's racing armour.

Farther north the First Army has made recorded penetrations of 90 miles.

The advance of First Army armour to a point only a few miles south of Paderborn enveloped the Ruhr in a great steel arc, cutting off all communications with German

Continued Back Page A

THEY LINKED UP, RACED ON

A BRITISH sergeant gives the O.K. sign as British tanks with American troops race on from Dorsten, where men of the British Second Army and the American Ninth Army linked up

Infantry clear one town after another

From COLIN WILLS
News Chronicle War Correspondent

WITH THE SECOND ARMY, Friday.

HUNDREDS of miles of roads eastward over the green Westphalian downlands are shaking day and night with the weight of British armoured columns rolling far into Germany.

Official statements speak of advances up to 40 miles, but official statements cannot keep pace with an affair like this.

It is as though Montgomery has spilled over the Rhine a great mass of quicksilver which is running out in all directions.

Reconnaissance elements range so far from their parent units that we do not know what new and sensational locations they will get in the next report.

Following them go tank columns, with infantry mounted on tanks or travelling on Bren-carriers, track vehicles and lorries.

Artillery chases the columns, but is barely able to set up guns and carry out shoots before it is time to move on.

Infantry columns

Behind these hurrying spearheads roll solid columns of infantry divisions going in to consolidate town after town.

And back in the bridgehead and on the west Rhine every road is laden with a vast weight of reinforcements and supplies that make each incursion part of an invasion—an occupation.

These brilliant advances are not made without opposition. The Germans have no front, no solid line, but they have thrown together groups of whatever men and guns they can muster to hamper each thrust.

I passed through one village today where a few hours before a unit of the British Sixth Airborne had been challenged by 350 Germans with a number of self-propelled guns.

The airborne men, in a fierce fight, killed 110 Germans and took the rest prisoners.

And, by the time I passed, the airborne men were already many miles ahead, fighting in another town.

Wait for News

Physical obstacles cause some delay—here and there a blown bridge, here and there a small minefield.

And in several towns our own bombing has created such masses of rubble that it is impossible for tanks to pass until bulldozers are brought up to plough through, or roll ruins flat, so that tanks can roll over.

It is at present impossible to name localities reached, owing to security silence, but, when the gains from the past few days are released, it will keep you busy with a map of Germany.

It is all keeping the German High Command busy, too—and keeping them guessing.

All Reich is being mopped up

From NORMAN CLARK
News Chronicle War Correspondent

BEYOND THE MAIN, Friday.

THE war, as a military operation, is coming to an end. The pursuit is petering out into the large-scale mopping-up of engulfed pockets.

Disintegration is setting in, but it is not in an advanced stage yet. There may still be local actions.

That is the picture of this front as we see it from this sector; it is 260 miles from the nearest Russian forces.

As on previous days this week Gen. Patton's tanks have been used as a rake, the infantry as the following-up roller.

Fanning out in three columns, the Third Army tanks are in the vicinity of Treysa and Alsfeld, 29 and 40 miles respectively south of Cassel, the Grebenau 50 miles north-east of Frankfurt.

These areas have been reached after advances of 21, 15 and 7 miles respectively. One column reported meeting no resistance at all; others small arms fire.

They filed in

Another story which illustrates the completeness with which the enemy has been surprised by the swift exploitation of fast-moving situations is the case of the train which steamed into Hanau Station.

As the train pulled up to stop singing came from the compartments from troops, many of them convalescents, who had come to stop the rot. The train should have pulled into Frankfurt, but was halted by signals. The reinforcements began to detrain, thinking in the dark that this was Frankfurt.

Through the booking-office turnstile they filed—to be made prisoners.

Low cloud, rain

Low, grey clouds and squalls of rain have followed the improved weather of the last day or two

One fortnight with Gen. Patton

With the U.S. Third Army, Friday.—Gen. Patton, in an Order to his troops tonight, disclosed that since they crossed the Moselle on March 16 they have:

Seized 6,484 square miles of enemy territory;

Captured 3,072 cities and towns;

Taken 140,112 prisoners and killed or wounded 99,000 other Germans; and

Eliminated practically the entire German First and Seventh Armies.

"History records no greater achievement in such a limited time," says the Order.

This morning's war map is devoid of arrows. So swift is the Allied advance, east and west, into the Reich that exact indications of their extent are impossible

TANKS' 100 MILES IN 40 HOURS

From STANLEY BARON, News Chronicle War Correspondent

WITH THE U.S. FIRST ARMY, Friday.

TANKS of the famous 3rd Armoured Spearhead Division, commanded by Maj.-Gen. Maurice Rose, today entered Paderborn, and after one of the most dramatic switches of the war turning north from Marburg, 104 miles by road from the Rhine (65 measured by air), they have travelled more than a hundred miles in 40 hours.

At 9.35 this morning leading elements reached Paderborn, great German defence depot, and at that point, where they were 65 miles to the east of the British 7th Armoured Division, it was possible to say that the whole of the Ruhr and all the country south of it to the line of the Sieg River had been outflanked.

Analogies for the great pocket thus created are impossible. Its area is 4,000 square miles. It wipes off the map Germany's greatest industrial area. It puts the cold hands of destruction or capture over every soldier of the German Fifteenth Army and every other unit which was brushed northwards by the First Army's advance or southwards by the British Second Army and American Ninth Army as they drove into and around the Ruhr.

Unwanted planes

These two days have seen the greatest and most successful turning movement in the history of warfare, and you can leave it at that.

Air support has been cut down to the minimum. Observation planes have been able to make their reconnaissance only seldom and with difficulty.

But this does not matter. The

Continued Back Page B

V-Day "within week"

With British Second Army, Germany, Friday.—There is a firm belief at this H.Q. tonight that though the Germans will never accept unconditional surrender, V-Day could conceivably be declared within a week and almost certainly within the next month.

Biggest raid on U-boats

IN the U.S. 8th Air Force's greatest attack on naval installations, five U-boat building yards were among yesterday's targets at Wilhelmshaven, Hamburg, Bremen and Farge.

Six jet Me.s were shot down and five grounded planes destroyed by some of the 900 Mustangs which escorted 1,400 heavies. Nine bombers and three fighters are missing.

Spitfires pinpointed many targets in the rocket zone.

Mosquitoes bombed Berlin last night for the 38th time in 39 nights.

Starlit Straits

Long sunny periods; at night starlit sky and rising barometer.

LATE NEWS

RELIEF SUPPLIES FOR EUROPE

Washington, Friday.—Over 400,000 tons of Unrra supplies will be delivered to the liberated areas of Europe by the end of June, L. B. Pearson, Canadian Ambassador to the United States and chairman of Unrra's Supply Committee, said in Washington today.

LONDON DIM-OUT

Tonight	Tomorrow
8.0—6.7 a.m.	8.2—7.5 a.m.

Moon rises, 10.28 p.m.; sets, 8.24 a.m. tomorrow. New Moon, April 12

GERMANS CLAIM TO BE MAQUIS

From WILLIAM FORREST
News Chronicle War Correspondent

IN THE RUHR, Friday.

SOON after the opening of the Military Government office the manager of the tramways of Hamborn (three miles north of Duisburg) called to say he was anxious to get the trams running again, but had only 20 employees left.

"The others," he said, "were all Poles and Frenchmen, and they have gone."

And there were five German workers who claimed to have belonged to an underground resistance movement. They confessed that their numbers were very limited.

Was a Communist

Remembering that the Ruhr was once a Communist stronghold, we asked them how many Communists are in their movement. The question seems meaningless to them.

"Communists?" said their spokesman, as if trying to recall something from the distant past.

Then, after a pause: "Ah, yes, we have one member who used to be a Communist leader."

The collapse of Hitler's Germany finds the workers without leaders, without organisation, and, it would seem, with the memory of their former State all but obliterated by twelve years of Nazi terror.

Clocks go on an hour on Monday

Double Summer Time comes into force next Monday morning, at 1 a.m. Greenwich mean time. The clock is at present one hour in advance of Greenwich mean time, and from Monday until Sunday, July 15, it will be two hours ahead.

All clocks and watches should be put forward one hour tomorrow night. Employers are asked specially to remind their workers to do this.

Nazis start plans to win the peace

WASHINGTON officially disclosed last night details of a Nazi plan to perpetuate the doctrines of the Hitler regime.

A State Department announcement said that the U.S. Government has photographic copies of German documents "clearly indicating" these plans, some of which have already been put into operation.

Others are ready for launching on a wide scale immediately hostilities end in Europe.

Guard for mayors

The disclosure dealt with German plans for rebuilding economic, financial, propaganda and military control.

Nazi Party members, German industrialists and militarists "are planning for the renewals of pre-war cartel agreements," the statement added.

Following the murder of the Burgomaster of Aachen, every mayor in Allied occupied towns behind the U.S. lines has been placed under continual guard.

ALL LIFE WAS DRAINED FROM DUISBURG

From RONALD WALKER
News Chronicle War Correspondent

DUISBURG, Friday.

DUISBURG is a dead city, but it has not been killed in the way Cologne has been killed.

Duisburg has had some 25,000 tons of Bomber Command's high explosive and incendiary bombs dropped on it, but the city has ceased to live more because of the bombs that have fallen farther east than because of those within the city limits.

It is badly damaged, but only, say, about one-third as badly damaged as Cologne.

Many of its factories are still fairly intact and there are plenty of houses without a pane of glass broken—a Ruhr phenomenon. With its satellite towns and suburbs, such as Ruhrort, Hamborn and Rheinhausen, the great industrial complex sector which constituted the administrative area of Duisburg made a scattered and difficult target, with many comparatively large open spaces.

Duisburg has not been battered to extinction. It has had the life drained out of it.

You wonder how the civilians existed in a city which has had no water, light or drainage for six months.

In Duisburg today is seen what is really meant by the phrase "isolating the Ruhr."

DANZIG (AND 45 U-BOATS) TAKEN: AUSTRIA INVADED

STORMING through the rest of Danzig Marshal Rokossovsky's troops yesterday completed the capture of the city—where the war began 5½ years ago—and seized 45 U-boats.

Ten thousand prisoners were taken and the booty included 140 tanks and self-propelled guns, 358 field guns, 84 planes, 15 armoured trains, 360 railway engines, over 6,000 trucks and 151 ships.

More than 39,000 Germans were killed.

The Order of the Day announcing its capture used the Polish name of Gdansk. The Polish national flag now flies over the city for the first time since 1772.

In the South Marshal Tolbukhin's troops crossed the frontier into Austria, north of Koeszeg, the Soviet communique stated last night.

A cable from Moscow said that heavy fighting was going on in the frontier zone on the direct approaches to Wiener Neustadt and that Tolbukhin was massing his troops for a break-through south of Vienna.

Meanwhile Marshal Malinovsky's armies, which are operating on both sides of the Danube, launched an offensive in Southern Slovakia on a 40-mile front and drove on for 31 miles towards the Bratislava Gap.

The new gains, announced in another Order of the Day, began with the forcing of the Rivers Hron and Nitra and the breaking of the defences on the western banks.

As the troops drove forward they captured the Slovakian side of the twin Danube town of Komarno (the Hungarian half of which fell on Wednesday) and four others, all of which were described as "powerful defence strong-points in the Bratislava direction."

More gains in Hungary by Marshal Tolbukhin's men were announced in a third Order of the Day. Keszthely, at the western end of Lake Balaton, and Zalaegerszeg, halfway to the frontier, were captured.

The Daily Sketch

CANDIDUS ON PAGE TWO

No. 11,194 ★★ WEDNESDAY, APRIL 4, 1945 ONE PENNY

Fighting Among The Rocket Sites

25 MILES FROM THE ZUYDER ZEE

Patton shortens Berlin 'Marathon'

WHILE General Patton's Third Army spearheads thrusting across the Werra River to the outskirts of Gotha, 18 miles east of Eisenach, are within 150 miles of Berlin and 65 of the Czechoslovak frontier, British and Canadian forces have reached a point 25 miles from the Zuyder Zee.

The Guards Armoured Division have captured Nordhorn, at the approaches to the Zuyder Zee, thus severing the last direct supply line connecting Germany with the V sites round The Hague.

German troops, estimated at 50,000, are getting out of Holland as quickly as they can by land and by the hundreds of evacuation barges massed in the Zuyder Zee.

Two bridgeheads were established yesterday by the Canadians over the Twenthe Canal, between Zutphen and Hengelo. They are now 20 miles into Holland. Half a mile north of the canal runs the "rocket" railway from Hanover.

General Crerar's troops have cleared the Germans from all the "Arnhem Island" between Nijmegen and Arnhem.

The only way the Germans can now transport rockets into Western Holland is by a circuitous route by a railway skirting Northern Holland, which is susceptible to attack.

An Associated Press correspondent placed Field-Marshal Montgomery's troops within 90 miles of Wilhelmshaven.

From LEONARD MOSLEY, Kemsley Newspapers War Correspondent, with the British Forces, Tuesday

THE battle for Osnabruck, vital Nazi rail junction and home of the most infamous concentration camp in Northern Germany, is on to-

Turn to Back Page, Col. 2

When the Ruhr pocket was sealed at Lippstadt, Germans, finding their police had gone, rejoiced with looted drinks in a distillery. More pictures on Page 5.

Fronts at a Glance

MONTGOMERY British and Canadian forces are fighting in the area of V-bomb sites in Northern Holland, and are 25 miles from Zuyder Zee. Canadians have established two bridgeheads over the Twenthe canal between Zutphen and Hengelo.

SIMPSON Hurling a tank column against the Weser defences, General Simpson's forces have raced to a point 175 miles from Berlin. Herford, ten miles east of Bielefeld, has been reached.

HODGES Siegen, one of the German strongholds dotted round the fringes of the Ruhr has been cleared.

PATTON Third Army men are 150 miles from Berlin, 150 miles from the Russian front, and 65 miles from the Czech border. An armoured division has reached the outskirts of Gotha, 26 miles from Weimar. Cassel has been captured.

PATCH Germans are fiercely resisting between Wurzburg and Heilbronn. A cavalry unit has captured the Giebelstadt airfield, seven miles south of Wurzburg. Aschaffenburg has surrendered.

V-DAY PLANS | Holiday (Paid) For (nearly) All

Two days' holiday with pay for workers in State service when the "cease fire" sounds in Europe was announced last night as part of the Government's V-day plans. It was given as a "lead to all industry." Peace-time lighting and a stand down of part-time Civil Defence may come before then.

Holidays

TWO days' holiday (with pay) will be given to all workers in Government factories and in Government service.

This official announcement was made by the Government last night in view of the development of the war and "also recognising that industry would be looking for a lead."

So far as Government factories and Government service are concerned, it has been decided that the day of the announcement of the European Cease Fire, irrespective of the hour upon which the announcement is made, together with the day immediately following shall be regarded as days of paid holiday.

The Government suggests that it would be appropriate that all schools should also grant holidays for those two days.

In addition there will probably be a desire throughout industry to give expression to the feeling of common effort that has carried us through the strenuous years of the war by setting aside, at a date to be determined according to local circumstances, a day of holiday at individual factories.

Workers in Government factories and establishments will, therefore, be given an additional day of paid holiday at some later date.

The statement points out that some workers in essential services, however, must be prepared to carry on, and special compensatory arrangements will be made in these cases.

Lights

THE Ministry of Home Security and the War Cabinet are awaiting the decision of the R.A.F. authorities before giving final approval to the plans to lift the black-out before the war in Europe ends, writes THE DAILY SKETCH Political Correspondent.

They propose to lift the black-out, to restore street lighting to normal strength and to allow full headlights on cars and public and commercial vehicles.

There will be a proviso that in the event of an alert the old restrictions will be reimposed with all their old rigour.

Civil Defence

IT is also intended to stand down the part-time Civil Defence personnel such as wardens.

Full-time wardens, heavy and light rescue parties, and ambulance and other Civil Defence workers will be retained for the present, in case of eleventh-hour attempts by the enemy to stage air raids on this country.

Shelters to remain open after the war.—Page Seven.

Russians Take Home Of 'Jets'

CAPTURE of Wiener Neustadt, home of the Messerschmitt jet-plane factories, was announced by Marshal Stalin last night in an Order of the Day to Marshal Tolbukhin.—Story on Page 8.

V2 GENERAL DEFIES HITLER

From VICTOR LEWIS, 'Daily Sketch' Air Correspondent

AIR-GENERAL FRITZ CHRISTIANSEN, commander of the German troops in Holland and the man responsible for the rocket bombardment of England, is believed to have openly defied Hitler and decided to evacuate the northern arm of Holland west of the Zuyder Zee.

It is known that a little less than a month ago he received strict orders from Hitler that in no circumstances was he to abandon the V2 assault.

No matter how great the pressure became, he was told he must defend his V2 troops and their equipment.

Abandoning His Men

A few days later his headquarters were burned to the ground by a rocket and incendiary attack by Typhoons of the 2nd Tactical Air Force. Christiansen "disappeared" for several days.

From a new "hide-out" he is believed to have issued orders to step up the V2 firing rate until all the rocket stocks were exhausted.

This one-time world-roaming, heavy-drinking sailor, who took to the air late in life and flew the giant ten-engined Do. X flying boat round the world, then told his staff that, despite the orders he had received, he proposed to abandon Holland if the Allies crossed the Lower Rhine.

Plans for a fighting retreat were put into operation several days ago.

Because the Special Gruppe troops launching the rockets were not fighting soldiers but technicians or elderly men useless to him in battle, it is believed he decided to leave them to their fate.

Killed In Mutiny

Dutch underground agents are said to have reported that the Special Gruppe troops got wind of this plan, and that four of the Air-General's staff and 20 technicians were killed in a mutiny which broke out in the village of Oud-Ade.

Twelve other rocket-launching troops, including one officer, were shot by Christiansen's orders.

Hated by the Dutch, the bullying, sneering Nazi general is said never to have left his headquarters without an enormous bodyguard.

TIMELY WORDS OF FAITH

The right hand of the Lord is exalted: the right hand of the Lord doeth valiantly.

Psalms, 118, 16.

DAILY MIRROR, Saturday, April 7, 1945.

Daily Mirror

APL 7

No. 12,885
ONE PENNY
Registered at the G.P.O. as a Newspaper.

Three Armies racing for Hanover

TANKS BY AIR TO WITHIN 40 MILES OF LEIPZIG

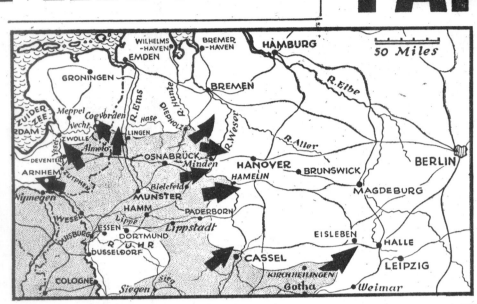

AS THREE Allied armies were racing last night on the last lap to Hanover, the Germans reported that American units, considerably reinforced with tanks brought by air, were only 40 miles from Leipzig and 110 from Berlin.

They said spearheads were near the town of Eisleben, eleven miles from Halle, city of 200,000 people, and nearly fifty miles from General Patton's last reported position.

Allied reports confirmed that behind those spearheads U.S. forces were fanning out on a wide front, while heavy bombers pounded Halle.

For Hanover, capital city of a province that for over 100 years was ruled by the Kings of England, the last hours have struck. The German radio was broadcasting warnings of the approaching armies.

General Dempsey's famous spearheads, the British 11th Armoured Division and the Sixth Airborne, pushing straight on from their several bridgeheads over the Weser, were surging across the last twenty miles to this city of 440,000 inhabitants 140 miles from Berlin.

Armour and infantry of the Ninth U.S. Army and First Army tanks were also racing for Hanover.

Men and material were being rushed up in support of the British spearheads and the Seventh Armoured Division (the Desert Rats) covered sixty miles in twenty-four hours, past the Duemmer See Lake towards the Weser.

It was a day of big advances on all Montgomery's fronts. The North Sea ports

Continued on Back Page

Nine V2s (with firing details) seized by tanks

IT was just an ordinary German goods train that tanks of General Hodges's Third Armoured Division brought to a standstill near Paderborn.

But when the tankmen inspected the wagons they found nine of the up-to-now super-secret V2 rockets—complete with instructions on how to use them.

The rockets, with their long, tapering shell of aluminium, were complete, with great tanks of fuel, but they did not have warheads, these being attached just before firing.

Encased in a sealed metal tube in the nose of each V2 was a set of instructions on:

How to fuel it;
How to set instruments and the radio control for range and direction; and
How to launch the rocket.

For transport the rockets were placed in goods wagons

The rockets are 45ft. long, with four fins on the tail. There were two fuel tanks with each rocket.

The front end of the V2 was divided by light wooden panels into four compartments in which were a set of instruments, including radio and power units controlling the flight.

The two lower compartments contained a compressed air power unit and small turbo-generators.

"There's a hell of a mess of wires in there," said an officer. "You'd be an old man with a long white beard trying to figure it out alone."

RED ARMY STORM VIENNA CITY—HEARD IN LONDON

LISTENERS in London last night heard the boom and clatter of battle over Vienna radio as Red Army troops stormed the city proper.

The Soviet communique claimed only that the Russians were within one mile of the city, but the Vienna announcer said that assault units had reached the city and that street fighting was going on.

"Women are to be brought out of the defence zone in the next available transport," he said.

"In an open square Vienna Volkssturm men are still undergoing rifle practice. To-night, however, they are going into the line."

Von Hammer, German News Agency military correspondent, reported that "a tremendous battle of machines" was raging outside the city.

Meanwhile on the Berlin front Russian troops are making good progress.

4,000 BRITISH CAPTIVES FREED

FOUR thousand British Commonwealth prisoners of war have been liberated from Stalag 9 Mulhausen, Germany.

There is evidence that the British prisoners of war at Oflags 9 AH, Spangenburg, and 9AZ, Rottenburg, were evacuated eastwards before the arrival of Allied forces.

No CD stand down yet, says Morrison

Civil defence must be kept up to a standard that is "reasonable and necessary" said Mr. Herbert Morrison, Home Secretary, speaking at Chatham last night.

There might, he said, be a possibility of the enemy re-deploying his V-weapons or increasing the range, while the possibility of raids by piloted aircraft must not be overlooked.

First picture of the rocket

The huge object in this rail wagon is a V2. It was captured—along with others—when American troops found a train in the German town of Bro[illegible]. For the first time Allied experts were able to examine the "terror" rockets which the Germans fired at London and "Southern England." (More pictures on Page Five).

WESTERN ITALY EDITION

UNION JACK

LATE SPECIAL

Friday, April 13, 1945 No. 458 Two Lire

DEATH OF PRESIDENT ROOSEVELT

WE deeply regret to announce the death of President Roosevelt, which occurred suddenly yesterday at Warm Springs, Georgia, from cerebral hemorrhage. He was 63.

In accordance with precedent, the Vice-President, Senator Harry Truman, becomes President.

President Roosevelt has died in the first months of his fourth term of office as President of the United States. For some time he had been under constant medical care.

HIS SMILE WAS FAMOUS

Vice-President Harry Truman, former lawyer and farmer, comes from Missouri. He defeated Senator Henry Wallace in the vice-presidential ballot. He is 61.

Key-note of his election campaign was his message: "As we march forward to certain victory we must make plans for a lasting and just peace . . . To lay a foundation in the post-war world that will secure for all men everywhere basic human rights."

An Architect Of Victory

FRANKLIN DELANO ROOSEVELT made American history by being the first President to have three full terms in office, and then to be triumphantly elected for a fourth. And it was those third and fourth terms which established him as not only a great American but a great figure in world history.

He will be for ever remembered as one of the chief architects of Allied victory, and in more ways than one his greatness was the product of adversity—first the infantile paralysis which threatened to end his political career when it was only half begun, and then the tremendous strains of world war, which brought out his highest qualities in his association with the other great war leaders on the Allied side.

Roosevelt was born at Hyde Park, New York State, on January 30, 1882, a descendant of a Dutch family which had been in the States for two centuries or more. He studied law, graduated in 1907, joined the Democratic party, and was elected to the New York State Senate in 1910.

In Woodrow Wilson's first Administration in 1912 he was appointed Assistant Secretary of the Navy, and he came to Europe at the end of the last war on army inspection work and to supervise the demobilisation of the American forces.

Defeated as a candidate for the vice-presidency in 1920, Roosevelt returned to his law practice. In the following year he was stricken with infantile paralysis, as the result of an unlucky swim in an ice-cold sea, and it was years before he could even shuffle along on crutches.

A man of less vigorous spirit would have been broken, but not so Roosevelt. His personality was far more than a charming way with people—valuable though that itself was in later years; he had in fact a temperament which banished all defeatism from the minds of his associates, and erased the very word from his own vocabulary.

Sheer spirit and will-power made him able to continue his political activity.

In 1928 he was elected Governor of New York, and again in 1930. Two years later he attained the Presidency, which he was to hold for more than 12 years.

On assuming office on March 4, 1933, he at once started on the policy of bold social and economic reforms which became known as the New Deal.

It was a policy which aroused great opposition among some powerful sections of American opinion, yet in 1936 Roosevelt was re-elected to the Presidency, and again in 1940—this time with the additional difficulty of creating a precedent in taking office for a third term.

It was said of Roosevelt even as long ago as his second election that ' everybody is against Roosevelt—except the electorate." That was certainly true of the great majority of the American Press. But his popularity among the mass of the people was enormous, and his own personal gaiety and resilience were inexhaustible. The famous smile of the photographs was the expression of an attitude to life, and not just a politician's pose.

Domestically, Roosevelt was a crusader for the common man. The President did not believe that one of the wealthiest countries in the world was so spiritually bankrupt that it could afford to support millions of unemployed.

Roosevelt gave new hope and courage to the little man, the under-privileged of the nation which he was to lead so brilliantly through the slough of depression into the bright days of the middle 30's across the abyss of Pearl Harbour and within hailing distance of complete victory over Germany.

He was one of the greatest internationalists as far as relations between the United States and other countries were concerned. His was the policy of the "Good Neighbour" towards the South American countries.

When Roosevelt took office great bodies of American citizens were, at best, natural isolationists, and some centres were definitely hostile to Europe and all its problems.

It was the genius of the President which gradually conveyed to the overwhelming majority of his people that just as peace is indivisible so a war in which European democracy was threatened with extinction was the business of all true and thinking Americans.

Roosevelt made so light of his physical handicap that all but his political enemies were inclined to forget it. One of these once said to his wife: "Don't you find that your husband's disability is inclined to affect his judgement?"

There was a murmur of disapproval from people who had overheard, but Mrs. Roosevelt held up her hand and answered gently:

"Why, yes. I've found that it makes him make more allowances and think more kindly of all the people who have difficulties of their own."

Roosevelt was the product of adversity in more than the physical sense. The economic tornado which struck the world in the early thirties threw up two men into power and ultimate conflict—Roosevelt in the new world and Hitler in the old. And Roosevelt was among the first to see the shadow of Nazism lengthening across the Atlantic's wide waters.

Throughout the years before

(Continued on Page Four.)

President Roosevelt has been present at twelve of the big meetings of the war. He met Mr. Churchill on eight occasions, at sea, in Washington, Casablanca and Quebec; met Mr. Churchill and Marshal Stalin at Teheran and the Crimea; Mr. Churchill and Generalissimo Chiang Kai-shek at Cairo; and Mr. Churchill and President Inonu at Cairo. The picture above was taken at the Teheran meeting in Nov-Dec., 1943.

War Fronts

WEST: **Ninth Army tanks are across the Elbe on the last lap for Berlin. Field-Marshal Montgomery has begun the battle for the North Sea ports. (Page Four).**

ITALY: **Eighth Army offensive goes well. Santerno river has been crossed in strength. Fifth are 14 miles from Spezia. (Page Four).**

RUSSIA: **With the Battle for Vienna almost over Marshal Tolbukhin's troops are already pouring west towards Linz and the Bavarian border. (Page Four).**

FAR EAST: **Super Forts blast Tokio in big daylight raid. 14 Army troops inflict heavy losses on enemy forces retreating East. (Page Three).**

Daily Mirror

APL 13

Friday, April 13, 1945
No. 12,890 ONE PENNY
Registered at G.P.O. as a Newspaper.

END IN A FEW DAYS, U.S. TOLD: BRIDGEHEAD IS 6 MILES LONG OVER ELBE

Paratroops drop near Berlin, say reports

A HIGH American General Staff Officer told the U.S. Senate Military Committee last night that the end of organised fighting in Germany will probably come within a few days.

As he spoke, Ninth Army troops who had crossed the Elbe fanned out across the Prussian Plain towards the outer defences of Berlin.

A midnight message disclosed that they hold a bridgehead six miles long and there was an unconfirmed report from French sources that paratroops have been dropped at Brandenburg, twenty miles from the capital.

INFANTRY WELL UP

It is not merely tanks which have come to the edge of this flat, treeless country across which Berlin lies. The infantry have kept pace with them to a great extent.

"A West Front in the former meaning of the word has ceased to exist," admitted Max Krull, chief military correspondent of the German News Agency. He pointed out that the danger is now that the Allies and the Russians, only 100 miles apart, will slice Germany in two.

But he maintained that before starting a big two-front drive on Berlin, the Allies would try to carve up the Nazi forces south of the capital.

GREAT LEAP BY PATTON

His fears were becoming reality last night as Patton's tanks leapt forward on a dash as spectacular as that which carried the Ninth Army to the Elbe.

They covered forty-five miles and crossed the Saale River on a stretch of thirty miles, and forged on under a news black-out. Infantry also reached the Saale and planes blitzed everything in the path of the advance.

U.S. First Army tanks also reached the Saale at a point only twenty-three miles from Leipzig.

A second big armoured punch by Patton was carried to within forty miles of the Czech frontier.

Weimar, a third of it smashed to the ground, sent an envoy on a bicycle to surrender and was occupied.

Bayreuth is threatened. The U.S. Seventh Army have captured Schweinfurt and Heilbronn and the French have taken Baden Baden.

BRITISH FRONT IS ON THE MOVE AGAIN

The British front in North Germany is on the move again.

Commandos, using knives, daggers and bayonets, yesterday extended their bridgehead over the River Aller towards Hamburg.

Thirteen miles away Celle, former gas warfare centre of the German Army, was captured by storm by Monty's crack 15th Scottish Division, which seized intact a bridge across the river.

Many gas and chemical warfare instructors were taken prisoners.

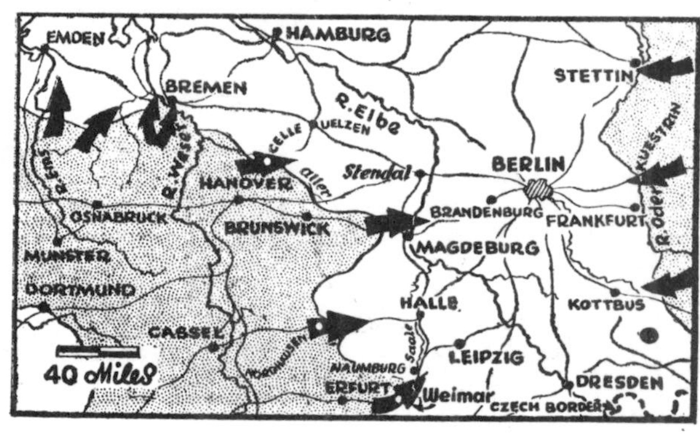

ROOSEVELT DIES ON EVE OF ALLIED TRIUMPHS

President Roosevelt—died in his sleep.

PRESIDENT ROOSEVELT died suddenly from a cerebral hemorrhage in his sleep at West Springs, Georgia, yesterday afternoon.

A White House statement said: "Vice President Truman has been notified. He was called to the White House and informed by Mrs. Roosevelt."

The White House announcement added that a Cabinet Meeting has been called.

"The four Roosevelt boys in the Services have been sent a message by their mother, which said that the President slept away yesterday afternoon."

"He did his job to the end, as he would want to," the statement continued.

The interment will be at Hyde Park (the President's New York estate) on Sunday.

Senator Harry Truman, the Vice President, Missouri County judge, and one-time Kansas City haberdasher, moves up to the highest office in the land, as a result of the President's death.

At Capitol Hill, Vice-President Truman's aides disclosed that he had left for the White House only a few minutes be-

Continued on Back Page

Daily Mirror

APL 21

Saturday, April 21, 1945.
No. 12,897 ONE PENNY
Registered at G.P.O. as a Newspaper.

Eisenhower says 'Enemy in the West is tottering to defeat'

RUSSIANS FIGHT AROUND THE EDGE OF BERLIN

AS two Russian spearheads fought last night less than eight miles from the outskirts of Berlin, General Eisenhower declared in an Order of the Day that Hitler's armies in the west are "tottering on the threshold of defeat." An Allied Supreme Headquarters announcement said we would link up with the Russians in a few days.

Admitting that a Soviet spearhead is only eight miles from the bounry of Berlin, the German military spokesman revealed that another spearhead has penetrated even nearer.

While the first force, with tanks in the lead, is fighting round the lakes of the Hangelsberg Forest, which reaches up to Berlin's eastern boundary, the second force, even nearer, is battling against tank buster formations among the trees of the Sternebeck Forest.

Berlin radio said Russia n tanks broke through the main defences but were checked and wiped out. The radio also said that 3,000,000 of the 4,000,000 Berliners are still there.

Moscow partially lifted the news black-out last night to confirm the capture of a semi-circle of towns twenty-five miles from the Berlin boundary.

Koniev's men meanwhile are twenty-six miles from Dresden and fifty-five from General Patton's Americans.

NUREMBERG CLEARED

Symbol of the Hun defeat, the Stars and Stripes, was raised last night—Hitler's birthday—over the ruins of the Nazi "holy city" of Nuremberg, where 3,000 S.S. troops became our prisoners.

The German Command is losing its grip on the great northern ports. A report flashed to Montgomery's headquarters last night indicated the start of a retreat. A surprise sweep by the Guards Armoured Division threatens the great naval port of Bremerhaven.

Submarines in the Elbe shelled British forces and our guns and planes hit back. In the battle with German warships bombers set a cruiser on fire.

The Germans in their counter-attack on the U.S. Ninth Army front, however, have gained more ground.

BLUE arrows—RED Army

For the first time since D-Day, SHAEF's great operational wall-map shows that blue arrows marking the Russian offensive have moved into the extreme eastern strip of the map beyond Berlin, says Associated Press.

The Russian positions are taken from the communiques of the previous day.

Link-up in few days, slaves told

A SPECIAL message from Allied Supreme H.Q. was broadcast last night to Russians and Poles in the gap between the Russian and Allied armies. It said: "Stay where you are. In a few days the gap will be closed.

"Keep discipline, suppress pillaging and looting. Elect leaders.

2 shot dead in Corner House

FIFTY-SEVEN-YEAR-OLD Mr. John B. Tratsart sat in his chair at the Corner House, Tottenham Court-road, London, and looked happily at his sons and daughters who had all turned up at the reunion dinner he had planned for them last night.

There was Clair, the eldest, aged 28, Jacques, who is 27, and 17-year-old Hugh and Anne, aged 13½, both holidaying in London and joking and laughing with the rest of the family.

They made a happy picture. Hundreds of people eating there gave them more than a first glance. Suddenly, above the buzzing of conversation the diners heard three revolver shots.

The blue smoke and smell of cordite hung over the Tratsarts' table where Mr. Tratsart, no longer the well-dressed smiling business man, stood poised above it with blood trickling from his mouth, then fell across the table, sliding to the floor like a drunken man.

Young Hugh collapsed in his chair as his father fell, while Clair slid from the table and slumped on the floor.

Looking at the silent diners was a man, wild-eyed, who held a smoking revolver in his hand.

For a second no one moved. Then an Army officer swung off his chair just as the man raised the revolver to shoot himself.

The revolver exploded as the officer grabbed the man and disarmed him.

Fighting his way through the crowd, a young medical student

Continued on Back Page

NOT SO GOOD

The barometer fell all day in the Straits of Dover yesterday, and the week's brilliant spell of summery weather may not last over the week-end.

British troops, sick with fury, drive SS to bury Belsen victims

LITANY for the nameless dead of Belsen—the pitiful victims pictured in yesterday's *Daily Mirror*—was the hoarse shouts of British soldiers, sick with disgust and fury, driving the infamous men and women of the S.S. to bury the bodies in graves ripped by bulldozers in the tainted earth.

From Allied correspondent last night came dispatches describing the ghastly scenes at the concentration camp which S.S. Fuehrer Josef Kramer and his sub-human accomplices turned into ahell.

Each of Belsen's dead got a ghastly burial. There were no flowers at this funeral, no tears of well-bred sympathy, no music.

The British soldiers who drove the S.S. brutes to their horrible task were beyond tears.

The British troops shudder at the sights they see. General Dempsey's men—Desert Rats, tankmen, "Red Devils"—have seen the war at its ugliest from Dunkirk, through Africa and Italy to the beaches of Normandy. But they have never before seen anything like Belsen.

A wave of hatred and horror has spread through the ranks of these British troops after visiting Belsen, the blackest indictment of

Continued on Back Page

Labour's plan

The Labour Party's election programme—a plan for Britain's future—is issued today.

The plan contains important proposals for nationalising fuel services, steel and transport, for key controls, and for social security and housing.

The programme is outlined on Page Five. Editorial comment is on Page Two.

21 DIVISIONS GONE

"Hun losses will never be known"

GENERAL EISENHOWER last night issued an Order of the Day to mark the end of the battle of the Ruhr pocket.

He said: "This victory of Allied arms is a fitting prelude to the final battles to crush the ragged remnants of Hitler's armies in the west, which are now tottering on the threshold of defeat."

The Supreme Commander disclosed that twenty-one German Divisions have been eliminated by the Allies, who captured more than 317,000 prisoners, including twenty-four generals

Many tanks and more than 750 guns were destroyed or taken.

General Eisenhower said that the booty, which was immense, was still being counted.

"The enemy's total losses in killed and wounded will never be accurately known," he declared.

BERLIN TARGETS

Out of the 800 U.S. bombers which took part in yesterday's operations, 600 Flying Forts went to the Berlin area, attacking rail facilities to the south-west, west, north-west and north.

A NAZI HAS WRITTEN TO ME

By The Editor

(SEE PAGE 6)

AIR FORCE NEWS

ITALY-BALKANS-N. AFRICA-EGYPT-LEVANT-IRAQ-PERSIA-E & W. AFRICA-SUDAN-ADEN-RHODESIA-MADAGASCAR-GIBRALTAR

MARRIED WAAF WILL BE FIRST OUT

(SEE PAGE 10)

No. 104 FREE TO ALLIED AIR FORCE PERSONNEL APRIL 24, 1945

M.P.s Fly To Germany At C in C's Call

BRITAIN ENRAGED BY NEW NAZI HORRORS

'High Authority's' New Evidence

PUBLIC opinion in Britain has never been so shocked and enraged in all the years of war as it has been over the terrible report of atrocities in German concentration camps. These hell-spots were captured by the advancing Allied troops, and following their discover, General Eisenhower immediately contacted Prime Minister Churchill, asking him to send a Parliamentary delegation to investigate.

The response was immediate, and the names of volunteers were submitted to the Speaker the same afternoon. Eight representatives of all political parties, flew to Germany at once.

The press at home has expressed its horror at the sickening evidence with grave leaders, and the evidence and pictures have been published without apology.

Some of the pictures have reached Air Force News office, including the two given on this page. We are not going to apologise for printing them either.

They are dreadful, and they will shock you. But this is a case where you should know the truth, coming as it does from unimpeachable sources.

You will share the anger of our folk at home that such things are possible in this century by a nation that called itself civilised.

1 These men are British soldiers. Four years ago they were fit, strong men, and they were taken prisoners by the Germans. This microgram picture from London shows them after their release last week at Gettingen by the advancing Allies. They were almost too weak and emaciated to smile. Broken through lack of food, they had been sent to a prison hospital. What they needed was not medicine but food.

2 These men, women, and children were Soviet citizens of the Lvov region. This picture has been released by the Russian Extraordinary State Committee just as it was discovered in the files of the Zolochev Gestapo. The committee which has been investigating German crimes in that area, declares that the Germans executed hundreds of thousands of Soviet civilians, war prisoners and slave workers. The dead bodies were heaped up like this after their murder before mass burial.

DAILY EXPRESS

No. 14,009 | Coast dim-out 9.48 pm to 6.7 am | SATURDAY APRIL 28 1945 | Moon rises 10.25 pm sets 7.51 am | One Penny

HITLER'S EMPIRE, SPLIT IN TWO, MAKES ITS LAST STRUGGLE

Allies from East and West unite, then turn to deliver the final blows

THIRD REICH IS DEAD

At 4p.m., April 25, in its 13th year

HANDSHAKE ON TWISTED GIRDER LINKS ARMIES

From SELKIRK PANTON: Torgau on the Elbe, Friday

THE Third Reich of Adolf Hitler is dead. It died in its 13th year at four o'clock on Wednesday afternoon, when General Courtney Hodges' First U.S. Army linked up with Marshal Koniev's First Ukrainian Army and cut Germany into two parts, north and south.

Two junior officers—Lieutenant William Robertson, of California, and Lieutenant Alexander Silvachko, the Russian, shook hands on a twisted girder of the wrecked Torgau railway bridge over the Elbe and arranged details for the meetings between the regimental and divisional commanders on both sides, which took place yesterday.

Soon, Hodges and Koniev will meet.

Torgau, which nearly 200 years ago saw the victory of Frederick the Great's Prussians over the Austrians, saw history made again while its shell-wrecked buildings burned in the fresh spring breeze and smoke overhung the town.

WINE, SONG AND MUSIC

Now the Russians—Rooskies as the Americans call them affectionately—are celebrating the momentous link-up with wine, song and music.

The wine, drunk in beer mugs, comes from the cellars of Torgau, and the music from the piano accordions "liberated" from the Wehrmacht storehouse in the almost deserted town.

I was one of three British journalists who were present at the headquarters of the 273rd Infantry Regiment, 69th Division, of General Hodges' Army when the first flash came in to say the link-up had been made.

We had just walked into the regimental command in a palatial manor house behind the lines, when the radio operator shot into life and cried: "I think we've contacted the Russians."

In an instant the headquarters sprang into action. Colonel C. M. Adams, the commander of the regiment, took the message. It ran: "Mission accomplished; making arrangements for meeting C.O.s; no casualties."

The flash came from Lieutenant Albert Kotzebue, of Texas, who had been sent out on patrol eastwards towards the Russians. The time was 3.20 p.m. He was told to stay put and await further instructions.

But his friend, Lieutenant William D. Robertson, of Los Angeles, of the same 273rd Regiment, had better luck. He went out on patrol and went further east than he should have done. And he met the Russians.

This is the story he told me: "I guess I must have gone too far. There were floods of people streaming back towards Wurzen, and German soldiers and officers were throwing away arms as my 20 men in four jeeps kept going along.

"I figured I could not stop to disarm these Jerries, so I kept going until suddenly I was in Torgau, and there were the Rooskies on the other side of the Elbe.

FLAG ON CASTLE TOWER

"I heard some firing, small arms stuff, so I got some white cloth and paint from a wrecked drug store and made a kind of Stars and Stripes.

"I went up on a tower of the old castle overlooking the river and waved the flag. They stopped firing. I shouted 'Tovarish (comrade), kamerad.'

"They fired flares. I shouted I did not have flares, but they could not hear. They started firing again. It turned out that they had been fooled only the day before by Germans with a home-made American flag.

"So I left the flag flying and started out on the wrecked bridge, climbing over the debris. At the same time a Russian armoured car came down their end of the bridge and a soldier started crawling towards me. When we came together we kind of said 'Hallo' and shook hands. We exchanged watches as mementoes"

Robertson then went across to the Russian side of the Elbe and met a Russian major and other officers. "We had a bottle of wine, a can of sardines, chocolates, and some biscuits. We drank a lot of toasts, and they filled my water-bottle with schnapps."

'THE RUSSIANS ARE HERE!'

On Wednesday night, as we were in quarters waiting news from the American front line, we were alarmed just before midnight and told: "The Russians are here at headquarters."

We raced round in the moonlight to divisional headquarters, and there followed one of the strangest Press conferences ever held—a mixture of news, wine, cognac, vodka, speeches, and interviews with the young American and Russian officers who made the first contact.

In the room of General Emil Reinhardt, C.O. 68th Infantry Division, more than 40 war correspondents, a dozen U.S. officers and four Russian officers crammed

BACK PAGE, COL. FOUR

Panton was a prisoner

REPORTING the historic link-up is the climax of an extraordinary war for SELKIRK PANTON.

Chief correspondent in Berlin for the Daily Express until the war, Panton was captured by the Germans in 1940 in Copenhagen.

He spent four years as a prisoner in Denmark and was repatriated two months ago.

After four weeks in London he was assigned to cover the U.S. First Army. And now on his journey back to Berlin he is the man on the spot for the cutting of Germany into two.

TWO ARMIES MOVE TO PINCER MUNICH

From MONTAGUE LACEY

SUPREME H.Q., Friday.—With the Allied link-up. vast forces have been released to turn to the destruction of the last pockets of Hitler's empire in north and south.

In the south American tanks crashed into the fortress of Austria.

The German First Army is reeling under the blows of both General Patch's Seventh Army and Patton's Third Army, sweeping down on Munich and the Austrian Alps.

German defences have been broken in many places. We are 25 miles from Munich and 70 from Salzburg, now reported to be the seat of the German Government.

The Third Army crossed the Austrian frontier two miles south of the junction with the Czech and German frontiers.

The 86th Division has captured Ingolstadt, on the Danube, and is astride the Munich-Nuremberg motor road, with the enemy showing little fight.

Two great steel pincers are closing now around Munich as the Third and Seventh Armies race to encircle the largest German city in the south.

GENOA IS CAPTURED, NEARING VENICE

From JAMES COOPER

ITALY, Friday Night.—Genoa, the most important port in Italy, was entered today by an American task force.

The way to the birthplace of Christopher Columbus was made for them by patriots, who had already captured a large part of the city and opened the way for the Americans and American-Japanese under Major-General Almond.

There is no report yet on what success the patriots had in preventing the fleeing Germans and Blackshirts from blowing up the port.

But the troops who had held us up by demolitions and coast guns disappeared overnight.

Elsewhere, we are pouring more troops over the Adige in the hope of trapping what German troops remain in North-East Italy after the Po debacle. We are still finding only rearguard opposition.

The Eighth Army, clearing Loreo, is now only 25 miles from Venice.

RED ARMY SEIZES BERLIN AIRFIELD

STALIN officially confirmed last night the capture of Spandau, north-west Berlin suburb which gives its name to the Spandau machine gun, and Potsdam.

The Russians also took the Tempelhof airfield. More than 11,500 of Berlin's defenders went into the prisoner cages. Eighty-five planes were captured.

Soviet troops have also advanced 45 miles west of Berlin.

In the north fresh advances are squeezing the Baltic pockets. The Russians swept 30 miles west of the Elbe at Stettin to take Prenzlau.

GERMANS FLEE EMDEN IN U BOATS

CANADIAN ARMY, Friday.—Fifty German submarines—500 and 250 tonners—have arrived at Emden during the past few days, and are believed to be setting up a shuttle service taking troops to Denmark or Norway.

Considerable sea traffic has also been seen around the Frisian Islands, whose big coastal guns are now trained on the Canadians.—B.U.P.

Won't-surrender general seized

BREMEN, Friday.—Captured in Bremen today were General Becker, the commander who refused to surrender the city: Major-General Werner Siber, garrison commander; and, in the port, a vice-admiral with 16 U boats and a destroyer.—Express News Service.

'THE YANKS ARE HERE'—'THE RUSSIANS ARE HERE'

INFANTRYMEN of the U.S. First Army have worked their way across a broken bridge over the Elbe; extend their hands to grasp the welcoming hands of Russian neighbours.... There was singing and dancing on the east bank of the river afterwards, much slapping-on-the-back between Americans and Russians and many toasts in the sunshine.

Petain sleeps by death post

From ROBIN DUFF: Paris, Friday

MARSHAL PETAIN and his wife slept tonight, in two low, narrow, oak bedsteads on the ground floor of the Fort Montrouge, south of Paris.

Their room, bare except for essentials, measures 13ft. by 10, and its window is iron-barred.

Outside is the post at which traitors condemned since the liberation of Paris have been shot.

To enter the Marshal's prison room you must pass through another, which is even smaller. In that room are two nuns, who are in permanent attendance on Petain. Two Army doctors, a captain and a lieutenant are on call.

Madame Petain asked to go to Montrouge with her husband. There is no charge against her.

In the passage outside their room in the fort, Paris gendarmes march slowly up and down. One hundred are on guard duty. No-one may enter the grounds without special authority of General Koenig, Military Governor of Paris.

'CLEMENCY' ROW

An official statement says the Marshal and his wife were given ordinary prison food. In fact they breakfasted off bread and butter and asked for beef tea instead of coffee. But most of the food was still on the tray when it was brought out.

For lunch they asked for an omelette.

The French Government tonight denied a Moscow radio report that most of the Council of Ministers favour liberty for Petain.

The State Prosecutor, M. Andre Mornet, has said of Petain: "His policy must be condemned, but in view of his great age I hope that his last days may be as free of pain as possible."

Commenting on this, the Left Radical Franc-tireur writes: "If it is confirmed, this statement is a pure scandal. We expect a denial or an explanation."

Mme. Marcelle Belle, who jumped on a chair at a Socialist election meeting last night and spoke in favour of Petain, was arrested

REDOUBT A MYTH SAYS DIETMAR

'When Berlin goes, all is over : Hitler is there'

Express War Reporter: Germany, Friday

GENERAL KURT DIETMAR, German High Command radio spokesman, has surrendered. He told his American captors in the Magdeburg sector that Hitler is still in Berlin, and will die there, that the Redoubt is a myth, and that the war will end within a few days.

Dietmar crossed the Elbe in a rowing-boat on Wednesday, and walked into the American lines on the Ninth Army front, accompanied by his 16-year-old son Bernhardt and his aide-de-camp, Major Werner Pluskat.

Dietmar's son carried a large Red Cross flag Like his father he was in German Army uniform.

To American officers Dietmar said that he had come to intercede for wounded civilians Questioned, he admitted he was afraid of falling into Russian hands.

He was asked if he wished to give himself up, and was given half an hour to decide.

Within a few minutes he had made his choice: "I will be safer with you," he said. "I surrender."

Dietmar told American officers, "Hitler is still in Berlin. But Berlin will fall, and Hitler will either be killed or will commit suicide. Then the war will end in a few days.

"One of three generals—von Brauchitsch, Guderian or von Rundstedt—will take control, and will make peace immediately on almost any terms.

"The Redoubt is a myth When Berlin falls it will be all over."

"Goering has probably been executed already."

'The man who knew'

Daily Express Radio Editor, G. W. Frerk, writes :—

Dietmar, who always "knew what was coming," was the most plausible among Nazi radio spokesmen His regular Tuesday evening war commentaries on the German home radio had a nation-wide audience

For a long time Dietmar was believed to be just a "voice" invented by Goebbels, until in summer 1943 the Germans provided a few biographical details to prove that he was a real, live general.

He is 57, and commanded a battalion in the last war. When this war broke out he was commandant of the Military Engineers' School in Berlin. He took part in the invasion of Norway, and in 1941 became radio spokesman for the German High Command.

He talks in a crisp, firm, sonorous voice, speaking slowly at times to emphasise a point.

Cancellations of his broadcasts were usually an indication of important developments. With the arrival of the Allied armies on German soil, his absence became more frequent.

He made his last personal appearance on March 15, when he said: "We have been pressed back to a new inner defence ring of the fortress Germany. The command of the hour is that we must fight hard for what is left."

Reynaud and Daladier free

TWO former French Premiers and the man who was Allied Commander-in-Chief before the German march on Paris have crossed from Germany into Switzerland, said Paris radio last night. They are :—

PAUL REYNAUD, the Premier of France to whom Mr. Churchill suggested an Anglo-French union in June 1940.

Reynaud favoured the plan, but the French Cabinet rejected it. He tried to reach Spain by car, but was badly hurt in a crash. He is 65.

GENERAL MARIE GUSTAVE GAMELIN, C.-in-C. of the Allied Armies in 1939, who placed his faith in the Maginot Line. He is 73.

EDOUARD DALADIER—known as the "strong man of France" until superseded as Premier by Reynaud in March 1940. He was Prime Minister in 1933 when Hitler came to power, and was one of the signatories of the Munich Agreement in 1938. He is 61.

Two other former French Premiers, M. Blum and M. Herriot, are near St. Margareten on the German-Swiss border.

The Germans are to release all Allied civilian internees, the French Minister for Prisoners confirms

This station is closing down . .

General Kurt Dietmar, the Wehrmacht radio commentator, lips tightly clamped together, is driven away in a jeep after crossing the Elbe to make his surrender.

Victory prizes for young composers

THE Daily Express announces today a Victory Music Contest, open to young British composers. Two prizes are offered—one of £250, the second £150.

The contest is sponsored by the Daily Express to herald the approach of victory and peace.

And it is in the spirit of these that composers should find their inspiration

The contest is for a symphonic work of one or more movements, fully orchestrated; playing time between 15 and 20 minutes.

It is open to British composers, male or female, who will be under the age of 35 on January 1, 1946.

BY OCTOBER

Scores must be submitted to the Daily Express, Fleet-street, London, E.C.4, not later than October 31, 1945, accompanied not only by the name and address of the composer, but also by a nom de plume.

Noms de plume only will accompany the scores when they are placed for adjudication before—

Mr. Arthur Bliss,
Dr. Malcolm Sargent, and
Mr. Constant Lambert,

who have agreed to act as judges.

A public performance of the prizewinning works under the baton of a well-known conductor will be arranged at the Albert Hall next winter by the Daily Express.

The Daily Express also undertakes to bring to the attention of leading conductors the six best compositions which do not win a prize.

Nazis worry about their poison gas

NEAR REGENSBERG, Friday.—Germans in Regensberg had huge stores of poison gas, but they made no attempt to use them, and sent positions to the Americans so that no shells would hit them.—A.P.

Missed—the 12.15

THIRD ARMY, Friday.—Kesselring's private 15-car train has been captured 20 miles from Regensburg.

Dried egg ration halved

The dried egg allocation will be cut from two packets to one a month from tomorrow until May 26, says the Food Ministry.

Improving

Straits: Day cold, showery; night improving.

Himmler men shoot Goering

SAYS GERMAN

ZURICH, Friday.—A German diplomat from Munich revealed today the background to Goering's "resignation."

He said: "Last Monday Goering sent Hitler an urgent letter asking him, with the Nazi Party, to accept the consequences of a lost war and prevent the further shedding of German blood.

"The same night Himmler sent his own bodyguard to Goering's home, and Goering's fate was sealed. His wife, Emmy, was present.

"One report says that Goering was ordered by the commandant of Himmler's bodyguard to execute his own death sentence, whereupon he first shot his two daughters and then himself.

"Another version is that the bodyguard mowed down Goering and his wife without warning."—Exchange.

4 a.m. LATEST

HITLER CALLS TO BERLIN WOMEN

Hamburg radio says Hitler has issued new appeal to all women and girls to take up arms to fight the Russians

Mussolini is held: wife turned back

From FREDERICK GLEANER

BERNE, Friday.—It is reported from inside Italy tonight that Mussolini has been captured by partisans at Nesso, on Lake Como, just south of the Swiss frontier.

Arrested with him are Graziani, his C.-in-C., Guido, his Minister of the Interior, Farinacci, former secretary of the Fascist Party, and Pavolini, secretary-general of the Republican Fascist Party.

One version of the capture is that the partisans surprised Mussolini and his henchmen at lunch.

They intended to try escaping into Switzerland by way of Chiasso.

It is known that Mussolini's wife, Donna Rachele, has already tried to get over the frontier.

She and her daughter asked at Chiasso for permission to enter Switzerland.

While Donna Rachele pleaded with the frontier guards, eight people who had come with her skulked in the back of closed cars, keeping well out of sight.

The head of the frontier post told Donna Rachele he had instructions from the Federal Council they could not enter. The cars turned back into Italy.

Italy is likely to claim the right to try Mussolini instead of sending him to an international court as a war criminal

THE STARS AND STRIPES
MEDITERRANEAN

Vol. 2, No. 147, Monday, April 30, 1945 ITALY EDITION * * TWO LIRE

MUSSOLINI EXECUTED

5th Enters Milan; 7th In Munich

Brazilians Take Nazi Division

(BULLETIN) WITH THE 15TH ARMY GROUP, April 29 — The 56th London Division of the British 8th Army, headed by the famous 169th Queens Brigade, has entered Venice.

The 2nd New Zealand Division has reached the the Piave River, scene of Italy's greatest victory in World War I.

WITH THE 15TH ARMY GROUP, April 29 — Organized German resistance in Italy was crumbling today under the paralyzing blows of two Allied Armies, gathering momentum for the knockout punch and there were signs that the complete disintegration of the German Armies had begun.

Dramatic developments were disclosed in tonight's communique

Milan nas been entered by 5th Army troops.

Negotiations were in progress for the surrender of the Liguarian Army, formerly commanded by Marshal Rodolfo Graziani, now a prisoner and under Allied military control.

The 148th German Infantry Division surrendered to the Brazilian Expeditionary Force, delivering up

(Continued on Page 8)

Himmler Statement Hints Hitler Death

SAN FRANCISCO, April 29 (UP) — The possibility that Heinrich Himmler may have killed Hitler, as cynical evidence to the Allies of his "good faith" in desiring to surrender Germany, was suggested in diplomatic quarters here today.

A high British source revealed first evidence in what was regarded in San Francisco as a desperate attempt by Himmler to save his own skin. These quarters assert that Himmler advised the Allies through Stockholm that Hitler "may not live another 24 hours."

The timing of the message was such that many believe Hitler may already be dead at the hands of his once trusted lieutenant."

Berlin 90 Percent In Russian Hands

MOSCOW, April 29 — The Red Army is now battling for a May Day victory in Berlin — 90 percent of which, according to United Press, is in Russian hands.

With less than 24 hours to go before the eve of the great Soviet holiday, Marshals Gregory Zhukov and Ivan Koniev have launched a crushing all-out assault on the center of the city where the Germans are now hemmed into an area roughly covering the oldest part of the Reich capital.

The Moabit section of Berlin, northwest of the Wilhelmstrasse, fell to the Red Army tonight, according to the Soviet communique.

The German High Command, gambling everything on the possibility of a last-minute "split" developing between the West and East Front Allies, has withdrawn its troops facing U. S. forces on the

(Continued on Page 8)

Yanks Push Into Shrine Of Nazism

SHAEF, April 29 — Munich, fourth largest city of Germany and birthplace of Nazism, was entered by troops of the 6th Army Group tonight. Entry into the great Bavarian city after a 20-mile advance from the west, was made by elements of Lt. Gen. Alexander M. Patch's U. S. 7th Army from the north and southwest.

Initial dispatches did not tell of any fighting within the city which for the past two days had been wracked by unrest and revolt.

Earlier today American armies had been reported converging on the city in an 80-mile arc extending from the northeast to the southwest, and dispatches tonight told of the liberation by the U. S. 3rd Army of 27,000 Allied prisoners of war from a camp at Moosburg on the Isar River, 27 miles northeast of Munich. A great number of those freed prisoners were reported to be American airmen.

There has been no indication yet that Allied Armies have reached the most notorious of German concentration camps at Dachau, eight miles northwest of Munich.

The situation within Munich remained uncertain following an apparent attempt yesterday by a group identifying itself as the "Free Bavarian Movement" and led by General Ritter von Epp, Hitler's 75-year-old commissioner for Bavaria, to take over the city's government.

Reuter's reported that a radio using the city's wave length had told of revolt within the city, and had called upon the advancing Allies to bomb Field Marshal Albert C. Kesselring's headquarters near Munich.

Later, Reuter's said, the south

(Continued on Page 8)

Patriots Also Kill Aides, Mistress

ROME, April 29—Benito Mussolini has been executed by Italian Patriots, Radio Milan, voice of the Committee of National Liberation of Northern Italy, said today.

The Radio said Mussolini was executed last night along with a number of his henchmen and his mistress.

Two British war correspondents, Christopher Lumby, of the London Times, and Stephen Barber, of the London News Chronicle, who went into Milan in advance of Allied troops, reported today that they had personally seen the bodies of Mussolini and 17 of his henchmen on display in the Piazza Loreto. They said that crowds of Italians swarmed to view the bodies, and revile them.

The correspondents reported that Mussolini and others, after having been captured near Lake Como, were taken to the village of Guilano di Mezzegere nearby. There they were tried and executed at 1620 hours on Saturday, April 28. Their bodies were carried in trucks to Milan for public display on the same spot where just a year ago 15 Patriots were executed.

Rome newspapers, like Il Giornale del Mattino and Libera Stampa, spread the news in bold, black headlines. Over all Rome quickly the report travelled, and crowds gathered around every newstand and great excitement stirred the people. At a rally being held near Piazza Venezia in honor of the northern Patriots, loud cheering greeted the announcement.

Radio Milan did not give details of the executions, nor of the summary trial which must have preceded them. Italians in Rome believed Mussolini and his followers were stood against a wall and shot by a firing squad of Partisans.

Among the others mentioned as executed were Alessandro Pavolini, Carlo Scorza, Fernando Messasona, Goffredo Coppola, Nicola Bombacci and Claretta Petacci, mistress of Mussolini.

Pavolini was probably the chief Fascist among them. He was once Mussolini's propaganda minister. As one of a group of seven in the Fascist Grand Council, he used

(Continued on Page 8)

BENITO MUSSOLINI
Reviled In Death

Truman To Tell When Nazis Fall

WASHINGTON, April 29 — Official confirmation of a German collapse—when and if it comes—will be proclaimed in person by President Harry S. Truman in a message over all radio networks, Stephen T. Early, presidential secretary, announced last night.

Early's announcement was made after the nation had broken out in a pandemonium of joy and exultation over a false report from San Francisco that Germany had surrendered.

Meanwhile, Secretary of State Edward R. Stettinius Jr. and Russian Commissar for Foreign Affairs V. M. Molotov met in a surprise session late yesterday to consider the contents of a note from Marshal Stalin to President Truman and Prime Minister Churchill.

The note, according to a Reuter's dispatch, recommended that the offer of Heinrich Himmler, chief of all Nazi defenses, to surrender Germany to the U. S. and Great Britain, be rejected.

That such an offer had been made was "confirmed in responsible Soviet quarters," Tass, the Soviet news agency, said it had been "authorized to state."

Reports from Washington and London that said that Himmler's offer had been turned down because only unconditional surrender to all three major powers would be acceptable.

The Soviet view, according to Reuter's, as expressed in Marshal Stalin's note was that Himmler might not have sufficient authority to make such an offer and that no surrender talks should be started before Nazi armed might is completely annihilated.

The Russians, Reuter's reported, are said to be determined that the Nazis should not have the slightest justification or the appearance of justification for a repetition of German propaganda after World War I that Germany could have fought on but agreed to give up.

The peace story which originated in San Francisco yesterday touched off celebrations which did not end until long after President Truman announced that rumors about the end of the war in Europe were groundless.

Radio networks throughout the

(Continued on Page 8)

Patriots Claim Fall Of Treviso, Turin

ROME, April 29 — Radio Milan from all indications firmly in the hands of Italian Patriots, claimed the liberation of Turin and of the province of Treviso, in northeast Italy today, Reuter's reported

The radio announcement said that Turin had been liberated by the Partisans, and all its military barracks occupied.

General Mark W. Clark, 15th Army Group Commander, broadcast the following instructions to the Partisans:

"You must by all means prevent the Germans from carrying out the destruction of industrial plants and machinery," General Clark said. "On this task depends the future of Italy."

The signal for a general rising of North Italian Partisans was given by Field Marshal Sir Harold R. L. G. Alexander, Allied commander in chief in Italy through the National Liberation Committee, the Milan Radio disclosed.

Nazi Civilians Get Diet One-Third of GIs

SHAEF, April 29—German civilians will be allowed a diet about one-third that of American soldiers and slightly more than half the standard for liberated Europe. It was announced here today, according to Reuter's.

The majority of Germans will be allowed 1,150 calories daily as compared with the 4,000 daily of American soldiers and with the consumption of between 2,500 and 3,000 in the U. S., and the 2,000 which is the standard of the liberated countries.

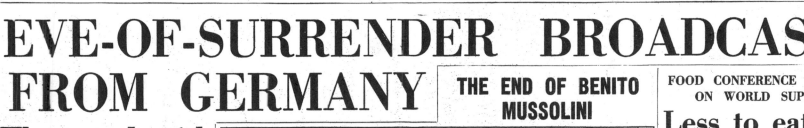

News Chronicle
No. 30,875 TUESDAY, MAY 1, 1945 ONE PENNY
4 a.m. EDITION

EVE-OF-SURRENDER BROADCASTS FROM GERMANY

War speeds with giant strides towards its end

FROM Hamburg radio, the only transmitter of any power left to the Germans, there came last night two remarkable eve-of-surrender broadcasts. One was a dirge for Berlin; the other was a farewell to the Reich. The principal speaker was Dr. Scharping, one of the leading German political commentators. These are his words:

"Everybody knows that this war is racing towards its end. The end may come tomorrow, and there will be hundreds of thousands, nay millions, of German children and German women standing at their windows and looking out into the empty streets towards the return of father and husband. But they will never come back.

"And thus the question arises: What was the meaning of this war? Looking back, we realise that both we at home and the men at the front have surpassed themselves in heroism and bold deeds.

"They have shown the world what Germany can do when she gathers all her strength.

"They have withstood with aching hearts but with set teeth the onslaught of three continents, and have stood fast as long as it was humanly possible.

"Fallen heroes"

"Now we are taking leave of this eerie trek of fallen heroes who march on to mount guard for the better future of Germany.

"Every German must firmly retain in his heart the faith that this war has had its meaning. He must be certain that each one of us will talk German also in future, though our country may be temporarily occupied. We shall remain loyal to our mother tongue.

German rivers

"The Elbe will also in future remain the German river, and so will the Rhine and the Oder. They will never be Germany's frontier.

"Let us embrace Germany, it is a force which grows and flourishes. I have found few words in the recent past to express the fortitude of the German people and I shall say little today at a moment when this war is speeding with giant strides towards its completion."

Berlin falling

And of Berlin, "over which at any moment now the enemy's flag may fly," this was said: "Now Berlin is a heap of ruined houses and smoking debris.

"We can hardly grasp what happened when we remember Berlin almost hidden under a sea of flags when Austria was incorporated into the Reich, when we remember Berlin as the centre from where the final decisions went out. We cannot understand that this field of ruins should be the same Berlin. Now there are only memories of Berlin."

Cabinet's night meeting

A meeting of all available Ministers, not merely the War Cabinet, was held at Downing Street late last night.

Another meeting will be held this morning before Parliament meets. It will then be decided what, if anything, is to be said in the House on Himmler's peace overtures.

— By VERNON BARTLETT

SUNDAY'S unbounded optimism about Germany's unconditional surrender was somewhat checked yesterday by a few awkward questions.

If Himmler were trying to make his own survival a condition, is there the slightest prospect that men so tough as Mr. Churchill and Marshal Stalin would listen to him?

Or that public opinion in any country would agree that the Nazi primarily responsible for the concentration camps should escape the ultimate penalty?

If he had no hope of gaining any such advantage for himself, would any consideration for his family or his compatriots lead him to order the surrender?

If Himmler is in Flensburg, or some other town near the German-Danish border—as is reported—how can he deliver to the Allies the body of Hitler? For Hitler, if still alive, is presumably in Berlin, since somebody is believed to have stolen the aircraft in which he was to have escaped.

Counter-order?

If Hitler cannot be produced, what guarantee is there that Himmler's order would be obeyed?

Might not Goebbels, or even Hitler himself, issue a counter-order, the effect of which would be to prolong the struggle after the Allied onslaught had been slowed down by the belief that the German war was ending?

Such questions are natural in view of the kind of men involved. But it still remains certain both that Himmler has been trying for months to bring the war to an end and that his order to surrender would be obeyed by most of the S.S., the only band of thugs which might otherwise galvanise large sections of the German people into further desperate resistance.

BERNADOTTE HAS COMPLETED TASK

STOCKHOLM, Monday.

AGAIN today rumours of peace negotiations flew thick and fast. Two facts emerge.

Count Bernadotte, who is now in Denmark, returns to Sweden tomorrow. His mission is completed. He will not go back to Denmark or to Germany.

A Swedish mission—two members of the Foreign Office and the chief of the military traffic section of the State Railways—left for Denmark and returned later to Malmoe.

Official circles have nothing to say about the task of this mission, but the Swedish transport system is an important link between German-occupied Norway and German-held Denmark.

These are the rumours circulating here during the day:

1—Himmler is believed to have given Count Bernadotte a capitulation offer addressed to the Soviet Union as well as to Britain and the United States The Soviet Legation confirms that no such offer has yet been handed over, although it is awaited.

2—The Danish Press Service issued this report: "It is reliably learned that Himmler and Count Bernadotte met at Aabenraa (on the Danish-German border) yesterday The negotiations lasted all day and are understood to be continuing today. Whatever the position, it is known that Himmler and Count Bernadotte are still at Aabenraa"

3—There are reports that Werner Best, with whom Count Bernadotte is reported to have had conversations in Denmark yesterday, is now in Stockholm Another message says that Himmler is in Stockholm, but he is also reported to be in Luebeck.

4—From Malmoe there is a report that a Danish radio station had said that Count Bernadotte had spent yesterday near Aabenraa, and after "several important telephone conversations had gone south"—presumably into Germany

In Denmark and Norway the people demonstrated openly yesterday and today. The Germans did not even attempt to disperse the crowds. In Denmark the Danish flag was hoisted.

THE END OF BENITO MUSSOLINI

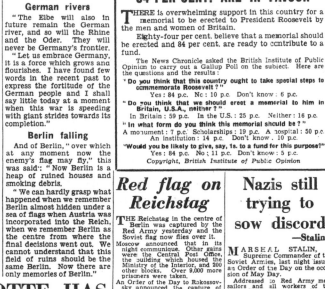

This was the end of Benito Mussolini. His body hangs head downwards suspended on a rope tied to his feet and pulled up to the roof of a garage runway in the Piazza Loreto, Milan. Hanging beside him is his mistress, Claretta Petacci. Shots were fired into Mussolini's body from the crowd pressing round the gibbet. This picture and others on Back Page were transmitted by radio specially to the News Chronicle from Berne last night

British memorial to Roosevelt
84 PER CENT. ARE IN FAVOUR

THERE is overwhelming support in this country for a memorial to be erected to President Roosevelt by the men and women of Britain.

Eighty-four per cent. believe that a memorial should be erected and 84 per cent. are ready to contribute to a fund.

The News Chronicle asked the British Institute of Public Opinion to carry out a Gallup Poll on the subject. Here are the questions and the results:

"Do you think that this country ought to take special steps to commemorate Roosevelt?"
Yes: 84 p.c. No: 10 p.c. Don't know: 6 p.c.

"Do you think that we should erect a memorial to him in Britain, U.S.A., neither?"
In Britain: 59 p.c. In the U.S.: 25 p.c. Neither: 16 p.c.

"In what form do you think this memorial should be?"
A monument: 7 p.c. Scholarships: 19 p.c. A hospital: 50 p.c. An institution: 14 p.c. Don't know. 10 p.c.

"Would you be likely to give, say, 1s. to a fund for this purpose?"
Yes: 84 p.c. No: 11 p.c. Don't know: 5 p.c.

Copyright, British Institute of Public Opinion

Red flag on Reichstag

THE Reichstag in the centre of Berlin was captured by the Red Army yesterday and the Soviet flag now flies over it.

Moscow announced that in its night communique. Other gains were the Central Post Office, the building which housed the Ministry of the Interior, and 200 other blocks. Over 9,000 more prisoners were taken.

An Order of the Day to Rokossovsky announced the capture of Greifswald, Terptow, Neu-Strelitz, Fuerstenberg and Granste, in North-Western Pomerania and Mecklenburg. His troops are within five miles of Peenemuende.

Another Order announced the capture of the Czech key town, Moravska-Ostrava, by Gen. Eremenko. Zlinka, 47 miles to the south-east, was also taken.

★

Highlights from other European sectors:

Elbe Front.—Gen. Simpson's U.S. Ninth Army has made contact with the Russians at Apollensdorf, near Wittenberg. Americans under British Second Army Command have made a new crossing of the Elbe.

Canadians.—The Germans' Oldenburg defence line has been turned.

Bavarian Redoubt.—Munich, cradle of Nazidom, has been completely cleared by the U.S. Seventh Army.

Italy—Gen. Mark Clark announced the destruction of 25 German Divisions. Japanese-American troops have captured Turin.

French landing on Gironde isle

From Our Own Correspondent

Shaef, Monday.—French troops with air and sea support landed on the Ile d'Oleron this morning to open up the port of Bordeaux

Before the landing—which was reported to be progressing satisfactorily—the 65 German batteries defending the island were heavily bombarded.

Nazis still trying to sow discord —Stalin

MARSHAL STALIN, as Supreme Commander of the Soviet Armies, last night issued an Order of the Day on the occasion of May Day.

Addressed to Red Army men, sailors and all workers of the Soviet Union, it said: "Today our country is celebrating May Day, the international holiday of the workers.

"This year the peoples of our country are celebrating it in an atmosphere of the victorious conclusion of the great patriotic war.

"By simultaneous blows from East and West the Allies and the Red Army were able to cut the German forces into two isolated parts and to effect a junction of ours and Allied troops to form a united front.

Days numbered

"There can be no doubt that this circumstance means the end of Hitlerite Germany. Its days are numbered.

"Seeking a way out of their hopeless plight the Hitlerite adventurers resort to all kinds of tricks, down to flirting with the Allies in an effort to cause dissension in the Allied camp

"These fresh tricks are doomed to utter failure. They can only accelerate the disintegration of the German Army.

"Mendacious Fascist propaganda intimidates the German population by absurd tales alleging that the armies of the United Nations wish to exterminate the German people.

"The United Nations do not set themselves the task of destroying the German people. The United Nations will destroy Fascism and German militarism, will severely punish war criminals and will compel the Germans to compensate for the damage they caused to other countries.

"But the United Nations do not molest and will not molest Germany's peaceful population if it honestly fulfils the demands of the Allied military authorities."

Man who shot ex-Duce tells story of the final scenes

MILAN, Monday.

IN a last melodramatic gesture before he died Mussolini offered to buy his life with "an empire," according to a Milan Communist newspaper in an interview with Mussolini's executioner, a member of the Communist Garibaldi.

Claretta Petacci, Mussolini's mistress, threw her arms round the ex-Duce's neck at the last moment and screamed "He must not die."

This was the account given in the newspaper "l'Unita":

"The command of the 52nd brigade, aware of the importance of the captured prisoners, divided them into three groups. Mussolini was taken with Petacci to Giulino di Mezzegera, in Como Province, and placed in a small windowless room in a peasant's cottage, guarded by two partisans.

His lost look

"I entered" (the executioner wrote) "with my sub-machine gun at the ready. Mussolini was standing near the bed. He was wearing a brown overcoat and the cap of the Republican National Guard without insignia. His boots were down at heel.

"He had a lost look in his eyes, which were protruding, and his lower lip was trembling—he was a terrified man.

"His first words were 'What's the matter?'

"I had planned to carry out the execution not far from the house. To get him there I had to resort to a stratagem. I said, 'I have come to liberate you. . . Hurry, we have little time to lose.'

Mussolini pointed to Claretta Petacci. "She must go first," he said. She seemed unable to understand what was going on, and rushed about gathering up her personal belongings. Mussolini kept urging her to hurry.

Thought he was free

"Losing patience, he eventually left the hut before her.

"Once in the open Mussolini turned towards me and said: 'I offer you an empire.' Instead of answering I told Petacci to come on. She drew level with Mussolini and, followed by me, they walked down a mule track towards the road where a car was parked.

"When we reached it Mussolini seemed convinced that he was a free man. He motioned to Petacci to precede him, but I told him: 'You go first. You are better concealed. But with that Fascist cap it is a little risky.'

"He took it off, and patting his bald head, said: 'And this?'

"I told him, 'Pull the peak low over your eyes.'

"Then we set off for the place I had chosen—a sort of small square formed by fences on both sides of the road.

"I stopped the car, motioning to Mussolini not to talk. In a low voice I told him, I heard a noise. I am going to investigate.'

"I jumped off the running board and walked to the end of the stone wall. 'Get over in that corner.' I said.

"Even though Mussolini obeyed promptly he no longer appeared to be convinced but obediently stood with his back to the wall at the place I indicated. Petacci was on his right. There was silence.

"Suddenly I pronounced sentence against the war criminal. 'By order of the general command of the Liberty Volunteer Corps I am entrusted with the task of rendering justice for the Italian people.

Terror-stricken

"Mussolini was terror-stricken. Claretta Petacci threw her arms round his shoulders and screamed: He must not die.

"I said: 'Get back in your place if you don't want to die too.

"The woman jumped back. From a distance of three paces I shot five bursts into Mussolini, who slumped to his knees.

"Then it was Pettaci's turn.

'Justice had been done."—A.P.

A voice in the wilderness

The Portuguese newspaper, "Voz," comments on the shooting of Mussolini: "We bow with respect before his memory. They have killed a great European and a great Latin."

Graziani trial opens

The trial of Marshal Graziani began in Milan yesterday, only a few hours after the bodies of Mussolini and his collaborators had been removed from public display.

Petain questioned

Paris, Monday.—The interrogation of Petain, which began today, is being held at Fort Mont Rouge to avoid the risk of demonstrations were he to be driven through Paris to the court.

FOOD CONFERENCE WARNING ON WORLD SUPPLIES

Less to eat this year and next

THERE will be less food available in many important categories in 1946.

This was indicated last night in a preliminary statement by Britain, Canada and the U.S. on the recent Washington conference on problems of world supplies and distribution.

The United Nations, the statement said, are faced this year not only with larger requirements but with supplies which in certain categories will be less than in 1944.

"The problem will extend not merely over the next few months but into 1946.

"The problem of food is one of the most urgent now facing the United Nations. It is another common struggle which must be won.

"Either they must find the answers to the food problem or millions of persons throughout the world will meet disillusionment and disappointment following the wake of victory.

Victory's price

"The present shortage of certain foods is part of the price it has been necessary to pay for the victories of the Allied Forces in Europe and the Far East. The problem grows greater, not less, with each victory."

The statement listed these causes:

Growing military requirements.

Our responsibility for the subsistence of the hundreds of thousands of German prisoners taken in N.W. Europe.

Making up deficiencies in the minimum requirements of the liberated countries.

The feeding of displaced persons and others deported into Germany by the Nazis until they can return to their homes.

German plunder of the food producing areas of Europe which they previously occupied.

Sowing impossible

"Sowing of crops in many battle-stricken areas is impossible this year.

"The food production of Europe will, for some time, be far below the pre-war level."

"In the face of these increased and essential requirements, the world output of many foodstuffs, notably meat, sugar, rice, and fats and oils, is lower this year than last. This reduced output is due to further withdrawals of man-power from the farms into the armed

Continued Back Page

LATE NEWS

ARGENTINA ADMITTED

San Francisco, Monday.—Argentina has been admitted to United Nations' Conference by 31 votes to 4 in plenary session.

(See Back Page)

LT. WINANT TAKEN TO SALZBURG

Third U.S. Army, Monday.—Lt. John G. Winant, son of U.S. Ambassador to Britain, was removed from Moosburg prisoners-of-war camp by Gestapo and taken to Salzburg a "political prisoner." Airmen liberated by U.S. troops reported today.

Moon sets 8.52 a.m., rises 1.41 a.m. tomorrow. New Moon, May 11.

Russia and Austria: U.S. disclaimer

From Our Own Correspondent

New York, Monday.—The United States does not recognise the Provisional Government of Austria, and is still without official confirmation that any such Government has been formed.

This was made clear this afternoon by Acting Secretary of State Joseph C. Grew, who told his Press conference that the question is being taken up with the Soviet Government, whose troops now occupy Vienna.

Decision on Austria may be delayed: Back Page

110,000 war prisoners freed

From NORMAN CLARK
News Chronicle War Correspondent

WITH THE THIRD ARMY, Monday.

THE U.S. Third Army, in capturing Moosburg, on the Isar River, liberated 110,000 Allied prisoners-of-war.

They are from all Services and include women and war correspondents. Three Russian women doctors are among them.

The prisoners include 11,000 Americans, British, Canadians, South Africans, Australians, New Zealanders, Poles, Russians, French and Serbs.

Moosburg is said to be Germany's biggest prisoner-of-war camp.

9,000 died at Dachau in three months: Page Three

Fuel warning

The Minister of Fuel and Power appeals to the public to be specially careful in the use of gas and electricity today, particularly between 8 a.m. and noon.

Daily Mirror

MAY 2

Wednesday, May 2, 1945
No. 12,906 ONE PENNY
Registered at G.P.O. as a Newspaper.

U-Boat chief claims he's new Fuehrer, tells Huns to fight on

HITLER DEAD

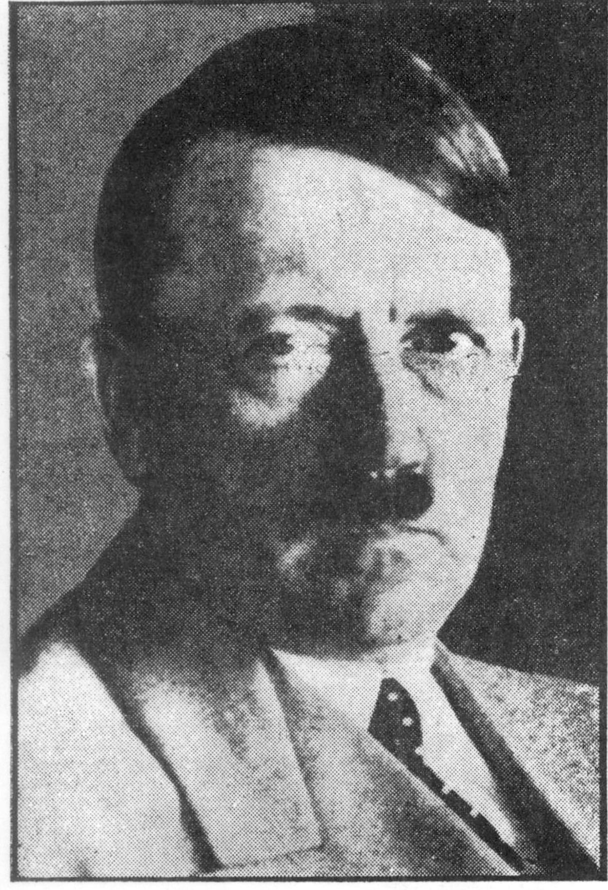

Adolf Hitler, leader of the Nazi Reich since January 30, 1933, the world's chief criminal, now dead at the age of fifty-six. His career appears on Pages 4 and 5.

"Fell at his post in battle of Berlin," says Nazi radio

HITLER is dead. He "fell for Germany" in the Reich Chancellery in Berlin yesterday afternoon, according to a broadcast from Hamburg at 10.30 last night.

Grand-Admiral Doenitz, 54-year-old inventor of U-Boat pack tactics, broadcast, claiming that Hitler had appointed him Fuehrer and Commander-in-Chief of the German Forces.

Doenitz came to the microphone and declared: "The military struggle continues with the aim of saving the German people from Bolshevism.

"We shall continue to defend ourselves against the Anglo-Americans just as long as they impede our aim."

A ghost voice broke in: "Rise against Doenitz. The struggle is not worth while if crime wins."

The announcement of Hitler's death at fifty-six, after being Fuehrer since January 30, 1933, was preceded by slow Wagnerian music and finally by a roll of drums.

During the announcement and Doenitz's speech from Hamburg, the southern German radio network went on broadcasting light music.

It was not until half an hour later that it put

Continued on Back Page

MYSTERY OF HIMMLER PUZZLES THE CABINET

By BILL GREIG

THE unexpected appearance of Admiral Doenitz as Fuehrer came as a shock to members of the Cabinet who have been in touch with the surrender discussions at all stages.

It had been assumed that Himmler would automatically succeed Hitler, and that this would be followed by complete surrender. What has gone wrong is not yet clear, but the belief is expressed officially that nothing has happened likely to lengthen the war appreciably.

The unknown factor is still Himmler. There are two possibilities.

That fanatical Nazis—of whom Doenitz is a fair specimen and one of the toughest—have seized Himmler to prevent surrender.

That Doenitz, as leader, is nothing more than a screen behind which still another attempt to negotiate will be made with Himmler holding the real power.

The possibility of Himmler also being dead was one which received some support last night, and the Government was making anxious attempts to find out the truth through neutral sources.

Despite his fighting speech Doenitz is not considered as really intending to stage a "fight to the last man" campaign. It is felt that behind his words lies no more than a desire to hearten the German people while he makes another effort . . . bound to be in vain . . . to get terms from the United Nations.

Doenitz and his friends may have believed that Himmler had succeeded in making a deal, safeguarding himself with Britain and America. Regarding themselves double-crossed, they turned the tables on him.

That Himmler tried to save his own skin is now admitted

It can now be revealed that it was Himmler and not Hitler who carried through all the arrangements regarding prisoners of war. He then gave the impression of being the real if not the titular head of Germany. At no time did Doenitz appear on the scene.

The possibility of Doenitz making some last desperate effort to hearten the Germans while he tries to negotiate is not overlooked here.

This might even include a renewal of air attacks on this country, but they could only be on a small scale.

The fact that the evacuation of Norway and Denmark had apparently begun before Doenitz spoke suggests that Himmler had actually given some orders regarding surrender earlier in the day.

Attention is drawn to the fact that although Doenitz tried to suggest that Hitler died in action he carefully avoided saying so in as many words.

From facts known in London it is certain that Hitler did not die so nobly, though his end may have been equally dramatic and not exactly from natural causes.

From one in close touch with the Government I was given this summing-up last night: "It is doubtful if whatever happened in Germany last night has lengthened the war by more than a week. The military position is as clear as that. Doenitz has no navy, no organised army and only the skeleton of an air force."

The new "Fuehrer" for how long?

Admiral Doenitz

Doenitz lived here —in an asylum!

WHEN 50-year-old Admiral Karl Doenitz, Germany's new Fuehrer, invented the U-boat pack, his order to crews was: "Sink without mercy."

He left his job as U-boat chief to become C.-in-C. of the German Navy in February, 1943, and his technical brilliance was always a more formidable weapon than Hitler's intuition.

"The German Navy will fight to a finish," he has boasted.

During the last war he spent a considerable time in England—as a prisoner of war in a Manchester lunatic asylum.

The British sloop Snap Dragon fished him out of the Mediterranean after sinking his U-boat in 1917.

By feigning insanity after his capture he qualified for a place among the first batch of prisoners to be repatriated to Germany.

He has shown himself capable of bluntly admitting the worst and fighting tenaciously in spite of it. Admitting in 1942 that U-boats had abandoned the deep Atlantic for attacks off the American coast, he declared:

"Operating in American waters is no easy matter.

DAILY EXPRESS

No. 14,013 Coast dim-out 9.56 pm to 5.58 am  THURSDAY MAY 3 1945 Moon rises 3.23 am (Fri) sets 11.34 am One Penny

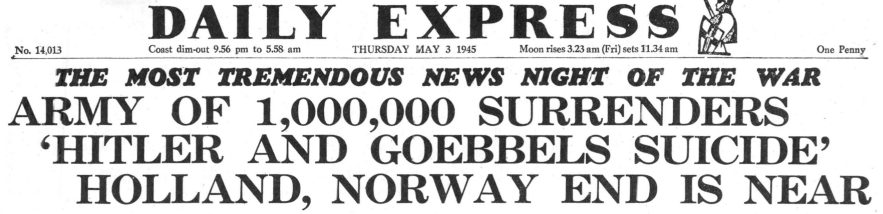

THE MOST TREMENDOUS NEWS NIGHT OF THE WAR

ARMY OF 1,000,000 SURRENDERS
'HITLER AND GOEBBELS SUICIDE'
HOLLAND, NORWAY END IS NEAR

All through last night the most dramatic news of the war was pouring into the Daily Express office, showing that the Nazi resistance is near its end:—

1–The enemy army of 1,000,000 men in Italy and Western Austria surrendered, yielding a vast area of the southern Redoubt.

2–Berlin fell to the Russians. Hitler and Goebbels are reported to have committed suicide.

3–German resistance in Holland was reported over. An early surrender in Norway and Denmark is expected.

4–Large German forces seeking to escape into Denmark have been cut off by a British drive to the Baltic.

Details of these triumphs are given on this page in Daily Express cables from Alaric Jacob, Cyril Ray, Alan Moorehead, Paul Holt, James Wellard, Gordon Young, and E. D. Masterman.

Berlin falls

Nazi boss tells Russians about Fuehrer's fate

From ALARIC JACOB: Moscow, Wednesday night

ADOLF HITLER, Josef Goebbels and General Krebs, newly-appointed German Chief of Staff, killed themselves in the last fortress in the last scene of the last act of the Battle of Berlin, according to a communiqué issued by Marshal Stalin just before midnight.

The authority for the statement is given as Hans Fritsche, Goebbels' deputy and star broadcaster, who talked after he was captured.

No details of the manner of the Nazi leaders' suicide are given. No mention is made of finding the bodies.

But it is most unlikely that Stalin would issue Fritsche's statement in a communiqué unless the Russians had absolute proof.

General opinion in Moscow today was that the Russian commanders would never believe the story of Hitler's death unless they found the body.

Goebbels appears to have made good the pledge he uttered in his last speech, that he would die rather than live under a Bolshevik occupation.

He said his wife and children were with him.

He was 48, the most cunning brain of all the Nazis and Minister of Propaganda and Enlightenment.

But a long list of lesser leaders were captured alive in Berlin today.

In a series of triumphant announcements tonight Stalin revealed that Berlin fell at 3 p.m. and that 70,000 Germans surrendered at the end.

South-east of Berlin a great pocket of Germans was wiped out with more than 60,000 killed and about 120,000 taken prisoner.

Among the chiefs of Berlin's defence who surrendered in the fortress were :—

General Kurt Wettag, General Walter Schliess-Dankwart, Vice-Admiral Voss (Chief of Staff of Berlin's Defence), Colonel Hans Melchior, Chief of Staff of the 56th German Tank Corps, Colonel Theodor von Wissling.

Voss was one of those reported

→ BACK PAGE, COL. SIX

'RESISTANCE IN HOLLAND OVER'

SAN FRANCISCO, Wednesday.—Authoritative sources today said that German resistance in Holland has ended, and that a formal announcement of the Nazi surrender there may be expected at any time.

The same sources forecast an early announcement of a German surrender in Norway and Denmark, but said that operations in those countries have not yet ceased.

4.30 a.m. LATEST

'ANY HOUR NOW'

U.S. broadcaster said on Moscow radio early today : "Complete collapse of German resistance west of Berlin and in Northern Germany can be expected any hour—if it has not already taken place."

BLITZ CHIEF CAPTURED

U.S. SEVENTH ARMY, Wednesday.—Field-Marshal von Sperrle, responsible for London blitz, and Field-Marshal von Weichs, former Baltic C.-in-C., were captured today.—Reuter.

War ends in Italy, most of Redoubt

ALPS MARCH-IN BEGINS

From CYRIL RAY: Allied H.Q., Caserta (near Naples), Wednesday

UNCONDITIONAL SURRENDER OF GERMANY'S SOUTHERN ARMY BEGAN AT NOON TODAY. THE TREMENDOUS NEWS THAT NEARLY A MILLION TROOPS, COVERING THE SOUTHERN REDOUBT IN AUSTRIA, HAD LAID DOWN THEIR ARMS TO FIELD-MARSHAL SIR HAROLD ALEXANDER WAS ANNOUNCED FROM THIS HEADQUARTERS TONIGHT.

This is the greatest unconditional surrender in military history. The Germans have signed away an area of 30,000 square miles, including the Brenner Pass, and Alexander's armies can advance unhindered under the terms of the agreement to the Swiss frontier and to within ten miles of Berchtesgaden.

ON VIENNA ROAD

The territory given up includes all Northern Italy (except Trieste) and the Austrian provinces of Vorarlberg, Tyrol, Salzburg and parts of Carinthia, and Styria, with the cities of Salzburg, Innsbruck and Linz.

And the great march-in to the Alps over the body of an army which for four years has held Italy in thraldom has begun.

It will bring troops of the Mediterranean Command within a few miles of the Russians west of Vienna. Red Army officers were present at the signing of the surrender in the Royal Palace of Caserta.

Only time separates Alexander's armies from those of Generals Patton and Patch in Bavaria and Northern Austria. German "cease fire" radio orders were being sent out tonight.

The surrender was signed on Sunday, one day after the death of Mussolini, one day before the reported death of Hitler.

HIMMLER MAN SIGNED

It was signed not only on behalf of the German commanders, but also most significantly by Himmler's great collaborator and ex-chief of his personal staff, S.S. General Karl Wolff. In other words, Himmler's associate acted on his chief's orders before Doenitz gave the counter-order to continue the fight.

Here is the text of the special communique :—

Enemy land, sea and air forces, commanded by General Vietinghoff-Scheel have surrendered unconditionally to Field-Marshal Sir Harold Alexander.

The terms of the surrender provide for the cessation of hostilities at 12 noon G.M.T. Wednesday, May 2, 1945.

The instrument of surrender was signed on Sunday afternoon, April 29, at Allied Force Headquarters at

BACK PAGE, COL. FIVE

FRANCO ARRESTS LAVAL

From D. J. ROBERTSON

MADRID, Wednesday.—Laval and his wife were arrested tonight in Barcelona after landing at the airfield in a Junkers 88.

Following representations by the American Ambassador, Mr. Norman Armour, Franco ordered Laval to leave at once. He refused.

Now he is interned in the Montjuich fortress pending the Spanish Government's final decision.

He is said to have asked for trial by an international tribune.

The American Consul at Barcelona informed Mr. Armour of Laval's arrival. He went to the Foreign Office and protested. The Foreign Minister, Lequerica, telephoned Franco.

Franco instructed Barcelona to give the plane enough petrol to take the craft to the nearest frontier, escorted by Spanish fighters.

With Laval were four Vichyites. They were flown by German pilots.

Laval tried several times in the past week to enter Switzerland or the pocket principality of Liechtenstein, but both refused him.

Petain's wife to be tried

PARIS, Wednesday.—Mme. Petain, who is 67, was told today that she is to be tried on charges of intelligence with the enemy. She protested vigorously and said that she had never taken any interest in politics.—Express News Service.

Portugal mourns

Hitler reaction yesterday :—

Two days' mourning were ordered by the Portuguese Government, with flags at half-mast.

Mr. de Valera, Eire Premier, last night called on the German Minister to express condolences. But Eire flags were at top mast.

Hotting up

Straits : Warmer.

The Surrender—in Italy

END of war in Italy. Representatives of all branches of the armed forces of Britain and America gather at one end of a long, polished table in the Royal Palace of Caserta. In the centre of the group—white-haired General Morgan, empowered by Field-Marshal Alexander to sign the unconditional surrender terms accepted by the Germans. The German plenipotentiaries, dressed in check sports coats and flannels, stand at the other end of the table. [illegible] holds the surrender document.

BRITON GETS INTO DENMARK

From GORDON YOUNG

First British reporter to enter Denmark since 1940.

DENMARK, Wednesday.—I am writing this despatch in a little house in a Danish town where gay red and white flags are hanging from the windows.

The wonderful young men of the Danish underground brought me here by their courier service today, but all I can say about the trip is that it is astonishing what they get away with.

After what seemed like an eternity tossing about in a small boat on a dark, cold sea, I stumbled ashore on to Danish soil and was guided by tall, shadowy figures through the complete black-out of the coast.

When we reached this house we entered by dimmed torchlight, and not until my host had made certain that the black-out was complete did he turn on the lights and make the introductions.

What seems to have been happening here is this : The Germans have moved from a number of provincial towns, but in others they have been ordered to stand firm.

In Copenhagen the Gestapo and S.S. troops are carrying on as usual, though large numbers of men have been moved to barracks outside the city.

Gen. Boehme on the phone

From E. D. MASTERMAN

STOCKHOLM, Wednesday.—Seeking to check reports that General Boehme, the German C.-in-C. in Norway, had left Oslo, I put in a telephone call to him today, saying I was a Daily Express reporter.

After a few minutes I heard a voice saying, "Hello. This is General Boehme. What do you want to know?"

"I want to know whether it is true that German troops are making preparations to leave Norway."

"If that is what you want to know, I can tell you——" Then his voice faded out. Obviously someone—probably Doenitz's Gestapo—severed the line.

After a few minutes a voice said : "Please hold the line. The general will be back at once." But he never came back.

Doenitz has called all German commanders to swear allegiance to him, but only Lindemann in Denmark, and Boehme in Norway, have responded.

Doenitz's Kiel hope vanishing

From ALAN MOOREHEAD

MONTGOMERY'S H.Q., Wednesday. — The news pouring in today makes it obvious that the hopes of Doenitz setting up a bastion in the north are vanishing every hour.

Both Himmler and Doenitz are reported tonight to be in the Danish peninsula, but the British have today raced across to Lubeck and cut it at its base.

The British and the Americans have completely paralysed this corner of Germany.

They have taken 5,000, perhaps 6,000, prisoners; nearly 100 guns and tanks, 1,000 vehicles.

The Germans had been fleeing back to Denmark. But now, within a few days or even hours, more mass surrenders are likely.

From the air, from the leading ground scouts, the messages are all the same—"The scene is chaotic, everything is breaking up."

Quarrel

In Denmark, it seems clear, Himmler and Doenitz are running rival camps. It was Doenitz who got to the Hamburg radio first and announced the death of Hitler and his own succession.

Yet Himmler was known to be in Hamburg a few days ago, and Hamburg is—or was until last Monday—the headquarters of the German S.S., Himmler's own corps.

Something must have happened between Doenitz and Himmler in the past four days.

Obviously Doenitz knew of Himmler's negotiations with the Allies. He must have opposed them and decided to seize control himself. And tonight he is said to be in Kiel preparing for a final stand.

Denmark is an obvious place to defend—a long, winding peninsula, with many islands and sea bases, a broad canal cutting its base and an untouched reservoir of Nazi divisions.

The German Navy alone has any real morale left. Most of its remaining craft have fled up to the harbours of Denmark and Schleswig Holstein.

All bewildered

Something like 13 army divisions are located there.

Senior German officers we have been capturing in the past 24 hours, say Denmark is the last Nazi hope. Like everyone else in the German army, they are bewildered by the rush of events, they cannot make out the details of the row between Doenitz and Himmler, but they think that anything that Doenitz tries to do by way of a protracted stand will be futile.

The general attitude seems to be "There is no-one left. Hitler, Goering, Rundstedt—all gone. So what is the use of carrying on? The Hitler Youth may carry on for a bit, but everyone knows it is hopeless."

Somone advances the idea that Doenitz and the navy are determined to wipe out the shame of the naval revolt in 1918 by being the last to surrender this time.

Germans trapped on rush to Denmark

From PAUL HOLT: Montgomery's H.Q., Wednesday

AFTER lunch today British armour and airborne infantry finished a motor ride of over 50 miles and came up at the Baltic coast in two places and completely sealed off Schleswig-Holstein and Denmark.

Tanks of the 11th Armoured Division reached Lubeck, where Count Bernadotte saw Himmler last week, without firing a shot and in time for tea.

This afternoon further east along the Baltic coast, British Sixth Airborne Division jeeps entered the port of Wismar, where they are only 30 miles away from the Red Army, who today captured Rostock. The British-Soviet link-up is expected in a matter of hours.

It has been a day of complete fantasy, and from the delirious reports coming to these headquarters all the afternoon these hard facts emerge :—

Three strong strands of the British Second Army have lopped off Schleswig-Holstein and Denmark from Germany.

Inside the area—a rough triangle between Lubeck, Wismar and Schwerin—there has been no fighting today, but every road, country lane and cart track is a solid mass of German columns fleeing from Germany towards Denmark.

All yesterday and today the 83rd Group of Typhoons and Spitfires have been "Falaising" this rout with grim result. So packed are the roads with refugees and marching Allied prisoners of war that no pilot has been allowed to strike without first going down low once for sure identification.

No horse-drawn or pedestrian traffic has been touched. Yet in the few hours of good flying weather yesterday and today 1,500 motor transport vehicles have been surely blitzed.

BIG HAUL

Where are these Germans going? Away from the Russians and into Denmark. They do not know that their escape route into the northern redoubt has been cut three times today. Tomorrow's prisoner bag will be huge.

Twice today pilots came across long marching columns of R.A.F. prisoners of war. The columns smartly halted on the roads and formed themselves into the shape of the letters RAF.

Hundreds swim Elbe to surrender

From JAMES WELLARD: Ninth Army, Wednesday

WHAT has happened in Italy, Austria and on other fronts is being repeated today and tonight on the Ninth Army front, where the German collapse has reached chaotic proportions.

German soldiers are swimming the Elbe in hundreds to surrender to the Americans as the Russians close in behind them.

Everywhere along the Elbe hundreds of thousands of German soldiers and civilians are pressing down to the banks, waving white flags.

The Russians, surging on in tidal wave proportions, have made still another contact with the Americans at Balow, on the Elbe, where they exchanged patrols with the U.S 84th Division.

German planes are landing on American airfields. Three came down today in the 16th Corps zone. The pilots asked only to see their families before being led away to prison cages.

Giles Romilly escapes

U.S. 7TH ARMY, Wednesday.—Giles Romilly, nephew of Mr. Winston Churchill, has reached the U.S. 6th Army in Bavaria after escaping from a prison camp.

Romilly, a member of the Daily Express staff, was captured when the Germans took Narvik.

UNION JACK

SPECIAL EDITION

Thursday, May 3, 1945 • • • No. 478 Two Lire

A Million Of The Enemy Lay Down Arms

FULL SURRENDER OF NAZIS IN ITALY

ALTHOUGH fighting continues in other parts of Europe, the entire enemy forces in Italy have surrendered unconditionally to the Allies under Field-Marshal Alexander. This triumphant end to the campaign was announced last evening.

Hostilities ceased at 14.00 Italian time yesterday, when nearly a million of the enemy laid down their arms in the surrender area, which includes part of Austria.

The Italian campaign, which began with Montgomery's landing at the base of the peninsula in September 1943, has thus resulted in the first mass surrender of a complete German front.

The grand climax came after the great break-through to the Po Valley by the Fifth and Eighth Armies, aided in their sweeping advance by Italian Partisans. In three weeks the German defending forces were torn to pieces. The last act is described in this special communique from AFHQ:

Enemy land, sea and air forces commanded by Col.-Gen. Heinrich von Vietinghoff-Scheel, German C-in-C S W and C-in-C Army Group "C," have surrendered unconditionally to Field-Marshal Sir Harold Alexander, Supreme Allied Commander, Mediterranean Theatre of operations.

The terms of surrender provided for the cessation of hostilities at 12 noon GMT Wednesday, May 2, 1945.

The instrument of surrender was signed on Sunday afternoon, April 29, at AFHQ Caserta, by two German plenipotentiaries and by Lt.-Gen. W. D. Morgan, Chief of Staff, AFHQ.

One German representative signed on behalf of Gen. Von Vietinghoff and the other on behalf of Ober-grupenfuehrer Karl Wolff, Supreme Commander of SS and Police and German General Plenipotentiary of the Wehrmacht in Italy.

After signing the document of unconditional surrender the two German plenipotentiaries returned by secret route to Gen. Von Vietinghoff's HQ in the High Alps to arrange surrender of the German and Italian Fascist land, air and naval forces.

Territory under Gen. Von Vietinghoff's South - Western Command includes all Northern Italy to the Isonzo River in the north-east, and the Austrian provinces of Vorarlberg, Tyrol, Salzburg and portions of Carinthia and Styria.

The enemy's total forces, including combat and rear echelon troops surrendered to the Allies, are estimated to number 1,000,000 men. The fighting troops include the remnants of

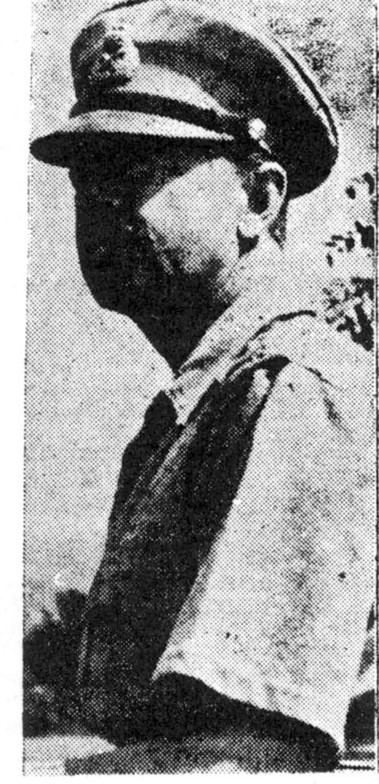

22 German and six Italian Fascist Divisions.

The instrument of surrender consists of six short paragraphs. Three appendices giving details appertaining to land, sea and air forces were attached to the instrument. The following terms are imposed :

1. Unconditional surrender by the German C.-in-C. South-West of all forces under his command or control on land, on sea, or in the air, to the Supreme Allied Commander Mediterranean Theatre of Operations.
2. Cessation of all hostilities on land, on sea or in the air by enemy forces at 1200 hrs. GMT, May 2, 1945.
3. The immediate immobilisation and disarmament of enemy ground, sea and air forces.
4. Obligation on the part of the German C.-in-C. South-West to carry out any further orders issued by the Supreme Allied Commander Mediterranean Theatre.
5. Disobedience of orders or failure to comply with them to be dealt with in accordance with the accepted laws and usages of war.

The instrument of surrender stipulates that it is independent of, without prejudice to, and will be superseded by any general instrument of surrender imposed by or on behalf of the United Nations and applicable to Germany and the German Armed Forces as a whole.

The instrument of surrender and appendices were written in English and German. The English version is the authentic text. The decision of the Supreme Allied Commander Mediterranean Theatre will be final if any doubt or dispute arises as to the meaning or interpretation of the surrender terms.

The signing took place in

(Continued on Page Four)

Special Orders Of The Day

Special Orders of the Day were issued by the Allied commanders in Italy to mark the surrender.

From Field-Marshal Sir Harold ALEXANDER, Supreme Allied Commander, Mediterranean Theatre :

SOLDIERS, sailors and airmen of the Allied Forces in the Mediterranean Theatre :

After nearly two years of hard and arduous fighting, which started in Sicily in the summer of 1943, you stand today as the victors of the Italian campaign

You have won a victory which has ended in the complete and utter rout of the German armed forces in the Mediterranean. By clearing Italy of the last Nazi aggressor you have liberated a country of over 40,000,000 people. Today the remnants of a once proud army have laid down their arms to you—close on a million men, with all their arms, equipment and impedimenta.

You may well be proud of this great and victorious campaign which will long live in history as one of the greatest and most successful ever waged. No praise is too high for you soldiers, sailors, airmen and workers of the United Forces in Italy for your magnificent triumph.

My gratitude to you and my admiration is unbounded, and only equalled by the pride which is mine in being your Commander-in-Chief.

From Gen. Joseph T. McNARNEY, Deputy Supreme Allied Commander, Mediterranean Theatre:

THE enemy in Italy has surrendered unconditionally.

Your magnificent victories in the spring offensive left him only two alternatives, to surrender or to die.

This hour is the glorious climax to one of the greatest triumphs in the long, hard-fought war in Africa and in Europe. Your triumph will live always in the hearts and minds of our people. The attack against the enemy's so-called inner fortress began in the Mediterranean. You have come from Alamein and from Casablanca to the Alps. After the successes in North Africa you smashed the enemy in Tunisia. You drove him from Sicily. You invaded Italy, and despite ferocious resistance and incredibly difficult terrain and weather you drove him back, always back. You have destroyed the best troops he possessed. At this moment of surrender he is against the Alps, helpless under your blows to defend himself.

The victory is yours—you of the ground, sea and air forces of many nationalities who have fought hard as a single combat team The surrender today is to you.

Now, with final and complete victory in sight, let us go forward until the last foe. Japan, is crushed. Then, and not till then, will freedom-loving men and women be able to enjoy lasting peace

From Gen. Mark W. CLARK, Commanding General, 15 Army Group:

TO the soldiers of the 15 Army Group : With a full and grateful heart I hail and congratulate you in this hour of complete victory over the German enemy and join with you in thanks to Almighty God.

Yours has been a long hard fight—the longest in the war of any Allied troops fighting on the continent of Europe. You men of the Fifth and Eighth Armies have brought that fight to a successful conclusion by your recent brilliant offensive operation,

(Continued on Page Three)

FALL OF BERLIN

Great news also came from Germany itself last night. Marshal Stalin announced the capture of Berlin and vast numbers of prisoners in a complete rout of the garrison. (See Page 4.)

Daily Mirror (MAY 4)

Friday, May 4, 1945
No. 12,908 ONE PENNY
Registered at G.P.O. as a Newspaper.

RAF attack "die-hard armada" making for Norway redoubt

500,000 MORE—HUN COLLAPSE IN REICH COMPLETE

Hamburg's radio now gives out OUR orders to Germans

IN Hamburg last night the British commander was using the German radio to broadcast "standstill" orders to the Nazi troops in the fallen city.

The German radio programme had ended in a "good bye" to listeners and a last "Deutschland Uber Alles" as the British Seventh Armoured Division — the "Desert Rats"—were marching in triumph into the city.

Hamburg, Germany's greatest port, had fallen to the British without a shot being fired. The German commander, General Wolff, declared it an open city, the first to be so declared by the Germans in this war.

With the Union Jack flying over the British Army's biggest prize since D-Day, the Desert Rats' commander took charge.

"No member of the German Wehrmacht is to leave the town," he ordered over the radio. "All must remain in their positions to await further orders.

Germans Rejoiced

"No motor-cars or other vehicles can leave the town. There must be no destruction of bridges or other installations.

"German commanders are responsible for the discipline of their units."

And Hamburg rejoiced at its own downfall.

The beer halls were full and the inhabitants appeared to be enthusiastic about the death of Hitler, which freed them from their oath.

Later the British commander imposed a curfew on the city, ordered all the population except employees at the electricity stations and waterworks, to stay in their homes.

The Germans surrendered Hamburg after the garrison realised that they had no hope of holding out after the first British patrols had reached the city.

Now the German Army is queueing to give themselves up.

Haw-Haw's talk—by another voice

Haw-Haw's daily feature on the German radio, "Views on the News," was broadcast last night by an unknown announcer.

How we met Russians

The first British-Russian link-up took place east of Wismar, and while our troops and the Red Army men were shaking hands, German prisoners were walking by—looking very scared.

Troops of the British Sixth Airborne Division broke into cheers when they saw the first Russian tank rumbling towards them. Then British and Russians ran towards each other.

General Boles, commander of the division, met the commander of the Russian tanks.

British troops are nearly into Denmark

LAST NIGHT DIE-HARD NAZIS HELD ONLY A FEW SQUARE MILES OF GERMAN SOIL ON WHICH THEY COULD STAGE SUICIDE BATTLES. ALMOST ALL THEIR ARMIES IN THE REICH HAD BEEN SMASHED BEYOND RECOVERY.

In the north hundreds of thousands of troops were stumbling, a broken mob, in a mass surrender to the British Second Army. In twenty-four hours at least 500,000 have given themselves up—a tremendous revenge for Dunkirk. This does not include the garrison of Hamburg, which surrendered yesterday.

The collapse in North Germany following the crack-up in Italy and Western Austria produced the surrender of 1,500,000 Huns in less than thirty-six hours.

Whatever German forces still in being are in Holland, Denmark, Czechoslovakia—and Norway. The situation regarding these pockets last night was:—

NORWAY.—RAF pilots yesterday sighted about 250 ships, including U-boats and sailing ships, making for Norway from Denmark. This armada of die-hards was protected only by two single-engined fighter planes.

The RAF pounced. Rockets sank ship after ship, some in the open sea and some in harbours. One 10,000-ton ship was left ablaze in Lubeck Bay (Germany).

Prague "Hospital City"

DENMARK.—The British Second Army has crossed the Kiel Canal, natural barrier to Denmark. Our guns are shelling Flensburg aerodrome, on the German side of the frontier. Situation inside Denmark is obscure. Swedish sources say the Danish police have been told to remain "underground" for the present.

HOLLAND.—New York radio announced surrender negotiations.

CZECHOSLOVAKIA.—"Fuehrer" Doenitz declared Prague, centre of this redoubt, a "hospital city," and announced a political reshuffle indicating the collapse of this redoubt.

Apart from the big news, there was a mass of reports from many sectors of the front underlining the salient fact—the Wehrmacht in Germany is finished.

Judging by their latest broadcasts, the Bremen and Wilhelmshaven radios, which sent out the same programme, may be under Allied control.

They said that until further notice news in German would be broadcast at 5 p.m., 8 p.m., 10 p.m. and midnight, and news in English would be broadcast at 8.30 p.m.

Two items broadcast by Wilhelmshaven were: The

Continued on Back Page

Through the mob came a lorry with boys of the old BEF

A GERMAN lorry with an inscription which told a story in five words forced its way through the milling mob of panic-stricken Germans which clogged the roads in Germany yesterday.

The words chalked on its side were: "Some of the original BEF."

Other German lorries, Volkswagens and private cars carrying Allied prisoners were labelled "RAF P.O.W.s" or "Aussies from Tobruk."

Military police sorting out the traffic jams gave these men from the prison camps priority to quicken their journey to the Elbe and home.

Smashed fighting vehicles—tanks and guns—lie everywhere.

German Generals, Red Cross nurses and civilians crushed into any sort of transport like sardines or clinging to the sides like flies, are moving westward seeking refuge from the Russians inside the Allied lines.

As one British officer put it yesterday: "We are taking prisoners by the acre."

There are fifty generals among the fleeing forces, whose number is estimated at between 100,000 and 250,000.

"We don't know where our men are," they said. "They are like chaff before the Russian tornado."

German troops and civilians alike say: "Now that Berlin has fallen the war is over."

German soldiers try to barter with the refugees for civilian clothing, offering money and their last stocks of food. Others have plundered villages and barns.

The fields are black with German troops who forsook the cluttered roads and are tramping through the meadows and ploughed fields which are already strewn with weapons.

Red Cross convoys with large numbers of wounded are

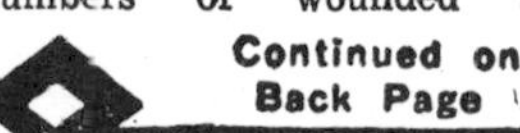
Continued on Back Page

GOING HOME

Men of the Sixth South African Armoured Division now in Italy are to return home as soon as transport is available, the South African Defence Department announces as they will not be required for garrison duties.

ITALIANS ASKING FOR MORE ROOM

Italian youths were busy yesterday pasting posters on walls all over the centre of Rome demanding that Italy should keep the Adriatic ports of Trieste and Fiume, the whole of Istria and the port of Zara.

All these territories are claimed by Marshal Tito for our Ally, Yugoslavia.

News Chronicle

No. 30,879 SATURDAY, MAY 5, 1945 ONE PENNY

LATE LONDON EDITION

MONTY'S JOB DONE

Britain's land war ends today in N.W. Germany, Holland, Denmark

CEASE FIRE AT 8 a.m.: OVER 1,000,000 GERMANS YIELD

FOR NORTH-WEST GERMANY, FOR HOLLAND, FOR DENMARK, THE WAR IS OVER. AT 6.10 LAST NIGHT THE GERMANS IN THESE AREAS SURRENDERED UNCONDITIONALLY TO FIELD-MARSHAL MONTGOMERY'S 21st ARMY GROUP H.Q.

SHORTLY AFTER EIGHT O'CLOCK SUPREME H.Q. ANNOUNCED:

"FIELD-MARSHAL MONTGOMERY HAS REPORTED TO THE SUPREME ALLIED COMMANDER THAT ALL ENEMY FORCES IN HOLLAND, NORTH-WEST GERMANY AND DENMARK, INCLUDING HELIGOLAND AND THE FRISIAN ISLANDS, HAVE SURRENDERED TO THE 21st ARMY GROUP, EFFECTIVE 0800 HOURS D.B.S.T. TOMORROW.

"THIS IS A BATTLEFIELD SURRENDER INVOLVING THE FORCES NOW FACING THE 21st ARMY GROUP ON THEIR NORTHERN AND WESTERN FLANKS."

THE FORCES INVOLVED NUMBER WELL OVER 1,000,000, OF WHICH A QUARTER ARE NAVAL PERSONNEL—THE BIGGEST GERMAN SURRENDER SINCE NOVEMBER, 1918.

THERE NOW REMAINS TO BE CLEARED IN THE NORTH AND WEST THE CHANNEL ISLANDS, THE POCKETS ON THE FRENCH COAST AND NORWAY.

LAST NIGHT A NORWEGIAN QUISLING LEADER BROADCAST AN APPEAL FOR CALM AND ORDER TO PREVENT NORWAY FROM BECOMING A BATTLEFIELD.

"WITH THIS END IN VIEW," HE SAID, "WE ARE PREPARED TO COLLABORATE WITH ALL FORCES WILLING TO DO SO."

MONTY TELLS THE GERMANS

Field-Marshal Montgomery in a tent at his headquarters on Thursday tells the German surrender delegates there were no "terms." He told them to return yesterday with unconditional surrender. They did. *More pictures Back Page*

Monty told other armies: yield to Soviets

AT last it has come, the great surrender that marks the end of the road which has led from Libya through Tunisia, Sicily, Italy and France to North Germany and the Baltic.

And this was the manner of its coming.

The story is told by Bill Downs, C.B.S. correspondent, broadcasting last night from Germany. These are his words:

The signing took place in a weather-beaten camp set up especially for the ceremony. In the words of Field-Marshal Montgomery, as he walked to the tent where the official signing took place, and grimly commented to the reporters, "This is the moment."

On Wednesday, May 2, Gen. Blumentritt, commander of the so-called "Army Group Blumentritt," hoisted a white flag and sent an emissary to the British Second Army.

He said he commanded all the forces between the Baltic and the Weser River and wanted to surrender his army group.

Gen. Dempsey replied that he should start moving, and a rendezvous was arranged for yesterday.

FIELD OF SURRENDER

The surrender was signed at an H.Q. set up by Field-Marshal Montgomery at the German Army training ground on the Luneberg Heath, south of Hamburg.

Gen. Blumentritt did not appear yesterday, but sent word that negotiations were going on at a much higher level than his military station. He could not negotiate.

It was yesterday that a forward party of four higher military officials again hoisted a white flag and drove into the British lines.

The head of the party was Gen.-Admiral von Freideberg, C.-in-C. of the German Navy, who replaced Admiral Doenitz when the latter assumed the title of Fuehrer.

Von Freideberg's rank also carried the title of General of the Army; thus he was able to negotiate for the ground forces as well.

With von Freideberg was Gen. Kienzl, the next ranking officer, who was Chief of Staff to Field-Marshal Busch, who is commander of the Northern German Army.

Next came Rear-Admiral Wagner, the staff officer to von Freideberg, and lastly Major Frieder, a staff officer to Gen. Kienzl. This was the party which helped to negotiate with Field-Marshal Montgomery.

They were taken to Field-Marshal Montgomery's field H.Q. on the Luneberg Heath. He stepped out, returned their military salute and asked: "What do you want?"

THREE ARMIES OFFERED

The Germans replied: "We come here from Field-Marshal Busch to ask you to accept the surrender of three German armies which are now withdrawing in front of the Russians in the Mecklenburg area."

These three armies, it was later revealed, were the Third Panzer Army, the German 12th Army, and the 21st Army.

"No," he said, "certainly not. Those German armies

Continued Back Page A

The defeated and the liberated trail west

From S. L. SOLON
News Chronicle War Correspondent

WITH THE RUSSIAN FORCES ON THE BALTIC, Friday.

IF you can imagine the chaotic retreat of Napoleon's army from Moscow, coupled with mass evacuation of civilians fleeing from the Mississippi Valley in flood-time, all this against a background of earthquake disaster and wreckage, you will have some picture of what we are observing in these delirious hours.

No emotion, no anguish, no gratification and no crime are absent in this panorama of victory and defeat, in which one is swirling as in a whirlpool.

Down the road come the endless trail of covered waggons, pails and household utensils dangling from the axles, children long since weary of the adventure of sleeping with heads bounding against furniture and crates stored in the back.

Mothers, bleary-eyed and frightened, are walking behind the waggons, shrinking back at the curt summons to clear the road as military vehicles roar by.

THE ROAD WEST

Thousands upon thousands of German soldiers are making their way westward, the trail of discarded equipment and personal gear along the roads marking the rising tide of exhaustion and demoralisation.

Then there are the great crowds of the liberated—our men, British, Americans, Canadians, French, Russians, Poles, Belgians—they are all there by the multitude—and it is in their faces, their pinched but happy faces, that the difference can be told.

For most of them are wearing a motley garb that might have been drawn at random from the props of a stock theatre—top hats, fancy waistcoats, comic opera uniforms.

THE GHOST WALKS

And sometimes through this great parade of the defeated, the homeless, the liberated, and the conquerors—for in this crushing traffic that extends mile upon mile our military vehicles must inevitably take their turn—there sometimes walks the skeleton figure of a political prisoner from one of the horror camps, unmistakable in his hunger and his weird, striped-flannel prison garb.

Even in liberty he has had to escape, for now the camps are sealed to prevent the spread of disease, and only authorised transfers are being allowed.

Continued Back Page B

Horthy writes

In the Swabian Jura, Friday.

ADMIRAL HORTHY, former Regent of Hungary, who was taken into protective custody by the U.S. Seventh Army on Sunday, told a group of war correspondents today that he planned to write to President Truman to ask that Hungary be represented at the peace conference.

Bus strike may end

The London transport strikers may return to work tomorrow, a representative of the Central Bus Committee of the Transport and General Workers' Union stated last night.

Branch meetings of the bus, tram and trolley sections of the union were attended last night by delegates from the committee, who recommended the resumption of work without delay.

IF NAZIS HIDE WITH NEUTRALS

Use force, declares 1 in 2

THE British public are resolved that we should try to get hold of all the Nazi leaders. Even if they try to take refuge in neutral countries the public consider we should go after them there.

These views are held by 94 per cent. of men and women throughout England, Scotland and Wales, as was revealed in the latest Gallup Poll in which was asked:

"If a neutral country gives refuge to Nazi leaders, should the Allies try to get hold of the Nazi leaders?"

Only 4 per cent. said "No," the remaining 2 per cent. being uncertain.

★

"What should the Allies do to try to get hold of the leaders?" was further asked of those who said that we should try to get hold of them.

50 per cent. said "Use force."

20 per cent. said "Use diplomatic pressure."

17 per cent. said "Use economic pressure."

15 per cent. said "Try persuasion."

(The total is more than 100 because some people made more than one reply.)

When a similar inquiry was made recently by the Gallup Poll in Canada the large majority agreed with the British, that the Allies should get hold of any Nazi leaders from neutral countries.

[British Institute of Public Opinion; World Copyright Reserved.]

Allied air power

From JAN YINDRICH

U.S. SEVENTH ARMY, Friday.

FIELD-MARSHAL VON RUNDSTEDT, in an interview today, attributed Germany's defeat firstly to "terrific" Allied air superiority.

This prevented the railways from operating and made the movement of troops with sufficient speed impossible.

Asked if he would agree that the basic reason for Germany losing the war was the attack on Russia, he replied: "It is hard to say. If the Russians had attacked us it would have been the same story."

He was asked why the German Army turned against Russian instead of England.

"No attempt was made in strength to invade England," he replied, "but a plan was drawn up and preparations made. It was then decided that it was impossible."

R.A.F. put 150 German ships out of action

IN their greatest week since their formation squadrons of Air Marshal Coningham's R.A.F. 2nd T.A.F. played a great part in bringing about the surrender of the German forces in Holland, Denmark and North-West Germany.

Germans fleeing from the Russians and British created a tremendous traffic jam in the Schleswig-Holstein peninsula.

Most of the troops were trapped, but some attempted a "Dunkirk" to Denmark and Norway from the Western Baltic ports.

Every available fighter and fighter-bomber was thrown in against the mass of road transport and shipping, which ranged from an obsolete battleship and luxury liners to tugs and sailing ships.

Massacre

It was a massacre.

Using rockets, bombs and cannon shells, aircraft of Second Tactical Air Force in the last five days put out of action 150 ships, including many U-boats, which were probably trying to get to Norway, destroyed or damaged 4,500 road transport, shot down 116 enemy aircraft, and put out of action 100 on the ground.

It was the greatest "kill" in such a short period since D-Day.

In addition one of the largest strike forces R.A.F. Coastal Command has ever dispatched against enemy shipping yesterday continued the great attack which the Command began on Thursday on ships attempting to escape from Kiel.

Enemy 'thoroughly whipped'

—EISENHOWER

Supreme H.Q., Friday.

IN a proclamation made available here tonight Gen. Eisenhower stated:

"The German forces on the Western Front have disintegrated. Today, what is left of two German armies surrendered to a single American division—the 102nd—commanded by Maj.-Gen. Frank Keating.

"Any further losses the Germans incur are due to their failure instantly to quit. They know they are beaten. Any further hesitation is due to their own stupidity or that of the German Government.

"On land, sea and in the air the Germans have been thoroughly whipped. Their only recourse is to surrender."

French ask Spain for Laval

Paris, Friday.—The French Cabinet decided today to send a Note to the Spanish Government demanding the extradition of Laval and other members of his party.

Laval is being held strictly incommunicado

"Haw Haw" fled to Denmark

Hamburg Radio Station, Friday.

WILLIAM JOYCE ("Lord Haw-Haw") left for Denmark by car on Wednesday night, said the chief censor at this radio station. The other British radio quislings joined the convoy. British troops missed them by 12 hours.

Joyce's "Views on the News" scripts—there are dozens of them—are here, all signed "William Joyce."

There are up-to-date copies of every British national newspaper—and a book, "Jewish Influence in British Life."—Reuter.

LATE NEWS

3,000 FREED IN BERCHTESGADEN

Shaef, Friday.—Between 3,000 and 4,000 British and American officers liberated from German prison camp in Berchtesgaden area.

Moon sets, 12.47 a.m.; rises 4.33 a.m. tomorrow. New Moon, May 11

Sunday Graphic
No. 1,570 (E) SUNDAY, MAY 6, 1945 A KEMSLEY NEWSPAPER TWOPENCE

3 MORE GERMAN ARMIES MAKE TOTAL SURRENDER

Norway C.-in-C. Also Reported 'Ready To Capitulate'

FINAL GERMAN CAPITULATION WAS BROUGHT NEARER LAST NIGHT BY THE UNCONDITIONAL SURRENDER OF THREE MORE GERMAN ARMIES.

All three armies fell to the group commanded by General Devers—two to the Americans and one to the French—and with them probably another 400,000 men passed into Allied hands.

At the same time there were unconfirmed reports from Stockholm that General Boehme, Nazi Commander in Norway, had decided to capitulate; that a British military mission had arrived in Oslo; and that Terboven, Nazi Governor in Norway, had resigned.

The day's surrenders in the South—apparently ordered by Kesselring—meant almost an end to the fighting on the American fronts except in Czechoslovakia.

There Patton's Third Army captured the German 11th Panzer Division in a new offensive over a 110-mile front in which they took 12,000 prisoners.

Simultaneously the Russians attacked from the East, while Czech Patriots wirelessed for help, saying German tanks were advancing on Prague.

Despite the Cease Fire at 8 a.m. yesterday, fighting broke out in Denmark, and Copenhagen was shelled.

FULL STORY ON BACK PAGE

SURRENDER

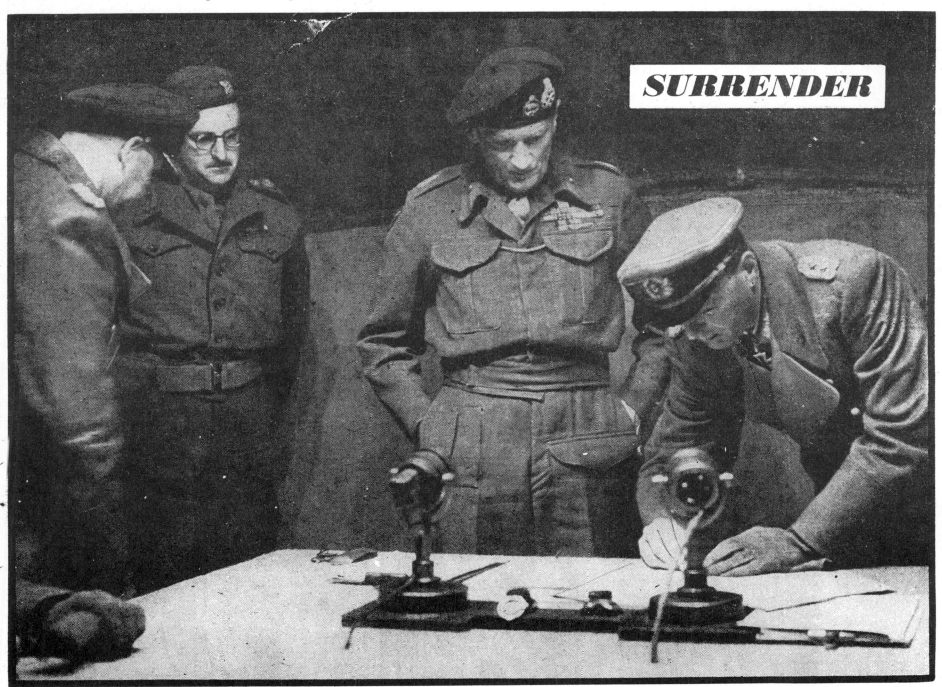

'Sunday Graphic' cameraman Reginald Clough records Field-Marshal Montgomery's greatest triumph as General Kinsel, German plenipotentiary, signs unconditional surrender.—*Full Picture Story and Document on Middle Pages.*

MONDAY, MAY 7, 1945

Closing Prices

LIGHTING-UP TIME 10.32
RADIO, PAGE SIX.

LATE NIGHT

THE STAR

No. 17,743 ** ONE PENNY

DOENITZ ANNOUNCES

COMPLETE SURRENDER

'We Succumbed To Overwhelming Power'

THE WAR IN EUROPE IS OVER. ALL THE GERMAN ARMED FORCES TODAY SURRENDERED UNCONDITIONALLY TO THE ALLIES.

First news that Peace had come was given by Flensburg Radio which has been broadcasting Nazi announcements since the German collapse began.

The broadcast was made by Count Schwerin von Krosigk, Foreign Minister in the Government set up by Doenitz, the new Fuehrer. Krosigk said:

"German Men and Women: The High Command of the Armed Forces has today, at the order of Grand-Admiral Doenitz, declared the unconditional surrender of all fighting German troops. As the leading Minister of the Reich Government, which the Admiral of the Fleet has appointed for dealing with the war tasks, I turn at this tragic moment of our history to the German nation.

"After an heroic fight of almost six years of incomparable hardness, Germany has succumbed to the overwhelming power of her enemies. To continue the war would only mean senseless bloodshed and a futile disintegration. The Government, which has a feeling of responsibility for the future of its nation, was compelled to act on the collapse of all physical and material forces and to demand of the enemy the cessation of hostilities.

"It was the noblest task of the Admiral of the Fleet and of the Government, supporting him after the terrible sacrifices which war demanded, to save in the last phase of the war the lives of a maximum number of fellow-countrymen. That the war was not ended simultaneously in the West and East is to be explained by this reason alone. We end this gravest hour of the German nation and its Reich."

Following Krosigk's statement, the radio said: "You have heard the address of the the Foreign Minister to the German people. We shall repeat this address tonight at 8." Earlier today Danish radio, which is now in Allied hands, had announced the surrender of the Germans in Norway.

CHURCHILL MAY NAME TOMORROW AS VE DAY

Mr. Churchill was expected to announce this evening that the Germans had surrendered fully and unconditionally. It was anticipated that he would name tomorrow as VE Day. The Premier's statement was being accompanied by similar announcements in Washington and Moscow.

Mr. Churchill was announcing the surrender over the radio. Later the King will thank all who have contributed to the victory in Europe. He will ask the people to brace themselves for the final phase of the war with Japan. In Downing-street this afternoon Mr. Churchill presided over a full meeting of the Cabinet, and at the same time telephone calls went on between Whitehall, Washington and Moscow. On Thursday, fifth anniversary of the formation of his Government, Mr. Churchill will make what he hopes will be his first broadcast as Prime Minister in a peace-time Europe.

Got Your Flag?

Encircling movement on an Oxford-street flag-seller in anticipation of the big news.

WE ENTER NAZI NAVAL BASES

THE Polish Armoured Division, who entered the North Sea naval base of Wilhelmshaven, found the port very badly damaged and the German cruiser Koeln in the harbour with her decks awash.

Merchant shipping was also much damaged, says Reuter, from 21st Army Group H.Q. today.

The Third Canadian Division have entered Emden, and the occupation of North West Germany between the Ems and the Weser is reported to be "proceeding satisfactorily."

The first troops of General Crerar's forces to move into Holland crossed the former front line today. The leading section was a reconnaissance unit of the 49th (West Riding) Division.

Prague: Patton 15 Miles Away

A few hours before the announcement of surrender was made, Prague radio—presumably the partisan-controlled transmitter—said that Gen. Patton's U.S. Forces were only 15 miles from the Czech capital.

The radio also said that two Red Armies had linked up 130 miles from Prague.

"Passive resistance," mainly by road blocks, was reported in the Austrian Tyrol.

GOEBBELS'S BODY FOUND?

Reports reaching Moscow today said that the bodies of Goebbels and his family had been found in an air-raid shelter near the Reichstag in Berlin, says Reuter.

BACK HOME IN DENMARK

M. Christmas Moeller, who escaped to Britain with his wife, in May, 1942, and who is Foreign Minister in King Christian's new Danish Cabinet, arrived in Denmark from Britain in a Mosquito plane today, Danish radio reported this afternoon.

King Christian signed preliminary laws at a Cabinet meeting today.

DAILY  NEWS

Copr. 1945 by News Syndicate Co. Inc. NEW YORK'S PICTURE NEWSPAPER Trade Mark Reg. U. S. Pat. Off.

Vol. 26. No. 272 | New York, Tuesday, May 8, 1945★ | 32 Main+8 Brooklyn Pages | 2 Cents IN CITY LIMITS | 3 CENTS Elsewhere

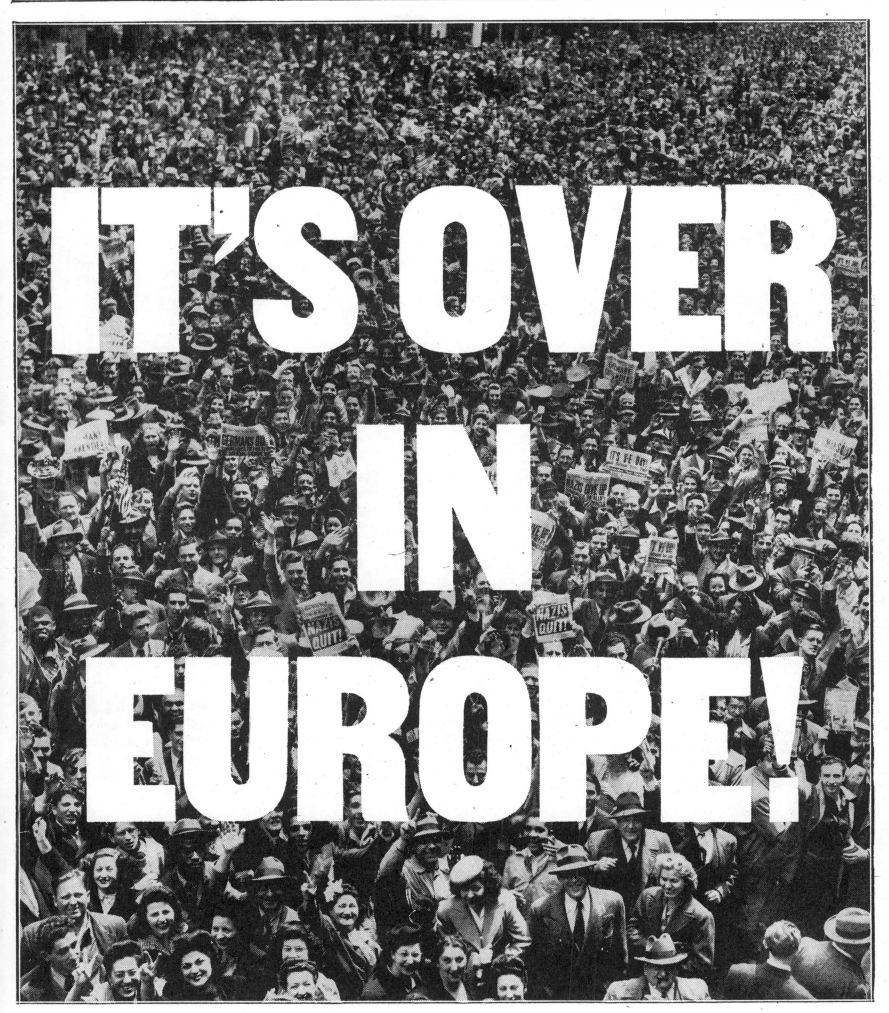

IT'S OVER IN EUROPE!

PROCLAMATION DUE AT 9 A.M.

—Stories on Pages 2 and 3

Daily Mirror

MAY 9

Wednesday, May 9, 1945
No. 12,912 ONE PENNY
Registered at G.P.O. as a Newspaper.

BRITAIN'S DAY OF REJOICING

Cheering their "Winnie"

Dense crowds in Whitehall, estimated by the police at 50,000—all cheering like mad—mobbed the Prime Minister when he emerged from Downing-street after his broadcast speech. With the broad grin of victory on his face—and a new cigar clamped between his teeth—Winston Churchill gave his famous V-sign.

Minute past midnight

THE final total surrender documents were signed by the Germans and the three Allies yesterday IN BERLIN. The Channel Isles were to be freed at once.

Hostilities in Europe ended officially at 12.1 a.m. today.

News Chronicle
No. 30,895 FRIDAY, MAY 25, 1945 ONE PENNY
LATE LONDON EDITION

HIMMLER COMMITS SUICIDE

Took poison at British H.Q.: Unrecognised when arrested

PHIAL OF CYANIDE WAS FASTENED INSIDE HIS MOUTH

From IAN BEVAN, News Chronicle War Correspondent

LUENEBURG, Thcrsday night.

THE body of Heinrich Himmler, one of the last of the Nazi leaders to be run to earth, tonight lies on the bare boards of a front room of a house in Lueneburg.

He committed suicide by taking potassium cyanide shortly before midnight on Wednesday, the day that von Friedeburg had poisoned himself at Flensburg.

HIMMLER

The room where the body is lying is a typical German front parlour, and the usual mass of furniture has been pushed aside while the body lies in the centre.

It is clad only in a torn British army shirt and a pair of grey socks covered with a grey army blanket.

Himmler had been stripped naked for the final medical examination and the search for poison. When an attempt was made to examine his mouth he made a quick movement of the head and bit open a small glass phial containing potassium cyanide. He died within 15 minutes, at four minutes past eleven. The phial had been in his mouth for some hours.

MOUSTACHE SHAVED OFF

I examined the body shortly after it had been viewed by a party of high-ranking Russian officers. The eyes had been shut and glasses, with light tortoise-shell frames, had been placed on the nose. The familiar moutache was missing, as he had shaved it off some days ago in an attempt to disguise himself.

The lips, even in death, were set in a cynical leer. The flabby body betrayed years of good living.

The house where the body is lying, guarded by a British soldier with fixed bayonet, is a semi-detached red brick villa.

It is being used by a defence company as an examination centre for prisoners.

Himmler was first taken into custody on Monday when he tried to cross a bridge at Bremervoerde (45 miles west of Hamburg). A Black Watch guard was on the bridge. Himmler, travelling under the name of Hizinger, had made some atempt at Disguise, including a black patch over the right eye.

He was accompanied by two adjutants, one of whom was a big, burly member of the S.S.

Himmler and his adjutants were on foot and were wearing civilian clothes. The papers which Himmler showed the guard aroused suspicions, and he was detained for investigation.

He was passed to a security camp at Westertimke and then back to another security camp about eight miles from Second Army headquarters.

Final examination

He was still unrecognised, but at this last camp he asked, through one of his aides, for an interview with the camp commandant.

This was granted, and he announced to the commandant: "I am Heinrich Himmler."

The commandant immediately telephoned the chief intelligence officer at army headquarters, who refused to believe the news but came to the camp immediately.

There he was amazed to see a man whom he recognised as Himmler sitting talking to the intterogating officer.

After questioning, Himmler was taken to the house in Lueneburg for a final medical examination.

During the car journey he was noticed to be rubbing his cheek, but this was thought to be merely a nervous mannerism.

At the house the medical officer made a minute examination.

Finally he ordered Himmler to stand under the light in the centre of the room and open his mouth and roll his tongue.

The end

Then the doctor inserted a finger inside the cruel lips and moved it around behind the gums to see is there was anything concealed.

Himmler realised the game was up and made a quick movement of his head.

A small blue spot appeared between his teeth. He bit this and the poison did its fatal work.

I have seen a duplicate of this suicide phial which Himmler must have kept in his mouth from the first detailed search until the end.

It is about half an inch long and a quarter of an inch wide.

It was big enough to kill the man whose life work had been death.

The greatest gangster of them all: See Page Two

Ribbentrop's papers found

South-East Germany, Thursday.—The records of the German Foreign Ministry, including von Ribbentrop's general papers, have been found in a castle 15 miles south of Regensburg.

DOENITZ: THE FINAL SCENE

German naval officer on right is Admiral-Gen. von Friedeburg. An hour after this picture was taken at Flensburg he committed suicide by taking poison. With Friedeburg on one side of a table in the bar of the liner Patria are Grand Admiral Doenitz (centre) and Col.-Gen. Jodl. On the other side of the table are members of the special Shaef mission. Their leader, Maj.-Gen. L. W. Rooks (wearing glasses), is telling the Germans that they were under arrest. Picture below shows the arrest of other members of the Flensburg "Government" They had apparently slept late

De Gaulle's pledge

Family grants in France

IN a broadcast over Paris radio last night Gen. de Gaulle said:

"We all knew that it would be not enough for the guns to be silent in Europe for all the difficulties and damages of the past to come to an end."

Urging "a population policy" for France, Gen. de Gaulle said that families must be aided and immigration must be regulated.

He promised that by the end of 1945 the French Provisional Government would:

1. Make decisions which would "organically place in the hands of the State, for the exclusive benefit of the nation," two key industries —coal and electricity—and also the control of credit.

2. Reorganise its administration to enable it to solve modern problems.

Price control

Gen. de Gaulle gave a warning that it was absolutely necessary to control prices and wages to avoid a dangerous spiral leading to inflation and the ruin of the French currency.

The Government would maintain the firm stand already taken in fixing prices and wages. [This was a reference to steps taken in the past few days to fix prices of food, especially of fruit and vegetables, by a daily schedule of prices in the wholesale markets.]

The "harbour is in sight," he declared. "Let us be united. A magnificent future awaits France."

General Strike in France averted

Paris, Thursday.—The threat of a general strike as a sequel to the Government's decision on Tuesday to take a firm stand against the demands of the C.G.T. (French T.U.C.) for a further rise in wages appears to be over, at least for the time being.

The strike order, which it was intended to issue today, has been withdrawn.

M. Benoit Frachon, one of the secretaries of the C.G.T., said tonight: "We consider that the demand for an increase from 20frs. (2s.) an hour to 23frs. is fully justified and feasible.

"We shall now plead our cause in the National Consultative Assembly."

This increase of three francs an hour was one of the demands the Government flatly refused.

Petain trial will start in June

The trial of Marshal Petain will probably begin on June 15, M. Francois de Menthon, French Minister of Justice, said yesterday, according to the French radio. M. Marcel Deat, former Vichy Minister, will be tried in his absence at the beginning of June.

Fine

Today's forecast for London and S.E. England:

Wind west or variable, light; fine; rather warm.

Further outlook: Fair.

German cruisers at Wilhelmshaven

SHAEF, Thursday.

The German cruisers Prinz Eugen and Nuremberg have sailed from Copenhagen to Wilhelmshaven because Copenhagen is a commercial port with few naval facilities.

Wilhelmshaven is a naval base with every necessary installation and no flow of mercantile traffic. There the Allies will be able to look after the prize warships more easily, and will be able to keep them in better condition than in Copenhagen.

When Labour may want Left unity

LASKI APPEALS TO CONFERENCE

"Do not tie our hands"

From IAN MACKAY, the Industrial Correspondent

BLACKPOOL, Thursday.

THERE is considerable speculation among the delegates to the Labour Party Conference here tonight on a cryptic declaration made during today's session by Professor Harold Laski on what the Labcur Party will do if it is returned as the largest party in the House of Commons but without a clear majority.

Many of the delegates interpret Professor Laski's statement as an intimation that in certain events the Labour Party will be prepared to form a United Front Government with the Liberals and other progressive parties.

Professor Laski was replying for the Executive in a debate on a resolution urging the party not to accept minority office or to join a Coalition with the Tories.

His answer was made in carefully selected words. "There is no possibility whatever of Labour joining in a Coalition with the Conservatives," he declared emphatically.

"But as to the other issue of joining with other people, I do urge this conference not to tie the hands of the party."

Effect of vote

It was emphasised tonight among the delegates that Professor Laski was speaking officially for the National Executive, and as Mr. Attlee, Mr. Morrison and Mr. Dalton are members of that body presumably his declaration represents the views of the Parliamentary chiefs as well.

It is probable that the Executive was induced to adopt this attitude as the result of the narrow vote on the Progressive Front resolution on the opening day of the conference, when the vote of one small union the other way would have turned the conference in favour of unity.

New U.S. envoys to prepare for Big 3

From Our Own Correspondent

New York, Thursday.—A Big Three meeting is "definitely in the works," White House Press Secretary Ross said today.

The London and Moscow missions of Joseph E. Davies and Harry Hopkins do not in any way take the place of the projected meeting of President Truman, Prime Minister Churchill, and Marshal Stalin, he told reporters.

Powers to recall ex-M.P.s

By STANLEY DOBSON, The Political Correspondent

SPECIAL legislation may have to be passed in the next three weeks to enable Parliament to be summoned after the dissolution should a crisis develop. In normal times Parliament ceases to exist after its dissolution and cannot meet again until after a general election.

If there were any unexpected development in the war against Japan or in national or international affairs in general during the period between dissolution and the recall of Parliament after the election, the Prime Minister and the "caretaker" Government might find it imperative to summon the "dead" Parliament.

It is a contingency that the Prime Minister is anxious to guard against, and discussions are now proceeding whether such a course could be taken and what constitutional changes would be necessary.

Emergency steps

If, for instance, Japan offered to surrender unconditionally before the end of July, the Prime Minister would naturally want to call Parliament together. Such a development is not expected, but world affairs are so unpredictable at the moment that, if possible, emergency arrangements for calling Parliament together again will be made.

Mr. Churchill has now drawn up his list of candidates for possible promotion to the "caretaker" Government. The list, I understand, contains a few surprises. So many posts have to be filled—108 in all—that a number of Conservative Ministers who had been displaced in recent years may be given another chance.

Simonite posts

The Prime Minister is said to be aiming at a blend of tried and trusted Ministers and more youthful back-benchers whose chances of promotion have been limited in the past five years because Labour and Liberal M.P.s had to take their proportion of posts.

In his choice he has been advised by the Chief Government Whip and by Mr. Ernest Brown, leader of the Simonites, who expects his allegiance to the Tory cause to be suitably rewarded by an increase

Continued Back Page A

OCCUPATION ZONES MUST BE SETTLED IN AUSTRIA

By VERNON BARTLETT

TWO proclamations to the Austrian people by Field-Marshal Alexander were published yesterday.

They emphasise, by implication, the urgent need for a rapid decision upon the respective areas of that country to be occupied by the British, Americans, Russians and French, and upon the establishment of the Central Control Commission in Vienna.

"Supreme legislative, judicial and executive authority and powers within the territory occupied by forces under my command," runs one sentence in the second proclamation, "are vested in me as Supreme Commander of the Allied forces and as military governor."

Possible conflict

It will be recalled that the Russians have already established an Austrian Government, under Chancellor Renner, whose writ runs in theory throughout the country. There might, therefore, be a conflict of authorities which would create the worst possible impression among our enemies.

This Austrian Government is not recognised in any way by the British and Americans. Nor will it be unless they decide, after their members of the Control Commission have been established in Vienna, that it is a thoroughly representative Government.

But when this Control Commission will start work is still undecided. At present the Russians are in Graz, which had been designated as headquarters of the British zone of occupation.

Similar problems arise in the case of control inside Germany. Berlin may not be the headquarters of the Central Control Commission. Damage to the city would probably justify that decision, although the Russians claim that conditions there have so improved that they have been able to reopen cinemas.

Vitally important

But there are also reports that there will be no Central Control Commission at all.

These matters are vitally important to every soldier and civilian in every Allied country. They are being discussed in the dangerously secretive atmosphere of the European Advisory Commission, whose members, being officials, are not in a position to make decisions.

They are, in effect, being decided by a series of unilateral actions for which there can be no excuse now that the European war has ended.

2,500,000 prisoners of war are being repatriated now

From Our Own Correspondent

SHAEF, Thursday.

SOVIET and Shaef representatives meeting near Leipzig this week drew up a plan which went into effect yesterday for the repatriation of 1,500,000 Russians from Western Europe and nearly 1,000,000 Western Europeans and Americans from Eastern Europe.

The Western Europeans include 30,000 British prisoners who were interned in the zone now occupied by the Red Army.

Reception-delivery camps have been established on both sides of the demarcation line between the Russian and Anglo-American zone. Wounded and sick have first priority in the reparation programme.

3,000 messages from China

Three thousand Red Cross messages from British civilians in civil assembly centres in Japanese-occupied China have reached the Foreign Relations Department of the Red Cross and St. John in London.

Herring catches may be thrown back to keep up price

THERE is so great a glut of herring on the East Coast that the catches may be thrown back into the sea.

The Herring Producers' Association, which has agreed with buyers at East Coast ports on a 78s. minimum, has advised Stornoway (centre of the greatest of the Scottish fishery districts) that, in view of the glut the only way for fishermen to maintain a fair price is to be ready to dump their catches.

The glut has brought fishing at Stornoway to a standstill. Despite the urgency of the food situation no boats will go to sea for the rest of this week. About 1,000 crans of herring were landed yesterday by 50 boats. A cran is 37½ gallons, or about 750 herrings.

Nets restricted

Although the fishermen had tried to avert a glut by restricting the number of nets in use by each boat, buyers pointed out that they could not possibly handle 1,000 crans for kippering.

Freshing is out of the question because there is a glut at the rail and road head ports of Mallaig and Gairloch and there is no Ministry of Food scheme for curing at Stornoway.

Stornoway fishermen are most reluctant to dump herring in the present situation. They complain that they have been let down by the Producers' Association and Ministry of Food because Stornoway has been left out of the agreement with the buyers, with the result that there is no guaranteed minimum and no scheme for curing.

Clothing shortage

The War Office requirements of 2,000,000 suits, hats, and undergarments to rig out the demobbed Service men are almost certain to result in a clothing shortage. A North-East retailer told the News Chronicle yesterday that he seriously doubted the ability of the retailers to meet the next issue of civilian clothing coupons later in the year.

Potatoes will cost more

THE Ministry of Food announced last night that the tonnage subsidy paid to keep potato prices low is being withdrawn and the retail price of old potatoes will go up on Sunday next.

In Great Britain the maximum price of Grade A varieties will be increased by twopence per 7lb., and that of Grade B varieties by threepence per 7lb., except in Scotland south of the Forth, where the increase is threepence-halfpenny.

V.C. killed Japs with sword that pierced him

GOING to help a Bren gunner during a company attack on a Jap position in Burma, an Indian Army corporal, Naik Fazal Din, who is awarded the V.C. posthumously, was run through the chest by a Japanese officer's sword, the point appearing through his back.

On the Jap officer withdrawing the sword Naik Fazal Din, despite his terrible wound, tore it from his grasp and killed him with it.

He then went to the assistance of a sepoy of his section who was struggling with another Jap and killed the Jap with the sword.

The position won, he reported to platoon headquarters, and died.

LATE NEWS

OKINAWA: ALLIES ENTER CAPITAL

U.S. forces on Okinawa sent troops into Naha, the capital, in force after building two bridges across the Asato River, said Guam communique last night.

JAP SHIPPING HIT

Three Japanese freighters and large ocean-going tug were sunk and nine landing craft set on fire in raids along Asiatic coast, said last night's communique from Gen. MacArthur's H.Q.

Moon rises 8.14 p.m., sets 5.56 a.m. tomorrow. Full Moon Sunday

Daily Mail
NO. 15,314 ONE PENNY ** FOR KING AND EMPIRE WEDNESDAY, JUNE 6, 1945
ADVANCE

Treat with care
for extra wear
Bear Brand
Utility Stockings

EISENHOWER, MONTGOMERY, DE TASSIGNY meet ZHUKOV in conference

FOUR CONQUERORS' TERMS ANNOUNCED FROM BERLIN

Germany split into zones: all action 'unified'

HITLER'S Third Reich, which was to have lasted 1,000 years, came to its official end at 4.40 p.m. yesterday. At that moment representatives of Britain, America, Russia, and France, meeting in Berlin, signed a "declaration regarding the defeat of Germany" under which the country passed to the rule of the Allied Control Council.

The declaration was signed by the four men who are to run Germany—General Eisenhower (U.S.), Marshal Zhukov (Russia), General de Lattre de Tassigny (France), and Field-Marshal Montgomery (Britain).

The declaration and three statements issued with it cover the terms of surrender, Allied policy towards Germany, and the methods of control.

Control is vested in the Control Council, consisting of the four Allied Commanders-in-Chief, each assisted by a political adviser.

The Council, whose decisions must be unanimous, will secure uniformity of action throughout Germany, which has been divided into five control zones:—

The **eastern zone** goes to Russia;
The **north-western** zone to Britain;
The **south-western** zone to the United States;
A **western** zone to France; and
Greater Berlin, which will be occupied by the forces of all Four Powers.

The controlling Power in each zone may, if it wishes, utilise the troops of any Power that has actively fought against Germany.

This assumption of control means that the Allies have supreme authority over all aspects of German life.

It means that all the powers of the German Government, of the High Command, and of any State or municipal authority have passed to the Control Council.

The declaration makes it clear that this assumption of power does not mean the annexation of Germany, whose boundaries and status are to be determined later.

OUR ORDERS

The declaration in effect is Germany's "armistice terms." No terms could be presented before owing to the complete collapse of Germany and the fact that fighting went on until she was virtually occupied.

Now, says the declaration, there "is no central Government or authority in Germany capable of accepting responsibility for the maintenance of order, the administration of the country and compliance with the requirements of the victorious Powers.

"It is in these circumstances necessary, without prejudice to any subsequent decisions that may be taken, to make provision for the cessation of any further hostilities on the part of the German armed forces, for the maintenance of order in Germany and for the administration of the country, and to announce the immediate requirements with which Germany must comply."

Under the 15 clauses of the declaration, which puts Germany back to its 1937 frontiers (before the Austrian *Anschluss* and the occupation of the Sudetenland), the Allies have told the Germans the "basic requirements" of unconditional surrender.

ALL IS OURS

These include the disarmament of all armed forces, the surrender of all ships planes, war equipment and factories, laboratories and experimental stations

All plans, blue-prints, inventions, and records are to be handed over: communications and transport come under Allied control: labour, utility services, and maintenance factories must be used as the Allies demand.

Many of the clauses—they range from prisoners of war to displaced persons, from political prisoners to war criminals—have already been fulfilled by the surender or defeat of German armies.

Of war criminals the declaration says: "*The principal Nazi leaders as specified by the Allied Representatives, and all persons from time to time named or designated by rank, office, or employment by the Allied Representatives as being suspected of having committed, ordered or abetted war crimes or analogous offences, will be apprehended and surrendered to the Allied Representatives.*

Article 13 of the Declaration lays down the future policy towards Germany in these terms:

"*. . . four Allied Governments will take such steps, including the complete disarmament and demobilisation of Germany, as they deem requisite for future peoce and security.*

"*The Allied representatives will impose on Germany additional political, administrative, economic, Gnancial, military, and other requirements arising from the complete defeat of Germany. . . . All German authorities and the German people shall carry out unconditionally the requirements of the Allied representatives.*"

And Article 14 declares that "In the event of failure on the part of

BACK PAGE—Col. FOUR

Leaders flew to Tempelhof

City of silence

From **DREW MIDDLETON**, Combined Press Correspondent

BERLIN, Tuesday.

GENERAL Ivan Sokolosvsky and General Polutnik greeted General Eisenhower on Tempelhof airfield in Berlin to-day.

A Red Army band struck up "The Star-spangled Banner" and the Russian anthem while the Americans and the Russians stood at the salute.

General Eisenhower inspected a guard of honour of Siberian infantry, and later Russian troops marched past while Eisenhower took the salute.

Afterwards he drove through the ruined suburbs to the area which the Russians have taken over to house the Allied visitors.

The city was so silent that the sound of the tyres in the streets sounded like the roar of an aeroplane.

The streets were dotted with propaganda signs containing excerpts from Stalin's broadcast, notably his statement that Russia did not want to enslave the German people.—*B.U.P.*

5 plane loads

A broadcast from Berlin to all U.S. radio networks last night said:

The Allied Control Council for Germany met to-day in Marshal Zhukov's headquarters in the south-eastern outskirts of Berlin.

The signature of the declaration took place at 4.40 p.m. (D.B.S.T.).

The U.S delegation reached the Tempelhof airfield in five planes shortly after 11 o'clock this morning.

The French arrived next, followed by Field-Marshal Montgomery shortly after noon.

Order of victory

Moscow radio interrupted the musical programme last night to announce that Montgomery and Eisenhower have been awarded the Order of Victory by the Supreme Soviet of the U.S.S.R.

The Order, the highest military distinction of the Soviet Union, was recently introduced, and only a few Soviet marshals, including Marshal Stalin hold it. The Order is studded with diamonds and is worth about £3,750.

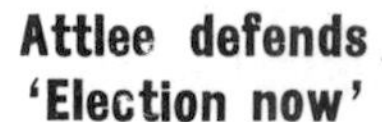

Attlee defends 'Election now'

Long-term planning split all parties

THE Labour Party's election broadcasts were opened last night by Mr. C. R. Attlee, its leader, who said:

"When I listened to the Prime Minister's speech last night, in which he gave such a travesty of the policy of the Labour Party, I realised at once what was his object.

"He wanted the electors to understand how great was the difference between Winston Churchill, the great leader in war of a united nation, and Mr. Churchill, the party leader of the Conservatives.

"He feared lest those who had accepted his leadership in war might be tempted out of gratitude to follow him further.

"I thank him for having disillusioned them so thoroughly. The voice we heard last night was that of Mr. Churchill, but the mind was that of Lord Beaverbrook.

Tribute to Premier

"BUT before turning to the issues that divide parties, I would like to pay my tribute to my colleagues in the late Government of all parties, or of none, with whom I have had the privilege of serving under a great leader in war, the Prime Minister.

"We concentrated our energies on the supreme need of winning the war, and were able to agree on all the practical measures required.

"It was, however, inevitable that when an approach was made to long-term policy in relation to the economic organisation of the country, there would be a divergence of view on the principles to be applied, which necessitated an appeal to the country.

"I should like to deal with the reason for having this election, because I notice that there is some misunderstanding and some deliberate misrepresentation.

Case for election

"THE point was very well put by the Prime Minister in introducing the Prolongation of Parliament Bill in 1944. He said:

"'*I can assure the House that in the absence of most earnest representations from the Labour and Liberal Parties I could not refrain from making a submission to the Crown in respect of a dissolution after the German war is effectively and officially finished.*'

"The calling of a general election involved the break-up of the Government, but has not in any way altered the firm resolve of the Labour Party to do its utmost to win the war against Japan.

"While Labour Ministers were still in office all preparations had been made to ensure that the men and materials necessary for this purpose should be made available.

"There are many other matters which the late Government dealt with to provide for the immediate situation after the ending of the war against Germany on which there is no difference between parties.

"I hope, too, that there may be continued agreement among us all on the main lines of foreign policy. After the last war the League of Nations was formed to maintain peace and the rule of law, and to prevent aggression.

"My generation that fought in the last war hoped much from

BACK PAGE—Col. SIX

SPY OF 16 WALKS TO DEATH

HEINZ PETRY, 16-years-old Nazi youth from Alsdorf, was caught spying on American troops. With him was 17-years-old Josef Schoner. Both were condemned to death. Here you see Petry marched off to execution.—Another picture in BACK Page.

'Bald' tyres on roads once more

Order revoked

By Daily Mail Reporter

THE war-time restriction on the use of badly worn tyres has been lifted.

A regulation which came into force on January 1, 1943, prohibited the use of tyres which were worn down to the canvas.

"The Order was made so that all owners of vehicles running on the roads should send their tyres for retreading before they got beyond repair, as rubber was in short supply," said a Ministry of Transport official last night.

The Order has been revoked as from last Monday, and police authorities were told yesterday that summonses already issued need not be proceeded with.

"However deplorable the condition of the tyre, no action can be taken against the driver unless an accident results," said a police authority.

Göring By Lord Wright

LORD WRIGHT, chairman of the War Crimes Commission, said in London yesterday that the commission, on evidence advanced by a national office, had found that there was a prima facie case on which Göring could be tried as a war criminal.

But Lord Wright said that he could not yet say whether Göring would be tried by a national court or, as a major criminal by an international court. He added:

"I should say of a man like Göring that the scope of his activities is very great. But they do involve robbery and murder and various other offences in which he was directly involved."

Sir James Grigg, War Minister, told M.P.s yesterday: "Field-Marshal Göring is not in the custody of the British Forces."

Haw-Haw By himself

WILLIAM JOYCE is saying "I have nothing to fear" as he lies in hospital awaiting his return to England, wires Richard McMillan, *B.U.P.* war correspondent.

He is apparently confident, and claims that there is no charge which the British authorities can prefer against him. He is progressing satisfactorily and is recovering from the wound inflicted on him when he was captured.

Superintendent Burt, of the Military Intelligence Department, returned by air to London yesterday after his interrogation of Joyce, and submitted evidence to the Director of Public Prosecutions,

Hopes to be MP

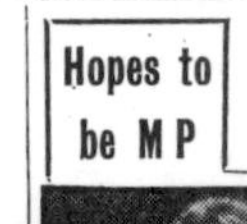

The HON. WILLIAM DOUGLAS-HOME. Released yesterday

Earl's son is freed, may fight election

By Daily Mail Reporter

RELEASED from Wakefield Prison yesterday, the Hon. William Douglas-Home, third son of the Earl of Home, travelled to London to make election arrangements.

He expects that these may result in his standing as an Independent candidate for Windsor.

He was cashiered and sentenced to 12 months' imprisonment by court-martial, in Belgium, last October.

The charge was that Capt. Douglas-Home "did not proceed to his squadron and act as liaison officer in the battle of Le Havre when ordered to do so."

Good conduct brought remission of part of his sentence.

As he left the prison yesterday he said that he hoped to stand in the election, adding: "If I can get the cash to stand the expense."

'RED ENSIGN'-WITH A HAMMER AND SICKLE

HERE you see the Royal Sovereign, British battleship, after she had been handed over to the Soviet Navy in 1944. with four British submarines.

THE Royal Sovereign, 35,000 tons, 620ft. long, with 8 15-inch guns and 12 16-inch guns, was the last battleship to be built in a naval dockyard. She was completed at Portsmouth in 1916.

De Gaulle was saved by Gen. Spears

WHEN FRANCE FELL

By Daily Mail Reporter

GENERAL DE GAULLE would have been arrested by Weygand, and the French resistance movement would have died almost as soon as it was born, but for the man General de Gaulle maligned—Major-General Sir Edward Spears.

Mr. Churchill hinted at this in the House of Commons yesterday when he said: "General Spears is the last person on whom General de Gaulle should make reflections, because he personally secured General de Gaulle's escape from France to "this country on June 18, 1940."

The story behind this was told last night by one of Brigadier-General Spears's associates:

When France capitulated, General Spears was acting as liaison officer with M. Paul Reynaud's Government.

De Gaulle was afraid that he would be arrested by order of the Commander-in-Chief, General Weygand.

IN HIS CAR

On June 17, 1940, General Spears was about to leave the aerodrome at Bordeaux. General de Gaulle was in attendance there, ostensibly to see the British liaison representative off to England. General Spears had brought de Gaulle to Bordeaux in his car.

A secret arrangement had been made between General Spears and General de Gaulle that at the take-off the French leader should try to board the plane.

De Gaulle was accompanied by his A.D.C. Solemnly and with an elaborate show of courtesy, the two generals played out the comedy of saying farewell; making arrangements for future meetings and discussing routine business.

Aboard the plane was a large box filled with papers and private luggage belonging to General de Gaulle. Just before the take-off the pilot of the plane shouted out that unless this box was securely roped he would have difficulty in taking off.

Realising that every second was vital and that Weygand's representatives might arrive at any moment to arrest de Gaulle, General Spears gave hurried orders to the mechanics to try to take some of the roping off the landing-blocks of the plane.

HAULED IN

Though the mechanics worked feverishly, they could not detach the rope. It was too stiff.

General de Gaulle's aide rushed off to fetch some rope. He was able to get enough to tie the box into the plane.

General Spears boarded the plane. He stretched his hand out as if to say a final good-bye to General de Gaulle, and then suddenly pulled him bodily into the plane.

De Gaulle's aide-de-camp jumped in after his chief, and the plane took off.

In his statement in the House of Commons yesterday Mr. Churchill denied that General Spears was recalled from his post in the Middle East at the request of General de Gaulle.

General Spears gave up the post because he wished to return to his Parliamentary duties before the election.

100 cents=192 pies

BOMBAY, Tuesday.—Under a contemplated decimal coinage system for India, the rupee would be divided into 100 cents instead of the present 192 pies.—*Reuter.*

France seeks Big 5 talks

PARIS, Tuesday.

THE French Government to-day proposed that the Big Five Powers should meet to seek a solution of "all Middle East problems."

The Cabinet reached this decision this morning before Mr. Churchill had made his statement on the Levant, in which he said that a Five-Power conference would "cause delay."—*Reuter.*

Premier's Statement on Syria—BACK Page.

Watch on sky 'hogs'

RAF WANT THE FACTS

By Daily Mail Air Correspondent

SPECIAL R.A.F. observers yesterday maintained their look-out over towns in Britain for low-flying "sky hogs" who frighten women and children and endanger life with unnecessary aerobatics.

At the same time Air Ministry officials were completing plans for re-routing aircraft to avoid flying over Central London.

The Air Ministry are determined to stamp out the "air hogging" that has provoked complaints.

There is a danger that the whole well-disciplined R.A.F. may get a bad name for the sins of a few irresponsible pilots—some of them civilian test pilots—who stunt over seaside beaches and crowded inland towns.

In the four weeks since VE-Day the R.A.F. have flown over 10,000 sorties to and from Britain.

Yet since the beginning of the year the Air Ministry have received only some 300 complaints about low flying.

Daily Mail readers are asked to help the R.A.F.'s "sky cops" in tracking down the low-flying pilots by sending to the Air Ministry or to Northcliffe House complaints of undisciplined flying.

MORE BRITISH SHIPS FOR PACIFIC

New Delhi radio says: "It is reported that a large British battle squadron and another cruiser squadron will soon join the British Pacific Fleet."—B.U.P.

'GHOST' BOMBER DOWN IN SEA

Halifax, Tuesday.—A Lancaster bomber of the R.C.A.F. "Ghost Squadron," bound from England to the Azores, crashed into the sea to-day. The nine members of the crew were rescued.—Exchange.

2

DAILY EXPRESS

No. 14,049 Lighting-up: 11.18 pm to 4.42 am FRIDAY JUNE 15 1945 Weather: Cool, windy, some rain One Penny

GESTAPO MEMBERSHIP MAY BE TREATED AS PROOF OF GUILT

Allies considering plan to speed up sentences on Himmler's lesser thugs

WAR CRIMINALS' TRIALS BEGIN NEXT MONTH

Goering will face court in Germany

TRIBUNAL OF ALLIES

Express Political Correspondent GUY EDEN

FIRST trials of lesser war criminals—men accused of such crimes as murder, torture and starvation of prisoners—will start early next month before Allied tribunals to be set up in Germany. Among these first criminals will be the guards and others at concentration camps such as Belsen, which is in the British zone.

A special Royal Warrant, to be issued today, will speed up the trials by empowering the tribunals—military courts staffed usually by five or six officers—to pass sentence at the end of the trial instead of having to wait for it to be confirmed.

As soon as the sentence, which may be death or imprisonment, has been confirmed by the Allied military commander-in-chief it will become effective.

Major war criminals like Goering will be tried by an inter-Allied court in Germany. In no instance will war criminals be dealt with by courts of their own nationality.

Plans are under discussion with the United States, Soviet and French Governments to proclaim all the Gestapo, the S.S. and similar organisations "criminal conspiracies," mere membership of which will be a war crime.

Each occupying Power will try war criminals in its own zone, according to military law or international code for the conduct of war.

Commissioned officers of any rank from lieutenant upwards will sit on the courts, and a number of courts will sit at once, to avoid delay in bringing accused men to trial.

In public

The trials will be held in public, and although every accused person will be given every chance to make a defence, no political speech-making will be allowed.

Those sent to jail will go to places under Allied control—never to German-run prisons. Death sentences will be carried out in the manner ordered by the courts, and may be either hanging or shooting.

Representatives of other Allies may attend as observers at the trials in the British zone.

If the plan to "proclaim" the Gestapo and SS is adopted, it will enable the Allies to get at members of these bodies against whom it may not be possible to prove specific crimes.

The procedure will be to try about a dozen of the leaders of those bodies before a superior court, whose decision would be binding on all other courts. Proof of membership will thus suffice to secure a conviction.

Big lists

Lists of members and other material are in Allied hands, and it will be possible to bring great numbers to trial.

The decision to make mere membership a crime is likely to be based on the facts that membership of these bodies was voluntary and that their whole object was criminal.

It will greatly speed up and simplify the task of ensuring that war criminals do not escape on some legal technicality.

The form of the inter-Allied courts which are to try the Big Men like Goering has not yet been fixed, but they will be military courts, and will sit in Germany.

It is not intended to condemn the major criminals out of hand, but to give them a full trial, with every opportunity of defence.

CHURCHILL AND THE LIBERALS

MR. CHURCHILL issued the following statement last night:—

IT has come to my notice that whereas in some parts of the country the Sinclair Liberal candidates are receiving the active support of the Socialists and the Communists, in other parts the Sinclair Liberal candidates are representing to the electors that they are standing in support of me, and are telling the electors that "a vote for them is a vote for Churchill."

I desire therefore to make it plain that the Sinclair Liberal candidates are standing at this election in opposition to me and the Government, and that a vote for a Sinclair Liberal candidate is in fact a vote not for me, but for the Socialist opposition.

I welcome all Liberal support for the National Government, and I am sure that there are many Liberals in this island who will give their votes to candidates fully pledged to support me.

In particular, the Liberal National candidates have made common cause with the Government, and I believe that they represent the bulk of Liberal opinion throughout the land.

For all, the motto should be. "Country before party."

The Liberals—

Six hours earlier, SIR ARCHIBALD SINCLAIR, leader of the Liberals, said in Manchester:—

I RESERVE complete freedom of action for the Liberal Party to decide for itself in the next Parliament where its duty lies.

Everything will depend on the composition of the new House of Commons, and the Liberal Party must have full discretion to decide what to do.

—and Churchill

Last night MR. ROY HARROD, Sinclair Liberal candidate for Huddersfield, said:—

I REGARD Mr. Churchill as one of the greatest Englishmen who have ever lived.

It would be proper for the Liberals to offer Mr. Churchill their support to cover the remainder of the Japanese war and the crucial stages of the Peace Conference, subject to an undertaking that he would put full pressure behind the Liberals' support of the Atlantic Charter, and repudiate entirely the views of Lord Beaverbrook and his friends, which guided the Conservative Party.

I suggest that Sir Archibald Sinclair should go to the Prime Minister with this precise condition.

DROPPED MINE: 600 DIE

At German dump

COPENHAGEN, Thursday.—Nearly 600 German naval personnel and civilians were killed today by two explosions at Flensburg, on the Danish-German frontier.

Mines were being removed from a big underground depot when one was dropped.

This caused the main explosion, which killed everyone within hundreds of yards and smashed windows for miles along the border.—Exchange.

Lost plane found on island

Express Staff Reporter

OBAN, Thursday.—It has taken five months to find a plane which was seen to crash in flames on the west side of Jura island, off the Argyll coast, 40 miles due west of Glasgow.

Parties of farmers, R.A.F. men and Italian prisoners combed the island for days last January until it was thought the plane must have crashed into the sea.

But yesterday Archibald McKechnie, a gamekeeper, saw something glittering in the sun high up on the island's 2,400ft. mountains.

He climbed for two hours, and there in a deep gully was the plane—and the men who died in it.

JOHN ENGLAND—1

ATTORNEY-GENERAL ORDERS INQUIRY

IN a written reply yesterday, Sir David Maxwell Fyfe, Attorney-General, replied to M.P.s' questions about the "John England" incident.

QUESTION NO. 1, by Squadron-Leader E. L. Fleming (Cons., Withington, Manchester) was whether the Attorney-General was aware

That a letter, signed John England, has been sent by the directors of the Manchester and Salford Co-operative Society to Servicemen inviting them to vote for Socialist candidates at the forthcoming General Election, and enclosing a gift of 5s. from the Co-operative War Comforts Fund; and if he will take steps to bring such gifts within the Corrupt Practices Act.

QUESTION NO. 2, by Mr. E. H. Keeling (Cons., Twickenham) asked

If the Attorney-General's attention has been drawn to the letter . . . and whether he proposes to take any action.

Replying to both questions, Sir David Maxwell Fyfe, said:—

"My attention has been drawn to this matter by the Director of Public Prosecutions (Mr. Theobald Mathew), and inquiries into it are proceeding."

9 CHILDREN KIDNAPPED

Swept off in two limousines in Paris boulevard

From PAUL HOLT: Paris, Thursday

NINE Polish children, rescued from the horror camp at Buchenwald, were kidnapped at noon yesterday in the busy Boulevard St. Michel, Paris.

The children, bathed and reclothed after a night's rest at a repatriation centre, were put in a lorry in charge of a French sergeant to be driven to Orly, outside Paris.

For some time the lorry was followed by two big black limousines. In the Boulevard St. Michel the first car, gangster fashion, slewed in front of the lorry and forced it to stop on the pavement.

A Polish officer made the children climb down from the lorry and pile into the limousines. When the French sergeant tried to break in he was knocked down by a Polish soldier driving one of the cars.

The limousines drove away and the French sergeant shouted to two American military police in a jeep.

'TO BARRACKS'

The jeep caught the second limousine just outside Paris, rescuing seven of the nine children. The leading car, with the other two got away.

The Polish soldier driving the second car gave his name as Labendz, and said that a Polish lieutenant named Pacheleis ordered him "to take the children to the Bessieres barracks, which is the headquarters of the Polish Military Mission."

The Polish Embassy say all they know is what they read in the Communist paper l'Humanité. This is what l'Humanité says:—

"The children were to be taken to the Bessieres barracks, which is the recruiting centre for Poles, to join the Fascist Polish Army at Inverkeithing, Scotland."

But the children, according to the few witnesses available, were all between ten and 14.

Krupp can still turn out tanks

Express Special Correspondent

BRUNSWICK, Thursday.—Germany's war potential was NOT destroyed by bombing.

Heavy industries and communications were knocked out by our strategic bombing. There were gaps in the intricate organisation needed to carry on the war. But knocking out an industry and destroying it, well, they are very different things.

Allied commissions are assessing the damage. Here is a likely pre-view on their reports: facts compiled in a tour of the major "target areas." This is the state of the German war machine:—

HAMBURG.—The Blohm and Voss plant can launch submarines within a month, be mass producing in three months. The firm's production of air transports can be on again in four months.

More than 1939

Battleship and cruiser-building yards can be repaired in nine months. Within a year Hamburg's war industries can be turning out more than they did in 1939.

MAGDEBURG.—Krupp's huge tank factory can produce 50 Mark IVs a week within two months given the raw materials. Some plant is destroyed, but many assembly lines are intact.

LEUNA, biggest German synthetic oil plant, in four months can be turning out a fifth of all the oil an army like the late Wehrmacht would need for mechanised war.

FALLERSLEBEN, biggest German motor-car plant, already producing 14 German versions of the jeep (Volkswagen) a day under U.S. supervision. The huge stamping machines are intact. In four months the plant can be repaired to produce 500 Volkswagen, 2,000 teller mines, and 300 wing structures for Junkers planes a day.

V2 in masses

NORDHAUSEN. This underground plant with its 25 miles of tunnels is untouched. Mass production of V1 and V2 can start immediately.

These estimates were given by managers still on the scene.

The Allies intend to strip these plants of vital machinery.

They will supervise all phases of German industrial life. After the Allied control commission has finished its work there may be no heavy industry left.

But this does not mean that Allied control can relax. The lesson from a ground inspection of our chief targets is that German powers of recuperation and resource are terrific.

(World copyright.)

Russia to try 16 Poles

The 16 Poles who were arrested by Russia are to be tried soon by the Soviet Supreme Military Court.

Moscow radio, announcing this last night, recalled that the men are accused of organising terrorist activities and having illegal radio transmitters in the rear of Soviet troops in Poland.

Among the 16 are M. Jan Jankowski, the London Polish Government's Vice-Premier and delegate to Warsaw, and General Okulicki who succeeded General Bor-Komarowski as Commander of the Polish Home Army.

News of the arrest, after the 16 had been missing for some time, was given by the Soviet on May 5.

Cook to 1,000 is leaving

All the cooking at St. James's Hospital, Leeds, which has 1,000 beds, is done by an 18-year-old assistant cook.

Now she is leaving to get married.

Wage of £3 to learn new job

By TREVOR EVANS

EX-FORCES men can earn £3 a week while they learn a new job.

That is the Government's scheme for those who wish to train for a new start in Civvy Street.

Mr. R. A. Butler, the Minister of Labour, announced yesterday that they will be paid allowances higher than unemployment benefit, but less than what they will get when they finish training.

The rates are £3 a week for an unmarried man above 20 if he lives at home while training, £1 15s. plus cost of lodgings if he trains away from home, an extra 10s. for a married man, and 5s. for the first child under 16.

If he has to maintain two homes while training he gets an additional allowance of 24s. 6d a week.

Thus, a man who is married and has one child gets £3 15s. if he lives near his training centre. His lodging and double-home allowances represent the average expenses he would have to meet.

Women's rates will be £2 7s. if they train near home, and lodgings and £1 5s. if away from home.

These new rates show an increase of about 10s. a week on the rates announced last year.

They recognise that Britain is moving towards a £5 a week standard for a full week's pay for men. (Average weekly earnings for men in 1938 were £3 9s a week.)

30,000 want to stay

Training centres are now being prepared to deal with about 75,000 men this year.

But a new factor is entering into the calculations.

Recently, the Services headquarters circulated their units inviting officers and men to volunteer for one or two years' extra service after the time for their release or until after the war with Japan ends.

Unofficial estimates now are that such volunteers might muster up to 30,000 men.

4.30 a.m. LATEST

HONGKONG HIT

MANILA, Friday.—U.S. planes dropped more than 25,000 gallons of jellied petrol on Hongkong causeway in the biggest fire raid on the Japanese in China.—B.U.P.

TANGIER MOVE

TANGIER, Friday.—Mr. Charles Peake, British Consul-General in Tangier and Mr. Rives Childs, the American representative, are flying to a London conference to discuss the return of Tangier to international status. It is at present under Spanish occupation.—Express News Service.

20 days to Polling Day

LAVAL GOES SUN BATHING

From FRANK ROSTRON

MADRID, Thursday.—Pierre Laval, tanned and nearly 10lb. heavier than when he arrived six weeks ago, sat sunbathing today in his de luxe prison at Montjuich fortress.

He is writing his memoirs and a statement for use in his defence if he is brought to trial.

From a source in daily contact with Laval I learn that he told the military governor last week he had decided to return to France.

But when he was asked to sign a request for air transport to Paris, he refused to do so.

He has more than £100,000 in Swiss francs.

POCKET CARTOON

"I admit you know more about the man Joyce than I do, but all the same I feel a mistake has been made somewhere."

JOHN ENGLAND—REPORT No. 2

'I AM TOO OLD TO BE CAUGHT OUT'

SAYS ALDERMAN FLOWERS

Express Staff Reporter: Manchester, Thursday

ALDERMAN W. H. FLOWERS, publicity chief for Manchester and Salford Co-operative Society, was asked yesterday: "Are you the author of the 'John England' letter that was circulated to the Forces?"

He replied: "I am far too old and experienced a campaigner to be caught out on such matters."

The question was put to him at his office in Downing-street, Manchester, following acceptance by Manchester Socialist Party's committee of the explanation that the sending of 5s. postal order gifts together with "Vote Socialist" appeals was a "technical error."

CUTTINGS FILE

Open before him was a file containing cuttings from the Daily Express referring to the "John England" letter.

He added: "You people have been trying hard for a long time to find out all about the matter—carry on. If you think you know all about it you don't need my help.

"At the proper time and place—when I feel so disposed—perhaps I'll have quite a lot to say about the letter but not until then."

Writing as secretary of the "Comforts for Troops" Fund in the current issue of the Manchester and Salford Co-operative Herald, Alderman Flowers says:—

"I feel that a rich dividend will be returned on all the efforts in connection with the scheme. In the post-war years these people will not forget that during this period of 5½ years of war, Manchester and Salford did something to help their boys and girls engaged in this struggle."

ALDERMAN W. H. FLOWERS

"If you think you know all about it, you don't need my help."

TORIES GET 56 CLEAR IN FORECASTS

MORE than 500 forecasts of how the constituencies will vote in the General Election have been received by the Daily Express Election Bureau.

These give the Conservatives a majority of 56 over other parties.

Including the Liberal Nationals and one Liberal pledged to support Mr Churchill the National Government would have a working majority of 86.

With 138 results still to come the state of the parties, according to the Straw Ballot, would be:—

Conservatives	279
Liberal Nationals	14
Socialists	185
Liberals	9
I.L.P	4
Independents	9
Communists	2

Taking new constituencies into account, net gains and losses of the principal parties are shown by the Ballot as follows:—

GAINS

Socialists	49

LOSSES

Conservatives	21
Liberal Nationals	9
Liberals	3
Other parties	3

Leopold 'to abdicate'

BRUSSELS, Thursday.—M. Van Acker, Belgian Premier, and a legal expert left by air for Salzburg today to confer with King Leopold.

The presence of the lawyer is interpreted by some as meaning that the king will abdicate.—B.U.P.

Mr. Eden: Going on well

Mr. Anthony Eden's duodenal ulcer is responding well to treatment, it was announced last night.

Mr. Eden has been advised to cancel all engagements for four weeks, except for a broadcast on June 27.

Haw-Haw on Monday

Express Staff Reporter

William Joyce, "Lord Haw-Haw," will appear before the Chief Metropolitan Magistrate, Sir Bertrand Watson, at Bow-street on Monday morning. Only formal evidence will be given.

A remand will be asked for and it is expected that Mr L. A. Byrne, leading Crown counsel, will open the prosecution's case at the next hearing—possibly on Monday week.

Haw-Haw is still in a British military prison in Brussels.

Patton going back to Germany

SHAEF, Thursday.—General Patton's Third Army and General Patch's Seventh Army will form the permanent occupation forces in Germany.

Patton, who was reported to be seeking a Far East command, will return to Europe soon.—B.U.P.

M.P.s now

PARIS, Thursday.—Forty-eight ex-prisoners of war and deportees to Germany were co-opted today on to the French Consultative Council.—Reuter.

Napoleon's sword too

PARIS, Thursday.—General Eisenhower was the guest of honour at a banquet tonight when General de Gaulle presented him with the sword worn by Napoleon when he was First Consul.

He flies back to America tomorrow.—Express News Service.

Woman gives home for wounded

Sir Walter Womersley, Minister of Pensions, announced last night that Gowrie House, Eastbourne, now an Australian Red Cross club, has been given as a home for disabled ex-servicemen. The donor is believed to be a woman who left Eastbourne early in the war.

To fix zones

SUPREME H.Q., Thursday.—Final occupation zones in Germany are expected to be decided at the next Big Three conference, said a high authority today.

Gandhi silent on India plan

BOMBAY, Thursday.—Neither Mr. Gandhi, Congress leader, nor Mr. M. A. Jinnah, President of the All-India Moslem League, would comment today on Britain's new offer of almost complete Indianisation of the Viceroy's Council.

Mr. Jinnah wanted time to study the offer, and Mr. Gandhi is waiting until he has consulted the Congress Working Committee, eight of whom are to be released today after three years' imprisonment.

The Working Committee is likely to meet in Bombay on Wednesday and accept the Viceroy's invitation to a conference on June 25.—Reuter.

The Tudor I. takes the air

The Avro Tudor I., first new British civil air liner to take the air since the end of the war in Europe, made a successful test flight at Ringway, the Manchester airport, yesterday.

It is scheduled to travel non-stop to Montreal in 12 hours with 24 passengers.

French call-up

France is to call up three new classes, mostly for the army.

UNION CHIEF ATTACKS PETTY DICTATORS

Express Staff Reporter: Sydney, Thursday

ADDRESSING the State Council of the Federated Engine-drivers' and Firemen's Association, Mr. Hugh Sutherland, president of the New South Wales branch, attacked the Federal Government for having given control of the nation to boards and departmental officers.

"It is now necessary to run a gauntlet of barrage, impudence and arrogance by these petty dictators, appointed and supported by a Government which was elected to give expression to the wishes of the great majority of the people.

"We see daily the pitiful sight of elected representatives going towards these boards and servilely conveying requests on behalf of the people who elected them to govern.

"I urge that the strongest possible action should be taken by the organised working-class to insist that members of these commissions and boards should be placed in some useful and productive employment and that their powers be handed back to the various legislative assemblies.

"If such action is not taken the existing form of Fascist control will not only continue for many years, but will be intensified. These control boards are like human fungus attached to a social body, and are causing rot and decay."

Cancelled

MONTREAL, Thursday.—All reservations by guests at Quebec's Chateau Frontenac Hotel, scene of two war conferences, have been cancelled for July. Everyone is asking why.—Express News Service.

GOOD DEED in a naughty world

London gets new potatoes

Four special trains carrying 729 tons of new potatoes from Cornwall arrived in London yesterday.

This is London's first large consignment, and the potatoes should be in the shops some time today.

They would provide a 2lb. ration for 816,000 families.

Share deals banned

The Stock Exchange Council yesterday banned dealings in the 2s. shares of British Coal Distillation, owners of an oil-from-coal process. No explanation was given.

Mr W. Wakefield Adam, who recently became chairman of the company, said last night he knew of no reason for the action.

SEAC

THE SERVICES NEWSPAPER OF SOUTH EAST ASIA COMMAND

No. 545 One Anna.

MONDAY, 9 JULY, 1945.

Printed by Courtesy of THE STATESMAN in Calcutta.

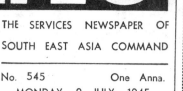

JAPS HALTED IN BATTLE OF SITTANG BEND

INTO BATTLE

Troops of 19 Ind Div—the Div which captured Mandalay—h a v e been fighting hard along the road towards Mawchi, east of Toungoo, in heavy monsoon rains.

Here Pathans of a Punjab Regt are pictured attacking a Jap position under cover of a smoke screen.

KANDY, Sun.—Troops of an Indian Div have beaten back the spearhead of the Japanese westward sally across the Sittang River. They have ejected the Japs from the village of Le-Einzu which represented the deepest announced Japanese penetration from the river and reopened a direct line of communication to Myipkyo.

This is only a minor reverse for the Japanese, writes Alan Humphreys, API war correspondent, and it appears that they are holding stronger footholds just west of the Sittang. Fighting in this area is going on under conditions which would seem to prohibit even the least movement.

The so-called roads are usually only banked-up tracks, which are so thick with mud and water that troops with difficulty are able to cover about half a mile in an hour.

Once off these raised tracks, the country floods often up to ten feet deep

53,000 Left

Narinder Sethi, API war correspondent at ADV HQ ALFSEA says though the Japs in Burma, are now reduced from an overall strength of 200,000 to a bare 53,000, their fighting morale is not diminished and they are continuing their attacks with the utmost fury.

According to today's SE Asia Command communique Japanese activity in the Sittang River bend is increasing.

The village of Nyaungkashe, 25 miles NE of Pegu, has been shelled on two successive nights, and the Japanese are reported to be established NE, NW and SW of the village.

Seventy miles north of Pegu, our troops are maintaining pressure on several hundred Japanese.

Artillery concentrations and air strikes are driving the enemy further north and east towards the Sittang.

Close Air Support

In the Mawchi-road area, one of our positions was shelled during the night. Elsewhere intensive patrolling continues.

AIR: Spitfires and Thunderbolts of Air Command yesterday gave close support to our troops in the Mokpalin-Nyaungkashe area:

Japanese positions and pillboxes were hit and an ammunition dump was blown up.

Liberators and Sunderlands sank a 120-ft. coaster laden with oil off the coast of Kra Isthmus and damaged **seven other coasters.—API.**

Good Morning . . .

An event in America, which may recur elsewhere, is worth watching.

More than 16,000 workers at Goodyear Tyre Company are on strike, and have been warned that unless they return to work they will be drafted for military service.

Many servicemen will see a rough justice in this. They hold that war-production workers should be subject to a war-time discipline, which in any case would be far lighter than that imposed on troops. And, equally, that employers should be under the same discipline, tho' they like "controls" no better.

After all, we have been assured both on high and low authority that "there is a war on."

*

The Charles Goodyear who began the rubber tyre business was one of the great inventors.

Like most inventors worth a hoot, he was fanatically in favour of his own invention, and was thus regarded by his neighbours as a bit barmy. His wife shared this view, especially when he had gone to the local cooler three times for debt.

She nagged him; but he kept on with his experiments, in her kitchen. He was trying to solve the problem of how to stop rubber softening and melting at high temperatures, and hardening and cracking at low temperatures.

One afternoon in 1837 his wife returned home early from shopping.

Hearing her familiar step, Charlie Goodyear hastily shoved the bowl of raw rubber he was experimenting with into the oven along with some sulphur.

Soon an acrid smell filled the house. With a sinking heart Charlie sneaked into the kitchen and furtively whipped out the bowl. To his astonishment there it was! Triumph! All he had worked for! The secret of vulcanisation—rubber plus sulphur plus heat.

Mrs Goodyear, however, gave him a really fine piece of her tongue.

*

We have now reached the point where we can make synthetic rubber And a good job we can, for when the Japs seized Malaya, the Dutch East Indies and Burma they got about four-fifths of the world's natural rubber sources.

But synthetic rubber cannot be used for all purposes, and in any case, requires a proportion of the real stuff.

That lies in territory still almost entirely in Jap hands. However, we have recaptured certain areas where the rubber tree grows. And depots where the processed rubber has been stored.

The value of this rubber—one of the most precious stores of modern mechanized war—cannot be exaggerated. Possession of it means shortening this campaign by uncounted months.

*

So at the risk or repetition (tho' not, we hope, of nagging like Charlie's Old Woman) we urge our long-suffering and good-tempered public to "Watch Your Tyres".

Bring back the worn ones for re-treading, and salvage the worn-out ones. Conserve any rubber stocks you find. Don't slash the rubber-bearing trees.

For the Lord helps those who help themselves, and as Bill Slim reminded some of the Fleet-st sahibs the other day, "Damn few others have helped us."

* *

Soldiers, airmen and a few sailors keep writing to SEAC asking us to decide whether they are entitled to this or that campaign medal. We'd like to answer every question, but we just cannot set up as interpreters of the rules.

If we get further official interpretation, we'll print it immediately.

DEFEATING MALARIA

HQ, SE ASIA COMMAND, Sun.—The never-ending battle against malaria is producing striking results in SE Asia Command, writes Major W. Martin.

Figures just released show that there were 240,000 malaria and fever cases last year, representing 46 per cent of the total sick.

Already, for the first four months of this year, it is down to 27 per cent. There has been a reduction of 62 per cent over the figures for the same period in 1944.

The overall rate for return to duty from medical units in the operational area is approximately 92 per cent. This compares with the figure of two years ago—70 per cent—when hospitals throughout Eastern India were flooded with patients.

100,000 Flown Out

Atebrin (Mepacrine) as a suppressive of, and treatment for malaria, came rapidly to the fore during 1944, and had a remarkable effect on reducing malarial figures.

A drug was imported by air to combat the dysentry-diarrhoea group of diseases and as a result, less than 50,000 cases were reported last year.

Scrub typhus drew the attention of the experts through its admission rates. With the help of world experts SE Asia Command pathologists have evolved effective preventive methods which are now in use in infected areas in Burma.

In 1943, few wounded were air evacuated. Last year, over 100,000 cases were carried by air from the front line to base hospitals.

STALIN—SOONG TALK

MOSCOW, Sun.—It was learned here that there has been a second meeting between Marshal Stalin and Dr T. V. Soong, the Prime Minister of China.—Reuter.

NAVY SWEEPS MALAY WATERS, Says TOKYO

NEW YORK, Sun.—A mighty Royal Navy task force was reported by Tokyo yesterday to be sweeping mines out of the invasion seaway to Malaya and Singapore in a move which has long been foreshadowed in New York as the next step in Admiral Lord Louis Mountbatten's campaign against Japan's dwindling South East Asia conquest, says William Hardcastle, Reuter's correspondent, in a radio despatch.

The news came at the end of a week in which Japan has been expressing mounting fears over the invasion threat to the great naval base and the rich colony area—fears underlined by the fact that all unnecessary civilians on this territory have been evacuated.

The Tokyo radio report declared that 16 warships took part, including two carriers, making up the "mainstay" of the force, indicating that other auxiliary vessels were operating there too.

The operation began, according to the Tokyo report, with the clearing of mines out of waters east of Car Nicobar Island, 300 miles north of Sumatra.

'Invade Any Time'

A feeling of great events to come—and soon—spread over the whole Pacific theatre today as senior Allied officers marked the eighth anniversary of China's war against Japan with authoritative statements on the future course of operations.

Proclaiming that a "final decisive stage" has been reached, Generalissimo Chiang Kai-shek declared: "We expect an Allied landing on Japan."

The man upon whom the brunt of such an operation will fall—commander of the Pacific Fleet Marine Force Lt-Gen Roy Geiger—confidently predicted that the Japanese homeland could be invaded "any time we want—the only thing now left is wading in and finishing the war."

JOHN AMERY IN TREASON CASE

LONDON, Sun.—John Amery, son of Mr Leopold Amery, Secretary of State for India, was arrested yesterday on his arrival in England.

An official statement from Scotland Yard last night announcing this said Amery will appear at Bow Street Police Court on Monday.

John Amery was flown under escort from Italy. He will be charged under the Treason Act.

Like William Joyce he is alleged to have made broadcasts in support of the Axis. John Amery married Miss Una Wing, a London actress, at Athens in 1933.

He was captured with his wife on 25 April, while driving from Milan to Como near the Swiss frontier.

FRENCH GIVE UP LEVANT TROOPS

PARIS, Sun.—The French Government has decided to hand over to the Syrian and the Lebanese Governments the command of "troupes speciales"—troops recruited locally in the Levant.

This decision was described by a Foreign Office spokesman here as "a gesture of conciliation and appeasement"—Reuter.

ELECTION WAITS ON HOLIDAYS

LONDON, Sun.—The General Election tumult has not yet died here. All parties are making a great effort in the 24 constituencies which have still to vote.

They are mostly in Scotland and Lancashire where holiday weeks have been observed. Now that some of the holiday-makers have returned, canvassing has begun in earnest and the parties are sending their "big guns."

CQMS Norman L. Moggs of the Pioneer Corps, surprise Independent candidate at Central Hull, has started his campaign. He says he wants to be a "spokesman for the service man."

The Evening Standard draws attention to another election. Since 1939, Britain's local councillors have known office but never the perils of the ballot, says this paper. In November they must retire and local democracy make an attempt to recapture its lost rhythm.

PM ON HOLIDAY

LONDON, Sun.—Prime Minister Churchill arrived at Hendaye, in the South of France, today accompanied by Mrs Churchill.

An official announcement said the Premier hoped to have a few days' rest before attending the Big Three conference.—Reuter.

SIMON APOLOGISES

LONDON, Sun.—Lord Simon, Lord Chancellor, has sent a letter of apology to Prof Laski for some "unpremeditated" remarks he had made at an election meeting at Carshalton, Surrey.—Reuter.

BLOCKADE PLANES HIT JAP SHIPS

GUAM, Sun.—Nine more Japanese ships have been set on fire or damaged in the Yellow Sea and south of Honshu during the past two days by blockading planes.

Up to last night Japan had suffered 33 days non-stop air attacks.

Day after day, from the Marianas, Iwojima, and Okinawa a force that totals, according to Tokyo, 11,000 aircraft will pound the Japanese homeland.

New Australian offensives have begun against the Japanese in the Wewak area of New Guinea and in South Bougainville in the Solomons after a period of consolidation.—Reuter and Globe.

JAP MERCY SHIP VISITS WAKE Is

GUAM, Sun.—The US Navy has permitted a Japanese hospital ship to evacuate 974 sick and wounded men from the enemy garrison on Wake Island.

The US destroyer Murray stopped and searched the hospital ship before and after it had called at Wake Island.—APA.

80,000 MORE TEACHERS

LONDON, Sun.—A total of 80,000 additional teachers will be needed when the 1944 Education Act comes into full effect, said Sir Maurice Homes, Permanent Secretary of the Education Ministry, giving evidence before Royal Commission on equal pay.

Sgt COMMISSIONED IN THE FIELD

ADV. HQ. ALFSEA, Sun.—After leading his platoon of Africans through two campaigns in the Kaladan, Arakan, Burma, Sgt K. T. West, 16, Glenesk-rd, Eltham, London, has been given a direct commission in the field.

THURSDAY, JULY 26, 1945

Latest Prices

ELECTION RESULTS

No. 17,811 ★ ONE PENNY

A LABOUR LANDSLIDE

Caretaker Govt. Leaders Fall Like Ninepins

TORY PARTY CHAIRMAN IS DEFEATED: MORRISON, BEVIN AND CHURCHILL IN

"STAR" REPORTER

RESULTS declared so far in the General Election show that there has been a virtual landslide in favour of Labour, with gains from the Tories registered in all parts of the country.

Heads fell rapidly among the Churchill Caretaker Government. The first to be defeated was Mr. Harold MacMillan, the Air Minister, at Stockton-on-Tees.

In quick succession there followed: Mr. Brendan Bracken, First Lord; Sir Walter Womersley, Pensions Minister; Mr. Hore-Belisha, Minister of National Insurance; Mr. Geoffrey Lloyd, Minister of Information; Mr. Amery, Secretary for India; Mr. Duncan Sandys, Minister of Works; Mr. R. K. Law, Minister of Education; Mr. William Mabane, Minister of State; Sir James Grigg, War Minister; Sir Donald Somervell, Home Secretary; and Mr. Gerald Spencer Summers, Secretary for Overseas Trade.

Shock followed shock for the Conservatives as the results poured in.

In the Tory stronghold of Birmingham, for instance, Mrs. E. A. Wills won the Duddeston Division with a majority of 4,954 against a Conservative majority of 3,262 last time. Another woman, Mrs. E. M. Braddock, captured the Exchange Division of Liverpool for Labour.

And in Rushcliffe (Notts), Mr. Ralph Assheton, chairman of the Conservative Party, was beaten by Mrs. Paton (Labour).

Labour's first London gain was in Hammersmith South, where Mr. W. T. Adams beat Sir J. Douglas Cooke, the Conservative member, who had a 6,068 majority in 1935. In South-West St. Pancras Mr. Haydn Davies captured the Tory seat with a majority for Labour of 3,671.

Mr. Bevin held Wandsworth and Mr. Herbert Morrison won East Lewisham, to which he had transferred from his old constituency of Hackney.

In the Mile End Division, Mr. Piratin won the seat for the Communists against Labour.

Mr. Churchill was returned for the new constituency of Woodford, where his former opponent, standing as an Independent, polled 10,488.

Mr. Churchill's son, Major Randolph Churchill, and Captain Julian Amery, the Conservative candidates in the double constituency of Preston, were both beaten.

☆☆ ABC list of results declared up to the time of going to press begins on Page Three.

MINISTERS IN

Winston Churchill, Prime Minister.
Quintin Hogg (Under-Secretary for Air).
Sir David Maxwell Fyfe (Attorney-General).
Oliver Lyttelton, President of the Board of Trade and Minister of Production.
Capt. Crookshank, Postmaster-General.
R. A. Butler, Minister of Labour.
R. S. Hudson, Minister of Agriculture.
Oliver Stanley, Colonial Secretary.
Lennox Boyd, Secretary Ministry of Aircraft Production.

MINISTERS OUT

Brendan Bracken (First Lord of the Admiralty).
Harold Macmillan (Secretary for Air).
Sir Walter Womersley (Minister of Pensions).
Gerald Spencer Summers (Secretary for Overseas Trade).
Leslie Hore-Belisha (Minister of National Insurance).
Geoffrey Lloyd (Minister of Information).
L. S. Amery (Secretary for India).
Duncan Sandys, Minister of Works.
Richard Law, Minister of Education.
William Mabane, Minister of State.
Sir Donald Somervell, Home Secretary.
Charles Waterhouse, Parliamentary Secretary Board of Trade.

STATE OF PARTIES

STATE of parties, compiled on the results declared up to the time of going to press, is as follows:—

GOVERNMENT

Conservative	62
National	1
Simonite	5
	68

OPPOSITION

Liberal	2
Labour	188
ILP	1
Communist	1
Common Wealth	1
Independent	4
	197

In the last Parliament the state of Parties at the Dissolution was:—Government: 358 Con., 27 Simonite, 6 Nat. Lab., 4 National; total 395. Opposition: 163 Lab., 19 Lib., 3 Ind. Lab., 3 ILP, 3 Common Wealth, 2 Irish Nat. Abstentionist, 1 Communist, 18 Independent, 1 Scot Nat.; total 213. Seven seats were vacant.

GAINS & LOSSES

	Gains	Losses
Conservative	1	92
National	0	1
Simonite	1	3
Totals for Government	2	96
Liberal	0	4
Labour	102	3
ILP	0	0
Communist	1	0
Common Wealth	0	0
Independent	1	3
Totals for Opposition	104	10

Shares Drop

"STAR" CITY EDITOR

Special arrangements were made in the Stock Exchange for announcing the Election results.

Early Labour gains influenced a cautious attitude in markets, and unsettled Industrials, several of which were 6d. to 1s. lower.

Home Rails were marked down about ½.

WAITING FOR 13

After tonight 13 election results will still remain to be declared.

Twelve of these are university seats, the results of which are expected during the next week.

The thirteenth seat is Central Hull, where the poll has been delayed by the death of a candidate. Polling will be on August 9.

New U.S. Coin

A new ten cent coin commemorating the late President Roosevelt is to be put into circulation shortly, reports Reuter from Washington. It will have a portrait of Roosevelt on one side.

Envoy To Chile Flies Home

Sir Charles William Orde, retiring British Ambassador to Chile, left Santiago today by air for Buenos Aires on his way home, said the Buenos Aires radio.

Belper, Derby—Brown, G. A. (Lab) Maj 1,881. Lab gain.

Rhondda E.—Mainwaring (Lab), maj. 972. No change.

Llandaff and Barry, Glam.—Ungoed-Thomas (Lab.), maj. 6,598. Lab. gain.

Torquay, Devon.—Williams (C.), maj. 11,889. No change.

Richmond, N. Riding Yorks.—Dugdale (C.), maj. 8,905. No change.

STATE OF PARTIES

Con. 102, Nat. 1, Simonite 9. Total for Government 112. Labour 227, Liberal 4, ILP 1, Commonwealth 1, Communist 1, Independent 4. Total for Opposition 238.

GAINS AND LOSES

Conservative gains 3, losses 113. Nat. gains 0, losses 1. Simonite gains 1, losses 5. Total for Government gains 4, losses 119. Labour gains 124, losses 3. Liberals gains 1, losses 6. Communist gains 1, losses 0. Independent gains 1, losses 3. Total for Opposition gains 127, losses 12.

ANOTHER WOMAN M.P.

Coatbridge, Lanark.—Mann, Mrs. (Lab) maj. 6,777. No change.

Romford.—Macpherson (Lab.), maj. 5,971. No change.

Wembley S.—Barton (Lab.), maj. 3,431. New division.

Coventry, West.—Edelman (Lab) maj. 15,013. Lab gain.

5¢ IN NEW YORK CITY AND SUBURBS
10¢ ELSEWHERE IN THE UNITED STATES

COMPLETE NEWS—MAGAZINE SECTION—COMIC FEATURES

New York Post

FOUNDED 1801, VOLUME 144, NO. 219. COPYRIGHT, 1945, NEW YORK POST CORPORATION.

BLUE 7 FINAL LATE SPORTS • BACK PAGE •

TWO SECTIONS NEW YORK, MONDAY, AUGUST 6, 1945 36 PAGES

EXTRA

ATOM BOMB

(2,000 Times as Powerful As Any Ever Made Before)

DROPPED ON JAPS

Story on Page 3

IMPEACH BILBO, VETERANS DEMAND

Story on Page 5

DAILY EXPRESS

No. 14,094 | Lighting-up: 9.39 pm to 4.33 am | TUESDAY AUGUST 7 1945 | Weather: Cool, showers | One Penny

Smoke hides city 16 hours after greatest secret weapon strikes

THE BOMB THAT HAS CHANGED THE WORLD

Japs told 'Now quit'

THE Allies disclosed last night that they have used against Japan the most fearful device of war yet produced—an atomic bomb.

It was dropped at 20 minutes past midnight, London time, yesterday on the Japanese port and army base of Hiroshima, 190 miles west of Kobe.

The city was blotted out by a cloud of dust and smoke. Sixteen hours later reconnaissance pilots were still waiting for the cloud to lift to let them see what had happened.

The bomb was a last warning. Now leaflets will tell the Japanese what to expect unless their Government surrenders.

So great will be the devastation if they do not surrender that Allied land forces may be able to invade without opposition.

20,000 tons in golf ball

ONE atomic bomb has a destructive force equal to that of 20,000 tons of T.N.T., or five 1,000-plane raids. This terrific power is packed in a space of little more than golf ball size.

Experts estimate that the bomb can destroy anything on the surface in an area of at least two square miles—twice the size of the City of London.

When it was tested after being assembled in a farmhouse in the remote desert of New Mexico, a steel tower used for the experiment vaporised; two men standing nearly six miles away were blown down; blast effect was felt 300 miles away.

And, at Albuquerque, 120 miles away, a blind girl cried "What is that?" when the flash lighted the sky before the explosion could be heard.

In God's mercy we outran Germany

This statement was prepared by Mr. Churchill before he resigned, and was issued from Downing-street last night.

By WINSTON S. CHURCHILL

BY THE YEAR 1939 IT HAD BECOME WIDELY RECOGNISED AMONG SCIENTISTS OF MANY NATIONS THAT THE RELEASE OF ENERGY BY ATOMIC FISSION WAS A POSSIBILITY.

The problems which remained to be solved before this possibility could be turned into practical achievement were, however, manifold and immense; and few scientists would at that time have ventured to predict that an atomic bomb could be ready for use by 1945. Nevertheless, the potentialities of the project were so great that his Majesty's Government thought it right that research should be carried on in spite of the many competing claims on our scientific manpower.

At this stage the research was carried out mainly in our universities, principally Oxford, Cambridge, London (Imperial College), Liverpool and Birmingham. At the time of the formation of the Coalition Government [May 1940] responsibility for co-ordinating the work and pressing it forward lay in the Ministry of Aircraft Production, advised by a committee of leading scientists presided over by Sir George Thomson.

At the same time, under the general arrangements then in force for the pooling of scientific information, there was a full interchange of ideas between the scientists carrying out this work in the United Kingdom and those in the United States.

A REASONABLE CHANCE

Such progress was made that by the summer of 1941 Sir George Thomson's committee was able to report that, in their view, there was a reasonable chance that an atomic bomb could be produced before the end of the war. At the end of August 1941 Lord Cherwell, whose duty it was to keep me informed on all these and other technical developments, reported the substantial progress which was being made.

The general responsibility for the scientific research carried on under the various technical committees lay with the then Lord President of the Council, Sir John Anderson. In these circumstances (having in mind also the effect of ordinary high-explosive which we had recently experienced), I referred the matter on August 30, 1941, to the Chiefs of Staff Committee in the following minute:—

> **GENERAL ISMAY FOR CHIEFS OF STAFF COMMITTEE.**—*Although personally I am quite content with the existing explosives, I feel we must not stand in the path of improvement, and I therefore think that action should be taken in the sense proposed by Lord Cherwell, and that the Cabinet Minister responsible should be Sir John Anderson.*
>
> *I shall be glad to know what the Chiefs of the Staff Committee think.*

The Chiefs of Staff recommended immediate action with the maximum priority.

I.C.I. MAN IN CHARGE

It was then decided to set up within the Department of Scientific and Industrial Research a special division to direct the work, and Imperial Chemical Industries, Ltd., agreed to release Mr. W. A. Akers to take charge of this directorate, which we called, for purposes of secrecy, the Directorate of "Tube Alloys."

After Sir John Anderson had ceased to be Lord President and became Chancellor of the Exchequer, I asked him to continue to supervise this work, for which he has special qualifications.

To advise him there was set up under his chairmanship a consultative council composed of the President of the Royal Society [Sir Henry Dale], the chairman of the Scientific Advisory Committee of the Cabinet [Lord Riverdale], the Secretary of the Department of Scientific and Industrial Research [Sir Edward Appleton] and Lord Cherwell.

The Minister of Aircraft Production, at that time Lord Brabazon, also served on this committee.

Under the chairmanship of Mr. Akers there was also a technical committee on which sat the scientists who were directing the different sections of the work, and some others. This committee was originally composed of Sir James Chadwick, Professor Peierls, and Drs. Halban,

CONTINUED ON PAGE THREE

Experts worked at Bushy Park

By GUY EDEN

THE final vital link in the chain of experiments that led to the atomic bomb is said to have been discovered largely by accident and to have been mainly the work of British scientists.

It was considered advisable to transfer the experiments to America's vast open areas because an explosion of the kind created by the new explosive force would have done vast damage in Britain—even if it were in some remote part of Scotland.

Many of the experiments were made at Teddington, Middlesex.

Underground

The scientists realised that they were dealing with a power so enormous that it might have wiped out the whole of that side of London

There were many close shaves during the experiments which went on throughout the blitz on Britain.

Sir Charles Darwin, director of the physical research laboratory at Teddington, lives literally on the job.

His house—a fine Regency mansion once occupied by King William IV.—stands in the middle of Bushy Park, and in the centre of the physical research laboratory grounds.

It is surrounded by experimental sheds, and there are underground laboratories below the mansion.

A hedge of security surrounds Sir Charles's home. A pass must be filled in before ringing his front-door bell.

Sir Charles has orders not to talk to any one—even his wife—about the atomic bomb.

'Under 400 lb.'

A REPRESENTATIVE of the Ministry of Aircraft Production said last night: "The atomic bomb is, speaking conservatively, ten times smaller than a block-buster (4,000lb.), but many times as powerful.

One bomb dropped on a town would be equivalent to a severe earthquake, and would utterly remove the place.

This invention will probably have a revolutionary effect on our future. It is impossible yet to measure its effects.

There is nothing more true than the passage in the official statement that by God's mercy Germany did not succeed first. If she had, none of us would now be here."

The men who knew

SIR JOHN ANDERSON
He supervised the work

SIR CHARLES DARWIN
He was called in

PROFESSOR BOHR.
The U 235 man—smuggled here from Denmark.

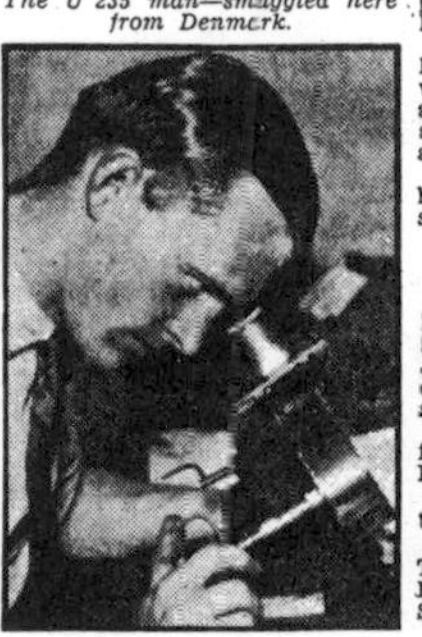

PROFESSOR FEATHER
Claims he was the first to split the oxygen atom.

SIR GEORGE THOMSON
Adviser to the Air Ministry on matters of science.

Canada helps

OTTAWA, Monday.—Uranium for the atomic bombs, is supplied by Canada. The Government established a plant in North Ottawa, and took over the Eldorado Mining and Smelting Company to guarantee supplies.

On the record

WASHINGTON, Monday.—A seismograph at Georgetown University registered a faint earth tremor at the time the first atomic bomb was dropped on Japan.—B.U.P.

BLAST FELT 300 MILES FROM BOMB TEST

Steel tower turned to vapour

From C. V. R. THOMPSON: New York, Monday

THERE is reason to believe that the vital part of the atomic bomb with its almost incredible power of devastation is not much bigger than a golf ball.

We have not seen it; all that is given officially—and this from the War Department—is that it is "a revolutionary weapon destined to change war, or which may even be the instrumentality to end all wars."

But something is known about the first test, made in heavy rain at 5.30 a.m. on July 16 in a remote area of New Mexico.

We know that the blast was felt nearly 300 miles away. Imagine feeling in Piccadilly-circus the effect of a bomb dropped in Penzance.

And there is this account, given by the U.S. War Department, of what happened in New Mexico.

"At the appointed time there was a blinding flash, lighting up the whole area brighter than the brightest daylight. A mountain range three miles from the observation point stood out in relief.

"There came a tremendous sustained roar, and a heavy pressure wave, which knocked down two men outside the control tower, 10,000 yards—nearly six miles—from the scene of the explosion.

Vaporised

"Immediately afterwards a huge multi-coloured surging cloud boiled to an altitude of more than 40,000 feet. Clouds in its path disappeared. Soon, shifting sub-stratosphere winds dispersed the narrow grey mass.

"The steel tower from which the bomb had been suspended had been entirely vaporised. Where the tower stood there was a huge sloping crater."

Specially equipped tanks were brought into the area to examine the crater.

General Leslie R. Groves, one of the key men in the project, who was in the observation post nearly 10 miles from the tower, said:—

"Two minutes before the scheduled firing time all people lay face down with their feet pointing towards the explosion. As the remaining time was called over the loud-speaker there was a complete, awesome silence.

Ball of fire

"Dr. Conant, president of Harvard University, said that he had never imagined seconds could be so long. Most of the observers, in accordance with orders, shielded their eyes.

"First came a burst of light of a brilliance beyond comparison. We all rolled over and looked through dark glasses at the ball of fire. About 40 seconds later came the shock wave followed by the sounds, neither of which seemed startling after our complete astonishment at the extraordinary lighting intensity.

"Two supplementary explosions of minor effect other than lighting occurred in the cloud—which reached the sub-stratosphere in

BACK PAGE, COL. ONE

PLANE KIDNAPS SCIENTIST

Snatched from Nazis to help us

A DANE who was smuggled into Britain and two Germans who were hounded out of their country helped the Allies to perfect the atom bomb.

PROFESSOR NIELS BOHR is the Dane; one of the men who isolated the rare form of uranium known as U.235.

When the Nazis invaded Denmark they wanted him to carry on the atomic research that had won him the Nobel prize. His answer—he closed his laboratory and vanished "underground."

The Gestapo hunted him. In October 1943, Resistance men whisked him past the Gestapo into Sweden.

Twelve days he stayed in Sweden; protected by squads of Swedish police from the ever-hunting agents and the Gestapo.

A Mosquito bomber flew through the "German air" over Norway to pick up the professor and bring him to England.

Here, and later in the U.S.A., Professor Bohr and his colleagues worked on the problems of the atom bomb, their whereabouts always secret; their laboratories always guarded.

Professor Bohr is in Britain now; his whereabouts are no longer secret. He is in London.

TWO GERMANS

PROFESSOR RUDOLF PEIRERLS and **DR. FRANZ EUGEN SIMON** are the Germans; Berlin Jews who fled from Hitler's persecution and repaid Britain for her sanctuary.

Professor Peirerls has been Professor of Applied Mathematics at Birmingham University since 1937.

Other scientists who worked on the bomb were:—

SIR GEORGE PAGET THOMSON, 53, Professor of Physics, Imperial College of Science since 1930.

A widower with two sons, two daughters; lives in Stanley-gardens, Notting Hill Gate, W.; likes ski-ing and sailing.

MR. WALLACE ALAN AKERS, 57, is a director of I.C.I.; educated Lake House School, Bexhill; Aldenham School; and Christ Church, Oxford.

A bachelor, yachtsman. Lives at the Royal Thames Yacht Club.

TWINS

SIR JAMES CHADWICK, Professor of Physics at Liverpool University. He startled science in 1932 by discovering an uncharged particle, the neutron, which completely changed conceptions of the constitution of matter. He is a Nobel Prize winner.

Married 1925, has twin daughters.

PROFESSOR J. D. COCKCROFT, Jacksonian Professor of Natural Philosophy, Cambridge.

Thirteen years ago he broke up the atom by machinery, heralding the use of atomic energy for war.

He is 48, married and has a son and four daughters.

PROFESSOR NORMAN FEATHER of the Cavendish Laboratory, Cambridge.

Claims he split the oxygen atom, the first man to do it, in 1932.

LORD CHERWELL, until 1941 Professor Frederick Alexander Lindemann; professor of Experimental Philosophy at Oxford since 1919, and Mr. Churchill's personal assistant in 1940.

Fission

Webster's Dictionary defines the noun "fission"—used by Mr. Churchill—as "a cleaving, a splitting, or breaking-up into two parts." The word is a little-used derivative of the Latin verb "findere," which means "to cleave."

This ends war as we know it

Express Staff Reporter

THE Allied discovery ends war as we know it, because not only bombs, but torpedoes, gun shells and infantry weapons can be filled with atomic explosive.

Here is the principle: when the atomic bomb strikes the ground a mechanism causes the uranium in it to disintegrate into millions of particles with enormous energy, moving at speeds like 186,000 miles a second.

These bombarding particles coupled with the sudden liberation of terrific heat cause a catastrophic explosion.

The bomb probably contains less than an ounce of the rare metal uranium, which, like radium, is constantly casting off high-speed particles, but in small numbers.

What the scientists have done is to find a way of setting free all the locked-up energy at once.

The world's supply of uranium is very small. But, using an apparatus called the cyclotron, scientists at Cambridge have been able to give to other substances the properties of uranium.

No battleship could stand a near-miss from an atomic bomb.

No plane could last in a sky of bursting atomic A.A. shells.

Tank armour could never be made to withstand the impact of a Piat bomb filled with the new explosive.

One ounce of atomic explosive probably liberates more energy in a flash than can be drawn from Niagara Falls in a week.

THE WONDER OF THE WORLD

JAPAN | TOKYO | YOKOHAMA | Hiroshima | KURE | KOBE | OSAKA | NAGASAKI | Pacific Ocean

HIROSHIMA (population 244,000) is one of the most important seaports of Central Japan.

It was famous before today—because in the bay outside the port is the sacred islet of Itaku-Shima—"Island of Light"—which is regarded as one of the three wonders of Japan. The island has a temple dating from 587.

THANKS, BRITAIN

Says Professor

From GUY AUSTIN

LOS ANGELES, Monday.—Professor R. Robert Oppenheimer, director of the work on the atomic bomb, told me tonight that any success he may have had is greatly due "to the magnificent job your people in Cambridge University—a wonderful, wonderful place—did in teaching me."

The professor was at Cambridge in 1926.

"We owe a profound debt of gratitude to our British colleagues," he said. "The whole development is probably the greatest example of the wonderful co-operation between American and British scientists and between nations."

From the laboratory where he had done most of his work, the professor said, with quiet confidence, "I think we have done remarkably well."

LEFT HIS FARM

Professor Oppenheimer goes in for large-scale farming as a hobby, and he has a ranch in New Mexico. "But for the past three years it has had to take care of itself. We have all had our noses too deep in the success of this bomb."

As for the credit for discovery, the professor insists that it be equally shared. The staff engaged on it were 98 per cent. American and two per cent. British, but, he said: "The contribution of my British colleagues was of paramount value."

4.30 a.m. LATEST

THE JAPANESE INVESTIGATE

Tokyo radio today said that the extent of the damage at Hiroshima "is now being examined."

JAP TOWN DESTROYED

GUAM, Monday.—The Japanese industrial town of Taramizu, on Kyushu, was completely destroyed in yesterday's raid by 580 Super-Forts.

Daily Mail

NO. 15,369 ONE PENNY ★★ FOR KING AND EMPIRE THURSDAY, AUGUST 9, 1945

'ALL OVER within a week,' says WASHINGTON

RUSSIA IN: THE FINAL ULTIMATUM TO-DAY

Truman to tell Tokio 'Last chance to escape annihilation'

SOVIET RUSSIA is at war with Japan to-day. Moscow radio flashed Marshal Stalin's decision to the world last night, 52 hours after the first big Japanese city had been "atomised."

The announcement said Russia was entering the war, "true to her Allies." Within a few minutes President Truman gave the news to hastily summoned reporters in Washington. Immediate reaction in high Washington circles was: "The war can be over within a week."

Moscow radio disclosed that the Japs had asked the Soviet Union to mediate with Britain and the U.S. But, said the statement, the proposal lost all validity when Tokio turned down the July 26 ultimatum from Potsdam.

President Truman is expected to give Tokio a final ultimatum when he broadcasts at 10 o'clock to-night, New York time (3 a.m. to-morrow British Summer Time). He will tell the Tokio War Lords that the full terror of atomic bombing will be unleashed on Japan unless they surrender unconditionally.

Feeling among the Allied nations last night was that the Far East war was in its last weeks—possibly days—now that Japan is faced with the overwhelming power of Britain, Russia, and America.

Stalin's decision was given by his Foreign Minister, Mr. Molotov, to Sato, Jap Ambassador in Moscow. Sato was peremptorily told to communicate the decision to the Tokio Government.

MEDIATION SCORNED

Molotov's statement to Sato, broadcast by Moscow radio, was:

After the rout and the capitulation of Nazi Germany, Japan remains the only Great Power which still stands for the continuation of the war.

The demand of the three Powers—the U.S.A., Great Britain, and China—on July 26 this year for the unconditional surrender of the Japanese Armed Forces was rejected by Japan.

Thus the proposal made by the Japanese Government to the Soviet Union of mediation in the Far East war has lost all foundation.

Taking into account Japan's refusal to capitulate, the Allies approached the Soviet Government with a proposal to join in the war against Jap aggression and thus shorten hostilities, decrease the number of casualties, and contribute towards the most speedy restoration of peace.

True to its obligation as an Ally, the Soviet Government has accepted the proposal of the Allies and has joined the declaration of the Allied Powers of July 26 this year.

The Soviet Government considers that this policy is the only means capable of bringing nearer the peace, and saving the peoples from further sacrifices and sufferings.

It gives the Japanese people the opportunity of ridding themselves of those dangers and destruction suffered by Germany after her refusal to accept unconditional surrender.

'THERE'S STILL TIME'

Moscow radio added: "Comrade Molotov also informed Mr. Sato that, simultaneously, the Soviet Ambassador in Tokio, M. Malik, had transmitted to the Japanese Government the declaration of the Soviet Government."

Moscow then quoted this statement by M. Molotov to the Ambassadors of Britain, the U.S., and China:

"On August 8, M. Molotov received the Ambassador of Britain, Sir Archibald Clark Kerr, the Ambassador of the U.S.A., Mr. Harriman, and the Ambassador of China, Mr. Chang Fu-ping, and informed them of the decision taken by the Soviet Government to declare a state of war between the Soviet Union and Japan as from August 9.

"The Ambassadors expressed their satisfaction with the declaration of the Soviet Union."

Mr. James F. Byrnes, U.S. State Secretary, said last night: "There is still time—but little time—for Japanese to save themselves from the destuction that threatens them."

Russia's Far Eastern base of Vladivostok is only 600 miles in a direct line from Tokio, which is already being hammered by Allied air armadas operating from bases south and south-east of the Japanese capital.

Russia's "Red Banner" armies along the Manchurian frontier are believed to have been substantially reinforced since the defeat of Germany, three months ago yesterday.

They will go into action against Japan's first-rate Kwantung (mainland) army based in Manchuria.

Attlee's statement

The following statement was issued by the Prime Minister from 10, Downing-street, last night:

"We in Great Britain have fully appreciated and understood the tremendous sacrifice and strain imposed on Russia by her heroic campaign against Nazi Germany, and we have always had confidence that, as soon as victory had been won in the West, Russia would take her stand with her Allies against the enemy on the Eastern Front.

"The unconditional surrender of Germany has now made possible the deployment of the forces of the U.S.S.R. against the last of the aggressors.

"The declaration of war made to-day by the U.S.S.R. upon Japan is a proof of the solidarity that exists between the principal Allies, and should shorten the struggle and establish conditions which will allow general peace to be brought about.

"We welcome this great decision of Soviet Russia."

LAST ROUND

THIS map shows how the entry of Russia into the Far East war hems in Japan from all sides. From great new air-bases, the Red Air Force will strike at Tokio, Osaka, and Yokohama.

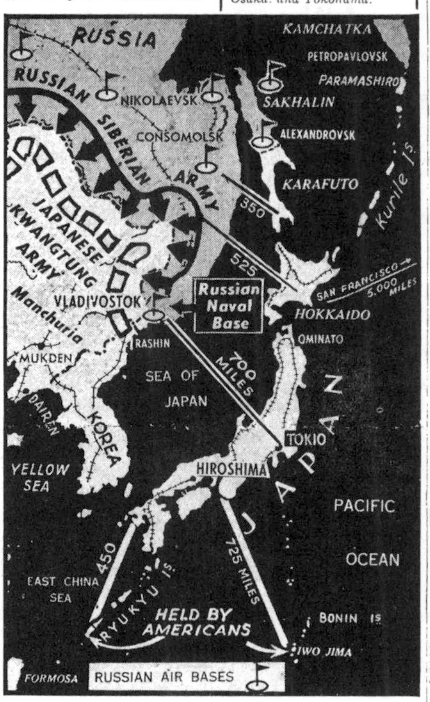

Leading march east

Koniev. *Zhukov.* *Blücher.*

Million Russians are moving on Japan

NEW YORK, Wednesday.

RUSSIA probably has an army of 1,000,000 veteran troops on the move to-day against Japan's outposts in Manchuria and Korea.

Most of these troops have had years of service in the two special "Red Banner" Far East Armies, which were maintained by Russia at almost full strength throughout the war, even at the times of the greatest crises on the Eastern Front.

The Russian commanders in the East will not be known until Marshal Stalin issues his first communiqués, but they will probably include some of the crack Marshals who led the armies in the West.

Many of these men, including Marshal Zhukov, won fame in fighting in the large-scale Manchurian frontier battles of Lake Khasan in 1938 and Lake Buir Nor in 1939.

Zhukov would be a likely commander, since it was he who crushed the Japanese Sixth Army in a full-scale battle at the Khalka River in 1939.

Marshal Koniev, who was number two man on the West Front, was with the "Red Banner" armies in the Far East when the Germans attacked Russia.

Koniev was last reported to be ill in Vienna, which may be a diplomatic way of masking his movement to Siberia.

The Russian declaration cannot come as a surprise to anybody who has been in Russia during the past 18 months.

There seems no doubt that the timing of the declaration was agreed upon at Potsdam, where the three steps to knock Japan out of the war were planned.

The first was the ultimatum from the Western Allies to Japan. The second was the atomic bomb. This is the third.

It can be revealed now that speculation in the U.S. Press on Russia's entry into the war has been restricted at the special request of the censors so that the terrific impact of the Allied blows against Japan should not be lost.

UNEASY PEACE ENDED

RUSSIA'S declaration of war against Japan ends 20 years of uneasy peace between the countries in which "secret war" has lasted for months at a time on the borders of Manchuria and thousands of men have been killed. A diary of the main diplomatic events in those years is:

1925.—Japanese recognise Soviet Government for first time and evacuate last part of Russian territory. After this there was little diplomatic contact for nearly ten years.

1925-35.—Soviets resentful at Japs' refusal to discuss the question of fishing rights in Russian waters, awarded Japan by Treaty of Portsmouth, 1905. Constant series of incidents on border of Manchuria.

1937.—Amur river clash. This was most important border battle, and Japs had 184 casualties. The fight preceded the intensification of their undeclared war against China. Russia lost the fight and did not react diplomatically.

Russians fortified Amur frontier, doubled track of the trans-Siberian railway to carry supplies in case of real war and reformed Soviet Far East Army.

1939.—Two months fighting at Nonmohon on the border costs the Japanese 18,000 casualties. A truce was declared on the outbreak of the European war.

1941.—In January M Matsuoka, then Japanese Foreign Minister, announced that important negotiations were about to begin. In April Russia and Japan signed a five-years non-aggression pact.

1945.—On April 15 Russia denounced the pact on the grounds that it had "lost its meaning."

Atom bomb fleets waiting for signal

Truman's choice

From JAMES BROUGH, Daily Mail Special Correspondent

WASHINGTON, Wednesday.

LIGHTS in the White House are burning late to-night. President Truman, fresh from his announcement of Russia's declaration of war, is wrestling with a problem more fearful, perhaps, than any which has faced other heads of State in all history.

In front of him are reports and pictures proving that one 400lb. missile can wipe out 60 per cent. of a city of 300,000 people.

Mr. Stimson, his War Secretary, has reported that the raid was more successful than scientists or military men had considered possible.

It is estimated that 150,000 Japanese died in four square miles of havoc.

From Guam, General Spaatz has cabled that a fleet of specially-equipped Super-Fortresses are ready to deliver Atobomb No. 2 on whatever target the President names.

From three great war plants in Tennessee and Washington State reports have been sent to the White House that production of atobombs is well up to schedule.

In 36 hours

At a command the President can send out a fleet of bombers to obliterate a nation, but with it thousands of American and British troops who have been held behind barbed wire in Japanese cities since Bataan and Singapore.

While he works people are praying in their homes that he may make the right decision.

Shall he end the war now with this crushing devastation, or shall he go ahead with present plans to use the lives of thousands more Allied soldiers, sailors, airmen who will tread the bloody road to peace from island to island until the shores of Nippon are reached?

What is President Truman holding in his hand? Is it Pandora's Box which, if opened wide, will release a whirlwind destroying first Japan but finally all the world?

Or is it a gift through science which, if used now, can end not only this war but the scourge of war for all time?

Within the next 36 hours the President will make his decision known to the world in a broadcast to the nation.

EIRE HITS AT 'DESERTERS'

No pension

Irishmen who deserted from the Eire Army and joined the British Forces will no longer be court-martialled if absent for 180 days or more. This was officially announced in Dublin last night.

As from yesterday, however, the deserters will be automatically dismissed from the Eire Army. They will forfeit all pension rights and will be prohibited for seven years from holding any employment under the State or in a local authority. They will also be ineligible for the "dole"

Army sources in Dublin admitted last night that "at least 1,000 men" had deserted from the Eire Army in the last five years; most of them had joined the British Forces.

'Davies as envoy to Britain'

From Daily Mail Correspondent

NEW YORK, Wednesday.—Mr. Joseph E. Davies, former U.S. Ambassador to Russia, was to-day reported to have been chosen as the next American Ambassador to Britain.

The present Ambassador, Mr. John Winant, will soon become the U.S. representative on the United Nations Economic Council.

ATTLEE PLANS STATEMENT

Moscow (and the atom bomb) bring the end near

TOKIO FANATICS TOTTERING

By WILSON BROADBENT, Political Correspondent

EVERYTHING points to Japan's early collapse under the threat of further atomic bomb raids, and Soviet Russia's declaration of war. In Whitehall, it is thought that the end of the war in the Far East is now only a matter of weeks.

"The end may come even sooner than that," was the cryptic comment of one high official yesterday, some hours before the Moscow announcement. Japan will now feel that she is cornered, and that capitulation is her only chance of survival.

Obviously, Russia's declaration was timed to fit in with the all-round pressure now being imposed on Japan.

Presumably it arises out of the Potsdam deliberations, although until last night Russia's attitude to the Far East war, and her share in the atomic bomb decision, were among the unrevealed secrets of the Big Three Conference which had caused general mystification.

All the information reaching London by way of the joint Chiefs of Staff Committee in Washington indicates that the fanaticism of the Japanese war leaders has been severely shaken.

Ever since the collapse of Germany the Japanese have been casting round for means to avert the inevitability of a crushing defeat, but they cannot have been aware of the impending use of the atomic bomb.

According to official opinion, this development will speed events inside Japan, where unrest is growing, and even the convention of saving face no longer has the same appeal to the masses.

The bomb

The Prime Minister is planning to make a statement on the Far East war as soon as the House of Commons reassembles next week.

He will be pressed to give some indication of the circumstances in which the decision was reached to use the atomic bomb; what was the attitude of the British Government in the first consultations; and if Russia joined in them.

Russia's declaration of war may be taken by most people as an explanation for her not being associated with the ultimatum sent to Japan before the first atomic bomb was loosed on that country.

But Mr. Attlee will also have to answer questions on this aspect of

BACK PAGE—Col. ONE

Peter issues challenge to Tito

'Dictatorship'

TWENTY-ONE-YEARS-old King Peter of Yugoslavia has quickly reacted to Marshal Tito's call for a republic. Last night he issued a proclamation dismissing his three Regents.

"Henceforth," he said, "the duty of defending the constitutional rights of my people reverts to me."

The proclamation, issued from 41, Upper Grosvenor-street, London, said:

"Yesterday's speech of Marshal Tito is the final repudiation of the agreement concluded between himself and Dr. Subasic, my Prime Minister, a process which he began almost immediately after it was signed.

"It is public knowledge that my assent to the agreement was given only at the advice of the great Allies in order that no obstacle should be placed in the way of the successful outcome of the war in Europe.

"In my country there exists on a full scale the dictatorship of the Tito régime.

'Terror'

"Every trace of law has been wiped out from the State organisation, thus taking away entirely the free will of the people.

"There are preparations for a plebiscite by forceful means and under terror of the special police organisation which replaced the Gestapo."

"As to the freedoms mentioned in the agreement, those of Press, public meetings, and forming of political parties, etc., have remained a dead letter. Only one voice is heard, that of Marshal Tito and his totalitarian movement.

"I consider that the Regents have not been allowed to perform my constitutional duties and that they have overlooked their oaths and obligations given to me.

"I proclaim that they can no longer represent me or work in my name. I have decided to withdraw the authority which I give to them.

"I cannot give my personal sanction to a state of affairs which is abhorrent to me."

The action of King Peter can have little practical or immediate effect on the general situation in Yugoslavia. The question of the Monarchy must remain over until a popular decision has been reached.

It was reported yesterday that Marshal Tito had called for a republican form of Government and the complete destruction of "reactionary bands" still hiding in the forests.

50,000 HOME THIS MONTH

ROME, Wednesday.

AT least 50,000 British soldiers serving in this theatre will be sent home for leave during this month, it was authoritatively stated here to-day.

By the end of the month age service groups 1 to 13 will have left the theatre. The average weekly rate at the moment for men going home for leave, discharge, and redeployment is about 21,000.

The men go home either by road, via Salzburg (Austria) and Calais; by rail, via Marseilles, Paris, and Dieppe; or Lausanne (Switzerland), Paris, and Calais; or by air, direct from Italy to England.—*Reuter.*

India solution hint

CALCUTTA, Wednesday.—Sir Stafford Cripps has replied to the message of good wishes sent by the President of Congress, Abdul Kalam Azad, with the following cable: "May our joint efforts soon solve the problem of India."—*Exchange.*

CELEBRATIONS IN BERLIN

Berlin, Wednesday.—Allied soldiers celebrated in Berlin when they heard the news of Russia's declaration of war on Japan.—B.U.P.

ALLIED PLANES HIT 59 JAP SHIPS

Allied planes destroyed or damaged 59 Japanese vessels in attacks in areas ranging from waters off Korea to the Netherlands East Indies, says Manila communiqué.—B.U.P.

2

Race to save blazing ship

HALIFAX, Nova Scotia, Wednesday.—Three Royal Canadian Navy minesweepers equipped with fire-fighting apparatus are to-night travelling at top speed to the 7,000-tons vessel Argos Hill which is blazing in the Atlantic, 385 miles out from Halifax.

Before being ordered to abandon ship, the English crew of 40 fought the flames for 24 hours.

All except one man, who is unaccounted for, have been taken off and are aboard the cargo ship Noah Brown, which is standing by.—*Reuter.*

FRIDAY, AUGUST 10, 1945

FINAL NIGHT EXTRA

Evening Standard

37,722 | 24-HOUR FORECAST: Brighter: warmer | MOON: Rises 8 a.m. Sets 10 p.m. LIGHTING-UP TIME: 9.33 p.m. | ONE PENNY

Tokyo accepts Potsdam ultimatum

SURRENDER ON TERMS

Last bid to save the Emperor

Japan offered conditional surrender to the Allies at twenty minutes to one o'clock this afternoon. The Japanese rulers are willing to accept the "give in or be destroyed" declaration issued by the Allies at Potsdam as long as the Mikado stays on the Throne.

The Japanese announcement, which was broadcast, came 110 hours after the dropping of the first atom bomb and 36 hours after Russia entered the war against Japan.

This offer has not yet reached London, but President Truman summoned members of the U.S. Cabinet in Washington to-day. Several days may be required for direct contact and surrender arrangements if the Allies accept.

Mr. James F. Byrnes, U.S. Secretary of State, said at 2.20 p.m. (London time) that the U.S. have not had any official surrender offer yet. The U.S. Government will take no action without consulting all other governments concerned, he added.

A Moscow message states that the Japanese Premier, Togo, informed the Soviet Ambassador in Tokyo, M. Malik, that Japan is ready to accept the Potsdam terms.

Japanese radio listeners had been warned to stand by for "a sensational message which the people of the war-torn world had been waiting for and longing to hear." Then came the announcement. And this is what it said:

"The Japanese Government to-day addressed the following communication to the Swiss and Swedish Governments for transmission to the United States, Britain, China and the Soviet Union.

"In obedience to the gracious command of His Majesty the Emperor, who, ever anxious to enhance the cause of world peace, desires earnestly to bring about an early termination of hostilities with the view to saving mankind from the calamities to be imposed upon them by the further continuance of the war, the Japanese Government several weeks ago asked the Soviet Government, with which neutral relations then prevailed, to render its good offices in restoring peace with the enemy Powers.

The Mikado's wish

"Unfortunately, these efforts in the interest of peace having failed, the Japanese Government, in conformity with the august wish of His Majesty to restore general peace and desiring to put an end to the untold sufferings entailed by the war as quickly as possible, have decided upon the following:

"The Japanese Government is ready to accept the terms enumerated in the joint declaration issued at Potsdam on July 26 by the heads of the Governments of the United States, Great Britain and China, and lately subscribed to by the Soviet Government, with the understanding that the said declaration does not comprise any demand which prejudices the prerogatives of His Majesty as a sovereign ruler.

"The Japanese Government hopes sincerely . . ."

At this point the transmission was interrupted, and after a moment was resumed with the service warning "Stand by."

After a few moments the news agency went off the air.

● Back Page, Col. One

Jubilation

As soon as the news of Japan's offer reached Australia House its windows opened and on Aldwych below torn papers and unused telegram forms showered down.

For 90 minutes the paper floated down, buses, taxis and cars carrying the paper along, white streamers catching on the shoulders of despatch riders.

Men of all Services from Australia House gave the "Digger" call—Coo-eee—and let off fireworks.

West End typists and clerks showered confetti like a snowfall on to the streets from office windows, and workers climbed out on to the balconies waving and shouting.

All work was suspended in offices in Kingsway, Aldwych and the Strand, and employees crowded on to the roofs and threw showers of paper down in the streets below.

Inveresk House, Bush House and other large buildings were festooned with ticker tape and paper streamers.

Policeman tossed

Showers of paper poured from top floor windows in Leicester-square, Piccadilly-circus and Regent-street. Then crowds began to pour into Piccadilly-circus till the traffic was forced to a standstill. All up Shaftesbury-avenue bus and car drivers gave it up, parked by the kerb.

A burly police-sergeant tried to get the traffic moving again out of Shaftesbury-avenue into Piccadilly-circus.

But a party of Americans led by a bearded submariner seized him carried him shoulder high round the circus, and tossed him time and again into the air until he was helpless with laughter and the crowd was roaring.

Towards three o'clock Trafalgar-square began to fill up. It looks as though London will go to town in a big way to-night.

At Portsmouth for nearly an hour after the news came through sirens and hooters of warships and tugs were shrieking.

Pictures—PAGES FIVE AND EIGHT.

FOURTEEN YEARS

Sept. 18, 1931.—Attack on Manchuria.
July 7, 1937.—Battle of Lukuochia, Peking.
Dec. 8, 1941.—Attack on Pearl Harbour.
Dec. 9, 1941.—At war with Britain.
Dec. 10, 1941. — H.M.S. Prince of Wales and H.M.S. Repulse sunk.
Dec. 25, 1941.—Hongkong surrendered.
Feb. 15, 1942.—Singapore surrendered.
Feb. 27, 1942.—Battle of Java Sea.
Sept. 13, 1942.—Turning point of war. Japan held in New Guinea.
Aug. 7, 1945.—Hiroshima obliterated.
Aug. 9, 1945. — Russia declares war.
Aug. 10, 1945. — Japan surrenders.

British Cabinet meet

A meeting of the British Cabinet was held this afternoon.

Evening Standard Political Correspondent

The march of events following the Jap offer will be in this order:

The official text will be decoded for submission to the Cabinet. This will take some time.

The Cabinet will decide whether the offer is acceptable to Britain. It is expected to take the line that as the offer makes special conditions about the Emperor, it does not represent "unconditional surrender," or fit in with the Potsdam declaration.

The British Government will communicate with the other powers, who will have considered the offer individually.

A joint reply will be prepared and sent to Japan.

Waiting period

Then there will be a period of waiting for the Japanese reply.

That too will be examined individually by the Powers and a joint decision will be taken.

Not until the end is certainly in sight will plans be considered for celebrations.

These will include two or three days' holiday, broadcasts by the King and the Prime Minister, thanksgiving services and organised celebrations throughout the country of the return of peace to the world.

An American report that the condition about the Mikado will not prevent Britain from agreeing to the Jap proposal is without authority.

IT WOULD BE LIKE LEAVING HITLER

Powers and the Mikado

From WILLIAM ALISON

Immediate reactions in well-informed quarters in London indicate that the attempt to preserve the Emperor Hirohito as ruler of Japan is bound to be rejected.

The Allies have all along insisted that the only act on the part of Japan which could end the war would be complete and unconditional surrender — as complete as it was in the case of Germany.

Any special protection for the Emperor and his prerogatives would not be unconditional surrender.

To accept terms which would leave the Emperor would be comparable to accepting German surrender and leaving Hitler, to carry on as head of the State.

On March 10, 1942, when Mr. Eden made a statement to the Commons about the Japanese atrocities in Hongkong he was asked by Sir Percy Harris:

"Is it clear that not only the Emperor, but the Government of Japan and the whole Japanese people are responsible for these atrocities and not merely the army?"

Mr. Eden replied: Yes, sir. That is certainly so.

There have been two views about Hirohito as a war criminal. One said that to execute him would prolong the war by increasing Jap fanaticism: the other that there could be no permanent peace as long as there was a "sacred" Mikado in Japan.

NAGASAKI

Nagasaki, second city hit by the Atom Bomb, vanished in a twisting column of smoke and flame visible for 250 miles. See PAGE THREE.

These are the Potsdam Terms

In the Potsdam Proclamation, issued on July 26, President Truman, Mr. Churchill and General Chiang-Kai-shek gave Japan the choice of surrender or prompt and utter destruction.

It was an ultimatum, couched in 13 strong paragraphs, signed in Potsdam by Mr. Churchill and President Truman before Mr Churchill left for London, and the next day it received the complete concurrence of General Chiang-Kai-shek.

President Truman then issued instructions to the Office of War Information in Washington to bring the Proclamation before the Japanese people.

'Poised to strike'

Paragraph 1 of the Proclamation stated that the United States, Great Britain, and China, representing hundreds of millions of their countrymen" had conferred and agreed that Japan should be given an opportunity to end the war.

Paragraphs 2 and 3 pointed out that the prodigious land sea and air forces of the three nations were poised to strike the final blows against Japan, and that the might converging on Japan was immeasurably greater than that which had been applied to the Nazis.

The full application of that military power would mean the inevitable destruction not only of the Japanese armed forces, but also of the Japanese homeland.

Paragraph 4 said the time had come for Japan to decide whether she would continue to be controlled by her militaristic advisers, who had brought the Japanese Empire to the threshold of annihilation, or whether she would follow the path of reason.

'We insist . . .'

The remaining paragraph gave the Allied terms: "There will be no deviation; there are no alternatives, and we shall brook no delay."

The terms were: "The authority and influence of those who have deceived and misled the people of Japan into embarking on world conquest must be eliminated for all time. We insist that a new order of peace, security and justice will be impossible until irresponsible militarism is driven from the world.

"Until such a new order is established, and there is convincing proof that Japan's war-making power is destroyed, points in Japanese territory designated by the Allies shall be occupied to secure the achievement of the basic objectives now set forth.

"The terms of the Cairo declaration shall be carried out and

▲ Back Page, Col. Three

TUESDAY, AUGUST 14, 1945

Evening Standard

37,725 24-HOUR FORECAST: Sunny; dull periods; warm. MOON RISES: 12.31 p.m. Sets 11.7 p.m. LIGHTING-UP TIME: 9.26 p.m. ONE PENNY

FINAL NIGHT EXTRA

AT LAST—IT'S NEARLY ALL OVER

A 'voluminous reply on basis of a statement by the Tokyo War Ministry.' But it means—

JAPS ACCEPT

The Emperor cries 'This is calamity'

Japan has given in to the terms imposed on her in the latest Allied Note, Swiss radio announced this afternoon. This, if confirmed, as it seems likely to be, means that the Japs have bowed to the Allied demand for unconditional surrender.

The Swiss radio said: "The Japanese information office this morning reported acceptance of the Allied capitulation formula, on the basis of a statement by the Japanese War Ministry."

A little before that Paris radio put out this message: "A last-minute despatch from Berne announces that the Swiss Foreign Office have received an answer from the Japanese Government to the American Note. The Japanese answer is a rather voluminous message, which is now being decoded. It is thought in Berne that the document will be handed to the U.S. and Chinese Ministers this afternoon."

At the same hour Tokyo was heard broadcasting emergency calls to Japanese ships at sea, and other Tokyo transmitters were contacting Japanese officials in Stockholm.

Hirohito's future

Terms sent to the Japanese Government on Saturday (in reply to the Japanese offer to accept the Potsdam Declaration on condition that the Emperor was allowed to remain) were as follow:

1. **—The Japanese Emperor and Government are to subject their authority to that of an Allied Supreme Commander. (General Douglas MacArthur has been unofficially mentioned for the post.)**
2. **—The Emperor is to order the surrender of Japanese troops in all theatres.**
3. **—The Japanese Government is to transport prisoners and civilian internees to places of safety immediately.**
4. **—The Japanese people are to be free to decide their ultimate form of government.**
5. **—Allied troops are to remain in Japan for a specified period.**

VJ COACH TRIPS

To the coast

The Regional Transport Commissioner for London has decided that the authority which was issued for coach journeys to the coast on August Bank Holiday Monday shall include also VJ public holidays.

Each operation must be confined to one day only, all passengers returning the same day.

Guard at Laval's gaol arrested

PARIS, Tuesday.—One of the guard at Fresnes Prison outside Paris, where Pierre Laval and other collaborators are held awaiting trial, has been arrested on a charge of trying to smuggle arms to the prisoners.

The man, Jean Malacenne, was arrested on the outskirts of the city while trying to make his escape. —A.P.

Governor killed

The Governor-General of Western Japan and the Lord Mayor of Hiroshima were killed in the Atom Bomb raid said Tokyo radio to-day.

No more food, says Minister

Sir Ben Smith, new Food Minister, said this afternoon: "There is no prospect of any improvement in the rations." He listed:

Meat. — Little likelihood of replacing corned beef with carcass meat this year

Bacon.—Serious difficulty; no restoration of the cut.

Sugar. — Further economy needed, but not cut in domestic ration.

Oils and Fats.—No increase.

Eggs.—More shell eggs, fewer dried eggs.

Fish.—The one bright spot—much more.

Fruit.—More tomatoes, more oranges.

(Details PAGE FIVE.)

THE LIGHTS GO UP

AT PEARL HARBOUR

NEW YORK, Tuesday. — The lights of Pearl Harbour, reinforced by 40 searchlights, went on again last night after the Japanese surrender forecasts had been picked up, said reports received here.

Rockets and flares filled the air for 20 minutes.—Reuter.

Rail wages may be fixed to-day

Final arrangements for the new agreement covering wages and conditions for railway workers throughout the country (apart from the shopmen) are expected to be announced to-day.

A further conference in London this afternoon is considering the fixing of differential rates for grades above the minimum rated grades, and the date from which increases will take effect.

A Japanese transmitter broadcasting to occupied Asia was heard announcing that it was closing down until 1 p.m. B.S.T., when a news announcement would be put on the air.

And soon after 1 p.m. a message from the Mikado to the people of occupied Asia was put out by the Japanese News Agency.

HIROHITO BLAMES U.S.

It began by expressing Hirohito's "extreme concern at the calamity caused by the United States."

The message was addressed to Japanese citizens assembled before the bridge leading to the parade grounds outside the Imperial Palace in Tokyo.

Hirohito said his concern had existed since war was declared on the United States and Britain in 1941.

While the Mikado's message was being transmitted by the Japanese News Agency, Tokyo radio announced: "A very important announcement will be broadcast at noon on Wednesday, Tokyo time (4 a.m. B.S.T.)."

When the United States Secretary of State, Mr. James F. Byrnes, reached his office he said he could add nothing to Press reports of the Japanese broadcast. He then had a 20-minute conference with President Truman.

When he left the White House Mr. Byrnes said, according to Reuter: "Yes, I am expecting some news." But he did not say when.

Indication that the Japs had decided there was nothing for them to do but to give in came in a Tokyo broadcast early to-day, which said: "The text of the Imperial message accepting the Potsdam proclamations will be coming soon." That announcement was repeated several times.

LATE CABINET SESSION

A little earlier Tokyo radio reported that the Japanese Cabinet had been in continuous session until late at night, and indicated that the reply to the Allied unconditional surrender demand would probably be available "as soon as legal procedures are completed."

The British Cabinet—like the Japanese Cabinet—were in session for an hour and a quarter at No. 10, Downing-street during the morning. But there was a world of difference between the atmosphere in which the two Cabinets met.

Cheering crowds were outside No. 10. It is hardly

● **Back Page, Col. One**

5000 TONS OF BOMBS ON JAPS

Strong sea and air attacks reinforced the warning to Japan that the war was still on.

Superforts, in their first raid since the Japanese surrender offer on Friday, flew from bases on Tinian to blitz Marifu rail yards and shipping to-day, said Reuter.

Marifu is 14 miles from Hiroshima, atom bomb target.

The Forts dropped 5000 tons of high explosive bombs, said A.P., and later it was disclosed that another force, continuing the day-long blasting of individual targets in the Japanese homeland, attacked the Hikari naval arsenal and the Osaka army arsenal.

Over 600 bombers and fighters—biggest air fleet ever sent out by Far East air forces—took part in this first phase of a new air campaign

Over 40 Japanese vessels were sunk or damaged, with direct hits on a cruiser, cables B.U.P.

Over 1000 British and American carrier airplanes from Admiral William Halsey's U.S 3rd Fleet struck at six airfields protecting Tokyo's metropolitan area.

U.S. warships, nearly 1100 miles away, bombarded three military positions in the Kuriles. Japan's northerly outposts

VJ DAYS probably Thursday and Friday

By WILLIAM ALISON

Final official news of the Jap acceptance of the Allied conditions was expected to reach London this afternoon.

As soon as possible the Prime Minister will go to the microphone.

Everything is ready in No. 10 Downing-street for him to speak from there

According to tentative plans the Prime Minister's speech is expected about 5 or 6 o'clock this evening.

The King will speak to the nation on the radio at 9 o'clock to-night.

A DAY'S WARNING

While no final decision has been taken about the VJ two-days' holiday, these are likely to be Thursday and Friday.

The view to-day was that a day's warning of the holiday would be more convenient alike to employers and employees.

With Thursday and Friday as holidays many workers will be able to look forward to four clear days.

The Prime Minister's first act when the news is final and definite will be to go to the Palace to see the King.

If the news comes to-day—and all the plans are, of course, conditional on that—Mr. Attlee will go to the Palace again to-night. It is expected that the King and Queen will appear to the crowds on the Palace balcony and that Mr. Attlee will accompany them.

MR. CHURCHILL

Mr. Attlee's further appearance before the crowds will be governed by circumstances.

I learn, however, that arrangements have been made so that the Ministry of Health balcony in Whitehall will be available for him to speak to the crowds as Mr. Churchill did in the VE celebrations.

What part Mr. Churchill will take in the celebrations is not yet known. There are certain to be demands from the crowds for the war leader, but Mr. Churchill will decide himself to what extent he will participate. There will be a welcome for him everywhere.

THANKSGIVING

To-morrow both Houses of Parliament will attend thanksgiving services. These are expected to take place after the State opening

▲ **Back Page, Col. Four**

London starts new celebration

Evening Standard Reporter

The news of the Japanese acceptance was received in Holborn, Oxford-street and other parts of the West End with great excitement.

There were fights in Tottenham Court-road, Oxford-street, Oxford-circus, and adjacent thoroughfares, for copies of the evening newspapers. People on buses clambered down with a rush to get copies.

Bunting appeared at the windows of shops and offices. Ticker tape floated down.

A great crowd gathered in Trafalgar-square, where loudspeakers had been installed in anticipation of an announcement.

People crowded the steps of the National Gallery,

POST THIS COPY TO A SERVICE FRIEND OVERSEAS POSTAGE ½d.

No. 9195

DAILY HERALD

WEDNESDAY AUG 15 1945

ONE PENNY

Midnight News Of Victory: Holidays Today And Tomorrow

IT'S OVER—OFFICIAL

Jap Surrender Will Be Signed At Once—To MacArthur

COMPLETE and final surrender of Japan, and the end of the war, was announced from London, Washington, Moscow and Chungking at midnight last night.

Arrangements have been made for signing of the surrender at the earliest possible moment. General MacArthur has been appointed Allied commander to receive the surrender.

Broadcasting the news to Britain from No. 10 Downing-street, Mr. Attlee announced that today and tomorrow would be victory holidays.

The Japanese reply was handed over to the Swiss Foreign Office in Berne at 8.10 p.m.

The Minister, Shunichi Kase, delivered it in person, and left at once.

Within a few minutes the Foreign Office sent for the United States Minister, Mr. Leland Harrison, who arrived shortly before 8.30 p.m., and the text was cabled to Washington at 9.5 p.m.

It was transmitted to the Swiss Legation there and delivered by the Minister, M. Max Grassli, to Mr. James F. Byrnes, the United States Secretary of State.

About a minute later, Mr. Byrnes left for the White House. He walked rapidly through a side door, carrying a bundle of papers.

Special Electric Supply

At 5 p.m. British Summer Time yesterday the following Tokyo Radio message in English was picked up in London and New York:—

"It is authoritatively learned that the Japanese Government's reply to the Four Powers' message is now on its way to the Japanese Minister in Berne."

It followed, by just over three hours, a report from the same station that a "very important announcement will be broadcast at noon on Wednesday"—4 a.m. today B.S.T.

The announcer read an order calling upon Japan's 100,000,000 people, without exception, to listen to the 4 a.m. broadcast.

Special arrangements were made later to supply electric current for radio sets "to places where daytime supplies would not otherwise be available."

"Long Vigil Ending"

Such confusion was caused by the spate of rumours that circled the world before the great news that the White House had to issue an official denial of a statement issued by President Truman's Press Secretary, Mr. Charles Ross.

Early yesterday American Government radio stations heard Tokyo transmitting a long code message to the Japanese Minister in Berne.

In the afternoon the White House announced that the Swiss Foreign Office, had received the Japanese reply, and that its contents would be disclosed simultaneously, some time during the day, in the capitals of the four Powers.

Mr. Ross, breaking the news to hundreds of reporters, commented: "It looks as if the long vigil is coming to an end."

Half an hour later the Swiss Legation in Washington flashed to the State Department the following message from its Foreign Office in Berne:

"Very urgent. Japanese Legation reports that the coded cables it received this morning do not contain the answer awaited by the whole world."

Attlee: Mikado Issues Order

MR ATTLEE, the Prime Minister, broadcasting at midnight, said:

Japan has today surrendered. The last of our enemies is laid low.

Here is the text of the Japanese reply to the Allied Command:

"With reference to the announcement of August 10 regarding the acceptance of the provisions of the Potsdam Declaration and the reply of the Government of the United States, Great Britain, the Soviet Union, and China, sent by Secretary of State Byrnes on August 11, the Japanese Government has the honour to reply to the Governments of the four Powers as follows:

"(1) His Majesty the Emperor has issued an Imperial rescript regarding Japan's acceptance of the provisions of the Potsdam Declaration.

"(2) His Majesty the Emperor is prepared to authorise and insure the signature by his Government and the Imperial Headquarters of the necessary terms for carrying out the provisions of the Potsdam Declaration.

"(3) His Majesty is also prepared to issue this communication to all military, naval and air authorities to issue to all forces under their control wherever located to cease active resistance and to surrender arms.—Signed Tojo."

Turn Of Tide

Let us recall that on December 7 1941, Japan, whose onslaught China had resisted for over four years, fell upon the United States and upon ourselves who were sorely pressed in our death struggles with Germany and Italy.

Taking full advantage of surprise and treachery, the Japanese forces quickly overran the territories of ourselves and our Allies in the Far East, and at one time it appeared as though these invaders would reach the mainland of Australia and advance into India.

But the tide turned.

With ever-increasing speed the mighty forces of the United States and the British Commonwealth and Empire and other Allies were brought to bear.

Their resistance has now everywhere been broken.

At this time we should pay tribute to the men from this country, from the Dominions, from India, and the Colonies, to our Fleets, Armies and Air Forces that have fought so well in the campaign against Japan.

We Rejoice

Our gratitude goes out to all our splendid Allies, above all to the United States, without whose prodigious efforts this war in the East would still have many years to run.

We also think especially at this time of the prisoners in Japanese hands, of our friends in the Dominions, Australia and New Zealand, in India and Burma, and in those colonial territories upon whom the brunt of the Japanese attack fell.

We rejoice that these territories will soon be purged of the Japanese invader.

Here at home you have earned

① Continued on Back Page

Communists Defy Chiang Kai-Shek

GENERAL CHU-TEH, leader of the Chinese Communist forces in North-West China, has sent a wireless message to Generalissimo Chiang Kai-shek, refusing to accept an order not to advance against the Japs.

The message, says Yenan radio, declares that the order to remain at posts and await instructions is contradictory to a second order also received telling officers and men in various zones to intensify their efforts.

The "await instructions" order, the message says, "does not conform to the national interest. We consider you have issued the wrong order, and we have to reject it resolutely."

EMPEROR HEARD ALLIED BOMBERS

From Arthur Webb
"Herald" Reporter,
Washington, Tuesday

THE roar of Twentieth Air Force planes putting out their maximum effort was heard today by the Japanese Emperor and his peace committee in the Imperial Palace at Tokyo.

Super-Forts dropped about 6,000 tons of demolition and incendiary bombs on military targets during daylight today and in the early hours (Japanese time).

Targets were Hikari naval arsenal, Osaka army arsenal, Marifu railway yards, near Hiroshima, the first atom bomb target,

Heavier air attacks than ever are in store, said a military authority in Washington.

More than 15,000,000 leaflets have been dropped on Japan during the past week. They dealt with the peace negotiations, atomic bombing and the entry of Russia into the war.

Russians In Jap Island

RED ARMY troops were last night inside Japanese territory on the island of Sakhalin, just north of the enemy's mainland tip.

Moscow's communiqué reported that the advance is being pushed forward after the smashing of the defences on the Soviet frontier which cuts across the island.

Away to the south-west the Red Fleet stormed the Korean port of Selshin, 125 miles from Vladivostok.

Malinovsky's crack troops, advancing 75 miles in a day, have swept to points 200 miles from the Bay of Liaotung, cutting the Manchurian escape gap to 200 miles.

On the eastern side of the country practically the whole Japanese communications network has been shattered with the capture of Mutankiang, 150 miles south-east of Harbin, the junction on the Harbin-Vladivostok line.

Anti-Queue Rally

Fewer than 70 London housewives turned up for an anti-queue meeting in Central Hall, Westminster yesterday.

7 Saved From Hotel

A turntable ladder was used by firemen to rescue seven people from the upper storeys of the Willmot Hotel, on Broadstairs seafront early yesterday.

RADAR 'EYES' SAVED BRITAIN

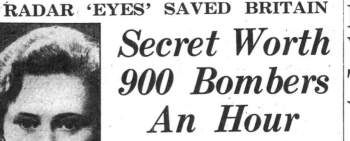

Secret Worth 900 Bombers An Hour

By CHARLES BRAY

FIVE years before the war broke out, harassed and sorely worried officials of the Air Ministry believed that only a death ray could save this country from the ever-growing air might of Germany.

In desperation they asked British scientists what were the chances of an early development of some such power. The answer was immediate and emphatic—there was no early hope of a death ray.

IN 1936 it was decided to use three girls as "guinea pigs" to test if women could be used on radiolocation work. The girls, on the clerical staff at the secret radar station in Suffolk, were (above) "Ginger" Girdlestone, she is now Mrs. M. Parry, and . . .

. . . Nellie Boyce, now Mrs. S. Jefferson . . .

. . . And Jenny Brooker.

Theirs was a weary job often just hour after hour in a darkened room waiting for light signals on an indicator tube.

But they proved that girls could do it, and though a cautious minute to the Air Minister said "it is not known how they will react when flustered," 12 more girls were added to the original three.

The hundreds of "Gingers" and Jennys and Nellies who worked on Radar during the war gave the answer to that.

But energy re-radiated from an aircraft ought to suffice for locating enemy planes and give warning to defences.

Grasping at this straw, a secret army of scientists was recruited, small in numbers at first. The brains of this country, of the Dominions and of America, were called to work unceasingly and exclusively on the problem.

Military resources were pooled, professors were banished to lonely hide-outs, men died without public mourning—an air crash which killed them could not be disclosed, their work was so secret.

So science gave to the United Nations not a death ray, but Radar, the system utilising bursts of radio energy which, when reflected from solid objects—say, an oncoming plane—enables their whereabouts to be fixed by measuring the time taken for the radio "echo" to return.

Today this war-winning idea is already being placed at the disposal of air and sea transport, for in peace we shall travel more safely through Radar.

250,000 Workers Kept Mum

The "Boffins," as Radar scientists are known throughout the Services, kept ahead of the enemy in radio development and its application to military use.

Until now the secret of ten years battle of wits has been well kept, despite the quarter of a million workers directly and indirectly employed. And much of the work is still secret.

It was the device produced by the "Boffins" that saved Britain when Germany threw her air might against us in 1940. It defeated every move made against us, with the exception of the V.2. It saved England from being starved by the U-boats, it protected convoys, it helped to break German industry.

In two months it changed the number of bombers we could send over a target in an hour from 100 to 1,000.

It was Radar, too, that gave bomber crews the "magic eye" which enabled them to see in miniature outlines of coast or town, despite darkness or fog.

Detected Crawling Infantrymen

It also played an escorting part on D-Day, guiding minesweepers, landing craft and the air fleets.

Radar even made it possible for the Army to detect an infantryman crawling along the ground many yards away.

By the end of the flying bomb attacks, Radar-aided AA guns were accounting for between 80 and 100 per cent. of the bombs reaching them.

And the scientists' later application of Radar on wavelengths down to a few centimetres paved the way for the airborne Radar "map" which led to Germany's disruption from the air.

(Full story of Radar on Page 2.).

PETAIN LAST DRAMA

"Herald" Reporter
PARIS, Tuesday.

THE 24 jurymen who have heard evidence in the Petain trial for the last 20 days tonight left the stuffy courtroom to consider their verdict.

Before they rose they heard Marshal Petain give his own evidence.

Then they adjourned—together with the three judges—and passed into a room with blue baize-topped tables.

There, under the protection of 12 guards armed with tommy-guns and revolvers, they began their deliberations.

The jury took time to have dinner before starting their deliberations shortly after 9 p.m. (B.S.T.). The dinner, which was served to the three judges as well as to the jury, was specially cooked and brought into the Law Courts from the kitchens of the Prefecture of Police near by.

The police refused to allow any private undertaking to prepare the food, presumably to eliminate any possibility of tampering with food following the anonymous threatening letters both judges and jurymen have received.

Feared Threats

Marshal Petain, in his special quarters, took a light meal with a glass of milk, and then half undressed and dozed on his bed. Two nuns who have been watching over him prayed in a corner of the room.

The verdict, it is anticipated, may be given by a majority of three to one. It was not expected until early today.

(Trial scenes: Back Page).

German Mines Kill Our Men

Four British soldiers have been killed and five injured clearing mines laid by the Germans on the Guernsey coast.

Helped by German prisoners-of-war, nine of whom have been killed and 15 injured, we have cleared more than 76,000 mines in this area since May.

These Roads To Close At 9.30

SCOTLAND YARD issued a warning last night that there will be a big traffic diversion for the opening of Parliament today.

Those who intend to gather near Parliament-square and Whitehall are advised to be there before 9.30 a.m. Anyone who need not go near the diversion area is asked to keep away.

Constitution Hill, The Mall, Birdcage Walk, Whitehall, Parliament-square, Millbank and Lambeth Bridge will all be closed from 9.30 a.m. till the Royal procession returns to Buckingham Palace—about 1 p.m.

Girl Who Vanished

A 23-year-old man will appear at Stratford, E., court this morning charged in connection with the disappearance a month ago of a 15-year-old London girl, Patricia Marian Ball. She was traced this week living in Birmingham.

P.M. WILL THANK YOU

By Ernest Jay
Political Correspondent

MR. ATTLEE, in the Commons this afternoon will thank Britain's fighting men and women and the nation's workers for their great share in the victory.

After the State opening of Parliament by the King the House will adjourn until just before 4 p.m.

Then M.P.s will reassemble in the usual Chamber, and will go in procession, headed by the Speaker, to St. Margaret's, Westminster, for a Thanksgiving Service.

On their return the Prime Minister will make a formal statement on the end of the war.

This will take the form of an Address to the King, and will express gratitude to the Forces and workers.

The King, accompanied by the Queen, will drive in State from Buckingham Palace for the opening of the Victory Parliament.

It will be the first pageant of peace and will provide a colourful spectacle although shorn of much of the pre-war ceremonial.

Thousands of people lining the route will have their first opportunity of seeing members of the new Labour Government.

Mr. Attlee is expected to leave Downing-street at 10.30 a.m., ten minutes before the royal procession starts from the Palace. It goes by way of The Mall, Horse Guards Parade into Whitehall and across Parliament-square to the Victoria Tower.

Crown Guarded

The King and Queen are due at the Victoria Tower at 10.50 and will be met by the ceremonial heralds, the Lord Chancellor and other officials responsible for the safety of the Crown.

The Crown, which will be carried immediately ahead of the King into the Robing Room, was brought from its war-time place of safety at Windsor yesterday.

It remained at St. James's under guard last night and will be taken to Westminster just befor the King and Queen leave.

The King's Speech will be delivered in the Lords' chamber.

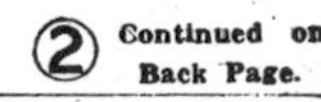
② Continued on Back Page.

STOP PRESS

HOLIDAY TODAY

Mr. Attlee announced today and tomorrow will everywhere be treated as days of holiday.

Weather Herald

Mainly fair at first, thundery rains later.

Further outlook: Unsettled.

Lighting-up Time: 9.24 p.m.

Last Day Of War Hour By Hour

TIME-TABLE of news, rumour and counter-rumour as the end-of-war drama developed yesterday:

6 a.m.—Tokyo radio began sending long code messages to Switzerland. Heard in New York.

7 a.m.—Japanese broadcast that an Imperial edict accepting the Potsdam declaration would be forthcoming soon.

9.15 a.m.—New York picked up Japanese radio report that "something important" would be available about 2 p.m.

11 a.m.—New York heard Japanese radio stations calling all Japanese ships at sea.

11.12 a.m.—Tokyo began sending radio code messages to Japanese officials in Stockholm.

11.13 a.m. — "Swiss Foreign Office has received a long Japanese reply."—Paris radio.

11.14 a.m.—Swiss Legation in Washington announced: "No message received."

11.15 a.m.—Paris radio said a reply was being decoded.

12.33 p.m.—"Japan has accepted the Allied capitulation formula."—Swiss radio.

12.47 p.m. — Japanese News Agency began transmitting to newspapers in occupied Asia the text of statement by Emperor, expressing "extreme concern for the calamity." Message was embargoed until 9 p.m.

1.48 p.m.—Tokyo radio stated that a very important announcement would be broadcast at noon (4 a.m. BST) today.

3.11 p.m.—President Truman's Press Secretary, Mr. Ross, announced that the Swiss Foreign Office had received the Japanese reply at noon

4.35 p.m.—Swiss Legation in Washington phoned the State Department to deny that the Swiss Government had received any message from Japan.

5 p.m.—New York picked up Tokyo broadcast: "The Japanese Government's reply is now on its way to the Japanese Minister at Berne."

5.51 p.m.—Downing-street announced "No official confirmation yet received of the many rumours circulating."

8.10 p.m.—Swiss communiqué: Japanese reply handed over in Berne.

9.5 p.m.—Reply cabled to Washington.

10.24 p.m.—United States radio: Reply received.

Midnight. — Mr. Attlee announces Japan's surrender.

Daily Mirror
WED AUG 15 1945
FORWARD WITH THE PEOPLE
No. 12,995 ONE PENNY
Registered at G.P.O. as a Newspaper.

PEACE

JAPAN SURRENDERS—ALLIES CEASE FIRE

Piccadilly, caught napping, woke up

"Daily Mirror" Reporter

PEACE news caught West End revellers napping — but only for an hour, and then Piccadilly went wild.

At midnight there were not more than a hundred people round Eros. By 1.30 this morning there were thousands—screaming, shouting, dancing and throwing their hats in the air.

When Mr. Attlee announced the Jap surrender there were twelve people outside Buckingham Palace—rearguard of the thousands who thronged the West End for five nights in succession for the great news. One man was shouting for the King.

But at two o'clock the march on the Palace had begun again, and great crowds packed The Mall and Trafalgar Square.

In the area between Marble Arch and Grosvenor Square American troops went delirious with delight.

Jeeps tore down Oxford-street and there was a continual hullabaloo of motor horns, klaxons, bells, police whistles, tin drums, dustbin lids—in fact anything which would make a noise.

A crowd of about 200 American soldiers and sailors with the Stars and Stripes at their head marched down Oxford-street singing "Yankee Doodle Dandy" and "Over There."

And a gigantic conga line of about a thousand Service men, women and civilians headed by a Scotsman in kilts, marched from Marble Arch, through Grosvenor Square, and continued on their way to Piccadilly.

At 3 a.m. police estimated that the crowds in Piccadilly Circus were as great as those on VE-Day.

For after the Premier's midnight broadcast thousands of people set out from the suburbs in lorries, horse-drawn carts, motor-cycles and cycles (some even walked) in an early morning effort to join in the West End celebrations.

Rockets and fireworks flashed and exploded over the heads of the merry-makers around Eros, and there were cheers for firemen who arrived to tackle a blaze in an office block hit by the rockets.

Sitting on the backs of the

Continued on Back Page

Troops had to rescue the police

TOWNSFOLK all over Britain got up in the middle of the night and lit bonfires. Servicemen fired Verey lights over the country side, sailors, soldiers, airmen and Service girls started mafficking in a big way.

And in America, hordes of celebrators—it was only 7 p.m. for them—set out to make a night of revelry that would go down in history.

Civil and military police had to hold back a Liverpool crowd which tried to mob a troopship at Prince's landing stage. Hundreds of bonfires turned the sky into a ruddy glow a few minutes after victory was announced.

Military police were posted to keep a huge crowd out of the White House at Washington. Then troops had to be sent to rescue the military police, who were being crowded against the fences and walls, and take them into the White House grounds.

Eight abreast, Servicemen and civilians marched through Gillingham, Kent, carrying the Union Jack, headed by an impromptu band of dustbin lids snatched from house fronts.

9 p.m. BROADCAST BY THE KING

The King will broadcast at 9 o'clock tonight. There will be a Thanksgiving Service on the B.B.C. at 8.15 p.m.

Today and tomorrow V-days "Enjoy yourselves" call by Attlee at midnight

"PEACE HAS ONCE AGAIN COME TO THE WORLD. LET US THANK GOD FOR THIS GREAT DELIVERANCE AND HIS MERCIES." IT WAS THE VOICE OF THE PRIME MINISTER, BROADCASTING FROM NO. 10, DOWNING-STREET AT MIDNIGHT TO TELL BRITAIN THAT JAPAN HAS SURRENDERED.

Japan has accepted the Allied terms without qualification. The Jap Emperor is to order all his forces to lay down their arms and obey all commands of the Allied Forces.

ALLIED ARMED FORCES HAVE ALREADY BEEN ORDERED TO SUSPEND OFFENSIVE OPERATIONS. AN ATTACK BY HUNDREDS OF PLANES WAS CALLED OFF IMMEDIATELY.

In his broadcast Mr. Attlee announced that today and tomorrow will be V-Day holidays.

"Let all who can relax and enjoy themselves in the knowledge of work well done," he said.

Arrangements have been made for the formal signing of the surrender at the earliest moment and President Truman has named General MacArthur as the Allied commander to receive the surrender.

Washington reports last night said that the surrender will probably be signed on a battleship, or on Okinawa, scene of one of the most savage battles of the Pacific war.

Emperor to Broadcast

It was announced in Tokio that the Japanese Emperor, breaking all precedent, would broadcast to the nation at midday (4 a.m. British Summer Time).

In his White House statement last night President Truman said: "The proclamation of VJ-Day must wait upon the formal signing of the surrender terms by Japan.

Soon afterwards, however, came an announcement that President Truman had proclaimed a two-day holiday for all Federal employees on Wednesday and Thursday throughout the United States.

Mr. Attlee went to the microphone in No. 10 to give the news of the surrender after a bewildering day in which the hopes of the world had been raised and dashed again

Continued on Back Page

PETAIN SENTENCED TO DEATH

MARSHAL PETAIN was sentenced to death at 3.30 this morning.

The verdict on the eighty-nine-year-old Marshal was announced after the jury had been conferring for six hours.

When the 20th and last day's session of the trial passed its eighth hour, food was sent in to the jury.

While the jury was deliberating, Madame Petain was informed that she was freed, with no charges against her,

Sunday Pictorial

No. 1,630 Twopence

All the Great Pictures:

SOUVENIR NUMBER

VICTORY SPECIAL

The moment that symbolises the pride of a nation. The King—with the Queen and Queen Mary—takes the Salute as the proud might of Empire passes by.

WAR PAPERS

LUDOVIC KENNEDY was born in Edinburgh and educated at Eton and Christ Church, Oxford. Since 1955 he has been well known on British television – first as a newscaster, then as presenter and interviewer on programmes such as *This Week, Panorama, Tonight, 24 Hours, Midweek* and *Did You See?* The maker of many successful documentaries, including *Battleship Bismarck* and *Great Railway Journeys of the World,* he has also written a number of naval books and travel anthologies, as well as four books on miscarriages of justice. His best-selling autobiography, *On My Way to the Club,* was published by Collins in 1989.

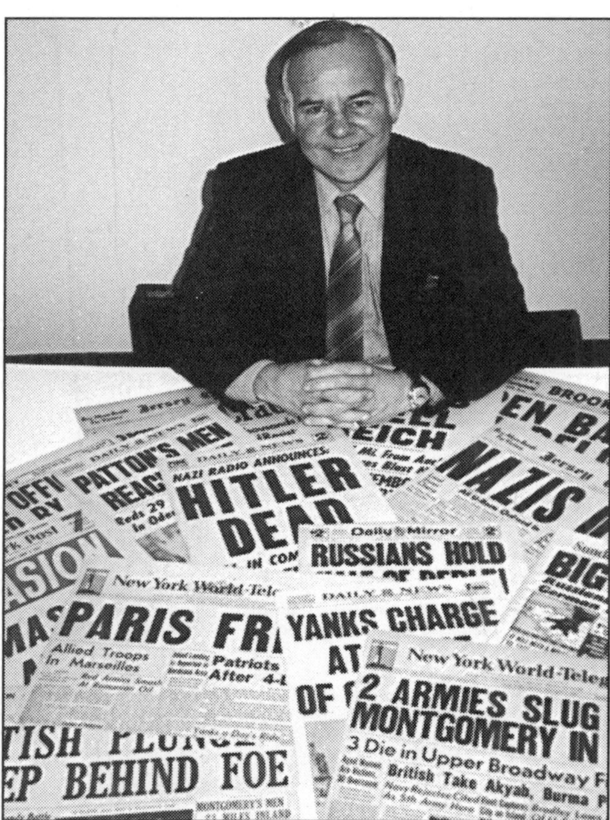

JOHN FROST has been collecting historic newspapers for 50 years, and his unique private library has an astonishing 40,000 editions dating back to 1630. His collection from the World War II period alone exceeds 10,000.
He saw active service from 1939-1945 with the 11th Armoured Division, and is a member of the Normandy Veterans Association. He was in Lubeck two days after the death of Adolf Hitler, and retrieved a Nazi newspaper reporting his death.
He is much in demand as a lecturer on Press history, with frequent TV and radio broadcasts, and supplies period newspapers to TV and film companies and book publishers. John Frost is married with two sons and lives in New Barnet, Hertfordshire.